I Can't Begin to Tell You

M16.

I Can't Begin to Tell You

Elizabeth Buchan

W F HOWES LTD

This large print edition published in 2015 by
W F Howes Ltd
Unit 4, Rearsby Business Park, Gaddesby Lane,
Rearsby, Leicester LE7 4YH

1 3 5 7 9 10 8 6 4 2

First published in the United Kingdom in 2014
by Penguin Group

A CIP catalogue record for this book is available
from the British Library

ISBN 978 1 47129 781 6

Typeset by Palimpsest Book Production Limited,
Falkirk, Stirlingshire

www.printondema~~nd-worldwide.com~~ of Peterborough, England

For Elizabeth, my Copenhagen companion

From 1940 to 1946 the Special Operations Executive (SOE) was a British secret service that supported Resistance in all enemy-occupied countries.

CHAPTER 1

Day One

Kay Eberstern was moving as unobtrusively as she could manage through the tongue-shaped wood of ash and birch which ran alongside the lake on her husband's Danish estate. It was five o'clock on an early November evening in 1942.

It was imperative not to be seen.

At this time of the evening the men working on the estate went home and they would be taken aback if they caught sight of Kay lurking here. They would ask: 'What is the master's wife doing?' If it were peacetime, they might conclude that she was meeting a lover. But it was not peacetime. It was war, Hitler's war, and British-born Kay had got herself caught up in it. If she was spotted, gossiped over, or betrayed, there could be, almost certainly would be, serious repercussions for the Eberstern family.

Her orders had been to wait for an hour every evening in the wood at Rosenlund, for up to three days. Here she was to rendezvous with 'Felix', a

1

British-trained agent who, if all had gone to plan, would have arrived in the area in order to set up resistance operations. She had also been warned that the plans might go awry and the mission aborted. The agent was being parachuted into Jutland and faced a difficult sea journey to Zealand and a subsequent cross-country one into the Køge area.

Kay could have no illusions as to what might happen to Tanne and Nils, her children, or to Bror, her husband. Everyone knew that the Danish police weren't backward in coming forward in rounding up anyone involved in this sort of activity and handing them over to the German *Gestapomen*.

Was outraged decency a sufficiently good reason to put Tanne and Nils, and her marriage to Bror, at risk? Was her refusal to tolerate evil, cruelty and a creeping fascism worth it?

Being seriously apprehensive was a new and unwelcome sensation and Kay was struggling to master it. If her task hadn't been so crucial, and in other circumstances, she might have set about analysing its effects. Damp palms and a queasy stomach were predictable. Less so, were the upsurges of bravado followed by the slump into panic. Like a disease, fear caused weakness and debilitation.

The winter was gearing up and, at this time of the evening, it was growing cold. She pushed her gloved hands into her pockets. Tomorrow, *if* there was a tomorrow, she would take pains to kit up

2

more warmly. It hadn't occurred to her until she was actually standing and freezing in the wood that she should think practically and prepare. For a start, she needed a torch.

Why was she here?

What was happening back at the house? Had she been missed yet? Birgit was preparing dinner and Kay had been careful to tell her that she hadn't been sleeping well – not an untruth – and would be taking a nap.

An owl hooted: a hollow, eerie sound.

Kay shifted uneasily.

Two years ago, on 9 April 1940, Hitler marched into Denmark and declared it a Protectorate with a special blood-brother relationship with the Reich, completely ignoring the non-aggression pact which he had signed with Denmark.

It looked as though the Danes had been caught napping.

Rumours of Hitler's intentions had been circulating for months. Kay had turned into an obsessive listener to the BBC while it reported what was happening in Austria, Czechoslovakia and Poland – but in Denmark, even with Germany just next door, events had seemed removed, almost remote. She and Bror took their places at the breakfast table early on that April morning, he pale and grim, she flushed and on edge. They gazed at each other and Kay imagined she heard in her head the appalled cries of protest at this new arrangement of Europe.

It had taken all day to get a phone connection to her mother in England. Fretful, anxious hours, and lipstick-stained cigarette butts were heaped in the ashtray by the time she got through.

'Kay . . .' Her mother was on the verge of weeping, which was unlike her. 'Your sisters and I have been desperate to hear from you. We've heard the news. Are you all right?'

'Are *you* all right?'

It was baffling how such important conversations could be reduced to the basics.

Kay searched to make the verbal connection mean something. 'We're getting over the shock.'

'Darling, couldn't you come home?'

Home.

She thought of Piccadilly Circus, of the lisle stockings she used to wear, of nips of sherry in meanly sized glasses and overdone beef for Sunday lunch, and of her mother standing in the passageway of her tiny cottage at the end of a waterlogged lane clutching the telephone receiver. She thought, too, of her mother's deferential, polite widowhood lived out on the edges of a society that didn't rate widows very highly.

Coming to live in Denmark, she had left all those things behind.

'Kay, I wish you didn't live so far away. I wish . . . I wish . . . I don't want to die without seeing you again.'

'You're not going to die, Mother. Do you hear me?'

Her mother pulled herself together, as Kay knew she would. 'I've taken in two little boys, evacuees. The bombing is so bad in London and they're sending all the children into the country. They had fleas! Imagine! They don't speak the King's English. But I'm getting used to it . . .'

The timed call limped to its three-minute limit. England was cut off.

Kay shook herself, determined not to dip into homesickness. Her life was here now, in Denmark.

How hard it had been to keep the homesickness and misery at bay when she first arrived as a nervous and badly dressed bride. Having met Bror at her friend Emily's twenty-first dance, she had married him only six months later. It had been a fast and exciting transition. Too rapid, perhaps? Although she was deeply in love and saw her new life as an opportunity to be grasped, she had been ignorant of the battle she would face in turning herself into a woman capable of running Rosenlund. The Ebersterns expected conformity and there were times when she had had to fight to subdue her rebellion. There had also been occasional clashes with Bror, whose politics were more old-fashioned than hers.

Yet in those early days her senses had been stoked and stroked by physical love, by the sights and scents and tastes of a different country, by the challenge of mastering the Danish language and customs. It had been a time of languor, of sensuality and of plenty, when the glittering mysteries of ice and fog during the long dark Danish winters offered some compensation for the occasional moments of sadness.

Inside Kay's walking shoes, her toes were cramping. Sweat had gathered at the bottom of her spine and the waistband of her skirt was unpleasantly damp. The truth was that she was frightened. Truly terrified she had made the wrong decision.

To steady herself, Kay started counting up to ten.

One . . . two . . .

They were lucky at Rosenlund. The war had not really hit them here yet – or in Køge, the ancient fishing port just three miles to the east. Only a short train ride from the capital, Rosenlund still could, and did, function along traditional rural lines. The seasons dictated its agenda. So it had been easy, and natural perhaps, to duck away from the worst and for family life to continue, not so much blithely, but removed.

All the same. All the same . . . was a refrain that ran frequently through Kay's mind.

Elsewhere, Danes who opposed the Directorate were being rounded up. There were reports of torture and of murder in the streets and in the cells of Vestre prison in København (as Kay had learned to call it). Others were holed up in houses which they trusted to be safe, only to be betrayed by fellow Danes, the so-called *stikker*.

In the early days of their love affair, Bror told

her: 'In Denmark it is a point of honour to care for our communities.'

Then, she believed him.

Anyone could see that in giving Bror possession of the eighteenth-century ochre-painted house, with its farmlands and woods occupying a fertile curve outside Køge, fate had dealt him a royal flush.

She had only to conjure the image of his tall, fair figure standing by the window in the elegantly proportioned drawing room, looking out across the lake to the fields and wooded clumps, to hear him say: 'As long as one field lies against another supporting it, there I shall be . . .' It was the voice of a man at ease with his task, caught up by an urgent, emotional, almost mystical, union with the land.

No one could accuse Bror of not caring for his inheritance.

'Three,' she muttered to herself. 'Four.'

Think of something else . . .

The early days . . .

Bror wooed Kay with stories of the Danes. Obviously. He told her of Vikings, of fishermen, artists, designers, navigators, wireless inventors, democrats. He told her of heroes and their voyages, of the Danes' ongoing tussle with the sea.

He described how the sea turned iron grey in winter and brilliant blue and amber in summer. He explained the geographical oddity which meant the Baltic froze in winter because it wasn't very salty. He singled out the pebble beaches, the pines, the wild myrtle and gorse and the tiny islands which peppered the coastline.

He told of being the small boy, then the teenager, who got up before light and went out with his father to shoot duck on the mist-shrouded marshes. The making of a crack shot.

The salt tang. The silence. The swoop of the birds. The beating of their wings.

Almost word for word, Kay remembered what he said.

Bror painted a land of cool, clean beauty and astringent winds . . . all of which Kay discovered to be true when it became her home and she found happiness.

Bror Eberstern, her husband. To outsiders he was a courteous landowner, with a laconic, sometimes brusque, manner of which they could be afraid or daunted. Only a few intimates knew of his gentleness and tenderness and the reserve which masked his feelings.

No man was an island and it followed that no woman was either. Habit, children, their shared bed, their shared days, their deep feelings for each other – these created the ties which had grown thicker and tougher over the years. Yet Bror had gone and made a decision, a political one, which had the power to change her life.

Kay was angry about it. Bitterly so.

She shifted position, kicking up the undergrowth which smelled of leaf mould mixed with recent

8

rain. So much of life had its scents and stinks: newborn babies, roasting pork, bad drains, fresh bread, the glamorous and addictive aroma of Turkish cigarettes, the tanning lorry, pink and white sweet peas. So did waking early in the morning to a world cleansed by the dark, to recently polished leather shoes, Bror's aura of tweed and tobacco . . . To be conscious was to engage with sensations in which she took endless pleasure. To be alive was a gloriously tactile experience, gloriously absorbing. Any eloquence she might summon to describe what she was experiencing faltered in the face of the shimmery intensity of her feelings.

Five forty-five. Fifteen more minutes before time was up.

In wartime, the senses were assaulted in new ways. People were less clean, less well fed. Poverty and scarcity smelled different.

If poverty smelled, did fear smell too? These days fear and suspicion were everywhere. Danish police were checking every traveller on trains and on boats and ferries. *Gestapomen* patrolled the ports. Then there were the *stikker*. Nosy. Officious. Highly dangerous. And you never knew where they were.

That *stikker* were a big problem wasn't surprising. Their equivalents would be everywhere, including Britain. No society was incorruptible and no one's motives were unadulterated. When Kay's father lay dying, he let slip to his daughter a little of what

9

he had learned amid the mud and the blood of the Great War: 'When you are cold and hungry and frightened . . . or wounded, you don't care about political philosophies or the passions which drive them. They fall away. You want to survive and you will sacrifice most things to do so . . .' Watching his features drain of life, she cried helplessly. At the time, her grief was too overwhelming for her to examine what her father had meant but the halting words must have rooted in her unconscious mind for she remembered them now.

A grey, insubstantial mist which had previously settled over the lake was shifting. The darkness folded down. There were noises which she half recognized, half not, for, in her state of heightened awareness, they appeared to be extra loud and ominous.

Time?

Five minutes to go. The knot in her chest slackened for she doubted Felix would turn up now – whoever he was. A hero? An opportunist? A non-conformist? A communist? It was common gossip that it was only the communists who demonstrated any open resistance in Denmark.

In the two years since Denmark had been occupied Kay had lived in a bubble. It had taken the lunch with Anton, Bror's cousin, for her to understand that some men and women were responding to the need to be decent and, believing their government to be supine, were taking matters into their own hands.

If that was so, what did Bror's actions make him?

Asking and answering the question made Kay feel dangerously out of kilter.

Crack.

What was that? Heartbeat accelerating, Kay whipped round. Nothing. Breathing out slowly, she refocused on the lake. The mist had now cleared and the light from the stars nipped and bobbed on the water.

Would Felix be tall, short, old, young? Was he Danish? Probably. Otherwise the language barrier would be too difficult. Even after twenty-five years in Denmark, Kay still spoke with a foreign inflection.

Time was up.

She was off the hook for today and, for all that she had resolved to be strong and resolute, she was thankful.

Glancing over her shoulder, she moved off in the direction of the house.

. . . 'Pack up your troubles in your old kit bag . . .' the ghost of her father sang in her ear in a cracked baritone. 'Can't you be quiet, dear?' said her mother . . .

Immersed in her marriage as Kay had been since she arrived here twenty-five years ago, occupied by motherhood and life at Rosenlund, she'd found that the power of England to evoke an intense response in her had diminished. Yet, since that April morning in 1940 when Hitler marched into Denmark, she had been winded at

11

odd moments by homesickness – its jolt speeding through her body in an almost physical manner. 'Plucky little Britain is punching above its weight,' said Anton and she wanted to cry out: 'My country!' Then she remembered. No, England wasn't her country any longer. Denmark was.

Remember that.

Even so, she found herself wanting to rap people on the chest and to say: 'Do you understand Britain has gone it alone?'

Here in this wood, where Danish sphagnum moss lapped around her shoes and the smell of water pricked in her nostrils, Kay would have given much for the sight of the damp ox-eyed daisies and rose-bay willow herb growing outside her mother's cottage . . . to be sitting with friends in a dark, smoky Gaumount cinema . . . to be rattling along in a red London bus, to be dancing to the band in the Savoy in someone's arms – preferably Bror's but those of any warm, handsome male would do for that moment. It would mean being part of a nation who knew where they were. *Fighting Herr Schicklgruber.*

Breathe in. Breathe out.

Go home.

CHAPTER 2

A couple of weeks ago, out of the blue, Anton
Eberstern, Bror's first cousin, had rung Kay
at Rosenlund to invite her to lunch at one
of København's most talked-about restaurants.

She went.

The restaurant was the sort of professional enterprise in whose cosmopolitan gloss was embedded
the famous Danish *hygge* – a cultivated cosiness
designed to shut out the world's troubles. *Hygge*,
Kay reckoned, was the Danish riposte to the wear
and tear of cruel winters, a fragmented territory
and an often hostile sea.

Bror was going off on a ten-day fishing trip on
Jutland with his cousins, the Federspiels, but he
dispatched Kay to act as his eyes and ears. 'Anton
must be up to something,' he said with the curious
expression that she could never get to the bottom
of. They occasionally discussed the antipathy
between Bror and Anton – or, at least, Kay tried
to discuss it, but she never got very far since Bror's
response tended to be anything but rational. 'I
don't think he's ever got over the fact that I have
Rosenlund,' he once admitted. 'And he's rotten to

13

women.' Kay had laughed and informed Bror that he had just made Anton seem twice as attractive. A womanizer with a slight grudge. 'Every woman in Denmark will make it her mission to heal him.'

The train had been crowded, as was usual these days, and the talk in the carriage had been of the watered-down milk which had become the norm and the difficulty of obtaining petrol. In København itself there were German soldiers in the streets, older and shabbier than might have been expected from the reputedly smart-as-paint *Wehrmacht*.

When Anton got up to greet her in the restaurant, she was startled by his neat blond moustache. 'That's new.'

'Admiring my beauty. Don't frown, darling. It's my tribute to Herr Hitler.' He smiled but not with huge amusement. 'Camouflage in war is sensible.'

She peered at Anton.

The cousins may have borne a family resemblance – the jawline, the blondness, a certain facial expression. That was deceptive. Temperamentally, they were chalk and cheese.

Anton was shorter and of slighter build than Bror. When not in his uniform, he displayed a fondness for cashmere coats, Savile Row tailoring and custom-made shoes. He loved political gossip and diplomatic intrigue and was well informed. He made the best of lunch companions.

In comparison to Rosenlund, Anton's house and land were modest – there being only a small acreage with which to enjoy a mystical relationship.

If he minded – as Bror suggested – he never gave the slightest indication to Kay. A bachelor, he concentrated on love affairs, good wine, cigars and the flowers which he grew in his famed hothouses. To receive one of Anton's bouquets was said to be a signal for seduction. Life was too serious to be serious, he told Kay. She believed him until she grew wiser and more sceptical. Anton was a colonel in Danish military intelligence and, presumably, somewhere in the mix of charm and conviviality was a professional.

Anton ordered for them both.

Over the fish soup, he regarded Kay with his customary combination of overt lust and admiration. As the bride, Kay had found Anton's behaviour unsettling. These days, she found his lightness of touch attractive. Once or twice she had asked herself if his obvious admiration pandered to her vanity. Just a little? More than a little?

Anton raised a glass of Chablis. 'The hat is good, Kay. Blue on blonde hair is magnetic. Did you buy it on one of your little trips to Paris?'

The hat was royal blue with a black feather and wispy netting and nestled on Kay's piled-up hair. The effect was particularly good with the Eberstern pearls round her neck, something she knew perfectly well when she dressed for this meeting.

'Yes,' she said and sighed, remembering wet streets, perfume, garlic soup, making love with Bror in a hotel room. 'I miss Paris.'

'Did you wear it to seduce me?'

'Oh, the masculine mind.'

'Are you sure you didn't? Anything can happen after lunch, you know.' He held her gaze. 'I love you, Kay, for how quickly you stopped being British and dowdy after you came here.' There was a tiny pause. 'How are things at dear old Rosenlund?' A further pause. 'And dear old Bror? How's he taken it all?'

Bror had been angry and unsettled by the German takeover of the country. 'Think of the numbers, Kay,' he'd said in response to her frantic question as to why no one had gone out and fought. 'There are seventy-five million Germans and only four and a half million of us. Who do you expect to win? Who? Tell me . . .' He'd grasped her by the shoulders. '*Tell me.*'

She'd looked up at him. 'But not too . . .' The words were stillborn.

Geography and politics did not make up the whole story for Bror. There was also a question of kinship. The Ebersterns had German relations and knew Germany well. It was logical, Kay told herself. Inevitable. Bror wasn't British or American and part of his psyche responded to the Germanic traditions. Over the generations, German wives and husbands had come to live at Rosenlund, leaving echoes in the house and on the land. No wonder Bror's reaction to the Reich's presence was complex and, almost certainly, fraught with tensions.

Discussing Bror with Anton was tricky and she

16

avoided it when possible. 'Making-do, like everyone else. Some of the men are trickling away to work in Germany.'

'Dear, oh dear,' said Anton.

She didn't mention that they had been forced to cut back on expenditure or, now short-handed, Bror got up earlier, held daily meetings with Arne, his foreman, and worked later to keep it all going.

The waiter topped up the glasses.

'Do you know what he has been up to?'

She sensed that this was a loaded question and instinct told her to keep her reply neutral. 'Business trips up here. Out in the fields. Talking to Arne. The usual.'

It wasn't quite true. With a touch of apprehension, she recollected Bror had – unusually – taken to closeting himself in the estate office to make phone calls. Once, she had answered the house telephone to an official-sounding voice asking to speak to her husband. That had been followed by an unexpected trip to København.

Anton chose his moment. 'Have you heard about the Declaration of Good Will?'

Something clicked. This lunch had been plotted out – a manoeuvre. More likely than not, she was being used to get at Bror for some purpose.

Anton continued: 'It's been drawn up by the Agricultural Ministry to keep the Germans quiet. Landowners have been asked to sign it. Has Bror mentioned it?'

The information came as a shock – and she was

forced to take a moment before asking: 'What are you trying to tell me?'

Anton took on board her reaction. 'Have you heard about it?'

'I haven't, no.' She ran her finger around the rim of her wine glass and it gave off a tiny shriek. 'But if I had . . .?'

He shrugged. 'If you sign a document such as the Declaration you are on the record. The Nazis are brilliant at records. I thought you should know.'

'Anton . . .?' He was making her uneasy. 'Why should I know this?'

'Ask Bror.'

'I will.' Kay hoped her smile would mask her sudden terror that Bror had done something stupid. 'And where do *you* stand?'

She expected . . . well, what? A riff on the virtues of keeping one's head down? The impossibility of Denmark doing anything but what it was doing. Perhaps even admiration and support for the Reich? It was what many Danes believed.

His gaze shifted around the room and then focused hard on her face. 'Kay, the situation in Denmark is dismal but there are alternatives.'

She could not have been more surprised. 'Meaning?'

'This is for your ears only.' He waited for the implications to fall into place. 'Understood?'

An astonished Kay nodded. Anton poured out the last of the wine with his usual dispatch.

'Danes can't fight in the conventional way,' he

said. 'But there are growing numbers of those opposed to the Nazis hiding up in Sweden and England. Some of them who've managed to reach London are being trained in undercover work. Intelligence-gathering, sabotage, mustering underground armies.'

It was as if an earthquake had shaken the restaurant and Kay was wandering, dazed, through the rubble. 'But isn't the Danish army working for the Nazis? Aren't you?'

'I'm working alongside . . .' Anton dropped his searchlight scrutiny. 'Everyone has to be very, very careful. They are not kind to what they call enemy terrorists.'

Kay dredged her memory. Not long ago, a story had done the rounds about a British-trained parachutist jumping out of a plane over Jutland and his parachute failing to open. His smashed body had been discovered by the authorities and the reprisals, once they had rounded up anyone they thought might have been involved, were very bad.

'So, in England . . .?' she murmured.

'You miss it?' Anton must have caught her confusion and nostalgia.

'Yes. When the war began, I was horrified, of course. But since the invasion of Denmark I feel differently.' She tucked a strand of hair back into her chignon. 'Not surprising, is it?'

He was sympathetic, almost tender. 'It makes you realize what it means to you?'

'Yes. Big events do.'

Anton lowered his voice. 'Denmark is not high on the Allies' agenda. Even so, the British, including these people I was talking about, will give some support if we can get organized here. Unfortunately, this means they will interfere in ways we don't necessarily like but . . .' He shrugged. 'Can't be helped.'

Her bewilderment more or less under control, Kay strove to understand the implications. 'Surely, if there's trouble in Denmark, it will tie up the German troops here even though they are needed elsewhere.'

It was a small triumph of strategic thinking.

'So . . .' Anton gave one of his smiles. 'You do keep up.'

'Anton, look at me.' He obeyed immediately. 'You know I could betray you.'

The handsome features darkened. 'But you won't, Kay. Because you're British. Because you're no fascist.' Again, the tender note sounded. 'Because your heart beats to an English drum.'

She flinched.

Two tables away a couple blew kisses at each other. Across the room a man in a loud tweed suit was eating a solitary meal.

'These people you talk about in England . . .?'

He got her gist. 'Who are they? A curious bunch. Bandits operating in the shadows. From what we can gather, and we are not supposed to know about it, there's an outfit based in London which trains men – and women – for undercover

20

operations and infiltrates them into occupied countries. It has Prime Minister Churchill's backing . . . being a bit of a boy scout himself, he's very keen on it. We've seen it referred to in one report as the "SOE".' He spread his hands as if to say: *God knows what that stands for.* 'But intelligence chatter has picked up talk about "The Firm". Its existence is top secret.'

'How did you make contact?'

'Darling Kay, the first rule is to never ask questions.'

'But you're taking a risk telling me. A big one.'

'Calculated, Kay.'

She stirred in her seat. Fingered the pearls at her neck. She had the oddest notion that Anton had unearthed an element in her of which she had not been aware.

'All sorts of things are needed. For instance, if we are going to work with the British we need safe houses for agents to hide up in. I've already organized one or two in Køge.' He stared at her and she felt, suddenly, older, more experienced, more laden with knowledge than she had ever imagined. 'You get the picture?'

She glanced up at the ceiling of the restaurant, its decorative plaster work reminding her of whipped cream. God only knew how it would survive if København was bombed like London.

Sense prevailed.

'If you're asking me, I can't,' she said. 'The children. Bror.'

'Tanne is twenty-four. Nils is twenty-two. Hardly children. And Bror . . .' Anton dismissed him with a gesture.

Bror had done something. But what?

Kay collected her wits. 'No,' she said.

Anton allowed a long moment to elapse into which she read disappointment, a slight contempt.

'I understand . . .'

It was clear that he didn't.

Anton snapped his fingers at the waiter, asked Kay if she wanted anything and ordered a double brandy for himself, then launched into a description of the *fester-kinder* party recently held by his neighbours . . . the buffet, the wines, the conversations, the nightmare of transport without petrol. He was at his most brilliantly diverting and it meant nothing.

'I must go,' she said at last. 'I'm sorry.'

'Don't be.' His lids dropped over his eyes. 'There is one thing . . . Some pamphlets need delivering to Lippiman's bakery in Køge.'

'That's simple,' she said and held out a hand. 'Give them to me.'

He raised his eyes. 'I don't think you understand, darling.'

Then she did.

'The previous courier was caught,' continued Anton. 'I need someone to pick up from the contact at the station and deliver them. Lippiman does the rest.'

The hidden parallel world in which Anton dealt

was beginning to piece together. 'Mr Lippiman!' She glanced down at her left hand where the ring with the Eberstern diamonds caught the light. 'How surprising people are. I thought I knew him.'

'You thought you knew me.'

Kay sat very still. 'This is really you, Anton. I had no idea.' Something was shifting in her mind . . . but what? 'Why did I have no idea?'

'No one ever knows anyone.'

'Anton, what is Bror up to?'

He sat back in his chair. Easy and amused. Malicious. 'Ask him.'

There was a silence.

'I *really* must go.'

'Of course.' He reached over and captured one of Kay's hands. 'Would you do this? Just this once? The courier will wait on the platform for the afternoon train with a basket. It's just a matter of you taking the basket and dropping it in at the bakery on the way back.'

What had Anton done to her? She felt newly connected, but also disorientated – as if she had been pushed out of the shadow into blinding sun.

'It's very simple, Kay.'

With an excitement that was almost erotic, Kay allowed her hand to remain in his. 'If I am caught?'

'Ah.' He retrieved his hand. 'Then I would deny everything and swear my undying support of the Reich. Which means I'm unreliable and you are on your own. Understood?'

★　★　★

The girl standing on the platform where the Køge train was waiting was roughly the same age as Tanne – far, far too young to be putting herself in danger.

Kay's excitement drained and a faint nausea replaced it.

Someone should tell her. Someone should take her in hand and explain what it would mean to be found out. Where was her mother?

A basket was parked by the girl's feet and she was wearing inadequate-looking boots which Kay feared would let in the cold and wet.

Still some distance away, Kay stopped and pressed a hand to a cheek flushed from the wine at lunch. A couple of German soldiers in their green-grey – *feldgrau* – uniforms swaggered past her. Knowing they were being watched, they talked loudly, made jokes and showed off. Halfway down the platform, they stopped to light up cigarettes.

The girl with the basket stiffened visibly.

No, Kay willed her. *Act normally*.

Grasping her handbag strap, Kay walked up the platform. The girl registered Kay's presence. Then she turned her head away.

The movement exposed a delicate neck and its pale vulnerability triggered a violent reaction in Kay. It was like the moment when she had first held Tanne in her arms and had been overwhelmed by powerful and, as she had discovered, ineradicable impulses to protect her child.

The girl could be Tanne.

And if she had been Tanne?

The image of Rosenlund took shape, with every breath growing brighter and clearer – its high windows, the terraces, the lake, the fields and woods. She heard the sound of the harvest being brought in, the squeal of the pigs herded up for slaughter, the clunk of the threshing machine. In a terrible old pair of linen trousers, Bror was climbing into the boat with a picnic basket, followed by the children. It was a sunny summer day, and the sun bounced off the water as they rowed over to Princess Sophia-Maria's island in the middle of the lake. She heard their shouts and the yell as one or other of them jumped into the always-freezing water.

Kay wasn't going to endanger them.

Denmark could hold its own. It would survive.

For God's sake.

Turning around abruptly, Kay made her way back down the platform, pushing against the tide of passengers heading for the train.

Common sense had triumphed – a powerful and protective shield which she had raised for the right reasons.

CHAPTER 3

Day Two

'So there you are,' said Bror. 'I wondered where you'd gone.'

Jacket in hand, Kay swivelled round. Bror was advancing down the tiled passage to the place where the family's outdoor clothing hung on labelled pegs – in Denmark it was important to keep track of warm clothing.

'Goodness, you startled me,' she said.

He observed the jacket in her hand and the brogues on her feet. 'Isn't it an odd time to be going out?'

She glanced at the pegs with the neatly stowed jackets and coats. There was Tanne's Norwegian hat, Nils's green Norfolk jacket bought on a trip back to England, Bror's hunter's jacket.

It was astonishing how, once the mind was made up, the lies slid as easily off the tongue as her breakfast *ymer*. 'The dogs seem restless and I need a bit of fresh air.'

'Do they?' Bror was surprised. 'They were out for hours with me this morning.' He pointed to

26

the door at the end of the passage where the fanlight displayed the intensifying dusk. 'It's too dark and cold, Kay. Leave it for this evening. I'll take them out tomorrow.'

This was the Bror whom she knew so well – whose sweetness and gallantry she knew so well too.

'I don't think you understand. I want a little time to myself.'

He stuck his hands in his pockets, bent his fair head and seemed to be absorbed by the sight of his shoes. 'You can't remain angry with me, Kay. We have to be clever, both of us. Sooner or later you must accept the changes.' She was silent. Bror persisted. 'You're still very angry.'

Yes, she was.

She wanted to tell him that, since their conversation by the lake when Bror had told her the truth, something had changed between them. And something had changed in her, Kay, too. In doing what he had done, Bror had displaced the subtle balance of love and loyalty which had existed between them for so long.

She pulled on her jacket and buttoned it up, tight and hard. 'Yes. Very. Go back to your newspaper, Bror.'

In response, Bror reached behind her for his jacket. Hooking it off the peg, he said, 'I'm not letting you go out on your own. I'll come with you.'

★　★　★

The day after the København lunch, Kay rang Anton from the hall in Rosenlund. A fuzzy image of herself was reflected in the polished hall table while she talked – and it was as if she was watching a stranger. 'I've been thinking things over. A lot of things. Particularly what you told me about Bror.' She gathered her resolve. 'I need more chapter and verse.'

'Talk to him yourself.' Anton's voice sounded hollow down the line.

'Anton . . .'

Anton considered. 'I've got an appointment in Køge,' he said. 'Can you meet me there?'

It was done.

'Kay . . .' Before she put down the receiver, Anton sounded a warning. 'Remember what we agreed?' He was reminding her to say nothing. 'And, Kay, never talk on the phone.'

They met 'by chance' in Køge's main square.

It happened to be market day. Stalls lined the square and seethed with shoppers. Butchers were doing a good business as was the milk stall. Under a striped awning, the baker had laid out a display of Bror's favourite gingerbread which caught Kay's attention.

In uniform, Anton always presented a dapper sight. Out of it, he blossomed into elegance. Today, since he was on home territory, he had slung a cashmere coat over his suit and a red silk scarf round his neck. Beside this magnificence Kay, in her second-best grey flannel costume with a grey felt hat which dipped over one eye, felt less modish than previously. He kissed her in a more or less cousinly fashion and as he led her to a bench he remarked that the hat wasn't a patch on the Parisian one.

He watched her fiddle with her gloves and waited patiently for her to begin.

'Those pamphlets? What was in them?'

He frowned. 'Don't waste my time, Kay.'

'I wouldn't do that,' she said.

'All right. It was a list of commandments. Don't work for Germany; or if you do, work badly. Join the fight for freedom. We're trying to get the message out to the outlying rural areas.'

After the positive feelings that resulted from not accepting the pamphlets, it had come as a shock to Kay to discover how one small non-action – as small as not stretching out a hand to pick up a basket – could so profoundly unsettle her equilibrium. For it had.

She laced her gloved fingers together. 'Anton, you do understand . . .?'

But he wasn't interested in her protestations. 'The author was a brave man. He hid the copies in a room full of deadly bacteria in the Serum Institute and risked his life.'

'And the girl? What's happened to her?'

Anton shrugged. 'Not my business. Nor is it yours.'

What was done was done. Kay looked up and over to the canvas awnings flapping in the wind. 'Tell me more about this declaration or whatever it is.'

She knew perfectly well that she had fed Anton an opportunity to indulge in a little malice. He took it. 'How peculiar. You're always at pains to tell me that you two are as thick as thieves. Don't you and Bror . . . er, discuss?'

'That's the point. I can't ask him. He's still away until next week, seeing the cousins in Jutland. Anyway, even you can appreciate it is difficult for us . . . for me.'

'*Are* you serious, Kay?'

She bit her lip and looked away. The twenty-four hours which had elapsed since her lunch with Anton had seen a crack opening in her loyalties to Bror. 'Yes,' she said.

He shifted closer to her on the bench. 'To repeat what I said at our . . . our delightful lunch . . . After the initial relief that Denmark's occupation would be relatively peaceful, unlike that in France or Poland, many Danes are increasingly questioning the situation. We don't want violence but no one can fail to notice that the British and Americans are both fighting. "Why aren't we in the fight?" these Danes will ask. And "What can we do?"'

A man in a trilby hat stopped to light a cigarette. He glanced at Kay and Anton. Anton fell silent and waited until he was out of earshot.

Touching her arm, he said, 'In your case, you might think: But I'm British and therefore I'm in the fight, but I'm not sure how. Because of the peculiar Danish situation, it isn't clear-cut.'

A woman in stout boots and carrying two milk churns clanked past.

'The British have made it clear to our contacts that they are too tight-arsed to fund an underground army here but they would, nevertheless, like us to provide intelligence and do lots of lovely sabotage. Railways, bridges, factories . . . you can imagine. Naturally, there's a problem. Intelligence and sabotage aren't always compatible because sabotage triggers reprisals and muddies the waters for the intelligence-gatherers.'

She stared at the houses on the opposite side of the square, the autumn sun illuminating the rich reds and burnt siennas of the painted facades. 'Surely it won't make any difference as it's likely there will always be reprisals?'

Anton raised an eyebrow. 'Kay, you've missed your vocation. Listen . . . German troops are constantly in transit to and from Norway. The Nazis also need to maintain garrisons here in case the Allies invade through this route.' He allowed the last point to sink in. 'Granted, it's unlikely, but the Allies will invade one day, you know. The Germans also need to patrol the shipping routes bringing in the Norwegian minerals which they badly need. Bauxite for aluminium, for example. All of which makes them vulnerable.'

Her eyes narrowed.

She could imagine lines of German troops waiting for trains. Temperatures plummeting. Snow in piles. Breath steaming. Cigarette butts raining down. Grey-green uniforms. The men talking – Suisse Deutsch. Southern dialects. Prussian vowels. A babble. But maybe for those men . . . those boys . . . the Danish skies where the stars and planets burnt in the velvety black would be a reminder of home . . .?

'You've gone quiet, Kay.'

She stirred. 'The people you're talking about . . . they are brave.'

'Yes.' For once Anton sounded completely sincere.

'Like the girl on the platform.'

'Stop thinking about her.'

She realized then that she envied these unknown people – for their commitment and their immunity to fear which, on some level, they had to have.

'Kay, I want you to think about something. I don't want you to make up your mind, just to think about it. In a few days' time there will be someone who will need a safe house in the area and a place to hide his wireless transmitter. Do you know what that is?'

'To send messages?'

'Good girl. I just want to point out that there are plenty of potential hiding places at Rosenlund.'

Yes. Yes, there were. Hundreds.

How many rooms were there? She could never remember. How many outhouses?

It was possible to spend more than a day combing through the estate and still not be entirely sure that all of it had been covered. On first arriving at Rosenlund she had existed in a state of constant astonishment and it had taken her a couple of years to adjust to it.

Places to hide a clandestine wireless transmitter?

Kay turned to Anton. 'You love Rosenlund, don't you?'

Anton held out his cigarette case to Kay. She shook her head. He extracted one and lit up. 'Of course I love it. Wouldn't anyone?'

There were the outhouses – lots of them. There were the woods. And the workers' cottages, some of which were already empty because the men had left to work for the Reich.

She combed through the possibilities.

There was the house. Recently repainted in its customary soft ochre, its main rooms faced south towards the lake but others were tucked up under the eaves, or built along corridors infrequently used.

There was the garden. There was the avenue of limes which cast its lure to the walker: *Come down through me to the water's edge.*

There was the lake with Princess Sophia-Maria's island rising out of the winter's green-grey ice or the bright, hard clarity of the summer's blue spectrum. There was the island's summer house – a little decayed, smelling of winter mould and spring rain, rotting a little and home to spiders and their victims but, viewed from the shore, as pretty as a Fragonard fantasy.

If she brought in the bandits from the shadows . . . what then?

She glanced sideways at Anton. He was peacefully smoking his cigarette, one leg hooked over the other. Over the years, she had got him wrong. Maybe, maybe, she had got the other things wrong, too.

'I'll come with you,' Bror repeated. He was already buttoning up his jacket. 'It's too dark for you to be out on your own.'

The heat rose to her face and she turned her head away. 'Like I said, go and read your newspaper.'

But he gave her no choice and, in the end, she whistled up Sif and Thor, who hauled themselves reluctantly from their baskets.

'They don't look restless to me,' he remarked.

They left the house by the back door and walked around the kitchen garden. Kay urged that they should make for the lake. 'The moonlight on the water will make it easier to see where we're going,' she said.

Bror made no comment.

They were used to walking side by side: talking, sometimes linked together and usually with the dogs. Kay couldn't count the times she had only to turn her head and Bror would be there . . . on the cold days when their eyes and noses streamed, in the flat yellow summer sunshine, or on the midsummer nights when the sky was almost too crowded with stars.

They left the gardens behind and struck out along the rough path which was the alternative to the lime walk down to the lake. Sure-footed as ever, Bror set the pace. In the dark, he loomed large and solid.

For the first time ever, she wanted him gone.

Bror sensed her mood. 'You don't have to speak to me . . .' She could tell from his tone that there was a hint of a smile.

When they reached the lake's edge, Kay turned east towards the tongue-shaped wood and Sif and Thor, having woken from their torpor, foraged enthusiastically up ahead. Kay walked rapidly, managing to leave Bror in her wake, and as she neared the edge of the wood she whistled and the dogs came bounding up.

Bending down, she whispered in Thor's tensed, silky ear, 'Rabbits, go.'

The effect was immediate. Thor leaped crabwise, turned and raced along the shore, barking ferociously, with Sif in hot pursuit. The noise was exactly as Kay wished: fit to raise devils.

Bror caught up. 'You're exciting them for no reason.'

No reason?

She imagined the agent who might be mounting vigil among the trees – a man trained into living a secret life, carrying with him a clandestine wireless transmitter. If he was there, and she hoped he wasn't, he was probably cold and hungry and exhausted.

There was nothing she could do about it.

Would his training kick in at the sound of the

dogs? Would he conclude: *I am being warned and I'd better get out?*

'Sorry,' she said. 'What's the time, Bror?'

He squinted down at his large square watch. 'Sixish.'

Sounding more conciliatory, she said, 'Perhaps we should go back.'

He caught her by the shoulders and pulled her to him.

Then he let her go.

It was then Kay understood: Bror was desperate to convince her that what he was doing was right. He needed her on his side.

She fell into step beside him. Day Two was over.

CHAPTER 4

Bror had returned from the fishing trip on Jutland in the late afternoon just over a week after Kay's meeting with Anton in Køge's market place.

Halfway down the lime walk, Kay heard the sounds of his arrival. The dogs did, too, and they set up a howling before circling behind Kay and disappearing back to the house.

Kay did not follow them to greet him as she once might have done.

Instead, she continued down to the lake and stood and watched the water, which always gave her great delight. An eddy at the water's edge – stirred by the colony of eider duck which had landed further out towards the island – shook the pebbles in a frail replica of a tide.

Undecided, anxious, unsure . . . was she being sucked back and forth over the pebbles like the lake water?

The slanting autumn sun struck its surface and the ray split into shades of white and blue. Underneath, the stones were outlined with extraordinary clarity.

It wouldn't be long before Bror came to find her.

Correct. Five minutes or so later the dogs came pattering up and his figure could be seen walking down the lime walk. It was a matter of moments before he reached her, caught her up and kissed her.

'I'm back,' he said unnecessarily. 'Miss me?'

'Yes.'

Good at reading her, he took a cue from her expression. 'What's wrong?'

'I want to talk to you.'

Placing a finger under her chin, he up-tilted her face. 'Do that. It's been a long, lonely journey. Lots of spot checks. Soldiers all over the place. Not much to eat.'

How familiar he smelled with the mix of his cologne – ordered regularly from the shop in Berlin, for nothing else would do – the rough tweed of his jacket and just the lightest tang of male sweat.

She stepped away from him, which alerted him.

'I take it this is serious.'

England, she thought. *Bandits in the shadows.* 'Did you sign the Declaration?'

The blue eyes narrowed. 'Who've you been talking to?' There was a pause. 'I see, Anton.'

'Not exactly. Why didn't you tell me?'

'Anton should be less loose-tongued. He has an axe to grind and he likes to cause trouble.'

'What axe?'

Bror said in level tone. 'He's also a womanizer.'

'Are you seriously telling me Anton thinks he'll seduce me by telling me that?' She squared up to Bror. 'Why didn't you tell me?'

'Isn't it obvious?'

'No, it isn't. Make me understand this . . . Why have you sold us to the Nazis? I understand your feeling and affections for Germany. I share many of them. I like your Munich relations. I know my children have German blood in them and I have always been proud of it . . . but Hitler is mad. And so are the idiots around him. Actually, I take that back. They can't be idiots because they seem to be quite effective. But they're evil.'

Tails at full mast, the dogs shot out from a clump of bulrushes. Bror snapped his fingers at Sif. 'Down, girl.'

Kay turned away. 'Don't put us in the wrong, too. Think about the Americans having come in with the Allies. The situation can't be that bleak for you to do this, not as bleak as it was at the beginning of the war.'

'But they are bleak,' he said. 'We can't ignore it. Communists are being rounded up—'

'And you agree with all that?'

That angered him. 'Don't treat me like a fool, Kay.' He stuffed his hands into his pockets. 'Listen to me, the Reich is a very efficient machine, perhaps the most efficient the world has seen. It will win. We Danes have an advantage because the Nazis think we share in their Aryan brotherhood rubbish. I think we have to capitalize on it to save lives.'

Up in the sky, flying low, a plane screamed across the house and lake. The noise was ear-splitting . . . and, somehow, barbaric. Furiously, she pointed at it. 'Your friends.'

Bror didn't bother to look up. 'Well, let's hope for everyone's sake it isn't a British bomber.' He paused. 'We will have to get used to the noise of planes.'

In spring, the patch of bulrushes which the dogs had taken themselves into was ring-fenced for the nesting birds, but now, in autumn, the huge spiky seed cases were stiffening in the cold. Bending down, Bror traced the outline of a seed head. 'I've signed the Declaration of Goodwill to the Occupier. The Minister of Agriculture drafted it and asked the landowners to endorse it.' He straightened up. 'I did it to protect you, the children, Rosenlund.' He was addressing her back. Almost pleading. 'It will keep us safe, Kay.'

At that, she turned and grabbed the lapels of his jacket. 'But you didn't consult me! I would never have said yes. Never.' She tugged hard. '*Why* didn't you ask me?'

'I didn't because it's difficult for you.' Kay was silent. 'Do I need to point it out? I wanted to spare you.'

She pushed him away and stamped her foot down hard. A shower of grit rose and pattered back to earth.

'Think about it, Kay. The minute war was declared we, the Danes, lost half our export market – our market with the British. How do we make it up? We have to eat and earn money. There's always the risk of social unrest if trade and production fall. People will starve. The Germans want our food, our meat, our expertise. That need will keep Denmark going until the war is over.'

'If the Nazis are beaten, your name will be on that document, Bror.' A piece of grit had fallen into her shoe and she concentrated on its sharp sting.

'Here . . .' He had noticed. 'Lean on me.' Kay unlaced the shoe, took it off and knocked out the grit. Bror continued: 'The community has to survive and I have to try to make sure it does. Not taking extreme positions will serve us better.'

She shoved her foot back into the shoe and knelt down. 'What about German morality? You can't just march about Europe invading every country that takes your fancy.' The bow wouldn't tie and she yanked at the laces.

'You British are special . . .' He was stepping carefully but not carefully enough. 'But you're islanders, Kay, and it influences how you see the rest of the world. The Germans and the British are always at each other's throats. Danes are more practical and less ambitious in that respect. We prefer to endure and put our heads down.'

The soil under her knee was brown and green, and strewn with pebbles, but they blurred with

41

the onset of her fury. Whipping to her feet, she said: 'Do you know what you have just done?'

'You're going to tell me.'

Her voice shook. 'You've just told me I don't belong here. But I've lived here longer than I lived in England. Remember that.'

'Kay . . .'

Bror put out a hand to restrain her but she dodged out of reach. Turning on her heel, she left him gazing over the flat, shiny water.

It was easy enough to avoid him for the rest of the day. Inviting herself to supper with an artist who was currently renting a cottage in Køge and with whom she had made friends, she made sure she was out of the house until bedtime as well.

Returning home at ten-thirty or so, she went straight upstairs to their pretty yellow-and-white bedroom. There she sat at the dressing table brushing her hair with hard, determined sweeps that set her teeth on edge.

Bror entered.

She glanced up. Ignoring her protest, he prised the brush away. 'My job, I think.'

When he brushed her hair, there was no need for explanations, or even talk. She had learned the signs. Short, sharp strokes indicated Bror was agitated – probably something to do with the farms or the house. Slow, hypnotic ones told her all was well. Often, the brushing of Kay's hair was the signal he wanted her.

By the same token, if Kay held herself stiffly, or

did not respond, he knew he had reparations to make. If she relaxed – easing back against the chair – he might abandon his task to kiss her neck.

These were the signals between them which made up a coded language they both understood. It contained their marital world: their jokes and teases, their angers, their desire for one another and, until recently, their mutual understanding.

She closed her eyes. Bror was so gentle – but then he always was with animals, with children, with her.

Drawing the bristles through the long, blonde strands, he said at last, 'Kay, it's war and we have Tanne and Nils to consider.'

'Oh, so it isn't Rosenlund that's your main concern?'

He slapped the brush down on the glass top of the dressing table.

'Do you mean to be so childish?'

She picked up the brush and pressed it back into his hand. 'Then don't tell me I don't belong here. Ever.'

It was Bror's turn to apologize. 'I was clumsy.'

'Thank you.' He caught up a handful of her hair and she asked in a low voice: 'Have you any idea how you hurt me?'

'Very much, I expect.' He teased the brush through a lock of hair – and the strokes seemed to replicate themselves up and down her body. He shifted closer. 'You and I must decide how to get through the war. Together.'

She got to her feet and folded back the lace-edged top sheet on the bed. The under sheet was pulled taut and inviting over the softest mattress topping that Denmark could manufacture. She looked up at him. 'Yes, we must.' She removed her dressing gown. 'But you have made it difficult.'

Bror shrugged. 'That's the burden I shall have to carry. I couldn't do otherwise.'

'Not even for me?'

'It was for you. And the children.'

She stared at him. 'But we have to think about the bigger issues.'

He sat down on the edge of the bed. 'Survival is a very big issue and I know you'll say, "But not survival at any price", and it's a good argument. We've never had to face starvation, or brutal retribution, and others do, but we have a duty to survive, too. Kay . . .' He was sad, sorry, determined, reasonable, and, suddenly, much older. 'Don't think I haven't thought about it. It's far harder to take what some might consider the coward's path.' He looked down at his clasped hands and said simply, 'I know that's what you think.'

There was a long, horrible silence.

Do I help Anton? Do I not?

Coward.

'Come here, Kay.'

After a moment, she obeyed. He stood up and began to ease off her nightdress.

'No,' she said, resisting. 'Not while we're like this.'

44

'Please,' he said. 'Let us try. It's a way of understanding.'

They knew so well how they both responded, and what they wanted from each other. This time, Bror was determined to make her part of who he was and what he felt for her – and she slipped into the old pleasures, as she had done so many times.

At the finish, however, Kay was no clearer on what to do.

Bror raised himself up onto an elbow. 'Kay, please remember . . .' He was searching for the right nuance. '. . . it hasn't just been me and Rosenlund. It's been you, too. You've been part of it and I couldn't have done it without you. We've been a partnership.'

' "Why aren't we in the fight?" these Danes will ask. And "What can we do?" ' reiterated Anton in her ear.

She turned her head on the pillow to look at him and the lazy, sensual, miasmic aftermath of sex disappeared. To her distress, she was looking at a man she wasn't sure she recognized. 'A war changes people and things. Bror . . . you signing the Declaration has changed the situation . . . That's what I feel . . .' She twisted the sheet between her fingers. 'I won't mention it again but, if we are to be truthful, I must say.'

He rolled over and kissed her. It was a rough, hard gesture. 'And you not supporting me,' he pointed out. 'That changes things, too.'

After he fell asleep, Kay remained awake, her

fingers bunched up into her palms. War had a long reach. Being innocent of what that meant did not spare anyone from its malignity. Bror had never disappointed her, never let her down . . . never let anyone down as far as she knew. Now, he had.

She must deal with it.

Her imaginings were as vivid and disturbing as they usually were in the small hours. She brooded over her weeping mother, the beatings, the violence, the Nazis' rape and pillage, the death of decency. In particular, she thought of the young girl standing on a platform on a railway station with her death warrant by her feet.

The mind could not absorb too much at once – or, at least, not hers. Picking through the pros and cons, she reminded herself that any big decision was riddled with conflict and, possibly, contradictions. When fear of being caught had to be added to the mix then . . . then the terrors and complications threatened to be overwhelming.

Early the next morning Anton telephoned and caught Kay at her most fatigued and fragile. 'I need help,' he said. 'You're my last resort. I was going to send flowers to someone but she's gone away. They are so beautiful that I don't want to waste them. Can I send them to you?'

Irresolute, she clutched the telephone receiver.

'Kay . . .?' Anton adopted the wooing tone. 'They will go to waste.'

Bror's pragmatism wasn't enough.

Bandits operating in the shadows.

46

She heard herself say in a perfectly normal voice: 'How lovely.'

'I'm not quite sure when. It could be tomorrow, or one of the following two days,' he said. 'Just as soon as I can get hold of the gardener. He usually manages to deliver things between five and six p.m. But if he hasn't after three days, then he won't because the flowers will be past their best.' There was a pause. 'By the way, darling, the birches down by the lake look very fine this year, particularly those just by the oak. You know the one.' There was another pause. 'I meant to ask you the other day if you've read Steinbeck's *The Moon is Down*? You should, it's very good, even in translation. Do ask your visitors about it and see if I'm right.'

The following afternoon, a bouquet of autumn blooms in arterial reds, marmalades and the deep black-red of a dahlia arrived for Kay.

Their spicy, piquant scent hinted of soil and sun, which never failed to delight Kay. She bore them off to the vase room and, while she arranged them, she tried to make sense of the intelligence which Bror had given her over the telephone.

One agent coming in. Wait for up to three days in the birch wood by the oak tree. The password is . . .

One by one, she placed the flowers into a glass vase. Catching up the black dahlia, she rolled it between finger and thumb and realized its stem was thicker than the others.

She understood.

Her fingers shook as she unwrapped the piece

47

of paper folded tightly round the stem and read: *Darling Freya, you have forsaken me for Felix.*

It was signed: *Odin.*

Carefully, she inserted the dahlia into the arrangement.

Her name was Freya.

By Day Three, she was better organized.

She had boots and a thick jacket, plus the torch. Letting herself out of the kitchen wing, she made her way down to the lake by the path she and Bror had taken on Day Two. It was the best route because it had the virtue of being out of sight of the house.

This time, she had made sure that Birgit served tea to Bror in the office, where he was labouring over accounts. 'Plenty of gingerbread,' she instructed Birgit. 'And make sure you refill the pot.'

Even a thicker jacket provided no real barrier to the cold snaking through her body. She tightened its belt. Soon, all too soon, the sun would disappear from the land and winter darkness would lock down over Denmark.

Then the real cold would arrive, catching Jutland, Zealand, Funen, Lolland and the hundreds of other islands in its icy grip. It would drive roots deep into buildings, into the sea, into the earth, and it would colonize water. As it intensified, ice fantasies would build, crystal by crystal, in rivers and streams and, under the freezing onslaught, even the toughest trees would stoop in homage to the cold.

Making stealthy progress through the trees, Kay kept a check on the time. Every so often she stopped to take stock. A deer startled in the under-growth crashed away, insects scuttled over the leaf fall. Halting finally at a curve in the path where three birches grew close to an elderly oak, she settled to wait.

What was that?

Three days of vigil. Had they sapped her courage and resolve? Had they strengthened them?

Five-thirty.

In the undergrowth there was movement. A twig snapped.

Kay held her breath.

A figure wheeling a bicycle materialized out of the darkness.

She breathed out.

He was tall, as tall as Bror, and whippet thin. As he drew closer, she could see that he was young, early thirties perhaps, and dressed in worker's overalls.

The figure stopped, hands clasped tight around the handlebars. 'What are you reading?'

The voice was hoarse and tired.

She couldn't answer immediately – for she was struggling with a sense of unreality. Pulling herself into order, she managed: 'Steinbeck's *The Moon is Down*.'

'Freya.'

'Felix, welcome.'

CHAPTER 5

For Felix – not his real name but he almost preferred it to Kasper – this rendezvous was the culmination of a profound change of heart, of philosophy, of a way of life.

Two years ago, as a committed pacifist, he was pursuing an ordered and predictable existence. Now he couldn't even be sure that he still had a life ahead of him. No one could have any illusions: doing what he was doing dramatically shortened life expectancy.

The morning on which the Nazis invaded Denmark, he and Jette, his girlfriend, were in bed in her København flat.

A neighbour banged on the door. 'Get up, the Germans are here.'

Jette didn't stir. Hers was always the deepest of sleeps.

Padding in bare feet over to the window, Kasper, as he then was, looked out. Scattered across the pavements and the square opposite were handfuls of leaflets which had been dropped by aircraft. One of them rested on the window ledge and he grabbed it. It was German propaganda and the message was clear: *accommodate, adjust, cooperate.*

Sitting down on the edge of the bed, he observed the tousled, unconscious Jette. Reaching over, he woke her and told her the news. Later on, they listened to the wireless and heard the announcement that the Danish Government was prepared to accept and to work with the new Protectorate.

'Kasper, don't look like that.' Jette was boiling water for much-needed coffee. 'We'll survive. We'll just keep our heads down and carry on as before. You have houses to build. With your status, it doesn't matter who the government is.'

She was complimenting him, the award-winning architect he had become after hard thinking and hard work . . . the architect who specialized in light, airy, practical social housing conceptually light years away from traditional Danish design.

'You believe that?'

She poured the water over the coffee grains. 'If you're a true democrat you can't reject the vast majority. The Danes want peace and the government has ensured that they have it.'

In her white wool blouse, pleated green skirt and a necklace of tiny glass beads, Jette looked so clean, so neat . . . so immovable. In that moment, irrationally, and certainly unfairly, for his beliefs on non-violence were as strong as hers, Kasper hated her.

'So you don't mind what has happened, Jette?'

A thoughtful person, she took time to answer.

'Of course I *mind*. But I'll live with it. So will you.'

The coffee grounds sifted through the boiling water to the bottom of the pot and Kasper reflected on Denmark's military weakness, on the geographical impossibility of fighting and on the two hundred and more Danes who lived on the border in North Schleswig, who would suffer if there was trouble.

'I'll live with it.'

The words did not sit easily on the tongue.

Later, he found they had spread like an ink stain. They were whispered in the office, on site, in his inner ear when in bed with Jette. They were repeated in other ways and in other places by those whose manner varied from the angry and resigned to the smug or subversive. Yet the unease grew.

Poor Jette. As Kasper was dragged increasingly into his preoccupation with the war, his temper shortened.

She tried to make sense of the puzzle Kasper now presented.

'I don't understand you, Kasper. I don't . . .'

Question to himself: why was he spending more and more time with the groups whose aim was to create 'a just anger' against the occupation, especially as quite a few in the groups were writing and printing underground literature? One of them – dark, Jewish and far too thin – asked Felix to help distribute them. Which he did.

'Living with the status quo,' he explained to the bewildered Jette, 'does not mean you approve.'

Question: why was he talking to those who had contacts with the tiny, still shaky, resistance in Denmark? And why was he so interested in the whispered accounts of escapes to Sweden and London?

Question: why was his vocabulary expanding to include words such as 'sabotage', 'infiltration'?

He was learning how powerful the unconscious was when it desired its own way – how it pushed and prodded. He went out of his way to seek out examples of Nazi brutality and repression. When fighting broke out in the København streets, he rushed to observe. When his friend, a communist journalist, was thrown into the Vestre prison, he bribed a guard to let him visit and came away seriously disturbed by what he had seen.

One morning in the spring of 1942, he woke up and told Jette that he was leaving.

She turned a gaze drenched in misery on Kasper. 'It's someone else.'

'No.'

She pulled together the tattered remnants of pride and her always predominant desire to be rational: 'If you go now you will never come back.'

He took in the peachy skin, the silky hair, the kind earnest expression, the anguish which lay under it. A mixture of relief that the matter had been brought to a head, guilt at the relief, affection and a giddy-making sensation of liberation, rooted in his chest. 'I understand.'

Half an hour later he let himself out of her apartment. She stood on tiptoe to kiss him goodbye. 'You've changed. You're not the man I first knew.'

Within days he had shut down the architectural practice, sold his flat and deposited the money in the bank. Instinct told him to cover his tracks, and Kasper observed it by cycling to Frederikshavn, where he bought a passage in a fishing smack over the Øresund. Once in Sweden, he made contact with 'Richard' in Stockholm, a fellow Dane to whom he had been directed by the daughter of his old professor. Richard, he was told, could put him on a plane to London to meet 'certain' people.

Richard was cautious. He wanted to know who Kasper was, what were his motives and contacts, and he forced him to kick his heels for a week while he ran a check. 'Don't speak to anyone while you're here and do your best to be unobtrusive. Spies are like rabbits in Stockholm, and it's impossible to tell which is which.' He grimaced. 'Most of them are probably double agents anyway. We'll get you out when a decision has been made.'

Then it was all systems go.

With masterly understatement, Richard warned Kasper of the rigours of the flight. 'You'll be rammed up the bum of a British Mosquito for the duration. Since the Luftwaffe also use the airport, it can be a bit tricky getting you on board but it shouldn't be too bad. It'll be bloody cramped. Use the oxygen mask. You can get brain damage at that altitude.'

'Who will I be meeting?'

'Can't answer that, old chap. You'll have to trust me, Kasper.'

That was the last time he answered to his real name.

Funny that. He didn't miss it.

As soon as the Mosquito landed he was bundled into a car and driven to London. Still groggy, he peered out of the window, sorting out impressions. His parents divorced when he was ten, and his mother fled from Odense to England, where she married an Englishman. The result was that he was shuttled between Britain and Denmark as a teenager, and he became familiar with England and London. Peacetime London, anyway: the prosperous and bourgeois one, smugly grand in places and more or less clean, if smudged with tar and smoke.

King's Cross, Marylebone Road . . .

Clearly, the war had changed the city in subtle, and not so subtle, ways. Two years into conflict, the dirty, pocked streets spilled out their innards and heaps of rubble lay all over the place. There was what he could only describe as a rot, miasmic and despairing.

The car crawled through the streets, swerving to avoid the potholes and the patches of water seeping from fractured water mains, and he longed for something reassuring, even a coffee, a good coffee. But that, as he later discovered, was nigh-on impossible in England.

Having arrived at his destination, he began the process of initiation into The Firm. 'Your name is Felix,' he was told. 'You will answer to no other.' At a series of meetings he was addressed by the heads of the intelligence, signals and Danish sections. Their briefings had been, more or less, unanimous.

Our organization specializes in the unorthodox and clandestine . . . Our approach is unusual, unconventional thinking is our point, and it is so secret that total silence is demanded of you.

He learned that there had been very little undercover activity in Denmark to date. A couple of radio operators had been smuggled in with their sets earlier in the year but both had gone silent. The worst was feared.

What we want you to do, Felix, is to light a flame of Danish resistance and stoke it into a sodding great bonfire.

He warned them of the extreme difficulties of operating under a puppet government with legions of informers on all sides.

To their credit, the section heads listened with care, then they issued their directives.

We will train you, and then you will go and do something about it.

So far, only the communists had made real efforts to resist and they paid the price by being frequently rounded up. To make headway, Felix would need to build alliances and coalitions with them.

Do deals with the Reds, make a few promises but don't offer too much . . .

Wasn't that just like normal politics? He would have to find ways of burrowing into an acquiescent population. Of course, it might prove to be easier than he estimated now the Nazis were busy draining the country of its meat and dairy, and pinching the able-bodied men to work in German factories.

After his induction in London, Felix was sent for training to a number of Special Training Schools, the STSs, run by The Firm.

One of his first tasks was to learn Morse code. That had been a pig. In The Firm's slang, Felix was not a natural 'pianist'. 'Pity you're not musical,' observed the Morse instructor. 'The musical ones do best.'

Forced to practise hard and often, tapping out the rhythms on any flat service, he found his dreams were invaded by its staccato bleeps.

'--..,-.--,.-' This was his call sign: ZYA. It belonged to him, and to him alone. He would use it to contact the Home Station, back at base.

ZYA.

Home Station allocated times for agents to make contact, and he'd been told that whenever his scheduled call, his 'sked', was due, the signals clerk allocated to him at Home Station would patrol the airwaves, waiting patiently for him to transmit his call sign. It would be a moment of trust, of faith that the letters oscillating through the frequencies were precise and faithful to the message.

A signals clerk would have no idea who Felix was, or where he was, and the not knowing was a requisite for this shadow existence. In fact, by the time The Firm had finished with Felix – driven its tentacles into his psyche and changed the patterns of his thoughts – he'd been hard put to know who he was as well.

Going into the field meant that an agent carried several identities stacked one on top of the other. Felix's call sign was ZYA but his code name, the one he would use to transmit his messages, was Mayonnaise. His field name was Felix – the name he would be known by as he worked to build resistance in Denmark. He was also in possession of a couple of aliases, complete with identity papers sewn into the lining of his jacket.

There was much to take in.

Learn every detail we've given you. Your birthplace, your background, your uncles, your first woman, your pet rabbit. This is not a joke.

So it was that, as a fully trained undercover agent working for what was known as The Firm, Felix found himself being driven by a FANY to a secret airfield somewhere in England. From there he would be parachuted back home into Denmark.

His right hand beat out a tattoo on the leather armrest: - -..,-.- -,.-

58

The FANY had dark hair bundled up under a cap and the back of her neck was clean, pearly with youth and inviting. Who was she? One of the hand-picked girls who were trained by the under-cover services to help with practical matters, to drive, courier and God knew what else. At the STSs, FANYs – the initials stood for First Aid Nursing Yeomanry, a hark back to the First World War – were everywhere. They were polite, even-tempered, necessary. Trained into absolute discretion, too. Neither she of the pearly neck, nor he, would talk on the journey other than in the barest of exchanges.

The car blinds had been pulled down but not quite far enough and, here and there, he caught flashes of buildings. Felix peered out to witness the weary and dun-looking population picking its way around the rubble in the street. Back to their homes? Out for the night? He spared a thought for the inconvenience and exhaustion of shopping, keeping clean, travelling . . . These were the topics he used to consider when he dreamed up onto paper his light and airy houses, back in the life which he had left behind.

At the final meeting with the chiefs, he had been given an unequivocal and bleak picture.

There is some activity on Jutland. We've managed a couple of arms drops there but not much else.

In the driver's seat, the FANY jabbed her foot on the brake. 'Sorry, sir,' she said as they jerked to a halt. 'Pothole.' She added, 'It wasn't there yesterday.'

Having headed north for approximately an hour the FANY turned right and drove along the road which, so pitted was it, clearly led to hell. The car axle shrieked in protest and the wheels rattled. Next, they appeared to be in an ordinary field with a farmhouse and a barn beside it. However, to their left, an aircraft taxiing down a runway suggested that this was no typical farm. The growl of its engines split the night's silence. A uniformed man emerged from the farmhouse, introduced himself as Felix's dispatching officer and ushered him inside the barn.

Inside, equipment was stacked on shelves lining the walls and a fire burned in the grate. A group of men checked over piles of stuff on the table.

'Now then,' said the dispatching officer, issuing Felix with overalls and a parachute. 'Here we go.'

There were a couple of other 'Joes' waiting to go in with Felix. Both Danish. The first was tall and sandy-haired, with the kind of flat features which Felix disliked. He gave the barest of greetings before demanding a drink and then a second, and paid no further attention to Felix. The second Joe appeared to be a different kettle of fish. Short, with thinning hair, slightly bandy-legged, he was nothing to look at. Schoolmaster or a clerk in an obscure ministry? Or something like that. Would he handle anxiety and fear well? He was not in the least heroic-looking, rather the reverse, cutting an unremarkable, almost anonymous figure.

Paradoxically, despite his obvious jumpiness and a dry little cough, he looked a better bet for the undercover life than his nervy companion.

Curious. The little man with his dry cough was the kind of person whom Felix found himself wishing to protect. Security reasons forbidding them to share their field names, they exchanged code names. 'Mine is Vinegar.' He trilled an arpeggio up Felix's sleeve with his fingers.

He was telling Felix he was a pianist. Well, that was two of them, at least. The section heads had promised that they would send in more pianists as soon as they could train them, but couldn't make any promises as to when that would be possible.

They warmed their bums in front of the fire, and having been chilly on the drive this made Felix almost too hot.

'I would kill for a drink,' Vinegar confided to Felix, 'but I daren't.' They were speaking in Danish. 'Are you scared?'

'Yes. You?'

'Shitless.' Vinegar articulated the word with great precision. He pointed to the third Joe patrolling the barn entrance with an empty glass clutched in his hand. 'So's that one. But he's choosing to drink instead of owning up.'

Felix smiled. Vinegar was nice.

The dispatching officer was professionally cheerful. 'No need to worry, you've got a top-hole pilot. The best. He'll fly just above the water and

61

Jerry won't clock you. Makes the old bus skim like a bird. Not many can do that.'

Ten minutes later they were led out to the waiting Halifax.

The dispatching officer had spoken with a forked tongue. It was a tricky journey flying low over the Skagerrak. They were crammed into the plane's fuselage. No leg room. Bodies rigid and the plane creaking and shuddering like a haunted house. Wrapped in shock-absorbent Koran fibre, the wireless sets – Felix's and Vinegar's – swung like demented pendulums from the strut to which they had been strapped.

Felix could make out Vinegar across the cramped space. As pianists, they had even more in common. To wit: their life expectancies were short. Less than short.

Both of them knew it.

He had just closed his eyes when the pilot made a ninety-degree turn and sent him crashing into Vinegar. Not a good move. Vinegar groaned, retched and vomited into a bag.

The smell was awful and it wasn't just the vomit. Petrol. Sweat. Flatulence. Stale burned-engine odours.

Sweat slid down between Felix's buttocks but his skin was as cold as ice.

Vinegar was glassy and sweating, too, like a pig. 'Sorry,' he murmured. 'Not what was ordered.'

Vinegar retained his precise inflection despite his palpable fear, which Felix judged to be of the knee-knocking, bowel-loosening variety. He cursed silently. That sort of fear was infectious and he didn't wish to catch it.

Again, without warning, the Halifax lurched upwards.

A shout through the speaker tube: 'Tracer flak. Hold on.'

A corkscrew dive.

Predictably, Vinegar was sick again. Afterwards, he pulled his knees up to his chin and bowed his head. He was a picture of wretchedness. Felix and the third Joe managed to keep sitting upright.

'For Christ's sake,' mouthed the dispatching sergeant into the speaker tube. 'Not so low. We're about to hit the water.'

Up they went again. This time in a scuddery ride across the sky towards the target drop zone.

The red light snapped on.

The dispatching sergeant hooked up the static lines of each of them in turn and jabbed Felix in the ribs to indicate what he had done. 'Ready?' Then he lined up the containers which would go in after the parachutists.

The light flared into green.

Vinegar jumped first. A small mercy, given the state of his stomach. His set was pushed out behind him.

Next out was the third Joe who disappeared into the night sky.

Don't forget what we have tried to ram into your heads . . .

The dispatching sergeant's hand pressed down onto his shoulder. 'It's a go,' was screamed into his ear.

A push.

Jumping.

My God, he was jumping . . .

The cold, heavy air slapped away the stinks of the Halifax but the shapes rearing up towards him were more menacing than he remembered from training, the slap and whine of the air in his ears was magnified to a louder roar and the tug on the parachute when he landed was tougher to control.

Moonlight splayed over the turf where he found himself, flat out and tangled up in lines, and he smelled mud and cold grass and just a whiff of brine. Raising his head, he spotted his wireless set with its parachute streaming out like a Portuguese man-of-war. The seconds spun by. Disorientated, head swimming, he thought: *I am home.*

A couple of figures pelted towards him.

Training kicked in. Felix scrabbled for the harness straps and hauled in the parachute. There was no sign of Vinegar or the third Joe.

'Welcome,' the first figure said as he loped up. 'I'm "Jorgen".' He grabbed at the parachute and helped Felix to roll it up. 'We have to get going. The police are moving in. A *stikker* has tipped them off.'

No time for passwords. No time for thinking. Felix was hustled towards the van parked at the edge of the field.

'The others?'

'Wind got them. We think they've landed a mile or so back. A couple of the men have gone to pick them up.'

At the very least, he needed to know if Vinegar and his set were safe. 'Can we check on them?'

'No,' said Jorgen. 'Don't you understand?'

Two other men loaded the wireless set into the van, hoisted in the containers with the guns and explosives which had come down safely with it, and shoved Felix inside. His legs and torso smarted from the hard landing. The engine choked into life.

He leaned out and said to Jorgen, 'Let me know about the other two. It's important.'

Jorgen ignored him. 'Hurry,' he said to the driver. Then he turned to Felix. 'You've been away too long, *ven*. Can't hang around. Everywhere is riddled with *stikker*. You can't trust anyone.' He added with menace: 'The fuckers.'

CHAPTER 6

The A Mark II* wireless set. Three compartments – receiver, transmitter and power supply – complete with headset, the crystal plus a spare, eight fuses, a screwdriver and sixty feet of antenna wire. The total weight when packed into a suitcase was approximately twenty pounds.

Felix looked at it. What had The Firm's boffins been thinking when they constructed this one? Not only was it cumbersome, but there was nothing quite as obvious as a man in wartime carrying a heavy-looking case.

But he had to deal with it. Having landed in the south of Funen, he was aiming to make for a safe house in Køge run by 'Jacob'. From there he would make contact with 'Freya'.

Making his way east, he needed his wits and his training as he was passed down the resistance line – men and women who fed him, sheltered him and handed him onwards – always heading towards Køge and the rendezvous. It took over a week. Days when he experienced fear and distrust – how could he not? – and became reacquainted with profound loneliness. It would be, The Firm's instructors promised him, an education in the ways of the self.

Do you trust yourself, sonny? Do you believe in yourself?

They knew what they were talking about.

He reached Køge in one piece. A skim of porridge ice was shuffling over the sluggish sea around the port, creaking and groaning with the currents. A thicket of masts poked up inside the harbour. Berthed boats thudded and clinked with the ebb and flow of the water. Apart from a solitary tanker out on the horizon, the sea was empty of vessels.

He permitted himself a moment to gaze up the coast towards København, only a short train journey away. Once he had established the Køge network, he would dig in there.

Back in London, Felix had been briefed on Jacob, who would be his main contact in the area. Jacob was unmarried and lived alone, which sounded ideal. But you could never be sure.

'Give me a percentage of how trustworthy Jacob is?' he demanded of the briefing officer.

'Reports are good. But you can only go so far with reports. Up to you to judge.'

The question of trust – how much, how little, where, was it plentiful or in short supply, had it run out? – had become everyday currency. It added a depth and provocation to the thought processes.

Located on the western outskirts of Køge, Jacob's cottage was a traditional building of the type Felix knew so well from his upbringing in Odense, with a slate roof and a large gable. On entering a small downstairs room, he was hit by a familiar stew of smells: tobacco, old rope, wet wool, a hint of sealing wax, wood smoke. In the rudimentary kitchen there were whiffs of salt fish, grease and rancid oil for the lamps – the things necessary for survival. But over and above these was the stink of what he knew so well from his work: grinding poverty, the elements of which he had striven to eradicate in his modern designs. The only thing from that childhood home which was missing in this cottage was the primitive odour of his own fear of his father, who had beaten Felix regularly as he grew up.

Jacob turned out to be in his early twenties: a fair-skinned acne sufferer, thin to the point of emaciation. Over a rough and ready meal of herring and bread, he brought Felix up to date. German and British aircraft had been busy in the skies, propaganda was being dropped by the British, Køge was riddled with *stikker*, local bus services were pretty much suspended and only the rich could afford petrol.

Felix got the message. Jacob was a communist who wanted to make it clear that Felix was the outsider. Still, he had courage and principle and gratitude was due to him.

Later, Jacob showed him the bicycle Felix could use. 'Do you know where you're going?'

Before he left the final training school, Felix had studied the map and the briefing notes.

Rosenlund. Three miles west of Køge. An estate of approximately 3,000 acres with the house at its centre, plus lake with wood.

Further intelligence revealed that lack of public transport ensured it was pretty much isolated, which made it ideal for Felix's purposes.

'Don't get caught with a map,' Jacob said, opening the chest under the window. 'Maps are hard to find, and if you do get caught with one the police will assume you're a terrorist and hand you over to the *Gestapomen*.' He shoved over an oilskin, a jacket and overalls. 'Take these.'

'Thanks.' The overalls were too short and smelled of sweat and God-knew-what. But they would do.

When Jacob went to fetch something else, Felix shrugged off his jacket and whipped out his penknife. Slitting open the cuff of the right-hand sleeve, he extracted a leather pouch and checked the contents. Ten diamonds.

Bloody guard with your life. They're White Africans and a couple are four carat.

The Danish section chief had been precise in his instructions. Again and again, Felix had been made to run through the names of contacts in København to whom he could sell them, then bank the money and use it to fund operations.

He readied himself. It was then Jacob sprang a surprise. Emerging from the lean-to by the cottage's back door, he thrust at Felix a leather box into which air vents had been cut. 'Pigeons. They were dropped a day ago.'

'What the—?' Felix eyed the box. 'I wasn't told anything about pigeons.'

Jacob wasn't having any of that. 'Apparently your contact is expecting them. I can't deal with them. The drop yesterday has stirred everything up locally so you would be wise to use them for messages until things have settled down again.'

The bicycle was a boneshaker. With the pigeons stowed in the basket under some carrots and cabbage leaves and the wireless set strapped onto the back he felt conspicuous in a bad way. 'Poor devils,' he informed the pigeons. 'Your life isn't your own. Neither is mine.'

A wind sliced into his cheek. Even the oilskin offered no real protection against the chill and he was taking time to warm up. Above him Mars was making its early evening debut. The ash trees, the larches, the wind in the pines, the flat fields and the shrieks of the birds . . . these elemental pieces of Denmark were seeded into the workings of his body and spirit. Without question, this was his country, and with every step, with every rattling cold breath he took into his lungs he was repossessing it.

He was beginning to feel better.

The journey to Rosenlund took longer than expected. His bloody fault. At a crucial junction, he forked right instead of left and was forced to retrace his route. So much for the map study. Half an hour into the agreed waiting period, he slipped into the Rosenlund estate via the gate and pedalled alongside the wood. When the lake came into sight, he dismounted and wheeled the bicycle into the tree cover. The pigeons protested at the jolting. 'Shut up,' he told them. All the same, he took pity, slinging the box around his neck to give them a softer ride.

He knew from the map that the wood formed a tongue-shaped clump which ran parallel to the lake. Cautiously – checking, always checking, to the right, to the left, over his shoulder – he manoeuvred through the trees.

Contact: Freya.

London told him that she had been set up by 'Odin' but nothing much more was known. She had to be taken on trust.

A glint of water through the trees rewarded him. So, too, did the figure of a woman waiting between three birches and the solid block of an oak. He clasped the handlebars tight. 'What are you reading?'

She didn't reply at once and Felix had a bad moment. Then she said: 'Steinbeck's *The Moon is Down*.' The answer sounded unpractised and there was a hint of a foreign inflection.

He breathed out a long breath. *Thank God.*

They sized each other up. She, awkward and, clearly, feeling her way.

'I'm sorry I took so long.'

'My instructions were to wait for three days.' She was sounding more confident. 'Then abandon it. I had almost given you up.'

He detected a note of regret. 'I've just made it, then.'

'We'll have to wait until the estate workers have finished their work and gone home . . .'

Again, he detected hesitancy. He propped the bicycle against a tree and settled the birds against his chest. 'It's cold.'

Unusually for him, a veteran of the Odense winters, the cold was bothering Felix. Perhaps it was tiredness? The instructors had warned of how low temperatures and too little sleep cranked the body down into second gear and sapped morale.

She glanced upwards. 'The snow is on its way. I hate to think it won't be warm again until spring. That's the worst thing. Not like—' She didn't finish the sentence.

He suddenly realized that she wasn't Danish. The foreign inflection had given her away, and he took a bet with himself that she had been going to say: *Not like England.*

He squinted down at her. Tall, forty-three, possibly forty-five, wearing woollen trousers, a belted suede jacket plus fur-lined boots. It crossed his mind that it wasn't fair that Freya looked fit and healthy while English women were battling with rationing. It kept them slender enough, but the lack of cream and butter meant that their hair didn't shine nor their skin glow. Plus, those battling English women had to make do with skimpy and badly fitting clothes.

'The pigeons . . .' He directed his thoughts on to the business in hand. 'Were you expecting them?'

'Ant—' She corrected herself. 'Odin sent me a second message after I got the one about you, warning me about them.' She didn't elaborate but glanced at her watch. 'Not long now. Leave the bicycle.' She crept forward to the point where the trees gave way to a stony shore.

Felix checked his Browning pistol in his jacket pocket, unloaded the wireless set, laid the bicycle down flat between two tree trunks and adjusted the strap of the pigeon box over his shoulder.

He edged forward.

Freya's hand shot out and stopped him in his tracks. 'Don't move.'

No need to be told twice.

For someone starved of feminine company, the voice in his ear was liquid honey. 'It's one of our farm workers taking the short cut home.'

Who was she?

Don't ask. That was the rule.

It hadn't taken more than a day undercover for Felix to discover that some of the rules talked up by Home Station were useless, and others hadn't been thought of. They needed thinking about. He would suggest them when . . . when he returned. Far more useful probably was the advice given by his instructor who taught him about enemy organizations.

The country you knew before the war will have changed. Spare a thought, too, for what's going to happen to it when the war is over. It will change again.

The breeze was strengthening and a strand of Freya's hair whipped across Felix's cheek. She brushed it away and, catching a hint of perfume, he felt a stab in his guts. Lust? They had been warned about that, too. Those tough, gifted instructors at The Firm's STSs had thought about most things.

The body has no discrimination. It muddles responses and very often equates desire with danger.

They moved forward. Felix strained to make out the terrain. He knew from his briefings that there was a large lake with an island more or less at its centre. This had a jetty and some sort of summer house on it. In the distance there were arable fields and cottages and, a mile or so away, a house perched above lawns which sloped down to the edge of the water.

Silence. Felix shifted from foot to foot.

Again, she whispered in his ear. 'I'm taking you to the pigeon loft. It hasn't been used in years but it's out of sight of the house and I've readied the cages for the birds. I'll go first.'

The path which she led him down wound away out of sight of the house and felt rough and little used under foot. After five minutes, they came to a row of outhouses, a couple of which were not

74

in good condition. Freya ignored them, slipped past rusting machinery housed under a lean-to and halted by a barn-like structure at the end of the row. Picking up a bucket, she tussled with the door and disappeared.

Felix checked to the right, to the left and over his shoulder.

Keep checking. Checking should be like breathing. Trust no one, sonny.

He followed her.

Inside, a bare bulb hung from a crossbeam and struggled to illuminate hay bales and a litter of farm equipment. Ancient pigeon dung smeared the mud floor below a couple of pigeon cages.

With her back to the door, Freya was scrubbing the top of the wooden bench. He sized her up. With delicate features and with a faint air of command, Freya did not look the kind of woman who did much scrubbing, rather the reverse. Felix set down the case. 'You know, you must always keep a watch on the door.'

She glanced round. 'Is that spy-speak?'

'Elementary security.'

'Listen—' she scrubbed harder '—I'm just helping out a friend. I'm not like you.' A sliver of soap dropped onto the floor and she bent down to deal with it. 'I'm just doing him a favour.' There was a pause. 'This is the only time.'

He was tempted to say that it didn't work like that. Once in, once you had stepped into the shadow, you were in it. It was a state of mind.

'I meant to do this earlier,' she said. 'If we are to have the birds, it has to be clean.'

The door was damp and took some forcing shut. He leaned back on it and observed Freya at work. In the end, he had gone into this war for a principle that had proved stronger than his pacifism. The need to fight evil, to save Europe and for the honour of Denmark. These were the big concepts which would, he hoped, offer something to cling to when things got bad – when faced with pain, gut-loosening fear or extinction. Even so, if he ever got back to London he would tell them that the big concepts weren't the whole story. It was small things that got you through long, lonely uncomfortable hours. The warmth of the sun after hiding for hours in the dark, the small kindness of a bag of heated cherry stones handed up to him while freezing in an attic, a bed with a mattress. For a man in his thirties, watching a good-looking woman such as Freya would also be high on that list.

Her movements were graceful and a pleasure to watch and gave him a sort of solace. Wasn't the relish he took in them proof that, if he was to die here in his torn-up homeland, at least he would not do so desensitized by war and violence?

'The birds could get ill, you know. I've looked it up,' she said.

Her Danish was excellent and the hint of foreign inflection distractingly attractive.

'I borrowed a book from Arne, my husband's

foreman. I told him that I was thinking of breeding pigeons for their meat. You know that the Nazis are pinching all our pork and beef?' She took the pigeon box from Felix and lifted it onto the bench. 'It's all right, boys,' she said in English. 'You're safe.'

A pigeon's protest reverberated around the barn.

'In the old days, there was a thriving pigeon colony here. It's in my husband's records. It was the sign of a gentleman's residence, apparently.'

The information dropped easily from her lips.

'Don't tell me any more,' he said. 'It's best.'

She shot him a look. 'I see.'

He helped her to undo the buckles and ease off the lid. The interior was divided into two sections, each one containing a bird with bottled water and grain pressed into a hard block.

After the initial flurry, the birds went quiet. Freya reached in and lifted out a big, buff male. The label on his section read: Hector. The second, a darker bird, was Achilles. 'Hello, Hector,' she said softly. The bird's eyes were bright and watchful. 'Easy now, boy.' She walked over to the cage and placed Hector inside. 'The books said they might be panicky and restless so we'll have to be nice to them and talk to them in English.' She went to lift out Achilles.

'Wait a minute,' said Felix. Extracting a box of cigarette papers, he teased out the one on which he had written a message in code.

Arrived safe. All agencies up and running.
Please confirm Vinegar is operational and
in place. Mayonnaise

Folding it up, he slipped it into the tiny tube to be fastened onto the pigeon's leg. 'It needs to go soon.'

'They need rest,' Freya said cheerfully. 'But I'll send Achilles off tomorrow morning.'

'What exactly have you been told?'

Her eyelids lifted revealing misty-grey eyes. 'Nothing much.'

'Right.' He took a decision. 'I have to hide something.'

There was a tiny pause, but one he knew was significant – as if she was gathering herself up to step into the shadow.

'If you mean the wireless transmitter . . .' Her gaze held his. 'I know about that.' She pointed to the floor. 'It's all arranged.'

Dropping onto one knee, she pulled back a tarpaulin. It was so old it was rigid. Underneath, a couple of boards had been slung over a hole in the dirt floor. 'It's not brilliant but it will have to do for the time being.' She assessed the case. 'It's not so easy to hide.'

He shrugged. 'I will be moving it about. But I will have to use it here very soon and, after that, from time to time.' He touched her arm. 'That *is* all right?'

She sat back on her heels. 'Yes.'

'Sure?'

She nodded and her hair swung against her cheek.

He stowed the case in the hole and, together, they manhandled the boards and tarpaulin back into place. Seizing a broom waiting in the corner, Freya swept dust over the hiding place.

She was breathing hard, her breath audible, nervy.

'A warning,' she said, pushing a heap of dirt across the furthest corner. 'Apparently the Nazis disguise the direction-finding vehicles as delivery vans. They give themselves away because they are always petrol-driven. Many people round here have to make do with gaz. So watch out.'

Again, he gave himself the pleasure of watching her. 'Is there anything else I should know?'

She considered. 'Did they tell you in London about the King and Hitler?'

Felix nodded. He had been briefed in as much detail as The Firm could muster. There had been much collective amusement when it was discovered that Hitler had sent the Danish King a fulsome telegram to congratulate him on his birthday in September and the king's reply had been terse to the point of insult. However, it hadn't been so amusing when a furious Hitler suspended diplomatic relations as a result and sent in General Werner Best, an SS man to his last shiny button, to take overall charge of his favoured Protectorate.

Freya propped the broom against the wall and

produced a packet of cigarettes from her pocket. 'Best's nickname is "Hitler's Revenge" and he's not a nice man. But for the consequences, someone ought to kill him.'

Her physical beauty was in sharp contrast to the notion of murder and assassination . . . her skin, the blondeness, the softness belonged to the mother smiling at a baby. It belonged to the lover. Beauty belonged to the deep, sweet ecstasies of the flesh and to the feelings which promoted life, not death.

She held out the packet of Escorts. 'Want one?'

Actually he did, more than anything, but he pushed the packet away. 'Not here. Smoke is a giveaway.'

Her gaze flew up to meet his.

Again, he felt that she was positioning herself. Pushing her mind towards acceptance? Readying herself for something which, she sensed, was inevitable?

Finally, she said, 'It seems I have a lot to learn.'

Was she telling him she was in?

Her gaze veered towards the door and the moment passed.

'I'll be back,' he said. 'Tomorrow.'

The bicycle ride back to Køge took it out of Felix. His body ceased to pump adrenalin, and the stiffness in his muscles slowed him down.

The priorities. Contact London. Check Vinegar and other Joe in place . . . He hoped to God that Vinegar had made it and was safe. Check safe houses. Hide weapons. Begin recruiting.

The list was a long one and the cold nearly bested him.

Doubt was a condition of life – his life at any rate. But he had learned to deal with it. Doubt was a spur. It made action leaner and fitter. More effective. Even so, on that hard journey back, Felix found himself asking: *Am I up to this?*

CHAPTER 7

Hidden in the back of Jacob's cottage, and almost felled by some hefty slugs of schnapps, Felix dozed on and off.
He was back in training at The Firm.

'My name is Major Martin . . .'

Major Martin, or DYC/MB, as he signed himself on his messages, welcomed Felix into a stuffy, cramped room, not much more than a cupboard really, in the building used by The Firm's Danish section, somewhere near London's Marylebone Road.

Felix was not a natural observer of human beings – he preferred buildings – but Major Martin's very dark brown, almost black, eyes made an instant impact. These rested on Felix thoughtfully. 'You are probably not going to love me much.'

During his training, Felix had become better acquainted with English humour, which took getting used to. 'Probably not,' he answered.

Major Martin indicated a chair. 'So why have we met? Because, as an agent in the field, you will need to send messages back here. In code, obviously.

These will be picked up by our signals clerks in one location, decoded by our decoders in another and then analysed in yet another. For security reasons, none of the departments are allowed to communicate with each other. So we have to try to make it all work. I am responsible, along with others, for the coding part and I am going to teach you how to do it.'

'Black days,' said Felix.

Major Martin tapped his finger on the table as if to say: *Steady on.*

'We use the poem-code system here,' he said, and Felix picked up an undercurrent, a reservation in the tone. A scepticism? 'Put simply, the code sender selects words from a previously agreed poem, numbers the letters of those words as the key and buries the message in a grid that combines the numbered code letters with a lot of useless letters.'

Felix was relieved. 'That sounds reasonably straightforward.'

The major then went on to give a detailed explanation of the system, describing the encryption, the transpositions, the indicator groups, the laying of traps in case the message was intercepted, the feints to fool the enemy, the counter-feints . . .

'Christ,' said Felix.

'Sending messages also requires you to include two security checks. A bluff one which you can use to fool the enemy and the real one which . . .' the major's voice held steady, 'we hope the enemy never get hold of. No one else will have yours.'

Rummaging in his briefcase, Major Martin produced a piece of paper. 'First off, I'm going to give you a poem.'

'I thought agents chose their own poems.'

Major Martin glanced up at Felix. 'Let's see . . . If you asked me to predict your choice I would plump for something from your Danish national poet. Failing that, Kipling's "If", because it's likely to be a British poem that you've heard of.' He sounded ultra dry. 'Good thinking. But if you have heard of it, so will the enemy.'

At this point, both of them lit up cigarettes.

Major Martin balanced his on the ashtray. Smoke rose between them. 'Why is it the intelligence services, not so aptly named, refuse to understand that the enemy reads poetry too? In fact, more than we do.' He sent Felix a wintry smile. 'But we are getting around this with our very own Ditty Box.' He pushed the paper across to Felix. 'We have fine minds working on them. Some of the ditties can be read by a maiden aunt without a blush. Most of them can't. Sad but true. It's easier to remember a filthy poem.'

Felix read aloud.

> Do you wish for a silver fish
> To leap through the stream?
> Do you wish for the light
> To shine on yours and mine?
> Do you wish for the peace of my kiss?

He grinned. 'Can't I have a dirty ditty?'

'They're all in use. But I'll get the FANYs on to it. They're ace.' Major Martin glanced at the ditty. 'Sorry, not one of our finest. But it was composed in the small hours. Could you memorize it?'

Felix was warming to Major Martin. 'I may be cold, hungry, in the dark and surrounded by the flower of the Gestapo closing in, but I promise to remember The Firm's second-best poem. But I have to say, it's not even a second best . . .'

'I apologize, I really do, but the enemy won't know it. Bonus?'

Felix dragged on the cigarette. The major watched him.

'Does it help to know that we will keep your test coding exercises? If you make a muddle and we can't decode the message – we call those the indecipherables – we will crawl all over your test coding exercises. They reveal your weaknesses, your lapses of speech, so to speak. We will use them to help us work out what has gone wrong.'

'Even if they've captured me and are making me send messages?'

A small silence.

Major Martin was wise enough not to comment. 'I'm here to persuade you that you possess the skill and competence to send these messages. In return, you must allow me to understand how you work.' He pushed another piece of paper in Felix's direction. 'Being Danish you might know about ice hockey.'

'A little.'

'I want you to tackle the exercise I am about to set you as if you were assembling an ice hockey team.'

'Major Martin, this gets better and better.'

Major Martin smiled. Again, there was a suggestion of deep anxiety behind the easy manner. He worries about us, Felix thought. Major Martin is responsible for sending us lot out into the darkness armed with not much more than doggerel, and he knows it.

'You have twenty minutes,' he said. 'Choose your words from the poem and encode: "Send explosives, guns, chocolate *stop*".'

It was hard work and Felix found himself sweating. Some idiot had suggested to him that there was poetry in encryption, in the silent stalking down of words, in transforming them, but for the life of him he couldn't see it.

Major Martin assessed the result. 'I detect a case of coding paralysis,' he commented. 'A word of advice. Always go back to the beginning.'

The session was proving to be a humiliating one.

'Stubborn is the word,' said Major Martin.

'Stubborn it is . . .' The words issued through Felix's gritted teeth.

Major Martin eventually wrapped it up. 'Good. But you have forgotten something vital.'

'The security checks.'

'Correct,' said Major Martin. 'If I, or one of my

formidable team, read this message we would assume you and the set *had* been captured.'

'What about the decoding?' asked Felix.

'Decoding will be for another session. Coding and encoding are different animals. It's rare to be good at both. Odd that, isn't it? But I'm going to make you practise until you beg for mercy. A few tips: free your language, vary your transposition keys. *Don't* fall into set patterns. Code as if you are . . . er . . . making love.'

Felix was shaken awake by Jacob shouting in his ear. 'Go, go. Police in the street.'

For precisely that reason, Felix had not undressed. It took only seconds to snatch up his boots, jacket and peaked hat and let himself out of the back of Jacob's cottage.

He wheeled the bicycle into the street, jammed on the cap and set off in the direction of the town centre, keeping the pace deliberately leisurely. At Sankt Nicolai Kirke he pushed the bicycle behind a bush, went inside, selected a pew at the back and bowed his head. For twenty minutes or so, he would sit it out in the church.

What he wouldn't give for a hot bath. For clean and basic things. For water washing between his legs and toes. For the smell of a good soap. This thought surprised him, for when had he ever cared about scented soap?

Jacob's overalls were too short in the crotch and, for all that he had extended the shoulder straps, they bit into his balls. Felix grinned. His first task in the service of Denmark? Save his balls.

Early morning light streamed in through the arched window above the high altar, glossing the circular altar rail. He noted how the arch was there to support the breadth of the wall, the keystone taking the strain while the Gothic line was meant to express the human aspiration to reach heaven . . .

Architectural vocabulary was second nature to him. Less so, the architecture of resistance. At the STS they taught the structures of an underground army and explained how it was modelled on the interlocking cells of a bee colony, which was the strongest and most efficient exemplar in nature. There would be one overall leader – himself – and three or four group leaders who knew nothing of each other. Their task would be to move around this area of Zealand, recruiting and training, but no action was to be taken without the overall leader's permission.

His ruff a startling white above his billowing black robe, the pastor walked down the aisle. His gaze rested on Felix. *Hostile?*

It was an error to assume that religious men would be on the side of the angels.

Get the hell out.

He abandoned the bicycle and made for the street running behind the *Torvet* – the main square. Here, the half-timbered houses, painted ochre or bull's-blood red, and the grey paving stones looked as serene as they must have done in peacetime. He bought a newspaper, found the café which Jacob had told him was a rendezvous, and settled at a window table with a coffee and a *kringle* pastry. Both were of bad quality but, his body craving fuel, he got them down.

Automatically, he kept a watch on the street. Automatically, he checked that there was a back entrance to the café.

Second nature, now.

A fishmonger pushed his cart heaped with herring and pink roe past the window. The sight reminded him powerfully of the time when his parents were still together and they still had a family life of sorts.

Remember Anders, Pastor Neuman's son and his best friend? What games they had played. Lanky pests, the pair of them, running alongside the fish carts, imitating the cries of the mussel vendors – and frequently having to scarper, hiding up in warehouses, watching the fishing boats go in and out of the harbour and taking bets on which one would get stuck on the sand bank. One sun-flecked summer's day they had built a fleet of Viking long ships with mussel shells and corks and sent it over the sea to Valhalla.

Sometimes, in the spring, he and Anders cycled past the hanging birches at the end of the street, past the red church and into the countryside. In the rye fields the larks sang, the cherry trees at their edges foamed white and blush-pink and the pair of them talked themselves hoarse. When the cold returned, they switched operations and went searching for treasure on the shoreline, the sea painting white salt hems on to their boots and, above them, gulls wheeling in big, watery skies.

Enough.

Felix read the paper thoroughly. There was news of the curfew in København, complaints about the lack of merchandise in the shops and the scarcity of cigarette papers. An editorial argued for keeping the peace. 'We don't want, or need, uprisings or sabotage.'

When Felix next looked up, Jacob was seated at the next table. Through dry, bitten lips, he said: 'Police everywhere. My neighbour, Lars, was found trying to make a gun in his house. They shot his daughter.'

'Dead?'

'She'll survive but minus her leg. Don't come back to me. They're watching.'

The waitress placed coffee and a pastry in front of Jacob and Jacob fell on them, licking his finger to scoop up every crumb and draining every drop of coffee like a man who was famished.

Some hours later Felix wheeled the bicycle into the Rosenlund estate, pushed it into some bushes and waited under the cover of the trees for dusk to fall. Out here, the silence was almost disconcerting, and the ground under his feet, layered with leaf mould, was heavy going.

The initial exhilaration at being back in his homeland had leached away. He ached all over. He was tired and he wasn't sure where he was going to hide up for the night.

Having made it to the pigeon loft, he found Freya was already waiting for him. This time, she wore a jacket with a fur-lined collar which framed her face. Like Anna Karenina, he thought.

Her greeting was friendly, and she touched him on the arm. 'Achilles went this morning.' She sounded a touch wistful. 'He seemed glad to go.'

Watched by a beady-eyed Hector, they dragged back the tarpaulin where the wireless set was hidden. 'Time's a bit tight,' he warned.

'Then I'll help you.'

'You should go. It's dangerous.'

'I know,' she said, calmly and without fuss. Even so, when she raised her eyes to his he caught a hint of turmoil.

Together, they set up the equipment on the bench and, on Felix's instruction, Freya looped the antenna wire over a rafter. 'You're a natural,' he said.

She gave a short laugh. 'Someone else said that to me.'

Felix plugged in the valves and headset, selected the correct crystal and connected the power pack. Using the calibration curve pasted into the lid of the case as a guide, he feathered the dial. 'Got it.' He had hit the correct frequency and a neon light glowed. He looked up at Freya. 'Last chance to leave. The German listening stations will be fixing on us this very moment. Somewhere in Berlin, or Augsburg or Nuremburg or—'

'Stop, Felix.'

She appeared to be torn between wanting to flee . . . and something else. What? A curiosity and an excitement which kept her rooted to the spot?

'You are about to talk to England,' she said. 'God only knows how it's possible but it's so good to know. A miracle of science.'

With the arrowhead pointing to 'Transmit', he waited until the bulbs glowed ever brighter and tapped out his call sign.

Immediately, scything through the ether, came the response: QVR. *Ready to receive.*

Home Station was there. Back in England, someone was listening out for him.

QTC1, he tapped. *I have one message for you.*

MESSAGE NUMBER 4 *stop* **SITUATION QUIET** *stop* **RESISTANCE MINIMAL** *stop* **REQUEST WIRELESS SETS, SMALL ARMS, EXPLOSIVES** *stop* **PLEASE CONFIRM VINEGAR SAFE AND OPERATIONAL** *stop* **REPEAT CONFIRM VINEGAR OPERATIONAL** . . .

Twenty minutes later he signed off: QRU. *I have nothing further for you.*

'Quickly,' he said, shutting everything down.

Working in silence, they packed up the equipment in the case and Felix snapped the locks into place. He looked across to her. She was tense and absorbed in the task. What unexpected collusions this work had got him into. Apart from a few facts, he knew nothing about Freya – except for one thing. She held his life in her hands.

'Can I stay here tonight? The safe house has turned out to be unsafe for the time being.'

Freya was dusting down her jacket and he detected a hesitation.

'*Gestapomen* shot a young girl this morning in the neighbouring house. She'll lose her leg.'

A flare of anger. 'Poor girl.' She was silent for a moment – clearly battling with the decision. 'All right. I'll bring . . . As soon as it's properly dark I'll organize food and a quilt. Otherwise you'll freeze.'

'Sorry to ask you.'

She gave him a straight look. 'Don't be.' Again, he sensed she was gathering the resolve to drive herself further along a road. 'You must ask if you need anything else done.' She sounded husky with strain. 'With the work . . .'

He showed his surprise. 'I thought this was a one-off?'

'One gets sucked in,' she said.

'Not good enough, Freya.'

She breathed in sharply. 'I've – I've changed my mind. I don't think one can stand back any longer. I thought I should. I thought I *could* . . .'

'Let me think about it.'

She nodded.

Freya left to fetch the food. Alone again, Felix inspected Hector's cage.

The men and women who can do this work are not necessarily the obvious ones.

What did he knew about her. Enough to trust?

The case for . . . He ran over it. The case against . . . ditto.

Fatigue seemed to wrap his mind in wet felt. He dropped down onto the floor, propped himself up against the wall by the bench and set about decoding the incoming message. The task ate up the last of his current stock of energy. Checking his knife was still strapped in place round his leg and his Browning pistol was in his right hand, he allowed his head to drop onto his chest.

The footsteps invaded the safe and warm silence of his sleep. Light, purposeful, cunning. *Wake up.* Rolling silently to his feet, he took a grip on the pistol.

Where am I?

This wouldn't do. He had to be sharper, quicker, more on the case than this.

Her voice sounded through the gloom. 'It's Freya.'

She proffered a bundle in both hands – rather as she might hold an offering in a temple. 'Food and a quilt.' She was wearing a scarf and strands of silky, blonde hair tumbled onto her shoulders under it.

He took the bundle and set it down.

She seemed to be waiting.

'About what you said earlier . . .' He couldn't be sure because the light was bad but she seemed to pale and, again, she gave a sharp intake of breath. 'I need a courier.'

She went very still.

'You can retract the offer,' he said.

'No . . .' she replied after a pause. '*No*. I mean, it's clear to me . . . I can't not act. I can't retract. I have to come in with you. I *have* to.'

Her vulnerability was almost painful to observe and Felix abandoned every rule about not asking questions. 'What about your husband? Children? You realize what danger you will be putting them in—'

'Stop . . . I know.'

He was tempted to shake her to make her see sense. 'You could just stay safe.'

'Safe? Yes, I suppose that is correct . . .' Her voice was strengthening. 'But not safe from conscience. Not safe from knowing for the rest of your life that you failed to act. Where does the family fit into this? I don't know, Felix, but I believe in decency, the sort where a young girl doesn't have her leg blown off for no reason.' She shrugged and the fur edging on her jacket rippled with the movement. 'Selfish? Perhaps it is but I've also discovered lately that I'm proud of what Britain is doing.' She gave a quick, nervous smile. 'Does that answer the question?'

Poking a finger through the bars of the bird cage,

Felix experimented with a waggle. The bird observed him with a complete lack of interest. 'I would have to inform London.' He glanced at her. 'Obviously you couldn't go to England to train, which would be the best . . . the safest . . . thing to do. But I can teach you some of what I know.' He fell silent for a moment. 'Do you understand how dirty this business is? It's dangerous . . . very dangerous. It will involve lying and almost certainly having to commit crimes. We have to eavesdrop and spy on people we know and sometimes love.'

'I'm not stupid.'

'Sorry.'

Extracting a scarf from her pocket, she handed it over to him. 'You'll need this.' She sounded collected and businesslike. 'And I do understand.'

'Then I'll do one more sked here. Any more and it'll be too dangerous. The big problem is there're not enough sets in the country. Pitifully few, in fact. I plan to ask London to drop in several. We'll hide them in various places and I can move between them. Much better than using couriers to transport the sets. But until London obliges we have to—'

She anticipated him. 'You want me to take this one somewhere.'

No one knew better than Felix what he was asking of Freya. 'Yes. I am. You're a woman and the Nazis aren't, as yet, so suspicious of women. They're stopped and searched less often. You would be a good cover. I imagine you visit København from

96

time to time? Frequently?' She nodded. 'Good.' He wound the scarf round his neck – and it felt like a noose. 'When I give the word, get on the midday train to København and find the newspaper vendor by platform five. A contact will meet you there and tell you where to take it.'

She gave a half smile. 'Any tips for the job?'

He glanced over to the spot where the set was hidden. His brain, starved of sleep and food, projected a pinkish-red aura over it.

'Behave absolutely naturally – and that can take some doing. You must work out, too, how to react if you're challenged.'

'I'll manage. You're not the only one with a cool head.'

If that was a tease, it wasn't funny, he found himself thinking. Sourly. Then, he felt ashamed and imparted a piece of news which he suspected would please her. 'Apparently Achilles made it.'

Her face lit up. 'I told him about the green fields and berries in the hedges, and the nice warm loft which was waiting for him. He got the message.' She laughed rather delightfully at her own joke. 'But Arne – I mean someone – told me that the Germans have orders to shoot anything that might be thought a homing pigeon.' She placed a hand on the door latch. 'You must eat your bread and cheese.'

'Is there butter by any chance?'

'There is.'

'I'm in paradise.'

He came and stood beside her. Freya was a reasonably tall woman but, since he topped her by a couple of inches at least, he was forced to look down. Her face was half in the shadow. She shifted a little and he caught sight of a long neck framed by strands of fur.

Outside, there was a noise. A crack of ice, or hardened wood? Freya froze. He bent over and whispered, 'Go.'

She didn't argue but vanished through the door.

Felix backed up against the wall and waited, pistol in hand, for a good twenty minutes.

Nothing.

So far, his war was playing out with alternating episodes of fear and pulsing adrenalin, then long cold stretches of boredom and – almost – dissatisfaction.

Not to mention the lack of a hot bath.

CHAPTER 8

The Firm had commandeered Henfold House, which was a couple of miles from the small town of Henfold in the Midlands. Inviting its owners to take up residence elsewhere for the duration, they turned it into Listening Station 53d. It was promptly named Gloom Towers by its disrespectful staff.

That much Mary Voss knew. But not much else about the outfit for which she found herself working. No one did – certainly not Nancy or Beryl, who were the two girls to whom she mostly talked. The others, her fellow FANYs who worked alongside Mary on the shifts, tended to ignore her. At forty-one, Mary was considered far too old to bother with. Mary got that. But Nancy and Beryl were less blinkered by their youth and Mary often shared a cup of tea with them in the canteen. Their odd friendship, which had developed as the months went on, was, for Mary, one of the unexpected pluses of a war.

As usual, the signals room where they worked – the former laundry in the Victorian kitchen wing – managed to be both cold and stuffy. The small

99

radiator fixed to the wall was worse than useless and the windows let in the gusty draughts.

'They'll be fixed. I swear by my mother's milk.' The corporal in charge of maintenance said that so often that no one listened any more.

'We dream on,' said Nancy. Even on the night shift, Nancy habitually wore bright lipstick and her hair in a complicated roll because 'we need to keep cheery'. Mary admired that battle spirit.

She located Number 33, her station, and sat down. No one acknowledged her, nor did she expect them to. Right from the beginning, they had been taught total concentration on the job in hand. The training had been hard. Sometimes she dreamed of the room filled with long wooden tables at which they practised Morse on the dummy keys. As a girl's speed got better, she was shunted up to the next table, ever closer to the instructor. Most of them got stuck on one letter or another. Funny that. Her particular stumbling block had been the letter R, but she had fought to smooth out every last jag and imperfection.

Anyway, here she was with Morse flowing in her bloodstream – so much so that she found herself automatically tapping out odd words when they caught her eye. 'Exit' and 'railway station' being among the most frequent. It was, she often reflected, quite extraordinary how she could translate everyday objects into a dot and a dash.

Mary looked up. On the wall opposite was a large poster with the words 'Remember the Enemy is Listening'. As if they didn't think about it morning, noon and night.

The wooden chairs had been designed to torment the signals clerks, so uncomfortable were they – and so roughly finished off that the girls' precious stockings snagged on them.

She embarked on her routines.

Check the clock.

Check the board on which had been written up the agents' call signs, their code names, the frequencies on which they transmitted and their skeds.

In the next hour, she had two skeds. Shifting around on the unforgiving chair to find a more comfortable position, she put on the headphones. Immediately, she was immersed in a clicking, hissing, gurgling world.

Close eyes to let hearing adjust. This was one of the golden rules.

Tune the dial to find the frequency.

If only, Mary thought, and not for the first time, if only they had the bang-up-to-the-minute American HRO receivers with their pinpoint accuracy instead of the old dinosaurs the Brits were lumbered with . . . Then she would be there on the button waiting for her agents. Instead, she was forced to keep one hand on the dial because the frequencies had a trick of melting away.

Easy now. Swivel the needle ever so slowly back and forth through the spectrum until the whole sweep had been covered.

'I think . . . what do I think? It's like searching the wireless for dance music on those foreign stations after the parents have gone to bed and Auntie BBC has shut up shop for the night,' said Nancy. Maybe. Mary wasn't sure she wished to consider something as serious as their work in Nancy's light-hearted way.

Final time check.

Who the agents were she had no idea. The signals clerks were not given even a hint. They were told nothing apart from the bare operational facts of the call signs and the skeds, and they were instructed not to speculate.

That she found hard.

All the girls agreed this was misguided policy. It showed that the bigwigs did not trust them and, considering how hard and exhausting the work was, the lack of trust made the signals clerks indignant. The long hard slog during the nights, when they were forbidden to break, even for a cup of tea, was especially taxing. 'If they didn't have us,' said Beryl. 'What would they do?'

Mary concentrated. Often the signals were weak but she had trained herself to be receptive to the merest drift of sound.

A bubble bursting.

Atmospheric music . . . the waltz of the wave bands.
Time?

Pencil poised in her right hand, she made another foray into the frequencies with her left.

It was forbidden to get close to their agents.

Those vulnerable, quixotic, brave pianists. The instructors had been precise. No little wireless exchanges. No sneaky transmission of the number 73, which meant 'best wishes' in any radio language and could be taken to mean 'keep your chin up' or 'we are thinking of you'. Mary wondered indignantly what difference it would make. What harm could there be in making a tiny human gesture across the ether?

When she had got to know them better, Mary talked it over one day with Nancy and Beryl as they sat drinking their tea in the canteen. The other two girls exchanged glances. Complicit.

'Can you keep a secret?' Nancy's red mouth curled at the corners. 'Sometimes me and Beryl slip in this . . .' She knocked out the letters on the table.

'My goodness!' Mary was taken aback. The letters spelled out the word 'shit' – but, in a flash, she understood why. They were the fastest letters to transmit.

Over the teacups, which sported scummy rims because the water was hard, Nancy and Beryl were regarding her in the way that was now familiar to Mary: cut the old girl some slack.

'We've shocked you,' said Nancy.

'No,' Mary replied hastily. 'No. Please don't think that. It's just rather a strange message of comfort.'

Beryl giggled. 'Too right.'

What they were expected to do was to learn their

agent's individual style of transmitting. 'Think of it as handwriting,' the instructor said. 'We call it the agent's "fist".' During the training, it was drummed into them that they must listen out for even the tiniest variants. Oh, the pleasure, both visceral and deep, it gave Mary to know that she turned out to be particularly good at it.

'Is your agent on the run? Surrounded by the enemy? Transmitting in fear, cold and darkness? Is he or she who they said they are?'

In her bones . . . *in her bones* Mary knew she could answer all those questions, and the more she considered and observed, the more she realized that the authorities didn't possess her expertise. They didn't have a clue. She and the girls *knew* their agents and understood. If asked, she could have told the authorities a thing or two about themselves which they hadn't dreamed of.

In some respects, she and the girls were operating just as subversively as the agents.

In the signals room, the intensity of the work had upped the humidity but it was still freezing. Mary's feet were turning numb but it was of no matter. Goodness knew what conditions were like for the men and women for whom she was straining every ounce of concentration. Where were they transmitting from? Deepest France? Poland, perhaps? Surely not Germany? Some were hesitant, some impetuous, some sloppy. Only that last shift, for instance, the agent had been frightened. Don't ask Mary how she knew. She just *did*.

Anxiety burned over the airwaves and she had the oddest notion that it seeped into her bone marrow. His or her distress affected her, and she had been forced to marshal all her reserves to transmit Home Station's message back.

Hang on . . . She had willed her faith, her support, her care to pour through her fingertips.

On schedule a high-pitched sound drilled into her ears and she snapped to needle-sharp attention.

ZYA

The agent would continue to transmit the call sign at one-minute intervals until she answered.

What power Mary possessed between that moment of receiving the signal and the moment when she placed her finger on the transmitter key and responded to it. Yes, it was a brief interregnum, but during it she held total sway – which was quite a thought for someone who had never had significant control over her hitherto unremarkable life.

Her finger pushed down the transmitter key. QRK. *What is my intelligibility?*

QSA4. Her signal readability was apparently four.

QTC1, tapped the agent. *I have one message for you.*

Mary's pencil travelled over the log paper.

QRU. *I have nothing further for you.*

After adding the sign-off from ZYA, Mary placed the paper in the basket from which it would be collected and taken to the decoders, and then, uncaring that the signalmaster might bawl at her, she slumped back against the chair.

What are you doing, Mary Voss?

I'm listening.

To the cries and whispers.

Of those I am forbidden to know.

Those in the dark.

Out there.

Hours later – and the end of the shift was in sight.

Her energies burned up, Mary was woozy and depleted, which meant she would need to take extra care not to make mistakes. All too aware that the present shift pattern was wreaking havoc with her constitution and her sleep, she felt permanently askew, as if she was sailing with a broken compass. Her dreams were particularly bad – vividly disruptive and alarming – and she awoke battered and exhausted.

The dreams were almost certainly her mind registering its protest at the upheaval to her body. Seven days on days. Seven days on nights. But she wasn't about to repeat the mistake of discussing the problem of sleeplessness to the others. When she had mentioned it to Beryl some months ago, Beryl had shrugged as if to say that working nights didn't bother her, which made Mary feel even older than she was.

Yet the fun she had in the canteen made up for a lot. To be united in camaraderie was a novel experience for Mary. In her previous job as supervisor at her local telephone exchange, she had had to respect the boundaries and keep herself to herself. But here she couldn't help over-hearing the chat and the free exchange of opinions. Oh, how they disliked the bosses, the predatory men, the rotten conveniences and the endless spam, but their collective admiration and loyalty for Mr Churchill gave them a nice warm glow. Before they went on shift there tended to be lots of jokes and chat at the tables. Post-shifts were more subdued occasions and the girls regarded each other through glazed eyes or stared at the exhortations pinned up on the canteen walls.

YOUR SILENCE IS VITAL
WALLS HAVE EARS
IF THE ENEMY DISCOVERS US THEY
    WILL BOMB US

Mary often wondered who it had been at the telephone exchange who picked up that she knew Morse. Whoever it was must have had connections and Mary found herself being interviewed by a woman in a severely cut suit in a vicarage in Kensington, who asked her all sorts of questions, including how she had learned Morse. The answer was simple: her father, who had been in Signals during the Great War, had taught it to her to help Mary out before she joined the Girl Guides.

The woman in the suit had looked very grave. 'Miss Voss, if you were instructed to keep a secret, and to keep it for the rest of your life, could you do it?'

Her answer must have been convincing because, before she knew it, Mary had joined the FANYs and signed the Official Secrets Act.

The shift ended and Mary fetched her coat from the room which in a previous life had had been designated for the house's vases – *an entire room for vases!* – and now did service as a cloakroom. She glanced in the meanly dimensioned mirror propped up on the windowsill. Hair still neatly rolled up. Tie straight.

It was eight o'clock in the morning and her day was ending.

When she stepped outside, figures were drifting up and down the drive, their faces pallid and ghostly in the quasi light of a December day – probably, like her, suffering from too little sleep. There were a couple of WRAAFs, an army sergeant and a stream of cipher and signals clerks.

Nancy came out behind her. 'Lucky sods,' she said. 'At least they can get to the pub when they come off duty.'

The sergeant from provisions, the one with a ridiculous handlebar moustache, passed them on the steps and gave a thumbs-up.

'I think he fancies me . . .' Nancy took her time to smooth her gloves over her hand. 'He can think again.'

A car drew up in front of the main door. A chauffeur sprang into action and a uniformed figure with many pips and braids emerged from its interior.

'Bigwig,' said Nancy. 'I could put up with him for the car.'

Mary focused on the bigwig, who was ruddy and portly with a mean little moustache. 'No, you couldn't.'

Mary's digs in Locarno Avenue were at number eight. Letting herself in, she placed the key on 'Lodger's Hook' and went into the best parlour, where Mrs Cotton left out a cold meal and a thermos.

The tiny room was unlived-in and felt it. Of symbolic status, it was rarely used and kept in aspic, while Clan Cotton huddled around the stove in the back kitchen and kept themselves to themselves. Mary knew that Mrs Cotton took enormous pride in the room's overstuffed furniture and starched antimacassars. Taking care, as always, not to drop a crumb, she ate her sliver of Woolton Pie and half a sliced carrot and drank the tea in the Thermos. Having finished, she stacked her used crockery on the tray and left it on the table. As soon as Mrs Cotton heard Mary go upstairs, she would dart out and deal with it.

Station 53d personnel were allocated only basic rent. Mrs Cotton's back bedroom contained a narrow bed, a chest and a chair. The single wall adornment was a grim picture of the martyrdom of a saint called Sebastian, about whom Mary knew little, but his death looked nasty. However taxing it must have been, Mrs Cotton kept the house spotless. 'It was what I was put on earth for,' she said when Mary complimented her. Hers was a life dominated by scruple and scrubbing, a life in which she fought against the odds to produce fresh laundry and provisions. Mary admired the stoicism.

Fatigue had beaten her and Mary sat down with a thump on the bed. Reaching under her skirt, she unhooked a suspender. The evenings were mornings and the mornings, like this one, were midnight. She had never been an early riser at the best of times. She had been a girl who rebelliously drowsed and dreamed until her mother told her off. How many lie-ins had she enjoyed in her life? She could count them on the fingers of one hand. Once – Mary fumbled for the second suspender as she recalled the sweet and funny memory – once she and her cousin, Mabel, saved up and took themselves off for a night (in separate rooms, of course) in the splendours of a hotel in West Wittering. They had hung the 'Do Not Disturb' signs outside their rooms. From time to time Mary thought wistfully of that deep, unbroken slumber and the long, luxurious return to consciousness.

Her stockings were not glamorous ones, but precious even if the darn rubbed on the right big toe. She rolled them down and her flesh shrank from exposure. Experimentally, she pinched a bit of inner thigh, the area which rarely saw light of day. Still soft and silky.

110

Oh, Mary.

No one had ever felt its softness and silkiness.

'Your fate is in the stars, dear,' her mother had had a habit of saying whenever the vexed subject of marriage came up. 'It's no use wishing otherwise.'

As time went by, Mary knew her chances of marriage and physical fulfilment grew fewer and, worse, with each passing year she felt elements in her spirit wither and deplete. She strove valiantly not to allow that atrophy.

'You can tell the difference between a woman who's been loved . . . and one who hasn't.' Her mother again, her beady eyes invariably fixed on her daughter as she spoke.

Wriggle out of suspender belt. Remove her one good vest on which – unfortunately – Mrs Cotton had launched some kind of military offensive, shrinking it into a felted garment of torture. Unfasten brassière.

Pour water from the ewer into the enamel basin. Wash face. Wash all over. 'Strive for cleanliness, inner and outer,' the vicar at their local parish had preached. 'It's marvellous, my brethren.'

Was it?

She glanced at the clock, a cheap buy from Woolworth's. Housed in red tin it was the brightest object in the room. *Hurry, Mary.* It wouldn't be long before she had to get up again.

Throwing back the sparsely feathered eiderdown and ancient blankets, she slid into bed. The cold sheets always gave her a bit of a shock but, forcing

111

herself to relax, she lay back and closed her eyes. She had to be rested for the next shift.

No mistakes. Ever.

She began to drift.

In another life, Mary would be warm. Her underwear would be made from silk and the finest cotton and she would be able to buy books whenever she wished. Currently, her budget permitted only one a year. What else? Good white bread every day. A proper dentist, because her teeth were a problem, always had been, and her mouth housed a catalogue of aches, some dull, some excruciating . . .

There was half an hour to the end of the shift.

Mary and Nancy exchanged looks and, under the bench, Nancy tapped out a Morse rhythm with a foot.

'Shut it,' hissed Beryl.

Mary realized that, increasingly, and however tired she might be, she dreaded signing off. It was true. Because in that fizzing, gurgling world to which she listened bubbled a wellspring from which she drank.

Check the clock.

There was one more sked to go. XRT, code name Vinegar.

Along with ZYA, code name Mayonnaise, he was one of her new agents, and therefore to be especially cosseted and nurtured and protected. She was the only one to know that Vinegar had been a bit iffy with his first transmission back to

Home Station. In fact, more than iffy. Plain out of control. He had used the wrong sign-off and muddled up a frequency. But he had got the hang of it. Actually, she was surprised at how quickly Vinegar had turned into an excellent keyer. By his fourth transmission Vinegar had got the hang of it and *she* had got the hang of him by then, too – his Cs (pointed, regular mountain peaks), and his Ms (a tiny dunce's cap).

It had bothered her a bit, that rapid transition. 'He's settled down very quickly,' she confided in Nancy. 'On those first transmissions he was so nervous. Next thing, he's as smooth and confident as you could wish.'

Nancy shrugged. 'Why are you so bothered about it? He just needed a bit of time, that's all.'

Nancy was right. Even so, Mary brooded over Vinegar. Eventually, she brought up the subject with Signalmaster Noble, who told her that she was being fanciful and over-cautious. 'Go and do your job, Voss,' he said. *Get out of my sight.*

Vinegar. How did he manage, out there in the darker areas of the war?

She was sure Vinegar was a 'he'.

She imagined him dark-haired, tall and perhaps very clever. Brave, anyway. Yes, heroic.

Was he alone?

Where in the many possible countries was he?

She pictured him keying in from, say, a barn, the wireless transmitter propped on a hay bale and the aerial threaded up into the rafters. Again and again, the signals clerks were warned not to speculate, and they weren't supposed to know the ins and outs of clandestine transmitting. But none of them were stupid. They all knew one end of a wireless transmitter from another, and if the powers that be didn't trust them, that was their look out.

She had never experienced extreme fear, only the dull thud of a vague but persistent anxiety about the future, and of how life would pan out for a forty-one-year-old spinster. Anxiety was trying enough, and sometimes in the past it had made her take to her bed with one of her headaches. But crippling, paralysing fear? She couldn't, and didn't, pretend to know about that.

The noise in her ears stuttered and faltered. She adjusted the dial and watched the needle swing.

This ugly, ungainly machine wove a secret network of sound. To use it was to risk death, and, worse, the demolition of body and spirit by torture. Yet maybe . . . maybe Vinegar knew that Mary was listening out for him, guarding him, pouring her reassurance down the airwaves. Maybe it made him feel better.

Foolish?

BRSTU XOSAR VOPYI . . .

She took down the message, basketed it and watched it being taken by the dispatch clerk in the direction of the cipher room.

CHAPTER 9

They had been summoned up from the bowels of Gloom Hall for yet another endless lecture on security.

Did the powers that be never let up?

It was ten a.m. on a winter's morning and the place was bloody freezing because no one, not even in the nineteen hundred and forty-two years since Christ was born, could work out how to keep a place warm, which, you might have thought, would not have been beyond the wit of man.

So reflected Ruby Ingram as, with a group of her fellow cipher clerks – not to be confused with the signals clerks with whom they were not allowed to fraternize – she trooped into the lecture room to which they had been ordered. There were forty of them. Girls with brains. Girls without brains. Girls from the Shires. Girls from the tenements. Some pretty, others not, some hiding behind the terrible spectacles which was all that seemed to be on offer these days. Average age: twenty-one.

Not surprisingly the noise was ear-splitting.

Ruby didn't blame them. Talking at full volume

helped the girls to ignore the calculated insult by the men in charge of failing to provide them with chairs.

'Who do they think they are?' said Frances.

Ruby eyed her. Along with salt-of-the-earth Janet, Frances had turned out to be a friend but she could sound as haughty as a duchess.

'They think they're men.' Ruby was at her most wry.

'They *are* men,' Janet pointed out.

This was the Janet who, late one night, had posed the question: 'Why should possessing a visible organ between your legs mean you rule the world?'

The lecture room, which had probably been a dining room or, possibly, a small ballroom before the war, smelled of damp and chalk, and reminded Ruby of the bathrooms at Newnham College.

No, she mustn't think about Newnham. Mustn't think about Cambridge. Mustn't think about the fact that, having achieved a brilliant Double First in Maths, she was not granted her rightful degree. Because? The answer beat out wearily in her brain. Because Cambridge University did not grant degrees to women.

Janet waved a hand in front of Ruby. 'You with us?'

Ruby bestowed a rare smile on Janet, who was an oft-time saviour. On the bad days when Ruby was crippled with pain from migraine, Janet was always there. Somehow she obtained hot-water bottles and aspirin and told her to shut up when Ruby railed at her affliction.

Ruby's chilblains itched. Frances shivered visibly.

'Why are we waiting?' sang Janet in her strong, confident soprano.

'Because,' a male voice announced from the door, 'you are waiting for me.'

Silence fell as swiftly as a tropical night.

Flanked by a sergeant, a uniformed man walked the length of the room to the lectern. Placing papers on it, he faced the girls. 'My name is Major Martin. Peter Martin. I'm sorry I've kept you waiting, but I did so on purpose. I had every intention of making you uncomfortable.'

That was one way of getting their attention. Ruby nudged Janet.

Major Martin was just above average height and slight. Late twenties? Possibly thirty? Dark hair. Dark eyes. Well-shaped hands. His uniform was pressed, his Sam Browne belt shone but, curiously, his shoes needed attention.

Balancing lightly on the neglected shoes, he leaned on the lectern. 'I was having you recorded.'

A collective gasp greeted this information and Ruby thought she saw a gleam of satisfaction light up the dark gaze.

'Sergeant Walker here is going to play it back to you.'

The silence turned into an embarrassed one as a babble of voices was released. It took a moment for

117

Ruby to unscramble the sounds issuing through the speakers on the ceiling.

Janet's voice sang out: 'Why are we stuck in this piss house?'

That was plain enough.

Beside Ruby, Frances coloured violently at the replay of her plummy tones lambasting – in terms no lady should utter – the sergeant who had ushered them into the lecture room.

It didn't take much for Ruby to be prodded into objecting and she spoke up. 'That's not fair, sir.'

Major Martin shifted. 'No, it isn't fair, Ensign . . .?'

Didn't he know that FANYs were only ever addressed by their surnames?

'Ingram.'

He held up a hand for silence and got it. Forty pairs of eyes focused on him. 'Thank you all for coming to see me in this . . . er, piss house. Your colleague here questions the fairness of the little trick that has just been played on you. A good challenge, but I'm going to demonstrate to you how fairness has nothing to do with it.' His gaze, thoughtful and professionally sceptical, raked over his audience. 'You lot have trained on pretty average material. The sort of stuff that streams in and out of base stations and embassies and is coded and decoded in relative safety. But you have a chance to progress.' Again, he held up a hand. 'Have I got your total attention? I hope so, otherwise you will be returning to your former, and

118

almost certainly duller, lives. With one difference. Your tongues will have been cut out.'

Major Martin clearly enjoyed the stir *that* created.

A joke. Ruby closed her eyes for one . . . two . . . three seconds. Well, it was something positive in their dull lives.

When she opened them, Major Martin sent her a look which suggested he was amused by her reaction.

He continued: 'We now know that you have all complained of the cold and discomfort in no uncertain terms. Let's take a look at this pitiful situation. You have been made to stand up for . . . twenty minutes, give or take? Very annoying, I grant you. The room is unheated and we didn't allow you to put on your greatcoats. Torture, you might agree.'

Frances muttered. 'Get on with it, man.'

'I want all of you to think about a different situation. You are hungry, cold and, worse, shaking with fear. You are on the run, and you have to get a message back to London. It's dark. You have no light and no shelter. And the message you have to get back to London is one that *you have already transmitted*. Why?'

He looked around his audience. Frances's handsome mouth had dropped open and a faint pink remained in her cheeks.

Audience enslaved, mission accomplished, Ruby concluded.

'I'll give you the answer. You are retransmitting

the same message because we here at Home Station *have not got our act together*. So, I'm going to ask you the question: What is fair about being tormented by fear, sleeplessness, hunger and discomfort, and by being on the run, when you are required to retransmit a message that you have already risked your life sending previously? The joke being that with every transmission Jerry gets a better fix on you.'

He suddenly switched tack and threw a question at Janet. 'Where were you before you fetched up here?'

'Typing pool, sir.'

'Well, I think I'd rather be in this piss house than a typing pool. And I'll tell you why. You have a chance to do something. Instead of running around making cups of tea for your male superiors, you can be on the front line of, admittedly, a secret theatre of war, so you can't boast about it, but what you do will make a difference. This is what I'm offering you.'

Now, why is he looking at me? Ruby returned Major Martin's scrutiny. No bashful avoidance.

'Women in particular should take their chance. They probably won't be thanked for it but that's beside the point.'

He can hold an audience, she thought. *I'll give him that. He can pull a stunt, too. I'll give him that as well.*

The FANY tribe stood as acquiescent as anyone could have wished. Ruby knew that under many

120

of the uniform-covered chests surged various difficult, even disobedient, emotions but they knew when not to misbehave.

Peter Martin checked his watch and held up a piece of the paper used for incoming signals. 'Since ten o'clock last night we have received two indecipherables. The first is from an agent in France, code name Abel. His cover is blown, the Gestapo are after him and he needs to be picked up fast, but we need to know the map coordinates. However, they are trapped inside the indecipherable. The second indecipherable is from an agent in Denmark. Denmark, as you will all know, is small and flat. If you are an agent, it is even smaller and flatter. It's easy to be spotted, particularly if you are walking around with a clandestine radio. In fact, you are about as inconspicuous as a lit-up Christmas tree. More radios are needed, therefore, to be dropped in and kept in hiding places so the agents can move unencumbered between them. Why? Because it is dangerous to transmit from one place only. The message contains details of a drop zone scheduled for tomorrow. Unfortunately, the agent was either bone tired, frightened or, possibly, under the influence of too much Danish beer and we can't read it. I can't go into any further details, but we can't miss the slot.' Major Martin paused. 'Let me remind you, an extra radio could make the difference between a dead agent and a live one.'

Ruby put up her hand. 'You want us to crack

121

these two?' She allowed a beat to elapse before adding: 'Sir.'

Twelve hours later Ruby missed the bus from her digs, where she had snatched four hours' sleep, which meant she had to kick her heels for a good twenty minutes.

She was paying for the five extra minutes in bed. But her sleep had been fretful, filled with the noise of teleprinters and jumbled letters and snippets of random information . . .

She'd woken exhausted, with a dry mouth and an incipient headache, knowing full well the duty sergeant would enjoy the tongue-lashing he would hand out. She'd fumbled for the remaining aspirin in the bottle and swallowed it down with a glass of water.

Now she was stuck here, in Henfold's town centre. Such as it was. Apart from an unremarkable market square, there was a W. H. Smith, a chemist, a jeweller (fat lot of good in a war), plus a butcher with the inevitable queue outside it. At each end of the shopping parade there was a pub and, miracle of miracles, a library housed in confident, high-Victorian municipal architecture.

Head still faintly throbbing, she walked towards it.

'Come on in . . .' The pale, male, malnourished-looking librarian at the desk dug into his limited energy reserves to welcome her. 'Please use us, but if you want to take out a book you will have to join.'

Ruby couldn't say to him, 'Can't do that. Top secret.' Instead, she gave him one of her smiles, designed to make the recipient's day. Crossing over to the reference section, she hauled out the *D* volume of the Encyclopaedia Britannica.

'Denmark is a tiny country with a population of under 5 million . . .' she read. For reference, she checked the publication date of the encyclopaedia: 1929. 'It is spread over some one hundred islands . . .'

She skimmed through descriptions of 'Northern Smorgasbord' and 'Southern Hideaways' where it was possible to feel 'you're far away from civilization'.

On further inspection, the pages, foxed and musty, offered a grand tour through Danish geography – gentle inclines, neat, bright-coloured houses, barns and woodpiles, the glint of a pale sea – and a little of its history.

Who exactly were the Danes?

Perhaps nothing encapsulates the essence of Danishness better than the idea of *hygge*, the companionship experienced by Danes when they gather together. To experience a sense of *hygge* is to retreat into a peaceful and cosy world . . .

The volume was heavy but she knew exactly how to balance it, an expertise acquired during the hours spent in the library at Cambridge.

123

She had learned wonderful things in that library.

Binary numbers make it possible to represent all computable numbers as infinite sequences of 0s and 1s alone . . .

How excited she had been on first reading the theory. She'd been like a girl with her nose pressed against a window pane through which she could make out the sweet and glistening enticements of the new mathematics, a girl who thought she could bring the world to her feet.

She could safely say that interested her far more than any human being.

Back to the encyclopaedia.

Denmark was 'very small and flat'. Given their work and what was going on there, the agents in place wouldn't have much in the way of camouflage. She recalled Major Martin's softly spoken and urgent injunctions. What a stunt he had pulled. He minded very much about those undercover men and women and was going to make the cipher clerks mind, too. Ruby liked that. There was none of that stiff upper lip, British-men-don't-display-feelings kind of approach to the situation but, rather, passionate engagement. Nor had there been any of that barely concealed patronage and the run-along-and-leave-the-grown-up-stuff-to-us attitude displayed to women by the majority of men she had encountered.

As Major Martin said, agents over there were trying to get the wireless sets from London delivered safely. They needed all the help they could get. Help which she, Ruby, knew she could give them because she was clever enough to do so. Granted, her contribution would be small but it would matter.

Think.

She stared at the books on the shelves and rehearsed the principles of encryption to refresh herself. Adding on and substituting letters were the simplest of the principles employed, the latter becoming more complex when a single letter was substituted with letter pair – but it was a process subject to mistakes.

Think, Ruby.

'In practical cryptography,' she had been told in her early training, 'part of the message transmitted does not make up the message itself but conveys instructions on how to decipher that message. The non-message letters are called indicators.'

All the basic stuff. Too basic for what was needed for the problem in hand? Perhaps she should consider the refinements and additional complications to encoding and decoding which had been thought up by fiendishly clever people.

Ruby corrected herself. Don't go too fast. Agents in the field were not necessarily fiendishly clever mathematicians. They functioned on the basic applications and possibly a level above, but not that much above.

Ruby replaced the encyclopaedia, wrote down the word *hygge*, which she liked the sound of, and went to catch the bus.

In the cipher room, the girls had divided them-selves up into teams and were continuing to work flat out on the two indecipherables. You could feel, measure almost, the tension.

So far they had made five thousand attempts.

'The crack teams haven't cracked it,' said Ruby taking her seat alongside the others.

'Shut up,' said Janet.

'If you say so.' Ruby reapplied herself. She checked the indicators, which would tell her which words of the poem had been chosen by the agent when he encoded the message, and focused on them. There were three immediate possibilities. One: the indicator groups were mutilated by trans-mitting conditions and taken down incorrectly because poor reception meant the signals clerk had not been able to make head or tail of them. Two: the agent had been badly trained and was muddled. Three: the agent had been captured and the radio was being played by the enemy, who did not know to include the indicator groups. Yet. An ominous word. Ruby knew little enough about what was going on but enough to know that if a radio operator fell into enemy hands, it was prob-ably only a matter of time before the indicators and codes were tortured out of him or her.

The first assault on the indecipherable proved useless.

Ruby massaged her fingers and settled down to the coding version of a long plod through the foothills before base camp even came into sight.

Depressingly quickly, she knew that this was going to be the equivalent of climbing the Himalayas without ropes.

Four hours later, shaky and exhausted, she waited by the bench of the duty officer in order to inform him that it was still a no-show. He was on the phone. 'This is not the five loaves and two fishes affair, you know,' he barked and put down the receiver. 'We don't have enough people.' He glared at Ruby. 'You're to report to office thirteen,' he said. 'Third floor.'

Ruby didn't move. Blimey, what was she wanted for?

'*Now*, Ingram.'

The third floor was reserved for Higher Beings, where the lucky buggers benefited from the light. Generally speaking Ruby nourished a healthy scepticism about the Higher Beings. All the same, she wouldn't have been human if she hadn't been curious to see what was up. More than curious.

However, it was Major Martin who waited by the window – and that did surprise her.

At her entrance, he turned round and she was shocked to see he had black circles under his eyes.

'Sir, are you all right?'

He raised one dark eyebrow. 'I could do with more sleep.'

'Sorry, sir. I didn't mean . . .'

The eyebrow returned to base. 'It's all right, Ingram. You are allowed to demonstrate normal

127

human responses.' He smiled grimly. 'Even if they remind us how awful we look.'

'I didn't mean that.'

'Yes, you did.'

She smothered a smile. Major Martin was nice. 'Yes, I did.'

'Good. Now we can exchange views without pretence. Sit down. We have twenty minutes precisely, and I want to talk to you about something.'

She was genuinely startled. 'You want to talk to *me*?'

'What's so extraordinary about that? Don't people talk to you, Ingram?'

She stifled a smile. 'Sorry, sir. We are used to being treated like pond life.'

'You shouldn't accept that,' he said.

What did he mean? Her? The girls? Had he singled her out? To Ruby's astonishment, she felt a faint flush steal over her face.

He continued: 'I don't want you to think like that any more. I want you on side and I want some proper work and hard thought from you.'

A tiny flutter of triumph went through her breast. *At last.*

He had noticed her. He knew she had brains.

Office 13 was at the corner of the house and enjoyed the advantage of two windows, the clear light exposing the tiredness etched into their faces. Perhaps the murk of the cipher room had its uses after all?

Martin regarded her thoughtfully before pushing

a piece of paper over the desk. 'On this, there's a message in code and another *en clair*. I'm going to give you ten minutes to decode and encode.' He glanced at his watch. 'Ready.'

She decided not to be annoyed by this lapse into the schoolmaster. 'I need something to write with, sir.'

He rootled around in his briefcase. 'Why don't you have a pen on you?'

'Because . . .'

A pencil now balanced on the flat of his hand. She looked up into his face: a nice face, an exhausted face.

'Come *on*,' he said.

Ruby accepted it. 'You're right, sir. I should be carrying a pencil.'

She didn't often back down but she could tell that he was a fair-minded person and fairness and a chance to prove herself was all she asked.

First off: take the frequency count. Think of it as feeling a pulse. The cryptographer's pulse.

She sensed his eyes were on her lowered head but refused to be hurried or flurried. After a while, she forgot about Major Martin. Ten minutes later she put down the pencil. Silently, she pushed the paper back over the table to him.

He barely glanced at it. 'Too simple?'

'One should never underestimate the task,' she said. 'But, yes.'

'How would you describe what you have just done?'

'I suppose you could say that I corralled the letters and brought them to heel. Then I applied some intuition.'

'How very female.'

'From time to time it works, sir. So do educated guesses.'

'That wasn't main-line traffic,' he said. 'That was an agent's message. It's baffled quite a few.'

She nodded. 'The first transposition had gone wrong.'

The light in the room had grown even more dazzling.

'Agents' coding and decoding require different aptitudes and casts of mind to the main-line coding activities. Wouldn't you say?' He smiled a smile which signalled one colleague's acknowledgement of another.

She felt a visceral thrill. Major Martin had unearthed what she longed for – to be in on the discussion. He had spotted that this was her territory. Wrestling with problems was her meat and drink, and just as necessary.

'Sir . . . can I say something? I know it's not my place but I think you should hear it. The indecipherables. I've been thinking around the problem. Why not dedicate a section of the cipher clerks to work solely on the indecipherables? Train us in the specifics.'

Major Martin sat back and interlocked his nice-looking fingers.

Had she gone too far? Had she been too quick

to push her luck? Well, hell, Ruby didn't care. He needed to know that people like her were not just ciphers themselves.

'Actually, we're on the same page,' he said. He sent her a half smile of approval and she wondered what lay behind all this. Because something did. 'Which doesn't surprise me,' he added.

Ruby took a deep breath. Something – the dark, expressive eyes, the sympathy reflected in them – told her that Major Martin was a man with whom she could take a risk. 'Sir, can I ask something else?'

He looked at her long and hard. *Was he going to take a risk?*

Yes, he was. 'Go on, Ingram.'

She shut her eyes for a second. This might be the end of the not-so-glowing career. 'The poem codes? Are they the most secure system?'

She had hit the nail.

For a moment, his expression was stripped naked, exposing a deep, harrowing anxiety. 'And why would you think that, Ingram?'

Ruby held out both hands. 'Even a fool, even . . .' He raised an eyebrow. 'Even a fool,' she rushed out, 'can see that a poem, particularly a well-known one, can be got out of someone. The method isn't – it can't be – foolproof.' *Idiot*, she thought. *Shut your mouth.* But shutting her mouth was not Ruby's way. 'It's wrong to send the agents off with something . . . so flimsy.'

She had trespassed. No one was supposed to

discuss these things. Especially not the pond life that she was.

She held her breath.

Major Martin leaned back in the chair. He was about to say something, checked himself and then decided to go ahead anyway. 'As I see it, we have no greater duty laid on us than to give the agents a secure coding system. Not just for the sake of our country but to give them a chance of survival.'

He spoke passionately.

I knew it. I knew it. He's worried sick.

So that was it. Agents were dying alone in that darkness out there, hunted, cornered and tortured, and he minded if the reason was Home Station's carelessness or stupidity. Major Martin minded very much – and so did Ruby.

There was a click. A connection. Emotional . . . intellectual . . . mathematical? She couldn't say what precisely but it was there.

They were on dangerous territory and she knew perfectly well that they should not be discussing this subject.

Peter Martin beat a retreat. He got to his feet and said: 'Shall I tell you what I think? You can't wait to be running a show. Am I right? So, I would like you to take charge of the indecipherable team. Pick out the brightest, or rather the best, girls, train them and keep tabs.'

Disappointed that that was it, Ruby decided to make do with what she had been offered. Making a rough computation, she said, 'We'll need rotating groups of at least twelve.'

He whistled softly. 'Fine. Personnel will go mad. Top brass will shout.' His mouth twitched. 'We're due a little well-earned entertainment.'

Again, he checked his watch. 'I've got you on board?'

She nodded.

'About coding security . . . Keep thinking, as I will at my end. Say nothing. I don't know what will happen. However, I think you have the kind of mind and aptitude which might be useful.' He picked up his briefcase. 'We'd have to sort out a promotion and you would have to come to London.'

'Wonderful,' she said.

Major Martin's smile was a wintry one. 'Some people might not like it but I imagine you could more than deal with office politics. This is not a good time for the Allies . . . and we just have to put up with that sort of stuff.'

Ruby liked the 'we'.

CHAPTER 10

On København's Bredgade a van shuddered to a halt and four Danish policemen threw themselves out of it.

They were armed.

Neither Tanne Eberstern nor her brother, Nils, paid it much attention.

Muffled up against the cold, the two of them were heading to a bar for a beer before Tanne went on to meet her friend, Grete, at the ballet.

A cigarette butt in the gutter caught Tanne's eye and she bent down and hoiked it up. A scavenger. But, these days, tobacco was like gold dust and, oh joy, she had discovered a stationer on the Bredgade who kept a stock of Bible paper which doubled up nicely for the roll-your-owns.

'Disgusting,' said Nils, his hand slapping in brotherly fashion onto her back. 'Stop it.'

Then she felt Nils's hand ball into a fist.

'Tanne . . . look up. Trouble.'

He shoved her against a shop window as policemen scythed through the pedestrians in the street.

'Stop.'

A youth in a navy-blue cap and worker's overalls had been heading towards Tanne and Nils but, at the sight of the police, he spun round and beat a retreat. Too late. A couple of the police seized him from behind and shoved him against the wall.

The majority of the onlookers shrank back – an animal reaction. None of them protested.

The youth looked wildly from side to side. *Help me? Patriots?* Tanne caught his expression: determined, full of hatred, on the brink. One of the police shouted at him. He shouted back. A second policeman, big and burly, stepped forward and hit him on the jaw with the butt of his gun.

There was a low mutter, a collective groan, from the onlookers.

Blood streamed.

His cry of pain was also one of protest.

Shameful. The thought tore through her.

The policemen squared up to their victim. Breathing heavily, some flecked with sweat.

'Name?'

'*Fuck off!*'

'Your papers?'

One of the policemen dug into the pocket of the youth's overalls.

It was then she noticed the *Gestapoman* sitting in the front of the policemen's van, watching events. He was smoking.

My God. Tanne realized with a flash of comprehension that the police were enjoying their new licence to unleash violence. The presence of a

Gestapoman whipped them up. The victim's arms were now spread out in crucifixion, the tendons in his wrists stretched like string under the pale skin. Blood dripped onto his collarless shirt.

Here was an especial shame. Danes were perpetrating war on fellow Danes.

'Let him go,' she shouted and Nils's hand clapped like a trap across her lower face.

'Shut up, Tanne.'

An alley ran down to the left of the shop they were standing outside. A cyclist emerged from it at speed. Poising at the junction, he readjusted his balance, put his head down and rode directly towards the knot of police. Wham! His wheel slammed into the legs of one policeman. The man bellowed and slumped to the ground.

The diversion gave the youth a chance. He wrested himself from their grip and took to his heels.

Run, run, Tanne willed him.

Weaving in and out of the shoppers and pedestrians, he pelted down the street and out of sight. One of the police gave chase. A second yelled at the onlookers to stand back while he attended to his fallen colleague.

The fourth?

The cyclist swung the bicycle round and pedalled furiously towards Tanne and Nils. Oh God, she thought. He was aiming to go back the way he'd come.

No.

In horror, she watched as the fourth policeman drew his gun, dropped to his knees. The gun jerked. There was a whistle – almost musical – and a tearing sound.

Tanne was standing a little in front of Nils and the blood spray hit her first, pattering over her feet, pooling onto the road. It was then she smelled it. Hot. Rank.

His head smashed in by a bullet, the cyclist hit the ground. Wheels spinning, his bicycle fell on top of him.

Inside her leather shoes, Tanne's feet were slippery, and a red stain oozed over her stockings. A single rivulet of blood ran down her left leg.

The scene burned into her vision.

The onlookers seemed frozen. Terror? Outraged and disgusted at the behaviour of their own police?

Shock made her incoherent. *His blood is on my legs. His blood is on my legs.*

The felled policeman cried out and cursed as his colleagues tried to move him.

'Don't get involved,' hissed the woman who was standing beside Tanne. She was clutching her shopping basket to her chest.

The injured policeman was manoeuvred into the back of the van, where they laid him flat, and the body of the cyclist was thrown in beside him. The van drove off in the direction of the hospital.

The street looked normal. *No, it didn't.* People moved in slow motion. The cobbles were hemmed with blood, which was trickling into the gutter.

An echo of the bullet's whistle, and the crump as it hit the skull, remained in the air. A life had been snuffed out.

She spoke through lips that didn't want to obey her. 'I must wash my legs.'

They were standing outside a well-known sausage bar. Nils hustled her inside it and they found a table. He asked for a bowl of water and helped Tanne to clean herself up.

A waitress, pale and on the verge of tears, slapped a menu on their table. There was a nervous clatter of cutlery. The phone by the till rang and was answered. The last rays of sun slanted in at the window, seeking out the shock and shadows on the diners' faces. The massy block of the Dagmuhaus building across the square was as ever, and the traffic in the street had returned to normal. Yet all was different. Witnessing that scene had changed her.

Nils nudged over a glass of beer. 'Drink.'

She steadied her hand. 'Do you think he was a communist?'

He shrugged. 'Possibly.'

'He was someone's son, brother.' The beer was good and she sucked in a second mouthful, then searched her bag for her tobacco stash and cigarette papers.

'I know.'

'Terrible things are happening in Denmark.'

'Yes, they are.' Nils was calm and matter-of-fact. 'But we have to carry on as best we can.'

Tanne shrugged. How come Nils was so . . . untouched? Clumsily, she resumed the task of rolling the cigarette and lighting it. 'Here, want one?'

'No.' Reaching over, he stilled the fingers that seemed to have lost their control. 'Don't take on. Don't let it get to you. Don't let anyone get to you.'

Blood. Brains on the road. Death.

'Aren't you upset about what we've just seen?'

'Of course. But you mustn't think about it. Otherwise it weakens you.'

'But we have to think about it. Nils, you can't not have an opinion.'

'I disagree.' Nils was his customary, infuriating, detached self. Her brother had a hide inches thicker than most and she could never make out if this was genuine or, for some psychological reason, he had cultivated imperviousness, and very successfully, too.

She and he were chalk and cheese. Nils was considered something of a mathematical genius, and his strengths, such as they were, could not be more different from Tanne's talents. He had taken his first degree at eighteen. Since then he had been sequestered at the university, adding a master's in symbolic logic, plus a PhD, to his academic achievements. So highly did the university rate him that they had given him a set of rooms over-looking the main quad and told him he could occupy them for as long as he wished.

The alcohol was working its way through Tanne's system – soothing and steadying. 'What's the latest project?'

Normally Nils brushed aside questions about his work because he knew most people didn't begin to understand. On this occasion, he was prepared to humour her. 'Electronic communications,' he said. 'We are working on a small revolution. Actually, a big one.' He grinned.

She flicked a shred of tobacco from her finger. 'Do your new German masters at the university know about it?'

Very soon after the Nazi takeover of the country, German academics from Heidelberg and Munich arrived at Nils's department at the university and muscled in on the research.

Nils glanced around. 'You mean my new *esteemed* colleagues?' He lowered his voice. 'Even I know you must watch what you say.'

Squinting at him through the cigarette smoke, she murmured, 'Your new and esteemed colleagues, then.'

'My brilliant German colleagues know all about me. They made it their business.'

Looking at Nils, she was struck by his innocence – his mad faith that everything could carry on regardless – and shivered. 'Nils, you will be careful?'

'Why wouldn't I be? I intend to stay in my rooms doing my work for the duration of the war, and I won't be prised out.'

She sent him a quizzical look. 'You really, really

are not going to take sides? You are not going to say the Germans are right or wrong?'

'No.'

'Not even after—' She stubbed out the cigarette. 'Not even—?'

'No.'

There it was: the shutter rattling down and cutting Nils off from the rest of humanity. It was an excellent tactic, giving him freedom to pursue his thoughts without the muddle and fuss of other considerations. It never occurred to him, nor would it have mattered to Nils, that others had to carry the can for a lot of things as a result.

The stains on Tanne's stockings seemed to her as bright as burning beacons. 'One day I might begin to understand what symbolic logic is.'

He looked at her with that contemptuous but affectionate look that she knew so well. 'There's no need.'

'I'm supposed to be at the ballet,' she said, after a pause. 'Grete will be waiting.'

Before they parted Tanne insisted that Nils returned with her the following day to Rosenlund, for dinner and to stay over for a night. 'The parents fret about you. You don't see enough of them. Let them check that you are all right.' She added, 'We are a family.'

Nils had a way of pushing Tanne into sounding so much older than was necessary. A hundred years older.

'The condition of being a parent is to fret. It

doesn't mean anything. Anyway, I don't want *Far* going on at me.'

'Nils, he doesn't. You choose to see it like that.'

The contemptuous but affectionate Nils was back. '*Far* and I don't understand each other, never have. I think he's blinkered. He thinks I am a peculiar species who has the misfortune to be his son.'

Aha, thought Tanne, picking up a touch of regret and resentment in Nils's tone. It wasn't all as cut and dried in her brother's mind as he would have her think.

'No need to look like that, Tanne. As the inheritor of his sacred Rosenlund, you get the special treatment.'

She frowned.

'And *don't* tell me that you find it a burden. You love the idea.'

Did she?

Despite all this, Nils allowed Tanne to persuade him and, the following day, they caught an early afternoon train to Køge.

Thick with cigarette smoke, the carriage was crowded but they managed to commandeer the last two seats. '*Mor . . . Mor . . .*' wailed a child, wanting the attention of its exhausted-looking mother, who couldn't rouse herself to respond. She wore a hand-knitted jersey in bright green which had been patched and re-patched. Her husband ate his way stolidly through a meat pie wrapped in greaseproof paper. Every so often the mother's gaze rested on the diminishing meat pie but her husband did not offer her even a crumb.

The train eased out of the station and, almost immediately, came to a halt. Tanne glanced at her watch. Stop-go. Stop-go. This was the way trains functioned in the war. Thank God, the child cried itself into exhaustion.

Yesterday's street scene had played, and replayed, in her head a thousand times – every small detail starkly etched. The blood-splattered cobbles. The splintering of bone. The tense huddle of spectators.

Horrible.

Wrong.

Nils dozed. Tanne diverted herself by looking out of the carriage window. She thought about the dress she had ordered from *Fru* Nielsen. Powder blue: designed to complement the ashy tones of her hair.

Bloodstains.

She concentrated on *Sleeping Beauty*, a ballet she knew inside out. A fragile Princess Rose, whose ankles looked as though they might snap at any minute, had been kissed passionately awake in a scene which usually evoked shivery, warm feelings. Not this time. Death in a street had shaken Tanne's assumptions and she was now beginning to understand that she had been living in ignorance of the realities – gulled by an upbringing in the innocent wilderness of Rosenlund.

As arranged, Arne was waiting at Køge station

143

with Loki harnessed into the pony trap. Nils seized Arne's hand and shook it. Arne was the one person to whom he showed obvious affection. 'How are you, Master Nils?'

'All the better for seeing you, Arne.'

Each ran a check on the other – her slight brother and big, burly Arne. They were friends: the sort who went fishing together and sat in contented silence for hours, firm in that friendship. Nils climbed up beside Arne. 'I'll take the reins.'

At Rosenlund, Tanne stopped in the hall to admire an arrangement of hothouse flowers. She checked the card beside the vase: 'To Kay, with love from Cousin Anton'.

Running up to her bedroom, it was impossible to miss the family tree placed at the turn of the stairs. No inhabitant of Rosenlund, no visitor, could ever be in doubt as to the Eberstern pedigree.

In 1777, Bertel Eberstern had been granted a patent of nobility. In 1798, his son, Carsten Eberstern, married Princess Sophia-Maria of Westphalia. And so it went on.

Those dead forebears, many of them German, still had the power to mould her existence. As the elder child she would one day step onto the estate and kneel to accept her future. Being the younger, Nils would not inherit, and from time to time he needled her about it. 'I can choose my own life,' he pointed out. Flatly. Unsympathetically.

Could Tanne?

When she inherited, it would be to care for the

144

land, the house, the farms, for the duration. A curious position to be in, but she enjoyed it and resented it, sometimes with the same breath. Adults of her parents' generation regarded her with approval, for she possessed future status. Yet if she confessed to her friends what her future entailed her words were met with indifference and, occasionally, contempt.

Nils was correct. She wasn't free.

But she could be. She could be.

Sometimes she lay in bed and plotted escaping to Rome or Paris. To live in an attic and behave disgracefully.

'Most women in the world don't even have the vote,' her mother had pointed out, more than once, when Tanne voiced her misgivings. 'Let alone the right to take possession of their inheritance. Denmark is ahead of the world.'

And I should be grateful?

At those moments she hated her mother, who was so settled, so in the mould. Had her mother ever rebelled? Or ever considered that there was another kind of life, that no one should be in thrall to bricks and mortar? Did she ever get angry, as Tanne so often did?

Who knew? Her daughter didn't.

Then, in the aftermath of strong emotion, stole the calm of passions spent, the familiar image of the beautiful house and land lodging uppermost in her mind. She remembered the times riding out with her father, rising at dawn for the duck shoot, the boating parties, the family eating and talking together. It was, she told herself, a Platonic ideal of rural life – a utopia, a benign autocracy – where it was possible to live the good fulfilling existence.

Pausing to look through the large window at the turn of the stairs, she saw the knife-sharp, frozen lines of winter had formed like the first exploratory strokes of a drawing. Where the late sun hit the lake there was an explosion of light and icy dazzle. She grimaced. Those summer vistas, the radiance of trees and lawn, were now only memories.

As usual, tea was served in the small sitting room overlooking the garden and lake. Nils was already installed in a chair by the window doing a crossword.

Tanne sat on the arm of the chair. 'Am I annoying you?'

He did not bother to look up. 'Yes.'

'Did you ring for tea?'

'No idea.'

'You probably did.'

The door opened and, in rubber boots over her bare legs, as was her wont, Arne's wife, Birgit, appeared with the tea tray. Nils leaped to his feet – he could be quick when he wished to be – and captured the tray. 'It seems I did.'

He put the tray down on the table, and flicked Birgit's plait. 'You're going grey, Birgit. It suits you.'

As she left the room, Birgit smiled at him over her shoulder and said: 'Go on, be as rude as you like.'

The habit of taking tea had been imported into the family by her mother. A silver teapot. Bone china so fine you could see your fingers through it. A plate of cake. Kay always specified Victoria sponges and boiled fruit cakes. So English. If Tanne had anything to do with it, Danish favourites such as *kekstorte* and Napoleon's Hats sneaked onto the cake stand and, of course, their father's favourite gingerbread. It was civilization, tricked out with lace napkins. A small ritual knitted up into the greater one of Rosenlund's daily existence.

Their father arrived. He had been out for hours riding the boundaries to check on the winter arrangements, which meant endless checking up on fodder, silage, fuel and cattle shelter.

He was still in his riding clothes and was moving a little stiffly. He went straight over to Nils and dropped a hand on his shoulder. 'Nice to see you, Nils. Are you staying long?'

Nils was not as tall as his father. The family joked about a distant troll ancestry sneaking into the warrior Ebersterns. Nils pretended he thought it was funny, too. The joke had rippled along through the years until the day their mother said, 'Have any of you considered that it might be my ancestry?' shocking them all into silence because their mother's background never seemed to come into it. 'Whoever it was,' said Nils, who minded about his lack of height, 'was no friend of mine.'

'Until tomorrow,' he answered. 'I've things to do.'

Translated, this meant Nils yearned to quit the

beauty and elegance of Rosenlund and return to his hermetic, dusty, comfortless set of rooms.

'Don't you want to know what's going on here?' her father asked.

'To be honest, not particularly.'

He was disappointed. 'It would be nice if you stayed,' he said. 'Won't you?'

Nils got up and wandered over to the window. 'No,' he said flatly.

'No interest at all in what's going on?'

'Why should I?' Nils turned round to face him. 'You and Tanne have it all sewn up.'

'But there's a war on.'

'I know,' said Nils in a very deliberate manner. 'I know.'

Nils may have been shorter than his father, but they shared the same colouring and cast of features and, when they were angry, similar expressions. There comparisons stopped and contrasts began, for their characters could not have been more dissimilar. Difficult people, both of them; difficult to gauge and, Tanne suspected, a mystery to most.

But she loved them.

She stepped into the breach. 'Nils, some of the stock died last winter because of the cold. We don't want that to happen again.'

'So? You've stocked up. Simple.'

'But the milk yields are down,' said her father.

Nils shrugged.

Don't push too hard, Far, Tanne told him silently.

He gave up. 'What's going in København?'

'The usual,' Tanne replied. 'Shopping, theatre, eating.' A man was shot dead. 'I went to the ballet. *Sleeping Beauty*. It's on all the time.'

'Of course it is,' said Nils. 'Denmark kissed awake by Prince Charming. The question is: who is Prince Charming?'

Something went click in Tanne's head. So? The arch of the ballerina's foot . . . she had been balancing not on an aesthetic pin but a political one. How stupid Tanne had been not to have seen that the ballet was being used as a coded message of defiance. No wonder *Sleeping Beauty* was being performed all the time, and how irritating that it was Nils who had pointed it out.

'København is stuffed with Danes eavesdropping on other Danes,' continued Nils. 'The *stikker* who report things to the Germans. The atmosphere is most peculiar and jumpy.'

'Surprised you notice.' Tanne was a little sour.

He flashed her a look as if to say: *That was not worthy of you.* 'No one feels safe to speak their mind. Even I've noticed.'

No, it wasn't worthy of her, and she was annoyed with herself for allowing point-scoring habits from their childhood to resurface. Tanne made a face at him. It was so unlike Nils to comment on anything other than his immediate concerns. These, he once informed her, were formulae, theories of computable numbers, academic papers.

Her father snapped his gingerbread in two. A

149

fine dust fell to his plate. 'Be careful what you say about the Germans.'

'We know what side you're on,' said Nils, goading. 'It must be increasingly difficult to square it with Mother.'

It wasn't like Nils to be malicious. Amused, disdainful, removed . . . yes, but malice did not often figure. It was the war, she thought, with increasing desperation.

Her father elected not to notice. 'Perhaps the *stikker* are necessary. Order must be maintained. Rebellion and resistance make life impossible.'

Tanne heard herself exclaim. '*Inform* on your fellow citizens?'

'We have to consider Denmark's position,' he said, not unreasonably.

She stared at him. 'But that's it, *Far*. We do have to consider.'

It was true – and she had not done so. Not properly. Not in depth. Worse, she did not possess the political vocabulary to describe what she felt.

'We have to deal with Germany,' her father was saying. 'It's not what Denmark asked for but we've done it. You must consider that the communists could be as much of a threat.'

'Overdoing it, *Far*,' said Nils from his perch by the window.

Her father swung round to face him and Tanne read in his expression both disappointment and a baffled irritation.

'Do you two understand anything? Have you

seen what Stalin is up to? First he joins in with Hitler and overruns Poland. Why? Answer: because he reckoned he could snaffle a piece of it. Now he's fighting on the side of the Allies, but it isn't for love of peace and democracy. It's because he has his own plans for expansion. Denmark might well be among them. Do you want to live in a communist country? Better the devil you know . . . And there is Rosenlund.'

'Oh, Rosenlund,' said Nils in a sarcastic voice. 'Rosenlund . . .'

There was a long awkward pause. Her father pushed his cup and saucer away and lit a cigarette. 'Whatever you think, Nils, it is worth saving. And I will.'

Why, oh why, did he say such things? He wasn't a fool and he certainly wasn't a bad man.

Her gaze sifted over familiar things: the secretaire with the bowed legs, the chair with the curling back, the long pier glass painted bronze and decorated with a lotus-plant design, the china pots under the window patterned with blue agapanthus and fiery geraniums, the bone china on the tray, the fine Danish landscape over the fireplace of a clearing in a birch wood covered by spring anemones.

'Hello, darlings.'

Their mother stood in the doorway, dressed in one of her pretty woollen afternoon frocks. She had a heightened colour and looked younger than Tanne had seen her for a long time.

151

'Sorry. I was out walking and I had to change.'

All three stared at her.

'What is it?' she asked. 'I can feel the atmosphere.' She snapped her fingers and the noise sounded like a gun shot.

'The war, of course.' Nils resumed his seat.

Tanne glanced down at her teacup and noticed that the saucer had a chip on its rim.

Her mother sat down in her usual seat behind the tea tray. With a deliberate movement, she lifted up the teapot. 'I think you were discussing politics.' She poured herself a cup of tea. 'Not a good idea.' She picked up the milk jug and the colour deepened in her cheeks. 'It's a subject we should leave well alone.'

Tanne's gaze shifted from her mother to her father. Neither of them was looking at the other. 'We can't,' she said flatly. 'The war is happening.'

To her surprise, her mother's hand whitened with tension as it grasped the milk jug. 'That's why we have to make sure we don't quarrel.'

'*Never forget . . .*' her mother used to say.

'*Never forget what?*'

'*We are a family.*'

It was possible to both love and hate at the same time. Yes, yes, it was. When Tanne hated her mother, she hated her more than she loved her. Sometimes it was vice versa. Her mother was her mirror image – all mothers and daughters were. Whereas her feelings for her father were fixed and constant, like the planets, and driven by the need to protect him, her feelings for her mother shifted like the tide.

Early-ish the following morning, Nils went back to København.

A year ago, the decision had been taken to train Tanne in the running of Rosenlund and she had been summoned to a session in the estate office, which was lined from floor to ceiling with the ledgers. The ledgers went back to the early nineteenth century, and contained a switchback narrative of bumper yields, harsh winters, golden summers and barren harvests but none, apparently, as bad as the past twelve months.

Checking over the accounts with him, she was shocked to hear her father swear under his breath. Dairy yields were down, plus the order had come through from the Town Hall to requisition a number of their precious pigs.

'What right do they have?' Tanne demanded.

Her father moved over to the window. A troubled silence followed before he explained that the German Reich and the Danish Protectorate were now one family. Families shared.

'*Sharing*, yes,' said Tanne.

This was a new world with new realities and again, Tanne felt ashamed that it had taken so much time for her to realize what was going on.

'If this winter is like the last one . . .' He turned to face her. 'Tanne, darling, promise me that you will never get involved in anything stupid.'

'Why?'

He looked at her as if she was mad. 'Why? Because—' He gestured at the ledgers. 'You know why.'

'I understand.'

He turned back to the window. 'More important . . . is your safety.'

Badly bruised from a tussle with a gate in the north field a couple of days ago, his hand rested on the blind. The flesh was green and yellow, the nail blackened. It must be hurting him. It was a reminder that her father could be wounded and her heart squeezed in her chest.

At university, she had talked politics endlessly and, she now acknowledged, carelessly. With Aage, Grete, Hannah, Gooda, all close friends, she had debated the overthrow of the monarchy, putting students into Parliament and turning pacifist. 'We are articulating Denmark's future,' they told each other and thrived on the noisy clash of viewpoints. She remembered Aage leaping up onto a table and managing to look both magnificent and ridiculous.

How pleasurable the long beach walks dodging salt-bleached driftwood had been, and the demanding summer bicycle rides and, when back at university for the autumn and winter, the exciting and messy sessions with printing machines and duplicators.

None of them had understood how their ideas would work in practice. Still less what a war meant.

154

Certainly not the *realpolitik* of guns and greed and killing.

She joined her father at the window and he reached out, put an arm round her shoulders and pulled her to him. Together, they looked out onto the winter landscape.

Very often at this time of year, a light, pretty snow was the first to fall. Then the winds arrived, the sky lowered, more snow fell, packing down the pretty and sparkling surface into a sullen, greyish layer over which could be seen the spoor of desperate deer weaving this way and that.

Arne had taught Nils and Tanne how to spot the signs of winter starvation. 'A hungry deer scratches up patches of snow to try to get at the leaves below. Watch for the scatters of urine in the snow that mean they are dying.'

'Promise me you won't get involved, Tanne?' her father repeated.

She sneaked a sideways look at him. Her father's fair hair was silvering up. Definitely, he was older, more careworn, slightly haunted. She had always felt that she knew him best of all, and considered him as 'hers'. She understood his handsome, slightly remote exterior hid passionate feelings. Perhaps a vulnerability? Her friends knew better than to criticize him in her presence because Tanne protected him, sometimes against her mother.

'I promise.'

CHAPTER 11

The snow fell for a day.

Kay received a message from Felix which had been tucked between stones in the wall that ran around the back of the estate. 'Please bring Aunt Agatha's present up on Thursday.'

So it begins, she thought.

How do I do it?

It was no use being indulgent, or weak. Having opted to walk this particular path, walk it she must. She was doing it for decency in the largest, widest sense, but that was not to say she didn't feel frightened, because she did.

She worked out her tactics.

On the Wednesday evening, she put on her black lace dress – a favourite with Bror – and made sure they ate a good dinner. Afterwards, they retired to the small sitting room. Birgit had lit the fire and the card table was pulled up in front of it.

Tanne was staying with a friend in Køge and they had the house to themselves.

'A game of Snap?' she suggested.

'The best of five.'

Bror played ferociously but not ferociously enough. Kay beat him three games to two. Good. 'Darling . . .'

Bror smiled his slow, rather sleepy smile which had so enchanted Kay on first meeting him. 'I know that tone. You want something.'

'Could I have the car tomorrow? I want to go and see Nils. I'll park it at the station and be back on the evening train.'

'But you don't like driving in the snow.'

'It wasn't that heavy a snowfall so the roads should be passable.'

Bror laid down his cards and made for the whisky decanter.

She felt a chill. 'Bad loser, darling?'

Glass in hand, he turned round and looked at her. Her smile faded.

'You're not going to København to meet Anton, are you?'

The breath seemed stuck in her lungs. Getting up from the card table, she said, 'I'll have one, too.'

Bror handed her a measure in a cut-glass tumbler. It tasted of Scottish peat bogs, of wild berries and mountain water – which she remembered from holidays in Argyll before marrying Bror. 'You haven't answered my question, Kay.'

Relief.

It was the wrong question and she could deal with it. Kay cradled the glass against her stomach. 'No. I'm not going to see Anton.' It occurred to

157

her that she should be more indignant and she added sharply: 'It's a ridiculous question.'

Bror considered the contents of his glass. 'You don't need me to tell you that Anton wants you, Kay. I notice he's been sending you flowers . . .'

'Look at me, Bror,' she said angrily.

'You see, I think . . .' He came over and placed a hand under her chin.

She was conscious of his energy – his strong, focused energy – flowing through his fingertips into her. 'Perhaps *you* should be thinking more clearly, Bror.'

He turned away.

'Look at me, Bror.'

He shrugged and took up a position by the fireplace. 'I think that you're still angry with me about signing the Declaration. Am I right?' Kay was silent while she worked out her next step. He continued: 'You forget how well I know you.'

'The Declaration's nothing to do with Anton. You're mixing up the two.'

'Anton would absolutely make the Declaration his business. It's a way of needling me. Anyway, he told me once that if there was a war it was best to be on the side which America was likely to support. Which I'm sure will be your position.'

'So?'

Bror dropped the subject of Anton. 'You and I have to be careful that we don't let all this divide us.'

She bit her lip – and the guilt which was becoming a companion settled over her.

'Nothing to say, darling?'

'This *is* ridiculous, Bror. You know how I feel about the Declaration and I am certainly not going to sleep with your cousin. Can we talk about something else?'

'Better we talk about it, than brood,' said Bror.

Clutching her whisky, Kay walked up and down, and the heavy material of her skirts swished in the uneasy silence. 'Haven't we enough to deal with at the moment?'

'Kay . . .'

It was the voice which had wooed her so many times.

The old feelings kicked in – and they also provided a solution to this particular conversation. 'Darling Bror . . .' Kay went over to him and pushed the glass against his chest. 'Sorry, I'm so sorry . . . this bloody war.'

He took her glass, set it down and pulled her to him. His hands slid over her shoulder blades. 'I'm sorry, too.'

When Bror apologized he meant it and she knew how difficult it was for him to do so. Within her armour of black lace, she was as tense as a coiled spring and she longed for the impossible – to return to the beginning. With a sigh, she pressed her face against his chest.

His grip tightened. 'Kay . . .?' He placed a finger at the base of her neck – precisely at the point where the pulse beat. 'Why do you want to see Nils? Is there anything wrong?'

'He's my son. Why wouldn't I want to see him?'

Nothing was normal any longer. The lie took shape as easily as the truth. It was then Kay understood that part of her had already broken away. Part of her was already on that train with the wireless transmitter, working out what to do, how to proceed.

He kissed the place on her neck where his finger had rested.

She murmured, 'You should want to see him, too. You must try to be closer to him, Bror. Promise me. You never know with a war . . .'

Her voice trailed away. Had she overdone it? Nils was always a slightly tricky subject.

He flinched. 'Nils has left home.' Bror allowed himself a note of regret. 'Which makes it easier as I don't have to think about him all the time.' He laid a hand on her breast and his touch set up familiar sensations in her pelvis. 'Kay . . .' Gently, he pushed her towards the sofa.

She looked up at him. 'Here?'

'Yes, here.'

'Goodness . . .' She laughed and dropped back onto the sofa.

Between them they fought with the folds of black lace, which they wadded around her hips. She undid his trousers. He engaged expertly with the button of her French lace knickers.

It was fierce, hot and relatively brief. At one

point he turned her over, at another she rose un-
inhibited above him. The moment appeared to
satisfy a need in both of them, and reminded them
of an element in their life together which was in
danger of being lost. It was, Kay thought, a stirring, salty reminder of the early days when lust
preoccupied them, and nothing was political.

Afterwards, they lay jammed together on the sofa
like a pair of teenagers.

'My dress! My poor dress,' said Kay.

They smiled at each other, broken and uneasy
smiles.

What next?

'Go to København,' Bror said. 'But if the weather
is bad, I insist you get Arne to drive you.'

The snowfalls had freshly iced the countryside,
and thrown soiled, sleety sheets over the towns
and villages.

On the journey from Køge, Kay rubbed a circle
out of the ice crystals on the train window. Then
she peered out across a white, shrouded landscape.
Was she prepared to die for this land?

Retrieved from the pigeon loft, the case was on
the rack above her.

Please . . . She sent a prayer up into the ether.
Please. Let me do this properly.

As instructed, she waited by the newspaper
vendor at the main station in København. A youth
in a peaked cap brushed up against her, slipped
a key into her hand and whispered the address,

161

adding: 'The flat has been checked out. No children. No maids.'

That was important. Children and maids posed a risk

On the pavements, the snow was piled six feet deep but, unusually, the authorities had made no move to clear it away. Carrying the case, Kay emerged from the station. A bitter wind blew from the north which bit into her exposed skin and swirled up her skirt. More than thankful for her boots and gloves, she adjusted her hat and headed for the tram stop.

The city was eerily silent. Cold always dulled her brain and, as Kay grew older, her aversion to it deepened. It crept into her bones and she dreaded the prospect of another vile winter like the previous one.

There were two other passengers at the tram stop, both of them bundled up into coats and scarves. Kay pulled off a glove and checked the key zipped into a compartment in her brown crocodile handbag.

The tram was only half full. Kay chose a seat in the middle of the carriage and tucked the case under her legs. Two German officers got on and sat down in the seats in front her. 'Thank you, thank you,' one of them said politely in bad Danish.

They were dressed in the *feldgrau* soldier's uniform but, at a pinch, they could have been taken for tourists. Kay was forced to study the back of their heads. One of them had a mole at his hairline, the other had fair acned skin. Their ordinariness made it difficult to feel anything stronger than mild distaste.

The tram hissed along the tracks.

The young girl in a threadbare brown coat seated beside Kay stood up and pushed her way to the standing area at the back.

A few seconds later an elderly man heaved himself to his feet and joined the girl. It wasn't long before the majority of the passengers followed suit and jammed the standing area, which meant Kay and the German soldiers were the only ones still seated.

More clacking of wheels, plus muffled conversation from the standing platform filtered towards Kay.

A cool head, Felix had instructed. *Act normally.*

Despite the tuition, Kay's foot anchoring the case trembled and a numbness crept up her right leg.

If she remained seated, she would be marked out. If she got up, it would be obvious that the case was heavy. Split-second decision. She concentrated on steadying her foot.

Get off the tram.

The next stop was in sight. She picked up the case. One of the soldiers looked round. He had a pleasant, unassuming face. 'Let me help you,' he said.

What was normal? What was normal? Certainly

not the cocktail of terror and disbelief flowing through her veins.

But this nice, ordinary-looking soldier had read the manual: 'Be polite to the natives of whichever country you are occupying.'

He held out his hand.

She thought rapidly, running through her experiences of fraternizing with Bror's German cousins and connections over the years.

What got the best response from them?

In a flash, she remembered sitting in a plush Munich café, the women at one end of the table, the men at the other and a violinist hard at work on a Strauss waltz. Plates of choux pastry larded with cream were piled high between them. The men smoked cigarettes and kept a close eye on their wives, Kay among them. Play the little woman, she thought. Like the English, German men liked to think that they held all the cards.

'Thank you,' she said and followed him to the back of the tram. 'You're so kind.'

As she pushed past a knot of passengers, a finger jabbed into her back. She flinched. Another drove painfully into her side.

'Nazi lover.'

The words were uttered softly but loud enough. Turning her head, she encountered blank faces.

The soldier deposited the case on the pavement and wished her a good day in bad Danish before getting back onto the tram.

The tram drew away. Shivering, Kay looked up at the group of hostile faces, ashamed that she minded what they thought of her.

A feeble sun emerged from the grey cloud but didn't do anything to raise the temperature. The case handle bit into her fingers and her feet were blocks of ice.

At a junction with Østergarde, she peered into a shop window in which was reflected a blurry, moving collage of other pedestrians checking for tails.

Her own face looked back at her.

Always, she had considered her features too non-descript, except for her chin, which Anton, in one of his flirtatious moments, insisted was a stubborn one. 'You look as soft as butter, darling, but your chin tells me you're a fraud dressed up in pearls.' She was wearing the substantial Eberstern pearls and an exquisitely cut suit under her coat which, along with the blue hat, was the fruit of one of her pre-war Parisian trips.

How was she managing the transition from well-to-do Danish matron into a secret operator who could be hunted and shot, along with her family?

Nothing will have prepared you for it . . . Felix again, instructing and cautioning.

Once more, she checked for a tail in a shop window. It was then she realized that the pearls were unwise. If anyone saw them under her coat, they would mark her out. Impatient with herself, she undid the clasp and dropped them into her bag. Lesson learned.

She quickened her pace, walking as fast as she could manage with the heavy case and without drawing attention to herself.

The safe house was reached through a courtyard at the centre of which the last of the hawthorn berries still clung to the trees. Looking neither right nor left, she skirted round the courtyard. Her nervousness intensified, driving acid into her stomach. God only knew how many pairs of eyes might be watching.

Inserting the key into the door, she pushed it open and stepped onto a pile of letters.

It was apparent at once that no one had been in the stale and unaired flat for some time. Setting the case down, she went on the prowl. In a room leading off the hall there was a vase of mummified flowers. Dead flies littered the windowsill. The floor-length drapes at the windows were coated in dust. The cushions on the sofa still bore the imprints of the people who last sat in them.

Back in the hall, she picked up the post addressed to Mr, Mrs and Master Frederick Mueller and stacked it in piles on the hall table, ready for the addressees to read the contents.

She knew in her heart that it was a useless gesture and something rotten had happened to the Muellers. All the same, she felt obliged to make it. Otherwise, it was to give up.

In the kitchen, a recipe book lay open on the

sideboard. 'How to make a garlic sausage,' Kay read. In the sink, dirty cutlery rested in scummy, stagnant water, but the shelves around the room were neatly arranged, the storage jars labelled in a clear hand. The family who had lived here had been proud of the place.

Something – and it wasn't difficult to figure out what it might have been – had gone wrong for the family.

Light the gas. Fill the kettle. Place it on the ring.

Exactly what had happened to the Muellers?

The net curtains at the windows were good quality. Parting them a fraction, Kay checked out the courtyard. Scarlet pinpricks of the hawthorn berries caught her eye in the gloom.

All clear. Except that it wasn't. Nothing was.

The gas popped, making her jump. Since there was no milk, Kay made herself sit down with a few leaves of tea floating in the hot water and smoked a cigarette to steady herself. Not having anticipated a nervous reaction to her new role, she had been surprised by the disruption to her sleeping and eating patterns.

The front door was opening. In a flash, she was on her feet and, for the first time in her life, she wished she had one of Bror's guns.

Dead on time, it was Felix. The overalls had been replaced by a thick coat, smart trousers and a jacket, with a Fedora pulled down over his face. He tossed the hat onto the table. 'Any tea spare?'

167

The cupboard was well stocked with china and Kay found a second mug. 'How are you?'

They were speaking in low voices.

'Fine.'

Felix wasn't fine but tense and preoccupied. Kay pointed to the case and he placed it on the table.

'Any trouble?' he asked.

'No.'

'Followed?'

'No.'

He snapped open the locks and eased up the lid. 'How's Hector, by the way?'

'Hector? He and I have become friends. But I think he's homesick.'

'He'll be home soon enough.' He surveyed the case's contents. 'I'm sorry I had to ask you to bring it here.'

'I thought London was supposed to train the sentiment out of you.'

He pointed a finger at his chest. 'Observe, I am still human.'

The flash of humour was reassuring. 'Felix, look at me.'

His lips twitched. 'Gladly. Very nice, too.'

'No one is going to suspect the British wife of Bror Eberstern.'

He turned on her. 'That's stupid, Freya. Don't be.'

It had been a long time since she had been addressed so tartly and her hands tightened round the mug. 'The Nazis know that I'm aware they

168

will be watching me because I am British. Therefore it's likely they'll conclude that, because I know they're watching, I won't dare to do anything.'

'The key word is "likely". Unreliable at best.'

It was then she realized that she was not the cause of his anger but bearing the brunt of it. 'Trouble?'

He was checking out the Send/Receive switch. 'Perhaps.'

She knew that he should not go into detail. But he did.

'The word is that . . . Well, reports have it that an agent up in Jutland is out of control.' He grimaced. 'Drinking heavily . . . Apparently, when he drinks, he talks. He's been warned. Many times.'

They were standing very close to each other, whispering.

'What will you all do?'

'Christ. Don't ask.'

In the heat of the moment, he had raised his voice.

'Shush.' She laid a finger on his lips.

He brushed her hand aside, but checked himself. 'There's been no word of Vinegar either at this end of proceedings. London tells me that he's up and running when I ask them to confirm. But I'm uneasy and I don't know why. My contacts on Jutland have not set eyes on him. They just leave the messages in the drop boxes and vice versa.'

'He could be being ultra cautious,' she said.

'Maybe.'

She imagined the resolution which needed to be scraped together before abandoning oneself to the unknown and the moment of terror before the opening of the parachute. 'He may have been injured and is lying low.'

'He's picking up the messages and sending them.' He wrapped a length of the aerial round his finger and stared at it. 'You can't be in this game without considering the possibilities. We have only London's word that he's not dead. But what do they know? Is Vinegar a traitor? Are the Germans playing back the wireless set? Or am I delusional?'

'If Vinegar was taken what could happen?'

Felix was playing with the handle of the case. 'Probaby tortured. The Jutland network would be compromised and there's a good chance we would be, too. If that was the case . . .' He looked up. 'If that was the case, dear Freya, we would have to take to the hills.'

'Not many hills in Denmark,' she pointed out.

Felix stared at her. Then he gave a short laugh. 'A lot depends on who's got him, if anyone has. Gestapo or the military. Whoever, they might run him until they want to pull us in. They could be using Vinegar to transmit to London . . .'

Kay was curious. 'What's he like?'

'No hero to look at, but I liked what I saw.'

Time was going slowly. Her jangled, snapping nerves, perhaps? 'More tea?'

Felix wasn't interested in the tea. 'We're under-funded and need people. London is clueless and, for all the protests to the contrary, doesn't care that much about Denmark. We need more sets and more pianists. London sent in a couple before me, but according to my contacts one of the sets was smashed up on landing, the other pianist was caught transmitting in a block of flats.'

She didn't need to ask what had happened to him. She didn't want to ask.

'Unless we have more back-up,' said Felix, 'I'm hindered from running the network because I'm always trying to reach the set, wherever it is.'

Clasping the mug, her hands sought to absorb the final vestiges of warmth from the hot water, and she heard herself say, 'I'll train.'

'Not in the mood for jokes.' Felix set down his mug on the table and, peering at her, realized it wasn't a joke. 'No.'

'Yes,' she countered.

There were things to be done and men were dying and girls were having their legs shot off. And here she was in a flat made terrible by its owners' enforced absence. And her husband . . .? Her husband could be considered a traitor.

'You don't know what you're doing.'

'Agreed, I can't go to London to train, but there must be someone over here who can teach me Morse?' She pushed for the *coup de grâce*. 'You can't afford not to take me up.'

'It's dangerous.'

'Self-evidently. Give me a proper reason.'

'You are more valuable as a courier.'

171

'The two aren't mutually exclusive.'

'Almost.'

'But not quite.' She was making headway. 'Get another wireless set sent in. Teach me Morse. We'll keep one set at Rosenlund and the other in safe houses here.' She thought of her recent journey and her travelling companions of anxiety and acid stomach. 'Get thee behind me,' her father used to say of his longing for brandy. It never worked but it was worth trying. 'Between us, we can keep up the skeds but ensure we never fall into a pattern. We just have to work out a system of communication and message drops.'

What was she doing? The voice she was hearing belonged to someone else.

Felix ran a finger along the edge of the case. 'You may be right. There's a push to develop new wireless sets over here. We're good at radio technology. London might be persuaded to allow us to train our own operators.'

He fished a cigarette stub out of his pocket. 'Do you know how long the average life expectancy of a wireless operator is?'

What was she doing?

'No point in asking, Felix, or in answering.'

'Six weeks.'

She looked away towards the window.

'*Why* would you do this, Freya?'

She thought – rapidly, longingly – of the place which had become her home . . .

Summer sun – how she loved it. Rosenlund's

172

long windows thrown open to expel the cold winter air trapped in its corners and to invite in the fresh, warm day. Clean bed linen. A book by the fire. The lake at Rosenlund frozen into a spectrum of exquisite colours. Good food . . .

She thought of her family.

Bror. Tanne. Nils.

Felix lit a match. As it flared into the gloom, she understood an odd truth: once you had committed, the urge was to commit further. Deeper.

He dragged at the stub of his cigarette and sucked in smoke. 'Freya, I'm trying to put you off.'

Smoke drifted between them. She wanted to remind him of his own rules. *Smoke is a giveaway.* But the sight of his tired, drained face shut her up.

'Someone has to do it. If it isn't me, perhaps someone with a young family will and that would be worse.' Her reasoning was taking shape, urgent and imperative. 'London wants and needs intelligence. Yes? It wants things to happen in Denmark. Yes? They haven't much to depend on except people like us. Denmark has not had a chance to prove . . . Well, what? That it can fight?' She leaned against the table. 'If we don't do our best, Denmark *will* go under.'

He clapped softly.

'I'm curious, Freya. You're not Danish.'

'Shut up, Felix. I'm as Danish as anyone. And British. And someone who is saying that action is necessary.'

Felix took a decision. 'Come with me to the bookshop on the Strøget in half an hour.'

It was a yes.

She glanced at her watch. 'Sked time?'

Felix snapped to attention and parted the net drapes at the window just a fraction. 'The lookouts should be in place by now.' The drapes dropped back into place. 'If you can, before you go on air make sure you have lookouts. They may save your life.'

He sat down, put on the headphones and flexed his right hand. 'Ready.'

She watched him, willing her heartbeat to return to normal.

ZYA. *The call sign.*

QRK. *What is my intelligibility?*

QVR. *Ready to receive.*

A good ten paces behind him, Kay trailed Felix through Tivoli Gardens. Like the other parks, it was crowded with people snatching some fresh air and daylight before the long night closed in.

Felix left Tivoli by the south gate and Kay followed him.

He had done his chameleon routine: hat pulled down over his face; wool scarf wrapped round his neck. Looking straight ahead and walking briskly, he managed to mimic most of the men in the city.

Crossing the street, he doubled back on his tracks and they retraced their route through the shoppers until they reached the fashionable and popular bookstore in the Strøget. Felix came to a halt and was apparently absorbed by the display in the front of the window. Kay walked past him and entered a boutique selling women's underwear. She spent ten minutes discussing the dearth of lace trimming and bought a couple of sweat pads for under the arms.

She went back to the bookshop.

Check the window, Felix had briefed. *If there's a Tolstoy on display, it's safe. If there is a copy of Homer's* Iliad, *it isn't.*

She peered through the window where frost patterns were gathering. Copies of the Bible, an illustrated volume of Norse Myths and a pre-war novel were arranged in the front of the display. Tucked into the back there was a luridly jacketed copy of *Anna Karenina* beside the latest edition of *Mein Kampf*. Someone had a sense of humour.

Kay went in.

A man with a prophet's beard was serving at the counter, and she asked him the name of the translator of the *Anna Karenina*. 'If you follow me,' he said, 'we can look it up.' He ushered her into the back of the shop.

The furiously untidy and stuffy room into which she was ushered stank of smoke and the white paintwork was tinged yellow from nicotine. Running across one wall were bookshelves, stacked from floor to ceiling with books and periodicals.

175

Felix already sat at a round table whose surface was pitted and stained with cigarette burns and water marks. Two other men sat opposite him.

The first was a raw-looking youth with a shaved head, in blue overalls. The second, attired in a business suit, was Anton.

It wasn't hard to pick up the tension in the room and, as Kay entered, Anton sent her look which she interpreted as a warning to shut up about knowing him.

She wished he wasn't there. Anton's presence added an unwanted complication.

Felix introduced the youth. 'Freya, this is Jacob.'

'*Hej*, Jacob,' she said.

Jacob didn't bother with niceties. He ran a hand over his head. 'Any chance you were followed?'

'No.'

Kay sat down and Felix surveyed the faces at the table. 'Last Monday, Jacob's friends in the Køge cell were rounded up. We've had reports from a contact working in the laundry who said she heard screams from the cells. Jacob's here because he needs to lie low for a few days.'

Jacob's pale features creased in anger. 'I want to try to get them out.'

'No,' said Felix. 'We can't.'

Jacob rounded on him. 'You don't give all the orders.'

'Yes, I do,' said Felix – and Kay saw a new side to him.

Anton held up a hand. 'Shush.'

Jacob rose to his feet, moved over to the door and listened. He looked awkward and ungainly but, Kay noted, he could move like a cat.

Jacob gave a thumbs-up and leaned back against the door. 'So you won't help?' His frown was now so deep it looked permanent. 'My mother would do more than you lot.'

Anton steepled his hands, pressing the tips of his fingers together. Kay could tell he was regretting this meeting, and disliking Jacob. 'Action cannot be taken in isolation,' he offered. 'Your communist friends are admirable, but not equipped. What would your mother prefer? Her son alive or dead? Or would she like to listen to your screams?'

'Listen, Jacob . . .' Felix listed a pitifully sparse inventory. Guns: ten Sten guns, ten Colt pistols. Ammunition: approximately two hundred rounds. A quantity of plastic explosive. 'But it's not enough.'

'So you won't do anything?'

'*Can't* . . .' said Felix. 'But if we could we would.'

Felix's obvious sympathy succeeded in calming Jacob down. Kay liked him the better for being patient with the younger man.

They discussed the position from all angles. The resistance could recruit an underground army, and would do so, but, without help, they could not lay hands on much in the way of weapons. London would have to send in regular drops by plane and the group would have to locate drop zones and weapons dumps.

'London holds the purse strings,' said Jacob. 'And Denmark has to obey.'

Jacob's resentments and prejudices were openly worn and Kay wondered if London knew how much it was resented?

Anton did not contribute much, which struck Kay as odd. Was it policy? Or was Anton sitting on the fence for some reason?

'We are agreed. London is the only way to get our hands dirty.' Felix touched Kay lightly on the shoulder and Anton frowned. 'Any thoughts?'

'I agree that we should work with London as much as possible.'

Felix glanced at Anton for confirmation. 'Any objections?'

'Only the old one,' replied Anton. 'My contacts don't want any trouble. They want everything quiet so they can pass on intelligence unobtrusively. Wrecking railway lines and factories stirs up the enemy who, of course, react badly. That makes it difficult for them.'

'Why are we here, then?' demanded Jacob.

It was a rhetorical question.

'At the moment, we only have British-made wireless sets in the country,' said Felix. 'We hope this will change. But one is mine and there is a second one in Jutland. They're pigs to carry around, plus they operate on alternate currents. He gave a wry smile. In Denmark we operate mostly on a direct one, so it is sometimes difficult to use them.'

'Trust the British not to check.' Anton snapped open his cigarette case.

'Our engineers are secretly working on a new prototype radio transmitter. It will be able to switch currents, and also transmit at high speed which means the message is virtually undetectable. But they need time and places to set up secret labs. And they will need the crystals from London.'

'Any idea when they will be ready?' asked Anton.

'Who knows?' said Felix. 'It's highly dangerous for them.'

Guns. Ammunition. Radio communication. Recruitment.

Kay had wandered into a mad, fractured universe.

Felix and Jacob left, and Anton and Kay remained seated at the table.

Kay picked up her bag. 'Do you agree with what has been decided?'

He shrugged. 'It's the best we can do.'

Kay took her lipstick and powder compact out of her bag. 'Are you serving several masters, Anton?'

'Don't you trust me?'

She applied lipstick to her bottom lip, angling the compact so that the mirror reflected Anton's face, but she couldn't read his expression. 'Should I?'

His hand snapped round her wrist. Startled, she almost dropped the lipstick. 'Never doubt me.'

She removed his hand and, slotting the lipstick and compact back into her bag, snapped shut the clasp. 'Why should I?' she said. 'Unless you give me reason.'

179

Anton took hold of one of Kay's hands, this time gently. 'How pretty and elegant.' Turning it over, he raised it to his lips and kissed it. His mouth was warm on her cool skin. 'The British secret services have their own jealousies and factions. Our information is that the British senior intelligence services consider the outfit which trained Felix to be filled with upstarts and amateurs, and they go out of their way to obstruct them.' He gave her back her hand. 'Enjoy the ironies, darling. The Brits are at war with Germany but fight each other.'

'Isn't that what people do in organizations? The Nazis fight each other like rats in a sack and Jacob and his communists have no love for us. Nothing's new.'

'I had no idea how wise you were, Kay.' He picked up his hat. 'We'll leave separately. Where are you going?'

'To see my son.'

CHAPTER 12

Ruby wrestled the word 'København' from the encrypted message, but that was more from an inspired guess than the result of her persuading the text to yield up its secrets logically.

It was a bugger, this one. A double-dyed, double-decker bugger.

It had been well over a month since her meeting with Major Martin and the dismal Christmas of 1942 had come and gone and nobody much rejoiced either at the arrival of the new year. It was bloody cold, too, her digs increasingly horrible and, even though she enjoyed heading up the teams, the work on the indecipherables was grinding and headache-inducing.

Sometimes she thought about Major Martin. Actually, if she was truthful, it was more than sometimes. What was it about him that so intrigued her? It didn't take long before she cottoned onto the fact that she liked him because he had asked her opinion.

Seated at their benches Attila Team shifted, sighed, muttered and scraped their chairs along the floor. Apart from the professional saints, most were jumpy and short-tempered. No doubt it was that time of the month – it was for her, and bugger that, too, because it hurt.

Curiously, Attila Team seemed to suffer it at the same time. Was this biological quirk worth examining? When a group of women gathered together on a regular basis, why did this synchronization happen? Was this another plank in the argument that, far from being an expression of divine will, humans were merely a collection of cells which obeyed only the laws governing physics and biology?

However, unless she was prepared to ask everyone, which she wasn't, or conduct a scientific sampling, her theory would, of course, remain just that.

But the notion of being suspended in primal space, without moral purpose, was intriguing, liberating.

It was important to concentrate on the text. To seek. To think.

After a bit, Ruby cheered up. She could feel her mind strengthening and improving. In this war, the scientists and mathematicians were proving to be the magicians, and she was one of them.

It had taken some weeks to get this unit up and running. With the patterns imposed by the work, the girls hadn't gelled instantly. There was some grumbling, some bad temper and one or two incipient rebellions which Ruby had nipped in the bud.

'A right bloody tyrant,' said Janet.

Then, without explanation, gears shifted. The unit fell into shape and had been operating beautifully ever since.

She was proud of herself.

She reapplied herself to the message. What could she tease from it?

She ticked off the list. Pair C and T was number 1 in the code groups. Pair N and B was number 2.

It was painstaking, exhausting work. Dull . . . dull . . . beyond dullness, but oh so important. The letter pairs were refusing to acknowledge one other. Each one of them had declared divorce and no amount of her counselling was bringing them together.

Ah, maybe that was it? She spotted and pounced on a hole below the water. During the numbering phase of constructing the code, the agent had made a mistake which meant the lettered phase, which depended on the accuracy of the numbered phase, was sailing merrily out to sea without the lifebelt of its indicators.

Letters netted in, corralled and tamed.

She pencilled 'Bluff check present' in the top left-hand corner and 'True check present' in the right-hand one, and placed the text in the relevant out-tray for Intelligence to weave their spells over.

The door opened. A rustle went through the room. Ruby looked up.

Major Martin.

'Surprise,' murmured Janet.

First off, his uniform could have done with a press and his belt a polish. Not that she cared. Second, the dark eyes were troubled.

The last, she did care about marginally. Only marginally.

'Can't keep him away, can we?' Frances directed a look at Ruby. 'Can we?'

Major Martin took up a position by the window for which the indecipherable teams gave daily thanks. Having a window reminded them that the world still existed.

Ruby speculated as to what was going through his head. What would she be thinking if she was in charge? Was this new set-up going to work? Was he wasting precious, precious resources? Had he got it right?

She was increasingly certain that it wasn't all straightforward for the chiefs – all men, naturally – in this war. It was a conclusion that would have pleased her mightily if the situation hadn't been so serious. Still, from time to time it was fun to indulge in a touch of *Schadenfreude* before calling herself to order.

'The chairs don't look too comfortable,' Major Martin said eventually.

This was astonishing. It was unheard of for anyone senior, or male, to consider their comfort.

'They aren't comfortable, sir,' said Frances in the confident plummy tones of her class. 'Could you get us some decent ones?'

Ruby hid a smile. Major Martin would live to regret his overture. They all knew there was nothing he could do about the bum-numbing chairs. Requisitions for equipment were nigh-on impossible. Like petrol, butter, pretty clothes and, oh, most things.

Still, he had a captive audience. Maybe that pleased him? 'I wanted to thank you all.' Was there a tinge of melancholy in his tone? 'The system seems to be up and running . . .'

Was it? Had she thought of every last detail? Had she thought through the systems?

'How many indecipherables?' Peter Martin was asking.

She snapped to attention and answered, 'Six last week. They were dealt with within twenty-four hours. Two yesterday.'

'Have you cracked these last two?'

'A minute ago. It was . . .' She pointed in the direction of the out-tray and rolled her eyes.

'She means it was a bugger, sir.' Janet wore her best smirk.

Ruby gave her the have-you-gone-off-your-tiny-head glare. 'It was.'

'How long did it take?'

'We launched a blanket attack on it for a day, sir,' she said, realizing she was sucking in more and more of the jargon every day. 'Then I spent two shifts on it.'

He frowned. Again, Ruby picked up a deep anxiety and knew what caused it. It would be the acidic, creeping worry that, cryptographically speaking, they were not solving the problems quickly enough for the men and women out there who were relying on them.

'Carry on,' he said and left the room. A second after the door shut behind him, Janet sniggered.

'Shut up,' said Ruby.

Yet when the sergeant poked his head round the door half an hour later with a summons, she wasn't surprised.

Peter was waiting for her in an airless cubby hole by the main entrance to the building. It had a tiny table and one chair.

He held up a warning finger. 'Top secret, Ingram, never to be talked about now, or in the foreseeable future.'

'I understand perfectly.'

Peter tucked a file into his briefcase. 'Goodness!' His lips cradled a smile. 'I'm not sure "meek" suits you.' Ruby frowned and then thought better of it. 'We had a conversation about your considerable underused abilities. I also suggested that I want you transferred to London.'

'The London bit hadn't escaped my notice.'

'Patience is a virtue.'

'Not in a war.'

'No.' He leaned back against the table and pointed at the chair. She shook her head. She wasn't going to sit while he lounged above her.

He gazed thoughtfully at her. Assessing? 'Until recently all agents' messages were received and distributed back to us by the so-called senior intelligence services, who do not like The Firm one little bit. But that's another story. Our top brass don't like SIS either and they went to work lobbying the powers in Whitehall. The result is . . .' At this point, Major Martin sat down, leaving

Ruby hovering. 'Well, The Firm has been allowed to form a new HQ Signals Office in Norgeby House in London. It has to be staffed twenty-four hours a day and will form a clearing house for agent traffic. The country sections will be told to maintain contact. Attached to it will be a newly formed Security and Planning Office whose function is to monitor the security of the agents' traffic, to identify any problems and to think strategically. That's where you would fit in. But I also need you to keep working on the indecipherables. I can't waste your talents.' He paused for emphasis. 'You will be busy. Fiendishly so.'

She said softly: 'Halleluiah.'

'Halleluiah, indeed,' he said, wry, dry and amused.

Nothing happened for a couple weeks until one morning when Ruby clocked onto her shift and was presented with her transfer orders.

She rushed to pack and to organize transport to the station.

Slow train. Filthy train. But a train going to London.

'Unheard of,' Frances had said when Ruby broke the news to her and Janet. 'You're sleeping with him.'

'Lucky sod,' said Janet. 'Is he good?'

'He's good,' replied Ruby. 'I trust him.'

'I meant in the sack, you fool.'

She was surprised that she minded about leaving the girls.

She glanced up at the netting luggage rack. What little clothing she possessed was packed into brown paper parcels and tied with string.

'For God's sake,' she heard Frances say in her ear. 'Don't you possess a suitcase?'

Her reply had been brief. 'No, my parents' house was bombed, and we lost everything.'

Barely any light managed to struggle through the gloom of the winter afternoon, a frost was closing in and, by the time the train steamed into the station, dark had fallen. The platform was dirty, the air was smutty and it was no warmer here than in Henfold. Welcome to London, she thought, feeling her spirits dip.

To her immense surprise she was met by a car and driven off to the Ritz, where she was told that a gentleman was waiting for her in the dining room. Without being told, Ruby knew who it would be.

She was right, which was brilliant and flattering and all that. Not so brilliant was the fact that she had no time to do her hair or to pull the seams of her stockings straight.

Heigh-ho.

'This is very good of you,' Peter Martin said to Ruby. 'To come, I mean.'

'Yes, isn't it?'

That obviously took him aback, and he peered at her to see if she was joking or not.

She allowed herself a smile.

'Oh, good.' He relaxed. 'I thought for a moment . . .'

'That I was a humourless man-eater, or something?'

He did not confirm. He did not deny.

'Tell me about Cambridge, Miss—'

He was about to say Miss Ingram. She didn't want that.

'Just Ingram, don't you think?'

'I do think. Or perhaps I don't. Perhaps Ingram suits you better?'

She surveyed the piece of fish that had been placed in front of her. God forbid it was snoek. Thank goodness the candles in the centre of the table threw a kindly light over her plate. 'Cambridge was interesting but a disgrace.'

'I'm sure you've let them know how you feel.'

Ruby hoped that she was managing to convey just how deep her anger was. 'When the war is over, I shall lobby for a woman's rights and I shall fight for my degree.'

Had she gone too far? Not that she cared. She was used to the anger which she carried around with her. Anger, plus the disinclination to be nice, or rather, to be feminine.

'I agree,' he said. Without irony, and seriously.

His response was not one that she was used to.

She pressed on. 'Women should fight more. We've been bred to be passive and accepting. We have to put up with the same as men . . . bombs, war, the lot, but the difference is we are second class. The war might change attitudes.' Her lips tightened. 'But I'm not holding my breath.'

189

He really was looking at her. 'Change will come.' To her surprise – or was it outrage? – he touched her hand as it rested on the table. 'But don't count on it happening overnight. Things will change because change is part of our human condition, but it takes time.'

'That's the sort of argument men employ when they know they're on the defensive.'

'I thought we were having a proper discussion,' Peter said. 'In which we consider the propositions and debate them.'

Ruby pulled herself together.

He continued. 'All revolutionaries want results now. Be careful. True change takes patience. But instant upheaval often results in things returning to the status quo. Think of the French Revolution.' He spread out his hands, palms upwards. 'Maybe you won't see it until your daughter grows up.'

Exasperated, she exclaimed, 'How have we ever evolved?'

Peter Martin laughed and poked at the food on his plate. 'By eating fish. It helps the brain.'

The fish had proved not too bad and, a while later, they left the Ritz to stroll towards Piccadilly Circus. It was dark, but in a few shops there was frantic last-minute blacking-out activity. As they strolled, not saying much, a large moon rose above the city throwing a gorgeous, hopeful light over it and doing its best to mask the dust and rubble, and the stink of coal, gas and rotting rubbish stirred up by a bombing raid two nights previously.

'The moon is lovely,' she said, 'but I can't help thinking its beauty is such a contrast with the anxiety and fear which most people are experiencing that it's almost cruel.'

He was silent.

'Don't you think?'

'I think it is better to have beauty at some cost than no beauty.'

Someone jostled against them and their hands brushed each other's.

'Ingram, how did they find you?' Major Martin sounded more relaxed.

'I won a crossword competition. Best time on record, apparently. The next thing I knew, I received a letter ordering me to an interview in London with a pompous man who told me precisely nothing except I would be bound to secrecy, even in the grave. And would I accept?'

'Why did you accept?'

By now they had reached Piccadilly Circus.

'It's funny being here with no Eros,' she said.

'You haven't answered the question.'

She turned to him. 'Everyone has to take a chance in life. It was the pompous man and whatever he was offering, or a terrible secretarial job.'

'I see.'

'No, you don't. You're male. Anyway, one life isn't enough. You have to try several.'

'Good God, I wonder if they know what they've taken on?'

His obvious amusement stung and she felt

191

patronized. 'And I wonder why you've taken me out?'

'Because . . . we have to continue our discussion.' He steered her away from the other pedestrians. 'Keep your voice low.'

They continued towards Leicester Square and while they walked Major Martin kept a wary eye on passers-by and explained that the poem-code method had come about because the intelligence powers that be considered it better security for the agent to carry the code in his head. 'But you and I,' he said, 'and some others know better.' It was a bad system for two reasons. One, the slightest mistake in the coding – 'and Ingram, just imagine some of the difficulties and dangers most agents will be operating under' – resulted in indecipherable messages. Two, the poem could be tortured out of the agent.

During the past few weeks, Ruby had had time to think over the implications. Even so, she was horrified. 'We can't let agents go into . . . into wherever they go with a flimsy set of tools.'

'That's my point.'

'Do we have any idea how many are being captured and giving away their codes?'

'Classified,' he said.

But she could tell from his tone that the numbers were significant. 'Can you tell me anything about what's happening?'

'No.'

She felt that omnipresent anger tie up her voice.

'Why would you bother with me, then? Why are you telling me this?'

Abruptly, he stopped and she almost collided with him. 'Because I'm offering you something to consider other than your anger, which is, I grant you, justifiable.' The moonlight brought the lines of his face into relief. 'But this is a war and you are a clever and gifted woman. Anything I manage to do will take persuasion and it will be inch-by-inch progression. We need unorthodox minds to get round these problems and I want to use you to help me get there. I can't reach the end of this war – I can't die – knowing I didn't try to help these agents. So, you see, it's your cleverness which I'm interested in, not your anger, or anything else. And the same should go for you.'

For a revelatory second, Ruby felt an acute . . . well, disappointment. About what, exactly? That he thought her clever? Wasn't that what she was always wanting? Needing? Demanding? He was giving her what she wanted. 'I apologize,' she said. Apologies never came easily to her and she repeated it.

He was amused. 'Did that hurt?'

She grinned. 'Almost.'

His hand rested on her shoulder for a couple of seconds. 'Not easy, is it?'

'No,' she admitted.

'But we agree?'

Yes, they agreed. And that was something.

Speaking in a low voice, he moved closer. But not too close. 'We don't live in a vacuum even in a war, when most things go by the board. Here on the Home Front we also have to think about how we fight and, if we can, square it with our conscience if the methods are not always the obvious ones.'

'Again, I agree.'

'Then how can we live with ourselves if we give those agents a coding system which can be tortured so easily out of them? Where is the morality in what we are doing? Why should we ask them to give their lives for nothing? Particularly as we don't witness the results of our complacency. The broken-up bodies. The blood. We only read about it in some bland report. If that. Agents will be tortured. We know that and there is no way to prevent that happening. But, if it is to happen, let's make it impossible for them to give up any information – by not giving it to them. Then, at least, they are . . . suffering for some purpose. It will have meaning.'

Would it? Did suffering ever have a purpose? Ruby found herself raising her face to look at him and an unfamiliar emotion tugged in her throat, in her chest, deep in her guts. The moonlight falling over their features played its tricks, too.

CHAPTER 13

When Ruby checked in at Norgeby House the following morning, she was allocated a space squeezed into the far end of a corridor alongside Peter Martin's secretary, a shapely blonde.

'I'm Gussie,' the latter informed Ruby as she sorted piles of paper into buff folders with TOP SECRET stamped on them. 'I expected you earlier.'

'I got lost.'

'From Waterloo?' The idea seemed to astonish Gussie.

Ruby edged into the space between the second desk and the wall and sat down. Gussie's pile of folders grew.

'How are the digs? Took me a bit of string-pulling but I got them in the end.' She looked up and Ruby found herself being assessed by a pair of very green eyes. 'They're much sought after.'

The 'sought after' bit must be the view of the river, not the grimy sheets and unappetizing breakfast provided by a surly landlady. 'I'm very grateful.'

Gussie transferred her attention back to the job in hand. 'I've been here since the off, and know the ropes. Anything you need, ask my permission and I'm sure I'll give it to you. If you need to talk to Major Martin, check with me first.'

Definitely not that friendly.

Gussie continued, 'I should warn you there's been some comment about your showing up here. Not everyone likes it.'

'Normal rules don't apply in wartime,' said Ruby.

Gussie took on board the message. Ruby didn't intend to be intimidated. 'No, they don't.'

Ruby shrugged. She pointed to an in-tray on her desk. It was already overflowing. 'These are for me, I take it.'

'They are.'

She glanced through the papers which included one on tightening up security procedures and an indecipherable marked 'Top Priority'. She hauled a couple of pencils out of her bag, plus her note-book. On the first page she had inscribed: 'Mathematics knows no races.'

Underneath she had written out a quotation from the great G. H. Hardy:

> Three hundred and seventeen is a prime number not because we think so, or because our minds are shaped in one way or another, but because it is so, because mathematical reality is built that way.

Yet the point about encryption and decryption was precisely because minds did shape them. They did not float in a mathematical ether. Someone decided on the message, and worked out how its components were connected. The circumstance in which it was composed mattered very much. Mathematical detachment, in the true sense, was not possible.

Questions needed to be asked of each message. Did this man or woman truly understand the system? Did they have a good memory? Were they careless? Did these agents have absolute confidence in the system? If captured, God forbid, had the wireless operator the sort of personality that could outwit and resist the Gestapo?

Ruby picked up her pencil.

As the days wore on, she found it lonely work. She missed the rudeness, the bottomless well of bad language and the humour of the girls. She marshalled the facts – as sparse as hen's teeth – which she knew about her employer. Not that anyone ever talked but, if asked, she reckoned most of those in its service would be hard pressed to tell you what The Firm was exactly, or what it did. Everyone knew about their little area within it but had no clue how to piece together the whole. Everyone tiptoed around hugging their secrets. If this behaviour wasn't vital, it would be funny.

Carry on, Ingram.

* * *

A couple of weeks later Gussie took a phone call. 'Get your skates on, Ingram. You're wanted at the Other Place.'

'Where?'

'You will be taken,' said Gussie.

It turned out to be a flat off Portman Square used by The Firm's French section. It was a top-secret location and, officially, Ruby didn't know about it.

As part of their induction, and before they moved on to one of the training schools, two French agents had come for a coding lesson. Major Martin wished Ruby to be there as an observer.

Was this going to be a waste of time? Far better that she got on with developing the ideas, the theory, the practice.

Major Martin caught her eye as the two agents filed into the room. *This is the human dimension*, he seemed to be telling Ruby. They were introduced by their current aliases, but not their code names.

On his previous mission, Augustine had been caught and tortured. Having managed to escape, he had been picked up by a Lysander from a field near Poitiers. He was pale, haunted-looking and had a wracking cough. Eloise was slender, with short dark hair and pale skin. Ruby judged her to be not much older than she was. Wearing a buttercup-yellow jersey, she seemed intelligent and spoke fluent, if accented, English.

They settled down to business. 'Augustine, I

want to pick your brains,' said Major Martin. 'You've been operating in the field for some time. What can we do to make coding and sending messages more secure?'

'*Tuez tous les Boches*.' Augustine's little aside was accompanied by a phlegmy cough.

Eloise touched him on the arm. '*Calme toi*.'

'Here's what I think,' said Augustine when he had his breath back. 'Having to keep to regular and predictable skeds adds to the danger. The Boches have direction-finding units all over the place. Once they have a sounding and they know the timing of the skeds, they surround the area. *Alors* . . . they sit and wait for the agent to come on air. *Voilà. C'est fini*. The skeds should be varied so they won't know when we come on air. It will also give us more time to move the sets about.'

'Agreed,' said Peter. 'I'll speak to Signals.'

Eloise fixed large eyes on Augustine.

She's sucking in every piece of information, stifling her nerves, Ruby thought, and her own jangled in sympathy.

'Anything else?'

Augustine shook his head. Then he tossed into the room: 'Sending messages is a joke. Except instead of laughing, you lose your life.'

There was a short heavy silence.

'It was bad out there,' said Major Martin. 'I know, and I'm sorry.'

Ruby swallowed.

Major Martin produced a set of coding exercises

and handed them to Augustine. 'For you, these are more a matter of brushing up. Don't worry if you're rusty. You can relearn quite easily. We can schedule several sessions before you go back in.' He focused on Eloise. 'This is the first session for you.'

Eloise plucked at the wrist of her yellow jersey with nervy fingers.

'First rule: you must never send a message of less than one hundred and forty letters. If you do, it will be to tell us that you are caught.'

How intense these two were . . . in the way they held themselves and how they spoke. Augustine already knew about cold and hunger, flight, distrust and betrayal. Eloise was anticipating them, and yet was still willing to go in.

Augustine began his exercise but was promptly poleaxed by a coughing bout. He started over again.

Eloise licked her pencil and got on with it, her jaw set. But her hand was unsteady.

Ruby's gaze collided with Major Martin's. *We are the lucky ones.*

Eventually, they were done. Ruby cast an eye over the results and it was obvious that Eloise's attempt was clumsy and riddled with mistakes.

'Could you take Eloise outside while I go over security checks?' Major Martin was asking.

There wasn't much room. The flat was stuffed with people and a spiral staircase took up a lot of hallway. Agents were presumably coming in and out and, for security reasons, Parks the door-woman hustled Eloise and Ruby into a room which turned out to be a bathroom with an exotic black marble bath.

'Don't you come out of here,' said Parks, shutting the door on them. In the corridor outside, masculine feet clattered up and down. There was a burst of Polish and a woman asked, '*À quelle heure, à quelle heure?*'

Ruby gaped at the bath. She had never in her life seen such a thing.

They perched on its edge. Eloise fiddled with the cuff of her yellow jersey again. '*Merde*,' she said as a piece of wool unravelled.

'Is there anything I can do to set your mind at rest about the coding?' Ruby asked her.

Eloise clutched the side of the bath, her knuckles almost bursting through the skin.

'It's not natural to me. I worry that if I'm under stress I'll forget how to operate.' She looked at Ruby. 'I *worry* . . . so much depends . . .'

'Practise. Every moment you have spare, practise. But, if you really don't think you can cope with this side of things you must say so.' She tapped the marble to emphasize the point. 'Please. It's not a failure.'

The advice seemed to calm Eloise. If you can give an agent an escape route, Ruby realized, coping with a situation was easier.

'Eloise, do you mind if I ask you a few questions?'

She shook her head.

'I am trying to understand how the codes we give you work for you. We need to know how you cope under different circumstances. For instance, when you're in a hurry, or in the dark, or frightened.'

'Oh that . . .' Eloise got to her feet. 'Forgive me, but I must use the lavatory.'

'I'm so sorry but I can't give you any privacy.'

Eloise shrugged. 'Do you think we care about privacy any more?' She raised her skirt and sat down on the lavatory. 'That is the least of the worries.' There was a modest rush of liquid into the pan and Eloise had finished. She washed her hands.

'The five words you chose from your poem when you did the exercise,' Ruby checked through the file, 'the ones which indicate your transposition key – can you tell me why you chose them? For instance, why did you choose "book"?'

'It's easier to spell than some of the other words in the poem. I know it. I won't forget it.'

'And "red"?'

'It was short. And when there is no time . . .'

'And "sunshine"?'

She brushed the feathery fringe away from her forehead. 'An indulgence. It reminds me of home.'

Ruby took notes.

'What if . . .' Eloise gave a shuddering sigh. 'What if I can't – I can't manage when I'm out there? What if I fail?' She held out her hands and

Ruby dropped her notes and seized them and held them tight.

'You won't fail. I promise.'

The words were inadequate, so inadequate, and the promise an empty one.

Soon afterwards, Major Martin called in Eloise, and Augustine joined Ruby in the bathroom. He lowered himself gingerly onto the edge of the bath.

'I know you had a bad time,' she said. 'Have you recovered?'

He turned a haunted gaze on her. 'I won't be forgetting, if that's what you mean. But, I was lucky. Fine people took care of me and I got away. Others weren't so lucky.' Now he looked anywhere but at Ruby. 'In prison one of ours was brought in with a broken leg. The Gestapo took great delight in twisting it at regular intervals. It was part of the torture . . .'

'*Part* of his torture?'

Ruby's hands clenched.

'Someone else had their eye taken out by a fork.'

There was nothing to be said.

'May I ask you something?' It was too difficult to dwell on the details and Augustine changed the subject. 'If an agent needs extra help with codes can they ask for it?'

'In theory, yes.' She eyed him thoughtfully, wondering if he was thinking about Eloise. 'Please, you realize you must not involve yourself with other agents?'

He shrugged as if to say: *You know nothing of what*

it's like. You know nothing of how it works. We need each other. We need each other to be strong and confident.

True. How could Ruby know what it was like? All she could say, all she could give in the way of comfort was: 'If you talk to Major Martin, I am sure something can be done.'

'*Merci.*'

'No. We should be thanking you.'

Never in her life had she felt so useless.

She ate and drank encryption. She dreamed it. She breathed it. She struggled with it.

But after the interviews with Eloise and Augustine, she had worked out something. The more they knew about how agents might work – dived into the recesses of their minds, mapped the nooks and crannies of human emotion – the better they would serve the men and women who went out, regardless, into the field.

A couple of days later Ruby came on shift and found Major Martin in the office. He was holding one of her decrypts.

He turned to Gussie. 'Would you mind?'

With exaggerated effort, Gussie got to her feet. 'I'll give you ten minutes.'

Peter cocked an eyebrow. 'Gussie is without price. Have you killed each other yet?'

'She's a good woman,' said Ruby.

He pushed the paper towards her. 'There's a query on the last grouping but one.'

'Sure.' She unlocked the drawer containing her

working papers and spread them out on the desk. Together they bent over them and she pointed to a numbered pair. 'There . . . that was the departure on this one.' She took him through the process. 'See, the agent made a mistake here and I traced it back. I can't make sense of the word. It's a foreign one. "Dan . . . k". There is one letter missing.'

'S,' he said.

'Dansk?'

'Danish.'

He did not elaborate and she did not ask.

Major Martin placed his hands on the desk and leaned towards Ruby. 'Any thoughts, Ingram?'

She was tempted to say that it was impossible to conclude anything useful unless one knew the whole story – but thought better of it.

'Ingram, don't waste time.'

Eloise's words flashed across her mind: 'What if I fail?'

'I want to say that I am completely behind the idea that the poem-code system should be dropped and replaced by one which the agents could not possibly remember.'

'Good. I agree. Others agree. That's why we want you to think about it.'

'If we are in agreement, why can't we do something?' She shut and locked her papers in her drawer. 'Hasn't The Firm co-opted the most dextrous and flexible minds around? Aren't we supposed to be unorthodox in our thinking?'

'That's the theory.' He sounded tarter than a

slice of lemon. 'Bear in mind we still have some chiefs whose mind-sets were formed when the Empire thrived. They take persuasion.'

This was funny, and not funny. 'Could you provide the agents with a print-out which has worked-out keys already on it? The agents would use this once and then destroy it. For the following sked they use a second set . . .'

Peter seemed genuinely pleased. 'That's been thought of, too.'

She sent him a look. 'I'm curious about why you need me? If it's all been thought of.'

'I wanted more than one mind on the problem. So, write me a report.'

'Will it happen?'

'I bloody hope so. There are problems. The top brass and their mind-sets . . . Another question: could you use paper? Or should it be some other material which would be easier to hide? Paper is bulky and detectable. But the far more serious consideration is—'

Ruby was ahead of him. 'If the enemy discovers we are using this one-use method, they will copy it and *we* won't be able to read their traffic.'

'That's it,' said Peter. 'That's the problem.'

'So giving the agents extra security means we shoot ourselves in the foot.'

'Isn't that like life?'

Huddled into her space at the end of the corridor, Ruby began work on a security dossier. By this time she had wised up to the system, had snaffled a typewriter from Stationery and hunted down spare typewriter ribbon.

She read extracts from a secret manual written by instructors who trained recruits at Beaulieu in the arts of covert warfare.

Do not deceive yourselves about enemy objectives. The orders are that enemies of the Reich should die, but not before everything possible has been squeezed out of them. They want your codes. They want information. Who trained you? And where? Coding practices. In some instances, they might try to talk you into becoming double agents or stool pigeons for a time, but it depends on who is holding you. We gather from debriefs that the German military intelligence, the Abwehr, have a softer approach. They begin friendly, then progress to greater threats and then torture. The Gestapo, however, will start with torture but they will keep you alive until they get what they want. In those circumstances we ask you to try to hold out for forty-eight hours, which should give your networks time to disperse.

No one is expected to withstand prolonged torture. Therefore a better strategy is to try to avoid third-degree interrogation during which you would almost certainly tell them most things. Feed them information in a controlled manner. If necessary, surrender your codes reluctantly; offering some cooperation in playing back the sets would give you temporary credit. This means you have a chance of keeping your security checks secret which, when they do play back the sets, will alert Home Station because the security checks won't have been included in the message.

'Where is the morality in what we are doing?' Peter's voice echoed in her head. Then it occurred to her: in this game morality is not enough. You had to be practical, inventive and bold.

Perhaps Peter was wrong in his emphasis?

She thought hard and long over the problem of coding security, forcing her mind down strange pathways. How do humans behave? What are their priorities in certain circumstances? Are the Germans so different? If so, in what ways?

Her typewriter clacked in tandem with Gussie's.

1. Agents are under huge pressure. Ergo, it is to be expected that at least one of their messages over a period of time would be classed 'indecipherable'.
2. Therefore, their messages must be regularly tallied and inspected.
3. Home Station must always insist on the Security Checks.

4. Training records should be kept and always available.

How high in German priorities would enemy agents be? Had the Germans been putting their top cryptographers on captured material? The questions were endless, the answers fewer, but she was always led to the same conclusion: The Firm's coding needed to be more secure.

The phone went on Gussie's desk. The typewriter cacophony diminished as Gussie answered it. When the call finished, she turned to Ruby. 'You're wanted on the fourth floor.'

'Sod it,' said Ruby.

'Yup, sod it,' said Gussie. 'On the other hand, I'm pleased because, for a few minutes at least, you won't be cluttering up my precious office space.'

'I love you, too, Gussie,' said Ruby.

In the stuffy office up on the fourth floor, two men hunched at the desk over a large flow chart annotated in green ink. A third, Peter, was seated opposite them. At Ruby's entrance, three pairs of eyes looked up. Two of them were unwelcoming. Cigarettes burned in the ashtray. Peter introduced his colleagues.

'This is Lieutenant-Colonel Nettlesham from Intelligence . . .'

The younger of the two men ran a professional eye over Ruby and nodded. He was smart, she decided, probably thoughtful.

'And this is Major Charleston from the Signals Directorate. Gentlemen, this is Ingram, whose work on the ciphers has been so useful.'

Pale and overweight, Major Charleston sighed audibly.

Ruby braced herself. Unorthodox minds . . . *Unorthodox minds?* Looking at the major, she thought not.

'I want Ingram to outline to you both the ideas I asked her to work on.'

Major Martin had not warned her he was going to do this.

Ruby muttered 'Hell' under her breath, opened her mouth and began. 'First, we should consider the context,' she said. 'We have to ask whether our traffic is considered important enough for the top German cryptographers to be unleashed on it.'

Major Charleston's mouth folded into a peevish line.

Ruby continued. 'Presumably, all the top code crackers are employed on military intelligence, so the odds are our traffic doesn't as yet receive priority attention from the enemy. But as soon as expert cryptographers are put on the case they will easily decode much of it. Perhaps they already have?' She shot a look at the men – tight-lipped and uneasy. 'I know I can't ask these questions or get any answers. But even with less expert enemy cryptographers working on intercepts, the system we currently use is dangerously insecure, and it is only a matter of time before they crack them.'

There was a pause. 'Not only that, but once agents are captured it is a near certainty that they will be able to get the coding information out of them.'

Major Martin asked: 'Are you all right, Charleston?'

The major, who looked as though he was in the throes of a minor heart attack, threw him a look designed to slaughter at three paces.

'Sirs,' Ruby's mouth was drying up. 'The poem code should be abandoned.' Peter was looking at her approvingly. 'As soon as possible.'

Major Charleston recovered his powers of speech. 'The poem code is used by many other organizations. Our *sister* organizations. They manage perfectly well.'

'May I remind you, this isn't about protocol . . .' Peter intervened. 'This is a matter of the highest urgency and also our duty.'

'And may I remind you, Martin, that we are fighting a war with no time or resources to fiddle about with half-proven theories.'

Colonel Nettlesham cleared his throat. 'We're not taking any decisions until we have debated the pros and cons.'

'The pros are that obviously our agents can use this system reasonably easily.' Peter said it coolly enough but she had an instinct that he was angry. 'The cons are that, almost certainly, any inter-cepted messages are being read. I hardly need remind you that the Germans read poetry, and write it. Rather well, as it happens.'

The colonel was rolling a bulldog clip over in his fingers. 'The possibilities exist. Of course they do. Logic tells us that, but what I have to do is to assess the balance of probabilities.'

'Sir,' said Ruby, 'doesn't logic also suggest that if an agent is caught his or her poem code can be tortured out of them?'

Major Charleston stood up and turned to the colonel. 'I don't think we require Ingram's thoughts any longer.'

She appealed to the colonel. 'Sir, would you like a report?'

'Yes,' he said curtly. 'You will write it within the next two days. It will be top secret and sent to me, and only me. That is an order.'

All of which meant the report would land on his desk and stay there. Stuck.

'I'm going to resign from this place,' she informed Gussie on returning to their office space. 'They need maths teachers out there. Schools are crying out for them.'

Gussie was highly amused. 'Ingram, you've no idea. No one ever resigns from The Firm. It can't be done. Either they dismiss you, which means they cut out your tongue. Or they lock you in chains for the duration.'

'Ah,' said Ruby. 'That clears things up.'

Chains of command. Stupidities. Ingrained bureaucracy and turf wars, even in an organization such as this one where the clever were given full rein. Closed minds. Towers built of paperwork. Dead ends.

In the academic world there were infinite numbers and letter combinations fighting to be freed up. The numbers created patterns, glorious patterns, which linked into an as-yet-imperfect understanding of the universe. She could be there, unlocking doors and windows.

She pulled herself up short. This was a war, not a hothouse for theories. Somehow she had to extract the humanity that was secreted in the selfish bits of her and use it.

'It's a man's world.' Gussie patted the unfortunate perm which had reduced her normally glossy hair to a frizz.

'Not for ever,' said Ruby. Pointing to the stack of paperwork Gussie had already dealt with that morning, she added, 'Furthermore, you run the place.'

'We'll keep that a secret, shall we?' Again, the pat on the damaged hair. 'Sit down and get on with it.'

Ruby translated this to mean: *We understand each other very well.*

CHAPTER 14

Kay picked up Felix's latest message: 'Could you bring my hat home on Tuesday? I left it in København.'

A sked was due and Felix was probably operating in the Køge area and couldn't make København in time. Checking the trains, Kay realized it meant an overnight stay.

As predicted, Bror didn't like it. Irritated and more than a little rattled, he asked: 'Why do you have to see Nils so much suddenly?'

'I like to see him. *You* should see him more often.'

Bror frowned. 'Is that the truth?'

She felt rotten. Bror was suspicious that she had an assignation with Anton and she was causing him pain.

Yet if Bror was disturbed, so was Kay. Deception was far more demanding than she had imagined and she found it hard to handle. Guilt weighed her down. It was omnipresent. She felt it in everything she did and she couldn't shake it off. As a result she was avoiding Bror, which did nothing to help matters between them.

Eventually, she said: 'I'll send Nils your love.'

Whenever she was in København on her own, Kay stayed at the Damehotellet, which was clean, convenient and for women only. The walls were painted in soft, pale colours, there were flowers everywhere, and it had good linen. Unlike Rosenlund, no country mice or rat dared to poke its nose in there.

Planning for this particular stay involved thought. She had packed her overnight things into a shopping bag and taken good care that Bror didn't see her leave otherwise he might have questioned the lack of a suitcase.

She arrived at Damehotellet with the wireless set, which she had picked up without trouble, plus a bundle of *Frit Danmark* for distribution in Køge. With the set and leaflets hidden in the wardrobe of her room, she prepared for her dinner with Nils. This involved dressing up the carefully chosen black suit she had been wearing all day with the Eberstern pearls and earrings.

Observing her image in the mirror, Kay was reassured. She looked what she hoped. A smart wife and mother. Better still, under control.

She returned to the hotel soon after ten-thirty. The maid had plumped up the quilt on the bed, laid out her satin nightgown and drawn the brocade curtains. The room was warm and comfortable and, for once, the war retreated into the background.

The phone rang.

'Kay,' said Bror.

'Darling . . .' Kay sat down on the edge of the bed and pleated the hem of the nightgown between her fingers. 'It's very late. Are you all right?'

At times like this she envied Felix his solitariness in his undercover life. His lack of family. The advantage he possessed in not having to account to anyone.

'Good dinner?'

She caught the undercurrent: *Do I trust my wife?* That hurt. It really hurt that her decisions were eroding a marriage which had been built up over so many years. But this was what happened. What did she expect?

'Nils took me to his favourite restaurant. He's working hard and I came back here. I was practically asleep when you rang.'

At his end, Bror cleared his throat. 'Nils told me you were having an early supper.'

'As it turned out we couldn't get a table until later.'

Be careful when lying, Felix had cautioned. *It's the small ones that catch you out.*

'Are you checking up on me, darling?'

He cleared his throat. 'I think I am.'

He sounded odd, troubled.

'Bror, this is not like you . . .' The words were clammy with her deceit. 'Something's happened. What?'

'Ove Poulsen has given in notice. He's going to work in Germany.'

'Ove!' Ove's family had been at Rosenlund for generations.

'A slap in the face for me,' said Bror.

Ah. Again, guilt raised its dark head. 'You mustn't take it personally.'

But Bror would take it personally. Of course he would. Rosenlund was his Arcadia, a tangible expression of a life philosophy, and he took pains to ensure the men were comfortably housed and their work arrangements were fair.

'I told him never to come back.' She heard him take a sharp breath. 'Kay, it's going to leave us very short-handed.'

'We'll manage,' said Kay.

He asked what train she intended to catch in the morning. Kay told him. 'I'll make sure Arne meets you,' he said, adding, 'Curious thing, Kay, when I took the dogs out – we found a pigeon in the old pigeon loft. Arne tells me that he found it and put it in there. He never mentioned it.'

Arne?

A finger ran down Kay's spine. 'Poor thing. It must be lost. I hope Arne took pity and tucked it up with some food.'

'We're not a care home for pigeons.'

'It's not in anyone's way, is it? Besides, if food gets short we could always eat it.' Bror laughed. At a beat, the atmosphere changed. Greedily, she grabbed the few seconds when it could be said that all was well between them. 'Couldn't we?'

'So you are turning into a good Danish wife. It's taken twenty-five years.'

★   ★   ★

217

Her handbag and shopping bag over one arm, carrying the wireless set in the case in the other hand, Kay made for the Left Luggage at the station. Having deposited the case, she bought a magazine at the newsstand and went to inspect the platform where the Køge train was waiting.

If there were security checks or soldiers, she would leave the case in Left Luggage. But the platform was clear and, in due course, she retrieved it and boarded the train.

The journey was straightforward but not comfortable. Sitting quietly in her seat, her coat draped over her shoulders, Kay hid a thumping heart and sweaty palms and tried to remember anything she had ever read about the art of relaxation. Fear of being frightened was worse than being frightened. Wasn't it?

Arne was waiting at the station with the car parked alongside a couple of grocery vans. A snow flurry was casting a fresh white layer over the grey-black slush.

Lifting the case into the boot, Arne's eyes widened as he registered the weight. 'Shall I cover this with a rug?'

Snapping to attention, she nodded.

Arne. One of them?

The snow was coating them both in ghostly feathers. 'I gather you found Hector – I've named him Hector – in the old pigeon loft. Isn't he superb? I've grown fond of him but I suppose I ought to send him on his way one of these days. Except that it's so cold.'

'He's a nice bird, *Fru* Eberstern. I would say he came from a good home.'

'Oh dear, they're probably mourning him.'

Arne tucked in the rug. 'I hope you know what you are doing.'

'Looking after a stray bird, Arne. That's all.'

The lock on the boot always required an effort and Arne gave it a good shove. 'That's very kind of you, *Fru* Eberstern.'

The train sounded its whistle and shunted out of the station, leaving the snowy platforms abandoned under a grey sky.

'Best to get going,' said Arne.

Even in Køge the roads were slippery. Arne nosed the car down the street and headed for the turn-off to Rosenlund. Kay leaned back in the seat and closed her eyes.

Suddenly, Arne swung the car off the road to the left and Kay was thrown against the door.

'What are you doing?'

'Roadblock ahead,' said Arne. '*Feldgendarmerie.* Lots of them.' He pressed the accelerator and the speedometer needle swung upwards.

'There was no need to do that.'

Arne's mouth set in a grim line.

There was no time to speculate. Either Arne was with her or not, and she took the calculated risk. 'Did they see us?'

'Can't say.'

They found themselves in a side street – where the car was conspicuous by being the only one amongst a scattering of pedestrians who were plodding through the snow. The grey light dulled the yellows, ochres and bull's-blood red of the buildings. Steam seeped up from a grating. Kay tapped his shoulder. 'Arne, slow down. We're drawing attention to ourselves.'

At the end of the street, Arne turned left into the road that led up to the market place. 'We should go around the back of the town,' he said.

Kay squinted up ahead. 'We can't. There's a second roadblock.' She shrank back – and, to her shame, felt a moment of debilitating terror. *What have I done?*

She forced herself to think.

'We're going to have to bluff it.' Mercifully, her mind began to work clearly. 'Arne, get the case out of the boot and put it on the back seat. I'm going to sit with it and pull the rugs over me. And I'm going to be ill.' She unwrapped the scarf round her neck and tied it over her hair, pulling it well down. 'Have you got a knife, something sharp?'

Arne didn't waste time on questions, but hunted in the dashboard compartment and handed her a penknife. Kay ripped off a glove and slashed the plump part of her thumb.

Blood bloomed like a pretty little pimpernel flower and grew obligingly into a small peony. She blotted it with her handkerchief.

Arne slid the case into the back and Kay climbed in, wedging it behind her legs. He threw two rugs over her. She rammed her glove back on, sat back against the leather upholstery and held her handkerchief up to her mouth.

They drove at a moderate speed towards the roadblock.

A young and blond *feldgendarme* stepped out into the road and indicated they should stop.

Arne obliged and rolled down the window. The *feldgendarme* stuck his head in and said, '*Raus,*' followed by some sentences in German.

'We don't understand,' said Arne in Danish.

Kay coughed. Inside her glove, her thumb smarted. The *feldgendarme* beckoned to a Danish policeman who was also manning the roadblock. Thank God she didn't recognize him.

The policeman was instructed to translate. Wooden-faced, he explained, 'You must get out. We wish to search the car.'

'What's happening?'

'There are reports that terrorists are operating in the area.'

Arne heaved himself out of the driver's seat. 'Of course.' He walked around to the boot and clicked it open. 'Please.'

The *feldgendarme* turned his attention to Kay and she sagged back against the upholstery. The Danish policeman opened the passenger door. 'Please get out.'

Kay murmured, made an effort to do so, coughed huskily and made a play with the bloodstained handkerchief at her mouth. 'I'm sorry . . .' She drew the words out. 'I don't feel well.'

The *feldgendarme* demanded of the policeman: 'Find out what's wrong with the woman.'

She spread out the handkerchief and pressed it to her mouth. The blood on the linen was a fresh scarlet.

The policeman looked horrified. 'TB?' He didn't have to translate it for the German.

Arne shrugged.

Sweat sprang onto her upper lip and spread under her arms. Her legs, clamped round the case, threatened to cramp.

The blond *feldgendarme* stepped backwards. 'Stay away. The woman should receive immediate medical attention.'

'Drive on,' the policeman instructed Arne.

Snow was beginning to fall in earnest. As they drove through the roadblock, great flakes of it settled on the policemen and soldiers. Handkerchief still pressed to her lips, Kay regarded them over it. These were men she had outwitted.

Once out of Køge, Arne was forced to drop his speed in order to negotiate the now treacherous roads. White spears of larger plants poked up through the snow blanket and the smaller branches on the trees were already sagging under the weight.

Did one talk?

'How did you know, Arne?' she asked eventually.

He shrugged.

'You haven't mentioned it to anyone?'

'No.' Arne shook his head. 'How did you know what to do, *Fru* Eberstern?'

She glanced down at the stained handkerchief. The blood had made the cotton stiffen. Is that what happened when people were shot? 'The Germans are terrified of TB. Well, everyone is, aren't they?' As Arne turned the car into Rosenlund's drive she added, 'I don't want to involve you in anything further. Arne, you can, and must, forget this incident.'

'I'll do that, *Fru* Eberstern.'

'It must not come between you and *Hr* Eberstern.'

She regarded her hands as they rested in her lap. 'I really am sorry.'

'I know what I am doing, *Fru* Eberstern.'

They exchanged wintry smiles.

'Arne, can you take the back entrance and drop me by the outhouses? I want to say hello to Hector.'

As soon as the car drove away, Kay slipped into the pigeon loft and slid the case into its hiding place.

Back in her bedroom, she was in her underwear and changing her stockings when Bror came in.

'Good trip?'

'Interesting.' Kay sat down and rolled one of her treasured sheer stockings up her leg. Bror watched her. She heard her voice rising a little higher than normal as she reported a mish-mash of gossip and hearsay, some of it diverting. There was the anecdote of the German officers who, having hung up their holsters and belts in a restaurant cloakroom, discovered at the end of the meal that they had vanished. There was the boy in Aalborg who had stolen six grenades but didn't know what to do with them and returned them.

She inserted her foot into the second stocking. 'It's almost funny.'

'I suppose it is.' He bent over and, keeping his eyes trained on her face, hooked the suspender into the stocking welt. In that past life together it would have been an erotic, intimate moment, probably resulting in the stocking being removed.

But that wasn't possible now. Bror jerked at the suspender, catching her flesh in the fastening.

She laid a hand over his. 'You're hurting me.'

'Sorry.'

She removed her hand.

'Kay, don't repeat those stories in public, will you?'

'If that's what you wish.'

It was anguish to realize that she no longer felt safe with him and he was no longer her refuge. And vice versa. And equally harsh was the understanding that total estrangement would be easier than stringing him along.

She stood upright. 'What are you angry about?'

'There's something going on, Kay. You're acting oddly. You . . . look different.' His eyes were as dark a blue as she had ever seen them. Moving over to the door, he made to leave, checked himself and swung round. 'You know there's nothing more important to me than you and the children?'

'Yes, yes. I do.'

'But I don't know whether you know that, any

more. I don't know what you're thinking. Or whether I can rely on you.'

'Is this about Anton? Or politics?'

'You tell me.'

'Don't you trust me?'

Her discarded blouse on the chair with one of its shell buttons hanging by a thread . . . a tiny drift of powder on the dressing table . . . the jewellery case with the Eberstern pearls on the bed . . . How curious that, at this moment, she would notice these things.

'I think Anton means something to you and you are . . . well, seeing him.'

Bror had handed her a solution on a plate. She trembled at the implications. How pernicious would it turn out to be if she took it? Enough to cause them profound pain. Possibly tear up their lives?

Nevertheless, a point had been reached.

'Is that what you think?'

'I do.'

She shifted her gaze to the floor – a guilty gesture. 'I refuse to answer.'

'I want to know.'

'Please get out of here, Bror.' Her hands were placed defensively on her chest. 'And don't come back. Not tonight.' She paused. 'Not for many nights. Go and sleep somewhere else. Until we sort this out. But, the way I feel, it won't be soon.'

His lips went white. 'It *is* Anton.' Kay was silent. 'Isn't it?'

She made herself look up into his face. 'It's true I like Anton very much.'

Without another word, he turned on his heel and left the bedroom.

Kay's knees gave way and as she sank onto the bed her bandaged thumb snagged on the coverlet. She had cut it deeper than she intended and the wound stung.

So did the internal wound.

The following morning, an exhausted Kay waited with twenty or so others outside Lippiman's bakery in Køge.

A queue for Lippiman's bread had become a feature of the war. If it was raining, it made for misery – and played havoc with the women's hair. Sometimes, however, unless it was bitterly cold, standing outside for a few minutes and enjoying the aroma of freshly baked bread was pleasant enough.

She thought of Tanne's birth. That had been another bitter winter's day. During her labouring, she had taken comfort from the sight of the ash tree, its branches rimed by a deep frost, outside the bedroom window at Rosenlund. Just before the moment of the baby's arrival, the setting sun tipped it with fire. Weeping from pain, she watched the light change and wondered if she would live to see the next day.

She recalled, too, a memory from the early days with Bror, when he drove her triumphantly into

Køge for the first time. 'But it's old,' she had exclaimed, then blushed when Bror teased her back: 'Darling, it's not only the English who have a history. We have a history. A distinct one.'

When they were small, Nils and Tanne badgered Arne to tell them the local stories. 'Let me see,' he would say. 'Do you mean the one about the naval battle in Køge harbour during which Sweden was trounced?' He had a chest-load of yarns: of monster fishing catches, of midsummer celebrations and, of course, of the Køge ghost that sailed a ghostly boat out to sea. In summer the boat was said to skim over the water. In winter it broke through the creaking, shape-shifting ice.

The queue shuffled forward. A couple of women with plaits pinned round their heads had forgone the customary headscarf, and they must have been regretting the cold. There was an elderly man in a coat too big for him and a girl with a shawl and no coat, who shivered visibly.

In the past, the queue would undulate with gossip but a wartime bread queue was different. There was no ongoing conversational murmur, and no jokes. Voices were hushed and muted and, as Kay observed, there were several in the queue who were keeping a sharp eye on the others.

Inside the bakery, the morning's bake of rye loaves had been set out on the shelves by the door, displaying a spectrum of browns, from light tan to burnished ebony.

'Good morning, *Hr* Lippiman.' She handed over to him her basket containing the bundle of *Frit Danmark* wrapped up in a napkin. 'Birgit asked me to buy four loaves.'

Lippiman placed the basket containing the bundle on the shelf below the counter. He appeared calm and focused. As she watched, he whipped out the package and dropped it into an empty bag of flour which he pushed with his foot further under the counter.

He put three loaves into the basket and held up the fourth one. 'It's a little soft,' he explained, packing it in. Only now did he look directly at Kay. 'I hope you have a good day, *Fru* Eberstern. My regards to *Frøken* Eberstern. Tell her I'll have her favourite gingerbread tomorrow.'

Kay laughed. 'If I know my daughter she'll be down.'

The roads had seemed clear and she had driven to Køge in the trap. Loki was bored and fidgety and Kay took extra care guiding him across the marketplace. Loki trotted past the Town Hall – built in 1552, as Bror informed her all those years ago – and the Monument on the harbour. She always forgot in whose honour it had been erected but, bearing a similarity to Cleopatra's Needle in London, it reminded her of home. As they passed the circular Water Tower genially presiding over the town, Kay looked up.

Why, oh why, did there have to be a war?

Arne's street fronted onto the canal. His house

was one of the older ones. A modest building with dimpled glass in the windows, painted the blue of a sunlit sea. Bror regularly urged Arne and Birgit to take up his offer to live on the Rosenlund estate. To no avail. The cottage having been in Arne's family for generations, the couple were not budging.

Kay brought Loki to a halt. Maintaining a tight hand on the reins, she knocked on the door with her whip. 'Arne, are you there?'

While she waited, a man and woman walked past. He was in a navy-blue pea jacket, she in a dun-coloured raincoat and a home-knitted wool hat. They seemed hurried. Awkward.

'Do you know them?' She pointed out the couple to Arne when he emerged from the cottage.

'I don't ask, *Fru* Eberstern. Nor should you. People come and go here these days. Spying for the Germans, or trying to escape from the Germans . . . who knows?' He swung himself up and kidnapped the reins from Kay. 'Shall we go?'

Kay fastened her jacket up tight and arranged the rug over them both. 'The roadblocks have been taken down.'

Loki wound himself up to a trot and, avoiding the main thoroughfares, Arne drove them through the side streets and onto the Rosenlund road.

They talked together comfortably in a conversation ranging over repairs to the house and farm matters and, because the Germans were taking as much of it as they could lay their hands on, how pork was at a premium. Arne let slip that pigs were being smuggled into the butcher for slaughter, and the wives of the workers on the estate were secretly making hams and salamis to be hidden away.

Eventually, he asked, 'Your thumb, *Fru* Eberstern?'

Kay stripped off her glove and poked under the dressing. 'Looks as though it will take time to heal.'

Arne peered down at the oozing scab. 'Don't let it become poisoned.'

At Rosenlund, the day was punctuated by Kay's usual commitments but, when it began to grow dark, she slipped away to the pigeon loft.

Hector fixed her with bright eyes. 'Hello, boy.' Kay checked over his water and feed. 'Don't you look sleek and rested? But you won't be put in danger if I have anything to do with it.' Her voice sounded ghostly in the cold loft. 'Just remember, you don't speak English.'

England . . .

Don't think about England. But she did. She did and it hurt. It hurt. And she thought how strange it was to be reminded so viscerally that the umbilical still stretched between her and her mother country.

On her return to the house, she paused for a moment to look at it. The light from the windows cast pathways across the lawn and gardens and, out on the lake, the winter ice was as thick as it could be. She knew it so well. The beads of air trapped in the frozen water created a white palette which sparkled on sunny days but turned grey and melancholy on the bleak ones.

It would be a long time until, once again, they heard the shuffle and roar of ice melt which heralded spring . . . until white anemones and snowdrops flowered under the maples and the smell of wild garlic sifted through the air.

She bit her lip.

Sif and Thor hoved into sight. Behind them came a familiar figure.

'Tanne!' Kay smiled. 'You gave me a fright.'

Tanne was wearing one of her father's heavy tweed jackets and a woollen hat with ear-flaps which, years ago, Kay had bought her on a trip to Norway. She was flushed with cold.

'Giving the dogs a run. What are *you* doing?'

'Walking.'

'You do a lot of walking these days.' Tanne fell into step. 'I'm curious.'

The wind was getting up and Kay shivered. 'Let's go in.'

Inside the house, Kay pushed Tanne towards the porcelain stove in the hall. 'Darling . . . quick, warm yourself up.'

The dogs clicked over the black and white marble tiles and made for their baskets.

The damp had made Tanne's fair hair curl round her ears in a way which always delighted Kay and annoyed Tanne. She looked gorgeous and healthy and very alive.

Grinning broadly, Tanne pulled Kay to her and

dug her hands into her mother's pockets. 'You're a warmer option.' There was a second or two of silence. '*Mor*, what's this?'

Too late.

Before Kay could stop her, Tanne opened up the folded copy of *Frit Danmark* she had extracted from Kay's pocket. 'What on earth have you got here?'

'Nothing. Give it back.'

But Tanne snatched it out of reach. Then she read out: '"The caterpillar of the pale tussock moth *dasychira pudibunda* is destroying the beautiful Vallo beech woods."' She frowned. '"Slowly but surely, the caterpillars are feeding on the body of the beech and sucking it dry."'

'*Mor!* Where did you get this?'

'I picked it up from the street in Køge. It's not worth reading.'

'So why pick it up?' Tanne ran her finger over it. 'It's not damp.'

'Some time ago. I forgot it was in my pocket.'

Tanne raised an eyebrow. 'Even I can see that this is political satire.' She folded the paper over. 'What are you going to do with it?'

'Burn it.'

Tanne ignored her. '"Denmark must retrieve its honour." So that's what you have been thinking about during the *walking*?'

Kay took the pamphlet out of Tanne's hand, opened the grill and dropped it into the stove. 'Most of us have to consider the war and how we feel,' she said as reasonably as she could manage. She brushed back the mass of Tanne's hair, and added: 'But we have to be careful.'

'Don't fob me off, *Mor*.' Tanne allowed Kay to fuss over the hair. 'Are you going to tell me about it?'

'Nothing to tell.'

Tanne stepped back.

It seemed that, in Kay's war, the people she had to trust were strangers, not her dearest and most loved. The conclusion was unsettling, queasy making.

Tanne changed the subject. 'You must be worried about Gran and the aunts.'

'Yes.' Kay took off her jacket. 'Yes, yes. I keep telling myself that they'll be safer in countryside. It's London and the cities that are being bombed.'

'But do you approve of what your country is doing?'

'Tanne! It's half your country, too.'

'So it is. I forget.' Tanne picked up her discarded hat and drifted towards the staircase. 'See you at dinner.'

Most people would imagine that the subject was closed but Kay was an expert in reading her daughter. She knew Tanne. It would not be the last that she heard on *Frit Danmark* and she knew that she would have to consider carefully how to handle Tanne's questions. Knowing that she must lie to her daughter gave her a desolate feeling.

She went in search of Birgit and discovered her

233

in the kitchen putting the finishing touches to the chicken pie. 'Arne is waiting for you,' she told her. 'Go home. I'll manage in the kitchen.'

Birgit looked scandalized. Kay realized that her instruction ran counter to the other woman's notions of order, and of how things should be done.

She prised the knife away from Birgit, saying, 'Arne needs you back in your own house.' She glanced at the window where the frost patterns were forming. 'It's getting colder. I've arranged for Frau Nielsen's Else to come in to serve.'

'Little Else?' Birgit sounded puzzled. 'She's better than me?'

'Birgit, I was trying to save you trouble.'

'*Fru* Eberstern, trouble is my job.'

'I know, Birgit. But this wretched war means we have to adapt.'

'The war, *Fru* Eberstern, means we must not let things go.'

'Go home, Birgit. Arne is waiting and you are tired. I know you are.'

For a moment Birgit was stilled in her perpetual bustle. Pink suffused her cheeks. 'Maybe. Just this once.' She took off her apron. 'But it is not good to let things go.'

On first arriving at Rosenlund, Kay had been introduced to a staff of twelve, including two housemaids, and instructed in all aspects of running a house, from the storeroom to the laundry to the menus. Every morning fires were laid, and the gravel in the drive outside was raked smooth.

These days the gravel remained churned up for long periods. The staff had been whittled down to Birgit and two of the wives from the estate who came in part-time, plus little Else.

That other life, predictable, ordered, innocent – above all the innocence – was now a long time ago.

Bror and Tanne had spent the morning together combing over the estate accounts and they talked dairy yields all through dinner that night.

Thank God, thought Kay, and she tackled Birgit's chicken pie in silence.

Sorting out the meat from the pastry on her plate, she made herself eat as much as possible. It wasn't easy. She chewed away and told herself that she was committed. She had to be. With its violence and retribution, the war threatened to invade Rosenlund's boundaries. No more pastoral idylls. In the light of events, Bror's Arcadia would prove to be only a dream, and as fragile.

Collapsed by the stove, the dogs snorted and snuffled in sleep. Then a vehicle crunched over the gravel. Thor shifted to his feet and Sif raised her head and barked.

'Are we expecting anyone?' Bror looked up from his slice of cherry flan.

Else appeared in the doorway. 'Sir—'

Before she could finish, she was pushed aside and two uniformed Danish policemen entered the dining room.

'Sergeant Wulf?' Kay exclaimed, recognizing the older of the two. 'Is everything all right?'

'*Fru* Eberstern, *Hr* Eberstern, I apologize.'

'I think you should.' Bror had remained seated – an unusual discourtesy which meant he was angry.

Sergeant Wulf tugged at his belt. It was a gesture well known to many in his jurisdiction. He had been in charge of the Køge police station for the last decade and the joke ran that his belt had to be let out a notch each year. By report, Kay knew him to be a kindly man and more or less effectual.

'This is Constable Juncker from København. He is here to act as liaison between us and our German colleagues.'

Juncker was still youthful enough to be at the gangly stage. His uniform was new and well pressed and, having hitched his career to the Nazi bandwagon, he looked eager to toe the line.

What had she done? What had she done to her family?

There was no time for regret. Nor for panic.

Shut up, Kay.

Bror was brusque and unwelcoming. 'Why are you here?'

'Sir . . .' Sergeant Wulf was not a happy man. 'Forbidden literature has been found in a baker's van. *Hr* Lippiman's. Constable Juncker and I are following up leads. *Fru* Eberstern was seen at the bakery this morning.'

This was her fault – for she had brought the war right into their dining room.

Fear. Guilt.

The air crackled with suspicion. But, all of a sudden, she was cool and focussed.

Think of the details. When, where, how? Get them right.

'Gentlemen, some coffee?'

Turning to Kay, Bror asked, 'Do you know anything about forbidden literature?'

'No,' she said.

'There's your answer,' Bror addressed the men. 'Now go.'

Constable Juncker ignored him. His young, righteous gaze drilled into Kay. 'You do know the baker?'

'I do. I've used the bakery for many years.'

'Is it normal for you to do the shopping? Doesn't your housekeeper buy the bread?'

Kay directed her answer to Sergeant Wulf. 'We've lost staff and I like to help out by doing some of the shopping.'

Sergeant Wulf was clearly reluctant to be involved, but he said, 'You handed the baker a basket.'

'Did I?' She smiled at him. 'Perhaps I did.'

He scrabbled at his belt again. 'According to our witnesses you did. Was the basket empty?'

'I think so. It may have had my scarf in it.'

The details. Which scarf? Do not look at Tanne.

Tanne interjected. 'What has happened to *Hr* Lippiman?'

Constable Juncker got in first. 'He's been arrested and will be taken to København.'

At that, Tanne took Kay completely by surprise, her words cutting through the atmosphere: 'You're going to hand over a *Dane* to the Germans? A fellow Dane?'

CHAPTER 15

Tanne spat out the words.

Sergeant Wulf looked like an animal that lacked the guts for the kill.

'A Dane!' Tanne repeated, her thoughts scurrying through a moral and patriotic maze. 'A fellow Dane?'

'Tanne, *quiet.*'

She had never seen her father so angry.

But she was past caring. 'Why?'

Constable Juncker said simply, 'Denmark needs to be healed.'

Tanne was speechless. On hearing this idiotic remark, the fragments of thought which had been swirling around in her head for months cohered and became clear. Herr Hitler was not only mad and bad, but capable of infecting the whole world with his madness and badness. She opened her mouth to object, then caught her mother's eye. *Don't.*

She heard Aage's voice replaying in her head their old university rhetoric. *Democracy. Freedom. New dawn.* What would Aage be making of the war? Tanne knew the answer. Aage would declare he was sickened to his guts and the country, supine and spineless, was damned. (Once upon a time, she had been a little in love with Aage until she realized that his passionate demagoguery disguised a bully.)

When the men first burst in on their dinner, Tanne reckoned that Constable Juncker might be stupid, an impression she held until she encountered his cunning, calculating gaze and revised her opinion. Juncker was unembarrassed and on the make. Very much on the make. Unabashed, he moved around the room – taking in the fine prints, the gilt pier glass, the Sèvres china on the shelves. At one point, he reached over to touch an antique Chinese *famille rose* plate. She nearly cried out: 'Don't you dare.' It was such a pretty plate, decorated with delicately painted roses and daisies, and one of her favourites. Then it occurred to her that it was possible he had never been so close to such a valuable object. Who wouldn't wish to touch a *famille rose* plate?

She heard herself asking, 'What will happen to *Hr* Lippiman now?'

'He will be taken to København and handed over to the German authorities.' Constable Juncker returned to his perusal of the plate.

Her mother's expression gave nothing away. She fixed her eyes on Sergeant Wulf. 'I assume you're holding him at the police station?' Without drawing breath she continued, 'I'm sure whatever *Hr* Lippiman has, or has not, done can be dealt with much more competently by you. Do you need to bother your German colleagues with something so insignificant?'

Denmark needs to be healed. Constable Juncker was checking his reflection in the pier glass which hung between the windows overlooking the garden. The spanking new uniform, the slicked-back hair, the prominent lower lip, the intelligent gleam: what he saw appeared to satisfy him.

'Sergeant Wulf!' Her father was icy. 'You will both leave. *Now.*'

Her mother placed a restraining hand on his arm. 'Darling,' she said. '*Darling*, I am sure Constable Juncker would like a brandy before they go out into the cold. Why don't we all go into the drawing room?'

Her father's protests were stilled. Deflected, he gestured to the door and he and Constable Juncker vanished in the direction of the drawing room.

Her mother spoke to Wulf in a low, urgent voice. 'Sergeant Wulf, Troels Lippiman is a friend of yours. Aren't I right in thinking you stood as a godparent for his son, and you serve together in the church?'

'Yes,' replied Sergeant Wulf, his hand shoring up his belt.

Something else was going on, but Tanne couldn't work out what.

Her mother turned the full force of her charm on Wulf. 'Whatever you decide, you must make sure that *Hr* Lippiman is permitted to visit the

241

pastor in the church. He would want to pray. I know you will allow this because you're his friend. A visit to the church would be important to him. Help him, Sergeant. Now—' she smiled at him '—what about that brandy?'

Sergeant Wulf said: 'Constable Juncker has already informed København that the baker will be coming in for questioning.'

'All the more reason for prayer,' said her mother.

When they had left, Tanne returned to the dining room and her unfinished *delikatesse*.

Because of the war . . . because of the bloody war, Birgit had been forced to be sparing with the dried cherries embedded in the almond sponge. Still, it meant Tanne could pay special attention to each one and she made herself relish every chew of the bitter-sweet, tough-skinned fruit.

The first-floor passage outside the bedrooms was nearly impossible to negotiate noiselessly but Tanne had a long familiarity with its creaks and groans as she sped along it to the bedroom which she thought of as her parents'.

Yet only the other morning she had caught Else ferrying her father's things down the corridor to the blue bedroom. 'What's going on?' she demanded of her mother, who explained that neither she nor her father had been sleeping well and they both needed a bit of peace and quiet. It was all very confusing, and Tanne had a nagging feeling that she was missing something but could not put her finger on it.

Always, her special love in her parents' bedroom was the summer lace curtains but they were changed every October for thickly-lined blue damask ones and these had been drawn across the window embrasures. The lamp beside the bed threw a tactful glow over the room. Earlier, Else had been into the bedroom to turn down the satin coverlet and to lay out her mother's nightgown. Pearl crêpe de Chine with a touch of lace: it spoke to her of married life, a sexual life and a day-to-day intimacy she had yet to experience.

She plumped down onto the bed and picked up a book. The curtain at the window overlooking the lawn moved a fraction. Leaping to her feet, she pulled it aside. *'Mor?'*

Dressed in corduroy trousers and a thick jacket, her mother was directing a torch beam onto the lawns outside.

'What on earth?'

'Shush.'

'But what are you *doing*?'

Her mother snapped off the torch and let the curtain fall back into place. 'You shouldn't be here.' She put her hands on Tanne's shoulders and pressed her down onto the bed. 'Tanne, darling. I don't ask you to do much for me but I'm asking you . . . no, ordering you to go to bed.'

She struggled to understand. 'Is this to do with Lippiman and the pamphlets?'

243

Her mother kept up the pressure on her shoulders. 'Whatever it is to do with, *you* are not involved.'

On another day, at another time, lured by the prospect of a warm bed, Tanne might have been persuaded.

'Tanne, for once in your life, *obey* me.'

Was her mother turning into a shape-shifter of the old Danish tales? This wasn't the *Fru* Eberstern who had charmed Sergeant Wulf, or the occasionally dull and overprotective parent. Or the sweet and funny mother she could be. This was a woman Tanne didn't entirely recognize.

'*Mor*, what's happening?'

'There's no time to talk now, Tanne. Just go.'

Had she ever heard her mother issue an order with such force? Tanne dug in her heels. 'Whatever you're doing, I'm coming with you.'

'Don't be stupid, Tanne.' Her mother knotted a scarf under her chin.

Then she understood. Or, some of it.

'*I'm* stupid?' Tanne twitched the curtain back and peered at the garden. 'What happens if *you* run into trouble?'

Their eyes collided. 'Then you can look after your father.'

She spat back: 'Good thinking. Someone has to.'

Her mother picked up her gloves.

Tanne caught her arm. 'If you're going out to help Lippiman, I can be your alibi.'

'The Germans don't bother with alibis, Tanne.'

'Lippiman is my friend, too.'

It worked.

'God forgive me . . .' Her mother was both sharp and fierce. 'But there's no time to argue.' Wrenching open the wardrobe, she thrust a pair of trousers at Tanne. 'Put these on. Leave your shoes off.' She fished out a sweater and pulled it down over Tanne's head, pressing her hands to Tanne's cheeks. 'This is secret, Tanne. Completely secret. Understand?'

Mesmerized by this new, strange mother, Tanne agreed.

Rosenlund's front door was locked and bolted at night and they avoided it, padding instead down the pantry passage to the back door, where they kitted up in thick jackets and boots. The dogs whimpered and whined. Tanne threw them a couple of biscuits to shut them up.

Her mother eased back the bolts. 'We're going by bicycle.'

Outside, the cold scoured Tanne's throat. But she was used to that. Even so, the going was fairly hard and, in places, treacherous and they were both panting by the time they had wheeled their bicycles down the drive.

On reaching the road, they mounted. A large moon aided visibility, but it was hard to keep up a good speed. The snow, which was heaped in unexpected and powdery drifts, was laced with ice, pockets of mist loomed up at them without warning and at times it was too dark to see.

'Where are we going?' Tanne's whisper was amplified in the brutal stillness.

'Arne's.'

'Why?'

'Juncker wasn't as clever as he thought he was. He told us what was going to happen, which means we have an advantage. Arne will take the message.'

'But Lippiman is in the prison.'

'Sergeant Wulf will take him to the church.'

'How do you know?'

'Because I told him to.'

Save for the crunch of the wheels over the road surface, silence coated them. Ghostly whiteness and patches of moonlight. Fear prickled down Tanne's spine. She was aware that she had a shaky hold on the situation and she felt ashamed of her ignorance. What, exactly, was her mother involved in?

How much did her father know?

Avoiding the main street, they detoured around the back ones which, since they were icier, brought their own dangers. But they got there. Unsurprisingly at this late hour, Arne's cottage was dark. Tanne held the bicycles as her mother knocked softly on the window. Eventually, it was eased open.

A whispered exchange followed.

She heard Arne say, 'Leave it with me.'

'Hide him in Ove's cottage if you have to,' said her mother.

Arne's window shut noiselessly.

The way back was colder and harder. Tanne's energies dwindled, and the exhilaration of the earlier journey vanished. She felt weary to the bone. 'Wouldn't it have been easier to phone?' she asked when they were back in Rosenlund and rubbing themselves down.

'Arne doesn't have a phone and I don't trust anyone else. The exchange might listen in.'

'But *Mor*, even if they did, they wouldn't say anything.'

Her mother hung up her damp jacket. Her silence was eloquent.

'But we *know* them.' Tanne was bewildered.

'I warned you not to come. But you did. You must know *nothing* and you must be clever. Lives depend on it.'

'Do you know what you're doing?'

'Yes.' Her mother sat down as if her legs wouldn't hold her up any longer. 'It took me a little time, but I do know what I'm doing.' She tackled her boots. 'I was never going to talk about it, and I didn't want you involved.'

Both of them wrestled with the laces which had been rendered uncooperative by the damp and cold.

Tanne tugged at hers. To her horror, tears of rage and frustration gathered behind her lids.

'Lippiman is a good man,' continued her mother, 'and I'm not going to let him be taken. Others agree. So we are doing something about it.'

'And *Far*?'

Her mother shook her head.

'So you are all . . . against *Far* and—'

'Not against *Far* but against *them*.'

A vision of a future came into Tanne's mind. One where they would be juggling lies, watching their backs (even with friends), and moving words carefully around like counters on the draughts board.

'What about *Fru* Lippiman?'

Her mother pushed back Tanne's damp hair. 'She'll have to go into hiding, too. The Danish police have instructions to hand over anyone who might be involved. You can see Sergeant Wulf's position.'

'Where can they go?'

Her mother shook her head. 'I've no idea and you won't ask.'

'And *Far*?'

'Tanne.' Kay pulled Tanne to her feet and held her close. Just like she used to when Tanne was a child. But the words which she hissed into her ear were neither gentle nor loving. 'You will say nothing. He has enough to deal with.'

She smelled faintly of sweat, a basic human odour that Tanne never normally associated with her elegant, feminine mother – and that small dissonance was almost the strangest thing about the evening.

In bed, Tanne took a long time to warm up and she slept badly. When she woke, she lay and looked around her room. She had imagined that she knew everything there was to know about her parents, about Rosenlund. About Køge.

But she didn't.

In the afternoon of the following day, Tanne went in search of her mother and discovered her in the storeroom.

She was faced by a familiar sight. Notebook in hand, Kay was shouting across the passage to Birgit, who was in the kitchen beating eggs. Every so often Birgit shouted back.

Rosenlund's large and airy storeroom was an important place – almost the heart of the house, supervised by her mother and Birgit. Between them, they kept the shelves stacked with canned meats and beans and bottles of fruit and tomatoes. The bottles always gave Tanne particular pleasure – the yellows, ochres, russets and purples creating an autumnal patchwork against the whitewashed walls.

Tanne leaned on the door frame and waited for the shouting to stop. 'I've been in Køge.'

Her mother bent over the record book. 'Roads bad?'

'Pretty bad.' Tanne picked up a jar of tomatoes and held it up to the light. As red as blood? '*Mor*, you might like to know there was a raid on the church while a prisoner was there. He escaped.' She handed the jar over to her mother.

Her mother slotted it onto a shelf and wrote in the notebook. 'That's good.'

Tanne whispered, 'We're deceiving *Far*. It's not right.'

'We can discuss whether it's right or not after the war.'

'But *Far*—'

Her mother raised her head and glared at Tanne. 'Don't you understand, it's dangerous for him?'

Tanne digested the reproof. Looking up at the shelves glowing with colour, she said, '*Mor*, this won't happen again, will it? I mean . . . you . . . doing things?'

'No, darling. No. But we had to do something for Lippiman.' She wrote a note in the book. 'Are you here to help?'

At university, any analysis of war had been along conventional lines. As far as Tanne had thought about it, war was a male affair. Politicians sent soldiers to the slaughter. There was marching, men hunkered over campfires, supply lines and latrines. Afterwards, the politicians took over and everybody forgot about the men who died.

She had never imagined that women were fighting in this war discreetly and, she was beginning to understand, ruthlessly.

'Tanne, darling.' Her mother was back to her normal sweet and loving self. 'Do me a favour and pass me that tin of beans.'

The strange, bewildering episode was over.

CHAPTER 16

Mary Voss was on a bus to Northampton – which was a bit of a triumph. If Signalmaster Cripps had had his way she wouldn't be taking this twelve-hour leave at all, despite Mary reminding him she had worked over Christmas.

Signalmaster Cripps was not unkind, merely overworked, and the situation wasn't helped by the fact that he currently had a cold. No one was at their best with a beacon nose, a painful crack in their bottom lip and stuffed sinuses. In the end, he had conceded reluctantly that Mary must take what was due to her.

'I will, sir.'

She had enjoyed the manner in which she had emphasized the words. Not too forceful, but sufficiently firm.

Having fought for them, she was determined to make her hours of freedom noteworthy and decided to go shopping for a new dress. Henfold did not have any of the right shops. To buy clothes therefore meant taking a bus to Northampton.

The bus was chilly and smelled of cigarettes

and sweat. Avoiding the seats which were stained, Mary secured herself a window seat and it was pleasant enough rumbling along, letting her mind drift this way and that.

A couple of men in the row behind discussed the progress of 'our boys' and the German defeat at Stalingrad – which came as something of a shock. It made her realize that she had been too immured in her own corner of the war and had neglected to keep an eye on the bigger picture.

In fact she hadn't kept up with events outside of work at all since the last time she had visited her mother in Brixton, when she had been shaken to discover that the terrace where she had grown up had been bombed. Houses gaped like open mouths with so many broken, blackened teeth. Like a hot knife slicing through butter, the bomb had cut through the terrace exposing drunken staircases and cross sections of bathrooms with all their private arrangements for everyone to gawp at. One of the ruins still smoked.

She had prayed that no bodies were still in the wreckage, that no limbs were scattered about, and made herself concentrate on things she liked. A frilly blouse – a fanciful thought since no clothes were made with frills these days. A bunch of lavender. A pat of butter all to herself.

Mary had grieved. Tossed so casually out of a bomb bay, the bomb had pulverized coal scuttles, wooden spoons, rose-patterned china tea services and an array of life's pots and kettles, each with its accumulated memories. Objects which the women who slaved away in these houses would have treasured and by which they measured out their lives.

The dust . . . the dust had nearly choked her. The bombing had released so much of it. It was everywhere – on surfaces, between the sheets, on window frames, sifting into everyone's clothes, hair, nose and ears. When would they ever be properly clean again? When they came to write a history of wartime, historians must write about the dust, she thought. London was buried in the stuff and it hung in the air – minute particles of brick, stone, wood . . . and other more terrible things she wasn't going to think about.

Altogether, that last trip had been a sobering one. Her mother was growing more immobile, her temper ever sharper. Undressing her for bed had taken all Mary's powers of persuasion and of restraint. Wrestling with the buttons on the ancient liberty bodice, a 'Whiteley's best'. Much to-ing and fro-ing with hot water. Her mother criticizing its temperature. Boiling up a kettle and watching the steam paint out the vista outside the tiny kitchen window. The soft pop of gas under the kettle. Watching an expansive yellow moon shine over the roofs while she waited for it to boil, Mary was reminded of the illustrations from a childhood book of fairy tales.

The smell of an elderly body was unmistakable. So, too, was the decay and neglect enforced by decrepitude . . . the creeping indignities of stiffening limbs, of toenails thickening and yellowing with age.

Mary dreaded the ageing process overtaking her. But it would, and in her case there would be no daughter to help her at the end.

What was she doing with her life? What purpose did she have on this earth? The questions slid under the defences of her common sense and unsettled Mary. And it was no use saying God would provide because, plainly, He didn't.

Once in Northampton, it quickly became obvious that she didn't possess enough coupons for a dress. However, the shop assistant informed Mary she could buy a pair of stockings with a single one so she invested in a couple of pairs, knowing they would have to last the year. Emerging from the haberdasher's, she spotted a restaurant across the road and she treated herself to the one-and-sixpenny lunch menu and a cup of tea.

Afterwards, she walked back in the direction of the bookshop she had spotted close to the bus station.

Flunn's Bookshop was enjoying a brisk trade. Stacked on a table in the centre of the shop were copies of a Penguin paperback entitled *Aircraft Recognition* and a cheap atlas. The piles of both were diminishing at a steady rate.

But it was the travel section to which she gravitated. Increasingly, that sort of book interested her because, even if it was a little late in the day, she craved to know more about the world. She knew so little, and regretted her ignorance. For all she knew, Europe might be shrouded in darkness – which, in a manner of speaking, it now was – and its natives went around with horns on their heads. Mary wouldn't know if they did or they didn't.

Her browsing yielded a couple of nuggets. Mary learned there were Baroque churches in Germany and a pope's palace in France. Back home from the Great War and his signals unit, her father had dropped hints here and there about his time in France. The natives were strange, he told Mary and her mother. They put garlic in stews and smoked strong tobacco. What is garlic? Mary had wanted to know. She wished now that she had made him tell her more. It would have been lovely, too, to have sat down with him and, as professionals, to have mulled over the more complex intricacies of Morse and of signalling. It would have been a companionship. Of course, she could never have let her father into the secrets of her work but there would have been a good chance that he would have guessed.

An hour passed and, soothed and stimulated at the same time, Mary was completely content. Finally, she drifted towards the poetry section and took down a volume of Wordsworth.

Its pages were particularly crisp and white and the words on them appeared very black. She rifled between the Preludes and shorter poems and then . . . and then Mary read:

Her voice was like a hidden bird that sang;
The thought of her was like a flash of light
Or an unseen companionship . . .

She knew of Wordsworth, of course, but not in depth. Yet that small piece of his verse told her that the poet, that grand old man, understood what she was, and what she was doing. It was a moment of pure epiphany, of excitement, of a kind of transcendence which, for a few seconds, lifted Mary above her life – her dull, obedient life – into an elemental being.

Unseen. The description chimed in so many ways with her. For Mary regarded herself as unseen. From bitter experience, she had discovered she was the sort of person who was overlooked. At first, she had chaffed against being unremarkable, and there *had* been occasions when she had quivered with the injustice of being neither pretty, nor clever nor educated. By her late twenties, she had accepted her lot and rescinded on the notion of making a big splash in life. Not that she complained, but there had been bad times when she imagined that it wouldn't take much for the ties that bound her to life to snap.

Yet, as the years passed, Mary grew stronger and took pride in her expertise at 'putting up with things'. It made sense to be a realist. The world was organized for men's convenience. 'Endurance' and 'submission' were important words in the female vocabulary – she could transmit them in

Morse in a flash. There were plenty of others in her position. Plenty were worse off, and she was fed and clothed and, from time to time, had a laugh with her friends and could, more or less, cope with her mother. She grew to understand that hope and anticipation were painful emotions. Unreliable, too, and she was better off without them.

Unseen companionship . . .

A radiance seemed to be flowing through Mary.

She would never know Mayonnaise and Vinegar and the others in the obvious way but, as she now perceived in this moment of revelation, the obvious was not the only way. Not the only way at all.

How ridiculous – she realized she was crying!

Mrs Cotton forgot to check up on Mary – 'Sorry, dear, I was busy getting Mr C's tea' – and the alarm clock from Woolworth's had never kept good time.

It meant that Mary was late for her shift.

'One more transgression and you're for it, Voss,' said Signalmaster Cripps. But he didn't mean it. Not in the way Signalmaster Noble, the bully of the station, would have done. Noble he is not, ran the joke.

'Sorry,' she said. 'But I am here and ready and willing.'

'What are you waiting for, Voss? Get on shift.' She turned to go but he called after her: 'Voss, you're a good worker. But don't let it go to your head.'

Tonight up at Station 53d, an urgency surged

through the ether. Mary couldn't explain how she knew, but she did. Someone was on the run. Or there was a big operation on the go. Whatever it was they, the listeners, got wind of something momentous happening in the shadowy areas of the war.

The frequencies were jumpy tonight, too. The call signs came and went. In between her skeds, she kept her earphones on, which helped the concentration.

ZYA calling. Mayonnaise.

Mary's heart lifted.

QVR. *Ready to receive.*

Write the message down.

Don't think about anything else.

The 'handwriting' was as ever. The dashing T, the emphatic M. Yet it was strange how Mayonnaise never spoke to her in the same way as Vinegar. Apart from those early, stumbling transmissions, Vinegar's keying was so smooth and assured. Unflappable. She admired it very much. It was stoic in the face of the enemy and, in Mary's opinion, stoicism encompassed everything: heroism, courage and, yes, imagination, too.

She sat back on the wooden chair to wait out the minutes until Vinegar was due.

Half dead with fatigue, Nancy slumped over her station and the sight of Nancy's exhausted shoulders and mussed hair troubled Mary. One second's inattention and a message could be garbled. In her old life as supervisor at the telephone exchange Mary would have told Nancy off. Looking back at her time there, she concluded she might have been harsh occasionally, but she would have defended herself by saying she expected no less from herself than from others.

Very gently, she nudged Nancy with her foot.

'Go and sneak a cup of tea,' she whispered. 'Tell the Führer you have to, you know, *go*.'

They weren't supposed to 'go', but sometimes they had to and the signalmasters had to put up with it.

Nancy sat bolt upright and sent Mary a feeble grin. 'Good thinking, Voss.' She heaved herself to her feet. 'I'll have his balls for dumplings if he tries to stop me.'

The frequencies were weak. Storms were fouling the atmosphere. Yet the calls sang sweetly in her ear. Wherever they were coming from, she was there to listen to a steady stream of birdsong freighted with hurry or anguish, or with love and terror.

Tonight, Vinegar was late.

Where are you?

Bent over your set? In a field? In a church? Have you lost faith?

Are you sorry? Are you afraid? Are you lonely?

She thought of a future without the agents, *her* agents, of an existence shorn of the intensity of waiting and hoping. And dreaming . . . One day it would happen.

She would have to make do as she had always had to make do. And a little humour about it wouldn't come amiss, she reminded herself.

The needle wavered. She adjusted the dial.

Liquid sounds.

Keep calm.

Outer darkness.

Unseen companionship.

Then . . . yes. Yes, here was XRT. Vinegar. Pulsing through the interference and static.

His was a strong signal tonight

Mary began to write.

Twenty minutes later the call finished. Mary glanced up at the clock. Twenty minutes almost to the second. One moment longer and Vinegar might have been in trouble.

Her finger hovered over the transmitter key. Could she break through the barrier of her natural reticence? Could she break through the upbringing which frowned on words such as this and send 'shit' . . . as a token of her feelings, of her empathy, of her *unseen companionship*?

She didn't.

At the finish, she placed the paper into the basket. In a flash, Signalmaster Cripps was onto her. 'All right, Voss? Anything to report?'

'Nothing, sir. The fist seemed normal.'

'Right, I'll get it to the cipher room.'

She watched his retreating figure. She would have given much to follow 'her' message and to know what was in it. Just a couple of words would do. But that would never happen. It would never, ever be permitted. Secrecy between the departments was absolute.

At the end of the shift, she went to put on her coat. The other girls often complained how bulky their uniform was, but she was grateful for its warmth and relative smartness.

The lavatories were backing up again in what was laughingly called the Ladies Rest Room. They can't cope with all the traffic, was the joke. Someone had filled a bowl with water and disinfectant to make the room more pleasant, but it wasn't a place to linger.

A shoelace was flapping and she bent down to retie it – but her foot appeared to vanish down a dark tunnel at the end of which was a pinprick of light.

Fatigue. One of the effects of her constant exhaustion was to make objects appear insubstantial, or even hallucinatory, and for the hundredth time she resolved that she had to sort out her sleeping. Maybe a doctor could help? Otherwise she was going to be no good on shift.

Outside in the drive, Mary stood for a moment and closed her eyes. The incipient dizziness which occasionally attacked her at the end of a shift swirled at the back of her skull. This was the moment she always questioned herself. Had she made mistakes?

Had she failed in any way?

Was she missing anything?

CHAPTER 17

It wasn't to her credit, but Tanne took to watching her mother and found herself questioning why she kept her bedroom light on so late. Why did she insist on going for walks at dusk? Why was she growing so thin?

On one of the harshest of February days she bumped into Arne on the back stairs. He was carrying a paint pot and brushes. Tanne followed him up to the room which, years ago, had been occupied by the English nanny. Since then, too far from the main family area and difficult to heat, it had remained empty. Besides, it was considered that the steps leading up to it from the garden posed a security risk. Its one advantage was its magnificent view of the lake.

'*Herregud!*' she exclaimed, then repeated herself in English: 'Good heavens.'

The room was freshly painted. Its woodwork gleamed, chintz curtains were at the windows and a larger curtain had been hung by the door that opened on to the garden steps.

This door had been propped open and the

unforgiving cold chased the smell of the paint out into the frozen landscape.

'Arne . . . what's going on?'

Arne kept his back to her. 'Ask your mother.'

The refusal to meet her eye was indicative. She knew Arne and evasiveness was not in his nature. Arne, therefore, had been drawn into a conspiracy – or an understanding – which had something to do with her mother's uncharacteristic behaviour.

Hovering in the bright, cold room, she felt impatient, bewildered and more than a little lost.

Returning to her room, she threw clothes into her case ready for a trip to København and the ballet. Suitcase in hand, she emerged, only to overhear her parents engaged in heated argument in the hall.

'How could you, Kay?' said her father.

A mutual bitterness and distrust rose like smoky breath . . . Tanne had never heard or witnessed the like before.

Turning away, she took herself down the back staircase. Elation and high spirits were things which now belonged to the past. The war was exposing weaknesses, drawing lines, pushing people into different camps.

As usual, she was welcomed in København by Grete and the others. But it didn't take five minutes for Tanne to see that the group was subdued and anxious, especially Hannah, who looked frighteningly gaunt and jumpy. Many of them had taken to smoking furiously, and drinking whatever they could lay their hands on.

They told her the latest news. The Hotel d'Angleterre had been requisitioned by the German military and the German flag hung over it. The previous October, the King had fallen from his horse and no longer rode out daily from the palace through the city. Instead, Grete told Tanne, there was a song now doing the rounds: '*Der rider en Konge*'. 'If you hear it . . .' She tapped her nose. 'It means you don't agree with putting up with the Germans.'

Worse, far worse, Hannah's brother had been arrested and she was in a bad way about it. 'You should have told me,' Tanne said. 'What was he doing?'

Hannah gestured with both hands. 'Can't say. Not safe.'

The lack of confidence stung. 'Hannah, are there things going on I don't know about? Please tell me.'

'Well,' said Hannah – and the implication was that Tanne's ignorance was shameful. 'There are people who are working for Denmark's freedom.'

'Who are they? What don't I know?'

Again the hand gesture.

Hannah also reported that there was to be a new German unit, the Waffen SS Division Nordland, which was to be recruited from the Danish people. 'They don't like Jews,' she whispered. Ministers were being sacked because their faces didn't fit.

Danish laws were being meddled with and Danish dairy products whisked out of the country.

Predictably, the ballet was *Sleeping Beauty*. To the accompaniment of Tchaikovsky's ravishing legato strings and harp glissandos, and poised on a superbly arched pointe, Princess Aurora made her choice in the Rose Adagio by refusing to select any one suitor before pricking her finger and falling asleep.

How differently Tanne interpreted it this time. It was quite clear to her now that Princess Rose's romantic confusion could be interpreted as resistance. Had Tchaikovsky understood this? Didn't his music reverberate with sadness and longing for a better life?

Returning to Rosenlund in the early evening and finding no one around, she mounted the back stairs to the nanny's old room to discover her mother on her hands and knees in front of a cupboard, stowing bandages and disinfectant in it. The curtains were drawn and the room had been made very attractive, with comfortable armchairs, a desk and a chair, a lamp, and a fire burning in the grate.

'I thought I'd find you here,' Tanne said from the doorway.

Her mother started.

'I don't often see you doing any housework, *Mor*.'

'Don't sound so suspicious, darling.' Her mother sat back on her heels. 'I've been meaning to organize myself an office for some time. I need somewhere to do my accounts.' She smoothed down her skirt. 'We talked about this before, but in future we're going to have to do a lot more for ourselves. And I need a bit of peace. You know how your father fusses.'

'Peace, yes. But bandages?'

'There's a war on, darling. You never know.'

Tanne held out a hand to help her up. 'You mustn't lose any more weight,' she remarked.

'My appetite's not so good these days.' She gave one of her little smiles. 'Perhaps I'm not so greedy?'

Tanne tried to analyse her mother's expression. Intense? Alive? Perhaps 'intense' was inaccurate. Perhaps 'excited' was a better term. Whatever . . . Kay appeared to be lit up by an inner conviction.

Was she jealous of her mother? Tanne hoped not.

Later, when they were drinking tisane after dinner, her father said, 'I wish we still had Lippiman's gingerbread.'

He fixed a cold eye on her mother.

'I do hope he's safe,' said her mother. 'No more apricot pastries.' There was a silence. 'Someone must take over the bakery.'

'No one made *brunkager* like Lippiman,' said her father.

Her mother addressed her father directly. 'Bror, I'm sorry about the gingerbread. I'll ask Birgit to find it somewhere else.'

Her failure to call her father 'darling' was very apparent. Rosenlund was a house from which endearments had been banished.

'You know the parents are sleeping apart and have been for a while?' Tanne had informed Nils when she visited him one afternoon in his unkempt, cluttered set of rooms at the university.

'Wouldn't you? You get a better night's sleep.'

'They don't talk to each other either.'

He wasn't that interested. 'A change is as good as a rest.'

That night, Tanne dreamed of her father eating the spicy, brittle gingerbread which he and she so favoured. Snap, it went. *Snap*. In her dream, she was trying to decide if she was becoming more like her mother, or not.

She woke hungry but not for food. Her body was crying out for something she could not name. Was it physical satisfaction? Emotional satisfaction? A sense of belonging? Overriding these confusing urges was the one which Tanne understood perfectly: the need to go out to walk the land which one day she would inherit. After breakfast, she pulled on her leather boots with the thick-ridged soles and a padded jacket, and went in search of Sif and Thor. But they were already out with her father.

It was chilly heading for the lake and she pulled her hat down over her ears.

A faint spring sunshine was beginning to penetrate the perpetual grey. The thaw was making inroads into the lake ice, which cracked and hissed, shuffled and shifted. On the island, the place Sophia-Maria had favoured for her summer picnics, all the vegetation had been fossilized with frost but Tanne could just make out emergent patches of brown. Ice puddles on the path were growing liquid hems.

Tanne liked to think that she knew everything there was to know about the estate . . . where the first tiny yellow flowers of spring were to be found, or where the birds nested and the deer rutted, where the winter ice was likely to be at its most treacherous.

Rounding the western point of the lake, she turned to head back up to the house. The seldom-used path that led up to the outhouses was slippery, forcing her to concentrate on where she was going. When she next looked up, it was to see a man with a cap pulled down over his face letting himself into the pigeon loft.

Strangers were not unknown at Rosenlund, particularly these days. From time to time a tramp or someone out of work pitched up, spent a night in an outhouse and everyone turned a blind eye. She made a note to tell Arne.

It was then that she spotted her mother. She was also heading for the pigeon loft. Every so often she stopped and looked around. On reaching it, she ducked inside.

There were . . . there could be . . . several explanations as to what her mother was doing with a strange man, but only one made sense.

The teenage emotions which, years ago, Tanne had so often battled to master now resurfaced. Rage, real rage, and disgust, and astonishment.

It was none of her business what her mother did.

Yes, it was.

Neglected for so long, the door to the pigeon loft was swollen and didn't want to budge but she pushed hard and it yielded.

Her mother and the stranger were crouched over some sort of instrument. He had exchanged his cap for a pair of headphones.

The scene was disconcerting enough. More frightening was the pistol the man snatched up and pointed at her chest.

Her mother interposed herself between Tanne and the gun. 'It's all right, Felix.'

'Who is she?'

To her astonishment, her mother, instead of revealing who Tanne was, said: 'I can vouch for her. I know her.'

'But who is she?'

This was ridiculous. Tanne said, 'She's my mother.' Turning to her, she demanded: 'What *are* you doing?'

'What are *you* doing, Tanne?'

Her mother's hostility shocked Tanne. 'I saw this man, and then you.' She shrugged. 'I thought you must be meeting him.'

'It could be put like that.' Sounding more like her normal self, her mother prised the gun away from her companion. 'You're to get out of here.' She snapped on the safety catch of the pistol, put it into her pocket and hustled Tanne over to the

269

door. '*Go.*' There was real fear and distress in her voice. 'Go.'

A pigeon called from the cage. Tanne shook herself free and swung round. A bird, its bright eyes gleaming in the shadow behind the bars, looked back at her. 'Whose is this?'

'Quiet.' The stranger held up a hand for silence and with the other adjusted a knob on the machine. A light glowed. He pulled the headphones over his ears and began writing on the paper in front of him.

A curious noise sifted through the loft. High-pitched.

Her mother looked from him to Tanne and Tanne thought she saw tears in her eyes. 'God forgive me, Tanne, you'll have to stay here for the moment.'

Tanne watched as the man, rigid with concentration, took down groups of letters.

'What—' she began but her mother put her finger to her lips, crossed over to the door and peered out.

Was it five hours later, or only ten minutes, when the stranger tossed aside the headphones and stood up? Older than Tanne – she guessed – he was dressed in overalls, unshaven and obviously angry.

'Who's this?' Tanne asked.

'Felix,' replied her mother, who seemed more composed.

She addressed him: 'Is that your real name?'

'The only one I answer to.' He was concentrating

on the piece of paper in his hand. 'You'll have to deal with her, Freya.'

Freya?

'You must be quiet,' ordered her mother.

Tanne asked herself if it was because an essential element of her brain had gone missing that she was failing to understand what was going on.

There was a whiff of ancient bird dung . . . there were tins of creosote and lime whitewash stacked under the bench, an abandoned rake . . .

Time shifted and she and Nils were back playing in the pigeon loft. Tanne pelting Nils from above with pebbles. Nils vowing instant death. The hay fight from which they had both ended up catching fleas.

Felix began to pack the equipment into the case.

'Freya, get her out.' He did not look at Tanne as he coiled a length of wire.

'I have every right to be here.' As soon as the words were uttered, Tanne regretted how childish she sounded.

He gestured to the instrument that she had – finally – realized was some sort of wireless set. 'Are you being deliberately stupid? You're putting yourself in danger. Think of your mother, if not yourself.'

Her brain was moving slowly, ponderously. She was trying to make connections, and trying to make sense.

'Are you sending messages?'

His eyes reflected irritation and impatience at her and her questions, but what did he expect?

'Felix,' her mother's voice held a warning.

Felix shut the case and snapped down the locks.

Her mother was checking the door. 'Someone's coming.'

Without warning, Felix grabbed Tanne and covered her eyes and mouth with his hands. He was strong, very strong. 'Not a word,' he breathed in her ear.

His feet braced, he held Tanne hard against his chest in a grip impossible to escape. She was both hot and cold with outrage, with fear and . . . with a strange excitement.

Inside the pigeon loft, she could hear her mother moving around. Then footsteps could be heard padding along the tamped-down mud path outside and the pressure on her mouth increased. No one moved.

Eventually, Felix released her and gave her a little push. She blinked and found her balance. He went to the door and peered through a crack. A little out of breath, her mother leaned on the broom.

Tanne scrubbed at her mouth. 'That was unnecessary.'

'No, it wasn't.' He did not bother to look round. 'Don't make the mistake of imagining anything is unnecessary if it keeps one safe.'

'What have you done with the . . . whatever . . . that thing . . . the set?'

'You don't know,' said Felix. 'Understand?' He turned his head. 'Freya, will the coast be clear?'

Freya.

'I'm pretty sure it was Arne. I recognized his coat. He will have gone.'

'I'm not moving until you explain,' said Tanne.

'Go, Felix,' said . . . Freya.

The light from the door illuminated unshaven features that were grey with fatigue. All the same, Tanne acknowledged, he was a good-looking man.

A nod. Then, without another word, he picked up his cap, stuck it on his head and disappeared.

She gazed after him. '*Mor*, have you gone mad? No, scrub that. Have *I* gone mad?'

Her mother took Tanne's arm, hustled her outside and fastened the door.

'Answer me.'

'Don't argue. Go back to the house and wait.'

In her bedroom, Tanne found herself peering into the mirror. Did she recognize herself? She backed away to the bed, sat down on its edge and went over what had happened. Her mother, her infuriating mother, was clearly caught up in resistance work.

How blind could you be? Why hadn't she considered what was going on out of sight months ago? The war was more than two years old and she should have been sharper and wiser. It wouldn't have taken much wit to realize that resistance must be there. From her mother's action over Lippiman, from what Hannah had told her last night, from what she had just witnessed, she now knew without a doubt that it *was* there.

She had been blind.

Tanne looked down at her hands. It was dawning on her that every person had to make up their own mind about where they stood.

It was then Tanne was assaulted by an unwelcome thought. Even worse than her political and moral myopia was the knowledge she had been outdone by her mother.

She dismissed that one as unworthy.

What was she to do?

Change out of her walking trousers, for a start.

Punctuated by long pauses during which she found herself staring glassily out of the window, she hunted out a wool blouse and serge skirt.

My mother is a liar?

Again, she consulted the mirror, then picked up her hairbrush and tackled the snarls in her hair.

She was attempting to fasten the buttons at her wrist when her mother came into the bedroom and shut the door quietly behind her.

Tanne didn't look up. 'Don't bother to lie to me, *Mor*.'

'I'm not going to lie.' Kay sat down in the antique chair upholstered in a blue-and-white stripe that had been given to Tanne by her Swedish godmother. 'I want you to listen carefully.'

Tanne slipped on her shoes. 'How long have you being doing this, *Mor*? This isn't just rescuing

Lippiman or distributing a few underground pamplets, is it? This is bigger, something organized.'

'I can't go into detail, Tanne, except to say that what you saw affects your safety and it won't happen again. But you must understand that absolute secrecy and discretion are imperative. *Do* you understand?'

'Last time I checked, I had a brain.'

'Don't joke, Tanne.'

'Where did you get the equipment? Where are these messages going?' She bent over to adjust her shoe. 'Why are they being sent?'

Her mother was twisting her wedding ring round and round her finger. 'The less you know, the less you can reveal under duress.'

'Duress?' Tanne's heart gave a massive thump. 'What are you talking about? Are you in trouble?'

'I thought you said you had a brain?'

Tanne shrugged.

'Use it, Tanne. What do you think men like Juncker are capable of? Or the *Gestapomen*. Or—' her mouth was set '—the SS? You've seen and heard what's happening on our streets, in the prisons and . . .' She sighed. 'You know what's being said.'

'I'm not blind or deaf.' Tanne was struggling with the cuff again. 'But are *you* playing politics to annoy *Far*?'

Her mother got up and took possession of Tanne's wrist to deal with the rogue button. Her hand was perfectly steady. 'You don't *play* politics in war.' It was a quiet, but deadly, rebuke.

Angry with her mother, but angrier with herself for being so slow, so uninformed, so out of control, Tanne couldn't resist saying, 'Have you thought that you are putting *Far* and Rosenlund in danger?'

'I think of nothing else.'

'So why do it? Just because you crave a bit of adventure with a stranger?'

'Take that back.'

There was a pause.

'Sorry, *Mor*.' Tanne swallowed. 'I'm being stupid. It's the shock of finding you . . . But why you?'

'Do you want the truth? I wasn't bold or brave or decisive. I was asked to help out once. I said yes but only the once. But it doesn't work like that. Let that be a lesson, Tanne. One tiny step and you are sucked in.' The grey eyes were troubled. 'In the end, I had gone too far to turn back. But I've had my life. You haven't and you *mustn't* get involved.' Raising Tanne's hand to her mouth, she kissed it and pressed it to her cheek. 'Listen to me, *min elskede*. Please.'

The gossip in København. Shootings. Killings. Prison. Torture. Death. Belief. Principle . . . All these were closing in on Tanne and she had to make sense of them.

Her mother was still talking: '. . . But I do believe the Nazis have to be stopped. I want to be able to say that I went to the aid of my country.'

It irritated Tanne. '*Your* country?'

Silence.

'I suppose I should have known that would be your reaction.' Her mother made for the door.

'Stop!' Tanne was beginning to feel desperate. 'Please. Let's start again. I am involved, *Mor*. I've seen what I shouldn't have done. That makes me so.'

'No, it doesn't.'

With a snap, she opened the door and almost collided with Bror. Having returned from his morning inspection of the grounds, he had washed and changed. His hair was damp, his eyes bright from the exercise and Tanne knew he would smell of his special Berlin cologne.

'Raised voices. Are you two quarrelling?'

He looked only at Tanne.

Tanne's eyes encountered her mother's. Her mother's secrets were bad enough. The danger was frightening. Worse, was the destruction of the perfect candour between herself and her father.

From now on, Tanne could not say anything. She had to be silent.

The strain told on Tanne. Her head pounded incessantly, her eyes were inflamed from interrupted sleep and she found it an effort to concentrate on even the simplest tasks.

A few days later she drew her father aside after breakfast.

'*Far*, the Germans are demanding a percentage

of what we produce on the farms. What if we don't declare the total dairy yields?'

They happened to be by the stairs, standing almost directly under the family tree.

Unusually, a lock of hair had fallen over her father's face which made him look younger. 'Are you turning militant?'

'No, only practical. Why should they take our hard-won yields?'

'I'm not going to discuss it.' His silver cigarette case was never far away, and he took it out of his pocket. 'Tanne, I'm planning a duck shoot. Do you want to come?'

Childhood memories springing up from the time when she craved nothing more than to be with her father, tucked up in a hide, or wading through the marsh. Riding across the fields, wind stippling the water, the ever-changing cloud shapes. Their whispered asides. Mud, salty marsh, sappy, whippy grass. At the end of a hard session, the exhaustion which flooded, sweet and lovely, through the body.

'No, thank you, *Far.*'

'Not shoot?'

She bit down on her lower lip. 'With everything that's going on, I don't see duck-shooting in the same way.'

He shrugged but she knew that he was offended. 'No discussion? Shooting duck is over? Just like that?' He turned away. 'If that is what you wish.'

She wasn't going to let this go. Calculating that, in the end, her father would not ignore anything which affected Rosenlund, she said, '*Far*, you haven't answered my question. The dairy yields?'

Tanne was right. He took a moment and then refused to answer the question directly: 'There're more ways of skinning a cat than the obvious. I was thinking of ploughing up the south meadow to try for extra crops next year to make up the shortfall.'

He smiled down at her. 'The Protectorate is not going away and, whatever the bad history between Danes and Germans, we remain cousins.' He pointed to the family tree. 'Think of Sophia-Maria.'

'Even if the Nazis are wrong, *Far*?'

'Ah, so . . . I can see what you are thinking. The wind is changing. Am I right?' He extracted a cigarette from the case and a fleck of tobacco drifted to the floor. 'Tanne, I could support your idea by falsifying the figures, but I would be putting Rosenlund at risk.'

Tanne forced herself to look at him but her thoughts were elsewhere.

Messages needed to be sent . . . to whom and when?

He continued, with a touch of impatience. 'It wasn't possible for Denmark to defend itself. We didn't have the troops and the border is easy to cross. Why not save lives and negotiate? Why not ensure that Rosenlund survives. For you.'

Perhaps her father was right and life could continue as normal? Practicality. Pragmatism. Wasn't the first duty of life to survive it? Planted in the human spirit was an ineradicable will to live. The images which now haunted Tanne rose in her mind . . . Hannah's pale contorted face as she described how her brother had fled from the police, the dead cyclist, his blood on her legs and trickling between the cobblestones . . .

'What if I don't want it?'

'Tanne. Please.'

'What if the price isn't worth it?'

'Because you're young, my darling daughter, you can't see it. When I die, you will be thankful for this.'

Tanne watched him take the stairs two at a time. At the top he turned round. 'But don't worry, I've got plenty of years left in me yet.'

For a moment, his hand rested on the rail.

How lonely he seemed. Even with her mother by his side, he had always been a bit of a stoic.

But it didn't make him right.

Tanne fled back to København for a few days, calculating that different faces, different places would give her breathing space.

Arriving in the afternoon, she discovered that Grete and Hannah were tied up until the evening. No matter. She made her way to a favoured spot: the gardens of the Rosenborg Palace.

Fireworks, bonfires and any midsummer celebrations had all been banned for the coming year, but the Københavners didn't appear to be too depressed about these restrictions on their national life. In fact, they appeared to enjoy flouting the regulations and had come out in droves to enjoy a pale spring sunshine and to mill about in large groups. Well wrapped up, Tanne settled herself on a sunny seat to watch one particular group drinking beer and singing songs of an increasingly patriotic nature, while elsewhere there were deals being done, arguments taking place, lovers meeting and families taking pleasure in being together.

She spotted a German soldier exchange a packet of cigarettes for shaving soap with a man in a brown suit, and a youth in a *HitlerJugend* shirt helping a mother with a screaming toddler.

Ordinary things. Ordinary life. Yet, not.

'Look at this . . .' cried a blonde girl in a green overcoat, clapping a beanie hat with British RAF colours onto her head.

Within seconds, a couple of Danish police surrounded the girl. One of the policemen grabbed her wrist. She tried to wrest it out of his grasp.

Tanne got up.

Move away, Tanne. Survive.

Not honourable. Pragmatic, though, if . . . if . . . she was to work for Denmark's freedom.

The girl's friend froze with a biscuit held halfway to her mouth, watching as a German *feldgendarme* materialized out of the crowd and ordered the blonde girl to her feet.

She was now sobbing.

The *feldgendarme* gestured towards the exit and the Danish police dragged the girl away, leaving an upended bottle of beer to soak into the grass where, only a moment ago, she had been happily chatting with her friend.

A veil dropped over the promise of the day. In its place was a sourness. Those closest to the incident were rattled and anxious. A woman in a headscarf hustled away her two children. Others headed out of the gardens.

Tanne edged her way towards the exit. At the Kronprinsessegade gate, a man stood aside to let her through. He was wearing horn-rimmed spectacles and his skin looked an unhealthy greyish colour. Even so, she recognized him.

'Felix.'

He turned on his heel and walked swiftly away but she ran after him. 'You were with my mother.' That brought him to a halt. 'Who are you? Tell me.'

His gaze shifted up and down the street. 'Shut up, please.'

'Tell me, then.'

Felix came to a decision. 'Turn down Dronningens Tværgade and at the junction with Bredgade there is the Café Amadeus. Order a coffee.'

This was a dream. This was real. She had strayed into a Hans Christian Andersen's fantasy. A bubble lodged itself in her chest. Excitement? Laughter? No, surely not laughter. More a sense that she was arriving at a place which she hadn't known existed.

The coffee was in front of her when Felix arrived and slid in beside her on the banquette. She circled it with her hands. 'You look different.'

'It's amazing what glasses and a bit of dust on the skin can do.' His eyes moved restlessly around the room. 'Don't make it obvious but the man who has just come in . . . what's he doing?'

'What?'

Gathering her wits, Tanne bent down to adjust her shoe and sneaked a look. The man? Elderly, almost befuddled-looking, with a wispy beard. He had ordered a beer. He was watching them. She fiddled again with her shoe and straightened up. 'He's watching us.'

Felix leaned towards her. 'Kiss me.'

Not for one second did she hesitate. His mouth was alien and not at all passionate. Up close, his skin under the dust was smooth and fresh and she breathed in an unfamiliar scent.

She forgot her wavering, confused politics, the fears for her mother, her *anger* with her mother, the plans for the future. *What future?* Just for those moments nothing mattered except this stranger's lips on hers. Nothing at all.

She could tell that he was taken aback.

For the first time, his smile was genuine. 'Sorry about this but you'll have to kiss me again.'

Better. Much better. When it was over, she murmured: 'Who are you and why are you seeing my mother?'

'Do you imagine I am going to tell you?' His mouth rested by her ear.

She drew back in order to look into his eyes – as intently as a true lover.

Felix locked his gaze with hers. 'Not bad.' He kissed the base of her neck – and a sweet and wild music struck up in Tanne's head. 'We have to get out of here. Put your arm round me.'

Tanne got to her feet, pulled Felix upright and said gaily: 'Let's go, *elskede*.'

Entwined, they left the café and walked down the street. At the junction, Felix halted. 'Sorry about that. I thought I had shaken off the tails.'

She kept her arm round Felix. 'I don't know anything about you, or where you come from. Certainly not your name. But please tell me what's happening.'

He placed his hands on her shoulders. 'Listen to me. Do not get tangled in this. Do not.'

How strange. Her mother had talked of the step by step. The tiny incremental changes. Of the waters washing over the head.

Recklessness, a wanton exhilarated recklessness, had Tanne in its grip. She reached up and kissed Felix again on the lips. 'But I am.'

CHAPTER 18

The dentist's surgery off the Strøget, København's main pedestrian street, had the advantage of a basement room, plus a door opening into the garden where a couple of scrubby laurel bushes offered sanctuary to the birds recovering from the winter.

Wearing headphones, Kay crouched over a dummy transmitter key, her finger tensed so tightly that the joint had whitened. With her was 'Johan', an employee of Bang & Olufsen, who was instructing her in the mysteries of Morse. A burly, balding, middle-aged man, with an unhealthy mottled complexion and customarily wearing a jacket and frayed bow tie which had seen better days, he was a good, patient teacher.

She had been at it for several weeks. It was now April and the learning process hadn't been easy.

The room was crammed with dentist materials: small boxes of cement, a discarded hand drill, mouthwash and, arranged on the shelves, row on row of plaster-of-Paris denture moulds. Every so often Kay looked up and encountered their macabre grins.

Upstairs, the dentist's drill stopped and started.

Dot dash dash, Freya tapped: W.

The drill fell silent. Johan held up his hand. They had agreed it was safer to wait for its whining cover.

Kay slipped the headphones round her neck. 'I'm sorry I'm not a natural, Johan.'

'I've had worse, my dear.'

The flutter and whirr of the birds busying themselves in the laurels was, she decided, delightfully reassuring.

The gnat-like whine recommenced. 'Go,' said Johan.

Replacing the headphones, Kay reapplied herself to the transmitter key. With a grinding effort, she translated another letter into dash dot dot dash: X. This was followed by dash dot dash dash.

'Y . . . good,' said Johan, 'and now Z.'

Dash dash dot dot.

'Not so bad,' was the verdict.

She felt as exhausted as if she had run a race. 'It was dreadful.'

Being versed and skilled, Johan could have been superior about Kay's stumbling progress. But, natural teacher as he was, he offered up useful pointers instead. 'Listen to the sound combinations, as you would do to music.'

'And I thought I was musical.'

Kay tried to stand up but Johan pushed her down. 'The only way forward is to keep going.'

She laughed and reapplied herself.

'Listen for the melody of the letter rather than counting the dits and dahs,' he said, tapping out air-rhythms. 'The human brain learns a language much more easily when meaning is attached to the sounds. Without it, the brain has no handles to make that attachment. So . . . if you take the letter D in Morse, it might be more readily remembered as "dog did it" instead of "dash dot dot". Imagine a picture of your favourite dog and, hey presto, the symbol becomes part of the mental furniture.'

A figure slipped through the garden and let itself into the room.

'Felix.'

'Johan.'

Kay did not look up.

He observed Kay's halting efforts. 'Progress?' he asked.

Johan leaned over Freya and adjusted her keying finger into a more natural arc. 'By and large, yes.'

Kay finally met Felix's eyes. 'I'm trying,' she said.

Despite looking grim, Felix flashed a smile. 'We got you the best instructor in the country.'

Kay redoubled her efforts while Felix and Johan exchanged the latest information on the progress of the new, portable wireless sets which were being secretly developed.

'It's risky, really risky,' said Johan. 'We are forced to keep moving locations and it's difficult to transport and hide the components. But when we're done,' he said, with justifiable pride, 'you'll be able to carry a set in something as small as a briefcase.'

'Any idea when?' Felix eased into a chair. 'God, I'm stiff.'

Johan shrugged. 'Who knows? Tell the Nazis to go home and I could do it tomorrow.'

'I'll have to give London some sort of steer.'

'Oh, London . . .' Johan's tone was becoming familiar to Kay – that of the Dane who didn't much care for British interference. 'Word has it they're hostile to us training our own radio operators here. Tell them from me to stuff it, and tell them we need the crystals. Soon.' He sighed. 'Before soon.'

Oh, London . . . Kay's instinct was to spring to its defence, but she kept quiet.

Johan picked up a briefcase which was stuffed with papers. At the door, he turned and said to Felix, 'We do *need* the crystals.'

After he had gone, Felix slumped back in the chair and closed his eyes.

'Are you all right?' Kay touched his shoulder.

His eyes flicked open. 'We need guns, we need explosives, we need money and recruits . . .' He grabbed her arm. 'And getting them depends on this fragile wrist tapping out the messages.' He ran a finger over the junction where the veins rose over the swell of the thumb. 'And mine.'

Felix's guard was down. Kay rubbed her keying

finger, which had swollen. 'Is it something in particular?'

Various expressions chased over his features, mostly caustic. 'It's a piece of cake to run an underground network.'

Kay had never seen this side of Felix. Was he frightened? Exhausted? Or, God forbid, ill? 'Talk to me. I'm here.'

He stared out into the garden. 'Sweet of you, Freya. But I can't tell you anything you don't need to know.'

'They must have discussed with you in London that the mind can only take so much stress?' She was sounding very maternal. 'You're under appalling strain.'

'I'll manage, but thank you.'

How much could one person cope with on his own? It was a question which, no doubt, she would explore.

'Actually,' she said. 'I want to ask a favour. Would it be possible to get a letter out to Sweden, where it could be posted on?'

'Probably.'

'It's my mother. She'll be worrying and I want to reassure her. She's quite elderly and not in good health. If she died . . . What I mean is that I don't want her to die without hearing that I'm fine.'

'What will you say?'

Would she tell her secrets to her mother . . . about Bror? Felix? Bloody Morse code?

My Darling Mother,

I hope above everything that you and the sisters are well. I have no idea where you are but I imagine you are at home.

This is to tell you that we are all well. Would you believe it, life is almost normal and the war has hardly touched us? In fact, we have had parliamentary elections so democracy is alive and well here. Bror is busy with the house and the estate. I help him as much as I can. Tanne is here with us, but goes to and from Copenhagen to see her friends. Nils is busy with his research at the university. So, you see, our life under the Germans is boring and uneventful . . .

I think of you often . . .

'You won't mention that the Germans have imposed the death sentence for sabotage?'

'No.'

'Or the suicide of a wireless operator, one of ours, when *Danish* police tried to capture him?'

'No.'

'Or that the election was a complete farce and we now have a puppet government?'

'Isn't truth the first casualty of war?'

He raised an eyebrow. 'I'll do what I can.'

Kay picked up her bag. It was happening slowly but their minds were beginning to mesh. She had become better at anticipating what was needed, at understanding the disciplines and demands of deceiving on a grand level. It was a question of perception, and the way her mind worked these days was changing. For one thing, she knew lies were necessary. So was questioning every move. Whom did one trust? Where were the safety nets and the escape routes?

Reaching for her lipstick, she made up her lips. 'Have I smeared any?'

'It's perfect.' Felix barely glanced at her, and mooched over to the door. 'Did I ever tell you I saw a photograph of you in the paper when I was hiding? After I first came in.'

'That must have cheered you.'

'You were wearing a lot of jewels at some function.'

'Ah, the jewels.' She put the lid back on the lipstick and dropped it into her bag. 'I'll be wearing those tomorrow. It's the dinner for the Knights of the Silver Sword.'

'Grown men dressing up?'

'The women are dressed up, too.' His reaction amused Kay. 'A lot of people who matter will be there. Also some Germans. What should I be listening out for?'

'Troop movements.' Felix snapped to attention and explained that intelligence was revealing the Germans had a big problem. Hydro-electric power sites were being sabotaged daily by the Resistance all over the Reich, so they were forced to rely on aluminium to get their electricity. 'But they need bauxite to make aluminium and guess where that comes from?'

Kay knew that. 'Norway.'

'So, anything about ship and troop movements which would indicate where it might be coming in,' he said. 'You never know, Jacob might get lucky and be allowed to blow it all sky high.' He laughed – but not with any humour.

The sound shivered down her spine. It was getting to Felix: the anxiety, the paranoia, the simple fact that you stood a good chance of not being there the next day.

'Something *is* wrong. I'm not leaving until we have it out.' She pointed to the grinning plaster casts. 'Deaf as posts.'

Her new assertiveness was pleasing to Kay but she also cared about Felix. Caring would make her vulnerable but there were limits to an agent's detachment.

'The agent on Jutland. The drinking one. We talked about him before.'

'It's still going on?'

Felix looked grim. 'He promised his leader that he would reform. He did for a while. But he's back on the booze and it's got the better of him. Reports have come in that the stupid bugger was overheard boasting about his training.'

'It must be so hard,' she said. 'To know yourself.'

'You watch them—' Felix spoke more to himself than to Kay '—they watch you. Day after day, week after week, it's cat and mouse. At first the body takes the brunt of the strain . . . aches, indigestion, stiffness, the need for a drink. Then the mind begins to play tricks. Holed up, you think you're safe. There is a knock on the door, a bullet's crack. They take someone else and your nerves snap with terror and . . . a terrible thankfulness. It isn't you this time. But next time?'

There was a silence and her thoughts went this way and that.

The need for a drink . . .

'How did London miss it?' she asked.

He shrugged. 'It happens. No one can predict what life in the field will do to you.'

'Get him out to Sweden.'

He looked at her as if she didn't know what she was talking about – which she didn't. 'Try persuading a full-grown recalcitrant drunk to do what he doesn't want to do. So . . .'

What exactly?

Reading what was written on his face, she felt a hard, sharp shock. 'We can't do that . . .' She noted she used 'we'. 'That's not justice. I mean due process.'

Before the words left her lips, she knew they were redundant.

Therein lay another, less specified, kind of danger.

'We're not in the playground, Freya.'

'We are fighting this war so we don't end up like the murderers and thugs, too. You can't put us on the same level.'

293

He cut through. 'This is war, Freya. You want to live. I want to live . . . and we could all end up dead. The point is that we might have to do things that put us on a level with them. It's debatable, morally speaking, but simple in practical terms. Who do you want to survive? Them? Or us?'

She thought about London and the little she knew about Felix's organization. Putting together a bunch of tricks, training agents, parachuting in weapons, planning sabotage, recruiting an army to create a resistance with bite . . . was it possible for London to understand what it entailed? Not really. It was Felix, she and the others who were the here-and-now . . . the watchers, the doers. Yes, even she, grafted-on Dane – Tanne's words – as she was.

'Did you think like this before . . . in the other life?'

'Of course not. Stupid question.'

He sounded sad.

'Then we can't do what I think you're thinking,' Kay said.

'It's him or us. Probably. You want to survive, don't you?'

Yes, *yes*.

It was as if she was physically stepping over a line. And she knew she could never go back. 'What can I do?'

He barely moved a muscle but she knew he was relieved.

'Contact Jacob. Tell him Holger Danske must act. That's all you need say.'

She had one last stab. 'And if I don't?'

'Then . . .' He was almost tender. 'You're no use to me, Freya.'

She turned away and encountered a grinning plaster-of-Paris upper and lower jaw that was out of alignment.

'I'd have to kill you, too.'

Joke.

Footsteps could be heard clattering down the stairwell. In a flash, Kay had packed the dummy transmitter key into a box labelled Periodontal Extractor. She pushed Felix into a chair. 'Open your mouth,' she whispered. 'Pretend you're a patient.'

But it was Lars, the dentist. He put his head round the door and said, 'The lookouts are signalling trouble. Get out the back.'

They fled.

The Knights of the Silver Sword held two dinners a year, in spring and autumn. The order dated from the Middle Ages and the reasons for its founding had almost certainly been forgotten by the influential guests who were there solely to promote their own interests. Some years back, Bror had been elected onto the committee, pleasing him greatly. He never missed a dinner and Kay was expected to be on his arm.

It involved dressing up, which – however demo-cratically minded they were – the Danes liked to do. White tie, medals, long gowns, jewels . . . the lot.

A couple of days previously, Bror had cornered Kay at Rosenlund. 'I need to talk to you.'

'Of course.'

They hadn't spoken properly for weeks – only the necessary exchanges of information and detail for day-to-day arrangements. Bror remained in the spare room. A great silence lay between them.

'The dinner,' he said.

She scanned his face. Blue, stormy eyes. 'I'd rather not come this year,' she said.

'You will, Kay.' She raised an eyebrow and he modulated his tone. 'Please. Whatever is happening, whatever you decide, I ask you to be there.'

She settled on the pale blue chiffon dress thrown over a silk shift that she had worn to a pre-war wedding. On putting it on, she discovered that she was thinner in the waist, with a flatter stomach and slightly bulkier shoulders. In the past . . . before their estrangement . . . Bror used to tease her about her *weiner-brød*, and she was delighted with her sleeker body.

Seated at the dressing table in the bedroom at the hotel, Kay dusted powder over her shoulders. There was a knock on the door.

It was Bror, resplendent in white tie and medals. 'Ready?'

'Just my earrings to fasten.'

Her hands trembled with nerves and she fumbled the process.

He was watching her – but there was no tenderness, nor indulgence in the regard.

'Let me.'

He bent over her and she smelled the familiar cologne and the starch he favoured for his boiled shirts. Deftly, he hooked the earrings into place.

'There.'

No extra loving, sexy touch.

She missed it. How she missed it.

Letting go was always hard, but this was the hardest thing Kay would ever ask of herself – the letting go of mutual delight, mutual trust, anticipation and intimacy.

She rose to her feet.

'You look beautiful.'

Why did Bror bother? The exchange was formal and underpinned with distrust and distance.

Last year, in this hotel room, it had been very different.

Then, she had looked at Bror and said, 'You've hardly changed since I met you.'

Bror had touched her bared flesh just above the cleavage. 'Will you marry me?'

She had given a soft laugh. 'Of course. But I should point out we are married.'

'But I like asking you, over and over.' He'd slid a tender finger into her cleavage. Do you remember that first time?'

She did.

It had been before their wedding but they couldn't wait. Bror undressed her and she trembled with the daring of what she was about to do. With each garment he dispatched to the floor, he paused to look. 'You're beautiful, Kay.'

So was he.

He'd drawn her close. 'I never thought I would say this to anyone but I can't live without you . . .'

Calling on memories was exhausting and a bad habit.

She looked around the comfortable hotel room, her eyes resting on the bedspread, puckered where she had sat on it, the half-open drawer of the dressing table and the sliver of the bathroom, with the towel thrown over the side of the bath, just visible through the door.

The coiffured, bejewelled and assured *Fru* Eberstern was still there. But she was only part of the story. The wife, mother and chatelaine now hid another being – a woman who was more than a little in love with the idea of being someone else. That had consequences.

Flicking up his tails, Bror sat down on the edge of the bed. 'We haven't talked, Kay.'

Kay eased a kid glove over her wrist and pulled it up her arm. 'You mean about Anton.'

'You more or less told me you were having an affair. Are you?'

'I'm not going to answer that.' The blood thudded in Kay's chest.

There was a silence.

'I haven't slept for weeks,' he said at last.

That hurt. Inflicting pain on someone you loved

did hurt. Of course. And this was to destroy their customary kindness to each other, their intimacy and the automatic assumption that the other was *there*.

'But Anton's only part of it, isn't he? We should be clearer about how we deal with this war.'

'You know what I feel about Hitler.' She reached for the second glove and plaited the fingers. 'Look, I'm here to support you tonight.'

'You've made that clear.' Bror's hands dropped between his knees. 'When we go home we must . . . we must sort out our lives. But I'm too weary and tonight let there be peace between us.'

The last tiny kid-clad button was wrestled through its buttonhole. 'Oh Bror . . .'

Her sadness almost overpowered her. In all probability, she had lost a lover, a friend and a husband.

And the life they had made together.

He looked down at his shoes, polished to brightness. 'It's only going to get worse. Isn't it? So tonight shall we be united?'

He rose to his feet.

She picked up her silk stole and draped it round her shoulders, contemplating the worst.

'You haven't said yes. Do we have a deal?'

She nodded. 'Agreed.'

He bent down and kissed her on the cheek – a perfunctory, businesslike gesture.

Could a heart break? The way she felt, she supposed it could.

On entering the reception, she was cornered by an old friend, Clara Ramussen.

'Kay! You look wonderful. And you've lost weight.' She sent Kay a look that asked: *Have you acquired a lover?* 'Tell me the secret.'

'It's all the walking, Clara. Petrol being so scarce.'

'Goodness, I shall have to take it up,' replied Clara. 'I might get myself a new husband.'

The reception was crowded. There was the usual collection of Danes, and some German and Swedish businessmen. But, this year, the number of uniformed German guests had swelled noticeably.

Dashing in his dress uniform, Anton spotted Kay. Picking up two glasses of champagne, he came over and gave her one. 'How are you?'

Kay accepted the glass. 'For once, I'm really pleased to see you. I need your knowledge.'

'Nonsense, you're always pleased to see me.'

The odds were that Bror was watching and Kay raised her glass to Anton's. 'Tell me what I should know.'

'Good idea,' he said, without shifting his gaze from her face. 'Most of the Germans are run-of-the-mill and probably of not much interest.' He gave her some details. 'But there is one, General Gottfried. I've arranged for you to sit next to him . . .'

The ballroom where dinner was served was impressively mirrored and panelled. The pennants and flags of the Knights of the Silver Sword, celebrating ancient battles and feats, had been brought in for the evening and hung up on poles. The effect was magnificent.

On Kay's left was Aksel Fog, one of the stuffier knights whom she had known for years and just about tolerated. On her right, as Anton had promised, was the Abwehr general, General Gottfried.

General commanding Abwehr Signals Unit . . . Anton had briefed her under his breath. *Almost certainly dealing with intelligence, too. Make friends. You know what to do, darling.*

Anton was sitting further down the table and sent her a little smile.

The general proved to be charming. He had a long clever face, a dress uniform stiff with medals and ribbons, and excellent manners. He told her that he was commanding the København unit. He lived in Koblenz and, although he could not admire København more, he missed his home town very much. 'I am very proud of its architecture and its fines wines. Both are essential for the civilized life, don't you think?'

He spoke without irony which, given his obvious intelligence, surprised Kay.

Judging her silence correctly, he said, 'You consider that invading other countries is uncivilized, but all empires come about because of invasion, including the British one.'

He went on to talk about the Romans, of whom he approved. 'Their discipline and military ethos were vital elements in a highly organized operation. Without them, there would have been no

301

empire.' He raised his glass to her. 'The British Empire is less a product of discipline and more the fruit of inspired amateurism, wouldn't you say?'

This was his second reference to the British, which she took to mean the general had done his homework on her.

A cramp shot through her stomach.

'I genuinely admire the British Empire,' he added.

What could she say? Suddenly, the room felt sickeningly claustrophobic, the set-up very unsafe.

She managed to collect her wits. 'I'm sure the British would be delighted by your compliment.' She touched her own glass. 'General, do you approve this Riesling? It has obviously been chosen with you in mind.'

He nodded. 'This is very agreeable company. If I said it's a privilege to be part of it would you believe me?'

Kay was startled but hid it. If her instincts were correct, the general spoke as the outsider wishing to join the inner circle – and that was a psychological position about which she knew something.

After coffee, Kay rose to her feet and said, 'Please excuse me for a moment or two.' She made her way towards the ladies' powder room.

But Anton ambushed her before she reached it. Tucking his hand under her elbow he pushed her into a small salon off the hotel foyer. 'Come.'

'Are you mad, Anton?'

He shut the door. 'Have you learned anything?'

'You're right. He's in Intelligence.'

'Any proof?'

'He's done his homework. Knows who I am.'

They were facing each other, whispering.

Anton was facing the door. Suddenly, he reached out and pulled her to him.

'What are you doing?'

He said very softly into her ear, 'Someone is at the door.' He raised his voice. 'You know that kiss I have waited for?'

Who?

She slid into the role.

'The kiss that would mean nothing?'

'That one.' He leaned over. His mouth on hers was confident and accomplished and quite, quite different from Bror's.

'Who was it?' she murmured eventually, disentangling herself.

Anton shrugged. 'No idea.' His eyes reflected amusement, malice – and surprise. 'Was it nice?'

'Nicer than a cold bath. Not as nice as good champagne.'

Anton changed tack. 'We've been in contact with London. They want more action and have sent over suggestions.'

'Does Felix know?'

'Probably.'

'He won't like it. He likes to do things his way.'

'None of us are in a position to have our own way. Regrettably.'

She laid a finger on his arm. 'But you do, Anton.'

That amused Anton. 'Not quite.'

She had barely set aside her breakfast tray the following morning when Bror appeared. He sat down on the bed. 'The general has telephoned and invited us to the theatre.'

How should she play this? As the British-born wife? Given her anti-German stance, appearing too eager to meet the general might make Bror suspicious. Calculating her next move, Kay got out of bed and reached for her dressing gown.

'You said no, I hope. You said that we're going home.'

'Didn't you like the general?'

'He's a cultured man.'

'You're angry about the idea, though. Kay, I don't often ask anything of you . . .'

She tied the dressing-gown belt tight round her waist. 'True. But I performed for you last night. I don't think I can do it again today. I'll arrange to go home on my own.'

Bror made for the door. 'Oh, go to hell, Kay,' he said angrily, and vanished.

She dressed carefully. Rolling up the precious silk stockings and attaching them with the suspender, dropping the skirt of her navy-blue costume over her head, and fastening an Eberstern diamond onto the jacket lapel. Last, but not least, she tipped the Parisian hat over one eye. Before her eyes, *Fru* Eberstern of Rosenlund was reassembled.

She gave Bror half an hour to stew. After that, she went downstairs to the lounge where he was reading the morning papers.

He didn't notice her and she was free to observe him for a moment. She loved him. There was no doubt about that, but the man whom she loved had signed the Declaration and was friendly with German intelligence officers.

He looked up. A light came into the blue eyes and she knew that her efforts to look nice had paid off.

'I'm sorry, Bror. I was over-hasty.'

That evening, the Ebersterns were ushered into a box at the theatre where the general waited with an elegant blonde woman. He kissed Kay's hand and said: 'May I introduce my wife, Ingrid, who arrived this morning?'

Ingrid was delightful and, in normal circumstances, Kay would have enjoyed meeting her. Speaking in German, they exchanged information. Ingrid was the mother of two boys, and her other passion was the local amateur opera company. 'In the summer we give performances on the river,' she said. 'Last year I took the main role in *Grafin Mariza*.'

They chatted on.

Kay revealed that she went to the theatre and opera as much as possible but her responsibilities kept her at Rosenlund more often than she would like. She told Ingrid about the estate and its history.

'We have much in common,' said Ingrid at last. She glanced at her husband. 'I often think that our insistence on being different nationalities is nonsense. In Europe at any rate we are one big family.'

Ingrid spoke sense.

'I agree with you,' Kay replied, before changing the subject. 'Will you be staying in Denmark?'

Touching her husband on the arm, Ingrid replied, 'For some time, I think.'

In the interval, champagne was served and the general turned to Kay.

'*Fru* Eberstern, you've told me about your delightful daughter. What does your son do?'

Kay explained that Nils was an academic who was developing advanced mathematical theories. 'He can read numbers as fluently as you or I might read a book.' She couldn't stifle the pride. 'He's quite celebrated in his way.'

Never offer details. Be drab. Be unremarkable.

'I can't tell you,' he said a little later, 'how pleasant this is.'

She felt a flicker of unease.

'I'm glad you feel comfortable here, General. Are you going to travel in Denmark? For pleasure, perhaps? Some of the towns are very pretty and the scenery on Lolland is especially praised.'

The general's gaze rested on Kay. There was a great deal of sharp and analytical intelligence and a trace of humour – which she hadn't expected. 'You know, and I know, that not everyone loves

us, *Fru* Eberstern, and I won't be welcome everywhere. But I will be visiting Jutland.' He looked
down his handsome nose. 'If it's safe. My friends
in the SS tell me they're fully occupied with terrorists and spies. I imagine you know what I'm talking
about.'

How best to use this encounter? Very gently, she
set down her champagne glass on the table. 'I've
often wondered what happens to spies if you
capture them.'

'Depends. If our friends in the SS are involved,
they can be brutal. Personally, I'm against waste
and I think that if you've a highly trained operative in your hands, you should make use of them.'

She smiled at the general.

Back at the hotel, Kay threw her handbag onto
the bed. 'Thank God that's over.'

Bror took out his silver cigarette case. 'It wasn't
so bad.'

'I'll have one of those, too.' She stretched over
and pinched one.

He opened the French windows and stepped out
onto the balcony. Grabbing her stole, she joined
him. He lit her cigarette and she inhaled
gratefully.

'Bror, do you know how many people must have
seen us having our cosy theatre party with the
enemy?'

'You charmed them both.'

She looked down over the hotel garden. Beyond
it the lights of the capital were spread out.

'The general asked if he and Ingrid could visit Rosenlund. Apparently, you were encouraging him to see something of Denmark. He also wants to meet Nils.'

'No,' she said. 'To both.'

'I've arranged it for next week.'

Message to Felix: *Avoid Rosenlund.*

Bror smoked in silence.

Keep tight hold of what matters.

CHAPTER 19

Ruby and Major Martin were drinking ersatz coffee in a café in Baker Street that was a favourite of The Firm's personnel. The windows fronted onto the street and were partly covered by net curtains which had seen better days. Every time the door opened or shut, the bell above it rattled.

But the café had a pleasant enough atmosphere – almost relaxed, gossipy, cosily steamed up on wet days.

As usual, he commandeered a table at the back of the café, saying that it was essential in their line of work because it gave them a good view of the comings and goings at the door.

She liked that – for, at her ripe old age of twenty-four, Ruby had discovered an interest in people. How they looked, what they were saying . . . and what they *really* meant. It was ironic, wasn't it? As a result of her work, which consisted of codes, letters and numbers, she had discovered courage and suffering in the most unexpected places, and this affected her. Plus, on a more simple level, she also took pleasure in knowing that, although she looked exactly like everyone else in uniform, she was nurturing secrets. Was keeping secrets and enjoying them a misuse of power? A road to fascism? If so, she didn't care.

No one seated at the tables acknowledged anyone else even though, as Ruby was now aware, they might know each other well. It was good, basic security practice which would not be understood by those not in the know.

Good security was the reason Major Martin and Ruby arranged their meetings: they needed to go over the procedures again and again. This was the latest of several encounters during the past few weeks, and, if Ruby was as precise about her personal life as she was with her work, she would have to admit to enjoying them all. Two of them had even been conducted over dinner – snatched but fun – before they headed back for night sessions at the office.

Had any other elements crept into the meetings? Well, yes, and Ruby was in two minds as to how to deal with it. In her previous dealings with it, lust had been a straightforward matter. Either you slaked it or you didn't.

Major Martin briefed her on the latest in the turf wars. Perhaps it was the arrival of spring that made him look less haggard and more optimistic, but he still hadn't managed to polish his shoes. Funny, but that little dereliction made Ruby like him all the more.

'I've been thinking,' she said.

He transferred his total attention onto Ruby. 'Should I be afraid?'

She liked his humour, too, the way his joke or wry comment was often delivered with the straightest of faces.

'Out with it, Ingram.'

She stirred the coffee. 'We have the practice papers of the agents, which tell us if they have any little coding tics and habits. But that doesn't tell us what they sound like or what their Morse 'handwriting' is like. What if, at the end of their training, we ask the pianists to key in every letter and number, at varying speeds, and we record them doing this? We wouldn't let on to them why we're asking them to do it, or they'd become self-conscious. But if we then transferred the results onto graph paper, the signalmasters would have a record that could be easily read and referred to if a signals clerk questions the fist.'

From under her lashes, she watched him process the idea. In so many ways, they thought alike. Just like she would do – *had done* – he would be turning the idea around and examining it from all angles. Drawing a mental diagram. Constructing a hypo-thesis. Was the idea possible to achieve? What were the likely unintended consequences – for everything had unintended consequences? Security problems?

'Yes,' he pronounced. 'That makes sense. Good sense. We should have thought of it earlier.'

'If you're too close, you sometimes don't see things until you see them,' she said.

He grinned. 'Is that a principle for life?'

'How are we doing, do you think?'

How were they doing? The answer was that they were doing the best they could under the circumstances. Battling the dearth of intelligence from a war-enshrouded Europe, they found themselves shuffling forward one step, falling back two as they struggled to piece together a picture of what was going on.

Major Martin drained his coffee. 'I want to ask you something.'

Ruby experienced a flash of excitement, followed by doubt. Did he want her to go away and head up some dreary team somewhere else? After all, they agreed it was her cleverness that he wanted.

'Go on.'

'I want to know if you'll call me Peter.'

She looked up. 'If you like.'

He gave one of his smiles and it was an almost unbearably intimate moment. Ruby looked anywhere but at him.

'And . . .' He called her back to attention.

He meant what should he call her?

'Shall we stick to Ingram?'

'Right.' He signalled to the waitress and, if he was disappointed, it didn't register. 'I've been trying to work why you're different.'

'Most women are taught to hide their feelings. They are conditioned not to be read *en clair*.' Ruby wasn't entirely joking.

The dark eyes rested on her face and she had

the uncomfortable feeling that he was seeing right into her. 'From this moment on, you're sworn to tell me what you're thinking and feeling. Plain text.'

Did he want sex? Probably. That she understood far better than intimacy *and* it was easier to deal with. Taking her boss into her bed would be part and parcel of her strange new existence.

Peter raised an eyebrow, a tiny movement but one that made her, despite herself, very happy. 'I don't want to rush things.'

Ruby was touched by the old-fashioned gallantry. She took a deep breath. 'Bombs are falling. We could be dead tomorrow.'

'I know.'

'The bombs are a reason for rushing things, don't you think?' She paused. 'I think about death a lot . . . I imagine everyone does. The idea of it makes me angry because I can't bear to think I might miss out on something important.'

'I thought we agreed plain text?'

There was a silence.

'We did.'

'All right . . . er . . . how do you feel about us finding a room?'

She smiled. 'I could blush. I could look away. I could refuse to answer. I could say that I've no idea what you're talking about. I could be shocked and angry.'

'Presumably at some point you'll let me know which.'

They could be dead tomorrow. That is what many thought and some said.

'Actually, I was hoping you would ask.'

Ruby and Peter were in bed, tangled together.

The hotel in which they had taken a room last night was dingy and run-down, a survivor in a terrace that had been bombed twice, one of them a serious 'incident' – as the idiom had it. The proprietor appeared to be past caring about any proprieties, and signed them in without a second glance.

'Mr and Mrs Smith,' Peter wrote.

Funnily enough, Peter's lack of originality over the name had triggered a moment of doubt in Ruby. How banal, she thought. The brilliant code master was not so brilliant at the logistics of the tryst. But even she, for all her boldness, had found some of the arrangements embarrassing – explaining to her surly landlady that she would be away for the night, among them.

In the end, their mutual uncertainties unlocked new feelings in Ruby and touched her deeply. Peter's uninspired choice of 'Smith' may have been unpractised but it was a telling indication of who he was.

As soon as they'd reached their room Peter kicked the door shut and threw his greatcoat onto the chair. 'Sure about this?'

She stood with her hands by her sides. 'Yes.'

He came and stood very close to her. 'Sure enough to tell me your name?'

The naked light bulb hanging from the centre of the ceiling shed an unflattering light over both of them.

'I'm not going to bed with a surname.'

She looked down at her khaki skirt and lace-up shoes. 'It's Ruby,' she said.

'Ruby.' His hands rested lightly on her shoulders. 'Ruby . . .'

Now, morning light showed between the blackout and the window frame. Ruby hadn't slept much, but she hadn't expected to. The sex and the unfamiliar person beside her in the unfamiliar bed saw to that.

Ruby turned her head to look at him. One arm thrown out, he was breathing quietly.

The sheets felt gritty.

'What are you thinking?'

Peter had woken with a sigh, and a slight snort which she would have fun teasing him about.

She turned her head. 'About dust. About how you can't get rid of it.'

'So glad your mind is on the job.'

'I was also thinking about how people must feel when they wake up in France or Poland or Denmark. They must despair. I wonder if they know we think about them.'

'They won't have much energy to spare.'

'Do they know that we're trying to help?'

He didn't reply. Instead, he placed his hand on her naked stomach, his fingers straddling her hip bones in a possessive gesture. 'Rumours . . .' he began. 'Rumours are . . . are trickling in of round-ups and death camps in Eastern Europe. And in France.'

His words erased the joy and the vivid sensations of the night. They emphasized the flatness of the early morning and the prospect of a long day ahead.

Propping herself on an elbow, she said, 'Can you tell me more?'

The corners of his mouth turned down.

'I see. Secret.'

Swinging her legs over the side of the bed, she hauled herself up. It wasn't that warm and her arms were covered in gooseflesh. She looked down at her body. From that unflattering angle, her breasts appeared more meagre than usual and the line of pubic hair very marked against her white skin.

'You're so delicate, Ruby.'

Delicate? She had never thought of herself in that way. It pleased her. 'If you mean thin, I suppose that's because of the war.'

'I mean delicate, like porcelain.'

'Fragile and breakable.'

He reached over and touched her thigh. 'I wasn't talking about your mind.'

They were still awkward together, which was normal for new lovers. What's more, they were at a disadvantage because they knew so little about each other, and couldn't ask. She imagined that he might well have a fiancée or a wife tucked away somewhere, but decided that she didn't wish to know.

Ruby wrapped herself in the chenille counterpane, praying that it wasn't too grubby. 'Have you ever thought about secrecy? What it does and what it will do? For us? We can never tell our lovers, our children, our parents. Not even when we're dying.'

'Come back to bed.'

She ignored his summons and moved over to the window. 'Isn't it a little disturbing that the state can command total obedience?'

'Yes, it is. But, given so much depends on it, I willingly agree to it.'

'Even so.'

Peter stuffed the pillow behind his head. 'We probably don't know the half of it.'

She was taking down the blackout. 'I think . . . I think official silence can be like an infection. You don't know how dangerous it is until you have it.'

'Not at all,' he said. 'Infection can kill. Silence saves lives.'

'Perhaps.'

Her foot encountered the stained and chipped china pot that had been thoughtfully stowed in the corner beside the window. The sight of it made her a little queasy.

'*Are* you coming back?'

She cast aside the counterpane and climbed into bed beside him, slotting her body alongside his. 'Two spoons in a drawer,' she murmured.

317

Shivering a little, he wrapped the covers round them both. 'One day I'll make love to you somewhere truly hot.'

Ruby closed her eyes.

We're lucky. We're alive. We're free.

She turned round and encountered his gaze.

'You *are* different. But wonderful, bloody wonderful, Ruby.'

Was she going to bat the compliment back? Something stopped her: a grudging anger in her heart that she had nurtured since childhood, when everything – love, attention and encouragement – had been given to her brother. She wasn't proud of it, but there it was.

'You must let me compliment you, Ruby.'

'I thought you said that I was different from other women?'

He rolled over and placed a hand between her thighs. 'But that's not different . . .' he pointed out. 'This still happens to you . . .' There was a silence. 'And this . . .'

Two hours later they arrived separately at headquarters. Ruby opted to go in first and was settled at her desk by the time Peter walked past into his office and shut the door.

Gussie could read the signs quicker than most.

'Heard the one about utility knickers?'

'No.'

'One Yank and they're off. Did you have a good evening?'

'Wonderful.'

Gussie's gaze was perfectly neutral. 'I keep a spare blouse, etcetera, in my drawer for the times when I have a good evening.'

Ruby did not blink. 'Good advice, Gussie.'

Gussie redirected her considerable energies onto the pile of paper in front of her. 'You're wanted at the briefing session this morning. It was decided before your "wonderful" evening. Otherwise I might have been tempted to think the worst.'

'Remind me after the war to make friends with you, Gussie.'

When they next checked into the dismal hotel, Peter was a man on edge.

Ruby was exhausted, too. In the office, traffic was piling up. No sooner had she decoded one incoming message than four more arrived.

They were too tired to make love. Instead, hands loosely clasped, they lay side by side in bed.

'The ceiling's cracked since we were last here,' she said.

'So it has.'

'Do you think the place is safe?'

'Good question.'

She kissed his shoulder and the pulse at his temple.

'It's very odd,' she murmured into his cheek, 'not being able to ask each other anything about our real lives.'

'When the war's over there will be plenty of time.'

She was startled. 'So this isn't just a fleeting thing?'

319

'No,' he said. 'Not.'

She wasn't sure about this development. The idea of being tied down was one she instinctively rejected. Sex was one thing – she thought of what had taken place in this room and the pleasure she took in Peter's company – but the issue of personal liberty was something to be considered long and hard.

'I imagined that, after the war, you would go home to a family.'

'I have no family,' he replied.

'Oh, I got that wrong.'

'You did. And it was the one question you could have asked.'

'I wasn't sure I wanted to.'

'I see.'

'No, you don't. It was a matter of . . . honour.'

'Is that what they call it?' he said. 'Isn't it that, despite your views on personal liberty and sexual freedom, you didn't want to sleep with a married man?'

She managed a tired smile.

They slept for most of the night. Ruby woke early to find Peter already awake. He was lying on his back and looking up at the ceiling.

'I'm not making headway,' he addressed it. 'How do you solve these turf wars?'

'Even in an outfit dedicated to the unorthodox?'

'Even in an outfit dedicated to the unorthodox.'

'Peter, have you considered you – we – may not be right?'

He turned his head and she read the gnawing doubts in his expression. 'All the time. But I always return to the same conclusion.' He gave an exhausted smile. 'So do you. I know you do.'

Considering someone else in a serious way did not come easily to Ruby. She had been too busy making her own way with mathematics, those sweet, non-temperamental mathematics, to expend much thought on others.

Now she was obliged to open up areas within herself – to delve into her mental boxes. Those tightly fastened boxes. Peter was making her see differently. 'Tell me.' She fumbled for the right words. '*If* it helps.'

'Ruby, Ruby . . .' What was he saying? That he needed her to listen to get it all crystal clear? 'One, we agree the poem code is insecure because it can be tortured out of agents. Two, we agree the alternative of worked-out keys is better. They can be printed onto silk squares, hidden in the agents' clothing and destroyed after use. Even though we agree – three – it would be disastrous if the Nazis begin using the same system.'

'And the idea isn't being taken up?'

Peter sighed. 'In any organization, in any group, there are always people who set their shoulder against change. In this case, our boss is the chief defender of the poem code.'

'He should be shot.' Ruby rolled over towards him. 'Listen, it beggars belief that this man won't see the benefit to agents. So, isn't the next step to make him see it would be to his own benefit? Convince him that there is something in it for him?'

'Go on thinking.'

'Is there any country you're particularly worried about whose traffic we could study?'

'Can't go into that.'

She caught a hesitation. There *was* somewhere.

'Why don't you organize production of the worked-out keys anyway?' she suggested. 'If the chiefs can't, or won't, deal with the turf wars, then we can. Because, as we have discussed, we know we're sending the agents off with faulty tools. And that's –'

'Criminal,' Peter finished the sentence for her.

For a while, there was silence in the cheap hotel bedroom. Ruby closed her eyes, opening them only when he added: 'I need proof, Ruby.'

'Let's get it, then.'

No reply.

She tried again. 'Why can't we analyse a country's traffic? It might tell us something. I don't know quite what, but something.'

'Not a prayer. Each country's traffic is top secret, guarded with dragons and classified.'

'Which country has the least traffic? You can answer me that. Surely?'

'Denmark.' He touched her breast. 'Don't even think of it, Ruby.'

'Who are we fighting? The enemy? Or idiots on our own side?'

After a moment, he answered, 'I'm exhausted.'

Ruby joined him in staring up at the crack in the ceiling. 'To produce the worked-out keys you would need a team of girls to shuffle the numbers, a place for them to work, a supply of silk and a photographer to photograph the numbers onto the silk.' She grinned feebly. 'Not much.'

'Have you ever tried to get silk in wartime?'

'Bet Gussie knows someone in a ministry somewhere.'

Propelled by an unvoiced desire, they turned to each other.

'Peter, would we get the go-ahead if we obtain proof that the worked-out key system works?'

He touched the corner of her mouth with a fingertip. 'If there's proof, I promise . . . I promise I will drive the change through.'

The day hadn't even begun and Ruby craved nothing but sleep. Instead, she lay with gritty eyes and growling stomach and thought about Augustine and Eloise.

How could she begin to understand the inner world of the agent, a world in which, with each breath, they would be thinking: *They'll be coming to get me soon?*

CHAPTER 20

Around midnight, as Felix and the team waited at the drop zone, a night wind sprang up and blew coldly across it. He cursed and, with his torch, looked at his watch. There was a chance the plane and its precious cargo could be blown off course. Equally, clouds could blow across the moon and bugger up the navigation.

He did some warm-up exercises, blew on his hands and fingered the Browning pistol slotted into his belt.

They were six miles south-west of Køge in the direction of Haslev. One advantage of this drop zone was that there was only one serviceable route from Køge but plenty of back roads criss-crossing the terrain. Felix had taken enormous care encoding and transmitting the map coordinates, and prayed that the signals clerk at Home Station possessed sharp ears and fingers faster than Freya's.

He? She? What if the listener at Home Station hadn't had their mind on the job? What if they had been bored? Anticipating their day off? He thought about the web of connection, so delicately constructed in sound. If that bored listener at Home Station but knew it, the Morse which bounced between them bound them together tighter than any embrace.

Second time check.

Responsibility for the operation was huge. In fact, it was the biggest thing Felix had ever undertaken. The make-up of the Resistance was too changeable to categorize easily and he wasn't going to try. Instead, he concentrated every ounce of his diplomacy on manipulating the undercurrents, the clashing factions, into working cooperatively.

What had happened to the pacifist architect? For sure, the Jette of the 'keep quiet and don't do anything' school wouldn't recognize him. What he did know was that the principles from that previous life didn't get you far in this one. Stealing, lying and killing did.

'*We are fighting this war so we don't end up like the murderers and thugs, too,*' Freya said. '*You can't put us on the same level.*'

The irony had not been lost on him. But ironies were for safe, peaceable times.

He shifted position. Underfoot, the soil was layered with slippery leaf mould that had accumulated over the winter.

His diet hadn't been so good lately and he had developed a mouth ulcer at the back of his cheek. Unwisely, he poked it with his tongue.

The minutes were passing.

Did she do her stuff? That listener at the listening

station. He was now fantasizing that it was a pretty blonde. Slender and thoughtful, stooped over her wireless transmitter. That made him think of Jette again.

To think about the past was bad practice. It weakened you.

The instructors at The Firm had known what they were talking about.

He closed his eyes.

'Thou shalt not kill . . .' went the Commandment.

As instructed, Freya had passed the message concerning the drunken, loose-tongued agent onto Jacob. A couple of weeks later the message filtered back down the line: *The mustard has been wiped off the plate.*

Now, when he and Freya met, or spoke, there was a shadow cast over their dealings: *We are murderers. Long-distance ones, but murderers.* They never discussed it, but it brought them closer, and yet at the same time, paradoxically, it made each of them wary of the other.

The last time they met, Freya informed him she wanted to be part of the group at the drop zone.

'You're a security risk,' he'd replied bluntly. 'If anyone spots you, the well-known *Fru* Eberstern, it will act as a light bulb. God forbid if you were captured.'

No fool, Freya understood the argument. 'I want to see a plane from England. I want to look up into the sky and think: *This plane has come for me. It's come from my country.*'

Her eyes were wet.

'That's sentimental.'

'Yes, yes, it is.'

'Sentimentality is no use to me, Freya. And you're no use to me if you indulge in it.'

She'd uttered a rude Danish word before turning away.

Time?

As planned, his men, including Jacob, were taking up their positions and fanning out along the perimeter of the field, which was fringed with woodland. The instructions had been to leave home at staggered intervals, to make their way along a back road out of Køge, and to rendezvous by the line of larches that ran between the road and the stretch of scrubby grassland.

It had taken months to reach this point. Getting a drop organized was a miracle of painstaking piecing together of intelligence and planning. Anyway, Felix had taken the decision to avoid the worst of the Danish winter. There had been a couple of drops in the new year on Jutland and Funen which he had known about, one of which had gone wrong when the material had been lost in snowdrifts – all of which hardened his determination not to go operational until everything was as watertight as he could make it.

Casting his net as wide as was practicable, Felix had pulled in the men. One step forward, one step back, observing security procedures to the letter. Each recruit had been interviewed, either by him or by Jacob, but they did not share any names. All he knew for certain was that they represented a mixed bunch of allegiances and vested interests: communists, members of the newly formed Danish Unity Party, loners, almost certainly a criminal or two. He had had to trust his instincts, which were pretty sharp by now, but it was impossible to be absolutely sure.

Further discreet surveillance had been mounted to find out who in the Haslev police force was loyal and who had gone over to the Reich. 'Some of those bastards,' reported Jacob, 'are serving up patriots to the *Gestapomen* like hot meals.' He swiped a finger across his throat. 'We'll be waiting for them.'

The men were jumpy. Nervous. One of them urinated into the bushes and farted copiously. Knud lit a cigarette, keeping his hand cupped over the tip as he smoked it. Felix decided to let him. In the field, the cattle were spooked by the un-accustomed activity and had gathered in a restless group.

The chill wind knifed through Felix's clothing.

ETA of plane: five minutes. Miraculously, the sky had cleared, revealing a gibbous moon.

'What do you think?' whispered Jacob in his ear.

'The pilot will probably use the river to navigate and turn left at the bend.' He glanced up. 'It would be the best approach with the wind.'

One of the men materialized out of the cover of the trees and hissed: 'Something's coming.'

The trees threw shadows too dark to make out exactly what was moving along the road but the clunk of metal as the vehicle hit the winter potholes travelled through the night silence. The men melted into the trees. Felix snapped off the safety catch of the Browning. What a pitifully small weapon it was. He thought lustfully of the guns that were coming in with the drop.

Crouched down, breath held, he and Jacob watched as a bicycle with a trailer came into sight. Thickset and well wrapped up, the rider parked and flashed his torch twice. Felix relaxed. 'It's "Erik".' He signalled back, but as the torch beam hit the trailer it illuminated a cartoon pig painted on the side. He swore under his breath. If the police spotted pigs on vehicles, painted or otherwise, they asked questions.

He rose to his feet and loped over to Erik. 'Don't you know transporting pigs is forbidden?'

'It's a joke.' Erik was out of breath and reeked of herring cut with beer. 'Nazis got your sense of humour?'

'Nazis don't get jokes painted on trailers,' Felix commented sourly. 'When they don't get things, they shoot.'

Erik's hand shot out and grabbed Felix's arm. 'Remember our bargain.'

It wasn't for nothing that the motley bunch of instructors at STS, Old Tiny Tim in particular, had insisted on parachute discipline. Hands like hams, complexion the colour of claret, with a couple of black Labradors at his heels, Tiny Tim had been emphatic.

Destroy parachutes. Parachute silk is your ticket to hell.

But Erik, who had three marriageable daughters all clamouring for wedding dresses, insisted that keeping the parachute was part of the deal. 'Do you want me, or don't you?'

A van pulled up in the road, followed by a horse-drawn covered cart and both of them parked in the shadows. Leaving its owner to deal with the horse, the men spread out.

Felix counted the shadowy figures. Eight. Good. Further down the road, two others were on lookout. He had the full compliment.

As he looked around the drop zone he recalled another piece of STS advice.

Adapt to the terrain.

Ja. Ja.

Other agents in other countries had mountains and valleys, which were kind to them and made it difficult for the enemy. But Denmark? Denmark was as flat as . . . as a piece of paper.

The wind freshened.

One of the men coughed and spat before being shushed by his companion.

For the past few weeks, messages had streamed back and forth over the ether. Felix had begged London for more of everything: guns, wireless sets, money. Begged them. Gone down on his radio knees.

IMPERATIVE WE BEGIN ACTION *stop*
MAYONNAISE

Later messages spelled out the situation on the ground more clearly.

DANISH ARMY REMOVED FROM JUTLAND *stop* **GERMANS TAKEN OVER ARMS DEPOTS** *stop* **MAYONNAISE REPORTS OF ALUMINIUM PLANT UNDER CONSTRUCTION AT HEROYA** *stop* **ENEMY WILL SHIP IT THROUGH DENMARK** *stop* **MAYONNAISE**

Plus the request.

DEVELOPMENT OF RADIO SETS PROGRESSING *stop* **URGENT NEED FOR CRYSTALS** *stop* **MAYONNAISE**

Finally, there was the one which was written, so to speak, in blood.

MUSTARD HAS BEEN WIPED OFF PLATE *stop* **MAYONNAISE**

Did they understand what he was trying to tell them? *God Almighty, did they understand?*

He imagined the conversations taking place at the London headquarters. *Is Felix a firebrand? Has he read the situation correctly? Has he proved able?*

Is he the right leader? Should we replace him? The bigger question: *Do we need Denmark on board?*

Smug bastards. Tucked up in London, they couldn't begin to understand how potent the mixture of rage and patriotism could be.

Were they as sleepless as he was? Did they function almost entirely on adrenalin? Did their confidence dip? He pictured them in their smoky offices littered with paper and army-issue pencils. With the blackboards and the chalk dust and the anti-shatter tape on the window panes.

Did he trust *them*?

And yet, of course, there should be a healthy gulf between the eminences at headquarters and the Joes in the field. Asking questions ensured survival.

The moon seemed to grow brighter.

ETA: minus three minutes.

There was a faint rumble, and Felix spun round. A mutter went up from the men.

The noise grew. The throb of engines sounded above them like an echoing drumbeat.

He had forgotten how much noise an aircraft made and, for a shameful second, he was stricken with panic and an urge to flee. Responsibility for the men's lives rested with him and, if anything went wrong, he couldn't bring himself to think of the women and children who might curse him into the future.

The area vibrated with sound. Where are you? *Where are you?* In answer, a Whitley lumbered into view: nose down, Rolls-Royce Merlin engines throttled back. It gave the horse the jitters so the owner had his work cut out controlling it.

In reflex action, three torches flashed: the letter S.

'What's he playing at?' growled Jacob as the pilot failed to acknowledge the signal, flew straight across the drop zone and swooped out of sight, leaving trails of sound.

'Taking a fix,' said Felix.

Correct. The Whitley returned and circled. Once. Twice.

The torches flashed in a concerto of light.

'Go,' ordered Felix. '*Go.*'

Two parachutes bucked and jerked down towards the drop zone. Two more followed. Dandelion seeds tumbling, shaking, falling through the moonlit sky.

The noise was fit to waken the dead.

The wind slapped at Felix's face as, along with the men, he ran over the tussocky grass towards this descending manna. One by one, the containers landed with a slap and crack.

The Whitley returned for its final run. It approached, throttled back but anyone could see that it was off target. A fifth and sixth parachute tumbled out of its belly and went sailing way past the drop zone in the direction of Haslev.

But there was nothing they could do about it.

Laboriously, noisily, the plane wheeled. Then it dipped its wings in a signal from pilot to agent, homage from warrior to warrior, before flying away into a glimmering velvet sky.

'Go, go,' shouted Felix.

The men got to work, untangling the webbing, rolling up the parachutes. Weighing up to two hundred kilos each, the containers were buggers to move. But he had thought out the problem ahead of time and had instructed the men to bring wooden battens. These were now strapped onto the containers so that they could be hoisted shoulder high. In places, the turf was wet and unstable and it was touch and go to keep the load aloft.

The men poured with sweat.

Two containers were loaded into the van but proved much too long. One of the men climbed into the back and fastened the doors from the inside with his belt.

'Go!' Jacob banged on the driver's partition.

The van's engines ground into life. Felix ran back to the field.

The wireless set? The precious additional wireless set which was so badly needed to supplement the one now hidden in the city. It had landed in the centre of the drop zone – a bulky thing with its own defenders and careful padding. Felix tugged and ripped at the wrappings to reveal the familiar case.

The men lifted the final container onto the cart but it was too heavy and the cart's wheels sank down into the soft ground. The horse baulked.

'*Bare rolig.*' Its owner talked to it softly.

Swearing, slipping, sliding, the men hauled the container back off the cart.

Having quietened, the horse was persuaded to wheel round to face the road while the men unpacked the container at top speed and stowed the contents in the back: guns, ammunition, plastic explosives, cigarettes.

Erik helped himself to a couple of cartons of cigarettes and threw them on top of the promised parachute which he had stuffed into his trailer. 'I've got to go.'

Upending a couple of bags of turnips, the men spread them out over the haul in the cart. The farmer swung himself onto his seat and snatched up the reins. He urged the horse into a trot and headed off towards the farm outside Haslev. There, for the time being, the arsenal would be hidden under bins of animal feed.

Felix helped to drag the abandoned container under the larches and dumped it in a patch of undergrowth – which was the best they could do for the moment.

A shout made him look up. One of the men sprinted towards Erik.

Trailer rattling, Erik was pedalling away. Far too fast. One hand rested on the handlebars while the other held aloft a flashing torch.

The hairs stood up on the back of Felix's neck. 'What the—?'

Jacob grabbed a fistful of Felix's jacket. 'He's a *stikker*,' he shouted into Felix's ear.

Without a second's hesitation, Felix whipped out the Browning. '*Stop* him.'

Erik turned round . . . a vital second, and his mistake. The bicycle slowed. There was no time for Felix to consider, no time for due diligence, only time to react as he had been taught. He grasped the pistol in two hands, aimed and squeezed the trigger. The bullet pulsed out of the barrel. He fired a second time.

Double tap. One to fell. One to finish.

Erik toppled to the ground. The bicycle and its trailer crashed beside him, the wheels spinning madly.

Jacob ran over, knelt down beside Felix, felt for Erik's pulse and gave a thumbs-down. He scooped up the cigarettes, leaped to his feet and ran back into the trees.

The lookout posted on the Haslev road hared towards them. 'Cars!' he shouted.

A posse of headlights was moving along the road from Køge fast enough to suggest the vehicles were petrol-fuelled.

'Go!' Felix snatched up the case containing the wireless set. 'All of you. Enemy.'

One or two of the men panicked and ran this way and that.

The final container was dumped in the wood. The remainder of the team melted away between the tree trunks from where they would make for the back roads.

Erik's body lay where it had fallen.

Felix assessed his options – he had worked out escape routes earlier from the map. The lie of the land was straightforward but his problem was the moonlight which flooded the drop zone. If he could get across without being picked off, there was an irrigation channel on the other side which would provide cover.

He ran, the case tugging his arm down, banging his legs hard.

Felix was lean and hardened physically. Nevertheless, by the time he arrived at the north edge of the drop zone and rolled down into a drainage ditch, he was near blown. Crouching, he fought for breath.

Short pants. Breathe only in the upper chest.

They had joked with the instructors that that kind of breathing was practised by women in childbirth.

A convoy of vehicles, some armoured, raced down the road and slewed to a stop. Their doors were flung open, equipment extracted and guns set up. Dogs sprang onto the road.

He rested for five more seconds. A searchlight was already arcing across the drop zone. The dogs bayed. The firing began.

He assessed what he was up against: small arms, machine guns, small pieces of artillery – textbook German tactics to throw the whole bloody lot into the melee.

He raised his head above the lip of ditch. The firing emanated from the road but he knew that it was only a matter of moments before the sharp-shooters fanned out in a circle.

Haslev was the obvious place to make for and, therefore, not an option. Felix dropped his head, turned west and moved cautiously along the ditch. The searchlight moved onwards. Using the dark as cover he upped his pace. Maybe he'd be lucky.

Something punched him in the arm so hard that his vision blackened.

He had been hit.

Clutching his arm, he staggered on a few paces. The strength in his legs drained away. His head buzzed. Death eyeballed him as he fought to stay sensible.

Adrenalin punched in. Thank God. Thank God.

Think, Felix. Keep feet submerged to lose the scent.

The heavy case dragged him down. The ditch water was thick with mud. On he went, one step after another, reckoning his odds. Against him: a traitor who had given them away; two containers lost; the area crawling with *Gestapomen* and Danish police; a gunshot wound. As yet, thanks to the adrenalin, he couldn't feel much.

Think.

The dogs wouldn't know which scent to pick up first at the drop zone. That gave him one advantage.

Make for Rosenlund.

How many miles?

Far too many.

The adrenalin was thinning and pain was beginning to fan out from a red-hot centre in his arm.

His breath coming and going in agonizing bursts, his heartbeat louder in his head than the Whitley's engines had been, his arm stiffening, tightening, losing blood, he stumbled on.

At daybreak, case clutched in his good hand, he slid through the entrance in the north wall of the Rosenlund estate and wove unsteadily beneath the tree cover towards the pigeon loft. Once there, he moved a white feed bucket from the left-hand side of the door over to the right.

He didn't have to wait too long – but long enough – before Freya discovered him slumped against the wall.

She dropped to her knees beside him. 'Where are you hurt?'

Felix squinted at her, the pain making it difficult to control his eyelids. Lo and behold, in a tweed suit shot through with soft blues, Freya was transformed into an angel of mercy.

Already she was rolling up his shirt sleeve to expose entry and exit wounds in his right arm. They were blackened at the rim, and the surrounding flesh had puffed up.

'Where?'

'At the drop.'

She bent over to inspect the wounds more closely. 'You've caused quite a stir. Apparently, some of the containers came down in a field belonging to a farmer called Nyeman, to the north of Haslev,' she said. 'He and his wife tried to hide them but they've been arrested. Does this hurt?' She touched the area above the entry wound and he flinched. 'What happened? There's uproar. A man was killed.'

'I shot him. A *stikker*.' He pushed out the word with difficulty. 'There was no choice. Did the other men get back?'

'I don't know any more details.' She was patting and probing, and it hurt like hell. 'I don't think the bone's broken. You should see a doctor.' Freya got to her feet. 'Listen, Felix. I'm going to get some things. You have to stay conscious. Do you understand?'

He couldn't keep his eyes open.

Silence in the pigeon loft.

Where was Hector? Had he flown, his small body battling wind and German potshots?

The flickering images came and went.

Erik with his pig-painted trailer. How had he failed to spot that Erik had been a *stikker*? Or had Erik been just a brainless idiot only after what he could get? But Felix should have sniffed that out, too.

He had taken another life without due process. How many would be necessary to beat the murderers and thugs?

One of the instructors was bending over him.

Felix! Felix! If you think our methods are not cricket, remember Hitler does not play this game.

340

He groaned.

Freya was back, holding a basket. She lifted a bottle of water to his mouth and he drank thirstily. Then she poured antiseptic onto a handkerchief. 'Are you ready for this?'

He nodded. She dabbed at the wounds and he felt the scream bubble in his throat.

'I'm being as gentle as I can.'

'You smell so good, and I smell vile,' he managed to croak.

'Well, *I* don't mind, so be quiet.'

Freya bound up his arm with a piece of white cloth. He eased himself into a more comfortable position. 'We need to inform London.'

'Not safe at the moment,' she said. 'The place is crawling with police.'

He was unable to think . . . pain and exhaustion inched through him. The odour of ancient ammonia from long-gone pigeons combined with his own stink was making him nauseous.

'Send Hector,' Freya said. 'It's time he went. Give me a message, I'll take it down.'

Felix searched for the last drops of energy. 'Paper?'

Freya produced paper and pencil. 'I've taken to carrying these around.'

Felix dictated: 'Drop partial success *stop* lying low *stop* injured *stop* non life threatening *stop* have wireless *stop* Mayonnaise.'

The coding took more energy. Light-headed from blood loss, he struggled with the first transposition.

341

What was he trying to say? What did he mean? *Partial success equalled bungle.*

Freya copied the letter groups onto the smallest piece of paper they could manage. Then she unlocked the cage. 'You're going home, Hector. It's been a long stay, but you must go.'

The bird's eyes were bright with apprehension. Somehow, she managed to slot the message into the carrier case and strap it round Hector's foot.

'Is he fed and watered?' he asked.

'It's a first-class hotel here.' With Hector cupped in her hands, she moved over to the door. 'Do you think he knows, Felix? Do you think he can sense England after all this time?' Her voice was hushed.

She slipped outside.

Felix rolled to his good side and peered through a crack in the slats.

It was still morning and the light was . . . he searched for the word . . . tender. Freya bent over Hector, and they seemed to be talking to each other. She touched the bird's glossy head, stroked his plumage, her finger coming to rest on the ruff at the base of the neck.

What was she saying to him?

Go well.

She tossed up her hands. For a second, Hector was in Felix's line of sight. Then, he had vanished.

Perfectly framed, Freya gazed after him and dashed a hand across her eyes.

She slipped back into the pigeon loft. 'You must stay here for the moment.' The tears had vanished and she was collected and practical. 'But you can't stay here like this.' She cupped his face between her hands. 'Listen to me, Felix. Are you taking this in? Wait here until nine o'clock tonight. Then make your way around the side of the house that overlooks the lake. The steps there lead up to my office. I'll be waiting. There's an attic above it which I've had cleared out. You can hide in there until I can make arrangements to take you over to one of our cottages on the other side of the lake.'

'I can't miss a second sked,' he said. 'Do you understand?'

'Transmit from the house?' Her voice faltered and she interlocked her fingers together tightly. 'Do you know what you're asking?'

'A lot.'

'No,' she contradicted. 'You're asking *everything* . . .'

The day passed. The pain came and went. Then it returned and stayed.

Felix tried to sort out the situation but his mind wouldn't work. He knew only three things. One: the drop hadn't gone well. Two: his arm was useless for the present. Three: he had killed a man.

When nine o'clock came, he hauled himself to his feet and began the long journey.

Spring sunlight filtered lightly through the attic window. Felix turned his head and focused on the flowered quilt that covered him. Poppies in every shade of red. The scarlet splodges floated across his vision.

How had he got here?

Concentrate.

He closed his eyes.

What could he remember?

Freya hiding the case in a chest under the window and tucking the quilt around him as he drops exhausted onto the floor.

'You must sleep.' She tilts back his head and gives him brandy from a glass. 'Drink as much as you can. I will fetch you in the morning.'

He is already a little drunk, and her touch soothes him. A little.

The image of Erik toppling over onto the road returns.

'Felix, the wireless set is in the chest. Do you understand?'

'Yes.'

Save for the pinpoint of torchlight, it is dark in the attic and Freya moves cautiously.

She bends over him. 'Felix?'

'Yes.'

'What was it like? The plane. Did it look – English?'

Opening his eyes again Felix looked at his watch: eleven o'clock. Avoiding putting pressure on his arm, he manoeuvred himself into a sitting position and propped himself against the wall.

Even in this state, the reflexes kicked in.

Never enter anywhere unless there is an escape route.

Low-ceilinged, narrow and, except for a window under the eaves, no obvious alternative route out. Sweating, he got to his feet, shuffled over to the chest under the window and stepped up onto it in order to see out of the window. A man could haul himself out onto the roof. Just. But its steep slope offered little cover.

He slumped back.

Eat. He must eat and he reached for the bread and cheese which Freya had left. At first, he retched but, after a couple of mouthfuls, his stomach quietened.

He wanted to weep. He wanted to laugh. Yesterday, he had killed. How easy it was to take a life. Send a message. Or just raise an arm and pull a trigger. But he had also flirted with death and survived.

His elation at his survival vanished when he thought of the mistake he had made with Erik. Persuaded by the neediness of the man, he forgot that the Germans paid well for information. 'My family is suffering . . .' Erik spun the story. Stinking of tobacco, his overalls threadbare, the man was obviously in trouble. 'Look at what the Germans are doing to us. I want to do something for Denmark.' It had been bad judgement on Felix's part.

Freya had left a couple of books with the food. Wincing, he picked up one – an edition of *Niels Lyhne* by Jens Peter Jacobsen, a Danish classic.

Keeping his injured arm tight against his body, he managed to flip the book open at random and read:

> Something had given way in him, the night his child died. He had lost faith in himself, lost his belief in the power of human beings to bear the life they had to live . . .

He put it aside. He had to bear his life, here and now. There was no one else to help him.

He returned to the chest and stepped onto it. Outside, in the near distance, the lake glittered around the island in its centre. Beyond the lake stretched fields of arable land, dotted with a few cottages and clumps of trees. A couple of song thrushes sat in the tree to his right.

Directly beneath him was a terrace, paved with limestone flags. Various seats were positioned to catch the best view of the lake.

Voices sounded and Freya came into view below him. A pair of dogs pattered behind her. She was remonstrating with a tall, fair man whom he took to be her husband. They remained talking on the terrace for some time. Once, she laid a hand on his arm and he moved away. They continued to talk but at a distance.

Once or twice, Freya glanced up towards the window. She couldn't have known that Felix was watching. All the same, it made him feel stronger.

Around noon, he manhandled the case out of

the chest. What he was doing was out of order. He was putting the house in danger. But it had to be. Those were the choices in war.

Setting it up took an age. The aerial refused to obey him, the wire coils were unruly and he had trouble adjusting the dials.

As a result, he was a few minutes late for his sked. Placing his finger on the transmitter key, he began a stumbling transmission.

Afterwards, slumped down on the makeshift bed, he told himself that he should not have done that.

CHAPTER 21

In København, Hannah asked Tanne to accompany her to a meeting. 'I can't tell you what it's about. Will you come?'

'I can't,' replied Tanne. 'We've guests coming to stay tonight. My mother has . . . what I mean is, I have to help out.'

A German general was staying overnight at Rosenlund and Tanne's presence had been requested.

'I see.' Hannah fixed scornful eyes on Tanne. 'Are you sure you want to run about after your mother? Don't you think you need to be here, with us?' She thrust a pamphlet at Tanne. 'Take it home. Read it. Think.'

When Denmark was defeated by the Prussians in 1864, the country mourned its lost territories like lost children. To many, the country was terminally weakened. Its rulers were left fractured and indecisive, a state of mind they attempted to mask by burying themselves on their estates.

Tanne winced on reading that sentence. It was close to home.

> It was a stance which underlined their refusal to face the realities. But today's younger generation refuses to accept the oppressor and will dedicate themselves to the fight. We will mount a vigil. We will take down our arms and use them. Only one path leads to freedom and **that is the path of action**.

It was signed: Nerthus, goddess of peace and fertility.

Back at Rosenlund, Birgit had spent the day taking down the damask curtains in the hall and re-hanging the antique lace summer drapes. Tanne stopped to admire the lace waterfall spilling over the newly waxed floor.

Up on the stair landing, she looked out of the window. Had she let Hannah down? Hannah thought so.

At this time of the year the outlines of the landscape were softening fast and sunlight traced gorgeous dancing patterns on the water.

Always . . . always . . . she loved the moment when new foliage unfurled and the spikes of wild narcissi and crocuses broke cover under the hedgerows and trees. They seemed almost unbearably green and vivid and this year, too, for some reason, she felt more aware of her surroundings, her eyes sharper. Her skin was more receptive to the texture of her clothes – the green wool skirt and tweed jacket that she favoured flowing coolly over her contours. Everything about her was mysteriously more sensitive to stimuli.

The sun was hitting the island. Apparently, in warm weather, Princess Sophia-Maria loved to be rowed out there, and in later years generations of Eberstern children had also made themselves master of its enchantments with picnics, games and sleepovers.

Presiding over the staircase, Sophia-Maria's portrait awaited its annual dusting. Her father would fuss. Her mother would fuss. Everyone would fuss. 'She's only a minor royal,' Tanne teased her father, more than once. 'Couldn't we have done better?'

Minor or not, Sophia-Maria – so splendid in her sumptuous court dress which, since Napoleon was ravaging Europe, was prudently embroidered with the imperial bees – held sway over this family. She had bestowed not only her ormolu clocks, jewels, furniture and china on future Ebersterns but also the constituents of her blood and her genes. In return, she apparently demanded from these innocent descendants an acknowledgement of the almost mystical link with Germany.

In her bedroom, Tanne closed the door and leaned back. Genuflecting to a past was no longer valid.

Instead, she thought of Felix.

Who was he? In one sense, the answer was easy. A man who carried a gun, transmitted messages clandestinely and disguised himself, was a spy or a soldier. But what sort of spy or soldier, and what sort of man?

Birgit knocked and entered. She had pressed Tanne's new blue dress and handed it over. '*Fru* Eberstern says you are to look your best.'

The German general and his wife were due to arrive at Rosenlund during the afternoon and to stay overnight with them. Everyone, including her mother, was tense.

Her mother . . .

Freya?

The English mother . . . with her strange quirks, such as her insistence on taking tea in the afternoons and her refusal to fight the cold in the Danish way – it had taken Kay years to accept that wearing two pairs of socks in winter boots was an efficient method of keeping the feet warm, just to cite one example. If she was honest, in her crueller moments Tanne enjoyed her mother's discomfort when she clashed against her children's innate Danishness and Danish sense of family.

Tanne hung up the frock in the cupboard, the wooden hangers on the rail clacking together. Then she checked herself. A sixth sense commanded her: *Hide Hannah's pamphlet.* Placing it in a cardboard shoe box, she stowed it at the back of the cupboard.

Her mother was nowhere to be found in the house. After a search, Tanne discovered her in the stable yard backing Loki into the shafts of the pony trap which was loaded with blankets and bottles of water.

'What on earth are you doing?'

Loki's hooves clicked on the stones. Her mother checked the harness. 'Thought I'd give Loki some exercise. He's like a buttered bun.'

'Have you got time before the exciting general arrives?'

'Would I be doing it otherwise?' said her mother.

Tanne smelled a large rat: 'I'll come with you.'

'If you want to go out, keep your father company, darling. He's driving into Køge for fertilizer, if he can get it.'

'I'm coming with you.'

'Tanne, I would like to be on my own for a bit.' Her mother threw the reins over Loki's head and hauled herself up into the trap.

Tanne looked up at her. 'The truth.'

Loki was proving skittish and her mother concentrated on controlling him. 'Tanne, you're meddling and you've no idea of . . . well, what you're doing.'

'Maybe. But try me.'

'Keep a hold on Loki.' Her mother put on her gloves and gathered up the reins.

Tanne grabbed at Loki's bridle and brought him to a standstill. 'No more evasion.' No more of the unspoken. 'I know and you know you're up to something.' She tightened her grasp on Loki. 'I'm not letting you go, *Mor*.' She paused for maximum effect. 'Or should I say *Freya*?'

'Stop it.' A tiny bead of sweat stood out on her mother's upper lip. 'Tanne, you and Nils are dearer than life,' she said. 'This is no game and I have no time. Go away, Tanne. *Go away* . . .'

'Move over.' So saying, Tanne swung herself up beside her mother. 'Why are you sweating?'

The reply was impassioned. 'Listen to me, Tanne. I brought you into this world, and my great responsibility in life is to you. I have to protect you, not lead you into danger.'

'Isn't it a bit late for all that?'

Her mother made a noise between a sob and a laugh.

Tanne reached over and kidnapped the reins from her mother. 'Walk on, Loki.' Loki moved forward. 'I'm learning that life is precarious . . .'

'You're too young, Tanne.'

'. . . Learning it fast, too. This war is dangerous. Therefore we can't avoid danger. Where are we going?'

Her mother sounded desperate. 'But you haven't lived yet, or even seen the world.'

Cunning and sophistry were what Tanne needed – certainly for the new kind of morality she was discovering. 'I was born to find my own feet.'

'Go back to the house. Please. I couldn't bear it if you were involved.'

Tanne shot her a look. She understood . . . or

thought she did . . . that, for a parent, to work alone was much easier because it would be unendurable to watch a child suffer.

'You have done your job, *Mor*.' Tanne pressed home her point. 'We can share this.'

'God help me,' she murmured.

It flashed across Tanne's mind that the balance of power between parent and child was never meant to remain constant and this was the moment when it shifted.

'Where to?'

Her mother stared ahead.

'Where to?'

Again the noise between a sob and a laugh. 'The steps to my office and then on to Ove's cottage. It's been empty since he left for Germany.'

'Listen to me,' said Tanne, as she concentrated on turning the trap round. 'I've no idea what you're doing but I can help and I *should* help. I know every building, every path, every fox and chicken here. Every pig. Every rut in the road. And I know them better than you.' Her mother's eyes glistened with sudden tears. 'You need me. I let you baby me, *Mor*. For too long, perhaps. But it's time to be realistic. Isn't it?' Her mother wiped a hand across her eyes. 'Isn't it?'

Her mother sighed raggedly and gave in. 'It is, Tanne.'

The die was cast.

'So what's happening?'

★   ★   ★

354

On viewing Felix, his arm swollen, slumped against the wall in the attic, Tanne was afraid. He looked dreadful: pallid, bruised under the eyes and unsteady on his feet. The pair of them took turns to keep watch and thus it was a slow, agonizing process to manhandle him down the steps and into the dog cart.

'Get the case, darling . . .' Her mother was hauling on the reins and Tanne gasped at its weight as she stowed it beside Felix.

Tanne took charge of the driving. 'Go, go, Loki.' She urged him into a brisk trot and followed the cart track around the perimeter of the lake. From time to time they hit a rut and Felix groaned. Tanne ached to hold him . . . help him . . . do anything.

Ove's cottage came into view. It was half a mile or so from any of the other cottages and partly hidden by trees. It had been a clever choice. Versed in Rosenlund's schedules, Tanne knew that change-over day for tenants was 1 November or 1 May so the cottage would remain empty until November.

If it was secluded, it was without running water or electricity. But Tanne was confident that, thanks to her father's insistence on a roster of building maintenance for the cottages, it would be in reasonable condition.

But for a table and a bench, it was empty of furniture. There was not even a bed. They coaxed a by-now-semi-conscious Felix inside and laid him in the downstairs area on the floor.

Tanne fussed with a rug. 'He needs a doctor.'

'Not safe.' Her mother cut her off.

Tanne was almost breathless at the thought of Felix's discomfort. 'But he *needs* one. Look at him,' she pleaded. 'Let me fetch Dr Hansen.'

'Too risky. We don't know what Hansen thinks.'

Fear sharpened Tanne's tongue. '*You* don't, *Mor*. We do. His family have worked with our family forever and he's known us all our lives. We live in the same community.'

Felix was muttering unintelligibly.

'Hand me the other rug, will you?' Her mother wrapped it round a restless Felix.

Tanne watched her. 'I know we could trust Hansen.'

Hustling her into a corner, her mother hissed into Tanne's ear: 'You said you wanted to grow up. Yes?' Her tone softened, and she caressed Tanne's cheek. 'I believe you. But have you any idea what war does to people? It's good that you have such faith, really good. But even the best can act completely out of character and do terrible things when they or their loved ones are threatened.'

'Doctors don't take sides,' Tanne said, stubborn and unconvinced.

'I am afraid we've no option.'

Her mother returned to Felix. Tanne watched as she gently inserted a third rug under his wounded arm to make him more comfortable and made him drink a mouthful of water.

Her terror was that he would die – of wounds, or infection . . . or exhaustion.

But this wasn't the time or place to get emotional. A flush spread over Tanne's face, a shamed one. She and her mother had to deal with the situation and, despite never having had to face such a challenge in her privileged life before, she must rise to it.

Felix drank gratefully. 'Do you think you can work the set?'

Her mother nodded. 'Just.'

'Listen carefully. "Fish, stream, light, shine and kiss".'

'Got them,' she said.

'Repeat.'

Her mother recited them almost gaily. 'See! It'll be fine, Felix.'

The sight of Felix trying to concentrate affected Tanne and she was forced to look away.

'This is against every rule in the book but it's yours now . . .' He had to pause between words. 'The poem they come from was handed to me by a bloody genius in London who would shoot me if he knew what I was doing. Use it until we organize something else, until I can get word to London.' He moved his head restlessly. 'But not from here. The listeners will have clocked the location. Do it somewhere else. Understand? Not here.'

'You're not to talk any more.'

'Tell them we're going off air for the time being.'

He looked so ill.

Her mother looked at her watch. Time to go. 'I'm going to hide the wireless,' she said. 'Stay here with him.'

Ten minutes later she reappeared. 'Done.'

They left Felix wrapped in the blanket.

'The general will be here in an hour,' said her mother as she steered Loki into the stable yard. 'Tanne . . . I've got to get ready.'

They looked at each other – two women with traces of blood on their hands and clothing. Tanne's throat constricted. Why hadn't she ever seen that she and her mother were cut from the same cloth?

'Go and change,' she said, her mind rapidly sorting out options. 'I'll see to things. Tell them you'd made a mistake about me and I had been invited out to a dinner in Køge all along which I could not get out of. I'll take food and aspirin over to him.'

Her mother raised a sceptical eyebrow.

'*Mor*, I'm in this now.'

Maybe she could make up for the fact that so far she had shamefully ignored the reach and compass of this war?

Her mother seized Tanne's hand. 'Lives depend on this. Yours, his, mine.'

An hour later Tanne cycled up Køge's main street and dismounted outside the chemist.

There was a queue for his services. On a normal

day, Tanne enjoyed watching the pharmacist deploy his dark blue medicine bottles and count out the pills.

The queue shuffled forward.

Eventually, the pharmacist turned to Tanne and she requested aspirin and antiseptic powder, explaining that the friend with whom she was having supper had cut her hand chopping the beetroot.

'It could be nasty,' she said.

The pharmacist listened to Tanne carefully. 'Could be *nasty*, *Frøken* Eberstern?' It was a marked emphasis. He paused. 'It's important you bathe the wound in boiled water, disinfect it and apply a sterile dressing.' Tanne piled the packages into her basket and he added, 'And *Frøken* Eberstern, if your friend is running a temperature, she must take aspirin every four hours.'

Startled, she looked up from her basket but the pharmacist was busy pouring out cough syrup for the next customer.

Mor, I do know these people.

Finding Dr Hansen was not easy. Tanne was forced to cycle several miles around the town, chasing his progress from patient to patient. She caught up with him on the outskirts of Køge.

He was getting into his car.

'Dr Hansen!'

He turned. Dapper as always with his bow tie, he was clearly exhausted with his work load yet, on seeing Tanne, he gave a little bow. Their friendship had been forged over chicken pox and split knees, not to mention the episode when, furious at a reprimand from her mother, she had climbed up the haystack and fallen out of it. '*Frøken Tanne?*'

'Dr Hansen, could you come and look at someone?'

'What's the matter with them?'

She glanced over her shoulder. 'It's urgent.'

He didn't reply at once but leaned up against the car.

'Dr Hansen?'

'It had better be urgent,' he said.

'It is. I'll cycle ahead.'

At the north entrance to the Rosenlund estate, she motioned for him to stop and wind down the window. 'I'm afraid you'll have to walk from here. I'll put your case in my bicycle basket.'

Dr Hansen fingered his bow tie. 'What is this?'

Suddenly, she was uneasy.

You don't know people in war.

'I thought you understood.'

'No,' he said flatly. 'I don't.'

'*Please.*'

'What makes you think I'm willing to participate in whatever this is? What makes you presume? I thought you must have a friend in trouble, drunk or something, who was anxious their parents weren't involved.'

She made an effort to open the car door. 'Dr Hansen, someone is in trouble.'

He prevented her. 'I'm a doctor and I can't take risks.'

'You're a doctor.'

'*Frøken* Tanne, you are very naive.'

'Not too naive to know when to help.'

Finally, white with rage, he got out of the car. 'You've put me in an impossible position. I'll ask no questions, and you will not talk to me except to tell me what is essential. And I don't want to know where I'm going. Understood?' He wrenched off the bow tie and fashioned a blindfold.

'If that's what you wish.' Tanne grabbed his doctor's bag, took him by the arm and led him through the trees.

The room in Ove's cottage was frowsy with the smell of infection but Felix was awake, if feverish. She helped him to take off his shirt and held his hand.

Dr Hansen worked in silence, examining and probing, and did not look at Felix in the face. Finally, he asked Tanne to pass him the scissors from his bag. 'This will hurt.'

As he cut the flesh away from around the bullet's entry and exit wounds, Felix's fingers crunched down on Tanne's.

She made herself watch.

Once he cried out.

'Look at me,' she commanded him, smiling, smiling. 'Keep looking at me.'

Dr Hansen addressed the floor. 'The wound's

infected but I think the bone's intact. I'll stitch you up.'

He poured surgical spirit over his handiwork, stood up and turned his back. 'You're lucky. Your arm functions will be fine. But you'll need to rest it for a month. You're likely to have a temperature for a day or two, then you should be fine. *Frøken* Tanne, scrub your hands in disinfectant and dress the wounds every twenty-four hours until the scars begin to turn pink. Then allow the air to get to them as much as possible.'

He packed his bag fast and furiously. 'Take me back to the car. I don't wish to hear from you again.'

'Dr Hansen?' This man was as removed from the pleasant, kind doctor from her childhood as it was possible to be. 'Dr Hansen?'

At the doorway, he stopped and put on the blindfold. 'You have been very stupid, *Frøken* Tanne.'

'Shush, he'll hear.' She pulled the doctor outside.

He hissed into her ear: 'There's only one doctor in this area and that's me. What happens if I go?'

Was he right? Was he wrong?

Her stomach lurched but the iron was creeping into her soul. 'I'm taking you back now,' she said and he would not mistake her contempt. 'There's no need for us to speak to each other again.'

On her return, Felix fixed his eyes on her. 'Get out of here.'

'Don't talk.'

She fetched a bottle of lemonade that she had bought in Køge and made him drink it down with two aspirins. 'You're to take two every four hours. It's not much, but something.'

He managed to smile through lips cracked with thirst. 'Do you know what I would love?'

She bent over him. 'Tell me.'

'A banana.'

Was he delirious? 'I'm going to leave you now to fetch food and drink.' She tucked the blanket back over him. 'You must stay quiet.'

As she promised him, she returned in the early evening, creeping into the cottage. Felix was asleep and the blanket had slipped to reveal the smooth, brown flesh of his uninjured shoulder.

She wanted badly to touch that smooth, brown flesh but she contented herself with kneeling down beside him and tucking the blanket around him. He was burning up. His eyes flicked open.

'It's only me.'

'Miss Only-Me,' he muttered. 'But you shouldn't be here.'

She had brought bread, cheese, a small pot of honey and some early strawberries. She shook out two aspirin and propped him up so he could swallow them. 'You need food. Sorry I took so long,' she added. 'My parents are giving dinner to a German general and his wife. I have to be careful. I should be up there entertaining him.'

'Oh, good,' he murmured. 'You can crack a joke, then.'

Carefully, she eased him up against the wall and fed him little hunks of bread and cheese, followed by the strawberries which she dipped in the honey. 'The honey should give you strength.'

'Thank you.' He tried to sit up but failed.

A little later he asked, 'Are you leaving me?'

'No,' she said. 'I'm staying.'

This was her vigil. For Denmark. For her call to arms.

For Felix.

During the night, his fever worsened. Tanne forced him to swallow more aspirin but he vomited them up almost immediately. At intervals, she bathed his face and wrists while he twitched and groaned. Once, he demanded her name. 'But not your real name.'

When she went outside to the water butt to refill the jug, an almost full moon dominated a star-filled sky and there was a beautiful velvety feel to the air. On a second trip, she gave herself a bad fright imagining that she heard footsteps moving through the undergrowth. Jug in her hand, she remained rooted to the spot. *Do not faint.* With a struggle she brought herself under control.

Back inside, she saw that Felix had woken up.

'Don't look,' she said as she took off her trousers and rolled them up to make a pillow for him.

She lay down beside him.

'Talk to me, Miss Only-Me, but nothing personal.'

How's that possible? she wanted to say. *Every single*

364

thing is linked. Me, you, my mother, the war . . . my father, Rosenlund.

'The other day a pig was due to be killed,' she began. 'The butcher called in was sworn to silence. He was so skilled the pig barely squealed. Everyone was concerned that someone would hear and tell the authorities. As you know, all pigs are supposed to go to the Germans.'

'I feel sorry for the pig.'

'But he died painlessly and he was useful. He was turned into hams, sausages and salami, and his blood was used for black pudding. Bits of him were salted and made into brawn. And soap. You've no idea how exciting that was. You boil the skin in the copper for several hours, and eventually it turns into liquid soap perfect for washing floors.'

Beside her Felix was shaking. Concerned, she propped herself up on an elbow. 'Are you feeling worse?'

He turned a drained face to hers. To her astonishment, he was laughing. 'What stuff to entertain a wounded man! Most women would have gone on about fluffy rabbits and Erik the Viking.'

After that, he seemed more comfortable and fell asleep again. His chin was stubbled and his lips fever dry – even so he appeared younger than when he was awake.

Tanne lay with her head turned towards him. She knew for a certainty that this was a precious night, a moment which she would wish to be stamped on her memory, and she refused to waste it in sleep. Her previous terrors had dissipated. She was young, and becoming increasingly bold, and the unknown and amazing adventure of life beckoned.

Carefully, so as not to disturb Felix, she fitted her body along the length of his, to prevent him from rolling onto his injured arm. Occasionally, she put out a hand to restrain him, permitting herself to let it rest on his torso . . . shoulder . . . hip.

Before she fell out of love with Aage, she had spent a night with him so she was not innocent. This wasn't the same. The interlude with Aage had been fun, very physical and transient. This . . . this guarding of Felix possessed an intimacy, almost a spiritual significance, and his weakness moved her profoundly.

She shifted position. A familiar pain lodged in her lower abdomen and dug in. Tanne grimaced. With immaculate timing, her period had arrived.

The pain growled. Illness. Doctors.

Dr Hansen?

Had she been stupid?

Despite her intentions, Tanne fell asleep. When she awoke, at dawn, she was stiff and exhausted. The floor smelled of pine and, for a second, she imagined it was the Christmas log burning at Rosenlund.

Then she realized she was the only one occupying the rug and she jerked upright. 'Are you all right?'

Incredibly, Felix had heaved himself over to the window and was keeping watch. 'I thought it best to let you sleep.'

He eased round and leaned against the wall.

Brushing back her hair, she reached for her trousers, and shielding her underwear as best she could she wriggled into them.

'Thank you for getting me through the night.'

She fastened her waistband. 'I wanted to make you as comfortable as I could.'

Scrambling up, she walked over to him and laid a hand on his forehead. He was still feverish. 'You must lie down again. You need to rest.'

He let her help him down to the floor and pull the blankets over him, then he swallowed the aspirins she gave him with a mug of water.

Tanne picked up her basket. 'I'm glad the doctor saw to you.'

'So am I. Thank you.'

'But I'm worried. I'm not sure he's on our side.'

Felix got it at once. 'So he might talk?'

'He might. I don't know. He wasn't pleased. Look, you might as well know. I had to bully him.'

If she expected anger she had got Felix wrong. 'It happens,' he said. 'More than you think.'

'I was so sure Dr Hansen was a friend. But now I'm not. I'm sorry.' The confession was pathetic, and she hated the sound of herself making it.

Felix moved restlessly and, crouching over, Tanne tried to still him. 'Is the pain bad?'

'Yes . . . yes . . .' He clutched at her hand. 'But

367

that's not the point. We have to get out.' He closed his eyes. He was gathering his forces. 'We've got to get out. *Now*. Do you understand?'

'Shush . . .' She stroked his cheek. 'Shush.'

He gazed up at her with fever-bright eyes. 'You don't understand. We can't stay here any longer.'

'*We?*'

Felix tested the injured arm, stretching it out and clenching his fingers. 'If you're right, you're compromised.' He winced. 'We'll have to get out and lie low.'

Tanne thought of the stories she had heard from her friends. Flight. Hiding. Capture. She shivered. The finger of war was now pointing at her.

CHAPTER 22

Leaving Tanne in the stable yard, Kay had got herself up to the bedroom to change. Punctual to the minute, the Gottfrieds arrived at Rosenlund and Kay gave them tea on the terrace. It was warm, the new foliage on the trees looked radiant and the birds were nesting. Afterwards, Kay took them on the promised tour of the house and the gardens.

The general studied the portrait of Sophia-Maria and turned to Bror. 'The Führer would appreciate the brotherhood between us.'

Down at the lakeside, Ingrid pointed over the bright sun patterns on the water to the island. 'It's like something out of a fairy tale,' she said.

As the party strolled back to the house, a car crunched over the gravel in the drive.

'Are you expecting more visitors?' asked the general.

'My cousin Anton,' replied Bror. 'He heard you were coming to dinner and we were delighted to ask him to join us. He's probably bringing over flowers . . . his are quite famous. He likes to supervise their arrangement.'

Bror sounded the genial host but, in fact, he had been livid. At the last minute, Kay told him that Anton had invited himself to the dinner, explaining that Anton was friendly with the general, too. In fact, she had rung Anton and given him the tip-off.

'You want him here, Kay? Is that it?'

It wasn't Anton who waited for them by the front steps but Sergeant Wulf, Constable Juncker and an unknown SS officer.

Had they found him?

Tanne? How could she protect her?

What if they searched the house?

More than anything, she wanted to hold Bror's hand and to feel safe once more.

Instead she masked her tumult with a serene smile. Stick to Felix's rules.

Be brief. Be boring. Speak pleasantly and say nothing.

If Constable Juncker was a youth on a self-declared sacred mission to heal Denmark, the shinily booted SS officer looked a far more serious proposition. He and General Gottfried exchanged the barest of unenthusiastic greetings. Kay took notice. She had been right: the Nazis fought each other.

Sergeant Wulf did his best with the introductions. 'May I introduce *Hauptsturmführer* Buch. He's joined us from København.'

Hauptsturmführer Buch inclined his head.

Whey-faced, a little shifty, Sergeant Wulf looked a wreck, and his uniform needed a press. It was noticeable that, having lost so much weight, his leather belt had been hitched in by several notches.

'*Hr* Eberstern, *Fru* Eberstern,' he began. 'Can you tell us where your daughter is?'

'Our daughter? Has something happened?' Kay needed to be astonished – and was.

'She's not here,' Bror replied. 'Although it's none of your business.'

Constable Juncker cut across Sergeant Wulf. 'Who with?'

Kay noted the *Hauptsturmführer* covertly observing the general.

Grab a few seconds to think. Kay patted her hair. 'She's with her cousins. But, really, our daughter is an adult and doesn't account to us for her movements.'

The general's gaze settled on Kay's face.

She willed herself not flush. She willed her heart to behave itself so she could remain cool and think quickly on her feet. This was what fear felt like. Primal fear. The dry mouth. A skipping heartbeat.

'Your reasons for this visit?' Bror was asking.

Hauptsturmführer Buch was polite. 'There has been a report that someone answering her description has been aiding a terrorist.'

'How outrageous,' Kay went to stand beside Bror.

Bror said, more or less pleasantly: 'I must ask you to leave.'

Ingrid turned to her husband. 'Franz, should we go in and change for dinner?'

'General, Ingrid, I apologize for this intrusion,' said Kay.

'Just a minute.' The general drew *Hauptsturmführer* Buch aside and the two men conferred. The evening sun slanted onto the braid and brass of the uniforms. In the trees, the birds were beginning to roost. The scene possessed a dreamy, shimmery, peaceful quality which Kay had seen a thousand times.

Bror shoved his hands into his pockets.

She thought of the evening ahead – and of the huge effort it was going to take to behave normally.

But do it she would.

Hauptsturmführer Buch broke away from the general and said, '*Hr* Eberstern, you will forgive us for disturbing you. The General has persuaded us that we must have made a mistake.'

The general's eyes rested thoughtfully on Kay.

Dressed in the lace dinner gown and the family pearls, Kay took a long look in the mirror to assess the results. Good enough to please a German general? Good enough to deceive Bror?

Reflected in the mirror, the bed caught her eye. It gave her painful pause. These days she was its only occupant. A half-occupied bed was, as she had discovered, full of ghosts.

Bror knocked, entered and went straight to the point. 'What's going on?'

Kay sprayed her neck with scent. 'A stupid mistake. It happens all the time, I imagine.'

'Is there something you're not telling me?'

She lifted her shoulders in a tiny shrug. 'Of course not.' She twisted round to look at him and fiddled with the hairbrush, which had not been touched by Bror for weeks. 'I wish we didn't have to entertain.'

'You mean entertain Germans.'

She allowed herself to say, 'No, I mean I wish we had the evening to ourselves.'

Bror's face softened momentarily. Did he remember that, in the old days, they often went out together into the evening sunlight? Very often he would make her laugh. She would take his arm.

She curled an escaped tendril of hair round her finger, tucked it into her chignon and searched for her evening handkerchief in the drawer. Mundane actions steadied her.

'So, where is Tanne?'

Where?

'I forgot to tell you. Mai Federspiel rang up. They're having a *fester-cousine* party and wanted Tanne. I told her to go. Tanne didn't want to have dinner with a stuffy general.' Kay stood upright and brushed down her dress.

'Why is Anton here?'

She didn't reply.

'He's here for you, isn't he?'

Still, she said nothing.

'Christ, Kay . . .'

Under her long gown, one of her knees trembled with the enormity of what she was doing. She folded up the evening handkerchief and tucked it into her sleeve. 'If you want to believe that, do.'

'Kay, I'm not prepared to go on like this.'

She would have done almost anything to avoid causing the pain in that blue, storm-filled gaze. She focused on his shoulder. 'Not now, Bror. I have the guests to see to. Your guests.'

He turned on his heel. 'You're right. I want to say that I'm aware that the Gottfrieds being here is the last thing you want to cope with, but I'm grateful.'

Bror was never less than generous.

'It's my job,' she replied. 'And it's Birgit's and that of the others who do the cleaning and iron the bed linen.'

He banged the door shut behind him.

She waited before following him. Fists scrunched. Pressing her nails hard into the fleshy part of her thumb. Summoning anger to conquer fear.

As dapper as ever, Anton arrived. Kissing Ingrid's and Kay's hands, he presented them each with a bouquet of peonies and roses. During drinks on the terrace, he drew the general aside and they talked intently.

When the party moved into the dining room, Kay managed to manoeuvre Anton aside. 'We might have a problem.' She outlined the situation and Anton's eyes narrowed.

They sat down at the table. With Birgit occupied in the kitchen, Else had been drafted in to serve. Nerves and inexperience made her clumsy and the pea soup that she was offering to the general slopped over the tureen. Kay took pity, rescued Else and offered it to the general herself. He wasn't at all put out.

'That was kind, *Fru* Eberstern.' He spooned up the soup. 'But I suspect you are a kind person.' He smiled most charmingly. 'Were you the sort of child who nursed wounded animals?'

'General, you're very sweet.'

Anton, Bror and Ingrid being deep in a hunting conversation, the general was free to turn his full attention onto Kay. As she had noted, he was an elegant eater with good manners and he apologized for the earlier visit of the police. 'I hope my colleagues didn't appear too heavy-handed.'

'They were doing their job,' said Kay. 'You can't blame them for that.'

'I was right. You are a kind person.'

It was almost amusing. The general – 'Why don't you call me Franz?' – shamelessly picked her brains about Britain. Did most people have a wireless set in their homes? Was it true that the iron railings in the cities had been smelted down to make weapons? Kay replied that he was probably better informed than she was.

The general picked up his wine glass. 'Perhaps.'

He talked a little of Germany and, reluctantly, of his childhood, saying: 'My upbringing was not what you might expect.'

'Have you seen any more of this country since we last met, General . . . er, Franz?'

She disliked using his Christian name.

'I've been to Randers and Aarhus. As you will know, we have a headquarters in Aarhus.'

'Oh, surely the headquarters is in København?'

'We have bases in a lot of places. As I mentioned before, we're not loved and it's necessary to have a full complement of staff in many places.'

Why was he giving her this information?

But he was and Kay listened carefully. 'Aarhus University is a good place for our archives . . . and that's no secret, by the way.' He smiled at Kay. 'No doubt terrorists will target it but I should say at once that, given the high calibre of our men, any resistance in the area is pretty much doomed.'

Else had better luck serving the beef medallions and the general helped himself to several pieces. Kay picked at hers while he talked in glowing terms about his unit. 'I have a pedigree team with hard soldiering and specialist training behind them. Unlike the cynical and sceptical reservists, they're committed.' He went on to say that reservists were a big problem for the crack units such as his.

So, she thought, the general was relying on reserves, which suggested there was a shortage of troops.

'It's not straightforward,' he continued. 'We're trying to pin down enemy agents who we know are operating on Zealand and elsewhere.'

Bror had been listening and cut in: 'We're too busy trying to keep the farms going for that sort of thing here.'

Ingrid looked uncomfortable and she laid down her knife and fork.

Kay pressed the general. 'How can you track the terrorists?'

He clearly enjoyed the technical aspects of the work. 'An agent gets hold of a wireless transmitting set. He, or she, is given a call sign, say, ABC, and a frequency on which to transmit. They are instructed to transmit four or five times a week but it takes them over five minutes to do that, which means we can get a fix on where they are holed up . . .'

What were the general's motives for coming to Rosenlund? Curiosity? He knew she was British and almost certainly held conflicting loyalties. It was possible he held intelligence on the Ebersterns. However, a simple explanation was also possible. Simple explanations should never be overlooked. Was it that, for some reason – perhaps the upbringing he had been reluctant to talk about – the general and his wife felt they were outsiders and warmed to Bror and herself, also the outsider?

At his end of the table, Anton kept a weather eye on them both.

'And if you capture an enemy terrorist?'

'As I believe I mentioned before when we spoke about this at the theatre,' he said, 'in Signals and Intelligence we never waste good material.' A finger tapped gently on the table. 'Most people have a price. It's a question of finding out what. How we do it is up for debate. But we had – we have – a captured terrorist who . . . er, has decided to cooperate, which means we can talk to each other as adult to adult. I have a different approach from my colleagues in the SS, who are more draconian.' He shot Kay a look – cunning, rueful, slightly apologetic. 'That's not to say we're soft.'

Kay touched her lips with her napkin.

A captured terrorist who decided to cooperate. Kay combed over her meagre stockpile of information. Who could it be? Besides Vinegar were there other wireless transmitters operating in Zealand? She didn't know for sure. But she did know that Felix had been trying to find out where he was.

'Kay . . .?' The general wanted to know if she needed her water glass filled.

'Thank you . . . no.'

She imagined one of those brutal concrete buildings in which the Gestapo operated, the rooms filled with those who did not cooperate – and those who did but who almost certainly ended up the same.

Under the table, she clenched her napkin between fingers that felt numb.

'Human beings are predictable, wouldn't you say? Whatever their philosophy or religion,' continued the general, 'they have an inbuilt desire to please. It's a question of finding the trigger. If you can convince an enemy agent that it would be better for the world, for their family, for them, if they cooperate, you can usually get results.'

'A sophisticated approach, General.'

She caught Anton's eye.

'We often know where an agent is operating but we don't bring them in because we like to watch them. If you're too quick, the network scatters, which is no use.'

Kay couldn't bear it any longer. 'Heavens,' she said, lightly. 'I'll have to be careful when I'm on the phone. Just in case your men are listening in.'

'I apologize. I have been talking shop.' He was all charm. 'Did you know I have been in touch with your son?'

'Nils! How did that happen?'

Anton intervened. 'I was in a position to help,' he said. 'I took Franz to see him.'

Anton. How dare he? How could he? Kay shot him a furious look. In reply, he raised an eyebrow. *Trust me.*

She pulled herself together. 'I hope Nils behaved himself.'

'Politeness itself. He agreed to help us.'

Very carefully, Kay placed her crumpled napkin on the table. 'Did he have any option, Franz?'

'We are not complete bullies, Kay. He's a very interesting, extremely brilliant young man, a credit to his parents.'

'Are you interested in mathematics?' she asked.

'Let us say only in its applications,' he replied.

'I knew it, Franz . . .' Kay sent him a sweet, but treacherous, smile. 'You are a Renaissance man.'

The phone rang in the hall. It was for the general.

'I'm so sorry,' he said on his return into the

room, 'but I've been summoned to Berlin. I'm afraid Ingrid and I will have to leave before dawn. A plane has been sent to København.'

The evening continued – a slow and heavy endurance test. Eventually, Anton kissed Ingrid's hand in the most charming fashion, complimented the general on his knowledge of wine and said goodnight to Bror. Kay accompanied him to the front door.

'Why introduce Nils to him?' she hissed. 'What are you doing?'

He pressed her hand meaningfully. 'I've cut the telephone line,' he said, kissing her cheek.

A little while later Kay and Bror escorted their guests to their bedroom. The Gottfrieds were effusive in their thanks. 'There's no need to wake you in the morning,' said Ingrid charmingly. 'Franz and I are quite used to early morning getaways.'

Kay led the way back down the corridor.

'Goodnight,' said Bror outside the bedroom. He glanced at his shoes, polished to mirror brightness. 'Thank you.'

'Goodnight, Bror.' She watched him walk away.

Kay awoke with a start. Downstairs there were noises signalling departure, followed by a car moving carefully down the drive. She peered at her clock. It was five a.m. and she sank into exhausted sleep.

Again, she was pulled abruptly back into consciousness. Someone was in the room, searching in her drawers.

'Tanne!'

Tanne whirled round. 'Sorry, *Mor*. Didn't mean to give you a fright. I need some underwear.' She frowned. 'You will know why . . . so inconvenient. I've taken some of your things. I thought I shouldn't risk going to my room if the general was in the guest room.'

'He's gone. Thank heavens.' In a flash, Kay was out of bed. 'Listen, darling, you can't be here. The police and an SS officer came looking for you yesterday.' She searched Tanne's face. 'Someone—'

'Dr Hansen . . .' Tanne sat down heavily on the bed. 'I knew it.' She clutched her stomach as she confessed what she had done. 'How stupid I've been. How—'

'No time for that now . . . Listen to me. Think. Did Hansen know which cottage?'

Tanne exhaled with an audible hiss. 'Not really. He may have an idea but he was blindfolded. But he didn't want to know, *Mor*. That's why I thought we would get away with it.'

Think.

'Dr Hansen . . . if it was him . . . will have told them it's one of the cottages on the estate but won't know which one. That buys time. An hour or so, three at the most, to get Felix up and running. Get back to the cottage and stay there until I can work out how to get you away.' She glanced at the clock. 'Birgit and Else will be here soon to make breakfast. No one must see

381

you. Understand? I've told them you were with cousins and explained to your father that you went to stay with the Federspiels at the last minute. Let's get you some food.'

So saying, Kay flung on a pair of trousers and a jersey and they made for the back stairs. In the kitchen, she stoked up the stove, put the kettle on and packed a basket with bread and cheese.

The kettle boiled and Kay made Tanne drink some tea.

Don't ever pass up the opportunity to eat or drink.

Tanne had never seemed so beautiful. Or so focused. Or so alive. Or so beloved.

Kay refilled the cup and, pressing Tanne to eat a slice of bread and honey, watched her like a hawk as she did so.

How did resistance work?

Intelligence.

Surprise.

Attack and get out. Never hang around to defend.

'Tanne, can you memorize this and tell Felix?' She ran over the conversations with the general – captured agents, the Aarhus archive . . . 'The RAF might want to bomb it. Tell Felix, too, that they may have Vinegar. Can you remember that?'

Tanne burst out laughing. '*Mor*, never in my wildest dreams did I imagine you and I would be doing this.'

'Don't make a noise.' She pulled Tanne to her and kissed the tousled head. 'You must take care, my darling daughter. You'll have to live differently now. Be watchful. Ultra careful and discreet. Get yourself to the Federspiels. They'll look after you. Promise.'

Tanne held up a hand. 'Listen,' she whispered.

Vehicles were rolling up the drive.

Kay edged over to the window. This time there was the black car plus a couple of military vehicles. They parked. The doors were opened to release a posse of soldiers with dogs.

A dreadful certainty hardened.

'You're blown, Tanne. Leave – now! Never, ever, come back here until the war is over. Get out of Denmark. Go to Sweden. Do you understand?'

Tanne dropped the slice of bread she was holding. 'It's my fault.'

Down the passage, Sif and Thor began to howl.

'*Do you understand?*'

Tanne had gone chalk white.

'Tanne, concentrate.'

'*Mor*, forgive me.'

Think, Kay.

Wireless set.

'Tell Felix I'll deal with the wireless set. Don't take it with you.'

Were there any traces of Felix in the attic room?

'Forgive me . . .'

'Go,' Kay hissed. 'Get out the side door. Leave the cottage. Felix will know what to do.'

'*Mor* . . .'

'Of course I forgive you.'

Tanne ran.

Kay slipped up the back stairs and into her bedroom, ripped off the trousers and jersey and got into bed.

She had only seconds to spare. Bror was already at the bedroom door. 'Kay, can you come downstairs?'

No need to hurry. She took her time to put on her dressing gown and to brush her hair. Descending the stairs, she was confronted by *Hauptsturmführer* Buch, Sergeant Wulf and Constable Juncker in the hall and, beyond them in the drive, the men and the dogs.

An enraged Bror was remonstrating with Buch. Looking wretched beyond belief, Sergeant Wulf had distanced himself from the Germans. Bror looked round. 'There you are. Darling, these men want to search the house.'

The morning sunlight threatened to dazzle every wit Kay possessed. Sif and Thor surged into the hall followed by a goblin-eyed Else, who took one look and bolted up the stairs. Where was Birgit?

'*Search* the house?' She frowned. 'Do they have the authority?'

Outside, the tracker dogs barked and strained at the leashes. These were dogs which lusted after their quarry. They were dogs that would run fast and fierce.

Sif and Thor joined in. Buch snapped his fingers at them and, to Kay's astonishment, they quietened. 'We won't take up too much of your time.'

'So I should hope,' said Bror. 'I've appointments on the farm, and we're short-handed.'

Buch was a man who could finesse a situation. 'For those who cooperate with us we are only too happy to supply more workers, *Hr* Eberstern.' There was a pause. 'If you are short-handed.'

'No,' said Kay sharply, immediately regretting it. *Be boring.*

'Let me explain again,' said *Hauptsturmführer* Buch. 'There has been enemy activity in the area and a terrorist is hiding in the vicinity. He's wounded and he probably can't get far. Our intelligence tells us he is on the Rosenlund estate.' He was polite. He was firm. He was – Kay thought with a touch of hysteria – taking pains to behave like a gentleman. 'The intelligence couldn't have been clearer.'

Juncker slapped his thigh with his gloves.

Buch continued, quiet and relentless: 'We have reason to believe it was your daughter who helped him.' He gave a polite, wintry smile. 'Probably out of misplaced pity.'

'No,' said Kay. 'As I told you, she's with her cousins. They live in Aarhus.'

Mistake?

'Name,' demanded Constable Juncker.

Kay gave it.

'May we use the phone?'

'If you must.'

Juncker tried it, only to report the line was dead.

385

'Oh Lord,' said Kay. 'It's always happening. It's the mice. They eat through the cables. We're always having to lay new ones. She appealed to them. 'Gentlemen, I assure you the reports are incorrect.'

'Tell them, Wulf,' ordered Buch.

'The doctor says otherwise.' Sergeant Wulf was reluctant.

'My daughter helping a terrorist?' Bror was incredulous.

'*Fru* Eberstern, *Hr* Eberstern,' Sergeant Wulf was almost begging them, 'I'm afraid we must search your daughter's room.' He took a look at Bror's thunderous expression. 'The sooner you allow me, the sooner this will be over.'

They all trooped upstairs to Tanne's room and discovered Else cowering inside. 'I wanted to know if *Frøken* Tanne wished for her tea.'

'But *Frøken* Tanne is away,' said Juncker.

'Oh.'

Tanne's bed, with an arched wooden bedhead and green and white quilt – green and white were Tanne's colours – dominated the room. Clothes were heaped on it. Scattered on the floor were books and the dance records that she played on her gramophone. By the window, housed in a Sèvres pot, was the tropical fern which, against the odds, Tanne managed to keep alive.

Kay explained who Else was.

'Have you seen *Frøken* Eberstern today?' Buch was brusque.

Else flushed. 'Yes, no, I mean no. No. It must have been yesterday.'

'Which?' Buch took up a position by the window.

Else endeavoured to hide her shaking hands in her apron.

'Please stop,' said Kay. 'At once. This is bullying.'

Hauptsturmführer Buch signalled to Constable Juncker. 'Take her down to the station.'

'No!' Else's scream of terror shocked the listeners. 'Please.'

'Let me talk to her,' said Kay. Turning her back on the men, she snatched up one of Else's hands. 'Did you see *Frøken* Tanne this morning?'

She pressed down on the clammy fingers.

Else, still a child really, struggled to speak. Her nose was running and Kay offered her a handkerchief.

Else blew into it. 'I can't remember.' The words were barely audible.

'We can make you remember,' said Juncker.

Buch pointed to the chest. 'Would you mind opening this drawer?'

Kay looked to Bror for back-up. '*Hauptsturmführer* Buch, that's private to my daughter.'

It was useless.

Opening the drawer to reveal Tanne's delicate lacy things was one of the hardest things she had ever done. Sergeant Wulf endeavoured to calm a hysterical Else. Buch and Juncker searched the room.

Kay was stiff with hatred in a way she never imagined she would ever feel.

Intent on impressing, Juncker exhibited rodent cunning. He opened Tanne's wardrobe, shuffled the clothes on their hangers and poked at the rows of shoes on the floor. Then, at the back of the cupboard, he unearthed the shoe box and removed the lid. 'Sir?'

Triumphant, he carried it over to the desk and displayed the contents.

Buch held up the pamphlet. If anything his voice had grown softer. 'An explanation, please.'

Naturally, Buch didn't believe Kay when she improvised and told him that they used any old pieces of paper to stuff into wet shoes. 'Shoes are often wet out here.'

Bror was silent.

She could almost read his thoughts: *My wife. My daughter.*

'This is seditious, dangerous rubbish. Why didn't your daughter burn it?'

'It's wartime. Probably she found it somewhere and didn't want to waste valuable paper.'

Constable Juncker spoke into *Hauptsturmführer* Buch's ear. Buch turned to Bror. 'I am afraid this confirms we must search the estate.' He picked up one of Tanne's sweaters which had been on the bed. 'I will use this. The dogs will need the scent.'

'I haven't given you permission.'

'I think you will,' replied Buch.

Wulf, Buch and Juncker returned downstairs. Orders were issued and the dogs set up renewed barking.

Bror hustled Kay into her bedroom. 'Where *is* Tanne?'

'I told you. In Aarhus,' she replied. 'Let me get dressed.'

'Don't lie to me.' He was almost too angry to speak. He paced the room. 'Is Tanne mixed up in something? She is. I sense it. What have *you* done? There must be a reason that some idiotic, but clearly dangerous, German turns up and suggests our daughter is a terrorist, and I think the reason must be you.'

'This is war. It happens.'

'Or Anton.'

'Stop it.'

'And what has Anton done to the telephone? It was him.'

Anton bought Tanne some time.

'Where could Tanne have got hold of that leaflet?'

'Maybe she's got views of her own.'

Bror grabbed Kay by the arm. It was a rough, angry gesture and introduced a brand-new element into their relations: hostility. 'What *are* you?'

'And what are you, Bror?'

'You know who I am. You've always known.'

'Aren't you disgusted by what's happening to Denmark? Disgusted by the newspapers, the industrialists and businessmen all falling over themselves to accept the German mark? How we collaborate with an occupying force?' His fingers dug hard into her flesh but she continued. 'How we entertain German generals?'

'Tell me what is going on.'

Kay's resolve wavered. On her back rested the burden of bringing suspicion down onto the house and those that lived in it.

'Go and get dressed, Bror.'

'I'm going into Køge to try to sort this out.'

'Listen to me, Bror,' she said, fierce and impassioned. 'Whatever you think you *must* act normally, as if there is nothing to worry about. We will have breakfast as we always do.'

For a second or two, she thought the appeal had failed. Then he said: 'If I find out that it's you who's put Tanne in danger by involving her in something unwise, I'll never forgive you.'

That was nothing.

It was impossible to tell Bror that Kay would never forgive herself.

A little while later they were in the dining room making a pretence of eating. From the lakeside, the barking of the dogs increased to maddened frenzy.

She glanced at Bror. As she had instructed, he was eating steadily, but with a heightened colour.

Thank God the Gottfrieds had gone. With piercing gratitude she thought again of Anton's forethought. No telephone meant they would be out of contact.

The barking reached a crescendo, followed by gunshots.

'Oh my God . . .' Kay couldn't help herself.

She closed her eyes and felt the blood drain from her face. When she opened them, Bror was staring at her.

'Are you all right?'

She shrugged. 'You know I never like to hear guns going off.'

'This is a manhunt, Kay,' said Bror – and she detected a menace which she had not heard before. 'Think about it.'

Silence fell. Bror had lit up his post-breakfast cigarette when Sergeant Wulf shuffled into the dining room.

'I'm so sorry . . . I'm so sorry . . .'

A drumming mounted in Kay's ears, and her head swam.

Bror rose to his feet. 'What is it, Wulf?'

Wulf had gone a pale green colour. 'Your dogs,' he said. 'They've been shot. By mistake.'

Bror was on his feet roaring with anguish and anger. 'My dogs . . . my dogs.'

CHAPTER 23

efer pain on. Or divert it.

Had those STS instructors ever experienced pain? Of course they had. Some of them were tough to the point of inhumanity, and a couple had operated in China in terrible conditions. No, the answer was that you, the sufferer, had to find your own individual way through pain.

He had dealt with it.

He seemed to have been dreaming a great deal, especially in the cottage. Colourful fantasies which he imagined were the result of his fever. At a point when he felt as if his body was melting with heat, he dreamed a woman was bathing his face. Freya? Then he realized he was being tended to by a younger version.

'Name?' he'd muttered. 'But not your real name.'

'What would you like it to be?'

Man and woman . . . Adam and Eve . . .

'Eva,' he said.

She pushed back a mane of hair. 'Eva, it is.'

It was Eva bathing his face and lying beside him. Or was that a dream, too? One memory was clear enough. It was of Eva sitting bolt upright, with her hair tumbling over her shoulders. She had taken off her trousers and put them under his head as a pillow. Underneath she wore wide-legged knickers and he caught sight of the top of her thigh, a red stain and a suggestion of blonde hair. The sight worked powerfully on him but not in the way he would have expected. It had made him feel unbearably, awkwardly tender – and protective.

Perhaps it was lust, which Felix welcomed. Despite the state he was in, he wanted to feel lust, satiation, hope – all the things that proved you were alive.

Eva had brought him food and water, but he wasn't sure when. A strawberry? Honey? He recollected her telling him that her parents were giving dinner to a German general and his wife, and that she was supposed to be up at the house entertaining them.

At first, he had reckoned she was joking.

The night was a terrible one. Very early, he had managed to manoeuvre himself upright and move over to the window to keep watch. Eva was sleeping, curled gracefully on one side.

Tousled blonde hair, a strong chin, long limbs . . . it was a sight to make him feel better. When she woke, she rolled over, looked up at Felix in a puzzled way and reached for her trousers. When she was dressed, she felt his forehead and made him take more painkillers and drink a mug of water.

It was then she'd confessed her misgivings about Dr Hansen.

★   ★   ★

393

Someone was shaking Felix and he awoke with a groan.

It was Eva. 'Get up. The police and the SS have arrived at the house. They're hunting you, and want to talk to me.'

In a flash, he was on his feet. Pain sliced through his arm, followed by a wave of nausea. The blood drained from his head. He swayed and fell against the wall. Eva pushed his head down on his chest. He gagged, and bile and saliva dripped onto his shirt.

At last he managed to ask: 'Do they know who they're looking for exactly?'

'A man with an injured arm.'

'The doctor?'

'Stop talking, Felix. Freya . . . Freya says to leave the wireless set.'

Christ. *The wireless.* His head felt as if someone had taken an axe to it and his mouth was as rough as a quarry. 'Have they got dogs?'

'Yes.'

Fieldcraft. The hunters would use something of Eva's for the scent.

'Is there a river or a ditch near here?'

'Yes.'

All at once, he felt steadier. Propping himself against the wall, he said, 'You're in it now, Eva. Be prepared. We'll have to get out of Denmark. We must get ourselves to the harbour at Gilleleje and make contact with Sven. If we pay him enough he'll take us across to Helsingborg.'

394

Eva was moving around the room, smoothing away signs of recent occupation. She attempted a joke: 'So that's easy, then.'

'Not quite. The Germans have laid minefields in the Sound and the Allies have dropped magnetic mines. Between them, they are giving the fishermen grief. So he might not be too keen. But he might be persuaded to transfer us to a boat just inside Swedish waters. Could be tricky, boarding in a bad sea. You'd have to climb a ladder.'

'Do I look as though I can't?' She sounded almost offended. 'Well, I've heard the Swedes are opening up the bonded warehouses and whoever goes in can help themselves. Everyone gets disgustingly drunk.' She picked up the bottle of water and handed it to him. 'Meanwhile, here's an alternative.'

She bundled up the blankets. There was nowhere to store them and she looked questioningly at Felix.

'They'll have our scent on them – we'll have to take them with us and get rid of them somewhere.'

Together, they left the cottage and headed for the tree cover.

It was hard going. The nausea came and went and his legs felt like putty. The adrenalin should kick in eventually but, until then, he concentrated on placing one foot in front of the other.

Press the heel down, follow it with the toe.

Have we forgotten anything? There is something missing . . .

Don't think about the arm.

Referred pain.

At the road, he made Eva stop while still under the tree cover. 'Which way?'

She pointed to a large field in the distance. 'Big drainage ditch at one end. With a drainage pipe.'

'We'll make for that.'

The drainage pipe was only just big enough, but they crawled into it. The bottom was an inch or so deep in water but they had no choice other than to lie in it.

'Could be worse,' said Eva.

Quiet.

Stay absolutely quiet.

Some time later Felix checked his watch but the dial swam in and out of focus.

'Eva, how long have we been in here?'

Her voice sifted back to him. 'A couple of hours?'

Freya may be in danger.

'You know you can't go back?'

She took her time to answer. 'I know.'

'I meant you cannot go back to the house.'

'I know. I'm coming with you to Sweden.'

There was a lilt in her voice, an excitement. Unbelievably, their hiding place was filled with a wildly inappropriate gaiety that tore at his conscience. Eva was Freya's daughter, a responsibility that he had never envisaged and did not want. Yet here she was, jammed into a drainage pipe with her head up against his feet.

They were silent. After a while, she asked, 'Felix, how are you feeling?'

'Terrific,' he answered. 'I love having a shot-up arm.'

He heard her laugh.

'There's a message from my mother which I must tell you in case we split up.' There was a pause. 'I must this get this right. This General Gottfried is Abwehr and commands the signals unit but *Mor* thinks he's got a long finger in Intelligence, too. Does that make sense?'

'Yes, it does.'

'Listen, resistance in the Aarhus area is getting torn up by the Gestapo, who are using the university as a headquarters. There're reports that Gestapo archives are being stored there. She says to tell London that the archives need to be destroyed.'

'Simple,' he murmured. 'I'll get on the phone to the British RAF.'

'Can you remember that?' She nudged his foot gently. 'I'll remember it for you, if not. Oh, I almost forgot – she said something about vinegar, but I didn't understand what she meant.'

Felix dropped his head onto his good arm. Jumbled images chased through his mind . . .

The containers from the drop. Are they still sitting in the wood? Who checked?

I must manage my arm.

Messages? How to contact London?

Freya says that a general may be running one of our wireless sets.

Mustard is wiped off plate.

Kill him. Kill Erik, too.

Their blood is on my hands.

Vinegar? Were they running him?

Organize. Talk to the communists. Talk to the nationalists. Stockpile arms and explosives. Fashion an underground army out of a population who prefer it to be quieter.

Which wireless is being run?

Stop talking.

Do something.

I wish I didn't feel so sick.

Crazy, it's all crazy . . .

He dozed.

Prodded awake by the cold and damp, he realized that important political and military considerations required his attention. Item: how was Denmark going to manoeuvre itself out of the reach of the Third Reich? Item: were the communists going to be the ones who called the shots? Item: when would the Allies come? Item: how was he going to survive?

The war was too big. How could a bunch of resisters possibly imagine they could create a running sore in Hitler's hide? Certainly not he – powerless and wounded – a Dane dreaming of victory but only running on the spot.

Denmark. What was it doing to itself?

'Eva, you're in danger.'

'So?' She actually chuckled.

'Are you very wet?'

'Soaking. But I've never felt better.' Her hand rested on his ankle, an infinitely comforting contact.

He licked his bottom lip and squared up to his weakness. 'I don't think I'll make Gilleleje at the moment. So, change of plan. We'll head for the rubbish dump at Amager harbour. We can get a boat from there.'

'Amager! That's in the middle of København.'

'That's the point,' said Felix with a touch of smugness. 'Under the nose of the enemy. They would never expect it so they wouldn't look for it. You'd be surprised. Quite a lot of people traffic goes in and out. We'll have to hide up in København while we make the contacts.'

'And you get your strength back.'

'That, too.' He gave her the address of a safe house, and made her repeat it twice.

Eventually, Eva said: 'I can't hear any dogs. I'm going to get help.'

He felt a deep reluctance to let her go, fearing the absence of her physical warmth in their in-hospitable lair. More worryingly, at this moment of profound frailty, he didn't want to be alone.

The training had taught him that weaknesses would surface at just this point and he had been warned of their insidious effects.

But you put your head down, sonny, and tread on through.

He concentrated on planning the next move.

Yet again, he fell into a doze, and woke to find

Eva crouched down by the entrance to the pipe. 'Felix, get up. I've got Arne with the pony trap. He's going to take us to the station at Vallø. We're too well known at Køge.'

He snapped into wariness. 'Who's Arne?'

'I trust him with my life. *Come on.*'

He emerged to find that she had changed into trousers and a jacket. A bag was slung over her shoulder and her hair was brushed, her mouth lipsticked. She held out a pair of workman's over-alls. 'I'm going to help you into these.'

He was stiff from his incarceration and his arm was awkward. 'How long have you been gone?'

'An hour or so. They seem to have given up and driven back into town.'

'They'll be watching. You went back to the house?'

'If I can't get back into Rosenlund without anyone noticing,' she was helping to fasten the overalls, 'then I don't deserve to inherit it. We needed clothes and money, and I needed to look tidier.'

She was right.

He remembered something important. '*Lort!* The pistol.'

Every bloody rule of training . . . broken.

'Aren't we better without it? If we are caught with it . . .?'

He summoned his energies. 'That's one way of looking at it.'

Arne was waiting with the trap on the road. Felix gave him the once-over. A big man with greying hair, he had the air of someone accustomed to taking charge. Prudently, he avoided looking at Felix.

'You're to lie down in the back,' said Eva. 'Oh, wait.' She produced a bottle of schnapps out of the bag, unscrewed the top and sprinkled him with it. 'Just so you know, you're drunk. Try to act it.'

Slumped in the back, he spent the journey nursing his arm. At one point, he overheard Eva say, 'Tell my mother I'm fine. Tell her not to worry.'

There was the bass note of Arne's reply that Felix could not make out. Eva replied, 'How can I thank you?'

Just before Vallø, they ran into a roadblock, manned by a couple of Danish policemen. Arne brought the cart to a halt.

The younger-looking, more nervous-looking one of the pair stepped forward. The weapon in his belt had a dull gleam. 'Where are you going?'

'Taking this man home,' replied Eva. 'He's supposed to have been working for us but has proved . . . unreliable.'

'Where?'

'Slotskro. His wife is waiting.' Eva was deliciously charming and polite. The policeman's eyes travelled from Eva to Felix.

Eva looked at her watch. 'I'm going to be late.'

A hint of steel crept into her voice which Felix could only admire: it suggested that she was not used to obstacles being put in her way.

It worked.

The policeman stood back and they were on their way. The castle, surrounded by cobblestone streets and houses painted in yellows and ochres, came into view. Beyond these lay the station and, once there, he knew the watching and the waiting would begin in earnest.

He was frightened and hated to admit it. Yet he was determined to savour these last moments of fresh air and to fight his weakness. Remember, remember the point of what they were doing – which was to get his country out of its mess. As they trotted past the gardens rustling with trees and plants, the message written in his fear and pain was: We must not fail.

So be it if he died.

They travelled in separate train compartments and in København Felix went on ahead. Check right, left. Don't hurry. Stay upright. It was strange, but he felt safer in the city, even in a debilitated state.

The safe house which he made for had been a doctor's surgery before the war and the doctor's brass plaque was still screwed into the gate. Inside, it was similar to many of the abandoned houses, with an air of despair and neglect. In this one, though, there was evidence the doctor had prospered for there were several pieces of good antique furniture and a handsome eighteenth-century French clock.

He was tempted to wind it up. It would have seemed right – a gesture of defiance.

Not long afterwards, Eva arrived. She dumped packages on the kitchen table. 'Bread, butter and milk. Couldn't get any cheese, but I got hold of some sausage. The milk looks terrible. All watered down.'

'A banquet.' There was a pause. 'Eva, I'm sorry but I'm going to have to send you out to make contact with the man with the boat.'

'Of course.' She looked around for a place to stow the milk. 'Is there anything else?'

'Nothing for you.'

She was pale and there was a suggestion of sweat glistening on her upper lip which made him feel extremely guilty. He gave her the instructions.

When she had gone, he eased aside the net curtain at the window. The street was less busy than he expected. Not for the first time, he realized that something had happened to the Danish. They walked around with their heads down. A German motor convoy eased down the street. No one paid it much attention.

He massaged his arm. A river of pain flowed up and down it.

Would they get out? Had Arne given the message to Freya?

Flexing and bending, his trigger finger needed exercise.

Could they still rely on the fact that the Germans – who were quartered there, for God's sake – apparently never noticed Danish boats slipping in and alongside the rubbish dump on Amager island?

Was the contact trustworthy?

Go deep inside yourself. There are deep places on which to call, sonny.

The net curtain dropped back into place.

He set himself to wait.

Later, having got themselves through København, Eva and Felix were met by a man dressed in a thick fisherman's jersey and rubber boots at the entrance to the harbour. 'Call me Jens.' He hustled them into the shadow thrown by the old fort which dominated the harbour. 'Listen, we have a hitch. There's a U-boat on the other side of the harbour. Turned up out of the blue. It's either damaged, or it's resting up from an operation. Either way, we didn't get the intelligence in time to warn you. We can't do it. It's too dangerous. You must go back.'

Eva gave a little gasp.

Felix looked at her. In the darkness of the summer night, fractured by the searchlights and the lights strung along the quays, she appeared insubstantial.

Denmark's ghosts were sleeping, hidden beneath a passive, cowed, splintered nation. He was going to do his best to wake them. He had also to look after Freya's daughter.

With his good hand, Felix grasped at Jens's jersey. 'We're going.'

'Take your hands off me.' Jens stepped back. He scuffed his rubber boot along the stones. After a moment, he said, 'It'll cost you.'

'Fine,' said Felix. 'But we're going. Do you understand?'

The tactic worked. Jens nodded, and handed over two navy wool balaclavas. 'Put them on.'

An ominous breeze tugged at the pennants and Felix prayed it wouldn't get any stronger.

Surefooted and silent, Jens led them through the network of crates, bales and canvas bags that littered the quay and halted by a couple of trolleys stacked with boxes. 'Sit behind those until we get the signal.'

The three of them crouched down.

The wind battered at the rigging, and the sea slapped against the stone quay.

Felix backed himself against a hawser coiled up by one of the trolleys, which gave him some support.

Jens licked his finger and held it up to the wind. 'Stay here. Don't move or say anything. Wait for the signal then make for the *Ulla Baden* over there.'

He padded back down the quay and they were alone.

Eva took hold of Felix's good hand and placed her mouth against his ear. 'There's the *Ulla Baden*.' She pointed to a fishing vessel moored almost directly in front of them. It was a no-nonsense-looking vessel which, no doubt, had done sturdy service.

Her breath filtered through the balaclava onto his cheek, and the fingers resting in his were damp. He held them fast. '*Lort!* She's small.'

'Bad sailor?'

405

''Fraid so.'

'You're no Dane.'

He managed a grin. 'Hit a man when he's down.'

Again, he heard her chuckle. She consulted her watch. 'Two and a half minutes between each sweep of the searchlight. Is that going to be enough for you?'

'Like I said, hit a man when he's down.'

After an hour or so, the wind backed around and its full force hit them. Felix's balaclava tasted of salt and the wool was stiff with it. Despite the late hour, it was still just light enough to make out the shapes of the boats in the harbour. Eva was pressed up close to him. 'Storm,' he said into her ear. 'Just our luck.'

They sat out the waiting, listening to the waves rolling beside the quay, water slapping against fenders, the sighing and creaking of the pontoons as they bobbed up and down.

The searchlight swept the quays. Round, dip, round . . .

It was after midnight when their contact zigzagged silently towards them. Stopping beside the trolleys, Jens pretended to check over a pile of fishing tackle close by. 'Listen up. When a light shows on the *Ulla*, you run to her one at a time and the captain will hide you in the hold where the catch is put. He'll pile the nets on top of you. A warning: it's small.'

He dumped the tackle on top of the hawsers and vanished into the murk.

Crouching, tensed, they readied themselves. One

minute. Two minutes. Five, six . . . 'Get on with it,' Felix growled. The searchlight directed its blinding arc down onto the quay and away, leaving pitch black behind.

At last, a pinpoint of light glowed on the *Ulla Baden*, and Eva was up and away.

Felix poised on the balls of his feet.

Again, the signal. He launched himself across the slippery stones, up the gangplank and onto the boat. His good elbow was seized and he was pushed down into the hold.

It was tiny, barely ten foot square, smelling of – oh God – rotten guts, fish and blood. This was no joke. Above their heads, a man issued a rapid command. Within seconds, the nets were piled on top and the hatch battened down.

The water slapped at the side of the boat. Felix retched noisily.

'You can't be sick yet,' said Eva.

'Yes, I can.'

Suddenly, there was noise: booted feet slapping onto the stones and running up the gangplank. Felix grabbed Eva's arm.

Footsteps trampled the deck above them. These were followed by the skitter and patter of dogs' paws.

Felix closed his eyes: *This is it, then.* Tension replaced his nausea. Eva clung to his good hand. He pulled her to him, buried his face in her neck and smelled flowers and spring and sun. All the things to live for.

Try to keep silent for forty-eight hours if taken.

'If they get you, feed them as little as you can manage,' he whispered, passing on the STS advice. 'Tell them that I abducted you.'

But the dogs didn't bark. Instead, they appeared to be running around in circles. Orders were issued. A bucket banged down. The wind sang through the ship's rigging. There was a babble of male voices, orders in German.

Eva's body moved within his clasp. He felt the curve of her waist and the slight swell of her hip. He felt that she belonged there and, even more curious, that he knew her, through and through. For the first time in his life, he experienced terror for someone other than himself, someone he wanted to protect.

If Eva was taken . . .? How would she have any idea of the protocols of interrogation? The games played by the interrogator? The techniques? Their objectives? The methodical deconstruction of an agent's mind and body? Starvation. Darkness. Freezing temperatures. All the persuasive methods which were oh-so-creative.

He shuddered.

Eva pressed closer.

More orders in German. Again, a symphony of heavy boots. A voice screamed, 'Go, go!' to the dogs. The dogs whimpered and whined.

'What are you doing?' barked a voice with a German accent. 'Who is he?'

There was a mutter. A scuffle. An oath.

'Get off me, you bastard,' screamed someone in Danish.

'Your papers,' roared the German voice. 'Open the lockers.'

The skipper shouted in Danish: 'This is my ship.'

'Open the hatches.'

Eva's nails dug into his hand. The lid was removed from the hatch above them. A tiny streak of light percolated down through the nets as something prodded at them.

Felix and Eva shrank back against the walls.

Jab.

Jab.

The dogs' paws clicked on the wooden deck.

There was a whimper. A second. Then, nothing more.

The lid was shoved back onto the hatch.

To Felix's astonishment, the only voices they could now hear were not German.

Engines wheezed into life. Orders were now being issued in Danish. 'Cast off.'

The boat slipped its moorings and nosed out of the harbour. Immediately, a swell caught it up, slamming them from side to side.

'This is hell.' Felix tried not to groan as he retched into a tin he'd found rolling on the floor. 'Don't you dare laugh.'

'Would I?'

At the best of times a smallish fishing boat on the Kattegat or Øresund was a hostage to fortune. With a wind, it was Thor's plaything.

Felix spent the next hour or so heaving up his guts. Fetid already, the air in the tiny space turned rancid, but he was past caring. After a while, Eva prised the tin out of his grip and held it for him. That took something. Every so often she dabbed at his face with a handkerchief. That took something, too, given that he stank of vomit and infected wound.

'Felix?' Her voice was almost drowned out by the sea. 'I've decided. When we get to Sweden, I'm coming with you to London.'

With difficulty, he raised his head. 'No, you aren't.'

'I'm going to offer to work like you do.'

'It's too dangerous,' he said.

'That's for me to decide.'

His thoughts were moving slowly. 'You don't know the half of it.'

'I know enough,' she said urgently. 'I know that we have to do something. It took me a bit of time, but I've got there in the end.'

She was whispering this into his ear and he longed to gather her up. 'It's too big a risk. Stay quietly in Sweden until it's all over. Then you can go back to your family.'

'I'm ashamed that my mother got there first.'

Another spasm hit him. He was being dragged down into overwhelming weakness and despair.

Arms went round him. 'Lean on me.'

'I'm too disgusting.'

'You *must*.'

Her cheek was against his, like a gentle pillow.

Do not go into death without remembering the things that matter. Do not go brutalized.

Memories he would never forget: Eva cradling him in the cottage; her semi-nakedness and the snatched, intimate glimpse of her femininity; her laughter in the drainage pipe; her embrace amidst the stink and offal; this moment.

No, he would not go brutalized.

She was his saviour, the other half of his soul. Greek philosophers wrote about that, the *eros* and *agape*. Sacred and divine.

He was gasping for air and for some respite.

'Felix, this is my fault,' Eva whispered. 'You must forgive me.'

'I want you to live,' he said. *'Please.'*

The second's silence which elapsed felt breathless.

'And you, too, Felix.'

At last, the hatch was opened and he found himself downing great lungfuls of fresh air.

The skipper, a great bear of a man, stuck his head inside. 'We've been blown off course and shipped water. Get up here and start bailing.'

'How far are we from Swedish waters?'

'Close. But there's a minefield.'

Shivering, Felix wedged himself into the bow and bailed like there was no tomorrow. The water hissed past them and, every so often, he was drenched by a wave. Eva was up there with him. Soaked to the skin, her hair plastered over her shoulders, she looked like a fallen angel and bailed like a navvy.

Jabbing a thumb in the direction of the hold, she grinned broadly. He understood her exhilaration and the pleasure of release because he felt it, too.

An ancient beret crammed down on his head, the mate was busy in the chart room. Every so often he poked out his head to take a look at the stars. On deck, the lookouts clung to the rails, scanning the waters.

'Mine to port,' screamed one. 'Now.'

The skipper swung the wheel and the boat lurched to starboard.

There was an agonizing wait. Eva had dropped her bailer and hung over the side.

'Get back,' he yelled.

She straightened up. 'Phew! That was close. The mine was this far away.' She held up her hands and, incredibly, she was grinning.

Felix liked that, too. 'Idiot,' he said.

The *Ulla Baden* swung about and headed north, weaving and tacking as the lookouts called out warnings. An hour or so later the wind dropped to a breeze. Then it was gone. A faint, shadowy line of land appeared on the horizon. Out of the clear dawn sky, a couple of enemy planes rose like gulls.

The sight of them triggered hot anger in Felix. He hadn't survived the fish hold just to die from a German fighter's strafe.

'Get down below,' he called to Eva.

But she stopped, frozen, mid-deck.

The skipper shouted: 'Run up the German ensign.'

On board there was a collective intake of breath before a frantic burst of activity got the ensign flapping at the top of the mast. The planes roared towards them, dipped their wings in salute and flew by.

Felix lurched over to Eva, who had sunk down onto the deck. 'In future, do as you're told.' Fury and fright made him extra brusque.

She huddled over and dropped her face onto her bent knees. Her shoulders shook.

'Eva . . .'

'This is my fault.' She lifted a pale, tear-stained face. 'I thought I knew my country, but I didn't. *Mor* warned me people did strange things in war. But a doctor . . .'

He sat down beside her and used his good thumb to blot a tear. 'I'm grateful, and your regrets are touching. But you're not going to help by getting killed. Nor by going over and over what happened. That's one of the things to learn. Regrets waste energy.'

'But think of the people I've put in danger. My mother.'

'You're having a reaction to having been in danger,' he said.

She wasn't listening. 'Maybe Arne. Maybe other people I don't know about, and who don't know me. Or you.'

'That's war.'

'Is that all you've got to say?'

'That's all there is to say.'

'War absolves one from blame, then?' She inched closer to him. 'Are you so sure about *that*?' Felix didn't bother to answer. 'Where do you come from, Felix? Is there anyone you're worrying about? Or maybe you don't mind.'

'Best that way.'

'But *anyone*, Felix? A mother? A girlfriend. A wife?'

He shrugged, and immediately regretted the gesture which sent pain shooting down his back. 'One day, maybe, I can tell you.'

'One day? I'll keep you to that.'

The nausea was again gaining a hold over him and he pulled himself upright and retched over the side.

Behind him, Eva continued talking, but more to herself than to him. 'Whatever you say, I was stupid.'

With an effort, he raised his head from the rail. 'You can't think like that or you'll go mad,' he said flatly. 'So don't.'

That silenced her.

By the time the *Ulla Baden* steamed into the harbour at Malmø, Felix wanted only to die. As they helped him down the gangplank and onto shore, Eva cornered the skipper: 'How did you stop the dogs finding us?'

The skipper's tense, salt-flayed features relaxed

414

a trifle. 'We throw a mixture of rabbit's blood and cocaine over the deck. It numbs their noses.' His huge shoulders shook. 'They can't smell a thing and they're off their heads.'

For the first time in weeks, Felix laughed properly.

'Hurry,' said the skipper. 'We're running guns back and we need to make the tides and outwit that out there.' He pointed out to sea.

Felix looked. To his amazement a belt of fog had appeared from nowhere to blot out the horizon. 'You're going back in that?'

'What else?'

'My God, I admire you.'

The last thing Felix managed to do before he passed out was to write the promissory note for their fare. 'There's a contract at the Danish Treasury,' he said. 'It will be repaid once the war is over.'

CHAPTER 24

At the first opportunity, Kay went up to the attic room to check it over.

The quilt was tangled on the floor beside a bloodied piece of rag. Looking at this evidence, Kay let out a long breath of there-but-for-the-grace-of-God.

Tanne, darling . . . where are you?

She picked up the quilt and jumped when something clattered to the floor.

The pistol.

They didn't even have that.

She pushed it into her pocket. Folding the quilt, she knelt by the chest and stowed it inside. A stale lavender aroma wafted up from the interior of the chest. She leaned over and a hard object pressed into her knee. It was a child's marble . . . which had probably belonged to Nils, or possibly to the small, tousle-headed Bror she had been shown in Eberstern family photographs.

Sitting back on her heels, she balanced the marble on her palm and asked it: What now?

The greens and blues to be found in Rosenlund's lake exploded at its frozen heart. Gazing into it, she knew that, if she could never argue that her previous existence had been monochrome, her life had now taken on different colours.

The marble rolled back and forth in her cupped palm, and the colours appeared to melt into one brilliant medley – just like the fusion of politics, action and emotion into which she had pitched herself.

Should she give it all up? Retrieve what peace of mind there was to be had by becoming a spectator?

Dropping the marble into the chest, she closed the lid and went downstairs to hide the pistol in her office.

Later in the morning she fetched her jacket and outdoor shoes and automatically whistled for Sif and Thor.

She was forgetting.

There were no answering barks. No clicking of paws over the black and white tiles.

Sif and Thor were dead. Shot in the melée. Apparently Sif had taken her time to die, which Kay could not bear to think about. But when she did think about it, she had the oddest notion that her heart was physically hardening.

It was nearing the end of May before Kay considered it prudent to travel up to København.

If she took a walk on the estate, she glimpsed figures flitting between the trees. Driving to Køge, a black saloon frequently nudged into her sightline in the mirror. Strange clicks could be heard on the telephone.

They were watching for Tanne.

How much of this surveillance fell under Buch's remit, and how much it was the decidedly more amateur operation of Sergeant Wulf she had, as yet, to work out.

Whoever it was, it was vital to establish in their eyes that she frequently visited København.

Checking into the Damehotellet in København, she phoned Anton in his office.

At half-past seven precisely, dressed for dinner in a long dress and light cape, she arrived at the Hotel d'Angleterre to find him already waiting at the hotel bar.

'We're in the lion's den,' she said, eyes flicking in the direction of a group of German officers who were at the other end of the bar.

'Hidden in plain sight,' he replied.

She glanced down at her feet. 'Anton, I'm still angry with you. Very. You should never have involved Nils.'

'He'll be fine, so stop it.' Anton placed a finger under her chin and tilted it up towards him. 'Now come and sit down.'

He ordered cocktails. Taking a sip of hers, she found herself shivering uncontrollably.

He slid his arm round her. 'Tell.'

Kay knew he knew about events at Rosenlund. 'I'm worried sick about Tanne. Most of the time, I cope. But sometimes . . . I don't.'

'I can't help you. I wish I could.'

'It feels far worse because she wouldn't have got into it but for me.'

'She might have done. Tanne is an adult. She makes up her own mind.'

'Tanne didn't make up her mind to be shot at or—' Kay could not bring herself to say what. 'You know what they do to prisoners?'

'As a matter of fact, I do,' Anton replied calmly. 'Tucked up in Sweden, she's probably worrying about you, too.'

She looked down at her glass. 'I've had my life. Tanne is only just beginning hers.'

'An irritating remark, darling. You've had *part* of your life. There's plenty more to come.'

'You haven't had children.'

There was a silence.

'Kay . . . Almost certainly, Tanne is in Sweden and there's no safer place for her.'

'Thank you for cutting the telephone line. It gave them a breathing space. I was able to say with perfect truth that mice had got at the cables. They do, from time to time.'

'It's a basic rule. Cut off the enemy's communications.'

Kay sipped her martini. 'That bloody doctor. I've trusted him all these years.'

Anton brushed her cheek with a finger. His expression was grim. 'He should be shot. I could arrange it.'

'Don't joke.'

'I'm not.'

She looked up into Anton's face. 'Help me find her.'

He removed his arm. 'No. And you must not look for her either. Kay, you have to stay in control. Otherwise we all go down. It's absolutely imperative we do nothing except look normal. They will be watching. The telephones will have been humming between Køge and here. Probably somebody's watching us at this moment.'

She glanced at the barman who was polishing the glasses. Him? 'Bror suspects I've put the family and the house in danger.'

'Have you considered that, if the Nazis lose the war, Bror will have placed you in just as much danger? His name is writ large all over the place.'

Kay fingered her frosted glass. 'Anton, Bror isn't corrupt. He isn't a fascist either. He wants what's best.'

'The road to hell, and so on.'

'Unfair.'

'Forgive me if I smile, darling. But are you sure you know Bror?'

'As sure as I am that I know you, Anton.'

'That's my point.'

So it was. 'Could I have another martini, please?'

Anton motioned to the waiter. 'You know, darling Kay, things might be about to get worse. The Jews . . . While he's in charge of Denmark, General Best reckons it's in his interest to keep the Danes sweet. But we've heard tell that his SS friends are

420

keen to go over Best's head. That will be a problem for the Jews.'

'How likely is it?'

'We've taken soundings in Berlin. It's on the cards.'

How had Anton got hold of the intelligence from Berlin? 'The Nazis can't do a France or Poland on us, surely?'

'They can.'

'Over our dead bodies.'

'That might not be a joke.'

Kay thought it over. 'Do you have to see a lot of General Best?'

'I make sure I do. It's my safety net.' Anton ate his olive.

'Be careful.' She felt for his hand. 'Anton . . . you will be careful?'

Anton glanced down. 'I like the hand-holding.'

'Listen to me. Bror might be in trouble but you might be, too. The army isn't popular either. Most people don't like it for supporting the government.'

'Keep your voice down, darling.' Anton shrugged. 'There's not much the Danish army can do publicly except resign our commissions. Not so clever because it draws attention to us for no good purpose. However, I do know that interested parties are slowly coming together.'

'Oh?'

A lot of talk. A lot of jostling. A lot of fractious, opposing interests. But was it possible?

Anton continued. 'Think of one united under-ground army.'

'I will.' She retrieved her hand. 'You must take care.'

'I make it my business to look after myself. It's not much good being dead.'

She nodded. 'About Bror and Tanne—'

'Forget Bror.' Anton cut her short in a voice she rarely heard. 'He has made his bed.'

The martini arrived, chilly and strong enough to pucker the insides of her mouth.

Anton pinched her olive. 'You say Tanne's with Felix. He trained in Britain so there's a good chance they'll make for London. The embassy would take care of her there. She won't starve, she could find a job, and sit the war out. It might be the very thing for her. She might meet an English duke or an earl. Wouldn't that cheer you up?' He became serious. 'What happens to you and Bror is another matter.'

The bar was filing up with well-dressed, animated men and women in evening dress and uniforms. The waiters clinked glasses, rattled the cocktail shaker, clattered ice. There was an agreeable hum of civilized conversation and laughter. It was a scene with which she was totally familiar, and yet from which she was estranged. Without realizing it, Kay had moved on from this kind of life, exchanging it for one in which she was out in the dark and the unknown, running the gauntlet.

What did they need in this new life? Guns. Explosives. Money.

She leaned over towards him. 'Listen . . .' she said very softly, 'I've an idea for a drop zone. The lake at Rosenlund. Not now maybe, but when things have died down.'

She had taken him completely by surprise. 'Have you gone mad?'

'Think about it. It's reasonably remote, has one good road, plenty of back ones, and would be recognizable from the air.'

Good: she had captured his attention.

'Attach a buoy to the containers, organize rowers to collect them and hide the stuff on the estate until it can be distributed. But not in winter, of course.'

'Wouldn't it take too long to get the stuff out of the water?'

'If it's done properly I am pretty sure we could get it out before any vehicle from Køge could get there. Anyway, we could probably leave one or two buoys in the lake. The odds are no one would notice them because they wouldn't be looking for them.'

Anton stared into his martini. 'High summer means light nights and the RAF won't fly. Sitting ducks. Obviously, winter is out. But we still have a few weeks in the early autumn or spring. What about Bror? Won't you be throwing him to the lions?'

'Plenty of planes fly over the house. It would be nothing new.'

'Wouldn't Bror notice if his dear wife wasn't in bed with him?'

She allowed the pause to drift on until it became a silence.

He cocked an eyebrow at her. 'Oh, he's not in your bed?'

'Actually . . . at the moment, he's sleeping on the other side of the house.'

'I see.' Naturally, this private information amused him.

'No, you don't see, Anton.'

'All right. I don't see.'

'I gave him to think that you and I were having an affair. It made it easier.' She glanced down at her ring. 'Estrangement is easier.'

The glint in his eye was less amused. 'Poor old Bror. What crosses he has to bear.'

Anton ordered a third martini for himself.

Kay waited until it arrived. 'Shall I get the drop zone coordinates to London?' She mimed playing the piano.

He nodded. 'They'll need to send over a reconnaissance plane and check it out before anything can be arranged.' He watched her over the rim of the glass. 'Kay, if you're ever in trouble, I can't help.'

Anton made such a meal of this. 'So you've said.'

'If you are in trouble, go to Café Amadeus on the Bredgade and ask for Oskar. Remember that.'

She nodded.

He edged closer and she tried to ward him off, but he said, 'We're having an affair, remember?' His mouth was close to hers. 'Anything else to report?'

'London still has to send over the crystals for

the new wireless transmitters. Felix thought they would be ready very soon.'

'Let's hope so. Never has anything been so keenly anticipated.' Anton raised Kay's hand to his lips. 'For the time being, I suggest you mend a few fences with farmer Bror. Keep on good terms.'

Another silence.

'Darling, you can swear that I'm a cad and it was my fault. Say whatever you like – you can think of something – but, if I know my cousin, he will fall over himself to give you the benefit of the doubt. Keeping him sweet gives you room for manoeuvre.'

Her hand remained in his both for comfort and for security. She needed to reassure herself that she could handle what was coming.

She phoned Bror from the Damehotellet to tell him she would be arriving at Køge the following day on the two o'clock train.

She slept fitfully, breakfasted on *ymer* sprinkled with brown sugar and drank two cups of bitter coffee. Checking out of the hotel, she took a taxi to the Gothersgade, where she bought a hat from a favourite milliner. It was a straw one, sufficiently frivolous to be diverting.

Leaving the milliner's, she flagged down a second taxi and instructed the driver to take her to the university. As she paid him, she glanced towards the university entrance and she almost dropped her purse.

Clutching a sheaf of papers, and accompanied by General Gottfried and a lower-ranking officer, Nils emerged out of the main doorway into the street, where the three men conducted an animated conversation. At one point, Nils stabbed his finger down on a paper. The general nodded. Finally, they shook hands and the Germans got into a car which drove off. Nils transferred his papers from one hand to the other, took the steps back up to the entrance two at a time and disappeared into the building.

The taxi driver's finger tapped on the wheel and the look on his face was unmistakable. *Stikker.*

Kay snapped her bag shut. That Nils was cooperating was unthinkable. Yet it *was* thinkable, for Nils had his own way of going about things. He lived by his own logic, and saw the world differently. That much was true.

One day there would be retribution. Glancing at the taxi driver's grim visage, she had a disturbing vision of post-war Denmark split by additional hatreds and vendettas.

Leaning forward, she instructed him to continue to the station. As he drove off, she did not allow herself to look back.

The road to Køge ran parallel to the railway track for a good portion of the way. Apparently there had been an explosion on it and, while the train did its customary crawl, Kay watched armoured German vehicles speeding to the scene.

Sabotage? She hoped so.

She pressed a finger against the pane. Who would be responsible for it? The communists? The nation-alists? The strange organization that she was working for? Felix would be pleased. 'Sabotage would put Denmark on the map and get London to sit up,' he had told her once.

She caught a glimpse of her pale, drawn face in the train window. Could Tanne send word? Had Felix got out? She was pretty sure he would head for Sweden if he had. Surely Tanne would have gone with him?

Shockingly, she felt dislike – revulsion almost – for Rosenlund creep over her: its night silence; its petrified winter forests; the obligations that came with its occupancy; the grip of its past. Bror's obsession with it.

They were approaching the outskirts of Køge and Kay collected herself.

The train was late. Behind a checkpoint manned by soldiers in German *feldgrau* uniforms was Bror, cigarette in hand. Pulling on her pale green gloves, she adjusted the frivolous straw hat. There was no rule to say that one shouldn't deal with the enemy well dressed. Trusting to fate that none of them recognized her from the roadblock incident with Arne, she walked towards them and joined the queue.

The train blew its whistle – a desolate sound, she thought – and clunked slowly out of the station.

The wait was tedious. The soldiers were perfectly well aware of this but made no effort to hurry over the searches and papers. A woman carrying a sick-looking child was ordered to empty her basket. Kay offered to hold the child while the mother was searched.

The man in front of Kay wore a long gaberdine mackintosh. He was given the once-over: inevitable, perhaps, because he looked Jewish.

'No, no . . .' A screech of terror rose from the man. '*No.*'

Two of the soldiers stepped forward, hooked their arms under his elbows and dragged him off, his knees buckling. 'Help me . . . help me . . .' he called.

No one moved.

The trio vanished out of sight.

She could hear the thoughts of the silent onlookers. *Bloody communist. Bloody Jew. Had it coming. Daren't do anything. Hate them . . .* A spectrum of unvoiced responses.

When it was Kay's turn, she handed over her papers. The younger German examined them and conferred with his officer.

'Open your suitcase,' ordered the officer in bad Danish.

Kay lifted it onto the table and watched the men go through it. One silk nightdress. A tin of cold cream. Underwear. Her black dress.

'Unlock this box, please.'

Kay took off her gloves and complied, opening the box which contained her pearl necklace and earrings.

From his position by the barrier, Bror was keeping a close eye on proceedings.

'Are you satisfied, gentlemen?' she asked eventually, in German.

'Not quite. Where have you been?' She explained and was asked to repeat herself. 'Are you sure?'

'Quite sure.'

'Take off your coat,' ordered the officer.

They searched the coat's pockets and patted the seams and hem.

Nothing.

'Take off your hat.'

Her hair snagged on the hat pin and she was forced to work it free. The German snatched it away and ran a finger around the headband.

Nothing.

He handed it back.

'You may go.'

She couldn't bear to put the hat back on. Stiff with hatred, she picked up her gloves and the case and made her way towards Bror. He made no move to kiss her, but handed her into the car and they drove mostly in silence to Rosenlund, where he parked by the front door.

Reluctant to make the first move, reluctant to break the deep ice, they both lingered by the car in the sunshine.

Bror gave in first. 'Wulf has been on the phone. He told me they pieced together some evidence. A girl answering to Tanne's description was seen catching a train to København.'

'A girl, you say. How many girls are there in Denmark? When did they see her?'

'The morning after Tanne vanished.'

'Why have they taken so long to tell us this amazing fact?'

'Because they're watching us, to see if she comes back. Kay, I want to know if you went up to København to see her?'

She calculated the odds. Would Wulf have relayed the information on? Or would an old loyalty keep him silent?

'No, I didn't.' She turned and walked towards the garden.

Tanne had probably got away. Yes? No? Yes . . .

Bror caught up with Kay. As they so often did, they walked through the garden, past the irises and blowsy-headed peonies, past the beds which later would bloom with white cosmos and brightly coloured zinnias, drawn as always down to the lake.

The water was calm and transparent and Sophia-Maria's island appeared to float on it.

For once, the light was dazzling.

Bror bent down to inspect the nesting area in the rushes. How often had she seen him do that? As he stood upright he asked, 'Have I lost you?'

Her eyes were watering because of the sun. 'I'm not sure.'

Bror unleashed some uncharacteristic bitterness. 'It's your doing that Tanne has gone.'

'No,' she contradicted. 'War did it.'

'Maybe,' he acknowledged.

When she first arrived in Denmark, Kay had no idea what was meant by a Danish winter, no idea how the landscape changed from one of greens, yellows and cobalt blue, to the uniform, freezing melancholy of Lutheran grey and dun. Some years, as the outer darkness closed in, she had caught herself falling into a matching inner darkness. Struggling to survive those episodes, she had learned that she must neither panic nor give in.

Kay picked up a stone, a grey one streaked with white. Unlike a stone from the seaside, it had a sharp edge. She heard Anton's voice in her ear: 'Keep on good terms.'

'Darling Bror, we must not be at odds.' Unfolding her hand, the stone balancing on the palm, she offered it to him. 'Can we build a bridge?'

Looking across the sparkling water, she fantasized that, one day, he and she might live together in harmony again.

'We can stay here, out of sight, and work to keep the farms as productive as possible. That can be our contribution.'

He thought about it.

Accepting the stone, he hefted it from one hand to the other before sending it skimming away over the surface of the water.

Before dinner, she went up to her office and encoded her message.

Do you wish for the peace of my kiss?

431

With extreme effort. Teeth clamped together. Nervous.

Remember the five words.

Indicators.

Transposition.

Double transposition.

She longed for Felix's help. For Nils's wizardry with mathematical patterns. For Johan, her Morse teacher, and his calm instructions. For a degree of competence.

Message number . . . what number had Felix got to? She grabbed one at random. Fifty. Felix couldn't have sent more than fifty?

SUGGEST NEW DZ 1004993 *stop* PLEASE CHECK IT *stop* NO MORE MESSAGES FOR FORESEEABLE FUTURE *stop* ON THE RUN *stop* MAYONNAISE

That done, she went down to dinner and talked to Bror about crop yields and the mystery illness which was plaguing a couple of the cow herds. Afterwards, she pleaded fatigue and said she was going to have an early night.

Bror was looking at her with a peculiar intensity. There was a question mark and a supplication.

Was he asking to join her in her bed?

Not now. Not now. Having calculated that the surveillance on the estate would not be so efficient at night, she had to use the night hours.

Deliberately, she turned away. 'I'll see you in the

morning, Bror,' she said, cool and distant. A second elapsed before she added, 'I sleep so much better on my own. Don't you?'

It was after midnight when she crept down the steps outside her office and, the torch beam muffled with a handkerchief, made her way as fast as possible to Ove's cottage.

In the outside privy, she placed the wireless set on the wooden lavatory seat and wedged the torch into the case lid so its light fell over the dials.

What next? Ready the set. Aerial out. Dial tuned. A cool mind. A steady hand. The normal sked time had long passed and she selected the night-time emergency crystal.

ZYA QTC1 . . .

From ZYA, I have one message for you.

Nothing.

Again, the arduous keying in: ZYA QTC1.

Somewhere, someone was patrolling the emergency frequencies.

Hurry up . . . please.

QVR.

Ah . . . she had been picked up.

A lump heaved into Kay's throat. *Home.* Home was where they knew what they thought, who they were fighting, and to whom they should listen. Not like here. Not like fractured Denmark.

She did her best. Her finger felt useless on the transmitter key. Clumsy. Slow. Sweat ran down from her armpits. My God, she was bad at it. And surely everyone within a radius of a hundred metres would catch the fizzing ether in her head-phones, the tap of the key.

Somewhere out there, General Gottfried's crack unit had almost certainly latched onto the stumbling transmission. Had they fixed on it yet?

When it was over, her hands dropped into her lap.

She had gone over the drill with Felix. He had taught her that, if the emergency frequency was used, a pianist had to wait seventy minutes for a reply.

He explained what happened at the listening station when the emergency frequency was used. With someone standing by to type into the tele-printer, a cipher clerk at Home Station would decode at top speed. At headquarters top-priority systems would swing into action. A reply from the bosses would be formulated, encoded and transmitted.

The Morse began to pulse in her ears.

QTC1. *I have one message for you.*

Headphones on, she strained to hear the incoming message.

It was done. Finally. QSL. *I acknowledge receipt.* AR. *Over and out.*

She ticked the boxes.

Pack up methodically. Stow aerial and flex. Disconnect headphones. Remove crystal.

Where should she hide the wireless set? In the pigeon loft? Or leave it here?

Here.

She tore the outgoing message into shreds and tamped it down into the earth under the trees, folded the incoming message into a spill and tucked it into the cotton scarf round her neck.

Back in her bedroom, Kay undressed, sat down at her dressing table and began to decode the incoming message. It was laborious, mind-numbing work and she wasn't sure she was going to be able to do it.

But she did.

ABANDON AREA *stop* RETURN LONDON FOR DEBRIEF *stop* USE SWEDISH BUS *stop* CONTACT RICHARD *stop*

The message was too late to get to Felix but it helped Kay. London was looking out for him and, if Tanne was with Felix, they would take care of her.

Her gloves lay on the dressing table. With a practised movement, she wedged the decoded message into the first finger of the right-hand one and dropped it back down on the dressing table.

Bed . . . sleep . . . at last.

She was drifting . . . drowsing. The door opened and in came Bror. Casting aside his dressing gown, he lay down beside her.

She lay stiff with surprise. 'Bror . . . why are you here?' The relief that he was there. The terror that he was.

'Kay . . . darling Kay . . . this can't go on.'

435

He was so familiar, and yet so alien. They had travelled so far apart – and she thought her heart would break.

After a while, he put out an arm. 'This is madness. How have we let this happen?' He stroked her cheek. 'I can't lose you and Tanne.'

A bridge was being built. Fragile and shaky, it might not stand too many shocks.

It was so dark, Kay could not see him, only feel him – the length of his limbs, the flexed arm and the butterfly trails made by his fingers on her skin.

Exhaustion seeped through her. She loved Bror. Because she loved him, she could give him one thing. She could grant him some peace of mind. 'Bror, I suspect Tanne's in Sweden.'

'Suspect or know?'

'I can't tell you for sure.'

The stroking on her cheek ceased. 'I wondered. Sweden was the obvious place.'

They were whispering into the dark, moving closer.

'I know people are getting themselves over there,' he said.

'Then you'll know it's the best thing? Tanne will be safe, particularly if her politics are changing. Once the war is over, she can come back and she will have a clean sheet. She won't be—' Kay laid her hand flat against Bror's chest '—contaminated, I suppose.'

'And I am?'

'Let's not think about that now.'

He fell asleep with his head on her shoulder. She listened to his steady breathing and cradled her arm carefully round his body, holding him as if she would never let him go.

My God, that was close. That was very close.

CHAPTER 25

In early May, Mary received an unexpected communication.

Years ago, Mary's cousin Vera had married 'up' and left London – leaving behind Mary and an assortment of other cousins in their cramped Brixton terraces – and vanished into the roomier domain of a detached house and garden near Henford. Vera had always been the brainier one, and more determined. Since then, the family had not seen much of Vera, certainly not since the outbreak of war. Her letter inviting Mary to tea therefore came as a surprise, particularly as Mary had not been aware that Vera knew she was in the area.

The bus drove past rows of houses and bungalows with their lines of washing and scrubbed front steps, past the post boxes, telephone kiosks and scrubby vegetable patches. Once outside Henford, buildings yielded to green stubbled fields, and to ditches and hedgerows where Queen Anne's lace foamed in profusion.

Everything on this late spring day was bright and fresh – which Mary appreciated. Truly she did, and it lifted her spirits.

Yet she couldn't forget that the world was in a mess. Could the politicians do anything about it? Reposing in Mary's bag was a copy of Mr Beveridge's report on social policy. Apparently, in a new post-war Britain, poverty, disease and squalor would be given their marching orders, backed up by a new contributory scheme which would offer a safety net from the cradle to the grave.

Mary liked the sound of Mr Beveridge's thinking. If implemented, it would mean she wouldn't need to be quite so anxious about her future. She also approved the idea that she would be contributing to that future. And other's. *Mary Voss . . .* she murmured. *You matter.*

The walk from the bus stop to Vera's house turned out be half a mile or so and it was warm. Mary's one good blouse was made of Viyella and, within minutes, she was perspiring. Her not-always-successful solution to this universal problem was to sew pads into her clothing and to use plenty of talcum powder – if she could get hold of it – or bicarbonate. Praying that her perspiration wasn't too obvious, she walked up the path to Vera's front door.

'Mary . . . you're here already.'

Vera, a harassed-looking redhead with a redhead's translucent skin, had emerged from a room at the back of the house, wiping her hands on her apron. 'The bus must have been quicker than usual.' She drew Mary into the parlour. 'Let me look at you. It must be a couple of years.'

They were interrupted by the telephone ringing in the hall. An odd, worried look whisked over Vera's face. Pushing Mary into a chair, she went to answer it. Mary heard her say: 'Darling, *six* at dawn . . .'

Mary was amused to note that Vera's accent fluted in a way it never had when she was a child in Brixton.

'. . . *before* dawn? I'd better make the beds but I haven't had a chance to wash the sheets from the last lot yet. Too bad. They'll be too tired to notice. Will the new butcher give me extra bacon? I'm sure he suspects. Is he the silent type, do you think? I'll lay the table now. I've got one for this evening. The one last night broke my heart. He had a wild and haunted look . . . I was worried sick that his nerves were shot. They will look out for him, won't they? I must go. Mary's arrived for tea . . .' There was a pause before Vera said: 'Mary Voss, my cousin. You remember Mary?'

Probably not, thought Mary a touch acidly.

Vera's feet beat a rapid path down the passage. Mary went after her and discovered Vera in the kitchen filling the kettle. At Mary's entrance, she wheeled round. 'You startled me.'

'Sorry.'

'No, no. Not at all. I'm just getting tea . . . I'm sorry to say that I'm a bit behind today, Mary. John and I have had a lot on. The hens, I'm so late with them . . . Trouble with animals is that they don't understand if they're not fed.'

'If you like, I'll do the hens.'

'Would you? That is *awfully* nice of you. I'm afraid I've got some unexpected visitors coming later.'

'Who?'

Vera shrugged. 'Just people. They're travelling here and there, you know, and John and I put them up.' She made a vague gesture. 'The war effort.'

'How mysterious.'

Vera whisked off a cloth covering a plate of sandwiches. They were curling just a touch at the edges. 'It's nice to see you, Mary.'

'How did you know where to find me?'

There was a pause. 'I think I saw you in Henford before Christmas. You were in uniform and I reckoned you were working at the big house.' Vera appeared cagey about the details. She thrust a bowl at Mary. '*Would* you?'

Mary found herself by the chicken coop scattering the grain. A hen orchestra tuned up as a cluster of hens scuttled towards the food. A tiny bantam, no more than a handful of feathers, clucked by Mary's feet and she bent over and touched it with a fingertip. The little thing was so warm and soft and, in contrast to the life Mary was now leading, real.

She straightened up. Vera *had* done well. Even if the hedges needed a trim, moles had been at work all over the lawn and the hens had churned up a great patch under the oak tree, there was a spacious and generous feel to the garden.

From one of the straggle of outhouses, pigeons were sounding. It was a good noise, especially on a lovely day like this one. Curiosity piqued, Mary strolled over to the shed and poked her nose inside.

To her astonishment, it contained a row of large cages, several of which were inhabited by birds. On a bench in the middle were stacked leather carrier boxes, water bottles and blocks of hard feed.

Since when had Vera and John kept racing pigeons? Mary drifted over to the cages. At her approach, a couple of the birds fluttered their wings and called out.

A big buff-coloured male caught her eye. He had bright eyes and a strong-looking neck but there was a sore on his leg as if something had rubbed up against it. A piece of paper had fallen onto the floor of his cage. Mary squinted at it and experienced a small electric shock.

It was impossible not to recognize what it was.

Mary had sent and received enough signals to know that the neat columns of apparently random letters were an incoming message from the field, or perhaps an outgoing one. She had no idea which. What she did know was that this was a bad security breach . . . and Vera was obviously involved in secret work using pigeons to send messages.

Up to her neck in it, Vera was.

'Mary! What are you doing?'

Vera had come up behind her.

Mary did not look round. 'I had no idea you kept pigeons.'

'Well, we do.' Vera was very short.

Mary indicated the paper in the cage. 'Vera . . . Should you?'

Quick as a flash, Vera interposed herself between Mary and the cage. 'You've seen *nothing*, Mary. Do you understand?'

'I do.' She thought of the long hours of listening. 'Believe me.'

Vera swallowed. 'It was a mistake. Do you understand?'

Secrets. They were everywhere. The war was being fought with secrets. Big ones, negligible ones . . . ones that people died to keep. Those in the know had to keep silence and were forbidden to link up any tiny nuggets of evidence to assemble a bigger picture, however tempting.

The equation balanced. Mary knew she must not let on that she knew the pigeons in Vera's back garden were probably flying messages to and from occupied Europe. In return, Vera must be ignorant of where Mary worked.

Vera succeeded in pushing Mary out of the shed and shut the door. She leaned back against it. 'Mary, I have to trust you. Can I?'

'Yes.'

Both of them sounded very self-conscious – which made Mary want to giggle. But it wasn't a joke. 'That message . . . you must hide it.'

Vera blushed bright red. 'An oversight.'

Oh Lord, Mary thought. *I'm relishing this.* During their childhood, Vera had always been the cousin held up as an example by the adults, and the rest of them had suffered from it.

Vera scuffed a patch of earth with the toe of her shoe. 'It hasn't ever happened . . . it won't happen again.' Vera's embarrassment rose in waves and Mary couldn't help but enjoy it. Just a little.

Vera had a go at turning the conversation to normal. 'Did you feed the hens?'

'Yes, I did.'

The little bantam chose that moment to cluck across their path. 'It's so sweet,' said Mary.

With obvious relief, Vera said: 'That's Meeny. Miny and Mo are over there. I'm afraid Eeny died.' She touched Mary on the shoulder. 'Kettle's boiled and you've earned your tea.'

Her moment of triumph shelved, Mary sought to break the tension. 'It's quite a haven here.'

Vera gave a strained laugh. 'Rabbits, squirrels, some frogs . . .'

'We have bluebottles in the canteen which we can't get rid of and one of the girls swears she's also spotted fleas.'

'The real enemy.'

The cousins' eyes met in a glancing exchange. How strange war was, how very strange. Its reach was like leaking water which appeared in surprising places and a long way from its original source.

After a lull, traffic was hotting up at Station 53d and Signalmaster Noble was in a bad temper. Having shouted at Nancy for inattention, he left

444

the room to deliver the latest messages to the decoders.

'*Men!*' Nancy dropped her head into her hands and tugged at her hair.

'Men have two feet, two hands and, sometimes, two women, but never more than one shilling or one idea at the same time,' Mary sat down and checked over her pencils.

Nancy raised her head. 'Not *bad*,' she said admiringly. She raised her voice. 'Here, Beryl! Listen to what Mary's just come up with.'

Mary wasn't displeased. Quite the opposite. The girls' reaction, and her satisfaction in it, was very pleasing.

'You're doing a lot of extra shifts.' Nancy's head was back in her hands.

'So are you,' Mary replied.

'I'm doing it for the extra pay.'

Pleasing though it was to bank, the extra pay wasn't the main reason Mary took on the additional shifts. Disciplined and seasoned as she was, the work flowed through her fingers. By her own efforts, she had turned herself into one of the most reliable of operators. She loved that and the reward in doing something well. Yet it was the bond with 'her' agents which was always at the back of Mary's mind. That bond – whose demands and imperatives pushed her into flights of feeling that could take her breath away.

Now the days were getting longer, Mary reckoned that the agents would be freer to move around and to plan operations. Not that she had any concrete evidence. Maybe – and she hoped they would – they would take pleasure and gain some respite and relief from the sight of wheeling swallows, meadows sweet with hay, sheep at pasture, from the arrival of fresh vegetables and fruit, the warmth of city streets . . .

'Voss!' Signalmaster Noble had returned. 'You have ten minutes before your next sked. Get me a cup of tea. Smartish.'

He was out of order. Mary knew it and he knew it. The difference: he could get away with it.

Ten minutes meant ten minutes. Taking the quickest route to the canteen, Mary had to pass a small office at the top of the stairs. The door to this office was ajar. A raised male voice sounded from inside.

'The situation is a mess.' The speaker was clearly exasperated. 'According to Mayonnaise, Copenhagen is stuffed with informers. He also reported that one of the agents on Jutland had to be eliminated and the last drop was a disaster. Everyone's furious. The RAF bods are threatening to withhold planes. Only Vinegar is up and running.'

'And uncompromised?'

'As far as we know . . .'

Vinegar. Mayonnaise. On hearing these names, Mary's heart quickened.

Her footsteps on the wooden floor gave away her presence and the door slammed shut.

'Spies Are Everywhere' ran the legend on the

446

latest warning poster in the canteen. Well, she wasn't a spy but, in a short space of time, she had stumbled across two pieces of interesting information.

Copenhagen.

Was it possible that Vinegar and Mayonnaise were operating in Denmark?

At the next opportunity, she visited the local library and scoured the papers for any hints of relevant activity, puzzling over the references to Sweden and 'flows of information'. At first, she took this to mean radio traffic. Having consulted a map, and read one or two articles which dropped broad hints, she revised her opinion. 'Flows of information' looked more likely to be the result of fishing boats slipping away from the Danish coast into the Øresund, or stealing around the minefields in the Kattegat, and making their way to Sweden.

How did intelligence work? Mary was groping towards understanding how important it was to possess the ability to sift random facts and to make sense of them. The ratchets in her mind clicked onwards. For example: Vera was keeping messenger pigeons, and was almost certainly involved in war work. She was also entertaining 'visitors' who might, or might not, be engaged in secret work, too. Was it possible it had been Vera who had recommended Mary for Morse training? Vera knew about her father . . .

During the second week in May, Mary realized she had lost Mayonnaise. Or rather, he had gone silent.

'Sir,' she reported to Signalmaster Noble. 'Mayonnaise has missed two skeds.'

He frowned. 'Right, then. We'll get that logged.'

Mary's frustration was intense at not being able to ask why Mayonnaise had gone silent – at not being able to make any kind of comment.

She was allocated another agent. Different call sign, different fist. 'Just do your best, Voss, and don't say anything.' Signalmaster Noble smiled sardonically. 'It's not your place.'

Mayonnaise's silence affected Mary badly. She was terrified he was captured or on the run without a wireless set.

Where did you hide in a country that, she knew from her research, was uniformly flat? Surely there had to be woods, even a forest? And there must be places to hide along the coastline?

The pain she felt at losing an agent took even her by surprise. It got to her in many ways. Music . . . she found herself unable to listen to Beethoven's Fifth on the radio, for example, or Schubert's Quintet, or even Vera Lynn, without choking up. Appetite . . . she had to force herself to eat. Sleep . . . that was a subject best left, so bad were her sleep patterns.

Thank God, Vinegar still observed his skeds to the second. Please, she sent him a silent message, keep to the rules. Keep your mouth tight shut and cover your traces and tracks.

In idle moments, Mary fleshed him out. Her mental construct was of a man who was not particu-

448

larly tall or good-looking, but someone who was generous, physically adept and clever. From time to time, the details altered but one thing was for sure: he was nothing like the men with whom she worked. Vinegar wouldn't be wearing uniform and there would be none of that strutting that went with it.

This, she knew, was to create a soft-focus image. Yet now that she could picture him in her mind, the moments of loss and despair, experienced so often by Mary, began to dissolve. Thus, she arrived at the beginning of another life.

All thoughts of anything else were driven from her head when, during one shift towards the end of May, Mary was making a routine patrol of the emergency frequency and Mayonnaise came back on the air.

Thank God. Thank God.

Every sense straining, she took down the Morse. The signal was good, the best she had heard it for some time. Then, quite suddenly, Mary's stomach lurched.

This wasn't Mayonnaise. Halting, uneven, and with none of his characteristic confidence.

This fist was quite, quite different.

CHAPTER 26

Ruby's frustration was growing. As far as she could make out, nothing was being done about the problems of the poem code.

She had learned one thing. Even an organization like The Firm became clotted with systems and bureaucracy, however much it protested that it was different.

'How does anything ever get done anywhere?' she demanded of Peter.

'By patience,' he replied. 'Cunning. Guile.'

'For God's sake', she whipped back, sharp and sarcastic. 'Changing the agents' coding practice isn't caprice. It isn't bloody-mindedness.'

Patience. Cunning. Guile.

First off: employ mathematical principles to clarify the position, define the problem and improve the reasoning.

Shifting onto the moral ground, she asked the question: Why rank knowledge that would save lives below obedience?

Thirdly . . . thirdly . . . it was more than the sum of those two. Weren't they – and by that

Ruby meant all of them who worked in The Firm – collectively responsible? On to their consciences would be stamped the pain and the terror of the agents.

If the agents were prepared to take risks, those on the home front were morally obliged to do so, too. Anyway, it would give her a great deal of satisfaction to force all those arrogant, blinkered males to look at the problems again.

Knowing all too well that if she was caught, or made a mistake, her life would disappear into a black hole, Ruby worked out a plan.

The timing was crucial. Calculating that, after a fiendish early morning start, the galley slaves in Intelligence would be gasping for tea and their guards would be down, she phoned at eleven o'clock precisely and requested all the Danish back traffic since 1942.

'Permission?' said the male voice at the end of the phone.

'Major Martin.' She was amazed how the lie tripped off her tongue. 'I can bring up a tray of tea.'

Pause.

Please do not ask for a signed memo.

'Not strictly allowed,' said the voice at the other end. 'But I'll give you an hour and a desk.' He laughed. 'We like visits from a cipherine.'

'Good.' She did not add, *you patronizing bugger.*

Having got herself there, Ruby was faced by a

desk, her two sharpened pencils, her notebook and a pile of messages. Now she had to get on with it, and she was terrified.

But she had her wits. Her sharp, twitching wits.

Compared to other sections, Danish back traffic turned out to be pitifully sparse. With regard to the agents and any intelligence it revealed that nothing much had flourished in Denmark until early 1943. It appeared that there had been four wireless sets in total operating for The Firm. Two had gone silent in the summer of 1942. The two pianists who remained, Mayonnaise (call sign ZYA) and Vinegar (call sign XRT), had been operating since the autumn of 1942.

Flexing her fingers, Ruby detailed the procedures and protocols in her head.

All agents were issued with two security checks which came in the form of deliberate mistakes – for example, they would make a mistake with every sixteenth letter. The first of these was a bluff security check which, if necessary, they could give to the enemy if they were captured and tortured. The second was the real security check which they should try to keep back.

Stacked in date order, the messages were crisscrossed in blue crayon by Intelligence.

Message Number: 8
25 November 1942
REGRET TO INFORM TABLE LEAF CAUGHT AT RADIO BACK IN JUNE *stop*

DIED BY OWN HAND *stop* SET CAPTURED *stop* MAYONNAISE

Both security checks included. One mistake in transmission which the signal clerk had corrected.

Message Number: 9
4 December 1942
URGENT NEED FOR RADIOS *stop* TOO DANGEROUS TO MOVE SETS AROUND *stop* RECRUITING GOING WELL *stop* MAYONNAISE

Both security checks in place.
And so on through a sequence of numbered messages.

Message Number: 38
27 April 1943
MUSTARD HAS BEEN WIPED OFF PLATE *stop* MAYONNAISE

Both security checks were present. Message had several coding mistakes.

Message Number: 39
2 May 1943
DROP PARTIAL SUCCESS *stop* LYING LOW *stop* INJURED *stop* NON LIFE THREATENING *stop* HAVE WIRELESS *stop* MAYONNAISE

Neither security checks were present.

Message Number: 50

50? Ruby noted the leap in numbering.

SUGGEST NEW DZ 1004993 *stop* PLEASE CHECK IT *stop* NO MORE MESSAGES FOR FORESEEABLE FUTURE *stop* ON THE RUN *stop* MAYONNAISE

This one was a mess. No security checks were present. There were seven coding mistakes and five mistakes in transmission. Intelligence had noted the omissions.

Ruby glanced at her watch. Her pencils were wearing down and the minutes were ticking by. From time to time, some of the clerks sent her a curious glance. Sweat sprouted under her arms but she pressed on.

She turned her attention to Vinegar, who had sent forty-five messages, many of them quite short. Having taken the precaution of looking at Vinegar's test coding exercises, she checked over a few of the more typical messages. She realized that something did not quite add up. Was it the content of the messages?

Vinegar's traffic suggested that, to all extents and purposes, he was having an easy time. He was almost lyrical about the smooth running of his network, repeatedly requesting an arms drop and money. He fed in snippets of information about train and troop movements – although nothing very substantial, Ruby noted. However, when he was requested to return to London for briefing, he refused on the grounds that it would compromise the circuit.

Of Mayonnaise's messages three were indecipherables – which was about the norm for agents in the field – and the final one was, frankly, a puzzle which would have to be investigated. Apart from the last two, both the bluff and real security checks were always present and correct.

A rapid check of Vinegar's back traffic revealed that both bluff and real security checks were always in place. Furthermore, in direct contrast to Mayonnaise, *there had not been one single coding mistake in the transmissions.*

This was highly unusual.

How would an agent never make a coding mistake, unless they were a demigod? Good question.

Another odd thing was that very often in the later transmissions Vinegar always spelled 'stop' incorrectly: *stip, stap, stup.* Why was that? Given his exactitude, it was uncharacteristic and odd. Atmospherics?

She ran a second check. None of the earlier transmissions showed this mistake.

Stubbornly, to the last second, Ruby continued to comb back through the traffic. What was nagging at her? What was she failing to see?

Time up.

Knees like jelly, she made her way back to her own desk and dropped her head into her hands.

Her mind was full of images . . . choking . . . fearful . . .

Shots. An agent fleeing. The darkness of a prison cell. Dying on the run. An agent dropping out of the sky while the enemy waited below. A broken leg being twisted round as a preliminary . . .

The air in the office was stale . . . almost stifling. Ruby sprang to her feet. 'I need some exercise,' she told Gussie.

'Is that what they call it?' Gussie did not raise her head.

Ruby paced up and down the corridor. Restricted, stuffy, dim and dingy the office may have been, but at least it was in the free world.

Think.

What was eluding her? What had she not understood?

What do agents do under pressure? How do agents behave under pressure?

She remembered that during one of their many meetings Peter had told her: 'No agent in the field is ever perfect, particularly if he has a variable training record.'

Use her knowledge. What did she know for sure? She recollected Eloise, so anxious and unsure and frightened that she would not match up to the task.

Human beings tended to plump for easy options

at the best of times, let alone when their confidence was low. Eloise had taught Ruby that lesson. Under pressure, agents were almost certain to choose: a) the shortest words, b) the easiest to spell, c) the words which held emotional meaning whether they were aware of it or not.

Above all, they made mistakes.

On the way back to her office, she stopped off in Stationery and requested typing paper.

'You need a docket,' said the clerk, a youth in badly fitting khakis. He was not only spotty but looked the obstinate type.

'Tell you what,' said Ruby. 'I'll take you out for a drink.'

She got the paper.

The hours came and went and Ruby typed on late into the evening.

As she did so, conclusions fell into place.

Eventually, the night duty officer, a bouncy type who always set her teeth on edge, sidled up to her desk. 'Time for the off, miss.'

Frowning she looked up. 'Two minutes.'

He gave Ruby the once-over. She could read his thoughts: *Double agent and/or conducting an affair with one of the top brass still in conference upstairs?*

Rumour had it that a major and a FANY lovely had been found *in flagrante* on a desk.

Had this charmer been the one who found them?

'Righty-ho,' he said, which meant: *Which one is going to get his hand up her skirt?*

At nine o'clock the following morning, she put

457

in a request to see Peter in his office and was allocated ten minutes. Gussie shut Peter's diary with an emphatic click. 'And not one second longer.'

She stepped into his office. It was dusty, smoky and stacked with files marked 'Top Secret'.

'You could do with a cleaner,' she said.

Peter was writing rapidly with a fountain pen. He held up a finger. The sight of the thick dark hair brushed back hard against his head stirred up feelings which Ruby had no wish to deal with at this moment.

Gussie stuck her head round the door. 'Sir, I'm booting her out in ten minutes.'

Ruby looked over to the map on the wall which was covered with different-coloured pins. Agents? Several clusters in France. Far fewer in Greece and Albania. A couple in Italy. One in Germany – how did anyone survive there? Not enough to constitute a cluster in Denmark.

This war had gone on for so long. Could anyone remember houses with lights shining through windows at night? Or a city without rubble? Although the situation had taken a turn for the better with Monty's progress in North Africa and with Italy's surrender, there didn't seem to be much comfort on the home front. Could the unsubstantiated, but persistent, hints of atrocities in Eastern Europe be true? Other than Peter, the one or two people with whom she had discussed it had been adamant that such things were not possible.

Surely they were possible. But probable?

'Ruby?' Peter looked up with a smile that said: *I'm glad you're here.*

She placed her typewritten report in front of him. 'Read this.'

He rifled through. The smile switched off. 'Christ Almighty, where did you get this information?'

She was perfectly straight with him. Peter leaped to his feet. 'They hang people for less.'

'So?'

He swung round to face her. 'I don't think you understand. Quite apart from the position this places you in, complete and utter secrecy between departments is crucial. If the wall is breached, the trust is gone.'

'The agents trust us.'

A shadow passed over Peter's features.

'Listen to me, Peter.'

Ruby extracted Vinegar's test coding exercises from a file and spread them out over the desk. 'We have to entertain the possibility that the Germans are playing back one of our radios. Vinegar's training records told us he is a reasonable wireless operator but a bad coder and decoder.' She stabbed a finger down on a training paper. 'Tell me honestly. How likely is it he will have improved in the field?'

'Not very likely.'

'We don't have a record of his fist so we can't make comparisons. I think . . . I think there is more than a possibility that the enemy have

459

tortured the poem code and the security checks out of Vinegar and are making him transmit their messages.'

For a second, Peter was stricken and she experienced an untidy mix of triumph and apprehension. He glanced at the data and his face darkened. 'You should have consulted me, Ruby.'

She was shocked by his fury, and the old resentments erupted. 'Because you're senior? Because you're a man? I've done important work for you. Good analysis. You should be pleased.'

'For God's sake.'

They glared at each other.

She couldn't help it. '*Is* it because I'm a woman?'

'Shut up.'

Peter was right. Her sex was irrelevant and she must think strategically. 'There *is* something wrong. You must see it there. Furthermore, I think he was trying to tell us something.' She banged her hand down on the papers.

Stip, stap, stup . . .

'That's not proof,' said Peter.

'There's a pattern. Patterns are what we look for.'

'I don't know what to say to you.'

The cold and objective part of her thought: *He's a fool like other men.*

'You could say that I have a point. You could say that I'm right,' she said.

'You haven't proved it.'

'That's the point. I'm trying to show it to you

but, because we deal in the shadows and with unknowns, I can't give it to you all wrapped in birthday ribbon. You, of all people, understand that.'

The dark eyes trained on her were bitterly angry.

'Go,' ordered Gussie, who had walked into the office. 'He's due at the meeting.'

'Can I come back?' she asked.

He was as icy as she was. 'No.'

Without another word, Ruby left.

That evening, she sat in the tin bath in her digs. The trains rattling past the house shook the bathroom window. She washed between her toes and legs and considered the theory of the unconscious. According to the psychologists, all humans possessed one, and it drove their inner and outer lives. An upheaval was taking place in Ruby's, but she couldn't force whatever it was to the surface.

She towelled herself dry, hoiked out the knickers with the braid edging, put on the one good frock she possessed, with three-quarter sleeves and a pretty neckline, and piled her hair on top of her head. Salt-of-the-earth Janet was in London on twelve-hour leave, and they were going to make an evening of it.

'Not bad, girl,' she informed the reflection in the small mirror.

At the Berkeley Hotel, Janet leaped to her feet when she saw Ruby at the entrance to the bar. 'Good to see you. We've got the drinks.' She

461

manhandled Ruby to the table where, to her surprise, haughty-as-a-duchess Frances was also seated.

Frances had been staring glumly into her glass but looked up. 'Nice to see you, Ruby.'

'And you,' said Ruby, and she meant it.

Looking back, Ruby reckoned it must have been something to do with the Joe Loss band pumping out its music, or the warm and spiced summer evening, but the spiky feelings took a back seat and Ruby relaxed.

Janet pushed a glass over to her. 'Down the hatch.'

'Let's make the evening one in the eye for Hitler.'

Several cocktails later they were picked up by three RAF pilots on 'bloody well-earned' twenty-four-hour leave.

The men were drunk and very tired, but more or less in control. 'Dance with us, girls,' said the tallest, a recent burn mark visible on his cheek. His name was Tony. 'Do your bit for the war.'

'War means sacrifice,' Ruby teased, 'but I never realized how much.'

She took to the floor with him while Janet and Frances were swept up by Robin and Hal. Dancing with Tony was far from unpleasant.

Getting to London had been a nightmare, Tony murmured in her ear, but he and the boys had been hell-bent on it. 'Because I end up dancing with someone like you. Just what the doctor ordered.'

Ruby laughed. It was fun. Tony was fun. And she could tell that he wanted her. Well, not *her* precisely but a female body. She certainly wasn't offended. Such a big deal was made about sex. Such a hum and furore and hypocrisy when, in fact, it was as straightforward as enjoying good food.

The band slowed the tempo. Out of the corner of her eye, she spotted Janet entangled with Hal. Frances was moving dreamily across the floor with Rob. You could tell she had had dancing lessons and the two of them looked good together, the kind of good which money bought.

Tony pulled her closer. 'Funny old life, isn't it?'

She touched his uniformed chest. 'At least we have this,' she said.

'Meaning?'

'Sensations. Music. Dancing. Drink.'

'You should try flying. It's euphoria like you can never experience on earth. A feeling of total liberty.'

'I'd like to. I've never done it.'

'Get yourself transferred to a bomber station. You could have a new boyfriend every night and someone would be sure to take you up. Be prepared for tears, though. We come and . . . go.'

The lightly uttered words touched her. Having never flown, she didn't *know* what Tony was really talking about but she could grasp that the pilots and the WAAFs lived close to the edge.

At the end of the evening Tony tucked a hand

under her elbow and steered her onto the dance floor for the final dance. 'Come to the hotel with me, Ruby? I'm flying tomorrow, and I would like it very much.'

An ache for Peter took her by surprise. Then she recollected the cold hostility with which they had parted.

Tony was smiling down at her. Oh God, he might die in the next few days and he knew it. 'Yes, I'll come.'

They said their goodnights to the others. Their bright lipstick now smudged, the girls exchanged complicit glances. One day they might share confidences about the evening and its various finales . . . Taxis. Awkward admissions into a hotel. Whisky in tooth mugs. Even more awkward, or drunken, moments in the hotel bed.

Halfway through their love-making, Ruby knew that this wasn't so much a mistake as a lapse in taste. Not that she wasn't enjoying it. Tony was nice, he made love with vigour and panache, and they had fun. And, understanding the neediness of a man about to fly into battle, she strove to give him what he wanted. But she sensed he craved more and she couldn't give it to him. Although her pity was powerful it was not as elemental as true desire.

Afterwards, she got up and went into the bathroom to sponge herself down. The water was tepid and she shivered with the late-night chill, and with a misery that she did her best to ignore.

She had used sex as revenge, and the experience turned out to be sour. And – she smiled wryly at herself in the mirror as she dried herself, her limbs pale in the dim light – how very old-fashioned the revenge lay was, too.

Hands behind his head, Tony watched her as she got dressed. 'Shall we meet again, oh Ruby?'

She smiled down at him. 'I think not. I don't make a habit of this, and there is someone else.'

He frowned. 'Heavens. An unvirtuous woman. And I had imagined you had succumbed to my charms. Didn't think most women did that sort of thing.' He beat the flat of his hand on the mattress. 'I thought . . . I had an idea . . . but never mind.' He looked up at her. 'Most girls I know aren't as cool.'

She sat down on the edge of the bed and took his hand. 'I liked you very much.'

'But it was just the sex. Or the champagne?'

'Or wartime?'

'How very honest, Ruby.' The remark didn't sound like a compliment. 'Money well spent, then.' He dropped her hand. 'You're an unusual woman.'

She picked at a thread on her handbag strap. 'Most women would think more like me if they had a chance.'

'Would they now?'

She left with Tony's derision in her ears.

She had her come-uppance. It was so late that the last bus back to her digs had gone and she was

465

forced to pick her way through the darkness and the bomb-pocked streets in her evening dress.

When she got back to her room, she shut the door, leaned against it and cried.

The next few days saw lockdown at the office. There was either a big push on, or an emergency, and endless meetings took place behind closed doors in smoke-filled rooms where the chiefs gathered.

Eventually, Peter returned to his office and asked for Ruby. He looked as though he had eaten nothing much for days and the black circles were back under his eyes.

'You look awful,' she said.

'A forty-eight-hour special. You'd have enjoyed it.'

Ruby said nothing and waited.

Peter propped his chin in his hand. 'Are we going to speak to each other?'

What had she done? The answer was nothing, and everything. She had never admired conventional mores. If she wished to sleep with a man, she would. All the same, she wished she hadn't done so with Tony.

'I searched for you the other night,' he said gently. 'I couldn't find you.'

'And?'

'I wanted to ask if you were still angry.'

She felt thwarted by his sweetness, and maddened. Her instincts had been right all along. Love, even sex, was too complicated a subject on which to waste time. The guilt, jealousy, despair, bewilderment were neither interesting nor *worth* it.

'I was. I think I still am,' she replied. 'I know dinosaurs roam these corridors, but we're here to think laterally. Isn't that our point? And when we try to do something that needs doing . . .' She didn't finish the sentence.

'Try to understand, Ruby.' The tension was ratcheting up between them again. 'This outfit's improvised. Nothing like us has existed before. We've no experience to draw on, no manuals.'

'I've heard enough.' She had her hand on the door handle.

He added: 'There have to be rules and, if you or I were found out, we could be keel-hauled.'

Despite everything, she felt a squeak of triumph. Peter was engaged. His comment revealed that he was thinking about it.

She turned round. 'We agree the agents trust us. We instruct them to have faith . . . in *us*. We have to justify that.'

Agents were melting into enemy territory with only hope and trust and a bit of fieldcraft to get them through.

Peter got to his feet and came over to Ruby. 'Where were you the other night? Tell me.'

In that moment her feelings did an infuriating volte-face. If she told Peter the truth, she knew, *she knew*, he would disappear. She couldn't let that happen. His dark eyes, his sweetness, his clever and subtle mind, his slight elegant body were hers.

'I went home to my digs,' she said.

She was compromised. Everything was compromised.

'Is that the truth?'

She didn't believe in lying and this one was one of the hardest lies she had ever told. 'Yes.'

He stared down into her face. He didn't believe her and she felt his hurt and distaste as if they were her own. 'I thought we trusted each other.'

The old intemperate demon got the upper hand. 'Then go to hell, Peter.'

Yet Ruby wasn't giving up.

The agents had no one else to trust.

CHAPTER 27

Mary was summoned by Signalmaster Falks. 'Our lords and masters have been playing silly buggers again.'

For once, she had to make an effort to concentrate. 'Oh?'

Signalmaster Falks was not an organized man and it took him several searches through his overflowing in-tray to produce the piece of paper he wanted. 'Yup. That's it.' He scanned the typewritten page. 'From now on, each agent is to produce a crib sheet of their fist before they go in. We're to keep copies here as reference. You're to refer to them at all times.'

'I don't need one,' she protested. 'I know them like the back of my hand.'

'*You* might not need one, Voss. But some of the fluffy bunnies that I'm unfortunate enough to have on my watch might.'

Mary wasn't having that. 'Sir, they do a good job.'

He eyed her up as if to say: *Not you, too.* 'As I said, our lords and masters like to stick a finger in where it don't belong and they've instructed us to keep physical records of all our agents.

And we are to—' he peered at the paper '—*consult* them.'

'If it keeps them happy, sir.'

Signalmaster Falks stood up. 'You're a good worker, Voss. I have put in a recommendation to headquarters. It was the least I could do.' He cocked an eyebrow. 'Never know where it might lead.'

Her astonishment was so great that words almost deserted her. 'Thank you, sir.'

Falks returned to the chaos of his in-tray. 'Don't stand about, Voss. Get on with it.'

Several days later she was ordered by the duty sergeant to report to the room at the end of the corridor. *Pronto, Voss.*

The corridor was bustling with uniformed personnel, all of them seemingly focused and in a hurry.

Wearing a lieutenant's insignia, the FANY who was waiting for Mary sat behind the cheap-looking desk on a chair which had seen better days. An equally battered one had been placed in front of the desk. She held out her hand. 'I'm Ingram. But I don't hold much with all that formality. Please call me Ruby.'

Ruby was a good fifteen years younger than Mary, with large eyes, dark hair and enviably clear skin. Her mouth could have been termed generous except for a pinched, almost angry, set at the corners, but she was vivid and arresting.

Pointing to the second chair, she said, 'And I don't hold with standing either. Please sit.'

The two women faced each other across the desk.

To Mary's surprise, Ruby smiled. 'I've been told that apparently you lot are the signal-ritas and my lot are cipherines.'

'Could be worse,' said Mary.

Ruby was amused and then turned serious. 'The reports are that you're the best in the group, so I've been sent down here to brief you and to pick your brains.'

'Well, that must be a first.' The words flashed from Mary before she could stop them.

Ruby's interest in Mary seemed to quicken. 'You've been informed about the crib sheets for the agents?'

'Yes.'

'And?'

'It's a good precaution,' Mary replied. 'And, for the new, er, signal-rita, invaluable. But, for the old hands, probably unnecessary.'

Ruby looked puzzled. 'Please explain.'

'We just know our agents.'

'Ah, the Morse-trained ear?'

'We know the characteristics that are always evident, whatever the conditions they are sent under.'

'Even when there's a problem with the signal?'

Mary had never been so sure of anything in her life. 'Yes.'

'And when they're frightened, or under pressure. Or exhausted?'

'Especially then,' said Mary. 'Because—' She stopped herself.

'Because?' Ruby leaned forward, sniffing up facts, rooting out doubts. 'Be honest. Be precise, if you can.'

Mary shed her diffidence. 'Because I . . . and the others . . . care about each and every one, personally. I . . . we . . . watch over them.'

There was a second's uncomprehending silence.

'Because you care about them.' Ruby was sceptical to the point of offence.

Mary took up the gauntlet. 'It sounds mad, but it's true. Unless you understand them, you can't read them. Or take the message properly.'

'That's irrational and unreliable.' Ruby sat back and stared at Mary, challenging her.

Mary folded her hands in her lap and said nothing.

'I don't believe in the irrational. I believe in evidence and careful analysis,' continued Ruby.

Mary heard herself say, 'Everything has its place.'

'Of course, you have no idea who they are.'

'None.'

Ruby shrugged. 'It's unusual. Or, put it this way, your approach is not the kind of analysis that the average man would accept.'

'Maybe not,' said Mary. 'But, as I say, it has its place. I know it does.'

Suddenly, Ruby grinned. 'I'm anxious, always, to debunk the average man.'

In the adjacent room, a telephone was ringing. On and on it went.

'Someone answer it.' Ruby rolled her eyes. 'Please.'

Someone did, and there was peace.

Ruby produced a file from the briefcase at her feet. 'These are the latest crib sheets we've taken from agents. These show us the basic characteristics of how an agent transmits, which never change, whatever the conditions.'

Mary nodded.

'These are from the newer agents, obviously. We've no records for the ones who were already in the field when the decision was taken to keep these crib sheets. But most of your section is here. I want you to check them before we put them on file. Take a look at this one.'

Mary looked at the sheet Ruby put on the table in front of her. What she saw was an in-depth exercise on square-rule paper of every single letter of the alphabet in Morse. She only needed to study it for a few seconds. 'Agent with the call sign DEV,' she said.

'And this one?'

'YEW.'

Methodically, Ruby took her through the next two pages and Mary supplied the information without any problem.

'Who else do you have who we don't have records for?'

'XRT,' said Mary. 'Vinegar.'

Ruby's chair scraped along the floor, and she got to her feet. Mary couldn't help noticing how thin she was. 'Tell me about Vinegar.'

Mary clicked back through her mental file. 'I

was assigned him . . . in early November 1942. Last year.'

Ruby checked the list. 'Correct.'

'He transmits like clockwork. There's never much trouble with the signal. In fact, he's been remarkably consistent.'

There was a tiny pause. Suggestive? A cloud appeared on Mary's horizon.

'Think. Have there ever been any problems?'

'Only with his first transmissions,' she replied. 'He was nervous. I could tell by the rhythm and he was all over the place. In fact, on the very first one he muddled the sign-off and his frequency. But I didn't have to worry because, after his first four skeds, he was trouble free.'

Mary looked at Ruby. Something was up. The cloud on the horizon grew darker, and a worm twisted and turned in her chest.

'So after that Vinegar never seemed under pressure? Or frightened? Or to be transmitting in difficult conditions?'

'No,' Mary replied. 'It's quite unusual. You could trust him for a perfect message each time. Is he in trouble?'

Ruby ignored the question. 'Anything else?'

'Occasionally, his messages are shorter than most agents'.'

'Right,' said Ruby in such a way that Mary knew that the information had been important. 'Anyone else?'

'ZYA . . . Mayonnaise.' There was a catch in her

throat. 'He went dark a few weeks ago and missed a couple of skeds, but I continued to search for him. Then he came back on the emergency frequency. Once. But his last message, number fifty, was odd. I reported it to the signalmaster and asked if the security checks were used.'

'What sort of odd?'

'His fist was almost unrecognizable . . . It could have been someone else transmitting. For example, Mayonnaise's H is always very dashing: full of energy and life. On that last message, the H was configured differently.' Her fingers twisted together. 'I'd like to know what's happened to him.'

Did Ruby understand how she felt? Peering at her, Mary rather thought that, despite the brisk manner, she did. At any rate, a little.

'You know I can't answer that. Even if I knew.' Her gaze was shrewd and – indeed – not unsympathetic. 'He or she is the one you care about?'

Mary stared at her. 'One of them,' she admitted.

Pushing her vacated chair tidily back under the desk, Ruby said carefully, 'Shall we just say there was an explanation for Mayonnaise?'

It was a small drop of information. But manna to Mary.

She looked down at her hands. 'I see.'

'You mustn't get involved, you know. Otherwise how do we fight the war? If you care too much then it becomes impossible.' She slotted her papers back into the briefcase.

Was Ruby giving this piece of advice to herself

as much as to her? *Pot and kettle*, Mary said to herself.

'Are you quite sure you don't get muddled between them all?' Ruby shot the question at Mary.

'Muddled! No. *Never.*'

That appeared to satisfy Ruby. 'My orders are to tell you that, if you ever suspect anything, you ask to talk to Major Martin. Understood?'

'Yes.'

Before she left, Ruby gave Mary a piece of paper with a telephone number on it. 'You and I know,' she said, 'who runs the shop and, if you ever need to get hold of me, use this. But don't let anyone else see it. Or tell anyone about it.'

Finish. End of session.

On the way back to her station, Mary glanced out of a window and spotted Ruby. Briefcase parked by her feet, she was leaning up against a wall and smoking what was probably one of those popular Turkish ciggies the girls fought over. One foot was tucked up behind her for balance and her skirt had ridden up above her knee. She smoked quickly and appreciatively, looking like a woman in charge of her life.

Mary glanced up at the clock. Two minutes. Her headphones hissed and fluted.

The minute hand reached twelve.

Where was Vinegar?

He was a few minutes late for his sked but, eventually, he checked in. She took up her pencil.

At the end of the message, Vinegar signed off as usual . . . *I have nothing further for you.*

Her pencil faltered. Had she got that correct? There was a change in the rhythm of Q, which should have been dash dash dot dash. Instead she transcribed: dash dot dash dot. The letter C.

It was followed by A instead of R.

Instead of reading QRU it read CAU.

He had done it again. It was exactly as had happened on his first transmission. Not only that, he also muddled the frequency.

After putting the message into the basket, Mary made a note in her notebook: 'QRU reading CAU'.

Checking twice to see if she had made a mistake, something she dreaded, she then made another comment in her notebook: 'Frequency change from LMS to GHT.'

What was eluding her? No one was supposed to read the messages. Indeed, she couldn't. But the Q system was a universal language which the girls had got to know. Any fool could.

Mary rubbed her tired eyes. She thought about her agents, about where they might be. Was Mayonnaise moving around a city where everyone watched everyone else? How tough it must be, unable to trust anyone. Perhaps he was hidden, perched in a barn, or shivering in an open field, or high up in a mountain?

Vinegar . . . Why would he change frequency?

Between skeds, she searched out the duty signal-master. It was, unfortunately, Signalmaster Noble.

'I'd like to request that you get in touch with Major Martin.'

He frowned. 'And why, may I ask?'

She held his gaze. 'I'm afraid I can't say.'

'I won't do anything unless you tell me what is going on.'

'I'm sorry, sir. I can't.'

This was a face-off. Noble opted for the usual tactic to resolve it. 'Get back to your bench, Voss.'

'Sir, this might be important.'

'I don't care if it's an invitation to Hitler's bloody birthday party. Get back to your station.'

It was a double-shift day and Mary spent the period between them at a table in the canteen with a cup of stewed tea in front of her, trying to work out what to do. After that, she took a walk in the grounds. These were extensive and had once housed a noteworthy rose garden but, since the house had been commandeered, the signal bods had stuck aerials everywhere, even among the flowerbeds. Lately, these had multiplied over the lawns, finally destroying what remained of the garden's elegance.

She wished she had someone with whom to talk things over and longed to be able to ask advice as to how to behave when she was so sure something was wrong.

She had always been obedient as a child, then as a daughter and an employee. Not unusual for a woman. Her mother had seen to that, drumming that way of being into Mary.

Clocking off, she walked into town. It was four

o'clock and the afternoon sun was shifting over the town's market square and settling on the window of the Currant Bun café. There was a scurry of schoolchildren and shoppers. The butcher was about to close down his stall for the day, and the man on the hardware stall was packing up his tin bowls and clothes pegs. She made her way to the post office and queued for twenty minutes until the phone box was free.

She dialled, waited for the call to be answered and inserted the coins. 'Lieutenant Ingram, please.'

'Who is this?' demanded a female voice.

She explained.

'And who gave you this number?'

'Lieutenant Ingram. She asked me to contact her if I thought I should.'

There was a long pause. Mary raised her eyes to the ceiling. She had only three minutes and at least one had elapsed.

'You're not supposed to have this number. You could be in serious trouble.'

Something snapped in Mary. 'I insist you give my message to Lieutenant Ingram.'

She had said it. *Insist*.

Afterwards, she took her time to walk back to Mrs Cotton. Her sense of relief was overwhelming.

There wasn't long to wait before the repercussions began.

Signalmaster Noble was standing by her station when she appeared for her next shift the following afternoon. 'I'll have your guts for garters, Voss.'

479

She held her gaze steady. 'Could I sit down, please?'

His grip on her arm was vicious. 'Not so fast. You're wanted in room thirteen.'

'My shift?'

'Don't you worry your head about that.' Fury made his Adam's apple seem more pronounced than usual.

'I'll come back as soon as possible.'

'If I have anything to do with it you won't.'

Room 13 was tiny. Mary squeezed through the door and saw Ruby leaning against the windowsill.

'Hello, Mary. I came as quickly as I could.'

'Thank you.' Opening her notebook, Mary passed it over to Ruby. 'Whatever else, this is definitely not like Vinegar.'

Ruby scrutinized Mary's note about the sign-off that read CAU instead of QRU, and the later note about the change in frequency.

'He did that once before. On his first transmission,' Mary said. 'But it's not like him.'

Ruby reached for the pencil and paper on the desk and began to take her own notes from Mary's.

'Vinegar knows the Q system backwards,' Mary pointed out. 'He's never made a mistake and could transmit it in his sleep. And why the frequency change?'

Ruby tapped her teeth with her pencil. 'I don't know.'

'Do you think he's in trouble?'

Ruby said: 'I want to thank you, Mary. You've been very helpful. You can go back to work.'

As her mother would have said: 'In for a penny, in for a pound.' Mary's hands clenched. 'Ruby, I'm afraid you'll have to sort it out with Signalmaster Noble. He told me that I'd lose my job.'

'I assure you that you won't.' Ruby gathered up her papers. 'I'll ask Major Martin to phone at once.'

Mary remained where she was and Ruby raised her eyebrows. 'Anything else?'

'Can you tell me *anything*?'

'No.' Ruby was regretful. 'I wish I could.'

'It's hard.' Mary couldn't prevent herself.

'I can imagine. But it's for their sake as well as yours.'

Mary nodded and left the room. Halfway along the corridor, she spotted Signalmaster Noble. Arms folded, he was clearly looking for trouble, but so was she. Squaring her shoulders, she walked past him and into the signals room, where her desk was waiting. She sat down and picked up the headphones.

'The old bully was swearing about you,' said Nancy.

'Let him.'

Nancy shot her a look

Mary sat down and prepared herself for work. Anxiety and doubt were like lumps of coal in her chest.

CHAPTER 28

In the late afternoon, Kay rowed back across the lake from Sophia-Maria's island. She had been doing a reconnaissance of its jetty and checking over the summer house.

Would the island be adequate as a hiding place? Could they camouflage the material? How much time would be needed to get there and back? The water tumbled over the blades, making lovely watery sounds, and she ran through the sequence of a drop until she was fact-perfect. Preparation was everything . . . She didn't know how likely this was but, if and when London ever gave the go-ahead to use the lake as a drop zone, she would be ready.

Anton promised to make contact with London. 'If Felix made it, he will have been debriefed pretty thoroughly. They will have a good idea of the situation here.'

Kay felt her new isolation, both mental and physical. With Felix gone and Rosenlund under surveillance, all activities had ground to a halt, a state which Kay had imagined she would relish. She didn't, which went to prove how contrary human beings were. Lying low and keeping quiet made their own demands. Yes . . . yes . . . she was grateful for having got away with it and for her sudden peace and the chance to enjoy the summer weather. But, if she was truthful, she also found herself yearning for the adrenalin rush and the comradeship between unlikely people. Resistance, she realized, had become a state of mind.

Shortly after Tanne fled, Juncker had been sent on a course to København, which left Sergeant Wulf to pursue the enquiries. For a couple of weeks after Tanne vanished, he drove up to Rosenlund every few days to ask about her. Either Bror or Kay would report that she was still staying with the cousins and Sergeant Wulf would solemnly note it down.

It seemed that Sergeant Wulf's old loyalties had held.

Kay missed Tanne badly and often lay awake picturing the worst.

Please be in Sweden.

Allied night-time bombers had taken to flying over the area in large numbers on their way to bombing missions in Germany. Their noise broke into her already fragile sleep and she wasn't sleeping well.

But that was good. The noise was the excuse she used to Bror to keep him out of her bed. 'I can't sleep,' she told him. 'And it's worse if you're there, too.'

He didn't like it and it meant that the patching

up of their relationship was additionally uneasy and, sometimes, fraught. The bridge that had been built was still shaky. But, for the moment, that was the way it must be.

The political landscape was changing. Incidents of sabotage in shipyards and factories all over the country had been stepped up, and the newspapers were full of reports of resistance activity. 'Railway line blown up,' said one. 'Factory demolished,' said another. A series of strikes had been rolled out. To no one's surprise, the Nazis did not like the behaviour of their so-called reliable Nordic brothers.

Talk in the Køge bread queues was of little else. Rumours solidified and circulated. Rumours of torture, of *stikker* going into hiding . . . of people being shot in the streets. It was said that the Allies would invade through Denmark. It was also said that Werner Best and his crew were planning to round up the Jews, which would put the Danish government in an untenable position.

Is Tanne safe?

Of course she is.

No, she isn't.

Kay rowed on, the boat slipping easily through the shiny water.

There was sunshine and a deep blue sky to enjoy. There was Nils to consider. He had not been home for some time.

And Bror?

She peered down into the lake.

In. Out . . .

After the bad nights, exercise made her feel better.

In. Out . . .

Nosing the boat up to the jetty, she was surprised to find Bror waiting by the mooring post.

He made no move to help her and, hauling herself up onto the jetty, she slipped and fell. Struggling upright, she peeled a tacky mess of wet and blackened silver foil strips away from her leg. Whatever these were, they seemed to arrive in the wake of the bombers. She held up one. 'What are these for?'

'Ask your British-loving friends, Kay.'

Don't get angry. Don't despair. 'Good idea.' She smiled to take away the sting from the exchange.

'Want to know the news?'

She tied up the painter. 'I'm listening.'

'The Allies have landed in Sicily.'

'Thank God.' She closed her eyes.

'I knew you would be pleased.'

But Bror wouldn't be. Or, might he be? Not possessing a way into his thoughts any longer, she did not know.

There was a flurry and a clatter of wings.

'Look!'

A flight of duck rose from the rushes and looped above the golden landscape.

'Are you going shooting this year, Bror?'

Bror did not even glance at the duck. 'Not until Tanne is safely back.'

The water was so still that the trees were perfectly reflected in it. Such soft colours, she thought.

The boat knocked gently against the jetty.

'Kay, you would tell me if you heard from Tanne?'

'How could you imagine I wouldn't tell you?'

'Very easily,' he said and that shocked her.

Later, after they had eaten supper, Bror picked up his book. 'I'm going to have an early night.'

'Sleep well, then.'

He had brushed his hair back and it gleamed like an otter's coat. Looking at him, it occurred to Kay that he had never looked so well, or to such advantage.

It was no good thinking about the future. Or, at any rate, it was no good thinking of it without a degree of fatalism. The war had done its worst. Given the context, theirs was only a small tragedy but a bitter one. Like so many others were bitter and cruel. The odds were that they could never restore their true, honest marriage, and the sense of bereavement was all the heavier because she had been the one who had brought it about.

'Bror, will you kiss me goodnight?'

Without waiting for an answer, she reached up and kissed him.

After a moment, he stroked her hair.

Up in her office, she closed the door, drew the curtains and crouched down by the radio to listen to the banned BBC.

'Josephine loves her grandmother.'

'The rabbit arrived this morning.'

486

'The river is flooding over the meadows.'

She knew enough to know that some of the messages were instructions to someone in the field. On hearing the relevant one, a team would swing into action and prepare to receive the arms and explosives descending from the belly of a plane.

For some reason she felt uneasy tonight. True, she was no longer actively involved. Nevertheless, she could not shake off a sense that danger lurked everywhere these days and the result was to sharpen in her an urge to corral her possessions, neaten her arrangements, order her affairs – it was a feeling she remembered well from the hours before going into labour with the children. Perhaps it wasn't surprising. Birth and death were allies.

She sat up late making a list. Bring accounts up to date. Burn letters. Make will.

Afterwards, restless and disinclined to go to bed, she sat at her desk. It grew chilly and she reached for the wrap that she kept on the back of the chair. Pulling aside the curtain, she looked out. It was a clear night and the summer constellations lit up the sky.

There was a noise on the steps outside, a shuffle and scrape of feet.

In a flash, she had extracted the pistol from the desk and rammed it into her pocket.

A soft tap, then a voice whispered: '*Fru* Eberstern.'

One hand on the pistol, Kay opened the door. 'Arne.'

'*Fru* Eberstern, we need medicines and bandages.'

She didn't require an explanation. 'Bad?'

'Very.'

She was already on her knees by the cupboard, handing supplies to Arne, including bandages, a small bottle of brandy, scissors and a suture kit which she had bought from the vet.

'Where?'

'Jacob's place. I have the bicycles ready. We'll go by the back road to dodge the curfew.'

It was approaching midnight by the time she and Arne wheeled their bicycles around the back of Jacob's cottage.

Jacob was waiting to let them in and she was struck by the difference in him. No longer the pale, gawky youth he had been when she and he first encountered each other, Jacob had grown into a bulkier, confident figure. 'Thank God,' he said.

As Arne parked the bicycles he warned, '*Fru* Eberstern, what you're going to see is not good.'

She girded herself. 'I know.'

The room into which Jacob conducted her was small, sparsely furnished and lit by one medium-sized oil lamp. At its centre, a man lay across a couple of chairs which had been pushed together as an improvised bed. A newspaper was spread out underneath to catch the blood which streamed from a slash on his chest. Its smell was sickening.

At her entrance, he turned his head and she

battled with herself not to run out of the room. He was covered in sores, as thin as a rake and his face was almost pulp.

She swallowed. 'Danish police?'

'Gestapo.'

'How did he get here?'

'We had a tip-off that prisoners were being transferred from Aarhus to København. An ambush was arranged.'

'Where are the others?'

Jacob shrugged. 'Round and about.'

Kay bent over the wounded man. 'I'll try to help you.'

Drawing her aside, Jacob said, 'He can't talk . . . but we think the Germans have had him for some time, which would suggest he's important to them.' His voice was husky with exhaustion. 'Maybe they've finished with him. Or they were going to kill him off. The plan was to get him and the others out to Sweden.' He gestured to the injured man. 'But I don't think so.'

She knelt down beside him. 'Name?' she asked.

The man was conscious but since his jaw was at an odd angle, he struggled to respond intelligibly. The effort, and the smashed jaw, proved too much.

Was he one of Felix's men?

After a moment, Kay laid a hand gently, oh so gently, on his shoulder. 'Don't try any more.'

She examined him as best she could – biting down on her lip when he cried out. 'He's been beaten all over,' she said at last. 'Systematically and brutally.' Except for his hands. They appeared to be untouched, although Kay couldn't be absolutely sure about that because he was filthy. Underlying the more recent wounds, including the one on his chest, were older yellow and purple scars and contusions. His shoulders were raw – that was recent. Some of his injuries indicated cigarette burns, or small knife slashes, and they oozed pus.

Clinically, Kay noted the tally of violence: the bruises, the rotting flesh, the attempt to destroy his face.

What good were a couple of aspirin in this situation? Angry and helpless, she sponged the man down with water from the bucket Jacob had fetched, and dabbed at the worst of the wounds with disinfectant.

As she worked, her anger intensified. If she had ever doubted her refusal to tolerate evil and cruelty, this was no longer the case. If she had ever had doubts about being involved, they vanished.

Jacob and Arne watched.

'I was warned about this,' she said. 'If he's British-trained, which is possible, the Abwehr would have tried to use him and get as much out of him as possible without killing him. Afterwards, the Gestapo probably took over.' She straightened up. 'His jaw's smashed. He's got a head injury and the socket of his right eye is possibly broken. He needs to be in hospital.'

'Our contact at the hospital says they can hide

him in the isolation ward. But not until tomorrow,' said Jacob.

'Right.'

But it wasn't all right.

The bleeding from the chest wound needed to be dealt with. At least Kay could do something about that. She pulled the suture kit out of her pocket. 'I'll have to stitch it.' After scrubbing her hands with disinfectant, she sterilized the needle by dipping it into the flame of the oil lamp, then threaded it. 'Could one of you get some brandy down him?'

Jacob did his best but not that successfully.

'Bring in the lamp as close as you can,' she instructed Arne. 'And Jacob, please hold him.'

Her hand shook only marginally. Thank God for that. Arne held the lamp up and Jacob pressed down on the man's raw shoulders. Grasping the edges of the wound, she pulled them together. *Pop.* The needle pushed into the flesh with an unexpectedly loud sound.

She had no idea that human skin was so tough.

The wounded man whimpered.

How far can humans go? When do you stop fearing pain?

Questions that Kay could not answer.

Pop.

Too far gone, he barely made a sound after that.

She sewed on, knotting the thread, snipping it, then pressing a dressing onto the wound until the bleeding slowed.

491

The man made one last-ditch effort to speak but only a gurgling, glottal noise issued from the battered mouth. She bent over and strained to make sense of it.

But it was useless.

Before she left, Kay handed the Browning to Arne. 'You might need it tomorrow morning.'

He accepted it reluctantly.

The wounded man never made it to the hospital. When Arne appeared at Rosenlund the following afternoon, he told Kay that he had died during the night. He and Jacob hid the body in a cart under piles of old sacks and buried it in the woods.

Kay wept.

It was another warm and sun-filled day. The sky was cerulean blue, the wisteria on the terrace bloomed uninhibitedly, bright greens stippled in the woods. The air was so still that Kay felt as if the universe was holding its breath.

After dinner, she and Bror were drinking their coffee when Birgit appeared. She was sobbing incoherently.

Kay got to her feet. 'Birgit, what on earth's the matter?'

'Arne's been arrested.'

Kay put her arm round the other woman. 'Tell us.'

'They've taken him to the police station.'

'Who have?'

Birgit merely shook her head.

Bror said wearily, 'The usual nonsense. I'll phone Sergeant Wulf.' He rested a hand on Birgit's shoulder. 'Don't worry.'

He vanished into the hall.

Kay led Birgit through the French windows and made her sit down in the drawing room. She crouched down beside her. 'Shall I get you some coffee? Or brandy?'

'*Fru* Eberstern . . .' Birgit was having difficulty speaking. 'Arne had this.' To Kay's horror, she produced the pistol from her pocket. 'He was trying to hide it when they came.'

Without a second's hesitation, Kay whipped it out of Birgit's hand and stuffed it into her sewing bag, which she kept on the floor beside her chair. She raised a finger to her lips to indicate silence.

In the hall, Bror could be heard saying, 'The accusations are ridiculous.'

Birgit clawed at Kay's arm. 'Arne told me to tell you . . .'

Kay took both of Birgit's hands in hers. 'Speak softly. What did Arne tell you to tell me?'

The look Birgit flashed Kay was one of dislike and suspicion of Kay – the Birgit whom Kay had known for so long. 'He said to tell you that someone at the hospital talked.'

They heard Bror say, 'Good. That's settled.'

Kay held up a finger. 'Listen. What did my husband tell you? He has sorted it out.'

Birgit refused to look at Kay.

Bror came back into the room. 'Birgit, Sergeant

Wulf says he's very sorry. There's been a mix-up. Arne will be home shortly.'

'I'm going to drive you home,' insisted Kay. 'No argument.' She turned to Bror. 'We have the petrol?'

When Kay bought the car to a halt outside the cottage, a dishevelled, exhausted-looking Arne emerged from the front door. Birgit choked up with fresh tears and threw herself out of the car.

Arne hugged Birgit hard. Then he pushed her inside.

Kay rolled down the window. 'They didn't hurt you, did they?' She could tell he was badly shaken.

'*Fru* Eberstern, you must leave the area. There's too much talk.' One of his big square hands rested on the door handle.

He was speaking rapidly, far too rapidly. Kay understood.

'You *are* all right?'

'I've known most of them at the station since they were babies. I just had to remind them that, after the war, they had to live here.' He added, '*Hr* Eberstern helped, too. Please thank him.'

Kay glanced through the cottage window. Birgit was feeding logs into the stove.

'Birgit has given me the pistol. You don't need to worry about that.'

'I would have buried it.'

'She was frightened for you, Arne. We all were.'

Arne moved his hand and she registered the age spots which mottled the skin.

'The family is at risk, *Fru* Eberstern. You, especially. They gossip about you.' He bent down until his face was on a level with hers. 'Køge isn't safe any more. Go and hide until the war is over. You and the master. I'll take care of Rosenlund.'

A sixth sense told Kay to abandon the car at the end of the drive and to approach the house with caution. For a moment she stood still, absorbing the colours and scents which she loved.

Moving as noiselessly as she could, she zigzagged through the trees which lined the drive until the house came into sight.

Parked by the front door was the black car.

Turning, Kay tracked around the side of the house and let herself in through the kitchen entrance. Kicking off her shoes, she padded down to the drawing room and peered through the crack between the door and its frame.

Hauptsturmführer Buch and Constable Juncker occupied the space in the middle of the room. From her restricted viewpoint she had a good view of Juncker, but Buch was partially hidden.

'I've no idea what you're talking about,' Bror was saying. 'I don't care what your informant says. My wife couldn't possibly have been planning to smuggle a terrorist into the hospital without me knowing.'

Constable Juncker honed in on the miniature tortoiseshell clock which was on the table beside her chair. Kay squeezed her eyes shut. *No.* With a booted toe, Juncker nudged over the sewing bag. Picking it up, he shoved his hand inside. 'Sir.' He held out the pistol.

One small second can contain an eternity. In it, Kay travelled from debilitating craven fear to ice-cold resolve, from the bitter, bitter sorrow of farewell to the explosive excitement that, at last, things were happening.

'What on earth—?'

No one could mistake Bror's genuine surprise.

Buch's response was instant. '*Hr* Eberstern, that particular gun is known to be a terrorist weapon.'

'My wife—'

Bror was struggling. That was good. His unfeigned, unmistakable astonishment was his best defence.

'Where's your wife?' *Hauptsturmführer* Buch was, as always, calm and polite.

There was nothing Kay could do except leave Bror to his ignorance. That was all she could do for him.

She fled up the back stairs to her office, where she had everything ready on stand-by. The rucksack by the door had been packed: underwear, dried raisins, bandages and a bundle of bank notes. She snatched up the jacket and, pausing only to take a final look at a photograph of Tanne and Nils and to touch the larger photograph of Bror with a fingertip, she let herself out onto the outside steps.

Then she was away through the trees and running like the wind.

CHAPTER 29

Tanne and Felix were flown in from Stockholm hidden in the bomb bay of a Mosquito, then driven up to London. They were met by a businesslike FANY who issued them with some badly fitting civilian clothes and money, and conducted them to a hotel near High Street Kensington. For the time being, she explained, they were to lie low and were forbidden to contact any relatives or friends.

There could have been few drearier places in which to hole up than the hotel but they made the best of it by exploring the streets and walking in Kensington Gardens. They spent a lot of time in a local pub, which was a fairly jolly, rowdy, sawdust-strewn place.

Having visited with her mother several times, Tanne was familiar with the pre-war city. What amazed both her and Felix was the variety of uniforms now visible in the streets: Americans and Free French, Poles, Italians and some Greeks. Anyone, they noted wryly, but the Danish.

On their walks they saw severed gas pipes and burst water mains. Here and there they came across pockets of escaped gas, and there was the constant hazard of live electric wires. Many streets and terraces were in ruins. Wherever Tanne looked, there was hardship. London was shabby and fatigued, with the look of a person pushed almost too far – but not enough to give up. It wasn't fair but its grimy dereliction contrasted badly with København's solid stone buildings and the jewelled colours of the houses and farms of the countryside.

Tanne had not wavered in her determination to join Felix in his work. 'Your mother would never forgive me,' he repeated, more than once.

And, more than once, it crossed Tanne's mind that Felix referred frequently to her mother . . . Freya's courage, her willingness to adapt, her physical endurance. *Did he love her?* Knowing enough to know that love could arrive in many forms, the question, nevertheless, troubled her and she struggled not to think about it.

She needed to be clever to win the argument about entering the fight and she banked on the fact that Felix was not a sentimental man but a patriotic one. 'Who do you put first? Your country or my mother?'

It did the trick. Tanne found herself attending interviews in anonymous-looking buildings where she was questioned – ruthlessly, minutely – on her background and motivation, and put through some searching personality tests. Eventually, she was commissioned into the FANYs as a cover, as most of the women agents were. She was issued with a temporary British passport, given details of the bank account opened in her name for her pay and informed that she was to be sent away for training. Her number was D42 and her training name was 'Pia'.

On a Monday morning, she and Felix caught the ten-twenty train from Paddington, with orders to alight at the third stop after Northampton. She was surprised by the instruction – until she realized that station names were blacked out, which meant that strangers would have no idea where they were.

The train was crammed and they ended up standing in the corridor. She and Felix smoked, and tried to ignore the small horror of the lavatory beside them.

'English plumbing. It's dreadful,' she said.

Such was the crush, her head was practically jammed into Felix's chest. To avoid pressing into his injured arm, she adjusted her position, only to find that her pelvis was pressing into his hip.

'You'll get used to it.'

Tanne was dealing with new and powerful feelings. Had they been stirred up by Felix's weakness, which she had kept watch over that night in Ove's cottage? Or perhaps on the journey on the *Ulla Baden*, during which she and Felix had seen things of each other, in each other, which in peacetime might have taken them a lifetime to discover. For those hours, they had been so physically close – closer than she had ever experienced with anyone

– and they had left in her a desire to protect, to hold . . . and . . . to love?

'Will we be seeing each other where we're going?'

'Probably not,' he said. 'And we won't be working together. We know too much about each other. Security.'

She knew that he was aware of the position of her pelvis on his hip.

'We don't know *everything*.'

He squinted down at her. 'Are you being funny or crude?'

Exhilarated and almost breathless from the changes in her life, she said, 'Both,' and had the satisfaction of hearing him laugh.

It was drizzling when they alighted at the station to be met by a uniformed sergeant from the Buffs – a regiment which played host to the Danish fighters who fetched up in Great Britain. The sergeant was Danish and a man of few words. 'You'll be walking. Leave your luggage.' He issued them with a map and coordinates. 'Two hours,' he said. 'If you don't make it on the dot, you'll miss the meal.'

Two hours later, almost to the minute, having negotiated fields, stiles and streams in her flimsy lace-up shoes, Tanne stumbled with Felix up the drive of an old manor house. She knew, she just knew, that it would be cold inside and badly plumbed.

It was.

At the end of the promised meal, the students

– as they were referred to – were told to get some sleep. As Felix got up from the table he sent her a look: *Goodbye, Eva*.

Nine students assembled the following morning. Information about the others was, for security reasons, limited, but she gathered that 'Lars' had escaped the previous winter by skiing over the frozen sound to Helsingborg, 'Otto' had flown in the same way as they had and two of the others had arrived by fishing boat. The rest had either been living in England or made their way from Europe via Spain to offer their services.

They were thrown in at the deep end.

Run six or so miles before breakfast.

Morning lessons. Morse code. Map-reading. Fieldcraft.

Lunch. In general, this proved marginally better than breakfast.

Afternoon lessons. The group was conveyed by a covered ten-ton truck to an unknown location and abandoned there with only a compass each. 'Find your own way back,' was the order. Each day the route grew harder.

Dinner. Sometimes Tanne was too exhausted to eat. Afterwards, drinks were dispensed from the plentiful drinks cabinet. Then bed.

Where was Felix?

Without him, she felt desolate – as if an element vital to her life had been sucked away. Enquiring after him was a mistake and she was brusquely informed it was none of her business.

501

'It's curious how angry you can become when you test your limits,' she confided to Major Petersen, who was mentoring her. 'Why?'

'Because you fail, usually at the beginning. Failure is important. So, too, is finding the anger that will drive you on. Both failure and anger have to be mastered.'

Morning lessons during the second week: how to handle a pistol, machine gun, Sten gun, tommy gun and rifle.

This is the breech. This, the cocking lever. This, the selector button. Get to know them as well as your face. Most of you have never handled a gun.

She thought of the early morning mist wreathing over the Rosenlund marshes. The shining lake. Gleaming, virgin snow and the squat, black shadows cast by the trees. She thought of how in that past life, with a shotgun in hand, she and her father waited for the ducks to skim over the marsh. Finally, she thought of how she had pulled the trigger without a second thought.

Tanne pointed to the Sten. 'A savage weapon.'

Major Petersen, who, as ever, was on hand, ran his finger along the skeleton butt. 'Savage times.' His voice was flat. 'But this isn't too bad for something so improvised. It's adaptable and deadly.'

He was issuing a challenge: *This is serious. Killing.*

Tanne had to consider the possibility. She must think about the smack of bullet on bone, of flesh torn into ribbons, of bubbling breath and of pain which could be inflicted by her.

502

Petersen continued: 'The magazine is inserted horizontally into the left-hand side of the gun, which means you can use it lying flat. But don't use more than twenty-eight cartridges in the mag, otherwise the automatic feed can jam.'

A mysterious alteration was taking place in her muscles, bones and blood. Leaner, fitter, more physically adept, she thrived on the exhilaration of prolonged exercise.

Who am I doing this for? Denmark?

Yes. Of course I am.

Not entirely.

As for her thoughts, these were changing, too. The old assumptions shared by Aage, Erika and others at university were fast fading. They were too facile, too unsophisticated. Discussing the situation with her fellow fighters, she unearthed in herself stronger political and patriotic allegiances than the easy passions of her student days.

The weather that summer was soft and equable. Whenever she had a moment, Tanne seized the chance to walk through the parkland and gardens, enjoying the vistas of oak trees, sheep, a bowling green, and a peaceful little Saxon chapel tucked into a corner of the park.

Once, homesick and low, she looked across the lawn to the trees which fringed it and saw someone walking towards her. *Felix.* Tears sprang into Tanne's eyes and a joy lit her up. She hurried forward to meet him, but it was only Otto.

They had been warned that not all of the intake

503

would survive to the next stage. Late one evening Tanne and four others arrived back from exercise to discover the mother of all rows emanating from the cellar. On investigation, they discovered the rest of the group, half-slaughtered on English beer, shooting pistols at a caricature of Hitler.

They had all passed.

The following morning the groggy group were summoned by Major Petersen. He briefed them that they would be embarking for Special Training School 45. 'You'll be allowed out only one day a week and you're banned from shopping or eating at restaurants within a five-mile radius of the school.'

STS45 turned out to be a castle somewhere in Gloucestershire – a name Tanne had trouble pronouncing – with a staggering number of windows and chimneys. In the grounds there was a shot-down German plane, complete with a swastika and a gaping hole in its fuselage.

Tanne regarded it thoughtfully. Men had probably died a horrible death in there.

A Major Spooner waited to interview the group. One by one, a sergeant marched them into his office.

Major Spooner immediately made plain his dislike of women. 'You're quite irregular for this section,' was his opener. 'We don't have to deal with many females.' He leaned as far back in his chair as possible and took off his glasses as if to blur the awful sight.

By now, Tanne had worked out that Denmark was low on the British agenda. Could the reason be that a dinosaur, masquerading as a man, had been allocated to run this section?

The major hooked the arms of his glasses round his ears. 'You realize that, at best, you have a ten per cent chance of survival?'

'Yes, sir.'

'Think about it. If it's too much for you, you have a duty to tell us.'

'Sir, do you ask the men the same question? Just out of interest.'

There was a silence. 'I do. And that is a stupid question.'

'You want to know about my nerves and my endurance. So do I. That's what I'm here for.'

He observed Tanne over the glasses. 'Be careful, number forty-two. You don't know the half of it.'

Curiously, she felt at home at STS45. There were big fireplaces and big furniture, if badly arranged, and the pictures and displays of china reminded her of Rosenlund. The canteen produced good meals and, in the library, there was a selection of Danish papers and magazines.

The lessons resumed.

Their group joined a number of Danes who, because there had been so few operations scheduled for Denmark, had been kicking their heels at STS45 for anything up to a year. The newcomers had to work hard to catch up with them. Arithmetic. Map-reading. Reconnaissance. Morse. Using German, Finnish and Swedish weapons. Demolition. Every kind of sabotage known to man, including

505

scuttling ships. Burgling. Writing letters in invisible ink. The use of pigeons.

'Apart from anything else, gentlemen and, er, miss, you will be going home to set up what you might call a sabotage university,' they were told. 'You'll be holding little workshops all over the place. In the fields. In sheds. In piggeries. Got it?'

Also featuring on the curriculum were Unarmed Combat and Silent Killing. Here, she was initiated into various methods, including the Bronco kick: take a flying leap at your opponent then disable him by driving both heels into his body. Or there was the Bone Crusher. Or Mouth Slitting: if you are in someone's grip, you can stick your thumb in the corner of his mouth and split his cheek.

Would she ever be able to bring herself to put these methods into practice? And what if she died in the attempt?

In Danish mythology, a heroine who lost her life was spirited away by the goddess Freya to her domain in Asgard, and all was well. How useful myth was. How it tidied and sanitized. In contrast, Tanne was being taught to see that death could be agonizing, violent, often inflicted without justice or due process. She didn't like to imagine her mother's grief, and the silence into which her father would retreat, if she were to meet hers.

Their instructor watched over them like babies. 'Those who fail the exam will have to go right back to the beginning again,' he warned. 'Now, you don't want that, gentlemen and, er, miss. Do you?'

Assassin, spy, saboteur. Tanne was adding to her list of accomplishments.

Her next assignment was STS51 and Parachute School.

The journey from STS45 took all day. A student in the know told them the names of the stations as they steamed past the blacked-out names.

Tanne sat with Lars and Otto, a couple of Poles and a Norwegian. Soon after the train pulled out of the station before their final stop the compartment door slid open. She looked up from her newspaper – and the blaze of light was there for real.

Felix.

He looked a new man. Plus his British officer's uniform suited him. He jerked a thumb towards the corridor and Tanne leaped to her feet.

'Whoa,' said Otto. 'Do I detect love's young dream?'

'Shut up,' said Tanne.

She and Felix leaned against the rail and regarded the passing English countryside. Tanne couldn't stop herself smiling. She turned her head towards him and thought she would die of happiness.

'I shouldn't be here,' he said, touching her arm. 'But there are always exceptions to be made.'

'Good.'

'How did it go?' He peered at her. 'You look different, Eva. Which is what happens, I suppose.'

'I am different, but so pleased you are here. Really, really so happy, Felix.'

'Don't look at me like that,' he said. But he moved closer. 'I wanted to see you before . . . well, before. I have much to thank you for.'

For a second she was panicked. Was it only gratitude that made him seek her out?

Their faces were very close together. His eyes seemed to pierce her through and through. In the old days she might have ducked her head away from such a truth-seeking scrutiny. But she was beyond the restraints of her previous existence. She knew how important this moment was. She knew, too, that he had risked the wrath of the instructors to talk to her.

'I couldn't go without this . . .' He placed a finger on her lips.

'You mean it?'

'Yes.'

'It's not my mother?' She took a breath. 'I have sometimes wondered.'

Felix understood what Tanne was asking. 'She's special . . .'

Tanne thought of her blonde, beautiful, scented mother. How could she match up?

'But no.'

Tanne smiled.

'So, you've survived what those sadists have thrown at you?'

She grinned. 'Ask me about the Bone Crusher!'

'Ah, the Bone Crusher. An old friend.'

'Your arm?' She could see that he was holding it a little stiffly.

'Good as new.' Felix wasn't being quite truthful. 'Are you ready for the parachuting?'

She grimaced. 'I dread it.'

The compartment door was open and, eavesdropping unashamedly, Lars and Otto were being vastly entertained.

Lars leaned over and said in a stage whisper: 'You should know there are multilingual psychologists on the train monitoring our conversations. You two will be for the chop.'

'Don't look at me,' said one of the Poles in a thick accent.

To the sound of ribald laughter, Felix reached out and shut the compartment door.

As the train approached their station, Felix said: 'This really is goodbye, Eva.'

'So soon.' She heard her voice falter. 'I thought you might be coming with us.'

'I'm brushing up on a few things for a couple of days.'

'But when do you go?'

He shook his head.

She stole a look at his face. She didn't know anything about Felix and perhaps she never would. She didn't know his name, or where he came from, or what he did. But she knew what mattered to her: the way he slept, the way in which he dealt with pain and discomfort. His courage.

Those were enough.

'Do you mean *på gensyn* or *farvel*?'

So long. Or goodbye for good?

'Your choice,' he said. 'Which do you prefer?'

He was asking her if she wanted him.

Conscious that they were being watched, she placed her hand on his uniformed chest, imagining she could feel his heartbeat. 'Not *farvel*, Felix.'

After a moment he nodded. '*På gensyn* it is, then.'

The sign greeting the group on their arrival at STS51 read: 'You Are No Bloody Hero'.

She pondered this welcome as she lay sleepless and longing in her bed that night.

Who were they all?

Who was Felix? Where was her faith that they would meet again?

She was far from Rosenlund, chilly and home-sick. No, lovesick. Eventually, she got up and pulled on a thick jumper over her pyjamas.

She imagined Felix in bed. Probably in one of the dark, narrow, attic rooms that were crammed with ancient iron bedsteads. She willed him to steal downstairs to her. *Please*. Forbidden, of course. Should she find him? Did the English always forbid sex in a crisis? Lars had told her that the whole nation had a peculiar relationship with it. How did he know?

Felix *was* going back into the field. He had made that clear. Would he see her mother? Despite their conversation, the thought of Felix with her mother introduced the tiniest speck of grit into her happiness.

Would he see Rosenlund?

She wished she could go with him.

When she got up the next morning, she felt in her bones that Felix had left.

The pace of the training ratcheted up to the relentless.

During this stage, the instructors paid no attention to the fact that she was a woman. They just made her run harder and tote a twenty-five-pound load on her back that much further.

'Keep your bloody feet together, number forty-two,' yelled the sergeant who was instructing them. 'It doesn't matter if the plane is burning. It doesn't matter if you are being popped at by Gerry. It doesn't matter if you're surrounded by the entire Luftwaffe. Keep your fucking legs together . . .'

The practice parachute drops were hell. With a parachute pack on her back, Tanne jumped twelve feet from a specially built wooden construction and practised jumping through a mocked-up Joe Hole. Next up, was a proper jump from a Halifax, which had sounded so easy when the instructors had outlined the procedure.

But when she sat on the edge of the hole, with the roar of the Halifax's engines ringing in her ears, fear reduced her to jelly. She couldn't do this. She would rather crawl to Denmark than do this.

The dispatcher stood over her with a raised arm. His arm fell and he shouted, 'Go,' and Tanne discovered there wasn't any choice.

There was a terrific rush, a savage jerk through her body, then a joyous silence and she found herself floating through the air, wishing she could stay there peacefully for a long time. For those few seconds, she ruled the world.

She landed perfectly. Feet together. The hardest part was battling to undo the straps and to keep the deflated parachute under control in the teeth of a stiff breeze.

The sergeant loped towards her. 'Well done, number forty-two.' He ran an expert eye over her. 'If I didn't know better, I'd say you were one of the chaps.'

She grinned.

'Listen, I have a pretty little ditty for you. I keep it for my favourites. Learn it.'

If you don't keep your feet together, you will
   hit the Joe hole as you go out.
If you don't keep your feet together, you will
   land on one leg and break it.
If you don't keep your head up, you will
   somersault and land head first.

'It *is* a pretty ditty,' she said.

Finally, they endured another punishing train journey across England to Finishing School: STS35.

Waking on the first morning in a bungalow with a view across the sea to the Isle of Wight, she heard aircraft haring out across the English Channel. They had disappeared by the time she had drawn back the curtains.

'Today,' said their new instructor, 'we'll teach

you the different German uniforms, ranks, regiments and so on. You'll also learn how to concoct an alibi when you're embarking on an operation.' He paused, milking the drama. 'I can't impress on you enough that it's the detail that counts.' A smile crossed his mouth. 'But tonight you are allowed to go into town. Eat, drink, enjoy yourselves.'

After an excellent night out in Bournemouth, and a little drunk, Tanne returned with the others. A dogfight was going on over the sea. She watched and wished she hadn't. Engines screamed and black smoke obscured the moon as one of the planes corkscrewed towards the water.

Halfway through the night, she woke with a start. A torch shone in her face.

'Get up.' The order was in German.

Three men in SS officer uniform had their guns trained on her. Groggy with sleep and beer, she moved slowly. Two of the men frogmarched her down to a small, fetid cellar lit by a spotlight. Lars was already there, tied to a chair. They did not look at each other.

The harsh light was directed onto their faces.

'*Sprechen Sie Deutsch?*' demanded one of the SS officers, his accent immaculate.

The SS uniforms looked authentic, too. Where did they get them from? Dead Germans?

Irrelevant thought. *Concentrate.*

She felt outrage beating below the surface of her calm exterior and a slight nausea from the evening's excesses.

'Answer.'

She thought rapidly. Her German was almost perfect but if she asked for an interpreter it would give her an extra few seconds to think.

'No.'

One of them, groomed and pale, switched into English.

'Where were you yesterday evening?'

'I went into town.'

Never give too much detail.

'How?'

'On the bus.'

'What did you do there?'

Be dull.

'I went to the cinema and ate fish and chips . . .'

'How many uncles do you have?'

Cunning. Slipped in.

'What time was the film?'

The interrogation lasted for hours. Her hands remained tied painfully behind her back and she wasn't allowed to move.

At first, she thought with a slight contempt: *I can cope with this. It's a lie.* But, as her discomfort increased, doubt insinuated itself. Was it going to be as easy to hold on as she had imagined?

Lars had been taken away to another room and she could hear sounds as if he was being beaten up. Would they really beat him up? Would he get through?

She could not be sure and she discovered that not being sure was almost as bad as the discomfort.

'I need to go to the lavatory.'

'Tell her to go in her knickers,' one of them ordered her interrogator in German.

Urine ran down her legs and she ground her teeth at the humiliation. It soaked her clothes, too, and very soon the tender places between her legs began to smart.

Again, she told herself that it was not real. It was a lie.

They shoved a map under her nose. 'Give us the detail of where you went.'

She obliged and they threw the same questions at her over and over again.

'What did the conductor look like?'

'Who served you the fish and chips?'

As the hours wore on, her body grew stiff with tension and ached from the strain of holding out. To her alarm, she felt herself weakening. What on earth was she doing in this strange organization? What did they want from her? How far would they go?

She told herself: *There is no point. Give up.*

Cancel all knowledge of the instructors and the techniques and mental tools which they had so carefully taught her. Cancel thoughts of the family. Cancel thoughts of Denmark and what was happening there. This exercise was pointless.

She smelled of urine.

She thought of walking through the streets of Køge. She thought of Felix.

Surrender?

She lifted her eyes and encountered those of the pale German-speaking officer. He didn't bat an eyelid. Getting to his feet, he walked over to Tanne and slapped her hard on the face.

Her mind was swept clean of everything except anger. If she had to die, she wouldn't give him the satisfaction of making a noise, or giving a reaction.

Her cheek burned with shock and the impact of his hateful hand on her flesh. Bending her head, she looked down at her lap and her jaw tightened. This was the moment she would summon her resistance to bullying, violence and a dictatorship of souls – plus, she was damned if she would let them know how much she hated them. She must strip away her feelings. Concentrate on being the operative – hard, unsentimental, clever.

She lifted her head.

It was late morning when, without a backward glance, the officers got to their feet and filed out, leaving Tanne, still tied to the chair, alone in the cellar for another couple of hours.

Exhausted, she permitted her head to slump over her chest.

This was only the beginning. From this moment on, Tanne knew she was required to dig into her reserves of body and spirit, to peel away the layers that made up who she was, and to step out of the skin of the girl she had been – that girl who had so blithely gone to fetch a doctor. She must understand what people did in war.

Never more, never again, would she whistle to the dogs at Rosenlund and set off with them, light and innocent of heart.

All gone.

These were the bitter lessons of this charade.

Later the instructors went over their respective responses piecemeal. 'You were inconsistent here . . . You were unconvincing there . . .'

Even later, discussing the 'interrogation' with Lars, who had been as shaken as she had been, they speculated about the real identity of the 'SS' officers. Lars thought they were agents probably destined for active service in Germany, but no one could be sure.

That idea was enough for Tanne to forgive them. But only just.

CHAPTER 30

The day before he went back into the field in early September 1943, Felix was summoned to The Firm's London head-quarters for a briefing with Colonel Marsh, head of the Danish section, and Major Iversen, a recently appointed senior Intelligence officer. Both looked unfit and had the waxen pallor of those who spent too much time indoors.

The colonel went straight to the point. 'We don't really know how the mass of the population thinks. But we have had some pointers. The general strike in August, being one. However, for us the balance is tricky. Significant resistance activity in Denmark will keep Jerry busy and preoccupied, which will give our Russian friends some relief on the Eastern front and is desirable. On the other hand, we don't want a mass uprising before . . .'

Felix helped him out. 'Before the Allies invade?'

'Something like that.'

Major Iversen moved restlessly around the room. He had large feet and his shoes creaked.

'So, you're telling me that the Allies might invade through Denmark?'

The two men exchanged glances. 'Who knows?' said the major.

Felix leaned over the desk. 'I don't believe you. You know, and I know, that it's highly unlikely. You're just giving me that to keep up the smoke-screen about the invasion.'

The colonel's expression was as blank as a virgin blackboard. 'We rule nothing in and we rule nothing out. Whatever the scenario, it's vital that you, and we, keep control of all resistance activities. Otherwise advantages may be lost and our grip weakened. But it is true . . . one of the things we want is for you to spread the idea that the Allies may invade through Denmark, which hopefully will result in large numbers of German troops being tied up there.'

'But I'm not to know the real situation.'

The colonel shrugged as if to say: *Don't be so naive.*

'Many Danes don't relish the idea of being directed from London,' Felix was very dry.

'Make 'em,' said Major Iversen from his position by the window.

Felix said, 'Throwing dust in our eyes is not always the best way.'

He was curt and dismissive and, in response, Iversen emitted a gusty sigh. 'You must remember that Denmark's official policy of neutrality gives us problems. But we must concentrate on the positives. Getting this organization up and running has taken a bit of effort. We've made mistakes. We have had to feel our way. But the time for heroic amateurism is over.' With a creak of shoes, he turned round to face Felix. 'We've done a good job so far. What we need now is a tough, professional fight using whatever means, however unconventional, to bring Germany to its knees. Your task is to coordinate and support that struggle.'

'Through the British?'

The two men looked at Felix. 'Well, if you're sitting here, it would suggest that's the case,' said the colonel.

There was a chilly silence eventually broken by Felix. 'Then bring me up to speed. I'm out of touch.'

The colonel coughed, a phlegmy unhealthy rasp. 'You probably know that on the twenty-ninth of August martial law was declared, the Danish government resigned and Danish military personnel were interned . . .' He laid out some facts, placing them in a narrative as carefully as if they were the pieces of a jigsaw puzzle. 'Intelligence reports suggest that the German defeat at Stalingrad has given new heart to the resistance in Europe.'

Felix nodded.

'We welcome the increase in the Danish resistance but that balance I spoke of is crucial.' Was there a touch of impatience? Hostility, even? Felix couldn't be sure. 'We don't want it to become so big that a mass uprising takes place which would sting the enemy into a complete lockdown. That's why we are so keen to control the resistance activity from London. But we're happy with sabotage directed against shipyards and factories producing materials for the enemy.'

Felix drummed his fingers on the desk. 'So far you have sent a total of four wireless operators into Denmark, two of whom have been taken out. Thirteen sabotage instructors, of whom one had to be eliminated. And thirty-two containers have been dropped in various locations. Hardly huge.'

The colonel sent Felix a long, cool look. 'We are doing our best.'

There was more discussion, and then Felix said: 'It's agreed, then, that I operate on Zealand and build up the circuit from København. My task is to bring together the resistance factions and weld them together. Until I get radio contact up and running, I will send messages to Sweden, via our fishermen friends. I understand other agents will shortly be sent into Jutland and they will make contact with Vinegar and use him.'

'That's about it,' said the colonel. 'The agents are being trained at the moment.'

'You are sure Vinegar is up and running?'

There was another silence. Three minds were working around tricky questions to which there were no sure answers.

The colonel asked sharply: 'Any reason why you are querying it?'

'The silence. A feeling.'

'He's transmitting.' The colonel sounded just a

touch patronizing. 'I understand how hard it must be not to become too paranoid in the field.'

You bugger, thought Felix.

Iversen intervened. 'Can you retrieve your wireless sets?'

Felix nodded. 'With a bit of luck. My first one's hidden up in København. The second I had to leave with Freya. I'm sure it will still be there.'

As Felix left the room, Colonel Marsh called out, 'Felix . . .'

Felix turned back. 'Yes?'

'*Tak.*'

Thank you.

Felix returned to Denmark with a couple of other Joes via a complicated route similar to the one he and Eva had taken to escape. They endured being stuffed into the back-end of a bomber that flew them to Stockholm, a train journey to the coast and a nightmare few hours in a fishing boat.

When the boat nosed discreetly into Rødvig harbour, he staggered ashore and breathed in the stink of fish, salt and seaweed. It was good to be back.

He and the Joes sat out the rest of the night under cover of the woods outside the town. Near dawn, a German vehicle appeared from nowhere, cruising down the road. The three men flung themselves flat in the undergrowth. The car halted. A searchlight beamed out of its back window. Felix's fingers clawed into the earth, digging deep into bark and pine needles. Digging into Denmark.

He was not fucking well going to be captured within a couple of hours of arriving.

The car moved on.

In the distance, dogs barked.

Once the sun was up, they filed down to the stream and shaved as best they could, taking turns with the razor. They dampened their hair and rubbed their shoes before separately making for the station, where they bought tickets to different destinations. They were all aboard their trains before the German guard turned up at seven-thirty for duty.

It was back to life on the move, never sleeping more than a couple of nights in the same place. No two days were the same, and he tackled this lack of routine by treating every move calmly, as if it was the most banal of activities. He became a master at scanning every face for clues. Who were they? Them or us?

In København, he tapped up his contacts and 'sleepers' and made plans to meet each one. Activating a funding arrangement that had been organized with the bank by London, he set about building necessary bridges with other resistance groups.

It was Jacob who told him Freya was on the run and moving between safe houses in Nørrebro, one of the districts of København and he sent a message to her. After that, he contacted Odin and asked for soundings on the state of the Danish army. Was it with the resistance or not?

Late one afternoon, he and Odin rendezvoused near the Torvegade bridge. Fog wisped over the water and there was an autumn chill in the air.

They walked along the waterfront.

Odin was as persuasive as ever. 'London's making a mistake by not taking us into their confidence. My contacts don't like it and the lack of trust compromises our relationships. Some of my army colleagues, very senior ones, were forced to do a runner to Sweden the other day.' Odin came to a halt. A tug was chugging slowly downstream and its hooter echoed across the flat grey water. 'Someone betrayed them. The interesting question is: who? Some idiot in London? Or in Sweden, which is even leakier? Or was it here?' He was twisting a packet of German cigarettes between his fingers. 'Your guess is as good as mine.'

Odin had changed. There was an edginess, a bitterness, which Felix had not seen before and it made him wary. It was true, he didn't know Odin . . . or what drove him . . . and, in this game, no one ever really knew what the other was up to. For that, you had to be led by instinct, your experience and your 'nose'. Plus, questions had to be asked. All the time.

He listened to Odin carefully – sorting out the details, storing away information, searching for the weak spots.

German intelligence-gathering had become

highly efficient, in particular the Direction-Finding Signals Unit, Odin reported. But, as far as he knew, he was still trusted by his contacts in the Abwehr. Occasionally, General Gottfried shared operational details with him and some of it was useful, including the intelligence that parachute drops in the Aarhus area were almost all ending in disaster for the agents.

'Betrayed?'

'What do you think?'

Felix considered. 'The Aarhus area, you say? It's possible.'

Vinegar?

'There are limits to what I can find out.' Odin's gaze travelled thoughtfully up and down the waterfront. 'What's happening with the new wireless sets?'

'Nothing to report.'

Not true but Odin didn't have to know that. On his return, one of the good pieces of news to greet Felix had been that Johan and his team had, after several bad setbacks, which included a raid on their underground workshop, almost completed the task to manufacture the smaller, lighter wireless transmitter.

'I dare say London won't be happy about the new wireless sets.'

'They took some persuasion,' Felix replied. 'The British like to think they're the best at everything.'

'Crystals? Transmission schedules? Codes? What about those?'

Again the evasion. 'We'll know in good time.'

'Pig shit,' said Odin. 'We don't have time.'

The fog was deepening over the waterfront. Water slapped monotonously against the moorings.

A group of students were walking towards them and Odin gestured that he and Felix should turn aside.

'I have a proposition. Our ever-tidy German cousins have decided to marry the archives in the German Chamber of Commerce here with those in Aarhus. It's planned for next Thursday. We should snaffle it before it's locked away in a Nazi stronghold.'

Again, they fell into step.

'We don't need the archive.'

'You're a fool, Felix. It's a treasure trove. It'll tell us who's cooperating and for how much.' He tapped Felix's shoulder. 'Think of the blackmail opportunities.' He flashed Felix an unpleasant grin. 'Get stuff on your enemy. I might even check up on the family and see what I can get on them.'

The joke was not funny and almost painful.

Yet Odin was right.

'One more thing,' Odin added. 'You should know that the word is the Nazis plan to round up the Jews quite soon.'

At the junction with Hans Christian Andersen Boulevard they parted. 'Get the archive,' were Odin's parting words.

Felix watched his retreating figure. The instructors on his refresher course had been emphatic.

526

Question every friend or foe. Especially every friend. Trust only very sparingly. Question motives thoroughly. Avoid a direct answer.

At three o'clock the following day, Felix entered the Café Amadeus and took a seat under a portrait of the young Mozart. He had dusted talcum powder onto his hair, parted it on a different side, and stuffed his cheeks with torn-up bits of sponge.

Seeing Freya would be a boon, and good for him, but it was her younger version – the wild-haired, bold, tender companion of his flight – who preoccupied him.

Felix's appearance was bad enough but when Freya slid onto the banquette beside him, he was shocked.

The long blonde hair had been replaced by a page-boy bob with a fringe. Worse, it had been dyed red-brown although, here and there, a few blonde streaks stood out from the brown. A pair of large, unflattering, dark-rimmed spectacles could not disguise that she had lost her healthy glow.

She wouldn't have it any other way, Freya assured Felix. Life had become difficult at Rosenlund. Impossible, even. She recounted the story of the dying tortured man – 'He haunts me,' she said – and told him what happened with the Gottfrieds, with Arne, her subsequent escape and life on the run. 'War has freed me,' she said.

That struck Felix forcibly. Maybe it was true for all of them. Maybe, in its subversion of ordinary life, war was liberating.

'And your husband?'

The grey eyes narrowed with distress. 'You always have to pay something, don't you?'

Freya was someone else now. Johan had procured forged papers identifying her as Lise Lillelund, infant school teacher. Born on Funen. Widowed. Currently recovering from a bout of TB that required frequent journeys into the country for recuperation.

'Tell me about the man who died. Was there any clue to his identity?'

Their table hugged the wall and there was no one within earshot but she moved closer. 'I *think* he was one of us. But who he was working for I don't know. He was being transferred from Aarhus to København.'

'Aarhus!'

'He was brave, Felix. They'd tortured him for a long time.'

'Anything that would give us a clue. Anything?'

'Despite being beaten up, his hands hadn't been touched. It struck me as odd. Don't they usually go for the fingernails?'

Piecing together intelligence required lateral thinking . . . the sixth sense which pounced on a tiny detail, the scantiest of hints, perceived its import and set it beside another tiny detail.

'Some of his injuries were months old,' Freya continued. 'I wondered whether it might have been Vinegar.'

During the silence that followed, Felix looked

around the café. To an onlooker, this was such a normal scene. The white coffee cups. The half-full ashtray. Waiters. Chatter. A man and a woman huddled together on a café bench.

He felt a sickening thud as he groped towards a conclusion.

'It's possible,' he said at last. 'Especially if the prisoners were being transferred from Aarhus. Vinegar operated there.'

He ran back over the events of that first drop. That funny, air-sick, brave little man. Vinegar going in first. Disappearing. The *stikker* on the loose. The rapid dispersal. If the Germans *had* captured Vinegar it would have been easy to run him. Why would the enemy not do so? Running an agent was a useful method with which to capture other agents and equipment, to snaffle up information and to transmit misleading intelligence back to London.

He added: 'If Vinegar had been picked up by Danes working for the Germans when he first came in, he could have been fooled into thinking he was among friends and cooperated.'

At STS they had been warned about how this might happen.

They begin with friendly talk, good treatment, promises. They progress to maltreatment. Use everything you have to avoid third-degree interrogation. Weakened resistance can cause you to reveal all sorts of things.

Freya asked: 'But London should have realized. Why didn't they?'

'You tell me.' Felix knew his anger to be irrational, for it was easier said than done. 'They assured me they had checked up on Vinegar.'

Freya helped herself to one of his cigarettes. 'Why keep Vinegar alive?'

'Possibly because they thought London would know his fist. They would assume that Vinegar's records would be kept and consulted. They wouldn't have wanted London taking fright and closing the transmitter down. In that way, they got information, masterminded any drops . . . you name it.'

He spoke bitterly and she laid a hand on his. 'Don't waste your energy on anger.'

'I am angry. Precisely at the waste.'

'Felix . . .' Her grip on his hand tightened. After a moment, she continued: 'What I can't bear is that he died more or less alone. I would have held his hand.'

Her expression reflected a kind of terror, which Felix understood – and shared. It was the fear of the void, the one where nothing was known or certain and an agent was abandoned by everyone to the misery, terror and torment of its nothingness. Warned to expect periods when it would attack him, he had found its corrosiveness shocking and enfeebling. So too . . . by the look of her . . . had Freya.

Regrets and sentiments were useless. 'Freya . . . don't.' He got back to business. 'The wireless transmitter?'

Freya lowered her voice. 'The cottage. I used it

to send one message after you left. Told them you were going dark.'

'London got the message.'

She breathed out a sigh of relief. 'That's something.'

'Freya . . .?'

She knew and he knew they needed the wireless transmitter. No question. A trace of colour crept back into Freya's cheeks as she weighed and measured the decision. 'I'll bring it to København.'

'Freya, why do you do this? You of all people.'

Cigarette smoke curled between them. She tamped down the butt end of hers with a finger and a tiny fleck of tobacco clung to it. 'Many complicated reasons. But, in the end, it's simple, really. If I don't, who will?'

Jacob slid into the café and the three of them sat under Mozart's portrait, smoking and drinking beer and coffee.

Jacob reported on the twenty-four hours of intensive reconnaissance which had been mounted on the German Chamber of Commerce. 'The concierge is one of us . . .' he said, nicotine-stained fingers curled around his glass. 'But we have to rough him up and lock him in. He's terrified his family will suffer. He knocks off at about six. So far, a night watchman hasn't been posted. He let me take a look at the room.' He downed a swig. 'Full of stuff.'

It was good to be thinking of practical matters. 'Right,' Felix said. 'Two vans and all the Stens and ammo we've got. We need lookouts, cover outside the building, plus a rifle with telescopic sights for the sniper. The weapons must be hidden in the area a couple of days ahead.'

Jacob tackled a second beer. Two days ago he had been on Funen, instructing a group in sabotage, and his voice was hoarse from the shouting. He didn't approve of this operation. 'What are we doing wasting lives on this one?'

A speck of foam clung to his upper lip and Freya leaned over and wiped it away. 'Beer moustache.' It was a fleeting moment of camaraderie and affection.

'Better by far to blow up the railways and stop Fritz using Denmark as a transport hub,' he said.

Felix ignored him. He found a pencil and paper and drew a diagram. 'Opposite the annex, is the commercial college. We need a couple of machine guns to cover that as well.'

'You don't ask much,' said Jacob.

They settled on the time of operation, and the routes, lookouts and the getaway.

The sceptical Jacob repeated: 'What's the point of getting killed or wounded for a load of papers when we could be blowing up a bridge?'

Felix grinned at Jacob. 'Your moment in the sun is coming. London has instructed us to step up the sabotage.'

Jacob snorted.

Before she left, Freya whispered, 'Do something for me, Felix. If you can.'

'If I can . . .'

Her mouth twisted painfully. 'If you see a file on Eberstern – on my husband – will you destroy it?'

Four days later.
6.00 p.m.
The sky was a uniform grey and darkening. At the north end of the Saxogade three men in dark clothing drifted into the doorways and took up positions.
6.05 p.m.
Chatting and smoking, ten men wearing loose overcoats strolled into the street from the Matthåusgade and spread out along the road. A large grey van drew up behind them.
More men appeared.
Sitting in the cab beside the driver, a raw-boned giant from the docks, was Felix, balaclava pulled down over his face. He counted up the men. He was expecting seventeen. All there. Good.
6.07 p.m.
In a headscarf and nondescript mackintosh, Freya walked down the street towards the annex. Outside, she stopped and retied the scarf under her chin. Then she bent down to fasten her shoelace.
It was the signal that it was clear.
6.09 p.m.
One of the men sprinted up the steps into the annex building, ran through the door and took up position at a first-floor window.
6.10 p.m.

The men who had waited in the doorways now approached from the other end of the street and covered the commercial college with the guns that they pulled from under their overcoats.

6.13 p.m.

A second grey van rounded the corner and parked by the entrance to the Chamber of Commerce. The men took out their weapons and trained them on the street.

6.15 p.m.

Felix leaped down from the van. Freya, Jacob and six others materialized from doorways and followed him, one of them peeling off to deal with the caretaker. The rest ran with him up to the first-floor archive room, where the leading man shot out the lock of the double doors. Guns levelled, they advanced into a room where boxes were stacked in rows, neatly labelled in German script.

Jacob whistled. 'There's too much.'

Felix checked over the nearest boxes. 'Form a chain. Take the Roneo as well.'

They worked in silence and at top speed. Felix had calculated on half an hour, max.

6.45 p.m.

A siren sounded in the distance.

'Time to go,' said Felix. 'Now.'

He watched as the final box was hefted into the back of the van and the doors banged shut. The second van ground its gears. Tyres spun. Freya and the team melted away up the street.

Felix swung himself up into the first van. The driver drove cautiously along the street and headed south over the Langebrø bridge. In the distance, sirens screamed. Felix turned round to take a look. So far, so good.

The driver drove fast but competently. He seemed an unflappable sort. 'What are you going to do with this lot?'

'Hide it. After the war we'll send it to the official archives,' said Felix.

Once over the river, they drove down the Amager Boulevard before turning right into a network of streets. They were heading for a gateway that led into a yard with a warehouse on one side. As they approached, the doors opened and the vans drove straight into the warehouse, one after the other. The doors smacked shut. The driver gave a thumbs-up to Felix. 'That was good.'

The warehouse was stacked with barrels, boxes and sacks of concrete. Six men, who had been waiting for their arrival, threw away their cigarettes and got to work.

Two of them changed the number plates on the vans and sprayed the words 'Kraft's Electricians' on the sides. The remainder of the men concentrated on unloading and stacking the boxes behind the barrels.

Felix gave the vans the once-over. 'Fine,' he said.

Within a short time, the drivers had backed them out of the warehouse and were away.

The final box stowed, the men dispersed with

instructions to take different routes back to the city centre.

Felix's balaclava was sodden with his sweat but he waited until the last man had left before removing it. All was quiet, the place stank of paint, but he allowed himself a moment's satisfaction at the success of the operation.

Picking up the nearest box file to hand, he rifled through it.

Immaculate. If this was the calibre and organization of the intelligence then it would be a big, creamy piece of cake to piece together a trail of information. He read on. German nationals living in Denmark were sending streams of business intelligence to Berlin – so far, so predictable. More surprising was the tally – and it was a sizeable tally – of Danish firms who were falling over each other to be appointed suppliers to Germany. Letters from them, plus letters from young men volunteering to undertake unpaid work in Germany in order to prepare for 'the new post-war Europe', letters begging for preference . . . They were all present in file after file.

Felix hunted on and unearthed a card index, which he set down on a box. Brushing a finger over the cards, he watched them waterfall forwards and backwards, revealing a fulsome *dramatis personae* of businessmen, bankers, landowners and farmers, together with the numbers of their files. Then, as he knew he would do because of Freya . . . because of Eva . . . he tamped down on the letter E.

Eberstern. Green file 257.

Time was short. Why should he bother? What on earth was it to him?

Shuffling through the boxes marked E, he retrieved file number 257. Stapled into it was the Declaration which bore the signature of Bror Eberstern.

He skimmed over it. Now he understood what Freya wanted.

War had taught him about . . . oh, hatred, vendetta, but also about the surprising modesty of some, and the heroism of others who were prepared to lose everything. Its uncertainties and violence had also taught him friendship – his friendship with Freya – which was why he was now going to take possession of this incriminating document.

Folding the certificate into a square, he slipped it down inside one of his socks and stowed the file back in the box.

War had made him love his country. It had also caused him to burn with longing for . . . Eva . . . who had held him fast in the fish hold of a bucking ship. It had given him intense emotional experiences. In its aftermath . . . if . . . *if* . . . he survived, he would give thanks for such inner grace.

Time to go.

At the far end of the warehouse there was movement in the shadows.

A *stikker*? One of his men come back to check up?

537

Felix reached for his pistol and ducked behind the boxes.

Don't blink. Wait.

'Felix?' Odin materialized out of the shadow. He was dressed in a suit, with a light cashmere overcoat, shoes of the best quality and a hat pulled low over his face.

He had been right. This man didn't entirely add up.

'How did you get here?' Felix was curt.

'I followed the convoy and waited.'

'A word of advice.' Felix put the pistol away. 'Don't creep up on me. I shoot first.'

Odin shoved his hands into his pockets. 'What were you looking for, Felix?'

'None of your business.'

Odin pointed to the squat shape of the card index. 'That's what I've been sent for. Our chaps will keep it safely hidden.'

Was he after something else?

Odin moved closer and Felix caught a blast of alcohol. 'Motives are not always straightforward. They may be the right motives but they are not straightforward.'

'Since you're here,' said Felix, 'help me drag the tarpaulins over the boxes. This lot would be better hidden.'

Odin glanced down at his expensive clothes and sighed. 'In war it's necessary to make sacrifices.'

With some difficulty, they manoeuvred the tarpaulins into place. Spotting a half-empty bag of concrete power, Felix took a fistful and scattered it over the tarpaulins.

Good. They looked as though they had been there, untouched, for months.

Odin brushed down his lapel. Then, without warning, he reached over and patted Felix's pockets.

In reply, Felix's hands clamped down on Odin's. 'What the hell do you think you're doing?'

'Have you been snaffling information?'

'Fuck off, Odin.'

'You know as well as I do that everyone's in it for themselves.'

Felix increased the pressure of his grip. 'While we are asking questions, are you here to "check up on the family", as you put it?'

Odin looked down at Felix's hands. 'Get off me.'

Felix pushed him away.

Wiping his hands on a handkerchief, Odin said, 'Let's do a deal, Felix. You let me have half an hour here and I'll do my best to see that the dogs are called off Freya.'

Felix whipped out the pistol from his pocket. 'Get out.'

'You're missing a trick, Felix.'

Who could one trust? Did it matter any more?

Felix calculated. He didn't want trouble which would draw attention to the warehouse. Also, Odin was an important link and it would be cleverer, more constructive, to let him have his head and to keep an eye on him.

'Maybe.' Felix dropped the pistol back into his pocket.

Odin hefted up the card index and slotted it under his arm. 'Don't bother with trying to protect the fat cats in here. It will come out in the end.'

To punch him or not? Felix was sorely tempted. 'We're not going through this war just to return to how things were. You won't be giving the orders.'

'Someone always gives the orders,' said Odin, pulling his hat down over his eyes. 'But maybe you're right and it's over for people like me. Rest in peace, the ruling class.' He peered through the gloom. 'For some reason we Danes see ourselves as one big, happy, democratic family, and maybe that will happen.'

At the door, he turned round. 'By the way, where is Freya?'

'Shut up.'

'I've seen the way you look at her. You should be careful.'

'Shut up.'

'Or is it the daughter that's taken your fancy? I'm told she's disappeared.'

Felix actually laughed. He adjusted the torch beam so it blazed onto Odin's face. 'Get out of here.'

'Aren't you forgetting that we are on the same side?' Odin patted the card index. 'My informant tells me that this little sweetie is kept bang up to date. Which is good for us, don't you think?'

He raised a hand and waved. 'So sorry I can't give you a lift.'

It was after nine o'clock. Time was catching up with him.

Felix hurried through the streets, always conscious that there might be something gaining on his back. His steps quickened. Hurry. *Hurry*. But don't look too hurried.

Making his way through the back gardens to avoid the curfew, Felix got himself to the safe flat near the Vesterbrogade.

Had he been followed? *Check*.

Escape route out of the house? *Check*.

The routines had been laid down in his brain like neural pathways.

He slid in through the door. At his entrance, a figure reared up at him in the darkness. His hand flew to his pistol.

'Easy!' Freya said. 'Easy.'

'What are you doing here?'

'I wanted to see you.'

He put the pistol away and placed his hands on her shoulders, 'Idiot.' Odin's words came back to him: 'I've seen the way you look at her.'

He moved away.

'Have you got a cigarette?' she was asking.

He chucked her a packet.

She smoked it in quick, nervous bursts. Watching her, Felix thought how lonely she looked. He understood perfectly. This life turned you into a solitary person and a solitary spirit. Spending nights alone in a room, a gun to hand, hardly remembering which name it was you had today, twitching at every sound, yet prepared to go out with weapons blazing – it changed you.

Looking at this room, who wouldn't feel depressed? In one corner a dispirited plant struggled for survival and the overstuffed furniture was upholstered in a dingy brown.

'Freya, what do you want?'

'Is there any news of my daughter and husband?'

'You know I can't tell you.'

'*Please.*'

Felix crossed to the window to check the street outside. Vulnerability was not permitted in an agent's arsenal. Yet who was he to deny Freya what she needed to know? 'All I can tell you is that she got to Sweden safely.' He turned round to face Freya. 'That's it.'

'I'm sorry to harass you.' She stubbed out the cigarette. 'One day, you might understand. When you have children. Loving them is the most powerful thing.'

Once she had been glossy and perfumed. Now she was thin, crop-haired and her clothes smelled, but the pair of them understood danger, exhaustion and lowness of spirit. Intimately. They had shared it. What existed between them now went beyond mere description and beyond measuring.

'Felix . . .' Freya laid a hand on his chest. 'If

anything should happen to me, will you look after my daughter, who I think – I'm sure, whatever you say or don't say – is out there somewhere? Or will be, knowing her. For the war, I mean. Bror can't.'

He squinted down at her. 'You know I can't make a promise like that. No one can.'

She pretended she hadn't heard. 'I know she would be safe with you.'

'You don't know anything about me.'

'I do.' She lit up a second cigarette. 'Don't ask me how. I know you're the sort of person who always prefers to work on his own. Yes?' She chuckled – and at the sound a lump climbed shamefully into Felix's throat. 'I imagine you as an only child, playing on the beach, haring about on a bicycle, being taken to a pantomime at Christmas and sitting uncomfortably between your parents. Am I right?'

'Maybe.'

'I may not know your name but I understand the important things. That's why I'm asking you.'

Felix was sharp: 'Don't invite death by entertaining it.'

Her eyes narrowed in triumph. 'My point, Felix. That's exactly what someone who doesn't have children says. But for those who do, they *have* to think about it.'

Outside in the street, a car slowed down. Felix pulled the curtains shut, dowsed the light then snatched the cigarette from her and stamped on it.

'There's a way out of the window and over the wall into someone's back garden,' he said.

'So will you?' Her whisper seemed to echo in the dark.

'I can't make promises.'

A faint sigh emitted from Freya.

He knew he had disappointed her.

They pressed back against the wall by the window. He edged close to her. Closer. Their shoulders collided and he said, 'Your daughter is pretty extraordinary.'

Again, the chuckle that tore at his heart. 'Tell me something I don't know.'

'I have something for you.' He reached down to his sock, pulled out the certificate and pressed it into her hand.

'What is it?'

He told her.

Cradling it between her hands as if it was one of the jewels that she had once worn, she said: 'You got it for me?'

Their faces were almost touching. 'Do what you will with it.'

He barely heard the whisper. 'I cannot thank you enough.'

Felix slid his arm round her shoulders. 'I'm not going to ask questions. Nor am I ever going to talk about what it contains.'

A sliver of light from the car's headlights poked through the slit in the curtain and he saw that tears were running down her cheeks.

'I'm frightened,' she said.

He took his time . . . the images running hither and thither in his head.

'So am I.'

'Not of this . . .' She gestured into the darkened room. 'But of not coming up to the mark . . . failing when it matters.'

Felix leaned over and kissed Freya on the cheek. 'Shush.'

He was tender. He was loving. Those were the things he had been anxious that he would lose.

Twenty minutes or so later they agreed to turn the lights back on. Freya slid the paper into the lining of her jacket and tied on a headscarf. 'I'll go.'

'It's after curfew. You'll have to stay here.'

'I was forgetting.' She pulled off the headscarf. 'How I long for a deep, hot bath,' she remarked. 'A scented one. Sometimes I dream of being back in the bathroom in Rosenlund.'

So saying, she almost broke Felix's heart.

CHAPTER 31

Jacob sent a message from Køge: 'Lie low. SS Schalburg Corps in area for next two weeks playing war games. Currently north of Rosenlund.'

'Whoa,' said Felix. 'We keep away.'

There was no question of retrieving the wireless set. Instead, Felix sent Kay with a message to the group leader in Roskilde. Having delivered it, Kay criss-crossed the town, doubling back more than once on her path, and finally she boarded the København train.

The carriages were crowded and she was pressed up against the window.

The landscape was familiar, plunging Kay into nostalgia for her former Danish life. Then she reached further back into memory, to the little English girl she had once been who had waved a Union Jack at the British King and Queen as they drove through her town.

Her mother would think of her often. Of that, Kay was sure. As for her sisters? They would be too busy with their families to spare her more than a passing recollection.

Bror would be thinking of her, too, inevitably with anger. Perhaps he was astonished at how twenty-five years of a good marriage could turn on a sixpence into . . . bitterness and absence.

She missed him with a painful, scratchy emotion and yearned to see him, knowing perfectly well that the best thing to hope for was that, as with all desires, it would fade with time.

Kay's instructions were to avoid Køge and the areas of København where she was known. She did her best to follow them and to observe the things Felix had taught her about the undercover life before he had fled to Sweden. Tips on where to sleep, how to walk, what to say. The art of deception. The art of subterfuge.

Living undercover was an intense and overwhelming experience, and she was working on how to handle it.

Items to be carried in a bag, or to be worn on top of one another: one vest, two pairs of underwear, two pairs of socks.

She wore a long-sleeved blouse, pleated skirt and a beige mackintosh which she tried to keep immaculate. More than once, she had been forced to wear wet clothes because it hadn't been possible to dry them overnight.

Obedient to Felix's diktats, she never stayed more than two nights in the same place. Her sleep was fitful. Plus, her stomach responded badly to being on the move and frequently played up. After a life of plenty, infrequent meals had taken some getting used to. Felix allocated her what he could but obtaining money was difficult, and she was forced to eke out every kroner. Unsure where the next meal would come from, she dreamed unsettling dreams of roast pork, cherry flans and the best bread and butter.

A mile or so outside Hedehusene, the train ground to a halt. Kay's hand tightened on her basket. They were at a standstill in a steep-sided cutting, which meant it would be impossible to escape.

The sturdy woman opposite, who looked like a farmer's wife, peered at Kay. She willed herself not to shift in her seat.

Who could you trust? Who couldn't you trust?

A dog barked. Kay tensed. *Gestapomen* searching the trains with dogs were a regular occurrence.

Remain on it or not? Instinct told her to run but, before she could decide, the train moved off. The barking faded into the distance. Even so, she decided to get off.

At Hedehusene station, Kay dropped lightly down onto the platform.

Walk as if everything is perfectly normal. Look neither right nor left. Do not hurry out of the exit.

At the taxi rank, she asked to be driven back to Roskilde's main square. There she paid the taxi driver, further reducing her ever-diminishing stash of kroner, walked to the library and enquired if Pernille was available.

A woman emerged from an interior office.

She was short, anxious and underweight. 'Yes?' She wasn't welcoming.

'Would it be possible to take a parcel of cabbages?' Kay asked.

Behind the spectacles, Pernille's eyes widened. 'I'll organize someone to deal with them.'

Half an hour later Kay was being driven towards København in a taxi which had appeared at the back entrance of the library. Approaching the suburbs, she felt a relief. City streets and crowds provided cover and in them she could be safer. Anonymous.

The taxi driver deposited her behind the main station in the Colbjørnsensgade. He refused to take any money but said that she should come back to Roskilde after the war and pay him then. 'You trust me?' she asked.

'Yes,' he said and drove off without looking back.

A good Dane.

Walking towards the town square, she noted the uneasy atmosphere. Unusually, huddles of people were gathered at the street corners. 'Is anything happening?' she asked a woman at the bus stop. The woman was carrying a tiny boy with a green woollen hat and refused to look at Kay. 'I don't want to say anything.'

'Whisper it,' said Kay. 'Please.'

Reluctantly, she muttered, 'Extra German SS have arrived in the city. And Nazi police.'

'Do you know why?'

The woman shook her head.

Locating a public phone, she dialled Anton's office. His secretary answered but was unwilling to put Kay through until Kay gave her name.

'All right,' Kay conceded. 'Tell him that Princess Sophia Maria wishes to see him.'

Back came the message to meet at the Café Tivoli in an hour's time.

The Café Tivoli was to be found down one of the smaller streets in the Frederiksstaden district and five minutes or so from the military head-quarters. Kay knew it. Expensive and discreet about the meetings and liaisons which took place in it, and with a reputation for the best hot choco-late in København, it was the sort of place Anton would favour.

He was already seated at a table at the back of the café, nursing a brandy. The lighting was dim and the table was set apart from the others. At her appearance he looked up. She sensed him recoil. 'You look terrible,' he said.

'Hello, Anton.'

'What on earth possessed you to contact me?'

She took in the uniform and the handsome face. 'Aren't you glad to see me?'

'Of course.' He looked her up and down and it was clear he wasn't.

In a flash, Kay understood she was no longer useful to Anton.

'You've caused a lot of trouble. General Gottfried was beside himself. It's taken me a lot of sweet-talking to keep in his good books. I suspect that he's worried he let you into his confidence. Did he?'

'Nothing you don't know already.'

'You've made an enemy of the enemy. A personal one, darling. Always a bad move. Fouled the nest. The bore is that the general isn't so keen to take my advice any more. You've tainted me and I'm having to work at it.' The corners of his mouth turned down. 'Paddling hard like a swan.'

The waiter placed coffee in front of Kay.

'And Bror?' She had difficulty saying Bror's name.

'If I didn't know him better, I would say Farmer Bror was grieving. But the old boy was always gloomy at the best of times. Not that I see much of him.' He added, 'I'm told he's been up and down to København since you vanished. He sees Nils. How they must enjoy each other's company.'

'Nils! How do you know?'

Since she last saw him, Anton's laugh had turned chesty. He was smoking too much but Kay couldn't blame him. 'Don't be naive, darling.'

So Bror was being followed.

'I would suspect—' Anton did not disguise his amusement '—that Farmer Bror thinks you and Tanne have made a fool of him and Nils is the only one left with any sense.'

The coffee was wonderful. It tasted of times long ago, of money and of luxury. Ravenous for it, she drank it down. 'Order me another one, please.'

Anton obeyed.

'Why the extra Gestapo and the Nazi police drafted in, Anton?'

He positioned his cigarette case carefully on the table. 'Politics. In-fighting. It's an open secret. Hitler makes sure that he keeps his top brass on tenterhooks over their positions.' His smile was not reassuring. 'As you once said, darling, they fight like rats in a sack. It's always a winning tactic.' He seized Kay's hand, turned it over and ran a finger along the blue vein at the wrist. She felt a familiar tug of sexual attraction, but it was a discordant, disturbing feeling.

'Something must be happening. You must know what.'

He released her arm and spoke in a low voice. 'In the past few days, two German ships have docked here,' he admitted. 'Despite denials, our contacts tells us that Werner Best and General von Hanneken have been ordered to obey the directive from Berlin to round up all Danish Jews onto the ships and take them to Theresienstadt concentration camp.'

Kay forced herself to make the second cup of coffee last. Bitter. Black. Hot. And badly needed.

The brandy glass was empty.

'What are you going to do, Anton?'

'There's nothing I can do.'

She met his eye. 'Yes, there is. You *must* do something.'

'Don't look at me like that.'

She gathered her wits. 'What we do now deter-
mines our future. This is the moment when Danes
can show who they are.'

'Spare me.'

He wasn't interested.

'You do have a choice,' she persisted. 'You can
warn the Jews and make arrangements to hide
them.'

Anton transferred his attention to the waiter.

'Anton, *Anton*. Think.'

'Shut up, darling.'

'How many Jews are there in Denmark?'

'Six or seven thousand. I don't know the precise
number.'

'It must be possible to get a good few out to
Sweden. Some could hide in the more remote
areas.'

The waiter was approaching. Anton raised a
finger. 'Another brandy.'

She recalled their relationship over the years –
the teasing, the oblique flirting and the efforts to
keep him and Bror on good terms whenever they
met. 'Has the general, with his highly efficient
signals units, corrupted you?'

'If you must joke, make it more subtle.'

She nursed her coffee. 'It's early to be drinking
brandy.'

He shrugged. 'It isn't easy keeping afloat. In fact,
it's quite a strain. Do you know how many of my
brother officers have been interned?' Anton
contemplated the refilled glass. 'War isn't black

and white, tempting though it is to think it is.' He pinged a fingernail against the glass and it gave off a haunted, watery echo. 'For instance, sometimes you have to surrender information in order to keep credible. How black or white is that?'

Kay cut off the echo with a finger. 'Losing faith?'

He shrugged again – it was becoming a familiar gesture. 'In the long run, it's probably irrelevant who wins or loses. The imperative is survival. I took the view the Reich wasn't going to survive. Empires are tricky to achieve. And America is too powerful. Plus, in my way, I'm a patriot.'

Something pushed its way to the surface of her mind. Doubt? She peered at Anton and realized she had been reading him wrong all these months. 'Anton, you're on the right side, but for the wrong reasons.'

'Survival is the best reason. Think about it.'

Kay ran her fingers through her hair, stiff and dry from the cheap dye. 'Perhaps we never understood each other.'

Anton's jaw tightened. 'Melodrama doesn't suit you.' He pointed to her hair. 'I long to have back the pretty, witty woman I used to know. You look terrible.' When she sighed impatiently, he added: 'You realize you can't go back to Rosenlund? Or to Bror.'

'That's between him and me.'

'You're on the wanted list.' Anton smiled grimly. 'Mind you, Bror will be, too, at the end of the war.'

'So be it.' She got to her feet. 'I never knew what went wrong between you.'

Anton swallowed down the brandy. 'Went wrong between us? We don't like each other, that's all.' But something slipped from him . . . an envy, a longing, regret. 'And it's true my brooding country cousin had everything I wanted. Rosenlund. A wife like you.'

'You could have married.'

He caught up her hand in the old way – and, once again, she was the perfumed Kay Eberstern wearing Parisian couture. 'Tell me honestly, darling. Were you happy with Farmer Bror?'

'Yes. I was. Very.'

'But you like me, too?'

She braced herself. 'Yes, I liked you, too.'

Anton digested the past tense. 'What a pity it's all in the past and we can't go back. Are you frightened?'

She thought of the stories about bodies being taken apart piecemeal, the shootings, the incarcerations, the tortured man in Jacob's cottage. She thought of what the Jews must be experiencing. She thought of the fragmentation which had taken place within herself. 'Yes.'

'Keep away from Rosenlund.'

She breathed in sharply. *Home.*

'Kay . . .' Anton picked up his cigarette case and got to his feet.

'Ssh, that's not my name.'

'Get out of here. *Please.* Go to Sweden. Sit it

out until the war's over.' Then, as once before, he pulled her to him and kissed her.

His kiss was a reminder. Of what? Of being desired? Or of the time when she knew who she was and her days had been sweetly prescribed and bounded by innocent sleep. He murmured into her ear. 'Go to Sweden. Bror will never have you back.' His hand tightened on her shoulder.

No one could be trusted. Nothing remained the same. Nothing was normal. Her affection and fascination for Anton was turning into dislike. War had done that. She now saw that Anton was a profoundly cynical man – and cynicism was a fatal weakness.

The lie left her lips. 'Perhaps you're right. We'll meet after the war. Make sure you survive till then, Anton.'

'I have every intention of doing so.'

She detached herself. 'Goodbye, Anton.'

'Where are you going?'

Kay raised an eyebrow. 'You don't expect me to tell you, do you?'

Dates no longer meant much to Kay but everyone else knew the first days in October were important.

Anton had predicted correctly. On 1 October the long-suspected edict went out to round up the Jews.

In her shabby skirt and coat, Kay slipped here and there through the streets of København with Felix's messages, moving through the crowds of grey-looking people – heads down, shuffling, depressed – her appearance as nondescript as theirs. No doubt, if she'd looked, she would also have found the usual quota of flourishing black marketeers, *stikker* and criminals.

Yet sniff the air, as Kay did, and it was obvious something had changed. A mysterious trigger had been pulled.

Reports filtered in from their underground contacts all over the country.

Overnight, many of the Jews disappeared. They had been secreted in barns, outhouses, attics, cellars and churches, and a huge effort had been mounted to smuggle out to Sweden as many as possible.

She and Felix worked frantically. Planning. Coordinating. Alerting.

On 4 October, Felix instructed Kay to get herself down to Dragør, eight miles south of København.

By six o'clock that evening she was ensconced in a café on the harbour front. The tide was on the turn, and it was changeover time for the fishing shifts. The port bustled with craft pushing in and out through the wind and rain.

She scanned the quay for one in particular. Eventually, a small shabby boat eased alongside and moored.

Kay left the café, picked her way over rain-slippery cobbles to a house with a blue door and knocked.

'Dr Muus?'

Almost immediately the doctor emerged into the street carrying a black bag. She beckoned and he followed her to a house several streets back from the harbour where they were greeted by 'Bent', middle-aged and short-sighted, and one of the most successful and reliable of their men.

'They're traumatized,' said Bent, leading Kay and the doctor upstairs into a bedroom. 'You'll need to handle them carefully. Her name is Miriam.'

A young woman, still almost a girl, a small boy and a baby were huddled on the bed. The woman's hair was hidden under a scarf, accentuating a complexion as pale as whey. The children were dirty and the toddler was tear-stained.

Kay recollected her own pampered babies. The funny little sounds they made when feeding, hands batting her breast, the soft wool around their tended bodies, their yeasty smell.

She hunkered down beside the girl. 'Try not to worry, Miriam.'

'I-I'll be all right.' She was having difficulty speaking. 'I'm getting over the shock, that's all. Everything . . . we had to leave everything.'

'Your husband?'

'We didn't have enough money to pay for the fare for all of us. He's trying to borrow more so he can come, too. He promised we would meet in Sweden.'

'Have you eaten?'

'Bent has been so kind and given us bread and cheese.'

'We going to get you on board and this is what's going to happen.' Kay outlined the plan. 'I'm sorry, but we must do it now.'

Miriam clasped her baby tighter to her. 'You're sure it's safe?'

The doctor unlocked his bag. 'As safe as I can make it.'

He drew out a hypodermic needle and prepared it.

'That needle looks so big.' She swallowed back her tears. 'It will hurt them.'

'Yes, it will,' said the doctor. 'But you must be brave.'

'Hurry,' said Kay.

As she rolled up her son's sleeve, revealing his little arm, so white and fragile, Miriam whispered, 'We're playing a funny game, Erik. Look into my eyes and tell me what you see.'

The doctor acted swiftly, sticking in the needle and depressing the plunger. The child screamed once, short and sharp, then his eyes rolled back into his head and he fell forward onto his mother's knees.

The baby girl took a little longer and screamed harder, but eventually she was silent, too.

Miriam held them both and sobbed.

The doctor picked up his bag. 'The drug will wear off after several hours. They might be sick when they wake up.' His hand hovered over the heads of the unconscious children. 'Good luck.'

Kay carried the boy down the stairs. Miriam followed, cradling the baby. As they slipped and slid over the cobbles towards the harbour, salty rain lashed their faces.

When they reached the harbour, Kay was alarmed by the frenetic activity on the quays. A queue of taxis by the moored boats was disgorging passengers, all bowed down with bags and suitcases. Figures ran here and there.

She grabbed one of the sailors unloading his catch. 'What's happened?'

He didn't look up from his task. 'Word got around that the Jews could get boats out of here.' He moved away.

Someone shouted, 'Save my family.'

Shut up, she prayed. You never knew who would pick up the phone to the German commandant.

She turned to Miriam. 'See the light on that boat? We are going to make for it as fast as you can manage.'

Her arms wrapped round her daughter, Miriam ran. So did Kay, terrified one or other of them would fall over with their burdens as gusts of wind threatened to topple them.

Kay was running, running, feet fighting for anchorage, struggling to keep upright, the boy a dead weight in her arms. She felt the muscles in her back and arms take the strain. Pressed up against the child's body, she felt the beat of her own heart.

At the boat, she hustled them up the gangplank. Miriam was sobbing with fear, with sorrow, with relief. She turned to look at Kay and her mouth moved but Kay couldn't hear what she said. On board, other hands reached out and took charge of them. Kay relinquished her burden and the trio vanished into the bowels of the boat.

She turned and fled back into the shadow of a house. Here she waited until the putter of the engine and the visibly widening gap of black water between the fishing boat and the harbour reassured her they were on their way.

When she returned to Bent, he served her heated-up soup and slices of bread, then sat quietly while she ate and drank. Afterwards he ushered her to the room which had been occupied by Miriam and her children. Opening the window, he showed her an escape route over the roofs.

A rope had been slung up as a handrail between two chimneys – but it looked precarious.

'Which way should I go?'

'It's possible to get over the roofs of the two houses to our right, there is a walkway for the repair men, but be especially careful over the second. I'm not sure what their politics are. A fire escape leads down into a garden.'

Bent wished her good night. Kay stretched out on the bed, fully dressed, nerves thrumming. Rain beat against the window and the wind rattled the frame, and she prayed the fishing boat was well under way.

She awoke with a start.

Bent was pounding on the door. 'Cars everywhere.

Probably German. Stay on the roof. Don't try to escape.'

She ran to the window which overlooked the harbour. A fleet of cars was driving at full speed towards the waterfront, followed by a bus. To the north of the harbour, there was gunfire.

Whirling round, she flung open the escape window to rid the room of any telltale warmth from her occupation, smoothed over the coverlet and grabbed her shoes.

Then she was up and over the sill.

Her bare feet made contact with the tiles outside with an unpleasant smack. Reaching up, she closed the window as quietly as possible. Within seconds, she was shaking with the cold. Not good for balance. She made the calculation. Take thirty seconds or so to put on the shoes which would aid her flight? Or go?

Think.

Who or what were the Germans after? Someone might have given them a tip-off about her. More likely, they were putting a stop to the escape of the Jews in the harbour.

Stay put, therefore.

Inching across the roofs, clinging to the rope for dear life, she reached the shelter of a chimney and, with the utmost care, lowered herself behind it.

Shouts.

Screams.

Vehicles stopping with a screech of brakes.

The dogs. Always the dogs.

The shouts in German and Danish.

Craning round the chimney, she caught the tail end of a searchlight moving in a huge arc. A whistle blew. There was more shouting. Feet raced over the cobbles in the street, apparently coming closer.

She clung to that rope. How was she going to get out of this one? The rain stung her face and seeped through her clothes. What she would have given for Felix's training: the toughening, no-mercy-shown, stripping-down-to-the-essence preparation that he had described. At the very least, she would have been better at negotiating rooftops.

If you're caught you must hold out for forty-eight hours. That will give us enough time to disperse.

Forty-eight hours to discover one's limits and to experience real fear. Except for childbirth, she had no real acquaintanceship with pain. But she was becoming intimate with fear. Fear was a companion and, if not exactly a friend, a counsellor which taught her wisdom, although sometimes it also drew her down to a debilitating place.

More shots.

Shooting.

Ducks rising over the salt marshes, winging over the lake.

Bror.

Her children.

Up here, on this roof, she must not think about them. Those thoughts only made her vulnerable.

Her hold on the slippery roof was increasingly

in doubt and Kay felt herself slipping. She wound the rope round her arms. Steady.

Better, much better, to think . . . of the Germans surrendering in North Africa, of the Allies landing in Sicily, of Mussolini being deposed. Inch by inch, *inch by gory inch*, the war was changing. Over there, in the heat and the mud and the blood . . . And here in Denmark, too, where the grey spumy sea lashed the shores.

Still, by the time the hubbub had died away she was almost at the end of her physical tether. Bent appeared at the window. 'Come.' He helped her back in, supporting her because her legs wouldn't obey. He had brought up a hot milk drink and an extra blanket. She had never been so glad of anything, *anything*, in her life before.

Kay shook as Bent spooned the hot milk up to her lips. 'Some bastard *stikker* gave the commandant a tip-off. A busload of soldiers arrived just as the Jews were boarding the ships. Dozens of them have been arrested.'

Thin and chalky as it was, the milk was blessedly reviving. 'We should be out there, helping.'

'Too dangerous and you should rest for a while.' He offered her a cloth to wipe her mouth. 'Drink up, Freya. You might need it.'

'You're a good man, Bent.'

He blinked short-sightedly. 'It's my duty.'

Impulsively, she reached over and kissed him. He smelled of onions and fish.

A little after midnight, when Kay was trying to

564

sleep, an explosion tore through Dragør. She leaped to the window. Out in the Sound, a ship was on fire, flames tearing into the sky.

Ambulances raced towards the quays.

Within minutes, she and Bent were running down to the port. Already a crowd had gathered. Someone shouted that a Danish ship had hit a German mine.

She and Bent fought their way through the onlookers to the edge of the harbour. On the quayside, a doctor was organizing medical help for the wounded sailors being rowed ashore. Some were screaming. Others lay charred and silent on the stretchers. The doctor worked on stabilizing the worst injured before they were loaded into the back of the ambulances.

'Take him.' The doctor gave the signal for a badly burned sailor to be put into the ambulance. 'Come.' As cool as a cucumber, the doctor beckoned to a couple clutching bundles who had shrunk back out of the spotlights. They hesitated and he repeated: 'Come.' So saying, he packed them into the ambulance along with the stretchers.

The whole thing happened very fast.

Kay whispered, 'Bent, he's loading up the Jews with the injured.'

More ambulances raced to a halt and formed a queue. One by one, the stretchered sailors were dealt with by the doctor, and men, women and children were plucked from the shocked, huddled mass and shovelled in alongside them.

No one said anything.

No one in that shifting, disturbed crowd.

But they knew.

Good Danes.

How admirable the doctor was. In the end, Kay thought, most . . . the majority . . . of people were good and acted justly. Kay's throat tightened. It was important to know that truth. It was important to see it. Here was a man who seized a chance to defy evil. A man who acted.

Shouts. Sirens. German cars were racing along the road. Reeking of fuel, smoke from the blazing ship drifted inland, folding over the watchers. To Kay, it seemed to summon up all that was dreadful about the conflict – a hell, both real and metaphorical.

The rowers on the lifeboats strained to reach the port. The craft banged against the jetties. Yet more injured were landed.

'Who's the doctor?' she asked Bent.

'Dr Dich. He's one of us.'

One of us.

Kay gathered her wits. *What would the trained agent do?* What anyone would do in this case, was the answer.

Working their way around the crowd, she and Bent pushed to the front those who they reckoned were on the run. Bent peeled off to collect any who might be wandering the side streets or sheltering in the local cafés.

'Don't be afraid. Look straight at the doctor,'

Kay instructed those she helped. 'Get close to the ambulances.'

Some were dazed. Some wept hopelessly. Others were defiant.

A fourth and fifth ambulance manoeuvred into the increasingly crowded area. More Jews were pushed inside them. The doctor fastened the doors. 'The hospital,' he ordered the drivers. 'Next.'

Sirens blazing, lights flashing, they raced off. Kay watched. Eventually, all the injured sailors had been dealt with and the crowd had begun to thin out. Now it was imperative to scoop up any Jews who hadn't made it.

Bent clutched at Kay's arm. 'It's a good night's work for us Danes,' he said. 'Wouldn't you say?'

Us Danes.

CHAPTER 32

Twenty-four hours later Kay returned to København from Dragør with two teenage boys in tow. Separated in the melee from their parents, they had been wandering around the harbour, clutching satchels full of their school books, when Kay found them. They were almost speechless with shock.

'Pretend I'm your mother,' she instructed, snatching up the youngest one's hand.

It lay in hers, icy with its owner's desolation.

Where to hide them in the city while she arranged a safe passage out of the country? She took a decision to make for the Mueller house, only to catch sight of SS cars in the street. Aborting, she hurried them away down a street which ran parallel. It was sullenly empty, with only a few bicycles chained to the lamp posts.

What next? Where to go, whom to trust? The answer arrived – and it drove the breath from her chest. Nils. *Nils* . . .?

A black car nosed down the street. Hustling the boys ahead of her, she rounded the corner and cut down a side street.

Could she trust her son?

A little later Kay led the boys across the university courtyard and up the stairwell leading to Nils's room. Instructing the boys to stay quiet outside, she entered without knocking.

The usual sight greeted her. The light from the desk lamp revealed piles of dusty books, the sparse furniture, and paper stacked into wire baskets. Nils was at the desk, transcribing formulae onto a piece of squared paper.

Her son.

The characteristics she knew so well were all on display . . . clothes in need of a press, shaggy hair, threadbare tie. Familiar things which she so loved, and so hated, in him.

None of that mattered, of course, only that he was there. He looked well and busy and she loved him beyond words.

'What the—?' He looked up but it took a good few seconds before he recognized her. 'Good God!'

She held a finger up to her lips. 'Say nothing. I'm Lise, an infant school teacher you met on holiday.'

Shock slowed him. But he got to his feet and made his way over to her. 'Where've you been? We've been out of our minds with worry.'

Tears came into her eyes. She dug her hands hard into her pockets. 'Don't make me cry.'

'Nor me.' He brushed the palm of a hand across his eyes – touching Kay to the quick. It was as loving a gesture as Nils would ever make. She longed,

longed, to kiss him but knew he probably wouldn't tolerate it.

Did he look well? Yes, he did. Why hadn't he had a haircut? On balance, though, longer hair suited him. Precious, precious pieces of information on which to catch up, and to mull over, later.

'*Mor*, *why* are you here?'

'I need to hide some people and I thought of you. Please don't ask questions, Nils. Will you let me?'

He stuffed a hand into a pocket. 'I always ask questions, *Mor*. I'm not doing anything unless you explain to me.' He added, 'Sensibly.'

He meant without emotion.

'Who are they?'

'Jews,' she answered.

Nils started.

'Will you do this? Not for me but for them.'

He gave a drawn-out whistle.

'Nils, you can't let this happen. You can't have listened to the rubbish that's being said about Jews? They're herding them up like animals.'

Nils smoothed his hand across the network of symbols and figures on the papers in front of him.

She hissed, 'There's very little time. There are two boys out in the corridor who don't know what's happening to them. They're terrified and they have no idea where their parents are. Or what's going to happen to them.'

He reached for his pencil and turned it round and round between his fingers.

Her beloved son was not a monster . . . no, never that . . . but, as she knew so well, he looked at things from a different angle to most people.

'I can't leave them in the corridor.' If she had to beg, beg she would. '*Please.*'

Nils put down the pencil.

'You have the chance to be part of something . . . big. Worthwhile. More importantly, Nils, something right.'

He frowned.

'Nils?' One last attempt. 'It *is* the right thing to do. The moral thing.' She searched for the words to which he might respond. 'I wouldn't ask you . . . I wouldn't put you in this position except I don't know where else to go.'

He looked up. 'All right.'

Love for Nils broke in a wave over her head. 'Pretend they're pupils and you're giving them extra tuition but the session ran over and they found themselves trapped by the curfew. Keep them here. It'll only be for one night while their passage is arranged.'

She ushered the boys into Nils's room. 'You're being given tuition in applied mathematics,' she briefed them. 'Tomorrow morning I'll take you to Gilleleje where I'll get you a boat to take you to Sweden. Until then, you have to be quiet. Very quiet. And very patient.'

The boys' dark eyes registered their bewilderment.

'No need to look like that,' said Nils. 'I'm not

going to eat you.' He pointed to the bedroom. 'In you go.'

Nils's no-nonsense approach appeared to cheer them. The older one flashed a reluctant grin. 'Where will you be?'

'Right here, working. So you'll have to shut up.'

He closed the door on the boys and retreated with Kay to his study, where she thrust a paper into his hands. 'Read it and then get rid of it.'

He glanced at the headline: 'The Danish Freedom Council sharply condemns the pogroms the Germans have set in motion against the Jews in our country'. Nils slotted it into the paper pile in a wire basket. 'What happens if you don't turn up for them tomorrow?'

'Get them to Rosenlund and Arne.'

'Arne!'

'Yes, Arne. He knows what to do.'

Nils's expression was a master study of shock. In a different time, in a different situation, she might have laughed. 'Nils, darling.'

He retreated behind his desk. '*Mor*, I'm only doing this once. Have you got that? The thing is . . .' He scratched his head. 'The Germans visit me. Regularly.'

The skin on her arms goosefleshed. With alarm. With dislike.

'Don't look like that, *Mor*. They come here to discuss mathematical problems. What do you expect me to do? If I tell them to get lost I'll be put on a list, or thrown into the Vestre.

Anyway, it's the mathematical problems we're interested in.'

Memories of Nils as a tiny boy. He and his German cousins were romping around a hay meadow near Munich. It was a scene full of sunlight, fragrance, happiness.

What *did* she expect him to do?

'I saw you with General Gottfried.'

'Did you now?'

'I was in a taxi on my way to see you but I left when I saw who you were entertaining.'

'He wants to pick my brains. I allow him to up to a point. But only up to a point.' He shrugged. 'Self-preservation, *Mor*.'

'I knew you couldn't really support what the Germans are doing.'

He turned away. 'It's tedious when people take sides. I don't approve of people who don't think for themselves, that's all.'

'But supporting them?'

'I don't support them. I tolerate them.'

The difficulties of understanding her son's thought patterns were never going to lessen. 'How's your father?'

'Completely at sea. He can't believe what you've done.'

Unable to stop herself, she reached over and caressed his cheek. 'I'm sorry, Nils, but I'm not sorry. Can you understand?'

'That you've placed us all in danger? That you've gone?'

573

The harshness was mitigated by Nils slipping his arm round her shoulders. With that unexpected, and rare, sign of affection he was telling her that, perhaps, there was some point of convergence, some level of complicity.

After a moment he said: 'Do you think you were spotted coming here?'

'Possibly. I was desperate. But you take quite a few students, don't you? I thought I could take the risk.'

It was a bad night, holed up in the boiler room of a hostel near the river.

She went over and over what she should do. What could go wrong? Everything. What was her plan? Get the boys to the station. The risk? Being caught on the train. She must coach them on behaviour. Find more money.

In the discomfort of the boiler room she felt her will to keep going under attack and her resolution splinter.

Up early, Kay adjusted her clothes, tied a different headscarf under her chin and went out into the street.

Everything was grey. Sky, streets, people . . . her forebodings. She walked quickly, but not too quickly. One day, the grey would lift and they would all be normal again.

Watch. Check.

Shortly after eight-thirty, she let herself into Nils's rooms. A sweep of the room revealed he was not at his desk and the door to the bed-room was shut.

But someone was standing at the window which overlooked the courtyard. Hands in pockets. Worsted suit. Fair hair swept back. A man whom she knew through and through.

She tried to back out into the corridor.

Too late.

He turned. 'What—?' There was a second's shocked silence. 'Kay!'

Bror grabbed her and kicked the door shut. 'What are you doing here? Are you mad? But you're safe, you're safe.' He pulled off her scarf. 'Oh my God! What have you done to yourself?' He cradled her face between his hands. 'Your beautiful, beautiful hair.'

She clung to Bror's suit lapels – as if she could tap into his strength. She had dreaded this meeting. She had longed for it. During those frequently claustrophobic hours hidden up in a lair some-where she had been riddled with hate for Bror, and shame for his rotten politics.

To see him in the flesh was different. 'Hello.'

'Is that all you have to say?'

The material under her fingers was so familiar, the best quality, totally reliable. She grasped it tighter. 'Are you going to give me away?'

'What do you think?'

They looked at each other.

Dane and Briton. The husband and the wife. The landowner and the terrorist.

Bror put his arms round her. 'There's a price on your dyed, obstinate, stupid head.' She looked up to see unfathomable sadness reflected in the blue eyes. 'I'm so glad to see you, Kay.'

'And I you.'

His chin rested on the top of her head. 'Each day I wake up and my first thought is of you. But today it was different. Perhaps it was the unfamiliar hotel room? Or perhaps it was because I'm seeing the bank manager?'

'Is that a joke?'

'I haven't made a joke for – oh, months. Yet something pushed me to see Nils . . . and I find you. Do you think I knew without knowing?'

She smiled. 'That's a nice idea.'

Rain began to lash against the windowpanes.

'Where is he?'

Bror released her. 'Sleeping. At least, so I presume.' He paused. 'Do you know what you've done?'

'I do.'

'Did you hate me that much, Kay?'

'It's not a question of hate, or love.' She gave a small smile. 'But, yes, at times I did hate you.'

'I see.' Bror's right hand had a half-healed cut on a knuckle. How many times had she dealt with his bashed-up fingers? 'Come back, Kay.'

'You know I can't.'

'I know,' he said. 'It's hopeless but I thought I'd say it. Despite everything, I dream that you've come back. I imagine I can hear you whistling to the . . . the dogs and we walk down to the lake together.'

There was no time for this.

Kay took in a deep breath of Bror's Berlin cologne. 'Bror, I can't explain but, if I promise to meet you, will you leave now?'

Too late. A tousled, blinking, but fully clothed Nils appeared at the bedroom door. '*Far?* Here again? Why?'

'To see how you were. Is that so odd?'

Kay made to close the bedroom door, but not fast enough. It swung back to reveal the boys sleeping face to toe on the floor.

Bror looked from Kay to Nils. 'What's going on?'

'None of your business,' she said.

Bror reached inside his jacket for his cigarette case and lit up. 'Have you any idea how dangerous this is? The authorities are searching everywhere for the Jews.' He gestured to the untidy human heap on the floor. 'I presume . . .?'

'Shush.' The boys stirred and Kay closed the door to the bedroom. 'They've enough to put up with. Don't make them more frightened than they already are. Please.'

Nils sat down at the desk and pulled the papers sitting on its top towards him. 'Don't start, you two.'

'Do you think I'm a monster, Kay?'

He was sad, desperately so. She knew the signs.

'No, I don't. But do you know what's going on? Bror, *do* you know?'

'Of course.' He sounded more like his old self. 'Anton rang. God knows why. I didn't ask him to. His excuse was that he wanted to know how things were at Rosenlund. He couldn't wait to tell me about the round-ups and arrests. But at the hotel last night the talk was that most of the Jews have got away.'

'Yes,' said Kay. 'People did the right thing.'

'They did.' Bror wandered over to Nils's desk and flicked ash into the ashtray. 'Which makes one proud.' He looked up from the ashtray, meeting Kay's gaze. 'Don't you think?'

'Thank God . . .' Kay felt almost happy with relief. 'Thank God you feel like that. I didn't know . . . I dreaded that . . .'

Bror looked as though he had received a punch in the guts. 'You dreaded that I would agree with people being rounded up?'

'No, no . . . of course not.'

'Christ,' he said.

This was the moment and she took a gamble. 'Bror, I'm going to ask you to do something. Have you got the car? Take me to Gilleleje. Please. We can't have these boys' blood on our hands.'

'*Mor*,' Nils rattled the papers. 'What are you doing?'

Bror said, 'I'm not a murderer, Kay, either. Of course we can't have their blood on our hands.'

She stood before Bror – and she knew that she had become a travesty of the woman he had married. 'Help me, then.'

Bror picked up his hat and turned it round between his fingers. Outside, in the quad, a clock struck the hour.

Every second of delay was dangerous.

'*Please*, Bror.'

Bror held out his hand to Kay. With a sense that she had come home, she took it.

The boys were woken, briefed and hustled out into the corridor. At the door, Kay hesitated. Then she turned and ran back to Nils. 'I'm going to kiss you goodbye.' Cradling his head between her hands – in the way she had so often done when he was small – she did so. He smelled of sleep and beer and benign neglect. 'Please, please take care of yourself.'

'*Mor* . . .' To her surprise and delight, Nils kissed her back.

She swallowed.

Then she was gone.

Arm in arm, Kay and Bror crossed the quadrangle, the boys tagging behind them as if they were an ordinary Danish family. Ten minutes or so later they were packed into the car. Kay was in the front and the boys were in the back with a rug tucked around them.

They headed north out of København.

Kay sank back in the seat – and it was to sink back into a past she almost couldn't remember. A past in which the rich veneer of a walnut dashboard and the smell of leather seats – so luxurious and pleasing – were taken for granted.

Bror kept his eyes on the road. 'What do you want me to do?'

'Just get us there. Please.'

They were leaving the outskirts of København behind. The road was more or less clear. A few cars and vans chugged along and some wet cyclists battled the wind. Driving past the last ribbon of housing, it was clear that some of the houses were unoccupied. People were disappearing so fast . . . families were disappearing. The Jews had gone.

She thought about Køge. The place where she had spent most of her life was a mishmash if ever there was one. Nazi lovers and supporters lived there and shopped in the market place. As did realists and waverers and the frightened. There were the Birgits who lived in a state of high anxiety and didn't know which way to think, and there were the Jacobs and the Arnes who did know what they thought and acted on it. As ever, it came as a shock to Kay to know that she was part of that group.

What could be said in the final analysis? Resistance was always a matter of principle and politics? Or was it that some human beings were intrinsically bloody-minded? Or did resistance achieve that almost impossible synthesis by marrying both at the same time?

Who knew? Who knew?

Rain lashed down and the windscreen wipers gave off a customary screech. She laughed. 'You've never got them fixed.'

'There were other things to think about.'

Bror went first. 'Tanne . . .?'

She had to tell the truth. 'She got to Sweden,' she said.

A nerve twitched at Bror's temple. 'But she's safe, you think?'

There was a long pause. 'If she's in Sweden . . . but I can't know for sure if she's safe, Bror.'

'At least that's honest.'

She flinched.

At this section of the road the surface grew unreliable and Bror dropped his speed. He spoke with a rare intensity. 'I can't let you go again, Kay. For one thing, I can't stand the not knowing and . . .'

'And?'

'I can't bear to hate you.'

'We don't have to hate each other,' she replied. 'Not now.'

He glanced at her. 'The old life has gone and we can't have it back. That's the one sure thing in all this. You can accuse me of wickedness, or short-sightedness, and some of it would be true.'

The exhilaration at seeing Bror was draining away to be replaced by a numbing exhaustion.

'But will you believe me when I say I didn't know the extent of the Nazis' brutality . . . None of us understood at the beginning of the war what was going to happen. Even you. In Denmark there *was* an argument for the practical. For being a pragmatist.'

'No one thinks of arguments in the aftermath,' she said sadly. 'You are either the winner or the loser.'

'But you must understand why I chose the side I did.'

'Do you regret it?'

His gloved hands tightened on the wheel. 'I can't regret what is part of me. I'm not English or American. I'm Danish and some of my roots are in Germany.'

It hurt her to reply: 'But aren't these decisions moral ones?'

He nodded. 'That was my mistake.'

She checked on the boys. They were dozing. One of them whimpered in his sleep. 'Bror, let's not talk about it. Let's just drive.' She crouched forward on the seat, willing him to push on faster.

For a fleeting moment his hand lay on her thigh and the car picked up speed. After a while, he said, 'I've moved back into our bedroom. It has your things, your scent. I like that. I like to look out to the lake as you always did.'

Kay's first thought was that Bror was more likely to hear the plane if they made a drop. Her second was: *I can't bear it.* Followed by: *I have to bear it.*

'Kay . . . I know you understand what you have done.' There was a hint of bitterness. 'But I want you to know that *I* understand why you did it.'

The generous Bror. 'It was gradual thing,' she found herself confessing. 'A growing conviction. I got sucked into it so I can't claim a road to

Damascus conversion. It was a little resistance here, then there . . . and suddenly . . .'

'Look at me, darling.' Reluctantly, she obeyed and when she encountered the blue eyes she knew that what had anchored them together was still there.

Suddenly Bror checked himself. 'Kay . . . roadblock.'

It was a hundred metres or so up ahead. Bror cut the car's speed and drew up in front of it. Kay ran an expert eye over the soldiers standing miserably in the rain. 'Danish,' she hissed. 'Not German.'

'I'll do the talking, Kay. Do you trust me?'

Did she?

'Trust me, Kay.'

It was an order.

She gave a quick nod. He smiled for a second. 'Good.'

She turned round to the boys in the back. 'Not a word. Do you understand?'

The youngest looked half dead with misery. The older one had bitten his lower lip almost raw.

Bror tipped his hat down further over his face and wound down the window. Wind and rain blasted into the car as he conducted a polite, respectful conversation. Yes, he was taking his family north to visit relations. They had all been ill with some strange germ. His friend, General Gottfried, had advised him that the family needed a bit of a holiday and some good Danish dairy food.

The Danish soldier, wet and miserable, stamped his feet. Rain glistened on his youthful face, boredom registering in the downturn of his mouth. His companion, older and tougher, took a bit more persuasion.

'General Gottfried is going to join us,' said Bror. 'We plan to walk a little before the bad weather sets in.'

They were nodded through.

Bror started up the engine and they were away.

Kay stared at the windscreen and her eyes filled.

'Don't cry, darling Kay.'

'I'm sorry, Bror. Very sorry. But I would do exactly the same if it happened all over again.'

'So would I,' he said. 'Given what I am.'

'Bror,' she whispered. 'I . . .'

'Shush, Kay. None of our differences matter now. I love you. That hasn't changed and I want you alive. Do you understand?'

The car gathered speed. A familiar landscape unrolled. Ahead lay a grey sea and a passage to Sweden. Safety?

The poor boys. She turned round. Hands clasped, they had fallen back into a twitchy sleep. God willing their parents were still alive. They must be mad with anxiety. How she ached to give their children back to them. If she couldn't do that, at the very least she had to try to save their lives.

A short while later they drove into Gilleleje.

They kept the boys in the car while they entered into negotiations. The sum of money which Sven demanded for the fare over the Øresund was more than Kay possessed and it was Bror who paid up. Sven pocketed it. 'You think I'm over-charging,' he said. 'But consider the risks I'm taking.'

They left the boys hidden in his harbour boat-house, Sven having promised that he would ferry them over at the turn of the tide. Huddled on a bench, the boys barely managed a goodbye.

They returned to the car. Bror started up the engine and drove along the sea road out of Gilleleje for a kilometre or so. 'We came here one summer with the children. Remember?'

'I do.'

'What do you remember?'

She laughed. 'The wind. Trying to get a barbecue going on the beach. A lot of beer.'

A small, sandy bay came into sight and he braked. 'Do you think it might have been here?'

'I'm not sure.'

'I am.' He stopped the engine, got out of the car and walked around to the passenger door. 'Come.'

'I can't. You must get me to the train at Helsinger.'

'Come, Kay.'

It flashed across her mind that he might be plan-ning to kill her – and she shuddered inwardly. This was to become too habituated to a life of distrust.

'Why?'

'Gilleleje is a tiny place. We will have been noticed. The car will have been noticed. Don't you think we should make a show of being lovers?'

Again she laughed and looked up into his face. 'The ironies . . .' she murmured.

The wind caught them in a hard grip and they slithered down the sandy slope of the dune onto the beach. Bror put his arm round Kay and placed his mouth against her ear. 'Make for the beach hut over there.'

It looked familiar and she had a dim recollection of walking past it with the children. But, from the state of it, no one had bothered with it for years. A bleached, salty and cracking hulk, its wooden clapboards were rotting and the lock on the door was broken.

Inside, it smelled of tar, fish and brine. Abandoned coils of fishing twine and rope, stiff with age and mould, were strewn across the floor. Draughts knifed between the cracks.

Kay pulled off her headscarf.

'Kay.'

She turned round to face Bror. 'Yes.'

He leaned against the flimsily fastened door and reached for a cigarette. 'I want to know . . .'

'What?'

'About what you've been doing?'

Trust no one.

He made no move to touch her.

'You owe it to me, don't you think?'

Tell no one.

She told him about running through the woods, of her limited wardrobe. Of carrying her possessions on her back and of eating one meal a day.

Of how one becomes an itinerant in spirit with such a regime. Almost addicted to it? She described clinging precariously to a roof. She told him of the sad little Jewish family she helped to put on the boat to safety. But she didn't tell him about Felix or Arne, or the meetings and the plans and the wireless set. She didn't tell him, either, about London and the activities of the strange outfit for whom she was working. Nor of the struggle of the resistance to convince London that they mattered.

Telling Bror. Not telling him.

'You were too busy to miss me.'

'Oh, I missed you.' She tapped her chest. 'In there, deep down. Always.'

They could have been in their bed at Rosenlund, their bodies fitting together under the duck down. Talking.

Bror opened the door and threw the cigarette stub outside. Then he was beside her. 'Is this the truth?'

'Yes. Yes.'

'We have really got to the truth . . . between you and me?'

'Yes.'

He placed his hands on her shoulders in such a way that they cradled the curve of them. She drew in a breath. 'Bror?'

His hand sought under the much-worn, non-descript blouse and found her breast. 'Do you know how much I have missed you?'

Oh my God, she thought. Here she was . . . dirty,

587

dyed, thin . . . and here he was, pulling up her clothes . . . and, now, pushing her to the ground . . . like an impatient teenager.

'Do you remember that time at Rosenlund? In the lace dress?'

'I don't want to think of the past.'

'I know,' she said. 'But I can't help it.'

He didn't answer but pushed her legs apart. 'And Anton is part of you?'

It so often led back to Anton.

No more lies.

'I missed him, too.' Kay wanted to be truthful. 'But the old Anton. He was never anything, Bror. He was part of a life in which we didn't take things too seriously.'

Bror hesitated. 'So you used him to put me off the scent?'

'I did.'

'Christ, Kay,' said Bror. 'Do you know what you did to me? Do you know what it's like to lie awake imagining . . . Do you know what jealousy does? What it is? It's cruel. It's bitter. It's murderous.'

'I'm sorry.'

Bror bore down on her with his full weight. Deliberately crushing and exerting what power he possessed. 'Are you really sorry . . .?'

She spread her arms out wide, her half-opened blouse revealing her breasts. 'I am here.' Stirring deep in her body was an excitement, a sharp – almost too sharp to bear – desire and the longing for resolution.

Tar, brine, old wood . . . the smells would be forever associated with this moment.

After that, they were mostly silent. Her rucked-up clothing made a dent in her back as Bror took out on her both his anger and his love – and she permitted him to do so.

A little later he asked: 'So he's no longer in your head?'

'He never has been.'

There was a long pause. 'You hurt me, Kay.' Then he bent over and kissed her hard on the mouth.

Afterwards, he lay spent on top of her, his face pressed into her shoulder. She turned her head and the grain of the wood walls seemed monstrously enlarged. If permitted, jealousy became stronger than love and the urge to forgive.

'Forget Anton, Bror. Forget him.'

'Tell me you love me . . .'

Bror had never asked that of Kay before. 'I do.' She breathed in a shuddery breath. 'I do.'

Their marriage? After all these years, this is where they were. Almost broken by war, battered, with vast areas of darkness, irrevocably altered . . . but still living, still breathing.

In the silence, they heard the beat of rain on the roof.

It was time to go.

Kay wriggled out from under Bror and tried to tidy herself up. 'I know I look awful. I'm sorry.'

Bror touched her mouth with a finger. 'You look terrible. You look wonderful.'

589

Outside, the wind was stronger and a sleety rain slanted over the beach. Leaving the beach hut to its debris and decay, they headed for the car.

They drove in silence until Bror said, 'I don't feel right abandoning you, Kay.'

'You must.' Deliberately, she hardened her tone. 'You *have* to.'

'I want you to live more than anything.'

'As it happens, so do I.'

'I don't know what's going to happen. Or whether or not we will be here by the end of this mess. And it isn't a question of forgiveness because there's nothing to forgive.' He negotiated a corner.

Bror's sweetness made her cry. 'Actually, I wanted to thank you.'

'But I'm not stupid. I realize nothing will be the same,' he continued. 'Can it?'

'No.' She groped towards the answer. 'I can't give up now, Bror. I have to go back to what I am doing and you must go back to Rosenlund.' She raised her hands. 'I don't feel there's any choice.'

His hand searched for hers. 'Was it the adventure that kept you going? I sometimes thought you were restless . . .'

Had she been drawn to the fire because something hidden in her demanded it? Whipped her on?

'Perhaps. Among other things. Among other important things.' She took a deep breath. 'Bror, I am so sorry for what I've done to you and what I've done to the family. I'm sorry. I'm sorry.'

The wind rattled the car windows.

She began searching in her pockets. 'Oh God, I need a brush or a comb. My hair. I can't look a mess.'

Bror stopped the car, reached over to the glove compartment and extracted the comb which had always been kept there for Kay. 'Here. Sit still.'

They were back to long ago.

Carefully, tenderly, Bror combed Kay's ruined hair. What was he telling her – the terrorist wife?

The slow, gentle strokes told her that he loved her. In the turmoil and confusion of loyalties and politics and violence, that was still true.

'There must be something I can do to help, Kay?'

She looked down at her hands clasped in her lap and considered the answer which had been hovering. To keep whole in the face of fear was a colossal demand on anyone. Fear splintered the resolution and muddled the objective. It made one craven. Of all things, Kay continued to fear her fear, however hard she battled against it.

'There is one thing.' With a sense of profound relief, she leaned over and kissed his cheek. Bror let the comb fall to the car floor. Kay kissed the corner of his eye where the lines were being etched, then his chin, then his mouth. 'Promise me something . . .?'

Bror dropped Kay at Rungsted station and drove on to Rosenlund.

At the station, she sat down on a bench next to a man who was reading the daily paper. He looked

591

nondescript enough – but you never knew. The paper's headlines were visible from where she sat. The mass escape of the Jews provided the main subject.

The man looked up as he turned the page – and, for a tense second, Kay thought she was in trouble. 'Holger awakes,' he murmured. 'Holger awakes.'

Holger Dansk . . . the legendary Danish hero. A symbol of resistance.

She sighed with relief.

Communists, freedom fighters, the new Freedom Council . . . how and where these factions would unite into one effective force depended on people like Felix, Jacob and those such as herself.

What had brought them together? The question would never cease to fascinate her.

In København, Kay made for the safe house on the Ny Kongensgade. On the way she stopped at a couple of shops, and with the money Bror had stuffed into her pocket she purchased a comb, soap and cold cream, bread, and also sausage and a bottle of watery, greyish milk. At the hairdresser's, she asked for dark-brown hair dye. 'For my mother,' she explained to the assistant. 'She so hates being grey.'

At the safe house, she applied the dye and waited patiently for it to dry. Framed by the atrocious haircut, the face which looked back at her belonged to a stranger.

She ran a bath. Undressing, she discovered that her period had arrived unexpectedly and she had not made provision for it. The stains on her clothes were going to take time and trouble to remove.

In the bath, she regarded her newly thinned-out body. Was her system trying to recapture the days of marriage and maternity? Perhaps it had been love-making with Bror? The inconveniences of being female and on the run struck her as both funny and sad. How she ached to talk to Tanne about it and to ask her how she was coping with being female.

The water was only lukewarm but better than nothing. Kay made herself sit there for as long as possible. In this new existence, being clean was not always possible.

Lying back, she closed her eyes.

Bror?

She cupped her hand and trickled water over her chest. Grains of sand sifted out into the water and sank to the bottom of the bath.

Bror?

Think of his cattle and pigs in the fields, the mounds of cheese and pitchers of cream. Think of fresh bread. Of the jewels she used to wear. Remember always the fresh colours and scents of new growth in the Rosenlund woods, the smell of paper-white narcissi in the garden, the duck-down quilts on the beds, Bror's silk dressing gown. And always, always, the mesmeric moods and reflections of the lake. Its dreamy summer sparkle. Its frozen secrets in winter.

CHAPTER 33

Ruby and Peter hadn't spoken properly for months – and it was now October. And, no, she hadn't counted the weeks.

In August, Peter disappeared. He had been seconded to The Firm's headquarters in Cairo and wasn't scheduled to reappear in the office until late September.

Ruby lectured herself that she didn't mind his absence. Nor was she bothered that they had clashed so bitterly. There were other, much bigger, worries as the war lurched on.

Quite apart from anything else, she was half dead with fatigue. The agent traffic was building. With Peter absent, she had to cope with the situation on her own, which often meant working around the clock for days on end. Every brain cell had been squeezed dry.

But from time to time, she would raise her head from her desk and . . . there he would be, a ghostly Peter hunched over the desk in his office. She despised herself for it, for she didn't wish to see him either as an apparition or in reality . . .

but he was there. Ever wayward, even obstinate, her psyche disagreed.

Peter returned on a bright autumn morning, reclaiming his office with a slam of the door and a shout to Gussie. He was tanned but painfully thin as a result of a bout of dysentery.

Ruby sat at her desk and didn't move.

Gussie enquired if he had fully recovered.

'I was banged up in hospital with a lot of pretty nurses,' he replied.

She offered him a cup of stewed tea. 'Here's a reward for all that deprivation.'

The routines slotted back into place. First, Peter and Gussie tackled the backlog. Only then was Ruby summoned.

She walked into his office, closed the door and leaned back against it. Despite her fine intentions, her heart beat faster.

'Things seem under control here,' he said, shuffling through papers. 'It's to your credit that you and Gussie managed so well.'

'Isn't it amazing?' said Ruby.

'Just one or two things that need to be corrected.'

The old irritation stirred. Gussie and she had got on fine without him. 'I know,' she replied. 'Gussie and I often said: "We need Peter to put us right."'

She had succeeded in gaining his full attention.

'Oh Lord . . .'

'Oh Lord?'

'Don't look like that, Ruby. It spoils it.'

She looked down at her feet shod in regulation lace-up shoes. 'Spoils what?'

'The image that kept me going in hospital. When my insides were threatening to dissolve and I couldn't sleep, and it was painful, I thought of you.'

'Why?'

'Because when you smile, the sun, er . . . comes out.'

Ruby frowned. 'And?'

'Because I reasoned that, if I thought of someone as obstinate and bloody-minded and angry as you, then I couldn't possibly give in.'

'Fair enough.'

He got to his feet. 'Can we start again?' A pause. 'Ingram?' The last was said tenderly, like the private joke it was. The dark eyes raked over her face. 'Now. Quickly.'

Were they . . . were they going to begin all over again?

She kept her voice brisk and professional. 'I've thought of a way of trying to prove how unsafe the poem-code method is and it involves Vinegar.'

Peter sat down again. 'Right,' he said coolly and steepled his hands. 'You think Vinegar is being run by the Germans.'

They stared at each other.

She began: 'As you know, I went through his back traffic and there are several things to consider about him. Or her. We know Vinegar is no good at coding and yet he has produced impeccably coded messages. At the very least, should this not be questioned?' She shot a look at Peter. He was listening. 'But we can do it, Peter. To test Vinegar, we could send a deliberate indecipherable to him. Not too difficult for a trained German cipher clerk to cope with, but too difficult for Vinegar. If he asks for it to be retransmitted, we can conclude that he's still at liberty because, bad at codes as he is, he won't be able to decode it. On the other hand, if he replies, we'll know that an expert has worked on it.' She paused. 'And the expert is likely to be German.'

Break open a hypothesis and deconstruct it against every possible eventuality and consequence.

That was what she had been taught at Cambridge. That was what Peter would be doing. He needed time to examine the idea. Rightly so.

Eventually, after a long week, Gussie jerked her head in the direction of his office. 'Sir wants you. But, for God's sake, keep him sweet this time. He's been like a bear with a sore head.'

At Ruby's entrance, Peter got to his feet, a courtesy which touched her.

He went straight to the point. 'The idea's a good one,' he said. 'Suicidal but a good one. We just need to find a way to work it.'

Ruby hadn't realized how strange she had been feeling – as if she had been holding her breath for weeks.

Moving a little stiffly, Peter sat down.

What was she going to do about her feelings for him?

He's still very thin. He needs care. Her guts twisted painfully and the question forced its way out of her: 'Did you work through the night?'

His expression lightened. With relief? 'Are you worrying about me? And the answer is yes, I did.' The old, wry Peter – and the old, sparky Ruby – were back and they welcomed each other with a big smile.

Enough. To the problem.

'You realize the security protocols are draconian,' he said. 'Every message is logged and checked, both here and in the signals office. If one goes missing, or someone tries to send one that isn't authorized, there's an immediate witch-hunt. How we get our message transmitted is going to take some thought.'

'In any defence, there's always a weakness.'

'True. But it's bloody small in this case. But we agree, Ruby?'

'We agree.'

'Meanwhile . . .' He pushed the message he was holding over to her. 'Could you take this to the signals office? The night squad broke an indecipherable. It took over ten thousand attempts. I want to teleprint them my thanks.'

She looked down at the piece of paper. Running and fetching for Peter?

'Please?' His eyes danced. 'I wouldn't ask you normally, but there's a war on and you look useful.'

'Bugger off.' She found herself stiffening.

'Has nobody ever teased you, oh lovely Ruby? They should, you know.'

She glanced at it. Automatically, she began working away to disinter the words hidden among the letter groups – a Michelangelo chipping away at the block of marble to reveal the figure in its depths.

Oh, habit.

Up in the signals office, Ruby hovered by a signals clerk. He was young, frazzled and looked extremely anxious. He barely glanced at Ruby when she handed over Peter's message. 'Put it with the rest.'

Something prompted her to ask, 'Are you having trouble?'

'I'm not sure what to do,' he confessed as he rifled through a stack of paper. 'Can you advise?' He held up one of them. 'There are new procedures for cancelling messages. I've orders to cancel this one but I'm not sure how to proceed. It's message number sixty for Vinegar.'

The signals clerk could be in for bad trouble if she did this – but Ruby didn't hesitate. 'Give it to me,' she said. 'I can deal with it for you.'

Inside, she was shaking.

Later she and Peter faced each other across the desk in his office. Message number sixty to Vinegar – in reply to message number fifty-nine – lay on the desk between them. It had taken them an easy fifteen minutes to decode.

STAND BY FOR DROP ON TWENTIETH *stop* DZ AS SPECIFIED BY US NOT YOU *stop* LETTER K REPEAT K SIGNAL *stop* BBC MESSAGE CANUTE GETS HIS FEET WET *stop* ACKNOWLEDGE AND PLAY BACK BBC MESSAGE *stop*

'Why have they cancelled this?' Ruby asked.

'Maybe the section heads want to add something, but need to break it up as it is a long message.'

It made sense.

'Let's go over this.' With each point, Peter tapped a finger on the table. 'What do we know about Vinegar? He's a rotten coder but turns out impeccably coded messages. He is also a highly relibable wireless transmitter operator. He keeps asking for money and more agents. He's also been very specific about drop zones and won't take London's suggestions. Finally, despite requests, he omits to give details to London of any of the agents he says he's recruited. But his bluff and real security checks are in place.'

'Our argument, therefore, is that London is being played by the Germans, who are operating Vinegar's set,' said Ruby. 'That is why he is never keen to answer their questions. It also means that it is possible that any agents and equipment dropped at Vinegar's request have been delivered straight into German hands. If that has happened, it would only be because Vinegar's poem code has been tortured out of him.'

If ever a man looked at breaking point, Peter did then.

He had held off smoking until now but gave in. 'Question: why haven't our other agents noticed? Answer: there're only two of our wireless operators in Denmark at the moment. One is Vinegar, who was allocated to Aarhus on Jutland. Mayonnaise, who is operating on Zealand, reported that Vinegar was missing from the initial drop when they all went in. But, when checked out, it appeared Vinegar was sending traffic regularly. London discussed it, dismissed the problem and informed Mayonnaise that all was well.'

'This would be because the Germans had got the bluff and real security checks out of Vinegar and so all seemed to be normal?'

Peter twisted a pencil round and round.

'But why didn't Mayonnaise check up on Vinegar?' asked Ruby.

Peter leaped to his feet and consulted the map on the wall. 'Getting between Jutland and Zealand is not a doddle. Probably impossible at times. The Germans will have mounted watches on ferries and sea traffic.'

'Couldn't they get messages to and from? The couriers?'

'Who knows?' said Peter. 'London is relaxed about it because the chiefs are convinced that their coding methods are foolproof and that the enemy can't possibly be reading our traffic.'

Ruby raised her eyes to his. 'So . . . we go back

to the initial proposition. We arrange for this message to be sent, but this time we encode it in such a way that only a very experienced crypto-grapher could read it. If Vinegar replies, it suggests very powerfully that an expert, who almost certainly won't be Vinegar and is probably a German, is working on the decoding. We can present this as evidence to your chiefs.'

'But *if* Vinegar isn't in German hands, he'll reply asking for a retransmission and then the balloon will go up, and we'll be found out.'

Ruby was feeling sick enough as it was. 'What would they do with us?'

Peter raised an eyebrow. 'I gather there's a cooler in the remotest part of Scotland. Odds and sods are sent there. If they don't kill us, that is.'

He opened his drawer and produced a piece of paper. 'Vinegar's poem. Taken from "Helge",' he read. 'Vinegar insisted on a poem he knew from childhood, which doesn't help one bit. Oehlenschläger is the national poet and everyone knows his poems.'

She trembled inwardly.

'Are you ready?' he asked. '. . . Ingram?'

They chose 'late', 'heart', 'night', 'more' and 'begin', and wrote them out with a couple of spelling mistakes, since tired cipher clerks were sometimes guilty of that, and numbered the letters sequentially underneath. Next they made the first transposition with four of the columns in the wrong order: hatting, as it was known in the trade, and chicken feed to an expert cryptographer to correct.

They argued – almost pleasurably – over the deviations in the second transposition.

'Final question,' said Ruby. 'If it's an indecipherable won't they just ask us to repeat it?'

'Fritz won't want to hold up a drop. It's rich pickings.'

'And if it is Vinegar who's transmitting all along?'

'Trust you like haggis and turnips?'

As she left the room with the message, he said, 'Ruby . . .'

She turned back.

'Ruby . . .'

Her heart jumped and fluttered.

He looked at her with love. Oh God. And with tenderness. And openness. Ruby returned his look but her previous treachery – so lightly done – felt as heavy as lead.

If Peter ever found out it would hurt him, and hurt him deeply. Equally, her discovery that her strongly held beliefs on sexual liberty lacked staying power troubled Ruby not a little. The payback from the Tony episode was to realize that she would be haunted by it for a long time – and that was stupid, time-wasting and ran against her grain.

But she loved Peter.

And that was the price.

Handing over the message to a different signals clerk, she lied: 'The chief encoded it himself.'

⋆   ⋆   ⋆

Twenty-four hours later Peter sent Ruby a note: 'He's missed a sked.'

Another day crawled past.

They met in the corridor and whispered to each other.

'Would it be an idea to talk to Signals Clerk Voss while we wait?' she asked.

A third day.

Nothing.

For much of the time, Ruby couldn't eat. She relied instead on cups of stewed tea which turned the inside of her mouth to cotton wool.

Eventually, Gussie took a telephone call. She tossed her head. 'There's a car outside and the orders are that you are to join His Majesty. You're going down to the listening station. Bring writing materials.'

Listening Station 53d looked picture-postcard perfect as they swept into its drive. The trees were just beginning to turn and the unspoiled areas of the garden were full of shrubs and creepers.

'Ready?' asked Peter.

Ruby ran her tongue around her mouth, wishing she could brush her teeth, and that she didn't feel so nauseous.

She nodded. 'As I'll ever be.'

After Security had done their bit, they were shown into the signals room and found Signals Clerk Voss, headphones on, at her station.

'Sir.' She acknowledged Peter by pushing back one ear of the headphones but kept the other in place.

604

Save for the necessary equipment of sharpened pencils and sheets of paper, her station was immaculate. Propped up against the transmitter was an encoded message from London, ready to go.

Peter checked the skeds pinned up on the wall. 'Mayonnaise, when is he due?'

'Tomorrow. He went dark for some weeks but he's back.'

Ruby was quick to pick up that she sounded strained.

Encountering Mary Voss for the third time, Ruby paid more attention to her, taking on board the slight lilt to her voice and her passionate involvement in her job. Almost a possessiveness. Ruby resisted fiercely the temptation to categorize women by their looks, but on further scrutiny Mary Voss was blessed with a lovely skin and kind eyes. Unshowy and modest, she looked like the type of Englishwoman who, having never been encouraged to consider her looks, didn't.

'I gather Vinegar missed two skeds?'

This was confirmed by Signals Clerk Voss, but with obvious anxiety. She was about to add something when Peter cut her off.

'Tell me what you told Lieutenant Ingram here about Vinegar's fist?'

Mary had been waiting for the question. 'He was nervous in his early transmissions. I could tell. His C and M dotted about a bit. Agents are like that sometimes. Then they settle down . . . more or less. But they can be quite changeable. Some days they'll be that nervous and one can understand it. Other days they're smooth and confident. But they settle into an acceptable pattern. It was different with Vinegar because his improvement was so marked.'

Ruby shifted closer to Mary. 'In what way? Can you give Major Martin every detail?'

Mary Voss looked up at her. 'Vinegar is always assured. Smooth. Easy.'

'Anything else? Anything at all about him?'

Mary took her time. She was very careful. And precise. 'As I told you, in the first message he transmitted QRU as CAU. After that, he used the normal QRU sign-off.'

'That suggests he relaxed a bit,' said Peter.

'*Relaxed?*' exclaimed Ruby.

Mary looked at Ruby, who nodded encouragement. 'There was another thing,' said Mary. 'He got his frequency wrong.'

'Could be nothing,' said Peter.

'Except,' said Mary, 'he's made both mistakes a second time. I've got the note here with the date and time.'

She handed it over to Ruby.

'Did you inform the signalmaster when you first noticed the variations?' Peter asked.

'I reported it to Signalmaster Noble.'

'And what did he say?'

'To get on with the job.' Suddenly she held up a hand. 'It's one of mine, sir.' Her expression looked as if dawn had broken after a long, freezing night. Replacing her headphones, she took up her pencil and began to take down the Morse. Everything about her was pure concentration and Ruby was startled by its fierceness.

A furious Peter went to find the signalmaster to give him one of his typically quiet, but deadly, dressing-downs.

Letters streamed from Signal Clerk Voss's pencil onto the message paper.

There was a pause. Then she tapped out a short phrase. She explained: 'That's AK/R. I'm acknowledging receipt. Now, I'll give him QTC1 which means I have one message for him.'

As she watched the message being dispatched as easily and professionally as the one received, Ruby's guts told her that Vinegar was definitely being run by the Germans.

'Mary, it's vital to say nothing to anyone else about our investigations. But, if there is anything else you can think of, however tiny, please will you contact me or Major Martin?'

She was apprehensive and troubled. 'Not through the signalmaster?'

'No.'

Mary's lips curved in an enigmatic little smile.

Although the FANY chauffeur would be subject to the Official Secrets Act, it was a security rule never to discuss matters in the car. As they approached Regent's Park, Peter ordered the driver to pull up. 'Out,' he said to Ruby. 'We need to walk.'

They set off at a lick through the cherry trees.

Barrage balloons swayed in the sky. An ambulance's bell sounded in the distance. Fallen leaves lay scattered over the grass.

'Ruby . . .' Peter was sounding a warning. 'Ruby—'

She knew without being told what he was going to say and swung round to face him. 'Vinegar has replied confirming arrangements for the drop in Jutland. Why didn't you tell me?'

'Because I wanted your mind clear when you made your judgements after talking to Voss.'

'Oh God, oh God, I was right.' Despite herself, Ruby let Peter take her hands in his.

'You were right.'

His grip on her hands began to drive the circulation from her fingers.

'Thoughts?' demanded Peter.

'We begin with this and use it to construct the case.'

How does a captured agent try to warn Home Station?

What do you do if Home Station is blind and deaf to your warnings?

'Peter, what if the security checks have been tortured out of him and he's been trying to tell us a different way? Say, you are made to transmit with the Germans watching you. There's no chance of leaving out the real check. Is there?'

A man came up behind them and Peter released her. Ruby rubbed her fingers while she waited for the man to move out of earshot.

She continued in the same impassioned under-tone: 'They keep him alive for as long as he is useful and make him do the transmitting, because they know we know his fist, but they read, compose and code the messages.'

Peter nodded. 'It could happen.'

Stip, stap, stup . . .

'Was Vinegar trying to tell us way back when he misspelled "stop"?' She grabbed his arm. 'I now think he was. I think it was his way of telling us and we weren't listening.'

Picture it: captured, roughed up. Tortured? Alone, so alone, but your every move watched.

'My God, Peter.'

Picture his despair, or rage, or both. Did he think: They have not kept their promises?

'Then the Germans are very clever. Having studied his fist, they gradually take over the actual transmissions and get rid of him when they have no more use for him.'

Did she or he die thinking: They did not listen to me?

'It's possible.' Peter searched Ruby's face. Thinking, probing, assessing.

'Right, Ruby, we have to go and deal with this.'

'To the Danish section?'

He paced up and down. 'If there's going to be a major row, and there will be, it should be with the top bosses.'

'If there was a drop planned, it should be stopped.'

They faced each other. 'Trust me,' he said. 'I know how it works.'

She shoved the strap of her handbag further up her shoulder. 'You're thinking bad, aren't you?'

'Very bad.'

'So am I.'

She reached out her hand and he took it. A simple enough gesture, but she sensed it was a life-changing one. He stroked her fingers. 'Are you ready?'

Dizzy with love and fear, Ruby inhaled a shaky breath. 'I think so. Yes.'

It happened quickly. Within an hour of their return to the office, Ruby was summoned.

'Busy little bee,' Gussie did not look up from her typing. 'Buzzing about.'

The hours the two of them underwent being grilled by the head of intelligence, head of signals, chief code master and Colonel Marsh, head of the Danish section, were not ones she would look back on with affection.

The lamp on the desk shone very brightly as the assembled men conducted their interrogation.

Why . . . what . . . how?

How did you get hold of this material?

The gravest indiscipline.

Courts martial . . .

The heat from the light caused beads of sweat to spring onto her upper lip.

'Sir—' it was easier to focus on one face and she chose Colonel Marsh's '—the probability was that our assumptions were wrong about Vinegar. I decided to investigate.'

These men were baffled and furious. More than that, she sensed they were also frightened: frightened because their systems and intelligence had failed them.

'You realize,' said the head of signals, 'that you used one of my staff who could have been accused and put in the dock?'

'I would have taken the blame, of course,' said Peter.

The head of intelligence was livid. As he talked, spittle flew. 'You bloody fool, Martin.'

Peter stood his ground. 'Perhaps. But how do we explain why Vinegar has never misnumbered his transposition key, or misspelled a word or made any of the coding mistakes which are perfectly normal in other agents?'

The head of intelligence folded his fingers together. 'They've been trained well.'

'What about the "stip", "stap", "stup"? Wasn't he trying to tell us something?'

A look of utter contempt was directed at Ruby.

'How many times did the misspelling occur?'

Ruby told them.

'Out of how many messages?'

'In approximately a quarter of his transmissions. There was a cluster early this year.'

'So why didn't he continue to use that device?'

Peter said: 'It's possible that he was being monitored extra closely. Perhaps he was weaker, more brutalized, less willing to take the risk. Perhaps the Germans took over the transmissions rather than dictating them to him. We don't know what is happening, or happened, to Vinegar. Will probably never know.'

The head of signals said: 'It's a just a tic. Other agents have them.'

Ruby thought: *No*.

Colonel Marsh had a Welsh lilt to his voice that dropped into a softer and softer register. 'This has been an outrageous breech,' he pronounced.

Peter was firm: 'But justifiable. It's my considered view that, as from today, Vinegar should be considered suspect and any drops arranged with him should be diverted elsewhere in Denmark. Plus, we *must* revisit the arguments for dropping the poem code.'

'You could have bloody jeopardized the whole set-up, Martin.'

The truth was that no one knew the truth. It was one step forward, one step back. As far as they were concerned, Europe was shrouded in darkness. There was no clear, luminous, steady light to shed understanding on what was really happening. No clarity.

'What to do?' Colonel Marsh posed the question delicately into the smoke-laden atmosphere.

'What's best,' answered Ruby. 'What's logical. We must consider the worst.'

The heads of intelligence and signals could barely bring themselves to look at Ruby.

The subtler Colonel Marsh reflected for a moment. Then he nodded. 'Yes,' he agreed. 'Let's begin.'

Towards the end of the exhausting session, while searching for further proof, Ruby rifled through the report worked up from the notes she had taken during the conversations with Mary Voss. Then . . . then . . . something obvious, so *blindingly* obvious, struck her.

'Sir,' she addressed Colonel Marsh. 'Sir, look at this.' She added angrily, 'I insist.'

Grudgingly, he cast a look at where her finger rested. It was on a section of the notes dated July 1943. His colour changed as he read out: ' "Variations in signalling: QRU reading CAU. Plus: Frequency change from LMS to GHT." '

The head of signals shoved his chair back with a screech.

Colonel Marsh lifted a now-ashen face. 'That spells CAUGHT.'

The balloon went up.

When Ruby returned to the office, she sank down onto her chair.

'For the record, Gussie, bees die once they've stung somebody.'

Gussie sniggered.

'My last request is that you give me a good funeral.'

CHAPTER 34

S o many things for Tanne to remember. So much information to store in an impregnable place in her mind until it was embedded and the lies sprang naturally onto her tongue.

Today you shoot with your left hand.

Today you shoot in the dark.

This light will dazzle you but you must keep shooting. Concentrate.

Describe your drop zone in detail. Remember you will have no map.

The addresses of your contacts. Who are they? What do they do?

You will pretend that I am Jens Borch of number forty-five Algarde, København. What do you say to me?

'Good day, Mr Borch. My aunt Karen sends her greetings. She says to tell you that she remembers the wonderful saddle-of-mutton dinner you shared before Christmas. She hopes that your wife has recovered from her miscarriage.'

You are to be dropped into the Aarhus region. Stand by.

'Are you ready to go?' asked her dispatching

officer. 'Do you understand what's required of you?'

Had her mind notched up a level? Did she understand that, *from now on*, nothing would be straightforward? Everything should be, would be, viewed obliquely and familiar things, places and people would have a question mark over them.

'Do you understand that your life may be at risk?'

She remembered running through the fields, stubble whipping at her ankles. Dogs baying.

Just as well to get used to it.

She glanced up at the sky which looked infuriatingly blue and settled – she wouldn't have minded if the drop was called off today. She hadn't been sleeping so well and needed to catch up on rest. Was the insomnia a way of telling her she was frightened?

They filed into the large drawing room. Calm and serious, the dispatching officer waited in front of the fire. 'Operation Table d'Hôte is on. You will be fed at four o'clock, and this is your lucky day, with wine.'

Before that came the fuss of the last-minute details. Hair? Tanne's had been cut short and dyed raven black. The result was awful. Spectacles? With great difficulty a Danish pair with heavy black rims had been obtained and plain glass lenses inserted. Clothes? Had a Danish label been sewn onto the waistband of the serge skirt? Correct laces in shoes? Check for London bus tickets, cigarette butts, the wrong kind of face powder – oh, for God's sake . . .

My code name is Serviette. My field name is Eva. My alias is Else Steen. I was born in Randers and came to study in København but decided studying was not for me. I am currently a waitress in the Casablanca Café in Aarhus. I have lodgings at number two . . .

Ready to go.

Nerves strung. Bowels twinging.

Then . . . phones started ringing. All over the house. There was a flurry of activity, the sound of rapid footsteps going in and out of rooms. Eventually, the briefing officer appeared. 'This is the final briefing and there is a last-minute alteration,' he instructed. 'The drop zone is shifted to Zealand. Jutland is out.'

Tanne started.

'Something has come up and the section heads have decided not to take any risks. You must deal with this as best you can and take evasive action.'

The briefing combed over the details.

Later a car with blinkered headlights nudged around the perimeter of a secret airbase heading towards a couple of buildings. It stopped outside what looked like a cowshed.

Appearances were deceptive. Inside, a fire burned, one uniformed officer checked over racks of equipment and a couple of others played poker in the corner. They smiled and nodded in their direction as Tanne and the others filed in.

'Hello, again.' A captain she recognized from

STS51 greeted them. 'I've been allocated as your dispatching officer.' His expression was of kindly concern. 'Hope you don't mind,' he continued, 'but I thought I'd see you off.'

It was good to see a familiar face. Tanne waited quietly while he handed out equipment to each of them: overalls, overshoes, gloves, a small flask of rum, a rubber crash helmet, a tin of sandwiches and five thousand kroner in used ten-kroner notes.

The flying suit was far too big, and she struggled to pull up the sleeves. The captain assisted her.

'Knife, dagger or pistol?' he asked.

'Pistol.'

Of the unpleasant, not to say awful, options they suggested, killing or wounding someone from a distance was distinctly better than one-to-one combat.

He handed it to her, plus ammunition. The butt fitted into the curve of her hand. *My lifeline*, she thought.

The captain must have noted the slight tremor of her hand. 'Rumour has it that one of the agents, nameless of course, hid a dog in these overalls and it jumped with him. He argued that a man with a dog who answered to its name was not likely to be suspected by the Germans as a parachutist. The man was a genius but God knows what the dog thought.'

The diversionary tactic worked and Tanne smiled.

'And this—' he held out his hand, palm uppermost '—is your cyanide pill.'

She had never, ever imagined that death would sit in a palm of the hand: a rubber-encased capsule.

'Use it if necessary.'

To die for the honour of her country? So that her soul would be snatched up by the goddess and borne away to Asgard?

'Thank you.' She stowed it carefully and tried to defuse the atmosphere with a joke. 'The helmet makes one look dreadful.'

The captain rested his hand briefly on her shoulder.

Leaving the barn, she turned to take a last look. The shelves of equipment. The men playing cards. The slightly fevered expressions. The map on the wall. The fire – a symbol of sanity and comfort. The captain lifting a hand in farewell.

Having climbed into the belly of the Hudson, she crawled into place. The others followed.

'I feel like a suppository.' Lars was squashed up against her.

'Eh?'

The roar of the plane's engines intensified as it began a lumbering progress down the runway, finally lifting up and over a ridge which hid the airfield from the village.

Very soon, the last of the land disappeared from view. She forgot about England – and it vanished into the past.

Lars looked almost as bad in his helmet as she did in hers. He shouted up to her. 'Denmark very soon.'

Was she being heroic?

She trusted that some part of her was.

Be truthful, Tanne. Be truthful, *Eva*. Heroism, she had learned, was almost certainly diluted by other impulses and desires that had been only briefly touched on at the training schools. In her case, if she was honest, she was eaten up with a love for Felix and it was quite, quite different from anything she had ever felt before.

She closed her eyes.

Concentrate on the immediate. The noise of the aircraft. The smell of the fuel. The tea sloshing around her stomach. The infuriating need to pee.

Tanne dozed.

Much later the red light glowed, and the dispatching sergeant snapped to attention. Within seconds she was positioned by the Joe Hole. Tanne glanced down. God Almighty . . . she was going down there? Terror gripped at her guts and her heart beat in a chest which felt as tight as a drum. *Go on, Tanne.* Trying not to flinch, she made herself look down again. Moving across her vision was a magic lantern of moonlit fields. Occasionally, among the dark, dense patches of woodland, there was the fractured glint of water.

Home.

The sergeant tapped her on the shoulder, pointed up to the static line to show he had attached it properly and gave her the thumbs-up.

The light switched to green.

'Go.'

Terror. Abject terror.

No time left to think . . . and there she was, suspended in the sharp, thin air, a shape billowing down to the moonlit field below, with four others above and beside her.

The earth reared up: a big flat plate that tilted alarmingly.

Keep your bloody legs together.

Tighter than a nun's.

For a couple of seconds she lay winded on the ground, smelling home: a mixture of turf and grass and the tiniest suggestion of salt. Feet ran towards her.

The wind tugged at the deflated parachute and she scrabbled for purchase by digging her fingers into the turf.

'Eva!'

Home.

No longer Tanne, she was Eva.

'Get up, Eva.'

Grinning broadly she got to her feet and held out her hand. '*Hej!*'

Two weeks later, keeping under cover as much as possible, Tanne hiked cautiously up the road from Køge in the direction of Rosenlund. Autumn's dropping temperatures were colouring the tree foliage and the silver birch and beech presented a fire dance of yellows and oranges shot through with sparks of red.

Stop.

Engines in the distance?

Dodging back among the trees, she dropped down flat into the undergrowth. A minute or so afterwards a convoy of Danish army trucks drove past in the Køge direction. Head down, she counted the number of trucks and staff cars. An entire unit? Furthermore, the fact that it was using this back road suggested their orders were to be inconspicuous.

She waited until the last vehicle was well out of sight and gave herself a few more minutes.

She thought of the other Joes who had come in with her. There had been no time for proper goodbyes, just farewell pecks on iced cheeks – before they were spirited away to separate locations. She had been driven to København where, as Else Steen, she had been given a room above a café and worked as a waitress. 'Wait for your orders,' was the instruction. When they came earlier that afternoon, Tanne felt the shock waves.

She checked her watch. Five p.m. Approximately an hour and a half until dark. She set off again. Her speed was good and she held it steady, enjoying the exhilaration that came with a fit body and a good pair of boots. In her backpack were bread, cheese and her pistol.

Slipping into the Rosenlund estate via the north gate, she made for Ove's cottage. The door was locked, but she swung herself up to the first floor and crept over to the window which had a faulty catch. Thank you to all the instructors at the STS. Once inside, she unlocked the door, propped herself against the wall and ate the bread and cheese.

So near to the family home . . . and yet as far away as it was possible to be. She tried not to think about her father. She knew what his distress at the absence of his daughter would be – and imagined his feelings of betrayal. No, no . . . to think of her father would be to induce weakness and that was out of the question.

Sleep when you can.

Tanne awoke with a start. Danger! Its proximity flashed through her warning systems. Groping for the pistol, her hand closed around the butt, its reassurance so welcome.

A footfall. Careful and almost noiseless. Expert.

The catch at the door moved . . . infinitesimally . . . but enough.

In a flash she rolled to one side and was up and crouching, pointing the gun with both hands. This was it. Her training had prepared her for this encounter, and this was the point when it translated into reality.

The door pushed open. Tanne took aim.

'Eva?'

'Felix.'

The pistol clattered onto the wooden floor.

She was so livid that she trembled. 'How dare you do that? Do you know what I could have done to you?'

He bent down and picked up the pistol. 'Actually, I do. Sorry.'

'Idiot, idiot, idiot.'

He grinned broadly. 'I like the temper.'

Now she was trembling not with fright or anger but from joy.

'I wanted to see you,' he said.

He was wearing a thick jersey, corduroy trousers and boots, and an ammunition belt was slung across his midriff. A Sten was tucked up under his armpit.

'Why aren't you at the rendezvous?'

'I have been.' He handed the pistol back to her. 'I came to say there's been plenty going on since my return . . . and it's going to get more intense.'

'And? Is that news?'

'The odds on us surviving shorten.'

He was matter-of-fact. Yet his words conjured a picture of them both, wrapped in the Danish flag, being rolled into a hasty grave.

It is important to understand that your life expectancy is short.

Until that moment . . . until Felix appeared in front of her, Tanne accepted the prospect of extinction. She had been taught. She had trained. Possible death was the deal. But now everything in her that could, cried out: *I want to live.*

That was a lesson, she thought, and she cringed at the feebleness of her resolve.

'But we're going to survive, Felix,' she told him.

As he had done once before, long ago, he placed

a hand over her mouth – and she knew she had come full circle. 'Don't tempt fate.'

'Superstition.' She pressed her chin against his hand. 'If we will ourselves to live then we stand a good chance.'

'Just shut up, will you?' Felix took Tanne roughly into his arms. 'But I applaud the principle.'

Tanne knew, she absolutely knew, that her life had been leading up to this point of revelation and understanding. The exhultation at having arrived rendered her speechless.

The ammunition belt was pressing painfully into her chest. 'There's no time now to say much,' he said. 'But afterwards it will be different.'

'Afterwards . . .' she murmured, and the promise danced like the reflection of the sun on Rosenlund's lake.

He ran his hand through her awful hair. 'I'll find you a good hairdresser.'

Tanne laughed. 'Go on.'

'I'll take you to a private place and we will take our time to get to know each other.' He was almost apologetic. 'Because I will want to be sure.'

She was smiling idiotically. 'Be sure of what?'

'That I have got to know every inch of you. And . . .'

That pleased her immensely. 'And?'

'I will learn about you. Properly.'

'Ah. You might have to practise a long time.'

Her feelings were new and unfamiliar. Certainly uncharted. They almost fell within the category of painful – by which she meant the depth and searing-ness of loving Felix. It's good, she thought. It's a miracle. About to go out into the dark and the danger, she had been granted this moment.

'I mean I want to know you, Eva.'

To reassure herself, she touched his face. This was real. He was solid. Felix was no dream. No.

She had no idea who he was, or where he came from. But she had no reservations about him and no reservations about what she wanted.

Holding her face between his hands, he peered at her through the gloom.

He kissed her.

She put her arms round his neck. *Remember*, she told herself. *Remember this.*

After a while he asked, 'Am I forgiven for startling you?'

'What do you think?'

After a while Felix disengaged himself and she gave a small groan of protest. 'We've just under two hours.' He laid the back of his hand against her cheek. 'There's no choice.'

It was time to be professional.

She briefed Felix on the army trucks she had spotted and he questioned her about the numbers, their direction. 'They've been around for a few weeks,' he said. 'It has held things up here.'

'I thought Rosenlund was compromised as a drop zone.'

'It is and it isn't.' Felix moved over to the window and took a look outside. 'It was Freya's idea and it ticked a lot of boxes. The RAF did a reconnaissance but we had to mothball it while the place was being watched. Then Odin sent word that the surveillance had been called off. The alternatives are few and far between, and for some reason London has suddenly banned drops in Jutland. Instructions were sent via Sweden to use this one.' He shrugged. 'We need the stuff. So . . .'

'Who's Odin?'

Felix pressed a finger against her lips. 'A mole deep in where it matters.' He didn't speak with any enthusiasm. 'But vital. He tells us when and where the Germans are likely to be busy.'

He explained the plan. Because of the last-minute switch, he had been forced to draft in men from København as well as Køge. 'We need everyone we can get hold of.'

'*C'est* on, *c'est* off . . .' she murmured, phrases she had picked up from one of the agents during training. She looked at Felix. *C'est* on. *C'est* very much on.

'There is one thing I have to ask you,' Felix said finally.

'Ask me, then.'

'The wireless set. Freya was forced to leave it here and we need it in København. It won't be any use here once this is over.' There was a long pause. 'You know what I'm asking.'

She was getting ready, checking the pistol, tying back her hair. 'Yes.'

'It's the last thing I want to ask you.'

'It's my job, Felix.'

She bent down to retie the lace on her boot. He knelt beside her and put his hands on her shoulders. 'Afterwards, Eva . . .'

'Afterwards,' she repeated.

She gazed into his face, trying to memorize every flicker of expression, everything about him.

She knew that he knew that they both knew the truth: the only thing certain was that nothing was certain.

Felix fetched the wireless set from its hiding place where Freya had left it and, moving like the trained agents they were, they went out together into the night.

CHAPTER 35

The sun set at approximately six-thirty but the large and brilliant moon ensured it was not totally dark. Observing their training, Felix and Tanne moved cautiously through the trees in the direction of the lake.

Felix carried the wireless transmitter. Tanne had her pistol at the ready.

The glorious autumn had dried out the undergrowth and they trod over layers of snapping, crackling leaf fall. Checking, always checking, they went carefully.

At the lakeside, Felix went ahead to rendezvous and Tanne, the wireless transmitter at her feet, kept watch under the tree cover.

Home.

But it was hard to make out the house, which was a good thing.

It was growing chilly and she was grateful for the long-sleeved woollen jumper she had on under her jacket.

Felix stole back through the trees. He reached out and took Tanne's hand. Their fingers locked.

'The others?'

'On their way,' he said.

A couple of men, in dark clothing and berets, materialized out of the undergrowth and joined them. Shortly afterwards four more followed. Finally, a tall, slender, black-clad figure in a beret crept up to the edge of the trees and crouched down.

The figure was familiar, and yet it wasn't.

Was it?

Tanne's sharply indrawn breath was audible in the hush. '*You!*'

Her mother quivered as if she had been hit.

Fury – because Felix should have warned her – mixed with relief at seeing her and gratitude that she was still alive, made Tanne clumsy and she lurched into her mother's arms.

They clung together.

The touch was the one from childhood – the touch that had anchored Tanne to her life, her family, her home.

Nuzzling Tanne's cheek as she had done so often over the years, her mother kissed her – once, twice, three times – and whispered, 'Remember that I'm Freya now . . .'

'And I'm Eva. How are you, Freya?' But she longed to say: *How are you*, Mor?

In the gloom, Tanne was able to make out that Kay was smiling. 'Better for seeing you.'

Hugging her, Tanne noted that her mother was very thin – thinner than Tanne could ever imagine – and her hair had been dyed into a dark mass.

She smelled different: of unlaundered clothes and sweat and a world away from the scented, powdered, soft-bodied woman of the past.

Kay turned away and grabbed Felix. Tanne heard her say: 'Your promise, Felix—'

Felix cut her off. 'Eva has been trained. She has chosen to do this. It's her job now.'

Kay looked from one to the other. 'You've been in England?' Tanne nodded. Her mother swung round and hit Felix hard on the chest. 'You've betrayed me, Felix.'

He caught her hand. 'Freya . . .'

'It was the one thing I asked of you.'

Felix the lover had vanished. In his place was the agent. 'I'm not going to stop anyone who wants to join in the fight—'

'Freya,' Tanne intervened. 'It was my decision.'

'Shut up now,' said Felix.

He checked the time and signalled to the team to gather round. They were passing around the hip flask. One of them was finishing the tail hunk of a sausage. Another cracked such a filthy joke that his companions hushed him.

'Five minutes. Listen carefully. Army vehicles are on the move in the area. It could mean nothing, it could mean trouble. Our intelligence suggested they were moving out of the area but we can't be sure. The noise will be bad but the British bombers fly over here frequently and, with a bit of luck, Fritz will take no notice.' He paused. 'Anyone who wishes can bugger off now.'

No one moved.

'Right, then.'

Close to the shore, the lake was stippled by clusters of underwater reeds. Further out, the water was calm and gleaming under the moon and stars.

Tanne wondered what the pilot would be thinking. Had he briefed himself sufficiently? Had he written a list: fly east, turn south, look for a lake? Did he believe the intelligence that would have reassured him there were no anti-aircraft guns nearby? Had the navigator memorized the towns, rivers and forests?

Felix was now briefing them individually for the final time.

There was a noise. A footstep . . .? It came from behind a clump of bushes.

'*Lort!*' One of the men swung round and took aim.

Nostrils flaring, they waited. Nothing. Placing a finger to her lips, her mother crept towards the bushes. The dark swallowed her up. Tanne's heartbeat quickened.

Kay returned. 'An animal, I think.'

She stood beside Tanne and drew her close. 'Promise me you won't take stupid risks,' she whispered. As she spoke, they heard the faint throb of an engine. 'Promise.' The noise increased in intensity and volume. She looked up into the sky and continued calmly, 'You have to make sure you live. For *Far*. For Nils. For me.'

Tanne said nothing.

'Eva . . . do you understand. Do you promise?'

On time. On cue. Silhouetted in the moonlight, the Halifax flew into view and her mother gasped. The Halifax could never be called a beautiful plane, yet, bathed in chalky pale moonlight, it was almost elegant, and it hung in the sky like a Chinese lantern.

Dodging flak, the Halifax had got here, the result of hours of meticulous planning. Tanne recollected the people she had met back at The Firm: the coding experts, the instructors, the good-mannered FANYs, the handling officer, the dispatcher, even the cook who had made the sandwiches to eat on board. All contributed to this moment.

Gut-churning, ear-splitting waves of sound.

The moonlight played over her mother's uplifted face. Impossible to know what Kay was thinking. Was it grief, or pride, or elation? 'Oh, well done,' she murmured. 'Well done.'

She sounded incredibly British and a lump edged into Tanne's throat. Moving closer, she made sure their shoulders touched. Whatever happened, they were in this together.

We are not going to be beaten, she wanted to shout up at the lumbering aircraft. *And you have made it possible.*

Felix knelt on the shoreline. The beam from his torch dotted and dashed the letter R.

The Halifax flew across the moon and Tanne whispered, 'We are going to be fine.'

Don't be negative.

Think of the task in hand. Go over it, piece by piece. Outwit the enemy with your mind.

Would she have the courage to take her pill?

Five hundred feet, that was the optimum flying height, no more, no less. The Halifax took a fix, grinding around in a circle before making a low pass over the water. A hot, fuel-laden wind buffeted the watchers below. From its belly fell six parachutes. Huge, ungainly jellyfish which the wind caught, slapping hard against the silk and snapping at the straps.

His job done, the pilot circled once more. The Halifax's wings dipped in farewell, and salute. *Look what we've managed.* Her mother gave a suppressed sob.

The plane rose, roared, set its course for home and drove on into the night sky.

The noise. The noise. It would waken the dead. An instinct made Tanne whip round and look towards the house.

Just in time. A light snapped on in her parents' bedroom.

'Felix . . .' She pointed to the house.

The group swung into action.

Six buoyancy flags bobbed in the water, each one marking a container. The first two men into the boat rowed out to the couple furthest away. Hauling the parachutes and containers on board, they rowed back to shore and unloaded. The scene was filmic, almost dream-like. The second team leaped into the boat, rowed hard and fast and picked up two more.

Once on shore, the wet parachutes were bundled up, and battens slotted through the container handles. The loads were lifted and the men disappeared in the direction of the road and the parked-up vans.

It was Kay and Tanne's turn. The oars settled like old friends into the palms of Tanne's hands – as they had so often done at the family's summer gatherings.

In the stern, her mother was positioned to catch up the containers. Reaching the first of the buoys, Tanne feathered the oars. Her mother bent over and hooked the buoy to the rope.

In the same way they netted the second container.

It was not easy. The rope was wet and tough to manipulate and Kay had to fight it. Time was passing.

Job done. Edging over to sit beside Tanne, Kay took an oar. Containers dragging behind them, they rowed as fast as they could towards the island.

The landing stage was tiny and rotten but they knew its tricks. Even so, hauling the containers onshore took all their strength. Tanne knelt and prised open the first, revealing tightly packed bundles in waterproof material. These they ferried up into their designated hiding place under the summer house.

Her mother searched for one in particular. Double-wrapped in protective material, the package was marked with a red dot. 'The crystals.'

Tanne unhooked the buoys, chucked them into the containers and stuffed the parachutes on top, piling in the stones which her mother had collected into a heap by the jetty. 'I shall dream of that lovely silk,' she said, shutting the lids down. Between them, they dragged the two containers back to the water.

How many minutes had elapsed?

'Team Eberstern?' In the boat, Kay positioned her oar. 'Are you ready?'

Water glistened on the feathering oars. Moonlight splintered onto the lake's surface. A couple of times the boat wallowed as, in their haste, they mistook their timing.

Halfway across, Tanne unhitched the rope from the containers and held each one down, waiting for the water to invade them. With a hiss they filled up and sank into the blackness, a trail of silver bubbles rising from their grave.

The two women rowed liked demons. As they neared the shore, Tanne sneaked a look at her mother. She looked pinched from the effort and her strokes were becoming uneven. The moonlight revealed an ill-fitting padded jacket and a thick fisherman's sweater underneath. Her mother would never normally wear that sort of sweater.

Tanne's eyes pricked.

At STS they had warned of the effects of adrenalin but they had not explained how an air of unreality could hover over an operation, or that feelings which should be safely buried could push and kick their way to the surface.

Forward. Pull. Feather. Forward. Their two

bodies worked in unison. Voices carried across water so they didn't speak until they reached the shore, where they moored the boat and ran into the trees.

They paused for breath.

Craning her head, Tanne spotted Felix carrying the case and moving towards them through the trees. He beckoned. Tanne grabbed the package with the crystals and the women ran over to him.

But, as she picked up speed, Tanne was aware of a familiar figure hanging back by the treeline, almost out of sight. But she could spot him.

Her father.

He was staring across to Sophia-Maria's island.

Tanne ran even harder.

Parked on the road, a van was waiting. As soon as they came into sight, the driver revved the engine. Hands reached out from the back and hauled them inside. Felix swung himself and the case up beside the driver.

The back was packed with the packages and sopping parachutes and Tanne, Kay and a couple of the men were forced to cling on as best they could.

They drove for about three minutes and then screeched to a halt. Tanne squinted through a slit in the bodywork. 'We've been flagged down,' she reported. 'The driver's talking to someone.'

There was a rapid exchange and the driver swore violently. Whoever had flagged them down now leaped up beside Felix. Gunning the van at top speed down the road, the driver swung it to the left and drove for another hundred metres or so and into a farmyard.

The driver sprinted around to the back of the van and hauled open the doors. 'The Germans are onto us. Word is they waited until we were on the move because they want to get their hands on the stuff. This is Tage Seest's place but he's in hiding. There's a slurry pit here. Shove it there.'

Working silently, they tipped the packages into the slurry. The parachutes were rolled up and pushed under hay bales. Tanne scattered straw over their footsteps.

'Get in,' ordered the driver.

Clutching the crystals, Kay scrambled back into the van. Felix swung up into the front. The driver coaxed the van out of the farm and back onto the road.

Tanne was conscious of every breath.

They headed down the lane and looped back on themselves.

Where does the enemy least expect to find you? Behind him.

The van halted. 'Out,' said the driver, barely waiting for them to disembark before driving off.

They were back on the northern perimeter of the Rosenlund estate. First Felix went over the wall, climbing with loose-limbed confidence. Then Kay handed up the wireless set and followed him. Tanne took charge of the crystals, slung them around her neck and went up and over.

They dropped down onto the scrubby turf and headed for the copse to their left, where they hunkered down.

Panting, Felix leaned back against a tree trunk. 'Time?'

Tanne peered at her watch. 'Three forty-five.'

There was nothing to be done but to wait it out.

Tanne was dozing when she felt Felix grip her arm. 'What?'

He pointed. Over in the Køge direction, a finger of light cut through the night sky.

Her mother shivered. With cold? With fright? 'Listen,' she said.

Vehicles were moving down the road in their direction.

'We split.' Felix leaped to his feet. 'When it's light, make your way to the station and catch the six-thirty train to København. Or the seven o'clock. I'll wait there for you with the set and hand it over. If you don't make either of those, I'll abort. At København, look for the blue taxi in the rank outside the station. He knows a safe house. The password's *skummet melk*.'

Hefting up the case, he disappeared out of sight, skilful and almost silent.

Tanne and Kay backed further into the copse. When they judged they were close to its centre, they dropped down into a sitting position against the tree trunks. In the silence, their breathing was audible.

Tanne's heart thudded. Easy now.

It was still very dark. Small animals were moving around in the undergrowth. *Snap.* There was a crackle in the undergrowth to their right. A rustle to their left.

Wait in silence. Listen. Silence can tell you more than noise.

Her mother's shoulders slumped. 'You're not to touch the wireless set,' she whispered. '*Understood?*'

'Shush.'

'If you won't think of me, think of *Far.*' Kay pulled Tanne to her. 'It's an order.'

Back to the nursery. Her mother's soft lap. The murmured endearments.

'How long since you've been home?' Tanne asked her.

'I left not long after you.'

'Any news of *Far?*'

'He's well. And safe.'

'Has he any idea of where you and I are?'

'It wouldn't be hard for him to work it out.' Her mother's mouth was close to her ear. 'Whatever happens I want you to remember that I love your father.'

Tanne was conscious of tiredness. Big, all-encompassing fatigue creeping right down to the soles of her feet. The cold nipped at her exposed skin.

'But is that enough?' How stupid was that? She, too, loved her father. But she, too, was sitting in a dark wood waiting to go on the run.

'If it wasn't for the war, it would have been

639

enough. But war changes people.' Kay detached herself, took Tanne's hand. She pulled at the little finger. 'We're different now from what we were. For you, this war will affect only a small part of your life. It doesn't seem like that at the moment . . .' Tanne could tell from her voice that she was smiling. 'But it's true. You will get over what's happened.'

What to say? What to think? '*Mor*, I swear I saw *Far* earlier. I think he came down to the lake to see what was going on.'

'The plane woke him, then. I thought it might. He told me he had moved back into our bedroom.' Her voice grew urgent. 'He mustn't find us, darling. Do you understand?'

They agreed to take turns to get some sleep and Tanne insisted on keeping first watch. Her mother must have been tired, too, for she dozed.

Her mother had forbidden her to touch the wireless set.

That heavy, bulky case which was impossible to explain away if challenged. Tanne supposed a brilliant actor might pretend it was a gramophone or . . . or a dictating machine, and get away with it. She wasn't an actor, but perhaps terror would make her so. If caught with it, there would be no question what would happen. Operationally, too, it acted like a flaring beacon, pulsing Morse and attracting every direction-finding unit in the universe, trapping its pianist in its crystals, aerials and headphones.

The cold filtered through the wood. Cold always smelled, Tanne found.

After an hour, she and her mother swapped. Tanne settled herself against the tree. Her body relaxed, her legs grew heavy.

She was woken by Kay pressing a finger over her mouth. With the other hand, she pointed in the direction of the road. 'Car stopped. Someone's coming.'

Cradling the pistols, they stood upright. There was a merest crack. A shuffle. A rustle of leaves.

Fieldcraft: muddle the enemy and, if necessary, surprise him from behind.

Tanne gestured to her mother: *Go right.*

She went left, moving stealthily, cautiously.

The footstep?

It was that of the experienced hunter. Easy. Assured.

Dawn was breaking, but it was still fiendishly difficult to make out shapes with any clarity.

Tanne froze. Three metres or so in front of her hiding place, a figure padded past. Male. Tall. She could just make out that he wore a long hunter's jacket, with a hat pulled down over his face. A rifle was slung over his shoulder, probably one used for game. On reaching the place where they had holed up, he dropped down and placed the flat of his hand on the earth.

Listening.

He was familiar, achingly so. At the same time he was alien and unknown.

Tanne wanted both to run towards him and to flee. Neither was possible.

The man straightened up and walked back towards the road.

Wait until you are sure.

Kay materialized like a ghost from her hiding place. 'A *stikker*?'

'Poacher, I think.'

'That would be it.'

The two women stared at each other. Kay placed her hands on Tanne's shoulders. 'Let's both believe that.'

This was complicity as strong as the umbilical cord. Neither of them was going to acknowledge that it had been her father. Neither would ask what the other thought he had been doing. *Please, please let it be a simple explanation . . . that he was up early to shoot duck as he has done so often before.*

Kay looked shattered. Tanne seized her hands. 'You're ill. You're shaking. This is too much for you. Please will you get yourself to Sweden? And let *Far* know.'

Her mother wasn't having any of that. 'I'm shaking because I'm tired, cold and hungry. So are you. I'll be up and running once I've eaten.'

Tanne said, 'We have to go.'

'Let me look at you, Tanne. Please.'

Hearing her name was odd.

Kay placed a hand under Tanne's chin. Familiar. Loving. 'You're filthy. We'll have to go into the washrooms and clean up. We'll be mother and daughter if anyone talks to us.'

'No,' said Tanne. 'Our papers are different.'

'Of course.' Kay shrugged. 'I was forgetting.'

First light was dawning and they prepared for the off. Unwrapping the crystals which were embedded in sponge, Kay buried all traces of the packaging under a clump of bushes. Tanne checked them over for damage. They looked fine.

They lay in her palm. So mundane and squat – the gateway to the ether which pulsed to a secret poetry and to the cries and whispers of those trapped behind the lines of the Reich.

Tanne slipped them into the pouch she wore round her waist under her trousers. The bulge was masked by her jacket.

'Tanne . . .' said her mother. 'Tanne, darling. I want you to take this.' And she pressed her beret down onto Tanne's head. 'It will get cold, very cold. You'll need it.'

Snatching it off, Tanne asked, 'What about you?'

Kay took the beret back again. 'It's for you.' She pulled it down over her daughter's ears, tucking her hair under the rim. 'There.' She leaned over and kissed her cheek. A butterfly touch. 'There.'

Her mother tucking her up in the bed with a red and white quilt. Her mother stroking her face. Her mother bathing a cut on her knee . . .

'*Mor*?'

Again, Kay's mouth brushed Tanne's cheek. 'Go well, my beloved daughter.'

They hiked into the town together but when they reached the Sankt Nicolai Kirke, they parted.

Tanne allowed herself to watch her mother

progress down the street. Dyed. Thin. Shabby. Kay did not look back once.

She set herself to walk purposefully.

Always look as though you know what you are doing.

Slipping inside a café she made for the wash-room. Here she sluiced her face and hands, combed out her hair and put on the glasses.

So what had *Far* been doing? She frowned at the face in the mirror. It hurt, it really hurt, to be questioning his motives, but she must acknowledge – she had to – that he supported the enemy. Would he . . . would he tip off the Danish police?

Of course she still loved him, but painfully, protectively, and with a new consciousness.

What secret decisions had been taken that meant she ended up here rather than in Jutland? And why? Coincidence? Fate? Bungling? Possibly all three. The more Tanne reflected on it, the more curious she found it. God knew how, but her life had been fused together with those of the war-makers, and interconnections made for political and strategic purposes.

Pinning up her hair, she extracted the crystals from her bag and tucked them into the scarf which she tied, turban fashion, round her head.

There was still time to order milk and a roll. She paid for them up front and ate them at a table facing the door. Afterwards, via the backstreets, she made her way to the station and bought a return ticket to Holte, the station after København. She would, however, alight in København.

Felix was already at the far end of the platform. He was sitting on a bench reading a paper, the case beside him. To see him . . . just to see him . . . Tanne was truly astonished by the strength of emotion that hit her like a hammer.

Four minutes until the train.

The passengers waiting on the platform projected a grey uniformity. The war, and worry, Tanne supposed. What, where, *who* were they in this war? These were questions that people must be asking themselves over and over. When peace came, how were they all going to live with one another again?

Escape route? Tanne noted a gap in the railings which ran alongside the platform and she checked it out. The aperture was large enough to squeeze through and gave access to the area where cars and carts parked. A couple of delivery vans near to the entrance could possibly provide temporary cover if necessary.

Two minutes to go.

One minute.

A convoy of trucks roared into the station fore-court, followed by a staff car.

Tanne swung round.

Soldiers in *feldgrau* uniform surged onto the platform, followed by two German officers, plus a man in Danish uniform.

She glanced at Felix. Routine?

No.

Felix's mouth had settled into a grim line.

The soldiers fanned out and corralled the

passengers waiting on the platform. A couple more blocked the exit. Tanne checked her escape route. *Lort!* A woman with a child clutching her skirt was peering through the gap, obstructing Tanne's getaway.

Lort! Lort!

Four soldiers advanced down the platform, followed by the officers. Tanne's training clicked in.

Learn to recognize the uniforms as well as you know your times tables.

The first wore the closed-collar uniform of the Waffen-SS, the second that of a high-ranking Abwehr officer. A general.

The general turned and beckoned to the Danish army officer who was lurking in the rear. Tanne stared. She knew who that was. Of course she did. It was Anton Eberstern.

On time, the train came into the station. The instincts in Tanne still untamed by her training screamed: *Flee!* With a supreme effort, she made herself walk up the platform towards Felix, timing it so she drew level with him as the train halted and its doors opened.

Check the getaway route.

At the gap in the railings, a man had joined the woman with the child. Hunter's jacket, hat pulled down and a rifle in a case slung over his shoulder. It was the man she and her mother had spotted in the wood.

Far.

It made sense. Alerted by the drop, he would

have tracked the pair of them as they walked into Køge. The accomplished hunter, *Far* was perfectly capable of it.

She knew then. She knew that, in his way, he had been watching over them.

He bent down, said something to the woman and pushed her gently away from the railings. That simple gesture told Tanne he would never betray them. No, her kind, loving father would be telling the woman to go, to be safe, to save her child from possible trouble.

Far.

Tanne patted her scarf to check the crystals were still in place.

Felix rose to his feet and joined the passengers surging towards the train doors. Head down, she edged in his direction.

Hand at the ready. *Give it to me.* Felix looked straight past her but a foot nudged the case over to her. Tanne reached down . . . but before she could pick it up, the case was snatched away and a piece of paper pressed into her hand.

What? *What?*

Tanne watched in horror.

At a steady, purposeful pace, her mother walked towards the carriage nearest to the engine. She was carrying the case as easily as if it weighed very little.

There was nothing Tanne could say or do.

Felix snarled into her ear: 'Get out.'

She hesitated – an absolute violation of the training. But leave her mother? 'Help her,' she whispered.

'I'm ordering you. Get out. Lie low until I make contact.'

'Halt!' The order was shouted by the German sergeant.

Her mother continued to walk down the platform – and with every step she was growing smaller, thinner, more insubstantial . . .

'*Halt!*'

Reckless, reckless *Mor*.

Please, please, Tanne prayed.

'Halt or we shoot . . .' The order was bellowed out but, at that precise moment, the train sounded its whistle and the first words of it were lost.

Only the word 'shoot' was audible.

One of the soldiers, a young keen one, took aim. Tanne watched his arm swing up in a rapid response, his finger adjusting on the trigger, the slight tensing of the muscles under his sleeve.

She heard the crack of the shot. Heads turned. She watched, unable to move, as her mother staggered. Blood flowered on the back of her blue jacket, spreading unevenly.

Kay stopped. She swayed, staggered, took another step forward before dropping to one knee.

The sergeant ran across and slapped her on the wounded shoulder. 'Get up.'

Tanne leaped forward. 'No.'

Felix hauled her back savagely.

'Let me go.'

His fingers dug into her arm – agonizingly, cruelly. 'No, you don't.'

'You can't leave her.'

'Yes, I can. So will you.'

A sound between a moan and a scream came from her mother as the sergeant pulled her to her feet.

The crystals were burning under Tanne's scarf. The crystals sent in for the new wireless sets that would help to win the war.

She glanced at the folded paper Kay had pushed into her hand. Written on it in her mother's writing was: 'Give to *Far.*'

She couldn't leave her. Felix must understand.

The passengers had formed a tight, frightened knot. The Waffen-SS officer walked towards Kay. His fellow officer stopped to brief one of the soldiers guarding the entrance to the platform.

She would never forgive Felix.

She hated him.

She loved him.

The war had to be won.

Her mother knew that.

Kay turned her head slowly, agonizingly slowly. Her gaze drifted towards Tanne, rested on her for an infinitesimal second and moved on.

Go well, my beloved daughter.

You can't cry, Tanne. You can't cry.

Felix jabbed a finger hard into her spine. 'Go.'

Tanne went.

CHAPTER 36

The sergeant in the hateful *feldgrau* uniform bellowed at Kay and she forced herself to look at him. *Who are you?*

She was growing faint. But it didn't much matter because she knew she didn't stand a chance.

The SS officer issued an order – and she knew that voice.

Her knees wouldn't hold her and she sagged between the soldiers who were holding her up. The sergeant grabbed her by the hair so she was forced to look directly at *Hauptsturmführer* Buch.

'Have you anything to say?' he asked.

She remained silent.

'We know who you are.' He articulated the words very precisely. 'This is the wanted terrorist, Kay Eberstern.' His face loomed towards hers. 'What are you carrying?'

She closed her eyes.

When she opened them again, it was to see Anton positioned behind Buch. Everything became clear. To give him credit, Anton had warned her in the København café: 'Sometimes you have to surrender information in order to keep credible.'

Anton had sold them out because, on the run, she was no longer useful to him. Or rather she was more use to him as a sacrifice. It was the perfect equation.

'Open it up.' At the order, one of the soldiers, a skinny, underfed lad, undid the clasp and swung back the lid. Dials, crystals, the coiled antenna of the wireless.

Aladdin's cave.

'What's this?' asked Buch.

'A gramophone,' she managed to get out between icy lips.

The soldiers were told to stand away and she was left swaying tipsily.

'Stand up,' he said.

Think of something to keep going, she told herself. Think of the grasses rippling in the fields at Rosenlund.

Again, the driver sounded the whistle – a harsh, despairing wail.

She was losing blood. It was running down her back and pooling in the waistband of her knickers. They would be ruined and she had only a couple of pairs.

'What is it?' he repeated.

The swimming sensation intensified. 'It's a gramophone.'

Buch pulled his pistol out of the webbing at his waist, levelled it and calmly shot her in the knee.

She went down flat without a sound.

Then, there was nothing.

No, there was something.

'*There must be something I can do to help, Kay?*'

'*There is one thing.*' *She leans over and kisses his cheek, the corner of his eye, then his chin, then his mouth.* '*Promise me something . . . Don't let them take me,*' *she says.* '*Promise. You don't know what they do to you. I do.*'

'*Kay . . .*'

'*Promise.*' *She rests her hand against his cheek.* '*Will you?*'

'*It's not a promise I can make.*'

She means to say all sorts of things. That she loves him.

Had Kay told him? She hoped so.

She became conscious of a singing in her ears. Through a slit in her eyelids a ribbon of sky appeared: the big, flat, white Danish sky at the periphery of which faces stared at her. One of them, a man, had eyes as round and terrified as those of a scared child in a cartoon. A woman had clapped her hand to her mouth.

The pain began in earnest. Waves of it, each wave mounting to a higher crescendo. She tried to control it by imagining herself in the lake at Rosenlund. Freezing water numbed sensation.

Time became elastic. Each second expanded infinitely.

General Gottfried's face swam into her vision. 'Get up.'

Why wasn't she surprised that he was here?

She focused on him. The intelligence that she

had marked on first meeting him was obvious. So was anger. He was a man who knew he had been duped and didn't like it. He would kill her whatever.

Enough. Why waste time on the general?

'So,' he said. '*Fru* Eberstern. I'm sorry to see you like this.' He paused. 'I'm sorry about a lot of things.'

He would be. It was a tiny grain of comfort to think she had run rings – or a ring – round him. She looked away.

'Get up,' he repeated.

Her limbs refused to obey.

The general was speaking in German. 'You thought you'd got away with it? Yes? But you weren't clever enough. We ran your colleague for months. London seemed wilfully blind. So many little things they ignored which we were sure they would pick up on. But no. The British are very self-satisfied.'

Security checks. Double security checks.

Summoning every ounce of her strength, every wit which remained, she managed to say, 'Are you sure they weren't playing you, General?'

He frowned.

Fear threatened to sap what was left of her strength. Kay knew what lay in store. Where had they hurt her so far? Her shoulder? She tried to flex her right arm. Useless. Her left leg wouldn't work either.

I'm going to make the fear go away.

I'm not going to die riddled and rotten with it.

She was dragged to her feet again. Nausea and pain warred with faintness.

She looked up. Smoke from the train filtered across the sky. She looked down to her shoes, now splattered with blood.

The onlookers were murmuring, shifting. A child cried.

'Shame,' said a woman. 'Shame on you.'

What did the woman mean? Shame on whom? She longed for Bror.

Painfully, she turned her head away from the general and his men. From Anton.

Was it so surprising that human beings were untrue to each other?

Concentrate on the sky instead, the same sky which stretched over England and Rosenlund.

Her chin dropped onto her chest. The sergeant yanked her head up and her gaze was jerked towards the railings.

And there he was. Bror. Dressed in his hunter's clothing with his rifle. Was he returning from the duck shoot? She ached to be there with him, ranging through the woods, matching his careful, loving progress and his delight in the land. She wanted to be beside him at the lake shore, watching the water as the sun set.

Her eyelids dropped down over her eyes.

He had kept his promise.

He had tracked them.

He was there . . . she was not alone . . . he would never abandon her.

With a monstrous effort, Kay lifted her head. Their eyes met.

They had shared their lives.

Do it, Bror. Please.

I can't.

You can. You must. They will torture me until I am nothing.

I want you to live, Kay, live.

Life was sweet with you, Bror. Remember that. And I don't want to die.

She watched him position the rifle and take aim.

Nils. Tanne.

She watched the tears roll down his face.

Then she closed her eyes.

Thank you, darling Bror.

They were in the drawing room at Rosenlund playing Racing Demon. Both of them were laughing. Kay looked up and out of the window to the lake.

CHAPTER 37

June, 1944

Mary battled her usual exhaustion.

The previous two shifts had been difficult, with shrieking atmospherics, and her ears were ringing.

Straightening her serge skirt, Mary glanced in the mirror. Was she dreaming it? Or was the face that looked back at her beginning to be the sort of face of which people might say: She looks good for her age? A face that looked as though its owner knew what she was doing.

She thought back to her training days – when everything had been alien and alarming.

'Speed in Morse', said the manual, 'can only be achieved when one ceases to "read" individual dots and dashes and the groups of dots and dashes which make up individual letters. With practice, all these become subliminal.'

Mary had never thought it would happen, but it had.

Nancy looked up as Mary came into the signals room. 'Okie dokie?'

She was trying out the new Americanism that was sweeping the country.

'Fine,' said Mary, and she took her seat.

'This bloody, bloody war,' said Nancy, and she regaled Mary with the story of a never-to-be-forgotten stay in a luxury hotel before the war. 'The bedroom had a bathroom attached to it, with soaps and towels. And—' Nancy's voice lowered dramatically '—there was a basket of fruit, a crystal bowl for face powder and a huge mirror over the bed.'

Another life.

Some of the girls were finding the snail's pace of the war difficult to cope with. It was all very well listening to Mr Churchill's speeches, which were designed to whip the heart into fiery resolution, but the truth was that when you were stuck into endless shifts, they had a limited impact. Patriotic and determined as the girls were, they needed encouragement sometimes.

She considered tackling her superiors and even rehearsed what she would say. 'Some acknowledgement would work miracles. And we know secrecy is crucial, but not being told anything is hard for the girls and it can grind them down. Of course, they realize they can't be told the real identity of the agents but they need to feel they're trusted by you.'

Perhaps she would say something.

For she so longed to know what had happened to her agents, where they were. She wanted to know partly because they were part of her . . .

partly because she needed to compensate for what she saw as her dereliction of duty towards Vinegar. Her particular Gethsemane.

Ruby had come to see her at the station, which was very kind of her. Mary had a premonition that it wouldn't be good news.

'Do you mind if I sit down?' she'd asked Ruby.

'Be my guest.'

Ruby lit a cigarette and, as she dropped her lighter back into her briefcase, Mary noticed a wedding ring. It was then that Ruby told her about Vinegar.

It had taken a while for Mary to respond. How could she – the best listener and one who loved her agents – have failed to see that Vinegar was being run by the enemy?

She *should* have known – and the knowledge that she had failed ate into her. It was bitter bread to eat. But that was the price of this war. And it was the price of life.

What had happened to him? Vinegar was almost certainly dead . . . but did he die knowing that someone back home was listening out for him? Could he have possibly intuited that she cared for him? That the Morse whispering and bouncing over the earth's curve carried her blessings?

If so, he might just have thought – a brief, flickering comfort – that his death would not be lonely, and certainly not in vain.

'Thank you for taking the trouble to tell me,' Mary said. 'No one else would have done.'

'This is strictly out of order.' Ruby smoked

thoughtfully. 'But something you said when we first met, about how you felt about your agents, affected me. You'll be pleased to know that the coding system has finally been changed to a much more secure system.'

'That's good news.'

Ruby flicked ash into the ashtray. 'You do understand that, if anybody finds out I've told you, I will be shot.'

Mary nodded. 'Understood.' She fixed on Ruby's ring. 'Forgive me, but have you just got married?'

A curious expression flitted across Ruby's face. Exasperation? Joy? 'Yes, last month.'

Later Mary wondered whether that last meeting with Ruby was linked to another encounter. A short while after Ruby's visit, on being ushered into an office at the station that she hadn't known existed, Mary was informed that after the war 'they' wanted to offer her a job. Somewhere near Pinner. 'Eastcote, actually,' her interviewer said. 'The country needs listeners like you.'

That was all she was told, but she had accepted the job nonetheless.

'Jamming's bad at the moment,' said Nancy. 'Never know where they get the sugar.'

A familiar bad joke. It helped with the exhaustion.

As usual the room was filled with benches, unwieldy wireless sets, people. Signalmaster Noble was on duty. The old joke – 'Noble he is not' – kept on running. His power complex made him far more energetic than the decent Signalmaster Falks. Noble made a point of patrolling between the desks. Every so often he would bend over a clerk's shoulder to check her progress.

'Bloody perv.' Nancy wrinkled her nose. 'Hasn't he had enough of looking down our blouses?'

Mary swept the frequencies, meticulously checking each one as well as the skeds. She had a new agent: BTU, code name Jelly. Dead on time, a message came in from him. She handed it up to Signalmaster Noble.

Nancy was frowning at the letters written on her log paper. Some of the girls were adjusting their dials, the precise and delicate articulation at which Mary excelled. Others were slumped over their benches, gathering their energy.

The hours limped on.

Sniffs. A cough.

'Oh, my lord!' Anne on Number 14 tore off her headphones and leaped to her feet. 'Listen to this.' She began to read, her voice young and hopeful, shaking with excitement: ' "*Vive la France! Vive l'Angleterre!*" '

It took fully ten seconds for the listeners to understand that the message had come in *en clair* and not in code.

'My God!' screamed Nancy. 'It's begun. Our boys must have gone in.'

The room erupted as Anne waved the piece of paper aloft and hurried off to find Signalmaster Noble.

Tears streamed down Mary's face.

She wept for the deaths, for the violence and for the darkness that had gripped humanity. Inexplicably, she wept for the pigeons who, carrying their messages and regardless of storm and flak, battled through to come home.

She wept for the sacrifice.

Nancy stood over her. 'For God's sake, Mary, the Allies have gone into France. Buck up.'

With a supreme effort, Mary wiped her face with her handkerchief and tucked it back into her sleeve.

She checked the clock. Time for the search.

Where are you?

Summoning her skill, she swept the dial.

The whisper of the sea in a shell . . .

As she checked and adjusted, the upheaval in her heart subsided for the time being.

The needle quivered. She steadied it. *The professional.* She owed her agents everything she possessed.

Time? It was time.

And . . . there he was. Mayonnaise. Tapping with his usual fluency. There they were: the upward slope of Z; the jagged pattern of Y; the simplicity of A . . .

The rush of emotion was anything but professional, but it was pure and sweet.

Do you read me?

We read you, Denmark.

I am here.

Employment Law

PEARSON

We work with leading authors to develop the strongest
educational materials in law, bringing cutting-edge thinking
and best learning practice to a global market.

Under a range of well-known imprints, including Longman,
we craft high quality print and electronic publications which
help readers to understand and apply their content, whether
studying or at work.

To find out more about the complete range of our
publishing, please visit us on the World Wide Web at:
www.pearsoned.co.uk

Employment Law

Fifth Edition

Malcolm Sargeant and **David Lewis**

Middlesex University

Longman
is an imprint of

Harlow, England • London • New York • Boston • San Francisco • Toronto
Sydney • Tokyo • Singapore • Hong Kong • Seoul • Taipei • New Delhi
Cape Town • Madrid • Mexico City • Amsterdam • Munich • Paris • Milan

Pearson Education Limited
Edinburgh Gate
Harlow
Essex CM20 2JE
England

and Associated Companies throughout the world

Visit us on the World Wide Web at:
www.pearsoned.co.uk

First published 2001
Fifth edition published 2010

© Pearson Education Limited 2001, 2010

ISBN: 978-1-4082-2925-5

British Library Cataloguing-in-Publication Data
A catalogue record for this book is available from the British Library.

Library of Congress Cataloging-in-Publication Data
Sargeant, Malcolm.
  Employment law / Malcolm Sargeant and David Lewis. – 5th ed.
    p. m.
  Includes index.
  ISBN 978-1-4082-2925-5 (pbk.)
  1. Labor laws and legislation – Great Britain.   I. Lewis, David, 1949 Mar. 24–   II. Title.
  KD3009.S27 2010
  344.2401–dc22

                                                          2010013773

10 9 8 7 6 5 4 3 2 1
14   13   12   11   10

Typeset in 9/12.5pt Giovanni by 35
Printed and bound in Great Britain by Henry Ling Ltd, Dorchester, Dorset

Contents

Visit the *Employment Law*, Fifth Edition **mylawchamber** site at **www.mylawchamber.co.uk/sargeant** to access valuable learning material.

Self study support

- Use the practice exam questions to test yourself on each topic throughout the course.
- Use the updates to major changes in the law to make sure you are ahead of the game by knowing the latest developments.
- Use the live weblinks to help you read more widely around the subject, and really impress your lecturers.

For more information please contact your local Pearson Education sales representative or visit **www.mylawchamber.co.uk/sargeant**

Preface

In recent years there have been many developments in employment law and regulation. All these developments are reflected in this edition.

The book is intended to be a comprehensive and supportive text for those studying employment law, whether they are law students or others. It emphasises the importance of the European Union in shaping employment protection in this country and other Member States of the Community. It also tries to reflect the continuing changes that are taking place in the subject and includes a summary of the Equality Act 2010. Mostly it will provide the reader with a good understanding of employment law and, hopefully, encourage them to further study and research.

Malcolm Sargeant
David Lewis
April 2010

Guided tour

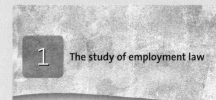

1 The study of employment law

1.1 Introduction

The subject of employment law is the regulation of the relationship between employer and worker or, put in another way, the relationship between the user of labour and the supplier of labour. This regulation takes place at an individual level and at a collective level. At an individual level the law takes the view that the contract of employment is like any other contract, namely a legally binding agreement that two equal parties have voluntarily entered into. At a collective level workers and employers have banded together into trade unions and employers' associations in order, partly, to give themselves greater bargaining power with each other.

The sources of this regulation are diverse and include:

1. Primary and secondary legislation initiated or supported by Government.
2. The EU Treaties and legislation, usually, but not always, in the form of Directives.
3. The decisions of the courts, including the High Court, employment tribunals and the

'The Study of Employment Law' chapter provides a comprehensive introduction to the main sources of employment legislation, and the best way of accessing them.

7.7 NATIONAL MINIMUM WAGE

4. Workers who are homeless or residing in a hostel for the homeless, are eligible for income support and are participating in a voluntary or charitable scheme.[272]
5. Share fishers.[273]
6. Workers employed by a charity or a voluntary organisation, or similar, who only receive expenses in respect of work done. These expenses can include subsistence income for the worker concerned.[274]
7. Workers who are residential members of religious or charitable communities in respect of work done for those communities. Exempt from this are communities which are independent schools or those that provide courses in further or higher education.[275]
8. Workers who are prisoners do not qualify for the NMW in respect of any work done in pursuance of prison rules.[276]

Work is also defined as excluding any work relating to the employer's family household if the worker lives in the employer's family home, is treated as a member of the family, does not pay for the living accommodation and, if the work had been done by a member of the employer's family, it would not have been treated as being work.[277]

7.7.2 Calculating the hourly rate

The hourly rate paid to a worker is calculated by finding the total remuneration paid in that period and dividing it by the total number of hours of time work, salaried hours work, output work and unmeasured work worked in the pay reference period (these categories are discussed below).[278] The total remuneration in such a period is calculated[279] by adding together:

1. All money paid by the employer to the worker in the pay reference period.
2. All money paid in the following reference period that relates to the pay reference period.
3. Any money paid by the employer later than the following reference period in respect of work done in the pay reference period.[280]
4. Any amount permitted to be taken into account for the provision of living accommodation.[281]

Clear headings and sub headings facilitate easy navigation around each chapter.

4.4 UNFAIR DISMISSAL

There are occasions when there is a dispute as to whether the individual has been dismissed or whether they have resigned. This was the case in *Morris v London Iron and Steel Co Ltd*[112] where the employee claimed that he had been dismissed and the employer claimed that there had been a resignation. After hearing evidence, the employment tribunal was unable to decide which was the truth. Bearing in mind that the onus of proof was on the employee, the complaint was dismissed. This approach was approved in the Court of Appeal:

... the judge should at the end of the day look at the whole of the evidence that has been called before him, drawing inferences where appropriate, and ask himself what has or has not been shown on the balance of probabilities, and then, bearing in mind where the onus of proof lies, decide whether the plaintiff or the defendant, or both, succeeds.

A radical alteration to an employee's contract of employment may amount to a withdrawal of that contract and a conclusion that the individual was dismissed. *Hogg v Dover College*[113] was a drastic example of this. A teacher was informed by his employer that he would no longer be head of department, that he would be employed on a part-time basis only and his salary was to be halved. The EAT concluded that:

both as a matter of law and common sense, he was being told that his former contract was from that moment gone . . . It is suggested on behalf of the employers that there was a variation, but again, it seems to us quite elementary that you cannot hold a pistol to somebody's head and say 'henceforth you are to be employed on wholly different terms which are in fact 50 per cent of your previous contract'.

This was not a variation of the contract which might give the employee the opportunity to accept or reject a potential repudiation, but amounted to an express dismissal by the employer. This approach was applied in *Alcan Extrusions v Yates*[114] where the imposition of a continuous rolling shift system in place of a traditional shift system, contained in the employees' contracts, also amounted to an express dismissal by the employer. Alternatively, the unilateral variation of an employee's contractual working hours might amount to a breach of a fundamental term entitling the employee to resign and claim constructive dis-

Short extracts from legislation and legal judgments ensure that you have access to primary material in all key areas.

FURTHER READING

Chapter summary

This chapter outlined the types of termination that amount to a dismissal at law and those that do not. It looked at the requirement of the parties to give notice and discussed the common law concepts of summary and wrongful dismissal. The law of unfair dismissal was described in detail with attention focusing on the potentially fair reasons for dismissal, the requirements of procedural fairness, the need to claim in time and the remedies available. Finally, the circumstances in which employees might be entitled to a redundancy payment were detailed.

Further reading

Anderman, S. 'Termination of Employment: Whose Property Rights?' in Barnard, C., Deakin, S. and Morris, G. (eds) *The Future of Labour Law*: Hart Publishing, 2004, Chapter 5.

Collins, H. 'Nine Proposals for the Reform of the Law on Unfair Dismissal': Institute of Employment Rights, 2004.

Deakin, S. and Morris, G. *Labour Law*: 5th edn, Hart Publishing, 2009, Chapter 5.

Incomes Data Services 'Unfair Dismissal', in *Employment Law Handbook*: IDS, 2005.

Korn, A. *Compensation for Unfair Dismissal*: Oxford University Press, 2005.

Lewis, P. 'Legal Aspects of Employment Change and Their Implications for Management' (2001) 32(1) *Industrial Relations Journal* 71.

www.acas.org.uk

www.berr.gov.uk

www.tuc.org.uk

Chapter summaries are located at the end of each chapter and concisely sum up the main points and focus to be taken from each chapter.

Further reading lists direct you to the most relevant resources with which to supplement your study. Use them for reading around a subject or for coursework preparation.

Visit the *Employment Law*, Fifth Edition **mylawchamber** site at
www.mylawchamber.co.uk/sargeant to access:

Self study support: Use the practice exam questions to test yourself on each topic
throughout the course. The site includes updates to major changes in the law to
make sure you are ahead of the game, and weblinks to help you read more widely
around the subject.

Abbreviations

AC	Appeal Cases
ACAS	Advisory, Conciliation and Arbitration Service
All ER	All England Law Reports
AMRA	Access to Medical Reports Act 1988
ASTMS	Association of Supervisory, Technical and Managerial Staffs
AUEW	Amalgamated Union of Engineering Workers
CA	Court of Appeal
CAC	Central Arbitration Committee
CBI	Confederation of British Industry
CEEP	European Centre of Enterprises with Public Participation
CHR	European Convention on Human Rights
CMLR	Common Market Law Reports
CO	Certification Officer
CPSA	Civil and Public Services Association
CRE	Commission for Racial Equality
DDA	Disability Discrimination Act 1995
DBIS	Department for Business, Innovation and Skills
DRC	Disability Rights Commission
DRCA	Disability Rights Commission Act 1999
EA	Employment Act 2002
EADR	Employment Act 2002 (Dispute Resolution) Regulations 2004
EAT	Employment Appeal Tribunal
EC	European Community
ECHR	European Court of Human Rights
ECJ	European Court of Justice
ECR	European Court Reports
EEA	European Economic Area
EEC	European Economic Community
EES	European Employment Strategy
EHRC	Equality and Human Rights Commission
EHRR	European Human Rights Reports
EIRR	European Industrial Relations Report
EOC	Equal Opportunities Commission
EPA	Equal Pay Act 1970
ERA	Employment Rights Act 1996
ERELA	Employment Relations Act 1999
ETA	Employment Tribunals Act 1996
ETEJO	Employment Tribunals (Extension of Jurisdiction) Order 1994

ETUC	European Trade Union Confederation
ETUI	European Trade Union Institute
EU	European Union
EWC	European Works Council
GCHQ	Government Communications Headquarters
GMBATU	General, Municipal, Boilermakers and Allied Trades Union
HASAWA	Health and Safety at Work etc. Act 1974
HC	House of Commons
HL	House of Lords
HMSO	Her Majesty's Stationery Office
HRA	Human Rights Act 1998
HSCE	Health and Safety (Consultation with Employees) Regulations 1996
ICE	Information and Consultation of Employees Regulations 2004
ICR	Industrial Cases Reports
IRLR	Industrial Relations Law Reports
LBPIC	Telecommunications (Lawful Business Practice) (Interception of Communications)
MHSW	Management of Health and Safety at Work
MP	Member of Parliament
MPL	Maternity and Parental Leave etc. Regulations
NALGO	National Association of Local Government Officers
NEC	National Executive Committee
NGA	National Graphical Association
NIRC	National Industrial Relations Court
NMW	National minimum wage
NMWA	National Minimum Wage Act 1998
NUM	National Union of Mineworkers
NURMTW	National Union of Rail, Maritime and Transport Workers
OJ	Official Journal
ONS	Office for National Statistics
OPSI	Office of Public Sector Information
PTW	Part-time workers
QB	Queen's Bench
RIP	Regulation of Investigatory Powers Act 2000
RRA	Race Relations Act 1976
SDA	Sex Discrimination Act 1975
SE	Societas Europaea
SI	Statutory Instrument
SNB	Special Negotiating Body
SOGAT	Society of Graphical and Allied Trades
SPA	State Pension Age
SRA	Standard retirement age
TGWU	Transport and General Workers Union
TICE	Transnational Information and Consultation of Employees
TUC	Trades Union Congress
TULRCA	Trade Union and Labour Relations (Consolidation) Act 1992

TUPE	Transfer of Undertakings (Protection of Employment) Regulations 1981
UEAPME	Union Européenne de l'Artisanat et des Petites et Moyennes Entreprises
ULR	Union learning representative
UNICE	Union of Industrial Employers' Confederations of Europe
WLR	Weekly Law Reports
WT	Working time

Table of cases

Table of statutes

Table of statutory instruments

Table of European legislation

Regulations

Recommendations

Publisher's acknowledgements

We are grateful to the following for permission to reproduce copyright material:

Tables

Table on page 4 from ACAS Annual Report & Accounts 2008/9, http://www.acas.org.uk/CHttpHandler.ashx?id=1626&p=0, © Crown Copyright 2009; Table on page 19 adapted from "Employment protection rights of employees and workers" DTI 2002 discussion paper on employment status, Department for Business Innovation & Skills, www.berr.gov.uk (C) Crown copyright 2002; Table on page 172 from 'Religious affiliations', Census 2001, http://www.statistics.gov.uk/census2001/census2001.asp, Crown Copyright material is reproduced with the permission of the Controller, Office of Public Sector Information (OPSI).; Table on page 199 adapted from 'The employment of people with disabilities in the European Union', Executive Summary of Research Paper; written by European Experts Group on employment for disabled people; commissioned by the DG Employment and Social Affairs., © European Communities, 2001.

Text

Extract on page 5 from ACAS areas of activity, www.acas.org.uk, copyright © Acas, Euston Tower, 286 Euston Road, London NW1 3JJ; Extract on page 6 adapted from What is The Central Arbitration Committee?, http://www.cac.gov.uk/index.aspx?articleid=2239, copyright © CAC 2009; Extract on page 7 from Information Commissioner's Office, www.ico.gov.uk, copyright © ICO; Extract on pages 6–7 from Certification Officer, www.certoffice.org; Extract on page 120 from *Disciplinary and Grievance Procedures, Code of Practice 1*, The Stationery Office (2009) pp. iii, v–xi, ACAS © Crown Copyright 2009.

In some instances we have been unable to trace the owners of copyright material, and we would appreciate any information that would enable us to do so.

1 The study of employment law

1.1 Introduction

The subject of employment law is the regulation of the relationship between employer and worker or, put in another way, the relationship between the user of labour and the supplier of labour. This regulation takes place at an individual level and at a collective level. At an individual level the law takes the view that the contract of employment is like any other contract, namely a legally binding agreement that two equal parties have voluntarily entered into. At a collective level workers and employers have banded together into trade unions and employers' associations in order, partly, to give themselves greater bargaining power with each other.

The sources of this regulation are diverse and include:

1. Primary and secondary legislation initiated or supported by Government.
2. The EU Treaties and legislation, usually, but not always, in the form of Directives.
3. The decisions of the courts, including the High Court, employment tribunals and the Employment Appeal Tribunal, but especially, as in other fields of law, decisions of the Court of Appeal and the Supreme Court (which replaced the judicial role of the House of Lords in October 2009).
4. The decisions of international courts, especially the European Court of Justice and the European Court of Human Rights.
5. Codes of practice and guidance issued by Ministers of the Crown and by individual bodies authorised by statute to do so. These latter include the Health and Safety Commission/Executive and the Equality and Human Rights Commission (EHRC).
6. The Advisory, Conciliation and Arbitration Service (ACAS) and the Central Arbitration Committee (CAC), which have been given a special role by governments in the field of dispute resolution between workers and employers, both individually and collectively.

A concern for students of employment law is how to access the large amount of information available in the most efficient and effective way. Books like this one are one source of information, but further study means accessing the law and its sources directly. The purpose of this chapter is to provide some information on accessing employment law and to show that a large amount of information is available free from the organisations mentioned above and others, much of which is accessible via the Internet.

1.2 Primary and secondary legislation

The Acts of Parliament most often referred to in this book are the Trade Union and Labour Relations (Consolidation) Act 1992 (TULRCA 1992) and the Employment Rights Act 1996 (ERA 1996). Both of these have been much amended by other statutes. There are other important Acts, such as the Equal Pay Act 1970, the Sex Discrimination Act 1975, the Race Relations Act 1976, the Disability Discrimination Act 1995 and the National Minimum Wage Act 1998. There are also a large number of statutory instruments which form an important source of employment law. For example, much EU legislation is introduced via regulations under s. 2(2) European Communities Act 1972.

Study sources for both Acts of Parliament and secondary legislation are:

1. Office of Public Sector Information (OPSI) – The Stationery Office, which is the official publisher to Parliament, prints copies for sale of all primary and secondary legislation. These can be expensive but are often available in libraries. All such legislation since, and including, 1988 is available on the OPSI website at: *www.opsi.gov.uk*

Click on 'Legislation' and you will be taken to a site from which you can access new legislation made available in the previous two weeks. If you then click on 'UK' under the heading 'Legislation' you will be taken to a further page which will enable you to access all Acts of the UK Parliament adopted since 1988. If you click on 'Statutory Instruments' you will be able to access subordinate legislation. Bear in mind that there are several thousand statutory instruments adopted each year, so it will help you if you know the year and the number that you are looking for. Thus SI 1998/1833 will lead you to statutory instrument number 1833 adopted in 1998, which will take you to the Working Time Regulations 1998.

2. Houses of Parliament – Hansard is the full verbatim report of debates in the Houses of Parliament and is kept by many libraries in microfiche format. There is also a large amount of information available on Parliament's website at: *www.parliament.uk*

If you click on this, you will be able to choose between the House of Commons and the House of Lords and explore at your leisure. Click on 'House of Commons' and you will see a section on 'Research Papers'. If you click on these you will be able to explore all the recent research papers written by House of Commons research staff. This will include papers on employment law issues and Bills before Parliament.

Alternatively, if, at the Parliament Home Page, you click on 'Site Map' this will give you access to the entire work of Parliament, including copies of Bills before Parliament and the current work of the House of Commons and the House of Lords. It will usefully give you access to the Committee System and the reports that Select Committees of both Houses have made. For example, you might follow this through to the Business Innovation and Skills Committee.

The Government department that has the most relevance to the study of employment law is the Department for Business, Innovation and Skills (formerly the Department for Business Enterprise and Regulatory Reform). Its website can be found at: *www.berr.gov.uk*

The site has copies of all the consultations that have been carried out concerning the introduction of many EU measures in the field of employment law and provides guidance on current legislation.

3. Other sources of statutes will be the same as for other law subjects studied, such as Halsbury's Statutes, Lexis and Lawtel.

1.3 The EU Treaties and legislation

Six countries adopted the Treaty of Rome in 1957 but the European Community has grown to 27 Member States at the time of writing. From December 2009 the two principle sources of EU law are the Treaty on the Functioning of the European Union and the Treaty on European Union. The scope of the EU's activities has also grown from being concerned with a number of primarily economic objectives to a Union that has an important social dimension as well as an economic one.

As a result of this, there is a large amount of EU material available and it seems to increase at a rate that alarms even specialist students of EU law. Ways of accessing this information will include:

1. European Documentation Centres – a large number of libraries contain European Documentation Centres, which will normally have a specialist librarian in charge. These keep paper copies of both current and historical EU material. They are most useful if you know what you are looking for rather than starting a cold search.

2. The EU has a website with an enormous amount of material. It is not the easiest site to navigate but will reward those who know which document they are looking for or those with patience. It can be found at: *http://europa.eu.int*.

   Once you have clicked on the language you require, the next page provides a subject list of what the European Union does. Click on 'Employment and Social Affairs' and you will come across a page divided into two sections which are 'Latest Developments' and 'A Comprehensive Guide to European Law'. Useful sites on this page include 'Employment and Social Affairs' which will take you to the page of the Directorate General that has responsibility for these matters. You might also try the 'European Foundation for the Improvement of Living and Working Conditions' which has extensive information about what is going on in the EU and individual Member States. Lastly you might also click on the page headed 'Legislation in Force' in order to access the piece of legislation that you are interested in.

3. A good library will have other sources, such as those contained on various CD-ROMs, as well as access to relevant information via other commercial bodies.

1.4 The courts

1.4.1 Employment tribunals and the EAT

Section 1(1) Employment Rights (Dispute Resolution) Act 1998 renamed industrial tribunals as employment tribunals so this is how they are referred to in this book. Unlike many other courts, employment tribunals and the Employment Appeal Tribunal (EAT) are created by statute[1] as is the subject matter in which they deal.[2] The composition of employment tribunals is set out in the Employment Tribunals Act 1996.[3] An interesting issue with regard to tribunals and the Human Rights Act 1998 was raised in *Smith* v *Secretary of State for Trade*

---

[1] See ss. 1 and 20 Employment Tribunals Act 1996.
[2] Sections 2–3 and 21 Employment Tribunals Act 1996.
[3] Sections 4 and 22–25 Employment Tribunals Act 1996.

and Industry.[4] Article 6(1) of the European Convention on Human Rights gives everyone the right to an 'independent and impartial' tribunal. The question raised was whether employment tribunals which were appointed by the Secretary of State could adjudicate in claims against the Secretary of State and still be an independent and impartial tribunal.

The work of employment tribunals is increasing partly because of new legislation on employment rights giving individuals the opportunity to make a complaint to an employment tribunal. Appeals from employment tribunals, on a point of law, are normally to the EAT, which sits in Edinburgh and London. The table below provides a breakdown of employment tribunal claims in 2008/9:[5]

Subject matter	Number and percentage of applications	
Unfair dismissal	55,000	23.3%
Wages Act	30,634	13.0%
Breach of contract	31,637	13.4%
Redundancy pay	10,234	4.4%
Sex discrimination	10,751	4.6%
Race discrimination	4,878	2.1%
Disability discrimination	6,442	2.7%
Equal pay	48,560	20.6%
Working Time Directive	17,844	7.6%
Flexible working	246	0.1%
Age discrimination	3,395	1.4%
National minimum wage	517	0.2%
Others	15,928	6.7%
Total	236,116	100%

Source: ACAS Annual Report & Accounts 2008/9 © Crown Copyright 2009

1.4.2 **Case reports**

Paper reports of proceedings at the EAT, the Court of Appeal (CA) and the Supreme Court are published in:

Industrial Cases Reports (ICR), and

Industrial Relations Law Reports (IRLR).

Wherever possible, these are the sources used in this book. Both carry good summaries of the cases in question. Cases may also be reported in non-specialist law reports, such as the All England Law Reports (All ER), the Weekly Law Reports (WLR), or in Appeal Cases (AC).

Other, more comprehensive, sources are:

1. *www.employmentappeals.gov.uk* (the EAT);

2. *www.courtservice.gov.uk* (the High Court and the Court of Appeal);

3. *www.supremecourt.gov.uk/index.html* (the Supreme Court).

[4] [2000] IRLR 6.
[5] See ACAS Annual Report 2008/9.

Apart from the EAT, these sources are not restricted to employment law cases only and can be found via a number of other links. The advantage of all these sites over the paper reports is that the judgment of the court is reported in full in all cases. The Employment Tribunals Service website also contains a lot of useful information and statistics. It can be found at: *www.employmenttribunals.gov.uk*

1.4.3 International courts

For employment law purposes, the two most important courts are the European Court of Justice (ECJ) and the European Court of Human Rights (ECHR). Significant and relevant cases in both are reported in the ICR and IRLR, but they both have their own paper and electronic reports. These are:

European Case Reports (ECR) for the European Court of Justice; and

European Human Rights Reports (EHRR) for the European Court of Human Rights.

Again, these reports cover all the work of the courts and will include a large number of cases which are not directly relevant to the study of employment law. In addition, both courts have websites which will provide access to the judgments of the court. These sites are:

1. *www.curia.eu.int* (the ECJ).
2. *www.echr.coe.int* (the ECHR).

1.5 Advisory, Conciliation and Arbitration Service

The Advisory, Conciliation and Arbitration Service (ACAS) was established by statute in 1975 to promote the improvement of industrial relations.[6]

It operates as an independent publicly funded body and is not subject to direct ministerial control. It is run by a committee of 12 individuals, which is made up of leading figures from business, unions, independent sectors and academics. ACAS operates in four key areas of activities. These are:

1. Preventing and resolving disputes by means of collective conciliation and advisory mediation.
2. Conciliating in actual and potential complaints to employment tribunals.
3. Providing information and advice.
4. Promoting good practice and training.

Examples of its success are:

1. 898 collective cases were completed in 2008/9,[7] of which 74 were subsequently withdrawn. Of the rest, conciliation was successful in 755 cases and unsuccessful in 69.
2. In the same period 74,777 applications to employment tribunals were dealt with. Of these 22,993 (30.7 per cent) were withdrawn and 31,843 settled (42.6 per cent), and only 19,941 made it to a tribunal hearing (26.7 per cent).

---

[6] See now s. 209 TULRCA 1992.
[7] See the latest annual report available on the ACAS website, *www.acas.org.uk*.

The ACAS annual report is a good source of statistical information and is free from its website. It also produces a wide range of publications which focus on good practice and explain the legal obligations of practitioners. Of considerable importance is its guide *Discipline and Grievances at Work* (see Chapter 4) and its codes of practice on:

- disclosure of information to trade unions for collective bargaining purposes 2003;
- time off for trade union duties and activities 2004; and
- disciplinary and grievance procedures 2009.

ACAS has authority to issue these codes of practice under ss. 199–202 TULRCA 1992. Sections 207 and 207A TULRCA 1992 provide that the contents of these codes will be taken into account at hearings before employment tribunals, courts or the Central Arbitration Committee (CAC). ACAS has a very useful website, which contains consultation and proposals on matters such as new codes of practice. It can be found at: *www.acas.org.uk*

1.6 Central Arbitration Committee

The Central Arbitration Committee (CAC) is a permanent independent body with a number of roles:[8]

1. To adjudicate on applications relating to the statutory recognition of trade unions for collective bargaining purposes (see Chapter 11).
2. To determine disputes between employers and trade unions over the disclosure of information for collective bargaining purposes (see Chapter 11).
3. To determine claims and complaints regarding the establishment and operation of European Works Councils in Great Britain (see Chapter 9).
4. To provide voluntary arbitration in trade disputes, in certain circumstances.

In the period 2008/9 the CAC did not receive any applications concerning voluntary arbitration. However, it did receive five applications concerning disclosure of information and 42 concerning trade union recognition.

The Committee consists of a chair and 11 deputy chairs, together with 56 members experienced as representatives of employers or workers. Any determinations of the Committee are made by the chair, or deputy chair, plus two members. The CAC has a useful website at: *www.cac.gov.uk*

This website contains information about the CAC and its statutory powers. It also contains information about decisions of the CAC and details about individual cases.

1.7 Certification Officer

The Certification Officer is appointed[9] to carry out particular functions[10] (see Chapter 10):

1. Maintaining a list of trade unions and employers' associations.

---

[8] See ss. 259–265 TULRCA 1992.
[9] Sections 254–255 TULRCA 1992.
[10] Part I TULRCA 1992.

2. Receiving, ensuring compliance with statutory requirements and keeping available for public inspection annual returns from trade unions and employers' associations.

3. Determining complaints concerning trade union elections, certain other ballots and certain breaches of trade union rules.

4. Ensuring observance of statutory requirements governing mergers between trade unions and between employers' associations.

5. Overseeing the political funds and the finances of trade unions and employers associations.

6. Certifying the independence of trade unions.

The Certification Officer produces a detailed and useful annual report which contains information on employers' associations and trade unions and on the work of the Certification Officer. The report and other material can be seen on the website at: *www.certoffice.org*

1.8 Information Commissioner

The Office of the Information Commissioner (previously known as the Data Protection Commissioner) was established by the Data Protection Act 1998, much of which came into effect on 1 March 2000.[11] The Commissioner oversees and enforces compliance with the Data Protection Act 1998 and the Freedom of Information Act 2000. It does this by, amongst other means:

1. Publishing guidance to assist with compliance.

2. Providing a general inquiry service.

3. Encouraging the development of codes of practice.

4. Maintaining the public register of data controllers under the Data Protection Act 1998 and the list of public authorities with approved publication schemes under the Freedom of Information Act 2000.

5. Prosecuting persons in respect of offences under the legislation.

There is an excellent website at: *www.ico.gov.uk*

This provides legal guidance and compliance advice as well as links to the Data Protection Act 1998, codes of practice and consultation documents, including the code of practice on the use of personal data in employer/employee relationships.

1.9 Equality and Human Rights Commission (EHRC)

The Equality and Human Rights Commission was established by s. 1 Equality Act 2006. In addition to assuming responsibility for the work of the previous anti-discrimination Commissions (i.e. the Equal Opportunities Commission, the Commission for Racial Equality and the Disability Rights Commission), it has the duty to combat unlawful discrimination on the grounds of sexual orientation, religion or belief, and age.

---

[11] Section 6(1) Data Protection Act 1998.

Section 8 Equality Act 2006 provides that the EHRC must:

(a) promote understanding of the importance of equality and diversity,
(b) encourage good practice in relation to equality and diversity,
(c) promote equality of opportunity,
(d) promote awareness and understanding of rights under the equality enactments,
(e) enforce the equality enactments,
(f) work towards the elimination of unlawful discrimination, and
(g) work towards the elimination of unlawful harassment.

It must also monitor the effectiveness of equality and human rights legislation and report on progress made every three years.[12] As part of its general powers the EHRC can provide advice and information, produce codes of practice, conduct inquiries, carry out investigations and issue unlawful act notices.[13]

The EHRC website is located at: *www.equalityhumanrights.com*

1.10 Other useful websites

Some sites are useful because they provide good links to other legal sites, such as:

University of Kent	*www.kent.ac.uk/lawlinks*
Industrial Law Society	*www.industriallawsociety.org.uk*

Other useful sites include:

British Employment Law	*www.emplaw.co.uk*
Cabinet Office	*www.cabinetoffice.gov.uk*
Chartered Institute of Personnel and Development	*www.cipd.co.uk*
Confederation of British Industry	*www.cbi.org.uk*
Employers Forum on Age	*www.efa.org.uk*
European Industrial Relations Observatory	*www.eurofound.europa.ev*
European Trade Union Confederation	*www.etuc.org*
European Trade Union Institute	*www.etui.org*
Federation of Small Businesses	*www.fsb.org.uk*
Health and Safety Executive	*www.hse.gov.uk*
Incomes Data Services	*www.incomesdata.co.uk*
International Labour Organisation	*www.ilo.org*
Labour Research Department	*www.lrd.org.uk*
Low Pay Commission	*www.lowpay.gov.uk*
National Statistics	*www.statistics.gov.uk*
Times Law Reports	*http://business.timesonline.co.uk*
Trades Union Congress	*www.tuc.org.uk*
UK Official Documents	*www.official-documents.gov.uk*
UNICE (European Employers' Organisation)	*www.unice.org*
Unison	*www.unison.org.uk*

---

[12] Sections 11–12 Equality Act 2006.
[13] Sections 13–16, 20–21 Equality Act 2006.

Chapter summary

This chapter has outlined the way in which employment law is made and the bodies that develop, supervise and enforce it. It described how employment law is created by primary and secondary legislation which is then interpreted by the courts, especially by employment tribunals and the Employment Appeal Tribunal. It also indicated the relevance of EU law and the decisions of the European Court of Justice. Finally, it looked at the major institutions created by Parliament to deal with employment and discrimination issues.

Further reading

Collins, H., Ewing, K. and McColgan, A. *Labour Law: Text and Materials*: Hart Publishing, 2005, Chapter 1.

Deakin, S. and Morris, G. *Labour Law*: 5th edn, Hart Publishing, 2009, Chapter 2.

Smith, I. and Thomas, G. *Smith and Wood's Employment Law*: 9th edn, Oxford University Press, 2008, Chapter 1.

Visit **www.mylawchamber.co.uk/sargeant**
to access legal updates, live weblinks and practice
exam questions to test yourself on this chapter.

2 The employment relationship

2.1 Introduction

The purely contractual approach to the employment relationship is unsatisfactory because it suggests that there are two equal parties agreeing the terms of a contract. The contractual approach was adopted by the courts in the 1870s, but it is still, in reality, an unequal relationship. One party uses the labour or talents of another in return for providing remuneration. The payment of that remuneration, except in unusual circumstances, creates a labour force which is dependent upon the employer's goodwill and desire to continue with that relationship. It may be made less one-sided by statutes which limit the freedom of employers to take action against workers and may be made more equal by collective bargaining arrangements between employers and trade unions. In 1897 the Webbs wrote that:

> Individual bargaining between the owner of the means of subsistence and the seller of so perishable a commodity as a day's labour must be, once and for all, abandoned. In its place, if there is to be any genuine freedom of contract, we shall see the conditions of employment adjusted between equally expert negotiators acting for corporations reasonably comparable in strength.[1]

This was a call for effective collective bargaining with trade unions being able to negotiate with employers as equals.

Otto Kahn-Freund[2] described contracts of employment as concealing the realities of subordination behind the conceptual screen of contracts concluded between equals. The reality, he concluded, was that such contracts were between institutions and individuals. Freedom of contract is seen as a voluntary act of submission by the individual.[3] Later, Lord Wedderburn suggested that:

> The lawyer's model of a freely bargained individual agreement is misleading. In reality, without collective or statutory intervention, many terms of the 'agreement' are imposed by the more powerful party, the employer, by what Fox has called 'the brute facts of power'.[4]

Despite these limitations, the courts have not allowed the power of the employer to overcome the freedom that the parties have to enter voluntarily into contractual relations.

---

[1] Sidney Webb and Beatrice Webb, *Industrial Democracy* (1897).
[2] Professor Otto Kahn-Freund, who died in 1979, was an eminent and influential labour law academic.
[3] See Paul Davies and Mark Freedland, *Kahn-Freund's Labour and the Law* (Stevens, 1983).
[4] Lord Wedderburn of Charlton, *The Worker and the Law* (Sweet & Maxwell, 1986), Chapter 2.

Nokes v *Doncaster Collieries*[5] concerned an individual miner working for Hickleton Main Colliery Ltd who was apparently unaware that the company had been dissolved by a court order and that his contract of employment had been transferred to Doncaster Amalgamated Collieries Ltd. The issue was whether, in the circumstances, the contract automatically transferred to the new employer, even though the employee was ignorant of the change. Lord Atkin stated:

> My Lords, I should have thought that the principle that a man is not to be compelled to serve a master against his will . . . is deep seated in the common law of this country.

The employee needed to have knowledge of the employer's identity and to have given consent to the transfer. Without such knowledge and consent it would not be possible to say that the employee had freely entered into a contractual relationship with the employer.[6]

Discussion about the importance of the contractual relationship also conceals the complexity and variety of working relationships that now exist. It is misleading to use a model of an employer/worker relationship consisting of a full-time employer and a full-time worker. Apart from the distinction between the employed and the self-employed, which in itself may be at times a difficult distinction (see below), contractual relationships will include those on part-time contracts, limited term contracts, zero hours contracts, casual contracts and so on.

The contract of employment is also an unsatisfactory way of describing the employment relationship because it does not reflect the often informal relationship between employers and workers. This informal relationship is reflected, for example, in the number of hours that are worked in the United Kingdom, which are longer than elsewhere in the EU (see Chapter 7). The hours that many people work are often in excess of their contractual obligations and suggest that there is an informal expectation that this amount of work is required. Similarly it is difficult to incorporate quality and quantity of effort into a contract. During peak periods of work, employees may perform at a much more demanding level than in normal periods in order to cope with the extra workload. The contract of employment is not able to describe or incorporate this aspect of the employer/worker relationship.

2.2 Parties to the contract – employers

2.2.1 Employers' associations

Employers' associations are potentially important in their role as:

1. A representative of a particular industrial or commercial sector, such as the Engineering Employers' Association, or as a representative of a particular type of employer, such as the Federation of Small Businesses, or as representatives of different employers working with common interests, such as the Business Services Association.[7]

2. A social partner, when they might be consulted by Government on proposed policies or legislation. They may also have an international role and be able to influence EU decisions. One example of this is the Confederation of British Industry (CBI) which is a member of

---

[5] *Nokes* v *Doncaster Amalgamated Collieries Ltd* [1940] AC 1014 HL.
[6] For the statutory approach to employee rights during transfers, see Chapter 9.
[7] Representing contracting businesses working in a variety of sectors.

UNICE, the European private employers' organisation, which is, in turn, a member of the Social Dialogue Committee in the EU.

3. A negotiator with trade unions on behalf of the members that they represent. It is perhaps less common than previously, with the decline in union membership, to have industry or sector-wide agreements on pay and conditions. They are more common in the public sector than the private one. Where they exist they may regulate the pay and conditions of large numbers of employees, such as in the education or health service sectors. There is also a likelihood that such agreements will be incorporated into individuals' contracts of employment.[8]

Part II TULRCA 1992 is concerned with the regulation of employers' associations. They are defined as temporary or permanent organisations which consist mainly or wholly of either employers or individual owners of undertakings; or consist of constituent bodies or affiliated organisations, which are, in themselves, collections of employers or owners of undertakings; whose principal purposes include the regulation of relations between employers and workers or trade unions.[9] The Certification Officer has an obligation to keep lists of employers' associations and make them available for public inspection at all reasonable hours, free of charge.[10] It is not mandatory, however, for associations to apply for listing.[11] According to the Certification Officer's annual report for 2008/9, there were 67 listed and 66 unlisted employers' associations at the end of March 2009.

An employers' association may be either a body corporate or an unincorporated association.[12] If the latter, it will still be capable of making contracts, suing and being sued, as well as being capable of having proceedings brought against it for alleged offences committed by it or on its behalf.[13] As for trade unions (see Chapter 10), the purposes of employers' associations, in so far as they relate to the regulation of relations between employers and workers, are protected from legal actions for restraint of trade.[14]

2.2.2 Identifying the employer

Section 295(1) TULRCA 1992 defines an employer, in relation to an employee, as 'the person by whom the employee is (or, where the employment has ceased, was) employed'. Section 296(2) offers a similar definition in relation to workers.[15] In this case the employer is 'a person for whom one or more workers work, or have worked or normally work or seek to work'. These definitions are repeated elsewhere, such as in s. 54 National Minimum Wage Act 1998.[16] The differences between employees and workers are important and are discussed below.

---

[8] For examples of such incorporation, see *Gascol Conversions v Mercer* [1974] IRLR 155 and *Whent v T Cartledge* [1997] IRLR 153.
[9] Section 122(1) TULRCA 1992.
[10] Section 123(1) and (2) TULRCA 1992; for information about the Certification Officer, see Chapter 1.
[11] The processes for applying to have a name entered on the list, removing it from the list and appealing against the Certification Officer's decisions are contained in ss. 124–126 TULRCA 1992.
[12] Section 127(1) TULRCA 1992.
[13] Section 127(2) TULRCA 1992. See *Barry Print v (1) The Showmen's Guild of Great Britain; (2) Bob Wilson & Sons (Leisure) Ltd*, unreported, 27 October 1999 where an unincorporated association was held to be without legal personality, save for s. 127(2) TULRCA 1992.
[14] Section 128 TULRCA 1992; issues related to the property of and to the administration of employers' associations are contained in ss. 129–134 TULRCA 1992.
[15] See also s. 230(4) ERA 1996.
[16] See Chapter 7.

The employer may be an individual, but is more likely to be a partnership or a business with limited liability. In equity partnerships the individual partners are likely to retain personal responsibility for the actions of the partnership. In a business with limited liability there may be a separation of identity between the management of a company or business and the legal person that is that company or business. Thus, in some situations, management may make decisions affecting an employee, who will then have recourse against the business itself. The contract of employment or statement of particulars of employment will normally identify the employer.[17]

It is possible for the natural or legal person who is the employer to be changed if there is a transfer of the contract of employment. As will be explained in Chapter 9, the Transfer of Undertakings (Protection of Employment) Regulations 2006[18] enable the identity of the employer to be changed in such a manner that the employee will retain continuity of employment.[19] Unlike the case of *Nokes* v *Doncaster Collieries*[20] (discussed earlier) this may happen, in situations protected by these Regulations, even without the employee's knowledge.[21]

2.2.3 **Employers as employees**

The separation of the identity of management and the owners of an undertaking has some consequences for employees. The courts are reluctant to lift the veil of incorporation to look into the reality of that which lies behind it. In *Catherine Lee* v *Lee's Air Farming Ltd*[22] the controlling shareholder was also the company's sole employee. The court decided that:

> There appears no greater difficulty in holding that a man acting in one capacity can give orders to himself acting in another capacity than there is in holding that a man acting in one capacity can make a contract with himself in another capacity. The company and the deceased[23] were separate legal entities.

Thus it is possible for a controlling shareholder to be an employee of the same organisation. The Court of Appeal considered such a situation in *Secretary of State* v *Bottrill*[24] where an individual was appointed managing director of a company and, temporarily at least, held all the share capital. At the same time the individual signed a contract of employment, which set out the duties of the post, the hours to be worked, holiday and sickness entitlement and details of remuneration. The issue was whether such a person was really an employee. The court did not accept a previous EAT decision which had concluded that a 50 per cent shareholder,[25] who was also a director, was not an employee. The EAT had concluded that

---

[17] Section 1(3)(a) ERA 1996.

[18] SI 2006/246.

[19] See also s. 218 ERA 1996 in relation to continuity of employment in certain changes of employer; discussed further below.

[20] [1940] AC 1014 HL.

[21] See *Secretary of State for Trade and Industry* v *Cook* [1997] IRLR 151 CA, which overturned a previous decision in *Photostatic Copiers (Southern) Ltd* v *Okuda* [1995] IRLR 12, and confirmed that such knowledge was not an essential prerequisite.

[22] [1961] AC 12.

[23] The applicant was the widow of the controlling shareholder and sole employee.

[24] *Secretary of State for Trade and Industry* v *Bottrill* [1999] IRLR 326 CA.

[25] *Buchan* v *Secretary of State for Employment* [1997] IRLR 80; the Court of Appeal preferred the decision of the Court of Session in *Fleming* v *Secretary of State for Trade and Industry* [1997] IRLR 682 where the court concluded that whether a person was an employee or not was a matter of fact and all the relevant circumstances needed to be looked at, rather than adopting a general rule of law.

a controlling shareholder could not be an employee because such a person would be able to control decisions that affected his or her own dismissal and remuneration and that there was a difference between an individual running a business through the device of a limited liability company and an individual working for a company subject to the control of a board of directors. The EAT stated that, in the context of employment protection legislation, *Lee's Air Farming* could not be relied upon to support the proposition that a shareholder with full and unrestricted control over a company could also be employed under a contract of service. The Court of Appeal, however, stated that all the factors that indicated an employer/employee relationship, or otherwise, needed to be examined. The fact that the person was a controlling shareholder was only one of those factors, albeit a potentially decisive one. Other factors to be considered were whether there was a genuine contract between the shareholder and the company, the reasons for the contract coming into existence and what each party actually did in carrying out their contractual obligations. The issue of control was important in deciding whether there was a genuine employment relationship: for example, were there other directors and to what extent did the employee become involved in decisions affecting them as employees.[26] More recently, in *Secretary of State* v *Neufeld*[27] the Court of Appeal thought that there was no reason why a shareholder and director cannot also be an employee. It does not matter that the shareholding provides total control of the company. Finally, in *Clark* v *Clark Construction Ltd*[28] the EAT identified three sets of circumstances where it might be legitimate not to give effect to what is alleged to be a binding contract of employment between a controlling shareholder and a company. First, where the company is itself a sham. Second, where the contract was entered into for some ulterior purpose, for example to secure a payment from the Secretary of State. Third, where the parties do not in fact conduct their relationship in accordance with the contract.

2.2.4 Associated, superior and principal employers

One of the concerns of employment protection legislation is to ensure that, when necessary, two or more associated employers are treated as if they were one. This is especially important where there are exemptions for small employers, such as in the requirements for statutory recognition of trade unions.[29]

Section 297 TULRCA 1992 and s. 231 ERA 1996 define any two employers as associated if one is a company of which the other has, directly or indirectly, control or if both are companies of which a third person, either directly or indirectly, has control.[30] This is a convenient definition when adding up numbers of employees to decide whether an employer or a group of employers crosses a threshold. However, it is important not to assume that groups of associated employers are to be treated as one employer for employment protection purposes in all situations. Each employer retains its distinct legal personality. In *Allen* v *Amalgamated*

---

[26] See also *Sellars Arenascene Ltd* v *Connolly* [2001] IRLR 222 CA which also considered the position of a controlling shareholder of a business that had been taken over. The court held that the tribunal had placed too much reliance upon the individual's interest as a shareholder rather than as an employee. The fact that he would gain if the company prospered applied to employees as well as shareholders.

[27] [2009] IRLR 475.

[28] [2008] IRLR 364.

[29] See Sch. A1 Part I, para. 7 TULRCA 1992 and Chapter 11.

[30] See also s. 82(1) Sex Discrimination Act 1975.

Construction,[31] for example, the ECJ held that a relevant transfer[32] of employees took place between two companies, who were distinctive legal entities, but who were part of the same group and would probably, under the statutory definitions, be treated as associated employers.

A superior employer, according to s. 48 National Minimum Wage Act 1998, is deemed to be the joint employer, with the immediate employer, of the worker concerned. This occurs where the immediate employer of a worker is in the employment of some other person and the worker is employed on the premises of that other person. This is a definition that seems to be aimed at stopping workers being sub-contracted to other workers so that the superior employer is liable for ensuring that the national minimum wage is paid.

Section 12(1) DDA 1995 makes it unlawful for a principal, in relation to contract work, to discriminate against a disabled person. Section 12(4) describes a principal as:

> a person (A) who makes work available for doing by individuals who are employed by another person who supplies them under a contract made with A.

There are similar provisions contained in s. 9(1) Sex Discrimination Act 1975 and s. 7(1) Race Relations Act 1976 aimed at making the hirer, rather than the recruitment agency or intermediary, liable for discrimination against contract workers. *Abbey Life Assurance Co Ltd* v *Tansell*[33] involved a computer contractor who hired himself out via a company he had established for that purpose. He was placed as a contractor by an agency, so that there were two organisations between him and the ultimate hirer. The Court of Appeal held that the ultimate hirer was still the principal for the purposes of the DDA 1995, as Parliament had probably intended that it should be the ultimate hirer who should be liable rather than the agency.

2.3 Parties to the contract – employees

2.3.1 Dependent labour

One of the features of employment law in the United Kingdom is the distinction between employees and workers. The latter tends to have a wider meaning. Section 230(1) ERA 1996 defines an employee as 'an individual who has entered into or works under (or, where the employment has ceased, worked under) a contract of employment'. Section 230(2) defines a contract of employment, for the purposes of the Act, as meaning 'a contract of service or apprenticeship, whether express or implied, and (if it is express) whether oral or in writing'. The meaning of worker can be the same, but it can also have a wider meaning, i.e. an individual who has entered into, or works under, a contract of employment or

> any other contract, whether express or implied and (if it is express) whether oral or in writing, whereby the individual undertakes to do or perform personally any work or services for another party to the contract whose status is not by virtue of the contract that of a client or customer of any profession or business undertaking carried on by the individual.[34]

---

[31] Case C-234/98 *GC Allen v Amalgamated Construction Co Ltd* [2000] IRLR 119 ECJ; see also *Michael Peters Ltd* v *(1) Farnfield; (2) Michael Peters Group plc* [1995] IRLR 190 where the Group chief executive failed to persuade the EAT that the chief executive's post transferred with a number of subsidiaries to the transferee employer.

[32] In relation to the Transfer of Undertakings (Protection of Employment) Regulations 1981, SI 1981/1794, replaced by new Regulations in 2006; see Chapter 9.

[33] [2000] IRLR 387 CA.

[34] Section 230(3) ERA 1996.

Thus there are some individuals who will not be under a contract of employment to a particular employer, but are under a contract to perform personally any work or services. Often they will be treated as self-employed, which means, for example, that they would not receive the benefits of employment protection measures applicable to employees. Nevertheless, these workers may be as dependent on one employer as employees are.

In *Byrne Brothers (Formwork) Ltd* v *Baird*[35] the EAT held that the intention[36] was to create an intermediate class of protected worker who, on the one hand, is not an employee and, on the other hand, cannot be regarded as carrying on a business. In this case the EAT concluded that self-employed sub-contractors in the construction industry fitted into this category. The court stated:

> There can be no general rule, and we should not be understood as propounding one; cases cannot be decided by applying labels. But typically labour-only sub-contractors will, though nominally free to move from contractor to contractor, in practice work for long periods for a single employer as an integrated part of his workforce.

Not all the self-employed are people engaged in business on their own account and one way of distinguishing between the two is to ask what is the dominant purpose of the contract.[37] Is the contract to be located in the employment field or is it in reality a contract between two independent businesses? In *Inland Revenue* v *Post Office Ltd*[38] the EAT decided that sub-postmistresses and sub-postmasters were not workers for the purposes of the National Minimum Wage Act 1998 because they had a choice whether or not to personally perform the work.

The numbers of self-employed workers has grown significantly in the last 20 years and, in 2008, amounted to approximately 4 million people, compared to over 27 million employees.[39] Over two-thirds of the self-employed have no employees themselves and are dependent upon using their own skills and labour.[40] For some workers, self-employment is an illusion. They will be dependent upon one employer for their supply of work and income, but may be lacking in certain employment rights because of their self-employed status. One study of freelancers in the publishing industry, for example, concluded that:

> Freelancers in publishing are essentially casualised employees, rather than independent self-employed . . . in objective terms they are disguised wage labour.[41]

There is then a real difficulty in distinguishing between those who are genuine employees and those who are self-employed, especially if they have the same dependence on one employer as do employees. To some extent this is recognised by the Government when certain employment protection measures are applied to workers and others to employees only. The Working Time Regulations 1998,[42] for example, refer, in reg. 4(1), to a 'worker's working

---

[35] [2002] IRLR 96.

[36] This case involved the definition of worker in reg. 2(1) of the Working Time Regulations 1998, which is identical to that contained in s. 230(3) ERA 1996

[37] See *James* v *Redcats (Brands) Ltd* [2007] IRLR 296.

[38] [2003] IRLR 199.

[39] Information supplied by the Office for National Statistics; see *www.statistics.gov.uk*.

[40] Julie Bevan, *Barriers to Business Start Up: A Study of the Flow into and out of Self Employment*, Department of Employment Research Paper no 71.

[41] Celia Stanworth and John Stanworth, 'The Self Employed without Employees – Autonomous or Atypical?' (1995) 26(3) *Industrial Relations Journal*, September.

[42] SI 1998/1833.

time', whilst the Maternity and Parental Leave etc. Regulations 1999 apply only to employees (see table on p. 19).[43]

2.3.2 The distinction between the employed and the self-employed

There are a number of reasons why it is important to establish whether an individual is an employee or self-employed:

1. Some employment protection measures are reserved for employees, although there are some which use the wider definition of worker, including the Working Time Regulations 1998,[44] the Sex Discrimination Act 1975 and the Race Relations Act 1976. An example of protection being offered only to employees is contained in *Costain Building & Civil Engineering Ltd* v *Smith*,[45] where a self-employed contractor was appointed by the trade union as a safety representative on a particular site. The individual had been placed as a temporary worker with the company through an employment agency. After a number of critical reports on health and safety he was dismissed by the agency at the request of the company. He complained that he had been dismissed, contrary to s. 100(1)(b) ERA 1996, for performing the duties of a health and safety representative. In the course of the proceedings he failed to show that he was other than self-employed. This proved fatal to the complaint, as the relevant regulations only allowed trade unions to appoint safety representatives from amongst its members who were employees.[46] As the EAT concluded that there was no contract of employment between the agency and the individual, he did not come within the protection offered to trade union health and safety representatives.

2. Self-employed persons are taxed on a Schedule D basis, rather than Schedule E which applies to employed earners. This allows the self-employed person to set off business expenses against income for tax purposes. A good example of the effect of this was shown in *Hall* v *Lorimer*.[47] Mr Lorimer had been employed as a vision mixer working on the production of television programmes. He decided to become freelance and built up a circle of contacts. He worked on his own and was used by a large number of companies for a short period each. He worked on their premises and used their equipment. The Inland Revenue (now Her Majesty's Revenue and Customs) had assessed his income as being earned under a series of individual contracts of service and thus chargeable to Schedule E income tax. He claimed that he was self-employed and should have been taxed under Schedule D. It was important to him financially. In his first year his gross earnings were £32,875 and he had expenses of £9,250. If assessed under Schedule E he would need to pay tax on the gross amount. If assessed under Schedule D he would be able to offset his expenses and only be liable for tax on £23,625. In the event Mr Lorimer was successful and the Court of Appeal held that he was self-employed.

---

[43] SI 1999/3312. See reg. 13(1) where employees with one year's continuous service, and responsibility for a child, are entitled to parental leave.

[44] See, e.g., *Quinnen* v *Hovells* [1984] IRLR 227, where the EAT concluded that the definition of employment contained in s. 82(1) Sex Discrimination Act 1975 enlarged the ordinary meaning of employment to include individuals outside the master/servant relationship.

[45] [2000] ICR 215.

[46] Regulation 3(1) Safety Representatives and Safety Committees Regulations 1977, SI 1977/500; employee is defined by reference to s. 53(1) HASAWA 1974, which defines employee as a person who works under a contract of employment.

[47] *Hall (HM Inspector of Taxes)* v *Lorimer* [1994] IRLR 171 CA.

3. Employers are vicariously liable for the actions of their employees and normally not for independent contractors. Lord Thankerton summed up the test for vicarious liability at that time:

> It is clear that the master is responsible for acts actually authorised by him; for liability would exist in this case even if the relation between the parties was merely one of agency, and not one of service at all. But a master, as opposed to the employer of an independent contractor, is liable even for acts which he has not authorised, provided they are so connected with acts which he has authorised that they may rightly be regarded as modes – although improper modes – of doing them.[48]

This liability of the employer has been extended so that it continues even for acts of intentional wrongdoing which the employer could not have approved. Thus the employer of a house warden who sexually abused boarders at a school for maladjusted and vulnerable boys was held to be vicariously liable for the actions of the employee.[49] The House of Lords held that the correct test for deciding whether an employee's wrongful act had been committed during the course of employment, so as to make the employer vicariously liable, is to examine the relative closeness of the connection between the nature of the employment and the employee's wrongdoing. In this case the employee's position as warden and the close contact with the boys that this entailed created a sufficiently close connection between the acts of abuse and the work which he had been employed to carry out.[50] Applying this test, the Court of Appeal has ruled that a club owner was vicariously liable for an act of violence committed by a security guard away from the club premises.[51] The House of Lords has subsequently stated that there is no relevant distinction between performing an act in an improper manner and performing it for an improper purpose or by improper means. Thus the mere fact that employees were acting dishonestly or for their own benefit is likely to be insufficient to show that they were not acting in the course of employment.[52]

4. The employer will also owe a duty of care to employees. This was demonstrated in *Lane* v *Shire Roofing*[53] where the claimant was held to be an employee (see below) rather than a self-employed contractor. As a result of this, damages in excess of £100,000 were awarded after a work-related accident which would not have been awarded if the claimant had been carrying out work as an independent contractor.[54] In *Waters* v *Commissioner of Police of the Metropolis*[55] a police constable complained that the Commissioner of Police had acted negligently in failing to deal with her complaint of sexual assault by a colleague and the harassment and victimisation that followed. The House of Lords held that:

> If an employer knows that acts being done by employees during their employment may cause physical or mental harm to a particular fellow employee and he does nothing to supervise or

---

[48] *Canadian Pacific Railway Co* v *Lockhart* [1942] AC 591 at p. 599 PC.

[49] *Lister* v *Hesley Hall Ltd* [2001] IRLR 472 HL.

[50] See also *Balfron Trustees Ltd* v *Peterson* [2001] IRLR 758 where an employee of a firm of solicitors acted dishonestly; the crucial factor, according to the High Court, relying on *Lister*, was whether the employer owed some form of duty or responsibility towards the victim; if the answer was yes, then the employer cannot avoid liability because the duty or responsibility was delegated to an employee who failed to follow the employer's instructions.

[51] *Mattis* v *Pollock* [2003] IRLR 603. See also *Gravil* v *Redruth RFC* [2008] IRLR 829 where a rugby club was held liable for a punch thrown by a player during a match.

[52] *Dubai Aluminium* v *Salaam* [2003] IRLR 608.

[53] *Lane* v *Shire Roofing Co (Oxford) Ltd* [1995] IRLR 493 CA.

[54] See also *Makepeace* v *Evans Brothers (Reading)* [2001] ICR 241 CA where a main site contractor was held not to have a duty of care to a contractor's employee who injured himself using equipment supplied by the main site contractor; responsibility rested with the employer alone.

[55] [2000] IRLR 720 HL.

prevent such acts, when it is in his power to do so, it is clearly arguable that he may be in breach of his duty to that employee. It seems that he may also be in breach of that duty if he can foresee that such acts will happen . . .

Thus the employer owes a duty of care to employees who may be at physical or mental risk or for whom it is reasonably foreseeable that there may be some such harm (see 2.4.3 below).[56]

2.4 Identifying the employee

The common law has developed a number of tests for distinguishing those who have a contract of employment from those who are self-employed. It is important not to see these tests as mutually exclusive, but rather developments in the law as a result of the courts being faced with an increasingly complex workplace and a greater variety of work situations.

Employment protection rights of employees and workers[57]

Employment right	Employees only	All workers (including employees)
Written statement of employment particulars	✗	
Itemised pay statement	✗	
Protection against unlawful deductions from wages		✗
Guarantee payments	✗	
Time off – for public duties, to look for work or arrange training in redundancy, ante-natal care, dependants, pension trustees, employee reps, for young person to study or train, for members of EWCs		
Ordinary or additional maternity leave	✗	
Parental leave, paternity leave, adoption leave	✗	
Right to notice	✗	
Written statement of reasons for dismissal	✗	
Unfair dismissal	✗	
Right to be accompanied		✗
Right to a redundancy payment	✗	
Right to an insolvency payment	✗	
Protection by the Transfer Regulations	✗	
Protection by the Fixed-term Work Regulations	✗	
Right to be informed and consulted about collective redundancies	✗	
Right to national minimum wage		✗
Right to rest breaks, paid annual leave and maximum working time		✗
Protection by Part-time Workers Regulations		✗
Rights connected with belonging to a trade union or time off for trade union duties and activities	✗	
Right to dispute resolution procedures	✗	

Source: Department for Business Innovation & Skills © Crown Copyright 2002

[56] See *Wigan Borough Council* v *Davies* [1979] IRLR 127 on bullying and harassment by fellow employees.
[57] Adapted from a DTI table contained in its 2002 discussion paper on employment status; available on the website *www.berr.gov.uk*; the Department for Trade and Industry (DTI) was renamed the Department for Business, Innovation and Skills in 2009.

2.4.1 **The control test**

An early test developed by the courts was the control test. In *Walker* v *Crystal Palace*[58] a professional footballer was held to have a contract of service with the club. He was paid £3 10s (£3.50) per week for a year's contract, in which he was expected to provide his playing services exclusively to the club. He was under the club's direction during training and was also expected to be available for matches. The club argued that he did not have a contract of service because, it asserted, it was essential that in such a relationship the master should have the power to direct how work should be done. In *Yewens* v *Noakes* Bramwell J had defined a servant as:[59]

> a person subject to the command of his master as to the manner in which he shall do his work.

It was argued that this definition could not be applied to professional footballers who were hired to display their talents and skills. The control of the club is limited to deciding whether the player is picked for the team or not. Farewell J dismissed this plea on the basis that many workmen displayed their own initiative, like footballers, but were still bound by the directions of their master. In this case the player had agreed to follow detailed training instructions and to obey his captain's instructions on the field:

> I cannot doubt that he is bound to obey any directions which the captain, as the delegate of the club, may give him during the course of the game – that is to say, any direction that is within the terms of his employment as a football player.[60]

The problem with this test for distinguishing the employed from the self-employed is that it is limited in its application. Employers, subject to statutory and common law restraints, are able to exercise considerable control over employees. This was recognised in *Market Investigations*[61] where the issue was whether a market researcher was employed under a contract of service (see below).

This test recognises the reality of many employment relationships and the level of control may still be a factor in deciding whether a person is working under a contract of employment or a contract for services. In *Lane* v *Shire Roofing Company* the Court of Appeal acknowledged this:[62]

> First, the element of control will be important; who lays down what is to be done, the way in which it is to be done, the means by which it is to be done, and the time when it is to be done? Who provides (i.e. hires and fires) the team by which it is to be done, and who provides the material, plant and machinery and tools used?

Although the concept of control is only one of a number of factors which might influence the final decision as to whether a person is an employee or not, it can still be crucial. In *Clifford* v *UDM*[63] the Court of Appeal approved the approach of an employment tribunal in deciding that in situations that lack clarity, control may be an important factor. The control

---

[58] *Walker* v *The Crystal Palace Football Club Ltd* [1910] 1 KB 87.
[59] [1880] 6 QB 530 at p. 532.
[60] [1910] 1 KB 87 at p. 93.
[61] *Market Investigations Ltd* v *Minister of Social Security* [1968] 3 All ER 732.
[62] [1995] IRLR 493 at p. 495.
[63] *Clifford* v *Union of Democratic Mineworkers* [1991] IRLR 518 CA.

need not be exercised directly. *Motorola Ltd v Davidson*[64] concerned an individual who was engaged by an agency to work at Motorola's premises. The individual was dismissed by the agency at the request of the company. This level of control, even though exercised via a third party, was sufficient to establish an employment relationship between the company and the individual.

2.4.2 The integration test

Early reliance on the control test alone proved inadequate, especially when considering more complex employment relationships. These relationships arise when there are highly skilled individuals carrying out work which, except in the most general sense, cannot be subject to any close control by an employer. Such examples might be a ship's captain[65] or the medical staff in a hospital, as in *Cassidy v Ministry of Health*.[66]

It is not entirely clear when a person is integrated into an organisation and when they are not. It was stated in *Stevenson, Jordan & Harrison v McDonald and Evans*[67] that:

> One feature that seems to run through the instances is that, under a contract of service, a man is employed as part of the business, and his work is done as an integral part of the business; whereas, under a contract for services, his work, although done for the business, is not integrated into it but is only accessory to it.

If an individual is integrated into the organisational structure he is more likely to be an employee. The less the integration, the more likely the person is to be self-employed. In *Beloff v Pressdram Ltd*[68] Lord Widgery CJ approved Denning LJ's statement in *Stevenson, Jordan & Harrison*[69] and stated:

> The test which emerges from the authorities seems to me, as Denning LJ said, whether on the one hand the employee is employed as part of the business and his work is an integral part of the business, or whether his work is not integrated into the business but is only accessory to it, or, as Cooke J expressed it, the work is done by him in business on his own account.

It is difficult to anticipate where the dividing line may be drawn: for example, what of the dependent contractor? If a person is self-employed, but works continuously for one organisation, are they to be treated as integrated into the organisation or not? Much work is now outsourced. To what extent, for example, is the catering assistant who works for an outsourced company to be treated as an integrated part of the organisation in which he is located?

The integration test seemed to be an attempt to cope with the difficulties posed by the growth of technical and skilled work which may not be the subject of close control by an employer. Although it may be used as an indicator of a person under a contract of service, it cannot be conclusive. Indeed the problem with this test and the control test is that they do not sufficiently distinguish between the employed and the self-employed. It is arguable that it is possible for workers without a contract of employment to be closely integrated into an organisation and closely controlled by that organisation. To some extent this has been

---

[64] *Motorola Ltd v (1) Davidson; (2) Melville Craig Group Ltd* [2001] IRLR 4.
[65] See *Gold v Essex County Council* [1942] 2 KB 293.
[66] [1951] 2 KB 343 CA.
[67] [1952] 1 TLR 101, *per* Denning LJ.
[68] [1973] 1 All ER 241.
[69] [1952] 1 TLR 101.

recognised by the Court of Appeal in *Franks* v *Reuters Ltd.*[70] In this case it was held that a person who had worked for Reuters on a full-time permanent basis for more than four years on an assignment from an employment agency could be an employee of Reuters. It is consistent with general legal principles that dealings between parties over a period of years are capable of generating an implied contractual relationship (see *Dacas* v *Brook Street Bureau* below).

2.4.3 The economic reality test

This test is considered in *Market Investigations Ltd* v *Minister of Social Security*,[71] where the court considered not only the amount of control exercised over a part-time worker but also the question whether she was in business on her own account. The case concerned a market researcher who was employed to carry out specific time-limited assignments. The issue was whether she was employed under a contract of service or a contract for services. The court cited the case of *Ready Mixed Concrete*[72] in which MacKenna J stated that a contract of service existed if three conditions were fulfilled. These were:

1. whether the servant agreed that they would provide their own work and skill in return for a wage or other remuneration;

2. the individual agreed, expressly or impliedly, to be subject to the control of the master; and

3. that the other provisions of the contract were consistent with a contract of service.

It was also stated in that case that an 'obligation to do work subject to the other party's control is a necessary, though not always a sufficient, condition of a contract of service'. In *Market Investigations* the court held that further tests were needed to decide whether the contract as a whole was consistent or inconsistent with there being a contract of service. The company argued that the researcher performed a series of contracts and that a master and servant relationship was normally continuous. This view was rejected by the court which doubted

> whether this factor can be treated in isolation. It must, I think, be considered in connection with the more general question whether Mrs Irving could be said to be in business on her own account as an interviewer.

It was concluded that she was employed by the company under a series of contracts of service. She was not in business on her own account, even though she could work for other employers (although she did not). She did not provide her own tools or risk her own capital, nor did her opportunity to profit depend in any significant degree on the way she managed her work.

This test of economic reality, i.e. looking at the contract as a whole to decide whether the individual was in business on his own account, was an important development in distinguishing between those under a contract of service and others. The element of control is still important, but there is a need to take into account the other factors that make up the contract of employment. Where there is ambiguity it is relevant to know whether the parties to the contract have labelled it a contract for services or a contract of service (see below). There is, as Cooke J pointed out in *Market Investigations*, no exhaustive list of factors which can be

[70] [2003] IRLR 423.
[71] [1968] 3 All ER 732.
[72] *Ready Mixed Concrete (South East) Ltd* v *Minister of Pensions and National Insurance* [1967] 2 QB 497.

taken into account in determining the relationship. More importantly, this test recognises the fact that the parties to the contract are independent individuals. The employee is not necessarily seen as merely someone under the control of another.

Thus a person who works for a number of different employers may be seen as an employee[73] or a self-employed contractor.[74] The economic reality test builds upon the control and integration tests and will view such matters as investment in the business or the economic risk taken as important considerations.

2.4.4 The multiple factor test

This test is a further recognition that there is no one factor that can establish whether a contract of service exists. In different situations, the various factors can assume greater or lesser importance. It is really a test that *Ready Mixed Concrete*[75] and *O'Kelly*[76] tried to come to terms with. In the first case, the court identified five factors which were inconsistent with there being a contract of service. In *O'Kelly* the court identified 17 possible factors which might influence the decision. More recently, the important factors appear to be that of personal performance and mutuality of obligation (see below). MacKenna J[77] illustrated the complexity of the decision:

> An obligation to do work subject to the other party's control is a necessary, though not always a sufficient, condition of a contract of service. If the provisions of the contract as a whole are inconsistent with it being a contract of service, it will be some other kind of contract, and the person doing the work will not be a servant. The judge's task is to classify the contract . . . he may, in performing it, take into account other matters than control.

The problem with this approach, which may be insoluble without a more precise statutory definition, is that it can lead to inconsistencies of approach. It is employment tribunals that will decide what weight is to be given to specific factors in particular circumstances. It is not always clear whether such a decision is a question of fact or of law, which, in turn, affects the appeal court's opportunities to intervene in tribunal decisions to create uniformity of approach (see below).

2.4.5 Mutuality of obligation

One important factor the courts have examined in order to decide whether a contract of service exists or not is that of mutuality of obligation between employer and individual. In *O'Kelly v Trust House Forte plc*[78] a number of 'regular casual' staff made a claim for unfair dismissal. In order to make this claim they needed to show that they were working under a contract of service. The tribunal had identified a number of factors which were consistent, or not inconsistent, with the existence of a contract of employment. These included performing the work under the direction and control of the appellants and, when they attended at functions, 'they were part of the appellants' organisation and for the purpose of ensuring the smooth

---

[73] See *Lee v Chung and Shun Shing Construction & Engineering Co Ltd* [1990] IRLR 236.
[74] See *Hall (HM Inspector of Taxes) v Lorimer* [1994] IRLR 171 CA.
[75] [1967] 2 QB 497.
[76] *O'Kelly v Trust House Forte plc* [1983] IRLR 369 CA.
[77] *Ready Mixed Concrete (South East) Ltd v Minister of Pensions and National Insurance* [1967] 2 QB 497 at p. 517.
[78] [1983] IRLR 369.

running of the business they were represented in the staff consultation process'. These elements of control and integration were, however, not enough. One of the factors on which the tribunal had placed 'considerable weight' was a lack of mutuality of obligation between the two parties. The employer was under no obligation to provide work and the individuals were under no obligation to perform it.

In *Carmichael*,[79] the House of Lords approved the conclusion of an employment tribunal, which had held that the applicant's case 'founders on the rock of the absence of mutuality'. The case was about whether two tour guides were employees under contracts of employment and therefore entitled under s. 1 ERA 1996 to a written statement of particulars of the terms of their employment. The House of Lords accepted that they worked on a casual 'as and when required' basis. An important issue was that there was no requirement for the employer to provide work and for the individual to carry out that work. Indeed, the court heard that there were a number of occasions when the applicants had declined offers of work. Thus there was an 'irreducible minimum of mutual obligation' that was necessary to create a contract of service. There needed to be an obligation to provide work and an obligation to perform it in return for a wage or some form of remuneration. Part-time home workers, for example, who had been provided with work and had performed it over a number of years could be held to have created this mutual obligation.[80] The obligation upon the employer is to provide work when it is available, not to provide work consistently. Thus a person who worked as a relief manager and had a contract which stated that there would be times when no work was available and he would not be paid on these occasions was still entitled to be treated as having a contract of employment. There was an obligation upon the employer to provide work when it was available.[81]

When this mutual obligation is absent in either party, then a contract of service, in some extreme cases, will not exist. In *Express and Echo Publications Ltd* v *Tanton*[82] the Court of Appeal stated that the test was a contractual one. It was necessary to look at the obligations provided, rather than what actually occurred. In this case an individual's contract enabled them to arrange, at their own expense, for their duties to be performed by another person when they were unable or unwilling to carry out their work. Such a term was incompatible with a contract of service, as it meant that the individual lacked the obligation to work themselves in return for the remuneration. The obligation to work personally for another is, according to the EAT in *Cotswold Developments*,[83] at the heart of the relationship. This approach was somewhat qualified in *Byrne Brothers (Formwork) Ltd* v *Baird*[84] which involved labour-only subcontractors in the construction industry, with a contract that allowed the worker to provide a substitute in limited and exceptional circumstances. This right was not inconsistent with an obligation of personal service. The same approach was applied to gymnasts working for a local authority who were able to provide substitutes for any shift that they were unable to

[79] *Carmichael* v *National Power plc* [2000] IRLR 43 HL.

[80] *Nethermere (St Neots) Ltd* v *Gardiner* [1984] ICR 612 CA; see also *Clark* v *Oxfordshire Health Authority* [1998] IRLR 125 CA where the position of a nurse in the staff bank was considered and it was held that there was an absence of mutuality of obligation.

[81] *Wilson* v *Circular Distributors Ltd* [2006] IRLR 38.

[82] [1999] IRLR 367 CA. See also *Stevedoring and Haulage Services Ltd* v *Fuller* [2001] IRLR 627 where the documentation expressly provided that the individuals were being engaged on an *ad hoc* and casual basis with no obligation on the company to offer work and no obligation on the applicants to accept it.

[83] *Cotswold Developments Construction Ltd* v *Williams* [2006] IRLR 181.

[84] [2002] IRLR 96.

work.[85] The local authority paid the substitutes directly and the gymnasts could only be replaced by others on the Council's approved list.[86]

Subsequently the Court of Appeal stressed that both 'mutuality of obligation' and 'control' are the irreducible minimum legal requirements for the existence of a contract of employment. *Montgomery* v *Johnson Underwood Ltd*[87] concerned a temporary agency worker who, despite being on a long-term temporary assignment of over two years, wished to show that she was employed by the agency which had placed her. She failed because the court held that there was little or no control or supervision of her by the agency, so that one of the essential prerequisites was missing.

On the other hand, in *Consistent Group Ltd* v *Kalwak*[88] the EAT found that there was sufficient mutuality of obligation between the worker and the agency to establish that the workers concerned were employees of the agency. Consistent Group Ltd provided staff from Poland to work in hotels and food processing. The recruits were given contracts headed 'Self-employed sub-contractor's contract for services'. It contained clauses which stated that the sub-contractor was not an employee of the agency and was not entitled to sick pay, holiday pay or pension rights. The sub-contractor was able to work for others provided that the agency did not believe that it would interfere with any work provided by the agency; the sub-contractor agreed to provide services personally and, if he could not, had to inform Consistent and find an approved replacement. The EAT warned that tribunals must be alive to the fact that armies of lawyers will simply place substitution clauses, or clauses denying any obligation to accept or provide work in employment contracts, as a matter of form, even where such terms do not begin to reflect the real relationship.

The reality was that these workers had come from Poland expecting to work for the agency and their accommodation depended upon doing such work. There was no realistic chance of them working elsewhere whilst the agency required their services. Although they were able to provide substitutes rather than do the work personally, this only arose if they were unable to work, not if they did not wish to accept the work.[89] The contract, therefore, bore no relationship to the reality and there was sufficient mutuality of obligation to establish that an employment relationship existed.

Subsequently the Court of Appeal has ruled that a sham may be found where the parties to a contract have a common intention that the document or one of its provisions is not intended to create the legal rights which they set out whether or not there is a joint intention to deceive third parties or the court.[90] It has also stated that tribunals have to consider whether the words of a written contract represent the true intentions or expectations of the parties not only at the inception of the contract but, if appropriate, as time passes.[91]

---

[85] *MacFarlane* v *Glasgow City Council* [2001] IRLR 7.

[86] See *Ready Mixed Concrete*, note 77 above, where the High Court had held that occasional and limited delegation was not inconsistent with a contract of service.

[87] [2001] IRLR 269 CA.

[88] [2007] IRLR 560. Subsequently, this case was remitted to the employment tribunal by the Court of Appeal: [2008] IRLR 505.

[89] This distinction between someone who was unable to work, as opposed to someone who was unwilling to work, was also considered in *James* v *Redcats (Brands) Ltd* [2007] IRLR 296; if the requirement is to provide a substitute when the individual was unable to work, this does not appear to suggest that there is no obligation to perform the work personally.

[90] *Autoclenz Ltd* v *Belcher* [2010] IRLR 70.

[91] *Protectacoat Ltd* v *Szilagyi* [2009] IRLR 365.

2.5 Question of fact or law

Appeals from an employment tribunal may be based either on a question of law, or against a decision that was so unreasonable as to be perverse. This means:

> that the primary facts as found by the fact-finding tribunal must stand, but also that the inferences of fact drawn by the tribunal from the primary facts can only be interfered with by an appellate court if they are insupportable on the basis of the primary facts so found.[92]

The reluctance of the appeal courts to interfere unless there is a point of law or a perverse decision may lead to inconsistencies between different employment tribunals. In a sense it seems rather odd that the EAT, which is composed of one lawyer and two experienced lay people, should be confined to appeals on the question of law. The problem of inconsistencies between the approaches of different employment tribunals was highlighted in *O'Kelly*[93] where the Court of Appeal stated:

> Without the Employment Appeal Tribunal being entitled to intervene where in its view the employment tribunal has wrongly evaluated the weight of a relevant consideration then it will be open to employment tribunals to reach differing conclusions, so long as they are reasonably maintainable, on essentially the same facts.

In such cases, the court concluded, it is only where the weight given to a particular factor shows a misdirection in law that an appellate court can interfere.

It is not always clear whether an issue is a question of law or a question of fact. In *Carmichael*,[94] for example, the Court of Appeal had held that the employment tribunal should have decided as a matter of law that an exchange of letters constituted an offer and acceptance which gave rise to a contract of employment in writing. The House of Lords disagreed[95] and stated that the employment tribunal was entitled to find, as a fact, that the parties did not intend the letters to be the sole record of their agreement. The oral exchanges could also be taken into account. This difference in interpretation allowed the Court of Appeal to reverse the decision of the employment tribunal and the House of Lords to restore it.

In *Lee* v *Chung*[96] the Privy Council had suggested that the decision whether a person was employed under a contract of service or not was often a mixed question of fact and law. It distinguished between those cases where the issue is dependent on the true construction of a written document[97] and those where the issue is dependent upon an investigation of factual circumstances in which the work is performed. This latter situation makes the decision a question of fact in which the appeal courts should not interfere.

This seems to be the approach adopted by the House of Lords in *Carmichael*, except that in this case one of the differences with the Court of Appeal rested on whether reliance should be placed on a construction of the written documents (a question of law) or on the factual circumstances surrounding the agreement (a question of fact). One can appreciate that there might be a public policy issue related to allowing appeals on any issue other than a legal one,

---

[92] *Nethermere (St Neots) Ltd* v *Gardiner* [1984] ICR 612 at p. 631, *per* Dillon LJ.
[93] [1983] IRLR 369.
[94] [1998] IRLR 301 CA.
[95] [2000] IRLR 43 HL.
[96] [1990] IRLR 236.
[97] See *Davies* v *Presbyterian Church of Wales* [1986] IRLR 194 HL.

which might result in increased numbers of appeals. It is difficult, however, to escape th
clusion that the issue is flexible and that, if an appeal court feels strongly enough, it wi
ways of reviewing an employment tribunal's conclusions.

2.6 The intentions of the parties

What is the effect of the parties to the contract deciding that, for whatever reason, it should
be for services, rather than of service? This clearly happens in different occupations, where
there is an acceptance that individuals are to be treated as self-employed contractors, rather
than employees. One study of the construction industry concluded that some 58 per cent of
the workforce, excluding local government, was treated as self-employed. This was some
45 per cent of the total workforce. The author concluded that there 'is the strongest indication that self-employment, as an employment status, is an economic fiction'.[98] In *Ferguson* v
Dawson & Partners[99] the claimant worked on a building site as a self-employed contractor. He
had no express contract of any kind, although the court accepted that implied terms existed.
Although the label of self-employment, as agreed by the parties, was a factor to be considered,
it could not be decisive if the evidence pointed towards a contract of employment.[100]

In the financial services sector, salespeople are traditionally treated as self-employed, yet
they have targets to meet and meetings to attend and cannot sell policies from businesses that
compete with their employing company. In this industry, as in others, the parties have come
to an arrangement based upon a particular employment relationship. In *Massey* v *Crown Life
Assurance*[101] a branch manager with an insurance company changed his employment status
from employee to self-employed, although he continued in the same job. Two years later, the
company terminated the agreement and he brought a complaint of unfair dismissal. He
could only make this claim if he was an employee. Lord Denning MR summed up the Court
of Appeal's approach:

> If the true relationship of the parties is that of master and servant under a contract of service,
> the parties cannot alter the truth of that relationship by putting a different label on it . . . On the
> other hand, if the parties' relationship is ambiguous and is capable of being one or the other,
> then the parties can remove that ambiguity, by the very agreement itself which they make with
> one another.[102]

Thus, the parties' views as to their relationship can be important if there is any ambiguity.
The House of Lords has held[103] that the intentions of the parties can be relevant, rather
than a more limited concentration on the written documentation, where this is not decisive,
although the meaning of documents should be that which would be conveyed to a reasonable person.[104]

---

[98] Mark Harvey, *Towards the Insecurity Society: The Tax Trap of Self-employment*, Institute of Employment Rights
(1995) October.
[99] [1976] 1 WLR 1213 CA.
[100] See also *Young & Woods Ltd* v *West* [1980] IRLR 201 CA and *Lane* v *Shire Roofing Company (Oxford) Ltd* [1995]
IRLR 493 CA where the courts relied upon the test in *Market Investigations Ltd*, note 61 above, to decide that
the applicants in both cases were employees, even though treated as self-employed for tax purposes.
[101] [1978] 1 WLR 676 CA.
[102] *Ibid.* at p. 679.
[103] *Carmichael* v *National Power plc* [2000] IRLR 43 HL.
[104] See *Investors Compensation Scheme Ltd* v *Hopkin & Sons* [1998] IRLR 896 HL.

2.7 Continuity of employment

Continuity of employment is important because a number of statutory rights, such as the right to claim unfair dismissal and the right to receive written reasons for dismissal, depend upon having continuous employment with an employer. Other rights, such as the right to take parental leave and the right to additional maternity leave, also depend upon the employee having one year's continuous employment with an employer.[105] The employment concerned must relate to employment with one employer,[106] although this can include associated employers. The test for control amongst such employers is normally decided by looking at who has the voting control, but there might be, in exceptional circumstances, a need to look at who has de facto control.[107]

2.7.1 Continuity and sex discrimination

The question of whether such a rule can amount to indirect sex discrimination or whether it can be objectively justified was considered in *R v Secretary of State for Employment, ex parte Seymour-Smith and Perez (No 2)*.[108] This case was brought when the qualifying period was two years and the complainants were individuals who were prevented from bringing a complaint of unfair dismissal because they did not have the necessary two years' continuous service. They claimed that the proportion of women who could comply with the two-year qualifying period was considerably smaller than the proportion of men. The House of Lords referred a number of questions to the ECJ.[109] The ECJ replied[110] that the entitlement to compensation and redress for unfair dismissal came within the scope of art. 119 EEC (now 157) and the Equal Treatment Directive,[111] but that the national court must verify whether the statistics showed that the measure in question has had a disparate impact between men and women. It is then up to the Member State to show that the rule was unrelated to any discrimination based upon sex and reflected a legitimate aim of its social policy. This case began with the dismissal of the applicants in 1991 and finally returned to the House of Lords for a decision in 2000. The court accepted that the qualification period did have a disparately adverse effect on women. In the period between 1985 and 1991 the number of men and women who qualified for protection was in the ratio of 10:9. The court held that objective justification had to be determined as at 1985, when the amendment was introduced, and at 1991, when the individuals made their complaint. The court held that the onus was on the Member State to show:

1. that the alleged discriminatory rule reflected a legitimate aim of its social policy;

2. that this aim was unrelated to any discrimination based on sex; and

3. that the Member State could reasonably have considered that the means chosen were suitable for attaining that aim.

---

[105] Maternity and Parental Leave etc. Regulations 1999, SI 1999/3312.
[106] Section 218(1) ERA 1996.
[107] *Payne v Secretary of State for Employment* [1989] IRLR 352.
[108] [2000] IRLR 263 HL.
[109] [1997] IRLR 315 HL.
[110] [1999] IRLR 253 ECJ.
[111] Directive 76/207/EEC; see Chapter 5.

The Government argued that the extension of the qualifying period should help reduce the reluctance of employers to take on more people. The court was sympathetic to the Government's case and accepted objective justification:

> The burden placed on the government in this type of case is not as heavy as previously thought. Governments must be able to govern. They adopt general policies, and implement measures to carry out their policies. Governments must be able to take into account a wide range of social, economic and political factors . . . National courts, acting with hindsight, are not to impose an impracticable burden on governments which are proceeding in good faith.

It was ironic that the judgment was arrived at after a new Government had reduced the qualifying period to one year.

2.7.2 **Continuity and the start date**

An employee's period of continuous employment begins on the day on which the employee starts work, although any period before an individual's 18th birthday does not count for the purposes of redundancy payments.[112] In *The General of the Salvation Army* v *Dewsbury*[113] a part-time teacher took on a new full-time contract which stated that her employment began on 1 May. As 1 May was a Saturday and the following Monday was a Bank Holiday, she did not actually commence her duties until the Tuesday, 4 May. She was subsequently dismissed with effect from 1 May in the following year. The issue was whether she had one year's continuous employment. The EAT held that the day on which an employee starts work is intended to refer to the beginning of the person's employment under the relevant contract of employment and that this may be different from the actual date on which work commences.

There is a presumption that an individual's period of employment is continuous, unless otherwise shown.[114] Thus the onus is on those who wish to argue the point to show that there was not continuous service within the Act's definition. It is likely, however, that the presumption of continuity only applies to employment with one employer, unless the tribunal accepts that a transfer of the business and, therefore, the contract of employment, has taken place.[115]

Section 212(1) ERA 1996 states that:

> Any week during the whole or part of which an employee's relations with his employer are governed by a contract of employment counts in computing the employee's period of employment.

A week is defined in s. 235(1) ERA 1996 as a week ending with Saturday or, for a weekly paid employee, a week ends with the day used in calculating the week's remuneration. Thus if a contract of employment exists in any one week, using this formula, that week counts for continuity purposes. In *Sweeney* v *J & S Henderson*[116] an employee resigned from his employment on a Saturday and left immediately to take up another post. The individual regretted the decision and returned to work for the original employer the following Friday. The employee was held to have continuity of employment as a result of there not being a

---

[112] Section 211(1) and (2) ERA 1996.
[113] [1984] IRLR 222.
[114] Section 210(5) ERA 1996.
[115] See *Secretary of State for Employment* v *Cohen and Beaupress Ltd* [1987] IRLR 169.
[116] [1999] IRLR 306.

week in which the contract of employment did not apply. This was despite the fact that the employee worked for another employer during the intervening period.[117] The employee worked under a contract of employment with the employer during each of the two weeks in question and thus fulfilled the requirements of s. 212(1) ERA 1996.

If there is a period in the employment where the contract is tainted by illegality, continuity may not be preserved. In *Hyland* v *JH Barker (North West) Ltd*[118] an employee was paid a tax-free lodging allowance even though the employee did not stay away from home. The period of four weeks in which this happened did not count towards continuity of employment. Unfortunately for the employee, as this period fell within the 12-month period prior to dismissal, he was held not to have the necessary continuity of service to make a complaint of unfair dismissal. The EAT stated that 'continuously employed' meant 'continuously employed under a legal contract of employment'.

2.7.3 Continuity and absences from work

Absence from work means not performing in substance the contract that previously existed between the parties. Such a definition applied to a coach driver whose work was greatly reduced by the miners' strike in 1984. A substantial part of the individual's work was removed, but the employee was able to claim a temporary cessation of work (see below).[119]

There are a number of reasons for which a person can be absent from work without breaking their statutory continuity of employment. These are:

1. If the employee is incapable of work as a result of sickness or injury.[120] Absences of no more than 26 weeks under this category will not break continuity.[121] There needs to be a causal relationship between the absence and the incapacity for work in consequence of sickness or injury. The absence from work also needs to be related to the work on offer. If an injured employee was offered different work from that which he normally did but it was nevertheless suitable, the tribunal would have to decide whether the employee was absent from that newly offered work as a result of the sickness or injury.[122]

2. If there is a temporary cessation of work. According to s. 212(3)(b) ERA 1996, absence on account of a temporary cessation[123] of work will not break continuity of employment. The word 'temporary' indicates a period of time that is of relatively short duration compared to the periods of work. However, the decision as to whether the cessation is temporary

---

[117] In *Carrington* v *Harwich Dock Co Ltd* [1998] IRLR 567 an employee resigned on a Friday and was re-employed on the following Monday. Despite a letter from the employer stating that, by resigning voluntarily, the employee's continuity of service was broken, the EAT held that there was continuity.

[118] [1985] IRLR 403.

[119] *GW Stephens & Son* v *Fish* [1989] ICR 324; the miners' strike lasted for about one year; the employee in this case had the normal duty of driving miners to work each day.

[120] Section 212(3)(a) ERA 1996.

[121] Section 212(4) ERA 1996; see also *Donnelly* v *Kelvin International Services* [1992] IRLR 496, where an employee who resigned on the grounds of ill health, but was then re-employed some five weeks later, was held to have continuity even though they had worked for another employer during the period.

[122] See *Pearson* v *Kent County Council* [1993] IRLR 165.

[123] Cessation of work means that work has temporarily ceased to exist; it does not mean that the work has been temporarily or otherwise re-allocated to another employee. See *Byrne* v *City of Birmingham* [1987] IRLR 191 CA where the employer created a pool of casual employees to share the work; the absence then was not because of a cessation of work but because the employee was not offered any.

is not a mathematical one only to be achieved by comparing an individual's length of employment with the length of unemployment in a defined period.[124] Although it is possible to look back over the whole period of an individual's employment in order to come to a judgment, 'temporary' is likely to mean a short time in comparison with the period in work. Thus seasonal workers who were out of work each year for longer than they actually worked did not have continuity of employment.[125] Other seasonal workers who were regularly out of work for long periods were in the same position, even though, at the beginning of the next season, it was the intention of both parties that they should resume employment.[126] In contrast, an academic who was employed on regular fixed-term contracts to teach was held to have continuity, even though the individual was not employed during August and September each year. During this time the employee prepared for the coming year's teaching and the EAT decided that this amounted to a temporary cessation of work.[127]

3. Absence from work in circumstances that, by custom or arrangement, the employee 'is regarded as continuing in the employment of his employer for any purposes'.[128] In *Curr* v *Marks and Spencer plc*[129] the Court of Appeal ruled that a four-year absence under a child break scheme broke continuity because the ex-employee was not regarded by both parties as continuing in the employment of the employer for any purpose. Similarly, in *Booth* v *United States of America*[130] the employees were employed on a series of fixed-term contracts with a gap of about two weeks between each contract. On each return to work they were given the same employee number, the same tools and equipment and the same lockers. Despite the employees arguing that this arrangement was designed to defeat the underlying purpose of the legislation, the EAT could not find an arrangement. This would have required, in advance of the break, some discussion and agreement that continuity could be preserved. It was clear that the employers did not want such an arrangement. Neither is it likely that an agreement made subsequent to the absence could be used to preserve continuity. Section 212(3)(c) ERA 1996 envisages the arrangement being in place when the employee is absent. Thus an agreement between an employer and an employee that a break in work would not affect continuity was ineffective because it was made after the employee's return.[131]

2.7.4 Continuity and industrial disputes

A week does not count for the purposes of computing continuity of service if during that week, or any part of it, the employee takes part in a strike.[132] In contrast, periods when the

---

[124] See *Ford* v *Warwickshire County Council* [1983] IRLR 126 HL.
[125] *Berwick Salmon Fisheries Co Ltd* v *Rutherford* [1991] IRLR 203; see also *Flack* v *Kodak Ltd* [1986] IRLR 255 CA, where a group of seasonal employees in a photo finishing department tried to establish continuity of employment.
[126] *Sillars* v *Charrington Fuels Ltd* [1989] IRLR 152 CA.
[127] *University of Aston in Birmingham* v *Malik* [1984] ICR 492; see also *Ford* v *Warwickshire County Council* [1983] IRLR 126 HL.
[128] Section 212(3)(c) ERA 1996.
[129] [2003] IRLR 74.
[130] [1999] IRLR 16.
[131] *Morris* v *Walsh Western UK Ltd* [1997] IRLR 562; see now *London Probation Board* v *Kirkpatrick* [2005] IRLR 443.
[132] Section 216(1) ERA 1996.

employee is subject to a lock-out do count for continuity purposes. However, in neither case is continuity itself broken.[133] *Bloomfield* v *Springfield Hosiery Finishing Co Ltd*[134] concerned a dispute which resulted in a strike by employees. They were summarily dismissed and the employer began to recruit replacement staff. As a result the strike ended and the employees returned to work. Subsequently the employees were dismissed for redundancy. Their claims for redundancy payments were rejected because, it was said, they did not have sufficient continuity of employment, as a result of being dismissed during the strike. The court held, however, that the term 'employee' should be given a wide meaning and that the strikers continued to be employees during the strike or until the employer engaged other persons or permanently discontinued the work that they were employed to do.

2.7.5 Continuity and change of employer

Although the continuity provisions normally apply to employment by one employer,[135] there are occasions where a transfer from one employer to another can preserve continuity of employment.[136] One such situation is when there is a relevant transfer under the Transfer of Undertakings (Protection of Employment) Regulations 2006[137] (see Chapter 9). These Regulations treat the original contract of employment as if it was agreed with the new employer. Thus an employee's period of service will transfer to the new employer.

Where the trade, business[138] or undertaking is transferred to a new employer, continuity is also preserved by s. 218(2) ERA 1996. The employee's length of service is deemed to be with the new employer, although, as pointed out in *Nokes* v *Doncaster Collieries*,[139] this is likely to require the knowledge and consent of the employee. There have been difficulties in identifying when a business has transferred rather than a disposal of assets taking place. In *Melon* v *Hector Powe Ltd*,[140] the employer disposed of one of two factories to another company. The disposal included the transfer of the work in progress and all the employees in the factory. The court held that there was a distinction between a transfer of a going concern, which amounted to a transfer of a business which remains the same business, but in different hands, and the disposal of part of the assets of a business.[141] It is employees in the former situation who are able to rely on s. 218 ERA 1996. There are a number of other specific situations where continuity is preserved:[142]

1. If a contract of employment between a corporate body and an employee is modified by an Act of Parliament so that a new body is substituted as the employer.

2. On the death of an employer, an employee is taken into employment by the personal representatives or trustees of the deceased.

---

[133] Section 216(2) ERA 1996.
[134] [1972] ICR 91.
[135] Section 218(1) ERA 1996.
[136] See s. 218(2)–(10) ERA 1996.
[137] SI 2006/246.
[138] Business is defined in s. 235 ERA 1996 as including a trade or profession and includes any activity carried on by a body of persons (whether corporate or unincorporated).
[139] [1940] AC 1014 HL.
[140] [1980] IRLR 477 HL.
[141] The court cited a speech to this effect by Lord Denning in *Lloyd* v *Brassey* [1969] ITR 199.
[142] Section 218(3)–(10) ERA 1996.

3. If there is a change in the partners, personal representatives or trustees that employ a person.[143]

4. If the employee is taken into the employment of another employer who is an associated employer of the current employer.[144]

5. If an employee of the governors of a school maintained by a local education authority is taken into the employment of the authority, or vice versa.

6. If a person in relevant[145] employment with a health service employer is taken into such relevant employment by another such employer.

Section 219 ERA 1996 provides that the Secretary of State may make provisions for preserving continuity of employment. The current regulations are the Employment Protection (Continuity of Employment) Regulations 1996,[146] which serve to protect continuity of employment where an employee is making a complaint about dismissal or making a claim in accordance with a dismissal procedures agreement.[147] Continuity is also protected as a result of any action taken by a conciliation officer or the making of a compromise agreement in relation to a dismissal (see Chapter 4).

2.8 Specific types of employment relationship

2.8.1 Agency staff

The employment agency industry is an important part of the United Kingdom economy. It grew from an industry that merely supplied domestic staff to the current-day one that supplies individuals with a wide range of skills. In November 2009 it was estimated that there were about 1.3 million agency workers in the UK labour market.[148]

2.8.1.1 The Agency Workers Regulations 2010

The Agency Worker Regulations 2010 are designed to implement Directive 2008/104/EC and are due to come into force in October 2011. They introduce the principle of equal treatment for agency workers after they have been in an assignment with the same hirer for a qualifying period of twelve weeks. Regulations 3 and 4 respectively provide definitions of 'agency worker' and 'temporary work agency'. Regulation 5 gives agency workers the right to the same basic working and employment conditions as he or she would have been entitled to if they had been engaged directly by the hirer. Regulation 6 makes it clear that it is terms and conditions relating to pay, the duration of working time, night work, rest periods, rest breaks and annual leave that are relevant. Regulations 7–9 deal with the completion of the qualifying period and the structuring of assignments as a method of avoiding the impact of this

---

[143] See *Stevens v Bower* [2004] IRLR 957.

[144] See *Hancill v Marcon Engineering Ltd* [1990] IRLR 51; a transfer from an American company to one in the UK, where both were controlled by a Dutch company, was enough to ensure that the employee had transferred to an associate employer.

[145] 'Relevant' means those undergoing professional training who need to move employers for that training; s. 218(9) ERA 1996; s. 218(10) defines health service employers.

[146] SI 1996/3147.

[147] See s. 210 ERA 1996.

[148] See *www.number10.gov.uk/Page21359*.

measure. Finally, Regulations 12–13 provide agency workers with rights in relation to access to employment and to collective facilities and amenities provided by the hirer.

2.8.1.2 Agency/worker relationship

One of the questions for the courts has been to identify the employer of the staff concerned. Although the particular facts of each case will be important, the possible options are:

1. The individual is working under a contract for services.
2. There is a global contract of employment between the individual and the agency, covering all the assignments on which a temporary worker may be sent.
3. There is a contract of employment for each individual assignment.

In *McMeechan* v *Secretary of State for Employment*[149] a temporary worker completed a series of individual assignments through an employment agency. He was given a job sheet and a standard written statement of terms and conditions for each assignment. The statement specified that he was providing services as a self-employed worker and was not operating under a contract of service, although the agency did deduct tax and national insurance contributions. When the agency became insolvent, the individual made a claim to the Secretary of State for wages owed. The claim was refused because, it was argued, the individual was not an employee of the insolvent company. The Court of Appeal examined two aspects of the relationship between the agency and the individual. The first was the general relationship covering the whole period during which the individual was used by the agency and the second was the relationship during any specific engagement on which the agency had used the individual. The court considered[150] *Wickens* v *Champion Employment*[151] which looked at the general relationship and involved an attempt to show that all temporary staff of an agency were working under contracts of employment. This failed because:

> the relationship between the employers and the temporaries seems to us wholly to lack the elements of continuity, and care of the employer for the employee, that one associates with a contract of service.

The question for the court on the individual assignment was whether this could amount to a contract of service or not. The arguments for there being a contract for services were that there was an express statement that the individual was self-employed and there was freedom to work for a particular client on a self-employed basis. On the side of there being a contract of service were the power reserved by the agency to dismiss for misconduct, the power to bring any assignment to an end, the establishment of a grievance procedure and the stipulation of an hourly rate of pay, which in turn was subject to deductions for unsatisfactory timekeeping, work, attitude or misconduct. The court concluded that:

> when those indications are set against each other, and the specific engagement is looked at as a whole in all its terms, the general impression which emerges is that the engagement involved in this single assignment gave rise, despite the label put on it by the parties, to a contract of service between the temporary worker and the contractor.

---

[149] [1997] IRLR 353.
[150] The court contrasted the judgments in *McLeod* v *Hellyer Brothers Ltd* [1987] IRLR 232, which concerned Hull trawlermen who worked on periodic agreements, and *Nethermere (St Neots) Ltd* v *Gardiner* [1984] ICR 612, which concerned home workers with no fixed hours who were paid by results.
[151] [1984] ICR 365.

In *Dacas v Brook Street Bureau*[152] it was stated that formal written contracts between a woman and an agency and between that agency and the end user relating to the work to be done for the end user did not necessarily preclude the implication of a contract of employment between the woman and the end user. As a matter of law, when an issue is raised about the status of an applicant in unfair dismissal proceedings, an employment tribunal is required to consider whether there is an implied contract between the parties who have no express contract with one another. This view was supported by the Court of Appeal in *Cable & Wireless plc v Muscat*.[153] The court stated that in cases involving a triangular relationship consisting of a worker, an employment agency and an end user, the tribunal should consider the possibility of an implied contract between the worker and the end user. In this case such a contract was held to exist as the individual had been employed and then, at the employer's request, become a contractor via an employment agency. The court held that the end user was under an obligation to provide work and the worker was under an obligation to attend their premises and do the work, subject to their control and supervision. In *James v London Borough of Greenwich*[154] the Court of Appeal stated that the real issue in agency worker cases is whether a contract should be implied between a worker and the end user rather than whether an irreducible minimum of mutual obligations exist. The mutuality point is important in deciding whether a contract is a contract of employment or some other kind of contract. However, in agency cases the issue is whether a third contract exists at all between the worker and the end user.

2.8.1.3 Employment agencies and businesses

The private employment industry has been regulated since 1973 when the Employment Agencies Act 1973 came into force. This contained a system for licensing and regular inspections by the (then) Department of Employment. The implementation of this Act was changed by the Conduct of Employment Agencies and Employment Businesses Regulations 2003,[155] and ss. 15–16 of the Employment Act 2008.

The 1973 Act and the 2003 Regulations distinguish between employment businesses and employment agencies. Employment businesses are those that are concerned with the supply of temporary staff, whilst employment agencies are those that are concerned with the supply of work seekers to fill permanent vacancies with clients.[156] Many organisations are both employment businesses and employment agencies.

The main provisions of the Act and the Regulations are:

1. Neither an employment agency nor employment business may charge fees to work seekers for finding them work, or seeking to find them work. Neither an agency nor an employment business may make help to a work seeker conditional upon using other services which require a fee. There is a limitation on the terms in contracts between employment businesses and hirers preventing temporary workers from taking up permanent jobs unless a fee is first paid to the employment business.

2. An employment business may not introduce a work seeker to a hirer to perform the normal tasks carried out by a worker who is taking part in an industrial dispute or other

---

[152] [2004] IRLR 358.
[153] [2006] IRLR 355.
[154] [2008] IRLR 302.
[155] SI 2003/3319.
[156] See s. 13(1)–(3) Employment Agencies Act 1973.

industrial action, unless it is an unofficial strike or industrial action, i.e. one that does not take place within the rules governing such actions contained in the Trade Union and Labour Relations (Consolidation) Act 1992.

3. Employment businesses are not able to withhold pay owed to a temporary worker just because the worker has not obtained a signed worksheet from the hirer.

4. When an agency or business first offers to provide services to a work seeker, then the agency or business must provide the work seeker with details of their terms of business and fees (if any). The agency or business will obtain the agreement of the work seeker about fees (if any) and the type of work the agency or business will try to find for the work seeker.

5. Employment businesses must agree whether the work seeker is, or will be, employed under a contract of service or a contract for services (see above). The work seeker will also be given an undertaking that the business will pay him for the work that he does, regardless of whether the business is paid by the hirer. Other terms of business will include the rate of remuneration paid to the work seeker and the minimum rate of remuneration to be paid to the employment business, details of any entitlements to holidays and to payment in respect of holidays.

6. Similar requirements are imposed upon employment agencies to explain to work seekers what services will be provided and details of any fees to be paid to the agency for work-finding services, although fees may only be charged to work seekers wanting work in such areas as sport, music, dance and theatre.

7. Agencies and businesses are required to keep documentation showing the work seeker's agreement to the terms of business and any changes to them. Neither an agency nor a hirer may introduce or supply a work seeker unless the agency or business has sufficient information about the hirer, the dates on which the work seeker is required and the duration of the work, the position to be filled and the experience, training and qualifications necessary to work in the position, including the rate of remuneration to be paid to the work seeker. There are similar conditions in relation to obtaining information about a work seeker before that person can be introduced to a hirer. Agencies and employment businesses must obtain references on job seekers wishing to work with vulnerable persons.

8. Every advertisement must carry the full name of the agency or business and state the nature of the work, its location and the minimum qualifications necessary when advertising rates of pay.

9. Employment agencies must not introduce an employer to a young person under the age of 18 years if that person is attending school or has just left school, unless that person has received vocational guidance from their local careers service.

10. There are strict rules on record keeping.

Anyone who contravenes the prohibition on charging fees to work seekers, fails to comply with regulations to secure the proper conduct of the agency or business, falsifies records or fails, without reasonable excuse, to comply with a prohibition order, will be guilty of an offence and subject to a fine not exceeding the statutory maximum (£5,000 in 2009). Section 16 EA 2008 has strengthened the powers of inspectors, and anyone obstructing an officer from carrying out enforcement functions can be fined.

An employment tribunal may make an order prohibiting a person (or company) from carrying on, or being concerned with, an employment agency or business for up to ten years on the grounds of the person being unsuitable because of misconduct or any other sufficient reason. In addition, terms of contracts with hirers or work seekers which are invalid in terms of the Act or Regulations will be unenforceable. Any contravention of the Act or Regulations which causes damage, including death or injury, will be actionable in civil law.

2.8.1.4 Gangmasters

Gangmaster is the word used to refer to individuals or groups of individuals who hire out 'gangs' of workers for the completion of certain tasks, most commonly in the agricultural and parts of the fisheries sector. Their activities have fallen outside the regulatory controls covering employment agencies and businesses. It appears that the individuals making up these gangs are often immigrants, sometimes illegal, who work long hours for low pay and are generally exploited. The worst incident in recent times was the drowning of 21 Chinese cockle pickers in Morecambe Bay in 2004. It has been estimated that there are up to 60,000 such workers living on very low pay in the United Kingdom.

In response to these issues the Government adopted the Gangmasters (Licensing) Act 2004. This Act makes provision for the licensing of activities concerning the supply of workers involved in:

- agricultural work;
- gathering shellfish;
- processing or packaging agricultural produce or shellfish or fish products.

The 2004 Act established the Gangmasters Licensing Authority which issues licences to gangmasters and keeps under review the activities of persons acting as gangmasters. A person or organisation may not be a gangmaster without a licence issued by the Authority and a register of licences is accessible to members of the public.

Persons who act as gangmasters without a licence or with false documents are guilty of an offence and can be fined plus imprisoned for up to 12 months. Similarly a person may not knowingly use an unlicensed gangmaster. Such a person will also be liable to a fine and imprisonment for a period up to 51 weeks. The 2004 Act also allows the Government minister to appoint enforcement officers who will ensure that only licensed gangmasters are operating. These officers have wide powers to inspect records and obtain information. Obstruction of such officers is a criminal offence, allowing fines and imprisonment of the obstructors.

2.8.2 Fixed-term contracts

According to the EU Labour Force Survey, during the period 2000–2005, the relative number of men and women employed in fixed-term jobs in the EU increased. Although the proportion of men and women employed on fixed-term contracts varies markedly across the Member States, in 2005, 14 per cent of male and 15 per cent of female employees were engaged in such jobs and a significant proportion of these had fixed-term employment because they could not get permanent work. It is also worth noting that almost a third of male and female employees aged under 30 were engaged on fixed-term contacts.[157]

---

[157] See *http://epp.eurostat.ec.europa.eu/*.

On 18 March 1999 the Social Partners at European Community level concluded a Framework Agreement on fixed-term work which became Directive 99/70/EC.[158] This Directive came after a lengthy period of the European Commission attempting to obtain agreement amongst the Member States. Proposals were first introduced in 1990 and, until 1999, only one measure had been adopted.[159]

The purposes of the Framework Agreement are to:

(a) improve the quality of fixed-term work by ensuring the application of the principle of non-discrimination;

(b) establish a framework to prevent abuse arising from the use of successive fixed-term employment contracts or relationships.[160]

A fixed-term worker is defined by clause 3 of the Agreement as:

A person having an employment contract or relationship entered into directly between an employer and a worker where the end of the employment contract or relationship is determined by objective conditions such as reaching a specific date, completing a specific task, or the occurrence of a specific event.

The Agreement introduces a principle of non-discrimination against fixed-term workers,[161] with stricter controls over the renewal of such contracts. That such workers need to be protected is illustrated in *Booth* v *United States of America*.[162] Despite arguing that the arrangement for two-week breaks between contracts was designed to defeat the legislation, the applicants were unsuccessful in their claim for a redundancy payment, even though, apart from three two-week breaks, they had some five years' service. One of the consequences of the Fixed-term Work Directive is to require some objective justification for continuing fixed-term contracts of employment.

Section 18 Employment Relations Act 1999 was a first step by the Government in implementing the requirements of the Fixed-term Work Directive. It removed s. 197(1) and (2) ERA 1996, which allowed individuals with a fixed-term contract of one year or more to opt out of the unfair dismissal provisions contained in Part X ERA 1996.[163]

Section 45 Employment Act 2002 provided authority for the introduction of the Fixed-term Employees (Prevention of Less Favourable Treatment) Regulations.[164] They define a fixed-term contract as either a contract of employment which is made for a specific term, or a contract that terminates automatically on the completion of a particular task, or the occurrence or non-occurrence of any specific event, except one resulting from the employee reaching normal retirement age or such conduct of the employee that might entitle an

---

[158] Council Directive 99/70/EC of 28 June 1999 concerning the Framework Agreement on fixed-term work OJ L175/43 10.7.99.

[159] Council Directive 91/383/EEC supplementing the measures to encourage improvements in the safety and health at work of workers with a fixed duration employment relationship or a temporary employment relationship OJ L206 29.7.91.

[160] Clause 1 Framework Agreement.

[161] Clause 4 Framework Agreement.

[162] [1999] IRLR 16.

[163] See Employment Relations Act 1999 (Commencement No 2 and Transitional and Savings Provisions) Order 1999, SI 1999/2830.

[164] The Fixed-term Employees (Prevention of Less Favourable Treatment) Regulations 2002, SI 2001/2034, which came into force on 1 October 2002.

employer to summarily dismiss that employee.[165] The ability of the parties to give notice to terminate does not prevent the contract from being for a fixed term.[166]

The scope of the unfair dismissal provisions in the ERA 1996 has been widened to include these 'task' contracts of employment.[167] The ending of these contracts will be regarded as a dismissal for the purposes of the Act. As a result an individual on such a contract obtains a number of statutory rights which are enjoyed by permanent employees. These include the right not to be unfairly dismissed, the right to a written statement of reasons for dismissal and the right to statutory redundancy payments. The ERA 1996 was also amended so that those on 'task' contracts of less than three months will have the right to minimum notice periods in the same way as permanent employees.

A number of important decisions have been taken about which individuals are to be protected and which are to be excluded. The Government has decided to apply the regulations to employees only. The approach is different from that taken by Part-time Workers Regulations (see 2.8.3 below). Those who are not treated as employees are to be excluded. Whilst recognising the problems associated with including non-employees, the decision does have the result of excluding significant numbers of individuals who work on fixed-term contracts and who, apart from their employment status, are indistinguishable from permanent employees or employees on fixed-term contracts.

The definition of comparator uses the same approach as that used by the Part-time Workers Regulations. The individual with whom a fixed-term worker is to be compared is someone who, at the time when the alleged treatment takes place, is employed by the same employer and is engaged on the same or broadly similar work, having regard to whether or not they have similar skills and qualifications, if this is relevant. The comparable permanent employee must work or be based at the same establishment, although other locations will be considered if there is no one appropriate at the same establishment.[168]

The Regulations provide that a fixed-term employee has the right not to be treated by the employer less favourably than a comparable permanent employee with regard to the terms of the contract or by being subject to any other detriment related to being a fixed-term employee.[169] This includes less favourable treatment in relation to: first, any period of service qualification related to a condition of employment; second, training opportunities; and, third, the opportunity to secure permanent employment in the establishment.

Importantly, however, the Government has decided to include less favourable treatment in relation to pay and pensions. As a result, the rules on statutory sick pay, rights to guarantee payments and payments on medical suspension are amended to ensure that fixed-term employees and comparable permanent employees are treated in the same way. Similarly, where there are qualifying rules for membership of pension schemes, then these rules should be the same for fixed-term and comparable permanent employees, unless the different treatment can be objectively justified. The Government believes that this will help reduce pay inequalities because the majority of fixed-term employees are women, so the inclusion of pay and pensions will help reduce the inequality between the sexes.

---

[165] Regulation 1(2).
[166] *Allen v National Australia Group Ltd* [2004] IRLR 847.
[167] For these purposes they are referred to as limited term contracts.
[168] Regulation 2.
[169] Regulation 3. In *Department of Work and Pensions v Webley* [2005] IRLR 288, the Court of Appeal ruled that termination by simple effluxion of time cannot, of itself, constitute less favourable treatment.

There is a defence of objective justification in the Regulations.[170] Interestingly, the Government has opted to allow the 'package' approach, as an alternative to the 'item by item' approach (compare Equal Pay below), when deciding whether an individual has been treated less favourably on the grounds of being a fixed-term employee. It will not be necessary to compare each part of the terms of employment and ensure that each individual part is comparable to the permanent employee, unless the employer so wishes. Such treatment is objectively justifiable if the terms of the fixed-term employee's contract of employment, as a whole, are at least as favourable as the permanent comparator. This presumably means that it will be permissible to pay a higher salary in compensation for other benefits such as holidays and pensions, so long as the value of the 'package' overall is equivalent or better than that of the permanent employee. It should be noted that the words 'objective grounds' in clause 4(1) of the Framework Agreement do not permit a difference in treatment to be justified on the basis that it is provided for by a general, abstract national norm, such as a law or collective agreement. According to the ECJ, unequal treatment must be justified by precise and concrete factors characterising the employment condition to which it relates, in the specific context in which it occurs and on the basis of objective and transparent criteria in order to ensure that there is a genuine need and that unequal treatment is appropriate for achieving the objective pursued and is necessary for that purpose.[171]

If an employee considers that he has been treated less favourably on the grounds of being a fixed-term employee, then he is entitled to request a written statement giving particulars of the reasons for the treatment. This must be provided by the employer within 21 days of the request. Such a statement will be admissible in any future employment tribunal proceedings.[172] A dismissal connected to enforcing an employee's rights under the Regulations will be treated as an unfair dismissal.[173]

Unfortunately, the Regulations seem unlikely to stop the repeated use of fixed-term contracts, which is a rather strange outcome. Where there is a succession of fixed-term contracts resulting in the employee being continuously employed for four years or more, the contract will automatically be deemed a permanent contract, unless there is objective justification suggesting otherwise.[174] The problem lies in the definition of continuous employment contained in the ERA 1996. Any week during which a contract of employment exists will count towards continuity of employment (s. 212(1) ERA 1996).[175] Thus any sort of break not covered by ERA 1996 is likely to sever continuity and make the Regulations ineffective. The European Court of Justice's decision in *Adeneler*[176] highlights the problems caused. This case involved workers employed by the Greek Milk Organisation, ELOG, who had been engaged on a number of fixed-term contracts. One of the issues in the case was that Greek legislation provided that continuity was broken if there was a gap of more than 20 days. The Court of Justice recognised that the decision as to what constituted continuity had been left to the Member State to decide. It held, however, that this discretion could not be exercised in such a way as to compromise one of the aims of the Directive, namely to prevent the misuse of

---

[170] Regulation 4.
[171] *Alonso* v *Osakidetza-Servicio Vasco de Salud* [2007] IRLR 911. In *Impact* v *Ministry for Agriculture & Food* [2008] IRLR 552 the ECJ confirmed that clause 4(1) has direct effect.
[172] Regulation 5.
[173] Regulation 6.
[174] Regulation 8.
[175] See *Sweeney* v *J & S Henderson* [1999] IRLR 306.
[176] Case C-21/204 *Adeneler* v *Ellinikos Organismos Galaktos* [2006] IRLR 716.

fixed-term contracts. It therefore held that a gap of 20 days allowed such misuse to continue and was not in accord with the aims of the Directive.

If an employee considers that he or she has become a permanent employee because of the Regulations, then he or she may request a written statement from the employer stating that he or she is now a permanent employee or, if not, the reasons why the individual is to remain a fixed-term employee. This statement must be given within 21 days and is admissible in future employment tribunal proceedings.[177] Provision is made for some flexibility as the maximum qualifying period can be varied by collective or workforce agreements. However, this may be of limited benefit because the agreement will be reached with employee representatives, the majority of whom are likely to be permanent employees. This may not be a problem for situations where the employees are represented by a trade union and reach a collective agreement on the issue. Yet it might be difficult where employees elect their own representatives, the majority of whom will not be affected. It is more likely to be a problem if the workforce agreement is reached by a majority vote of the workforce (this can be done where there are fewer than 20 employees). It is questionable whether employees in such situations will resist management demands for a more flexible approach if the majority are unaffected by the proposals.

Employees will be able to claim unfair dismissal if they are dismissed for exercising their rights under the Regulations. They can take their claim for less favourable treatment to an employment tribunal which has the power to award compensation to the claimant and recommend that the employer takes action within a specific period in order to obviate or reduce the adverse effect complained about. The compensation is limited, however, as the tribunal is specifically forbidden to award damages for injury to feelings. The matters that will be taken into account will be the loss of benefit arising from the infringement and any reasonable expenses of the complainant as a result of the infringement.

2.8.3 **Part-time contracts**

The European Directive on part-time work[178] was adopted as a result of a Framework Agreement reached by the social partners as part of the Social Dialogue process.

2.8.3.1 **Discrimination against part-time workers**

The treatment of part-time workers is a discrimination issue because the great majority of part-time workers are female.[179] According to the Labour Force Survey, between March 1992 and August 2006, full-time employment increased by 10 per cent whilst part-time employment increased by 23 per cent. By August 2006, part-time work amounted to 25 per cent of total employment but the rate was much higher for females (42 per cent) than for males (10 per cent). Part-time employment was more common amongst women across all major occupational groups, although the rate was much lower for females in management jobs (20 per cent compared with 4 per cent of males in managerial occupations). In August 2006 the average number of hours worked in full-time main jobs was 37.2 and 15.6 in part-time main jobs.[180]

---

[177] Regulation 9. See *Duncombe* v *Secretary of State for Children, Schools & Families* [2010] IRLR 332.
[178] Directive 97/81/EC of 15 December 1997 concerning the Framework Agreement on part-time work concluded by UNICE, CEEP and ETUC OJ L14/9 20.1.98.
[179] See *R* v *Secretary of State, ex parte Equal Opportunities Commission* [1994] IRLR 176 HL.
[180] *www.statistics.gov.uk.*

According to the former Equal Opportunities Commission,[181] some considerable progress was made as a result of the Employment Protection (Part-time Employees) Regulations 1995.[182] These Regulations removed the rule that employees were required to work a minimum number of hours before they were entitled to certain employment protection rights enjoyed by full-timers. They followed the decision of the House of Lords in *R* v *Secretary of State for Employment, ex parte Equal Opportunities Commission*,[183] which held that aspects of the minimum number of hours rule were incompatible with art. 119 EEC (now 157), the Equal Pay Directive[184] and the Equal Treatment Directive.[185] The 1995 Regulations extended protection to an estimated 689,000 part-time employees, of whom 574,000 (83 per cent) were female.

2.8.3.2 The Framework Agreement on part-time work

The purpose of the Agreement, according to clause 1, is to provide for the removal of discrimination against part-time workers and to improve the quality of part-time work, as well as to facilitate the development of part-time work on a voluntary basis. A part-time worker is defined in clause 3.1 as:

> An employee whose normal hours of work, calculated on a weekly basis or on average over a period of employment of up to one year, are less than the normal hours of work of a comparable full-time worker.

Justification for the measure is contained in the preamble to the Agreement. It is a measure that:

- Promotes both employment and equal opportunities for men and women.
- Helps with the requirements of competition by creating a more flexible organisation of working time.
- Facilitates access to part-time work for men and women in preparation for retirement.
- Reconciles professional and family life.
- Facilitates the take-up of education and training opportunities.

The Agreement applies to part-time workers, but there is an express provision (clause 2.2) permitting Member States to exclude casual part-time workers for objective reasons.

The comparable full-time worker is narrowly defined. It is someone who is a full-time worker in the same establishment, having the same type of employment or employment relationship and who is engaged on the same or similar work as the part-timer. Due regard is to be given to other considerations which include seniority, qualifications and skill. Where there is no full-time comparator, there is still a comparison to be made. It is to be done by reference to:

> the applicable collective agreement or, where there is no applicable collective agreement, in accordance with national law, collective agreements or practice.

It is difficult to give this any meaning in the United Kingdom where consultation with the social partners takes place less often than in many other countries in the European

---

[181] Hansard HC vol. 2 col. 346, session 1998–99.
[182] SI 1995/31.
[183] [1994] IRLR 176 HL.
[184] Directive 75/117/EEC.
[185] Directive 76/207/EEC.

Community. Importantly, however, there is no suggestion that there should be a situation where there are no comparators. The Agreement states that the comparison should be with the full-time comparator and, if there is no such person, then in accordance with national law, collective agreements or practice. It does not appear to suggest that, in the absence of a full-time comparator, there should be no comparison at all.

Clause 4 establishes the principle that part-time workers should not be treated less favourably than their full-time comparators merely because they work part-time, unless the difference in treatment can be objectively justified. Objective justification presumably will mean a reason for the difference in treatment that is not related to the individual working part-time. In *Bilka-Kaufhaus*[186] the ECJ considered the position of part-time shop sales assistants who were excluded from an occupational pension scheme that included full-timers. The Court concluded that an employer may be able to justify the exclusion of part-timers, in relation to a sex discrimination claim, where it represents a real need on the part of the undertaking and the means chosen to meet this need are appropriate to achieving that objective.

Where appropriate the principle of *pro rata temporis* should apply and, after consultation with the social partners, Member States may, where justified by objective reasons, make access to particular conditions of employment subject to periods of service, time worked or earnings. Opportunities for part-time work are to be encouraged. These would include the removal of obstacles to part-time work and giving consideration to requests from workers to transfer from full-time to part-time work and vice versa. A worker's refusal to transfer from full-time to part-time work, or vice versa, is not to be treated as a valid reason for termination of employment.

2.8.3.3 The Part-time Workers Regulations

The Part-time Workers (Prevention of Less Favourable Treatment) Regulations (the PTW Regulations) came into force on 1 July 2000.[187] The (former) Department of Trade and Industry's press release that accompanied the Regulations quoted the Secretary of State as saying that:

> The proposals I am putting forward today will ensure that part-timers are no longer discriminated against. This revised package safeguards the position of part-timers whilst avoiding unnecessary burdens on business.

In an attempt to achieve these two somewhat contradictory aims the Secretary of State stated that:

> the regulations will be introduced with a light touch by ensuring that comparisons can only be made between part-time and full-time workers with the same type of contract.

The effect of this is seen in the summary of the Regulatory Impact Assessment which accompanied the Regulations. The Assessment stated that there are some six million part-time employees in Great Britain. Of these the DTI estimated that one million have a comparable full-time employee against whom it is necessary to compare the terms and conditions of part-timers. It was also thought that some 400,000 will benefit from the equal treatment provisions. Large numbers of low-paid part-time workers will be excluded because there are no full-time comparators. It is difficult to understand how this justifies the Secretary of

---

[186] Case 170/84 [1986] IRLR 317 ECJ.
[187] SI 2000/1551.

State's assertion that the Regulations will 'ensure that part-timers are no longer discriminated against'.

Regulation 2(1) of the PTW Regulations identifies a full-time worker as someone who is paid wholly or partly by reference to the time worked, and, having regard to the custom and practice of the employer in relation to their other workers, is identifiable as a full-time worker. Regulation 2(2) has the same definition for part-time workers, except that they must be identifiable as part-time workers. The definition of a full-time comparator follows closely the one in the Directive, although, in terms of stating where the comparator needs to be based, it does have a wider coverage.[188] Full-timers, in relation to the part-timers, need:

1. To be employed by the same employer under the same type of contract.

2. To be engaged in the same or broadly similar work having regard, where relevant, to whether they have similar levels of qualifications, skills and experience.

3. To be based at the same establishment or, if there is no full-time comparator at the same establishment, at a different establishment.

In *Matthews* v *Kent Fire Authority*[189] part-time retained fire-fighters alleged that they were treated less favourably than full-time fire-fighters. The Court of Appeal had concluded that although they were employed under the same type of contract they did not carry out the 'same or broadly similar work'. The House of Lords disagreed and stated that, in making the assessment, particular attention should be given to the extent to which the work was exactly the same and to the importance of that work to the enterprise as a whole. If a large component of the work was the same, then the issue was whether the differences were so important that the work could not be regarded as the same or broadly similar. If part-time and full-time employees carry out the same work, but the full-timers do extra duties, this does not necessarily mean that the work is not the same or broadly similar.

It is a very demanding test for establishing whether an individual's job can be used as a comparator on which to base a claim for discrimination. The first issue is what happens if there is no full-time person who can meet the criteria. Where a workforce is made up entirely of part-time employees in a particular category, the regulations will be of no assistance in enabling them to claim discrimination on the basis of being a part-timer.[190] One example might be a contract cleaning operation. All the employees concerned with cleaning might be part-time and all the supervisory, management and administration employees might be full-time. The result is that there is no full-time comparator on whom the cleaning staff can base a claim. These employees may be low paid because they are part-time and, perhaps, because they are not organised collectively. However, they are unable to base a claim using the PTW Regulations. Although there may be a *prima facie* case of discrimination, it could not be based upon the PTW Regulations. Even the Government's own figures suggest that 80 per cent of part-time workers will not have a full-time comparator available to them.

Regulations 3 and 4 provide an exception to the need for such a comparator. Where a full-time worker, following the termination or variation of the contract of employment, works

---

[188] Hypothetical comparators are not permitted: see *Carl v University of Sheffield* [2009] IRLR 616.
[189] [2006] IRLR 367.
[190] In *Wippel v Peek & Cloppenburg GmbH* [2005] IRLR 211 the European Court of Justice suggested that a part-time casual worker might be covered by the Framework Agreement. However, Ms Wippel could not find a full-time comparator who worked on a casual basis.

fewer hours, the worker will be able to use himself or herself as the comparable full-timer for the purpose of deciding whether there has been less favourable treatment. The same rule applies if a full-time worker returns to work and performs fewer hours in the same job or a job at the same level, for the same employer, after an absence of less than 12 months. This is regardless of whether the absence followed a termination of employment or not.[191]

Regulation 5 establishes the principle of non-discrimination. A part-time worker has the right not to be treated less favourably than the employer treats a comparable full-timer as regards the terms of the contract or by being subject to detriment by any act, or failure to act, by the employer. The right only applies if the treatment is on the grounds that the worker is part-time and cannot be justified on objective grounds. In determining whether a part-timer has been treated less favourably, the principle of *pro rata temporis* applies. The one exception to this is overtime. Not paying overtime rates to a part-time worker until they have at least worked hours comparable to the basic working hours of the comparable full-timer is not to be treated as less favourable treatment. *McMenemy v Capita Business Services Ltd*[192] involved a part-time worker who worked only on Wednesdays, Thursdays and Fridays at a call centre which operated seven days a week. All employees had a contract of employment which entitled them to time off in lieu when statutory holidays coincided with one of their work-ing days. This meant that Mr McMenemy was not entitled to time off for statutory holidays that occurred on Mondays. As other colleagues who worked full-time received this time off, he complained that he was being treated less favourably than a comparable full-timer. He failed in his claim because the court held that the reason why he was not given time off for Monday statutory holidays was not solely because he was a part-timer, but because he did not work on Mondays. In order to show less favourable treatment he had to show that the employer intended to treat him less favourably solely because he was a part-time worker. The reason here for the less favourable treatment was that he had agreed not to work on Mondays. A full-time worker who worked from Tuesday to Saturday would also not be entitled to statutory holidays that fell on a Monday. Subsequently, in *Sharma v Manchester City Council*,[193] the EAT has ruled that the part-time nature of the claimant's work does not have to be the sole reason for the less favourable treatment. Additionally, the fact that not all part-timers are treated adversely does not mean that those who are cannot bring proceedings if being part-time is a reason for the discrimination experienced.

In the Government's compliance guidance, accompanying the PTW Regulations, the following examples are given:

- Previous or current part-time status should not of itself constitute a barrier to promotion.

- Part-time workers should receive the same hourly rate as full-timers.

- Part-time workers should receive the same hourly rate of overtime pay as full-timers, once they have worked more than the normal full-time hours.

- Part-time workers should be able to participate in profit-sharing or share option schemes available for full-timers.

- Employers should not discriminate between full-time and part-time workers over access to pension schemes.

---

[191] See also the provisions of flexible working contained in the EA 2002 – Chapter 8.
[192] [2007] IRLR 400.
[193] [2008] IRLR 236. This approach was followed in *Carl v University of Sheffield* [2009] IRLR 616.

- Employers should not exclude part-timers from training simply because they work part-time.
- In selection for redundancy part-time workers must not be treated less favourably than full-timers.

These examples apply only if the employer cannot objectively justify a distinction in treatment or if there is no full-time comparator meeting the criteria provided to whom the employee can be compared.

2.8.3.4 **Remedies**

As with other discrimination measures, the employer or agent of the employer will be liable for anything done by an employee in the course of their employment.[194] There is a defence of having taken all reasonable steps to prevent the worker doing the act.[195] There is the right not to be dismissed or suffer detriment as a result of exercising any rights under the regulations.[196] Interestingly, before a complainant brings a case to an employment tribunal they may request in writing from the employer the reasons for the less favourable treatment. The worker is entitled to a reply within 21 days and that reply, or lack of it, is admissible in tribunal proceedings.[197] There may be conciliation by ACAS which will try to arrange a settlement.[198] The tribunal can award compensation, although not for injury to feelings, and make a recommendation for action by the employer to rectify the situation.

2.8.4 **Apprentices**

Section 230(2) ERA 1996 defines a contract of employment as a contract of service or apprenticeship. The purpose of a contract of apprenticeship is to 'qualify the apprentice for his particular trade or calling'.[199] The execution of work for the employer is secondary.[200] Apprenticeship is distinct from an ordinary contract of employment because:

> although a contract of apprenticeship can be brought to an end by some fundamental frustrating event or repudiatory act, it is not terminable at will as a contract of employment is at common law.[201]

Edmunds v *Lawson QC*[202] was a case that was of great interest to students wishing to progress to the Bar. It raised the question whether a person who was offered and accepted an unfunded pupillage at a barrister's chambers was under a contract of apprenticeship with the chambers. If this were so, then the consequence would be that the pupil would be entitled to be paid at least the national minimum wage.[203] It was accepted that there was an offer of a pupillage and an acceptance of that offer. The consideration was the claimant's promise to

---

[194] Regulation 11(1) PTW Regulations 2000.
[195] Regulation 11(3) PTW Regulations 2000.
[196] Regulation 7 PTW Regulations 2000.
[197] Regulation 6 PTW Regulations 2000.
[198] Introduced by the Part-time Workers (Prevention of Less Favourable Treatment) Regulations 2001, SI 2001/1107 as an amendment to s. 18(1) ETA 1996 and s. 203(2)(f) ERA 1996; reg. 8 PTW Regulations 2000.
[199] *Wiltshire Police Authority* v *Wynn* [1981] 1 QB 95 CA. See *Flett* v *Matheson* [2005] IRLR 412 on the status of modern apprenticeship agreements.
[200] See *Wallace* v *CA Roofing Services Ltd* [1996] IRLR 435.
[201] *Ibid.* at p. 436.
[202] [2000] IRLR 391 CA.
[203] Section 54(2) and (3) National Minimum Wage Act 1998 offers a definition of worker and a contract of employment for the purposes of the Act.

act as a pupil and this was held to be of value not only to the pupil but also to the chambers and the individual pupil masters. The last requirement to establish a contractual relationship was an intention to enter legal relations. The High Court, in the absence of any express provisions, implied this intention from the subject matter of the agreement. There is a distinction between agreements which regulate business relations and those which regulate social arrangements. The former were likely to have legal consequences.[204] An offer, as in this case, to provide professional training, was therefore likely to be a business relationship, thus establishing the necessary intent. The Court of Appeal agreed with the views of the High Court, except that it held that the resulting contract was not a contract of apprenticeship. The pupil could not therefore be treated as a worker for the purposes of the National Minimum Wage Act 1998. Such a relationship would require a mutual obligation on the part of the pupil master to provide training and on the part of the pupil to serve and work for the master and carry out all reasonable instructions. This latter obligation was missing from the relationship.

Chapter summary

This chapter described the parties to a contract of employment, the tests that have been used by the courts to distinguish employees from other types of worker and the legal significance of having employment status. It also discussed the statutory provisions which determine the length of a person's continuous service. Finally, attention focused on specific types of employment relationship, namely agency, part-time and fixed-term workers.

Further reading

Deakin, S. and Morris, G. *Labour Law*: 5th edn, Hart Publishing, 2009, Chapter 3.

Painter, R. and Holmes, A. *Cases and Materials on Employment Law*: 7th edn, Oxford University Press, 2006, Chapter 2, Sections 1–3.

Wynn, M. and Leighton, P. 'Will the Real Employer Please Stand Up? Agencies, Client Companies and the Employment Status of the Temporary Agency Worker' (2006) 35(3) *Industrial Law Journal* 301.

http://www.direct.gov.uk/en/Employment/Employees/EmploymentContractsAndConditions/index.htm for the official page on employment contracts, including employment status.

http://www.hmrc.gov.uk/employment-status/index.htm for the view on employment status of HM Revenue and Customs.

Visit **www.mylawchamber.co.uk/sargeant**
to access legal updates, live weblinks and practice
exam questions to test yourself on this chapter.

---

[204] See, for further consideration of this, *Rose and Frank Company* v *JR Crompton Brothers Ltd* [1925] AC 445.

3 The contract of employment

3.1 Express terms

The Contracts of Employment Act 1963 required employers to give each employee a written statement setting out certain particulars of the employee's terms of service. This Act, subsequently amended and now contained in the ERA 1996, preceded an EEC Directive[1] on this issue and, rather unusually, the adoption of European legislation required little change in domestic law. The Directive required Member States to ensure that all employees received information 'of the essential aspects of the contract or employment relationship'.[2]

The express terms of a written contract will normally be conclusive in the event of a dispute. In *Gascol Conversions Ltd* v *JW Mercer*[3] the Court of Appeal held that:

> it is well settled that where there is a written contract of employment, as there was here, and the parties have reduced it to writing, it is the writing which governs their relations. It is not permissible to say they intended something different.

In this case the employees had signed a written statement accepting a new contract of employment. By way of contrast, in *Systems Floors (UK) Ltd* v *Daniel*,[4] the EAT concluded that a statement of terms and conditions of employment, given to the employee as a result of the employer's statutory obligations,[5] was only evidence of a contract of employment. In this case the individuals had signed a document which, it was held, was an acknowledgement of the receipt of the statutory statement. The EAT held that this statement did not constitute a written contract between the parties. It was merely a document that stated the employer's view of the terms. It may provide strong *prima facie* evidence of what the terms are but it is not conclusive of the terms of the employment contract. However, it will place a heavy burden on the employer to show that the actual terms of the contract are different from those contained in the statement.

---

[1] Council Directive 91/533/EEC on an employer's obligation to inform employees of the conditions applicable to the contract or the employment relationship OJ L288/32 18.10.91.
[2] *Ibid.* art. 2(1).
[3] [1974] IRLR 155 at p. 157 CA.
[4] [1981] IRLR 475.
[5] Now s. 1 ERA 1996.

Article 2(2)(c) of the Directive specifies that the information given to the employee must include the title, grade or nature of the post and give a brief specification or description of the work. The ECJ has held that this provision is sufficiently precise and unconditional to allow individuals to rely on it before the national courts. Although the written statement of terms is important evidence, employers must be allowed to offer evidence that they have made a mistake and provided incorrect terms.[6]

3.2 The statutory statement

Section 1 ERA 1996 provides that employees should receive a written statement of the particular terms of employment not later than two months after the beginning of employment. This statement may be given in instalments but must be complete not later than the two months, even if the employment ends within that period.[7] If a person, before the two months have passed, is to work outside the United Kingdom for a period of at least one month, then the statement must be given to them before they leave the country.[8]

The EA 2002[9] inserted new sections 7A and 7B into the ERA 1996. These provide that employers need not give a separate statement if they provide a letter of engagement or a contract of employment containing the information that would have been given if it were contained in such a statement.[10] This document still needs to be given within the two-month period or it can be given in the form of a letter of engagement prior to the start of employment. In such a case the effective date of the document will be the date on which employment begins.[11]

Section 11 ERA 1996 allows an employee to make a reference to an employment tribunal if a statutory statement or an alternative document is not received or if it is incomplete, or the employer has failed to provide a statement of any changes that take place.[12] If the employment has ceased, the reference must be made within three months of the cessation or such further time as the employment tribunal thinks was reasonably practicable. If the lack of, or incompleteness of, a statutory statement or alternative document becomes evident upon a claim being made under certain employment tribunal jurisdictions, such as unfair dismissal or disability, sex or race discrimination, then the tribunal is required to increase the compensation awarded by an amount equivalent to between two and four weeks' pay.[13] Where compensation is not awarded the employment tribunal must award a minimum of two to four weeks' pay.[14]

The ERA 1996 provides the following minimum list of contents for the statement of terms and conditions.

---

[6] Joined cases C-253/96 to 258/96 *Kampelmann v Landschaftsverband Westfalen-Lippe* [1998] IRLR 334 ECJ.
[7] Section 2(6) ERA 1996.
[8] Section 2(5) ERA 1996.
[9] Section 37 EA 2002.
[10] The information contained in ss. 1(3), 4(a)–(c), (d)(i), (f) and (h).
[11] Section 7B ERA 1996.
[12] Section 4(1) ERA 1996.
[13] Section 38 EA 2002; the complete list of such jurisdictions is contained in Sch. 5 to the Act; it includes, apart from those mentioned above, a wide range of issues such as those relating to the national minimum wage, working time and redundancy payments.
[14] Subject to the maximum for a week's pay specified in s. 227 ERA 1996.

3.2.1 Names and addresses of employer and employee[15]

The identity of the employer may be the subject of dispute. This may be true of individuals who are placed by one employer to work in the premises and under the control of another employer, such as agency staff.[16] It may also be true of changes resulting from a reorganisation or a transfer of employees between employers. However, a transfer of a contract of employment needs the employee's knowledge and, at least, implied consent.[17] In a case where two disabled employees were sponsored by Royal British Legion Industries to work in a 'host' organisation and remained there for nine years,[18] there was a dispute as to the identity of the employer. The EAT concluded that the correct approach was to start with the written contractual arrangements and decide whether these represented the true intentions of the parties. If they did, then the tribunal needed to discover if the situation had changed and when. There was a need to look at the reality of the situation in order to come to the correct conclusion.[19]

3.2.2 Date when employment began[20]

The date when employment begins can be important in establishing whether an employee has the minimum length of continuous service required for entitlement to various employment protection rights (see Chapter 2). For example, those individuals who are employed as temporary staff via an employment agency and are then employed on a permanent basis by the host company at which they work may need to clarify the precise start date of the new employment. The *Systems Floors*[21] case (see 3.1 above) involved a dispute about the employee's start date with the ability to make an unfair dismissal claim depending on the outcome.

3.2.3 Date on which continuous employment began[22]

For the purposes of assessing length of service, a person 'starts work' when their contract of employment commences rather than the date when they first undertook duties. This principle is likely to have a particular impact when the first day of the month is a Bank Holiday.[23] There is a requirement to take into account employment with a previous employer if that counts towards continuity. If there is a change of employer and a transfer of employment in accordance with s. 218 ERA 1996 or a relevant transfer takes place in accordance with the Transfer of Undertakings (Protection of Employment) Regulations 2006,[24] then service with the previous employer is likely to be added to the period of service with the new employer (see Chapter 9).

---

[15] Section 1(3)(a) ERA 1996.
[16] See *Dacas* v *Brook Street Bureau* [2004] IRLR 358 (Chapter 2 above).
[17] See *Bolwell* v *(1) Redcliffe Homes Ltd; (2) O'Connor* [1999] IRLR 485 CA.
[18] *Secretary of State for Education and Employment* v *Bearman* [1998] IRLR 431.
[19] See *Clifford* v *Union of Democratic Mineworkers* [1991] IRLR 518 CA.
[20] Section 1(3)(b) ERA 1996.
[21] [1981] IRLR 475.
[22] Section 1(3)(c) ERA 1996.
[23] See s. 211(1) ERA 1996 and *General of the Salvation Army* v *Dewsbury* [1984] IRLR 222.
[24] SI 2006/246.

3.2.4 **Remuneration**[25]

The statement will need to contain information on the scale or rate of remuneration or the method of calculating it and the intervals at which it is paid. Remuneration can have a wider meaning than the payment of wages, although the term 'wages' itself is capable of a broad definition. It need not be confined to the payment of regular wages, but may include payment relating to work done.[26] Wages, according to s. 27(1) ERA 1996, means 'any sums payable to the worker in connection with his employment' (see below).[27]

Employees also have the right to receive a written itemised pay statement from the employer. This is to be given before or at the time of payment and must contain information about: the gross[28] amount of wages or salary; the amount of any variable or fixed deductions and the purpose for which they are made; the net amount of wages payable; and, where different parts are payable in different ways, the amount and method of each part-payment.[29] The employer may give the employee a statement which contains an aggregate amount of fixed deductions, provided that the employer has given, at or before the time at which the pay statement is given, a standing statement of fixed deductions.[30] Such a standing statement must be in writing and contain details of the amount and purpose of each deduction and the intervals at which the deduction will be made. The statement can be amended in writing by the employer and must be renewed with amendments at least every 12 months.[31]

An employer may not receive payments from one of their workers, in their capacity as an employer, unless there is a pre-existing a contractual agreement for such payments to be made, or there is a statutory provision authorising such payment.[32] The exceptions to this rule are contained in s. 16 ERA 1996. These exceptions are:

1. Any payments that are a reimbursement of overpayment of wages or expenses paid to the worker.

2. A payment made by a worker as a consequence of any disciplinary proceedings resulting from a statutory provision.

3. Any payments required by the employer as a result of the worker taking part in industrial action.

4. A payment whose purpose is the satisfaction of an order of a court or tribunal requiring the payment to the employer.[33]

The employer does not have complete freedom to regulate remuneration as there is statutory regulation of wages. For example, the National Minimum Wage Regulations 1999[34]

---

[25] Section 1(4)(a) ERA 1996.
[26] See *New Century Cleaning Co Ltd* v *Church* [2000] IRLR 27 CA.
[27] Section 27(1) ERA 1996 lists a number of items that are included in the term 'wages', such as statutory sick pay and statutory maternity pay; s. 27(2) lists a number of items that are excluded from the definition, such as payments for expenses and redundancy pay.
[28] Gross amount is defined in s. 27(4) ERA 1996 as the total amount of wages before deductions of whatever nature.
[29] Section 8 ERA 1996.
[30] Section 9(1) ERA 1996.
[31] Section 9(2)–(5) ERA 1996.
[32] Section 15 ERA 1996.
[33] Section 16 ERA 1996.
[34] SI 1999/584.

provide for a statutory minimum wage; the Equal Pay Act 1970 attempts to stop discrimination in pay between women and men; and the Maternity and Parental Leave etc. Regulations
1999[35] define remuneration during maternity leave. Other sources of regulation may include
collective agreements incorporated into the contract of employment as well as custom and
practice within a particular industry.

3.2.5 Hours of work[36]

Any terms and conditions relating to hours of work, including those relating to normal
hours of work, need to be included.[37] Normal working hours are where there is a fixed
number or a minimum number of hours stated.[38] Where there are no normal working hours,
there is a formula for calculating a week's wage for statutory purposes. This involves
averaging over 12 weeks, although weeks in which remuneration is not due are excluded from
this period.[39]

An example of the issues that might arise when there is a lack of clarity on working hours
occurred in *Ali* v *Christian Salvesen Food Services Ltd*,[40] which involved a dispute over an
annualised hours contract of employment. Employees were paid on a notional 40-hour week,
but were not entitled to overtime until they had worked 1,824 hours in one year. The
problem arose for employees who were terminated during the course of the year and wanted
payment for hours they had worked in excess of the notional 40 hours per week. The Court
of Appeal refused to imply a term to deal with this issue, because there was a likelihood that
such a term had been deliberately left out of the agreement on annualised hours.

The Working Time Regulations 1998[41] also have an important bearing on the hours
worked (see Chapter 7). An employee is given a contractual right not to be required to work
more than a maximum of 48 hours work per week, averaged over a reference period, unless
there has been agreement otherwise in writing. Thus, in *Barber* v *RJB Mining (UK) Ltd*[42] the
High Court issued a declaration that the employees, who had been required to work in excess
of this during the reference period, were not required to work again until the average fell to
the maximum permitted.

The Part-time Workers (Prevention of Less Favourable Treatment) Regulations 2000[43] raise
an important issue in relation to working time. They introduced the principle of non-
discrimination between part-time workers and full-time comparators. Regulation 5 establishes
the principle of non-discrimination (see Chapter 2). A part-time worker has the right not to
be treated less favourably than the employer treats a full-time comparator. The principle of
pro rata temporis applies, so a part-timer should receive a proportion of the benefits enjoyed
by the full-time comparator in relation to hours worked. However, the one exception to this

---

[35] SI 1999/3312.
[36] Section 1(4)(c) ERA 1996.
[37] According to the ECJ in Case 350/99 *Lange* v *Georg Schünemann GmbH* [2001] IRLR 244, Directive 91/533 on
proof of the employment relationship requires employers to notify employees of any term which obliges the
employees to work overtime.
[38] See s. 234 ERA 1996 which is concerned with the calculation of a week's pay as in Part XI ERA 1996.
[39] Section 224 ERA 1996.
[40] [1997] IRLR 17 CA.
[41] SI 1998/1833 as amended by the Working Time Regulations 1999, SI 1999/3372.
[42] [1999] IRLR 308.
[43] SI 2000/1551.

concerns overtime. Part-timers are not entitled to premium overtime rates until they have at least worked hours which are the same as the basic full-time hours of the comparator.

3.2.6 Entitlement to holidays and holiday pay[44]

The statement of terms and conditions must enable the employee to calculate any entitlement to accrued holiday pay on termination of employment. The minimum amount of holidays is regulated by the Working Time Regulations 1998 (see Chapter 7).[45] Regulation 13 provides for a minimum of 5.6 weeks' paid[46] leave during a leave year. The Regulations also contain detailed provisions for dealing with individuals who terminate their employment during the year, enabling the employee to receive payment for leave not taken.[47]

3.2.7 Sickness, injury and pensions[48]

Employees are entitled to know the arrangements for absence through sickness and incapacity, including sickness pay. This information can be included in a separate document, as can information about pension schemes.[49] The statement of terms and conditions need merely direct individuals to the appropriate document, which must be 'reasonably accessible to the employee'.[50] There is no requirement for the employer to provide information about pensions if the employee's pension rights derive from any statutory provision, when those statutory provisions provide for another body or authority to give the employee information about pension rights.[51]

In *Mears v Safecar Security Ltd*[52] the written terms of employment did not contain any reference to sick pay. The Court of Appeal concluded that where there was a gap in the terms of employment and the tribunal had insufficient information to fill that gap, then the question should be settled in favour of the employee. However, in this case the court held that, taking into account all the circumstances and evidence, there had been no intention to provide pay during periods of absence through sickness and that such a term should have been included in the written terms of employment.

3.2.8 Length of notice[53]

The statement needs to reflect the notice that the employee is required to give and is entitled to receive on termination of employment. Minimum periods to which an employee and an employer are entitled are contained in s. 86 ERA 1996. These are related to the length of continuous employment. After one month's employment an individual with less than two years' continuous service is entitled to a week's notice. Thereafter one week is added for each year of service up to and including 12 years (see Chapter 4).

[44] Section 1(4)(d)(i) ERA 1996.
[45] Note 41 above.
[46] Regulation 16 Working Time Regulations 1998 concerns payment for periods of leave.
[47] Regulation 14 Working Time Regulations 1998.
[48] Section 1(4)(d)(ii) ERA 1996.
[49] Section 1(4)(d)(iii) ERA 1996.
[50] Section 2(2) ERA 1996.
[51] Section 1(5) ERA 1996.
[52] [1982] ICR 626 CA.
[53] Section 1(4)(e) ERA 1996.

3.2.9 **Title of job or job description**[54]

There is a need to provide the job title or a brief job description of the work to be done by the employee. The reliance that can be placed upon this job title or brief description was tested before the ECJ in *Kampelmann*.[55] Here the employers realised that a mistake had been made in the job information. The ECJ held that the job title or description could be factual evidence of the job duties, but that proof of the essential aspects of the relationship cannot depend solely upon the employer's notification. Employers must therefore be allowed to bring evidence to show that the notification is wrong.

3.2.10 **Temporary contracts**[56]

Where a position is not intended to be permanent, there is an obligation to include the period for which it is expected to continue and the date, if it is a fixed-term contract, upon which the contract is expected to end. This type of contract can include agency workers, who may be engaged on a week-to-week or even day-to-day basis, as well those individuals who are employed directly on fixed-term contracts. Issues arise for the latter when either the term is extended or the contract is not renewed (see Chapter 2).

3.2.11 **Place of work**[57]

The location of the place of work needs to be written down. If the employee is required or permitted to work at various locations there needs to be a note to this effect, together with the address of the employer. The precise place of work can be extremely important. For example, the consultation requirements for collective redundancies depend upon the number of employees to be dismissed 'at one establishment'.[58] Many employers will have a requirement for flexibility[59] and a requirement for the employee to be mobile written into the contract of employment. In *Aparau* v *Iceland Frozen Foods plc*[60] an employee was transferred to another branch after having several disagreements with the store manager. The employee disputed the employer's right to insist on the transfer and resigned, claiming constructive dismissal. The question was whether a mobility clause had become incorporated into the contract of employment. The EAT held that it had not and that it was not necessary to imply such a term. In certain occupations there may be an implication that mobility is necessary, but not in the contract of employment of a cashier working in a shop, where the nature of the work did not make such a clause necessary.[61]

3.2.12 **Collective agreements**[62]

Any collective agreements which directly affect the terms and conditions of employment are to be included in the statement. This includes, where the employer is not a party to the

---

[54] Section 1(4)(f) ERA 1996.
[55] Joined cases C-253/96 to 258/96 *Kampelmann* v *Landschaftsverband Westfalen-Lippe* [1998] IRLR 334 ECJ.
[56] Section 1(4)(g) ERA 1996.
[57] Section 1(4)(h) ERA 1996.
[58] Section 188(1) TULRCA 1992 and see Chapter 9.
[59] See *Deeley* v *British Rail Engineering Ltd* [1980] IRLR 147.
[60] [1996] IRLR 119 EAT.
[61] See also *Jones* v *Associated Tunnelling Co Ltd* [1981] IRLR 477 and *White* v *Reflecting Roadstuds Ltd* [1991] IRLR 331.
[62] Section 1(4)(j) ERA 1996.

agreement, the identities of the parties by whom the agreement is made requirement will apply to collective agreements that are, for example, reached b associations and trade unions. It is apparent from s. 2(3) ERA 1996, which allc to a collective agreement on periods of notice, that the terms of the collectiv should be reasonably accessible to the employee (for issues relating to the incorporation of collective agreements into contracts of employment, see below).

3.2.13 Periods working outside the United Kingdom[63]

If an employee is to work outside the United Kingdom for a period of more than one month, the statement will need to contain information about the period they are to be working outside the country, the currency in which they are to be paid, any additional remuneration payable and any terms and conditions relating to their return to the United Kingdom. This information was of particular importance when certain rights, such as those connected with making a claim for unfair dismissal, were dependent upon a person not ordinarily working outside Great Britain. Although this requirement no longer applies, the courts still expect an employee to be working in Great Britain at the time of dismissal.[64]

The Government introduced regulations[65] to implement the Posted Workers Directive[66] in 1999. The purpose of the Directive was to ensure that any legislation concerning the employment relationship in a Member State should be extended to include workers posted to that State. This protection is in relation to maximum working hours, paid holidays, minimum pay rates, rules on temporary workers, health and safety at work, the protection of pregnant women and provisions for ensuring equality of treatment between men and women. In the United Kingdom the Government amended the Sex Discrimination Act 1975, the Race Relations Act 1976 and the Disability Discrimination Act 1995 by ensuring that they cover all individuals apart from those who work wholly outside Great Britain.[67]

3.2.14 General provisions

If there are no particulars to be described under any of the headings above,[68] there needs to be a statement to that effect.[69] All of the information needs to be contained in a single document with the exception of: s. 1(4)(d)(ii) and (iii) relating to incapacity for work, including sick pay provisions, and pension schemes; s. 1(4)(e) relating to periods of notice; s. 1(4)(g) relating to temporary contracts; s. 1(4)(j) relating to collective agreements; and s. 1(4)(k) on employment outside the United Kingdom. Thus these matters can be dealt with in separate documents. In relation to incapacity for work, pensions, periods of notice and the impact of collective agreements, all there needs to be is a reference to some other document which is readily accessible to the employee.[70]

---

[63] Section 1(4)(k) ERA 1996.
[64] See *Lawson* v *Serco Ltd* [2006] IRLR 289.
[65] Equal Opportunities (Employment Legislation) (Territorial Limits) Regulations 1999, SI 1999/3163.
[66] Council Directive 96/71/EC concerning the posting of workers in the framework of the provision of services OJ L18/1 21.1.97.
[67] Section 10 SDA 1975, s. 8 RRA 1976 and s. 68(2) DDA 1995.
[68] Under s. 1(3) or (4) ERA 1996.
[69] Section 2(1) ERA 1996.
[70] Section 2(2) and (3) ERA 1996.

3.2.15 Disciplinary and grievance procedures[71]

The statement also needs either to specify the disciplinary and dismissal[72] rules and procedures relevant to an individual or refer them to a reasonably accessible document containing the rules and procedures. For the purposes of statutory statements, 'reasonably accessible' means that the employee has reasonable opportunities to read the documents in the course of employment, or the documents being made reasonably accessible to the employee in some other way.[73] There also needs to be reference to a person to whom the employee may apply if dissatisfied with any disciplinary or dismissal decision relating to him. Additionally any rules concerning the steps necessary for the purpose of seeking redress of any grievance need to be stated as well as specifying the person to whom the employee should address grievances. The disciplinary, dismissal or grievance requirements do not apply if the complaint relates to health and safety at work.

A failure to provide and/or implement a procedure may amount to a breach of contract entitling the employees to make a claim for constructive dismissal. In *W A Goold (Pearmak) Ltd v McConnell*,[74] two salespersons had their method of remuneration changed, which resulted in a substantial drop in their income. There was no established procedure for dealing with such grievances, but they talked to their manager initially. Nothing was done as a result of this. They then approached a new managing director, with whom they had a number of discussions. They were promised that something would be done, although nothing happened immediately. They then sought an interview with the chairman of the company, but were told that such interviews could only be arranged through the managing director. As a result they resigned and claimed constructive dismissal. Having considered Parliament's intentions in requiring employers to provide information about whom employees might approach if dissatisfied with a disciplinary matter or any grievance, the EAT concluded that the employer was in breach of the implied term to promptly afford a reasonable opportunity to obtain redress for a grievance.

Similarly an attempt to use different procedures from those contractually agreed may entitle the employee to seek an injunction to stop the employer's action.[75] In *Raspin v United News Shops Ltd*[76] an employee was dismissed after the failure of the employer to follow agreed disciplinary procedures. The employee was awarded compensation by the employment tribunal to compensate for the period that would have been worked if the procedure had been followed.[77]

3.3 Implied terms

Guidance about the implication of terms was given in *Mears v Safecar Security Ltd*.[78] First, one needs to see if there is an express term. If not, one should decide if there was a term which

---

[71] Section 3 ERA 1996.
[72] Section 3(1)(aa) ERA 1996.
[73] Section 6 ERA 1996.
[74] [1995] IRLR 516.
[75] See *Peace v City of Edinburgh Council* [1999] IRLR 417 and *Deadman v Bristol City Council* [2007] IRLR 888.
[76] [1999] IRLR 9.
[77] See also *Harper v Virgin Net Ltd* [2004] IRLR 390.
[78] [1982] ICR 626 CA.

could be said to have been agreed by implication. If this is not the case, then one looks to see whether such a term can be derived from all the circumstances, including the actions of the parties in the period during which the employment lasted. Finally, if none of this is possible, the employment tribunal may be required to invent a term. This last point was strongly disagreed with by the Court of Appeal in *Eagland* v *British Telecommunications plc*.[79] The case concerned a part-time cleaner who disputed her statement of terms and conditions. It omitted any terms relating to paid holidays, pay during absence for sickness and membership of a pension scheme which were included in the contracts of other part-time cleaners. The court held that it was not the task of employment tribunals to invent terms which had not been agreed between the parties. It distinguished between those terms which were mandatory and those which were non-mandatory. Amongst the latter are arrangements for disciplinary rules, pensions and sick pay schemes. Included in the former would be those legal necessities that arise out of a contract of employment, for example minimum periods of notice. Although the employment tribunal will have the opportunity to include those terms arising out of legal necessities, they have no power to impose non-mandatory terms where there is no evidence of the parties' intentions.

3.3.1 Terms implied by statute

Employment legislation is often designed to affect the terms in contracts of employment. One group of statutes and regulations are those concerned with non-discrimination. The most overt example of such implication of a term is contained in s. 1(1) Equal Pay Act 1970, which states that:

> If the terms of a contract under which a woman is employed at an establishment in Great Britain do not include (directly or by reference to a collective agreement or otherwise) an equality clause they shall be deemed to include one.

Other pieces of legislation that impose a non-discrimination requirement include the Sex Discrimination Act 1975, the Race Relations Act 1976, the Disability Discrimination Act 1995, the Part-time Workers (Prevention of Less Favourable Treatment) Regulations 2000 and the Employment Equality (Age) Regulations 2006.[80] All these pieces of legislation are concerned, in part, with preventing discrimination in employment against particular groups of workers.

A second group of statutes and regulations is concerned with specific terms and with setting minimum standards. These include the Working Time Regulations 1998,[81] which, for example, impose rules about maximum working hours and holiday entitlement, and the NMWA 1998 which requires minimum rates of pay for certain workers.

The third category is concerned with allowing statutory bodies to regulate the contents of the contract. This will include the Central Arbitration Committee (CAC), which has powers under s. 185 TULRCA 1992 to deal with disputes over disclosure of information. The CAC may require the employer to observe certain terms and conditions that it specifies. The CAC also has extensive powers to require collective bargaining arrangements between employers and trade unions in relation to the contents of certain aspects of the contract of employment.

[79] [1992] IRLR 323 CA.
[80] See Chapters 5 and 6 below.
[81] SI 1998/1833.

3.3.2 **Terms implied in fact**

These are intended to determine the true intentions of the parties. It is not a matter of law, but a matter of fact which the parties intended to be included in the contract. The two standard tests used to decide whether a term can be implied are the business efficacy test[82] and the officious bystander test, although these may be used as one. In *Shirlaw v Southern Foundries*[83] McKinnon LJ suggested that a term could be implied where it was so obvious that 'it goes without saying':

> If, while the parties were making their bargain, an officious bystander were to suggest some express provision for it in the agreement, they would testily suppress him with a common 'Oh, of course'.

Lord Wright in *Luxor (Eastbourne) Ltd v Cooper*[84] suggested that these tests allowed the implication of a term

> of which it can be predicated that 'it goes without saying', some term not expressed but necessary to give to the transaction such business efficacy as the parties intended.

One example in the employment context is *Jones v Associated Tunnelling Co Ltd*,[85] where there was a dispute about whether an employee was required to work at a particular location. Browne-Wilkinson J stated that, in order to achieve business efficacy, the starting point must be that a contract of employment cannot simply be silent on the place of work:

> . . . in such a case, it seems to me that there is no alternative but for the tribunal or court to imply a term which the parties, if reasonable, would probably have agreed if they had directed their minds to the problem.[86]

In *Ali v Christian Salvesen Food Services Ltd*[87] the court refused to imply a term into an annualised hours contract, even though there was an apparent gap, because the parties may have intended to leave that gap in the agreement. The Court of Appeal concluded:

> The importation of an implied term depends, in the final analysis, upon the intention of the parties as collected from the words of the agreement and the surrounding circumstances.

The desirability of putting into effect the intentions of the parties was also illustrated in *Aspden v Webb Poultry & Meat Group (Holdings) Ltd*.[88] Here an employer introduced a generous permanent health scheme for employees, allowing incapacitated employees to receive an amount equivalent to 75 per cent of their annual salary, beginning 26 weeks after the start of the incapacity. The employee was dismissed during a prolonged absence as a result of a serious illness. He claimed that there was an implied term in his contract that he would not be dismissed during incapacity for work as this would frustrate the benefits of the health insurance scheme. Although there was an express term in the contract allowing the employer

---

[82] See *The Moorcock* (1889) 14 PD 64.
[83] [1939] 2 KB 206 CA.
[84] [1941] AC 108.
[85] [1981] IRLR 477.
[86] See also *Courtaulds Northern Spinning Ltd v Sibson* [1988] IRLR 276 CA, which also concerned a change of work base for an employee.
[87] [1997] IRLR 17 CA, see text to note 40 above.
[88] [1996] IRLR 521. See also *Briscoe v Lubrizol Ltd* [2002] IRLR 607.

to dismiss as a result of prolonged incapacity, the court implied a term that a dismissal would not take place to stop an employee benefiting from the health scheme. This was because the contract was not written with the scheme in mind and if the parties had stopped to consider the issue it would have been their mutual intention not to frustrate the operation of the health scheme.[89]

3.3.3 Terms implied by law

These differ from implied terms of fact because they are not the result of identifying the intentions of the parties. In *Scally* v *Southern Health and Social Services Board*[90] the House of Lords stated:

> A clear distinction is drawn . . . between the search for an implied term necessary to give business efficacy to a particular contract and the search, based on wider considerations, for a term which the law will imply as a necessary incident of a definable category of contractual relationship.

In *Malik and Mahmud* v *BCCI*[91] the court stated that such implied terms operated as 'default rules'.

3.4 Duties of the employer

3.4.1 Duty of mutual trust and confidence

There is a duty on the part of both the employer and the employee not to act in a manner which undermines an implied term of trust and confidence which enables the contract of employment to continue in the manner envisaged.[92] In *United Bank Ltd* v *Akhtar*[93] an employee had a mobility clause in his contract of employment which provided that he could be transferred to any of the bank's locations in the United Kingdom at short notice with only the possibility of a discretionary relocation payment. He was asked to move to Birmingham from Leeds with less than one week's notice, although he had difficult personal circumstances. The court held that this amounted to a fundamental breach of the implied term that employers will not conduct themselves in such a manner that will harm or destroy the relationship of confidence and trust between employer and employee. It was possible to imply a term which controls the exercise of discretion in a contract of employment. In this case there was an implied requirement that reasonable notice should be given in exercising the power to relocate the bank's employees.

---

[89] See also *Takacs* v *Barclays Ltd* [2006] IRLR 877.
[90] [1991] IRLR 522 HL.
[91] [1997] IRLR 462 HL.
[92] See, for example, *Bliss* v *South East Thames Regional Health Authority* [1985] IRLR 308 CA, where the requirement that a consultant undergo a psychiatric examination was described by the court as an act which was calculated to destroy the relationship of confidence and trust which ought to exist between employer and employee.
[93] [1989] IRLR 507; see also *Woods* v *WM Car Services (Peterborough) Ltd* [1982] IRLR 413 CA, where continual attempts to change an employee's terms and conditions of employment amounted to a breach of the duty of trust and confidence.

An extreme example of employer behaviour can be found in the cases involving ex-employees of the Bank of Credit and Commerce International. This bank collapsed in 1991 after a period of trading insolvently and corruptly. In a series of cases, ex-employees claimed that the bank had been in breach of an implied term not to operate their business in a corrupt and dishonest manner. The House of Lords, in *Malik*,[94] accepted this argument and stated that:

> The conduct must, of course, impinge on the relationship in the sense that, looked at objectively, it is likely to destroy or seriously damage the degree of trust and confidence the employee is reasonably entitled to have in his employer.

Here the House of Lords concluded that the manner in which the bank conducted itself impacted on the employment relationship and that the individuals were able to treat the employer's conduct as a repudiatory breach of contract, enabling them to leave and claim constructive dismissal. The court then went on to approve in principle a claim for what became known as 'stigma' damages. The employees' job prospects had been so damaged that they were entitled to compensation for the damage done to their job prospects elsewhere. Many ex-employees of BCCI had signed compromise agreements[95] excluding further claims against the employer. However, the House of Lords would not allow the employer to rely upon these agreements in order to exclude claims for stigma damages. The agreements were signed some eight years before the House of Lords held that such claims were sustainable and the parties could not have intended to provide for the release from rights which they could never have contemplated as possible.[96]

Malik was further considered in *Johnson* v *Unisys Ltd*,[97] where an employee claimed damages for loss allegedly suffered as a result of the manner in which he was dismissed. The House of Lords stated that a common law right in relation to the manner of dismissal could not co-exist alongside the statutory right not to suffer unfairness. It was not possible to imply a separate term into the contract of employment that a power of dismissal would be exercised fairly and in good faith. Thus the employee could not rely upon the fact that he was dismissed without a fair hearing and in breach of the employer's disciplinary procedure to establish a claim for a breach of the implied term of trust and confidence. The court also stated that it was not appropriate to apply this implied term to dismissals, because it was about preserving the relationship between employer and employee and not about the way that the relationship is terminated.[98] Although it has a number of undesirable consequences, for example requiring courts and tribunals to decide whether an employer's wrongful conduct formed part of the process of dismissal, this approach was followed in *Eastwood* v *Magnox Electric plc*.[99] In this case the claimants alleged that they had been victims of their employer's campaign to deprive them of their jobs by fabricating evidence and encouraging other employees to give false statements for the purpose of disciplinary proceedings. The House of Lords held that in these circumstances the employees were not excluded from

---

[94] Consolidated cases *Malik* v *Bank of Credit and Commerce International SA, in liquidation*; *sub nom Mahmud* v *Bank of Credit and Commerce International SA* [1997] IRLR 462 HL.

[95] See Chapter 4.

[96] *Bank of Credit and Commerce International* v *Ali* [2001] IRLR 292 HL.

[97] [2001] IRLR 279 HL.

[98] See *Addis* v *Gramophone Company Ltd* [1909] AC 488 HL, which prevents an employee in a case of wrongful dismissal from recovering damages for injured feelings, mental distress or damage to reputation arising out of the manner of the dismissal.

[99] [2004] IRLR 733.

bringing common law claims for psychiatric injury based on a breach of trust and confidence prior to dismissal.

In *Malik*,[100] Lord Steyn stated:

> It is true that the implied term adds little to the employee's obligations to serve his employer loyally and not act contrary to his employer's interests. The major importance of the implied duty of trust and confidence lies in its impact on the obligations of the employer[101] . . . and the implied obligation as formulated is apt to cover the great diversity of situations in which a balance has to be struck between an employer's interest in managing his business as he sees fit and the employee's interest in not being unfairly and improperly exploited.

The affected employees still needed to establish that the bank's wrongdoing had stigmatised them in a way which undermined their prospects of finding alternative employment. In a subsequent decision,[102] the Court of Appeal held that the question to be asked was: but for the breach of duty, what would the prospective employer have done and what would have been the result for the employee? This might mean looking at the whole history of a person's search for new employment, such as considering how many jobs have been applied for, how many interviews obtained and what the results were. It is for the claimant to show causation, but the judge should look at the whole picture in reaching a conclusion.

In *French v Barclays Bank plc*[103] the action of the employer in stopping an interest-free bridging loan to a relocated employee, as a result of the length of time it took to sell the employee's old house, was held to be a serious breach of this implied term. This was despite the fact that the loan facility was at the discretion of the employer. Similarly the provision of a reference to a potential employer revealing information about which the employee was unaware is also likely to be a breach. In *TSB Bank plc v Harris*,[104] when a prospective employer approached the current employer for a reference, the latter revealed that 17 customer complaints had been made about the employee. It was the employer's practice not to discuss these with the employee concerned, which meant that the information, as a result of which a job offer was withdrawn, was unknown to the individual at the time of the reference. This failure to inform the employee and to discuss the complaints with her prior to revealing the information to a prospective employer amounted to a breach of the implied term of mutual trust and confidence.

It should also be noted that this implied term is dependent upon the alleged conduct of the employer being without reasonable and proper cause. Thus if an employer has justifiable suspicions that an employee was dishonest, it would not be a breach of trust and confidence to remove responsibilities for cash from that individual's duties. This was the case in *Hilton v Shiner Ltd*,[105] where the EAT stated that a two-stage process had to be completed. First, whether there had been acts which seem likely to seriously damage or destroy the relationship of trust and confidence. Secondly, whether there is no reasonable or proper cause for those acts.

Sexual harassment by a senior male employee against a female employee is also likely to amount to a breach of the implied term. If the actions were such that, over a period of time,

---

[100] [1997] IRLR 462 at p. 468.
[101] The court cited Douglas Brodie, 'The Heart of the Matter: Mutual Trust and Confidence' (1996) 25 *ILJ* 121.
[102] *Bank of Credit and Commerce International SA v Ali (No 3)* [2002] IRLR 460 CA.
[103] [1998] IRLR 646 CA.
[104] [2000] IRLR 157; see also cases under duty of care below.
[105] [2001] IRLR 727.

an employee found the workplace intolerable and felt that they had to resign over the unwanted harassment, that individual may then be entitled to make a claim for constructive dismissal because of the breach.[106] More generally, the contract of employment requires the maintenance of self-esteem and dignity. Thus the use of foul and abusive language could be a breach of trust and confidence[107] as could allegations about the employee made to others if they are calculated to seriously damage the employment relationship.[108]

The process by which an employer deals with an employee who is to be investigated can itself lead to a breach of mutual trust and confidence. Thus the suspension of a care worker pending an inquiry about allegations of sexual abuse against a child in her care was interpreted as a breach of the implied term of trust and confidence.[109] The court held that just because an investigation was to take place, it did not follow automatically that the employee must be suspended. The court described the employer's response as a 'knee-jerk reaction'.

It remains to be seen how far the duty of trust and confidence imposes positive obligations on employers to ensure that employees are treated fairly. For example, the House of Lords has accepted that in certain circumstances it will be necessary to imply an obligation on an employer to take reasonable steps to bring a contractual term to the employee's attention.[110] Similarly, in *Transco* v *O'Brien*[111] the Court of Appeal held that there was a breach of trust and confidence when, without reasonable excuse, an employee was denied the opportunity given to everyone else of signing a revised contract with enhanced redundancy payments. On the other hand, a failure to warn an employee who was proposing to exercise pension rights that the way he was proposing to act was not the most financially advantageous was not seen as breaching trust and confidence.[112]

Employees who believe that their employer has breached the duty of trust and confidence must decide what course of action to take. A resignation, which amounts to an acceptance of the employer's breach and the ending of the contract, may give rise to a claim for constructive dismissal. However, continuing to work and receive pay does not entitle the employee to disregard lawful and legitimate instructions from the employer because the duty to perform work and obey instructions is not dependent upon the employer's performance of its obligations.[113] If the employee resigns, the likely remedy for a successful claim will be compensation. Where there is a breakdown in mutual trust and confidence it may be difficult for a tribunal to order reinstatement or re-engagement of the employee. In *Wood Group Heavy Industrial Turbines Ltd* v *Crossan*[114] an employee was dismissed for a genuine belief by the employer that the employee had been dealing in drugs at the workplace. The employment tribunal ordered re-engagement in the belief that the employers had not carried out sufficient investigations. The EAT allowed the employer's appeal against this remedy because it decided that:

---

[106] See *(1) Reed; (2) Bull Information Systems Ltd* v *Stedman* [1999] IRLR 299.

[107] See *Horkulak* v *Cantor Fitzgerald* [2003] IRLR 756.

[108] See *RDF Group plc* v *Clements* [2008] IRLR 208 where the High Court acknowledged that garden leave alters the nature and content of this implied term.

[109] *Gogay* v *Hertfordshire County Council* [2000] IRLR 703 CA. See also *King* v *University Court of the University of St Andrews* [2002] IRLR 252, where the Court of Session confirmed that the duty of trust and confidence subsisted during an investigation into allegations of misconduct which might result in the employee's dismissal.

[110] *Scally* v *Southern Health Board* [1991] IRLR 522.

[111] [2002] IRLR 444.

[112] *University of Nottingham* v *Eyett* [1999] IRLR 87. See also *Outram* v *Academy Plastics* [2000] IRLR 499.

[113] See *Macari* v *Celtic and Athletic Football Club Ltd* [1999] IRLR 787 at p. 795.

[114] [1998] IRLR 680.

it is difficult to see how the essential bond of trust and confidence that must exist between an employer and an employee, inevitably broken by such investigations and allegations, can be satisfactorily repaired by re-engagement. We consider that the remedy of re-engagement has very limited scope and will only be practical in the rarest cases where there is a breakdown in confidence as between the employer and the employee.

3.4.2 **Duty to provide work and pay**

In *Beveridge* v *KLM UK Ltd*[115] an employee informed her employers that, after a long period of absence through sickness, she was fit to return to work. However, they refused to allow her to return until their own doctor had certified her fitness to do so. This process took six weeks, during which she was not allowed to work and was not paid. When she claimed that this amounted to an unauthorised deduction from her wages, the employment tribunal held that the employer was under no obligation to pay her as there was no express term of the contract to this effect. However, the EAT ruled that an employee who offers services to her employer is entitled to be paid unless there is an express provision of the contract providing otherwise. There was no such term in this case and the employee could do no more than attempt to fulfil her side of the contract.

There is also the question of whether there is an implied term in the contract of employment that the employer has a duty to provide work as well as pay. The traditional common law view was stated in *Collier* v *Sunday Referee Publishing Co Ltd*.[116] Here a newspaper sub-editor was retained by his original employer after the newspaper for which he worked was taken over by another organisation. When he was not given any work to do, he claimed that his employer had breached his contract. Asquith J illustrated the general point graphically:

> Provided I pay my cook her wages regularly she cannot complain if I choose to take any or all of my meals out.

However, the court recognised that there were exceptions when there was an obligation to provide work. This would be the case where individuals earned their income from commission and where publicity is part of the bargain, for example, in the case of actors or singers.[117] This is especially important when employers seek to insist on employees serving out lengthy periods of notice whilst keeping them idle, in order to stop them going to work for what is perceived to be a rival organisation.[118] The purpose is to prevent the employee going to a rival company with up-to-date knowledge of the existing employer's business. This period of enforced idleness is sometimes referred to as 'garden leave'. It particularly affects individuals who are reliant upon continuing to work in order to maintain their skills or stay in the public eye. In *Provident Financial Group plc and Whitegates Estate Agency Ltd* v *Hayward*[119] there was a specific term in the contract of employment which provided that the employer need not provide work. Taylor LJ stated that:

[115] [2000] IRLR 765.

[116] [1940] 2 KB 647.

[117] See also *Breach* v *Epsylon Industries Ltd* [1976] IRLR 180 which emphasised that it was necessary to look at the background to the contract to consider how it should be construed, in order to decide whether there was a term to be implied concerning the provision of work.

[118] The court is unlikely to give injunctive relief to an employer if the restriction stops the employee on 'garden leave' taking up employment with a non-competing organisation; see *Provident Financial Group plc and Whitegates Estate Agency Ltd* v *Hayward* [1989] IRLR 84 CA.

[119] *Ibid.*

employee has a concern to work and a concern to exercise his skills. That has been recognised some circumstances concerned with artists and singers who depend on publicity, but it applies equally I apprehend, to skilled workmen and even to chartered accountants.

Thus the need to exercise and maintain skills could be widely interpreted as including those who are experts in their field. In *William Hill Organisation Ltd* v *Tucker*[120] an employee was put on six months' garden leave. The individual held a unique position with specialist skills. In this case the court decided that the contract could be construed so as to give rise to an obligation on the employer to allow the employee to carry out his duties. This was not only because the individual held a 'specific and unique post' and needed to practise his skills regularly, but also because the terms of the contract pointed towards this conclusion; especially the obligation which required the employee to work the hours necessary to carry out the duties of the post in a full and professional manner. More recently, the High Court has introduced a qualification to the right to work. In *SG & R Valuation Service* v *Boudrais*,[121] the judge stated that those who have the right to work hold it subject to the qualification that they have not, as a result of some prior breach of contract or other duty, demonstrated in a serious way that they are not ready and willing to work. For these purposes, the breach of contract or other duty must amount to wrongdoing by reason of which they will profit. In this case there had been evidence of poaching customers and the use of confidential information by two senior employees on garden leave whilst serving out their notice before joining a competitor.

3.4.3 Duty of care

This is a duty that might cover a variety of responsibilities. There are certain statutory requirements relating to health and safety matters. Section 2(1) HASAWA 1974 requires an employer 'to ensure, so far as is reasonably practicable, the health, safety and welfare at work of all his employees'. Similarly there is an obligation on employees to inform the employer, or any other person responsible for health and safety, of any work situation which might present a 'serious and imminent danger to health and safety'.[122]

There is an implied duty in every contract of employment that an employer will take all reasonable steps to provide and maintain a safe system of work so as not to expose the employee to unnecessary risks of injury. In *Wilsons and Clyde Coal Co Ltd* v *English*[123] Lord Thankerton listed a number of duties of the master towards servants:

> If the master retains control, he has a duty to see that his servants do not suffer through his personal negligence, such as (1) failure to provide proper and suitable plant, if he knows, or ought to have known, of such failure; (2) failure to select fit and competent servants; (3) failure to provide a proper and safe system of working; and (4) failure to observe statutory regulations.

This obligation extends to responsibility for actions taken by employees and agents of the employer. The employer may be liable even if, centrally, it had taken all precautions as were 'reasonably practicable' but this had not been done by its employees elsewhere.[124] This

---

[120] [1998] IRLR 313 CA.
[121] [2008] IRLR 770.
[122] Regulation 14(2) Management of Health and Safety at Work Regulations 1999, SI 1999/3242.
[123] [1938] AC 57 HL; see also *Morris* v *Breaveglen Ltd* [1993] IRLR 350 CA.
[124] *R* v *Gateway Foods Ltd* [1997] IRLR 189 CA.

general duty also extends to persons who are not directly employed.[125] However, provided that the employer had taken all steps that are reasonably practicable, they should not be held liable for the acts of their careless or negligent employees or agents. In *R v Nelson Group Services (Maintenance) Ltd*[126] gas fitters had not completed their tasks correctly and had thereby exposed customers to danger. The Court of Appeal allowed an appeal on the grounds that the judge's directions had not allowed the employer's defence of reasonable practicability to be decided by the jury.

Section 2(2)(e) HASAWA 1974 states that an employer has a duty to provide and maintain a working environment that is, as far as is reasonably practicable, safe and without risk to health. This is similar to the implied term in every contract of employment that employers have a duty to provide and monitor, as far as is reasonably practicable, a working environment which is reasonably suitable for employees to perform their contractual duties. This includes the right not to be required to work in a smoke-filled atmosphere, as in *Waltons & Morse v Dorrington*.[127] In this case a secretary objected to working in poorly ventilated accommodation with a number of smokers. Although the employer took some measures, they proved inadequate to solve the problem and the employee resigned and successfully claimed unfair constructive dismissal. In *Dryden v Greater Glasgow Health Board*[128] the introduction of a no-smoking policy by the employer, after consultation, had an adverse effect on a nurse who smoked 30 cigarettes a day. The EAT concluded that, where a rule is introduced for a legitimate purpose, the fact that it has an adverse effect on an employee does not enable that individual to resign and claim constructive dismissal. There was no implied term in the employee's contract of employment which entitled her to continue smoking.

The employer's duty of care is owed to the individual employee and not to some unidentified ordinary person. This is especially true in relation to psychiatric illness caused by stress at work. The stages in deciding whether employers have carried out their responsibilities are: first, whether the harm was foreseeable; secondly, what the employer did and should have done about it; and, thirdly, where a breach has been shown, whether there is a causal relationship between the breach and the harm.

According to the House of Lords,[129] the best statement of general principle remains that of Swanwick J in *Stokes v GKN Ltd*:[130]

> The overall test is the conduct of the reasonable and prudent employer taking positive thought for the safety of his workers in the light of what he knows or ought to know.

The test is the same whatever the employment. It is not the job that causes harm but the interaction between the individual and the job. There needs to be some indication to the employer that steps need to be taken to protect an employee from harm. Thus if an employee returns to work after a period of illness and does not make further explanation or disclosure, then the employee is implying that he is fit to return to work. The employer is then entitled to take this at face value unless there is reason to think the contrary.[131] More recently, the

---

[125] Section 3(1) HASAWA 1974 and *R v Associated Octel Co Ltd* [1997] IRLR 123 HL.

[126] [1999] IRLR 646 CA.

[127] [1997] IRLR 488. See the Smoke-free (Premises and Enforcement) Regulations 2006, SI/2006 3368 which came into force in England and Wales on 1 July 2007.

[128] [1992] IRLR 469.

[129] *Barber v Somerset County Council* [2004] IRLR 475.

[130] [1968] 1 WLR 1776.

[131] See *Young v Post Office* [2002] IRLR 660.

Court of Appeal has emphasised the importance of distinguishing signs of stress and indicators of impending harm to health.[132]

Factors that are relevant to the question of foreseeability include: the nature and pressures of the job; is the workload more than normal for that job?; is the work particularly demanding for the employee?; are there signs of stress amongst others doing the same job?; is there a high level of absenteeism? The next stage is to consider whether there are signs of impending harm for the individual employee concerned, such as whether there are frequent or prolonged absences and whether the employee or his doctor has warned the employer about the risk of harm.[133]

Once harm is assessed as being foreseeable, attention focuses on what the employer should have done about it.[134] The actions that are reasonable will depend upon the employer's size and resources. It is then necessary to show that the breach was at least partly responsible for the harm. Thus in *Corr* v *IBC Ltd*[135] the House of Lords held that depression was the direct and foreseeable consequence of the accident and that suicide was the direct result of the deceased's depression.

The duty of care does not extend to medical practitioners who carry out health assessments on behalf of employers seeking to recruit staff. In *Baker* v *Kaye*[136] a medical practitioner concluded that an applicant was likely to consume excessive amounts of alcohol in a stressful work-related context. The employer withdrew a conditional offer of employment after receiving the medical report. Unfortunately the applicant had already resigned from his previous post because he had not anticipated any problems with the report of the medical examination. The High Court was asked to consider whether there was a duty of care owed by the doctor to the applicant. The court relied upon *Caparo Industries*[137] and *Hedley Byrne & Co Ltd* v *Heller & Partners Ltd*[138] to reach the conclusion that it was clear that economic loss was a foreseeable consequence of a breach of this duty and that there was a sufficient proximity between the parties to give rise to a duty of care. However, in this case the court decided that the defendant was not in breach of that duty. In a subsequent decision the Court of Appeal disagreed with this conclusion and held that there was no duty of care owed by a medical practitioner to a job applicant in these circumstances, even though the applicant might suffer economic loss as a result of a careless error in a doctor's report.[139] There was not sufficient proximity, as the duty of care will generally be owed to the person who commissions the report, not the subject of it. A medical practitioner is likely to be viewed, therefore, as an agent of the employer.[140]

In *Spring* v *Guardian Assurance plc*,[141] the House of Lords held that an employer was under a duty of care to a former employee when providing a reference to a prospective employer. The duty was derived from the previous contractual relationship between the employer and

---

[132] *Dickins* v *O2 plc* [2009] IRLR 58.
[133] See *Hone* v *Six Continents Ltd* [2006] IRLR 764 and *Intel Corporation* v *Daw* [2007] IRLR 355CA.
[134] See *Pratley* v *Surrey County Council* [2003] IRLR 794.
[135] [2008] ICR 372.
[136] [1997] IRLR 219.
[137] *Caparo Industries plc* v *Dickman* [1990] 2 AC 605 HL.
[138] [1964] AC 465 HL.
[139] *Kapfunde* v *Abbey National plc* [1998] IRLR 583 CA.
[140] See *London Borough of Hammersmith & Fulham* v *Farnsworth* [2000] IRLR 691, where the doctor's knowledge of an individual's disability was held to be enough for the employer to be held to have such knowledge.
[141] [1994] IRLR 460 HL.

the ex-employee. In this case the applicant sought damages for economic loss as a result of a failure to obtain work resulting from a reference written by a former employer. The question was whether the employer owed a duty of care to the applicant in the preparation of the reference. The House of Lords decided that employees had a remedy in negligence if they could establish that the inaccurate reference was a result of the employer's lack of care. However, this does not mean that every reference needs to be full and comprehensive. In *Bartholomew* v *London Borough of Hackney*[142] the Court of Appeal needed to consider both the employer's duty to provide a reference for the individual and the obligation towards potential employers to provide a reference without being misleading or unfair.[143] The court accepted that a reference must not give 'an unfair or misleading impression overall, even if its discrete components are factually correct'. According to the High Court in *Kidd* v *Axa Equity & Law Life Assurance Society plc*,[144] it was not in the public interest to impose an obligation on employers to provide a full, frank and comprehensive reference. The court further held that to show a breach of the duty of care the claimant needed to show:

1. That the information provided in the reference was misleading.

2. That the provision of such misleading information was likely to have a material effect on the mind of a reasonable recipient of the reference to the detriment of the claimant.

3. That the defendants were negligent in providing such references.

The employer providing the reference is also under an obligation to carry out any necessary inquiries into the factual basis of any statements made in the reference. Unfavourable statements should be confined to matters which had been investigated and for which there were reasonable grounds for believing that they were true.[145]

Finally, if the employee has a safety grievance, there is an implied term that employers will act promptly and provide a reasonable opportunity for employees to obtain redress. This view was put forward in *Waltons & Morse* v *Dorrington*,[146] where a non-smoker's attempts to have grievances about air quality were frustrated.

3.5 Duties of employees

3.5.1 Duty of obedience and co-operation

There is an implied duty to obey an employer's lawful and reasonable instructions and an employee's failure to do so might amount to a fundamental breach of contract.[147] However, it is possible for the failure to obey an unlawful instruction to result in a fair dismissal, for example when an employer reasonably but mistakenly believed that they were giving a lawful instruction.[148] Certainly a belief by the employee that the employer has breached an

---

[142] [1999] IRLR 246 CA.
[143] The reference needs actually to have been given to a third party: see *Legal and General Assurance Ltd* v *Kirk* [2002] IRLR 124 CA.
[144] [2000] IRLR 301.
[145] *Cox* v *Sun Alliance Life Ltd* [2001] IRLR 448 CA.
[146] [1997] IRLR 488.
[147] See *Laws* v *London Chronicle Ltd* [1959] 2 All ER 285 CA.
[148] *Farrant* v *The Woodroffe School* [1998] IRLR 176.

implied term is not justification for failing to obey other lawful and legitimate instructions.[149] This duty to obey might include the need to adapt to new technology. For example, in *Cresswell* v *Board of the Inland Revenue*[150] the introduction of computers into the administration of the PAYE system was held not to fall outside the job descriptions of the employees concerned. More recently, the EAT has ruled that there can be an implied term that an employee may be obliged to perform duties which are different from those expressly required by the contract or to perform them at a different place. However, an implied obligation to undertake work which is outside the express terms is only likely to be imposed where: the circumstances are exceptional; the requirement is plainly justified; the work is suitable; the employee suffers no detriment in terms of contractual benefits or status; and the change is temporary.[151]

The implied term to serve the employer faithfully also applies to managers who supervise others and exercise discretion in the carrying out of their duties. If the manager exercises that discretion in order to disrupt the work of the employer, then there may be a breach of this implied term. In *Ticehurst* v *British Telecom*,[152] as part of an industrial dispute, a supervisor refused to sign a declaration that she would work normally. This was seen as an intention not to perform the full range of duties and amounted to a breach of the implied term to serve the employer faithfully. In *Wiluszynski* v *London Borough of Tower Hamlets*[153] local authority employees took partial industrial action and refused to answer queries from Members of the Council. Despite warnings, the employees carried on attending the place of work and completed all their other tasks. The employer refused to pay them for the period when they were not fulfilling all their contractual obligations. The Court of Appeal held that the employees were in repudiatory breach of their contracts, but that the employer had alternatives to accepting the breach and dismissing the employees. One of these alternatives was to tell them that they would not be paid during the period when they failed to carry out all the terms of their contracts.

This obligation to carry out duties in a full and professional manner was an issue in *Sim* v *Rotherham Metropolitan Borough Council*.[154] The National Union of Teachers instructed its members not to provide cover for absent colleagues. The union claimed that the system had operated on the basis of goodwill only. The High Court rejected this argument and stated that the teachers had a professional obligation which they owed to their pupils and the school in which they worked. The court accepted that there was no statement in the teachers' contracts to this effect but held that this was not to be expected in professional contracts of employment. Such contracts specified the nature of the work and these extra duties were simply part of the professional obligations of teachers.

3.5.2 Duty of fidelity

There are two aspects of the duty of fidelity. The first is the implied duty not to compete with the employer and the second is not to disclose certain confidential information, except in

---

[149] See *Macari* v *Celtic and Athletic Football Club Ltd* [1999] IRLR 787.
[150] [1984] IRLR 190.
[151] *Luke* v *Stoke City Council* [2007] IRLR 305. However, see also the Court of Appeal's approach at [2007] IRLR 777.
[152] [1992] IRLR 219 CA.
[153] [1989] IRLR 259 CA.
[154] [1986] IRLR 391.

certain circumstances. A further issue is the use of restrictive covenants to deter employees from working for competing businesses and using the knowledge and skills gained whilst in previous employment.

3.5.2.1 **Not competing**

There is no general rule which, in the absence of an express term, restricts ex-employees from competing with their previous employer. If the former employer did not include an express term restricting the employees' activities, then they are unlikely to be able to claim that there is any sort of implied term that achieves the same result.[155] The position is more complicated when considering existing employees who are contemplating or actively setting up a business to compete with their present employer. In *Lancashire Fires Ltd v SA Lyons & Co Ltd*,[156] the Court of Appeal cited with approval a judgment of Lord Greene MR[157] in which he warned against the danger of 'laying down any general proposition and the necessity for considering each case on its facts'. However, the High Court has recently ruled that where a contact address list is maintained on the employer's email system and is backed up, that information belongs to the employer. Thus it cannot be removed or copied by employees for use outside.[158]

The obligations may be more extensive for some types of employees than others. In *Lancashire Fires* the younger brother of the company owner had obtained a loan from the company's principal supplier to set up in competition. He had also started to purchase the necessary premises and equipment. As a result he was held to have been in breach of the duty of fidelity. An individual does not breach an implied term of loyalty merely by indicating an intention to set up in competition with the employer, especially if any of the steps taken are in their own time. Thus two employees who wrote to a limited number of customers suggesting that they were about to start a competing business were held not to be in breach of such an implied term.[159] Other employers might find this a strange decision and understand why the employer in this case, having heard about the letter, dismissed the employees concerned. In *Adamson v B & L Cleaning Services Ltd*[160] an employee asked a customer to be put on a tendering list for a contract on which they were working when it was due for renewal. The EAT held that these actions amounted to a breach of the implied duty of fidelity.

Related to the issue of not competing is the making of secret profits from employment. Thus if an employee acts in such a way that the employer loses trust and confidence in them, summary dismissal may be justified. In *Neary and Neary v Dean of Westminster*[161] the claimants were dismissed for using their positions in the organisation to make secret profits. This conduct was held to undermine fatally the relationship of trust between the parties. In *Nottingham University v Fishel*[162] the court distinguished between an individual's fiduciary

---

[155] *Wallace Bogan & Co v Cove* [1997] IRLR 453 CA.
[156] [1997] IRLR 113 CA.
[157] *Hivac Ltd v Park Royal Scientific Instruments Ltd* [1946] Ch 169.
[158] *Pennwell Publishing Ltd v Ornstien* [2007] IRLR 700.
[159] See *Laughton and Hawley v Bapp Industrial Supplies Ltd* [1986] IRLR 245 and *Helmet Systems Ltd v Tunnard* [2007] IRLR 126.
[160] [1995] IRLR 193; see also *Marshall v Industrial Systems & Control Ltd* [1992] IRLR 294, where a company director making plans, and inducing another to join in those plans, to deprive their employer of their best customer, was held to have breached the duty of loyalty.
[161] [1999] IRLR 288.
[162] [2000] IRLR 471.

duty and the individual's obligation to maintain trust and confidence. This case concerned the earnings of a university academic from organisations other than his employer. A feature of a fiduciary relationship is the duty to act in the interests of another. This is not necessarily the case in an employment relationship, where there is no obligation on the employee to pursue the employer's interests above their own.[163] To decide whether the employment relationship and the fiduciary relationship coincide requires an examination of the particular circumstances. In this case the individual did not have a fiduciary relationship because there was no contractual obligation to seek work on behalf of the university, rather than for himself.[164]

3.5.2.2 Restrictive covenants

The proper approach to the issue of restraint of trade was summarised by Lord Parker in *Herbert Morris* v *Saxelby Ltd*,[165] when he stated:

> . . . two conditions must be fulfilled if the restraint is to be held valid. First, it must be reasonable in the interests of the contracting parties, and, secondly, it must be reasonable in the interests of the public. In the case of each condition [there is] a test of reasonableness. To be reasonable in the interests of the parties, the restraint must afford adequate protection to the party in whose favour it is imposed; to be reasonable in the interests of the public it must in no way be injurious to the public.
>
> With regard to the former test, I think it is clear that what is meant is that for a restraint to be reasonable in the interest of the parties it must afford *no more than* adequate protection to the party in whose favour it is imposed.

The court also drew a distinction between 'objective knowledge', which is the property of the employer, and 'subjective knowledge', which is the property of the employee. This latter might consist of information in a person's memory, rather than confidential information kept by the employer. Even this subjective knowledge is capable of being protected, although the court will look at each case on its own facts. The names and addresses of customers may be legitimate information to be protected, even if it is innocently remembered by the ex-employee, rather than deliberately taken from the employer.[166] However, there is a distinction between those covenants against competition which follow a sale of a business, including its goodwill, and those covenants designed to prevent ex-employees entering into competition with their previous employers.[167] Covenants concerning the latter are more likely to be interpreted strictly by the courts.

The view that a restraint clause must not provide more protection than is necessary is illustrated in *TSC Europe (UK) Ltd* v *Massey*.[168] In this case an ex-employee was subject to a clause that stopped the inducement of employees to leave the company. The clause was held to be unreasonable and unenforceable for two reasons. First, it applied to all employees and not just those who had particular skills or knowledge that were important to the business. Secondly, it applied to any employee who joined the company during the prohibited period,

---

[163] On the duty of employees to disclose their own misconduct see *Item Software Ltd* v *Fassihi* [2004] IRLR 928.

[164] However, he did have such a relationship in relation to other employees of the university out of whose work he made a profit. See also *Shepherd Investments* v *Walters* [2007] IRLR 110.

[165] [1916] AC 688 at p. 707 HL; see now *TFS Derivatives Ltd* v *Morgan* [2005] IRLR 246.

[166] See *SBJ Stephenson Ltd* v *Mandy* [2000] IRLR 233.

[167] See *Office Angels Ltd* v *Rainer-Thomas* [1991] IRLR 214.

[168] [1999] IRLR 22; see also *Wincanton Ltd* v *(1) Cranny; (2) SDM European Transport Ltd* [2000] IRLR 716 CA.

including those who joined after the plaintiff had left. The test of reasonableness is applied by considering the substance and not the form of the transaction, and by reference to all the facts and surrounding circumstances.[169] In this case, it was held to be too wide[170] and, therefore, unenforceable.[171]

The same approach is taken with respect to contractual clauses which limit an individual's ability to compete with their ex-employer. According to the Court of Appeal, the employer needs to establish that at the time the contract was made the nature of the relationship was such as to expose the employee to the kind of information capable of protection beyond the term of the contract.[172] Thus a clause which, on its true construction, prohibited an employee engaging in any business in the same industry, rather than from any business competing with the ex-employer, was wider than necessary to protect the legitimate interests of that employer. It should also be noted that it is only possible to remove an offending part of a covenant if it is a separate obligation to that which can be enforced.[173]

In *Rock Refrigeration*[174] a restrictive covenant which took effect upon the ending of the contract of employment 'howsoever arising' was not necessarily unreasonable. Nevertheless, in the event of the termination resulting from the employer's repudiatory breach of the contract, the employee would be released from their obligations under the contract. Similarly, a covenant which 'restricts individuals from competing in any aspect of a company's business being carried on at the date of the termination in which the employees were actually involved during their employment' was held to be reasonable.[175] A non-solicitation clause which prevented an ex-employee from dealing even with potential clients who were negotiating with the employer at the time the individual left employment was also held not to be too vague to be relied upon. This was the situation in *International Consulting Services (UK) Ltd* v *Hart*,[176] where an ex-employee approached a potential customer who had held some preliminary discussions about the provision of services. In this context, the discussions were held to be negotiations and were caught by the non-solicitation clause.

3.5.2.3 Confidential information

In *Faccenda Chicken*[177] employees set up a business delivering chickens to butchers, super-markets and catering operations and competed directly with their previous employer who had an identical operation. None of the employees had a restrictive covenant in their

---

[169] Reasonableness must be interpreted in accordance with what was in the contemplation of the parties at the date the contract was made: *Allan Janes LLP* v *Johal* [2006] IRLR 599.

[170] By way of contrast, a similar clause was held to be reasonable in *SBJ Stephenson Ltd* v *Mandy* [2000] IRLR 233, because the protection of the levels of investment in training employees and the stability of the workforce was a legitimate subject for a restrictive covenant.

[171] See also *Dawnay, Day & Co Ltd* v *de Braconier d'Alphen* [1997] IRLR 442 CA where a clause which purported to stop the solicitation of employees of all sorts, including junior staff, was held to be too wide to be enforceable.

[172] *Thomas* v *Farr plc* [2007] IRLR 419.

[173] *Scully UK Ltd* v *Lee* [1998] IRLR 259 CA; see also *Hollis & Co* v *Stocks* [2000] IRLR 712 CA, where a restriction on an employee not to work within ten miles of the ex-employer's office (a firm of solicitors) was interpreted as a restriction on working as a solicitor, rather than any employment, and was therefore not an unreasonable restraint of trade.

[174] *Rock Refrigeration Ltd* v *Jones and Seward Refrigeration Ltd* [1996] IRLR 675 CA.

[175] *Turner* v *Commonwealth & British Minerals Ltd* [2000] IRLR 114 – the fact that the employees were paid extra in return for agreeing to the restrictive covenant is not decisive, but is a legitimate factor to be taken into account; see also *Ward Evans Financial Services Ltd* v *Fox* [2002] IRLR 120 CA.

[176] [2000] IRLR 227.

[177] *Faccenda Chicken Ltd* v *Fowler* [1986] IRLR 69 CA.

previous contracts. The Court of Appeal addressed the apparent conflict between the duty of an employee not to disclose confidential information which had been obtained in the course of employment with the *prima facie* right of any person to exploit the experience and knowledge which they have acquired for the purpose of earning a living. Neil LJ set out the following legal principles:

1. Where the parties were, or had been, linked by a contract of employment, then the obligations of the employee are to be determined by that contract.

2. In the absence of express terms, the obligations of the employee with respect to the use of information are the subject of implied terms.

3. Whilst the employee remains in the employment of the employer, these obligations are included in the implied term of good faith or fidelity.[178]

4 The implied term which places an obligation on the individual as to conduct after the ending of the employment is more restricted in its application than that which imposes a general duty of good faith.[179]

5. In order to decide whether a particular item of information falls within an implied term to prevent its use or disclosure after employment has ceased, it is necessary to consider all the circumstances of the case.

In considering all the circumstances, a number of issues will be taken into account. First, the nature of the employment: if it is one that habitually uses confidential information there may be a higher standard of confidentiality required. Secondly, the nature of the information itself: only information that can be regarded as a 'trade secret' can be protected, rather than looking at the 'status' of the information. Thirdly, the steps that the employer had taken to impress upon the employee the confidentiality of the information. Finally, whether the relevant information can be isolated from other information which the employee is free to disclose or use.

For information to be classified as a trade secret, and therefore not to be disclosed, it is not incumbent upon an employer to point out to an employee the precise limits of what is sought to be made confidential. However, the closer an employee is to the 'inner circles' of decision-making, the more likely they are to know that information is confidential.[180] This issue presents particular problems for employees who wish to work elsewhere. There is a distinction between knowledge which an employer can show to be a trade secret, and therefore the employer's property, and information which is the result of the skill, experience and know-how accumulated by an individual in the course of their employment.[181] To be protected the information needs to be precise and specific enough for a separate body of objective knowledge to be identified, rather than a general claim to an accumulated body of knowledge which an employer claims to be confidential.[182]

---

[178] The duty of good faith will be broken if the employee makes, copies or memorises a list of the employer's customers for use after the end of employment.

[179] The court relied upon the judgments in *Printers & Finishers Ltd* v *Holloway* [1965] RPC 253 and *E Worsley & Co Ltd* v *Cooper* [1939] 1 All ER 290 to distinguish between those secrets which are really trade secrets and not to be revealed and those matters which are confidential whilst the employment subsists.

[180] As in *Lancashire Fires Ltd* v *SA Lyons & Co Ltd* [1997] IRLR 113 CA.

[181] See *Crowson Fabrics Ltd* v *Rider* [2008] IRLR 288.

[182] See *FSS Travel and Leisure Systems Ltd* v *Johnson* [1998] IRLR 382 CA and *Brooks* v *Olyslager OMS (UK) Ltd* [1998] IRLR 590 CA. On springboard relief until trial see *UBS Ltd* v *Vestra LLP* [2008] IRLR 965.

It is clear that an employer may be able to enforce an obligation of confidentiality against an individual who has made an unauthorised disclosure and used documents acquired in the course of employment. In *Camelot v Centaur Publications Ltd*[183] a copy of the draft accounts of the company which ran the National Lottery was sent by an unknown employee to an interested journalist. The information revealed, amongst other matters, increases in remuneration for some of the company's directors. The company asked the court to ensure that the leaked documents were returned, so that they could identify the individual who caused the leak. The Court of Appeal accepted that the case was not a whistleblowing one and held that it was in the public interest to enable the employer to discover a disloyal employee in their midst.

3.5.2.4 Public Interest Disclosure Act 1998

The Public Interest Disclosure Act 1998 amended ERA 1996 to provide some protection to workers who disclose information about certain matters. Section 43J ERA 1996 makes void any provision in an agreement, including a contract of employment, which attempts to stop the worker from making a protected disclosure. Section 43A ERA 1996 provides that a 'protected disclosure' is a 'qualifying disclosure', as defined in s. 43B, which is made in accordance with ss. 43C–43H. The qualifying disclosures defined in s. 43B are information about criminal offences, failure to comply with a legal obligation,[184] a miscarriage of justice, a danger to health and safety and damage to the environment. A likelihood of any of these events occurring is also a qualifying disclosure, as well as any information about concealment, or attempts to conceal, such information.

These disclosures must normally be made in 'good faith'[185] to an individual's employer or to some other person who has responsibility for the matter disclosed. The disclosure needs to be to these persons, to a legal adviser or to a prescribed person.[186] Sections 43G and 43H ERA 1996 impose strict rules about making disclosures in other circumstances. For example, apart from making the disclosure in good faith, the worker must reasonably believe that the information is true and not make disclosures for private gain. It must also be reasonable for the worker to make the disclosure.

Protection is given to a wide group of workers as defined in s. 43K ERA 1996.[187] Those who make a protected disclosure have the right not to be subject to detriment by any act, or failure to act, on the part of the employer by reason of the individual making the disclosure.[188] A dismissal for the same reason will be automatically unfair[189] as will selection for redundancy.[190] One of the problems for workers seeking to rely on this legislation is that there are

---

[183] [1998] IRLR 80 CA.
[184] See *Parkins v Sodexho Ltd* [2002] IRLR 109, *Babula v Waltham Forest College* [2007] IRLR 346 and *Hibbins v Hesters Way Project* [2009] IRLR 198.
[185] See s. 43C ERA 1996.
[186] See ss. 43D–43F ERA 1996 and the Public Interest Disclosure (Prescribed Persons) Order 1999, SI 1999/1549.
[187] See *Croke v Hydro Aluminium* [2007] ICR 1303.
[188] Section 47B ERA 1996. On the vicarious liability of employers see *Cumbria County Council v Carlisle-Morgan* [2007] IRLR 314. On compensation for injury to feelings see *Virgo Fidelis School v Boyle* [2004] IRLR 268.
[189] In *Miklaszewicz v Stolt Offshore Ltd* [2002] IRLR 344 an individual was dismissed, after the legislation came into effect, for making a disclosure some six years before. He was still held to be protected as the court held that it was the date of dismissal that triggered the employee's entitlement to protection, not the date of the disclosure. On the burden of proof see *Kuzel v Roche Ltd* [2008] IRLR 530.
[190] See ss. 103A and 105(6A) ERA 1996; Public Interest Disclosure (Compensation) Regulations 1999, SI 1999/1548 on the level of awards that may be given; there is no maximum figure set for compensation in such cases.

a number of hurdles which have to be overcome, including showing that one is acting in good faith[191] and had a reasonable belief in the existence of wrongdoing.[192]

3.6 Other sources of terms

3.6.1 Custom and practice

It is possible for terms to become incorporated into the contract of employment as a result of custom and practice. In *Sagar* v *Ridehalgh & Sons Ltd*[193] a weaver challenged a long-accepted practice in the textile industry of deducting pay for poor work. The weaver failed in the complaint because the court held that the practice had prevailed at the place of work for over 30 years. The practice was judged to be 'reasonable, certain and notorious' and, therefore, to have legal effect. There was a question about whether the practice could have effect if the individual was unaware of its existence. In *Sagar*, the court found it difficult to believe that the complainant did not know of its existence.

In *Duke* v *Reliance Systems Ltd*[194] it was held that a management policy could not become incorporated into a contract of employment on the grounds of custom and practice unless it had been shown that the policy has been drawn to the employees' attention and had been followed without exception for a 'substantial period'. These factors were later referred to as 'to be among the most important circumstances to be taken into account', but that all the other circumstances needed to be looked at. These included whether the 'substantial' period should be looked at in relation to these other circumstances to justify the inference that the policy had achieved the status of a contractual term. Additionally the issue of communication with the employees was one of the factors which supported the inference that the employers intended to become contractually bound by it.[195]

The need for the custom and practice to be reasonable, certain and notorious was further illustrated in *Henry* v *London General Transport Services*.[196] In this case the trade union came to an agreement with the employers about changes to terms and conditions of employment in preparation for a management buy-out. These changes resulted in reductions in pay and other less advantageous terms and conditions. There had been a tradition of at least annual negotiations between the employer and the trade union and agreement on changes. However, there was no express agreement that changes would automatically be incorporated into employees' individual contracts of employment. A number of employees, unhappy at the reductions, claimed unlawful deductions from their wages. The EAT held that, once the reasonableness, certainty and notoriety of the custom and practice was established it was to be presumed that the term represented the wishes and intentions of the parties concerned. This was not undermined by the fact that some individuals did not know of the practice or did not support it. Thus, in this case, the agreement was held to have become incorporated into the employees' individual contracts of employment.

---

[191] See *Street* v *Derbyshire Unemployed Workers Centre* [2004] IRLR 687.
[192] See *Bolton School* v *Evans* [2007] IRLR 140.
[193] [1931] 1 Ch 310 CA.
[194] [1982] IRLR 347.
[195] *Quinn* v *Calder Industrial Materials Ltd* [1996] IRLR 126.
[196] [2002] IRLR 472.

3.6.2 **Collective and workforce agreements**

Collective agreements are defined in s. 178(1) TULRCA 1992 as 'any agreement or arrange-ment made by or on behalf of one or more trade unions and one or more employers or employers' associations' concerning matters listed in s. 178(2) TULRCA 1992 (see Chapter 11). The first item on the list, in s. 178(2)(a), includes terms and conditions of employment. Collective agreements are presumed not to be legally enforceable contracts unless the agree-ment is in writing and contains a provision to that effect.[197] The result is that the vast majority of such agreements are not legally binding in themselves (see Chapter 11). However, they achieve legal effect if they become incorporated into the contract of employment. If the contract states, for example, that:

> The basic terms and conditions of your employment by this company are in accordance with and subject to the provisions of relevant agreements made between and on behalf of the Engineering Employers' Federation and the trade unions . . .[198]

then this is likely to be interpreted as an express provision incorporating the collective agreements negotiated between the employers and the trade unions (this issue is further considered in Chapter 11).[199]

Workforce agreements are an alternative mechanism for consulting and negotiating with employees when there is no trade union recognised for collective bargaining purposes (see Chapter 11). The specific requirements for reaching such agreements are contained in the Working Time Regulations 1998[200] and the Maternity and Parental Leave etc. Regulations 1999.[201] In both cases they are aimed at creating an opportunity for the parties to agree a more flexible approach to the implementation of the requirements of the regulations. A workforce agreement[202] must apply to all the relevant members of a workforce or group and the agreement needs to be signed by all the individual members of the workforce or the group, or their representatives. The exception being in the case of smaller employers with 20 or fewer employees. In this case the agreement can be signed either by the appropriate representatives or by the majority of the workforce.

3.7 **Variations in terms**

Section 4 ERA 1996 provides rules for notifying changes in the s. 1 ERA 1996 statement of terms and conditions. The employer is required to give the employee a written statement of the changes at the earliest opportunity and, in any event, not later than one month after the change.[203] Section 4(3)(b) ERA 1996 provides for this to be done earlier if the person is required to work outside the United Kingdom for a period of more than one month. If the

---

[197] Section 179(1) TULRCA 1992.
[198] Quoted in *Alexander* v *Standard Telephones & Cables Ltd* [1991] IRLR 286.
[199] Collective agreements can be arrived at, and incorporated into the contract of employment, by individual employers or by employers' associations negotiating with individual trade unions or groups of unions; see, e.g., *Hamilton* v *Futura Floors Ltd* [1990] IRLR 478.
[200] SI 1998/1833.
[201] SI 1999/3312.
[202] See Sch. 1 Maternity and Parental Leave etc. Regulations 1999.
[203] Section 4(3)(a) ERA 1996.

change relates to a change of employer and continuity of employment is not broken, then the new employer is not required to give a new statement, but merely to inform the employee of the change in circumstances,[204] specifying the date on which continuous employment began.[205]

There are a number of ways in which an employer may seek to change the terms of a contract of employment. The most straightforward would be to achieve mutual agreement to the changes with the employees and/or their representatives. If an employer is unable or unwilling to obtain this agreement, they may attempt to do so unilaterally. One way is to dismiss the employees and then offer them new contracts of employment containing the new terms. The employer will have satisfied their common law obligations if they give the contractually required period of notice of termination to their employees. The danger with this approach is that employers may leave themselves open to claims for unfair dismissal and redundancy and a lack of consultation concerning potential redundancies (see Chapter 9). In *GMB* v *Man Truck & Bus UK Ltd*[206] the respondent company had been formed by a merger of two other businesses. In order to harmonise terms and conditions the employees were given notice of dismissal and then offered immediate re-employment on new terms and conditions. The EAT held that the employer had failed to consult as required by s. 188 TULRCA 1992, which applies where there are collective dismissals.[207]

If the employer seeks to impose new terms then this may be interpreted as a repudiatory breach of contract, which the employee may decide to accept or not. One exception to this would be if the employer has a contractual right to make unilateral changes.[208] In *Farrant* v *The Woodroffe School*,[209] the employer tried to alter the job description of an employee on the mistaken advice that they were entitled to do so under the terms of the contract of employment. Even though the advice from the local authority was incorrect, the subsequent dismissal of the employee was held to be fair because it was reasonable for the employer to act on the advice received.[210] A second exception might be if the courts were willing to imply a term into the contract which permitted the employer to make a change. In *Jones* v *Associated Tunnelling Co Ltd*[211] the EAT concluded that there was an implied term to the effect that the employer had the right to change the employee's place of work to another location within reasonable daily commuting distance. The nature of the work required this change and the term was implied in order to give the contract business efficacy.

In *Jones*,[212] the employer also unsuccessfully claimed that the employee had assented to the change in the contract by continuing to work for another 12 months and not objecting. This argument was also used in *Aparau* v *Iceland Frozen Foods plc*,[213] where the EAT adopted the same approach. There was a need for

---

[204] Section 4(6) ERA 1996.
[205] Section 4(8) ERA 1996.
[206] [2000] IRLR 636.
[207] See Chapter 9.
[208] See *Airlie* v *City of Edinburgh District Council* [1996] IRLR 516.
[209] [1998] IRLR 176.
[210] See also *Port of Sheerness Ltd and Medway Ports Ltd* v *Brachers* [1997] IRLR 214, where the employer's legal advisers were held liable for giving negligent advice on handling redundancies.
[211] [1981] IRLR 477.
[212] *Ibid.*
[213] [1996] IRLR 119 EAT; see also [2000] IRLR 196 CA on a separate point.

great caution in reaching the conclusion that an employee has, by merely continuing an employment without any overt change or overt acceptance of terms which the employer is seeking to impose, truly accepted those terms so as to vary the contract.

In this case a shop worker was issued with a new contract containing a mobility clause, which was not activated for a further 12 months. It could not be said that the employee accepted the change by continuing performance when the impact of the change was some time away. Similarly, continuing to work under protest should not be construed as acceptance.[214] More recently, in *Harlow v Artemis Ltd*[215] the High Court confirmed that where an employer purports to change terms unilaterally that do not immediately impinge on the employee, then the fact that the employee continues to work does not mean that he can be taken to have accepted the variation. Here it was decided that an enhanced redundancy policy formed part of the contract of employment.

In some situations it may be vital to distinguish between the variation of an existing contract and the creation of a new one; for example, for the purposes of making a claim within a time limit which runs from the date of termination. According to the EAT, the task in each case is to determine the parties' intentions. Where it is clear from the documentation that the parties have agreed to implement changes via a fresh contract, that is decisive. However, if the change is not of a fundamental nature the proper inference is that there is a variation unless the court or tribunal is satisfied that there was, objectively viewed, an express agreement that the mechanism to be adopted was the termination and new contract route.[216] Subsequently the EAT has confirmed that fundamental as well as minor changes can be effected by consensual variation.[217]

In cases of pressing need the employer may be justified in changing the employees' terms and conditions. In *Catamaran Cruisers Ltd v Williams*[218] a company was in financial difficulties and wanted to introduce less favourable terms and conditions. The EAT thought that they were able to do this but the lay members were obviously concerned about the outcome and stated that they wished

> to record that much of recent employment law has been to protect employees against arbitrary changes of their terms and conditions of employment and that this, as a principle, must stand . . . and that an employer must demonstrate . . . if he dismisses an employee for failing to accept changes of their terms and conditions of employment his actions must fall within the bounds of reasonableness.

Sometimes employers make changes which are the result of management policy rather than a change in the contract of employment. If an employer has a code of practice on staff sickness which, for example, included procedures for monitoring different types of absence, a decision to alter the procedure so that there were more frequent checks might amount to a change of policy which the employer could carry out unilaterally.[219] Lord Woolf summed up the approach:[220]

---

[214] *Rigby v Ferodo Ltd* [1987] IRLR 516 HL.
[215] [2008] IRLR 629.
[216] *Cumbria County Council v Dow (No 2)* [2008] IRLR 109.
[217] See *Potter v North Cumbria Acute NHS Trust* [2009] IRLR 900.
[218] [1994] IRLR 386.
[219] *Wandsworth London Borough Council v D'Silva* [1998] IRLR 193 CA.
[220] *Ibid.* at p. 197.

The general position is that contracts of employment can only be varied by agreement. However, in the employment field an employer or for that matter an employee can reserve the ability to change a particular aspect of the contract unilaterally by notifying the other party as part of the contract that this is the situation. However, clear language is required to reserve to one party unusual power of this sort. In addition, the Court is unlikely to favour an interpretation which does more than enable a party to vary contractual provisions with which that party is required to comply.

Chapter summary

This chapter examined the express and implied terms that can be found in contracts of employment and identified the types of information that an employer is required by law to provide in writing. It also outlined the possible individual and collective sources of obligations and discussed the particular duties imposed by statute and the common law on both employers and employees. Finally, it mentioned the process by which contractual terms can be lawfully varied.

Further reading

Barmes, L. 'The Continuing Conceptual Crisis in the Common Law of the Contract of Employment' (2004) 67(3) *Modern Law Review* 435.

Collins, H., Ewing, K. and McColgan, A. *Labour Law: Text and Materials*: Hart Publishing, 2005, Chapter 2.

Deakin, S. and Morris, G. *Labour Law*: 5th edn, Hart Publishing, 2009, Chapter 4.

Freedland, M. *The Personal Employment Contract*: Oxford University Press, 2003.

www.acas.org.uk

www.berr.gov.uk/

Visit **www.mylawchamber.co.uk/sargeant**
to access legal updates, live weblinks and practice
exam questions to test yourself on this chapter.

mylawchamber
unrivalled support for legal education

4 Termination of employment

4.1 Introduction

There are a number of ways in which a contract of employment, like any other contract, can be brought to an end. It can occur because the performance of the contract becomes impossible or because one of the parties brings it to an end. This may be done by voluntary notice given by the employee or by his employment being terminated, by notice or otherwise, by the employer. In addition, statute provides some protection for employees who are dismissed.

4.2 Termination of the contract not amounting to dismissal

4.2.1 Frustration

The common law doctrine of frustration deals with situations where, as a result of some event outside the control of the parties, the contract becomes impossible to perform, at least in the way that the parties intended. This view was stated by Lord Radcliffe in *Davies Contractors Ltd* v *Fareham Urban District Council*:[1]

> . . . frustration occurs whenever the law recognises that without default of either party a contractual obligation has become incapable of being performed because the circumstances in which performance is called for would render it a thing radically different from that which was undertaken by the contract.

In *Paal Wilson & Co* v *Partenreederei Hannah Blumenthal*[2] the court held that there were two essential factors which must be present to frustrate a contract. These were that:

1. There must be some unforeseen change in the outside or extraneous circumstances, not provided for by the parties, which stopped the performance of the contract.
2. The outside or extraneous event should have occurred without the fault or default of either party to the contract.

Such a situation might be a custodial sentence. In *FC Shepherd & Co Ltd* v *Jerrom*[3] a contract of apprenticeship was held to be frustrated when an individual was sentenced to a

---

[1] [1956] AC 696 HL at p. 728.
[2] [1983] 1 AC 854 HL.
[3] [1986] IRLR 358 CA; see also *Four Seasons Healthcare Ltd* v *Maughan* [2005] IRLR 324.

period in a young offenders' institution for his part in a motorcycle gang fight. This was an event that was capable of rendering the performance of the contract impossible. The fact that the frustration must have occurred without the fault of either party means, according to the court, that the party who asserts that the performance of the contract has been frustrated must show that the frustration was not caused by his own act, and the person against whom frustration is asserted cannot rely on his own misconduct as an answer.

The following principles can be derived from these and other cases:[4]

1. The court must guard against too easy an application of the doctrine.

2. Although it is not necessary to decide that frustration occurred on a particular date, it may help the court to decide whether or not there was a true frustration situation.

3. There are a number of factors which may help to decide the issue:[5] the length of the previous employment; how long the employment would have continued;[6] the nature of the job; the nature, effect and length of the illness or disabling event; the needs of the employer for the work to be done and the need for a replacement to do it; the risk to the employer of incurring obligations related to redundancy or unfair dismissal of the replacement employee; whether wages have continued to be paid; the acts of the employer in relation to the employment, including dismissal of the employee; and whether in all the circumstances an employer could be expected to wait any longer.

4. The party alleging frustration should not be able to rely on that frustration if it were caused by that party.

Long-term sickness is capable of frustrating the contract of employment. However, an assessment needs to be made about whether any long-term incapacity has become a disability, thus providing the individual with protection under the Disability Discrimination Act 1995 (see Chapter 6). If there are provisions in the contract about long-term sickness, it may be difficult to argue that the incapacity is an unforeseen event,[7] although it is unlikely that a total incapacity arising from an illness could have been foreseen.[8] Frustration takes place because of events that have happened so it is not possible to argue that a contract has been frustrated by the likelihood of an event happening in the future. Thus when an employee returns to work after a heart attack, it is not possible to argue frustration on the grounds that he might have a second heart attack in the future.[9]

4.2.2 Death of the employer

The death of either party may frustrate a contract, but certain tribunal proceedings may continue and be defended by the personal representative of the deceased employer.[10] These include claims for itemised pay statements, guarantee payments, protection from detriment,

---

[4] See *Williams* v *Watson Luxury Coaches Ltd* [1990] IRLR 164.

[5] Some of which derive from *The Egg Stores (Stamford Hill)* v *Leibovici* [1976] IRLR 376, which considered the issues connected with the fairness of dismissing absentees.

[6] This is not to say that short-term contracts are not capable of being frustrated; see *Hart* v *RN Marshall & Sons (Bulwell) Ltd* [1977] IRLR 50.

[7] See *Villella* v *MFI Furniture Centres Ltd* [1999] IRLR 468.

[8] *Nottcutt* v *Universal Equipment Co (London) Ltd* [1986] IRLR 218 CA.

[9] *Conform (Darwen) Ltd* v *Bell* [1981] IRLR 195.

[10] See art. 9 Employment Tribunals (Extension of Jurisdiction) Order 1994, SI 1994/1623.

time off work,[11] maternity rights, the right to a written statement of reasons for dismissal and those rights relating to unfair dismissal, redundancy payments and insolvency protection.[12] Where a claim under these headings accrues after the employer's death, then it will be treated as a liability of the deceased employer and as having accrued before the death.[13]

4.2.3 Voluntary resignation

This refers to a situation where the employee voluntarily resigns with or without notice.[14] It is not always clear whether an employee has resigned voluntarily or as a result of pressure from the employer.[15] As was held in *Sheffield v Oxford Controls Co Ltd*,[16] there is a principle of law which states that:

> where an employee resigns and that resignation is determined upon by him because he prefers to resign rather than be dismissed (the alternative having been expressed to him by the employer in the terms of the threat that if he does not resign he will be dismissed) the mechanics of the resignation do not cause that to be other than a dismissal.

This approach was followed by the Court of Appeal in *Jones v Mid-Glamorgan County Council*,[17] which described it as a 'principle of the utmost flexibility which is willing . . . to recognise a dismissal when it sees it'.[18] There was no dismissal, however, in *International Computers Ltd v Kennedy*,[19] which also involved a redundancy situation. Advice to employees to make every effort to find other jobs as quickly as possible was not equivalent to saying 'resign or be dismissed'. The invitation to resign was too imprecise in relation to the ultimate dismissal of individuals. It would also appear that there is no dismissal when an employee resigns on terms offered by an employer's disciplinary subcommittee. In *Staffordshire County Council v Donovan*[20] the EAT stated:

> It seems to us that it would be most unfortunate if, in a situation where the parties are seeking to negotiate in the course of disciplinary proceedings and an agreed form of resignation is worked out by the parties, one of the parties should be able to say subsequently that the fact that the agreement was reached in the course of disciplinary proceedings entitles the employee thereafter to say that there was a dismissal.

Two issues here are the extent to which employees must make clear their decision to resign and whether the employer has any obligations arising out of that decision. Often contracts of employment require a resignation to be effected in a certain way, for example by putting it in writing or directing it to a certain individual. *Ely v YKK Fasteners*[21] involved an employee

---

[11] Excluding ss. 58–60 ERA 1996 for time off for occupational pension trustees.
[12] Section 206(1) ERA 1996.
[13] Section 207 ERA 1996.
[14] This may, in certain circumstances, amount to constructive dismissal: see below.
[15] See *Martin v MBS Fastenings (Glynwed) Distribution Ltd* [1983] IRLR 198 CA; this was not the issue at the Court of Appeal, but in the lower courts there was a question as to whether the employee had resigned in anticipation of the result of a disciplinary hearing or had been invited to resign by the employer.
[16] [1979] IRLR 133 at p. 135. See now *Sandhu v Jan de Rijk Transport Ltd* [2007] IRLR 519 CA.
[17] [1997] IRLR 685 CA; [1997] ICR 815 CA.
[18] See also *Allders International Ltd v Parkins* [1981] IRLR 68, where an employee was given the option of resigning or the employer calling in the CID to investigate allegations of theft.
[19] [1981] IRLR 28.
[20] [1981] IRLR 108.
[21] [1993] IRLR 500 CA.

who was considering emigrating to Australia. The employee told his employer of his plans and that he had applied for a job there. Eventually the employer took steps to replace him. When the individual decided not to emigrate he informed his employers. By then he had been replaced and the employer regarded the individual's employment as being at an end. The question was whether there had been a resignation or a dismissal. It was held that there was a dismissal and that the reason for this was the employee's late notification to the employer that he had changed his mind about resigning. This dismissal was for 'some other substantial reason' (see below) within the meaning of s. 98(1)(b) ERA 1996.

Sometimes employees resign on the spur of the moment because they have become angry or discontented about some actions of the employer. This occurred in *Kwik-Fit (GB) Ltd v Lineham*[22] where, after an argument, the employee threw his keys down on to a counter and walked out. The EAT held that there was no ambiguity in the words used by the employee. When a resignation occurs there is no obligation, except in special circumstances, for the employer to do anything but accept that decision. Words spoken in the heat of the moment or as a result of pressure on an employee may, however, amount to special circumstances. Where there are such special circumstances the employer should allow a day or two to elapse before accepting the resignation at face value. During this time information may arise as to whether the resignation was really intended. Not to investigate may open the employer to the risk of new facts emerging at an employment tribunal hearing which may cast doubt on the intention to resign. Where there are no special circumstances arising out of a decision made in the heat of the moment or as a result of employer pressure, the employer is entitled to take the employee's words at face value and is not required to look behind them or interpret them as a 'reasonable employer' might. Thus, in *Sothern v Franks Charlesly & Co,*[23] the words 'I am resigning' could be taken at face value, but in *Barclay v City of Glasgow District Council,*[24] the resignation by an employee with learning difficulties was held to constitute a special circumstance even though unambiguous words of resignation had been used.[25]

4.2.4 **Termination by agreement**

Termination by mutual consent is an important concept that has been widely used by employers in order to reduce the number of staff. It will usually take the form of a financial inducement in excess of any statutory entitlement to make leaving attractive. One common form is that of early retirement, where older workers are induced to leave the workforce by the offer of enhanced retirement packages. This was the situation in *Birch and Humber v The University of Liverpool,*[26] where the employer invited applications for early retirement as part of a staff reduction exercise. The two applicants were amongst those who applied and were accepted. Subsequently they sought redundancy payments. The employment tribunal was first faced with the question of whether they had been dismissed. It was held that, because

---

[22] [1992] IRLR 156.

[23] [1981] IRLR 278 CA.

[24] [1983] IRLR 313.

[25] See also *Sovereign House Security Services Ltd v Savage* [1989] IRLR 115 CA, where the words 'jacking the job in' spoken in a heated moment were held not to be a resignation.

[26] [1985] IRLR 165 CA; see also *Scott v Coalite Fuels and Chemicals Ltd* [1988] IRLR 131 which also involved individuals taking voluntary early retirement; the EAT followed *Birch and Humber* in holding that the decision as to whether someone had been dismissed was a question of fact for the employment tribunal to decide.

the retirement of any individual was subject to the employer's approval, then it was that approval which amounted to a dismissal, i.e. when the employer wrote to the employees stating when their employment would end, a dismissal took place. The appeal to the EAT was successful and the Court of Appeal also held that there had been a mutual agreement to terminate. The acceptance of the applications could not be divorced from the formal applications to retire. Purchas LJ stated that, 'in my judgment, dismissal . . . is not consistent with free, mutual consent, bringing a contract of employment to an end'.

The important question is whether the employer and the employee have freely agreed to end the contract of employment. In *Igbo* v *Johnson Matthey Chemicals Ltd*[27] there was a clause in a contract which an employer required an employee to sign before extended leave was granted. This stated that a failure to return on the due date would lead to the contract being automatically terminated. The employee was ill at the time she was due to return and, despite the submission of a medical certificate, the employer took the view that this failure terminated the contract. It was argued that there was no dismissal, but a consensual termination. The Court of Appeal rejected this because of its impact on (now) s. 203(1) ERA 1996, which provides that any agreement designed to exclude or limit the operation of the Act or stopping an individual from bringing proceedings before an employment tribunal was void. The clause that the employee had been required to sign attempted to limit her potential claim for unfair dismissal under the ERA 1996.[28] In *Logan Salton* v *Durham County Council*[29] an employee who, after he became aware that a report recommended his summary dismissal, negotiated a written leaving agreement with the employer. He subsequently claimed that this agreement was made under duress. The EAT refused to accept this and distinguished the case from *Igbo* by holding that the agreement was not part of the contract of employment or a variation of it, but a separate contract that was entered into willingly, without duress and after proper advice and for good consideration.

4.3 Termination of the contract by dismissal

4.3.1 Meaning of dismissal

For statutory purposes s. 95 ERA 1996 provides that a person is dismissed by the employer if:

1. The contract under which the individual is employed is terminated by the employer with, or without, notice.

2. The person is employed under a limited-term contract which terminates by virtue of the limiting event without being renewed under the same contract (see Chapter 3). There are three types of limiting event: the expiry of a fixed term; the performance of a specific task; or the occurrence of an event or failure of an event to occur.[30]

3. The employee terminates the contract, with or without notice, as a result of the employer's conduct. This last situation is commonly referred to as constructive dismissal.

[27] [1986] IRLR 215 CA.
[28] See also *Tracey* v *Zest Equipment Co Ltd* [1992] IRLR 268, where the clause stated that 'the company will assume that you have terminated your employment with us' if there was a failure to return to work on the due date; this was held to be too imprecise to be legally binding.
[29] [1989] IRLR 99.
[30] 'Limited term contracts' and 'limiting event' are defined in s. 235(2A) and (2B) ERA 1996 respectively.

As with issues concerning voluntary resignation and mutual agreement (see above), employment tribunals may be asked to decide whether words used by an employer constitute dismissal. For example, in *Tanner* v *DT Kean*[31] an employer used the words: 'That's it, you're finished with me.' The employee claimed that this was a dismissal, but the employment tribunal held that the words were an expression of annoyance and a reprimand. They considered what a reasonable employee would take the words to mean in the circumstances. The EAT stated that, in order to arrive at the correct meaning of the words, one could look at events that preceded the words spoken as well as those which followed, in order to determine whether the employer intended to bring the contract to an end.

4.3.2 **Wrongful dismissal**

The common law concept of wrongful dismissal may not be a fruitful avenue for employees to follow, unless, as in *Clark* v *BET plc*,[32] the individual is entitled to a long period of notice.[33] This is because damages will normally be limited to those losses arising out of the breach of contract, i.e. the loss of the notice period. However, this may include the loss of benefits that might have accrued during that notice period. In *Silvey* v *Pendragon plc*[34] the employee was dismissed for reasons of redundancy some 12 days before his 55th birthday, when certain pension rights would have accrued to him. Although the employee was given 12 weeks' pay in lieu of notice there was no provision for such a payment in his contract of employment. The failure to give him 12 weeks' notice was held to be a repudiatory breach of the contract. The court held that he was not only entitled to damages consisting of wages or salary, but also to the value of any pension rights which would have accrued during the period of notice. There was no difference in principle between lost pension rights and lost pay. Secondly, any entitlement to non-contractual damages will be limited by the common law duty to mitigate one's losses. It may, however, be the only action possible if an employee has less than one year's continuous employment and is thus debarred from pursuing a claim for unfair dismissal in accordance with Part X ERA 1996.

It is not entirely clear what the effect of an employer's breach is. The alternatives seem to be, first, that it results in an automatic termination of the contract of employment. This might seem reasonable as a breach which consists of a wrongful dismissal is likely to have the effect of destroying the basis of mutual trust and confidence between the employer and employee. The problem with this approach is that it makes wrongful dismissal a special case when compared to the way that the law of contract would normally treat a breach of contract. This 'normal' route is the second alternative, which is that it is the innocent party's choice as to whether to accept the repudiation and terminate the contract. In *Sanders* v *Ernest A Neale Ltd*[35] it was explicitly held that a repudiation of the contract of employment was an exception to the 'normal rule' that an unaccepted repudiation did not discharge the contract. Wrongful dismissal is a breach of the employee's contract of employment and terminates the contract without the need for acceptance by the employee.

---

[31] [1978] IRLR 110.

[32] [1997] IRLR 348; the notice entitlement was three years.

[33] See also *University of Oxford* v *(1) Humphries; (2) Associated Examining Board* [2000] IRLR 183 CA, which was a case where a university employee had a tenured post which would continue until he retired.

[34] [2001] IRLR 685 CA.

[35] [1974] ICR 565.

Although an employee might refuse to accept that the contract is at an end, the reality is that they may have little choice in the matter. This dilemma was exemplified in *Gunton* v *London Borough of Richmond upon Thames*,[36] where it was held that the employer had repudiated the contract of employment and a wrongful dismissal had taken place. The Court of Appeal thought that the individual ought to be able to decide whether to accept the repudiation of the contract, but stated that:

> this practical basis for according an election to the injured party has no reality in relation to a contract of service where the repudiation takes the form of an express and direct termination of the contract in contravention of its terms. I would describe this as a total repudiation which is at once destructive of the contractual relationship.

The problem for the wronged individual is that the court will not allow them to claim pay for work not done, i.e. after their contract has been repudiated.[37] Moreover the claim for damages for wrongful dismissal cannot continue beyond the time when the employer could lawfully have brought the contract to an end.[38] This contrasts with the approach of the courts when an employer unilaterally varies a term of the contract of employment, such as a reduction of wages. Such an event is likely to be a repudiatory action by the employer. In *Rigby* v *Ferodo Ltd*[39] an employee elected to continue working after the employer reduced his wages. Although the employer's action was a repudiatory breach of the contract of employment, the contract did not automatically end unless the employee accepted the breach as a repudiation. The employee had made known his objections and so it could not be held that there was an implied acceptance of the breach. Unlike cases of outright dismissal and an employee walking out, there was no reason why the contract of employment should be treated any differently from any other contract. Generally an unaccepted repudiation leaves the contractual obligations of the parties unaffected.

4.3.3 **Notice**

At common law employment is liable to be determined by 'reasonable' periods of notice.[40] If there is no express term to that effect in the contract of employment then it may be implied.[41]

Statute has limited the freedom of action of employers in giving, or not giving, notice of dismissal to their employees. The employee has statutory rights to a minimum notice period.[42] These are an entitlement to one week's notice for employees who have been continuously employed for at least one month and with less than two years' continuous employment, with an extra week for each year of continuous employment up to not less than 12 weeks' notice for continuous employment of 12 years or more. By way of contrast, employers are entitled to at least one week's notice of termination from employees who have been continuously employed for at least one month.[43] Additionally, any requirements for consultation with employees or their representatives, in redundancy or transfer situations

---

[36] [1980] IRLR 321 CA.
[37] See *Alexander* v *Standard Telephones and Cables Ltd* [1991] IRLR 286.
[38] See Ralph Gibson LJ in *Boyo* v *London Borough of Lambeth* [1995] IRLR 50 CA.
[39] [1987] IRLR 516 HL.
[40] See *McClelland* v *Northern Ireland Health Services Board* [1957] 2 All ER 129 HL.
[41] See, e.g., *Masiak* v *City Restaurants (UK) Ltd* [1999] IRLR 780.
[42] Section 86(1) ERA 1996.
[43] Section 86(2) ERA 1996.

(see Chapter 9), may inhibit the employer from giving notice until the appropriate time. None of this affects more generous contractual arrangements or the rights of either party to treat the contract as terminated without notice as a result of the other's conduct.[44]

The contract of employment continues to subsist during the notice period. The statutory rules contemplate the contract being brought to an end by one of the parties. It follows, therefore, that the ending of the contract through the doctrine of frustration, which occurs through no fault or design of the parties, will exclude any rules relating to notice periods.[45] Employees have the right to be paid during their notice period even if there is no work for them, provided that they are ready and willing to work. Pay is also protected if the notice period coincides with absence from work because of sickness, pregnancy, childbirth, parental or adoption leave or holiday leave.[46] An employer is not required, however, to pay for absences due to time off taken in accordance with Part VI ERA 1996,[47] or for trade union duties and activities specified in ss. 168 and 170 TULRCA 1992, or for taking part in strike action during the notice period, if it is the employee that has given notice.[48]

The ERA 1996 does not prevent an employee from accepting a payment in lieu of notice but an employer must have contractual authority for insisting on such a payment. Without such authority a payment in lieu of notice will be construed as damages for the failure to provide proper notice.[49] Thus a payment in lieu can properly terminate a contract of employment if the contract provides for such a payment or the parties agree that the employee will accept a payment in lieu, provided the payment relates to a period no shorter than that of the notice to which the employee would be entitled either under the contract of employment or s. 86(1) ERA 1996.[50] The date of termination at common law is the day notice expires or the day wages in lieu are accepted.

4.3.4 Summary dismissal

The right to dismiss summarily, i.e. without giving notice, may be an express or an implied term of the contract of employment. If it is an express term then the reason for the dismissal needs to come within the contractual definition of gross misconduct. Thus, in *Dietman* v *London Borough of Brent*,[51] a clause in the contract defined gross misconduct, for which instant dismissal would result, as 'misconduct of such a nature that the authority is justified in no longer tolerating the continued presence at the place of work of the employee who commits the offence'. After an inquiry the employee was found grossly negligent in her duties. The court held, however, that gross negligence did not come within the contractual definition of gross misconduct and that, therefore, the employee had been wrongfully dismissed.

The fact that a dismissal is without notice, or without sufficient notice, does not in itself render it unfair in statutory terms, but the lack of notice may render it a breach of the terms of the contract and a wrongful dismissal.[52] It is likely that the summary nature of the

---

[44] Section 86(6) ERA 1996.
[45] *GF Sharp & Co Ltd* v *McMillan* [1998] IRLR 632.
[46] Sections 88–89 ERA 1996. See *Burlo* v *Langley* [2007] IRLR 145.
[47] Such as time off for public duties, looking for work and care of dependants.
[48] Section 91(1)–(2) ERA 1996.
[49] *Cerberus* v *Rowley* [2001] IRLR 160.
[50] *Ginsberg Ltd* v *Parker* [1988] IRLR 483.
[51] [1988] IRLR 299 CA.
[52] See *BSC Sports & Social Club* v *Morgan* [1987] IRLR 391.

dismissal can only be justified as a response to actions which breach an important term of the contract in such a way as to undermine the employment relationship, including the duty of mutual trust and confidence. In *Laws v London Chronicle (Indicator Newspapers) Ltd*[53] Lord Evershed MR stated that the question was 'whether the conduct complained of is such as to show the servant to have disregarded the essential conditions of the contract of service'. A more modern view was expressed in *Neary and Neary v Dean of Westminster*[54] where Lord Jauncey stated that:

> conduct amounting to gross misconduct justifying dismissal must so undermine the trust and confidence which is inherent in the particular contract of employment that the master should no longer be required to retain the servant in his employment.

The conduct affecting the basis of mutual trust and confidence between the parties needs to be serious.[55] A situation where an employee appeared to be provoked into swearing at an employer and was then dismissed was held to be a wrongful dismissal, because the employer had already decided to dismiss the employee prior to the incident.[56] An example of where the courts have held a summary dismissal for gross misconduct to be acceptable is when an employee accesses confidential information, to which they are not entitled, for illegitimate purposes. In *Denco Ltd v Joinson*[57] an employee, who was a trade union representative, obtained information relating to the employer's business and other employees' salaries. The EAT held that this was no different from going into an office, for which he had no authorisation, picking up a key off the desk and unlocking a filing cabinet to take out confidential information.

If employers do not invoke the right to end the contract within a reasonable period, they will be taken to have waived their rights and can only seek damages. What is a reasonable period will depend on the facts of the particular case. In *Allders International v Parkins*[58] it was held that nine days was too long a period to be allowed to pass in relation to an allegation of stealing before deciding what to do about the alleged repudiatory conduct.

Finally, there may be an issue as to whether an individual is entitled to payment in lieu of notice after an instant dismissal. In *T & K Home Improvements Ltd v Skilton*[59] a contractual term entitled the employer to terminate an employee's contract 'with immediate effect' if he failed to reach his sales targets in any one month. However, such a phrase was held not to deprive the employee of the right to the three months' notice to which the contract entitled him. There was evidence elsewhere in the contract of terms which specifically deprived him of the right to a payment in lieu in certain situations, but these did not apply in this case.

4.3.5 Remedies for wrongful dismissal

A wrongful dismissal is a dismissal without notice or with inadequate notice in circumstances where proper notice should have been given. The expression also covers dismissals which are in breach of agreed procedures. Thus where there is a contractual disciplinary procedure, an

---

[53] [1959] 2 All ER 285 CA.
[54] [1999] IRLR 288.
[55] The gross misconduct must be examined in relation to the particular job and does not necessarily mean that the employee could not be employed elsewhere: see *Hamilton v Argyll and Clyde Health Board* [1993] IRLR 99.
[56] *Wilson v Racher* [1974] ICR 428 CA.
[57] [1991] IRLR 63.
[58] [1981] IRLR 68.
[59] [2000] IRLR 595 CA.

employee may be able to obtain an injunction (interdict in Scotland) or declaration from the courts so as to prevent a dismissal or declare a dismissal void if the procedure has not been followed.[60] However, an injunction will only be granted if the court is convinced that the employer's repudiation has not been accepted, that the employer has sufficient trust and confidence in the employee, and that damages would not be an adequate remedy.[61]

The problem with seeking an injunction to prevent an employer taking steps which might lead to a repudiatory breach is that it might have the same effect as an order for specific performance, i.e. stopping certain actions might have the same effect as ordering the employer to behave differently. This did not inhibit the granting of an interlocutory injunction in *Peace v City of Edinburgh Council*.[62] The case involved a teacher who was subject to a disciplinary procedure. The employer was stopped from introducing a new procedure which would have been in breach of the contract of employment. The court concluded that they were intervening in a choice between alternative schemes, rather than enforcing mutual co-operation. The individual was suspended, but the employment contract remained in existence.[63] In *Anderson v Pringle of Scotland Ltd*[64] the employers wanted to change the method of selecting individuals for redundancy from a 'last in first out' basis to a more discretionary one. The 'last in first out' formula had been part of a collective agreement which was incorporated into the employees' contracts of employment. The court granted an interim interdict (injunction) prohibiting the employers from using any other method for selection. It acknowledged the issue of specific performance but held that the employment relationship continued and the decision was about the mechanisms of dismissal rather than the principle. Lord Prosser stated that:

> In the contemporary world, where even reinstatement is a less inconceivable remedy, intervention before dismissal must in my view be seen as a matter of discretion, rather than an impossibility.[65]

Since the courts are reluctant to enforce a contract of employment, in the vast majority of cases the employee's remedy will lie in damages for breach of contract. A person who suffers a wrongful dismissal is entitled to be compensated for such loss as arises naturally from the breach and for any loss which was reasonably foreseeable by the parties as being likely to arise from it. Hence an employee will normally recover only the amount of wages lost between the date of the wrongful dismissal and the date when the contract could lawfully have been terminated.[66]

The principle that damages resulting from a wrongful dismissal should put an individual in the same position as if the contract had been performed does not apply where the failure to give contractual notice results in the loss of opportunity to claim unfair dismissal.[67] If an employer has the option of paying for the notice period whilst it is being worked or paying

---

[60] See *Jones v Gwent County Council* [1992] IRLR 521.

[61] See *Dietman v London Borough of Brent* [1988] IRLR 299.

[62] [1999] IRLR 417.

[63] See also *Robb v London Borough of Hammersmith* [1991] IRLR 72.

[64] [1998] IRLR 64.

[65] *Ibid.* at p. 67. See also *Irani v Southampton and South West Hampshire Health Authority* [1985] IRLR 203, where an interlocutory injunction was granted to restrain the employer from implementing an employee's notice before they had followed the disputes procedure.

[66] See *Marsh v National Autistic Society* [1993] IRLR 453.

[67] See *Harper v Virgin Net Ltd* [2004] IRLR 390.

a sum of money in lieu of notice, then the employer is able to pay this, even if it means that the employee will be stopped from having enough continuous employment to qualify to make a claim.[68] The courts will make the assumption that the employer will choose to perform the contract in the least burdensome way and that, had the contract been performed lawfully, the employee would have been dismissed at the earliest opportunity.[69] When looking at the failure to follow a disciplinary procedure, attention does not focus on whether or not an employee would have been dismissed if the procedure had been adhered to. The issue is how much longer the employee would have been retained before the employer could contractually give notice. It is this that will determine whether or not there has been a loss of opportunity.[70]

Damages are not awarded for distress or hurt feelings. In *Bliss v South East Thames Regional Health Authority*[71] Dillon LJ stated the general principle:

> The general rule laid down by the House of Lords[72] is that where damages fall to be assessed for breach of contract rather than in tort it is not permissible to award general damages for frustration, mental distress, injured feelings or annoyance caused by the breach. Modern thinking tends to be that the amount of damages recoverable for a wrong should be the same whether the cause of action is laid in contract or tort. But in *Addis* Lord Loreburn regarded the rule that damages for injured feelings cannot be recovered in contract for wrongful dismissal as too inveterate to be altered.

It was argued, in *French v Barclays Bank plc*,[73] that a loan contract providing low-interest mortgage facilities should fall within the exceptions. Thus it was asserted that when an employer varied the terms of the loan there ought to be damages awarded for anxiety and stress. This argument was not accepted by the court who felt constrained by the authorities, such as *Addis* and *Bliss*.[74]

Employees have a duty to mitigate their losses, although there should be no set-off of any sums to which they are contractually entitled. This issue was considered in *Cerberus Software Ltd v Rowley*.[75] The contract of employment provided for the termination of the contract upon the giving of six months' notice by either side. The contract also allowed that the employer *may* make a payment in lieu of notice to the employee. In the event the employee was dismissed without notice or payment in lieu. After five weeks he obtained alternative work at a higher salary. He then claimed damages for wrongful dismissal. One issue was whether he was entitled to six months' pay in lieu of notice as a contractual right or whether the measure of damages was the amount that the employee would have earned if the contract had continued. In the latter case the employee would have a duty to mitigate losses. The court held that the contract gave the employer a choice of whether to make the payment in lieu or not, so the employee did not have a contractual right to the six months' pay and the normal rules concerning minimising losses should apply.[76] The distinction between a claim for payments

---

[68] *Morran v Glasgow Council of Tenants Associations* [1998] IRLR 67.
[69] *Lavarack v Woods of Colchester Ltd* [1967] 1 QB 278 CA.
[70] See *Janciuk v Winerite Ltd* [1998] IRLR 63.
[71] [1985] IRLR 308 CA.
[72] In *Addis v Gramophone Company Ltd* [1909] AC 488 HL.
[73] [1998] IRLR 646 CA.
[74] See also *Johnson v Unisys Ltd* [2001] IRLR 279.
[75] [2001] IRLR 160 CA.
[76] See also *Gregory v Wallace* [1998] IRLR 387 CA.

due under the contract and those which are damages for wrongful dismissal is important. In the former situation the court or tribunal is being asked to set a sum to be paid to the claimant, irrespective of any damage suffered as a consequence of the breach.[77] Where there is a failure to mitigate, the court will deduct a sum it feels the employee might reasonably have been expected to earn. As regards state benefits, it would appear that any benefit received by the dismissed employee should be deducted only where not to do so would result in a net gain to the employee.[78] Finally, the first £30,000 of damages is to be awarded net of tax, but any amount above this figure will be awarded gross since it is taxable in the hands of the recipient.

Proceedings may be brought before an employment tribunal in respect of:[79]

1. damages for a breach of contract of employment or other contract connected to employment;[80]

2. a claim for a sum due under such a contract;[81] and

3. a claim for the recovery of any sum, in pursuance of any enactment relating to the performance of such a contract.[82]

Provided the claim arises or is outstanding on the termination of the employee concerned, such actions can be taken by both the employer and the employee.[83] Breach of contract claims are excluded if they are based on terms which:[84]

1. Require the employer to provide living accommodation for the employee.

2. Impose an obligation on the employer or the employee in connection with the provision of living accommodation.

3. Relate to intellectual property.[85]

4. Impose an obligation of confidence.

5. Are a covenant in restraint of trade.

Employees must present their claim to the employment tribunal within three months of the effective date of termination, or, if there is no such date, the last day on which the employee worked in the employment. The tribunal has discretion to lengthen this period if it decides that it was not reasonably practicable for the employee to present their complaint in time.[86] It is not possible to bring a claim for breach of contract to an employment tribunal before the effective date of termination.[87]

---

[77] See *Abrahams* v *Performing Rights Society* [1995] IRLR 486 CA.

[78] See *Westwood* v *Secretary of State* [1984] IRLR 209.

[79] Excluding those related to personal injuries (arts. 3 and 4 ETEJO 1994).

[80] This includes the ability to enforce compromise agreements on terms connected with the end of employment: see *Rock-It Cargo Ltd* v *Green* [1997] IRLR 581.

[81] In *Sarker* v *South Tees Acute Hospitals NHS Trust* [1997] IRLR 328 an employee was dismissed before she commenced work, but the court held that she was still entitled to make a claim for damages as the contractual relationship had come into existence.

[82] Section 3(2) Employment Tribunals Act 1996.

[83] Articles 3 and 4 ETEJO 1994. See *Peninsula Ltd* v *Sweeney* [2004] IRLR 49 and *Miller Ltd* v *Johnston* [2002] IRLR 386.

[84] Article 5 ETEJO 1994.

[85] Defined as including copyright, rights in performance, moral rights, design rights, registered designs, patents and trade marks (art. 5 ETEJO 1994).

[86] Article 7 ETEJO 1994.

[87] *Capek* v *Lincolnshire County Council* [2000] IRLR 590.

4.4 **Unfair dismissal**

The statutory concept of unfair dismissal was first introduced in the Industrial Relations Act 1971 and the right to claim is now contained in Part X ERA 1996. Section 94(1) ERA 1996 states that employees have the right not to be unfairly dismissed by their employer. In examining whether or not a dismissal is unfair, the following stages need to be completed. First, there is the issue of eligibility for protection. Second, it must be shown that a dismissal has taken place and the effective date of termination must be identified. Third, the reason for dismissal must be established. Finally, the question of reasonableness must be considered.

4.4.1 **Eligibility**

Before individuals can make a complaint of unfair dismissal they need to qualify for the right by overcoming some initial hurdles. These relate to their employment status and length of continuous service. Also considered here are contracts that are tainted by illegality.

4.4.1.1 **Only employees qualify**

Section 94(1) provides that it is employees that have the right. An employee is an individual who works under a contract of employment.[88] With an increasing number of rights accruing to workers[89] it may seem less logical for those working under a contract to perform services personally to continue to be excluded from Part X ERA 1996.[90] Employment status is considered in Chapter 2.

4.4.1.2 **Illegality**

As has been stated before, the general rules of contract apply equally to contracts of employment and there is a general principle that the courts will not enforce an illegal contract, the *ex turpi causa non oritur actio* rule.[91] It is necessary not only to examine whether the contract of employment was performed legally but also to look at its purpose. If the contract has an illegal purpose, then it may not be relied upon. In *Colen* v *Cebrian Ltd*,[92] Waller LJ summarised the position as follows:

> . . . an analysis needs to be done as to what the parties' intentions were from time to time. If the contract was unlawful at its formation or if there was an intention to perform the contract unlawfully as at the date of the contract, then the contract will be unenforceable. If at the date of the contract the contract was perfectly lawful and it was intended to perform it lawfully, the effect of some act of illegal performance is not automatically to render the contract unenforceable. If the contract is ultimately performed illegally and the party seeking to enforce it takes part in the illegality, that *may* render the contract unenforceable at his instigation. But not every act of illegality in performance even participated in by the enforcer, will have that effect. If the person seeking to enforce the contract has to rely on his illegal action in order to succeed then

---

[88] Section 230(1)–(2) ERA 1996.
[89] Section 230(3) ERA 1996.
[90] There are specific groups excluded from the right: these are the police (s. 200 ERA 1996) and share fishers (s. 199(2)) as well as those affected by a little-used opportunity to opt out of the provisions and replace them with a dismissal procedure agreement; see s. 110.
[91] Action is not available on an illegal contract.
[92] [2004] IRLR 210; see also *Wheeler* v *Quality Deep* [2005] ICR 265.

the court will not assist him. But if he does not have to do so, then in my view the question is whether the method of performance chosen and the degree of participation in that illegal performance is such as to 'turn the contract into an illegal contract'.

Knowledge of the illegality does not always appear to be relevant. In *EuroDiam Ltd v Bathurst*[93] the Court of Appeal indicated that the issue of illegality should be approached pragmatically and with caution, especially where the defendant's conduct in participating in an illegal contract was so reprehensible, in comparison with the plaintiff, that it would be wrong to allow the defendant to rely upon it. Such a situation occurred in *Hewcastle Catering Ltd v Ahmed and Elkamah*.[94] This case involved a number of employees who were dismissed after co-operating with HM Customs & Excise in an investigation of a fraud about VAT on customers' bills, for which their employer was prosecuted. The employees had participated in the fraud but only the employer had benefited. The court concluded that it would be wrong to allow the employer to rely on the argument that the fraud made the employees' contracts of employment illegal and prevented them bringing unfair dismissal claims.[95]

Thus the consequences of a strict application of the rules on illegality can be severe. *Salvesen v Simmons*[96] involved an employee who, at his request, was paid partly through an annual salary, with all the normal deductions for income tax and national insurance contributions, and partly through a consultancy which he operated with his wife. These latter payments were made without deductions. When a change of employer occurred, the new employer declined to continue with this arrangement. This was one of the issues that led the individual to resign and claim constructive dismissal. The EAT held that the contract had an illegal purpose, namely to defraud the Inland Revenue of tax. The result was that the employee was unable to rely upon it for the purposes of his claim even though the amount of tax lost to the Inland Revenue was small.[97] In *Hyland v JH Barker (North West) Ltd*[98] the giving of a tax-free lodging allowance for four weeks, whilst the employee commuted daily, was enough to taint the contract of employment with illegality. As a result the employee was unable to establish sufficient length of continuous employment to make an unfair dismissal claim. However, there is a difference between tax evasion and tax avoidance. Thus in *Lightfoot v D & J Sporting Ltd*[99] an arrangement to pay part of the salary to the employee's wife was held to be legitimate tax avoidance and did not make the employee's contract illegal.

It seems that such payments need to be part of an individual's regular remuneration and be more than occasional one-off payments without deductions. In *Annandale Engineering v Samson*[100] the occasional tax-free payments to a kennel hand by a greyhound trainer, made whenever one of their dogs won a race, could not be classified as part of the kennel hand's regular remuneration. The employer was not able to rely on the defence of illegality.

---

[93] [1988] 2 All ER 23 CA.

[94] [1991] IRLR 473 CA.

[95] See also *Broaders v Kalkare Property Maintenance Ltd* [1990] IRLR 421, where the EAT stated that a fraud against an employer was quite different from one concerned with fraud against the tax authorities. The former did not make the contract illegal, even though the employee was receiving unofficial payments without the employer's knowledge.

[96] [1994] IRLR 52.

[97] On the argument that the European Convention on Human Rights is infringed in these circumstances see *Soteriou v Ultrachem Ltd* [2004] IRLR 870.

[98] [1985] IRLR 403.

[99] [1996] IRLR 64.

[100] [1994] IRLR 59.

An exception to this approach was established in relation to claims for unlawful sex discrimination. In *Leighton* v *Michael*[101] an ex-employee in a fish and kebab bar made a claim for sex discrimination. She had taken on extra work, and payment for this was made gross, i.e. without any deductions for income tax and national insurance contributions. The employment tribunal had decided that it could not make a decision on sexual harassment claims because the contract was tainted with illegality. In the employment tribunal's view the individual needed to show that the discrimination was in the field of employment. In order to do this the claim had to be founded on the contract of employment, which was tainted. The EAT distinguished between actions based on dismissal, including constructive dismissal, and those based on discrimination. The former claims were concerned with enforcing rights based upon the contract of employment and in order to rely on the statutory rights the claimant had to establish not only that they were an employee, but also that they had been dismissed on the termination of a contract. By way of contrast, in a sex discrimination case, although there needs to be a reference to the contract to show that the claimant was employed, the right not to suffer unlawful discrimination does not involve relying upon, or basing a claim upon, the contract of employment. It is conferred by statute on persons who are employed.[102]

This distinction may seem artificial. Indeed, in *HM Prison Service* v *Miss M Chilton*,[103] which concerned another sex discrimination claim, Judge Peter Clark observed:

> We have grave reservations as to the correctness of *Leighton*. We are unable to appreciate the distinction between statutory claims of unfair dismissal and sex discrimination for the purpose of applying the public policy doctrine of illegality. Both statutory causes of action depend upon the contract as a prerequisite for the claim.

Despite this, because they had not heard full argument on the issue, the EAT again followed *Leighton*.

Hall v *Woolston Hall Leisure Ltd*[104] concerned an employee who was dismissed on the grounds of pregnancy and therefore had a claim under the Sex Discrimination Act 1975. She was paid part of her salary without the deduction of tax or national insurance contributions and she was aware of this illegality. The Court of Appeal confirmed the approach in *Leighton* and held that public policy grounds, that she should not be able to rely on the contract because of her knowledge of the illegality, were insufficient to defeat her claim. The court stated that it was undoubtedly correct that, where the complaint is of a discriminatory dismissal, the claimant must establish that she was employed and was dismissed from that employment, so that reliance must be placed on the contract. It further stated:

> It is the sex discrimination that is the core of the complaint, the fact of the employment and the dismissal being the particular factual circumstances which Parliament has prescribed for the sex discrimination complaint to be capable of being made . . . and the awareness of the employee that the employer was failing to deduct tax and NIC and to account to the Revenue does not of itself constitute a valid ground for refusing jurisdiction.

More recently, the EAT has stated that it does not consider that the authorities

---

[101] [1995] ICR 1091.
[102] Rights to protection in employment under the Sex Discrimination Act 1975 accrue to the wider definition of workers, rather than just employees; see Chapter 5.
[103] Employment Appeal Tribunal judgment delivered on 23 July 1999; not reported.
[104] [2000] IRLR 578 CA.

support the proposition that if the arrangements *have the effect* of depriving the Revenue of tax to which they were in law entitled then this renders the contract unlawful . . . there must be some form of misrepresentation, some attempt to conceal the true facts of the relationship, before the contract is rendered illegal . . .[105]

Where there is some illegality in the performance of the contract, the question for the court or tribunal is whether the right solution is to treat the whole contract as illegal or whether it is possible to sever the unlawful elements and allow the claimant to recover for the remainder. Thus in *Blue Chip Ltd* v *Helabawi*[106] a foreign student was only entitled to the national minimum wage for the weeks he was not in breach of a visa condition that prevented him working more than 20 hours a week.

4.4.1.3 Continuous employment

Normally, employees must be continuously employed for a period of not less than one year, ending with the effective date of termination,[107] in order to qualify for the right not to be unfairly dismissed.[108] However, this does not apply if the reason or principal reason for dismissal was automatically unfair (see below). The length of this qualifying period has changed on a number of occasions. Initially, in 1971, the period was two years. It then became one year and subsequently six months. The Employment Act 1980 lengthened the period to two years again for smaller employers.[109] In 1985 this was extended to all employers and remained at this level until 1999. Continuity is to be calculated up to the effective date of termination in accordance with ss. 210–219 ERA 1996 (see Chapter 2).

4.4.2 The dismissal

4.4.2.1 Whether a dismissal has taken place

Having established that an individual is an employee with at least one year's continuous service and not otherwise excluded, progress can be made to the next stage, i.e. to establish that a dismissal has taken place. Section 95 ERA 1996 specifies the circumstances in which a dismissal takes place. The first of these is when a contract under which the individual is employed is terminated by the employer. Where there is a dispute as to whether a dismissal has taken place, the onus of proof is on the employee. Thus it is vitally important not to confuse a warning of impending dismissal – for example, through the announcement of a plant closure – with an individual notice to terminate.[110] For the giving of notice to constitute a dismissal at law the actual date of termination must be ascertainable. Where an employer has given notice to terminate, an employee who gives counter-notice indicating that he wishes to leave before the employer's notice has expired is still to be regarded as dismissed.[111]

---

[105] *Enfield Technical Services Ltd* v *Payne* [2007] IRLR 840. The Court of Appeal upheld this decision: see [2008] IRLR 500.

[106] [2009] IRLR 128.

[107] Subject to the provisions in s. 97 ERA 1996 on the effective date; see s. 213(1) on continuity being preserved in accordance with that section.

[108] Section 108(1) ERA 1996 as amended by the Unfair Dismissal and Statement of Reasons for Dismissal (Variation of Qualifying Period) Order 1999, SI 1999/1436.

[109] Those employing fewer than 20 employees.

[110] See *Doble* v *Firestone Tyre Co Ltd* [1981] IRLR 300.

[111] Section 95(2) ERA 1996.

There are occasions when there is a dispute as to whether the individual has been dismissed or whether they have resigned. This was the case in *Morris* v *London Iron and Steel Co Ltd*[112] where the employee claimed that he had been dismissed and the employer claimed that there had been a resignation. After hearing evidence, the employment tribunal was unable to decide which was the truth. Bearing in mind that the onus of proof was on the employee, the complaint was dismissed. This approach was approved in the Court of Appeal:

> . . . the judge should at the end of the day look at the whole of the evidence that has been called before him, drawing inferences where appropriate, and ask himself what has or has not been shown on the balance of probabilities, and then, bearing in mind where the onus of proof lies, decide whether the plaintiff or the defendant, or both, succeeds.

A radical alteration to an employee's contract of employment may amount to a withdrawal of that contract and a conclusion that the individual was dismissed. *Hogg* v *Dover College*[113] was a drastic example of this. A teacher was informed by his employer that he would no longer be head of department, that he would be employed on a part-time basis only and his salary was to be halved. The EAT concluded that:

> both as a matter of law and common sense, he was being told that his former contract was from that moment gone . . . It is suggested on behalf of the employers that there was a variation, but again, it seems to us quite elementary that you cannot hold a pistol to somebody's head and say 'henceforth you are to be employed on wholly different terms which are in fact 50 per cent of your previous contract'.

This was not a variation of the contract which might give the employee the opportunity to accept or reject a potential repudiation, but amounted to an express dismissal by the employer. This approach was applied in *Alcan Extrusions* v *Yates*[114] where the imposition of a continuous rolling shift system in place of a traditional shift system, contained in the employees' contracts, also amounted to an express dismissal by the employer. Alternatively, the unilateral variation of an employee's contractual working hours might amount to a breach of a fundamental term entitling the employee to resign and claim constructive dismissal. In *Greenaway Harrison Ltd* v *Wiles*[115] the threat to end the contracts of employment if the change of hours was not accepted, amounted to an anticipatory breach giving rise to a constructive dismissal.

If an employer acts as a result of a genuine, but mistaken, belief that an employee has resigned, it may not be enough to prevent the conduct from amounting to a constructive dismissal. In *Brown* v *JBD Engineering Ltd*[116] an employer appointed a new employee and told customers that the previous employee was no longer employed, in the mistaken belief that the original employee had left as a result of an agreement. The mistake might be a relevant factor, but could not be enough to prevent the employee claiming that a dismissal had taken place.

4.4.2.2 Limited-term contracts

See 4.3.1 above and Chapter 2 on fixed-term contracts.

---

[112] [1987] IRLR 182 CA.
[113] [1990] ICR 39.
[114] [1996] IRLR 327.
[115] [1994] IRLR 380.
[116] [1993] IRLR 568.

4.4.2.3 **Constructive dismissal**

Section 95(1)(c) ERA 1996 provides that an employee is to be treated as dismissed if the employee terminates the contract as a result of the employer's conduct. This is known as constructive dismissal. Lord Denning[117] provided a clear definition:

> If the employer is guilty of conduct which is a significant breach going to the root of the contract of employment; or which shows that the employer no longer intends to be bound by one or more of the essential terms of the contract; then the employee is entitled to treat himself as discharged from any further performance. If he does so, then he terminates the contract by reason of the employer's conduct. He is constructively dismissed.

Lord Denning went on to state that the employer's conduct must be sufficiently serious so as to entitle the employee to leave at once.[118] However, once a repudiatory breach has occured, it cannot be cured by the contract breaker.[119]

An example of serious conduct which amounted to a repudiatory breach is shown in *Weathersfield* v *Sargent*.[120] The employee was given instructions to discriminate against ethnic minority customers. She was so upset by this policy that she telephoned the employer and told them that she was resigning, although she did not explain why. It was asserted that this failure to give a reason amounted to a failure to accept any repudiatory breach by the employer and so there could not be a constructive dismissal. The Court of Appeal did not accept this argument and held that it was quite clear what the real reason for the employee's departure was and the fact that the employee left for this reason amounted to an acceptance of the employer's repudiation.[121] By way of contrast, *RDF Group plc* v *Clements*[122] involved an individual who was subjected to a campaign of vilification in the press whilst on garden leave. However, the High Court ruled that, since Clements' own disloyalty amounted to a repudiatory breach of contract, he was not entitled to accept the employer's repudiation.

The Court of Appeal has held that a series of acts can cumulatively amount to a breach of the implied duty of trust and confidence and thus a constructive dismissal. The 'final straw', however, does not have to be of the same character as earlier acts. It must contribute something to the breach, but what it adds may be relatively insignificant so long as it is not utterly trivial. In *London Borough of Waltham Forest* v *Omilaju*,[123] the complainant was employed by a local authority and issued five sets of proceedings alleging race discrimination and victimisation. These were heard in July and August 2001 but the employer refused to pay Mr Omilaju his full salary when he was absent without leave in order to attend the employment tribunal. It was the authority's rule that employees in his position were required to apply for special unpaid leave or annual leave. In September 2001 Mr Omilaju resigned and claimed unfair dismissal. The Court of Appeal upheld the tribunal's decision that the refusal to pay for the time attending the tribunal could not be regarded as the 'final straw' in a series

---

[117] *Western Excavations (ECC) Ltd* v *Sharp* [1978] IRLR 27 CA.
[118] See also *Woods* v *WM Car Services (Peterborough) Ltd* [1981] IRLR 413 CA, which followed *Western Excavations* in this respect.
[119] See *Bournemouth University Higher Education Corporation* v *Buckland* [2010] EWCA Cio 121.
[120] [1999] IRLR 94 CA.
[121] In *Moores* v *Bude-Stratton Town Council* [2000] IRLR 676 a local authority councillor's abusive conduct towards an employee of the authority amounted to a breach of the duty of trust and confidence, such as to justify the employee resigning and claiming constructive dismissal.
[122] [2008] IRLR 208.
[123] [2005] IRLR 35.

of actions which together amounted to a breach of trust and confidence. According to the Appeal Court, a 'final straw' does not have to be of the same character as earlier acts. However, it must contribute something to the breach of the implied term even if what it adds may be relatively trivial.

It is not necessary for an employee to leave immediately in order to show that their departure is as a result of an employer's breach of contract. However, there is a need to establish that the breach (or breaches) was the effective cause of leaving. In *Jones* v *F Sirl & Son (Furnishers) Ltd*[124] the employee left some three weeks after the final event in a series of breaches of contract by her employer. She had obtained another job and left to take up the new position. The EAT concluded that the main cause of her leaving was the employer's actions, not because she had found another position to go to. A delay also occurred in *Waltons & Morse* v *Dorrington*[125] where the employer was held to be in breach of implied terms to provide a safe working environment and that the employer would reasonably and promptly afford employees a reasonable opportunity to obtain redress for any grievances.[126] In this case the employee strove to establish the right to sit in a smoke-free work environment. The failure of the employers to deal with her grievance led to the employee leaving and claiming constructive dismissal. She continued to work until she found alternative employment and it was argued that she had affirmed her contract in doing so. In rejecting the view that a delay in leaving negated the constructive dismissal, the EAT took into account her length of service and the fact that she needed to earn an income.[127] Similarly, continuing to work is not necessarily an affirmation of contractual changes. In *Aparau* v *Iceland Frozen Foods plc*[128] new contracts of employment were issued which contained a mobility clause. Some 18 months later the employee was given instructions to move to another branch. The employee denied that the employer had the right to issue such an instruction and successfully claimed that she had been constructively dismissed. The EAT accepted that the mobility clause had not been incorporated into her contract and a summary instruction to relocate was a repudiatory breach. By way of contrast, *White* v *Reflecting Roadstuds Ltd*[129] was about the transfer of an employee to an area of work where he earned less income. The employee resigned and claimed that he had been constructively dismissed. The claim failed because the EAT held that there was an express flexibility clause which permitted the employer to do this. There was no necessity to imply a reasonableness term into the clause as this would introduce a reasonableness test into the area of constructive dismissal.

An employer is not entitled to alter the formula whereby wages are calculated, but whether a unilateral reduction in pay or fringe benefits is of sufficient materiality to entitle the employee to resign is a question of degree. A failure to pay an employee's salary or wage is likely to constitute a fundamental breach if it is a deliberate act on the part of the employer rather than a mere breakdown in technology. In *Gardner Ltd* v *Beresford*,[130] where the

---

[124] [1997] IRLR 493 EAT.

[125] [1997] IRLR 488.

[126] See also *WA Goold (Pearmak) Ltd* v *McConnell* [1995] IRLR 516 and *Robins UK* v *Triggs* [2007] IRLR 857.

[127] In contrast, *Dryden* v *Greater Glasgow Health Board* [1992] IRLR 469 concerned an employer's introduction of a no-smoking policy; the EAT held that there was no implied duty to provide facilities for smokers and no breach as a result of which the employee could claim constructive dismissal.

[128] [1996] IRLR 119 EAT.

[129] [1991] IRLR 331.

[130] [1978] IRLR 63.

employee resigned because she had not received a pay increase for two years whilst others had, the EAT accepted that in most cases it would be reasonable to infer a term that an employer will not treat employees arbitrarily, capriciously or inequitably in relation to remuneration. However, if a contract makes no reference at all to pay increases, it is impossible to say that there is an implied term that there will always be a pay rise.[131]

The conduct complained about does not need to be taken by the employer. In *Hilton International Hotels (UK) Ltd* v *Protopapa*[132] a supervisor was severely reprimanded by her immediate superior in front of other employees. She resigned and claimed constructive dismissal. On appeal, the employer argued that there could not be a constructive dismissal because the immediate superior had no authority to sack her. The EAT did not accept this and reaffirmed the principle that an employer is to be held liable for the actions of employees for acts done in the course of their employment.[133] Finally, it should be noted that it is possible for an employer's repudiatory breach to be the result of the behaviour of the employee. In *Morrison*,[134] for example, the employer suspended an employee without pay as a result of the employee's behaviour. They had no contractual authority to suspend the employee who resigned and successfully claimed that she had been constructively dismissed. The employment tribunal decided that there should be a 40 per cent reduction in her compensation, because she had provoked the employer's unlawful reaction.

4.4.2.4 The effective date of termination of employment

The date on which a contract of employment terminates is important not just for reasons of calculating payments owed but also for calculating the start of the three-month period in which employees must make their complaint to an employment tribunal. The common law approach to the date of termination is that this will be when the notice given by the employer or employee expires, or the date that payment in lieu of notice is accepted. If an employer has given notice to an employee and, during that period, the employee resigns with the intention of leaving at an earlier date, the employee will still be treated as dismissed[135] but the effective date on which the contract ends will be that indicated by the employee's notice.[136]

Section 97(1) ERA 1996 provides a definition of the 'effective date of termination' in differing circumstances:

1. When a contract of employment is terminated by notice, the effective date is the date on which the notice expires. In *Hutchings* v *Coinseed Ltd*[137] an employee resigned and was told by her employer that she would not be required to work during her period of notice. She then

---

[131] See *Murco Petroleum* v *Forge* [1987] IRLR 50.

[132] [1990] IRLR 316.

[133] See also *Warnes* v *The Trustees of Cheriton Oddfellows Social Club* [1993] IRLR 58, where an invalid resolution passed at a club's annual general meeting took away the secretarial duties of the club steward. Despite the invalidity of the resolution, this act amounted to a fundamental breach of contract allowing a claim for constructive dismissal.

[134] *Morrison* v *Amalgamated Transport and General Workers Union* [1989] IRLR 361 CA.

[135] Section 95(2) ERA 1996.

[136] See *Thompson* v *GEC Avionics Ltd* [1991] IRLR 488, where an employee was given notice that her employment would cease on 9 November and she subsequently resigned and gave notice terminating her employment on 21 September, which was held to be the effective date of termination.

[137] [1998] IRLR 190 CA.

started work for a competitor at a higher salary. The court rejected the employer's claim that this amounted to a repudiatory breach of contract entitling them not to pay the employee during the notice period, given the fact that they had not required her to do work for them during this period. Where there is a mutual variation of the notice to terminate, the notice and the contract of employment expire on the new date.[138]

2. Where a contract of employment is terminated without notice, then the effective date is the date on which the termination takes effect.[139] This is regardless of whether the employer followed all the contractual procedures to which the employee was entitled[140] or whether the dismissal was done in the correct manner.[141] In *Kirklees MBC v Radecki*[142] the Court of Appeal confirmed that the effective date of termination is the date of summary dismissal as long as the employee knows it. Thus the employer's communication that the employee was being taken off the payroll unequivocally conveyed that the employment was being terminated.

Where an employee is dismissed and no longer has the right to work and where the employer no longer has the obligation to pay, then the contract is at an end, unless there is an agreement to continue the relationship during any appeal proceedings.[143] *Drage v Governors of Greenford High School*[144] involved the dismissal of a school teacher. The question at issue was whether the effective date of termination was the date when he was told of the initial decision to dismiss him or the date when he was notified that his appeal against dismissal had failed. The Court of Appeal held that:

> The critical question arising, as in any similar case where contractual provision is made for an internal appeal, is whether during the period between the initial notification and the outcome of the appeal the employee stands (a) dismissed with the possibility of reinstatement or (b) suspended with the possibility of the proposed dismissal not being confirmed and the suspension thus being ended.

Thus if a contract is held to have been suspended during the appeals procedure, then the effective date will be the notification ending that procedure. The terms of the initial notification are likely to be important, although not necessarily decisive.[145]

Even if the employee was contractually entitled to further payments, this may not delay the effective time or date of termination. Thus, as in *Octavius Atkinson & Sons Ltd v Morris*,[146] if an employee was summarily dismissed during the day, the effective time of the dismissal was when it was communicated to him. This was so even though the employee was entitled to further payments for travel to and from work.

---

[138] See *Palfrey v Transco plc* [2004] IRLR 916.

[139] *BMK Ltd and BMK Holdings Ltd v Logue* [1993] IRLR 477 considered the effective date of termination in constructive dismissals; the question to be asked is when did the termination take effect?

[140] See *Batchelor v British Railways Board* [1987] IRLR 136 CA.

[141] See *Robert Cort & Son Ltd v Charman* [1981] IRLR 437, which considered a summary dismissal without the contractual notice being given.

[142] [2009] IRLR 555.

[143] See *Savage v J Sainsbury Ltd* [1980] IRLR 109 CA.

[144] [2000] IRLR 315 CA.

[145] See *Chapman v Letherby & Christopher Ltd* [1981] IRLR 440, where the EAT held that the construction to be put on a letter of dismissal should not be a technical one, but one which an ordinary, reasonable employee would understand by the words used.

[146] [1989] IRLR 158 CA.

3. Where there is a limited-term contract which terminates as a result of the limiting event without being renewed under the same contract, the effective date is the date on which the termination takes effect.

Where the notice period is shorter than that required by s. 86 ERA 1996,[147] for the purposes of the qualifying length of service required to claim unfair dismissal and calculating the basic award for unfair dismissal,[148] the effective date of termination will be at the end of the period stipulated by s. 86 ERA 1996.[149]

Whether in a particular case the words of dismissal evince an intention to terminate the contract at once or only at a future date depends on the construction of those words. Such construction must not be technical but reflect what an ordinary, reasonable employee would understand by the language used. Moreover, words should be construed in the light of the facts known to the employee at the time of notification. If the language used is ambiguous, it is likely that tribunals will apply the principle that words should be interpreted most strongly against the person who uses them. It should also be observed that, where a dismissal has been communicated by letter, the contract of employment does not terminate until the employee has actually read the letter or had a reasonable opportunity of reading it.[150] Thus in *McMaster* v *Manchester Airport*,[151] the employer had posted a letter of dismissal to the applicant and had presumed that it was received and read. This was not an altogether unreasonable assumption, given that the employee was absent from work through sickness and might reasonably have been expected to be at home where the dismissal letter was sent. In fact he was away on a day trip to France and did not read the letter until the next day. The court held that it was the day that the employee read the letter which was the effective date of termination.

4.4.3 The reasons for dismissal

Having established that a dismissal has taken place and when it took effect, the next stage is to decide whether the reasons for dismissal can be treated as coming within those permitted by the ERA 1996, or whether they should be regarded as unfair.

4.4.3.1 Statement of reasons for dismissal

If an employer gives an employee notice of dismissal or terminates the employee's contract without notice, then the employee is entitled to be given a written statement giving particulars of the reasons for the dismissal. Employees engaged under a limited-term contract which expires without being renewed under the same contract are also entitled to such a statement.[152] There are a limited number of conditions attached to this right:

---

[147] The minimum periods of notice required; see above.

[148] Sections 108(1) and 119(1) ERA 1996.

[149] Section 97(2)–(5) ERA 1996; in *Lanton Leisure Ltd* v *White and Gibson* [1987] IRLR 119 two employees were dismissed without notice for gross misconduct and, consequently, failed to have enough continuous service to qualify for making an unfair dismissal claim. The employees claimed that they were entitled to the protection of (now) s. 97(2) ERA 1996. The EAT concluded that the employment tribunal had a duty to consider first whether there had been conduct warranting a dismissal for gross misconduct, which had the effect of removing the employees' contractual rights to notice.

[150] See *GISDA Cyf* v *Barratt* [2009] IRLR 933.

[151] [1998] IRLR 112.

[152] Section 92(1) ERA 1996.

1. It only applies to employees.

2. The employee must, at the effective date of termination,[153] have been continuously employed for a period of one year.[154]

3. The employee is entitled to the statement only if the employee requests it. Once requested, the statement must be provided within 14 days of the request.[155]

It is acceptable for the statement to refer unambiguously to other letters already sent which contain the reasons for dismissal.[156] Special provision is made for those who are pregnant or who are on maternity or adoption leave, if this leave is brought to an end. If they are dismissed, there is no continuous service requirement before they are entitled to a statement, neither do they need to request it.[157] Written statements provided by the employer are admissible in evidence in subsequent legal proceedings.[158]

An employee may make a complaint to an employment tribunal if the employer unreasonably fails to provide the written statement or if the reasons given are inadequate or untrue.[159] The obligation on employers is to state what they genuinely believe to be the reason or reasons for the dismissal. There is no requirement for the employment tribunal to decide whether they were good reasons or justifiable ones.[160] This would happen at a later stage if unfair dismissal proceedings were brought. If the employment tribunal finds the complaint well founded, then it may make a declaration as to what it considers the employer's reasons for dismissing were and also make an award that the employer must pay the employee a sum equal to two weeks' pay.[161] Somewhat bizarrely this right to complain only relates to letters that have been requested. If the employer gives the ex-employee an unrequested letter stating the reasons for the dismissal, then the employee is unlikely to be able to complain about the adequacy or truthfulness of such a letter.[162]

4.4.3.2 **Automatically unfair reasons**

Dismissals for automatically unfair reasons do not require an employee to have worked continuously for a period of one year.[163] These dismissals relate to such matters as the following:[164]

1. Family reasons[165] – these are reasons relating to the Maternity and Parental Leave etc. Regulations 1999[166] and include reasons related to (a) pregnancy, childbirth or maternity,

---

[153] Section 92(6)–(8) ERA 1996 describes the meaning of effective date of termination; these provisions are identical to those in s. 97(1)–(2) described above.

[154] Section 92(3) ERA 1996.

[155] Section 92(2) ERA 1996.

[156] See *Kent County Council* v *Gilham* [1985] IRLR 16 CA.

[157] Section 92(4)–(4A) ERA 1996.

[158] Section 92(5) ERA 1996.

[159] Section 93(1) ERA 1996.

[160] *Harvard Securities plc* v *Younghusband* [1990] IRLR 17.

[161] Section 93(2) ERA 1996; see Part XIV Chapter II ERA 1996 for the meaning of a week's pay; considered below.

[162] See *Catherine Haigh Harlequin Hair Design* v *Seed* [1990] IRLR 175, where the EAT held that an employment tribunal could not hear a complaint about just such an unrequested letter.

[163] Section 108(2)–(3) ERA 1996.

[164] This should not be taken as a comprehensive list; the number of automatically unfair reasons seems to grow with each new piece of employment legislation.

[165] Section 99 ERA 1996.

[166] SI 1999/3312.

(b) paternity, parental or adoption leave. They also include the right to time off for dependants contained in s. 57A ERA 1996.

2. Health and safety matters[167] – where the reason for dismissal was that the employee:
   - Carried out, or proposed to carry out, activities designated by the employer in connection with preventing or reducing risks to the health and safety of employees.
   - Performed, or proposed to perform, any of his functions as a safety representative or a member of a safety committee.
   - Took part or proposed to take part in consultation with the employer pursuant to the Health and Safety (Consultation with Employees) Regulations 1996 or in an election of representatives of employee safety within the meaning of those Regulations.
   - Where there was no safety representative or committee or it was not reasonably practicable to raise the matter in that way, brought to the employer's attention, by reasonable means, circumstances connected with his work which he reasonably believed were harmful or potentially harmful to health and safety.
   - Left or proposed to leave, or refused to return to (whilst the danger persisted), his place of work or any dangerous part of the workplace, in circumstances of danger which he reasonably believed to be serious and imminent and which he could not reasonably have been expected to avert.
   - Took, or proposed to take, appropriate steps to protect himself or herself or other persons, in circumstances of danger which he reasonably believed to be serious and imminent. Whether those steps were 'appropriate' must be judged by reference to all the circumstances, including the employee's knowledge and the facilities and advice available at the time. A dismissal will not be regarded as unfair if the employer can show that it was, or would have been, so negligent for the employee to take the steps which he took, or proposed to take, that a reasonable employer might have dismissed on these grounds.

3. Protected shop workers and betting shop workers[168] who refuse to work on Sundays.

4. Working time[169] – where the reason for the dismissal is that an employee has refused to comply with instructions contrary to the provisions of the Working Time Regulations 1998,[170] refused to give up any rights under these Regulations, failed to sign a workforce agreement or is performing, or proposing to perform, the duties of an employee representative in relation to Sch. 1 to those Regulations.

5. Pension scheme trustees[171] – performing, or proposing to perform, the duties of a trustee of a relevant occupational pension scheme, which relates to the individual's employment.

6. Employee representatives[172] – being, or taking part in the elections for, an employee representative for the purposes of consultation on collective redundancies[173] or transfers of undertakings.[174]

---

[167] Section 100 ERA 1996. See *Balfour Fitzpatrick* v *Acheson* [2003] IRLR 683.
[168] Section 101 ERA 1996.
[169] Section 101A ERA 1996. See *McClean* v *Rainbow Ltd* [2007] IRLR 15.
[170] SI 1998/1833.
[171] Section 102 ERA 1996.
[172] Section 103 ERA 1996.
[173] Part IV Chapter II TULRCA 1992.
[174] Transfer of Undertakings (Protection of Employment) Regulations 2006, SI 2006/246.

7. Protected disclosures[175] – an employee dismissed for making a protected disclosure (see 3.5.2.4 above).

8. Assertion of a statutory right[176] – where an employee brings proceedings to enforce a statutory right or alleges that an employer has infringed a statutory right. These are rights associated with bringing complaints to an employment tribunal; rights to minimum notice;[177] matters concerned with deductions from pay, union activities and time off for trade union duties and activities;[178] matters connected with the right to be accompanied at disciplinary or grievance hearings;[179] and rights conferred by the Working Time Regulations 1998.[180] It is irrelevant whether the employee has the right or whether it has been infringed, as long as the employee acts in good faith.

9. The national minimum wage[181] – any action taken by, or on behalf of, an employee in connection with enforcing rights relating to the national minimum wage. Again it is irrelevant whether the employee has the right or whether it has been infringed, so long as the employee is acting in good faith.

10. Working family tax credits or disabled persons tax credits[182] – any action taken, or proposed to be taken, by or on behalf of the employee in connection with rights requiring employers to make payments and requiring employers to provide employees with information.

11. Participation in protected industrial action[183] – where an employee took part in protected industrial action and is dismissed within the protected period. This protection does not extend to those who take part in unofficial industrial action (see Chapter 11).

12. Part-time work – where employees bring proceedings to enforce their rights under the Part-time Workers (Prevention of Less Favourable Treatment) Regulations 2000.[184]

13. Redundancy[185] – where the principal reason for a dismissal is redundancy and it is shown that the same circumstances apply to other employees in the same undertaking in similar positions and who have not been dismissed and it is shown that any of (1) to (12) apply.

14. Spent offences – where a conviction of less than two-and-a-half years is spent[186] the employee is not under an obligation to disclose it. Section 4 of the Rehabilitation of Offenders Act 1974 stops employers from dismissing someone for not revealing the information to them. Certain sensitive occupations, such as nurses, police and social service workers are excluded from these provisions.[187]

---

[175] Section 103A ERA 1996.
[176] Section 104 ERA 1996. See *Mennell* v *Newell & Wright* [1997] IRLR 519.
[177] Section 86 ERA 1996.
[178] Sections 68, 86, 146, 168–170 TULRCA 1992; see also s. 152 TULRCA 1992.
[179] Section 12(3) Employment Relations Act 1999.
[180] SI 1998/1833.
[181] Section 104A ERA 1996.
[182] Section 104B ERA 1996; see Sch. 3 Tax Credits Act 1999.
[183] Section 238A(2) TULRCA 1992. See 11.14.3 below.
[184] SI 2000/1551; see reg. 7.
[185] Section 105 ERA 1996.
[186] Meaning a period of time since the sentence was served; the length of this period depends upon the severity of the sentence.
[187] See *Wood* v *Coverage Care Ltd* [1996] IRLR 264 which was about an employee, whose post was redundant, being refused alternative work because of a conviction which excluded her from the social work alternative positions.

15. Transfers of undertakings – reg. 7(1) of the Transfer of Undertakings (Protection of Employment) Regulations 2006[188] makes a dismissal by reason of relevant transfer automatically unfair, unless the reason for the dismissal was an economic, technical or organisational one.[189]

16. Fixed-term work – where employees do anything to act on their rights under the Fixed-term Employees (Prevention of Less Favourable Treatment) Regulations 2002.

17. Flexible work – s. 104C ERA 1996 provides protection for a qualifying employee who applies, in accordance with s. 80F ERA 1996,[190] to change their hours, times or place of work to enable the employee to care for a child.

Other instances of automatically unfair dismissal are those which constitute discrimination made unlawful by the Sex Discrimination Act 1975,[191] the Race Relations Act 1976[192] and the Disability Discrimination Act 1995.[193]

4.4.3.3 Fair or unfair reasons for dismissal

Having established that a dismissal has taken place, it is then for the employer to show that the reason for it was fair.[194] This is to be done by showing that the reason (or the principal reason if there is more than one), for the dismissal is that:

1. It relates to the capability or qualifications of the employee for performing work of the kind for which the employee was employed.

2. It relates to the conduct of the employee.

3. It is the retirement of the employee.

4. The employee was redundant.

5. The employee could not continue to work in the position for which the employee was employed without breaching a duty or restriction imposed by an enactment.[195]

There is a distinction between the first two of these reasons and the last three. It is a distinction, defined by the EAT, as that between the language of actuality and that of relationship. In *Shook* v *London Borough of Ealing*[196] the EAT considered this distinction:

> Two of them are couched in the language of actuality: the employee must be redundant or engaged under an unlawful contract, as the case may be. The other two are expressed in the language of relationship: the reason must *relate* to the capability for performing the work of the relevant kind or must *relate* to the conduct of the employee, as the case may be.

If the reason, or principal reason, does not fall into one of the five categories above it may still be fair if the dismissal takes place for

---

[188] SI 2006/246.
[189] Regulation 7(2) Transfer of Undertakings (Protection of Employment) Regulations 2006; see *Dynamex Friction Ltd* v *AMICUS* [2008] IRLR 515 where the Court of Appeal accepted that employees had been dismissed for an economic reason when an administrator decided that he had no option but to sack them because the company had no money.
[190] Inserted by s. 46 Employment Act 2002.
[191] Section 6(2)(b) SDA 1975.
[192] Section 4(2) RRA 1976.
[193] Section 4(2)(d) DDA 1995.
[194] Section 98(1) ERA 1996.
[195] Section 98(2) ERA 1996.
[196] [1986] IRLR 46.

some other substantial reason of a kind such as to justify the dismissal of an employee holding the position which the employee held.[197]

It follows that where no reason is given by the employer, a dismissal will be unfair simply because the statutory burden has not been discharged. Equally, if a reason is engineered in order to effect dismissal because the real reason would not be acceptable, the employer will fail because the underlying principal reason is not within s. 98(1) or (2) ERA 1996.[198]

No account is to be taken of any pressure exerted upon an employer to dismiss unfairly. If the employer is under pressure to dismiss an employee resulting from threats of, or actual, industrial action this will not be taken into account. The tribunal will consider fairness as if there was no such pressure.[199] The exception to this rule is where an employer has been pressurised to dismiss an individual for not joining a trade union. In such a case the employer may request the tribunal to add the person whom it is alleged exercised the pressure as a party to the proceedings. The effect of this is that the tribunal may order that part of any compensation owed is paid by the third party.[200]

The reason for the dismissal is the one known to the employer at the time of the dismissal. It is not acceptable for a tribunal to take into account matters which were not known to the employer at the time of the dismissal.[201] In *W Devis & Sons Ltd* v *Atkins*[202] the employer attempted to introduce new evidence of a dismissed employee's serious misconduct. This failed because it was information that came to light after the dismissal had taken place for another reason, namely a failure to obey instructions. The court approved the approach taken in *Abernethy* v *Mott, Hay & Anderson*[203] where it was ruled that:

> A reason for the dismissal is a set of facts known to the employer, or it may be of beliefs held by him, which cause him to dismiss the employee. If at the time of the dismissal the employer gives a reason for it, that is no doubt evidence, at any rate as against him, as to the real reason.

Any extra information could, however, be taken into account when assessing compensation. The exception is information that may become available during an internal appeals procedure, although this material must relate to the original decision. To exclude this information would be to ignore important parts of the case, either in favour of the employer or the employee. Lord Bridge stated in *West Midlands Co-operative Society Ltd* v *Tipton*:[204]

> The apparent injustice of excluding . . . misconduct of an employee which is irrelevant to the real reason for dismissal is mitigated . . . by the provisions relating to compensation in such a case. But there is nothing to mitigate the injustice to an employee which would result if he were unable to complain that his employer, though acting reasonably on the facts known to him when he summarily dismissed the employee, acted quite unreasonably in maintaining his

---

[197] Section 98(1)(b) ERA 1996.
[198] See *ASLEF* v *Brady* [2006] IRLR 76.
[199] Section 107 ERA 1996.
[200] Section 160 TULRCA 1992.
[201] This includes considering the reasons throughout the notice period: see *Parkinson* v *March Consulting Ltd* [1997] IRLR 308 CA.
[202] [1977] AC 931 HL.
[203] [1974] IRLR 213.
[204] [1986] IRLR 112 HL.

decision to dismiss in the face of mitigating circumstances established in the course of the domestic appeals procedure . . .[205]

Section 98(4)(a) ERA 1996 provides that once the employer has shown that the reason for the dismissal comes within the terms of s. 98(1) or (2), then the issue for the tribunal is whether the employer acted reasonably or unreasonably in treating it as a sufficient reason for dismissing the employee. This will partly depend upon the size and administrative resources of the employer's undertaking[206] and will be decided 'in accordance with equity and the substantial merits of the case'.[207]

4.4.3.4 **Capability or qualifications**

Capability is assessed by reference to skill, aptitude, health or any other physical or mental quality.[208] Assessing capability may well be subjective and an employer will need to be able to show that they had reasonable grounds for their belief. In *Taylor* v *Alidair Ltd*,[209] which concerned the competence of an airline pilot, Lord Denning MR stated:

> In considering the case, it must be remembered that . . . [the Act] contemplated a subjective test. The tribunal have to consider the employer's reason and the employer's state of mind. If the company honestly believed on reasonable grounds that the pilot was lacking in proper capability to fly aircraft on behalf of the company, that was a good and sufficient reason for the company to determine the employment then and there.

There are special considerations applicable when the individual could put people's safety at risk but the question as to when it is fair to dismiss an incompetent employee is an important one for employers.

(a) Incompetent employees

The employer has a right not to have their business harmed by an incompetent person, but the employee also has a right to be treated fairly. In *Whitbread & Co* v *Thomas*[210] three employees were dismissed as a result of their lack of competence in failing to prevent stock losses. This was despite the fact that the employer did not know which of the three might be responsible for the losses. The employer had, however, done everything possible to prevent the losses, including issuing warnings and transferring, temporarily, the staff to other locations. The EAT accepted that the employer had fulfilled three necessary conditions. These were, first, that if the act had been committed by an identified individual it would have led to dismissal. Secondly, that the act was committed by one or more of the individuals in the group and, thirdly, that there had been a proper investigation to try to identify the person or persons responsible for the act.[211] Treating an employee fairly does not necessarily mean not

---

[205] Similarly defects in the disciplinary or dismissal procedures can be remedied on appeal: see *Whitbread & Co* v *Mills* [1987] IRLR 18.

[206] Section 98(4)(a) ERA 1996.

[207] Section 98(4)(b) ERA 1996.

[208] Section 98(3)(a) ERA 1996.

[209] [1978] IRLR 82 CA.

[210] [1988] IRLR 43.

[211] See *Monie* v *Coral Racing Ltd* [1980] IRLR 464 CA where this principle was established in situations of dishonesty. The EAT, in *Whitbread*, suggested that it would apply to situations concerning incompetence only exceptionally.

dismissing when they have many years of service. In *Gair v Bevan Harris Ltd*[212] a foreman was dismissed for unsatisfactory performance and this was held to be fair, even though the employee had 11 years' service. An unreasonable procedural delay, however, might turn an otherwise fair dismissal into an unfair one.[213]

According to para. 1 of the ACAS Code of Practice on Disciplinary and Grievance Procedures:[214]

> Disciplinary situations include misconduct and/or poor performance. If employers have a separate capability procedure they may prefer to address performance issues under this procedure. If so, however, the basic principles of fairness set out in this Code should still be followed, albeit that they may need to be adapted.

In addition, paras. 18–20 provide:

> Where misconduct is confirmed or the employee is found to be performing unsatisfactorily it is usual to give the employee a written warning. A further act of misconduct or failure to improve performance within a set period would normally result in a final written warning.

> If an employee's first misconduct or unsatisfactory performance is sufficiently serious, it may be appropriate to move directly to a final written warning. This might occur where the employee's actions have had, or are liable to have, a serious or harmful impact on the organisation.

> A first or final written warning should set out the nature of the misconduct or poor performance and the change in behaviour or improvement in performance required (with timescale). The employee should be told how long the warning will remain current. The employee should be informed of the consequences of further misconduct, or failure to improve performance, within the set period following a final warning. For instance that it may result in dismissal or some other contractual penalty such as demotion or loss of seniority.[215]

It should be noted that in *Airbus Ltd v Webb*[216] the Court of Appeal held that an expired warning does not make the earlier misconduct an irrelevant circumstance under s. 98(4) ERA 1996. Indeed, para. 22 of the Code points out that:

> Some acts, termed gross misconduct, are so serious in themselves or have such serious consequences that they may call for dismissal without notice for a first offence. But a fair disciplinary process should always be followed, before dismissing for gross misconduct.

(b) Ill health and absenteeism

A second and important aspect of capability is how employers deal with those who are absent from work as a result of ill health. Appendix 4 of the ACAS Guide provides advice on how to deal with persistent short-term absence, longer-term absence through ill health and special health problems.

According to the EAT, the cause of ill health is not a concern of the tribunal, only the question as to whether the employer was reasonable in dismissing the employee because of their

---

[212] [1983] IRLR 368.

[213] See *RSPCA v Cruden* [1986] IRLR 83, where an employee was dismissed for what was described, by the employment tribunal, as 'gross misjudgment and idleness quite incompatible with the proper performance of his duties'. The dismissal was unfair, however, because of a long delay in instituting proceedings.

[214] 2009. On the status of the Code see 4.4.4 below.

[215] Paragraphs 8–15 of the ACAS Guide *Discipline and Grievances at Work* describe the benefits of informality and paras. 76–78 deal with the first formal action for unsatisfactory performance.

[216] [2008] IRLR 309.

unfitness for work. Thus even when the employer may have some responsibility for the employee's lack of fitness for work, the matter is not relevant when considering whether the dismissal was fair on the grounds of capability.[217]

It is likely that a dismissal for ill health will not be fair if the employee has not been consulted. Discussions and consultation with the employee may bring out new facts which may influence the employer's decision. This is so even where the employer has received an independent medical report on the employee's state of health.[218] In *First West Yorkshire Ltd* v *Haigh*[219] the EAT ruled that where an employer provides an enhanced pension on retirement through ill health, it is expected to take reasonable steps to ascertain whether the employee is entitled to benefit from this scheme. There is a difference between situations where an employee becomes permanently unfit to carry out duties required by their post and occasions when the employer decides to dismiss as a result of a poor attendance record.

The issue of an individual becoming permanently unfit for work may also be an issue under the Disability Discrimination Act 1995 (DDA 1995) (see Chapter 6).[220] In *Seymour* v *British Airways Board*,[221] for example, a registered disabled person was dismissed after the employer prepared and implemented a policy in relation to 'non-effective' staff, who might be restricted in their work for medical reasons. The EAT held that, although the disabled person was entitled to special consideration, this was not sufficient to give them priority over others in a redundancy situation. After the passing of the DDA 1995, much has changed. In *Kent County Council* v *Mingo*[222] a disabled employee was held to have been discriminated against because priority was given to other redundant or potentially redundant employees who were not so disadvantaged. The unfitness needs to be in relation to the particular work which the individual was employed to undertake. Even where a contract gives the employer the right to transfer an employee to any other work at a similar level, the fitness of the individual needs to be assessed in relationship to the particular kind of work.[223]

Continued periodic absences may be a considerable problem for some employers. It is important that the individual is aware of the possible consequences of their absenteeism record. Formal warnings may not always be appropriate, nor will medical evidence where it is not possible to provide an accurate prognosis for the future. In *Lynock* v *Cereal Packaging*[224] the EAT held that the approach of the employer must be based upon 'sympathy, understanding and compassion'. Each case must depend upon its own facts, and important considerations will be:

> The nature of the illness; the likelihood of it recurring or some other illness arising; the length of the various absences and the spaces of good health between them; the need of the employer for the work done by the particular employee; the impact of the absences on others who work with the employee . . . the important emphasis on a personal assessment in the ultimate decision and, of course, the extent to which the difficulty of the situation and the position of the employee has been made clear to the employee.

---

[217] See *McAdie* v *Royal Bank of Scotland* [2007] IRLR 895 CA.
[218] See *East Lindsey District Council* v *GE Daubney* [1977] IRLR 181.
[219] [2008] IRLR 182.
[220] *Eclipse Blinds Ltd* v *Wright* [1992] IRLR 133 is an example of a case, prior to the DDA 1995, which concerned a disabled person with deteriorating health.
[221] [1983] IRLR 55.
[222] [2000] IRLR 90.
[223] See *Shook* v *London Borough of Ealing* [1986] IRLR 46.
[224] [1988] IRLR 510.

In *Trico-Folberth Ltd* v *Devonshire*[225] an employee received a formal warning about her number of absences from work due to ill health. After further monitoring showed no improvement in attendance she was dismissed, initially because of an unacceptable attendance record. During the internal appeal procedure, an appellate body changed the reason for dismissal on compassionate grounds to one of being medically unfit to work. The tribunal stated that a dismissal for the original reason may well have been fair but not on grounds of being medically unfit. There had been insufficient investigation of her condition and inadequate consultation with the employee to justify dismissal on these grounds.[226] Consultation with the employee is necessary, so that the matter can be discussed personally. Only in the rarest of circumstances is a dismissal on the grounds of health likely to be fair if there has not been adequate consultation between the employer and the employee.[227]

(c) Qualifications

Qualifications means any degree, diploma or other academic, technical or professional qualification that is relevant to the position held.[228] The qualifications need to be considered in the light of the particular position that the employee held. Thus, depending upon the circumstances, even a failure to pass an aptitude test can be a reason for a dismissal under this heading.[229] Such qualifications might include the need for a driving licence as in *Tayside Regional Council* v *McIntosh*.[230] When the local authority advertised for vehicle mechanics they stipulated, in the advertisement, that applicants should have a clean driving licence, although this was not mentioned in the written offer of employment. The successful applicant met this criterion, but, three years later, was disqualified from driving as a result of a motoring offence. The employer dismissed him as there was no alternative work available. Despite the lack of an express term in the contract, the EAT held that the need for a licence could be inferred and that it was an essential and continuing condition of the individual's employment.

4.4.3.5 Conduct

There may be a relationship between competence and conduct. For example, poor attendance at work might be seen as a lack of competence or a result of the employee's conduct.[231] In *Whitbread & Co* v *Thomas*[232] (above) the recurring stock losses in an off-licence raised issues about both the employees' competence in controlling the stock and their conduct in relation to their honesty or otherwise. Prior to the tribunal considering whether the employer acted reasonably in treating a reason as sufficient for dismissing an employee, it must first establish what the reason for dismissal was.[233] Issues about employee conduct are also issues about how an employer reacts to that conduct, so employee awareness of the conduct that is expected of them is important in establishing the reasonableness of the dismissal. *Lock* v

---

[225] [1989] IRLR 396 CA.

[226] See also *Grootcon (UK) Ltd* v *Keld* [1984] IRLR 302 for a further case where lack of medical evidence was important and where the real reason for dismissal may have been the insistence of a major customer.

[227] See *East Lindsey District Council* v *GE Daubney* [1977] IRLR 181 for a fuller discussion of consultation requirements in such situations; this case was followed in *A Links & Co Ltd* v *Rose* [1991] IRLR 353.

[228] Section 98(3)(b) ERA 1996.

[229] See *Blackman* v *The Post Office* [1974] IRLR 46 NIRC.

[230] [1982] IRLR 272.

[231] See, e.g., *Trico-Folberth Ltd* v *Devonshire* [1989] IRLR 396 CA.

[232] [1988] IRLR 43.

[233] See *Wilson* v *Post Office* [2001] IRLR 834.

Cardiff Railway Co Ltd[234] involved the dismissal of a train conductor who asked a teenage boy to leave the train when it was discovered that he had no ticket or money to pay. In this case the employer had failed to follow the ACAS Code of Practice by not making it clear which offences would be regarded as gross misconduct justifying summary dismissal.

As a general rule, if an order is lawful, a refusal to obey it will be a breach of contract and amount to misconduct even though similar refusals have been condoned in the past. Nevertheless, in disobedience cases the primary factor to be considered is whether the employee is acting reasonably in refusing to carry out an instruction.[235] Thus in *Robinson v Tescom Corporation*[236] the employee had agreed to work under the terms of a varied job description whilst negotiations were ongoing. His subsequent refusal to do so was held by the EAT to amount to disobedience of a lawful instruction.

Another area where there might be grounds for a fair dismissal is when a worker is dishonest. In *British Railways Board v Jackson*[237] a train buffet supervisor was dismissed because the employer believed that he was about to take his own goods on board the train to sell to customers, thus depriving the employer of revenue. There were no tills on train buffet cars, so the employer relied upon the honesty of its employees. The employer's action was held to be reasonable and the employer was entitled to take into account the prevalence of this type of dishonesty amongst employees and whether the dismissal would be a deterrent to others from following the same course. Dishonesty by employees against the employer is likely to be a breach of the fundamental relationship of mutual trust and confidence and a repetition of such a breach might lead to dismissal being within the range of reasonable responses (see below).[238] Providing evidence of the employee's dishonesty may be a problem but if the employer has reasonable grounds for sustaining a genuine belief about the employee's guilt, after carrying out an investigation, this is likely to be sufficient.[239] Thus in *Rhondda CBC v Close*[240] the EAT accepted that it was not outside the band of reasonableness (see below) for the employer to choose not to carry out its own independent questioning in a disciplinary procedure but to rely instead on police statements. The Appeal Tribunal also expressed the view that it is not generally incumbent on an employer to allow the cross-examination of witnesses.

It may not be immediately apparent to an employee that their actions are dishonest. Using an employer's telephone to make personal calls, for example, may be viewed as dishonest by an employer but not by an employee. There may be a need for a proper investigation as to the purpose and circumstances of such calls. In *John Lewis plc v Coyne*[241] the court seemed to prefer a subjective approach rather than any absolute definition of dishonesty. An employee was dismissed for breaching company rules on the use of telephones but the lack of a sufficient investigation by the employer made it unfair. The court considered that there was a two-stage process in judging whether dishonesty had occurred. The first was that it must be decided whether, according to the ordinary standards of reasonable and honest people, what

---

[234] [1998] IRLR 358.
[235] See *UCATT v Brain* [1981] IRLR 224.
[236] [2008] IRLR 408.
[237] [1994] IRLR 235 CA.
[238] See *Conlin v United Distillers* [1994] IRLR 169 CA where a repeated act of dishonesty led to such a dismissal.
[239] See *British Leyland (UK) Ltd v Swift* [1981] IRLR 91 CA and *British Home Stores Ltd v Burchell* [1978] IRLR 379, considered further below.
[240] [2008] IRLR 869.
[241] [2001] IRLR 139.

was done was dishonest. The second stage was to consider whether the person c must have realised that what he was doing was, by those standards, dishonest.

There is a distinction between misconduct at work and misconduct outside of it which no relationship to the employment. What, for example, is the position of an employer wh has an employee facing criminal charges? In *Lovie Ltd* v *Anderson*[242] an employee was charged by the police with two separate offences of indecent exposure. It might be natural for an employer not to wish to retain an individual who faces such charges but there is still an obligation to carry out an investigation and give the employee an opportunity to state their case. Similarly, in *Securicor Guarding Ltd* v *R*[243] an employee was charged with sex offences against children, which he denied. The employer was concerned about the reaction of important customers and, after a disciplinary hearing, the employee was dismissed. This was held to be unfair, partly because the employer had not considered other options, such as suspension with full pay, in accordance with the company's own disciplinary code, or moving the individual to less customer-sensitive work. By way of contrast, an assistant schools groundsman who pleaded guilty to a sexual offence against his daughter was dismissed because of the possible risk to other children. According to the Court of Appeal, the employer had no choice but to dismiss the employee despite the lack of further investigation. The plea of guilty and the nature of the job were sufficient.[244] In *Mathewson* v *RB Wilson Dental Laboratories Ltd*[245] a dental technician was arrested during his lunch break and charged with being in possession of cannabis. The employers were held to have acted reasonably in treating this as a sufficient reason for dismissal, even though the offence was unconnected with his work. The employer argued that it was not appropriate to employ someone on highly skilled work who was using drugs, and that there was concern about the effect on younger staff members of continuing to employ him. A conviction itself, unless for a trivial or minor matter, would normally be sufficient to provide the employer with adequate grounds for believing that the employee had committed the offence and might be enough to dismiss the individual.[246]

Examples of misconduct at work include those that involve relationships with colleagues. *Hussain* v *Elonex*[247] concerned an allegation of head-butting and was part of a number of incidents between the complainant and another employee. This was considered grounds for dismissal, although there was an appeal on procedural grounds. The same result occurred in *Fuller* v *Lloyds Bank plc*[248] where, after an employer's investigation into an incident at a Christmas party that involved smashing a glass into another employee's face, the complainant was dismissed.

An employer is entitled to expect an employee not to compete for customers or contracts (see Chapter 3 on implied duties). Such competition may amount to a sufficient reason for

---

[242] [1999] IRLR 164.
[243] [1994] IRLR 633.
[244] *P* v *Nottinghamshire County Council* [1992] IRLR 362 CA; compare *ILEA* v *Gravett* [1988] IRLR 497, where the lack of a sufficient investigation was sufficient to render a dismissal unfair. The employee was a swimming instructor accused of a sexual offence against a girl, but the police decided to take no action.
[245] [1988] IRLR 512.
[246] See *Secretary of State for Scotland* v *Campbell* [1992] IRLR 263, where a prison officer who was also treasurer of the officer's social club was found guilty of embezzling the club funds; this verdict was sufficient to justify his dismissal.
[247] [1999] IRLR 420.
[248] [1991] IRLR 336.

v *B & L Cleaning Services*[249] a foreman for a contract cleaning firm ... e would not compete for a cleaning contract with his employer. The ...veen competing with the employer, which is more likely to be a ...erely indicating an intention to compete in the future,[250] or applying ...itor. The stage the plans for competing have reached may well be ...nent tribunal in reaching a decision. Thus a managing director who ...another senior manager and attempted to induce another employee ...sm was held to have gone beyond merely indicating a plan to compete in the future and was held to have been fairly dismissed.[251]

4.4.3.6 Retirement

See Chapter 6 below.

4.4.3.7 Redundancy

In *Williams* v *Compair Maxam Ltd*[252] the EAT laid down some principles that a reasonable employer should follow if they were planning to dismiss on the grounds of redundancy. The EAT pointed out that these were not principles of law but standards of behaviour. The approach has, however, been widely followed, even if the judgment now appears to reflect an industrial relations landscape that no longer seems to exist. The principles are:

1. The employer would try to give as much warning as possible, to employees and their representatives, of impending redundancies.

2. The employer would consult the employees' representatives and agree criteria for selection.

3. The criteria for selection would not, as far as possible, depend upon the personal opinion of the individual making the selection, but on objective criteria.

4. The employer would seek to ensure that the selection is made fairly against these criteria.

5. The employer would try to offer alternative employment, rather than dismissal.

In selecting for redundancy a senior manager is entitled to rely on the assessments of employees made by those who have direct knowledge of their work. Employers may need to show, however, that their method of selection was fair and applied reasonably.[253] An absence of adequate consultation with the employees concerned or their representatives might affect their ability to do this (consultation issues are considered below). It will not always be possible to call evidence to show that adequate consultation would not have made a difference to the decision about selection for redundancy. If the flaws in the process were procedural, it might be possible to reconstruct what might have happened if the correct procedures had been followed. If, however, the tribunal decides that the defects were more substantive, such a reconstruction may not be possible.[254]

---

[249] [1995] IRLR 193.

[250] See *Laughton and Hawley* v *Bapp Industrial Supplies Ltd* [1986] IRLR 245 where the EAT held that an employee did not breach his duty of loyalty by indicating a future intention to compete.

[251] *Marshall* v *Industrial Systems & Control Ltd* [1992] IRLR 294.

[252] [1982] IRLR 83.

[253] In *Northgate Ltd* v *Mercy* [2008] IRLR 222 the Court of Appeal ruled that the ET had been wrong to conclude that a glaring inconsistency produced in good faith could not amount to unfairness in the administration of a selection procedure.

[254] See *King* v *Eaton (No 2)* [1998] IRLR 686.

Thus reasonableness will normally require a warning to and consultation with affected employees and/or their representatives, the establishment of a fair selection procedure and an attempt to avoid or minimise the redundancies. A defect in this process is not necessarily fatal to the employer. In *Lloyd v Taylor Woodrow Construction*,[255] for example, there was failure to inform the employee of the selection criteria before the decision to dismiss was taken. This flaw was corrected at the appeal stage when the employee was given the opportunity to challenge the criteria. In these circumstances the EAT agreed that the dismissal had not been unfair. In *John Brown Engineering Ltd v Brown*[256] an employer agreed the selection criteria with the employees' representatives but then refused to publish the marks allocated to each employee. This was held to make the appeals procedure a sham, as individuals could not appeal against their selection without knowing their marks, and the dismissals were held to be unfair.

An employer will normally be expected to provide evidence as to the steps taken to select the employee for redundancy, the consultation that has taken place with the employee or their representatives and the attempts to find alternative employment. Similarly, a tribunal would be expected to consider all these issues when reaching a decision on the reasonableness of the dismissal.[257]

'Last in, first out' is still used as a criterion for selection and it is assumed to be based on periods of continuous rather than cumulative service.[258] Arguably, this form of selection indirectly discriminates against women and needs to be objectively justified. Selecting employees on part-time and/or fixed-term contracts may also be potentially discriminatory. Section 105 ERA 1996 makes it unfair to select for redundancy on a variety of impermissible grounds (see 4.4.3.2 above). In addition, s. 152 TULRCA 1992 offers special protection to those who are members of a trade union or take part in its activities.[259] Section 153 TULRCA 1992 provides that where the reason, or the principal reason, for the dismissal of an employee was redundancy, but the circumstances constituting the redundancy applied equally to other employees holding similar positions and those employees have not been selected for redundancy, and the reason, or the principal reason, was that the employee was a member of an independent trade union, or taking part in its activities, then that dismissal will be unfair. In *O'Dea v ISC Chemicals Ltd*[260] it was argued that an employee who spent half his time on trade union activities was in a special position and that, as a result, there were no other employees in a similar position with whom he could be compared. The Court of Appeal held that the trade union activities should be ignored when deciding whether the circumstances of the redundancy applied equally to others in a similar position.

It is well established that employers have a duty to consider the alternatives to compulsory redundancy.[261] As regards alternative employment, 'the size and administrative resources' of the employer will be a relevant consideration. Nevertheless, only in very rare cases will a tribunal accept that a reasonable employer would have created a job by dismissing someone else.

---

[255] [1999] IRLR 782.
[256] [1997] IRLR 90.
[257] See *Langston v Cranfield University* [1998] IRLR 172.
[258] *International Paint Co v Cameron* [1979] IRLR 62.
[259] This section also covers those who wish to make use of a union's services and those not wishing to be members or take part in the union's activities; see Chapter 10.
[260] [1995] IRLR 599 CA.
[261] See Advisory Handbook on Redundancy Handling 2008, p. 5.

Consultation may be directly with the employees concerned or with their representatives (see Chapter 9 for specific requirements in relation to collective redundancies). In *Mugford v Midland Bank plc*[262] the EAT held that a dismissal on the grounds of redundancy was not unfair because no consultation had taken place with the employee individually, only with the recognised trade union. The EAT described the position with regard to consultation as follows:

● Where no consultation about redundancy has taken place with either the trade union or the employee, the dismissal will normally be unfair, unless the reasonable employer would have concluded that the consultation would be an utterly futile exercise.

● Consultation with the trade union over the selection criteria does not of itself release the employer from considering with the employee individually his being identified for redundancy.

● It will be a question of fact and degree for the tribunal to consider whether the consultation with the individual and/or the trade union was so inadequate as to render the dismissal unfair.

In deciding whether the employer acted reasonably or not, the tribunal must view the overall picture at the time of termination. The consultation must be fair and proper, which means that there must be:

● Consultation when the proposals are still at a formative stage.

● Adequate information and adequate time to respond.

● A conscientious consideration by the employer of the response to consultation.[263]

Although proper consultation may be regarded as a procedural matter, it might have a direct bearing on the substantive decision to select a particular employee because a different employee might have been selected if, following proper consultation, different criteria had been adopted. It is not normally permissible for an employer to argue that a failure to consult or warn would have made no difference to the outcome in the particular case. It is what the employer did that is to be judged, not what might have been done. Nevertheless, if the employer could reasonably have concluded in the light of the circumstances known at the time of dismissal that consultation or warning would be 'utterly useless', he might well have acted reasonably. Whilst the size of an undertaking might affect the nature or formality of the consultation, it cannot excuse lack of any consultation at all. Finally, it should be noted that the EAT has taken the view that warning and consultation are part of the same single process of consultation, which should commence with a warning that the employee is at risk.[264]

4.4.3.8 **Contravention of an enactment**

An example of a statutory ban on employment might be the rules contained in the Immigration, Asylum and Nationality Act 2006.[265] Sections 15 and 21 provide penalties if an organisation employs an adult subject to immigration control if he has not been granted leave to

---

[262] [1997] IRLR 208.
[263] *King v Eaton* [1996] IRLR 199.
[264] See *Elkouil v Coney Island Ltd* [2002] IRLR 174.
[265] See *Kelly v University of Southampton* [2008] ICR 357 and *Hounslow London Borough Council v Klusova* [2008] ICR 396.

enter or remain in the UK or such leave is invalid, has ceased to have effect or is subject to a condition preventing him from entering employment. However, a dismissal for the reason that the employer could not lawfully continue to employ someone without contravening a restriction under an enactment is not necessarily fair.[266]

4.4.3.9 Some other substantial reason

Section 98(1)(b) ERA 1996 includes a sixth potentially fair reason for dismissal. This is:

Some other substantial reason of a kind such as to justify the dismissal of an employee holding the position which the employee held.

This provides flexibility for employers to introduce reasons other than the specific ones provided for in the Act. In *RS Components Ltd v RE Irwin*,[267] which concerned the dismissal of a salesperson who refused to accept a new contract of employment containing a restrictive covenant, the court held:

There are not only legal but also practical objections to a narrow construction of 'some other substantial reason'. Parliament may well have intended to set out . . . the common reasons for a dismissal but can hardly have hoped to produce an exhaustive catalogue of all the circumstances in which a company would be justified in terminating the services of an employee.

Thus 'some other substantial reason' is a general category which enables the courts to accept reasons that are not related to those in s. 98(2) ERA 1996 as potentially fair. In Irwin's case the court was sympathetic to the employer's desire to protect its business by introducing non-competition covenants for its sales staff. The burden is on the employer to show a substantial reason to dismiss. The law is designed to deter employers from dismissing employees for some 'trivial or unworthy' reason.[268] However, if an employer can show that there was a fair reason in the employer's mind at the time the decision was taken, and that the employer genuinely believed it to be fair, then this might make it a dismissal for some other substantial reason.[269]

This desire to help employers make difficult decisions for sound business reasons has typified the approach of the courts. *St John of God (Care Services) Ltd v Brooks*[270] involved a charity-owned hospital whose National Health Service funding was reduced. As a result the employer proposed to cut pay and benefits to staff in order to make the necessary savings to stop them getting into financial trouble. The proposals were eventually accepted by 140 of the 170 employees. The complainants were four of those who did not accept the changes and were dismissed. The EAT held that it was insufficient to look at the proposals alone. They were only one consideration and the reasonableness of the employer's actions had to be looked at in the context of sound business reasons and other factors, for example that the majority of the employees had accepted the changes. The employees were, therefore, dismissed for some other substantial reason.[271] The acceptance of new terms and conditions by

---

[266] *Sandhu v (1) Department of Education and Science; (2) London Borough of Hillingdon* [1978] IRLR 208.

[267] [1973] IRLR 239 NIRC. See now *Willow Oak Ltd v Silverwood* [2006] IRLR 607.

[268] *Kent County Council v Gilham* [1985] IRLR 16 CA.

[269] On the removal of an incumbent chief executive following a takeover see *Cobley v Forward Technology* [2003] IRLR 706.

[270] [1992] IRLR 546.

[271] The EAT followed the approach adopted by the Court of Appeal in *Hollister v National Farmers' Union* [1979] IRLR 238 CA.

the majority of employees was also a factor in *Catamaran Cruisers Ltd* v *Williams*.[272] In this case the employers wished to make substantial changes to improve safety and efficiency. The EAT held that:

> We do not accept as a valid proposition of law that an employer may only offer terms which are less or much less favourable than those which pre-existed if the very survival of his business depends upon acceptance of the terms.

The EAT remitted the matter back to the employment tribunal with an instruction that it should not look solely at the advantages and disadvantages to the employees – it was also necessary to look at the benefit to the employer of imposing the changes in the new contract of employment. In *Farrant* v *The Woodroffe School*[273] an employee was dismissed for refusing to accept organisational changes. The employer mistakenly believed that the employee was obliged to accept a new job description and that the dismissal was therefore lawful. The EAT held that dismissal for refusing to obey an unlawful order was not necessarily unfair. Of importance was not the lawfulness or otherwise of the employer's instructions but the overall reasonableness. In this case it was not unreasonable for the employer to act on professional advice even if that advice was wrong.

4.4.3.10 **Reasonableness**

According to s. 98(4) ERA 1996, the employment tribunal will need to decide whether in the circumstances the employer acted reasonably or unreasonably, having regard to the size and administrative resources of the employer, in treating the reason as sufficient to dismiss the employee. This is to be determined 'in accordance with equity and the substantial merits of the case'. At this stage the burden of proof is neutral.[274]

As a matter of law, a reason cannot be treated as sufficient where it has not been established as true or that there were reasonable grounds on which the employer could have concluded that it was true. Under s. 98(4) ERA 1996, tribunals must take account of the wider circumstances. In addition to the employer's business needs, attention must be paid to the personal attributes of the employee – for example, previous work record. Thus when all the relevant facts are considered, a dismissal may be deemed unfair notwithstanding the fact that the disciplinary rules specified that such behaviour would result in immediate dismissal. Conversely, employers may act reasonably in dismissing even though they have breached an employee's contract. In appropriate cases the test of fairness must be interpreted, so far as possible, compatibly with the European Convention on Human Rights.[275]

Employers will be expected to treat employees in similar circumstances in a similar way. The requirement that the employer must act consistently between employees means that an employer should consider truly comparable cases which were known about or ought to have been known about. Nevertheless, the overriding principle seems to be that each case must be considered on its own facts and with the freedom to consider both aggravating factors and

---

[272] [1994] IRLR 386.

[273] [1998] IRLR 76.

[274] See *Boys and Girls Welfare Society* v *McDonald* [1996] IRLR 129 which concerned a residential social worker who allegedly hit a boy in his care, and emphasised the error of placing the burden of proof on the employer.

[275] See *X* v *Y* [2003] IRLR 561 on art. 8 and respect for private life.

mitigating circumstances. The words 'equity and the substantial merits' also allow tribunals to apply their knowledge of good industrial relations practice and to ensure that there has been procedural fairness (see below). In *West London Mental Health Trust* v *Sarkar*[276] the EAT observed that where a disciplinary process includes an investigation, negotiation, disciplinary hearing and appeal, all material up to and including matters raised at the appeal are relevant in determining fairness.

In *Polkey* v *AE Dayton Services Ltd*[277] Lord Bridge stated that there might be exceptional circumstances where an employer could reasonably take the view that these normal procedural steps would be futile and could not have altered the decision to dismiss. In such circumstances the test of reasonableness may have been satisfied.[278] This approach did not imply that the employer must have taken a deliberate decision not to consult.[279] The test of reasonableness was based on what the employers knew at the time of the dismissal, irrespective of whether the decision not to consult was deliberate.[280]

British Home Stores v *Burchell*[281] concerned the dismissal of an employee for allegedly being involved in acts of dishonesty with a number of other employees. The EAT provided some guidance on the steps that need to be taken by employers who suspect one or more employees of misconduct:

> First of all, there must be established by the employer the fact of that belief; that the employer did believe it. Secondly, that the employer had in his mind reasonable grounds upon which to sustain that belief. And thirdly . . . that the employer, at the stage at which he formed that belief on those grounds, at any rate at the final stage at which he formed that belief on those grounds, had carried out as much investigation into the matter as was reasonable in all the circumstances of the case.

This three-step test has been used extensively since this judgment.[282] In *Linfood Cash & Carry Ltd* v *Thomson*,[283] for example, two employees were dismissed on suspicion of theft. The dismissals were held to be unfair because, applying the *Burchell* test, the court concluded that even though the employer genuinely believed in the employees' guilt, they had no reasonable grounds for that belief and had not carried out a sufficient investigation.[284]

Having taken these steps the test is then whether it was reasonable for the employer to dismiss. *British Leyland UK Ltd* v *Swift*[285] involved an employee dismissed after being found guilty in a magistrates' court of fraudulently using a road fund licence belonging to a company vehicle on his own car. The question was whether a reasonable employer would have dismissed the employee. The court stated:

---

[276] [2009] IRLR 512.

[277] [1987] IRLR 503 HL.

[278] In *Warner* v *Adnet Ltd* [1998] IRLR 394 CA a failure to consult as a result of the appointment of a receiver, the dire financial straits of the company and the need to find a buyer urgently made the normal requirement to consult unnecessary; consultation could not have made a difference.

[279] In *Ferguson* v *Prestwick Circuits Ltd* [1992] IRLR 266 the employers took a deliberate decision not to consult, claiming that the workforce had stated a preference for this approach after a previous redundancy exercise; this was held not to be a sufficient reason for failing to consult.

[280] See *Duffy* v *Yeomans & Partners Ltd* [1994] IRLR 642 CA.

[281] [1978] IRLR 379.

[282] It was approved by the Court of Appeal in *Weddel* v *Tepper* [1980] ICR 286 CA.

[283] [1989] IRLR 235.

[284] See *Sainsburys Ltd* v *Hitt* [2003] IRLR 23 CA.

[285] [1981] IRLR 91 CA.

It must be remembered that in all these cases there is a band of reasonableness, within which one employer might reasonably take one view; another quite reasonably take a different view . . . If it was quite reasonable to dismiss him, then the dismissal must be upheld as fair; even though some employers may not have dismissed him.

Thus there developed a test based on a band of reasonable responses. *Iceland Frozen Foods v Jones*[286] concerned the dismissal of a night-shift foreman at a warehouse.[287] The employee had failed to secure the premises after the shift and was held responsible by the employer for slow production on the shift. The tribunal held that the dismissal was unfair both for the reasons given and on procedural grounds. At the EAT Browne-Wilkinson J summarised the legal position:

1. The starting point should always be the words of the statute.

2. In applying the statute the tribunal must consider the reasonableness of the employer's conduct, not simply whether the members of the tribunal thought the dismissal fair.

3. In considering the reasonableness of the employer's conduct, the tribunal must not substitute its own decision as to what was the right course for the employer to take.[288]

4. In many cases there was a band of reasonable responses to the employee's conduct with one employer taking one view and another employer a different view.

5. The function of the tribunal is to decide whether the decision to dismiss the employee fell within a band of reasonable responses which a reasonable employer might have adopted. If the dismissal falls within such a band then it is fair.

This approach was questioned in part by the EAT in *Haddon*,[289] *Wilson*[290] and *Midland Bank*.[291] The defects identified by the EAT were twofold. First, the expression 'range of reasonable responses' had become a mantra, so that nothing short of a perverse decision would be outside such a range. Second, it prevented members of employment tribunals from approaching the test of reasonableness by reference to their own experience in deciding what should be done. However, in *Post Office v Foley*,[292] the Court of Appeal reaffirmed the previous approach. The range of reasonable responses test does not become one of perversity because the behaviour of an employer has to be extreme before it falls outside the range. There are cases where it will not apply and the court gave two examples. First, where an employee, without good cause, sets fire to the factory, burns it down and is dismissed. Secondly, where an employee says good morning to the line manager and is dismissed. In these cases there is unlikely to be a need to use the range of reasonable responses test as the first dismissal would be reasonable and the second not. It is in the range between these two examples that there is the possibility of disagreement about what action a reasonable employer would take. That is when the employment tribunal must apply the test. As for the suggestion that the members of the tribunal ought to be able effectively to substitute their own views about what was the reasonable decision, the court held that:

---

[286] [1982] IRLR 439.

[287] See also *Neale v Hereford and Worcester County Council* [1986] IRLR 168 CA.

[288] See *Anglian Homes Improvements Ltd v Kelly* [2004] IRLR 793.

[289] *Haddon v Van den Bergh Foods Ltd* [1999] IRLR 672.

[290] *Wilson v Ethicon* [2000] IRLR 4.

[291] *Midland Bank plc v Madden* [2000] IRLR 288.

[292] *Post Office v Foley; HSBC plc (formerly Midland Bank) v Madden* [2000] IRLR 827 CA; see also *Beedell v West Ferry Printers Ltd* [2000] IRLR 650.

It was also made clear in *Iceland Foods* that the members of the tribunal must not simply consider whether they personally think that the dismissal is fair and they must not substitute their decision as to what was the right course to adopt for that of the employer. Their proper function is to determine whether the decision to dismiss the employee fell within the band of reasonable responses which a reasonable employer might have adopted.[293]

4.4.4 Procedural fairness (1): ACAS Code of Practice

The Code was first introduced in 1977 and the current version came into effect in April 2009.[294] It was issued under s. 199 TULRCA 1992, which provides for the revision of the Code to bring it into line with statutory developments. Failure to observe the Code will not in itself render an employer liable to any proceedings.[295] However, it will be admissible in proceedings before employment tribunals and the Central Arbitration Committee and any relevant parts will be taken into account.[296] In addition, s. 207A TULRCA 1992 allows such tribunals to adjust compensation by up to 25 per cent for unreasonable failure to comply with any provision of the Code. The Code covers disciplinary and grievance procedures and the right to be accompanied (see below).

The foreword to the Code emphasises that 'Employers and employees should always seek to resolve disciplinary and grievance issues in the workplace . . .'. Paragraph 2 suggests that 'rules and procedures for handling disciplinary and grievance situations . . . should be set down in writing, be clear and specific . . .'.[297] An example of the dangers of not ensuring that employees know what amounts to misconduct occurred in *W Brooks & Son v Skinner*.[298] After problems at a Christmas party for employees at which a number became drunk, the employer and the trade union negotiated an agreement that in future such behaviour would result in instant dismissal. Although normally such a collective agreement would be enough to show that the information had been communicated to the employees, it was not held to be so in this case. The following Christmas some employees became drunk and the complainant was sacked. The dismissal was held to be unfair because the complainant did not know of the agreement and it did not relate to conduct which any reasonable employee would realise would result in dismissal.[299]

Paragraph 4 of the ACAS Code identifies the following aspects of fairness:

- 'Employers and employees should raise and deal with issues promptly and should not unreasonably delay meetings, decisions or confirmation of those decisions.
- Employers and employees should act consistently.
- Employers should carry out any necessary investigations, to establish the facts of the case.
- Employers should inform employees of the basis of the problem and give them an opportunity to put their case in response before any decisions are made.

---

[293] On the approach to be taken when human rights issues are raised see *X v Y* [2004] IRLR 625 and *McGowan v Scottish Water* [2005] IRLR 167.

[294] It is important to note that, according to para. 1, this Code does not apply to dismissals owing to redundancy or the non-renewal of fixed-term contracts.

[295] Section 207(1) TULRCA 1992.

[296] Section 207(2)–(3) TULRCA 1992; see also the ACAS Guide on Discipline and Grievances at Work 2009 which does not form part of the Code.

[297] See also ACAS Guide paras. 16–28. Appendix 2 of the Guide provides sample disciplinary procedures.

[298] [1984] IRLR 379.

[299] Unlike that in the contrasting case of *Gray Dunn & Co Ltd v Edwards* [1980] IRLR 23.

- Employees should allow employees to be accompanied at any formal disciplinary or grievance meeting.

- Employers should allow an employee to appeal against any formal decision made.'

The foreword to the Code advises employers to keep written records of the disciplinary cases they deal with. In addition, paras. 5–28 discuss the following key steps to handling disciplinary issues in the workplace: [300]

- Establish the facts of each case.

- Inform the employee of the problem.

- Hold a meeting with the employee to discuss the problem.

- Allow the employee to be accompanied at the meeting.

- Decide on appropriate action.

- Provide employees with an opportunity to appeal.

Paragraphs 29–30 of the ACAS Code suggest that special consideration be given to the way in which disciplinary procedures operate in relation to trade union officials and those charged or convicted of a criminal offence.

Finally, we must consider the impact of appeal procedures. In *West Midlands Co-op* v *Tipton*[301] the House of Lords confirmed that a dismissal is unfair if an employer unreasonably treats the reason for dismissal as sufficient, either when the original decision to dismiss is made or when it is upheld at the conclusion of an internal appeal. A dismissal may also be unfair if the employer refuses to comply with the full requirements of an appeal procedure.[302] Whether procedural defects can be rectified on appeal will depend on the degree of unfairness at the original hearing.[303]

4.4.5 Procedural fairness (2): the right to be accompanied

Section 10 Employment Relations Act 1999 (ERELA 1999) introduced the right for workers[304] who are required or invited by the employer to attend a disciplinary or grievance hearing to be accompanied by a single companion if the worker makes a reasonable request in writing. According to para. 15 of the ACAS Code of Practice on Disciplinary and Grievance Procedures:

> To exercise the statutory right to be accompanied workers must make a reasonable request. What is reasonable will depend on the circumstances of each individual case. However, it would not normally be reasonable for workers to insist on being accompanied by a companion whose presence would prejudice the hearing nor would it be reasonable for a worker to ask to be accompanied by a companion from a remote geographical location if someone suitable and willing was available on site.
>
> *Source*: ACAS © Crown Copyright 2009

[300] Further advice is contained in paras. 35–103 of the ACAS Guide.

[301] [1986] IRLR 112.

[302] See *Tarbuck* v *Sainsburys Ltd* [2006] IRLR 664.

[303] See *Taylor* v *OCS Ltd* [2006] IRLR 613.

[304] With the exception of those in the security services, which includes the Security Service, the Secret Intelligence Service and Government Communications Headquarters: s. 15 ERELA 1999.

A disciplinary hearing, according to s. 13(4) ERELA 1999, is a hearing that could result in:

- The administration of a formal warning to a worker by the employer.
- The taking of some other action in respect of a worker by his employer.
- The confirmation of a warning issued or some other action taken.[305]

The right to be accompanied does not extend to more informal interviews which will not result in a formal warning. In *Harding v London Underground*,[306] where the employee had received an 'informal oral warning', the EAT ruled that a disciplinary warning becomes a formal warning if it becomes part of the employee's disciplinary record.

The right applies to workers, who are defined[307] as including those that come within the meaning of s. 230(3) ERA 1996 plus agency workers, home workers[308] and persons in Crown employment. It excludes those in the naval, military, air or reserve forces, and relevant members of the staff of the Houses of Parliament. Where this right is exercised, the employer must permit the worker to be accompanied at the hearing by a single companion chosen by the worker. The companion is to be permitted to address the hearing and confer with the worker during it. However, the employer does not have to allow the companion to: answer questions on behalf of the worker; address the hearing if the worker indicates that they do not wish the companion to do so; or use their position in a way that prevents the employer from explaining its case or prevents another person from making a contribution to the hearing.[309] Thus the companion is more than a witness to the proceedings but less than an advocate.[310] The companion can be:

1. An individual who is employed by a trade union and is an official[311] of that union.
2. An individual who is an official of a trade union whom the union has reasonably certified in writing as having experience of, or having received training in, acting as a worker's companion at such hearings.
3. Another of the employer's workers.[312]

An employer must also permit a worker to take paid time off during working hours for the purpose of accompanying another of the employer's workers to a hearing.[313] In addition, a worker has the right not to be subjected to detriment by the employer for exercising the right to ask for a companion or for being a companion. Any dismissal resulting from the assertion of these rights will be automatically unfair (see above).[314] A worker may present a complaint to an employment tribunal if the employer fails, or threatens to fail, to comply with these provisions. This complaint must be made within three months beginning with the date of the

---

[305] A grievance hearing is one which concerns the performance of a duty by the employer in relation to a worker: s. 13(5) ERELA 1999. On redundancy meetings see *Heathmill Ltd v Jones* [2003] IRLR 856.

[306] [2003] IRLR 252; see also *Skiggs v South West Trains Ltd* [2005] IRLR 459.

[307] Section 13(1) ERELA 1999.

[308] Further definition of agency and home workers is provided in s. 13(2) and (3) ERELA 1999.

[309] Section 10(2B)–(2C) ERELA 1999.

[310] On the appropriateness of legal representation see: *Kulkarni v Milton Keynes Hospital Trust* [2009] IRLR 829 (C/A) where it was held that a medical practitioner was entitled to be represented by a lawyer at his disciplinary hearing.

[311] Within the meaning of ss. 1 and 119 TULRCA 1992.

[312] Section 10(3) ERELA 1999; s. 10(4) provides an obligation on the employer to arrange alternative times for hearings if the companion has difficulties in attending.

[313] Section 10(6) ERELA 1999.

[314] Section 12(1)–(6) ERELA 1999.

failure or threat, unless the tribunal is satisfied that it was not reasonably practicable to do so. If the employment tribunal finds the complaint well founded, it may order the employer to pay compensation to the worker, not exceeding two weeks' pay.[315]

4.4.6 Claiming unfair dismissal

Unless the 'time limit escape clause' applies,[316] claims must normally arrive at an employment tribunal within three months of the effective date of termination. A complaint can also be presented before the effective date of termination provided it is lodged after notice has been given. This includes notice given by an employee who is alleging constructive dismissal.[317] What is or is not reasonably practicable is a question of fact and the onus is on the employee to prove that it was not reasonably practicable to claim in time. The meaning of 'reasonably practicable' lies somewhere between reasonable and reasonably capable of physically being done.[318] The tribunal will look at the issue in all the surrounding circumstances.

The courts have dealt with this jurisdictional point on several occasions and have taken the view that, since the unfair dismissal provisions have been in force for many years, tribunals should be fairly strict in enforcing the time limit. Nevertheless, the issue of reasonable practicability depends upon the awareness of specific grounds for complaint, not upon the right to complain at all. Thus there is nothing to prevent an employee who is precluded by the passage of time from claiming on one ground from proceeding with a second complaint on another ground raised within a reasonable period. According to the Court of Appeal, if employers want to protect themselves from late claims presented on the basis of newly discovered information they should ensure that the fullest information is made available to the employee at the time of dismissal.[319]

4.4.7 Conciliation, arbitration and compromise agreements

ACAS has an important role in conciliation and arbitration (see Chapter 1). In 2008/9, 42 per cent of unfair dismissal applications[320] to employment tribunals were settled before reaching the stage of a formal tribunal hearing. These are not all a response to the intervention of ACAS, but clearly the organisation plays a significant part in reducing the burden on employment tribunals. Copies of unfair dismissal applications and subsequent correspondence are sent to an ACAS conciliation officer who has the duty to promote a settlement of the complaint:

- if requested to do so by the complainant and the employer (known as the respondent), or
- if, in the absence of any such request, the conciliation officer considers that he could act with a reasonable prospect of success.

---

[315] Section 11(1)–(6) ERELA 1999.

[316] Section 111(2) ERA 1996. The question of jurisdiction must be considered by an employment tribunal if it considers that the issue is a live one: see *Radakouits v Abbey National* [2010] IRLR 307.

[317] Section 111(4) ERA 1996.

[318] *Palmer v Southend Borough Council* [1984] IRLR 119. On the effect of the advice received see *Marks & Spencer plc v Williams-Ryan* [2005] IRLR 562.

[319] See *Marley Ltd v Anderson* [1996] IRLR 163.

[320] See ACAS Annual Report 2008/9.

In *Moore* v *Duport Furniture*[321] the House of Lords decided that the expression 'promote a settlement' should be given a liberal construction capable of covering whatever action by way of such promotion is appropriate in the circumstances. Where the complainant has ceased to be employed, the conciliation officer may seek to promote that person's re-employment (i.e. reinstatement or re-engagement) on terms that appear to be equitable. If the complainant does not wish to be re-employed, or this is not practicable, the conciliation officer must seek to promote agreement on compensation.[322] In addition, s. 18(3) Employment Tribunals Act 1996 (ETA 1996) requires conciliation officers to make their services available before a complaint has been presented if requested to do so by either a potential applicant or a respondent. It should be noted that, according to the EAT, an ACAS officer must never advise on the merits of a case and has no responsibility to ensure that the settlement terms are fair to the employee.[323]

Where appropriate, a conciliation officer is to 'have regard to the desirability of encouraging the use of other procedures available for the settlement of grievances', and anything communicated to a conciliation officer in connection with the performance of the above functions is not admissible in evidence in any proceedings before a tribunal except with the consent of the person who communicated it.[324] It should be noted that an agreement to refrain from lodging a tribunal complaint is subject to all the qualifications by which an agreement can be avoided at common law – for example, on grounds of economic duress.

Section 203(1) ERA 1996 states that a provision in an agreement is void in so far as it attempts to exclude the operation of any part of the ERA 1996 or stops a person from bringing proceedings under the Act.[325] Exceptions to this are found in s. 203(2) and include a provision that any agreement to refrain from instituting or continuing proceedings has been reached where an ACAS conciliation officer has taken action under s. 18 ETA 1996.[326] If an agreement is reached with the help of the conciliation officer, then it will be treated as an exception to s. 203(1) ERA 1996. Another exclusion is where an agreement to refrain from instituting or continuing proceedings has been reached in accordance with the conditions regulating compromise agreements.[327] The provisions on compromise agreements are contained in s. 203(3), (3A), (3B) and (4) ERA 1996 and are as follows:

1. The agreement must be in writing.

2. The employee or worker must have received advice from an independent adviser.

3. There must be an insurance policy in force to cover any claims from the complainant or the employer in respect of any losses in consequence of the advice.

4. The agreement must identify the adviser.[328]

---

[321] [1982] IRLR 31.

[322] Section 18(3)–(5) ETA 1996.

[323] *Clarke* v *Redcar Borough Council* [2006] IRLR 324.

[324] Section 18(6)(7) ETA 1996.

[325] In *Sutherland* v *Network Appliance Ltd* [2001] IRLR 12 the EAT held that it was only those parts of the agreement that were in contravention of s. 203(1) ERA 1996 that would be void; not necessarily the whole agreement.

[326] Section 203(2)(e) ERA 1996.

[327] Section 203(2)(f) ERA 1996. On the possible effects of a void compromise agreement see: *Gibb* v *Maidstone and Tunbridge Wells NHS Trust* [2009] IRLR 709. On misrepresentation see: *Industrials Ltd* v *Horizon Ltd* [2010] IRLR 204.

[328] See *Gloystarne & Co Ltd* v *Martin* [2001] IRLR 15, where the individual concerned denied having appointed a trade union official as his representative or agreeing to the compromise reached.

5. The agreement must state that these conditions regulating compromise agreements have been satisfied.

A person is an independent adviser if he is a qualified lawyer;[329] an officer, official, employee or member of an independent trade union who has been certified by the trade union as authorised and competent to give advice; an advice centre worker who is similarly certified by the advice centre, or some other persons identified by the Secretary of State. The effect of following this procedure is to stop any further proceedings and is something that employers may use if they wish to take action that might otherwise end up in a complaint to an employment tribunal. According to the Appeal Court, the requirement that in order to constitute a valid compromise an agreement must 'relate to the particular proceedings' should be construed as requiring the proceedings to be clearly identified. Although one document can be used to compromise all proceedings, it is insufficient to use the expression 'all statutory rights'.[330]

Section 212A TULRCA 1992 is an attempt to provide an alternative to employment tribunals in unfair dismissal disputes. It allows ACAS to devise a scheme for arbitration in such cases.[331] The characteristics of the scheme are:

1. The arbitrators are independent individuals, at least some of whom will not be lawyers.
2. Parties to a dispute would both need to agree to go to arbitration.
3. In so agreeing, they would give up all their rights to go to an employment tribunal.
4. The parties would submit their cases in writing and legal representation would be discouraged at the hearing, which would take place locally.
5. The decision of the arbitrator, who would have all the relevant powers of an employment tribunal, is to be binding, with no appeal to the EAT.

The arbitrators will be heavily influenced by the ACAS Code of Practice on Discipline and Grievance Procedures. The advantage of the scheme is that it should, if used, speed up the process and be less formal than employment tribunals have become.

4.4.8 Remedies

The remedies following a finding of unfair dismissal by an employment tribunal are reinstatement, re-engagement or compensation. There is also the opportunity to obtain interim relief.

4.4.8.1 Interim relief

An employee may apply for interim relief[332] if they have presented a claim for unfair dismissal by virtue of:

1. Dismissal on the grounds of trade union membership or activities.[333]
2. Being a designated employee to carry out activities connected with health and safety, or being a health and safety representative.[334]

---

[329] Section 203(4) ERA 1996 contains further definition of who is a qualified lawyer. On legal executives see Compromise Agreements (Description of Person) Order 2004 (Amendment) Order 2004, SI 2004/2515.
[330] *Hinton v University of East London* [2005] IRLR 552.
[331] See ACAS Arbitration Scheme (Great Britain) Order 2004, SI 2004/753.
[332] Section 128 ERA 1996.
[333] Section 161(1) TULRCA 1992.
[334] Section 100(1)(a)–(b) ERA 1996.

3. Being an employee representative, or a candidate to be such a representative, for the purposes of the Working Time Regulations 1998.[335]

4. Being a trustee of an occupational pension scheme relating to the individual's employment.[336]

5. Being an employee representative for the purposes of consultation on collective redundancies or transfers of undertakings.[337]

6. Being a reason connected with obtaining or preventing recognition of a trade union.[338]

7. Being a reason connected with making a protected disclosure.[339]

The application to the tribunal needs to be made within seven days immediately following the effective date of termination and the employer will be given seven days' notice of the hearing together with a copy of the application.[340] If it appears to the tribunal that it may, after a proper hearing, make a declaration of unfair dismissal, it will ask the employer if the employer is willing to reinstate or re-engage the employee. If the employer refuses or the employee reasonably refuses an offer of alternative employment,[341] the tribunal is able to make an order for the continuation of the contract.[342] It will stipulate the level of pay to be given to the employee, based on what the employee would normally have expected to earn in the period, but will take into account any payments already made by the employer as payments in lieu of notice or by way of discharging the employer's liabilities under the contract of employment.[343] Section 132 ERA 1996 enables the employment tribunal to award compensation if the employer does not comply with an order for continuation.

4.4.8.2 Reinstatement or re-engagement

If the employment tribunal finds the complaint well founded, it will explain to the complainant about its power to make an order for reinstatement or re-engagement and ask whether the complainant wishes the tribunal to make such an order. If the complainant expresses a wish for such an order, the tribunal will consider it.[344] An order for reinstatement is an order that the employer treat the employee as if he had never been dismissed. Thus the employee will return to the same job on the same terms and conditions as if there had been no interruption. The employer will pay any amounts due, less any sums already paid to the employee in connection with the dismissal.[345] An order for re-engagement is an order that the employee be taken back by the employer into a position comparable to that from which he was dismissed, or other suitable employment. The employment tribunal will specify the terms and conditions upon which the employee will return.[346]

---

[335] Section 101A(d) ERA 1996.
[336] Section 102(1) ERA 1996.
[337] Section 103 ERA 1996.
[338] Section 161(2) and Sch. A1 TULRCA 1992.
[339] Section 103A ERA 1996.
[340] Section 128(2) and (4) ERA 1996.
[341] Section 129 ERA 1996. There are issues about what terms and conditions might be offered on re-engagement.
[342] Section 130(1) ERA 1996, but not an order that ensures the employee actually goes back to work.
[343] Section 130(2)–(7) ERA 1996; this includes any payments made as damages for breach of contract.
[344] Sections 112–113 ERA 1996.
[345] Section 114 ERA 1996.
[346] Section 115 ERA 1996; the tribunal will, as far as is reasonably practicable, specify terms as favourable as reinstatement, the exception being where there is contributory fault by the employee (s. 116(4) ERA 1996).

If at least seven days before the hearing the employee has expressed a wish to be re-employed but it becomes necessary to postpone or adjourn the hearing because the employer does not, without special reason, adduce reasonable evidence about the availability of the job from which the claimant was dismissed, the employer will be required to pay the costs of the adjournment or postponement.[347] In addition, s. 116(5) ERA 1996 states that where an employer has taken on a permanent replacement, this shall not be taken into account unless the employer shows either:

- that it was not practicable to arrange for the dismissed employee's work to be done without engaging a permanent replacement; or
- that a replacement was engaged after the lapse of a reasonable period without having heard from the dismissed employee that he wished to be reinstated or re-engaged, and that when the employer engaged the replacement it was no longer reasonable to arrange for the dismissed employee's work to be done except by a permanent replacement.

The employment tribunal has considerable discretion about making such orders and there are tests of practicability and justice. The tribunal will take into account the complainant's wishes and whether it is practicable for the employer to comply with an order for reinstatement. It will also take into account whether such an order would be just in circumstances where the employee contributed towards the dismissal.[348] In *Rao v Civil Aviation Authority*[349] an employee with an extremely poor attendance record was dismissed. The dismissal was held to be unfair on procedural grounds and the employment tribunal refused to order reinstatement or re-engagement because there was no evidence that, if he were re-employed, his absences would not continue, he would require retraining and his return might not be welcomed by his fellow employees. The EAT approved this decision and stated that 'practicable' is not the same as 'possible' or 'capable' and that the task of the employment tribunal was to look at what had happened and at what might happen and reach a decision on the basis of what would be fair and just for all parties. The issue of practicability was considered in *Port of London Authority v Payne*,[350] which involved a number of dockers who had been unfairly selected for redundancy because of their trade union activities. The employers claimed that it was not practicable for them to comply with the orders for re-engagement because they were going through a period of large-scale redundancies and there were no available job vacancies.[351] The court held:

> The employment tribunal, though it should carefully scrutinise the reasons advanced by the employer, should give due weight to the commercial judgment of the management . . . The standard [for re-engagement] must not be set too high. The employer cannot be expected to explore every possible avenue which ingenuity might suggest.

In *Wood v Crossan*[352] an employee was suspected of various offences, including dealing in drugs. The employers formed a genuine belief that he was guilty of the allegations and, after

---

[347] Section 13(2) ETA 1996.
[348] Section 116 ERA 1996.
[349] [1992] IRLR 303 EAT; the finding of the new tribunal on compensation was appealed at *Rao v Civil Aviation Authority* [1994] IRLR 240 CA.
[350] [1994] IRLR 9 CA.
[351] See *Clancy v Cannock Chase Technical College* [2001] IRLR 331, where the EAT confirmed a tribunal decision to decline to make a re-engagement order because of a worsening redundancy situation with the employer.
[352] *Wood Group Heavy Industrial Turbines Ltd v Crossan* [1998] IRLR 680.

an investigation, the employee was sacked. The employment tribunal held that the dismissal was unfair because of an inadequate investigation and other procedural defects. The complainant's job had disappeared, so there was no possibility of reinstatement. Taking into account that the individual had 16 years' service and that there was no apparent animosity between him and the employer, the employment tribunal ordered that the complainant be re-engaged at the same salary. The appeal against this was allowed by the EAT, who held that the employer's belief in the guilt of the employee resulted in a breakdown of mutual trust and confidence. Without this bond the employment relationship could not exist. The EAT further concluded:

> We consider that the remedy of re-engagement has very limited scope and will only be practical in the rarest cases where there is a breakdown in confidence as between the employer and the employee. Even if the way the matter is handled results in a finding of unfair dismissal, the remedy, in that context, invariably to our mind will be compensation.

Where a person is reinstated or re-engaged as the result of a tribunal order but the terms are not fully complied with, a tribunal must make an additional award of compensation of such amount as it thinks fit, having regard to the loss sustained by the complainant in consequence of the failure to comply fully with the terms of the order.[353] It is a matter for speculation how long re-employment must last for it to be said that an order has been complied with. If a complainant is not re-employed in accordance with a tribunal order, he or she is entitled to enforce the monetary element at the employment tribunal.[354] Compensation will be awarded together with an additional award unless the employer satisfies the tribunal that it was not practicable to comply with the order.[355] According to s. 117(3)(b) ERA, the additional award will be of between 26 and 52 weeks' pay. Within this range, the tribunal has discretion as to what additional compensation should be awarded but it must be exercised on the basis of a proper assessment of the factors involved. One factor would ordinarily be the view taken of the employer's conduct in refusing to comply with the order. Conversely, employees who unreasonably prevent an order being complied with will be regarded as having failed to mitigate their loss.

4.4.8.3 Compensation

Compensation for unfair dismissal is divided into two parts. The first is a basic award which, like redundancy payments, is related to age, length of service and pay. The second is a compensatory award, which is related to the actual loss suffered.

The basic award is arrived at by calculating the number of years of continuous service and allowing the appropriate amount for each year. This appropriate amount is:

- One and a half weeks' pay for each year of employment in which the employee was not below 41 years of age.
- One week's pay for each year of employment in which the employee was not below the age of 22 years.
- Half a week's pay for each year of employment in which the employee was not within either of the above.

[353] Section 117(2) ERA 1996.
[354] Section 124(4) ERA 1996.
[355] Section 17(3)–(4) ERA 1996.

Only 20 years' service can be taken into account, which results in a statutory maximum of 30 weeks' pay. A week's pay is to be calculated in accordance with Part XIV Chapter II ERA 1996 (see Chapter 7).[356] In certain cases there is a minimum award of £4,700.[357] This is where there has been unfair selection for redundancy or dismissal related to one of the reasons listed above in relation to interim relief. The basic award can be reduced by such proportion as the tribunal considers just and equitable on two grounds:

- The complainant unreasonably refused an offer of reinstatement (such an offer could have been made before any finding of unfairness).

- Any conduct of the complainant before the dismissal, or before notice was given.

This does not apply where the reason for dismissal was redundancy unless the dismissal was regarded as unfair by virtue of s. 100(1)(a) or (b), 101A(d), 102(1) or 103 ERA 1996. In that event the reduction will apply only to that part of the award payable because of s. 120 ERA 1996.[358]

A compensatory award is that which a tribunal 'considers just and equitable in all the circumstances having regard to the loss sustained by the complainant in consequence of the dismissal insofar as that loss is attributable to action taken by the employer'.[359] Thus tribunals will normally have to assess how long the claimant would have been employed but for the dismissal.[360] However, the mere fact that the employer could have dismissed fairly on another ground arising out of the same factual situation does not render it unjust or inequitable to award compensation.[361] Employment tribunals will also have to consider whether the effect of subsequent employment was to break the chain of causation or not.[362] Thus in *Dench* v *Flynn & Partners* [363] an assistant solicitor was able to claim compensation for unemployment after a subsequent short-term job because it was attributable to the original dismissal.

Section 123(3) ERA 1996 specifically mentions that an individual whose redundancy entitlement would have exceeded the basic award can be compensated for the difference, whilst a redundancy payment received in excess of the basic award payable goes to reduce the compensatory award. The compensatory award can be reduced in two other circumstances: where the employee's action caused or contributed to the dismissal, and where the employee failed to mitigate his loss. Before reducing an award on the ground that the complainant caused or contributed to the dismissal, a tribunal must be satisfied that the employee's conduct was culpable or blameworthy – i.e. foolish, perverse or unreasonable in the circumstances. Thus there could be a finding of contributory fault in a case of constructive dismissal on the basis that there was a causal link between the employee's conduct and the employer's repudiatory breach of contract.[364] According to the EAT, tribunals must consider the issue of

---

[356] Section 119 ERA 1996; the maximum week's pay in 2010 is £380, so the maximum basic award would be £11,400.
[357] Section 120 ERA 1996; the amount is for 2009.
[358] Section 122 ERA 1996.
[359] Section 123 ERA 1996.
[360] See *Software 2000 Ltd* v *Andrews* [2007] IRLR 568.
[361] See *Devonshire* v *Trico-Folberth* [1989] IRLR 397.
[362] See *Aegon UK Corp Services Ltd* v *Roberts* [2009] IRLR 1042.
[363] [1998] IRLR 653.
[364] See *Polentarutti* v *Autokraft Ltd* [1991] IRLR 457.

contributory fault in any case where it is possible that there had been blameworthy conduct, whether or not this issue was raised by the employer.[365]

In deciding whether to reduce compensation the tribunal must take into account the conduct of the complainant and not what happened to some other employee – for example, one who was treated more leniently. Not all unreasonable conduct will necessarily be culpable or blameworthy; it will depend on the degree of unreasonableness. Although ill-health cases will rarely give rise to a reduction in compensation on grounds of contributory fault, it is clear that an award may be reduced under the overriding 'just and equitable' provisions.[366] Having found that an employee was to blame, a tribunal must reduce the award to some extent, although the proportion of culpability is a matter for the tribunal. According to the Court of Appeal, tribunals should first assess the amount which it is just and equitable to award because this may have a very significant bearing on what reduction to make for contributory conduct.[367] The percentage amount of reduction is to be taken from the total awarded to the employee before other deductions, for example offsetting what has already been paid by the employer.

Complainants are obliged to look for work but the tribunal must go through the following stages before it can decide what amount to deduct for an employee's failure to mitigate his or her loss:[368]

- Identify what steps should have been taken by the applicant to mitigate loss.
- Find the date on which such steps would have produced an alternative income.
- Reduce the amount of compensation by the sum which would have been earned.

The onus is on the employer to prove that there was such a failure. Whilst acknowledging that the employee has a duty to act reasonably, the EAT has concluded that this standard is not high in view of the fact that the employer is the wrongdoer.[369]

Section 123(5) ERA 1996 stipulates that no account is to be taken of any pressure that was exercised on the employer to dismiss the employee and s. 155 TULRCA 1992 provides that compensation cannot be reduced on the grounds that the complainant:

- Was in breach of (or proposed to breach) a requirement that he: must be, or become, a member of a particular trade union or one of a number of trade unions; ceases to be, or refrains from becoming, a member of any trade union or of a particular trade union or of one of a number of particular trade unions; would not take part in the activities of any trade union, of a particular trade union or of one of a number of particular trade unions; would not make use of union services.
- Refused, or proposed to refuse, to comply with a requirement of a kind mentioned in s. 152(3)(a) TULRCA 1992.
- Objected, or proposed to object, to the operation of a provision of a kind mentioned in s. 152(3)(b) TULRCA 1992.
- Accepted or failed to accept an offer made in contravention of s. 145A or 145B TULRCA 1992 (see Chapter 10).

---

[365] *Swallow Security Services Ltd* v *Millicent* [2009] Lawtel 25/3/09.
[366] See *Slaughter* v *Brewer Ltd* [1990] IRLR 426.
[367] See *Rao* v *Civil Aviation Authority* [1994] IRLR 240.
[368] See *Savage* v *Saxena* [1998] IRLR 102.
[369] *Fyfe* v *Scientific Furnishings Ltd* [1989] IRLR 331.

The maximum compensatory award is £65,300 in 2010, but it should be noted that this figure is linked to the retail price index. The limit applies only after credit has been given for any payments made by the employer and any deductions have been made,[370] but any 'excess' payments made by the employer over that which is required are deducted after the amount of the compensatory award has been fixed. As regards deductions, normally an employer is to be given credit for all payments made to an employee in respect of claims for wages and other benefits. Where an employee has suffered discrimination as well as unfair dismissal, s. 126 ERA 1996 prevents double compensation for the same loss.

It is the duty of tribunals to inquire into the various grounds for compensation, but it is the responsibility of the aggrieved person to prove the loss. The legislation aims to reimburse the employee rather than to punish the employer. Hence employees who appear to have lost nothing – for example where it can be said that, irrespective of the procedural unfairness which occurred, they would have been dismissed anyway – do not qualify for a compensatory award. However, if the employee puts forward an arguable case that dismissal was not inevitable, the evidential burden shifts to the employer to show that dismissal was likely to have occurred in any event.[371] Additionally, a nil or nominal award may be thought just and equitable in a case where misconduct was discovered subsequently to the dismissal.

The possible heads of loss have been divided into the following categories:

1. *Loss incurred up to the date of the hearing*

Here attention focuses on the employee's actual loss of income, which makes it necessary to ascertain the employee's take-home pay. Thus, tax and national insurance contributions are to be deducted, but overtime earnings and tips can be taken into account. Any sickness benefits received may be taken into account although, in *Sheffield Forgemasters Ltd v Fox*,[372] the EAT decided that the receipt of incapacity benefit (as it then was) did not preclude claimants from claiming compensation for loss of earnings during the same period. Being eligible for such benefits did not mean that the individual could not obtain paid work during that period.

It should also be noted that the loss sustained should be based on what the employee was entitled to, whether or not he was receiving it at the time of dismissal.[373] As well as lost wages, s. 123(2) ERA 1996 enables an individual to claim compensation for the loss of other benefits – for example a company car or other perks. Similarly, 'expenses reasonably incurred' are mentioned in the statute – so, for example, employees will be able to recover the cost of looking for a new job or setting up their own business. However, complainants cannot be reimbursed for the cost of pursuing their unfair dismissal claims.

2. *Loss flowing from the manner of dismissal*

Compensation can be awarded only if the manner of dismissal has made the individual less acceptable to potential employers. There is nothing for non-economic loss, for example hurt feelings. However, economic loss may arise where the person is not fit to take up alternative employment as early as he would otherwise have done (or ever); or where by virtue of stigma

---

[370] Section 124(5) ERA 1996.
[371] See *Britool Ltd v Roberts* [1993] IRLR 481.
[372] [2009] IRLR 192.
[373] For example, the minimum wage: see *Pagetti v Cobb* [2002] IRLR 861. On the issue of pay that should have been received during the notice period, the Court of Appeal has drawn a distinction between express and constructive dismissals: see *Peters Ltd v Bell* [2009] IRLR 941.

damage, loss of reputation or embarrassment no suitable employer was prepared to engage him, at least on terms that would not cause continuing loss.[374]

3. Loss of accrued rights

This head of loss is intended to compensate the employee for the loss of rights dependent on a period of continuous service. However, because the basic award reflects lost redundancy entitlement, sums awarded on these grounds have tended to be nominal. Nevertheless, tribunals should include a sum to reflect the fact that dismissed employees lose the statutory minimum notice protection that they have built up.

4. Loss of pension rights

There are two types of loss: the loss of the present pension position and the loss of the opportunity to improve one's pension position with the dismissing employer. When an employee is close to retirement, the cost of an annuity which will provide a sum equal to the likely pension can be calculated. In other cases the starting point will be the contributions already paid into the scheme, and, in addition to having their own contributions returned, employees can claim an interest in their employer's contributions, except in cases of transferred or deferred pensions. However, in assessing future loss the tribunal must take into account a number of possibilities – for example, future dismissal or resignation, early death, and the fact that a capital sum is being paid sooner than would have been expected. Although employment tribunals have been given actuarial guidelines on loss of pension rights, in each case the factors must be evaluated to see what adjustment should be made or whether the guidelines are safe to use at all.[375]

5. Future loss

Where no further employment has been secured, tribunals will have to speculate how long the employee will remain unemployed. Here the tribunal must utilise its knowledge of local market conditions as well as considering personal circumstances. According to the EAT, employees who have become unfit for work wholly or partly as a result of unfair dismissal are entitled to compensation for loss of earnings, at least for a reasonable period following the dismissal, until they might reasonably have been expected to find other employment.[376] However, in *Robins Ltd* v *Triggs*[377], the Court of Appeal decided that the tribunal had erred in holding that the employee could claim for future loss of earnings resulting from illness that had been caused by the employer's breach of contract. In this case the illness pre-dated the constructive dismissal. If another job has been obtained, tribunals must compare the employee's salary prospects for the future in each job and estimate as best they can how long it will take the employee to reach the salary equivalent to that which would have been attained had he or she remained with the original employer. Where the employee is earning a higher rate of pay at the time compensation is being assessed, the tribunal should decide whether the new employment is permanent, and, if so, should calculate the loss as between the date of dismissal and the date the new job was secured.

---

[374] See *Dunnachie* v *Hull City Council* [2004] IRLR 727.
[375] See *Port of Tilbury* v *Birch* [2005] IRLR 92.
[376] See *Kingston upon Hull City Council* v *Dunnachie (No 3)* [2003] IRLR 843.
[377] [2008] IRLR 317. In *Sheffield Forgemasters Ltd* v *Fox* [2009] IRLR 192 the EAT held the receipt of incapacity benefit did not preclude claimants from obtaining compensation for loss of earnings during the same period.

Finally, mention must be made of the Employment Protection (Recoupment of Jobseeker's Allowance and Income Support) Regulations 1996,[378] which were designed to remove the state subsidy to employers who dismiss unfairly. Such benefits had the effect of reducing the losses suffered by dismissed persons. These Regulations provide that a tribunal must not deduct from the compensation awarded any sum which represents jobseeker's allowance or income support received, and the employer is instructed not to pay immediately the amount of compensation which represents loss of income up to the hearing (known as the 'prescribed element'). The National Insurance Fund can then serve the employer with a recoupment notice which will require him or her to pay the Fund from the prescribed element the amount which represents the jobseeker's allowance or income support paid to the employee prior to the hearing. When the amount has been refunded by the employer, the remainder of the prescribed element becomes the employee's property. It is important to note that private settlements do not fall within the scope of these Regulations.

4.5 Redundancy payments

Dismissal as a result of redundancy is a common feature of economies which are constantly changing and developing. Statutory protection for workers was first introduced by the Redundancy Payments Act 1965 and was seen as a way of encouraging mobility of labour. This Act provided for the establishment of the Redundancy Fund and for employees, with sufficient continuity of employment, to be entitled to a redundancy payment. The Employment Protection Act 1975 also introduced collective consultation requirements as a result of the then newly adopted EEC Directive (see Chapter 9). The provisions concerning the right to a redundancy payment are now contained in Part XI Chapter I ERA 1996.

Subject to various provisions (see below) an employer is obliged to make a payment to any employee who is dismissed by reason of redundancy or is eligible for a redundancy payment by reason of being laid off or kept on short-time.[379] Dismissal for redundancy purposes has essentially the same meaning as in cases of unfair dismissal[380] and includes the death of the employer.[381] A prerequisite to a claim for a payment is that there has been a dismissal and the reason for it is redundancy. In *Birch and Humber* v *The University of Liverpool*[382] the employer invited staff to apply for early retirement as a means of reducing numbers. The employees in this case applied and were accepted. They subsequently claimed that they had been dismissed by reason of redundancy, alleging that acceptance of their applications for early retirement amounted to dismissal. The Court of Appeal did not agree that the acceptances could be isolated from the formal applications to retire. There had not been a dismissal but a mutual determination of the contracts of employment, even though the situation might conveniently be called a redundancy situation.

Once notice has been given by the employer, the relevant date can be postponed by agreement without prejudicing the original reason for dismissal. Thus, in *Mowlem Northern Ltd* v

---

[378] SI 1996/2439.
[379] Section 135(1) ERA 1996.
[380] See section 136 ERA 1996.
[381] Section 136(5) ERA 1996.
[382] [1985] IRLR 165 CA.

Watson[383] an employee was given notice of dismissal by reason of redundancy, but was then kept on for a further three months on a temporary basis to help try to win another contract. When this failed the employee left and the employer denied liability for making a redundancy payment on the grounds that there was no dismissal. The EAT held that the employee was entitled to the payment as the delay in leaving had been a result of a mutual agreement to postpone the date of termination by reason of redundancy.

According to s. 139(1) ERA 1996, employees are to be regarded as being redundant if their dismissals are attributable wholly or mainly to:

- the fact that the employer has ceased, or intends to cease, to carry on the business[384] for the purposes for which the employees were employed; or
- the fact that the employer has ceased, or intends to cease, to carry on that business in the place where the employees were so employed; or
- the fact that the requirement of that business for employees to carry out work of a particular kind, or for employees to carry out work of a particular kind in the place where they were so employed, has ceased or diminished or is expected to cease or diminish.

In this context 'cease' or 'diminish' means either permanently or temporarily and from whatever cause.[385]

In *High Table Ltd* v *Horst*[386] three waitresses worked for an agency and could be transferred to a variety of locations. In practice they worked for some years at one place. When a redundancy situation arose at that location, the employees sought to rely on their mobility clauses to argue that they were unfairly selected for redundancy. The Court of Appeal held that it defied common sense to expand the meaning of the place where an employee was employed. As these waitresses had worked permanently at that one location, that was their place of employment.

Lord Irvine LC, in *Murray* v *Foyle Meats Ltd (Northern Ireland)*,[387] stated:

[The statutory definition of redundancy] asks two questions of fact. The first is one of whether one or other of various states of economic affairs exists. In this case, the relevant one is whether the requirements of the business for employees to carry out work of a particular kind have diminished. The second question is whether the dismissal is attributable, wholly or mainly, to that state of affairs. This is a question of causation. In the present case, the Tribunal found as a fact that the requirements of the business for employees to work in the slaughter hall had diminished. Secondly, they found that that state of affairs had led to the appellants being dismissed. That, in my opinion, is the end of the matter.

This case was about the fact that some meat operatives from one part of the business were considered for dismissal by reason of redundancy and not operatives from the other parts who were less affected by the situation. The House of Lords approved the EAT decision in *Safeway Stores plc* v *Burrell*,[388] which had considered different approaches to whether a dismissal for redundancy had taken place, specifically the 'function test' and the 'contract test'.

---

[383] [1990] IRLR 500.
[384] 'Business' is defined in s. 235(1) ERA 1996.
[385] Section 139(6) ERA 1996.
[386] [1997] IRLR 513 CA.
[387] [1999] IRLR 562 HL.
[388] [1997] IRLR 200.

The question arises as to whether there is a need to identify specific individuals, the requirements for whose work has ceased or diminished, or whether it is sufficient to state that there has been a reduction in the need for the numbers of employees needed. This latter approach might mean dismissing some employees whose work continues.

The function test required the tribunal to look at the work that the employee was required to do, and actually did, in order to decide whether or not the job has disappeared. The contract test required the tribunal to consider whether there was a diminishing need for the work which the employee could be required to do under the contract of employment. In *Safeway Stores* the EAT concluded that both these approaches were incorrect. There was a three-stage process:

- The first question was: was the employee dismissed?

- If so, the second question was: had the requirements of the employer's business for employees to carry out work of a particular kind ceased or diminished?

- If so, the third question was: was the dismissal of the employee caused wholly or mainly by that state of affairs?

Thus the third stage is one of causation and in this case the court approved a method of selection known as 'bumping'. For example, if a fork-lift driver who was delivering materials to six production machines on the shop floor, each with its own operator, is selected for dismissal on the basis of 'last in, first out', following a decision of the employer that only five machine operators were required, and one machine operator with longer service is transferred to driving the fork-lift truck, the truck driver is dismissed for redundancy. This is the case even though the job of driving the fork-lift truck continues. There has been a diminished need for employees to carry out work of a particular kind and the dismissal of the employee was caused by this state of affairs.

The expiry of a limited-term contract may be a dismissal for reasons of redundancy. Thus the lecturers in *Pfaffinger* v *City of Liverpool Community College*,[389] who were employed during each academic year only, were dismissed for redundancy at the end of each academic term. Business reorganisations can lead to dismissals which are related to redundancy. Alternatively, they might be dismissals for 'some other substantial reason'.[390] An employer cannot, however, argue a case based on redundancy and when this fails turn to some other substantial reason.[391]

4.5.1 Qualifications and exclusions

In order to qualify for a right to a redundancy payment an employee must have been continuously employed for two years at the relevant date.[392] There are a number of situations where employees will lose their right to a redundancy payment:

---

[389] [1996] IRLR 508.

[390] See *Murphy* v *Epsom College* [1984] IRLR 271 CA for an example of a situation where a dismissal as a result of new technology might have been for reasons of redundancy or for some other substantial reason.

[391] *Church* v *West Lancashire NHS Trust (No 2)* [1998] IRLR 492.

[392] Section 155 ERA 1996. In most cases the relevant date is to be ascertained in the same way as the effective date of termination for unfair dismissal purposes (see above). However, where a statutory trial period has been served (see below), for the purpose of submitting a claim in time the relevant date is the day that the new or renewed contract terminated.

1. Employees who are dismissed with or without notice for reasons connected to their conduct.[393]

2. If an employee gives notice to the employer terminating the relationship with effect from a date prior to the date upon which the employer's notice of redundancy is due to expire, then the employee may lose their right to a redundancy payment.[394] This is provided that the employer serves a notice on the employee requiring him to withdraw his or her notice and to stay in employment until the employer's notice expires and warning the employee that he or she will lose their right to a payment.[395] An employee may ask an employment tribunal to decide whether it should be just and equitable to receive a payment, taking into account the reasons for which the employee seeks to leave early and the reasons for which the employer requires the individual to continue.[396]

3. If, before the ending of a person's employment, the employer or an associated employer makes an offer, in writing or not, to renew the contract or to re-engage under a new contract which is to take effect either on the ending of the old one or within four weeks, then s. 141 ERA 1996 has the following effect:
   - the provisions of the new or renewed contract as to the capacity and place in which the person would be employed, together with the other terms and conditions, do not differ from the corresponding terms of the previous contract; or
   - the terms and conditions differ, wholly or in part, but the offer constitutes an offer of suitable employment; and
   - in either case the employee unreasonably refuses that offer, then he will not be entitled to a redundancy payment.

The burden is on an employer to prove both the suitability of the offer and the unreasonableness of the employee's refusal. Offers do not have to be formal, nor do they have to contain all the conditions which are ultimately agreed. However, supplying details of vacancies is not the same as an offer of employment[397] and sufficient information must be provided to enable the employee to take a realistic decision.

The suitability of the alternative work must be assessed objectively by comparing the terms on offer with those previously enjoyed. A convenient test has been whether the proposed employment will be 'substantially equivalent' to that which has ceased. Merely offering the same salary will not be sufficient but the fact that the employment will be at a different location does not necessarily mean that it will be regarded as unsuitable. By way of contrast, in adjudicating upon the reasonableness of an employee's refusal, subjective considerations can be taken into account – for example domestic responsibilities. In *Spencer and Griffin v Gloucestershire County Council*[398] the employees had refused offers of suitable employment on the grounds that they would not be able to do their work to a satisfactory standard in the reduced hours and with reduced staffing levels. The Court of Appeal held that it was for employers to set the standard of work they wanted carried out

---

[393] Section 140(1) ERA 1996; s. 140(2)–(3) provides protection for those dismissed, in certain circumstances, as a result of the employee taking part in a strike.

[394] If the employee leaves early by mutual consent, then the redundancy entitlement will not be affected; see *CPS Recruitment Ltd v Bowen* [1982] IRLR 54.

[395] Section 142(1)–(2) ERA 1996.

[396] Section 142(3) ERA 1996.

[397] See *Curling v Securicor Ltd* [1992] IRLR 548.

[398] [1985] IRLR 393.

but it was a different question whether it was reasonable for a particular employee, in all the circumstances, to refuse to work to the standard which the employer set. This is a question of fact for the tribunal.

If the new or renewed contract differs in terms of the capacity or place in which the employee is engaged or in respect of any other terms and conditions of employment, then the individual is given a trial period of up to four weeks in which to decide whether to accept the new or renewed contract.[399] If the employee or the employer terminates this new or renewed contract, then the entitlement to a redundancy payment for the original dismissal remains.[400] The four-week trial period is calendar weeks and not necessarily 'working' weeks. Thus if public or other holidays come within the four-week period they do not extend that period.[401] This trial can be extended by agreement if a period of retraining is necessary, provided that the agreement is in writing and specifies the date on which the retraining ends and the terms and conditions which will apply at the end of the retraining.[402] In *Cambridge & District Co-operative Society Ltd v Ruse*[403] a long-serving employee managed a butcher's shop which was eventually closed. The employee was then offered the position of butchery department manager in a larger store. He refused because he considered this to be a loss of status and therefore not suitable alternative employment. The argument was whether this was an unreasonable refusal. The EAT accepted that the offer of employment was to be assessed objectively but the reasonableness of an employee's refusal was more subjective and depended upon personal factors important to that person. The reasons did not necessarily need to be connected with the employment itself.

4. If an employee takes part in strike action after having received notice of termination, the employer is entitled to issue a notice of extension. This notice, which must be in writing and indicate the employer's reasons, may request that the employee extends the contract beyond the termination date by a period equivalent to the number of days lost through strike action. Failure by the employee to agree to this, unless they have good reasons, for example, sickness or injury, may justify the employer withholding a redundancy payment.[404]

5. The Secretary of State may make an exemption order excluding certain employees from any right to a redundancy payment. These are employees who, under an agreement between one or more employers and one or more trade unions or their associations, have the right to a payment on the termination of their contracts. The Secretary of State may act after receiving an application from all the parties to an agreement that an order be made. A condition of such orders is that any disputes about the right of an employee to a payment or a dispute about the amount should be submitted to an employment tribunal for resolution.[405]

---

[399] See *Elliot v Richard Stump Ltd* [1987] IRLR 215 in which an employer's mistaken refusal to consider a four-week trial period was sufficient to enable an employee to reject an offer of alternative employment and claim an unfair dismissal on the grounds of redundancy.

[400] Section 138(2)–(4) ERA 1996.

[401] See *Benton v Sanderson Kayser Ltd* [1989] IRLR 19 CA, where an employee lost their right to a redundancy payment because they gave their notice after a four-week period had ended, even though the period had included a seven-day Christmas break.

[402] Section 138(6) ERA 1996.

[403] [1993] IRLR 156.

[404] Sections 143–144 ERA 1996.

[405] Section 157 ERA 1996.

6. Section 158 ERA 1996 enables the Secretary of State to exclude those receiving a pension from the right to redundancy payments.[406] Those employees who have a right or a claim to periodical payments or lump sums resulting from pensions, gratuities or superannuation allowances, which are paid with reference to the employment or on the leaving of the particular employment, can be excluded.[407]

4.5.2 Lay-offs and short-time

For the purposes of the legislation, a person is laid off for a week if they work under a contract of employment where the remuneration depends upon work being provided by the employer and the employer does not provide any work during the week in question.[408] An employee is taken to be kept on short-time for a week if they earn less than half a week's pay as a result of a diminution of work provided by the employer during that week.[409] Employees are entitled to a redundancy payment by reason of being laid off or being kept on short-time if they are laid off or kept on short-time for a period of four consecutive weeks or for a series of six or more weeks within a period of 13 weeks.[410] In order to claim the employee must resign[411] and give notice of the intention to seek a redundancy payment. An employer may resist the claim by issuing a counter-notice to the employee within seven days of receiving the notice of intention. In such circumstances the matter will be decided by an employment tribunal.[412]

4.5.3 Time off[413]

Section 52 ERA 1996 provides that an employee, with at least two years' service, who is given notice of dismissal by reason of redundancy, is entitled to time off to look for new employment or to make arrangements for training (see Chapter 7). An employee who is permitted such time off is entitled to be paid at the appropriate hourly rate.[414]

4.5.4 Level of payments

For those entitled to payment, once the number of years' service has been calculated[415] the 'appropriate amount' is calculated by allocating a certain sum of money to each of those years' service. The formula to be applied is:

1. One and a half weeks' pay for each year of employment in which the employee was not below the age of 41 years.

---

[406] See Redundancy Payments (Pensions) Regulations 1965, SI 1965/1932.

[407] Sections 159–161 ERA 1996 also exclude the right to redundancy payments in respect of certain public offices, service in overseas government employment and certain domestic servants.

[408] Section 147(1) ERA 1996.

[409] Section 147(2) ERA 1996.

[410] Section 148 ERA 1996.

[411] Section 150 ERA 1996.

[412] Section 149 ERA 1996; if there is a likelihood of full employment for a period of at least 13 weeks within four weeks of the employee's notice, then there is no entitlement to a redundancy payment: s. 152 ERA 1996.

[413] See Chapter 7 on working time.

[414] Section 53 ERA 1996.

[415] Section 162(1) ERA 1996.

2. One week's pay for each year of employment (not in (1) above) in which the employee was not below the age of 22 years.

3. Half a week's pay for each year of employment not within (1) or (2).[416]

This calculation is subject to a number of restrictions. First, there is a maximum amount to a week's pay as defined in s. 227 ERA 1996.[417] This amount is £380 per week in 2010. There is also a maximum of 20 years' service to be taken into account.[418] Thus the maximum amount that can be claimed for a redundancy payment in 2010 is £11,400. It should be noted that s. 163(5) ERA 1996 enables employment tribunals to provide compensation for workers who suffer financial losses as a result of non-payment of redundancy payments.

Any questions as to the right of an employee to a redundancy payment, or the amount of such payment, are to be referred to an employment tribunal. There is a presumption in any such case that the individual employee has been dismissed by reason of redundancy.[419] An employee does not have any right to a redundancy payment unless, before the end of a period of six months beginning with the relevant date:[420]

1. The payment has been agreed and paid or the employee has made a claim for the payment by notice in writing given to the employer.

2. A question as to the employee's right to, or the amount of, the payment has been referred to an employment tribunal or a complaint has been made to a tribunal for unfair dismissal under s. 111 ERA 1996.[421]

The written notice to the employer does not have to be in a particular form. The test is whether it is of such a character that the recipient would reasonably understand in all the circumstances that it was the employee's intention to seek a payment. In this context the words 'presented' and 'referred' seem to have the same meaning – i.e. an application must have been received by the employment tribunal within the six-month period. Nevertheless, if any of the above steps are taken outside this period but within 12 months of the relevant date, a tribunal has the discretion to award a payment if it thinks that it would be just and equitable to do so. In such a case a tribunal must have regard to the employee's reasons for failing to take any of the steps within the normal time limit.[422]

When making a redundancy payment,[423] otherwise than as a result of an employment tribunal decision, the employer is required to give the employee a written statement showing how the amount of the payment has been calculated. If the employer fails to do this, the employee may give the employer notice in writing requiring the employer to give the written statement within a period of not less than one week. Failure by the employer to provide such a notice, without reasonable excuse, will open the employer to the possibility of a fine.[424]

---

[416] Section 162(2) ERA 1996.
[417] See Chapter 7 for further discussion on the concept of a week's pay.
[418] Section 162(3) ERA 1996.
[419] Section 163 ERA 1996.
[420] See section 145 ERA 1996 for the meaning of the relevant date.
[421] Section 164(1) ERA 1996.
[422] Section 164(2) ERA 1996.
[423] If the employer fails to make the payment, then the employee may apply to the Secretary of State for payment: see ss. 166–170 ERA 1996.
[424] Section 165 ERA 1996.

Chapter summary

This chapter outlined the types of termination that amount to a dismissal at law and those that do not. It looked at the requirement of the parties to give notice and discussed the common law concepts of summary and wrongful dismissal. The law of unfair dismissal was described in detail with attention focusing on the potentially fair reasons for dismissal, the requirements of procedural fairness, the need to claim in time and the remedies available. Finally, the circumstances in which employees might be entitled to a redundancy payment were detailed.

Further reading

Anderman, S. 'Termination of Employment: Whose Property Rights?' in **Barnard, C., Deakin, S. and Morris, G.** (eds) *The Future of Labour Law*: Hart Publishing, 2004, Chapter 5.

Collins, H. 'Nine Proposals for the Reform of the Law on Unfair Dismissal': Institute of Employment Rights, 2004.

Deakin, S. and Morris, G. *Labour Law*: 5th edn, Hart Publishing, 2009, Chapter 5.

Incomes Data Services 'Unfair Dismissal', in *Employment Law Handbook*: IDS, 2005.

Korn, A. *Compensation for Unfair Dismissal*: Oxford University Press, 2005.

Lewis, P. 'Legal Aspects of Employment Change and Their Implications for Management' (2001) 32(1) *Industrial Relations Journal* 71.

www.acas.org.uk

www.berr.gov.uk

www.tuc.org.uk

Visit **www.mylawchamber.co.uk/sargeant**
to access legal updates, live weblinks and practice
exam questions to test yourself on this chapter.

Discrimination on the grounds of race, sex, religion or belief, and sexual orientation; the Equality Act 2010

5.1 Introduction

The principle of non-discrimination is a fundamental principle in Community law. The Community has taken a number of initiatives to further this principle:

1. Council Directive 2000/78/EC established a general framework for equal treatment in employment and occupation.[1] The purpose of the Directive is to put into effect in the Member States

> the principle of equal treatment as regards access to employment and occupation . . . of all persons irrespective of racial or ethnic origin, religion or belief, disability, age or sexual orientation.[2]

There is a further Directive proposed to extend this protection to activities outside the field of employment.[3]

2. Council Directive 2000/43/EC implements the principle of equal treatment between persons irrespective of racial or ethnic origin.[4] This helps bring to an end the imbalance in the EU's anti-discrimination programme. In contrast to the EU's action on sex discrimination, it has taken many fewer initiatives to combat race discrimination. It was not until the Amsterdam Treaty and the adoption of the new art. 13 that the Community had the authority to take such action. In its guide to the Directive the European Commission accepts that racial discrimination is widespread in everyday life and that legal measures are of 'paramount importance for combating racism and intolerance'.[5]

The purpose of the Directive, contained in art. 1, is

> to lay down a framework for combating discrimination on the grounds of racial or ethnic origin, with a view to putting into effect in the Member States the principle of equal treatment.

Article 2 is concerned with the meaning of direct and indirect discrimination and follows the Equal Treatment in Employment and Occupation Directive closely, including the addition

---

[1] OJ L303/16 2.12.2000.
[2] Article 1 of the Directive.
[3] Proposal for a Council Directive on implementing the principle of equal treatment between persons irrespective of religion or belief, disability, age or sexual orientation COM2008 426.
[4] OJ L180/22 17.7.2000.
[5] See also Council Regulation 1035/97 establishing a European Monitoring Centre on Racism and Xenophobia OJ L151 10.6.97.

of harassment. Its scope, of course, is wider than just employment, but those areas that are related to employment are also similar to the Equal Treatment in Employment Directive. In *Firma Feryn*,[6] for example, one of the directors of the respondent company made a statement to the effect that, although the company was seeking to recruit, it could not employ 'immigrants' because its customers were reluctant to give them access to their private residences for the duration of the works. The ECJ held that such a statement concerning candidates of a particular ethnic or racial origin constituted direct discrimination under art. 2(2)(a) of Directive 2000/43. Such a public declaration was clearly likely to dissuade some candidates from applying for jobs with the employer.

3. The Community has a long and effective record of measures combating sex discrimination and promoting equal treatment and equal pay. The original treaty establishing the European Economic Community, signed in Rome in March 1957, contained art. 119 which committed each Member State to the principle of 'equal remuneration for the same work as between male and female workers'. This was undoubtedly a far-reaching principle to have adopted in the 1950s. This commitment was contained in art. 141 EC and is now in art. 157 of the Lisbon Treaty. It includes the adoption of the principle of equal pay for male and female workers for equal work or for work of equal value. It also provides for the Community to

> adopt measures to ensure the application of the principle of equal opportunities and equal treatment of men and women in matters of employment and occupation, including the principle of equal pay for equal work or work of equal value.[7]

The Equal Opportunities and Equal Treatment Directive[8] provides, in art. 1, that its purpose is

> to ensure the implementation of the principle of equal opportunities and equal treatment of men and women in matters of employment and occupation.

Article 2 states that, for the purposes of this Directive, discrimination includes:

- Harassment and sexual harassment, as well as any less favourable treatment based on a person's rejection of or submission to such conduct.
- Instruction to discriminate against persons on grounds of sex.
- Any less favourable treatment of a woman related to pregnancy or maternity leave within the meaning of Directive 92/85/EC.

The extent to which the social objectives of art. 157 (141 EC) and, consequently, the Equal Treatment Directives, could influence the development of equal opportunities has been considered by the ECJ. One issue was whether this included positive discrimination in favour of women in terms of access to work. This was tested in *Marschall*,[9] where the complainant was a male comprehensive school teacher who had applied for promotion to a higher grade. He

---

[6] Case C-54/07 *Centrum voor Gelijkeid van Kansen en voor Racismebestrijding v Firma Feryn NV* [2008] IRLR 732.
[7] Article 157(3).
[8] Directive 2006/54/EC on the implementation of the principle of equal opportunities and equal treatment of men and women in matters of employment and occupation OJ L204/23 26.7.2006; this Directive recast seven previous sex equality Directives, including the Equal Pay Directive 75/117, the Equal Treatment Directive 76/207 as amended by Directive 2002/73 and the Burden of Proof Directive 97/80, into one consolidated Directive from 15 August 2009.
[9] Case C-409/95 *Marschall v Land Nordrhein-Westfalen* [1998] IRLR 39 ECJ.

was told that an equally qualified female applicant would be given the position as there were fewer women than men in the more senior grade. The ECJ considered previous judgments[10] which concluded that the Equal Treatment Directive did not permit national rules which enabled female applicants for a job to be given automatic priority. Article 2(4) of the the Equal Treatment Directive 76/207, however, provided that the Directive should be 'without prejudice to measures to promote equal opportunity for men and women' and the ECJ considered whether this could alter the outcome. It distinguished between those measures which were designed to remove the obstacles to women and those measures which were designed to grant them priority simply because they were women. The latter measures, as in *Kalanke* and *Marschall*, conflicted with the Directive. There was a difference between measures concerned with the promotion of equal opportunity and measures imposing equal representation. This situation appears unchanged despite art. 157(4) (141(4)) of the Treaty which states:

> With a view to ensuring full equality of practice between men and women in working life, the principle of equal treatment shall not prevent any Member State from maintaining or adopting measures for providing for specific advantages in order to make it easier for the under-represented sex to pursue a vocational activity or to prevent or compensate for disadvantages in professional careers.

In *Abrahamsson and Anderson v Fogelqvist*[11] the ECJ held, somewhat disappointingly, that this did not permit measures positively to discriminate in favour of women in a selection process. Preference could not be given to one sex merely because they were under-represented. There had to be an objective assessment of the relative qualifications for the job in question in order to establish that the qualifications of the two sexes were similar before any preference could be given to one sex over the other.[12]

Article 3 of the Equal Opportunities and Equal Treatment Directive now states simply that:

> Member States may maintain or adopt measures within the meaning of Article 141(4) (157(4)) of the Treaty with a view to ensuring full equality in practice between men and women in working life.

The cumulative effect of art. 157 (141) and the equality Directives has been to influence considerably the decisions of the courts in the United Kingdom when interpreting its anti-discrimination legislation. Two of the principal statutes concerned with discrimination are the Sex Discrimination Act 1975 (SDA 1975) and the Race Relations Act 1976 (RRA 1976).[13] They are considered together as the approach, and often, the wording, of each statute is similar.

5.1.1 Types of discrimination

5.1.1.1 Direct discrimination

In relation to discrimination in the employment field and vocational training, direct discrimination is described in s. 1(2)(a) SDA 1975. A person discriminates against a woman if:

> On the ground of her sex he treats her less favourably than he treats or would treat a man.

---

[10] See Case C-450/93 *Kalanke v Freie Hansestadt Bremen* [1995] ECR 660 ECJ and Case C-312/86 *Commission v France* [1998] ECR 6315 ECJ.

[11] Case 407/98 [2000] IRLR 732 ECJ.

[12] See Case 158/97 *Application by Badeck* [2000] IRLR 432 ECJ.

[13] Two other important statutes are considered separately; these are the Equal Pay Act 1970 and the Disability Discrimination Act 1995.

Section 2(1) SDA 1975 provides that this discrimination can be reversed, so that men are discriminated against if treated less favourably than women on the grounds of their sex. This is qualified in s. 2(2) so that any special treatment given to women in connection with child-birth or pregnancy should not be taken as being discriminatory against men (see Chapter 8).

Thus the two essential features of direct discrimination, in the SDA 1975, are, first, that it takes place on the grounds of sex and, secondly, that it takes place when a person is treated less favourably than a person of the other sex. Thus a comparative model of justice is used. The treatment given to A is relative to the treatment given to the comparator B.

The 'less favourable treatment test' also applies in situations of gender reassignment[14] and discrimination against married women and civil partners in the field of employment.[15]

The question to be asked under s. 1(1)(a), according to the House of Lords, is:

> Would the complainant have received the same treatment from the defendant but for his or her sex?[16]

This test can be applied where the treatment given derives from the application of gender-based criteria and where the treatment given results from the selection of the complainant because of his or her sex. Thus, when a local authority gave free use of its swimming pools to persons of pensionable age, then a male of 61 years who has not reached pensionable age is discriminated against in comparison with a woman who reached it at the age of 60 years.[17] There need be no intention to discriminate and motives are not relevant. In *R v Birmingham City Council, ex parte Equal Opportunities Commission*[18] the local authority offered more places in selective secondary education to boys than to girls. This was held to be treating those girls less favourably on the grounds of their sex and the fact that the local authority had not intended to discriminate was not relevant.

In the absence of an actual comparator the court will need to construct a hypothetical one, in order for the complainant to show that she was treated less favourably than the hypothetical male. Inferences as to how this hypothetical male would have been treated can be gained from the surrounding circumstances and other cases which might not be exactly the same but would not be wholly dissimilar. An exact comparator is not, of course, needed as it might be impossible to prove less favourable treatment, especially in isolated cases, if this were the case.[19]

The provisions on direct discrimination are mirrored in the RRA 1976, so that interpretations of provisions in one Act, by the courts, can lead to the same interpretation being applied to the other Act. Section 1(1)(a) RRA 1976 provides that a person discriminates against another if, on racial grounds, they treat that person less favourably than they would treat another person. Thus here there is also a twofold test to be applied. The first is that the discrimination should be on racial grounds and the second is that the person concerned is treated less favourably than another person. This is not to suggest that there is a hypothetical reasonable employer who treats employees reasonably, so that it is possible to identify those treated less reasonably on racial grounds. In *Zafar v Glasgow City Council*[20] Lord Browne-Wilkinson stated that:

---

[14] Section 2A(1) SDA 1975. See 5.1.2.4 below.
[15] Section 3(1) SDA 1975.
[16] *James v Eastleigh Borough Council* [1990] IRLR 288 HL.
[17] *Ibid*.
[18] [1989] IRLR 173 HL.
[19] See *Balamoody v UK Central Council for Nursing* [2002] IRLR 288 CA.
[20] [1998] IRLR 36 HL.

In deciding that issue, the conduct of a hypothetical reasonable employer is irrelevant. The alleged discriminator may or may not be a reasonable employer. If he is not a reasonable employer, he might well have treated another employee in just the same unsatisfactory way as he treated the complainant, in which case he would not have treated the complainant less favourably for the purposes of the Act of 1976.

Thus if an employer behaves in the same unreasonable way to all their employees it may not be possible for one individual to say that they have been treated less favourably, no matter how unreasonably they were treated. This situation also occurred in *Laing* v *Manchester City Council*[21] where a white supervisor was held not to have acted appropriately in her supervisory role to a subordinate who was black and of West Indian origin. The claimant failed to establish a *prima facie* case of discrimination because the supervisor's behaviour was not the result of any bias against the employee or other black employees, but was the result of her lack of experience, which resulted in her treating all employees in the same manner.

The test to be applied in race discrimination cases is the same as that applied in sex discrimination claims. The court will need to ask the question whether the complainants would have received the same treatment but for their race. This question needs to be asked when a choice is to be made between a non-racial explanation offered and a racial explanation offered by the complainant.

5.1.1.2 Indirect sex and race discrimination

In relation to sex discrimination in the employment field and vocational training, indirect discrimination is described in s. 1(2)(b) SDA 1975. A person discriminates against a woman if:

He applies to her a provision, criterion or practice which he applies or would apply equally to a man, but –
(i)   which is such that it would be to the detriment of a considerably larger proportion of women than of men, and
(ii) which he cannot show to be justifiable irrespective of the sex of the person to whom it is applied, and
(iii) which is to her detriment.

This revised definition became effective in October 2001.[22]

The previous definition still applies to discrimination on the grounds of colour and nationality.[23] A person discriminates against another if:

He applies to that other a requirement or condition which he applies or would apply equally to persons not of the same racial group as that other but –
(i)   which is such that the proportion of persons of the same racial group as that other who can comply with it is considerably smaller than the proportion of persons not of that racial group who can comply with it; and
(ii) which he cannot show to be justifiable irrespective of the colour, race, nationality or ethnic origins of the person to whom it is applied; and
(iii) which is to the detriment of that other because he cannot comply with it.

---

[21] [2006] IRLR 748.
[22] Sex Discrimination (Indirect Discrimination and Burden of Proof) Regulations 2001, SI 2001/2660. This gives effect to art. 2(2) of Council Directive 97/80/EC on the burden of proof in cases of discrimination based on sex OJ L14/6 20.1.98.
[23] Section 1(1)(b) RRA 1976.

In relation to race, ethnic or national origins, indirect discrimination occurs where a provision, criterion or practice applies or would apply to persons not of the same race, ethnic or national origins but such people would be put at a particular disadvantage and this cannot be shown to be a proportionate means of achieving a legitimate aim.[24] This apparent difference in treatment between colour and nationality and the other related grounds has been sorted out by the new Equality Act, which adopts a uniform definition (see pp. 190).

The process for deciding whether indirect sex discrimination has taken place is, therefore, to examine the 'provision, criterion or practice' and assess, first, whether it would be to the detriment of a considerably larger proportion of women than of men, and, secondly, whether it is to the individual's detriment.[25] This is provided that the application of the 'provision, criterion or practice' cannot be shown to be justifiable irrespective of the sex of the person to whom it is applied. Each situation needs to be looked at on its own merits. Just because a policy might be gender-neutral in some situations, it does not follow that it will be so in all situations. *Whiffen v Milham Ford Girls' School*,[26] for example, concerned a school which followed its local educational authority's model redundancy policy. This required that the non-renewal of temporary fixed-term contracts should be the first step to be taken. In this particular case, however, the result was indirectly to discriminate against female employees because 100 per cent of male employees could satisfy the condition that an employee needed to be on a permanent contract in order not to be terminated early, but only 77 per cent of female employees could satisfy this condition.

A 'requirement or condition' (provision, criterion or practice) can be the necessity for previous management training or supervisory experience,[27] a contractual requirement that required employees to serve in any part of the United Kingdom at the employer's discretion,[28] or the imposition of new rostering arrangements for train drivers.[29] One might conclude that merely the imposition of such requirements under these circumstances would be sufficient for an employee to show that the employee had suffered a detriment, but there is a need for a detriment to be shown. In *Shamoon*,[30] for example, a female chief inspector was stopped from doing staff appraisals after some complaints about the manner in which she carried them out. When she complained of sex discrimination, the House of Lords ruled that a detriment occurs if a reasonable worker would or might take the view that they had been disadvantaged in the circumstances in which they had to work. However, it is not necessary to demonstrate some physical or economic consequence.

In *Seymour-Smith*[31] the House of Lords gave judgment in a long-running case that had begun with the dismissal of the applicants in 1991. The House of Lords had referred the case to the ECJ for guidance, amongst other matters, on the legal test

> for establishing whether a measure adopted by a Member State has such a degree of disparate effect as between men and women as to amount to indirect discrimination for the purposes of

---

[24] Section 1(1A) RRA 1976.

[25] As with direct discrimination, s. 2(1) SDA 1975 enables this provision to be reversed in order to provide similar protection for men.

[26] [2001] IRLR 468 CA.

[27] *Falkirk City Council v Whyte* [1997] IRLR 560, where in practice the need for such experience became obligatory rather than desirable as at the beginning of the selection for promotion process.

[28] *Meade-Hill and National Union of Civil and Public Servants v British Council* [1995] IRLR 478 CA.

[29] *London Underground v Edwards* [1998] IRLR 364 CA.

[30] *Shamoon v Chief Constable of the RUC* [2003] IRLR 285.

[31] *R v Secretary of State for Employment, ex parte Seymour-Smith and Perez (No 2)* [2000] IRLR 263 HL.

Article 119 [now 157] of the EC Treaty unless shown to be based on objectively justified factors other than sex.

The ECJ responded[32] by stating that the first question, when attempting to establish whether there was indirect discrimination, was to ask whether the measure in question had a more unfavourable impact on women than on men. After this it is a question of statistics. This means considering and comparing the respective proportions of men and women that were able to satisfy the requirement of the two-year rule. The ECJ further stated:

> it must be ascertained whether the statistics available indicate that a considerably smaller percentage of women than men is able to satisfy the condition of two years' employment required by the disputed rule. That situation would be evidence of apparent sex discrimination unless the disputed rule were justified by objective factors unrelated to any discrimination based on sex.

In this case the House of Lords decided that the statistics did not indicate a significant difference, although it was accepted that such measures should be reviewed from time to time.[33] The Government argued, as objective justification for the measure, that it would encourage recruitment as some employers were reluctant to employ new staff because of the lack of such a rule. This argument appeared to be accepted by the court, although it is somewhat ironic that the final decision was given some time after the qualifying period was reduced to one year with little apparent effect on recruitment. In *Rutherford* v *Secretary of State (No 2)*[34] the issue of statistics was considered in a case where a man complained that the inability to claim unfair dismissal and redundancy payments[35] after retirement age were indirectly discriminatory on grounds of sex. His argument was that a considerably higher proportion of men worked after the age of 65 years compared to women and that, therefore, these rules indirectly discriminated against men. The Court of Appeal followed the approach taken in *Seymour-Smith* by insisting that the employment tribunal should have primarily compared the respective proportions of men and women who could satisfy the age requirement.

Although these cases concern sex discrimination, the same rules apply in cases of racial discrimination. The justification for any measure needs to be irrespective of the colour, race, nationality or ethnic or national origins of the persons concerned. In *JH Walker Ltd* v *Hussain*[36] an employer had banned employees from taking non-statutory holidays during its busy period of May, June and July. Their justification for this was a business-related one. About half the company's production workers were Muslims of Indian ethnic origin. The holiday period ban coincided with an important religious festival when many of the employees traditionally took time off. Seventeen employees took the day off despite the ban. When they returned to work they were given a final written warning. The 17 employees successfully complained of indirect racial discrimination. The employment tribunal and the EAT held that the rule was discriminatory and that the business justification put forward was not adequate (on religious discrimination see 5.2.1).

---

[32] Case C-167/97 [1999] IRLR 253 at p. 278.
[33] The need to assess provisions periodically in the light of social developments was made by the ECJ in *Commission* v *United Kingdom* [1984] IRLR 29.
[34] [2004] IRLR 892. This conclusion, for different reasons, was subsequently upheld by the House of Lords; [2006] IRLR 551.
[35] Sections 109 and 156 ERA 1996.
[36] [1996] IRLR 11.

5.1.1.3 **Victimisation**

Section 4 SDA 1975 provides that a person is discriminated against (victimised), in respect of any provisions in the Act, if the person victimised is treated less favourably than other persons would be treated in those circumstances, and the reason that the person is victimised is because that person has:

1. Brought proceedings under the SDA 1975, the Equal Pay Act 1970[37] or ss. 62–65 Pensions Act 1995.[38]

2. Given evidence in such proceedings.

3. Done anything else with reference to these Acts in relation to the discriminator.

4. Alleged that the discriminator has committed an act which contravenes any of these pieces of legislation.

The RRA 1976 also provides protection from victimisation on the same basis in s. 2. Both the SDA 1975 and the RRA 1976 remove this protection, however, in the treatment of a person who makes allegations that are false or not made in good faith.[39] A complaint of victimisation on sex or race grounds is different from a complaint of sex or race discrimination. The latter is about showing less favourable treatment on the grounds of sex or race, whilst a victimisation claim is about showing less favourable treatment as a result of doing a protected act.[40] In *HM Prison Service* v *Ibimidun*[41] the complainant had a successful claim for discrimination against the employer; he then launched a number of other claims, some of which resulted in cost orders being made against him (five cost orders in total). He was eventually dismissed by the prison service and brought claims of victimisation and unfair dismissal. His claims failed because, although the bringing of the claims were protected acts, the reason for his dismissal was that he had brought the claims in order to harass the employer. The provisions of the RRA were designed to protect bona fide acts, not ones brought with a view to harassment.

Conscious motivation by the employer to treat someone less favourably as a result of their previous actions was not necessary, which was the situation in *Nagarajan* v *London Regional Transport*,[42] where an applicant for a post claimed victimisation when the application was unsuccessful. The individual concerned had made a number of previous complaints against London Regional Transport. The House of Lords held that the reason why a person is discriminated against on racial grounds is not relevant when deciding whether an act of racial discrimination has occurred. There was, therefore, no good reason for adopting a different approach to motivation when applying s. 1(1)(a) or s. 2(1) RRA 1976.

This approach appeared to be somewhat qualified by the House of Lords in *Chief Constable of West Yorkshire Police* v *Khan*.[43] In this case a sergeant in the police applied for promotion in another force at the same time as having an outstanding employment tribunal application

---

[37] See *St Helens MBC* v *Derbyshire* [2004] IRLR 851.

[38] These sections introduce an equal treatment rule into occupational pension schemes.

[39] Section 4(2) SDA 1975 and s. 2(2) RRA 1976.

[40] See *(1) Air Canada; (2) Alpha Catering Services* v *Basra* [2000] IRLR 683, where a complainant was not allowed to raise the question of victimisation during the employment tribunal hearing of her race discrimination complaint; she was subsequently able to start completely fresh proceedings on the victimisation complaint.

[41] [2008] IRLR 940.

[42] [1999] IRLR 572 HL.

[43] [2001] IRLR 830 HL.

alleging racial discrimination by his employer. The employer refused to give a reference until the proceedings were completed. The employee then complained that he had been unlawfully victimised contrary to s. 2 RRA 1976. The court acknowledged that such references were normally given on request, but decided that in this case the reference had not been withheld because the employee had brought proceedings. It had been withheld so that the employer's position could be protected with regard to the proceedings. This was a legitimate action for the employer, acting honestly and reasonably, and should not result in a charge of victimisation. In contrast, the failure of an employer to provide a reference to an ex-employee who had settled a complaint of sex discrimination after alleging that she had been dismissed because of her pregnancy was entitled to bring a complaint of victimisation against her previous employer.[44]

In *St Helens Metropolitan Borough Council* v *Derbyshire*[45] a number of staff had brought an equal pay claim. About two months before the equal pay claims were due to be heard the employers sent letters to the staff stating that they were concerned about the impact of the claim on staff. The House of Lords agreed with the court in *Khan* (see above) that employers acting honestly and reasonably ought to be able to take steps to preserve their position in discrimination proceedings, but it emphasised that it was primarily from the perspective of the alleged victim that one decides whether any detriment has been suffered, not from the perspective of the alleged discriminator.

5.1.1.4 Harassment

Section 3A RRA 1976 defines harassment on the grounds of race, ethnic or national origins. This occurs when a person engages in 'unwanted conduct which has the purpose or effect of violating that other person's dignity, or creating an intimidating, hostile, degrading, humiliating or offensive environment'. However, conduct will only be regarded as having this effect if 'having regard to all the circumstances, including in particular the perception of that other person, it should reasonably be considered as having that effect'.

In *Reed and Bull* v *Stedman*[46] the bullying behaviour of a manager towards a secretary was held to amount to sexual harassment in breach of s. 6(2) SDA 1975. This behaviour resulted in, according to the EAT, a breakdown of mutual trust and confidence. When the secretary was forced to leave her employment as a result of this breach, she was entitled to make a claim for constructive dismissal, resulting from discrimination within the meaning of s. 6(2) SDA 1975. The EAT considered that sexual harassment was a form of 'shorthand for describing a type of detriment'. The question to be asked was whether the applicant had been the subject of a detriment and whether this detriment was on the grounds of sex. Motive and intention is not essential, although it may be relevant, but lack of intent is not a defence. The EAT held that:

> The essential characteristic of sexual harassment is that it is words or conduct which are unwelcome to the recipient and it is for the recipient to decide for themselves what is acceptable to them and what they regard as offensive. A characteristic of sexual harassment is that it undermines the victim's dignity at work. It creates an 'offensive' or 'hostile' environment for the victim and an arbitrary barrier to sexual equality in the workplace.

[44] *Coote* v *Granada Hospitality Ltd (No 2)* [1999] IRLR 452. See now s. 20A SDA 1975 and s. 27A RRA 1976 on discrimination after the employment relationship has ended.
[45] [2007] IRLR 540.
[46] *(1) Reed; (2) Bull Information Systems Ltd* v *Stedman* [1999] IRLR 299.

It follows from this that because a tribunal would not find an action or statement offensive, but that the applicant does, the complaint should not be dismissed. There still needs to be evidence of the harassment however. In a one-to-one counselling interview between a male manager and a female clerical officer, it was alleged that the manager was sexually aroused and that she was effectively trapped in the interview room with him.[47] She claimed that this amounted to sexual harassment. The employment tribunal accepted that the manager was not sexually aroused, but decided that the atmosphere at the interview was sexually intimidating. There was, for example, only one copy of the appraisal report, so that it had to be read jointly. The EAT allowed the appeal. Proof of sexual harassment would cause a detriment, but having rejected the evidence on which the claim was made, i.e. that the manager was sexually aroused, it could not be said that there was sexual harassment. The EAT did not think that it was necessary or desirable for all female employees to be required to have a female chaperone every time they had an interview with a male manager.

Driskel v *Peninsula Business Services Ltd*[48] provides a useful summary by the EAT of the approach to be taken by employment tribunals. Having adopted the categorisation of sexual harassment in *Reed and Bull* the EAT then stated:

1. A finding of less favourable treatment leading to 'detriment' was one of fact and degree, and a single act may justify such a complaint.[49]

2. Although the ultimate judgment is an objective one, the employment tribunal can take into account the employee's subjective perception of the subject matter of the complaint as well as the understanding, motive and intention of the alleged discriminator. Thus an isolated incident, without complaints, may not amount to harassment, but taken together with other such incidents may amount to discrimination.[50]

3. The employment tribunal should not lose sight of the significance of the sex of the complainant and the alleged discriminator; there is a difference in banter between heterosexual males and between persons of opposite sexes.

4. Reliance should be placed on *King* v *The Great Britain-China Centre*[51] in that sex discrimination may well be covert and not readily admitted, as in race discrimination cases.

Employers are likely to be held liable for subjecting their employees to detriment if they fail to take action, or permit harassment of employees where they had the ability to control the situation. This happened in one particularly distasteful case where two waitresses were subjected to racial and sexual abuse whilst they were clearing tables during an after dinner speech by a well-known comedian.[52] There is still, however, a need to show that the employer treated the employee less favourably than they would have treated a man or a person from a different racial group in similar circumstances.[53] The word 'subjecting' in s. 4(2)(c) RRA 1976 implies control. A person subjects another to detriment if they cause or allow that detriment

---

[47] *British Telecommunications plc* v *Williams* [1997] IRLR 668.

[48] [2000] IRLR 151.

[49] See also *Insitu Cleaning Co Ltd* v *Heads* [1995] IRLR 4.

[50] See *Moonsar* v *Fiveways Transport Ltd* [2005] IRLR 9.

[51] [1991] IRLR 513 CA.

[52] See *Burton and Rhule* v *De Vere Hotels* [1996] IRLR 596.

[53] See *Home Office* v *Coyne* [2000] IRLR 838 CA, where the fact that the employer regarded the harassment as the female employee's fault was not something that could be related to her sex as opposed to her relations with some other employees.

to happen in circumstances where they can control whether it happens or not. If the abuse or harassment comes from a third party, the question for a tribunal is whether the event or situation was sufficiently under the control of the employer that good employment practice could have eliminated or reduced the detriment. In this case it was clear that the management should have withdrawn the employees from their waitressing duties in order to protect them from racial abuse and harassment.

The EAT stated that there were three elements to the liability of the employer under s. 3A (dealing with harassment) of the RRA. In *Richmond Pharmacology Ltd* v *Dhaliwal*[54] Ms Dhaliwal was British and had lived in England all her life. She resigned and, during her notice period, relationships with the employer deteriorated. Her manager made the statement: 'We will probably bump into each other in future, unless you are married off in India.' She brought proceedings for racial harassment and was successful but was only awarded £1,000. The three elements of liability under s. 3A RRA, according to the EAT, were:

1. Whether the employer engaged in unwanted conduct.
2. Whether the conduct had (a) the purpose, or (b) the effect of either violating the claimant's dignity or creating an adverse environment for her.
3. Whether the conduct was on the grounds of the claimant's race (or ethnic or national origins).

There is much overlap between these three elements, but a tribunal should look at each in turn. The EAT further stated that not every racially-slanted adverse comment or conduct may violate a person's dignity; whilst it is important that employers and tribunals are sensitive to the hurt that can be caused by racially offensive comments or conduct it is also important not to encourage a culture of hypersensitivity or the imposition of legal liability in respect of every unfortunate phrase. The tribunal had indicated that this case was close to the border in the size of the payment made.

5.1.2 Sex discrimination – the subject matter

The gender pay gap (as measured by the median hourly pay excluding overtime of full-time employees) appears to have actually widened in recent times. In 2008 the gap between men and women's median hourly pay was 12.8 per cent, compared to 12.5 per cent the previous year. If one compares the mean levels of hourly pay (rather than the median) then the gap in 2008 was actually 17.1 per cent, compared to 17 per cent a year earlier. These figures hide some striking extremes: for example, the Equality and Human Rights Commission reported that men received bonus payments in the City (of London) at a rate which was five times the amount received by women.[55] The result is that women earn 87.4 per cent of the rate earned by men, using the median figure, and 82.8 per cent using the mean.

5.1.2.1 Women and men

Although the SDA 1975 has, as a primary purpose, the removing of gender imbalances between men and women, it does not necessarily require the same treatment as between men and women. The aim is to ensure that one gender is not treated less favourably than another. One area of contention in the employment field has been the imposition of dress codes that

---

[54] [2009] IRLR 336.
[55] See BBC News website 6 September 2009.

might have the effect of discriminating against one particular sex. In *Smith v Safeway plc*,[56] for example, a male employee was dismissed because his ponytail grew too long to keep under his hat. The store had a code which required men to have hair not below shirt collar level, but female employees were permitted to have hair down to shoulder length. Phillips LJ stated that:

> I can accept that one of the objects of the prohibition of sex discrimination was to relieve the sexes from unequal treatment resulting from conventional attitudes, but I do not believe that this renders discriminatory an appearance code which applies a standard of what is conventional.

The result was that the court held that the employer was imposing a dress code that reflected a conventional outlook and that this should not be held to be discriminatory. The effect of such a decision was, however, that a male employee was dismissed because of the length of his hair, which would have been permissible in a female employee.[57]

5.1.2.2 Married people

Section 3(1) SDA 1975 provides substantially the same definition of direct and indirect discrimination as s. 1(2). In this case, however, the rules protect married people and those in civil partnership from discrimination on the grounds of their marital or civil partnership status. This is so unless, of course, any action can be shown to be justifiable irrespective of the marital or civil partnership status of the person to whom it is applied.

This may be a rule originally designed to stop discrimination against married women in employment, although it also applies to men.[58] However, there is no corresponding rule that states that it is unlawful to discriminate against people because they are unmarried or not in a civil partnership.[59] *Bavin v NHS Pensions Trust Agency*[60] considered issues concerned with the rights of transsexuals (see below), but was primarily concerned with the entitlement of dependants on the death of a member of a pension scheme. The rules stated that only widows or widowers were entitled to benefits. This excluded all other dependants who were not married, for whatever reason, to the deceased pension scheme member. The issue of discrimination for this reason did not even arise in the case.

Section 3 also acts to stop discrimination in favour of single parents. In *Training Commission v Jackson*[61] a married mother was refused a child care payment to help her take up a place on an employment training scheme. She was refused on the basis that the scheme was intended to help lone parents attend such a scheme. The Training Commission relied upon the defence, in s. 3(1)(b)(ii), that the restriction was justifiable. It was argued that lone parents were a particularly disadvantaged group in the labour market and that this was the best use of limited resources. The EAT dismissed an appeal against the employment tribunal's decision that this reason was insufficient to justify the indirect discrimination against married people.

---

[56] See *Smith v Safeway plc* [1996] IRLR 457 CA.

[57] In *Burrett v West Birmingham Health Authority* [1994] IRLR 7 female nurses were required to wear caps but male nurses were not. The EAT held that the important issue was that they both had to wear uniforms, not that those uniforms differed. See also *Department for Work & Pensions v Thompson* [2004] IRLR 348.

[58] Section 3(2) SDA 1975.

[59] Although one might argue that art. 2(1) Equal Treatment Directive might provide protection to single people when it requires there to be no discrimination 'by reference in particular to marital or family status'.

[60] [1999] ICR 1192.

[61] [1990] ICR 222.

In considering issues between a married couple, outdated assumptions that the man is the breadwinner might also amount to unlawful discrimination against the woman in the marriage. In *Coleman* v *Sky Oceanic Ltd*,[62] for example, two competing travel firms employed one member each of what became a married couple. There was a concern about confidentiality of each business's information. The two companies consulted and decided to dismiss the female because the man was assumed to be the breadwinner. Such an assumption, according to the Court of Appeal, was an assumption based upon sex and amounted to discrimination under the SDA 1975. *Chief Constable of the Bedfordshire Constabulary* v *Graham*[63] also concerned a married couple. Inspector Margaret Graham had a promotion rescinded by the Chief Constable because she was married to a chief superintendent in the same division. It was considered that there would be difficulties arising from having the couple working together at these levels. The EAT upheld the employment tribunal's decision that the complainant was treated less favourably than a single person would have been, for reasons connected to her marital status. Interestingly, the EAT also supported the tribunal's view that there was also indirect discrimination. This was because there was a higher proportion of female officers in relationships than men.

5.1.2.3 **Pregnancy and maternity**

The period during pregnancy and maternity leave is a specially protected one. The dismissal of a female worker on account of pregnancy can only affect women and therefore constitutes direct discrimination.[64] Article 10(1) Pregnant Workers Directive[65] provides that dismissal should be prohibited during the period from the beginning of pregnancy to the end of maternity leave, save in exceptional circumstances unrelated to the worker being pregnant, breastfeeding or having recently given birth.

Section 3A[66] SDA 1975 is concerned with discrimination on the grounds of pregnancy or maternity leave. Prior to 2005, it stated that a person discriminated against a woman if:

(a) at a time in a protected period, and on the ground of the woman's pregnancy, the person treats her less favourably than he would treat her had she not become pregnant.

This wording was criticised by the High Court in *Equal Opportunities Commission* v *Secretary of State for Trade and Industry*.[67] The court stated that this section impermissibly introduces a requirement for a non-pregnant comparator and that the statute needed to be recast to remove this requirement. The court also criticised aspects of s. 6A which is concerned with 'exceptions relating to terms and conditions during maternity leave'.[68] In particular this section provides that, subject to exceptions, it is not unlawful 'to deprive a woman who is on additional maternity leave of any benefit from the terms and conditions of her employment'. The court stated that this part needed to be recast so that there was no difference between

---

[62] [1981] IRLR 398 CA. On assumed ethnic characteristics see *Bradford NHS Trust* v *Al-Shahib* [2003] IRLR 4.
[63] [2002] IRLR 239.
[64] See, e.g., Case C-177/88 *Dekker* v *Stichting Vormingscentrum voor Jonge Volwassen* [1991] IRLR 27 ECJ and Case C-32/93 *Webb* v *EMO Air Cargo (UK) Ltd* [1994] IRLR 482 ECJ.
[65] Directive 92/85/EEC on the introduction of measures to encourage improvements in the safety and health of pregnant workers and workers who have recently given birth or are breastfeeding OJ L348/1 28.11.92.
[66] Inserted by the Employment Equality (Sex Discrimination) Regulations 2005, SI 2005/2467.
[67] [2007] IRLR 327.
[68] Also inserted by the Employment Equality (Sex Discrimination) Regulations 2005, SI 2005/2467.

ordinary statutory maternity leave and additional statutory maternity leave.[69] As a result of Regulations made in 2005[70] the need for a comparator was removed from s. 3A and s. 6A was amended in 2008 so that there was equal treatment for women on ordinary or additional maternity leave.[71]

This protection does not just apply to permanent employees, but will also apply to others. In *Patefield v Belfast City Council*,[72] for example, a contract worker was replaced by a permanent employee whilst she was on maternity leave. The fact that the employer could have replaced her at any time when she was actually working was not relevant. Of importance was that she was replaced whilst on maternity leave and the employer was, therefore, guilty of direct sex discrimination. Similarly a loyalty bonus scheme introduced to keep people at work until an office closed down was held to be discriminatory when it was paid to only those employees that attended work, thus excluding two employees on maternity leave.[73]

In *Brown v Rentokil Ltd*[74] the ECJ considered the dismissal of a female employee who was absent through most of her pregnancy and was dismissed under a provision of the contract of employment which allowed for dismissal after 26 weeks' continuous absence through sickness. The court held that arts. 2(1) and 5(1) of the Equal Treatment Directive:

> preclude dismissal of a female worker at any time during her pregnancy for absences due to incapacity for work caused by an illness resulting from that pregnancy.

Absences after pregnancy and maternity leave are to be treated in the same way as any other sickness is treated under the employee's contract of employment. Measures which impose length of service conditions before an employee is eligible for promotion, when time spent on maternity leave is excluded from the calculations as to that length of service, will also be excluded by art. 2(3) Equal Treatment Directive.[75] The Directive will allow national provisions which give women specific rights because of pregnancy,[76] but the provision of such rights is intended to ensure the principle of equal treatment.

> Therefore, the exercise of the rights conferred on women under Article 2(3) cannot be the subject of unfavourable treatment regarding their access to employment or their working conditions. In that light, the result pursued by the Directive is substantive, not formal, equality.[77]

Thus the refusal to appoint a pregnant woman to a permanent position because there was a statutory restriction on her employment in that position during her pregnancy amounted to sex discrimination. This was the situation in *Mahlberg v Land Mecklenburg-Vorpommern*[78] where a pregnant woman was refused an appointment as an operating theatre nurse because German law banned pregnant women from being employed in areas where they would be exposed to dangerous substances. The financial loss that the employer might suffer

---

[69] The court relied upon the case of *Land Brandenburg v Sass* at the ECJ, Case C-284/02 [2005] IRLR 147.
[70] Employment Equality (Sex Discrimination) Regulations 2005 SI 2005/2467.
[71] Sex Discrimination Act 1975 (Amendment) Regulations 2008 SI 2008/656.
[72] [2000] IRLR 664.
[73] *Gus Home Shopping Ltd* v *Green and McLaughlin* [2001] IRLR 75.
[74] Case C-394/96 [1998] IRLR 445 ECJ.
[75] Case C-136/95 *Caisse Nationale d'Assurance Vieillesse des Travailleurs Salariés v Thibault* [1998] IRLR 399 ECJ.
[76] See Case C-179/88 *Handels og Kontorfunktionærernes Forbund i Danmark (acting for Herz) v Dansk Arbejdsgiverforening (acting for Aldi Marked A/S)* [1991] IRLR 31 ECJ.
[77] See note 75 above.
[78] Case C-207/98 [2000] IRLR 276 ECJ.

because they could not employ the woman in the position for the duration of her pregnancy was not an acceptable reason for the unfavourable treatment. Similarly, in *P & O Ferries Ltd v Iverson*[79] a woman was stopped from going to sea once she reached week 28 of her pregnancy. Pregnancy was one of a number of lawful reasons for stopping an individual going to sea, but it was the only one for which, with this employer, there was no pay. All the other reasons, including sickness, resulted in suspension with pay. The fact that this was not available to pregnant women was held to be discriminatory.[80] Whether the employee concerned is on a permanent contract or a fixed-term contract is of no consequence. In *Tele Danmark A/S*,[81] for example, the ECJ held that art. 5 of the Equal Treatment Directive and art. 10 of the Pregnant Workers Directive precludes a worker who was recruited for a fixed period who failed to inform her employer that she was pregnant even when she was aware of this when recruited, and then was unable to work during much of the period because of her pregnancy, from being dismissed on the grounds of her pregnancy. Expiry of the fixed term would not amount to a dismissal, according to the ECJ, but a non-renewal of the fixed-term contract on the grounds of pregnancy would.[82]

5.1.2.4 Gender reassignment

Gender reassignment is defined in s. 82(1) SDA 1975:

> Gender reassignment means a process which is undertaken under medical supervision for the purpose of reassigning a person's sex by changing physiological or other characteristics of sex, and includes any part of such a process.

Section 2A SDA 1975[83] provides that a person A discriminates against person B and treats person B less favourably than they would other persons, on the grounds that B intends to undergo, is undergoing or has undergone gender reassignment.[84] This section was added after the ECJ decision in *P v S and Cornwall County Council*.[85] This concerned an employee who informed the employer of an intention to undergo gender reassignment. The first part of this was to undertake a 'life test' which consisted of spending a year living in the manner of the proposed gender. Whilst on sick leave for initial surgery, the employee was dismissed. The employment tribunal decided that the individual had been dismissed because of the gender reassignment, but decided that the SDA 1975 did not apply to these circumstances. They referred the matter to the ECJ with the question as to whether the Equal Treatment Directive provided for this situation. The ECJ held that the Directive sought to safeguard the principle of equality and applied, although not exclusively, to discrimination on the grounds of sex. The court held that discrimination on the basis of gender reassignment was to treat a person less favourably than persons of the sex to which the individual had been deemed to belong before the gender reassignment and was therefore contrary to art. 5(1) Equal

---

[79] [1999] ICR 1088.

[80] See also *British Airways (European Operations at Gatwick) Ltd* v *Moore and Botterill* [2000] IRLR 296 for a similar approach in relation to air crew grounded because of pregnancy.

[81] Case 109/100 *Tele Danmark A/S v Kontorfunktionærernes Forbund i Danmark* [2001] IRLR 853 ECJ.

[82] Case 438/99 *Jiménez Melgar v Ayuntamiento De Los Barrios* [2001] IRLR 848 ECJ.

[83] Inserted by the Sex Discrimination (Gender Reassignment) Regulations 1999, SI 1999/1102.

[84] Section 2A(1) SDA 1975 provides that this is in relation to employment; ss. 35A and 35B SDA 1975 concerning discrimination by, or in relation to, barristers or advocates; and discrimination in other fields in so far as it relates to vocational training. See *Gender Reassignment – A Guide for Employers, www.womenandequalityunit. gov.uk.*

[85] Case 13/94 [1996] IRLR 347 ECJ.

Treatment Directive.[86] The Gender Recognition Act 2004 now gives transsexuals the opportunity to obtain legal recognition of their acquired gender.

Section 2A(2)–(4) SDA 1975 also provide that a person is treated less favourably if the reason concerns any arrangements[87] or absences concerned with the reassignment and there is an obligation not to treat the absences less favourably than absences through sickness or injury. In *Chessington World of Adventures Ltd v Reed*[88] an individual announced a change of gender from male to female and, as a result, was subjected to continuous harassment from her work colleagues. She eventually was absent through sickness and then dismissed. The EAT confirmed the employment tribunal's view that the employer, who had known of the harassment, was directly liable for the sex discrimination that had taken place.

5.1.3 Race discrimination – the subject matter

The ethnic minority population of Great Britain has grown during the post-war period. In 1984 there were 2.3 million people classified as ethnic minorities. By 2006 this had grown to 4.7 million. There was a growth in the white population, during the same period, from 51 million to 52.5 million.[89]

Any consideration of the Race Relations Act 1976 must take into account the fact that race discrimination (as with sex discrimination) continues to exist, despite the fact that the Act was adopted over 30 years ago. Unemployment remains higher amongst black and ethnic minority groups, when compared to the white population.[90] In 2002, for example, employment rates for all ethnic groups was 69 per cent, including for black African people 49 per cent and for Pakistani workers 24 per cent, as compared to 71 per cent for white people.[91] This discrimination extends to earnings, especially with regard to Pakistani/Bangladeshi male workers who, according to one report, earned about two-thirds of the earnings of their white counterparts.[92] Nor is it entirely possible to isolate the effects of the Act from the effects of other legislation, especially successive Immigration Acts which have been aimed at restricting the rights of immigrants (ethnic minorities) from entering Great Britain.[93] The first Race Relations Act was enacted in 1965, but did not include employment or the concept of indirect discrimination. There was a further Race Relations Act in 1968, which was eventually followed by the 1976 Act, which distinguished between direct and indirect discrimination.

5.1.3.1 Racial grounds

Section 1 RRA 1976 provides that discrimination can take place on racial grounds or against persons of a racial group. Section 3(1) defines racial grounds as meaning 'colour, race, nationality or ethnic or national origins'.[94] It also defines racial group as a group of persons

---

[86] See *A v Chief Constable of West Yorkshire Police* [2004] IRLR 573.

[87] On access to toilet facilities see *Croft v Royal Mail Group* [2003] IRLR 592.

[88] [1997] IRLR 556.

[89] Equal Opportunities Commission *Facts about Men and Women in Great Britain 2004 and 2006*; see now *www.equalityhumanrights.com*.

[90] Although there is considerable variation as between ethnic groups.

[91] Labour Force Survey 2001/2; see Office for National Statistics website – *www.statistics.gov.uk*.

[92] Figures drawn from CRE publications.

[93] Such as the Commonwealth Immigrants Acts 1962 and 1968; the latter was aimed at restricting the immigration of East African Asians.

[94] Discrimination on the grounds of race, ethnic or national origins is now treated differently from colour and nationality as a result of the Race Relations Act 1976 (Amendment) Regulations 2003, SI 2003/1626.

'defined by reference to colour, race, nationality or ethnic or national origins'. *Mandla* v *Dowell Lee*[95] resulted from a school refusing to change its school uniform policy to allow the wearing of turbans. This stopped a boy's application to join the school, because his father wished him to be brought up as a practising Sikh, which in turn required the wearing of a turban. The boy's father complained to the Commission for Racial Equality (CRE) which took up the case which finally went to the House of Lords to consider. In order to establish that racial discrimination had taken place, in terms of the Act, it was necessary for Sikhs to be defined as a racial group. The argument centred on whether they were an ethnic group. The court decided that there were a number of conditions to be met before a group could call itself an ethnic group. Lord Fraser stated:

> The conditions which appear to me to be essential are these: – (1) a long, shared history, of which the group is conscious as distinguishing it from other groups, and the memory of which it keeps alive; (2) a cultural tradition of its own, including family and social customs and manners, often but not necessarily associated with religious observance. In addition to those two essential characteristics the following characteristics are, in my opinion, relevant; (3) either a common geographical origin, or a descent from a small number of common ancestors; (4) a common language, not necessarily peculiar to the group; (5) a common literature peculiar to the group; (6) a common religion different from that of neighbouring groups or from the general community surrounding it; (7) being a minority or being an oppressed or a dominant group within a larger community.

Such a group could include converts to it or persons who have married into it. Thus the term 'ethnic' could have a wide meaning.

Surprisingly, this definition did not extend to Rastafarians (discrimination on the grounds of religion or belief is discussed at 5.2 below). In *Dawkins*[96] an applicant for a job was turned away because he was a Rastafarian and would not comply with a requirement for short hair. His complaint of discrimination was rejected by the Court of Appeal on the grounds that Rastafarians could not be defined as a racial group within the definition of s. 3(1) RRA 1976. They did not fulfil the criteria laid down in *Mandla* v *Lee* because they did not have a long shared history,[97] and could not be compared as a racial group to the Jamaican community or the Afro-Caribbean community in England. By way of contrast, the Scots and English could be held to be separate racial groups as defined by reference to their national origins, as both Scotland and England had been separate nations in the past,[98] although an attempt to define English-speaking Welsh people as a separate ethnic group from Welsh-speaking Welsh persons failed. This was because it was insufficient to identify a separate group on the basis of language alone.[99]

It is possible for a person to be unfavourably treated on racial grounds even if the claimant is not a member of the group being discriminated against. In *Weathersfield* v *Sargent*[100] a person of white European ancestry was instructed to discriminate against black and Asian people in the hiring out of vehicles. She resigned and claimed constructive dismissal on the grounds that she had been unfavourably treated on racial grounds. The Court of Appeal held

---

[95] [1983] IRLR 209 HL.
[96] *Dawkins* v *Department of the Environment; sub nom Crown Suppliers PSA* [1993] IRLR 284 CA.
[97] Only 60 years was suggested by the court.
[98] See *Northern Joint Police Board* v *Power* [1997] IRLR 610; applied in *BBC Scotland* v *Souster* [2001] IRLR 150 CS.
[99] *Gwynedd County Council* v *Jones* [1986] ICR 833.
[100] [1999] IRLR 94 CA.

that it was appropriate to give a broad meaning to the expression 'racial grounds'. It was an expression that should be capable of covering any reason or action based on race. In *Redfearn v SERCO Ltd*[101] a white man was employed as a bus driver and escort for children and adults with special needs. It emerged that he was a candidate for the British National Party at the local elections. Membership of this party was restricted to white people only. Some 70–80 per cent of the bus passengers were of Asian origin and also some 35 per cent of the employer's workforce in this instance. He was dismissed on health and safety grounds because of the feared reaction of other employees and passengers. The Court of Appeal supported the view that he had not been dismissed on racial grounds, although it did state that discrimination on racial grounds is not restricted to less favourable treatment on the grounds of the colour of the applicant. White persons could be treated less favourably than other white persons on the grounds of colour, for example in the case of a white person being dismissed after marrying a black person or a white publican refusing to admit or serve a white customer on the grounds that he is accompanied by a black person. The court also held that although the circumstances leading to the dismissal included racial considerations, this did not necessarily mean that the dismissal itself was 'on racial grounds'.

5.1.3.2 Asylum and immigration

The rules on employing those who are subject to immigration control and who do not have permission to stay and work in the United Kingdom are strict. Section 15 of the Immigration, Asylum and Nationality Act 2006 provides that it is not permitted to employ an adult subject to immigration control if the person has not been given leave to enter or remain in the United Kingdom; or the person's leave is invalid, ceased to have effect or is subject to a condition preventing him from accepting employment. An employer will be liable to a penalty if they break this rule. An employer may be excused the penalty if he can show that he has complied with the prescribed requirements in relation to the employment of such persons. An employer who knew, at any time during the period of employment, that the person was subject to the limitations in s. 15 cannot be excused the penalty.

Section 21 of the Act provides that a person who employs another knowing either that the individual concerned is subject to immigration control and has not been given leave to enter or remain in the United Kingdom, or that the individual's leave is invalid, ceased to have effect or is subject to a condition preventing him from accepting employment will be subject to the possibility of both a fine and a term of imprisonment. It is important, however, to treat all candidates in the same way in order to avoid any actions that might constitute unlawful discrimination.

5.1.4 The general duty to promote racial equality and gender equality

The Race Relations (Amendment) Act 2000 came into effect in April 2001. It amended the 1976 Act and, amongst other matters, it placed a statutory duty on a wide range of public authorities to promote racial equality and to prevent racial discrimination. This duty is now contained in s. 71(1) RRA 1976, which states that:

> Every body or other person specified in Schedule 1A or of a description falling within that Schedule shall, in carrying out its functions, have due regard to the need –

---

[101] [2006] IRLR 623.

    a. to eliminate unlawful and racial discrimination; and

    b. to promote equality of opportunity and good relations between persons of different racial groups.

Similarly, the Equality Act 2006[102] inserted ss. 76A to 76E into the SDA 1975. Section 76A(1) provides that a public authority, in carrying out its functions, shall have due regard for the need:

    (a) to eliminate unlawful discrimination and harassment, and

    (b) to promote equality of opportunity between men and women.

This came into effect on 6 April 2007.

The Schedules each contain a large list of public authorities. The CRE published a statutory Code of Practice to give guidance to authorities in carrying out their duty.[103] Failure to observe the provisions of the Code may be admissible in evidence in legal proceedings.[104] Paragraph 3.2 of the Code provides that there are four guiding principles that should govern the implementation of this duty. These are:

1. Promoting race equality is obligatory for all public authorities listed in the Schedule. It is a general duty that will underpin all policy and practice.

2. Public authorities must meet the duty to promote race equality in all relevant functions. Relevance is about how much a function affects people, as members of the public or as employees of the authority.

3. The weight given to race equality should be proportionate to its relevance. Section 71(1) RRA 1976 (above) states that authorities must have 'due regard' to its duty to promote race equality. This means that the weight given to race equality must be proportionate to its relevance to a particular function.

4. The elements of the duty are complementary, which means that the duties to eliminate unlawful racial discrimination, promote equality of opportunity and promote good relations between people of different racial groups are all necessary to fulfil an overall duty.

Section 71(2) and (3) RRA 1976 enable the Secretary of State to impose specific duties to ensure the better performance of the public authorities in fulfilling their duties. The Race Relations Act 1976 (Statutory Duties) Order 2001[105] required the listed bodies to produce a Race Equality Scheme by May 2002. Such a scheme must state the functions and policies which the organisation has decided are relevant to its performance of its duty and include arrangements for consulting, monitoring, publishing results and training staff.[106]

If the Equality and Human Rights Commission is satisfied that a person has failed to comply with its duty, it can issue a compliance notice instructing the organisation to comply and report its actions back to the Commission. Failure to comply with this may result in the Commission's gaining a County Court Order to force the body to supply the information.[107]

---

[102] Sections 84–86.
[103] Statutory Code of Practice on the duty to promote race equality (CRE 2002); now the Equality and Human Rights Commission.
[104] Section 71C(11) RRA 1976.
[105] SI 2001/3458.
[106] Ibid., reg. 2.
[107] Sections 71D and 71E RRA 1976.

The Equal Opportunities Commission also published a Code of Practice on the Gender Equality Duty,[108] describing it as the biggest change in legislation since the Sex Discrimination Act itself over 30 years ago. The effect of this duty is similar to that of the race equality duty. There is a further duty in relation to disability (see Chapter 6).

5.1.5 Discrimination in employment

Parts II SDA 1975 and RRA 1976 are concerned with discrimination in the employment field. Employment is defined in s. 82(1) SDA 1975 and s. 78(1) RRA 1976 as meaning employment under a contract of service or apprenticeship or a contract personally to execute any work or labour. However, in *Allonby* v *Accrington & Rossendale College*[109] the ECJ decided that the word 'worker' in art. 141 has a Community meaning and cannot be defined by Member States. According to the ECJ, for these purposes a 'worker' is a person who, for a certain period of time, performs services for and under the direction of another for which they receive remuneration. Except for those who do not qualify, such as those who work wholly outside Great Britain, there are no restrictions imposed, such as a minimum length of continuous service[110] or an upper age limit, to stop an individual making a complaint of discrimination.

In a rather strict interpretation of sex discrimination in recruitment advertising, the Court of Appeal held that an act of discrimination had taken place when a magazine refused to accept an advertisement for a housekeeper/cook based in Tuscany.[111] The advertisement was placed in the magazine by a single man. The journal's reason for refusing was that it only accepted advertisements for overseas positions where the employer was a woman and that this was a way of protecting young females from exploitation. The court decided that this approach was unacceptable. The motive, in accordance with the decision in *James* v *Eastleigh Borough Council*,[112] was not a valid justification for discrimination.

Section 4(1) RRA 1976[113] makes it unlawful for a person, in relation to employment at an establishment in Great Britain,[114] to discriminate:

1. In the arrangements that are made for the purpose of determining who should be offered employment.[115]

2. In the terms that are offered in that employment.

3. By refusing or deliberately omitting to offer employment.[116]

---

[108] See now *www.equalityhumanrights.com*.

[109] [2004] IRLR 224.

[110] For example, in *Weathersfield* v *Sargent* [1999] IRLR 94, the employee left work on her second day of employment.

[111] *Bain* v *Bowles* [1991] IRLR 356.

[112] [1990] IRLR 288 HL.

[113] Also s. 6(1) SDA 1975.

[114] Section 10 SDA 1975 and s. 8 RRA 1976 state that employment is to be regarded as in an establishment in Great Britain unless the employee does their work wholly outside Great Britain. Prior to the Equal Opportunities (Employment Legislation) (Territorial Limits) Regulations 1999, SI 1999/3163, which transposed the Posted Workers Directive (Directive 96/71/EC), the exclusion was those who worked wholly or mainly outside Great Britain; see *Carver* v *Saudi Arabian Airlines* [1999] ICR 991 CA.

[115] In *Rihal* v *London Borough of Ealing* [2004] IRLR 642 the Court of Appeal held that the employment tribunal had been entitled to take into account its finding that a 'glass ceiling' operated in the housing department.

[116] Section 14 RRA 1976 and s. 15 SDA 1975 apply these provisions to employment agencies except for where the agency reasonably relies upon an employer's statement that the discrimination is lawful.

5.1.6 Burden of proof

One of the problems with discrimination cases is the ability of the complainant to show that discrimination has actually taken place. According to the Court of Appeal, very little direct discrimination is overt or deliberate. There is a need to look at the surrounding circumstances which may demonstrate that an apparently fair-minded act or decision was or was not influenced by racial bias.[117] Often the employment tribunal will need to draw inferences as to the conduct of individuals in a particular case. In *King v The Great Britain-China Centre*[118] an applicant who was Chinese, but educated in Britain, failed to be short-listed for a post of deputy director of the Centre, even though her qualifications on paper seemed to meet the selection criteria. In such a situation the tribunal was entitled to look to the employer for an explanation. In this case none of the five ethnic Chinese candidates was selected for interview and the Centre had never employed a person with such an ethnic background. The Court of Appeal supported the approach of the employment tribunal in inferring that there was discrimination on racial grounds.[119] In *King*, Neill LJ set down some principles and guidance that could be obtained from the authorities.[120] These were that:

1. It is for the applicant who complains of racial discrimination to make out his case.

2. It is unusual to find direct evidence of racial discrimination.

3. The outcome of a case will therefore usually rely upon what inferences it is possible to draw from the primary facts as found by the tribunal.

4. There will be some cases where it is possible to draw the inference of discrimination and in such cases the tribunal is entitled to look to the employer for an explanation.

5. It is unnecessary to introduce shifting evidential burdens of proof. Having adopted this approach then it is open to the tribunal to reach a conclusion based on the balance of probabilities.

Whether it is possible to draw an inference of discrimination on the basis of sex or race depends upon whether it is possible to show that a person has been subject to less favourable treatment than another person of a different sex or different racial group. In *Martins v Marks & Spencer plc*[121] an applicant of Afro-Caribbean ethnic origin applied, unsuccessfully, four times for a post as a trainee manager with Marks & Spencer. She settled a race discrimination claim on the last occasion and as part of the arrangement was allowed to take a selection test and was given an interview. She failed her selection interview with poor marks. The employment tribunal had found the selection panel 'biased' in its treatment of the candidate. This, the Court of Appeal decided, was not a meaningful conclusion. The real question was whether they were treating this candidate less favourably than they would treat another candidate in the same circumstances, and, secondly, whether one could infer that this less favourable treatment was on racial grounds. The Court of Appeal found that

---

[117] See *Anya v University of Oxford* [2001] IRLR 377 CA, where a black Nigerian resident in the United Kingdom complained of racial discrimination when he was rejected, following an interview, in favour of a white candidate.

[118] [1991] IRLR 513 CA.

[119] See *Igen Ltd v Wong* [2005] IRLR 258.

[120] See now s. 63A SDA 1975 and s. 54A RRA 1976.

[121] [1998] IRLR 326 CA.

there was insufficient evidence for this. The employer had established a defence under s. 32(3) RRA 1976.[122]

There is a need to establish a causal relationship between the detriment and the racial or sexual discrimination. Mummery J discussed causation in *O'Neill*:[123]

> The basic question is: what, out of the whole complex of facts before the tribunal, is the 'effective and predominant cause' or the 'real or the efficient cause' of the act complained of? As a matter of common sense not all the factors present in a situation are equally entitled to be treated as a cause of the crucial event for the purpose of attributing legal liability for consequences.

The tribunal's approach to the question of causation should be 'simple, pragmatic and commonsensical', although this approach needs to be qualified by the fact that the event complained of need not be the only or the main cause of the result complained of.

Section 4(2) RRA 1976[124] states that it is unlawful for a person to discriminate against an individual employed by them:

1. In the terms of employment given.
2. In the way that access to opportunities for promotion, transfer or training is afforded.
3. By dismissing them or subjecting them to any detriment.

In relation to discrimination on the grounds of race, ethnic or national origins, dismissal specifically includes the non-renewal of a limited-term contract or a constructive dismissal.[125] Additionally, where there has been a dismissal involving unlawful harassment or discrimination on the grounds of sex, race, ethnic or national origins, it is unlawful to inflict further harassment or discrimination if it 'arises out of and is closely connected to the employment relationship'.[126]

Issues related to promotion and development are important for removing both race and sex discrimination in employment. Jobs which require previous supervisory or management experience[127] can be indirectly discriminatory simply because there may be many fewer opportunities for women to obtain this sort of experience. In *British Gas plc v Sharma*[128] an employee with an MA was employed in a junior clerical post and was, apparently, unable to obtain promotion. She made a claim for race discrimination when she was not selected for two posts that carried a requirement for GCE 'O' levels.[129] In the event neither of the successful candidates had this level of education. The employment tribunal was entitled to draw an inference of race discrimination as a result of the employer's changing of the selection criteria during the interviewing process. One of the remedies available is that under s. 56(1)(c) RRA 1976.[130] An employment tribunal is able to make a recommendation for action within a specified period, which appears to be practicable, to obviate or reduce the adverse effect of the act of discrimination. The EAT held, however, that a recommendation by the tribunal that the applicant should be promoted at the next available opportunity was

---

[122] See also s. 41(3) SDA 1975.
[123] *O'Neill v Governors of St Thomas More Roman Catholic Voluntarily Aided Upper School* [1996] IRLR 372.
[124] See also s. 6(2) SDA 1975.
[125] Section 4(4A) RRA 1976.
[126] Section 20A SDA 1975, s. 27A RRA 1976.
[127] As in *Falkirk City Council v Whyte* [1997] IRLR 560.
[128] [1991] IRLR 101.
[129] A predecessor of GCSEs.
[130] See also s. 65(1)(c) SDA 1975.

outside their powers as it might be seen as an act of positive discrimination. There may have been better qualified applicants at the next promotion opportunity.

In order to make the task for complainants of sex discrimination less onerous Council Directive 97/80/EC on the burden of proof in cases of discrimination based on sex[131] was adopted by the other Member States in 1997. It was adopted by the United Kingdom, via an extension Directive,[132] in 1998. The purpose of the Directive is summarised in art. 1:

> The aim of this Directive shall be to ensure that the measures taken by the Member States to implement the principle of equal treatment are made more effective, in order to enable all persons who consider themselves wronged because the principle of equal treatment has not been applied to them to have their rights asserted by judicial process after possible recourse to other competent bodies.

The Directive took effect in national law in October 2001.[133] Section 63A was inserted into the SDA 1975. It provides that where, on a hearing of the complaint, the complainant proves facts from which the tribunal could conclude, in the absence of an adequate explanation, that the respondent:

1. has committed an unlawful act of discrimination against the complainant, and

2. is someone who is to be treated as having committed such an act against the complainant,[134]

then the employment tribunal will uphold the complaint unless the respondents prove that they did not commit such an act, or that they should not be treated as having committed it.

Subsequently the Race Relations Act was amended[135] so that similar provisions apply in cases covered by that Act.

Igen Ltd v *Wong*[136] was a case where the Court of Appeal considered a number of questions in relation to the interpretation of the statutes concerning the shifting of the burden of proof. The court held that the provisions required an employment tribunal to go through a two-stage process. The first stage is for the applicant to prove facts from which the tribunal could conclude, in the absence of an adequate explanation, that the respondent has committed an act of discrimination against the applicant. The second stage, which only comes into effect if the complainant has proved these facts, requires the respondent to prove that he did not commit the unlawful act. This case actually contains a 13-point guidance to the decision-making process in relation to the burden of proof. It includes:

1. The claimant must prove on the balance of probabilities facts so that, in the absence of an adequate explanation, the tribunal could conclude that the act of discrimination had taken place against the applicant.

2. It is unusual to find evidence of direct discrimination.

3. It could mean that at this stage the tribunal does not have to have reached a final conclusion.

---

[131] OJ L14/6 20.1.98 (Burden of Proof Directive).

[132] Council Directive 98/52/EC OJ L205/66 22.7.98.

[133] The Sex Discrimination (Indirect Discrimination and Burden of Proof) Regulations 2001, SI 2001/2660.

[134] Sections 41 and 42 SDA 1975 refer to the liability of employers and principals as well as those aiding such unlawful acts.

[135] In relation to employment tribunals s. 54A was inserted into the RRA 1976 by the Race Relations Act 1976 (Amendment) Regulations 2003, SI 2003/1626.

[136] [2005] IRLR 258.

4. The respondent must prove, on the balance of probabilities, that the treatment was in no way whatsoever on a discriminatory ground.

It is not always necessary to go through this two-stage procedure. In *Brown v LB of Croydon*[137] the court held that it was not obligatory, but good practice to do so. In some circumstances it was possible to go straight to the second stage. In this case the emphasis was on the reasons for the treatment, so it was natural to do so.

The importance of shifting the burden of proof to the respondent once a *prima facie* case of discrimination has been established is of great importance. In *Madarassy v Nomura International plc*[138] the Court of Appeal stated:

I do not underestimate the significance of the burden of proof in discrimination cases. There is probably no other area of civil law in which the burden of proof plays a larger part than in discrimination cases.

The burden of proof, however, does not shift just by showing that there was a difference in status (sex in this case) and a difference in treatment. 'Could conclude' means that 'a reasonable tribunal could properly conclude' from all the evidence put before it. This could include evidence from the complainant and evidence from the respondent contesting the complaint. The absence of an adequate explanation is not at this stage relevant as to whether there is a *prima facie* case of discrimination. It only becomes relevant if a *prima facie* case is proved. Thus the *prima facie* case has still to be shown.

5.1.7 **In the course of employment**

According to s. 32(1) RRA 1976,[139]

anything done by a person in the course of his employment shall be treated for the purposes of this Act . . . as done by the employer as well as him, whether or not it was done with the employer's knowledge or approval.

In *Jones v Tower Boot Co Ltd*[140] the employer argued that the acts of racial harassment were outside the normal course of employment. The employment tribunal took the view that this would amount to saying that no act could become the liability of the employer unless it was expressly authorised by the employer. The Court of Appeal supported this approach and took the view that the words ought to be given their everyday meaning. In *Sidhu*[141] the event, which consisted of a racially motivated assault on an employee by another employee, took place at a family day out organised by the employers. This was held not to be 'in the course of employment', but subjecting a female police officer, by a male police officer, to inappropriate sexual behaviour during an after work gathering of police officers in a pub and during a leaving party for a colleague, amounted to actions done in the course of employment.[142] When there is a social gathering of work colleagues, it is for the employment tribunal to decide whether the gathering was an extension of employment. Whether a person was, or was

---

[137] [2007] IRLR 259.
[138] [2007] IRLR 246.
[139] Section 41(1) SDA 1975.
[140] [1997] IRLR 168 CA.
[141] *Sidhu v Aerospace Composite Technology Ltd* [2000] IRLR 602 CA.
[142] *Chief Constable of the Lincolnshire Police v Stubbs* [1999] IRLR 81.

not, on duty and whether the events occurred on the employer's premises are just two indicators that need to be considered. In this case the two police officers could not have been said to be merely socialising with each other.[143]

5.1.8 Taking all steps that are reasonable and practicable

Section 32(3) RRA 1976 and s. 41(3) SDA 1975 provide an opportunity for employers to deny liability. The employer needs to show that they have taken such steps as are reasonably practicable to prevent the employee from doing the act or other acts of a similar description. In *Martins* v *Marks & Spencer plc*[144] (see above) the Court of Appeal held that:

> There can be no doubt that Marks & Spencer made out the defence on the findings of fact about the effective arrangements made for the 'special interview' to ensure that the members of the panel had no knowledge of the reason for the interview; their equal opportunities policy; their compliance with the Code of Practice issued by the Commission for Racial Equality in relation to selection procedures, criteria and interviewing; and their selection of the interviewing panel to include Mr Walters as a person with an interest in recruiting from ethnic minorities.

All these actions amounted to a sufficient defence for the employer. It is no defence to say that all possible steps were not taken because the taking of those steps would not have made any difference. This might be true in some extreme forms of harassment such as the sexual assault that took place in *Canniffe* v *East Riding of Yorkshire Council*.[145] Even though there may have been little the employers could have done to stop this action, the fact that they did not take further possible measures was enough to stop them being able to rely on s. 41(3) SDA 1975. The proper approach for the employment tribunal, according to the EAT, was:

1. to identify whether the respondent had taken any steps at all to stop the employee from committing the act or acts complained of and then,

2. having identified what steps, if any, had been taken, to decide whether there were any further steps that could have been taken which were reasonably practicable.

Whether these further steps would have stopped the acts is not decisive.

5.1.9 Aiding unlawful acts

Section 42(1) SDA 1975 and s. 33(1) RRA 1976 provide that a person who knowingly aids another to do an act which is made unlawful by the SDA or RRA will be treated as if they committed that act themselves. This includes an employee or an agent for whose acts the employer is liable.[146] The exception to this is when a person reasonably relies upon a statement made by the other person that the acts which are being aided are not unlawful.[147]

The concept of 'knowingly aiding' was considered in *Anyanwu and Ebuzoeme* v *South Bank Students Union*.[148] This concerned two black students who were elected as paid officers of the

---

[143] The matter was also considered in *Waters* v *Commissioner of Police of the Metropolis* [2000] IRLR 720 HL where an alleged sexual assault in a section house was deemed to be in the course of employment; see also *Lister* v *Hesley Hall Ltd* [2001] IRLR 472 HL, section 2.3.2.

[144] [1998] IRLR 326 CA.

[145] [2000] IRLR 555.

[146] Section 42(2) SDA 1975 and s. 33(2) RRA 1976. See *Yeboah* v *Crofton* [2002] IRLR 634.

[147] Section 42(3)–(4) SDA 1975 and s. 33(3)–(4) RRA 1976.

[148] *Anyanwu and Ebuzoeme* v *South Bank Students Union and South Bank University* [2001] IRLR 305 HL.

students' union. They were subsequently expelled from the university for other reasons and barred from the students' union building. This led to the termination of their employment with the students' union. They complained that, amongst other matters, their employer had discriminated against them in terminating their employment. They also complained that the university had knowingly aided this unlawful act. The House of Lords held that the word 'aids' did not have any special or technical meaning in this context and that there was an arguable case that the university had 'knowingly aided' the students' dismissal from employment by the students' union. The university had brought about a state of affairs in which the employment contracts were bound to be suspended. In *Gilbank* v *Miles*[149] a pregnant hairdresser was subject to a campaign of bullying and discrimination which led to the salon manager being made jointly and severally liable with the company employer as she had helped create the growth of a discriminatory culture.

In *Hallam* v *Cheltenham Borough Council*[150] the police had concerns about a wedding reception that was to be held at a council-owned hall. The father of the bride was of Romany origin. The Council reacted by imposing new contractual conditions, including admittance only to those with pre-issued tickets. The hirer treated this as repudiatory conduct and held the reception elsewhere. The Council were subsequently found to be guilty of racial discrimination. One further question was whether the police officers concerned had knowingly aided the Council in this discriminatory act. The House of Lords held that each situation should be looked at on its merits. In this case the police officers had not been a party to, neither had they been involved in, the Council's decision. There were a number of ways in which the Council could have reacted to the information, some of which would have been lawful, so more than a general attitude of helpfulness and co-operation was required.

5.1.10 Genuine occupational qualification or requirement

Both the SDA 1975 and the RRA 1976 provide for a situation where being of a particular sex or of a particular racial group is a genuine occupational qualification.[151] There are certain situations where it is permissible to use sex or racial origin as a criterion in the selection of an applicant or in providing access to promotion and training. The SDA provides a listing in s. 7(2) of those situations where being a man may be a genuine occupational qualification. These exceptions apply where only some of the duties of a job fall within the categories, as well as when all the duties do so.[152] These are:

1. Where 'the essential nature of the job would be materially different if carried out by a woman'. These can be situations where a man is needed for physiological reasons, although reasons related to strength and stamina are excluded. There is no further elaboration except for the specific exception of dramatic performances or other entertainment where there is a requirement for authenticity reasons.

2. Where there are decency reasons for a job to be held by a man such as those involving physical contact with men where they might reasonably object to the job being carried out by a woman or where the men are likely to be in a state of undress or using sanitary

---

[149] [2006] IRLR 538.
[150] [2001] IRLR 312 HL.
[151] Section 7 SDA 1975 and s. 5 RRA 1976.
[152] Section 7(3) SDA 1975.

facilities. Such a situation arose in *Lasertop Ltd v Webster*[153] where a male applicant failed to obtain an interview for a sales/trainee manager position with a women-only health club. The job entailed showing potential members around the club, including the changing rooms, saunas, sun-bed room and toilet. The EAT concluded that the club could rely upon a genuine occupational qualification defence in such circumstances.

3. Where the job concerns working in, or living in, a private home and the job needs to be held by a man because of the degree of physical or social contact and the knowledge of the intimate details of a person's life.[154]

4. Where the nature or location of the establishment make it impracticable for the job holder to live anywhere but on the premises supplied by the employer and there are no separate sleeping or sanitary provisions for men and women, nor is it reasonable to expect the employer to provide them.

5. Where the nature of the establishment, or the part in which work is done, requires the job holder to be a man. This can be a single-sex hospital, prison or other establishment for persons requiring special care and attention, where it would not be reasonable for the job to be done by a woman.

6. Where the job holder provides individuals with personal services promoting their welfare or education, or similar services, and this can best be done by a man.

7. Where the job needs to be done by a man because it is likely to involve the performance of some of the work in a country where a woman would not be able to effectively perform the duties.

8. Where the job is one of two held by a married couple.

If there are already sufficient numbers of male employees who are capable of carrying out these duties, and whom it would be reasonable to employ on these duties without causing the employer undue inconvenience, then the exceptions would not apply.[155] Rather than recruit a new employee using a genuine occupational qualification exception, the employer would be expected to cover these duties with existing employees. In *Lasertop Ltd v Webster*[156] the applicant claimed that the employer could not rely on the genuine occupational qualification defence for this reason. It was a new women-only health club. The EAT held that the relevant time for s. 7(4) SDA 1975 to operate was at the time when the discrimination takes place. As this was a new club recruiting staff, the position envisaged by s. 7(4) could not exist, as there were few existing employees at the time. The EAT was concerned that this would create a lacuna in the law, but still held that the employer could rely unhindered on the genuine occupational qualification defence.

Section 7A SDA 1975 provides similar rules to be applied in situations relating to gender reassignment and s. 7B provides that there is a further genuine occupational qualification concerning those who are planning a gender reassignment or are undergoing the process of gender reassignment. This exception includes jobs that are concerned with, first, being called upon to conduct intimate searches; secondly, living or working in a private home; thirdly, where the location or establishment requires the person to live on the premises and there are

---

[153] [1997] IRLR 498.
[154] This provision was added by the Sex Discrimination Act 1986.
[155] Section 7(4) SDA 1975.
[156] [1997] IRLR 498.

not separate facilities for preserving decency and privacy; and, finally, where the job holder is providing personal services to vulnerable individuals, promoting their welfare or similar and where the employer decides that the services cannot be provided by someone undergoing gender reassignment.

Under the RRA 1976 there are fewer situations in which a genuine occupational qualification applies. These are:

1. Where authenticity in drama or other entertainment requires a person of a particular racial group.
2. Where the production of visual imagery in art or photography requires a person from a particular racial group for reasons of authenticity.
3. Where the job involves working in a place where food and drink is served to the public and membership of a racial group is required for authenticity.
4. Where the job holder provides persons of that racial group with personal services promoting their welfare, and where those services can be most effectively performed by a person of that racial group.

In relation to (4), it should be noted that the test is whether the services can 'most effectively' be performed by a person from a particular racial group. It is not where they 'must be' or 'can be' provided by such a person. In *Tottenham Green Under Fives' Centre* v *Marshall (No 2)*[157] the EAT held that the 'desirable extra' of having a nursery worker being able to read and talk in dialect was sufficient to justify a genuine occupational qualification exception. Secondly, the services need to be performed personally. This means that employers filling managerial positions might find it more difficult to establish a genuine occupational qualification. When considering two management positions in a local authority housing department, Balcombe LJ stated:

> The critical questions may be put thus: 'Would the holders of these two jobs provide persons of the particular racial group with personal services promoting their welfare?' The Industrial Tribunal found not. The EAT found that they did not. The reason for the finding was quite fundamental, that is that the holders of managerial posts in the housing benefits service did not provide a personal service at all. Their contact with members of the public was either negligible or non-existent.[158]

The concept of a genuine occupational requirement was introduced to the statute book in 2003. This applies where, 'having regard to the nature of the employment or the context in which it is carried out', being of a particular race, ethnic or national origin is a 'genuine and determining occupational requirement'. It must also be proportionate to apply the requirement and either the person to whom it is applied does not meet it or 'the employer is not satisfied, and in all the circumstances it is not reasonable for him to be satisfied, that that person meets it'.[159]

5.1.11 Discrimination by other bodies

Section 12 SDA 1975 and s. 11 RRA 1976[160] provide that it is unlawful for

---

[157] [1991] IRLR 162.
[158] *London Borough of Lambeth* v *Commission for Racial Equality* [1990] IRLR 231 at p. 235 CA.
[159] Section 4A(1)–(2) RRA 1976.
[160] Section 11 SDA 1975 and s. 10 RRA 1976 provide that discrimination is unlawful for partnerships, in relation to arrangements for appointing a person as a partner in the firm; in s. 10(1) RRA 1976, however, the partnership needs a minimum of six or more partners before this aspect of the legislation applies.

an organisation of workers, an organisation of employers, or any other organisation whose members carry on a particular profession or trade for the purposes of which the organisation exists

to discriminate on the grounds of sex or racial grounds against those applying for membership in the terms for admittance or in refusing or omitting to accept the application for membership. Similarly, in s. 12(3) SDA 1975 and s. 11(3) RRA 1976, discrimination against members by depriving them of access to membership benefits or of membership itself or some other detriment is made unlawful.

The words 'organisation of employers' are to be given their ordinary and natural meaning. Thus an organisation like the National Federation of Self-employed and Small Businesses would qualify as an employer's organisation. This despite the organisation's own claims that it did not qualify on the grounds that a minority of members were self-employed, rather than employers, and their purposes were not related to their members as employers, but rather to their interests as business people.[161] Section 13 SDA 1975 and s. 12 RRA 1976 make it unlawful for bodies which can confer an authorisation or qualification which is needed for engagement in a particular trade or profession to discriminate. In *Arthur* v *Attorney General*[162] it was held that the body which sifted recommendations to the Lord Chancellor on appointments to become Justices of the Peace did not fall within the terms of s. 12 RRA 1976, because it only provided a filtering function, rather than conferring approval. Neither were Justices of the Peace an 'occupation' within the definition of 'profession' as defined in s. 78(1)[163] RRA 1976. *Tattari* v *Private Patients Plan Ltd*[164] distinguished between those bodies which granted qualifications or recognition for the purposes of practising a profession and those which stipulated a particular qualification for the purpose of its commercial agreements. In *Triesman* v *Ali*[165] the Court of Appeal held that the Labour Party was not a body within the meaning of s. 11 RRA 1976. However, there might be a remedy under s. 25 RRA 1976 which deals with associations not within s. 11.

The issues become more complicated when there is a dispute between members of an organisation. In *Fire Brigades Union* v *Fraser*[166] one member accused another of sexual harassment. In this case the trade union decided to represent the harassed woman, rather than the man accused of harassment. The employment tribunal compared the treatment received by the man with that of the woman concerned. The EAT accepted that the trade union had failed to provide an explanation for the difference in treatment, so that the employment tribunal had been correct in inferring sex discrimination contrary to s. 12(3) SDA 1975. The responsibilities in s. 12(2) SDA 1975 and s. 11(2) RRA 1976, concerning organisations of trade unions, employers and others, to non-members relate only to questions of admission or non-admission to the organisation. In another case concerning a trade union[167] an ex-member complained that they had been victimised and subjected to detriment by the union and three of its officials. The complaints referred to alleged verbal abuse and physical threats

---

[161] *National Federation of Self-employed and Small Businesses* v *Philpott* [1997] ICR 518.
[162] [1999] ICR 631. See also *Patterson* v *Legal Services Commission* [2004] IRLR 153.
[163] Section 82(1) SDA 1975. In both statutes, 'profession' is defined as including any vocation or occupation.
[164] [1997] IRLR 586 CA.
[165] [2002] IRLR 489.
[166] [1997] IRLR 671.
[167] *Diakou* v *Islington Unison 'A' Branch* [1997] ICR 121.

when the individual crossed a picket line and to the alleged dissemination of misinformation about the individual's conduct by the trade union. The claim failed because the individual was no longer a member and was unable to pursue a complaint that extended beyond admission and non-admission matters.

Discrimination against contract workers by a person other than the one with whom they have a contract is also unlawful where the contract worker is doing work for the other person (the principal) under a contract arranged between the principal and the contract worker's employer.[168] The Court of Appeal gave this a wide interpretation where an employee of a concessionaire in Harrods store was dismissed because the store withdrew its approval of her for reasons that she did not comply with the store's dress code. She made a successful claim of racial discrimination against the store.[169] The court held that s. 7 RRA 1976 is not limited to cases where those doing the work are under the direct management or control of the principal. It also applies when an individual is doing work for their employer, but also work done for the principal. In this case it was held that the concessionaire was supplying employees under the terms of its contract with Harrods to do work for Harrods in accord with s. 7 RRA 1976.

5.1.12 Remedies

Article 6 Equal Treatment Directive provides that all individuals have the right to obtain an effective remedy in a competent court against measures that infringe on the right to equal treatment between men and women.

Section 63 SDA 1975[170] provides that individuals may bring a complaint of discrimination, in relation to Part II of the Act, to an employment tribunal. The complaint may be as a result of discrimination by the other party or because the other party is liable under ss. 41 and 42 SDA 1975.[171] Such liability may be as a result of things done in the course of employment (see above) or as a result of a person knowingly aiding another person to do something that is unlawful under the Act.[172] An employment tribunal will not consider the complaint unless it is presented within a period of three months of when the act complained of was done,[173] unless the tribunal 'considers that it is just and equitable to do so'.[174] A broad approach was shown in *Derby Specialist Fabrication Ltd v Burton*,[175] where an employee resigned after a period of racial abuse and harassment. Although the discriminatory acts took place before this constructive dismissal, the EAT approved of the tribunal's decision that the three-month period ran from the date of the resignation. If the employee is making a complaint as a result of suffering a detriment from the employer, then the three months

---

[168] Section 9 SDA 1975 and s. 7 RRA 1976.

[169] *Harrods Ltd v Remick* [1997] IRLR 583 CA. See also *Jones v Friends Provident* [2004] IRLR 783.

[170] Section 54 RRA 1976.

[171] The provisions concerning the liability of employers and principals for acts done in the course of employment and the liability of a person who aids another person in carrying out an unlawful act under the SDA 1975; see also ss. 32 and 33 RRA 1976.

[172] See *Anyanwu and Ebuzoeme v South Bank Students Union and South Bank University* [2000] IRLR 305 HL.

[173] Section 76(1) SDA 1975 and s. 68(1) RRA 1976. On acts extending over a period see s. 76(6) SDA 1975, s. 68(7) RRA 1976 and *Hendricks v Commissioner of Police for the Metropolis* [2003] IRLR 96.

[174] Section 76(5) SDA 1975 and s. 68(6) RRA 1976. Note also that employees must first submit a statement of grievance to their employer: Sch. 2 paras. 6 and 9 EA 2002.

[175] [2001] IRLR 69.

commences from when he heard of the detriment.[176] Where an employment tribunal finds that a complaint was well founded, then it has a choice of what action to take:

1. It may make an order declaring the rights of the claimant and the respondent in relation to the act complained of.

2. It may make an order requiring the respondent to pay compensation to the claimant.

3. It may make a recommendation that the respondent takes action, within a specified period of time, for the purpose of obviating the adverse effect on the complainant of any act of discrimination to which the complaint relates.[177]

In *Prestcold Ltd v Irvine*[178] it was held that actions (2) and (3) above were exclusive. The first should take care of losses of wages, whilst the second is concerned with taking steps other than payment of wages in order to obviate or reduce the adverse effects of discrimination. If the respondent fails, without reasonable justification, to comply with the recommendation, then the tribunal may increase the level of compensation.[179] It is important to observe that there is no upper limit on compensation that can be awarded.

In *Essa v Laing Ltd*[180] the Court of Appeal ruled that a victim of racial abuse was entitled to be compensated for the loss which arises naturally and directly from the wrong. It was not necessary for the particular type of loss to be reasonably foreseeable. Individuals can recover for both physical and psychiatric injury[181] and obtain aggravated damages.[182] In relation to injury to feelings, the Court of Appeal has suggested that there are three broad bands of compensation – the minimum sum being £5,000 and the maximum being £25,000.[183]

Section 76 SDA 1975 provides for various time limits in which an employment tribunal may consider a complaint under the Act (see below). Proceedings in *Mills and Crown Prosecution Service v Marshall*[184] commenced after the decision in *P v S and Cornwall County Council*[185] and were out of time. These proceedings concerned an individual who was offered a post in the Crown Prosecution Service. The offer was withdrawn after the applicant informed the Director of Public Prosecutions that they were intending to reassign their gender. The Court of Appeal approved the approach of the employment tribunal in hearing the case out of time. They held that the wording in s. 76(5), which allowed the tribunal to hear such cases if it was 'just and equitable to do so', should be given the widest possible meaning as they were different from the words used in allowing tribunals discretion to hear complaints of unfair dismissal out of time.[186]

---

[176] Delays in internal procedures do not necessarily justify delaying the presentation of the complaint to an employment tribunal: it is one factor that will be taken into account; see *Robinson v Post Office* [2000] IRLR 804.

[177] Section 65(1) SDA 1975 and s. 56(1) RRA 1976.

[178] [1980] IRLR 267.

[179] Section 65(3)(1) SDA 1975 and s. 56(4)(a) RRA 1976.

[180] [2004] IRLR 313.

[181] See *Sheriff v Klyne Tugs* [1999] IRLR 481.

[182] See *British Telecom plc v Reid* [2004] IRLR 327.

[183] *Vento v Chief Constable of West Yorkshire Police (No 2)* [2003] IRLR 102.

[184] [1998] IRLR 494.

[185] Case 13/94 [1996] IRLR 347 ECJ.

[186] See also *Afolabi v London Borough of Southwark* [2003] IRLR 220; *Apelogun-Gabriels v London Borough of Lambeth* [2002] IRLR 116.

As an aid to complainants, s. 74 SDA 1975[187] permits the Secretary of State to prescribe a means by which a respondent can be questioned about the reasons for doing any relevant act.[188] The answers will be admissible in the tribunal proceedings and a failure to respond, or the giving of evasive or equivocal answers, may enable the tribunal to draw inferences that it considers just and equitable to reach, including an inference that the respondent committed an unlawful act. In *D'Silva* v *NATFHE*[189] a claimant alleged that a failure to respond to a discrimination questionnaire raised an inference of discrimination. The EAT said this was not automatically so; one needs to consider the particular circumstances and whether they were capable of constituting evidence supporting the inference that the employer had acted discriminatorily.

Additionally a complainant may apply to the Equality and Human Rights Commission for assistance, which may include giving advice, trying to procure a settlement, and arranging legal advice or representation.[190]

5.1.13 Codes of practice

The Equality and Human Rights Commission (EHRC) may issue codes of practice whose purpose is the elimination of discrimination in the field of employment or for the promotion of equality in that field between, first, men and women and, secondly, for persons intending to undergo, or who have undergone, gender reassignment.[191] The Code of Practice for the elimination of racial discrimination and the promotion of equality of opportunity in employment was first issued by the Commission for Racial Equality in 1983.[192] It is now the Code of Practice on racial equality in employment and came into force on 6 April 2006.[193] Similarly, the Code of Practice on sex discrimination, equal opportunities policies, procedures and practices in employment was first issued by the EOC in 1985.[194] The purposes of the Code, stated in its introduction, are: the elimination of discrimination in employment; to give guidance as to what steps employers should take; and to promote equality of opportunity.

Section 56A(10) SDA 1975[195] provides that a failure on the part of any person to observe the provisions of the Code will not, in itself, render them liable to proceedings. The failure will, however, be admissible as evidence in any proceedings before an employment tribunal and may be taken into account in determining the question. The EHRC is also entitled to conduct formal investigations[196] and make recommendations. Sections 67–73 SDA 1975 provide for the issue and enforcement of non-discrimination notices by the EHRC in relation to Part IV of the Act, which deals with discriminatory practices.

---

[187] Section 65 RRA 1976.

[188] Sex Discrimination (Questions and Replies) Order 1975, SI 1975/2048; see also the Race Relations (Questions and Replies) Order 1977, SI 1977/842.

[189] [2008] IRLR 412.

[190] Section 75 SDA 1975 and s. 66 RRA 1976.

[191] Section 56A(1) SDA 1975; in addition, the European Commission has issued guidance from time to time, e.g. Commission Recommendation 92/131/EEC and Code of Practice on the protection of the dignity of women at work OJ L249/1 24.2.92.

[192] The Code of Practice was made under s. 47 RRA 1976 and came into effect on 1 April 1984; see the Race Relations Code of Practice Order 1983, SI 1983/1081.

[193] See now *www.equalityhumanrights.com*.

[194] The Code of Practice was made under s. 56A SDA 1975 and came into effect on 30 April 1985 by the Sex Discrimination Code of Practice Order 1985, SI 1985/387.

[195] Also s. 47(10) RRA 1976.

[196] See Sex Discrimination (Formal Investigations) Regulations 1975, SI 1975/1993; also ss. 48–52 RRA 1976.

5.2 Discrimination on the grounds of religion or belief, or sexual orientation

Regulations forbidding discrimination on these grounds in employment were introduced in 2003. They were subsequently amended in 2006 by the Equality Act which extended the provisions to include goods, services and facilities.

5.2.1 Religion or belief

Religious discrimination can be closely linked to racial discrimination, but it was not expressly made unlawful until 2003. A good example was the case *Ahmad* v *ILEA*.[197] This concerned a Muslim school teacher who required a short time off on Friday afternoons to attend prayers at a nearby mosque. He resigned and claimed unfair dismissal when his employers refused him paid time off. They had offered him a part-time position working $4\frac{1}{2}$ days per week. The United Kingdom had not at the time incorporated the European Convention on Human Rights into national law, but, as Lord Denning stated in this case, 'we will do our best to see that our decisions are in conformity with it'. In this case it still meant rejecting the claim as it would give the Muslim community 'preferential treatment'. The court held that art. 9(2) of the Convention did not give an employee the right to absent himself from work in breach of the contract of employment. Lord Scarman dissented, stating that the issue began, but did not end, with the law of contract. The judgment would mean that any Muslim, who took their religious duties seriously, could never be employed on a full-time contract as a teacher. This is an old case and one must doubt whether the same decision would be reached today. It does, however, illustrate how it is possible to penalise someone for carrying out the activities and ritual connected to their religious beliefs. Another example is *Mandla* v *Lee*[198] where the Sikhs were identified as an ethnic group, and were thus protected under the Race Relations Act 1976.

The 2001 census asked a question about religion. It was a voluntary question and over 4 million people did not answer it. Of those that did, their professed religious loyalty was as follows:

Religious affiliations 2001 census	
Christian	41,014,811
Muslim	1,588,890
Hindu	558,342
Sikh	336,179
Jewish	267,373
Buddhist	149,157
No religion/religion not stated	13,030,008

Source: Crown Copyright material is reproduced with the permission of the Controller, Office of Public Sector Information (OPSI)

[197] [1977] ICR 490.
[198] [1983] IRLR 209.

There are wide geographical differences. The highest proportion of Christians in England was the north-east with about 80 per cent. In London this figure fell to 58 per cent. Approximately 38 per cent gave their religion as Muslim as well as 12 per cent of the population of the East Midlands. The London Boroughs of Westminster and Harrow had the highest concentration who stated that they were Hindu and in Barnet the figure for the Jewish population was around 15 per cent. On a lighter note, at the time of the census there was a campaign to persuade people to answer the religious question with 'Jedi Knight'. As a result some 370,000 people (0.7 per cent of the population) declared their religion as Jedi Knight![199]

The Framework Directive was transposed into national law by the Employment Equality (Religion or Belief) Regulations 2003 (hereafter the Religion or Belief Regulations).[200] These Regulations were amended by Part 2 of the Equality Act 2006, which, importantly, extended the scope of non-discrimination on this ground to goods, facilities and services.

Religion means 'any religion', belief means any religious or philosophical belief, and references to both religion and belief include references to a lack of religion or belief.[201] This is not a helpful definition as it provides no meaning to the terms religion or belief. It has been deliberately left to the courts, relying on art. 9 ECHR,[202] to decide whether any particular religion or belief meets this definition. The Government guidance on these Regulations[203] states that this definition is a broad one and will clearly include those religions that are widely recognised, such as Christianity, Islam, Hinduism and Judaism. Equally it will apply to groups within religions, such as Roman Catholics and Protestants. There is a difficulty with outward manifestations of religious belief, as shown in *Eweida* v *British Airways plc*.[204] Mrs Eweida was a devout Christian who regarded the cross as the central image of her belief; she wanted to wear it over her uniform in her role as a part-time check-in member of staff. The Company's rules only permitted the wearing of visible religious symbols where there was a 'mandatory' religious requirement. Mrs Eweida complained that this amounted to indirect discrimination contrary to Regulation 3 of the Religion or Belief Regulations. The Court of Appeal held that BA had not acted in a way that amounted to indirect discrimination. In order to show this there would have to be evidence of group disadvantage, not just the particular individual. This could not be done in this case.

5.2.2 Sexual orientation

In order to meet its obligations under the Equal Treatment in Employment and Occupation Directive,[205] the Government adopted the Employment Equality (Sexual Orientation) Regulations 2003 (the Sexual Orientation Regulations).[206] These came into force on 1 December 2003. Prior to these Regulations there were few provisions protecting people at work from being discriminated against because of their sexual orientation.

---

[199] This will only mean something to those who have watched the *Star Wars* movies.
[200] SI 2003/1660.
[201] Regulation 2(1).
[202] Article 9 of the European Convention on Human Rights states: 'Everyone has the right to freedom of thought, conscience and religion, this right includes the freedom to change his religion or belief . . .'
[203] Explanatory Notes for the Employment Equality (Religion or Belief) Regulations 2003 (DTI, 2003).
[204] [2010] IRLR 322.
[205] Directive 2000/78/EC.
[206] SI 2003/1661; the Government estimates that between 1.3 and 1.9 million people are affected by the Regulations.

The European Court of Justice concluded in *Grant v South-West Trains Ltd*[207] that discrimination based on sexual orientation was not contrary to Community law. The complaint was that the employer gave travel concessions to employees plus their spouses or partners of the opposite sex, but refused them to a long-term partner of the same sex as an employee. The ECJ held that there was no discrimination under art. 119 EEC (now 157) or the Equal Pay Directive. The problem was that a condition such as this applied to male and female employees. The court considered the judgment arrived at in *P v S*[208] and accepted that the decision in that case had been based upon gender discrimination. In *Grant*, however, a female same-sex partner would apparently have been treated in the same way as a male same-sex partner, so there could be no discrimination between the two. This approach meant that a person subjected to homophobic abuse and dismissal would not have been able to sustain a claim based upon sex discrimination or harassment.[209]

Until the Government relaxed its approach in 2000 this absence of protection posed a particular problem for members of the armed services. The Court of Appeal refused to construe the Equal Treatment Directive in order to include sexual orientation and suggested that any proscription of discrimination on the grounds of sexual orientation might need to be achieved by a specific Directive.[210] The Government's change of approach occurred after the European Court of Human Rights reached a decision in *Smith and Grady*.[211] Prior to this decision the policy of the Ministry of Defence had been that 'homosexuality, whether male or female, is considered incompatible with service in the armed forces'.[212] After the European Court of Human Rights held that the rights of the individuals under art. 8 (right to privacy) and art. 13 (right to an effective domestic remedy) of the European Convention on Human Rights had been violated, the ban on homosexuals in the armed forces was lifted. The Ministry of Defence issued a new Code of Social Conduct[213] which banned unacceptable social conduct, which applied to heterosexuals as well as homosexuals. The 'service test' was introduced to determine when it was necessary to intervene in the personal lives of employees. This test consists of the commanding officer considering whether

> the actions or behaviour of an individual adversely impacted or are likely to impact on the efficiency or operational effectiveness of the service.

There is a distinction between discrimination against homosexuals on the grounds of their sexuality and discrimination on the grounds of their sex. In *Smith v Gardner Merchant Ltd*[214] a male homosexual complained that he was subjected to threatening and abusive behaviour by a female colleague. He was subsequently dismissed and the employment tribunal decided that it did not have jurisdiction to hear claims of discrimination on grounds of sexual orientation. The appeal was won at the EAT and upheld by the Court of Appeal who concluded

---

[207] Case 249/96 [1998] IRLR 206 ECJ.
[208] *P v S and Cornwall County Council* Case 13/94 [1996] IRLR 347 ECJ.
[209] See *Smith v Gardner Merchant Ltd* [1998] IRLR 510 CA where a bar person was subjected to such abuse prior to dismissal.
[210] See *R v Secretary of State for Defence, ex parte Perkins (No 2)* [1998] IRLR 508 where a medical assistant was discharged from the Royal Navy because of his sexual orientation; see also *Secretary of State for Defence v MacDonald* [2001] IRLR 431 CS, which concerned a member of the RAF who was excluded because of his sexual orientation.
[211] *Smith and Grady v United Kingdom* [1999] IRLR 734 ECHR.
[212] *Ministry of Defence Guidelines on Homosexuality*, December 1994.
[213] *The Armed Forces Code of Social Conduct: Policy Statement*, 1999.
[214] [1998] IRLR 510 CA.

that such discrimination against a male homosexual could amount to discrimination against him as a male. In this case the correct comparator, under s. 5(3) SDA 1975,[215] in relation to the treatment by the work colleague could be with a homosexual woman and whether she would have been treated in the same way. For comparison concerning a complaint about the employer's handling of the situation, the female colleague could be used as the comparator. This approach did not help a lesbian school teacher who was subject to homophobic verbal abuse by pupils at the school. *Pearce* v *Governing Body of Mayfield Secondary School*,[216] followed the approach in *Smith* v *Gardner Merchant Ltd* to conclude that it could not be said that she had received less favourable treatment than a hypothetical homosexual male teacher, as there was no evidence that such a teacher would have been treated any differently. The change brought about by the Regulations is illustrated in *English* v *Thomas Sanderson Blinds Ltd*[217] where Mr English claimed that for many years he had been subject to homophobic abuse as a result of having attended a public school and living in Brighton. He was not homosexual and he accepted that his work colleagues did not really believe him to be homosexual. The Court of Appeal held that a person being tormented by homophobic abuse could rely on Regulation 5 of the Sexual Orientation Regulations even though he was not gay or perceived as being gay by his colleagues.

Regulation 2(1) of the Sexual Orientation Regulations defines sexual orientation as a sexual orientation towards:

- Persons of the same sex; thus covering both gay men and gay women.
- Of the opposite sex; which provides for heterosexual relationships.
- Of the same sex and opposite sex; which covers bisexual men and women.

Sexual orientation means an orientation towards a person of the same sex, the opposite sex or both sexes. It does not include sexual practices or sexual conduct.

5.2.3 Discrimination and harassment

Both sets of Regulations cover employees, contract workers, trustees and managers of pension schemes, office holders, the police, barristers, advocates, partnerships, trade organisations, qualifications bodies, providers of vocational training, employment agencies and institutions of further and higher education.[218]

Regulation 2(3) defines employment as meaning employment under a contract of service or of apprenticeship or a contract personally to do any work. Thus there is a broader definition of employment, adopting the same approach as the SDA 1975 and RRA 1976. A contract worker is someone doing contract work and the protection is against the 'principal'. This is a person who makes work available for doing by individuals who are employed by another person. Thus agency workers are protected against discrimination by the employer to whom they are sent to work by their employment agency.

---

[215] Section 5(3) SDA 1975 provides that a comparison of persons of different sex or marital status or of the cases of discrimination and gender reassignment must be such that the relevant circumstances in the one case are the same as, or not materially different from, those in the other.

[216] [2001] IRLR 669 CA.

[217] [2009] IRLR 206.

[218] Regulations 8–20 of both sets of Regulations.

Discrimination may take place:

- on the grounds of religion or belief, or
- by way of victimisation.

Regulation 3(1)(a) defines direct discrimination as:

> For the purposes of these Regulations, a person (A) discriminates against a person (B) if –
>
> (a) on the grounds of religion or belief (sexual orientation) A treats B less favourably than he treats or would treat other persons.[219]

Thus there is a need to show less favourable treatment compared to another person of a different religion or belief (or sexual orientation). The relevant circumstances of the person discriminated against and the comparator need to be the same, or 'not materially different'.[220] A simple example of direct discrimination given in the Government explanatory notes on religion or belief[221] is if an employer refused to allow a prayer break for Muslim employees at certain times. This would not amount to direct discrimination if the employer refused breaks for all employees at that time.[222]

The protection is against discrimination on the 'grounds of religion or belief' (or sexual orientation). Thus a person who is not a Jew, for example, but is discriminated against because the employer perceives him as being Jewish is equally protected. Similarly a person who is not gay but is discriminated against because the employer perceives him as being gay is also protected. There is no defence of justification in direct discrimination as there may be for indirect discrimination.

Indirect discrimination is provided for in reg. 3(1)(b). Thus discrimination occurs when:

1. A applies to B a provision, criterion or practice which A applies equally to other persons not of the same religion or belief (or sexual orientation) as B, but

2. which puts persons of the same religion or belief (or sexual orientation) as B at a particular disadvantage when compared with others, and

3. which also puts B at a disadvantage, and

4. A cannot show it to be a proportionate means of achieving his legitimate aim.

Thus the stages in showing that A's application of the provision, criterion or practice amount to indirect discrimination, are, first, that there needs to be a 'particular disadvantage' suffered by the group who share B's religion or belief or sexual orientation. This is different from the 'considerably smaller' definition used in the SDA 1975 and the RRA 1976 and is intended to be less reliant on statistical evidence than those measures concerned with sex and race discrimination.[223] The second stage is then to show that the complainant, B, is also put at that disadvantage. Clearly this has to be the same disadvantage suffered by the group in the first stage, but it does mean that cases can only be brought by people who suffered the disadvantage themselves. There is then an opportunity for the employer to show that the

---

[219] The reference to religion or belief here does not include A's religion or belief; see reg. 3(2).

[220] Regulation 3(3) Religion or Belief Regulations and reg. 3(2) Sexual Orientation Regulations; the Government guidance accompanying the Regulations suggests that this means that the relevant circumstances need not be identical.

[221] See *www.bis.gov.uk.*

[222] It might, however, amount to indirect discrimination if not justified.

[223] DTI explanatory notes; see now *www.bis.gov.uk.*

application of the provision, criterion or practice is justified because it concerns achieving a legitimate aim by proportionate means. An example might be an advertisement for a leader of a playgroup for Muslim children, which specifies that applicants must be familiar with the teachings of the Koran. A Jewish applicant might be able to show a group disadvantage, in that this would disadvantage all Jews, as well as an individual disadvantage to himself. It would then be for the employer to show that this provision, criterion or practice had a legitimate aim and was a proportionate means of achieving it.[224]

The second means by which discrimination can take place is by way of victimisation.[225] In this case a person, A, discriminates against another person, B, if he treats B less favourably than he treats or would treat other persons in the same circumstances because B has:

1. Brought proceedings against A under the Religion or Belief (or Sexual Orientation) Regulations.
2. Given evidence or information in connection with any proceedings brought against A under the Regulations.
3. Done anything else to A or any other person under the Regulations.
4. Alleged that A or any other persons have committed an act contrary to the Regulations.

The same applies if A treats B less favourably because B plans to do any of the above. Thus workers will be protected from less favourable treatment for taking action under the Regulations, even if any allegations made or information given are later shown to be false, so long as the allegations were made in good faith.

The definition of harassment is the same as that contained in other anti-discrimination statutes and regulations. Harassment on the grounds of religion or belief is defined as unwanted conduct which has the result of either violating a person's dignity or creating an intimidating, hostile, degrading, humiliating or offensive environment for the worker. Thus it is unwanted conduct, although it is clear that the worker need not express the view that the conduct is unwanted whenever it happens. There will be conduct which is self-evidently unwanted. The harassment does, however, need to be on the grounds of religion or belief. If a person is bullied for some other reason, it may not be possible to show that it took place because of an individual's religion or belief.

5.2.4 Discrimination and employment

Part II of the Religion or Belief (or Sexual Orientation) Regulations deals with discrimination in employment and vocational training. It is unlawful for an employer, at an establishment in Great Britain, to discriminate against applicants on the grounds of their religion or belief (or sexual orientation):

1. In the arrangements made for the purpose of deciding who should be offered employment.
2. In the terms of the offer.
3. By refusing to offer, or deliberately not offering, employment.[226]

---

[224] DTI guidance; see now *www.bis.gov.uk*.
[225] Regulation 4.
[226] Regulation 6(1).

It is also unlawful for an employer to discriminate against employees, employed at an establishment in Great Britain:

1. In their terms of employment.

2. In the opportunities afforded for promotion, a transfer, training or in receiving any other benefit.

3. By dismissing the employee or subjecting the employee to any other detriment.[227]

This includes constructive dismissal as a result of the employer's conduct.[228]

An example may be whether an employer needs to consider whether his pay arrangements, which include double pay on Sundays, are discriminatory. Such an arrangement might constitute indirect discrimination if not justified, as they may disadvantage employees whose faith recognises Sunday as a day of rest.[229] *Azmi* v *Kirklees Metropolitan Borough Council*[230] concerned a school support worker who was a devout Muslim. She was used to wearing a long dress and a veil which covered all her head and face apart from her eyes. After much consultation she was instructed not to wear the veil in school as it restricted the visual signals that children would normally receive from a person not wearing a veil. Her claim of direct discrimination failed because she was held not to have been treated less favourably compared to another person, who was not a Muslim, but who had her face covered.

Regulation 6(3) also provides that it is unlawful for an employer to harass applicants or employees. There is, however, no requirement for the employer to ask an applicant or employee about their religion or belief (or sexual orientation), especially as many individuals may regard the matter as a private one which they do not wish to discuss with the employer or potential employer.

Acts committed after the employment relationship has ended will also be unlawful if the discrimination or harassment arises out of, or is closely connected with, that employment relationship.[231] Anything done 'in the course of employment' shall be treated as if it was done by the employer, whether the employer had knowledge of the act or not. As in other areas of discrimination law the employer will have a defence if the employer can show that all steps as were reasonably practicable were taken to prevent the employee from doing the act, or, at least, from doing the act during the course of employment.[232]

There are some exceptions from Part II. These are, in the Regulations on Religion or Belief:

1. National security – reg. 24 provides that an act done for safeguarding national security, so long as it was justifiable in that context, is not unlawful.

2. Positive action – this may be taken where it reasonably appears to prevent or compensate for disadvantages linked to religion or belief suffered by persons of that particular religion or belief.[233]

---

[227] Regulation 6(2).
[228] Regulation 6(5)(b).
[229] See DTI guidance; see now *www.bis.gov.uk*.
[230] [2007] IRLR 484.
[231] Regulation 21.
[232] Regulation 22; reg. 23 deals with aiding unlawful acts, so an agent or employee acting as an agent for the employer or other for whom the employer is liable will be assumed to be doing the act itself unless the agent or employee reasonably relies on a statement from the principal that the act is not unlawful under the Religion or Belief Regulations.
[233] Regulation 25.

3. Special arrangements for Sikhs working on construction sites. If the employer has no reasonable grounds for believing that the Sikh worker would not be wearing a turban at all times, then the application of any provision, criterion or practice that stops the Sikh worker from doing this will not be one which can be shown to have a proportionate means of achieving a legitimate aim.[234]

In the Regulations on Sexual Orientation the exceptions are:

1. National security – reg. 24 provides that an act done for safeguarding national security, so long as it was justifiable in that context, is not unlawful.
2. Marital status – anything that prevents or restricts access to a benefit by reason of marital status is not unlawful, so it is perfectly lawful to discriminate in favour of married persons for access to some benefits.[235]
3. Positive action – this may be taken where it reasonably appears to prevent or compensate for disadvantages linked to sexual orientation suffered by persons of that particular sexual orientation.[236]

5.2.5 Genuine occupational requirement

In relation to applicants and employees, the provisions concerning discrimination do not apply if there is a genuine and determining occupational requirement for being of a particular religion or belief and it is proportionate[237] to apply that requirement in the particular case.[238] Thus there are a number of factors:

- It must be a *requirement* of the job, which means that it must be essential for a person to be able to carry out the job.
- It must be a *determining* requirement; something that is crucial to the job.
- It must be an *occupational* requirement, meaning a close connection with the job in question.
- It must be a *genuine* occupational requirement and not one just created to try to avoid the Regulations or because the employer does not like people of a particular religion or belief or specific sexual orientation.[239]

This may justify dismissal from a post where, for example, an employee changes their religion or belief (or sexual orientation) and this change means that he can no longer perform the functions of the post. If, on the other hand, an employee changes their religion or belief (or sexual orientation) and this has no effect upon performing the job functions, then the change in orientation would not be a justification for dismissal. There are likely to be only rare genuine occupational requirements for a person to be of a particular religion or belief or sexual orientation.

The above rules apply to any employer, but there are similar rules which apply if the employer has an ethos based on religion and belief.[240] This situation will relate to a limited number of employers. The differences are that:

---

[234] Regulation 26(1).
[235] Regulation 25.
[236] Regulation 26.
[237] Proportionate, according to the guidance, means the appropriate means of achieving the aim in question.
[238] Regulation 7(1) and 7(2).
[239] See Government guidance.
[240] Regulation 7(3).

- the employer will need to show that they have an ethos based upon religion or belief;
- the genuine occupational requirement will need to have regard to that ethos; and
- the genuine occupational reason does not have to be the determining requirement.

Thus it is a broader exception because the employer does not need to show that the genuine occupational requirement is a determining factor. It will still have to show that the genuine occupational requirement for an employer with a particular religious ethos applies to the particular job. *Glasgow City Council* v *McNab*[241] concerned a teacher who was turned down for an interview as acting principal teacher of pastoral care in a Roman Catholic school. It was established that had he been a Roman Catholic he would have been given an interview. The education authority failed to establish that being a Roman Catholic was a genuine occupational requirement as the post had not previously been covered by an agreement to reserve certain posts. The education authority also claimed that it was an employer which had an ethos based on religion or belief in accord with reg. 7(3) as it was responsible in part for schools which did have that ethos. This claim was also unsuccessful because such an authority, according to the EAT, could be one which had responsibility for schools with a number of different and possibly contradictory ethos at the same time.

One important issue here may be a potential clash between the protection given under the Sexual Orientation Regulations (see below) and those concerned with religion or belief. What is the situation if an organisation has a religious ethos that excludes homosexual people because it is against its ethos? Regulation 7(3) provides that if the employment is for an organised religion, then the employer may be permitted to apply a requirement related to sexual orientation:

- so as to comply with the doctrines of the religion, or
- to avoid conflicting with strongly held religious convictions of a significant number of the religion's followers.

In this latter case the exception refers to the nature of employment and the context in which it is carried out. This suggests that the exception applies to jobs whose purposes are to do with religion, rather than the religious organisations as such. Therefore it will be permissible for an exception to be made with the appointment of imams, priests, rabbis, etc., but perhaps not for all jobs within a religious organisation.

In *Ladele* v *London Borough of Islington*,[242] Lilian Ladele was a registrar of births, deaths and marriages; she was a strongly committed Christian and believed marriage was a union between a man and a woman for life. In 2005 the Civil Partnership Act 2004 came into force and allowed same-sex couples to enter into a civil partnership. She made it plain that she would have difficulties conducting civil partnership registrations because of her beliefs. All the registrars were expected to carry out civil partnership registrations. As a compromise she was offered the chance to just do those that required a signing event as opposed to a ceremony. She did not accept this compromise. She changed rosters with colleagues to avoid doing the civil partnership events. Management tolerated this but two gay colleagues objected. She was eventually subjected to disciplinary proceedings, as a result of which she complained to a tribunal of religious discrimination. The EAT stated that direct evidence of

[241] [2007] IRLR 476.
[242] [2010] IRLR 211 where the Court of Appeal approved of the decisions made by the EAT.

discrimination is rare and tribunals often have to infer discrimination from all the material facts. There is a two-stage test: first, the claimant needs to prove a *prima facie* case of discrimination; second the employer has to prove on the balance of probabilities that the treatment was not on the prohibited ground. If he cannot do this, then the tribunal must find that there is discrimination. It is not always necessary to go through the two stages however. In some circumstances it might be appropriate to focus on the reason given by the employer. Mrs Ladele claimed that she had been directly discriminated against because of her religious beliefs, but this was unsustainable. She was not complaining about being treated differently from others, but about not being treated differently. It was a complaint about a failure to accommodate her difference, rather than that she was being discriminated against because of that difference. The Council had been entitled to say that she could not pick and choose what duties she would perform based on her religious beliefs. The Court did say, however, that it would have been legitimate for them to take a pragmatic view and not designated as civil partnership registrars those who would have objections on religious grounds.

A further case highlighting this apparent conflict between religious belief and sexual orientation was *McClintock* v *Department of Constitutional Affairs*.[243] Mr McClintock was a Justice of the Peace who was also a practising Christian. He felt that he could not place children with same-sex couples. He wanted to be relieved of the possibility of having this role, but this was not to be permitted. As a result he resigned and claimed indirect discrimination on the grounds of his beliefs. The EAT held that to constitute a belief there must be a religious or philosophical viewpoint in which one actually believes; it is not enough to have an opinion or perceived logic. The kind of objection could not properly be described as a philosophical belief.

5.3 Equal pay

The Equal Pay Directive[244] built upon art. 119 (157) EC and established that the principle of equal pay meant:

> . . . for the same work or for work to which equal value is attributed, the elimination of all discrimination on grounds of sex with regard to all aspects and conditions of remuneration.[245]

Pay is given a broad definition and actions which have been held to be discriminatory include when retired male employees receive travel concessions not available to female retirees;[246] when part-time employees do not receive pay during sickness when it was paid to full-time employees;[247] and when men and women receive different payments, including pensions, resulting from compulsory redundancies.[248]

The Equal Pay Act was passed by Parliament in 1970, but there was a long introductory period before it came into effect in 1975. Although one cannot doubt that the legislation has had an impact on the relative pay of men and women, a significant gap still remains.

---

[243] [2008] IRLR 29.
[244] Council Directive 75/117/EEC of 19 February 1975 on the approximation of the laws of the Member States relating to the application of the principle of equal pay for men and women OJ 1975 L45/19.
[245] Article 1 Directive 75/117/EEC.
[246] Case 12/81 *Garland* v *British Rail Engineering Ltd* [1982] IRLR 111 ECJ.
[247] Case 171/88 *Rinner-Kühn* v *FWW Spezial-Gebäudereinigung GmbH* [1989] ECR 2743 ECJ.
[248] Case C-262/88 *Barber* v *Guardian Royal Exchange Assurance Group* [1990] ECR 1-1889 ECJ.

Section 1(1) EPA 1970 implies an equality clause into all contracts of employment which do not already contain one. An equality clause, according to s. 1(2) EPA 1970, is a provision relating to the terms, not just pay, of a contract under which a woman is employed. The clause has effect where a woman is employed:

1. On like work with a man in the same employment.

2. On work rated as equivalent with that of a man in the same employment.

3. On work which, not being work in (1) or (2), is, in terms of the demands made upon her, of equal value to that of a man in the same employment.[249]

In these situations any term of the woman's contract, apart from the equality clause, that is less favourable to the woman than the comparable man should be modified so as to be not less favourable. Similarly, if the woman's contract does not contain a term conferring a benefit on her that is contained in the comparable man's contract, then the woman's contract shall be deemed to include the term.[250] Equal pay must, therefore, be calculated not on the basis of the worth of the overall contract in comparison with the man's contract, but on the basis of each individual item taken in isolation. In *Brunnhofer*,[251] for example, two bank employees were employed in the same grade and on the same basic salary. The comparable man, however, was paid a higher supplement than Mrs Brunnhofer. This was subsequently justified on the grounds that the man carried out more important functions and was said to do work of a higher quality. The higher supplement, however, was paid from when they were recruited. It was not possible to justify the differences in pay by factors that became known only after the employees had taken up their employment and had been assessed.

In *Hartlepool Borough Council* v *Dolphin*[252] the EAT summarised the approach to be applied to equal pay claims:

(i) The complainant must produce a gender based comparison showing that women doing like work, or work rated as equivalent, or work of equal value to men, are being paid or treated less favourably than men; this would produce a rebuttable claim of sex discrimination.

(ii) The employer must then show that the variation between the woman's contract and the man's contract is not tainted with sex, i.e. that it is due to a material factor that is not the difference of sex. To do this the employer must show

(a) That the explanation for the variation is genuine.

(b) That the more favourable treatment of the man is due to that reason.

(c) That the reason is not the difference of sex.

(iii) If the employer cannot show that the reason was not due to the difference of sex, he or she must show objective justification for the disparity between the woman's contract and the man's contract.

The rules establish the need to make a claim based upon an inequality of terms between the complainant and a male comparator and not on the concepts of direct and indirect discrimination contained in the Sex Discrimination Act 1975.[253] The principle of equal pay

---

[249] The Equal Pay Act 1970 was amended by the Equal Pay (Amendment) Regulations 1983, SI 1983/1794 in order to ensure that the ability of an employee to claim equal pay for work of equal value was not dependent upon an employer consenting to a job grading system.

[250] Section 1(2)(a), (b) and (c) EPA 1970.

[251] Case 381/99 *Brunnhofer* v *Bank der Österreichischen Postsparkasse AG* [2001] IRLR 571 ECJ.

[252] [2009] IRLR 169.

[253] See *Ratcliffe* v *North Yorkshire County Council* [1995] IRLR 439 HL.

presupposes that the men and women whom it covers are in comparable situations.[254] Succeeding in a claim will entitle the female complainant to receive the same terms as that comparator.[255] This, in itself, may not always seem fair. *Evesham v North Hertfordshire Health Authority*[256] was an appeal against the remedy awarded by an employment tribunal as a result of a long-running claim by speech therapists that their work was of equal value to that of a district clinical psychologist. The claimant was a district chief speech therapist with six years' experience in her post. The comparator was a newly appointed clinical psychologist in his first year and near the bottom of the pay scale. Ms Evesham argued that she should be placed at a point on the incremental scale that reflected her experience. The Court of Appeal held that to do this would be to entitle her to pay in excess of that received by the male comparator, with whom she had established equal value. The EPA 1970 requires an identified comparator with whom the value of the applicant's work can be compared. It was a comparison between the work of individuals, rather than a comparison between what speech therapists do and what clinical psychologists do.[257]

5.3.1 The comparator

The comparator needs to be selected by the complainant[258] and be in the same employment as the claimant. This does not mean that the claimant can just choose an artificial or arbitrary group, although, in principle, the comparison should be between the advantaged and the disadvantaged group. In *Somerset County Council v Pike*,[259] for example, a retired teacher who came back to work part time found that the part-time work was not pensionable. The question was who the correct comparator should be. The employment tribunal said that it should be the entire teaching profession, and therefore the statistical evidence did not show disparate impact. The EAT said the pool should not consist of people who have no interest in the advantage or disadvantage in question; it should consist of retired teachers who had returned to work and then disparate impact could be shown.

The claimant and the comparator must be 'employed', which means being employed under a contract of service, a contract of apprenticeship or a contract personally to execute any work or labour.[260] However, in *Allonby v Accrington and Rossendale College*[261] the ECJ held that the word 'worker' in art. 141 (now 157) has a Community meaning and cannot be defined by Member States. For these purposes a 'worker' is a person who performs services for and under the direction of another for which they receive remuneration. In this case the requirement of having a contract of employment as a precondition of membership of a

---

[254] See Case 218/98 *Abdoulaye v Régie Nationale des Usines Renault* [1999] IRLR 811 ECJ, where employees absent through pregnancy were held to have occupational disadvantages which entitled them to an extra payment.
[255] According to *Hayward v Cammell Laird* [1988] IRLR 257 HL it is each item contained in the contract of employment that should be the same, not the overall terms and conditions.
[256] [2000] IRLR 257 CA.
[257] The ECJ held, in Case 236/98 *Jämställdhetsombudsmannen v Örebro Läns Landsting* [2000] IRLR 421 ECJ, that the proper comparison between the two groups is the basic monthly pay, excluding supplements; no account is to be taken of different working hours, although these might constitute reasons unrelated to sex.
[258] See *Ainsworth v Glass Tubes and Components Ltd* [1977] IRLR 74, where an employment tribunal was held to have erred by selecting the comparator they wished to use.
[259] [2009] IRLR 870.
[260] Section 1(6)(a) EPA 1970.
[261] [2004] IRLR 224.

pension scheme set up by statute had to be disapplied unless it was objectively justified. This was because a much higher percentage of women fulfilled all the conditions of membership except that of having a contract of employment as defined by national law.

The comparators need to be employed by the same employer as the claimant at the same establishment or other establishments in Great Britain which, including the one at which the claimant is employed, have common terms and conditions of employment generally or for particular relevant classes of employees.[262] This appears to be interpreted widely, so if there is a sufficient connection in a 'loose and non-technical sense' between the different employments then this might be sufficient. *Dumfries and Galloway Council v North*[263] concerned a claim by classroom assistants and others employed at the council's schools under a set of terms and conditions deriving from a collective agreement known as the 'blue book' agreement. They sought to compare themselves to male manual workers such as road workers and refuse workers, who were employed in various depots and governed by a separate collective agreement contained in the 'green book'. The question was whether the claimants and their comparators were employed in the 'same employment' as required by s. 1(6) EPA 1970. The EAT stated that where a woman seeks to use a male comparator who is not employed at her establishment, she has to show a real possibility that he would be employed there in the job he carries out at the other establishment, or in a broadly similar job. Having the same or associated employers does not mean necessarily that they are in the same employment. The purpose of s. 1(6) was to allow a woman to compare herself with a man in another of her employer's establishments, but only where there are factors which show a commonality or uniformity of employment regime between them. If there is no possibility of a person being employed to perform the comparator's job at the complainant's establishment, then this would suggest that there is no commonality of regime; thus here it would be wrong to conclude that the claimant and the comparator were in the same establishment.

A claimant cannot compare herself with a successor in her job.[264]

5.3.2 **Like work**

A woman is to be regarded as employed on like work with a man if her work is of a 'broadly similar nature' to his.[265] It may not be enough that the two groups being compared appear to do identical work. In a case that considered a health authority which employed both graduate psychologists and medical doctors as psychotherapists, the ECJ held that a difference could be identified between the two groups even though they carried out similar functions. In treating their patients both groups drew upon their training and experience. The doctors had a very different training and experience. That, combined with the ability to employ doctors on a greater range of duties, was sufficient to justify a difference in treatment in their remuneration.[266] The level of responsibility, together with the severity of the consequences of one's actions, may be a factor that distinguishes two jobs where the work may otherwise be identical. In *Eaton Ltd v J Nuttall*,[267] for example, although the complainant and the

[262] Section 1(6)(c) EPA 1970, added by the SDA 1975.
[263] [2009] IRLR 915.
[264] *Walton Centre for Neurology and Neurosurgery v Bewley* [2008] IRLR 588.
[265] Section 1(4) EPA 1970.
[266] Case C-309/97 *Angestelltenbetriebsrat der Wiener Gebietskrankenkasse v Wiener Gebietskrankenkasse* [1999] IRLR 804 ECJ.
[267] [1977] IRLR 71.

male comparator were employed on like work, the consequences of an error by the male comparator were much more serious than the consequences of an error by the female complainant.[268]

Often jobs done are not precisely similar and employment tribunals have been called upon to assess the importance of small differences which might distinguish the job of the applicant from that of the complainant. It may be necessary to examine what individuals actually do, rather than what their contract of employment obliges them to do, if different.[269] There is likely to be a two-stage approach:

1. An examination to decide whether, generally, the work that a complainant does is the same or broadly similar to the work done by a male comparator.

2. If it is work of a similar nature, are the differences between the things she does and the things he does of practical importance in relation to the terms and conditions of employment.

Without this approach a tribunal may fail to recognise that, although a woman and a man may be doing work of a broadly similar nature, they may not actually be employed on like work.[270] All the duties done by a complainant and a comparator need to be examined and it is unlikely that some duties could be ignored even if they take only a little time.[271] Nevertheless, the final conclusion may be based upon a broader view:

> It is clear from the terms of the subsection that the work need not be of the *same* nature in order to be like work. It is enough that it is of a similar nature. Indeed, it need only be broadly similar. In such cases where the work is of a broadly similar nature (and not of the *same* nature) there will necessarily be differences between the work done by a woman and the work done by the man.[272]

5.3.3 Work rated as equivalent

A woman is to be regarded as employed on work rated as equivalent with that of a man only if her job has been given an equal value with his job in a job evaluation study undertaken with a view to evaluating the jobs in an undertaking or group of undertakings.[273] Alternatively it would have been given an equivalent rating if the evaluation system was not flawed by having a system which gives different values for men and women under the same heading. The factors used in the assessment of any job under a job evaluation system need to be objective. The criteria used should be common to both men and women, but must also not be such as to discriminate against women. This does not necessarily mean that criteria involving physical strength, viewed as a male characteristic, should be excluded. If a job is

---

[268] See also *De Brito v Standard Chartered Bank* [1978] ICR 650 which also compared a trainee to more experienced employees.

[269] *E Coomes v Shields* [1978] IRLR 263; see also *Redland Roof Tiles Ltd v Harper* [1977] ICR 349, which took into account the fact that the male comparator was also a trainee manager and, for five weeks in a two-year period, acted as a supervisor.

[270] *Waddington v Leicester Council for Voluntary Service* [1977] IRLR 32.

[271] In *Dance v Dorothy Perkins Ltd* [1978] ICR 760 the EAT held that, where a comparator was chosen as a representative of a wider group, then it was important to examine the duties in the context that they were a representative.

[272] *Capper Pass Ltd v Lawton* [1977] ICR 83.

[273] Section 1(5) EPA 1970.

seen objectively as requiring a certain amount of strength, then this may be included as a criterion. It is important, however, to view the overall picture to ensure that any particular attributes, conventionally seen as female, needed for the job are also taken into account. Not to do this and leave, as part of the criteria, a factor associated with one sex might open the door to a discrimination claim.[274]

There is a problem when jobs are just slotted in against benchmark jobs and given a consequent grading. It might be possible to claim that such jobs have not properly been considered against the various criteria. The onus is upon the employer to show that there had been a job evaluation study which satisfied the requirements of s. 1(5) EPA 1970.[275]

In *O'Brien* v *Sim-Chem Ltd*[276] the three appellants complained that a job evaluation study had given their jobs an equal rating with that of their male counterparts. Apparently because of a Government incomes policy the employer did not apply the new job grade or salary range to the individuals in question. Although a job evaluation study required the co-operation of both employees and an employer, the consequences of a study were that, where jobs were found to be rated as equivalent, there should be a comparison of the respective terms and conditions. The job evaluation system does not, in itself, determine any terms of the women's contract. This is done in the subsequent comparison. Even where the results of the job evaluation study are not entirely accepted by the parties to the study, the existence of a *prima facie* valid job evaluation study would be enough for an employment tribunal to be bound by s. 1(5).[277]

5.3.4 Work of equal value

This category applies if a woman is employed on work which, not being work falling into the categories of like work or work rated as equivalent, is nevertheless, in terms of the demands made on her, of equal value to that of a man in the same employment. Examples given in s. 1(2)(c) EPA 1970 include demands under headings such as 'effort, skill and decision'. It will not be enough for an employer to cite the presence of workers, amongst the comparators, who fall into the categories of s. 1(2)(a) or (2)(b) EPA 1970 in order to argue that they therefore cannot fall into s. 1(2)(c). This is the situation that existed in *Pickstone* v *Freemans Ltd*[278] where female warehouse operatives claimed work of equal value with male warehouse operatives. To deprive the female employees of their right to a comparison for these reasons would be to deprive them of their rights under art. 141 EC (now 157).

If a complaint is made to an employment tribunal, then that tribunal has the option of appointing an expert from an independent panel to prepare a report on the equal value issue. Section 2A(1A) EPA 1970 allows an employment tribunal to determine the question of equal value itself and the circumstances in which the parties can choose to adduce expert evidence are restricted. Section 2A(2) and (2A) EPA 1970 provide that if a job evaluation study has attributed different values to the work of the claimant and the comparator, the tribunal must conclude that the work is not of equal value unless it has reasonable grounds to suspect

---

[274] See Case 237/85 *Rümmler* v *Dato Drück GmbH* [1987] IRLR 32 ECJ.
[275] See *Bromley* v *H and J Quick Ltd* [1988] IRLR 249 CA.
[276] [1980] IRLR 373 HL.
[277] See *Greene* v *Broxtowe District Council* [1977] ICR 241.
[278] [1988] IRLR 357 HL.

that the study discriminated on the grounds of sex or that there are other reasons why it is unreliable.[279]

5.3.5 Material factor defence

Section 1(3) EPA 1970 provides a 'material factor' or 'material difference' defence to an equal pay claim. This defence will assist an employer if they are able to show that the difference in pay is genuinely due to a material factor which is not the difference of sex.[280] In cases involving like work or work rated as equivalent, the factor 'must' be a material difference between the woman's case and the man's. However, in equal value claims the material factor 'may' be such a material difference.

Glasgow City Council v *Marshall*[281] concerned an equal pay claim between instructors and teachers in certain specialist schools. A number of female instructors claimed that they were employed on like work with male teachers and a male instructor claimed that he was employed on like work with a female teacher.[282] After a long hearing, over some 52 days, the instructors won their case at an employment tribunal. The employers appealed against the tribunal's decision on their defence under s. 1(3) EPA 1970. Their case was based upon the fact that the sets of employees had their terms and agreements settled by different collective bargaining structures. The employers also, with the help of statistics, sought to show an absence of sex discrimination. This latter argument was not appealed against. It was this presumed lack of sex discrimination that undermined the instructors' case, however. The House of Lords held that to exclude matters of sex discrimination would mean that the EPA 1970 was concerned with one employee being paid less than another, rather than with arguments about whether a female employee was paid less than a male comparator. Lord Nicholls stated:

> The scheme of the Act is that a rebuttable presumption of sex discrimination arises once the gender based comparison shows that a woman, doing like work or work rated as equivalent or work of equal value to that of a man, is being paid or treated less favourably than the man.

The burden of proof, according to the court, then passes to the employer who needs to show that the reason for the differences is not tainted with sex. In order to satisfy the employment tribunal the employer must show that:

1. The explanation or reason offered is genuine, and not a sham or pretence.

2. The less favourable treatment is due to this reason, i.e. it is a material factor.

3. The reason for the difference is not the difference of sex. In order to do this, the employer will need to show that there is an absence of direct or indirect sex discrimination. Finally, the employer will need to show that the factor relied upon is a 'material difference', i.e. a significant and relevant difference between the woman's case and the man's case.[283] If

---

[279] See Employment Tribunals (Constitution and Rules of Procedure) (Amendment) Regulations 2004, SI 2004/2351, Sch. 6 which sets out the procedural rules which apply in equal value cases.

[280] See *Ministry of Defence* v *Armstrong* [2004] IRLR 672.

[281] [2000] IRLR 272 HL.

[282] Section 1(3) EPA 1970 applies the Act to a reverse situation where a male employee may make a claim against a female comparator.

[283] See *McGregor* v *GMBATU* [1987] ICR 505 which considered that the work of the applicant was of equal value to the comparator, but that the comparator's long experience and exceptional knowledge was a material factor which justified the difference in pay.

there is evidence of sex discrimination the employer will need to show that the difference in pay can be objectively justified. If, however, as in this case, the employer shows an absence of sex discrimination, then the employer will not be required to justify the pay disparity.[284]

A material factor is said to be a 'significant and relevant' factor which is 'material' in a causative sense, when considering a pay difference.[285] Thus an employer can establish a s. 1(3) defence by identifying the factors causally relevant to the pay disparity and showing that they are free of sex discrimination. One result of this was the somewhat surprising decision of the ECJ in *Cadman*[286] where the court held that where there was a disparity of pay between men and women as a result of using length of service as a criterion, then the employer did not need to establish specifically that using this criterion was appropriate in order to achieve a legitimate objective. The court did add that where a worker can show evidence that casts serious doubt as to whether recourse to the criterion of length of service was appropriate in the circumstances, then the employer may have to justify in detail how length of service leads to experience which enables the worker to perform his duties better. The problem of course is that generally women are often unable to achieve the same length of service as men, because it is women who are more likely to have career breaks as a result of caring responsibilities.

In *Strathclyde Regional Council* v *Wallace*[287] a group of nine female teachers claimed to be doing like work with higher paid principal teachers. They were part of a group which consisted of 134 teachers, comprising 81 men and 53 women. The difference in sex was not a factor that could be relied upon. The material factor was, amongst other matters, the financial constraints that the education authority found itself under. There is nothing, according to the court, in s. 1(3) that requires the employer to justify the factors causing the disparity by showing that there was no other way in which they could have taken action to avoid the difference.

Nevertheless, if a sexually discriminatory practice is the cause of the disparity, the employer may still be able to rely on objective justification. In *Seymour-Smith*,[288] the effect of the, then, two-year continuous service qualification before a claim for unfair dismissal could be made was held to have had a disparate effect on women and amounted to indirect discrimination for the purposes of art. 141 EC. It could, nevertheless, be objectively justified as a legitimate method of encouraging employers to recruit.[289] It will not be enough for the employer to show that they had no intention of discriminating against a woman on the grounds of her sex. Thus an employer who mistakenly placed a male employee at a point on

---

[284] See *Nelson* v *Carillion Services Ltd* [2003] IRLR 428 and *Parliamentary Commissioner for Administration* v *Fernandez* [2004] IRLR 22.

[285] See *Rainey* v *Greater Glasgow Health Board* [1987] IRLR 26 HL.

[286] Case C-17/05 *Cadman* v *Health and Safety Executive* [2006] IRLR 969.

[287] [1998] IRLR 146 HL.

[288] *R* v *Secretary of State for Employment, ex parte Seymour-Smith and Perez (No 2)* [2000] IRLR 263 HL.

[289] See also Case 170/84 *Bilka-Kaufhaus* v *Weber von Harz* [1986] IRLR 317 ECJ where excluding part-timers from membership of a pension scheme was held to be justifiable on the grounds that the employer wished to discourage part-time recruitment; this decision would now have to take into account Directive 97/81/EC on part-time work; in Case 96/80 *Jenkins* v *Kingsgate (Clothing Production) Ltd* [1981] IRLR 228 the ECJ also stated that the differences between the pay of part-timers and full-timers was only contrary to art. 119 if it also amounted to indirect sex discrimination.

a salary scale higher than that to which they were entitled could not use this mistake as evidence of a material factor when a female employee made a claim for equal pay.[290]

5.3.6 Enforcing equal pay

Any claim, including a claim for arrears of remuneration and damages, relating to equal pay may be made to an employment tribunal.[291] Compensation for non-economic loss is not recoverable in an equal pay claim, unlike claims under the Sex Discrimination Act. Thus there can be no damages for injury to feelings under the Equal Pay Act.[292] An employer may also apply to an employment tribunal, where there is a dispute about the effects of the equality clause in s. 1(1) EPA 1970, for a declaration as to the rights of the employer and employees.[293] Section 2(4) EPA 1970 provides that claims must be lodged before a qualifying date. This is normally six months after the last day on which the claimant was employed. Where the proceedings relate to a period during which a stable employment relationship subsists, the qualifying date is six months after the day on which that relationship ended.

The Employment Act 2002 (EA 2002) introduced a questionnaire procedure into equal pay claims, as already existed in those relating to sex, race and disability discrimination claims.[294] The questions and replies can be admitted as evidence in any subsequent employment tribunal proceedings. If the employment tribunal considers that the respondent deliberately, or without reasonable excuse, failed to reply to the questions in the time limit, then it can draw any inference that it thinks just and equitable.

Section 2(5) EPA 1970 had provided that a successful complainant could only be awarded remuneration or damages in respect of the two years prior to the time when proceedings were instituted. The limitation period was challenged and referred to the ECJ, who held that the two-year period was a restriction on the right to have a full and effective remedy for breach of art. 119 EEC (now 157) and the Equal Pay Directive. The time limit under the Sex Discrimination Act 1975, the Race Relations Act 1976 and the Disability Discrimination Act 1995 was six years. Section 2(5) EPA 1970 was, therefore, a unique restriction and the period for equal pay claims should also be extended to six years.[295] Sections 2(5) and 2ZB EPA 1970 now provide that sums can be awarded back to the 'arrears date' in respect of any time when there was unequal pay. Normally, the arrears date will be six years before the date on which the claim is made.

5.3.7 Code of Practice

The most recent version of the Equal Opportunities Commission Code of Practice on equal pay came into effect on 1 December 2003. A failure of any person to observe any provision

---

[290] *McPherson v Rathgael Centre for Children and Young People* [1991] IRLR 206 CA; it was suggested, *obiter*, that the employment tribunal might have considered whether the applicant was able to select an anomalous employee, rather than four other male employees who were on the same salary as her.

[291] Section 2(1) EPA 1970.

[292] *Council of the City of Newcastle upon Tyne v Allan* [2005] IRLR 504.

[293] Section 2(1A) EPA 1970.

[294] Section 7B EPA 1970, introduced by s. 42 EA 2002. See Equal Pay (Questions and Replies) Order 2003, SI 2003/722.

[295] *Levez v TH Jennings (Harlow Pools) Ltd (No 2)* [1999] IRLR 764.

of the Code will not render that person liable to any proceedings, but the failure will be taken into account in any proceedings before an employment tribunal.[296] Its purpose is to provide practical guidance and to recommend good practice to those with responsibility for the pay arrangements within organisations.

5.4 The Equality Act 2010

At the time of writing this edition a new Equality Bill was progressing slowly through Parliament. It is designed to bring a more uniform approach to all the unlawful grounds of discrimination both in employment and in the provision of facilities, goods and services. It will replace much of the previously existing anti-discrimination legislation, including the Equal Pay Act, the Sex Discrimination Act, the Race Relations Act, the Disability Discrimination Act and the Regulations concerned with stopping discrimination on the grounds of age, religion or belief, and sexual orientation. There is uncertainty about when the Bill will actually be implemented, even when it has passed all its parliamentary stages. Up-to-date information can be found on this book's associated website at *www.mylawchamber.co.uk/sargeant*

5.4.1 The protected characteristics

The Bill lists the nine 'protected characteristics' with which it is concerned. These are:

1. Age – a person belonging to a particular group is protected. Age group means persons of the same age or persons of a range of ages.

2. Disability – this defines who is to be regarded as having the protected characteristic of disability. The provisions are similar to the Disability Discrimination Act 1995, so the Bill provides that a person has a disability if he has a physical or mental impairment that has a substantial and long-term adverse effect on his ability to carry out normal day-to-day activities.

3. Gender reassignment – a person has this protected characteristic if the person is propos-ing to undergo, is undergoing or has undergone a process (or part of a process) for the purpose of reassigning the person's sex by changing physiological or other attributes of sex. The Bill provides that all transsexual people are included. These provisions are similar to those in the Sex Discrimination Act 1975, except that there is no longer a need for the person to be under medical supervision in order to come within the definition.

4. Marriage and civil partnership – this applies to those that are married or in a civil part-nership, so just living together is not enough.

5. Pregnancy and maternity – traditionally discrimination against women who are pregnant or have recently given birth has amounted to sex discrimination.

6. Race – this includes colour, nationality and ethnic or national origin. Those who have any of these characteristics can be described as a 'racial group' and such a group can consist of more than one racial group.

[296] Section 56A(10) SDA 1975.

7. Religion or belief – religion means any religion or lack of religion; belief means any philosophical belief or lack of such belief. The guidance states that atheism or humanism would be included but not beliefs in communism, Darwinism, fascism, socialism or 'adherence to a particular football team'.

8. Sex – people having the protected characteristic of sex are men or women; men share this characteristic with other men and women with other women.

9. Sexual orientation – this is similar to the Employment Equality (Sexual Orientation) Regulations 2003, so sexual orientation means a sexual orientation towards people of the same sex, the opposite sex, or either sex.

5.4.2 Prohibited conduct

5.4.2.1 Direct discrimination

The new Equality Act will provide that a person (A) discriminates against another (B) if, because of a protected characteristic, A treats B less favourably than A treats, or would treat, others. The term 'on the grounds of' used in previous legislation is replaced by the term 'because of'. The guidance to the Act explains that this means the same but is designed to make it more accessible 'to the ordinary user of the Bill'. The guidance also states that this definition is broad enough to include those treated less favourably because of their association with someone who has the characteristic or because the victim is thought to have it.

The Act provides that direct discrimination in relation to age can be justified if shown to be a proportionate means of achieving a legitimate aim. Thus age continues to be the only protected characteristic where it is possible to justify direct discrimination. It also provides that, in relation to disability, it is not unlawful to treat a person with a disability more favourably than a person without a disability; racial segregation is always discriminatory; discrimination because of religion or belief can happen even where both discriminator and discriminated against are of the same religion or belief; in non-work situations treating a woman less favourably because she is breast-feeding a baby who is more than six months old amounts to direct sex discrimination.

The Act deals with specific situations of direct discrimination, as follows.

Discrimination arising from disability

The provisions here effectively reverse *LB Lewisham* v *Malcolm* (see below) but in words that are much more straightforward. The intention is to make disability-related discrimination unlawful and there is no need for a comparator. The Bill states that a person (A) discriminates against a disabled person (B) if A treats B in a particular way because of B's disability, provided that the treatment amounts to a detriment and A cannot show that it is a proportionate means of achieving a legitimate aim. This does not apply if A did not know, or could not reasonably be expected to know, that B had a disability. Whether A had complied with the duty to make reasonable adjustments or not is not relevant.

Gender reassignment discrimination: cases of absence from work

If a person is absent because they are undergoing the process of gender reassignment, then, in relation to absences from work, they may not be treated less favourably than the way they would have been treated if their absence was for sickness or injury, or for some other reason and it is not reasonable for them to be treated less favourably.

Pregnancy and maternity discrimination: work cases

There are a number of situations where less favourable treatment amounts to discrimination. These are because: of pregnancy or of any resultant illness (during the protected period); the woman is on compulsory maternity leave; or because she seeks to exercise rights related to ordinary and additional maternity leave. The protected period is the period of maternity leave to which the woman is entitled or two weeks after the end of the pregnancy if she has no rights to maternity leave.

5.4.2.2 Indirect discrimination

Indirect discrimination is defined as:

> A person (A) discriminates against another (B) if (A) applies to (B) a provision, criterion or practice which is discriminatory in relation to a relevant protected characteristic of (B)'s.

The Bill explains that a provision, criterion or practice is discriminatory if, in relation to a protected characteristic of B's:

- A applies, or would apply, it to persons with whom B does not share the characteristic;
- it puts, or would put, persons with whom B shares a characteristic at a particular disadvantage when compared with persons with whom B does not share it;
- it puts, or would put, B at that disadvantage; and
- A cannot show it to be a proportionate means of achieving a legitimate aim.

The guidance to the Equality Bill gives the following examples of indirect discrimination.

Examples

(a) A woman is forced to leave her job because her employer operates a practice that staff must work in a shift pattern which she is unable to comply with because she needs to look after her children at particular times of the day, and no allowances are made because of those needs. This would put women (who are shown to be more likely to be responsible for childcare) at a disadvantage, and the employer will have indirectly discriminated against the woman unless the practice can be justified.

(b) An observant Jewish engineer who is seeking an advanced diploma decides (even though he is sufficiently qualified to do so) not to apply to a specialist training company because it invariably undertakes the selection exercises for the relevant course on Saturdays. The company will have indirectly discriminated against the engineer unless the practice can be justified.

Thus indirect discrimination occurs when a policy which applies in the same way for everybody has an effect which particularly disadvantages people with a protected characteristic. Where a particular group is disadvantaged in this way, a person in that group is indirectly discriminated against if he is put at a disadvantage, unless A can show that it is a proportionate means of achieving a legitimate aim. Indirect discrimination applies to all the protected characteristics except for pregnancy and maternity.

5.4.2.3 **The duty to make adjustments**

There are special provisions relating to the duty to make adjustments for persons with a disability. The new Equality Act will provide that the duty to make adjustments has three requirements (in the definition 'A' is the person, such as the employer, on whom the duty is placed):

1. The requirement, where a provision, criterion or practice of A's puts a disabled person at a substantial disadvantage in relation to a relevant matter in comparison to persons who are not disabled, to take such steps as it is reasonable to have to take to avoid the disadvantage.

2. The requirement, where a physical feature puts a disabled person at a substantial disadvantage in relation to a relevant matter in comparison with persons who are not disabled, to take such steps as it is reasonable to have to take to avoid the disadvantage.

3. The requirement, where a disabled person would, but for the provision of an auxiliary aid, be put at a substantial disadvantage in relation to a relevant matter in comparison with persons who are not disabled, to take such steps as it is reasonable to have to take to provide the auxiliary aid.

A failure to comply with any of these requirements amounts to a failure to comply with the duty to make reasonable adjustments.

The guidance to the Act gives an example:

Examples

A bank is obliged to consider reasonable adjustments for a newly recruited financial adviser who is a wheelchair user and who would have difficulty in negotiating her way around the customer area. In consultation with the new adviser, the bank rearranges the layout of furniture in the customer area and installs a new desk. These changes result in the new adviser being able to work alongside her colleagues.

5.4.2.4 **Harassment**

The new Equality Act deals with harassment in relation to the relevant protected characteristics of age, disability, gender reassignment, race, religion or belief, sex and sexual orientation.

A person, A, harasses another person, B, if A engages in 'unwanted conduct related to a relevant protected characteristic, which has the purpose or effect of violating B's dignity, or creating an intimidating, hostile, degrading, humiliating or offensive environment for B'. This includes any form of unwanted verbal, non-verbal or physical conduct of a sexual nature which has the same purpose or effect. A person also harasses another if, because of B's rejection of or submission to conduct (whether or not of A), A treats B less favourably than A would treat B if B had not rejected or submitted to the conduct.

In deciding whether the conduct has that effect, each of the following must be taken into account:

1. The perception of B.

2. The other circumstances of the case.

3. Whether it is reasonable for the conduct to have that effect.

The guidance gives these two examples.

Examples

(a) A white worker who sees a black colleague being subjected to racially abusive language could have a case of harassment if the language also causes an offensive environment for her.

(b) An employer who displayed any material of a sexual nature, such as a topless calendar, may be harassing his employees where this makes the workplace an offensive place to work for any employee, female or male.

5.4.2.5 **Victimisation**

The Equality Act provides that person A victimises person B if A subjects B to a detriment because B has done a protected act or A believes that B has done, or may do, a protected act. A protected act is:

- Bringing proceedings under the Equality Act.
- Given evidence or information in such proceedings.
- Doing anything else for the purposes of, or in connection with, this Act.
- Making an allegation that A, or another person, has contravened the Act.

Giving false evidence or making a false allegation is not a protected act if the evidence is given, or the allegation made, in bad faith.

5.4.3 **Positive action**

The Act deals with the subject of positive action. It provides that if a person (P) reasonably thinks that persons who share a particular protected characteristic suffer a disadvantage connected to the characteristic, or have needs that are different from those others who do not share the characteristic, or have a low level of participation in an activity, then P is not prohibited from taking action which is proportionate to achieve the legitimate aim of enabling or encouraging persons who share a protected characteristic to overcome or minimise a disadvantage or to participate in an activity. It is likely that the Government will issue more detailed regulations concerning this subject. There is a more specific provision in the Bill, which refers to positive action in relation to recruitment and promotion. This allows an employer to take into account a protected characteristic when deciding who to recruit and who to promote, when people with that particular protected characteristic are at a disadvantage or under-represented. This is only possible where the candidates are equally qualified.

The guidance to the Equality Bill provides these examples:

Examples

(a) A police service which employs disproportionately low numbers of people from an ethnic minority background identifies a number of equally qualified candidates for recruitment and gives preferential selection to a candidate from an ethnic minority background. This would not be unlawful, provided the comparative merits of other candidates were also taken into consideration.

(b) An employer offers a job to a woman on the basis that women are under-represented in the company's workforce when there was a male candidate who was more qualified. This would be unlawful direct discrimination.

These sections are really a clarification of the legal situation existing before the Equality Act and reflect decisions of the European Court of Justice.

5.4.4 Multiple discrimination

The Bill, for the first time in UK equality legislation, provides the possibility of complaining about multiple discrimination, i.e. being discriminated against on more than one ground at once. There is provision for complaining on a maximum of two grounds.

5.4.5 The public sector equality duty

Prior to the Equality Act there was such a public sector duty in relation to disability, race and sex. The Bill now provides for this public sector equality duty to also include the other protected characteristics. The duty is set out so that a public authority must, in the exercise of its functions, have due regard to the need to:

1. Eliminate discrimination, harassment, victimisation and any other conduct prohibited by the Act.
2. Advance equality of opportunity between persons who share a relevant protected characteristic and persons who do not share it.
3. Foster good relations between persons who share a relevant protected characteristic and persons who do not share it.

The last two points do not apply to the protected characteristic of marriage and civil partnership.

The public authorities affected by this measure are listed in Sch. 19 to the Act, but it does include a wide range of bodies, including local authorities, health boards and trusts, education authorities, government departments, the armed forces and the police.

Interestingly, Part 1 of the Act extends this duty for some parts of the public sector to include socio-economic inequalities. The authorities affected will need to exercise their functions in 'a way that is designed to reduce the inequalities of outcome which result from socio-economic disadvantage'. The guidance to the Act suggests that such inequalities could include inequalities in education, health, housing or crime rates. The public sector affected includes Government departments, local authorities, health authorities and primary health care trusts as well as the police force in England.

5.4.6 Remedies

The Act provides that individuals may bring a complaint of discrimination to an employment tribunal. An employment tribunal will not consider the complaint unless it is presented within a period of three months of when the act complained of was done, unless the tribunal 'considers that it is just and equitable to do so'. Where an employment tribunal finds that a complaint was well founded, then it has a choice of what action to take:

- It may make an order declaring the rights of the claimant and the respondent in relation to the act complained of.
- It may make an order requiring the respondent to pay compensation to the complainant.
- It may make a recommendation that the respondent takes action, within a specified period of time, for the purpose of obviating the adverse effect on the complainant of any act of discrimination to which the complaint relates.

In a claim concerning indirect discrimination, where the respondent proves that there was no intention to treat the claimant unfavourably, a tribunal may not award damages to a claimant unless it first considers making a declaration or recommendation. Examples of recommendations that an employment tribunal might make concerning the respondent are given by the guidance to the Act:

- Introduce an equal opportunities policy.
- Ensure its harassment policy is more effectively implemented.
- Retrain staff.
- Make public the selection criteria used for transfer or promotion of staff.

If the respondent fails, without reasonable justification, to comply with the recommendation, then the tribunal may increase the level of compensation. It is important to observe that there is no upper limit on compensation that can be awarded.

Chapter summary

This chapter has been concerned with considering what is meant by direct and indirect discrimination, as well as victimisation and harassment, in the context of discrimination on the grounds of sex and race. It then looked at the same concepts with regard to the regulations that prohibit discrimination on the grounds of sexual orientation and religion or belief. In particular it considered the potential conflict between religious belief and the need to stop discrimination on the grounds of sexual orientation. It then proceeded to examine the Equal Pay Act 1970 and how it seeks to ensure equality in pay between men and women. Finally it briefly considered the Equality Act 2010 and how it may impact upon equality law in the UK.

Further reading

Deakin, S. and Morris, G. *Labour Law*: 5th edn, Hart Publishing, 2009, Chapter 6.

McColgan, A. *Discrimination Law: Text, Cases and Materials*: Hart Publishing, 2005, Chapters 6, 7, 9 and 10.

http://www.berr.gov.uk/employment/discrimination/index.html for the Department for Business, Innovation and Skills website on discrimination at work.

http://www.equalityhumanrights.com for the website of the Equality and Human Rights Commission.

Visit **www.mylawchamber.co.uk/sargeant**
to access legal updates, live weblinks and practice
exam questions to test yourself on this chapter.

mylawchamber
unrivalled support for legal education

6　Age and disability discrimination

6.1 Introduction

Discrimination on the grounds of age and disability are considered separately from the grounds of sex and race because they are both more recent statutory innovations and because there is a close link between the two. The Disability Discrimination Act was not adopted until 1995 and the Employment Equality (Age) Regulations did not take effect until October 2006.

The likelihood of disabilities and chronic conditions increases with age. Older workers with disabilities have traditionally been more likely to lose their jobs in workplace reorganisations as a result of fewer opportunities to train and upgrade their skills. Age and disability are a barrier when trying to get a job, according to research by the Ontario Human Rights Commission.[1] The number of people aged over 50 who are long-term sick or disabled has been increasing. This is somewhat paradoxical because there has also been a continuing increase in life expectancy and in the health status of older people.[2] In the UK 10.3 per cent of men in the 20–24 years age band are disabled compared with 33.9 per cent of men in the 50–64 years age group, suggesting a high correlation between age and disability.[3]

The European Experts Group on employment for disabled people reported that:[4]

Disability is much more prevalent among older people: 63 per cent of people with disabilities are older than 45. For non-disabled people the corresponding percentage is only 34 per cent. So the disabled population is relatively old. This is particularly so in Germany, Greece, Italy and Spain.

This pattern is mainly due to individuals' health condition deteriorating with age. Furthermore, many impairments leading to disability are acquired during a person's life. There may, in addition, be a 'generation factor', in so far as younger age groups experience better health and working conditions in their early working life and better health care and rehabilitation provisions, than their predecessors in older generations.

---

[1] See *www.ohrc.on.ca*.

[2] House of Lords Select Committee on Economic Affairs, *Aspects of the Economics of an Ageing Population*, November 2003, HL Paper 179–1, para. 5.3.

[3] For further consideration of this see Malcolm Sargeant, 'Disability and Age – Multiple Potential for Discrimination' (2005) *International Journal of the Sociology of Law*, 33, 17.

[4] *The Employment Situation of People with Disabilities in the European Union*, Executive Summary of Research Paper 2001; written by European Experts Group on employment for disabled people; commissioned by the DG Employment and Social Affairs.

Men	Disabled	Not disabled 16–29
16–29	9.2	90.8
20–24	10.3	89.7
25–34	12.1	87.9
35–49	17.5	82.5
50–64	33.9	66.1
Total	19.3	80.7
Women		
16–29	8.4	91.6
20–24	10.6	89.4
25–34	13.6	86.4
35–49	19.5	80.5
50–64	33.6	66.4
Total	19.3	80.7

Source: © European Communities, 2001

The Framework Directive on Equal Treatment in Employment and Occupation[5] included discrimination on the grounds of disability and age.

6.2 Age discrimination in employment

People of all ages can suffer from age discrimination, but it manifests itself mostly in discrimination against older people and young people. Article 1 of the Equal Treatment in Employment and Occupation Directive provides that the Directive's purpose is to lay down a general framework for combating discrimination in relation to a number of grounds including that of age. This is to be, according to art. 3, in relation to conditions for access to employment, access to vocational training, employment and working conditions and membership of employers' or workers' organisations. The approach is the same as other measures in relation to disability, sexual orientation, religion or belief. The Directive aims to introduce the 'principle of equal treatment' into all these areas, including age.

Article 4 provides for the possibility that a difference of treatment may be justified where there is 'a genuine and determining occupational requirement, provided that the objective is legitimate and the requirement is proportionate'. Article 6 refers to the justification of differences of treatment on the grounds of age. Differences in treatment on the basis of age may be justified if 'they are objectively and reasonably justified by a legitimate aim including legitimate employment policy, labour market and vocational treatment'. Examples given of such differences are:

[5] Directive 2000/78/EC.

- The setting of special conditions for access to employment and training, including dismissal and remuneration for young people, older workers and persons with caring responsibilities in order to promote their integration into the workforce.

- The fixing of minimum conditions of age, professional experience or seniority for access to employment or certain advantages linked to employment.

- The fixing of a maximum age for recruitment which is based either on the training needs of a post, or the need for a reasonable period before retirement.

It is interesting that it was felt necessary to spell out these exceptions to age discrimination in the Directive. It is perhaps symptomatic of the way that age discrimination is treated differently from other forms of discrimination. These provisions effectively state that some age discrimination is benign. There appears to be an economic or business imperative that suggests that more harm will be done if discrimination does not take place, rather than an imperative that states that age discrimination is wrong and can only be justified in exceptional circumstances. Effectively, discrimination is not to be allowed to continue except those forms which are held to be for the economic good of business.

The Directive was due to be transposed into national law by December 2003, but there was a provision, in art. 18, for Member States to have an additional period of three years. The United Kingdom took advantage of this flexibility and finally transposed the Directive in October 2006 by adopting the Employment Equality (Age) Regulations 2006.[6]

6.2.1 The ageing population

The population of the United Kingdom is ageing. The percentage of the population aged 65 and over increased from 15 per cent in 1983 to 16 per cent in 2008. Over the same period the percentage of the population aged 16 and under decreased from 21 to 19 per cent. This trend is likely to continue and, by 2023, 23 per cent of the population will be aged 65 and over compared to 18 per cent aged 16 or younger. The fastest population increase has been in the number aged 85 and over. By 2033 this group is predicted to more than double and make up some 5 per cent of the population.[7]

The relevance of these statistics here is that whilst the population is ageing, the proportion of older workers is also increasing. The numbers in employment for those aged between 50 and the State Pension Age (SPA) have increased from just under 65 per cent in 1997 to just over 72 per cent in 2008. The figure for those over the SPA who have continued to work increased during the same period from 8 to 11.8 per cent. Older workers are, however, much more likely to be self-employed and/or working part-time compared to other groups. In 2008, for example, some 12.6 per cent of those aged 25 to 49 were self-employed, compared to a figure of 17.3 per cent for those aged between 50 and SPA and 22.6 per cent for those over SPA. The figures for part-time work are 20.5 per cent for 25- to 49-year-olds; 24 per cent for those aged 50 to SPA and 68.1 per cent for those over the SPA. Thus, although the trend is for larger numbers of older people to stay in the workforce, they are less likely to be in full-time employment than younger age groups.[8]

---

[6] SI 2006/1031.

[7] Figures from Office for National Statistics at *www.statistics.gov.uk*.

[8] Information taken from *Older Workers Statistical Information Booklet*, 2008, Department for Work and Pensions.

The Government consultation document on its Code of Practice on Age Diversity in Employment[9] concluded that 'it is clear that age discrimination against older workers does exist'. It is interesting to speculate at what age a person becomes an older worker. One study asked this question of organisations.[10] Five companies put 40 years as the starting point, four suggested 45 and five said 50 years. One company stated that anyone over 30 years was in the category of older worker. Further information suggested that these generalisations were qualified by consideration of occupation and gender. Forty-something was not necessarily old for a management position, but might be for another occupation. Similarly women seemed to become 'older' at an earlier age. One respondent suggested that when women returned to work after children in their mid-thirties that they might be classified as an older worker.

6.2.2 The Employment Equality (Age) Regulations 2006

6.2.2.1 The meaning of discrimination

As with the other Regulations, protection is offered against direct and indirect discrimination, harassment and victimisation. The definition of direct and indirect discrimination is the same. The difference is that, unlike other forms of discrimination,[11] it is permissible to directly discriminate on the grounds of age in some circumstances. There is a requirement to show that the less favourable treatment is a 'proportionate means of achieving a legitimate aim'.[12]

In 2005 the Government had proposed some examples where direct discrimination could be justified as a proportionate means of achieving a legitimate aim. These were, first, the setting of age requirements to 'ensure the vocational integration of people in a particular age group'. This might include, presumably, the lower rate of the national minimum wage paid to those under the age of 22 years. Secondly, the fixing of a minimum age to qualify for certain employment advantages in order to recruit or retain older people. Thirdly, the fixing of a maximum age for recruitment or promotion based on the training requirements of the post and 'on the need for a reasonable period in post before retirement'. All three of these exceptions are, of course, debatable, but they do effectively permit direct discrimination on the grounds of age in the interests of both diversity and, perhaps, acceptability. Some examples of where these rules have been tested are:

1. *Hampton* v *Lord Chancellor*[13] which concerned the retirement age of Recorders. It was decided that maintaining a reasonable flow of new candidates for promotion was a reasonable aim of the retirement policy, but the means in this case were not proportionate (appropriate and necessary).

2. *West Yorkshire CC* v *Homer*[14] had a requirement for a law degree for candidates who wished to be promoted. It was claimed that this amounted to indirect discrimination against

---

[9] First published in 1999 and subsequently updated.
[10] Hilary Metcalf and Mark Thompson, *Older Workers: Employers' Attitudes and Practices*, Institute of Manpower Studies, Report No 194, 1990.
[11] Except in relation to genuine occupational qualification.
[12] Regulation 3(1).
[13] [2008] IRLR 258.
[14] [2009] IRLR 263.

older workers as this would be more challenging for them to achieve in time, but this claim failed.

3. *Seldon v Clarkson, Wright and Jakes*[15] concerned the principle of compulsory retirement in a partnership. The court accepted that the principle was justified, but that the reason for adopting it at age 65 was not acceptable, namely that this was the age at which performance would begin to drop off.

The further matter for concern is that this was not an exhaustive list. The 2005 consultation document stated that 'we would not want to prevent employers or providers of vocational training from demonstrating that age-related practices could be justified by reference to aims other than those in such a list'. An example contained in the 2005 consultation document was that 'economic factors such as business needs and considerations of efficiency may also be legitimate aims'. It is not conceivable that these exceptions would be allowed for sex, race or disability discrimination or on the grounds of sexual orientation or religion or belief.

6.2.2.2 Further exceptions

Part 2 of the Regulations deals with discrimination in employment and vocational training and provides that it is unlawful to discriminate against applicants and employees, including harassment, on the grounds of age. However, reg. 7(4) provides that applicants who would become employees[16] can be excluded from protection if they are older than the employer's normal retirement age or, if the employer does not have such an age, 65 years. It also excludes those who, at the date of application, are within a period of six months of such an age. The justification for this is that there would be little point stopping an employer discriminating on recruitment if the same employer could legitimately discriminate (without it amounting to discrimination) under reg. 30 (exception for retirement). All applicants over the age of 64$^1/_2$ years may be turned down on the grounds of their age only. Difficulties in obtaining work are amongst the most common forms of discrimination suffered by older people and some discrimination in this area is allowed to continue under the new Regulations.

Part 2 also contains an exception, as do other grounds of discrimination, for genuine occupational requirement. The Government has stated that it was likely to be construed narrowly and in one consultation gave the example of the acting profession. Part 4 of the Age Regulations is devoted to 'general exceptions to parts 2 and 3'.[17] These are in addition to those already mentioned in respect of direct discrimination. There are exceptions for complying with statutory authority, safeguarding national security and positive action.[18] There are also exceptions relating to the national minimum wage, certain benefits based on length of service, retirement, the provision of enhanced redundancy payments and the provision of life assurance to retired workers.[19]

Service related pay and benefits may include salary scales, holiday entitlement, company cars, etc., all or some of which may be related to length of service. Without some action,

---

[15] [2009] IRLR 269.

[16] Which in this case means those defined in s. 230(1) Employment Rights Act 1996 and Crown and parliamentary staff.

[17] Part 3 is concerned with 'other unlawful acts', including aiding unlawful acts and the liability of employers and principals.

[18] Regulations 27–29.

[19] Regulations 30–34.

benefits linked to length of service may amount to age discrimination as younger people who have not served the necessary time required may suffer detriment. Regulation 32 provides that an employer may award benefits using length of service as the criterion for selecting who should benefit from the award. First, there is no need to justify any differences related to service less than five years. Where it exceeds five years it needs to fulfil 'a business need of the undertaking':

> for example, by encouraging the loyalty or motivation, or rewarding the experience, of some or all of his workers.[20]

The argument is that having pay scales of a certain length is justified to recognise experience and, perhaps, seniority. It can also be argued strongly that workers who have been with an employer for five years should receive some preferential treatment compared to those who have just joined an organisation. These are, however, exceptions to a rule requiring the principle of equal treatment. It has been an important issue in relation to redundancy payments and there have been a number of cases concerning whether relating redundancy payments to length of service amounts to discrimination in favour of older workers at the expense of younger ones.

1. *Rolls Royce* v *Unite the Union*[21] considered two collective agreements which had an agreed matrix to be used to choose who should be selected for redundancy. There were five criteria against which an individual could score between 4 and 24 points. In addition there was a length of service criterion which awarded 1 point for each year of continuous service. Thus older employees would have an important advantage over younger ones. It was, unusually, the employer who claimed that the age elements amounted to age discrimination and the union which, successfully, resisted this claim.

2. *MacCulloch* v *ICI plc*[22] concerned a redundancy scheme which had been in existence since 1971. The amount of payment was linked to service up to a maximum of ten years, and the size of the redundancy payment increased with age. The claimant was 37 years old and received 55 per cent of her salary as a payment, but she claimed that someone aged between 50 and 57 years would have received 175 per cent of salary under the scheme.

3. *Loxley* v *BAE Systems*[23] had a contractual redundancy scheme in which each employee received two weeks' pay for the first five years of employment, three weeks' pay for each of the next five years and four weeks' pay for each year after ten years. There was also a further age related payment of two weeks' pay for each year after the age of 40 years. All this was subject to a maximum of two years' pay. The scheme was amended for older workers approaching retirement when the retirement age was raised, but essentially the claimant, who was 61 years of age, was not entitled to any enhanced payments for voluntary redundancy as he had an entitlement to a pension. Indeed the EAT stated that preventing such a windfall could be a legitimate aim.

There is also a general exemption concerning the national minimum wage so that employers can pay the lower rate for those under 22 and under 18 years without it amounting to age

[20] Regulation 32(2).
[21] *Rolls Royce plc* v *Unite the Union* [2009] IRLR 576.
[22] *MacCulloch* v *ICI plc* [2008] IRLR 846.
[23] *Loxley* v *BAE Systems (Munitions and Ordnance) Ltd* [2008] IRLR 853.

discrimination.[24] It is, of course, age discrimination against the younger person, but he will be prevented from claiming this. The intention is to help younger workers to find jobs, by making them more attractive to employers. One question is whether such a measure is a proportionate response to the problem. In *Mangold v Helm*[25] the European Court of Justice considered a German law which restricted the use of fixed-term contracts, but did not apply these restrictions to those aged 52 years and over. The court accepted that the purpose of this legislation was to help promote the vocational integration of unemployed older workers and that this was a 'legitimate public-interest objective'. It is not only the objective that needs to be legitimate, but the means used to achieve the objective need to be 'appropriate and necessary'. The problem with the German law was that it applied to all workers of 52 years and above, whether unemployed or not. The result was that a significant body of workers was permanently excluded from 'the benefit of stable employment' available to other workers. The court then stated:

> In so far as such legislation takes the age of the worker concerned as the only criterion [for the application of a fixed-term contract of employment], when it has not been shown that fixing an age threshold, as such, regardless of any other consideration linked to the structure of the labour market in question or the personal situation of the person concerned, is objectively necessary to the attainment of the objective [which is the vocational integration of older workers], it must be considered to go beyond what is appropriate and necessary in order to attain the objective pursued.

There must be a question about whether the application of a universal lower minimum wage for younger people is an appropriate and necessary response to the problem of youth unemployment.

One of the difficult issues for the Age Regulations was the question of what to do about the age related aspects of redundancy payments. The Government had proposed removing these and paying a uniform rate for all. Presumably when faced with the prospect of levelling upwards, so that no group would be worse off, the Government decided that the age related aspects can be objectively justifiable. The lower and upper age limits to entitlement have therefore been removed and employers are allowed to enhance payments.[26]

6.2.2.3 **Retirement**

The Framework Directive does not say a great deal about retirement ages. Paragraph 14 of the Preamble states that the Directive shall be 'without prejudice to national provisions laying down retirement ages'. Article 6.2 allows for the fixing of ages for invalidity and retirement schemes, and the use of ages for actuarial calculations, without it constituting age discrimination. Article 8.2 provides that any measures implementing the Directive shall not lessen the protection against discrimination that already exists in the Member State.

The United Kingdom, in implementing the Directive, adopted a default retirement age of 65 years. Retirement below the age of 65 years will need to be objectively justified and presumably this will be entirely possible and proper in some cases. Section 98 of the Employment Rights Act 1996 was amended to add another fair reason for dismissal which will be

---

[24] Regulation 31.
[25] Case C-144/04 [2006] IRLR 143.
[26] Regulation 33.

'retirement of the employee'. There was, however, no requirement to go through any statutory dismissal procedure. This is replaced by a statutory retirement procedure as outlined in ss. 98ZA–98ZF of the Employment Rights Act.

For retirement to be taken as the only reason for dismissal, it must take place on the 'intended date of retirement'. There is still the opportunity for the employee to claim that the real reason for dismissal was some other reason and that the planned retirement would not have taken place but for this other reason, or if the dismissal amounts to unlawful discrimination under the Regulations. The operative retirement date is 65 years unless there is an alternative date which is the normal retirement age, in which case it is that date.[27] There is then a procedure in which the employer and employee must participate. Failure on the employer's part in this regard may render the dismissal unfair.

The statutory retirement procedure comprises a duty on the employer to consider a request from the employee to work beyond retirement.[28] There is a duty upon the employer to inform the employee of the intended retirement date and the employee's right to make a request. There is then a statutory right for the employee to request that he be not retired on the intended retirement date. The employer then has a duty to consider this request. This is done by holding a meeting with the employee, unless not reasonably practicable. There is also an appeal procedure for the employee if turned down and timescales for meetings and decisions. Most notably there is an absence of criteria to be used by the employer in their consideration of the employee's request. Their only duty is to follow the procedure and consider it.

Thus the situation will be that where there is no consensual retirement, the employer may dismiss the employee and this dismissal will be a 'fair' dismissal provided it takes place on the retirement date and the employer has followed the statutory retirement procedure for consideration of any request from the employee not to retire. The most likely outcome of any decision by the employer not to require the employee to retire at the intended retirement date is for the employer to agree a new date. In effect this will allow the employee to continue his contract for a fixed term.[29]

Thus older workers, i.e. those over 65 or the normal retirement age, will continue to be discriminated against. This will be as a result of the Age Regulations which were, perhaps ostensibly, intended to stop age discrimination. Older workers will have no security, knowing that their employer can legitimately dismiss them at each new retirement date, provided a procedure of information and consideration is followed. The NGO Age Concern challenged whether these measures were compatible with the aims of the Directive.[30] The Government argues that the concept of a retirement age was based upon a social policy of maintaining confidence in the labour market. The High Court, after referring the matter to the ECJ,[31] agreed that the designated retirement age was not a disproportionate way of giving effect to the social aim of labour market confidence. It did say, however, that if the age of 65 had been adopted for the first time in 2009 (the time of the hearing) then it would not have been proportionate.

---

[27] Sections 98ZA–98ZE ERA 1996 as amended.
[28] Schedule 6 to the Age Regulations; Sch. 7 makes provision for transitional arrangements.
[29] Schedule 6 to the Age Regulations.
[30] *R (on the application of Age UK) v Secretary of State for Business, Innovation & Skills* [2009] IRLR 1017.
[31] [2009] IRLR 373.

6.3 **Disability discrimination**

The Framework Directive on Equal Treatment in Employment and Occupation included proposals to combat discrimination on the grounds of disability 'with a view to putting into effect in the Member States the principle of equal treatment'.[32] In particular it provided[33] that employers should have a duty of 'reasonable accommodation'. This means that employers are obliged to take steps, when needed, to ensure that a person with a disability could have access to, participate in, have advancement in and undergo training. The only possible exception to this duty, according to the Directive, is if this places a 'disproportionate burden' on the employer. Thus the Directive permits, in certain circumstances, positive discrimination in favour of the disabled employee or applicant.

The Disability Discrimination Act 1995 (DDA 1995) was the first measure to outlaw discrimination against disabled people in the United Kingdom and included an obligation upon the employer to make adjustments (see below).[34] The Act, which preceded the Framework Directive, gives disabled people rights in employment and other areas. The Act provided originally for a National Disability Council,[35] whose task was to advise the Government 'on matters relevant to the elimination of discrimination against disabled persons and persons who have a disability'. One of the criticisms of the Act was that this was an advisory body, which did not have the powers of investigation and enforcement held by the Equal Opportunities Commission and the Commission for Racial Equality. The position was changed with the Disability Rights Commission Act 1999 (DRCA 1999), which abolished the National Disability Council and replaced it with a Disability Rights Commission[36] (see below). The Disability Rights Commission itself has now been absorbed into the new Commission for Equality and Human Rights, which was established by the Equality Act 2006. The DDA 1995 was further amended by the Disability Discrimination Act 1995 (Amendment) Regulations 2003,[37] much of which took effect from 1 October 2004, and the Disability Discrimination Act 2005, which included a duty on public authorities to have regard to the need to eliminate disability discrimination in the carrying out of their functions.[38]

The need for action is illustrated by the fact that there are over 6.8 million disabled persons of working age in Great Britain,[39] who account for nearly one-fifth of the working age population, but only for one-eighth of all those in employment. When employed they are more likely than non-disabled people to be working part-time or as self-employed. Disabled people are over six times as likely as non-disabled people to be out of work and claiming benefit. Employment rates do, however, vary with the type of disability. Some types, such as those concerned with diabetes, skin conditions and hearing problems, are associated with relatively high employment rates. Other types, such as those associated with mental illness and learning disabilities, have much lower employment rates.

[32] Council Directive 2000/78/EC OJ L303/16.
[33] Article 5.
[34] The approach prior to the DDA 1995 had been to establish quotas of disabled people in an employer's workforce: see Disabled Persons (Employment) Act 1944; this approach failed.
[35] Section 50 DDA 1995.
[36] Section 1 DRCA 1999.
[37] SI 2003/1673.
[38] Section 49A DDA 1995.
[39] Disability Rights Commission Disability Briefing January 2004 (figures compiled from the Labour Force Survey). See now *www.equalityhumanrights.com*.

One survey on the effectiveness of the employment provisions of the DDA 1995 shows that, at the time of the report, only 23 per cent of the claims disposed of at employment tribunal hearings were successful. Those claimants who were legally represented did better, with a 39.7 per cent success rate for those represented by a barrister and 32.1 per cent for those represented by a solicitor. In contrast only 15.6 per cent of applicants in person were successful. Of all the DDA cases, some 68.6 per cent concerned dismissal compared with 9.2 per cent which concerned recruitment. Medical evidence was considered in just over 50 per cent of cases. In 33.9 per cent of cases where it was claimed that the employer should have made a reasonable adjustment (see below), the adjustment in question was a transfer to an existing vacancy.[40]

Section 53A provided for the Disability Rights Commission to give practical guidance on how to avoid discrimination in relation to the DDA 1995 and to promote equality of opportunity. The current Code of Practice was issued by the Disability Rights Commission and took effect in October 2004 (hereafter referred to as the DRC Code of Practice; now taken over by the EHRC).[41] Failure to observe the provisions of the Code does not in itself make a person liable to proceedings, but any provision of the Code that appears to be relevant to any question arising in any proceedings will be taken into account.[42] In addition further clarification is given in the Disability Discrimination (Meaning of Disability) Regulations 1996 and the Disability Discrimination (Employment) Regulations 1996.[43]

6.3.1 Meaning of disability

A disabled person is a person who has a disability,[44] or has had a past disability.[45] According to s. 1(1) DDA 1995 a person has a disability if he has a

> physical or mental impairment which has a substantial and long-term adverse effect on his ability to carry out normal day to day activities.

Thus the tests are, first, that there must be a physical or mental impairment; secondly, that it must have a substantial adverse effect; thirdly, that it must have a long-term adverse effect; and, finally, this adverse effect must relate to the ability to carry out normal day to day activities. Schedule 1 DDA 1995 provides some meaning to these terms. Certain addictions and conditions are not to be treated as impairments for the purposes of the DDA 1995. These include:[46]

1. Addictions to alcohol, nicotine or any other substance, unless the addiction was originally the result of medically prescribed drugs or treatment.

2. A tendency to set fires, to steal or to physical or sexual abuse of other persons.

3. Exhibitionism and voyeurism.

---

[40] Incomes Data Services, *Monitoring the Disability Discrimination Act 1995. First Interim Report to the DFEE*, March 2000.
[41] The Disability Discrimination Codes of Practice (Employment and Occupation, and Trade Organisations and Qualifications Bodies) Appointed Day Order 2004, SI 2004/2302.
[42] Section 53A(8) and (8A) DDA 1995.
[43] SI 1996/1455 and SI 1996/1456.
[44] Section 1(2) DDA 1995.
[45] Section 2 and Sch. 2 DDA 1995.
[46] See SI 1996/1455 above.

4. Seasonal allergic rhinitis (asthma), although it can be taken into account where it aggravates other conditions.

5. Severe disfigurement which results from tattooing or piercing.

In *Goodwin* v *The Patent Office*[47] the EAT held that the DDA 1995 requires the employment tribunal to look at the evidence by reference to four different conditions or questions:

1. Whether the applicant has a mental or physical impairment. 'Mental impairment' includes an impairment resulting from or consisting of a mental illness only if the mental illness is a clinically well-recognised illness.[48] One route to establishing the existence of a mental impairment is to show proof of a mental illness classified in the World Health Organisation International Classification of Diseases (WHOICD). Many parts of its classification require specific symptoms to manifest themselves over a specified period. Thus just claiming 'clinical depression' without further clarification is unlikely to be sufficient.[49] Similarly a failure to establish that back pain was the result of a physical or mental impairment put it outside the scope of the DDA. The word impairment is to have its ordinary and natural meaning and may result from an illness or consist of an illness. The onus is on the employee to show an impairment.[50] *Greenwood* v *British Airways plc*[51] considered a complaint from an employee who was told that one of the reasons for a failure to gain promotion was the employee's sickness record. The employee suffered flashbacks which could prevent him from working and affected his ability to concentrate. After a failure to gain promotion the employee was absent through depression. The employment tribunal decided to look only at matters at the time when the employee was rejected for promotion. The tribunal held that the applicant was not disabled at the time of the act complained of. The EAT concluded that the employment tribunal had erred in law and had wrongly decided that events subsequent to the act complained of were not relevant. The EAT concluded that one needed to look at the whole period up to the employment tribunal hearing to assess whether a person had a long-term impairment. Considering the whole period does not necessarily mean an investigation of the causes of the disability. In *Power* v *Panasonic UK Ltd*[52] an areas sales manager had the geographical area for which she was responsible expanded, following a reorganisation. She became ill and was eventually dismissed after a long period of absence. It was not disputed that during her long absence she was both depressed and drinking heavily. The tribunal concerned itself with whether the drinking or the depression came first, but the EAT stated that it was not necessary to consider how the impairment was caused. What was relevant was to discover whether the person had a disability within the meaning of the DDA at the relevant time. Even if the applicant were not held to be disabled under s. 1(1) DDA 1995, then he could be held to have had a past disability in accord with Sch. 2 DDA 1995. Schedule 2 para. 5(2) provides that where an impairment ceases to have a substantial adverse effect, then it may be treated as continuing if the effect recurs. This modifies Sch. 1 para. 2(2) which provides that where an impairment

---

[47] [1999] IRLR 4.
[48] Schedule 1 para. 1(1) DDA 1995.
[49] *Morgan* v *Staffordshire University* [2002] IRLR 190.
[50] *McNicol* v *Balfour Beatty Rail Maintenance Ltd* [2002] IRLR 711; in this case a trackman claimed that the vehicle that he was driving had gone over a pothole and jolted his back. He could not, however, show a mental or physical impairment that was the cause of the back pain that he then continued to suffer.
[51] [1999] IRLR 600.
[52] [2003] IRLR 151.

ceases to have a substantial adverse effect on a person's ability to carry out normal day to day activities, it is still to be treated as continuing to have that effect if it is likely to recur.[53]

2. Whether the impairment affects the applicant's ability to carry out normal day to day activities. The fact that an applicant can still carry them out does not mean that the individual's ability has not been impaired. If the individual can only carry them out with difficulty, then there may be an adverse effect. This can be seen in *CC of Dumfries and Galway*[54] where a policeman had difficulty in carrying on night work because he had ME. Nightwork was held to be a 'normal day to day activity'. An impairment is said to have an effect upon a person's ability to carry out normal day to day activities only if it affects mobility; manual dexterity; physical co-ordination; continence; the ability to lift or move everyday objects; speech, hearing or eyesight; memory or ability to concentrate, learn or understand; perception of the risk of physical danger.[55] This will include the impairments that affect the individual's ability to carry out duties at work, particularly if they include these 'normal day to day activities'.[56] In *Hewett v Motorola Ltd*[57] the complainant, an engineer, was diagnosed as having autism in the form of Asperger's Syndrome. He argued that, without medication or medical treatment, his memory would be affected and he would have difficulties in concentrating, learning and understanding.[58] The EAT held that one had to have a broad view of the meaning of understanding and that any person who had their normal human interaction affected might also be regarded as having their understanding affected. What is 'normal' may be best defined as anything that is not abnormal or unusual. It does not depend upon whether the majority of people do it, for example there may be some activities that only women usually do and the fact that men do not do them does not stop them being 'normal day to day activities'.[59] The DRC Code of Practice gives guidance as to what constitutes 'day to day' activities,[60] but this guidance is intended to be illustrative and not exhaustive. It is for the employment tribunal to arrive at its own assessment, rather than relying too much on this or medical opinions about what constitutes such activities.[61]

3. Whether the adverse effect is 'substantial'. If an impairment is likely to have a substantial adverse effect upon the ability of the person concerned to carry out normal day to day activities, but does not do so because of measures taken to treat or correct it, it is still to be treated as having the adverse effect.[62] Such measures can include counselling sessions for an individual who was suffering from a form of depression. This was held to be the case in *Kapadia v London Borough of Lambeth*[63] where an employment tribunal failed to find that a person was

---

[53] Schedule 1 para. 3 provides that an impairment consisting of a severe disfigurement is to be treated as having a substantial adverse effect, although this does not include a tattoo which has not been removed or a non-medical piercing of the body; see SI 1996/1455.

[54] *Chief Constable of Dumfries and Galloway Constabulary v Adams* [2009] IRLR 612.

[55] Schedule 1 para. 4 DDA 1995.

[56] *Law Hospital NHS Trust v Rush* [2001] IRLR 611, where the work of a nurse was stated to include some normal day to day activities.

[57] [2004] IRLR 545.

[58] See Sch. 1 para. 4g DDA 1995 which includes in the list of day to day activities, 'memory or ability to concentrate, learn or understand'.

[59] *Ekpe v Commissioner of Police* [2001] IRLR 605.

[60] Appendix B.

[61] See *Vicaray v British Telecommunications plc* [1999] IRLR 680.

[62] Schedule 1 para. 6(1) DDA 1995; see *Abadeh v British Telecommunications plc* [2001] IRLR.

[63] [2000] IRLR 14.

disabled within the terms of s. 1(1) DDA 1995, despite uncontested medical opinion. The EAT held that the employment tribunal had erred in doing so and had arrived at a judgment based on how the complainant seemed when giving evidence, although in *Goodwin* the EAT stated that this was something that the employment tribunal could take into account. The Court of Appeal, in this case, confirmed this approach and held that just because the symptoms are kept under control by medication, this does not stop a person suffering a substantial adverse effect on their day to day activities,[64] although there is a need for the individual to show that he would suffer from this effect without the medication or treatment.[65] The DDA 1995 was amended by the DDA 2005 to ensure that those suffering from a progressive condition, specifically cancer, HIV infection or multiple sclerosis, are deemed to have a disability. This means that they would not, as previously, need to show that it had a substantial adverse effect on their ability to carry out day to day activities.[66]

4. Whether the adverse effect was long term. According to Sch. 1 para. 2(1) DDA 1995, the effect of an impairment is long term if it has lasted at least 12 months or is likely to be at least 12 months or if it is likely to last for the rest of the affected person's life.

The House of Lords, in *SCA Packaging Ltd* v *Boyle*[67] concluded that the word 'likely' means 'could well happen', rather than 'probable' or 'more likely than not'. The Court stated, *obiter*, that where someone is following a course of treatment on medical advice, in the absence of any indication to the contrary, an employer can assume that, without the treatment, the impairment is 'likely' to recur. Similarly if it had a substantial effect on the individual's day to day life before it was treated, the employer can also assume that, in the absence of any contra-indication, if it does recur, its effect will be substantial.

There is also an important issue concerning 'associative' discrimination. *Attridge Law* v *Coleman*[68] concerned a legal secretary who had a son suffering from disabilities. She alleged that she had suffered discrimination under the DDA as a result of being a carer for her disabled son. She was not disabled herself. She argued that the Framework Directive offered protection from discrimination on 'the grounds of disability' and that the DDA 1995 should be construed broadly so as to implement this, and thus provide her with protection. The issue was referred by the tribunal to the European Court of Justice, which stated that it even though the person who alleged that she was the victim of direct discrimination was not herself disabled, it was the disability which was the ground for the less favourable treatment. The principle of equal treatment therefore also applied to her.[69]

6.3.2 Discrimination

Part II of the DDA 1995 concerns employment. Prior to 2004 there was an exemption for small employers, employing fewer than 15 employees, but this was subsequently removed.[70]

---

[64] [2000] IRLR 699 CA; see also *Leonard* v *Southern Derbyshire Chamber of Commerce* [2001] IRLR 19 where the EAT held that a tribunal should concentrate on what a person could not do or had difficulty doing.

[65] *Woodrup* v *London Borough of Southwark* [2003] IRLR 111 where an individual failed to produce medical evidence that the discontinuation of her psychotherapy treatment would have a substantial adverse effect.

[66] See para. 6A Sch. 1 DDA 1995.

[67] [2009] IRLR 746

[68] [2007] IRLR 89.

[69] Case C-303/06 *Coleman* v *Attridge Law* [2008] IRLR 722.

[70] Regulation 7 Disability Discrimination Act 1995 (Amendment) Regulations 2003, SI 2003/1673.

Employment is defined as being under a contract of service or apprenticeship or a contract personally to do any work.[71] Thus there is a wider definition than just employee, following the approach in the SDA 1975 and the RRA 1976.

It is unlawful for an employer to discriminate against a disabled[72] person in:

1. the arrangements which are made for the purpose of determining who should be offered employment;[73]

2. the terms in which that person is offered employment; and

3. refusing to offer, or deliberately not offering, employment.[74]

It is also unlawful for an employer to discriminate against a disabled person who is employed in, first, the terms of employment offered; secondly, in the opportunities afforded for promotion, transfer or training; thirdly, by refusing, or deliberately not affording, any such opportunity; and, finally, by dismissing the individual or subjecting them to any other detriment.[75] These provisions apply in relation to an establishment in Great Britain.[76]

In *British Sugar plc* v *Kirker*[77] an individual selected for redundancy claimed that they had been discriminated against because of a visual impairment, suffered since birth. The employers had carried out an assessment exercise in order to select those to be dismissed. This had consisted of marking employees against a set of factors. The complainant claimed that the marks attributed to them were the result of a subjective view arising out of the disability. The employee had scored 0 out of 10 for promotion potential and 0 for performance and competence. The EAT observed that such marks would indicate that the employee did not always achieve the required standard of performance and required close supervision. Yet the employee had never been criticised for poor performance and did not have any supervision. There was no need to consider the scores of other employees as the DDA 1995 did not require comparisons. It was clear that this individual had been under-marked by reason of their disability. The fact that many of the relevant events took place before the coming into force of the DDA 1995 did not stop the employment tribunal from looking at them in order to help draw inferences about the employer's conduct.[78]

Similar provisions apply to contract workers.[79] It is unlawful for a 'principal', in relation to contract work, to discriminate against a disabled person. In *Abbey Life Assurance Co Ltd* v *Tansell*[80] the principal was described as the 'end user' in a situation where there was an

---

[71] Section 68 DDA 1995; see *South East Sheffield Citizens Advice Bureau* v *Grayson* [2004] IRLR 353 where CAB volunteer workers were held not to be employees and thus the employer fell outside the scope of the DDA 1995 under the old rule that exempted employers with fewer than 15 employees.

[72] It is also unlawful to instruct or pressurise another person over whom the employer has authority to discriminate or harass on the grounds of a person's disability: s. 16C DDA 1995.

[73] Section 16B DDA 1995 also makes unlawful discriminatory advertisements.

[74] Section 4(1) DDA 1995.

[75] Section 4(2) DDA 1995; s. 4(4) provides that subsection (2) will not apply to any benefits, including facilities and services, that are offered to a section of the public that includes the employee, when those benefits are different from those offered by the employer to employees.

[76] Section 4(6) DDA 1995; see also ss. 68(4) and 68(4A) concerning the meaning of 'Great Britain'.

[77] [1998] IRLR 624.

[78] See also *Kent County Council* v *Mingo* [2000] IRLR 90 where a redeployment policy that gave preference to redundant or potentially redundant employees, in preference to those with a disability, amounted to discrimination in accordance with the DDA 1995.

[79] Section 4B DDA 1995.

[80] [2000] IRLR 387 CA.

unbroken chain of contracts between a person 'A' who makes work available for doing by individuals who are employed by another person who supplies them under a contract made with 'A'. In this case a contract computer person was employed by their own limited liability company which had a contract with a consultancy who supplied their services to an end user. Taking a purposive approach to the statute, the EAT and the Court of Appeal concluded that it was the end user who should be the target for the complaint as the agency would simply justify their actions by reference to the instructions of 'A'. Similar rules apply to office holders,[81] partnerships,[82] barristers and advocates.[83]

The DDA 1995 makes a number of forms of discrimination unlawful.[84] These are:

- Direct discrimination.[85]
- Disability related discrimination.[86]
- Victimisation.[87]
- Failure to comply with a duty to make reasonable adjustments.[88]

6.3.2.1 Direct discrimination

Direct discrimination results from treatment of a disabled person when:

1. it is on the grounds of the person's disability;
2. it is treatment which is less favourable than that given to, or that would have been given to, a person not having that particular disability; and
3. the relevant circumstances, including the abilities, of the person being used as the comparator are the same as, or not materially different from, those of the disabled person.

Thus the treatment must be on the grounds of the person's disability. There is no requirement for it to be a deliberate and conscious decision to discriminate. Indeed much discrimination may be the result of prejudices about which the discriminator is unaware.[89] The comparator must be someone who does not have the same disability and may be someone who is not disabled. It is important, however, that the comparator's relevant circumstances, including his abilities, are the same as, or not materially different from, those of the disabled person. It is not necessary to identify an actual person to use as a comparator. Where one with similar relevant circumstances is not available, then a hypothetical comparator can be used.

An example of direct discrimination given in the DRC Code of Practice is one where a person who becomes disabled takes six months' sick leave because of his disability, and is dismissed by the employer. A non-disabled fellow employee also takes six months' sick leave, because of a broken leg, but is not dismissed. The non-disabled employee is an appropriate comparator because the relevant circumstances are the same, i.e. having six months'

---

[81] Sections 4C–4F DDA 1995.
[82] Sections 6A–6C DDA 1995.
[83] Sections 7A–7D DDA 1995.
[84] See also Chapters 4 and 5 of the Code of Practice which gives a very good description of these types of discrimination with many examples, some of which are used here.
[85] Section 3A(5) DDA 1995.
[86] Section 3A(1) DDA 1995.
[87] Section 55 DDA 1995.
[88] Section 4A DDA 1995.
[89] The Code of Practice gives examples of this in its Chapter 4.

sick leave. Direct discrimination has occurred because of the less favourable treatment of the disabled person.

In relation to direct discrimination there is no justification defence for the employer. Treatment that amounts to direct discrimination cannot be justified, as it can in some other circumstances (see below).[90]

6.3.2.2 **Disability related discrimination**

Section 3A(1) DDA 1995 states that an employer discriminates against a disabled person when:

1. it is for a reason related to his disability;

2. the treatment is less favourable than the treatment given, or that would have been given, to others to whom the reason does not or would not apply, and;

3. the employer cannot show that the treatment in question can be justified.

The phrase 'disability related discrimination' is not used in the Act, but is used in the DRC Code of Practice to describe discrimination that falls under s. 3A(1) DDA 1995, but which does not amount to direct discrimination. It therefore has a wider scope and includes less favourable treatment which does not amount to direct discrimination. A good example of this was given in the DRC Code of Practice:[91]

> A disabled woman is refused an administrative job because she cannot type. She cannot type because she has arthritis. A non-disabled person who was unable to type would also have been turned down. The disability related reason for the less favourable treatment is the woman's inability to type, and the correct comparator is a person to whom the reason does not apply – that is, someone who can type. Such a person would not have been refused the job. Nevertheless, the disabled woman has been treated less favourably for a disability related reason and this will be unlawful unless it can be justified.

The whole effectiveness of the concept of disability related discrimination was thrown into doubt by a decision of the House of Lords in a housing related disability discrimination case. In *London Borough of Lewisham* v *Malcolm*[92] an individual suffering from schizophrenia sublet his council home. The Council took possession proceedings against him and he claimed that this was contrary to the DDA as it was the disability that made him decide to sublet, i.e. a disability related reason. The Court, however, said that the correct comparison was with a non-disabled person who had decided to sublet. The result was to considerably weaken the effectiveness of protection from disability related discrimination. In *Child Support Agency* v *Truman*[93] the EAT confirmed that the approach in *Malcolm* should equally apply in the employment context.

Any justification under s. 3A(1)(b) needs to be material to the circumstances of the case and substantial.[94] There are strict limitations to any justification defence. First, it cannot be used in cases of direct discrimination.[95] Secondly, it cannot be used to justify any failure in

---

[90] Section 3A(4) DDA 1995.
[91] Chapter 4 DRC Code of Practice 2004.
[92] [2008] IRLR 700.
[93] [2009] IRLR 277.
[94] Section 3A(3) DDA 1995.
[95] Section 3A(4) and (5) DDA 1995 define direct discrimination as treating a disabled person less favourably than the employer treats or would treat a person not having that particular disability whose relevant circumstances, including abilities, are the same as, or not materially different from, those of the disabled person.

the employer's duty to make adjustments (see below).[96] There may be situations when the employer will still not be able to justify the treatment, even if there are material and substantial justifications for the less favourable treatment. This may occur if the employer has failed in the duty to make reasonable adjustments. The employer will, in such circumstances, need to show that the material and substantial circumstances would have applied even if the adjustments had been made.[97]

There is a need to establish a causal link between any discriminatory act and an employer's justification. Having no knowledge of a disability may not be a sufficient justification, given that the discriminatory act relates to the way in which the employer treats the employee.[98] In *London Borough of Hammersmith & Fulham v Farnsworth*,[99] an employer had failed to inquire further about an applicant's health record on the grounds of confidentiality. The EAT concluded that this failure was not relevant, but, in any case, the applicant had been examined by a doctor on behalf of the employer. This examination put the doctor into the position of being the employer's agent, so the doctor having knowledge was the same as the potential employer having it. The relationship between the disability and the treatment received by the employee is not a subjective one, i.e. based on what the employer perceived. It is an objective test as to whether there is a relationship between the treatment and the disability. If such a relationship exists, the employer's knowledge, or lack of knowledge, is not relevant. Thus an employer who dismissed an employee after the individual had been absent for almost a year really ought to have considered the possibility of disablement, rather than claiming a lack of knowledge about the disability.[100]

The correct process for showing justification is, first, the disabled applicant shows less favourable treatment, such as dismissal, including constructive dismissal;[101] secondly, the employer shows that the treatment is justified if the reason for the decision is both material to the circumstances of the case and substantial, and that he has not, without justification, failed to comply with any duty under s. 4A (duty to make adjustments). 'Material circumstances of the case' can include the circumstances of both the employer and the employee.[102]

Consideration of the statutory criteria may involve an assessment of whether there was evidence on the basis of which a decision could properly be taken by the employer. This may consist of appropriate medical evidence or undertaking a risk assessment. If the decision was not based upon such evidence or was irrational in some other way, the employment tribunal may hold the reason for the decision to be insufficient or unjustified.[103]

The Court of Appeal also stated that the function of employment tribunals under s. 5(3) DDA 1995 is not very different from the task that they have to carry out with respect to unfair dismissals (see Chapter 4). In the latter they are required to adopt the range of reasonable

---

[96] Section 3A(6) DDA 1995.
[97] See Chapter 6 of the DRC Code of Practice 2004.
[98] See *Callagan v Glasgow City Council* [2001] IRLR 724.
[99] [2000] IRLR 691.
[100] See *HJ Heinz Co Ltd v Kenrick* [2000] IRLR 144.
[101] Section 4(5) DDA 1995 provides a definition of dismissal which includes constructive dismissal; see also *Catherall v Michelin Tyre plc* [2002] IRLR 61, where the EAT held that giving an employee the choice of early medical retirement or redundancy effectively gave the employee no choice and could be said to amount to a dismissal.
[102] See *Baynton v Saurus General Engineers Ltd* [1999] IRLR 604.
[103] *Jones v Post Office* [2001] IRLR 384 CA.

responses test in deciding whether a dismissal was reasonable. In the case of s. 5(3) they have to decide on the materiality and substantiality of the employer's decision. In both cases the employment tribunal might have come to a different decision themselves, but the need is to consider the opinion of the employer as to whether the decision was, in the one case, within the range of reasonable responses, and, in the other, whether the reason was both material and substantial.

6.3.2.3 Victimisation

An employer discriminates against an employee or another person if the employer treats that employee or other person less favourably than he treats or would treat other employees in the same circumstances because the employee or other person:

1. brought proceedings against the employer or any other person under the DDA 1995; or
2. gave evidence or information in connection with such proceedings brought by any other person; or
3. otherwise does anything under the DDA 1995 in relation to the employer or any other person; or
4. alleged that the employer or other person has contravened the DDA 1995.

Treating the employee or other person less favourably because the employer believes or suspects that the employee or other person has done or intends to do any of these actions is also unlawful.[104] Unlike the other forms of discrimination provided for by the DDA 1995, this form can be claimed by non-disabled people as well as disabled people. The treatment, however, will not amount to less favourable treatment if any allegation of the employee or other person was false and not made in good faith.[105]

There is also protection for ex-employees in a situation where there has been a relevant relationship between an employer and a disabled person and that relationship has come to an end. A relevant relationship is where there has been an employment relationship during which there was an act of discrimination or harassment. In such a situation it is unlawful for the ex-employer to discriminate or harass the disabled person concerned.[106]

6.3.4 Duty to make reasonable adjustments

The employer also discriminates against a disabled person if the employer fails to comply with a duty to make reasonable adjustments in relation to the disabled person.[107] A failure to make reasonable adjustments over a period of time would be almost bound to lead to a breach of the implied term of trust and confidence, which would then entitle the employee to treat it as a repudiatory breach of contract (see Chapter 3).[108] *Nottinghamshire County Council* v *Meikle*[109] concerned a local authority school teacher. Her vision deteriorated until she lost the sight in one eye and some vision in the other. She made a number of requests for

---

[104] Section 55(1) and (2) DDA 1995.
[105] Section 55(4) DDA 1995.
[106] Section 16A DDA 1995.
[107] Section 3A(2) DDA 1995.
[108] *Greenhof* v *Barnsley Metropolitan Borough Council* [2006] IRLR 99.
[109] [2004] IRLR 703.

adjustments, including to her classroom location, the amount of preparation time she was given, and that notices and written materials should be enlarged. There were delays in responses from the employer and eventually Mrs Meikle resigned. The Court of Appeal agreed with her that the continuing failure of the local authority to deal with the disability discrimination amounted to a fundamental breach of contract and that she had been constructively dismissed.

The importance of the need to make reasonable adjustments is shown in one survey,[110] which stated that over 25 per cent of people who left their job because of their disability said that adaptations would have enabled them to stay in work, but less than 20 per cent of these people were offered such changes. Thus, where the disabled person is placed at a substantial disadvantage compared to persons who are not disabled because of:

- a provision, criterion or practice applied by or on behalf of an employer; or
- any physical feature of premises occupied by an employer,[111]

it is the duty of the employer to take reasonable steps, in all the circumstances of the case, to prevent the provision, criterion, practice or feature from having that effect.[112] This obligation applies in respect of applicants for employment as well as in respect of existing employees. There is, however, no obligation placed upon the employer if the employer does not know, or could not have reasonably been expected to know, that the applicant or employee had a disability. The position was summarised in *Eastern and Coastal Kent Primary Care Trust* v *Grant*[113] which concerned an applicant with dyslexia. The EAT stated that an employer is exempted from the duty to make adjustments if each of four matters can be satisfied. These were that the employer:

1. Does not know that the disabled person has a disability.

2. Does not know that the disabled person is likely to be at a substantial disadvantage compared with persons who are not disabled.

3. Could not reasonably have been expected to know that the disabled person had a disability.

4. Could not reasonably be expected to know that the disabled person is likely to be placed at a substantial disadvantage in comparison with people who are not disabled.

These matters are cumulative and not alternatives.

'Provision, criterion or practice' includes any arrangements.[114] The arrangements referred to include, first, the arrangements for determining who should be offered employment, and, secondly, any term, condition or arrangements on which employment, promotion, transfer, training or any other benefit is offered. The arrangements referred to are strictly job related. Employers are required to make adjustments to the way that the job is structured and

---

[110] See Office for National Statistics, 'Disability and the Labour Market', *Labour Market Trends*, September 1999, p. 467.

[111] Physical feature includes any feature arising from the design or construction of a building, approaches to it, access or exits, fixtures, fittings, furnishings, furniture, equipment or material in the building: s. 18D DDA 1995.

[112] Section 4A(1) DDA 1995.

[113] [2009] IRLR 429.

[114] Section 18D DDA 1995.

organised so as to accommodate those who cannot fit into the existing arrangements. This appears to exclude providing assistance with personal arrangements and care so as to enable an individual to attend work.[115] Examples of steps which may need to be taken are:[116]

1. Making adjustments to premises.

2. Allocating some of the disabled person's duties to another person.

3. Transferring the disabled person to an existing vacancy.

4. Altering his hours of work or training.

5. Assigning him to a different place of work or training.

6. Allowing him to be absent during working or training hours for rehabilitation, assessment or treatment.

7. Giving, or arranging to give, training or mentoring.

8. Acquiring or modifying equipment.

9. Modifying instructions or reference manuals.

10. Providing a reader or interpreter.

11. Providing supervision or other support.

The question of whether an employer had made sufficient arrangements in the light of their knowledge is one of fact for the employment tribunal. *Ridout* v *TC Group*[117] concerned an applicant with a rare form of epilepsy who may have been disadvantaged by the bright fluorescent lighting in the interview location. The EAT held that no reasonable employer could be expected to know, without being told, that the arrangements for the interview might place the applicant at a disadvantage. The EAT held that the DDA 1995:

> requires the tribunal to measure the extent of the duty, if any, against the assumed knowledge of the employer both as to the disability and its likelihood of causing the individual a substantial disadvantage in comparison with persons who are not disabled.

The extent of the adjustments needed is subject to a reasonableness test. This first requires an employer to carry out a proper assessment of what is needed to eliminate a disabled person's disadvantage. This might include a proper assessment of the individual's condition, the effect of the disability on her and her ability to perform the duties of the post and the steps that might be taken to reduce or remove the disadvantages to which she was subjected.[118] In deciding whether it is reasonable for an employer to have to take a particular step, regard may be had to the nature of the employer's activities and the size of the undertaking, as well as the extent to which the step would prevent the effect or barrier that existed and the practicability of taking the step in the first place. It may mean creating a new job for an individual, such as in *Southampton City College* v *Randall*[119] where a reorganisation of work would have enabled the employer to create a new job for a lecturer whose voice had broken down. The

---

[115] See *Kenny* v *Hampshire Constabulary* [1999] IRLR 76.
[116] Section 18B(2) DDA 1995.
[117] [1998] IRLR 628.
[118] *Mid Staffordshire General Hospitals NHS Trust* v *Cambridge* [2003] IRLR 566.
[119] [2006] IRLR 18.

employers were guilty of disability discrimination because they did not consider this option and others as possible reasonable adjustments.

The size of an employer's resources are also important because regard needs to be had for the financial and other costs, the possible disruption of the employer's activities, the extent of the employer's financial resources and the availability of any financial or other help.[120] Failure to comply with the duty to make adjustments is not in itself actionable. It is a duty imposed for the purpose of determining whether an employer has discriminated against a disabled person.[121]

A further example of the scope of the duty to make reasonable adjustments arose in *Archibald v Fife Council*.[122] This concerned an employee of Fife Council who was employed as a road sweeper. As a result of a complication during surgery she became virtually unable to walk and could no longer carry out the duties of a road sweeper. She could do sedentary work and the Council sent her on a number of computer and administration courses. Over the next few months she applied for over 100 jobs within the Council but she always failed in a competitive interview situation. Eventually she was dismissed as the redeployment procedure was exhausted. The issue for the court was the limits of the duty to make reasonable adjustments. It was agreed that the DDA 1995 required some positive discrimination in favour of disabled people, but did this include finding them another job if their disability stops them from performing their current one? The court held that the DDA 1995, to the extent that the provisions of the Act required it, permitted and sometimes obliged employers to treat a disabled person more favourably than others. This may even require transferring them to a higher level position without the need for a competitive interview.[123]

6.3.5 Harassment

It is unlawful for an employer to harass a disabled employee or a disabled job applicant.[124] Harassment has the same meaning as in other regulations concerning discrimination on the grounds of sexual orientation and religion or belief (see Chapter 5). A person subjects a disabled person to harassment if he engages in, in relation to the disability, unwanted conduct which has the purpose or effect of:

(a) violating the disabled person's dignity, or

(b) creating an intimidating, hostile, degrading, humiliating or offensive environment for him.[125]

Conduct will be seen as harassment only if, having regard to all the circumstances, especially the perception of the disabled person, it can reasonably be considered as having the effect of harassment. Thus, although there is a reasonableness test, it is not necessarily an objective test as the view of the disabled person affected by the conduct is important.

---

[120] Section 18B(1) DDA 1995.
[121] Section 18B(6) DDA 1995.
[122] [2004] IRLR 651 CA.
[123] This was one of the problems for the employer. Most positions were at a higher level than that of a road sweeper and the local authority assumed that it had an obligation to make all promotion interviews competitive.
[124] Section 4(3) DDA 1995.
[125] Section 3B DDA 1995.

6.3.6 **Enforcement and remedies**

When a person considers that they may have been discriminated against in relation to Part II DDA 1995, that person may question the respondent, or potential respondent, by using prescribed forms for this purpose.[126] The questions will be admissible in evidence only if they are raised within a period of three months beginning when the act complained of was done.[127] If it appears to the employment tribunal that the respondent deliberately, and without reasonable excuse, failed to reply within a period of eight weeks or that the respondent's reply was 'evasive or equivocal', it will be free to draw inferences, including that the respondent has contravened the employment related part of the DDA 1995.[128]

Like the SDA 1975 and the RRA 1976, anything done by a person in the course of their employment is to be treated as also being done by the employer, whether or not it was done with the employer's approval,[129] although it will be a defence for the employer if they can show that they took all steps as were reasonably practicable to prevent the employee doing the act or doing such acts in the course of their employment.[130] Similarly, according to s. 57(1) DDA 1995 a person who knowingly aids another person to do an act made unlawful by the DDA is to be treated as doing that act themselves. The defence is that they reasonably relied upon a statement from that other person that the act done was not unlawful in terms of the DDA 1995.[131]

A person may make a complaint to an employment tribunal within three months of the act complained of.[132] A tribunal may consider an out of time complaint if it is 'just and equitable' to do so.[133] Where the complainant proves facts from which the tribunal could conclude, in the absence of an adequate explanation, that the respondent has acted in a way which is unlawful within the terms of the Act, then the tribunal can uphold the complaint, unless the respondent proves that he did not act in the way complained of. The tribunal may make a declaration as to the rights of the complainant and the respondent, order the respondent to pay compensation[134] to the applicant and/or recommend action to be taken by the respondent, within a specified period, for the purpose of obviating or reducing the adverse effect on the complainant.[135] If the respondent fails, without reasonable justification, to comply with the recommendation, then the tribunal may award compensation or increase the level of compensation already ordered.[136]

---

[126] Section 56 DDA 1995 and Disability Discrimination (Questions and Replies) Order 1996, SI 1996/2793.

[127] Article 3(a) Disability Discrimination (Questions and Replies) Order 1996, SI 1996/2793.

[128] Section 56(3) DDA 1995.

[129] Section 58(1) DDA 1995.

[130] Section 58(5) DDA 1995.

[131] Section 58(3) DDA 1995, but s. 58(4) provides that a person who knowingly or recklessly makes the statement which is false or misleading is guilty of an offence.

[132] Schedule 3 DDA 1995; the time limit applies equally to attempts to amend existing claims by adding on a complaint related to disability discrimination; see *Harvey* v *Port of Tilbury London Ltd* [1999] IRLR 693.

[133] See Sch. 3 para. 3 DDA 1995; s. 9 DDA 1995 provides that any term in the contract of employment that contravenes any provisions of the Act is void, but also contains rules for conciliation and compromise agreements regarding proceedings.

[134] See *Buxton* v *Equinox Design Ltd* [1999] IRLR 158 which considered the care that needs to be taken in assessing compensation where the amount is uncapped as in cases relating to the DDA 1995.

[135] Section 17A(2) DDA 1995; according to s. 17A(4), compensation can include injury to feelings.

[136] Section 17A(5) DDA 1995.

Chapter summary

The examination of measures to prohibit discrimination in employment continued in this chapter, where it considered discrimination on the ground of disability and on the ground of age. With regard to disability it looked at what is meant by disability and how the courts have given guidance to its meaning. In particular it looked at the law with regard to direct discrimination and disability related discrimination, as well as victimisation and harassment. It then looked at the important positive measure of the duty on employers to make reasonable adjustments. It examined the effect of the Employment Equality (Age) Regulations 2006 and especially the possibilities of justifying exceptions to the principle of non-discrimination.

Further reading

Deakin, S. and Morris, G. *Labour Law*: 5th edn, Hart Publishing, 2009, Chapter 6.

McColgan, A. *Discrimination Law: Text, Cases and Materials*: Hart Publishing, 2005, Chapter 8.

Sargeant, M. *Age Discrimination in Employment*: Gower Publishing, 2006.

Sargeant, M. 'Disability and Age – Multiple Potential for Discrimination' (2005) 33 *International Journal of the Sociology of Law* 17.

Sargeant, M. 'The Employment Equality (Age) Regulations 2006: A Legitimisation of Age Discrimination in Employment' (2006) 35(3) *Industrial Law Journal* 209.

http://www.berr.gov.uk/employment/discrimination/index.html for the Department for Business, Innovation and Skills website on discrimination at work.

http://www.equalityhumanrights.com for the website of the Equality and Human Rights Commission.

Visit **www.mylawchamber.co.uk/sargeant**
to access legal updates, live weblinks and practice
exam questions to test yourself on this chapter.

7 Time and pay

7.1 Working time

The discussion about the regulation of a person's working time encapsulated the arguments about the degree to which Governments should intervene in the employment relationship and the extent to which such regulation should originate with the EU. The British Government, in *United Kingdom* v *Council of Ministers*,[1] argued that such matters were an issue of subsidiarity and should be settled within Member States rather than by the Community. The Council argued that the justification for the Working Time Directive[2] was a health and safety one and that the Community had competence in this field. In the event, the United Kingdom finally transposed the Directive into national law some two years late.[3]

7.2 Young Workers' Directive

The Working Time Regulations include the transposition of parts of the Young Workers' Directive[4] into national law. This Directive came into effect on 22 June 1996, but the United Kingdom was permitted to delay this process. The final parts of the Directive were transposed into national law in 2002. This Directive was also adopted under art. 137 EC concerning health and safety. It applies to any person under the age of 18 years who has an employment contract or an employment relationship. Subject to minor exceptions, the Directive prohibits the employment of children. These are defined as persons of less than 15 years of age, or the minimum school leaving age, whichever is higher. The minor exceptions include work experience, work in the theatre and light work.[5]

Articles 6 and 7, which describe the general obligations placed upon employers and the prohibition of certain types of employment of young people, were implemented by the Health and Safety (Young Persons) Regulations 1997.[6] Those parts concerning the employment of children were implemented by the Children (Protection at Work) Regulations 1998

---

[1] Case C-84/94 [1997] IRLR 30 ECJ.
[2] Council Directive 93/104/EC concerning certain aspects of the organisation of working time OJ L307/18 13.12.93. This was significantly amended by the European Parliament and Council Directive 2003/88/EC.
[3] Working Time Regulations 1998, SI 1998/1833.
[4] Council Directive 94/33/EC on the protection of young people at work OJ L216/12 20.8.94.
[5] Articles 4–5 Young Workers' Directive.
[6] SI 1997/135.

(see below).[7] The provisions on working hours, night work, rest periods, periodic and annual breaks are included in the Working Time Regulations.[8]

The number of young people working is significant, despite the expansion of numbers in further and higher education. Many will be part-time workers helping to finance their education.[9] According to the Management of Health and Safety at Work Regulations 1999 (MHSW Regulations 1999),[10] an employer of a young person[11] must carry out a risk assessment which takes particular account of a number of factors.[12] These are:

1. The inexperience, lack of awareness of risks and immaturity of young persons.

2. The fitting-out and the layout of the workplace and the workstation.

3. The nature, degree and duration of exposure to physical, biological and chemical agents.

4. The form, range and use of work equipment and the way in which it is used.

5. The organisation of processes and activities.

6. The extent of the health and safety training provided or to be provided to young persons.

7. The risks from agents, processes and work listed in the annex to the Young Workers' Directive.

Regulation 10(2) of the MHSW Regulations 1999 provides that, before employing a child,[13] any employer must provide a parent[14] of the child with 'comprehensible and relevant information' on any risks to the child's health and safety that have been identified by the risk assessment and the preventive and protective measures that have been taken. Employers have a general responsibility for protecting young persons from any risks to their health and safety which are

> a consequence of their lack of experience, or absence of awareness of existing or potential risks or the fact that young persons have not fully matured.[15]

The Children (Protection at Work) Regulations 1998 amended the Children and Young Persons Acts 1933 and 1963 to give effect to the Young Workers' Directive. They impose restrictions on the working hours and the type of work that can be undertaken by individuals under the compulsory school leaving age.

7.3 Working Time Directive

The justification for the Working Time Directive in 1993 was art. 118a EC (now 137), which stated at the time that:

---

[7] SI 1998/276.

[8] There were also provisions relating to young people working on sea-going ships, which were dealt with by the Fishing Vessels (Health and Safety) (Employment of Children and Young Persons) Regulations 1998, SI 1998/2411.

[9] See Chapter 2 on the Part-time Workers Regulations 2000.

[10] SI 1999/3242.

[11] Young person means any person who has not attained the age of 18 years; see reg. 1(2) MHSW Regulations 1999.

[12] Regulation 3(5) MHSW Regulations 1999.

[13] Someone who is not over compulsory school leaving age.

[14] A parent is someone who has parental responsibility according to s. 3 Children Act 1989; the same definition as in the Maternity and Parental Leave etc. Regulations 1999; see Chapter 8.

[15] Regulation 19(1) MHSW Regulations 1999.

Member States shall pay particular attention to encouraging improvements, especially in the working environment, as regards the health and safety of workers, and shall set as their objective the harmonisation of conditions in this area, while maintaining the improvements made.

It was also justified, in the preamble to the Directive, by the following extract from the Community Charter of the Fundamental Social Rights of Workers:[16]

The completion of the internal market must lead to an improvement in the living and working conditions of workers in the European Community. This process must result from an approximation of these conditions while the improvement is being maintained, as regards in particular the duration and organisation of working time . . .

Thus the measure was intended to harmonise the approach of Member States to 'ensure the safety and health of Community workers'.[17] One problem for the United Kingdom was that many other Member States already had statutory rules on weekly and daily hours, which preceded the Working Time Directive. Belgium, France, Greece, Ireland, Italy and Portugal all had existing rules which limited working hours.[18] One of the consequences of using art. 118a EC (now 137) was that it could be adopted using the 'co-operation procedure' in art. 189c EC (now 252). This needed only a qualified majority by the Council of Ministers to adopt a common position with regard to the proposal. In the event the United Kingdom abstained, but indicated that it would challenge the legal basis for the Directive.

The subject matter of the Directive related to minimum periods of daily and weekly rest, breaks in work, annual leave, maximum weekly working time and patterns of work, such as night work and shift work. Subject to certain derogations permitted in art. 17, the Directive applies to the same public and private sectors as the Health and Safety at Work Directive.[19] There were a number of specific exceptions to this, which included air, rail, road and sea, as well as the activities of doctors in training.[20]

The Directive was due to be transposed into national law by 23 November 1996 but, partly because of the United Kingdom Government's legal challenge, it came into effect with the Working Time Regulations in October 1998. This challenge[21] was through proceedings for annulment of the Directive, or of certain parts of arts. 4, 5, 6 and 7. The action was brought under art. 173 EC (now 230), which gives the ECJ jurisdiction in actions brought by Member States or certain EU institutions, to review the legality of acts of the EU

on grounds of lack of competence, infringement of an essential procedural requirement, infringement of this Treaty or any rule of law relating to its application, or misuse of powers.

The UK action was based on the following four claims:

1. The Directive had a defective legal basis, i.e. it should have been adopted on the basis of art. 100 EC (now 94) or art. 235 EC (now 308), which required unanimity in the Council of Ministers.

---

[16] Adopted on 9 December 1989 by all the then Member States with the exception of the United Kingdom.
[17] The preamble states: 'Whereas, in order to ensure the safety and health of Community workers, the latter must be granted minimum daily, weekly and annual periods of rest and adequate breaks . . .'
[18] *European Industrial Relations Review* 280, May 1997, p. 18.
[19] Council Directive 89/391/EEC on the introduction of measures to encourage improvements in the safety and health of workers at work OJ L183/1 29.6.89.
[20] Article 1 Working Time Directive; see below for current exclusions.
[21] Case C-84/94 *United Kingdom* v *Council of Ministers* [1997] IRLR 30 ECJ.

2. The Directive did not comply with the principle of proportionality, because its provisions went beyond the minimum requirements permitted under art. 118a EC (now 137). Specifically, overall reductions in working hours or an overall increase in rest periods were not 'minimum requirements', the desired level of protection could have been attained by less restrictive measures and the proposed measures were not justified by scientific research. Additionally, it had not been shown that the Directive's objectives could be better achieved at Community level, rather than at Member State level.

3. The Directive contained a number of measures which were unconnected with its purported aims and were, therefore, a misuse of powers.

4. Finally, it was claimed that there was an infringement of essential procedural requirements. This arose because there was a failure to show a causal relationship between the proposals and health and safety, which meant that it had failed to state the reasons on which it was based. Alternatively, it was argued, the reasoning was flawed as there was a failure to explain that many of the measures were concerned with matters other than health and safety.

The United Kingdom lost on every point, except where the ECJ annulled a proposal that, in principle, the weekly rest period should be on a Sunday. The ECJ held that the principal purpose of the Directive was the protection of the health and safety of workers and that it was, therefore, adopted under the correct part of the Treaty and that it was not in breach of the principle of proportionality. It stated that the concept of 'minimum requirements' is not about setting minimum standards but refers to the individual State's ability to impose more stringent standards than that set by Community action. The Council also dismissed the claims of misuse of powers or inadequate reasoning.

As a result, there was a period when the United Kingdom had failed to transpose the Directive. In *Gibson* v *East Riding of Yorkshire Council*[22] a local authority employee claimed that she could rely on art. 7[23] of the Directive having direct effect during the period between 23 November 1996, the date by which it should have been implemented, and 1 October 1998, the date when the Working Time Regulations came into effect. She was an employee of an emanation of the State and the EAT held that she could rely on the Directive, as art. 7 in particular met the requirements for having direct effect[24] by being sufficiently precise and unconditional. The Court of Appeal disagreed with this approach, however, and allowed the appeal.[25] The court held that certain provisions were not sufficiently precise, especially the definition of working time itself. The court stated:

> The first basic question for the national court is: what is the period of 'working time' for which the worker must have worked before he becomes entitled to annual leave under Article 7? Annual leave is leave from 'working time'. The concept of 'working time' is not precisely defined. To what period of 'working time' does the specified period of annual leave relate? The question is not answered by Article 7 itself or by any other provisions in the Directive. How then is it possible for a national court to decide which workers are entitled to annual leave?

---

[22] [2000] IRLR 598 CA.
[23] Concerning annual leave; see below.
[24] See also *R* v *Attorney General for Northern Ireland, ex parte Burns* [1999] IRLR 315 which also considered this issue in relation to night work.
[25] *Gibson* v *East Riding of Yorkshire Council* [2000] IRLR 598 CA.

7.4 **Working Time Regulations**

The Working Time Regulations 1998 have been amended on a number of occasions.[26] One effect of these amendments is to weaken the 1998 Regulations even further, making it much easier for the employer and worker to agree to exclude the provisions of the maximum weekly working time of an average of 48 hours. There were also fresh exclusions from certain provisions for those whose working time is not measured or predetermined.

7.4.1 **Scope and definition**

The 1998 Regulations, which apply to Great Britain, offer protection to workers who are defined, in reg. 2(1), as those having a contract of employment or any other contract where the individual undertakes to do or perform personally any work or services for another party.[27] 'Young worker' is someone who is over the compulsory school age but is under 18 years of age.[28] Regulation 36 of the Regulations 1998[29] specifically provides for agency workers to be included. Where an individual is provided by an agency to do work for another, unless there is an agreement to different effect between the agency and the principal, the person who pays the agency worker in respect of the work is to be treated as the employer.[30]

The following three conditions must be satisfied for a period to constitute 'working time':

1. any period during which the worker is working;

2. any period when the worker is at the employer's disposal; and

3. any period when the worker is carrying out his duties and activities.

The definition of working time also includes any period during which the worker is receiving relevant training.[31] Relevant training is defined as meaning work experience which is part of a training course or programme, training for employment, or both of these. It does not include work experience or training provided by an educational institution or a person whose main business is the provision of training or courses provided by such bodies. Presumably this is conditional upon the employer's relationship with the training provider. If an institution provides a training course, defined by the employer as relevant to work, on the employer's premises and during normal working hours, it is difficult to see how this could not be 'relevant training', even though provided by this third party.

Lastly, working time means any additional period which is to be treated as working time under a 'relevant agreement'.[32] A 'relevant agreement' is any workforce agreement or any

---

[26] The Working Time Regulations 1999, SI 1999/3372; the Working Time (Amendment) Regulations 2001, SI 2001/3256; the Working Time (Amendment) Regulations 2003, SI 2003/1684. The 2003 Regulations are concerned with finally implementing the working time provisions of Directive 94/33/EC on the protection of young people at work.

[27] See s. 230(3) ERA 1996. See *Byrne Brothers (Formwork) Ltd v Baird* [2002] IRLR 96 and *Redrow Homes Ltd v Wright* [2004] IRLR 720.

[28] On the position of children see *Addison v Ashby* [2003] IRLR 211.

[29] Regulations 37–43 Working Time Regulations 1998 concern the position of other groups of workers, such as those in Crown employment and the armed forces and the police service.

[30] Regulation 36(2) Working Time Regulations 1998.

[31] Regulation 2(1) Working Time Regulations 1998.

[32] Regulation 2(1) Working Time Regulations 1998.

contractually binding part of a collective agreement or any other legally enforceable agreement between the worker and the employer (see below).

7.4.2 Exclusions

The 1998 Regulations follow the Directive closely in listing the exceptions to its coverage. Regulation 18 (as amended) excludes certain categories entirely. These are seafarers covered by Directive 1999/63 and those on board a sea-going vessel or a ship or hovercraft 'employed by an undertaking that operates services for passengers or goods by inland waterways or lake transport'. In addition, mobile staff in civil aviation who are covered by Directive 2000/79 and those performing mobile road transport activities who are covered by Directive 2002/15 are excluded from certain provisions. Other special categories are doctors in training[33] and those occupations where the characteristics of the activities are likely to be incompatible with the regulations, such as the armed services or the police.[34]

7.4.3 The 48-hour week

Regulations 4 and 5 are concerned with placing a 48-hour limit on the average amount of time worked per week. Unless an employer has first obtained the person's agreement in writing, a worker's working time (including any overtime) in any reference period must not exceed 48 hours for each seven days.[35]

Regulation 2(1) defines a day as a period of 24 hours commencing at midnight. The fact that working time is averaged means that it is possible for people to work long hours for sustained periods. In *King* v *Scottish & Newcastle*,[36] an individual was required to work for between 50 and 60 hours over the Christmas period, but there was no breach of the regulations as her hours were to be averaged over the reference period. The reference period is normally 17 weeks but can be varied by a collective or workforce agreement up to a maximum of 52 weeks.[37] This extension must be for 'objective or technical reasons'. It is not clear what these are likely to be but reg. 4(2) imposes an obligation on employers to take all reasonable steps 'in keeping with the need for health and safety of workers' to ensure that the limit specified is adhered to.[38] The obligation in reg. 4(2) is a separate obligation from the limit of 48 hours imposed by reg. 4(1). This was discussed in *Barber* v *RJB Mining (UK) Ltd*[39] where a trade union asked the High Court for a declaration that its members need not work again until their average working week fell to the 48-hour level. The trade union succeeded because the right in reg. 4(1) is a contractual obligation upon the employer.

The reference period can also be lengthened to 26 weeks for a number of special cases contained in reg. 21. These are situations where, for example, continuity of services needs to be maintained, for example in hospitals or airports, or where there are peaks of work, such

---

[33] On doctors' maximum hours see below.
[34] On emergency workers see *Pfeiffer* v *Deutsches Rotes Kreuz* [2005] IRLR 137.
[35] Regulation 4(1) Working Time Regulations 1998. On time spent 'on call' see *Landeshaupstadt Kiel* v *Jaeger* [2003] IRLR 804.
[36] IDS Brief 641, 10 May 1999.
[37] Regulation 23(b) Working Time Regulations 1998.
[38] It does mean that annualised contracts are catered for within the 1998 Regulations.
[39] [1999] IRLR 308.

as in agriculture or tourism, or where the workers' activities are affected by events or accidents outside the control of the employer. Finally, for new workers, who have worked for less than the reference period, the period to be counted will be the actual time worked.[40]

The 1998 Regulations provide a formula for calculating the hours worked for each seven days during a reference period.[41] They are calculated as

$$\frac{A + B}{C} = \text{average hours per week during reference period}$$

The purpose of this formula is not to count the days that are not worked during the reference period, but to include an equivalent number of days from the next period in order to make up for those lost days. In this formula:

A is the aggregate number of hours in the worker's working time during the course of the reference period.

B is the aggregate number of hours in the worker's working time in the period immediately after the end of the reference period, equivalent to the number of days excluded in A.[42]

C is the number of weeks in the reference period.

Example

An individual has two periods of employment during the 17-week reference period as follows: working ten hours per day for five weeks, then a break of two weeks before a further period of eight hours per day for ten weeks (working a five-day week). In the next reference period the individual works an average of nine hours per day. Thus

A = (10 hours × 5 days × 5 weeks) + (8 hours × 5 days × 10 weeks) = 650 hours worked;
B = 9 hours × 5 days × 2 weeks = 90.
The formula is now

$$\frac{650 + 90}{17} = 43.53 \text{ hours}$$

If the employee has agreed in writing to perform their work outside the scope of the regulations, then this formula cannot apply. If there is agreement to exclude for a limited period of time, then that period will count as excluded days. According to reg. 5, the agreement may apply for a specific period or for an indefinite period. It may also be subject to termination by the worker via the giving of notice, subject to a maximum of three months. If there is no such provision, then reg. 5 applies a seven-day notice period by default. Formerly, employers were required to maintain records of those who had opted out, specifying the numbers of hours worked during each reference period. All that an employer must now do is keep up-to-date records of the employees who have signed such an agreement.[43]

---

[40] Regulation 4(4) Working Time Regulations 1998.
[41] Regulation 4(6) Working Time Regulations 1998.
[42] Regulation 4(7) Working Time Regulations 1998; excluded days means days taken for the purposes of annual leave, sick leave, maternity leave and any days in which the limit does not apply as agreed in writing between employer and worker; see below.
[43] See Working Time Regulations 1999, SI 1999/3372.

7.4.4 **Night work**

Regulations 6 and 7 are concerned with limits on night working and related obligations placed upon the employer.[44] As with the rules on the 48-hour average week, the employer has a duty to take all reasonable steps, in keeping with the need to protect the health and safety of workers, to ensure that the limits specified are complied with.[45] Night work is defined as being work during 'night time'. Night time has a specific meaning, which is a period of at least seven hours that includes the period between midnight and 5 am. There are two alternative meanings given to the term 'night worker':

1. An individual who, as a normal course, works at least three of the normal daily working hours during night time. 'Normal course' means if the individual works such hours on the majority of days they work. This is said to be without prejudice to the generality of the expression, which suggests that there might be circumstances when 'normal course' can mean something else, such as working for at least three hours every day, rather than just the majority of days.

2. A worker who is likely, during night time, to work at least such a proportion of annual working time as may be specified in a collective or workforce agreement.[46]

In *R v Attorney General for Northern Ireland, ex parte Burns*[47] the High Court in Northern Ireland considered the meaning of the term 'normal course' as defined in art. 2(4) of the Working Time Directive. The employee had been asked to change to a shift system, which meant working a night shift between 9 pm and 7 am one week in three. The court held that the requirement for someone to work at least three hours during night time as a normal course meant no more than that this should be a regular feature of their work. According to the court, it was inconceivable that the protection should be confined to someone who works night shifts exclusively or predominantly.

In any applicable reference period, a night worker's normal hours must not exceed an average of eight hours for each 24 hours. There is a default reference period of 17 weeks and it is possible to agree to successive periods of 17 weeks[48] via a collective or workforce agreement. Where the individual has worked for the employer for less than 17 weeks, the reference period is the period since they started the employment.[49]

There is a formula for calculating a night worker's average normal hours for each 24 hours during a reference period. It is:

$$\frac{A}{B - C} = \text{average normal hours for each 24 hours}$$

A is the number of hours during the reference period which are normal working hours for that worker.

B is the number of days during the reference period.

[44] Regulation 6A Working Time Regulations 1998 deals with young workers.
[45] Regulations 4(2) and 6(2) Working Time Regulations 1998.
[46] Regulation 2(1) Working Time Regulations 1998.
[47] [1999] IRLR 315.
[48] Regulation 6(1) and (3) Working Time Regulations 1998.
[49] Regulation 6(4) Working Time Regulations 1998.

C is the total number of hours during the reference period comprised in rest periods spent by the worker in pursuance of entitlement under reg. 11,[50] divided by 24.[51]

Example[52]
A night worker normally works four 12-hour shifts per week. With a 17-week reference period,

A is 17 × (4 days × 12 hours) = 816 hours.

B is 17 × 7 days = 119 days.

The number of 24-hour weekly rest periods to which the worker is entitled under reg. 11 is 17; thus

C is (17 × 24 hours) divided by 24 = 17.

The formula will now look like this:

$$\frac{816}{119 - 17} = 8 \text{ hours}$$

The important difference between this formula and that applied to the 48-hour average is that this one deals with with a worker's normal hours rather than their actual hours.

7.4.4.1 Special hazards

There is an additional obligation on an employer contained in reg. 6(7) and (8). This is to ensure that no night worker whose work involves special hazards or heavy physical or mental strain works for more than eight hours in any 24-hour period in which the worker does night work. Thus the focus is on actual rather than normal working hours. A worker is to be regarded as being involved in such hazards and strain either if it is identified as such in a collective or workforce agreement which takes into account the specific effects and hazards of night work, or it is recognised in a risk assessment carried out in accordance with reg. 3 MHSW Regulations 1999.

7.4.4.2 Health care

The other aspect of an employer's obligations with regard to night work relates to the worker's health and well-being. An employer must not assign an adult to night work without ensuring that the worker has the opportunity of a free[53] health assessment prior to taking up the assignment, unless the worker has had a health assessment on a previous occasion and the employer has no reason to believe that it has been become invalid. The employer also has a duty to ensure that each night worker has the opportunity for a free health assessment at regular and appropriate intervals.[54] Young workers are entitled to a free assessment of their 'health and capacities' before being assigned to work during the restricted period,[55] unless they had one on a previous occasion and the employer had no reason to believe that it has been become invalid[56] and unless the work is itself of an exceptional nature.[57] It is not

---

[50] Weekly rest periods; see below.
[51] Regulation 6(5) Working Time Regulations 1998.
[52] Taken from the DTI guidance to the Regulations.
[53] Free means being of no cost to the workers to whom it relates: reg. 7(3) Working Time Regulations 1998.
[54] Regulation 7(1) Working Time Regulations 1998.
[55] The restricted period is between 10 pm and 6 am: reg. 7(2)(a) Working Time Regulations 1998.
[56] Regulation 7(2) Working Time Regulations 1998.
[57] Regulation 7(5) Working Time Regulations 1998.

clear if there is a difference between 'health assessment' and an 'assessment of health and capacities'. Health assessment does not appear to mean the same as a medical examination. In its guidance to the Working Time Regulations 1998, the DBIS suggests that a health assessment should take place in two stages. First, workers should be asked to complete a questionnaire which asks specific questions about their health which are relevant to the type of night work which they will be doing. Second, if the employer is not certain that they are fit for night work following the questionnaire, the worker should be asked to have a medical examination.

There is an obligation of confidentiality associated with the health assessment. There is to be no disclosure of an assessment, apart from a statement that the worker is fit to be assigned to or continue with night work, to anyone but the worker to whom the assessment relates. The only exception is if the worker has given permission for disclosure.[58] If a registered medical practitioner advises an employer that a worker is suffering from health problems associated with night work then the employer is under an obligation to transfer that person. There are two conditions attached to this obligation. First, it must be possible to transfer the individual to work which is not categorised as night work and, secondly, it must be work to which that person is suited.[59]

The employer must keep adequate records relating to regs. 4(1), 6(1), (7), 7(1) and (2).[60] These records must relate to each worker employed and must be kept for a minimum of two years from the date that they were made.[61]

7.4.5 Time off

Regulation 8 imposes a general obligation on an employer to give workers adequate rest breaks where the pattern of work is such that the health and safety of the individuals may be put at risk, in particular if the work is monotonous or its rate is predetermined. Apart from this general obligation on an employer, regs. 10–17 Working Time Regulations 1998 give the worker a number of specific entitlements to different types of breaks. These are entitlements only and there is no obligation upon the worker to take advantage of them.[62]

7.4.6 Daily rest periods and rest breaks

According to reg. 10(1) Working Time Regulations 1998, an adult worker is entitled to a rest period of at least 11 consecutive hours in each 24-hour period during which the person works for the employer.[63] The 24-hour period rather than an 11 hours per day rule means that, if necessary, the 11 hours can be over two working days. There is special provision for young workers who are entitled to a rest period of 12 consecutive hours in any 24-hour period that

---

[58] Regulation 7(6) Working Time Regulations 1998.
[59] Regulation 7(6) Working Time Regulations 1998.
[60] Maximum weekly working time, length of night work, length of night work involving special hazards or strain, health assessments for adult and young workers.
[61] Regulation 9 Working Time Regulations 1998; reg. 25 excludes this requirement in relation to workers in the armed forces.
[62] On the status of official guidance see *European Commission* v *UK* [2006] IRLR 888.
[63] On the impact of periods spent 'on call' see *McCartney* v *Overley House Management* [2006] IRLR 514.

the young person works for the employer, although this period may be interrupted in the case of activities that are split up during the day or are of short duration.[64]

Additionally, where an adult worker's daily working time exceeds six hours, then the individual will be entitled to a rest break which can be spent away from the workstation if they have one.[65] This break can be agreed by a collective or workforce agreement but, in default of such an agreement, it will be for 20 minutes. In *Corps of Commissionaires Management Ltd* v *Hughes*[66] the EAT held that the entitlement was to one rest break of 20 minutes no matter how much longer than six hours the individual worked. The rules for young workers are that where their daily working time is more than four and a half hours[67] they will be entitled to a rest break of at least 30 minutes. This break should be continuous, if possible, and can be spent away from the workstation. Interestingly, and perhaps impracticably, there is a provision that where the young person works for more than one employer, then the daily working time should be aggregated for the purposes of determining the entitlement to a rest break.[68]

7.4.7 **Weekly rest periods**

Adult workers are entitled to uninterrupted rest of not less than 24 hours in each seven-day period during which they work for an employer.[69] At the employer's discretion, this can be taken as one uninterrupted period of 48 hours in each 14-day period. Young people are entitled to a rest period of not less than 48 hours in each seven-day period that they work.[70] Unlike adults, this period is not required to be uninterrupted. According to reg. 8, the period may be interrupted in the case of activities involving periods of work that are split up over the day or are of short duration and may be reduced where it is justified by technical or organisational reasons.[71]

The 7- or 14-day periods can begin on a day established by a relevant agreement. If there is no such agreement, then at the commencement of the week (or every other week) beginning at the start of the week in which employment began.[72] A week starts at midnight between Sunday and Monday.[73] Note that there is no requirement for a Sunday to be part of the rest period.

7.4.8 **Annual leave**

The Working Time Regulations 1998 introduced a statutory entitlement to paid annual holidays. In *Craig* v *Transocean Ltd*[74] the EAT noted that:

---

[64] Regulation 10(2) and (3) Working Time Regulations 1998.
[65] See *Gallagher* v *Alpha Catering Services Ltd* [2005] IRLR 102 on the difference between 'downtime' and rest breaks.
[66] [2009] IRLR 122.
[67] Note that there is no requirement for these hours to be consecutive.
[68] Regulation 12 Working Time Regulations 1998.
[69] This is not to include any rest periods to which the worker is entitled under reg. 10(1) (daily rest periods) unless justified by objective or technical reasons concerning the organisation of work: reg. 11(7) Working Time Regulations 1998.
[70] Regulation 11(1)–(3) Working Time Regulations 1998.
[71] It may not be reduced for technical or organisational reasons to less than 36 consecutive hours.
[72] Regulation 11(4) and (5) Working Time Regulations 1998.
[73] Regulation 11(6) Working Time Regulations 1998.
[74] [2009] IRLR 519.

'annual leave' (now 5.6 weeks) was not defined in either the Directive or Regulations but connoted an entitlement to be absent from work and not at the employer's disposal during that period as well as being free from all employment duties. Under the Directive it is a type of 'rest period'.

Regulation 16 Working Time Regulations 1998 specifies that a worker is entitled to be paid in respect of their annual leave. Sections 221–224 ERA 1996 apply for the purpose of determining a week's pay, except for any references to a maximum limit.[75]

The leave year begins on the date on which employment starts and subsequent anniversaries, unless otherwise fixed by a relevant agreement.[76] If a worker joins during the leave year, they have a pro rata entitlement. The leave may be taken in instalments but cannot be replaced by a payment in lieu. Any statutory leave in excess of four weeks can be carried over into the following year.[77] It should be noted that there is no statutory entitlement to bank or public holidays in addition to the leave arrangements in the Working Time Regulations 1998. Thus it is possible for an employer to count bank or public holidays against the entitlement to leave. However, a unilateral decision by one employer to reduce the hourly rate of its employees in order to assist in meeting the costs of paid holidays introduced by these regulations was held to be impermissible by the EAT.[78] In *Caulfield* v *Marshalls Products*[79] it was accepted that a contractual provision for 'rolled up' holiday pay, which identifies an express amount or percentage by way of addition to basic pay, does not infringe the regulations. According to the Court of Appeal, there is nothing in the Directive which imposes an obligation to pay workers in respect of their holiday at the time it is taken. Nevertheless, a reference was made to the ECJ for its opinion. In the subsequent case of *Robinson-Steele* v *RD Retail Ltd*,[80] the ECJ ruled that 'rolled up' holiday pay was precluded by the Directive. However, it suggested that such payments could be offset against a worker's entitlement if the employer could prove that the sums were paid transparently and comprehensibly. Thus, in *Lyddon* v *Englefield Ltd*,[81] the EAT allowed 'rolled up' holiday pay to be set off. According to the Appeal Tribunal, the fundamental question is whether there is a consensual agreement identifying a specific sum properly attributable to holiday periods.

A worker may take their leave entitlement by giving notice to the employer. This is subject to the employer being able to give notice to the worker when to take leave or not to take leave.[82] A notice given by the worker or the employer must fulfil three conditions. These are that:

1. It may relate to all or part of the leave to which the worker is entitled in a leave year.

2. It shall specify the days on which leave is to be, or not to be, taken.

3. It shall be given to the employer, or the worker, by the 'relevant date'.[83]

---

[75] See *Sanderson* v *Excel Ltd* [2006] ICR 337 and *Evans* v *Malley Ltd* [2003] IRLR 156 where a sales representative's commission payments were not included in the calculation of a week's pay.

[76] Regulation 15A Working Time Regulations 1998.

[77] See *FN* v *SDN* [2006] IRLR 561 and the Working Time (Amendment) Regulations 2007, SI 2007/2079.

[78] See *Davies* v *MJ Wyatt (Decorators) Ltd* [2000] IRLR 759.

[79] [2004] IRLR 564; see also *Smith* v *Morrisroes Ltd* [2005] IRLR 72.

[80] [2006] IRLR 386.

[81] [2008] IRLR 198.

[82] Regulation 15(1) and (2) Working Time Regulations 1998. See *Sumsion* v *BBC (Scotland)* [2007] IRLR 678 and BERR's 'Your Guide to the Working Time Regulations'.

[83] Regulation 15(3) Working Time Regulations 1998.

The 'relevant date' is a date which is twice as many days in advance of the earliest day specified in the notice as the number of days or part-days to which the notice relates. If the notice relates only to the employer requiring the worker not to take leave, then this notice needs to be given as many days in advance of the earliest day specified as the number of days or part-days to which the notice relates.[84] It should be observed that employers are not required to consult with a worker before refusing a request for leave and the whole notice period may be varied or excluded by a relevant agreement.[85] If a worker is entitled to a rest period, rest break or annual leave under the provisions of the Working Time Regulations 1998 and also has a contractual right, the worker may take advantage of whichever right is more favourable.[86]

In *Stringer* v *HM Revenue & Customs*[87] the ECJ established that the right to paid annual leave cannot be made subject to a condition that the worker has actually worked during the leave year. Thus the right continues to accrue during sick leave and, on termination of employment, a worker who has been on sick leave and unable to take paid annual leave is entitled to payment in lieu. More generally, the ECJ stated that the Directive does not preclude national legislation prohibiting workers on sickness absence from taking paid annual leave during that absence, provided they can exercise their right during another period. Equally, national legislation could allow workers on sickness absence to take paid annual leave during this absence. Subsequently the ECJ has ruled that workers who are off sick must be allowed to carry over their holiday even if that is to a different leave year.[88]

7.4.9 Special cases

Regulation 19 excludes those employed as domestic servants in a private household from the provisions on the maximum working week and those concerning night work and health assessments for night workers.

Those whose working day is not measured or predetermined or decide their own hours are also excluded.[89] Examples of this last category are managing executives, family workers or those officiating at religious ceremonies in churches and religious communities. Also excluded are those who partly decide their own hours and partly have them determined for them. This group only have that part of their work which is predetermined counting for the purposes of the Working Time Regulations 1998, which seems to undermine the protection afforded.

There are a number of situations, in addition to the other exclusions, to which the regulations on night work, daily rest periods and weekly rest periods do not apply.[90] These exclusions are subject to compensatory rest periods being given.[91] There are six such situations:

1. Where the worker's activities are such that the place of work and the place of residence are distant from each other, or there are different places of work which are distant from each other.

---

[84] Regulation 15(4) Working Time Regulations 1998.
[85] Regulation 15(5) and (6) Working Time Regulations 1998. See *Lyons* v *Mitie Security Ltd* [2010] IRLR 288.
[86] Regulation 17 Working Time Regulations 1998.
[87] [2009] IRLR 214.
[88] *Pereda* v *Madrid Movilidad SA* [2009] IRLR 959.
[89] Regulation 20 Working Time Regulations 1998.
[90] Regulation 21 Working Time Regulations 1998.
[91] Regulation 24 Working Time Regulations 1998.

2. Where the worker is engaged in security and surveillance operations, requiring a permanent presence to protect property and persons. Examples of this may be security guards or caretakers.

3. Where the worker's activities require continuity of service or production. This results in a large number of exceptions.[92]

4. Where there is a foreseeable surge in activity, such as in agriculture, tourism and the postal services.

5. Where the worker's activities are affected by unusual and unforeseeable circumstances, exceptional events, accidents or the imminent risk of accidents.

6. Where people work in railway transport and their activities are intermittent, they spend their working time on board trains or their activities are limited to transport timetables and to ensuring the continuity and regularity of traffic.

Regulation 22 provides that shift workers changing shift are excluded from the provisions on daily and weekly rest periods when it is not possible for them to take such rest between those shifts.[93] Neither do these rest periods apply to workers whose activities involve work split up over the course of the day. An example of this may be cleaning staff.[94] In addition the rules about daily rest periods and rest breaks for young workers[95] can be varied if the employer requires a young person to undertake work for which there is no adult available[96] and the need is the result of unusual or unforeseeable circumstances beyond the employer's control or occasioned by exceptional events which could not have been foreseen. The need for the young person's services must also be immediate and of a temporary nature. In such circumstances the worker is entitled to compensatory rest to be taken within the following three weeks.

7.4.10 Relevant agreements

Regulation 2(1) defines 'relevant agreement' as a

> workforce agreement which applies to him, any provision of a collective agreement which forms part of a contract between him and his employer, or any other agreement in writing which is legally enforceable as between the worker and the employer.

The term is therefore an umbrella one which includes collective and workforce agreements as well as any other written agreements such as a contract of employment. A collective agreement is one within the meaning of s. 178 TULRCA 1992 and is an agreement between an employer and an independent trade union within the meaning of s. 5 of that Act.[97] In a

---

[92] Regulation 21(c) Working Time Regulations 1998 states that this is in relation to services provided by hospitals, residential establishments and prisons; work at docks or airports; press, radio, television, cinema, postal and telecommunications services and civil protection services; gas, water and electricity production, transmission and distribution; household refuse collection; industries that cannot be interrupted on technical grounds; research and development; agriculture.

[93] Regulation 25(2) and (3) Working Time Regulations 1998 also exclude, subject to compensatory rest, young workers serving in the armed forces.

[94] Regulation 22(1)(c) Working Time Regulations 1998.

[95] As in regs. 10(2) and 12(4) Working Time Regulations 1998.

[96] Regulation 27 Working Time Regulations 1998.

[97] Regulation 2(1) Working Time Regulations 1998.

move opposed by the TUC but supported by the CBI, the 1998 Regulations introduced the concept of workforce agreements, the requirements for which are set out in Sch. 1 (see Chapter 9). The importance of these requirements is that reg. 23 provides that collective or workforce agreements may modify or exclude the application of certain regulations. These are:

- Regulation 4 – the possible extension of the reference period to a maximum of 52 weeks.
- Regulation 6 – length of night work.
- Regulations 10, 11 and 12 – minimum daily and weekly rest periods and breaks in relation to adult workers.

Regulation 24 provides for compensatory rest when rest periods or breaks are excluded or modified.

7.4.11 Enforcement

The provisions of the Working Time Regulations 1998 which impose obligations upon employers[98] are generally to be enforced by the Health and Safety Executive.[99] An employer who fails to comply with any one of the relevant requirements will be guilty of an offence and subject to a fine. The Health and Safety Executive has wide powers for their inspectors to enter premises and investigate and it is an offence to obstruct them in their investigations.[100]

A worker may present a complaint to an employment tribunal relating to an employer's refusal to permit the exercise of those parts of the Working Time Regulations 1998 which provide entitlements,[101] or an employer's refusal to pay for all or any part of the annual leave.[102] The complaint must be presented within three months, or such further period as the tribunal considers reasonable, beginning with the date on which the exercise of the right should have been permitted or payment made.[103] Where the employment tribunal finds such a complaint well founded, it will make a declaration and award compensation or order the employer to pay the worker the amount the tribunal finds is due to the individual. The amount of compensation will be such as the employment tribunal finds just and equitable and will take into account the employer's default in refusing to permit the worker to exercise the right and any loss sustained by the worker in relation to the matters complained of.[104]

Any agreements to exclude or limit the operation of the regulations, including limiting the right of a worker to bring proceedings before an employment tribunal, will be void unless

---

[98] Regulations 4(2) (48-hour week), 6(2) and (7) (night work and special hazards), 7(1), (2) and (6) (health assessment provisions), 8 (pattern of work) and 9 (record keeping).

[99] Regulation 28(2) Working Time Regulations 1998; although, in relation to workers employed in those premises for which local authorities are responsible, by the Health and Safety Commission issuing guidance to the local authorities.

[100] See reg. 29 Working Time Regulations 1998 referring to parts of s. 33(1) HASAWA 1974.

[101] These are the provisions concerning daily and weekly rest periods, rest breaks and annual leave.

[102] Regulation 30 Working Time Regulations 1998. In *HM Revenue & Customs* v *Stringer* [2009] IRLR 677, the House of Lords held that a failure to pay holiday pay can also constitute an unauthorised deduction from wages under ERA 1996 (see 7.6.1 below).

[103] In *Miles* v *Linkage Ltd* [2008] IRLR 60, which involved the denial of rest periods, the EAT decided that the period of default begins when the employer refuses to permit the exercise of the right rather than when the employee starts the relevant working pattern.

[104] Regulation 30(3)–(5) Working Time Regulations 1998.

it results from action taken by an ACAS conciliation officer under s. 18 Employment Tribunals Act 1996 or it meets the statutory requirements for compromise agreements.[105]

7.4.12 Protection from detriment

Section 45A ERA 1996 provides that a worker has the right not to be subjected to any detriment by an act, or failure to act, by the employer on a number of grounds. These are:

1. That the worker refused, or proposed to refuse, to comply with a requirement imposed by the employer in contravention of the Working Time Regulations 1998.
2. That the worker refused, or proposed to refuse, a right conferred by the 1998 Regulations.
3. For failing to sign a workforce agreement, or any other agreement, with the employer in relation to the 1998 Regulations.
4. For performing, or proposing to perform, any of the functions or activities of an employee representative for the purpose of the 1998 Regulations.
5. That the worker brought proceedings against the employer to enforce a right conferred by the 1998 Regulations.
6. That the worker alleged that the employer had infringed such a right.

If the detriment is dismissal within the meaning of Part X ERA 1996 and the person is an employee, then those who are qualified must claim unfair dismissal rather than claiming a detriment under s. 45A. Dismissal for relying on the rights conferred by the regulations as an employee or an employee representative will be automatically unfair.[106] Otherwise a worker may complain to an employment tribunal that they have been subjected to a detriment.[107] If the claim is well founded, the tribunal will make a declaration and award compensation. If the claim relates to the termination of a worker's contract, which is not a contract of employment, then the compensation must not exceed the maximum amount that can be awarded to an employee under Part X ERA 1996.[108]

7.5 Statutory right to time off work

There are a number of reasons for which an employee is entitled to time off work, sometimes with pay. These are, apart from time off for trade union duties and activities and for being a union learning representative, contained in Part VI ERA 1996.

7.5.1 Time off for public duties

There are a large number of statutory bodies that rely on part-time contributors. This in turn is dependent upon employees obtaining leave of absence in order to take part in the

---

[105] Regulation 35 Working Time Regulations 1998; see also Chapter 4.
[106] Section 101A ERA 1996; similarly s. 105(4A) makes selection for redundancy on these grounds an unfair dismissal.
[107] Section 48(1ZA) ERA 1996. Workers must first submit a statement of grievance to their employer: see Sch. 2 paras. 6 and 9 Employment Act 2002.
[108] Section 49(5A) ERA 1996.

activities of these bodies. As a matter of public policy and to help ensure a mixture of people that reflect the make-up of the population, it must be in the interests of Government to ensure that it is possible for individuals to take time off work to perform public duties.

Section 50(1) ERA 1996 provides that an employer must permit an employee who is a Justice of the Peace to take time off during working hours to carry out any of their duties. There are no conditions as to length of service with an employer before an employee may take time off during working hours but there is no right to be paid for this activity. Working hours are defined as any time, in accordance with the contract, that the employee is required to be at work.[109] Section 50(2) describes other bodies whose members qualify for time off. These include members of a local authority,[110] a statutory tribunal, a police authority, a board of prison visitors or a prison visiting committee, a relevant health body,[111] a relevant education body,[112] the Environment Agency, Scottish Water or a Water Customer Consultation Panel. Time off in relation to these bodies is for the following purposes: (i) attendance at a meeting of the body or of any of its committees or sub-committees; (ii) the doing of something approved by the committee or body for the purpose of the discharge of the functions of the body or committee.[113] Section 50(10)(a) provides the Secretary of State with the power to add organisations to the list in order to bring attendance at their meetings and other work into these provisions.

The amount of time off that an employee is to be permitted to take is that which is reasonable having regard to all the circumstances; in particular, to how much time is required, how much the employee has already been permitted under ss. 168 and 170 TULRCA 1992,[114] and the circumstances of the employer's business and the effect of the employee's absence on the running of that business.[115] In *Borders Regional Council* v *Maule*[116] the EAT considered the situation of a school teacher who was a member of a number of public bodies, including the Borders Social Security Appeal Panel. During the previous year she had taken 22 days' leave of absence for such duties and 24 days in the year preceding that. The employer tried to regulate and limit the absences to two days a month. During one month when she had already taken two days, her request for an extra day to attend training was turned down. The EAT held that all the circumstances needed to be taken into account, including the number and frequency of other absences permitted by the employer, in order to assess whether there was a breach of the statute. The EAT also observed that where an employee was undertaking public duties to which the statute applies, there should be a discussion between the employer and the individual to establish a pattern of absences by agreement. An employee who was undertaking a number of such absences also had a duty to plan their level of commitment and produce a schedule that was reasonable in the circumstances.

An employee may present a complaint to an employment tribunal that an employer has failed to permit them to take time off. The complaint needs to be made within three months beginning with the date on which the failure occurred, unless it was not reasonably practicable

---

[109] Section 50(11) ERA 1996.
[110] Section 50(5) ERA 1996 offers a definition of a local authority.
[111] A National Health Service trust or health authority: see s. 50(8) ERA 1996.
[112] The managing or governing body of an educational establishment: see s. 50(9) ERA 1996.
[113] Section 50(3) ERA 1996.
[114] Time off for trade union duties and activities.
[115] Section 50(4) ERA 1996.
[116] [1993] IRLR 199.

to do so. If the tribunal finds the complaint well founded, then it will make a declaration to that effect and award compensation.[117] The amount of compensation will take into account the employer's default and any attributable loss suffered by the employee.[118]

7.5.2 Time off to look for work or arrange training[119]

An employee who has been given notice of dismissal by reason of redundancy is entitled to take reasonable time off during working hours[120] for the purpose of looking for new employment or making arrangements for training. This applies to those who have two years' continuous service at the time the notice was due to expire or would have expired if given in accordance with s. 86(1) ERA 1996.[121]

An employee who has time off under s. 52 ERA 1996 is entitled to be paid at the appropriate hourly rate. The hourly rate is arrived at by taking the amount of one week's pay divided by the number of normal working hours for that employee under the contract in force at the time notice of dismissal was given. If the working hours vary from week to week, then the average over a 12-week period, ending with the last complete week before the day on which notice is given, is taken.[122]

If the employer unreasonably refuses to allow an employee to take time off, the latter is entitled to make a complaint to an employment tribunal within three months of the date on which time off should have been given. The tribunal, if it finds the complaint well founded, may make a declaration and order the employer to pay an amount equal to the remuneration the individual would have received if they had taken the time off, provided that this does not exceed 40 per cent of a week's pay for the employee concerned.[123]

7.5.3 Time off for ante-natal care

A pregnant employee is entitled to time off during working hours if she has, on the advice of a registered medical practitioner, a registered midwife or a registered health visitor, made an appointment for the purposes of receiving ante-natal care. The woman may be required to produce a certificate from one of the above stating that she is pregnant as well as an appointment card or some other document showing that an appointment has been made.[124] This evidence is not required for the first appointment during the pregnancy. A woman is entitled to be paid by her employer during the period of absence from work.[125] It is important that pregnant women are not treated less favourably than others in the period before maternity leave begins. In *Pederson* v *Kvickly Save*[126] Danish employees absent from work through pregnancy-related sickness prior to their maternity leave were paid less than other workers

---

[117] It may not make conditions about what time off an individual may be permitted to have in the future: see *Corner* v *Buckinghamshire County Council* [1978] IRLR 320.

[118] Section 51 ERA 1996.

[119] Section 52 ERA 1996.

[120] Defined in the same way as for time off for public duties: see s. 52(3) ERA 1996.

[121] This provides for minimum levels of notice to be given.

[122] Section 53(1)–(3) ERA 1996.

[123] Sections 53(4), (5) and 54 ERA 1996.

[124] Section 55(1)–(2) ERA 1996.

[125] Section 56(1) ERA 1996.

[126] Case C-66/96 [1999] IRLR 55 ECJ.

who were absent for non-pregnancy-related illnesses. The ECJ held that to treat pregnant women in this way was contrary to art. 141 EC (now 157) and the Equal Pay Directive and thus discriminatory.

If time off is refused or if the employer fails to pay the whole or any part of any amount to which the employee is entitled, then the latter may complain to an employment tribunal. This claim must be made within three months of the appointment, or longer if an employment tribunal is satisfied that it was not reasonably practicable for the complaint to be presented within the three-month deadline. The tribunal may award compensation equivalent to the amount that the woman would have received if she had taken the time off, or an amount equal to the non-payment or underpayment of remuneration due.[127]

7.5.4 Time off for dependants

Clause 3 of the Framework Agreement on parental leave[128] states:

> Member States and/or management and labour shall take the necessary measures to entitle workers to time off from work, in accordance with national legislation, collective agreements and/or practice, on grounds of *force majeure* for urgent family reasons in cases of sickness or accident making the immediate presence of the worker indispensable.

The provisions implementing this are contained in ss. 57A and 57B ERA 1996.[129] They permit an employee to take a 'reasonable' amount of time off during working hours to deal with specified emergencies in relation to designated people. No definition of the word 'reasonable' is offered in the legislation and it is likely that the reasonableness of the amount of time taken off will vary according to circumstances.

There is no indication in the statutory provisions as to whether this time off should be with or without pay. There is also no requirement to keep records of the time off taken by employees. However, employers might feel that it is wise to do so because such records might be of assistance in showing that the amount of time taken was reasonable or not.

Section 57A ERA 1996 refers to employees being permitted to take a reasonable amount of time off 'in order to take action which is necessary'. *Royal Bank of Scotland plc v Harrison*[130] involved a mother who worked three days a week and cared for two young children. She learned on 8 December that her regular child-minder would not be able to care for her children on 22 December. When her attempts to make alternative arrangements failed she asked to take one day's leave. This was turned down but she took it anyway. The question for the EAT was whether an event that was known about and would not happen for another two weeks could be called 'unexpected'. The Appeal Tribunal held that the word 'unexpected' did not necessarily require the event to be sudden or an emergency so Ms Harrison was covered by the legislation.

Generally the right is for the care of dependants, although this is given a generous meaning in the statute. For these purposes dependants are: a spouse; a child; a parent; a person who lives in the same household as the employee and is not employed by the employee, tenant, lodger or boarder; any person who reasonably relies on the employee either for assistance on

---

[127] Sections 56–57 ERA 1996.
[128] See Chapter 8.
[129] Added to the ERA 1996 by Sch. 4 Part II ERELA 1999.
[130] [2009] IRLR 28.

an occasion when the person falls ill or is injured or assaulted, or relies on the employee to make arrangements for the provision of care in the event of illness or injury. Section 57A(6) also makes it clear that illness or injury in the above definitions includes mental conditions.

7.5.4.1 Situations which qualify

The ERA 1996 specifies the following situations which entitle the employee to time off:[131]

1. to provide assistance when a dependant falls ill, gives birth or is injured or assaulted;
2. to make provision for the care of a dependant when they fall ill or are injured;
3. as a result of the death of a dependant;[132]
4. to deal with unexpected disruption or termination of care arrangements made for a dependant; and
5. to deal with any incidents involving a child of the employee whilst at school.

The DBIS has given examples of situations that are likely to qualify. For example, when a dependant falls ill or has been involved in an accident or assaulted, including where the victim is hurt or distressed rather than injured physically, or when a partner is having a baby, or to make longer-term care arrangements for a dependant who is ill or injured.

It is clear that the Government's view was that such a right to time off should be linked to genuine emergencies, rather than a need to deal with more mundane domestic issues, for example, awaiting the arrival of a plumber to carry out repairs. During the report stage of the Employment Relations Bill, Lord Sainsbury stated on behalf of the Government:

> The statutory right will be restricted to urgent cases of real need. The emergency must involve a dependant who is either a family member or someone who relies upon the employee for assistance in the particular circumstances.

He then gave some examples of what the right to time off was intended to cover:

> We intend the right to apply where a dependant becomes sick or has an accident, or is assaulted, including where the victim is distressed rather than physically injured . . . reasonable time off if an employee suffers a bereavement of a family member, to deal with the consequences of that bereavement . . .
>
> Employees will be able to take time off in the event of the unexpected absence of the carer, where the person is a dependant of the employee. So if the childminder or nurse does not turn up, the employee will be able to sort things out without fearing reprisals at work . . .
>
> Employees may have to take time off to attend to a problem arising at their children's school or during school hours . . .
>
> A father will have the right to be on hand at the birth of his child . . .[133]

The ERA 1996 gives no indication about the length of time that should be permitted. It is likely to vary according to the type of incident and the only condition is that the employee is entitled to a 'reasonable' period of time off work. There will clearly be difficulties for employers in defining what is reasonable and whether each incident needs to be looked at on its merits or whether one can take into account the number of absences taken by an employee.

---

[131] Section 57A(1) ERA 1996.
[132] See *Foster* v *Cartwright Black* [2004] IRLR 781.
[133] HL Report stage, HL Deb, 8 July 1999, cols 1083–1089.

7.5.4.2 **Notice requirements**

Employees qualify for time off to deal with these emergencies if they tell their employer the reason for the absence and how long they plan to be away as soon as is reasonably practicable.[134] Failure to allow an employee time off may result in a complaint to an employment tribunal. The employee must claim within three months beginning with the date when the refusal occurred or longer if the tribunal considers that it was not reasonably practicable to do so.[135] If the tribunal upholds the complaint it must make a declaration to that effect and may award compensation. The amount will take into account the circumstances surrounding the employer's refusal and any loss sustained by the employee.[136]

7.5.4.3 **Protection from detriment and dismissal**

According to reg. 19 Maternity and Parental Leave etc. Regulations 1999, an employee is entitled not to be subjected to any detriment[137] by any act, or failure to act, by the employer for taking time off under s. 57A ERA 1996. Additionally, an employee who is sacked when the reason (or the principal reason) for the dismissal is taking time off under s. 57A ERA 1996 will be regarded as unfairly dismissed.

Similarly, if an employee is dismissed for reasons of redundancy and it is shown that the circumstances constituting the redundancy applied equally to one or more employees in the same business holding similar positions who have not been made redundant, and the reason (or principal reason) for the employee being selected for dismissal was connected with taking time off under s. 57A ERA 1996, the dismissal will be unfair.

In *Qua v John Ford Morrison Solicitors*[138] the claimant was a single mother whose young son had medical problems. As a result she was away from work for 17 days until she was dismissed ten months after her employment started. According to the EAT, s. 57A(1)(a) ERA 1996 is dealing with something unforeseen and does not allow employees to take time off in order to provide care themselves beyond the reasonable amount necessary to enable them to deal with the immediate crisis.[139] To determine whether action is 'necessary', factors to be taken into account include: the nature of the incident; the closeness of the relationship between the employee and the dependant; and the extent to which anyone else was available to assist. However, the EAT thought that for these purposes the inconvenience caused to the employer's business was irrelevant.

7.5.5 **Time off for pension scheme trustees**[140]

Employees who are trustees of the employer's 'relevant occupational pension scheme'[141] must be permitted time off during working hours[142] for the purpose of: (i) performing any of the

---

[134] Section 57A(2) ERA 1996. See *Truelove* v *Safeway* [2005] IRLR 589.
[135] Section 57B(2) ERA 1996.
[136] Section 57B(4) ERA 1996.
[137] See s. 47C ERA 1996.
[138] [2003] IRLR 184.
[139] Section 57A(1)(b) ERA 1996 permits reasonable time off to make longer-term arrangements for care.
[140] Sections 58–60 ERA 1996.
[141] Relevant occupational pension scheme is one defined in s. 1 Pensions Act 1993 and established under trust: s. 58(3)(a) ERA 1996.
[142] Working hours is any time, in accordance with the contract of employment, that the employee is required to be at work: s. 58(4) ERA 1996.

duties of a trustee; (ii) undergoing training relevant to the performance of those duties.[143] The amount of time off and any conditions attached to it must be reasonable having regard to how much time is required for the performance of the duties or training, as well as the circumstances of the business and the effect of the employee's absence on the running of that business.

An employer who permits an employee to take time off under s. 58 ERA 1996 must pay the employee for the time taken off, for which permission had been given, as if they had been at work. If the remuneration for the work which they would normally be doing varies with the amount of work done, the employee must be paid by calculating the average hourly earnings.[144] An employee may make a complaint to an employment tribunal that there has been a failure to allow time off or to pay for it within three months beginning with the date when the failure occurred, unless the tribunal decides it was not reasonably practicable. The tribunal may make a declaration and award compensation to be paid. Again the amount will depend on the extent of the employer's default and any attributable loss suffered by the employee.

7.5.6 Time off for employee representatives[145]

In certain circumstances, an employee elected for the purpose of representing employees in discussions with the employer has a statutory right to be paid reasonable time off during working hours for the purpose of carrying out the functions of a representative. Section 61 ERA 1996 provides that the employee representatives with whom an employer should consult when proposing collective redundancies[146] and a transfer of an undertaking[147] are entitled to time off. Candidates for election as employee representatives also have such an entitlement. Similarly the Transnational Information and Consultation of Employees Regulations 1999 (TICE Regulations 1999)[148] provide that an employee who is a member of a Special Negotiating Body, a member of a European Works Council, an information and consultation representative, or a candidate in an election for any of these, is also entitled to reasonable time off with pay. Working hours are any time that the employee is required to be at work in accordance with his contract.[149]

Employee representatives or candidates for election are entitled to be paid at the appropriate hourly rate for the time off. This rate is a week's pay divided by the normal working hours specified in the contract in force on the day that leave is taken. Where there are no normal working hours or the number of hours varies, then the average over a 12-week period is taken. Where an employee has been employed for less than 12 weeks, then reference is made to the normal working hours of other employees of the same employer in comparable employment.[150]

---

[143] Training can be on the employer's premises or elsewhere: s. 58(3)(c) ERA 1996.

[144] The average hourly earnings of the employee or of persons in comparable employment with the same employer; if none of these, then an average figure which is reasonable in the circumstances: s. 59(4) ERA 1996.

[145] Sections 61–63 ERA 1996.

[146] See Part IV Chapter II TULRCA 1992.

[147] See regs. 10 and 11 Transfer of Undertakings (Protection of Employment) Regulations 1981, SI 1981/1794.

[148] SI 1999/3323 regs. 25–27; see Chapter 9.

[149] Section 61(2) ERA 1996; reg. 25(2) TICE Regulations 1999.

[150] Section 62 ERA 1996; reg. 26 TICE Regulations 1999.

An employee may make a complaint to an employment tribunal that the employer unreasonably refused time off or failed to pay the whole or part of the remuneration to which the individual was entitled. The complaint must be made within three months of the day when time off should have been permitted, unless it was not reasonably practicable to do so. If the tribunal finds the complaint well founded, then it must make a declaration to this effect and order the employer to pay the employee an amount equal to that which would have been paid if the time off had been permitted. Where the complaint is about non-payment, the employer will be required to pay the amount due to the employee.[151]

7.5.7 Time off for a young person for study or training[152]

Certain employees are entitled to time off with pay during working hours for the purpose of undertaking study or training leading to a relevant qualification. If the employee is someone supplied to another employer (the principal) to work in accordance with a contract between the employer and the principal, then the obligations under the regulations fall upon the principal.[153] The employee must: (i) be 16 or 17 years of age; (ii) not be receiving full-time secondary[154] or further[155] education; and (iii) not have attained such standard of achievement as is prescribed by regulations made by the Secretary of State.[156] A 'relevant' qualification is an external[157] qualification which would contribute to the attainment of the standard prescribed in the regulations issued by the Secretary of State and would be likely to enhance the individual's employment prospects (whether with their employer or otherwise). Where an employee is 18 years of age and began study or training leading to a relevant qualification before that age, then the provisions as described continue to apply.[158]

The amount of time to be permitted needs to be reasonable in all the circumstances, taking into account the requirements of the employee's study or training, the circumstances of the business of the employer or the principal and the effect of the time off on the running of the business.[159] Pay is to be at the appropriate hourly rate. This rate is a week's pay divided by the normal working hours of the employee according to the contract in force on the day that leave is taken. Where there are no normal working hours or the number of hours varies, then the average over a 12-week period is taken. If an employee has been employed for less than 12 weeks, then reference is made to the normal working hours of other employees of the same employer with relevant comparable employment.[160]

An employee may make a complaint to an employment tribunal that the employer or principal unreasonably refused time off or failed to pay the whole or part of the remuneration to which the employee was entitled. The complaint must be made within three months

---

[151] Section 63 ERA 1996; reg. 27 TICE Regulations 1999.
[152] Sections 63A–63C ERA 1996.
[153] Section 63A(3) ERA 1996.
[154] Secondary as in the Education Act 1996.
[155] Further as described in Sch. 2 Further and Higher Education Act 1992.
[156] Right to Time Off for Study or Training Regulations 2001, SI 2001/2801; reg. 3 specifies standards of achievement.
[157] An external qualification is an academic or vocational qualification awarded or authenticated by a body as specified by the Secretary of State in the Schedule to reg. 4 Right to Time Off for Study or Training Regulations.
[158] Section 63A(4) ERA 1996.
[159] Section 63A(5) ERA 1996.
[160] Section 63B ERA 1996.

of the day when time off should have been permitted, unless it was not reasonably practicable to do so. If the tribunal finds the complaint well founded, it must make a declaration to this effect and order the employer or principal to pay the employee an amount equal to that which would have been paid if the time off had been permitted, or, if the complaint is about not being paid, order the employer or principal to pay the amount due to the employee.[161]

Since April 2010 employees in organisations with 250 or more employees have had a new right to request time off to undertake training. This is modelled on the flexible working provisions (see Chapter 8) which means that employers must consider requests seriously but can refuse time off if there is a good reason for doing so.[162]

7.5.8 Time off for trade union duties, activities and union learning representatives

Sections 168–170 TULRCA 1992 provide that an employer must permit officials and members of independent trade unions, recognised by the employer, to take time off during working hours for the purpose of carrying out the duties[163] of, or taking part in the activities of, the trade union.[164] There is a distinction between carrying out union duties and carrying out union activities. The former relates to duties carried out by officials, whilst the latter is concerned with the activities of union members. The statutory provisions allowing trade union officials a right to a reasonable amount of time off with pay to carry out their trade union duties and to undergo trade union training originated in the Employment Protection Act 1975. The right for an employee who is an official of an independent trade union recognised by the employer to take time off during working hours[165] is now contained in s. 168 TULRCA 1992. Official means either an officer[166] of the union, or of a branch or section of the union, or a person elected or appointed to be a representative of the members or some of them.[167] The right is to enable the official to carry out duties relating to the following:

1. Those duties concerned with negotiations or matters related to collective bargaining[168] for which the trade union is recognised by the employer.[169] This appears to be a test of proximity, i.e. to what extent are the duties undertaken by the official related to negotiations or collective bargaining. In *Adlington* v *British Bakeries*,[170] union officials wanted time off to attend a workshop on Government proposals to repeal 1954 legislation which regulated working

---

[161] Section 63C ERA 1996.

[162] Part VIA ERA 1996.

[163] This includes accompanying workers, at their request, to disciplinary and grievance hearings: see s. 10(7) ERELA 1999.

[164] The employee needs to ensure that a request for time off has been made and that the employer has refused the request, ignored it or failed to respond before they can establish a right to compensation: see *Ryford Ltd* v *Drinkwater* [1996] IRLR 16.

[165] Working hours are those hours when, in accordance with the contract of employment, the individual is required to be at work: s. 173(1) TULRCA 1992.

[166] Officer means any member of the governing body of a trade union or any trustee of any fund applicable for the purposes of the union: s. 119 TULRCA 1992.

[167] Section 119 TULRCA 1992.

[168] Section 168(2) TULRCA 1992. See *Beal* v *Beecham Group Ltd* [1982] IRLR 192 CA where duties connected with collective bargaining were held to include duties in preparation for that bargaining. See also *London Ambulance Service* v *Charlton* [1992] IRLR 510.

[169] See s. 178 TULRCA 1992 and Chapter 11.

[170] [1989] IRLR 218 CA.

hours, etc. The employer had agreed to give them time off but not with pay. The Court of Appeal held that the proximity of meetings to actual negotiations was a matter of degree and therefore a question of fact. In this case the purpose of the workshop was to acquaint union representatives with the implications of repeal, which would lead to negotiations, rather than any attempt to prevent the repeal. In contrast, an unofficial preparatory meeting of shop stewards was held to be outside the scope of the statute. It was not convened or authorised by the union, neither did the union ask that its shop stewards be given leave to attend.[171]

2. Those duties[172] connected with the performance, on behalf of the employees, of functions related to collective bargaining matters to which the employer has agreed. Section 199 TULRCA 1992 provides that ACAS has a duty to provide practical guidance on the time off to be permitted by an employer.[173] Paragraph 9 of the ACAS Code of Practice gives a number of examples of trade union duties for which time off should be given. These include functions connected with terms and conditions of employment, matters of discipline and the machinery for negotiation or consultation. However, time off to attend a conference about collecting information from employers may not fall within the terms of the legislation where there is already a means for obtaining that information.[174]

3. Those duties[175] concerned with the receipt of information from the employer and consultation by the employer concerning collective redundancies and transfers of undertakings.[176]

4. For the purpose of undergoing training in industrial relations.[177] This training needs to be relevant to the carrying out of the duties for which recognition is given and needs to be approved by the TUC or the union of which the individual is an official. Paragraph 24 of the ACAS Code of Practice gives examples of the types of training that might be included, such as the structure of the union or the role of the official. Paragraph 26 of this Code also makes it clear that an official will be more effective if they possess the skills and knowledge that might come from this training.

The time off for officials is with pay on the basis that the individual should receive what they would have earned if they had worked during the time off.[178] The guidance given by ACAS[179] on this subject is that there is no statutory requirement to pay for time off where training is undertaken at a time when the official would not normally have been at work. This was a problem especially for union officials who were part-time employees or worked shifts because they appeared to be excluded from receiving pay for union duties during the hours when they were not at work. In *Hairsine* v *Kingston-upon-Hull City Council*[180] a swimming pool attendant was a shop steward who worked a shift system. The employee was given time off with pay to attend a training course, only some of which clashed with the working hours.

---

[171] *Ashley* v *Ministry of Defence* [1984] IRLR 57, where, in addition, a union/MOD advisory committee was held to be too remote from the actual negotiations.
[172] Section 168(2)(b) TULRCA 1992.
[173] ACAS Code of Practice on Time Off for Trade Union Duties and Activities 2009.
[174] See *Depledge* v *Pye Telecommunications Ltd* [1981] ICR 82.
[175] Section 168(2)(c) TULRCA 1992.
[176] Section 188 TULRCA 1992 and Transfer of Undertakings (Protection of Employment) Regulations 2006, SI 2006/246; see Chapter 9.
[177] Section 168(2) TULRCA 1992.
[178] Section 169 TULRCA 1992.
[179] Paragraph 19 the Code of Practice.
[180] [1992] IRLR 211.

This individual was unable to substitute the daytime hours spent on the course for the evening shift hours they were expected to work. However, part-timers are more likely to be protected.[181] *Davies v Neath Port Talbot Borough Council*[182] concerned a council employee who worked a 22-hour week. The individual was a health and safety representative who was given time off to attend two five-day courses run by the union. The employer agreed to pay for the usual working hours, not the 40 and 32$\frac{1}{2}$ hours actually spent on the courses. In these circumstances the employee made an equal pay claim under art. 119 EEC (now 157). The EAT agreed that part-time workers had a right, under art. 119, to be paid on the same basis as full-timers when attending union-run courses. As the great majority of part-timers are female, to do otherwise would amount to indirect sex discrimination. The EAT concluded that s. 169(2) TULRCA 1992 which provides for the individual to be paid what they would have earned if they had been at work was, in so far as it applied to part-timers, in conflict with art. 119 and therefore could not be relied on.[183]

7.5.8.1 Taking part in trade union activities

Section 170 TULRCA 1992 provides that employees who are also members of an independent trade union recognised by the employer are entitled to time off during working hours for the purpose of taking part in any activities of the trade union or any activities in relation to which the employee is acting as a representative of the union. This right excludes time off for activities in relation to industrial action, whether or not in contemplation or furtherance of an industrial dispute.[184] There is no statutory right to pay during this period of time off. Examples of trade union activities are contained in paras. 37–38 ACAS Code of Practice. They include attending workplace meetings to discuss and vote on the outcome of negotiations or voting in union elections. Examples of acting as a representative are attending branch, area or regional meetings of the union to discuss union business or attending meetings of official policy-making bodies, such as the union's annual conference. In some way the activity needs to be linked to the employment relationship and the union. Thus a TUC lobby of Parliament against an Education Reform Bill was not an activity which entitled a number of teachers, who were members of the National Union of Teachers, to time off under s. 170 TULRCA 1992. Such a lobby was to express political and ideological objections to the proposed statute and was not part of the employment relationship.[185]

Sections 168(3) and 170(3) TULRCA 1992 state that the amount of time off, and the purposes for which it is taken, should be 'reasonable in all the circumstances' having regard to the relevant provisions of the ACAS Code of Practice. In *Wignall v British Gas Corporation*[186] the EAT held that each application need not be looked at in isolation. It would be reasonable for an employer, when considering a request for time off, to consider this in the light of time off already taken. The Code states that trade unions should be aware of the variety of difficulties for employers and take into account the size of the organisation, the number of workers, the production process, the need to maintain a service to the public and the need for safety

---

[181] See the Part-time Workers (Prevention of Less Favourable Treatment) Regulations 2000 (Chapter 2 above).

[182] [1999] IRLR 769.

[183] The EAT also refused to follow *Manor Bakeries v Nazir* [1996] IRLR 604, which had held that attendance at a union conference was not 'work' under art. 119.

[184] Section 170(2) TULRCA 1992; see Chapter 11.

[185] *Luce v London Borough of Bexley* [1990] IRLR 422.

[186] [1984] IRLR 493.

and security at all times. Equally, employers should be aware of the difficulties for trade unions in ensuring effective representation for a variety of workers, such as those who are shift workers, part-timers, employed at dispersed locations and workers with particular domestic commitments.[187] Trade union officials and members requesting time off should give as much notice as possible, giving details of the purpose of the time off, the intended location and the timing and duration of the time off.[188]

The remedy for employees is to present a complaint to an employment tribunal.[189] The claim needs to be made within three months of the date when the failure occurred, unless the tribunal finds that it was not reasonably practicable to do so.[190] If the tribunal finds the complaint well founded, it may make a declaration and award compensation. This compensation will be such as the tribunal decides is just and equitable and will take into account any losses suffered by the employee as a result of the employer's actions, including unpaid wages.[191]

7.5.8.2 Union learning representatives

Section 168A(1) TULRCA provides that an employee who is a member of an independent trade union recognised by the employer, must be given time off with pay to perform the duties of being a union learning representative (ULR).[192] The employer has this obligation if notice has been received from the trade union that the employee is a ULR and has undergone (or will undergo) sufficient training for the role.[193] The employee is also to be permitted time off to undergo training for the role.[194]

The functions of a ULR are, in relation to members of the trade union and others, to:

1. analyse learning or training needs;

2. provide information about learning or training matters;

3. arrange learning or training; and

4. promote the value of learning or training.

This will include consultations with the employer about carrying out these activities and any necessary preparations.[195]

7.6 Protection of wages

One major aspect of the relationship between the worker and the employer is payment for the work carried out, or time spent at the employer's disposal. Section 27 ERA 1996 provides a statutory definition of the meaning of wages etc. Wages include any fee, bonus,[196]

---

[187] Paragraph 45 ACAS Code of Practice.
[188] Paragraph 50 ACAS Code of Practice.
[189] Sections 168(4), 169(5) and 170(4) TULRCA 1992.
[190] Section 171 TULRCA 1992.
[191] Section 172 TULRCA 1992; see *Skiggs* v *South West Trains Ltd* [2005] IRLR 459.
[192] Paras 28–33 of the ACAS Code of Practice on Time Off for Trade Union Duties and Activities provides guidance on time off for union learning representatives.
[193] Section 168A(3) TULRCA 1992.
[194] Section 168A(7) TULRCA 1992.
[195] Section 168A(2) TULRCA 1992.
[196] In *Farrell Matthews and Weir* v *Hansen* [2005] IRLR 160 the EAT held that an employee suffered an unlawful deduction when the employer refused to pay the balance of a non-contractual discretionary bonus which was payable in monthly instalments. See now *Small* v *Boots plc* [2009] IRLR 328.

commission,[197] holiday pay,[198] or other emolument relating to the employment, whether or not payable under the worker's contract. It can also include statutory sick pay[199] and statutory maternity pay.[200]

7.6.1 Unauthorised deductions

Workers have a right not to suffer deductions of pay by their employer, unless the deduction is authorised by statute,[201] a relevant provision of the worker's contract or by the worker previously signifying their agreement in writing.[202] A 'relevant provision' of a contract is a term of the contract which has been notified to the worker prior to the employer making the deduction.[203] In *Kerr* v *The Sweater Shop (Scotland) Ltd*[204] it was held that an individual need not agree in writing to the deduction because it was possible for consent to be given through continuing to work once the change had been brought to the individual's attention.

The deduction in wages is to be treated as the difference between the amount owed to the worker[205] and the amount actually paid.[206] This can be calculated on each occasion that wages are paid. Thus where a person receives a regular salary, each occasion that the salary is paid can be considered for the purposes of whether there has been an unlawful deduction of wages.[207] The conditions that must be satisfied in order to show that workers have given their consent to deductions are: (i) there must be a document which clearly states that the deductions are to be made from wages; (ii) it must be clear that the worker agrees to the deduction.[208]

Section 14 ERA 1996 provides a list of deductions which are excluded from s. 13 ERA 1996.[209] These are if the deduction is:

1. A reimbursement of overpayment of wages or expenses[210] paid by the employer.[211]

2. Made as a result of disciplinary proceedings resulting from a statutory provision.[212]

---

[197] See *Kent Management Services Ltd* v *Butterfield* [1992] IRLR 394, which held that the withholding of commission was an unlawful deduction, even though the commission might be on a discretionary and non-contractual basis.

[198] See *HMRC* v *Stringer* [2009] IRLR 677 (H/L).

[199] See *Taylor Gordon Ltd* v *Timmons* [2004] IRLR 180.

[200] For a full list of what is included and excluded see s. 27 ERA 1996.

[201] For example, income tax and national insurance contributions.

[202] Section 13(1) ERA 1996; s. 15(1) ERA 1996 is similarly concerned with the rights of employees not to have to make payments to an employer.

[203] Section 13(2) ERA 1996; 'to the worker' means some written notification, not just the displaying of a notice; see *Kerr* v *The Sweater Shop (Scotland) Ltd* [1996] IRLR 424; also see s. 15(2) on 'relevant provision' concerning the right not to have to make payments to an employer.

[204] [1996] IRLR 424.

[205] This can be what is 'properly payable' in terms of employee expectations.

[206] Section 13(3) ERA 1996.

[207] See *Murray* v *Strathclyde Regional Council* [1992] IRLR 396, where a deduction in one month for a series of alleged overpayments was held to be a deduction in salary in terms of the statute.

[208] See *Potter* v *Hunt Contracts* [1992] IRLR 108, which concerned the deduction of the balance of a loan made to the employee from wages due on termination of employment.

[209] Section 16 ERA 1996 provides similar exceptions concerning the right of an employee not to have to make payments to an employer.

[210] Expenses are not to be subject to too much scrutiny; if there is a profit element in expenses, this would not necessarily stop the whole amount from being expenses; it is not the tribunal's job to try to apportion sums in order to be precise about what are expenses and what are not: *London Borough of Southwark* v *O'Brien* [1996] IRLR 420.

[211] See *Murray* v *Strathclyde Regional Council* [1992] IRLR 396.

[212] It has been suggested that this provision refers not to private employers, but to such services as the police or fire service: see *Chiltern House Ltd* v *Chambers* [1990] IRLR 88.

3. As a result of a statutory requirement to deduct sums and pay them over to a public authority.[213]

4. Where there is prior contractual agreement, or other prior written agreement, for the deduction of money to be paid over to a third person, after notification by the third person of the amount owed by the worker.

5. As a result of the worker taking part in industrial action.[214]

6. A deduction, made with prior written consent of the worker, resulting from the order of a court or tribunal.

There are special provisions for dealing with cash shortages and stock deficiencies in retail employment.[215]

It is not permissible to make a complaint about a threatened deduction from wages.[216] Section 23(1) ERA 1996 states that a worker may present a complaint to an employment tribunal that the employer *has made* a deduction from wages in contravention of s. 13 ERA 1996 or received a payment in contravention of s. 15 ERA 1996.[217] The complaint must be made within three months of the date of the deduction or payment. This date is the last date on which the payment could have been made in accordance with the contract, rather than from the date when it was actually made.[218] Where the complaint relates to a series of deductions or payments, then it must be within three months of the last deduction or payment, subject to the employment tribunal being satisfied that this was not reasonably practicable.[219] If the tribunal finds the complaint well founded it may issue a declaration and order the employer to repay the unauthorised deductions or payments to the worker. It can also provide compensation for workers who suffer financial losses.[220]

A failure to make a payment in lieu of notice is unlikely to be treated as a deduction in wages, although it might amount to a breach of contract. In *Delaney v Staples t/a De Montfort Recruitment*[221] the House of Lords dealt with a case where an employee was summarily dismissed and given a cheque as payment in lieu of notice. The employer subsequently stopped the cheque, claiming that the employee had taken confidential information with her. The employee then claimed an unlawful deduction had been made from her wages. The court held that a payment in lieu was not wages where it relates to the period after employment. Wages are payments in respect of rendering services during employment. All payments relating to the termination of the contract are excluded unless expressly provided for in the legislation. However, payments paid after termination in relation to work done before the termination are wages. In *Robertson v Blackstone Franks Investment Management*

---

[213] See *Patel v Marquette Ltd* [2009] IRLR 425.

[214] See *Gill v Ford Motor Company Ltd* [2004] IRLR 840.

[215] Sections 17–22 ERA 1996.

[216] See *Mennell v Newell & Wright (Transport Contractors Ltd)* [1997] IRLR 519 CA.

[217] An employer shall not receive a payment from a worker employed by them unless it is required by statute or has the worker's prior agreement in writing.

[218] See *Group 4 Nightspeed Ltd v Gilbert* [1997] IRLR 398; also *Taylorplan Services Ltd v Jackson* [1996] IRLR 184.

[219] Section 23 ERA 1996. See *List Design Ltd v Douglas & Catley* [2003] IRLR 14.

[220] Sections 24–26 ERA 1996.

[221] [1992] IRLR 191 HL.

Ltd[222] the payment of commission earned during employment but paid after the employee had left was held to be wages within the meaning of the Act.

Any variations in contractual terms to allow deductions does not provide authorisation for a deduction until the variation takes effect.[223] If there is a variation in pay resulting from a change in work patterns permitted by the contract, then a related variation in pay may not be treated as a deduction. Thus when there is a change in shift patterns permitted by the contract which results in the payment of a lower shift premium, this could not be treated as an unauthorised deduction from wages.[224] If the contractual variation is a result of the employer's unilateral decision, then any resulting reduction in wages may contravene s. 13 ERA 1996. In *McCree* v *London Borough of Tower Hamlets*[225] the employer introduced a new bonus system which absorbed a previously paid supplement to an employee. The unilateral abolition of this supplement resulted in a breach of these provisions.[226]

Where the employer makes an error in calculating the gross amount of pay due to a worker, the shortfall is not to be treated as a deduction.[227] For these purposes, an error is not one that is based upon a misunderstanding of the law. In *Morgan* v *West Glamorgan County Council*[228] an employee was demoted for disciplinary reasons and suffered a reduction in salary. The employer wrongly thought that they had the contractual authority to do this. This was not an error in terms of s. 13(4) ERA 1996 but the result of a deliberate decision to demote and reduce salary. Thus the shortfall in salary was to be treated as a deduction for these purposes.[229]

7.6.2 Normal working hours and a week's pay

Sections 220–229 ERA 1996 define a week's pay. For such purposes as the basic award of compensation for unfair dismissal[230] and the calculation of protective awards resulting from a failure to consult in collective redundancy situations,[231] a week's pay is subject to a maximum. This was set at £380 per week in 2010.[232]

Normal working hours are usually determined by reference to the contract of employment. If the contract stipulates a minimum number of fixed hours, then those are to be taken as the normal working hours.[233] If the contract requires overtime to be worked, these may become part of the normal working hours provided that there is an obligation to work the hours and they are guaranteed by the employer.[234] It is not enough to show that an employee

---

[222] [1998] IRLR 376 CA.
[223] Section 13(5) ERA 1996.
[224] See *Hussman Manufacturing Ltd* v *Weir* [1998] IRLR 288.
[225] [1992] IRLR 56.
[226] See also *Bruce* v *Wiggins Teape (Stationery) Ltd* [1994] IRLR 536, where there was a unilateral reduction in overtime rates; the EAT stated that no distinction was to be drawn between a deduction and a reduction in wages.
[227] Section 13(4) ERA 1996.
[228] [1995] IRLR 68.
[229] See also *Yemm* v *British Steel* [1994] IRLR 117, which also concerned a mistaken belief that the employer could change contractual duties with a resulting reduction in pay.
[230] Section 119 ERA 1996.
[231] Section 190 TULRCA 1992.
[232] See s. 227(1) ERA 1996.
[233] Section 234 ERA 1996.
[234] *Tarmac Roadstone Holdings Ltd* v *Peacock* [1973] IRLR 157 CA.

regularly worked extra hours. There needs to be an obligation upon the employer to pay for the hours and a duty on the employee to carry them out. This was the case in *Lotus Cars Ltd v Sutcliffe and Stratton*[235] where employees were expected to work a 45-hour week but contractually had a basic working week of 40 hours. They were paid a premium rate for the extra five hours worked each week. The court followed *Tarmac*[236] and concluded that the element of obligation was absent for these purposes.

The calculation date depends upon the purpose of the calculation.[237] There are a number of different categories:

1. If the employee's remuneration for normal working hours does not vary with the amount done in that period, then the amount of a week's pay is the amount payable by the employer under the contract in force on the calculation date if the employee works the normal working hours.[238] There are additional rules for those who do not have regular hours or are not paid according to the time they work (see below).

2. In cases where the remuneration varies in relation to the amount of work done, remuneration will be calculated by using the average hourly rate paid by the employer in respect of the 12 weeks ending with the last complete week before the calculation date or, if the calculation date is the last day of the week, then that week. This can include those whose remuneration includes commission or similar payment which varies in amount, but will exclude overtime premium rates.[239]

3. Where the normal hours worked vary from week to week, perhaps as a result of shift work, then the amount of a week's pay is the amount of remuneration for the average number of weekly normal working hours at the average hourly rate of remuneration. The average number of hours is to be calculated by totalling the number of hours worked over the previous 12 weeks and dividing by 12.[240]

4. Where there are employments with no normal working hours, then the weekly pay will be the average weekly remuneration in the period of 12 weeks ending with the calculation date. This is the last complete week before the calculation date or, if the date is the last day of the week, then that week. No account is to be taken of weeks when there was no remuneration and, in such cases, earlier weeks will be used to bring the total to 12.[241]

5. If an employee does not have sufficient service to calculate the 12 weeks, then there are a number of factors to help in the calculation of an amount 'which fairly represents a week's pay' contained in s. 228 ERA 1996. Those employees who have maintained continuity of employment may use time served and remuneration earned with the previous employer if necessary.[242]

---

[235] [1982] IRLR 381 CA.
[236] [1973] IRLR 157 CA.
[237] See ss. 225–226 ERA 1996.
[238] Section 221(2) ERA 1996.
[239] Section 221(3)–(4) ERA 1996; see *British Coal Corporation v Cheesebrough* [1990] IRLR 148 HL.
[240] Section 222 ERA 1996; the hourly rate and calculation date is as for s. 221(3) above; if there has been no pay in any of the weeks for the purposes of ss. 221 and 222, then earlier weeks are to be used to bring the total to 12, but any overtime hours included will not take into account any premium rates paid: see s. 223.
[241] Section 224 ERA 1996.
[242] Section 229 ERA 1996.

7.6.3 **Guarantee payments**

An employee is entitled to be paid an amount by the employer for any day,[243] or part of a day, during which they would normally be required to work in accordance with the contract, and they have not been provided with work. The workless days must be as a result of:

1. a diminution in the requirements of the employer's business for work of the kind that the employee was hired to do; or

2. any other event affecting the normal working of the employer's business in relation to such work.[244]

There is a statutory maximum payable to an employee, which makes the provision of little value to many people. The maximum daily figure set in 2010 was £21.20[245] and the maximum number of days for which payment must be made is five in any three-month period.[246] This right does not, however, affect any contractual rights to payment and any such payment can be offset against the statutory requirement.[247] In practice, this provision is of most use to those who have a contract which allows them to be laid off without pay or those who are paid by the amount of work that they produce (piece workers, commission-only workers).

There are a number of exceptions to entitlement:[248]

1. An employee must have been continuously employed for at least one month ending with the day before the day for which a guarantee payment is claimed.

2. Employees are not entitled to payment for 'workless days' if the failure to be provided with work results from a strike, lock-out or other industrial action[249] involving any employee of the employer or associated employer.

3. If the employee has been offered suitable alternative work by the employer for that day and has unreasonably refused that offer.

4. If the employee has not complied with reasonable requirements of the employer ensuring the employee's availability for work.

5. Situations where there is a collective agreement or an agricultural wages order concerning guaranteed payments and the Minister to whom an application is made issues an order excluding the obligation under s. 28 ERA 1996.

An employee may complain to an employment tribunal if the employer fails to pay all or part of the entitlement. The complaint must be made within three months of the failure to pay unless the tribunal accepts that it was not reasonably practicable to do so. In the event of the tribunal finding the complaint well founded, it may order the employer to pay to the employee the amount due.[250] No sanctions are applied to an employer who fails to pay.

---

[243] Section 28(4) ERA 1996; day means the 24-hour period between midnight and midnight; see also s. 28(5) dealing with situations where the day extends through midnight.

[244] Section 28(1) ERA 1996.

[245] Section 31(1) ERA 1996.

[246] Section 31(2)–(6) ERA 1996; see s. 30 for guidance in calculating the amount due, subject to this maximum.

[247] Section 32 ERA 1996.

[248] Sections 29 and 35 ERA 1996.

[249] 'Other industrial action' is to be given its natural and ordinary meaning, e.g. it can include a refusal to work overtime: see *Faust* v *Power Packing Casemakers Ltd* [1983] IRLR 117 CA.

[250] Section 34 ERA 1996.

7.6.4 **Suspension from work on medical grounds**

Employees have the right to be paid by the employer if they are suspended from work on medical grounds.[251] A person is suspended on medical grounds if the suspension is as a result of a requirement or provision imposed under any enactment, or a recommendation in a code of practice issued or approved under s. 16 Health and Safety at Work etc. Act 1974.[252]

This suspension, with the right to remuneration, is subject to a maximum of 26 weeks. An employee is to be regarded as suspended only for as long as employment continues and the employer does not provide work or the individual does not perform the work normally performed before the suspension.[253] There is no entitlement to payment if:

1. Employees have not been continuously employed for at least one month ending with the day before the suspension begins.

2. In respect of any period during which the employee is incapable of work because of a disease or other physical or mental impairment.

3. The employee has been offered suitable alternative work and has unreasonably refused that offer.

4. The employee does not comply with reasonable requirements imposed by the employer to ensure that the employee is available for work.[254]

Complaints about a failure to pay the whole or part of the amount due may be made to an employment tribunal within three months of the failure, unless the tribunal accepts that this was not reasonably practicable. Where the tribunal finds the complaint well founded it will order the employer to make the payment. There are no provisions for any other sanctions against the employer.[255]

7.7 **National minimum wage**

Section 1(1) of the National Minimum Wage Act 1998 (NMWA 1998) places an obligation upon employers and provides that any person who qualifies should be remunerated, in any pay reference period, at a rate which is not less than the national minimum wage.[256] The pay reference period is one month, or a shorter period if the worker is paid at shorter intervals.[257] Employer is defined in s. 54 NMWA 1998 as the person by whom the employee or worker is employed, but there are provisions to ensure that a superior employer is identified as the

---

[251] Section 64(1) ERA 1996. On maternity grounds see Chapter 8.

[252] Section 64(2)–(3) ERA 1996; the Health and Safety Commission has the power to issue or approve codes of practice relating to health and safety regulations.

[253] Section 64(5) ERA 1996.

[254] Section 65 ERA 1996.

[255] Section 70(1)–(3) ERA 1996.

[256] In *Revenue and Customs Commissioners* v *Annabel's Ltd* [2008] ICR 1076 it was decided that customer tips had become the property of a 'troncmaster'. Thus the payments to employees from the tronc were not 'payments paid by the employer'.

[257] Regulation 10(1) NMW Regulations 1999, SI 1999/584; financial arrangements when a worker's contract terminates are assumed to be done in the worker's final pay reference period: reg. 10(2).

real employer.[258] The Act was brought into effect on 1 April 1999 with the adoption of the National Minimum Wage Regulations 1999 (NMW Regulations 1999).[259]

The Act established the Low Pay Commission,[260] which is given responsibility for advising the Government on the amount to be paid. However, it is HM Revenue & Customs which has the role of enforcing the payment and prosecuting offenders (see below). The minimum wage was set at £5.93[261] per hour from October 2010 although three groups of workers are only entitled to a reduced rate. First, those workers who have attained the age of 18 years and are less than 21 years old are entitled to £4.92 in 2010. Second, the hourly rate for those under 18 years is £3.64 in 2010.[262] The third group is apprentices (see below).

7.7.1 Who qualifies for the national minimum wage

An individual qualifies for the national minimum wage (NMW) if they are a worker[263] who is working, or is ordinarily working, in the United Kingdom under a contract and who has ceased to be of compulsory school age.[264] Agency workers and home workers qualify. In the case of agency workers, if there is confusion as to who is the employer because of the lack of a contract between the worker and the agency or the principal, the person providing the wages or salary has the responsibility for paying the NMW.[265] Home workers are defined as individuals who contract to carry out work in a place not under the control or management of the person with whom they have contracted.[266]

The following groups do not qualify:

1. Workers who are under 26 years of age, who are employed under a contract of apprenticeship[267] and who are within the first 12 months of that employment.[268]

2. Workers participating in schemes to provide training, work experience or temporary work, or to assist them in finding work.[269]

3. Workers attending a higher[270] education course who are required before the course ends to complete a period of work experience not exceeding one year do not qualify for the NMW for work done as part of that course, for example sandwich students who spend part of their course gaining work experience.[271]

---

[258] Section 48 NMWA 1998; see also s. 34 NMWA 1998 on the employer of agency workers.

[259] SI 1999/584.

[260] Sections 5–8 NMWA 1998.

[261] Most benefits in kind, apart from living accommodation, are not to be treated as payments to the worker for the purposes of calculating the NMW: reg. 9 NMW Regulations 1999.

[262] Regulation 13(1) NMW Regulations 1999.

[263] Worker is defined in s. 54(3) NMWA 1998 and is given the same meaning as in s. 230(3) ERA 1996.

[264] Section 1(2) NMWA 1998.

[265] Section 34 NMWA 1998.

[266] Section 35(2) NMWA 1998.

[267] Contracts of apprenticeship include Modern Apprenticeships: reg. 12(3) NMW Regulations 1999; further definition is given by reg. 4 NMW Regulations 1999 (Amendment) Regulations 2000, SI 2000/1989 (NMW Amendment Regulations 2000); see *Edmunds* v *Lawson QC* [2000] IRLR 391 CA.

[268] Regulation 12(2) NMW Regulations 1999. From October 2010, apprentices who are under 19 or over this age but in the first year of their apprenticeship, will be entitled to a minimum wage of £2.50 per hour.

[269] Regulation 12(5) NMW Regulations 1999.

[270] Higher education course as in Sch. 6 Education Reform Act 1988: reg. 12(9) NMW Regulations 1999.

[271] Regulation 12(8) NMW Regulations 1999, as amended by the NMW Amendment Regulations 2000.

4. Workers who are homeless or residing in a hostel for the homeless, are eligible for income support and are participating in a voluntary or charitable scheme.[272]

5. Share fishers.[273]

6. Workers employed by a charity or a voluntary organisation, or similar, who only receive expenses in respect of work done. These expenses can include subsistence income for the worker concerned.[274]

7. Workers who are residential members of religious or charitable communities in respect of work done for those communities. Exempt from this are communities which are independent schools or those that provide courses in further or higher education.[275]

8. Workers who are prisoners do not qualify for the NMW in respect of any work done in pursuance of prison rules.[276]

Work is also defined as excluding any work relating to the employer's family household if the worker lives in the employer's family home, is treated as a member of the family, does not pay for the living accommodation and, if the work had been done by a member of the employer's family, it would not have been treated as being work.[277]

7.7.2 Calculating the hourly rate

The hourly rate paid to a worker is calculated by finding the total remuneration paid in that period and dividing it by the total number of hours of time work, salaried hours work, output work and unmeasured work worked in the pay reference period (these categories are discussed below).[278] The total remuneration in such a period is calculated[279] by adding together:

1. All money paid by the employer to the worker in the pay reference period.

2. All money paid in the following reference period that relates to the pay reference period.

3. Any money paid by the employer later than the following reference period in respect of work done in the pay reference period.[280]

4. Any amount permitted to be taken into account for the provision of living accommodation.[281]

Then various reductions are to be made, before the final figure can be arrived at, in accordance with regs. 31–37 NMW Regulations 1999. These include money paid during

---

[272] Regulation 12(12) NMW Regulations 1999.
[273] Section 43 NMWA 1998.
[274] Section 44 NMWA 1998.
[275] Section 44A NMWA 1998.
[276] Section 45 NMWA 1998.
[277] Regulation 2(2)–(4) NMW Regulations 1999; work by members of the family is not defined as work if the worker lives in the family home and shares in the tasks of the family or participates in the running of the family business.
[278] Regulation 14 NMW Regulations 1999.
[279] Regulation 30 NMW Regulations 1999.
[280] There are further conditions related to whether a worker is obliged to complete records of the amount of work done: reg. 30(c)(i)–(iii) NMW Regulations 1999.
[281] Defined in reg. 36 NMW Regulations 1999.

absences from work and during industrial action[282] and any money payments made by the employer representing tips and gratuities paid by customers, but not paid through the payroll.[283]

We now discuss the meaning of time work, salaried hours work, output work and unmeasured work.

7.7.2.1 **Time work**[284]

Time work is when workers are paid[285] for the number of hours that they are at work. It also applies if a worker is contracted to perform a particular job but is paid for the hours done each week or month and where a person is on piece work but is expected to work a certain number of hours per day. Whatever the level of the piece work, the worker must receive, on average, at least the NMW for each hour during the pay period.

Time work includes[286] time when the worker is available at or near the place of work (other than at home) for the purpose of doing time work. Regulation 15(1A) provides that if the worker is permitted to sleep, by arrangement, at or near the place of work, it is only the hours when they are awake for the purpose of working that count as time hours. This does not apply to situations where an employee is required to be on the premises for a specific number of hours and who may sleep, if he chooses to, when the designated tasks have been completed. It only applies where the employer gives specific permission to the employee to take a particular amount of time off for sleep.[287] Similarly, in *British Nursing Association* v *Inland Revenue*[288] staff providing a night-time booking service from home were entitled to have the entire period that they were available to answer the phone counted as time work. This was so even though they were able to undertake other activities during these hours, such as watching TV or reading. The Court of Appeal stated that it would make a mockery of the national minimum wage to conclude that the employees were only working when they answered the telephone and that all the time spent waiting for a call should be excluded. Time spent travelling can also be time work, unless it is incidental[289] to the worker's duties or is concerned with travelling to and from work. Travelling to an assignment or between assignments might be time work.[290] Time work does not include periods when the worker is absent or taking part in industrial action. According to the DBIS guide to the NMW, most workers who are not on an annual salary will be on time work.

---

[282] Regulation 31(1)(b)(i) NMW Regulations 1999.

[283] Regulation 31(1)(e) NMW Regulations 1999. On deductions for gas and electricity in tied accommodation, see *Revenue & Customs* v *Leisure Management Ltd* [2007] IRLR 450 CA.

[284] Regulation 3 NMW Regulations 1999.

[285] Regulation 8 NMW Regulations 1999 provides a definition of payments as being payments made before deductions, except for a limited number of payments including advances, pension payments, court or tribunal awards, payments relating to redundancy and payments as an award for a suggestions scheme.

[286] Regulation 15 NMW Regulations 1999.

[287] *Scottbridge Construction Ltd* v *Wright* [2003] IRLR 21. In *Burrow Down Ltd* v *Rossiter* [2008] ICR 1172 the EAT held that since the employee was required to undertake tasks during the time when he was otherwise permitted to sleep, he was actually working and engaged in time work for the whole of the shift.

[288] [2002] IRLR 480 CA.

[289] Travelling is incidental unless the worker needs to travel for the purposes of work, e.g. a bus driver or a catering worker on a train: reg. 15(3) NMW Regulations 1999.

[290] Assignment work is time work if it consists of assignments of work to be carried out at different places between which the worker is obliged to travel that are not places occupied by the worker's employer: reg. 16(3)(b) NMW Regulations 1999.

7.7.2.2 **Salaried hours work**

Salaried hours work is where a worker is paid under a contract for a set number of hours worked per year, is entitled to an annual salary and is paid in equal weekly or monthly instalments during the year regardless of the number of hours worked. Variations as a result of the payment of a performance bonus, a pay increase, excess hours payments or because the worker left part-way through the week or month do not stop the hours being salaried hours.

The provisions relating to salaried workers are similar to those for time workers[291] except that absences count if the worker is paid the normal pay during the absence. Absences such as lunch breaks, holidays and sickness absence count if they form part of the worker's basic minimum hours. Periods paid at a lesser rate do not count, for example when the worker is absent as a result of long-term sickness; neither do periods of unpaid leave and time on industrial action.[292] The basic number of hours for a salaried worker is the basic number of hours in respect of which a worker is paid, under the contract, on the first day of the reference period.[293]

7.7.2.3 **Output work**

Output work is work that is paid for by reference to a worker's output, be it the number of tasks performed or the value of sales made.[294] It is sometimes known as piece work or can be work that is paid by commission. Time travelling can be included except for travelling to the premises from which work is performed and, in the case of a home worker, the premises to which the worker reports. Again, time spent in taking industrial action does not count.[295]

There are two ways in which the hours of an output worker can be calculated. These are: (i) by counting the number of hours spent in output work,[296] or (ii) by applying a complicated system called 'rated output work'. This requires employers to give their workers a notice containing specified information and to test them in order to identify 'the mean hourly output rate'. The number of hours taken by a worker in producing the relevant pieces or performing the relevant tasks during a pay reference period is deemed to be the same number of hours that a person working at the mean hourly output rate would have taken to produce the same number of pieces or perform the same number of tasks during the pay reference period. Employers must pay their workers producing that piece or performing that task an amount per piece or task which, given that the workers are deemed to have worked at the mean hourly output rate, is at least equivalent to the hourly national minimum wage. Since April 2005, the number of hours spent by a worker on rated output work has been treated as being 120 per cent of the number of hours that a person working at the mean hourly output rate would have taken.

7.7.2.4 **Unmeasured work**

Unmeasured work is work that is not time work, salaried hours work or output work. It is work that has no specified hours and the person is required to work when needed or when

---

[291] Regulation 16 NMW Regulations 1999.
[292] Regulation 21(3)–(4) NMW Regulations 1999.
[293] Regulation 21(2)–(3) NMW Regulations 1999; regs. 22 and 23 are concerned with determining the salaried hours when the basic hours have been exceeded and when the employment terminates.
[294] Regulation 5 NMW Regulations 1999.
[295] Regulation 17 NMW Regulations 1999.
[296] Regulations 24–26 NMW Regulations 1999.

work is available, for example a carer.[297] There are two methods of identifying the number of hours to be worked and for which the NMW should be paid. These are, first, to pay the NMW for every hour worked. The second is for the employer and the worker to come to a 'daily average' agreement, to determine the average number of daily hours the worker is likely to spend on unmeasured work. The agreement must be made before the start of the pay reference period that it covers, be in writing, set out the average daily number of hours, and ensure that the daily average is realistic.[298] Where there is a dispute about the number of hours worked, no account will be taken of hours for which the worker has not submitted records, if that is what is required before payment can be made.[299]

7.7.3 Record keeping

An employer of a worker who qualifies for the NMW has a duty to keep records.[300] These records need to be sufficient to establish that the worker is being remunerated at a rate at least equal to the NMW. They must also be kept in such a way that the information relating to a worker in a pay reference period can be produced in a single document. In addition, the employer is required to keep copies of any agreements entered into with the worker concerning regs. 13(2) (accredited training), and 28(1) (unmeasured work).[301] These records must be kept for at least three years beginning with the day upon which the pay reference period immediately following that to which they relate ends.[302] The records may be kept on computer.[303]

If workers believe, on reasonable grounds, that they are being remunerated, in any particular reference period, at a rate less than the NMW, they have the right to request that the employer produce any relevant records and have the right to inspect them.[304] The inspection can be by the worker alone or accompanied by another person of their choice. The request to inspect records must be done by the worker giving a 'production notice' to the employer requesting the production of relevant records[305] relating to a specific period. If the worker is to be accompanied this must be stated in the 'production notice'. When this notice has been given, the employer must give the worker reasonable notice of the place[306] and time when the records will be produced. However, the records must be produced within 14 days of the employer receiving the 'production notice' unless otherwise agreed with the worker.[307]

If the employer fails to provide some or all of the records requested or fails to allow the worker to inspect the records or be accompanied by another person of the worker's choice, then the worker may make a complaint to an employment tribunal.[308] The complaint must

---

[297] Regulation 6 NMW Regulations 1999. See *Walton v Independent Living Organisation* [2003] IRLR 469.
[298] Regulations 27–29 NMW Regulations 1999.
[299] Regulation 29A NMW Regulations 1999 as amended.
[300] Section 9 NMWA 1998 and reg. 38 NMW Regulations 1999.
[301] Regulation 38(3) NMW Regulations 1999.
[302] Regulation 38(7) NMW Regulations 1999.
[303] Regulation 38(8) NMW Regulations 1999.
[304] Section 10 NMWA 1998.
[305] Relevant means those records which will establish whether or not the worker has been remunerated at a level equivalent to the NMW in any pay reference period: s. 10(10) NMWA 1998.
[306] The place must be the worker's place of work, any other place that is reasonable for the worker to attend or any further place agreed with the worker: s. 10(8) NMWA 1998.
[307] Section 10(9) NMWA 1998.
[308] Section 11 NMWA 1998.

be made within three months of the end of the 14-day period allowed for the provision of the records, or at the end of any other period agreed by the worker and the employer according to s. 10(9) NMWA 1998, unless the tribunal accepts that this was not reasonably practicable. Where an employment tribunal finds the complaint well founded, it may issue a declaration and make an award that the employer pays the worker a sum equal to 80 times the amount of the NMW in force at the time.

7.7.4 Enforcement

HM Revenue & Customs has the task of ensuring that workers are remunerated at a rate at least equivalent to the NMW. HM Revenue & Customs officers are given wide powers to inspect and take copies of records, require relevant persons to provide information[309] and to enter any relevant premises for the purpose of exercising their powers.[310] According to s. 14(4) NMWA 1998, a relevant person can be the employer or the employer's agent, the supplier of work to the individuals or the workers themselves. Relevant premises means the premises at which the employer carries on business or premises that the employer, or employer's agent, uses in connection with the business.[311]

The Employment Act 2008 amended s. 17 NMWA 1998 in order to provide a fairer method of calculating arrears for workers and a penalty for employers who fail to pay the NMW. If a notice of underpayment is not complied with, HM Revenue & Customs is able to take civil proceedings for the recovery of the money or present a complaint to an employment tribunal, on behalf of the worker, that there has been an unlawful deduction of wages in contravention of s. 13 ERA 1996 (see above).[312] In such proceedings the burden of proof is on the employer to show that the worker was remunerated at the appropriate level.[313]

A failure to comply with certain requirements of the NMWA 1998 can lead to prosecution for a criminal offence and can result in a fine. The offences in question are a refusal or wilful neglect to pay the NMW; failing to keep NMW records; keeping false records; producing false records or information; intentionally obstructing an enforcement officer; and refusing or neglecting to give information to an enforcement officer.[314]

7.7.5 Right not to suffer detriment

Section 104A ERA 1996 provides that the dismissal of an employee shall be unfair if the reason, or the principal reason, for the dismissal is entitlement to the NMW or any reason related to the enforcement of it. It is immaterial whether the employee has the right or whether the right has been infringed, although any claim must be made in good faith.

Section 23 NMWA 1998 provides that workers have the right not to be subjected to detriment because of entitlement to the NMW or any reason related to the enforcement of it. Again good faith is required for complaints and it is immaterial whether the worker has the

---

[309] Although no person may be required to provide information that will incriminate themselves or their spouse: s. 14(2) NMWA 1998. On disclosure of information by officers see s. 16A NMWA 1998.
[310] Section 14(1) NMWA 1998.
[311] Section 14(5) NMWA 1998.
[312] Section 19D NMWA 1998.
[313] Section 28 NMWA 1998.
[314] Sections 31–33 NMWA 1998.

right or whether it has been infringed. Detriment here will include workers who are not protected from unfair dismissal by Part X ERA 1996. The complaint to an employment tribunal must be made within three months beginning with the act, or failure to act, that is to be complained of, unless the tribunal considers that it was not reasonably practicable to do so. If the tribunal finds the complaint well founded it may make a declaration and award compensation.[315]

Chapter summary

This chapter started by describing issues related to working time. It outlined the impact of the 1998 Regulations, paying particular attention to maximum hours, breaks and minimum holiday entitlements. It also discussed the main statutory provisions impacting on the ability of employees to take time off work. Attention then turned to pay issues in the form of a detailed analysis of the law on authorised deductions and entitlement to and enforcement of the national minimum wage.

Further reading

Collins, H., Ewing, K. and McColgan, A. *Labour Law: Text and Materials*: Hart Publishing, 2009, Chapter 4.

Deakin, S. and Morris, G. *Labour Law*: 4th edn, Hart Publishing, 2005, Chapter 4.

Simpson, R. 'The Employment Act 2008's Amendments to the National Minimum Wage Legislation' (2009) 38 *Industrial Law Journal* 57.

Simpson, R. 'The National Minimum Wage Five Years On' (2004) 33 *Industrial Law Journal* 22.

www.acas.org.uk

www.lowpay.gov.uk

www.tuc.org.uk

Visit **www.mylawchamber.co.uk/sargeant**
to access legal updates, live weblinks and practice
exam questions to test yourself on this chapter.

mylawchamber
unrivalled support for legal education

---

[315] Sections 48–49 ERA 1996.

8 Parental and maternity rights

8.1 The Pregnant Workers Directive[1]

The Pregnant Workers Directive identified pregnant workers and workers who have recently given birth, or who are breastfeeding, as workers who face particular risks in the workplace. The Directive makes such workers a particular case for protection and makes provisions regarding the health and safety of this group, and adopted certain employment rights connected with pregnancy.

All Member States of the European Community already had laws for the protection of pregnant workers prior to this Directive. In the United Kingdom, for example, there had been a long tradition of offering such protection: for example, s. 34 Employment Protection Act 1975 provided that a dismissal would be unfair if the reason or the principal reason for the dismissal was pregnancy or a reason related to that pregnancy.

One of the purposes of the Directive was to create minimum standards throughout the Community. Before its introduction, there was considerable variation between the Member States on measures taken. As a result of the Directive there were a number of changes, although the variety remains. There were changes such as increases in maternity leave in Portugal and Sweden. In the United Kingdom there was a reduction in the qualifying period for maternity leave. There were amendments to Irish legislation and the introduction of paid time off for ante-natal examinations in Austria, Belgium, Denmark, Finland and Ireland.

8.1.1 Definition

The Directive[2] defines a pregnant worker as a woman who informs her employer of her condition, in accordance with national laws and practice. Most Member States require the worker to inform her employer of her pregnancy, or of the fact that she has recently given birth or is breastfeeding, before the protective measures can begin. In Belgium, Finland, France and the United Kingdom, for example, there is no general requirement for a woman to inform her employer that she is pregnant, but it is unlikely that there would be an entitlement to maternity rights and protection until the employer is informed. In Spain it is enough for the

---

[1] Directive 92/85/EC on the introduction of measures to encourage improvements in the health and safety at work of pregnant workers and workers who have recently given birth or are breastfeeding OJ L348 28.11.92 p. 1.
[2] Article 2(a) Pregnant Workers Directive.

employer to be aware of the pregnancy, even though not officially informed. In Luxembourg a woman needs to send a medical certificate to her employer by registered post, whilst in Austria the Labour Inspectorate needs to be informed, as well as the employer, of the pregnancy. There is a similar diversity in how long a woman can be defined as breastfeeding and, as a result, receive special protection. In Ireland women receive protection for six months for breastfeeding; in Spain it is nine months and in Greece it is one year.

A refusal to employ results in direct discrimination when the most important reason for the refusal applies only to one sex, rather than to employees, without distinction, of both sexes. Only women can be refused employment because of pregnancy, so a decision not to employ someone because they are pregnant is directly discriminatory against the woman concerned. *Dekker*,[3] which was a reference to the ECJ from the Dutch Supreme Court, concerned a woman who had applied for a post of training instructor in a youth centre. She was pregnant when she applied and she informed the selection committee of this. The committee recommended her as the most suitable candidate, but the board of the youth centre declined to employ her. The reason given was that their insurer would not compensate them for payments which would be due to Ms Dekker during her maternity leave. The ECJ concluded that the refusal to employ had been a reason connected with the pregnancy and that this was contrary to the Equal Treatment Directive (see below). As only women can be refused employment because of pregnancy, the fact that there were no male candidates for the post was not seen as relevant. In *Mayr*[4] the ECJ considered the case of a woman undergoing *in vitro* fertilisation treatment. She was dismissed during the treatment period, but before the fertilised ovum was transferred to her uterus. That procedure was carried out three days after her dismissal. The ECJ stated that the purpose of art. 10 was to protect pregnant women at the earliest possible moment from dismissal for reasons linked to the pregnancy. In the case of *in vitro* treatment, however, the protection commenced when the ovum was actually transferred. To do otherwise might give protection over a period of many years as there can be a gap of years before the actual transfer.

8.1.2 Risk assessment

The employer is required to complete an assessment of the risk of exposure to a non-exhaustive list of agents,[5] processes or working conditions and then to inform the worker or her representatives of the results and the measures intended to be taken concerning health and safety at work.[6] All countries have health and safety legislation which takes particular account of pregnant workers and a variety of means of informing them of those risks. In most countries it is the responsibility of the employer alone, but in some Member States statutory bodies become involved, such as in Finland, where occupational health experts carry out an investigation, and in Ireland, where the National Authority for Occupational Safety and Health has a role in ensuring employee awareness. There should not be measures, however, that go so far in their attempt to protect pregnant women that they breach the Equal Treatment Directive.

---

[3] Case C-177/88 *Dekker* v *Stichting Vormingscentum voor Jonge Volwassen* [1991] IRLR 27 ECJ.
[4] Case C-506/06 *Mayr* v *Bäckerei und Konditorei Gerhard Flöckner OHG* [2008] IRLR 387.
[5] Article 4 Pregnant Workers Directive.
[6] A failure to carry out a risk assessment amounts to sex discrimination: *Hardman* v *Mallon* [2002] ICR 510.

8.1.3 **Night work**

There are various approaches to issues related to night work in the Member States. The Directive[7] ensures that pregnant workers should not be obliged to carry out night work if it is detrimental to their health or safety. If there is such a risk then the woman concerned should be moved to day work or given leave from work if day work is not possible. Some countries had a policy of not allowing such workers to work at nights at all. In *Stoeckel*,[8] an individual was the subject of prosecution for infringement of a section of the French labour code which prohibited the employment of women on night work except in certain situations. The ECJ ruled that a provision that banned women from performing night work, when there was no such provision for men, was contrary to art. 5 of the Equal Treatment Directive.[9] Most countries require a medical certificate to show that working at night would be bad for the worker's health, although the certificate is not needed in Denmark or Greece. In Germany, Austria, Italy and Luxembourg there are still restrictions against night work which make it very difficult for such workers to work at nights at all.

8.1.4 **Maternity leave**

Workers must be permitted to take, as a minimum, at least 14 weeks' continuous maternity leave with at least two weeks' compulsory leave taken before or after confinement.[10] The duration of maternity leave in practice varies from 90 days in Portugal to 16 weeks in Greece and Austria and 20 weeks in Italy. Denmark has 14 weeks with a further ten weeks which either parent can have or share between them. In some countries, such as France, the leave entitlement is longer if the woman already has children. During maternity leave, entitlement to pay may vary from 100 per cent of salary, as in Belgium, Germany, Greece, Spain, Luxembourg, the Netherlands, Austria and Portugal, to 90 per cent in Denmark, 84 per cent in France, 80 per cent in Italy and 70 per cent in Ireland. Most countries impose rules for entitlement to benefits.[11]

In *Ulrich Hofmann* v *Barmer Ersatzkasse*[12] the ECJ was asked to consider a claim that the giving of leave to women alone did not accord with the terms of the Equal Treatment Directive. The claimant was a man who looked after a child whilst the mother returned to work as a teacher shortly after the birth. He was denied a claim for maternity benefit by the German social security service. The argument, in the legal proceedings that followed, was that the introduction of maternity leave was concerned, not with the protection of the mother's health, but exclusively with the care that she gave to the child. If this argument was correct, it was said, then the leave should be available to either parent and become a form of parental leave. The ECJ rejected this approach and stated that the Equal Treatment Directive was not intended to 'settle questions concerned with the organisation of the family'. If national legislation had been only concerned with the care of the child, then it ought to be non-discriminatory. The court held that maternity leave came within the scope of art. 2(3)

---

[7] Article 7 Pregnant Workers Directive.
[8] Case C-345/89 *Criminal proceedings against Alfred Stoeckel* [1991] ECR-1 4047 ECJ.
[9] Directive 76/207/EEC on equal treatment for men and for women with regard to access to employment, vocational training and promotion, and working conditions OJ L39 14.2.76 p. 40; see also Case 158/91 *Ministère Public et Direction du Travail* v *Levy* [1994] ECR 4287 ECJ.
[10] Article 8 Pregnant Workers Directive.
[11] European Commission, *The Regulation of Working Conditions in the Member States of the European Union*, 1999.
[12] Case 184/83 [1984] ECR 3047 ECJ.

Equal Treatment Directive, which 'seeks to protect a woman in connection with the effects of pregnancy and motherhood'. Thus maternity leave could legitimately be reserved for the mother, as it is only she that is likely to suffer from undesirable pressures to return to work prematurely.

8.1.5 Protection against dismissal

Member States are required to 'take the necessary measures to prohibit the dismissal of workers . . . during their pregnancy to the end of their maternity leave . . . save in exceptional cases not connected with their condition . . .'[13] As a result all countries provide protection against dismissal for pregnant workers or those that have recently given birth, although much of this protection emanated from previous anti-sex discrimination legislation. One issue for the national courts was whether there was a necessity to compare a pregnant woman's absence with that of a man to show that discrimination had taken place. *Webb* v *EMO*[14] was a case where an applicant was employed initially to cover for another employee who was to go on maternity leave. It was envisaged that the new employee would continue to be employed after the pregnant employee returned from her maternity leave. Shortly after starting work, the new employee discovered that she was pregnant also and the employer dismissed her. She complained of sex discrimination contrary to s. 1(1) Sex Discrimination Act 1975. When the case reached the House of Lords it was referred to the ECJ for a decision on whether the dismissal constituted sex discrimination. The ECJ held that it was contrary to the Equal Treatment Directive and that one could not compare a pregnant woman who was not capable of performing the task for which she was employed with a male who was absent through sickness and incapable therefore of carrying out his tasks.

In the Danish case of *Hertz*,[15] the male comparator was of importance, however. Ms Hertz was a part-time cashier and saleswoman. She gave birth to a child after a difficult pregnancy during which she was mainly on sick leave. When her statutory maternity leave period ended she returned to work. After a further period of about six months she was ill and was absent for 100 days. The illness had arisen out of her pregnancy and confinement. Eventually her employers dismissed her on the grounds of repeated absence due to illness. A question for the ECJ was whether this dismissal contravened art. 5 of the Equal Treatment Directive as the illness had resulted from the pregnancy. The court held that dismissal because of absence during maternity leave would constitute direct discrimination. With regard to an illness that appears some time after, however, there was no reason to distinguish between an illness that had its origin in pregnancy and one from any other cause. If such sickness absence would have led to the dismissal of a male worker under the same conditions, then there is no discrimination on the grounds of sex.[16]

The Equal Treatment Directive 2002[17] provides now that no comparator is needed in pregnancy discrimination and this is put into effect in the UK by amendments to the Sex

---

[13] Article 10 Pregnant Workers Directive.

[14] Case C-32/93 *Webb* v *EMO Air Cargo (UK) Ltd* [1994] ICR 770 ECJ.

[15] Case 179/88 *Handels og Konturfunktionærernes Forbund i Danmark (acting for Hertz)* v *Dansk Arbejdsgiver-forening (acting for Aldi Marked A/S)* [1991] IRLR 31 ECJ.

[16] See Case 394/96 *Brown* v *Rentokil Ltd* [1998] IRLR 445 ECJ, which also distinguished between the protected period during pregnancy and maternity leave compared to the period after that leave.

[17] Directive 2002/73/EC on the principle of equal treatment of men and women as regards access to employment, vocational training and promotion and working conditions.

Discrimination Act in 2008.[18] There is therefore no requirement for a comparator who is not pregnant or not on maternity leave in order to show discrimination has taken place.

8.1.6 Employment rights during maternity leave

Article 11(1) Pregnant Workers Directive provides for rights under the employment contract including the maintenance of a payment whilst a woman is granted leave from work because of risks to her health or that of her baby, or when she is granted leave from night work. Article 11(2) provides similar rights for workers during maternity leave as exist for health and safety reasons. The case of *North Western Health Board* v *McKenna*[19] at the ECJ concerned a sickness scheme which guaranteed full pay for the first 183 days of sickness in any one year and half pay for the remaining period. The scheme also expressly stated that sickness related to maternity related illness prior to the taking of maternity leave would be treated in the same way as sickness for any other reason. Mrs McKenna was absent because of maternity related sickness for virtually the whole of her pregnancy and also after her maternity leave. She spent some time, as a result, on half pay. She claimed that this was sex discrimination. The Court of Justice did not agree with this and stated that Community law does not require the maintenance of full pay for absences related to maternity related illness, provided that the payment is not so low as to undermine the Community law objective of protecting female workers, especially before giving birth.

8.2 The Parental Leave Directive[20]

The Parental Leave Directive implemented a Framework Agreement on parental leave reached by the social partners. The social partners are the European representatives of employer and trade union organisations.[21] As part of a process called the 'Social Dialogue', these representatives were invited by the European Commission to reach an agreement on parental leave. This agreement, called the Framework Agreement, was subsequently adopted in its entirety as a European Directive. The Social Partners reached a revised Framework Agreement in June 2009. This has resulted in a proposed new Parental Leave Directive in 2010 extending the amount of parental leave to be given and ensuring that the position of adoptive parents is considered. This Directive will need to be put into effect in the Member States within two years.

The proposals for having Community rules on parental leave had been in existence for some time. They were first introduced as a proposed Directive in 1983,[22] but the British Government opposed them and was able effectively to veto them as adoption required a unanimous vote in the Council of Ministers. In 1994 the proposals were again put forward, but this time under the Social Chapter, from which the United Kingdom had excluded itself.

---

[18] Regulation 2 of the Sex Discrimination Act 1975 (Amendment) Regulations 2008 SI 2008/656.
[19] Case C-191/03 [2005] IRLR 895.
[20] Council Directive 96/34/EC on the Framework Agreement on parental leave concluded by UNICE, CEEP and the ETUC OJ L145 19.6.96 p. 4; applied to the United Kingdom by Directive 97/75/EC OJ L10 16.1.98 p. 24.
[21] The organisations are UNICE, the European private employers' federation, CEEP, the European public employers' federation, and ETUC, the European trade union confederation.
[22] Proposal for a Directive on parental leave and leave for family reasons COM(83) 686 as amended by COM(84) 631.

These led to the Framework Agreement which was adopted by all the other Member States (excluding the United Kingdom) in 1996. After the 1997 general election, and a change of government, the United Kingdom 'signed up' to the Social Chapter. As a result, Directive 97/75/EC was adopted on 15 December 1997 extending the Parental Leave Directive to the United Kingdom. In order to comply, the Maternity and Parental Leave etc. Regulations[23] and ss. 57A and 57B Employment Rights Act 1996 came into effect on 15 December 1999.[24]

8.2.1 Scope of the Directive

Men and women workers are given the individual right to parental leave on the grounds of the birth or adoption of a child,[25] in order to enable them to take care of that child, for at least three months (this will be extended to four months by the new Directive), until an age of up to eight years. The actual age was left to individual Member States. Article 2(2) states that, in principle, these rights should be given on a non-transferable basis. Thus one parent could not transfer their right of up to three months' leave to the other parent, even if they had no intention of making use of the right.

The detailed rules and qualifying conditions on parental leave have been left to individual Member States to decide. This may include, for different countries, rules on the minimum length of service required to qualify, the arrangements for taking leave and the employer's ability to postpone leave for operational or other reasons. There is no requirement in the Directive that leave should be paid and any decisions on financing or social security arrangements are left to the individual Member States.[26] There are also provisions for countries to:

1. Protect workers against dismissal for taking parental leave.
2. Ensure that workers are able to return to the same job, or an equivalent, at the end of their leave period.
3. Ensure the maintenance and continuation of rights accrued to the start of the leave period.
4. Define the status of the contract of employment during the leave period.

In the *Hofmann*[27] case, the European Commission pointed out that a number of Member States were moving towards the granting of parental leave which, they stated, was 'to be preferred to leave which is granted to the mother alone'. Rules on parental leave have existed in other countries for many years, making the impact of the Directive substantially less than its possible impact in the United Kingdom.

8.2.2 Force majeure

Clause 3.1 of the Framework Agreement, implemented by the Parental Leave Directive, provides that Member States should take measures to entitle workers to time off from work on grounds of '*force majeure* for urgent family reasons in cases of sickness or accident making the immediate presence of the worker indispensable'. This led to the rules on the right to time off

---

[23] SI 1999/3312; subsequently amended by the Maternity and Parental Leave (Amendment) Regulations 2002, SI 2002/2789.
[24] See Employment Relations Act 1999 (Commencement No 2 and Transitional and Savings Provisions) Order 1999, SI 1999/2830.
[25] Clause 2(1) Framework Agreement on parental leave.
[26] Clause 2(8) Framework Agreement on parental leave.
[27] Case 184/83 [1984] ECR 3047 ECJ.

for dependants being introduced in the Employment Relations Act 1999.[28] Thus an employee is entitled to take a reasonable amount of time off in order to take action which is needed:

1. To provide assistance when a dependant falls ill, gives birth, is injured or assaulted.

2. To make arrangements for care for a dependant who is ill or injured.

3. As a result of the death of a dependant.

4. As a result of the unexpected disruption of arrangements for the care of a dependant.

5. To deal with unexpected incidents resulting from a child being at school.[29]

The definition of dependant is restricted to a spouse, a child, a parent or a person living in the same household as the employee who is not an employee, lodger, tenant or boarder.[30] There is an obligation for the employee to tell the employer the reason for the absence and the likelihood of its length as soon as is reasonably practicable.[31] Complaints for a failure to grant reasonable time off are made to an employment tribunal within three months of the date the refusal was made, unless not reasonably practicable. The tribunal may make a declaration and award compensation that it considers just and equitable.[32] *Qua v John Ford Morrison Solicitors*[33] concerned a legal secretary who had a large number of absences during a relatively short period of employment. She stated that most of these absences were due to medical problems experienced by her son. The EAT held that there was no statutory maximum to the number of occasions that an employee could be absent in accordance with s. 57A ERA 1996, but there was no entitlement to an unlimited amount of time off. The right to time off was to deal with the unexpected. When it was known that the employee's dependant was suffering from a medical condition which was likely to result in regular lapses, then it no longer came within the provisions of s. 57A, because it was no longer unexpected.

8.3 Maternity leave in the United Kingdom

Special measures to benefit pregnant women and women who had recently given birth were first introduced in the United Kingdom during the post-Second World War period. The National Insurance scheme, in 1948, introduced a maternity allowance for women contributors who gave up work to have a baby. This was paid for 13 weeks. The period was increased to 18 weeks in 1953. In 1975 the Employment Protection Act introduced six weeks' maternity pay for women who contributed to the Maternity Fund. This maternity pay equalled 90 per cent of normal weekly earnings less the amount of the maternity allowance. Maternity allowance and maternity pay were amalgamated in 1987 and became statutory maternity pay.[34] This is paid by employers, who then recover their costs by deductions from their tax and national insurance contributions. Small employers can claim an additional amount in respect of such pay.[35]

---

[28] Now contained in ss. 57A and 57B ERA 1996.
[29] Section 57A(1) ERA 1996.
[30] Section 57A(3) ERA 1996.
[31] Section 57A(2) ERA 1996.
[32] Section 57B ERA 1996.
[33] [2003] IRLR 184.
[34] See House of Commons Research Paper 98/99, *Fairness at Work*.
[35] See Statutory Maternity Pay (Compensation of Employers) (Amendment) Regulations 1999, SI 1999/363.

The Employment Protection Act 1975 also introduced the right to return to work for up to 29 weeks after confinement for women who had been employed for two years continuously with the same employer. In 1994, changes were made as a result of the Pregnant Workers Directive. These changes concerned the right for women to have at least 14 weeks' maternity leave, regardless of their length of service or hours of work. Two weeks of this were to be compulsory. They also concerned the payment to women of an 'adequate allowance', equal at least to State rules on sickness benefit, during their maternity leave period, although this could be limited to those with at least one year's continuous service. The changes were made in ss. 23–25 Trade Union Reform and Employment Rights Act 1993 and various regulations.[36]

Prior to the Employment Relations Act 1999 and the Maternity and Parental Leave etc. Regulations 1999 all women were entitled to 14 weeks' maternity leave, although confusingly they were also likely to be entitled to 18 weeks' maternity pay. Some, with two years' continuous employment, were also entitled to extended maternity leave. One of the aims of the Government in making the changes contained in the 1999 legislation, and subsequently, was to remove some confusion, especially with respect to the procedures for giving notice, arrangements for return to work and the definition of remuneration. Importantly, the number of women likely to benefit is large. It is estimated that there are about 370,000 pregnant employees in any one year in the United Kingdom.

8.4 Maternity and Parental Leave etc. Regulations 1999

The Maternity and Parental Leave etc. Regulations 1999,[37] were amended in 2002,[38] 2006[39] and 2008[40] (the MPL Regulations). Further provision was also made by the Work and Families Act 2006. These provide for three types of maternity leave: ordinary maternity leave, compulsory maternity leave and additional maternity leave, although the distinction between ordinary and additional maternity leave have been somewhat reduced by the 2008 Regulations. These are periods of leave, before and after childbirth, to which a pregnant employee, or one that has recently given birth, is entitled. The dates of leave are calculated as being periods before or after the 'expected week of childbirth'. Regulation 2(1) MPL Regulations defines this as the week, beginning with midnight between Saturday and Sunday, in which it is expected that childbirth will occur. This regulation also defines childbirth as 'the birth of a living child or the birth of a child whether living or dead after 24 weeks of pregnancy'. This means, of course, that a woman who gives birth to a stillborn child after 24 weeks of pregnancy will be entitled to the same leave as a person who gave birth to a live child.

Similar rules exist for ordinary and additional adoption leave and are contained in the Parental and Adoption Leave Regulations 2002.[41]

---

[36] Maternity Allowance and Statutory Maternity Pay Regulations 1994, SI 1994/1230 and Social Security Maternity Benefits and Statutory Sick Pay (Amendment) Regulations 1994, SI 1994/1367.

[37] SI 1999/3312.

[38] SI 2002/2789.

[39] The Maternity and Parental Leave etc. and the Paternity and Adoption Leave (Amendment) Regulations 2006, SI 2006/2014.

[40] The Maternity and Parental Leave etc. and the Paternity and Adoption Leave (Amendment) Regulations 2008 SI 2008/1966.

[41] SI 2002/2788, as amended by the 2006 Regulations – see above.

8.4.1 **Statutory maternity leave**[42]

The rules on maternity and parental leave apply to employees only. Regulation 2(1) MPL Regulations defines an employee as an individual who has 'entered into or works under (or, where the employment has ceased, worked under) a contract of employment'. A contract of employment is further defined as a 'contract of service or apprenticeship whether express or implied, and (if it is express) whether oral or in writing'. This is the same definition as in s. 230(1) and (2) ERA 1996 and is narrower than the definition of worker. It is the narrower definition that applies in the case of maternity or parental leave.

The MPL Regulations define employer, simply, as the person by whom an employee is (or, where the employment has ceased, was) employed.[43] The regulations also define associated employer, which assumes importance in certain respects, such as rights in a redundancy situation during maternity leave (see below). Two employers are treated as associated if one is a company of which the other (directly or indirectly) has control, or both are companies of which a third person (directly or indirectly) has control.[44]

An employee may be entitled to ordinary and additional maternity leave if she satisfies certain conditions. These are:[45]

1. No later than the end of the 15th week before her expected week of childbirth she notifies her employer of her pregnancy, the expected week of childbirth and the date on which she intends to start her ordinary maternity leave. If it is not reasonably practicable to inform the employer by that time, then she must inform the employer as soon as is reasonably practicable.

2. The employee must give this notice in writing if the employer so requests.[46] The employee is entitled to change her mind about the date for commencement of her maternity leave, provided she notifies the employer at least 28 days before the new date or the date varied.[47]

3. The employer is able to request, for inspection, a certificate from a registered medical practitioner or a registered midwife stating the expected week of childbirth, and the employee is required to provide it.

4. As a response to the notice the employer must, within 28 days, notify the employee of the date when her additional maternity leave will end.[48]

5. If the leave period commences because of absence from work on a day after the fourth week before the expected week of childbirth (see below),[49] then the employee is not expected to have given the required notice, but she will lose her entitlement if she does not inform her employer as soon as is practicable that she is absent from work wholly or

---

[42] Regulation 2(1) of the MPL Regulations states that statutory maternity leave means ordinary and additional maternity leave.

[43] Regulation 2(1) MPL Regulations.

[44] Regulation 2(3) MPL Regulations.

[45] Regulation 4(1)(a) MPL Regulations.

[46] Regulation 4(2)(a) MPL Regulations.

[47] Regulation 4(1A) MPL Regulations.

[48] Regulation 7(6) and (7) MPL Regulations.

[49] See Case C-411/96 *Boyle v Equal Opportunities Commission* [1998] IRLR 717 ECJ, which held that a rule which required a woman who is absent on a pregnancy related illness within six weeks of the expected date of childbirth should take paid maternity leave, rather than be given sick pay, was not precluded by the Pregnant Workers Directive.

partly because of her pregnancy.[50] This notice must give the date upon which her maternity leave now commences and must be in writing if the employer requests it.

6. If the leave period commences on the day which follows the childbirth (see below), then she is not required to give the specified notice in order to keep her entitlement. Whether or not she has given that notice, however, she is not entitled to ordinary or additional maternity leave unless she notifies the employer as soon as is reasonably practicable after the birth that she has given birth and the date on which this took place.[51] This notice must be in writing if the employer requests it.

Ordinary maternity leave can be started in a number of ways.[52] First, the employee may choose the start date, provided the notice requirements are met and provided that she does not specify a date earlier than the beginning of the 11th week before the expected week of childbirth.[53] Secondly, if the employee is absent from work on any day after the beginning of the fourth week before the expected week of childbirth, for a reason wholly or partly because of the pregnancy, then the ordinary leave period will automatically begin on that day. Thirdly, when the child is born. If the ordinary maternity leave period has not begun by this time, then it will begin on the day after childbirth occurs.

Ordinary maternity leave continues for a period of 26 weeks from its commencement, or until the end of the compulsory maternity leave period, whichever is later.[54] This period can be further extended if there is a statutory provision that prohibits the employee from working after the end of the ordinary maternity leave period, for a reason related to the fact that she had recently given birth. The period of leave may end early if the employee is dismissed during the period of her leave. In the event of such a dismissal, the period ends at the time of that dismissal.[55]

An employee's additional maternity leave period commences on the day after the last day of her ordinary maternity leave period and continues for 26 weeks, meaning that all affected employees are entitled to a total of 52 weeks' leave.[56] The period of leave may end early if the employee is dismissed during the period of her leave. In the event of such a dismissal, the period ends at the time of the dismissal.[57]

8.4.2 Compulsory maternity leave

Section 72 ERA 1996 provides that an employer must not allow a woman who is entitled to ordinary maternity leave to work during the compulsory leave period. The compulsory leave period is for two weeks commencing with the day on which childbirth occurs.[58] These two weeks fall within the ordinary maternity leave period, so are part of the 26 weeks permitted for such leave. An employer who contravenes this requirement will be guilty of an offence and liable to a fine if convicted.[59]

---

[50] Regulation 4(3)(b) MPL Regulations.
[51] Regulation 4(4)(b) MPL Regulations.
[52] Regulation 6 MPL Regulations.
[53] Regulation 4(2)(b) MPL Regulations.
[54] Regulation 7(1) MPL Regulations.
[55] Regulation 7(5) MPL Regulations.
[56] Regulation 6(3) MPL Regulations.
[57] Regulation 7(4)–(5) MPL Regulations.
[58] Regulation 8 MPL Regulations.
[59] Section 72(3)(b) and (5) ERA 1996.

8.5 Employment rights before and during maternity leave

Certain special rights are accorded to pregnant workers and those who have recently given birth or are breastfeeding.

8.5.1 Time off for ante-natal care

Sections 55–57 ERA 1996 provide that an employee who is pregnant and has, on the advice of a registered medical practitioner, registered midwife or registered health visitor, made an appointment to attend at any place for ante-natal care is entitled to time off with pay during the employee's working hours in order to keep the appointment.

8.5.2 Suspension from work on maternity grounds

Regulation 3(1) Management of Health and Safety at Work Regulations 1999 (MHSW Regulations 1999)[60] requires an assessment by the employer of the risks to health and safety of employees and others. Regulation 16(1) MHSW Regulations 1999 requires special attention in the event of there being female employees of childbearing age. The assessment is to decide whether the work is of a kind which would pose a risk, by reason of her condition, to the health and safety of a new or expectant mother or that of her baby. The obligation to carry out this risk assessment is not confined to situations where the employer has a pregnant employee. The employment of a woman of childbearing age should be enough to set off the need for such an assessment.[61] If it is reasonable to do so, the employer can change the working hours or working conditions in order to avoid the risks.[62] If it is not reasonable to do so then the employer must suspend the pregnant employee for as long as the risk persists. This suspension can only take place where a risk cannot be avoided. Avoiding risk does not mean the complete avoidance of all risks, but their reduction to the lowest possible level.[63]

Sections 66–68 ERA 1996 provide that an employee who is suspended from work as a result of a statutory prohibition or as a result of a recommendation contained in a code of practice issued or approved under s. 16 Health and Safety at Work etc. Act 1974, is entitled to be paid during that suspension, or offered alternative work. The alternative work needs to be both suitable and appropriate given the employee's circumstances and the terms and conditions offered to her must not be substantially less favourable than her previous terms and conditions.

Failure to provide alternative work and/or remuneration[64] can lead to a complaint to an employment tribunal by the employee. *British Airways (European Operations at Gatwick) Ltd*

---

[60] SI 1999/3242.

[61] See *Day* v *T Pickles Farms Ltd* [1999] IRLR 217.

[62] Regulation 16(2) MHSW Regulations 1999.

[63] See *New Southern Railway Ltd* v *Quinn* [2006] IRLR 267, where managers became concerned about the safety of an employee who had been appointed to the post of station manager. The tribunal stated that the managers had jumped to the conclusion that the employee could not continue in this role because of their personal feelings and had then attached a health and safety label to it.

[64] See Case C-66/96 *Handels og Kontorfunktionærernes Forbund i Danmark (acting for Høj Pedersen)* v *Fællesforeningen for Danmarks Brugsforeninger (acting for Kvickly Skive)* [1999] IRLR 55 ECJ, which held that national legislation which permitted the sending home of a pregnant woman, in such a situation, without paying her salary in full was contrary to the Equal Treatment Directive; legislation that only affects pregnant employees is in breach of art. 5 of the Directive.

v *Moore and Botterill*[65] concerned cabin crew who could not fly during their pregnancies and who succeeded in their claim for their full allowances whilst employed on alternative work. They were employed on alternative ground-based work, but were not given the flying allowances to which they had previously been entitled when working as cabin crew. If a statutory prohibition were to prevent the employment of a pregnant woman from the outset and for the duration of the pregnancy, then that prohibition might be held to be discriminatory.[66]

The complaint about pay is required to be made within three months, unless not reasonably practicable, of the day on which there was a failure to pay. Complaints about not being provided with alternative work need to be made within three months, unless not reasonably practicable, of the first day of the suspension.[67] The amount of compensation to be paid will be such as the tribunal decides is just and equitable in all the circumstances.

8.5.3 The contract of employment during maternity leave

The status of the employment contract during maternity leave has not always been clear. *McPherson* v *Drumpark House*[68] was a case that concerned an employee who went on maternity leave without fulfilling all the statutory requirements for taking such leave and returning afterwards. When she indicated to her employers that she was returning to work, they informed her that, in their view, she was no longer employed under a contract of employment. The issue for the EAT was whether the contract of employment continued during the period of maternity leave. The EAT concluded that it was not clear and that the payment of maternity pay was not in itself enough to show a continuation of the contract without some express or implied agreement to that effect.

8.5.3.1 Work during the maternity leave period

An employee may carry out up to ten days' work for her employer during her statutory maternity period (excluding the compulsory maternity period)[69] without bringing her maternity leave period to an end.[70] This is part of a policy designed to encourage employers and those on maternity leave to keep in touch with each other and, of course, to ease the moment of return to work. Any work carried out on any day shall constitute a day's work and the work can include training or any activity designed for the purpose of keeping in touch with the workplace.[71] Regulation 12A(6) MPL Regulations makes it clear that this does not mean that the employer has the right to require this work or that the employee has a right to work. It clearly needs to be a mutually agreed option, but one which many employers and those on maternity leave may be interested in using. The period spent working does not have the effect of extending the total duration of the maternity leave period.[72]

---

[65] [2000] IRLR 296.
[66] Case C-207/98 *Mahlberg* v *Land Mecklenburg-Vorpommern* [2000] IRLR 276 ECJ.
[67] Section 70 ERA 1996.
[68] [1997] IRLR 277.
[69] Regulation 12A(5) MPL Regulations.
[70] Regulation 12A(1) MPL Regulations.
[71] Regulation 12A(2) and (3) MPL Regulations.
[72] Regulation 12A(7) MPL Regulations.

8.5.3.2 **Employment rights**

Section 71(4) ERA 1996 provides that an employee on ordinary maternity leave is, first, entitled to the benefit of the terms and conditions of employment which would have applied had she not been absent. This does not include terms and conditions about remuneration,[73] although reg. 9 MPL Regulations limits the definition of remuneration to sums payable to an employee by way of wages or salary.[74] A failure to reflect a pay increase in calculating earnings related statutory maternity pay, for an employee on maternity leave, was likely to be a breach of art. 141 EC on equal pay and the employee would have an entitlement to make a claim for unlawful deduction from her wages.[75]

Secondly, the employee is bound by obligations arising out of those terms and conditions, and, thirdly, she is entitled to return from leave to the job in which she was employed before her absence (for discussion on the right to return to work, see below).[76] Indeed, where the contract of employment continues during pregnancy, to afford a woman less favourable treatment regarding her working conditions during that time would constitute sex discrimination within the terms of the Equal Treatment Directive.[77]

The rules for the period of additional maternity leave changed for employees whose expected week of childbirth began on or after 5 October 2008. Section 73(4) ERA 1996 provides that those on such leave are entitled to the benefit of the terms and conditions which would have applied had they not been absent, and are bound, subject to any regulations, by obligations arising under those terms and conditions and entitled to return to a job of a prescribed kind. The 2008 Regulations removed the distinction between ordinary and maternity leave so that an employee taking additional maternity leave is also entitled to the benefit of (and bound by any obligations arising from) all the terms and conditions of employment which would have applied had she not been absent. This does not include remuneration, as defined in reg. 9 MPL Regulations. The employee is entitled, like the person returning from ordinary maternity leave, to protection of her seniority, pensions and similar rights on her return.

All contracts of employment have an implied term of mutual trust and confidence which the employee and employer have a duty to maintain. This continues during the period of additional maternity leave.[78] The authors of the Regulations obviously had a concern that employees might use periods of additional maternity leave or parental leave to participate in rival businesses (see Chapter 2). These provisions ensure that contractual obligations restricting this continue during the period of absence, as well as the employer's and the employee's rights and obligations concerning notice periods. An example of a situation where an employer's treatment of an employee returning from maternity leave amounted to a breach of the duty of mutual trust and confidence can be seen in *Shaw* v *CCL*.[79] Mrs Shaw became

---

[73] Section 71(5) ERA 1996.

[74] Case C-333/97 *Lewen* v *Denda* [2000] IRLR 67 ECJ where a voluntarily given Christmas bonus was held to be 'pay' within the meaning of art. 119 EEC (now 157); thus an employer may not take into account periods when a mother was prohibited from working in order to reduce proportionately the amount awarded.

[75] See *Alabaster* v *Woolwich plc and Secretary of State for Social Security* [2000] IRLR 754.

[76] Following s. 17(2) EA 2002, this is changed to the right to return 'to a job of a prescribed kind'.

[77] See, e.g., Case C-136/95 *Caisse National d'Assurance Vieillesse des Travailleurs Salariés* v *Thibault* [1998] IRLR 399 ECJ, where a woman on maternity leave was not given an annual appraisal and was, as a result, deprived of a merit pay award.

[78] Regulation 17 MPL Regulations.

[79] *Shaw* v *CCL Ltd* [2008] IRLR 284.

pregnant and took maternity leave. Whilst on leave she submitted an application to return to work on a part-time basis. She was flexible about which days and what hours to work but wanted the total to be no more than 14 hours per week. Her application was refused by her employer. She brought claims which included direct and indirect sex discrimination and that she had been constructively dismissed. The Tribunal found in her favour on the discrimination claims. She had suffered direct sex discrimination as a result of not being allowed to return to work on a part-time basis and indirect discrimination as a result of the rule requiring her to work full time on her return from maternity leave. The EAT also held that this discrimination amounted to a fundamental breach of contract, specifically the duty of mutual trust and confidence (see Chapter 3) and thus allowed her claim for constructive dismissal.

8.6 Protection from detriment

Regulation 19 MPL Regulations provides that an employee is not to be subjected to any detriment by any act, or failure to act, by her employer[80] for a number of specified reasons. It is important to note that deliberately failing to act can also be a detriment, such as giving benefits to employees, but failing to give those benefits to persons included in the categories below. The specified reasons include that the employee is pregnant, has given birth to a child, took, or sought to take, the benefits of ordinary maternity leave, took, or sought to take, additional maternity leave or failed to return after a period of ordinary or additional maternity leave and undertook, considered undertaking or refused to undertake work that is allowed (see 8.5.3.1 above) during the maternity leave period. (According to reg. 19(6) if the act that leads to a detriment in this case takes place over a period of time, then the date of the act is the last day of the period. A failure to act takes place on the date it was decided upon.)[81]

In *Abbey National plc v Formoso*[82] an employee was held to have suffered detriment when her employer proceeded to hold a disciplinary hearing without the attendance of the employee, who was absent on a pregnancy related illness. The employee had given notice of the date when she wished her maternity leave to begin, whilst she was absent through pregnancy related sickness. The employers wished to resolve the matter prior to the maternity leave and proceeded with the hearing even though the employee's doctor considered that she was unfit to attend the meeting and would be so until the end of her pregnancy. The EAT confirmed the employment tribunal's view that pregnancy was the effective cause of the disciplinary hearing and that her treatment had amounted to sex discrimination. Similarly, in *Gus Home Shopping Ltd v Green and McLaughlin*,[83] two employees who were absent from work because of their pregnancy were held to have been discriminated against when they did not receive a discretionary loyalty bonus payable to all employees who remained in their posts until a business transferred to a new location. The different treatment meant that they had been unlawfully discriminated against on the grounds of sex.

---

[80] See s. 47C ERA 1996.

[81] Regulation 19(7) MPL Regulations states that, in the absence of any other evidence, a failure to act is when the employer does an act which is inconsistent with doing the failed act or, if no inconsistent act takes place, when the period expires in which the employer might reasonably have been expected to do the failed act.

[82] [1999] IRLR 222.

[83] [2001] IRLR 75.

8.7 Protection from dismissal

8.7.1 Redundancy

It may be that, during an employee's ordinary or additional maternity leave periods, it is not practicable for the employer to continue to employ her during her existing contract of employment, by reason of redundancy (see Chapter 4). If this happens then the employee is entitled to be offered any suitable alternative vacancy before the end of her employment under a new contract of employment, which takes effect immediately upon ending employment under the current contract. This applies to vacancies with the employer, their successor or an associated employer (see above). The new contract of employment must be such that the work to be done is of a kind which is both suitable in relation to the employee and appropriate for her to do in the circumstances, and the terms and conditions of employment and the capacity and location in which she is to be employed are not substantially less favourable than had she continued to be employed under her previous contract of employment.[84] If the employee is not offered available alternative employment then she may be regarded as being unfairly dismissed for the purposes of Part X ERA 1996.

Regulation 20(2) MPL Regulations provides that if an employee is dismissed for reasons of redundancy and it is shown that the circumstances constituting the redundancy applied equally to one or more other employees in the same undertaking who held similar positions to the dismissed employee, and those other employees have not been dismissed, and the reason, or the principal reason, for the employee being selected for dismissal was related to her pregnancy (as in protection from detriment above), then the dismissal will be unfair for the purposes of Part X ERA 1996 (unfair dismissal).

8.7.2 Unfair dismissal

There are a number of relevant reasons for dismissal which will be regarded as unfair. If the reason, or the principal reason, for the dismissal is:

1. the pregnancy of the employee or the fact that she has given birth to a child, during her ordinary or additional maternity leave period; or

2. the application of a relevant requirement, or a relevant recommendation in accordance with s. 66(2) ERA 1996 (see suspension from work on maternity grounds above); or

3. the fact that she undertook, considered undertaking or refused to undertake work in accordance with reg. 12A (see 8.5.3.1 above);[85] or

4. the fact that she took or availed herself of the benefits of ordinary maternity leave, or the fact that she took additional maternity leave;

then the dismissal is unfair.[86] A dismissal during pregnancy for reasons connected with the pregnancy is likely to amount to direct sex discrimination. In *Brown* v *Rentokil Ltd*[87] the

---

[84] Regulation 10(2)–(3) MPL Regulations.
[85] Regulation 19 MPL Regulations.
[86] Regulation 20 MPL Regulations.
[87] Case 394/96 [1998] IRLR 445 ECJ.

employers dismissed a female employee for sickness absences related to her pregnancy. The employer was applying a rule which meant that any male or female employee could be dismissed if absent for more than 26 weeks. The ECJ held that the situation of a pregnant worker absent because of her pregnancy could not be equated to the absences of a male worker due to incapacity for work.[88]

8.8 The right to return to work

An employee who wishes to return early from her additional maternity leave period must give her employer at least eight weeks' notice of the date on which she intends to return. If the employee tries to return early without giving this notice, then the employer may delay her return for eight weeks.[89] 'Job' is defined, in relation to a person returning to work after additional maternity leave, as meaning 'the nature of the work which she is employed to do in accordance with her contract and the capacity and place in which she is so employed'.[90]

An employee's right to return from leave to the job in which she was employed before her absence[91] means that she has a right to return both with her seniority, pension and other similar rights intact, as if she had not been absent, and with terms and conditions no less favourable than those that would have applied had she not been absent.[92] Except where there is a genuine redundancy situation leading to the dismissal, an employee who takes ordinary or additional maternity leave is entitled to return to the job in which she was employed before her absence.[93] If it is not reasonably practicable for an employer to permit her to do so, then she may return to another job which is both suitable and appropriate for her in the circumstances. This right to return is to return on terms and conditions no less favourable than would have been applicable had she not been absent from work at any time since the beginning of the ordinary maternity leave period. This includes returning with her seniority, pension rights and similar rights as if she had been in continuous employment during the periods of leave and not any less favourable than if she had not been absent through taking additional maternity leave after the ordinary maternity leave period.[94] There is not necessarily a right to return to a different job or to a job with different hours. Women of newly born children might need, for example, flexible working arrangements or part-time hours. Except in so far as they are affected by the Part-time Workers (Prevention of Less Favourable Treatment) Regulations 2000[95] or the Flexible Working Regulations 2002[96] the legislation does not provide this flexibility as a legal right. An example of the problems experienced in the past is that contained in *British Telecommunications plc* v *Roberts and Longstaffe*,[97] which concerned two full-time employees who wished to return to work after their maternity leave on a job-share basis. They were unable to comply with an 'operational requirement' that the work should

---

[88] See also Case C-32/93 *Webb* v *EMO Air Cargo (UK) Ltd* [1994] IRLR 482 ECJ.
[89] Regulation 11 MPL Regulations.
[90] Regulation 2(1) MPL Regulations.
[91] Section 71(4)(c) ERA 1996.
[92] Section 71(7) ERA 1996.
[93] Regulation 18(2) MPL Regulations.
[94] Regulation 18(5) MPL Regulations.
[95] See Chapter 2.
[96] Flexible Working (Eligibility, Complaints and Remedies) Regulations 2002, SI 2002/3236.
[97] [1996] IRLR 601.

include Saturday mornings, and complained of indirect sex discrimination. On the issue of whether they had a right to return to work on a job-share arrangement, it was held that this was not covered by the special protection given to women during their pregnancy and maternity leave. When a woman returns to work the statutory protection is ended.

If the employer offers an alternative post with an associate employer and this is unreasonably turned down by the employee, then the employee is likely to lose her protection from unfair dismissal under these regulations. In both these cases, the onus is on the employer to show that the provisions in question were satisfied in relation to any individual in question.[98]

If an employee has a statutory right to maternity leave as well as a contractual right, in her contract of employment, to such leave, then she is able to take advantage of whichever right, in any particular respect, is the more favourable.[99] Employees are not permitted to take advantage of the statutory right in addition to the contractual right. The regulation does suggest, however, in the use of the term 'in any particular respect', that an employee is able to select those aspects in each which are most favourable to her.

Regulation 22 MPL Regulations also provides an amendment to Part XIV Chapter II ERA 1996 in respect of a week's pay. When, for the purposes of that section, a calculation is being made on the basis of 12 weeks' average pay, then weeks in which the employee is taking ordinary or additional maternity leave and is paid less than her normal entitlement will be disregarded for the calculation purposes.

8.9 Flexible working

Section 47 EA 2002 amended the ERA 1996 to make provision for flexible working arrangements for the care of children. A qualifying employee may apply to his employer for a change in the terms and conditions of employment, in relation to:

1. The hours that are required to be worked.
2. The times when work is required.
3. Whether the work should take place at home or the place of business.
4. Any other aspect that might be specified in regulations.

The purpose of the application must be the care of a child.[100] Such an application must be made before the day on which the child reaches the age of 17 (or 18 if the child is entitled to a disability living allowance).[101] No more than one application every 12 months is permitted and the rules specifically exclude their application to agency workers, which may seem surprising in a wider context of making non-standard work attractive (see Chapter 2).

An employee is entitled to request a contract variation to care for a child if he has been continuously employed for a period of not less than 26 weeks and is either the mother, father, adopter, guardian or foster parent of the child, or is married to or a partner or civil partner[102]

---

[98] Regulation 20(7)–(8) MPL Regulations.
[99] Regulation 20(2) MPL Regulations.
[100] Section 80F ERA 1996.
[101] Regulation 3A Flexible Working (Eligibility, Complaints and Remedies) Regulations 2002 as amended by SI 2009/595.
[102] Regulation 2 defines partners as a man and a woman who are not married to each other but are living together as if they were husband and wife or two people of the same sex who are not civil partners of each other but are living together as if they were civil partners.

of one of these.[103] The request must be in writing, be dated and state whether a previous application has been made to the employer and, if so, when.[104] Within 28 days[105] of the request, the employer, unless he agrees to the request, must hold a meeting with the employee to discuss the application.[106] The employee has the right to be accompanied by another employee of the same employer. This companion has the right to address the meeting and confer with the applicant employee during the meeting.[107] After this meeting there are a further 14 days for the employer to give the employee notice of the decision reached. This decision needs to be in writing and can either be an agreement to the employee's request, specifying the contract variation which is to take place, or a rejection of the request. In the latter case the employer must give the grounds for refusal together with a sufficient explanation. *Commotion Ltd* v *Rutty*[108] concerned an individual who was employed as a warehouse assistant. After she became legally responsible for the care of her grandchild she made an application to work three days a week instead of five. Her request was turned down on the grounds that it would have a detrimental impact on performance in the warehouse. The EAT, however, supported her claim that the employer had failed to establish that they had refused the request on one of the grounds permitted by s. 80G(1)(b) ERA 1996. Tribunals were entitled to investigate to see whether the decision to reject the application was based on facts and whether the employer could have coped with the change without disruption. In this case the EAT found that the evidence did not support the employer's assertion and the employer had not carried out any investigations to see whether they could cope with what the claimant wanted.

Regulation 3B[109] introduced an entitlement to request a contract variation for the care of an adult. Thus an employee can request such a variation for a person over the age of 18 years if the employee has been continuously employed for a period of not less than 26 weeks and is, or expects to be, caring for a person in need of care who is either married to or the partner or civil partner of the employee, a relative of the employee, or living at the same address as the employee. In this case 'relative' means:

> a mother, father, adopter, guardian, special guardian, parent in law, step parent, son, step son, daughter, step daughter, brother, step brother, brother in law, sister, step sister, sister in law, uncle, aunt or grandparent, and includes adoptive relationships and relationships of full blood or, in the case of an adopted person, such of those relationships as would exist but for the adoption.

One of the oddities resulting from this much-needed amendment to the regulations is that the only people now for whom one cannot make a statutory request for flexible working are those between the ages of 17 years and 18 years. The parents of such an age group might feel that this is unfair as most people between these ages are still in need of adult care.

Section 80G(1)(b) ERA 1996 provides that an employer may refuse such a request only if one or more of the following grounds applies:

---

[103] Regulation 3 Flexible Working (Eligibility, Complaints and Remedies) Regulations 2002.
[104] Regulation 4 Flexible Working (Eligibility, Complaints and Remedies) Regulations 2002.
[105] All the periods referred to here can be extended by mutual agreement between the employer and the employee: reg. 12 Flexible Working (Procedural Requirements) Regulations 2002, SI 2002/3207.
[106] Regulation 3 Flexible Working (Procedural Requirements) Regulations 2002.
[107] Regulation 14 Flexible Working (Procedural Requirements) Regulations 2002.
[108] [2006] IRLR 171.
[109] Added by the Flexible Working (Eligibility, Complaints and Remedies) (Amendment) Regulations 2006, SI 2006/3314.

- The burden of additional costs.

- Detrimental effect on ability to meet customer demand.

- Inability to reorganise work amongst existing staff.

- Inability to recruit additional staff.

- Detrimental impact on quality.

- Detrimental impact on performance.

- Insufficiency of work during the periods the employee proposes to work.

- Planned structural changes.

- Such other grounds as may be specified by regulations.

An employee is entitled to appeal against any refusal by the employer. This appeal needs to be in writing, set out the grounds for the appeal and be dated. It must be done within 14 days after the date of the employer's notice giving the decision on the original application. Again within 14 days of this meeting the employer must give the employee a decision. If the appeal is dismissed, then the employer must state the grounds for dismissal and give a sufficient explanation as to why those grounds apply.[110]

Failure of an employer to respond in relation to one of these grounds or a decision by an employer to reject the application on incorrect facts may lead to a complaint to an employment tribunal and the award of compensation of up to eight weeks' pay.

8.10 Parental leave

Two important features of parental leave are, first, that it is available to fathers as well as mothers and, secondly, that it is unpaid.[111] This latter feature affects the take-up of the benefit, especially amongst those who cannot afford the cost of taking time off from work on an unpaid basis. The European Commission published a survey in 2004 on attitudes towards parental leave throughout the EU.[112] This showed that generally the level of awareness amongst men was quite high. Some 75 per cent of male respondents were aware that men could take parental leave. There were some variations between countries. In Sweden, for example, some 97 per cent of men were aware of this, whilst the figure fell to 57 per cent for Irish and Portuguese men. Some 84 per cent of male respondents, however, replied that they had neither taken parental leave nor were they thinking of doing so. This figure did not fall below 70 per cent for any country except Sweden and Finland. At the other extreme were the Spanish male respondents where 95 per cent said that they had not taken and were not thinking of taking parental leave. When the survey looked at the reasons stopping fathers from taking parental leave, the main responses were: insufficient financial compensation (42 per cent); not enough information about parental leave (34 per cent); and careers would be affected (31 per cent). Some 13 per cent of men gave a fear of having to do housework as a reason for not taking up the benefit! This included some 21 per cent of German male respondents, but only 5 per cent of the Greeks and Italians.

---

[110] Regulations 9 and 10 Flexible Working (Procedural Requirements) Regulations 2002.
[111] See 8.11 below for provisions relating to paid paternity leave.
[112] Directorate General Employment and Social Affairs, *Europeans' Attitudes to Parental Leave*, May 2004.

The issue of sufficient finance is not, of course, a male preserve. The average duration of extended maternity leave (which preceded the MPL Regulations 1999) actually taken was less than 30 weeks (40 weeks' entitlement). The main reason given for women returning to work early was that they needed the money (73 per cent of those returning).

8.10.1 Entitlement

Certain employees are entitled to parental leave. This is in addition to any entitlement to statutory maternity or paternity leave. The employees who qualify for parental leave are those who have been continuously employed for a period of not less than one year, and have, or expect to have, responsibility for a child.

The second condition raises the question of who has responsibility for a child. A 'traditional view' of children with a male and a female parent sharing responsibility for a child is not an acceptable model. The MPL Regulations go some way towards offering a definition. Regulation 13(2) states that an employee has responsibility for a child if they meet one of the following tests:

1. If the employee has parental responsibilities for a child.
2. If the employee has been registered as the child's father under any provision of ss. 10(1) or 10A(1) Births and Deaths Registration Act 1953 or of s. 18(1) or (2) Registration of Births and Deaths and Marriages (Scotland) Act 1965.

8.10.2 Meaning of parental responsibility

Parental responsibility is defined in s. 3 Children Act 1989. Section 3(1) provides that:

> . . . parental responsibility means all the rights, duties, powers, responsibilities and authority which by law a parent of a child has in relation to the child and his property.

Section 2(1) Children Act 1989 states that where a child's father and mother were married to each other at the time of the birth, they shall each have parental responsibility for the child. Thus parental responsibility is automatically acquired by both parents if married at the time of birth. It can also be automatically acquired by both parents if they marry subsequent to the birth.[113] Where they are not married the mother has parental responsibility, unless the father acquires that responsibility in accordance with the provisions of the Act.[114]

Section 4 Children Act 1989 deals with the acquisition of parental responsibility by the father. Where the child's father and mother were not married to each other, parental responsibility can be achieved by the father on an order of the court resulting from an application by the father, or by entering into a parental responsibility agreement with the mother, which provides for the father to have parental responsibility for the child.

Parental responsibility is therefore automatically acquired by the mother, but this cannot be said of the father if not married to the mother at the birth or subsequently.

Parental responsibility does not necessarily mean that a father is making day-to-day decisions about a child or, indeed, having the same responsibility for a child's welfare as the

---

[113] See s. 1 Family Reform Act 1987.
[114] Section 2(2) Children Act 1989.

mother may have. It suggests, as stated by Lady Justice Butler-Shloss[115] in a case concerning a father's application for a parental responsibility order:

> A father who has shown real commitment to the child concerned and to whom there is a positive attachment, as well as a genuine *bona fide* reason for the application, ought in a case such as the present, to assume the weight of those duties and cement that commitment and attachment by sharing the responsibilities for the child with the mother. This father is asking to assume that burden as well as that pleasure of looking after his child, a burden not lightly to be undertaken.

As the MPL Regulations make clear, this includes having responsibility for an adopted child or a child who is placed with the employee for the purposes of adoption.

8.10.3 **Leave entitlement**

An employee is entitled to 13 weeks' leave in respect of any individual child and 18 weeks in respect of a child who is entitled to a disability living allowance.[116] The leave entitlement is of 'any individual child', so that an employee/parent of multiple-birth children will be entitled to 13 weeks in respect of each. Similarly employees/parents with more than one child, of differing ages, will be entitled to 13 weeks' leave in respect of each child. Section 76(1) ERA 1996 states that the absence from work is with the 'purpose of caring for a child'. Although the ERA 1996 suggests that the regulations may 'specify things which are, or are not, to be taken as done for the purpose of caring for the child',[117] they do not. It is, presumably, left to the employer and employee to decide.

A week's leave has different meanings in different circumstances. First, it can mean that where the employee is required, under the contract of employment, to work the same period each week, then a week's leave is equal in duration to that period. Thus if an employee works from Monday to Friday each week, then a week's leave will be a period from Monday to Friday. Secondly, where the employee is required, under the contract of employment, to work different periods in different weeks, or works in some weeks and not others, then a week's leave is calculated by adding the total periods that the employee is required to work in a year and dividing by 52. Thus, for example, if an employee works for five days every alternate week, then a week's leave will be 5×26, divided by 52, making it 2.5 days.[118] If an employee takes leave in shorter periods than a week, according to the definitions, then an employer will need to total the leave taken to aggregate it into weekly periods.

The entitlement to 13 weeks' leave is dependent upon one year's continuous employment with the same, or an associated, employer, so, if an individual changes employers, that individual will be required to establish one year's continuous service with the new employer before being able to acquire rights to parental leave again. This raises the question of transferring the balance on an employee's entitlement between employers. If an individual, for example, takes four weeks' parental leave with employer A and then moves to employer B, they will have a balance of nine weeks' leave to which they will be entitled after one year's

---

[115] *Re S (A Minor) (Parental Responsibility)* [1995] 3 FCR 225.
[116] Regulation 14(1) MPL Regulations and reg. 14(1A) added by the Maternity and Parental Leave (Amendment) Regulations 2001, SI 2001/4010.
[117] Section 76(5)(a) ERA 1996.
[118] Regulation 14(2)–(3) MPL Regulations.

continuous service with employer B. The problem for employer B is to know how much of an entitlement the individual has left. This information can only come from employer A or from the employee. There is no requirement for employers to keep records of parental leave taken, although it will surely be a matter of good practice to do so.

8.10.4 **When there is entitlement to parental leave**

The entitlement to parental leave is in respect of a child who is less than five years old. When the child reaches its fifth birthday the entitlement ceases in respect of that child. The three exceptions to this are, first, when there are adopted children or children placed with an employee for adoption. In these cases the entitlement ceases on the fifth anniversary of the date on which the placement began. In such cases the upper age of five years cannot apply. The regulations provide an absolute upper age limit of the date of the child's 18th birthday. Secondly, an employee with a child who is entitled to a disability living allowance will be able to use their leave over a longer period, until the 'child' is 18 years of age.[119] Disability living allowance is defined as the disability living allowance provided by Part III Social Security Contributions and Benefits Act 1992.[120] Thirdly, if an employer exercises their right to delay parental leave (see below) and this results in the child passing the fifth birthday, the entitlement can still be taken at the end of the period for which leave had been postponed, even though the child will now be over five years old.

8.10.5 **Procedural rules**[121]

If there are no contractual rules to the contrary or any collective or workforce agreements affecting the procedures, then the MPL Regulations lay down a number of default procedures which apply before the employee can take their parental leave entitlement. There are essentially three conditions that an employee needs to comply with before their parental leave may commence. These are the evidence condition, the notice condition and the postponement condition. It should be noted that, under the default arrangements, employees may not take leave in periods of less than one week, except where the child is entitled to a disability living allowance. To fulfil the evidence condition an employer may request from the employee such evidence as may be reasonably required of the employee's responsibility or expected responsibility for the child in question, the age of that child or, if the request for leave is in connection with a child entitled to a disability living allowance, then evidence of that entitlement. It is interesting that the employee is not required to show any evidence of leave previously taken in respect of that child.

To fulfil the notice condition employees are required to give notice to the employer specifying the dates on which the period of leave is to start and finish. This notice is to be given to the employer at least 21 days before the start date. There are special rules for certain employees. The first applies to an employee who is the father and wishes his parental leave to commence on the date on which the child is born. In this situation the employee must give at least 21 days' notice before the beginning of the expected week of childbirth, specifying

---

[119] Regulation 15(1)–(3) MPL Regulations.
[120] Regulation 2(1) MPL Regulations.
[121] Schedule 2 MPL Regulations.

when the expected week of childbirth is and the duration of the period of leave. The second is where the leave is in respect of a child to be placed with the employee for adoption; then the notice needs to specify the week in which the placement is expected to occur and the duration of the leave. It needs to be given to the employer at least 21 days before the beginning of the placement week, or, if that is not reasonably practicable, as soon as is reasonably practicable.

Employers are able to postpone parental leave, except in relation to the leave requested in the special cases above, once the employee has given the required notice. The employer may take such action

> if the employer considers that the operation of his business would be unduly disrupted if the employee took leave during the period identified in his notice.

This is an important safeguard for employers who may be faced with a number of employees wishing to take time off at the same time of the year (for example, school holidays). The employer may postpone leave for up to six months as long as, at the end of the postponement period, the employee is permitted to take the same length of leave as originally requested. The employer is required to give notice to the employee of the postponement, in writing, stating the reasons for the delay and specifying the dates on which the delayed leave may commence and end. The employer's notice of postponement must be given to the employee not more than seven days after the employee's notice was given to the employer. This means, of course, that employees will have a minimum of 14 days' notice of the employer's decision to postpone the leave.

8.10.6 Limitations on parental leave

There are two important limitations contained in the default procedures. First, an employee may not take more than four weeks' leave in respect of a particular child in any one year and that leave must be taken in periods of at least one week, unless the child in respect of whom leave is taken is entitled to a disability living allowance.[122] This is rather an inflexible approach and can mean that a person will need to take a week's parental leave when they actually need less. This happened in *Rodway* v *South Central Trains Ltd*[123] where an employee needed a Saturday off in order to look after his son. His application for parental leave was turned down because of the lack of available cover. In the event he took the day off anyway and was subsequently disciplined. The EAT held that the individual could not have suffered a detriment because of a reason related to parental leave, because such leave could only be taken in periods of one week and not just for one day.

A week is here defined as in reg. 14 (see above). The definition of a year is interesting. It is a 12-month period commencing with the date, except in certain cases, on which the employee first became entitled to parental leave in respect of the child in question. This presumably means, for example, 12-month periods from the birth of a child. Alternatively, where a period of continuous employment is interrupted, then at the date when the employee newly qualifies after a further period of continuous employment.

---

[122] Schedule 2, paras. 7–8.
[123] [2005] IRLR 583.

It is important to note that these procedural rules can be varied by agreement between employers and employees or their representatives, in the form of collective or workforce agreements.[124]

8.10.7 Complaint to an employment tribunal

Section 80(1) ERA 1996 provides that an employee may complain to an employment tribunal if the employer has unreasonably postponed a period of parental leave or has prevented, or attempted to prevent, the employee from taking parental leave. The complaint needs to be made within three months beginning with the date of the matter complained about, or such further period as the tribunal agrees if this was not reasonably practicable. If the tribunal agrees with the complaint it may make a declaration to that effect and award compensation to the employee, having regard to the employer's behaviour and any loss sustained by the employee as a result of the matters complained of.

8.10.8 Employee rights during parental leave

An employee who is absent on parental leave is entitled to the benefit of the terms and conditions of employment which would have applied if they had not been absent. This includes any matters connected with the employee's employment, whether or not they arise under the contract of employment, except for matters relating to remuneration.[125] The employee is also entitled to the benefit of the employer's implied obligation of trust and confidence and any terms and conditions of employment relating to notice of the termination of the employment contract by his employer, compensation in the event of redundancy, disciplinary or grievance procedures.

The absent employee is bound by any obligations arising under their terms and conditions of employment. Additionally reg. 17(1) MPL Regulations states that the employee is bound by an implied obligation of good faith and any terms and conditions of employment relating to notice of the termination of the employment contract by the employee, the disclosure of confidential information, the acceptance of gifts or other benefits, or the employee's participation in any other business.[126]

There may be a problem in differentiating between when the employee is on parental leave and when occupying their own spare time. Generally, the spare time activities of employees are no business of the employer, although it may be possible to prevent employees working for competitors during their spare time if it can be shown that the employer's business would be seriously damaged. In *Nova Plastics Ltd* v *Froggat*[127] the EAT rejected the argument that there was a general implication that any work for a competitor should be regarded as being a breach of trust or a failure to give loyal service. The intention to set up in competition with the employer is not necessarily a breach of the implied duty of fidelity, although the renting

---

[124] For collective agreements, see Chapter 11.
[125] In Case C-218/98 *Abdoulaye* v *Régie Nationale des Usines Renault SA* [1998] IRLR 811 ECJ, the trade unions claimed that new fathers should be entitled to the same bonus given to women taking maternity leave; this view was rejected by the ECJ who held that they were not comparable situations.
[126] Section 77(1) ERA 1996.
[127] [1982] IRLR 146.

and equipping of premises, in an employee's spare time, and arranging financial backing to set up in competition may be construed as a breach.[128]

8.10.9 The right to return to work

There are important differences in this right, depending upon the length of leave taken:

1. An employee who takes parental leave for a period of four weeks or less, other than immediately after additional maternity leave, is entitled to return to work to the job in which they were employed before the absence.

2. An employee who takes more than four weeks' parental leave is also entitled to return to the job in which they worked prior to the absence. If, in this latter case, it is not reasonably practicable to return to that job, then an employer must permit the employee to return to another job which is both suitable and appropriate in the circumstances. The exception to this will be as a result of a redundancy situation.

3. An employee who takes parental leave of four weeks or less immediately after additional maternity leave is entitled to return to the job in which she was employed prior to the absence, unless it would not have been reasonably practicable for her to return to that job at the end of her additional maternity leave, and it is still not reasonably practicable for the employer to permit her to return to that job at the end of parental leave. In such a situation she will be entitled to return to another job which is both suitable and appropriate in the circumstances. There is also an exception for redundancy situations.[129]

This right to return is on terms and conditions, with regard to remuneration, which are no less favourable than those which would have applied if the employee had not been absent from work on parental leave, with seniority, pension rights and similar rights preserved as if the employee had been in continuous employment; otherwise on terms and conditions no less favourable than those which would have applied if there had been no period of absence.

The MPL Regulations also make provision for a person who takes parental leave immediately after the period of additional maternity leave. In that case they are entitled to return with all the above as if they had not been absent during the period of ordinary maternity leave, additional maternity leave and parental leave combined.

8.10.10 Protection from detriment and dismissal

An employee who has taken parental leave is not to be subjected to detriment by any act, or any deliberate failure to act, by the employer.[130] An employee who is dismissed for reasons connected to the fact that they took parental leave is to be treated as unfairly dismissed in accordance with Part X ERA 1996 (the provisions relating to unfair dismissal).[131] If there is a complaint of unfair dismissal and the question arises as to whether the reason, or principal reason, is related to the fact that the employee took, or sought to take, parental leave, then it is for the employer to show that the provisions have been complied with.[132]

---

[128] See *Lancashire Fires Ltd* v *SA Lyons & Co Ltd* [1997] IRLR 113 CA.
[129] Regulation 18(1)–(3) MPL Regulations.
[130] Regulation 19(1) MPL Regulations.
[131] Regulation 20(1)(a) MPL Regulations.
[132] Regulation 20(8) MPL Regulations.

An employee shall also be regarded as unfairly dismissed if the reason, or the principal reason, for their dismissal is that they were redundant and it can be shown that the circumstances causing the redundancy applied equally to one or more employees in the same business and holding similar positions to that held by the dismissed employee, and who have not been dismissed by the employer, and the reason, or the principal reason, for the selection of the employee for dismissal was that they had taken parental leave.[133] Thus an employee selected for redundancy, where it can be shown that other employees in similar positions were not selected for redundancy and the selected employee was chosen because of their parental leave, will automatically be entitled to make a claim for unfair dismissal. If, however, the employer, or an associated employer, offers the employee a position that is both appropriate and suitable, but the employee unreasonably turns it down, then the employee will lose any right to claim unfair dismissal by reason of taking parental leave.[134]

8.10.11 Additional provisions

If an employee has a statutory right to parental leave and also a contractual right, in their contract of employment, to parental leave, then they are able to take advantage of whichever right, in any particular respect, is the more favourable.[135] He is not permitted to take advantage of the statutory right in addition to a contractual right. The regulation does suggest, however, when it uses the term 'in any particular respect', that it is permissible to 'cherry-pick', i.e. pick out the best features of both schemes and take advantage of those.

Regulation 22 MPL Regulations also provides an amendment to Part XIV Chapter II ERA 1996 in respect of a week's pay. When, for the purposes of that regulation, a calculation is being made on the basis of 12 weeks' average pay, then weeks in which the employee is taking parental leave should be ignored.

8.11 Paternity leave

The Paternity and Adoption Leave Regulations 2002[136] provide the qualification rules for paternity leave. An employee is entitled to paternity leave if:

1. He has been employed for at least 26 weeks prior to the 14th week before the expected week of childbirth.

2. He is either the child's father or, if not, is married to or a partner of the child's mother.

3. He is to have responsibility, along with the mother, for the upbringing of the child.

An employee will still have satisfied the requirements if the child is born before the 14th week before the expected birth, or if the child is stillborn after 24 weeks of pregnancy, or if the child's mother dies.[137]

---

[133] Regulation 20(2) MPL Regulations.
[134] Regulation 20(7) MPL Regulations.
[135] Regulation 21(2) MPL Regulations.
[136] SI 2002/2788; these were amended by the Maternity and Parental Leave etc. and the Paternity and Adoption Leave (Amendment) Regulations 2006, SI 2006/2014 and by the Maternity and Parental Leave etc. and the Paternity and Adoption Leave (Amendment) Regulations 2008, SI 2008/1966.
[137] Regulation 4 Paternity and Adoption Leave Regulations 2002.

An employee may take either one week's leave or two consecutive weeks' leave. This must be taken before the end of a period of at least 56 days beginning with the date of the child's birth. In the event of multiple births only the first born will count for leave and date purposes.[138] Similar rules apply to the entitlement to paternity leave as a result of adopting a child, except that the key date is the date on which the child is expected to be placed with the adopter.[139]

Other rules, such as the evidential requirements and protection offered, are similar to those concerned with parental leave (see above). An example of a dismissal during paternity leave took place in *Atkins* v *Coyle Personnel plc*.[140] Mr Atkins had taken paternity leave but still carried out work and was available for contact by phone whilst at home. One phone call was from his manager on an issue related to his commission earnings. He was asleep at the time, having only had 3 hours' sleep the previous night because of the new baby. He was not pleased at being woken up; there was an escalating and angry email correspondence and a heated telephone call with his manager which resulted in Mr Atkins being sacked. His unfair dismissal claim included the claim that he had been dismissed for a reason connected with the taking of paternity leave. Regulation 29 of the Paternity and Adoption Leave Regulations 2002[141] provides that an individual is unfairly dismissed in accord with s. 99 ERA 1996 if the reason or principal reason for the dismissal was one connected with taking, or seeking to take, paternity leave. He failed in his claim because the employment tribunal decided that the reason for the dismissal was the frustration of his manager which had grown during the heated exchange between the two. Although he was dismissed during paternity leave, there was no evidence that the reason for the dismissal was connected with the taking of that leave.

8.12 Adoption leave

The right to adoption leave was introduced by the Employment Act 2002 and the Paternity and Adoption Leave Regulations 2002. Some amendments were made by the 2006 Regulations, and in addition the Work and Families Act 2006 provided for regulations to introduce additional adoption leave under certain circumstances. An employee who meets the necessary conditions and complies with the notice and evidential requirements is entitled to adoption leave. As with maternity leave this is divided into ordinary and additional adoption leave, although, of course, there is no equivalent of compulsory maternity leave.

An employee is entitled to adoption leave if the employee, if he is the child's adopter, has been continuously employed for a period of not less than 26 weeks ending with the week in which the employee was notified of being matched with the child, and has notified the agency that he agrees that the child should be placed with him on the date of placement.[142]

An employee's entitlement to adoption leave is not affected by the placement for adoption of more than one child as part of the same arrangement.

---

[138] Regulation 5(1)–(2) Paternity and Adoption Leave Regulations 2002.
[139] Regulations 8–11 Paternity and Adoption Leave Regulations 2002.
[140] [2008] IRLR 420.
[141] SI 2002/2788.
[142] Regulation 15(2) Paternity and Adoption Leave Regulations 2002.

Ordinary adoption leave and additional adoption leave will normally last for 26 weeks each. It may be less, of course, if the employee were dismissed before the end of this period. It may also end early if the placement is disrupted. The other matters concerning adoption leave are identical to those concerning maternity leave, which are outlined earlier in this chapter. These matters concern the right to return to work, notice periods for early return matters concerning terms and conditions during adoption leave, and contact between the employer and employee during adoption leave, including the right to carry out up to 10 days' work with the employer without bringing the statutory adoption leave period to an end.

Chapter summary

This chapter has been concerned with a variety of measures which give rights to parents and pregnant women, as well as protect them from discrimination. It began by looking at the special position of women who are pregnant or who have recently given birth. It examined their rights to maternity leave and their rights during that leave and when they decide to return to work, including the right to ask for flexible working patterns. Then the rights of both men and women to parental leave were considered and the relative rigidity of the default arrangements for such leave. Finally it examined the law with regard to both paternity and adoptive leave.

Further reading

Deakin, S. and Morris, G. *Labour Law*: 5th edn, Hart Publishing, 2009, Chapter 6.

http://www.direct.gov.uk/en/Employment/index.htm for the Government website on employment rights, which includes the topics in this chapter.

Visit **www.mylawchamber.co.uk/sargeant** to access legal updates, live weblinks and practice exam questions to test yourself on this chapter.

mylawchamber
unrivalled support for legal education

9 Business restructuring

9.1 Introduction

One of the occasions when a worker is perhaps at his most vulnerable, in relation to work, is when the business is reorganised in some way. The reorganisation may be the result of a takeover by another employer, or because the worker's own employer has become insolvent or there is a perceived need to reduce the number of employees. In such situations a worker's security of employment and their terms and conditions are often at risk.

The European Community recognised this at an early stage. There was a concern that the development of the single market would lead to a large number of mergers and acquisitions as industry and commerce became more European based, rather than nationally based. In order to make these changes more acceptable to workers and their representatives, a number of initiatives emerged from the Community's Social Action Programme of 1974. These were initiatives concerned with consultation in collective redundancy situations, protection during transfers of undertakings and for those whose employer had become insolvent. In particular there were three Directives that have long been part of national law and provide some protection for employees as a result of business restructuring. These Directives were the Collective Redundancies Directive,[1] which is incorporated into Part IV Chapter II TULRCA 1992; the Acquired Rights Directive,[2] which was originally transposed by the Transfer of Undertakings (Protection of Employment) Regulations 1981;[3] and the Insolvency Directive,[4] which is incorporated into Part XII ERA 1996. Subsequently, the Community has adopted two Directives concerned with information and consultation. These are the European Works

---

[1] Council Directive 75/129/EEC on the approximation of the laws of the Member States relating to collective redundancies OJ 1975 L48/29; amended by Directive 92/56/EEC OJ L245/3; consolidated by Directive 98/59/EC OJ L225/16.

[2] Council Directive 77/187 on the approximation of the laws of the Member States relating to the safeguarding of employees' rights in the event of transfers of undertakings, businesses or parts of undertakings or businesses OJ L61/26; amended by Directive 98/50/EC OJ L201/88; now consolidated into Directive 2001/23/EC OJ L82/16 22.3.2001.

[3] SI 1981/1794; now the Transfers of Undertakings (Protection of Employment) Regulations 2006, SI 2006/246.

[4] Directive 2002/74/EC amended Council Directive 80/987/EEC on the approximation of the laws of the Member States relating to the protection of employees in the event of the insolvency of their employer OJ L270/10 23.9.2002.

Council Directive,[5] whose purpose was the establishment of formal consultation processes in transnational undertakings, and the Information and Consultation Directive[6] which provides for the establishment of information and consultation procedures in all undertakings employing at least 50 employees in one Member State. These Directives were transposed into national law by the Transnational Information and Consultation of Employees Regulations 1999 (TICE Regulations 1999)[7] and the Information and Consultation of Employees Regulations 2004 (ICE Regulations).[8]

9.2 Consultation and information

The European Commission has a long history of introducing measures to encourage employee involvement and employee consultation in the enterprises in which they are employed. The Commission's attempts to adopt measures which included employee involvement, rather than measures aimed at consultation and information, have not been successful. The measures concerning employee involvement were associated with the Community's attempts to set up new legal instruments such as the European company statute.[9] This was one of a number of statutes aimed at setting up European legal entities, which would help organisations to carry out their business in different Member States within the Community without being hindered by a legal organisation based on the rules of just one Member State. Other entities included a European co-operative society and a European mutual society. The Commission included proposals for employee involvement in these organisations. Initially a German model of two-tier company boards was proposed, so that employee representatives would have membership of the supervisory board and have, therefore, some involvement in the running of the business. At various times since then the Commission has modified its proposals, but, as the Commission accepted, the proposals were never accepted because they were suggesting worker participation, rather than worker consultation.[10] It was only after, finally, adopting a much more flexible approach that Directives were adopted, providing for a range of employee involvement in new legal entities, known as a European company (or Societas Europaea)[11] and a European co-operative society.[12] The European Commission has two levels on which it has proposed to harmonise the approach of Member States to the issues of consultation of employees. These are, first, at the transnational level, as exemplified by the introduction of European Works Councils, and, secondly, at the national level, with the adoption of the Information and Consultation Directive.

---

[5] Council Directive 94/45/EC on the establishment of a European Works Council or a procedure in Community-scale undertakings and Community-scale groups of undertakings for the purpose of informing and consulting employees OJ L254/64.

[6] Council Directive 2002/14/EC establishing a general framework for informing and consulting employees in the European Community OJ L80/29 23.2.2002.

[7] SI 1999/3323.

[8] SI 2004/3426.

[9] See OJ C176 8.7.91.

[10] See Communication from the Commission on worker involvement and consultation COM (95) 547.

[11] Council Directive 2001/86/EC supplementing the Statute for a European company with regard to the involvement of employees OJ L294/22 10.11.2001.

[12] Council Directive 2003/72/EC supplementing the statute for a European Co-operative Society with regard to the involvement of employees OJ L207/25 18.8.2003.

9.3 **The transnational model**

The European Works Council Directive[13] (EWC Directive) was finally adopted after some 14 years of debate. It was originally adopted under the Agreement on Social Policy 1992 and so did not bind the United Kingdom. After the 1997 general election, and a willingness of the United Kingdom to accept the Social Policy Agreement, the Council adopted an extension Directive with a requirement for it to be transposed into national law by 15 December 1999.[14]

The purpose of the Directive was

to improve the right to information and to consultation of employees in Community-scale undertakings and Community-scale groups of undertakings.[15]

A Community-scale undertaking is one that has at least 1,000 employees within the Member States and at least 150 employees in each of at least two Member States. A Community-scale group of undertakings is one where a group of undertakings[16] has at least 1,000 employees within the Member States with at least two group undertakings in different Member States employing at least 150 employees.[17] These measures were due to be transposed into the rest of the Community within two years and, perhaps, their lack of effectiveness was shown in the 'Vilvoorde' crisis in 1997. This was where the French car maker Renault announced the closure of its Belgian plant without any consultation whatsoever with its Belgian workers or its European Works Council. The Renault EWC met once a year, but was not called together until after the company had announced the closure. Although Renault subsequently agreed amendments to its EWC agreement to consult on future transnational structural changes, the whole process perhaps reflects the weakness of the requirements and of any potential sanctions. A similar lack of consultation appeared to take place when BMW of Germany sold its Rover car making subsidiary in the United Kingdom in 1999. Consultation appeared to take place with German workers represented on the company's supervisory board, but not with British workers represented by eight members of its EWC.[18]

On 20 December 2000 the Council of Ministers reached agreement on a Regulation establishing a European Company Statute. This gives companies operating in more than one Member State the option of establishing themselves as 'European companies' (Societas Europaea or SE) operating under EU rules rather than a variety of national rules as at present. An SE can be established by the merger or formation of companies with a presence in at least two different Member States.

One concern in establishing this procedure was that companies previously based in countries with strong requirements for information and consultation might be able to avoid these requirements by establishing themselves as an SE, especially if they were merging with companies from countries with weak consultation requirements. As part of this agreement,

[13] Council Directive 94/45/EC on the establishment of a European Works Council or a procedure in Community-scale undertakings and Community-scale groups of undertakings for the purpose of informing and consulting employees OJ L254/64.

[14] Council Directive 97/74/EC OJ L010/22.

[15] Article 1(1) EWC Directive.

[16] Meaning a controlling undertaking and its controlled undertakings: art. 2(b) EWC Directive.

[17] Article 2(a) and (c) EWC Directive.

[18] The workers employed at Luton by Vauxhall Motors also complained about the absence of consultation when the company announced the plant's closure in December 2000.

therefore, there is a Directive[19] establishing rules for information, consultation and, possibly, participation of workers employed by the SE.

Information is defined as informing the representatives of the employees

> in a manner and with a content which allows the employees' representatives to undertake an in-depth assessment of the possible impact and, where appropriate, prepare consultations with the competent organ of the SE.[20]

Consultation is defined as:

> The establishment of dialogue and exchange of views between the body representative of the employees . . . and the competent organ of the SE, at a time, in a manner and with a content which allows the employees' representatives, on the basis of information provided, to express an opinion on measures envisaged by the competent organ which may be taken into account in the decision-making process within the SE.[21]

When the SE is created there will need to be a special negotiating body to discuss the arrangements for employee involvement. In the absence of any agreement there will be standard rules established by the Directive which will need to be followed. These require information and consultation on matters such as:

- The structure, economic and financial situation.
- The probable development of the business and of production and sales.
- The situation and probable trend of employment and investment.
- Substantial changes concerning organisation, introduction of new working methods or production processes.
- Transfers of production, mergers, cutbacks or closures of undertakings, establishments or important parts thereof.
- Collective redundancies.

There are also provisions for employee participation for those SEs which include companies from countries where there are such rules. Participation can include the right to elect or appoint, or oppose the election or appointment of, members of the supervisory or administrative board.

9.3.1 Transnational Information and Consultation of Employees Regulations 1999

The EWC Directive was transposed into national law by the TICE Regulations 1999, which came into effect on 15 January 2000.[22] By this time many British employees were already represented in EWCs set up by multinational companies, influenced by the law of other Member States which had already transposed the Directive. The Regulations do not have effect

---

[19] Directive 2001/86/EC.
[20] Article 2(i).
[21] Article 2(j).
[22] SI 1999/3323; the Regulations are some 57 pages long, so what follows can only be regarded as a summary of the main points; the Regulations themselves should be consulted for a more detailed understanding; see *www.opsi.gov.uk* and Chapter 1.

if there is already in existence an art. 6 or an art. 13 agreement, unless the parties have decided otherwise.[23] An art. 6 agreement is one that establishes an EWC in accordance with the Directive. An art. 13 agreement is one that established their own information and consultation procedures before the Directive was transposed into national law.

Consultation is defined in the TICE Regulations 1999 as meaning the exchange of views and the establishment of a dialogue in the context of an EWC or in the context of an information and consultation procedure.[24] The central management of an undertaking is responsible for creating the conditions and the means necessary for setting up an EWC, where the central management is situated in the United Kingdom; where it is situated outside the country, but has its representative agent based in the United Kingdom; or, if neither of these, has its biggest group of employees in the United Kingdom.[25] The number of UK employees is to be calculated by taking an average over a two-year period, with provision for counting some part-timers as a half number. The number of employees in undertakings in other Member States is to be calculated in accordance with whatever formula that State has adopted in its law transposing the EWC Directive. Employee representatives are entitled to information on these calculations so that they can decide whether the employer qualifies. If the information given to them is incomplete or inadequate, they may present a complaint to the Central Arbitration Committee (CAC).[26]

If central management does not act on its own initiative, the whole process of establishing an EWC can be started with a request from 100 employees, or their representatives, in two undertakings in two Member States. If there is a dispute as to whether a valid request has been made, this can be referred to the CAC for a decision.[27]

The first stage is the establishment of a special negotiating body (SNB), whose task is to negotiate, with central management, a written agreement covering 'the scope, composition, functions and terms of office' of an EWC or the arrangements for implementing an information and consultation procedure.[28] The SNB must consist of at least one representative from each Member State and there is a weighting formula to increase representation from bigger units in different States. The United Kingdom representatives are to be elected by a ballot of United Kingdom employees and any complaints about the ballot are to be made to the CAC. Where there is already an elected body in existence with whom consultation takes place, then that body can nominate the representatives from its membership.[29]

The contents of the agreement to be reached between the SNB and the central management are set out in art. 6 EWC Directive and are reflected in Part IV TICE Regulations 1999. The two parties are to negotiate in 'a spirit of co-operation with a view to reaching an agreement'.[30] They may negotiate an agreement to set up an EWC or to establish an information and consultation procedure.[31] The EWC agreement must include agreement on:

---

[23] Regulation 42 TICE Regulations 1999.
[24] Regulation 2 TICE Regulations 1999.
[25] Regulation 5 TICE Regulations 1999.
[26] Regulations 6–8 TICE Regulations 1999.
[27] Regulations 9–10 TICE Regulations 1999.
[28] Regulation 11 TICE Regulations 1999.
[29] Regulations 12–15 TICE Regulations 1999; the BMW EWC Agreement mentioned above, e.g., had a membership of eight German representatives, eight British representatives and four Austrian representatives.
[30] Regulation 17(1) TICE Regulations 1999 which copies the wording in art. 6(1) EWC Directive.
[31] Regulation 17(3) TICE Regulations 1999.

1. The undertakings which are covered by the agreement.

2. The composition of the EWC.

3. The functions and procedures for information and consultation.

4. The venue, frequency and duration of meetings.

5. The financial and material resources to be allocated to the EWC.

6. The duration of the agreement and the procedure for renegotiation.[32]

If the parties decide to establish an information and consultation procedure instead of an EWC, then this agreement must specify a method by which the information and consultation representatives[33] 'are to enjoy the right to meet and discuss the information conveyed to them'. The information conveyed to the representatives must relate in particular to 'transnational questions which significantly affect the interests of employees'.[34] If negotiations do not start within six months of a valid request by employees or fail to finish within three years from the date of that request, the regulations provide for a default agreement, which is contained in the Schedule. These provide for an EWC of between three and 30 members, with at least one member from each Member State where there are undertakings. This representation is weighted according to the relative size of the undertakings in different States. The rules cover the election or appointment of United Kingdom delegates and provide that the EWC should meet at least once per annum.[35]

Complaints about the failure of the negotiating process, either because of lack of agreement or a failure to start the process, or because of a failure to keep to the agreement, are to be referred directly to the EAT. The EAT may order the defaulter to remedy the failure and impose a fine of up to £75,000. Central management will have a defence if they are able to show that the failure resulted 'from a reason beyond the central management's control or that it has some other reasonable excuse for its failure'.[36]

One concern related to statutory rights to information is the revealing by management of 'confidential' information. Regulation 24 TICE Regulations 1999 provides that central management is not required to disclose any information or document which, 'according to objective criteria', would seriously prejudice or harm the functioning of the undertaking concerned. It is interesting to speculate as to what this actually means. Would the sale of a subsidiary undertaking in one Member State be such information, if it would prejudice the price received, even though it might have important effects for employees? There is an obligation for a representative, or an adviser to a representative, not to disclose confidential information unless it is a protected disclosure under s. 43A ERA 1996.[37] The CAC has the responsibility of settling disputes about confidentiality and can order information to be disclosed by management or order a representative not to disclose information.

Information and consultation representatives, members of EWCs, SNBs and candidates for relevant elections have certain rights. These are:

---

[32] Regulation 17(4) TICE Regulations 1999.

[33] Defined in reg. 2 TICE Regulations 1999 as a person who represents employees in the context of an information and consultation procedure.

[34] Regulation 17(5) TICE Regulations 1999.

[35] Regulation 18 TICE Regulations 1999.

[36] Regulations 20–22 TICE Regulations 1999.

[37] Regulation 23 TICE Regulations 1999.

1. The right to reasonable time off with pay during working hours.[38]

2. Protection against unfair dismissal; dismissal as a result of performing any of the functions or duties related to any of these bodies will make the dismissal automatically unfair in terms of Part X ERA 1996, the exception to this being where the reason or the principal reason for dismissal is a breach of confidentiality contained in reg. 23(1), unless the employee reasonably believed the disclosure to be a protected disclosure within the meaning of s. 43A ERA 1996.

3. The right not to be subject to detriment as a result of performing any of the duties or functions related to the bodies.

Complaints about any infringement of these rights are to be made to an employment tribunal.

9.4 The national model

Models of consultation vary between the Member States of the European Community. In many, works councils are an established way of channelling information, consultation and, sometimes, negotiation between management and employees.

In the United Kingdom, prior to the Information and Consultation with Employees Regulations 2004[39] (ICE Regulations), there were only a limited number of occasions during which there was a statutory requirement to consult. These included those concerned with collective redundancies and transfers of undertakings (see below). Prior to 1995 the only requirement was for this consultation to take place when there were trade unions recognised for the purpose. Following on from *Commission* v *United Kingdom*,[40] when the ECJ held this to be an inadequate application of the relevant Directives, this liability to consult was widened to include appropriate representatives.[41] Thus, in certain situations there is a requirement to consult even if there is not a trade union recognised for that purpose. A similar requirement is imposed by the Health and Safety (Consultation with Employees) Regulations 1996 (HSCE Regulations 1996).[42] Prior to these regulations there was a requirement for health and safety representatives nominated by the recognised trade union.[43] The 1996 Regulations were intended to provide for situations where there were no such safety representatives. The employer has a duty to consult, in good time, on a range of safety matters, including the introduction of any measure at the workplace which might substantially affect the health and safety of the employees.[44] The consultation must be with the employees directly or their elected representatives.[45]

---

[38] Regulations 25–26 TICE Regulations 1999.
[39] SI 2004/3426.
[40] Cases 382/92 and 383/92 [1994] IRLR 392 ECJ and [1994] IRLR 412 ECJ.
[41] Collective Redundancies and Transfers of Undertakings (Protection of Employment) (Amendment) Regulations 1995, SI 1995/2587, as amended by regulations of the same name in 1999, SI 1999/1925.
[42] SI 1996/1513.
[43] Safety Representatives and Safety Committees Regulations 1977, SI 1977/500.
[44] Regulation 3(a) HSCE Regulations 1996.
[45] Regulation 4(1) HSCE Regulations 1996.

The result of this approach has been extended to other regulations concerned with the transposition of Community law. These include the Working Time Regulations 1998[46] and the Maternity and Parental Leave etc. Regulations 1999.[47] In both sets of regulations there is a default agreement, one concerned with varying aspects of the rules on working time and the other concerned with the rules on parental leave. These default arrangements may be varied by a collective agreement or by a workforce agreement. The former occurs where there are independent trade unions recognised for the purpose. The latter occurs when there are employee representatives, either elected or appointed by the workforce.

Thus an employer has an obligation to consult employee representatives if they wish to adopt a more flexible approach to working time or parental leave. These consultations can result in workforce agreements.[48] An agreement is a workforce agreement if:

1. It is in writing.

2. It has effect for a specific period not exceeding five years.

3. It applies to all the relevant members of the workforce or all those who belong to a particular group.

4. It is signed by the representatives of the workforce; if the employer employs less than 20 workers, then there is the option for the majority of the workers to sign the agreement.

5. Before the agreement is made available for signature, the employer provides all of the workers to whom it is intended to apply with a copy of the agreement and such guidance as the workers might reasonably require in order to understand it fully.

The two Schedules also contain provisions for the election of employee representatives. These 'representatives of the workforce' are workers who have been elected to represent the relevant members of the workforce.[49] Thus, even prior to the 2004 Regulations there existed within the United Kingdom an alternative model for employee consultation. It applied to a very limited number of circumstances and was introduced as a result of the requirement imposed by the appropriate Directives to consult on specific issues.

9.4.1 The Information and Consultation Directive

Directive 2002/14/EC of the European Parliament and of the Council establishing a general framework for informing and consulting employees in the European Community[50] was finally unanimously adopted by the Council of Ministers in December 2001 after some years of debate. It suffered delays because of opposition from a number of countries, including the United Kingdom. The final version was much weaker than the original 1998 proposal, especially in terms of sanctions and of the implementation timetable. Nevertheless it is likely to have an important impact on employer/employee relations in the United Kingdom.

---

[46] SI 1998/1833.

[47] SI 1999/3312.

[48] See Sch. 1 Working Time Regulations 1998, SI 1998/1833 and Sch. 1 Maternity and Parental Leave etc. Regulations 1999, SI 1999/3312.

[49] Relevant members of the workforce are all those workers employed by a particular employer, excluding any worker whose terms and conditions of employment are provided for, wholly or in part, by a collective agreement: see Sch. 1 para. 2 Working Time Regulations 1998; para. 3 contains rules concerning the election of such representatives.

[50] OJ L80/29 23.3.2002.

It is the first EU Directive to introduce a generalised requirement to provide information and to consult with employees or their representatives. All other information and consultation measures have been concerned with specific situations, such as collective redundancies, transfers of undertakings or in situations where companies have a European Works Council. The Directive applies to all undertakings with 50 or more employees. This represents less than 3 per cent of all EU companies, but about 50 per cent of all employees.

In the preamble to the Directive the European Commission provides the justification for the measure. Some of the reasons given are that:

1. The existence of current legal frameworks at national and Community level concerning the involvement of employees has not always prevented serious decisions, that affect employees, from being taken and made public without adequate consultation.[51]

2. There is a need to strengthen dialogue in order to promote trust within undertakings. The result of this will be an improvement in risk anticipation, making work organisation more flexible, and to facilitate employee access to training within the undertaking. It will also make employees more flexible in their approach and involve them in the operation and future of the undertaking, as well as increasing its competitiveness.[52]

3. Timely information and consultation is a prerequisite for successful restructuring and adaptation of undertakings to the needs of the global economy, especially through the new forms of organisation at work.[53]

4. The existing legal frameworks for employee information and consultation are inadequate, because they 'adopt an excessively *a posteriori* approach to the process of change, neglect the economic aspects of decisions taken and do not contribute either to genuine anticipation of employment developments within the undertaking or to risk prevention'.[54]

There are perhaps some, even amongst those who support the aims of the Directive, who might be a little sceptical about such grand claims for the result of the introduction of employee consultation procedures. Nevertheless these justifications give rise to the purpose of the Directive. This is to establish minimum requirements for information and consultation, whilst not preventing Member States from having or introducing provisions more favourable to employees. The Directive only applies to undertakings with a minimum size of 50 employees or establishments with at least 20 employees. This is to avoid any action which might hinder the creation and development of small and medium-sized undertakings.[55]

The purpose is set out as being to establish a general framework for the right to information and consultation of employees in undertakings or establishments within the European Community. The practical arrangements for defining and implementing this are to be left to the Member States, who must carry out their obligations in such a way as to ensure their effectiveness. In doing this the employer and the employees' representatives must work 'in a spirit of co-operation'.

There are some interesting definitions, particularly with regard to the distinction between undertakings and establishments.

[51] Preamble para. (6).
[52] Preamble para. (7).
[53] Preamble para. (9).
[54] Preamble para. (13).
[55] Preamble paras. (18) and (19).

An *undertaking* is a public or private undertaking carrying out an economic activity (whether or not for gain) which is located within the territory of the Member States. An *establishment* is a unit of business where an economic activity is carried out on an ongoing basis with human and material resources. It remains to be seen whether the UK Government further defines these definitions when it eventually introduces regulations to transpose this Directive into national law. It might be worth considering this in order to avoid the possibility of further litigation about the precise meaning of these terms.

Information means transmission by the employer to the employees' representatives of data to help them acquaint themselves with the subject matter and to examine it. *Consultation* means the exchange of views and establishment of dialogue between the employer and the employees' representatives.

The importance of the definitions of undertaking and establishment are relevant because the Directive will apply either to undertakings employing at least 50 employees in any one Member State or to establishments employing at least 20 employees in any Member State. The method for calculating the thresholds of employees is left to the Member State.

It may be possible to make special arrangements for political, religious and charitable bodies where special rules already exist in the Member State and, as ever, Member States may exclude crews of ships 'plying the high seas'.

As mentioned above, the practical arrangements are to be left to the individual Member State. There are, however, rules concerning what information and consultation will cover, when it is to take place and what its objectives are. The subject matter is to be:

1. Information on the recent and probable development of the undertaking's or establishment's activities and economic situation.

2. Information and consultation on the situation, structure and probable development of employment and on any anticipatory measures envisaged, especially those that threaten employment.

3. Information and consultation on decisions likely to lead to substantial changes in work organisation or in contractual relations (including those covered in art. 9 below).

Information shall be given at such time, and in such fashion, as to enable employee representatives to conduct an adequate study and, where necessary, prepare for consultation. *Consultation* shall take place:

- Whilst ensuring that timing, method and content are appropriate.

- At the relevant level of management, depending upon the subject under discussion.

- On the basis of information provided by employer and of the opinion of employee representatives.

- In such a way as to enable employee representatives to meet the employer and obtain a response, and the reasons for that response, to the employee representatives' opinion.

- With a view to reaching agreement on decisions within the scope of the employer's powers.

As with the European Works Council Directive, there is the opportunity for management and labour to negotiate their own information and consultation arrangements, provided that they meet the requirements of the Directive and national legislation. Thus any agreements existing at the transposition date of 23 March 2005 were able to continue as were any other agreements subsequently negotiated. Presumably the UK regulations will provide a framework for such individually negotiated arrangements.

Confidential information has always been an important concern of employers, and the question of what is confidential and what is not will be part of the interest in watching this Directive put into practice. There are two aspects to confidentiality. One is imposing an obligation upon the parties to maintain a confidence. The second is the decision as to what material is so confidential that it cannot be revealed at all. In dealing with the first of these, Member States may provide that employee representatives, and any experts who assist them, may not reveal information to employees or third parties if provided in confidence 'in the legitimate interest of the undertaking or establishment', unless that other party is bound by a duty of confidentiality. This obligation may continue after the expiry of a term of office.

Member States may also provide that the employer need not provide information or consult when the nature of the information or consultation is such that, 'according to objective criteria', it would seriously harm the functioning of the undertaking or establishment or would be prejudicial to it.

Member States shall provide for judicial review of situations where the employer requires confidentiality or does not provide information or consult in accordance with above. This is the case with the TICE Regulations implementing the European Works Council Directive. The independent body is the Central Arbitration Committee.

Article 8 obliges Member States to have suitable judicial processes in place to enable the obligations of employers and employees to be enforced. It also requires adequate sanctions to be available for infringement of the Directive. These sanctions must be 'effective, proportionate and dissuasive'. This is going to be an interesting provision of any UK regulations. There are potentially large sums of money which may be involved in, for example, a merger or an acquisition. If an employer decided that it wished not to consult the employees, is a fine of the sort contained in the TICE Regulations going to be a sufficient deterrent? If it is not, then there might be an issue related to a bigger fine as to whether it would be proportionate.

9.4.2 The Information and Consultation of Employees Regulations[56]

Although art. 11 of the Information and Consultation Directive stipulated 23 March 2005 as the deadline for transposition, there was an extension for Member States who did not have a general, permanent and statutory system of information and consultation, such as the United Kingdom. The ICE Regulations took effect over a period of three years. For employers with at least 150 employees in the United Kingdom they came into effect on 6 April 2005, for those with at least 100 employees the date was 6 April 2007 and employers with at least 50 employees were included from 6 April 2008.[57] There is a narrow definition of employee, so only those who work under a contract of employment are included.[58] The number of employees is worked out by taking the average number employed in the previous 12 months.[59] Employees, or their representatives, have the right to ask for the data on employee numbers[60]

---

[56] SI 2004/3426.
[57] See Sch. 1 ICE Regulations 2004.
[58] Regulation 2 ICE Regulations 2004.
[59] Regulation 4 ICE Regulations 2004.
[60] Regulation 5 ICE Regulations 2004.

and if the employer fails to provide the information, or provides incorrect information, within one month, then the employee, or the employee representatives, can complain to the CAC. After this the CAC can order the employer to produce the information.[61] This information is, of course, crucial. It settles if and when the employer is covered by the Regulations.

The Regulations are complex and the process has a similar approach to that which is used in the statutory recognition of trade unions (see Chapter 11). The process can begin in one of two ways. Either the employer can initiate the process or it starts with a request from the employees. There is a duty of co-operation as stated in reg. 21:

> The parties are under a duty, when negotiating or implementing a negotiated agreement or when implementing the standard information and consultation provisions, to work in a spirit of co-operation and with due regard for their reciprocal rights and obligations, taking into account the interests of both the undertaking and the employees.

According to *Darnton v Bournemouth University*[62] the duty to co-operate was placed on the parties once the negotiating representatives commenced negotiations. In this case it was concluded that the employer was under no obligation to disclose its own legal advice not to make arrangements for the employees to receive such advice.

Stage 1 The request

At least 10 per cent of the employees, either together or separately, need to make the request to the employer to open negotiations to reach an Information and Consultation Agreement in order for it to be a valid request. This 10 per cent is subject to a minimum of 15 employees and a maximum of 2,500. Thus an employer with only 50 employees could require at least 15 employees to make the request, and, in larger organisations, of 25,000 or more, there is a cap on the numbers who need to be involved.[63] The request or requests must be in writing and sent to the employer's head office or principal place of business. It can be sent to the CAC if the employees wish to act anonymously.[64] If there is already an Information and Consultation Agreement in operation the employer may decide to hold a ballot of all employees to find out if they endorse the application for a new agreement.[65] In *Stewart v Moray Council*[66] the employer claimed that three existing agreements covered all employees, even though each only covered part of the workforce. The EAT accepted this argument but then stated that one of the agreements, that covering teachers, was not detailed enough. Where more than one agreement is relied upon, each of them has to cover all the requirements of the Regulations. In this case there was not sufficient information on one of the agreements concerning reg. 8(1)(d) where there is a requirement to set out how the employer is to give information and seek the views of the employee representatives.[67]

---

[61] Regulation 6 ICE Regulations 2004.
[62] [2009] IRLR 4.
[63] Regulation 7(1), (2) and (3) ICE Regulations 2004.
[64] Regulation 7(4) ICE Regulations 2004.
[65] Regulations 8–10 ICE Regulations 2004; the employer can only initiate a ballot if less than 40 per cent of the employees had endorsed the original request.
[66] [2006] IRLR 592.
[67] In *Amicus v Macmillan Publishers Ltd* [2007] IRLR 378 the employers had a pre-existing agreement covering only one site. The CAC held that this could not be relied upon to meet the requirements of the Regulations.

Stage 2 The negotiations

The employer may initiate negotiations without waiting for the employees to request action.[68] Whether it is done on his own initiative or as a result of an employee request the obligations upon the employer are the same. Regulation 14 sets out the procedure. As soon as is reasonably practicable the employer must make arrangements for the appointment or election of 'negotiating representatives'. The employees need to be informed of who these representatives are (in writing) and then invite the negotiating representatives to enter into negotiations to reach a negotiated agreement. All employees need to be entitled to take part in the appointment or election of representatives and all employees in the undertaking need to be represented by a representative.[69] As with the statutory recognition procedures for trade unions, there are strict time limits to be applied to the process. The negotiation must not last more than six months, unless both sides agree, from a time of three months after the employee request was made or the employer initiated the process.[70]

Stage 3 The negotiated agreement

A negotiated agreement must be in writing, be dated and cover all employees. It must set out the circumstances in which the employer must inform and consult the employees.[71] It must provide for the appointment of the Information and Consultation Representatives who are to be informed or consulted. Alternatively it may provide for the information and consultation of all employee representatives.[72] It must be approved by all the negotiating representatives signing it or at least 50 per cent of them if a ballot of all employees is held which approves the agreement.[73]

9.4.2.1 Standard information and consultation provisions

If the employer fails to initiate negotiations then the standard provisions will apply from six months of the date the employee request was made or within six months of the date that representatives were appointed or elected (whichever is sooner). Similarly if the parties fail to reach agreement within the allowed time limit then six months from that time limit expiry the standard provisions apply.[74] In practice this means that the standard provisions will normally be the minimum provisions agreed in any negotiated agreement. There is no need for the information and consultation representatives to agree to anything less as all they need do is wait for the period to expire and the standard provisions will automatically apply.

The standard provisions first itemise what information must be provided to the representatives.[75] These are:

(i) the recent and probable development of the undertaking's activities and economic situation;
(ii) the situation, structure and probable development of employment within the undertaking and on any anticipatory measures envisaged, in particular, where there is a threat to employment;

---

[68] Regulation 7(1) ICE Regulations 2004.
[69] Regulation 15 ICE Regulations 2004 provides for complaints about these requirements to the CAC.
[70] This period does not take into account the delays caused by a ballot or by complaints to the CAC.
[71] Regulation 16(1) ICE Regulations 2004.
[72] Regulation 16(1)(g) ICE Regulations 2004.
[73] Regulation 16(2) ICE Regulations 2004; Sch. 2 specifies the electoral process for the election of representatives.
[74] Regulation 18(1) ICE Regulations 2004.
[75] Regulation 20(1) ICE Regulations 2004.

(iii) decisions likely to lead to substantial changes in work organisation or in contractual relations.[76]

Where there is a failure to comply with any of the terms of a negotiated agreement or a standard provision, a complaint may be made to the CAC within three months beginning with the date of the failure.[77] The CAC may then issue an order for compliance. Failure to carry this out within three months may lead to a further complaint, this time to the EAT which has the power to issue a penalty of up to £75,000.[78]

9.4.2.2 Confidential information

Regulations 25 and 26 deal with the issue of confidentiality. If the employer issues material to employees that is confidential, then the employee owes the employer a duty not to disclose the information.[79] This is always a difficult issue for employee representatives, when they are given information that they are not allowed to disclose to the people who elected or appointed them in the first place. If the recipient does not believe that it is genuinely confidential then he may apply to the CAC to decide whether it was reasonable for the employer to impose a confidentiality condition.

Similarly the employer need not disclose information at all where 'according to objective criteria, the disclosure of the information or document would seriously harm the functioning of, or would be prejudicial to, the undertaking.' Again any information and consultation representative or, where there are no representatives, any employee or their representative, may apply to the CAC for a declaration as to whether it is confidential or not.

9.4.2.3 Employee protection

An employee who is a negotiating representative or an information and consultation representative is entitled to reasonable paid time off during working hours.[80] Employees may take a complaint to an employment tribunal for an employer's failure in this regard within a period of three months beginning with the day of the alleged wrongdoing.

A dismissal of any employee for carrying out activities in relation to the ICE Regulations will be an automatically unfair dismissal. The rules on minimum service or maximum age do not apply in these circumstances.[81] Similarly employees or representatives are protected from detriment.[82]

9.5 Collective redundancies

Redundancy is one of the potentially 'fair' reasons for dismissal listed in s. 98(2) of the ERA 1996. It is therefore dealt with in Chapter 4.

[76] The employer need not inform or consult under these regulations in relation to this section if the employer tells the representatives that he will be complying with the information and consultation obligations under s. 188 TULRCA on collective redundancies or reg. 10 of the TUPE Regulations 1981 on transfers of undertakings.
[77] Regulation 22 ICE Regulations 2004.
[78] Regulation 23 ICE Regulations 2004.
[79] Unless the recipient reasonably believes the disclosure to be a 'protected disclosure' under s. 43A ERA 1996.
[80] Regulations 27–28 ICE Regulations 2004.
[81] Regulation 30 ICE Regulations 2004.
[82] Regulation 32 ICE Regulations 2004.

Council Directive 98/59/EC on the approximation of the laws of the Member States relating to collective redundancies (the Collective Redundancies Directive) is a consolidation Directive. It consolidated Directives 75/129/EEC as amended by Directive 92/56/EEC on the same subject. The original Directive was adopted in 1975 and transposed into British law very quickly. It was included in the Employment Protection Act 1975 and has been part of national law, subject to various amendments, ever since. The provisions are now contained in Part IV Chapter II TULRCA 1992, which outlines the procedure for handling collective redundancies. The legislation has been targeted towards consultation and information, as distinct from negotiations, on the subject. The duty to consult rests upon an employer who is proposing to dismiss 20 or more employees at one establishment within a period of 90 days or less for reasons of redundancy.[83] This may include situations where the employer is proposing to dismiss a workforce and then immediately re-employ them as part of a reorganisation.[84]

This consultation shall begin 'in good time' and in any event at least 30 days before the first dismissal takes effect, or at least 90 days before the first dismissal takes effect if the employer is proposing to dismiss 100 or more employees at one establishment within a period of 90 days.[85]

A debatable issue here, of course, is at what point in time is the employer 'proposing to dismiss'. It is likely that, except perhaps in a disaster situation, there is a period of time over which the decision to dismiss employees by reason of redundancy is reached. There is, perhaps, first the decision in principle to dismiss employees. There may be a second stage where the parts of the organisation in which the redundancies are to take place are identified, followed by a further stage when particular employees are identified. In *R v British Coal Corporation and Secretary of State for Trade and Industry, ex parte Price*[86] the court approved an approach to fair consultation which meant that it began when the proposals were still at a formative stage. Glidewell LJ cited the tests proposed in *R v Gwent County Council, ex parte Bryant*:[87]

Fair consultation meant:

(a) consultation when the proposals are still at a formative stage;
(b) adequate information on which to respond;
(c) adequate time in which to respond;
(d) conscientious consideration by an authority of the response to consultation.

The court in *Griffin v South West Water Services Ltd*[88] disagreed with this, expressing instead the view that the employer's obligation arose only when the employer was able to identify the workers and be in a position to supply the information required by the Directive.

This issue was considered in *Hough v Leyland DAF Ltd.*[89] This case concerned security staff at a number of the employer's premises. The security manager was asked to prepare a report

---

[83] Section 188(1) TULRCA 1992; s. 195 defines dismissal for redundancy as dismissals not related to the individual and there is a presumption of redundancy in any proceedings unless the contrary is shown.
[84] See *GMB v Man Truck & Bus UK Ltd* [2000] IRLR 636.
[85] Section 188(1A) TULRCA 1992. According to *Vauxhall Motors Ltd v TGWU* [2006] IRLR 674 this period of 90 days is only the starting point; it does not mean that the consultation should end within this period. In this case it extended over 22 months.
[86] [1994] IRLR 72.
[87] [1988] COD 19.
[88] [1995] IRLR 15.
[89] [1991] IRLR 194.

on the possibility of contracting out the security function. The manager produced a report recommending that it should be contracted out. It was a further six months before the employer approached the trade union informing them of the employer's intention to contract out security services. The issue was at what stage the employers could be said to have been proposing to dismiss. The EAT held that this occurred at the time of the security manager making his report recommending the contracting out. The employers had argued that the proposals needed to be at a far more advanced stage before the statutory obligation to consult took effect. The EAT held:

> We agree that [s. 99] read as a whole contemplates that matters should have reached a stage where a specific proposal has been formulated and that this is a later stage than the diagnosis of a problem and the appreciation that at least one way of dealing with it would be by declaring redundancies.

The EAT then went on to state that it would not be more helpful to seek a more precise definition because of the large variety of situations that might arise. Article 2(1) Collective Redundancies Directive states that consultation should begin when the employer is 'contemplating' collective redundancies. This was considered in *Re Hartlebury Printers Ltd*.[90] The court held that proposing redundancies cannot include merely thinking about the possibility of redundancies. Contemplating redundancies in the sense of proposing them meant 'having in view or expecting' them. It is, therefore, likely to be at an early stage, but not so early that it is merely an idea that the company is thinking about.[91] If, however, the employer's decision making has progressed to the stage of contemplating two options for the future, one of which is closing down the business and the other is selling it as a going concern, then the employer has reached the stage of 'proposing to dismiss as redundant'.[92]

There are additional complications when an employer is part of a group of companies and the decisions leading to the redundancies are taken elsewhere, such as in the holding company. In *Akavan*[93] the parent company decided to close a factory and consultations were begun by a subsidiary company which was the employer. The ECJ held that the employer's obligation to consult arises when strategic decisions are made within a group of undertakings compelling the employer to contemplate or plan collective redundancies. Consulting prematurely may defeat the purpose of the Directive; by restricting the flexibility available to businesses when restructuring, creating heavier administrative burdens and causing unnecessary anxiety to workers about the safety of their job. It is the employer that has the responsibility for consultation, not the holding company, so the obligation is triggered when the strategic decision compels the employer to contemplate or plan redundancies.

The European Court of Justice[94] held that the notice of dismissals shall not take place until after some of the consultation had taken place. The court suggested that art. 2 meant

---

[90] [1992] ICR 704.

[91] See also *National Union of Public Employees* v *General Cleaning Contractors Ltd* [1976] IRLR 362, which considered the position of a contractor who unexpectedly lost a contract on retendering. The industrial tribunal held that it was sufficiently early to begin consultations after news of the lost contract, not before, even though there was a possibility of losing a contract at retendering; see also *Association of Pattern Makers & Allied Craftsmen* v *Kirvin Ltd* [1978] IRLR 318 where the EAT held that proposing means a state of mind directed to a planned or proposed course of events; in this case on the appointment of a receiver.

[92] See *Scotch Premier Meat Ltd* v *Burns* [2000] IRLR 639.

[93] Case C-44/08 *Akavan Erityisalojen Keskusliitto AEK RY* v *Fujitsu Siemens* [2009] IRLR 944.

[94] Case C-188/03 *Junk* v *Kühnel* [2005] IRLR 310 ECJ.

that consultation with a view to reaching an agreement really meant 'negotiation'. Such negotiation would not be meaningful if it took place entirely after the notice period had commenced. This resulted in an amendment to s. 193 TULRCA which ensures that notification of any proposals takes place prior to notice being given.[95]

9.5.1 Meaning of establishment

The obligation to consult rests upon 20 or more people being made redundant at one establishment. The ECJ considered the meaning of this term in *Rockfon A/S* v *Specialarbejderforbundet i Danmark*.[96] This case considered the Danish legal interpretation of the term 'establishment',[97] which provided that an establishment needed an independent management 'which can independently effect large-scale dismissals'. The ECJ held that the existence of such separate management was not necessary. The term applied to the unit to which the workers who have been made redundant are assigned to carry out their duties. This was further developed by the Court of Justice in a Greek case, *Athinaiki* v *Chartopoiia AE*,[98] where it was stated that an establishment

> may consist of a distinct entity, having a certain degree of permanence and stability, which is assigned to perform one or more given tasks and which has a workforce, technical means and a certain organizational structure allowing for the accomplishment of those tasks.

The link is not necessarily a geographical one, but one concerned with the employment relationship. In a much earlier case[99] the EAT had held that one should adopt a commonsense approach and use the word in a way in which ordinary people would use it. In this case this meant that 14 building sites administered from one base amounted to one establishment, rather than 14 separate ones. Establishment and employer are not synonymous, so if three distinct employers are making employees redundant, albeit at one location, the numbers cannot be aggregated to come within the terms of the statute.[100] In contrast, two field forces being restructured as a result of the merger of the two parent companies were held to be assigned to their branch offices, rather than to the field force as a whole. This meant that, when calculating whether the 20-person threshold had been exceeded, the establishment should be the field office rather than any other.[101]

9.5.2 Appropriate representatives

The employer must consult with the appropriate representatives of any of the employees who may be affected by the proposed dismissals or by any measures taken in connection with those dismissals.[102] The appropriate representatives are the employees' trade union representatives if an independent trade union is recognised by the employer.[103] If there is no such

---

[95] The Collective Redundancies (Amendment) Regulations 2006, SI 2006/2387.
[96] Case C-449/93 [1996] IRLR 168 ECJ.
[97] Used in art. 1(1)(a) Collective Redundancies Directive.
[98] Case C-270/05 *Athinaiki* v *Chartopoiia AE* v *Panagiotidis* [2007] IRLR 286.
[99] *Barratt Developments (Bradford) Ltd* v *UCATT* [1977] IRLR 403.
[100] *E Green & Sons Ltd* v *ASTMS* [1984] IRLR 134.
[101] *MSF* v *Refuge Assurance plc* [2002] IRLR 324.
[102] Section 188(1) TULRCA 1992.
[103] The Secretary of State may, on the application of the parties, vary the statutory provisions in favour of a collective agreement concluded by the parties themselves: s. 198 TULRCA 1992.

trade union then they may be either employee representatives appointed or elected by the affected employees for some other purpose, but who have authority to receive information and be consulted about the proposed dismissals, or they may be employee representatives elected by the employees for the purpose of such consultation.

The choice of which of these two alternatives should be consulted is left to the employer.[104] Prior to 1995 there had only been a requirement to consult trade union representatives if they were recognised by the employer. Where there were no recognised trade unions, there had been no requirement to consult. This approach had been challenged by the European Commission in *Commission* v *United Kingdom*.[105] As a result the ECJ held that the United Kingdom had not adequately transposed the Directive. The legislation was then amended in 1995 to allow the employer to choose whether to consult a trade union or other appropriate representatives.[106] This was then amended again in 1999, so that an employer could choose between the alternative appropriate representatives only if there was not a recognised trade union with whom to consult.[107]

Section 188A TULRCA 1992 sets out the requirements for the election of employee representatives where this is necessary. The onus is on the employer to make such arrangements as are reasonably practical to ensure fairness. The election is to be conducted, so far as is reasonably practicable, in secret. The employer's duties include deciding on the number of representatives to be elected, what constituencies those representatives should represent and the term of office of those representatives. The term needs to be long enough to enable the information and consultation process to be completed. The candidates for election must be affected employees at the date of the election.[108] All affected employees have the right to vote and no affected employee must be unreasonably excluded from standing for election. Employees must be entitled to vote for as many candidates as there are representatives to be elected. The elected representatives are to be allowed access to the affected employees and given such accommodation and other facilities as are necessary.[109] They are also entitled to reasonable time off during working hours to carry out their functions as a representative or candidate, or in order to undergo training for the performance of these functions.[110] Where, after the election, one of those elected ceases to be a representative, then there may be a need for the election of a replacement.[111]

The consultation itself is to include consultation about ways of avoiding the dismissals, reducing the number of employees to be dismissed, and mitigating the consequences of the dismissals. It is necessary for the employer to consult on each of these three aspects and not on just some of them. Thus, if an employer genuinely consults with employee representatives about ways of reducing the numbers involved and mitigating the consequences of the

---

[104] Section 188(1B) TULRCA 1992.

[105] Case 383/92 [1994] IRLR 412 ECJ.

[106] Collective Redundancies and Transfers of Undertakings (Protection of Employment) (Amendment) Regulations 1995, SI 1995/2587.

[107] Collective Redundancies and Transfers of Undertakings (Protection of Employment) (Amendment) Regulations 1999, SI 1999/1925.

[108] They must also be employed by the employer at the time when they were elected: s. 196(1) TULRCA 1992.

[109] Section 188(5A) TULRCA 1992.

[110] Section 61 ERA 1996.

[111] Note that s. 47 ERA 1996 provides protection against detriment for employee representatives and s. 103 ERA 1996 makes their dismissal unfair if it is related to their candidacy or position as an employee representative.

dismissals, they will still have failed in their duty if they have not also consulted about ways of avoiding the dismissals.[112] There is an obligation for the employer to undertake such consultations with a view to reaching agreement with the appropriate representatives.[113] There is certain information that the employer must disclose in writing to the appropriate representatives. This information consists of:

1. the reasons for the proposals;

2. the numbers and descriptions of employees whom it is proposed to dismiss;

3. the total number of employees of any description employed by the employer at the establishment;

4. the proposed method of selecting those to be dismissed and the proposed method of carrying out the dismissals; and

5. the proposed method of calculating payments if different from those required by statute. This information must be delivered to each of the appropriate representatives.[114] Whether sufficient information has been given is a question of fact for the employment tribunal to decide, although there is no rule that states that full and specific information under each of these heads should be given before consultation could begin.[115] It is not sufficient, however, for the employer to argue that the information can be gleaned from the surrounding circumstances and other documents and that any consultation would have had no effect upon the decision to close the workplace.[116]

9.5.3 Special circumstances

There are two 'escape' clauses for employers unable to comply with their obligations under s. 188 TULRCA 1992:

1. Where there are special circumstances which make it not reasonably practicable for an employer to comply with the consultation and information requirements, they are to take all steps towards compliance that are reasonably practicable in the circumstances.[117]

2. Where they have invited affected employees to elect representatives and the employees have failed to do so within a reasonable time, then the employer must give all the affected employees the information set out above.[118]

In *The Bakers' Union* v *Clarks of Hove Ltd*[119] the court held that there were three stages to deciding whether there was a defence in any particular case. First, were there special circumstances; secondly, did they render compliance with the statute not reasonably practicable; and, thirdly, did the employer take all the reasonable steps towards compliance as were reasonably practicable in the circumstances? In this case even an insolvency was not a special enough circumstance in itself to provide a defence against the lack of consultation.

---

[112] *Middlesbrough Borough Council* v *TGWU* [2002] IRLR 332.
[113] Section 188(2) TULRCA 1992.
[114] Section 188(4)–(5) TULRCA 1992.
[115] See *MSF* v *GEC Ferranti (Defence Systems) Ltd* [1994] IRLR 113.
[116] See *Sovereign Distribution Services Ltd* v *TGWU* [1989] IRLR 334.
[117] Section 188(7) TULRCA 1992.
[118] Section 188(7B) TULRCA 1992.
[119] [1978] IRLR 366 CA.

The shedding of employees in an attempt by a receiver to sell the business was not a sufficient justification in *GMB* v *Rankin and Harrison*.[120] The facts that the business could not be sold and that there were no orders were common to insolvency situations and not enough in themselves to justify being special. Special circumstances means something out of the ordinary or something that is not common. In any complaint to an employment tribunal, the onus is upon the employer to show that there were special circumstances or that they took all reasonably practical steps towards compliance.[121]

In *UK Coal Mining Ltd* v *NUM*[122] a coal mine closed because of damage resulting from sea water entering the mine and it was declared unfit. The employer decided not to go through the consultation procedure because the inrush of water could not have been foreseen. The EAT held that there was still an obligation to consult even when there was to be a closure of an operation; this would include the reasons for the dismissals. The reasons for the closure, rather than the closure itself, were the reasons for the dismissal and the true reasons here were the financial difficulties of the employer.

9.5.4 Failure to comply

Where an employer has failed to comply with the requirements to consult, a complaint may be made to an employment tribunal.[123] If the tribunal finds the complaint well founded it will make a declaration to that effect and may make a protective award. A protective award to those who have been dismissed as redundant or whom it is proposed to dismiss and the protected period, up to a maximum of 90 days, begins with the date on which the first dismissals take effect or the date of the award, whichever is earlier. The length is that which the tribunal decides is just and equitable.[124] There is a time limit for complaints. They must be presented to the tribunal before the date on which the last of the dismissals takes effect, or during the three months beginning with that date, or within such further period as the tribunal considers reasonable if it is satisfied that it was not practicable for the complainant to present their complaint during that period.[125] During the protective period all the employees who are covered will receive a week's pay[126] for each week that he would have been paid by the employer during that period.[127] Parts of weeks are paid proportionately. Tribunals are required to state their reasons for the length of the award made.[128] Protective awards resulting from a claim by a trade union can only be awarded in respect of employees for which the trade union has been recognised. Other employees must make their own complaints.[129] The purpose of the award is to ensure that consultation takes place by providing a sanction

---

[120] [1992] IRLR 514; neither were a local authority's financial difficulties a 'special circumstance': see *Middlesbrough Borough Council* v *TGWU* [2002] IRLR 332.

[121] Section 189(6) TULRCA 1992.

[122] [2008] IRLR 4.

[123] Section 189(1) TULRCA 1992; the onus of showing compliance with respect to questions about the election of appropriate representatives, or whether the employee representative was an appropriate representative, rests with the employer: s. 189(1A)–(1B) TULRCA 1992.

[124] Section 189(2)–(4) TULRCA 1992.

[125] Section 189(5) TULRCA 1992.

[126] A week's pay as defined by Part XIV Chapter II ERA 1996.

[127] Section 190 TULRCA 1992; s. 191 deals with certain situations, such as a fair dismissal and offers of alternative employment which might stop the employee continuing to receive payment.

[128] *E Green & Sons* v *ASTMS* [1984] IRLR 134.

[129] *TGWU* v *Brauer Coley Ltd* [2007] IRLR 207.

against employers who fail to do so properly. The focus of the award is not on compensating the employees but on the seriousness of the employer's failure to comply with their statutory obligations[130] and the employer's ability to pay is not relevant.[131] An employee may bring a complaint to an employment tribunal if they have not been paid their protective awards in part or entirety. This complaint must be brought within three months of the last date on which the employee claims they were entitled to payment which is likely to be the last day of the protected period,[132] unless the period is extended by the tribunal if it considers that it was not reasonably practicable to do so. If the tribunal finds the complaint well founded it can order the employer to pay the award.[133]

Employers have an obligation to notify the Secretary of State of their proposals to dismiss employees for redundancy.[134] Proposals to dismiss 100 or more employees within 90 days or fewer are to be notified at least 90 days before any notice is given to employees in respect of any of the dismissals. Proposals to dismiss 20 or more within such a period require at least 30 days' written notice to the Secretary of State.[135] The written notice must contain details of where the employees are employed, identify the representatives to be consulted and when consultation with them began. The Secretary of State may give a written notice requiring more information.[136] There is also a special circumstances defence for the employer if it is not reasonably practicable for the employer to comply with these notification requirements. Failure of a controlling employer to provide the information does not constitute a special circumstance.[137] Failure to comply with these requirements may lead to a fine and individuals can be prosecuted if their actions had led to a corporate body not complying with these statutory requirements.[138]

9.6 Employer insolvency

Many redundancies and transfers of undertakings (see below) are likely to arise out of the insolvency of employers. The precise effect on employees will depend upon the action taken by creditors in order to secure their assets. If a winding up order is made by a court, the effect is, from the date of its publication, to bring the contracts of employment to an end with immediate effect. If the court were to appoint a receiver, the effect would be the same. Receivers appointed by creditors, by way of contrast, do not constitute a change in the legal identity of the employer and no automatic termination of the contracts of employment takes place. The effect of the appointment of an administrator is the same as a creditor appointed receiver. This is because they act as agents of the company and do not replace the

---

[130] *Susie Radin Ltd* v *GMB* [2004] IRLR 400 where the employers unsuccessfully argued that the tribunal should have taken into account a separate decision that consultation would have been futile anyway. The Court of Appeal stated that the futility of the consultation was not relevant to the making of a protective award.

[131] In *Smith* v *Cherry Lewis Ltd* [2005] IRLR 86 the employer was insolvent, but this was held not to be relevant in making the award.

[132] *Howlett Marine Services Ltd* v *Bowlam* [2001] IRLR 201.

[133] Section 192 TULRCA 1992.

[134] Requirements of arts. 3 and 4 Collective Redundancies Directive.

[135] Section 193(1)–(2) TULRCA 1992 as amended by the Collective Redundancies (Amendment) Regulations 2006, SI 2006/2387.

[136] Section 193(4)–(5) TULRCA 1992.

[137] Section 193(7) TULRCA 1992.

[138] Section 194 TULRCA 1992.

legal entity.[139] Without statutory intervention such employees, if the insolvent business is not taken over or sold to a new employer, would merely join other creditors hoping to receive at least part of that which is owed to them.

Council Directive 80/987/EEC[140] on the approximation of the laws of the Member States relating to the protection of employees in the event of the insolvency of their employer (the Insolvency Directive) was the European Community's attempt to harmonise the approach of Member States. The purpose of the Directive was to add to employee protection by ensuring that each Member State had a guarantee institution which would guarantee, subject to limits, payment of employees' outstanding claims resulting from their contracts of employment and employment relationship.[141] Provisions providing this protection in Great Britain are contained in Part XII ERA 1996.

Section 182 ERA 1996 provides that employees may write to the Secretary of State to apply for payment of debts, owed to them by their insolvent employer, from the National Insurance Fund.

In *Everson and Barrass v Secretary of State for Trade and Industry and Bell Lines Ltd*[142] the ECJ was asked to settle the issue as to which country's guarantee institution should compensate the employees of an employer from a different Member State. In this case the Irish courts made a winding up order on the company in Ireland and the British employees of that company made a claim against the Secretary of State in Great Britain. In a previous case[143] the ECJ had held that it was the guarantee institution of the country of the parent company that was liable. This concerned employees who did not work from a registered office in the country where they were employed. In *Everson and Barrass* the ECJ held that, because the employees worked from a branch office from which all the employees worked, the guarantee institution of the country in which the branch was established should be liable for the payments. In *Svenska Staten*[144] the Court accepted that modern technology meant that an organisation did not need to have a fixed establishment in another State in order to have a stable economic presence there.

The Secretary of State will need to be satisfied that the employer has become insolvent,[145] the employee's employment has been terminated and that the employee was entitled to be paid the whole or part of the debt. Section 183(3) ERA 1996 provides that an employer which is a company is to be treated as insolvent if:

1. a winding up order or an administration order has been made; or

2. a receiver or manager has been appointed or possession has been taken of any of the company's property by debenture holders; or

3. there is a voluntary arrangement under Part I Insolvency Act 1986.

---

[139] See *In the matter of Maxwell Fleet and Facilities Management Ltd* [2000] IRLR 368 for an example of how administrators tried to use the Transfer of Undertakings Regulations 1981 in order to shed the employees and sell the business without inherited debts.

[140] Directive 2002/74/EC amended Council Directive 80/987/EEC on the approximation of the laws of the Member States relating to the protection of employees in the event of the insolvency of their employer OJ L 270/10 23.9.2002.

[141] Articles 3 and 4 Insolvency Directive.

[142] Case C-198/98 [2000] IRLR 202 ECJ.

[143] Case C-117/96 *Mosbæk (Danmarks Aktive Handelsrejsende) v Lonmodtagernes Garantifond* [1998] IRLR 150 ECJ.

[144] Case C-310/07 *Svenska Staten v Holmqvist* [2008] IRLR 970.

[145] Section 183 ERA 1996 defines insolvency for employers who are individuals and for employers who are companies.

If the employee cannot show that one of these events has taken place, then it is unlikely that the individual will be entitled to payment from the National Insurance Fund. Even though, as in *Secretary of State for Trade and Industry* v *Walden*,[146] the employer is in financial difficulties and the company has been dissolved, this will not be enough in itself. The absence of any one of these three definitions was sufficient to stop the employee from successfully making a claim.

There is only liability for debts which the employee was entitled to receive from the employer.[147] The debts which are protected by statute are:[148]

1. Arrears of pay up to a maximum of eight weeks, although there is likely to be an entitlement to choose the best eight weeks;[149] this includes[150] guarantee payments, payments for time under Part VI ERA 1996[151] and for time off for carrying out trade union duties,[152] remuneration on suspension on medical grounds[153] and any amounts due from a protective award under s. 189 TULRCA 1992.

2. Any amount payable to fulfil the statutory notice requirements in s. 86 ERA 1996.

3. Any holiday pay outstanding at the appropriate date[154] from the previous 12 months, up to a maximum of six weeks.[155]

4. Any basic award of compensation for unfair dismissal.[156]

5. Any reasonable sum by way of reimbursing the whole or part of a fee paid by an apprentice or articled clerk.[157]

In addition, s. 166(1)(b) ERA 1996[158] provides that employees whose employer is insolvent may apply to the Secretary of State for any statutory redundancy payments due.[159]

9.6.1 Occupational pensions

Article 8 of the Directive provides that Member States must ensure that all the necessary measures are taken to protect the interests of employees and ex-employees at the date of the employer's insolvency in respect of rights under occupational pension schemes. This is an important measure because it affects situations where not only the employer becomes insolvent, but also the pension scheme. *Robins* v *Secretary of State*[160] concerned two pension

---

[146] [2000] IRLR 168.

[147] See *Mann* v *Secretary of State for Employment* [1999] IRLR 566 HL.

[148] Section 184(1) ERA 1996.

[149] See *Mann* v *Secretary of State for Employment* [1999] IRLR 566 HL.

[150] Section 184(2) ERA 1996.

[151] Time off for public duties, looking for work, ante-natal care, dependants, occupational pensions and for employee representatives.

[152] Section 169 TULRCA 1992.

[153] Section 64 ERA 1996.

[154] See s. 185 ERA 1995 for the meaning of 'appropriate date'.

[155] This includes pay for holidays actually taken and accrued holiday pay: s. 184(3) ERA 1996.

[156] Or an award under a designated dismissal procedure, so long as it is not greater than the basic award.

[157] A rare event in modern times.

[158] See generally Part XI Chapter VI ERA 1996 on the rules regarding these and other payments by the Secretary of State.

[159] See *Secretary of State for Trade and Industry* v *Lassman* [2000] IRLR 411 CA, where employees were mistakenly paid redundancy payments. This was held to break their continuity of employment and they were unable to claim for the same period again when their new employer became insolvent.

[160] Case C-278/05 *Robins* v *Secretary of State for Work and Pensions* [2007] IRLR 271.

schemes which had a combined deficit of over £140 million. The pensioners therefore faced significant reductions in their pensions from these schemes. The question was whether the UK Government had an obligation, under art. 8, to make up the difference between what the funds would pay and what they would have been entitled to if they had not been in deficit. In the event the Court of Justice held that there was no requirement on the Government to provide a full guarantee. The Directive allowed a certain latitude to Member States. On the other hand, the amounts guaranteed in this case (between 20 and 49 per cent) did not amount to the minimum degree of protection that the claimants were entitled to.

9.6.2 Controlling directors

One issue concerns individuals who are controlling directors of companies as well as having contracts of employment with those companies. If an individual can have an influence upon whether a company is insolvent or not, is it possible for that same individual to have a claim against the Secretary of State for redundancy pay and other contractual emoluments?[161] In *Fleming* v *Secretary of State for Trade and Industry*[162] an individual was refused a claim for redundancy and statutory notice payments on the grounds that he was not an employee. He owned 65 per cent of the company's shares and, when the company got into difficulties, he had given personal guarantees to the company's two main suppliers and had elected not to take a salary for a time. This was enough for the employment tribunal to decide that he was not an employee. The appeal courts accepted that the decision as to whether an individual was an employee or not was a question of fact for the tribunal. The Court of Session held, therefore, that the tribunal was entitled to reach the decision that it did, but that the fact that a person was a controlling director was only one of the factors that should be taken into account. The significance to be given to that factor would depend upon the surrounding circumstances.

This view was supported in *Secretary of State for Trade and Industry* v *Bottrill*[163] which concerned the managing director of a company who held all the shares in that company. In this case he was also held to be an employee as the shareholding was only intended to be temporary. The court confirmed the approach that the controlling shareholding was only one of the factors to be taken into account. Other factors might be the degree of control exercised by the company, whether there were other directors and whether the individual was answerable to himself only and incapable of being dismissed.

9.6.3 Complaints to employment tribunals

The total amount payable in respect of any debt, where that debt refers to a period of time, is, currently, £380 per week[164] and even this is subject to deductions such as national insurance contributions.[165] If the Secretary of State fails to make a payment that has been claimed, or

---

[161] See *Lee* v *Lee's Air Farming Ltd* [1961] AC 12 for the classic approach to the relationship between an individual as a controlling director and an individual as an employee; also *McMeechan* v *Secretary of State for Employment* [1997] IRLR 353 CA, where an employment agency worker established their employee status and was able to claim against the Secretary of State.

[162] [1997] IRLR 682.

[163] [1999] IRLR 326 CA.

[164] Section 186 ERA; this is the figure for 2009/10.

[165] See *Titchener* v *Secretary of State for Trade and Industry* [2002] IRLR 195.

only makes it in part, then the individual may make a complaint to an employment tribunal. This complaint needs to be submitted within three months, beginning with the date on which the Secretary of State's decision was communicated, or such further period as the tribunal considers reasonable. If the complaint is upheld, the tribunal may stipulate the amount that should be paid.[166]

Where a 'relevant officer' has been appointed in connection with the insolvency, then the Secretary of State may wait for a statement of the employer's debts to employees from that officer before making any payments. The relevant officer is a trustee in bankruptcy, a liquidator, an administrator, a receiver or manager, or a trustee under an arrangement between the employer and the creditors or under a trust deed.[167] The Secretary of State also has the power to require, by giving notice in writing, an employer, or any other person having control of the necessary records, to provide any information necessary for the Secretary of State to deal with the claim. Failure to co-operate or the provision of false information can lead to a fine.[168]

Once the Secretary of State makes a payment, then all the rights and remedies associated with that debt accrue to the Secretary of State. If, for example, an employment tribunal makes an award after the payment has been made, then the debt is paid to the Secretary of State.[169]

9.7 Transfers of undertakings

The Transfer of Undertakings (Protection of Employment) Regulations 1981 (the Transfer of Undertakings Regulations 1981)[170] were the Government's belated transposition of the Acquired Rights Directive[171] into national law. These regulations were amended on four different occasions.[172] The Directive itself was amended in 1998 and was subsequently consolidated into Directive 2001/23/EC. The 1981 Regulations were finally replaced by the Transfer of Undertakings (Protection of Employment) Regulations 2006 which came into effect in October 2006.[173]

9.7.1 The meaning of a transfer of an undertaking

The application of the Directive has been much discussed at the European Court of Justice. The Court's decisions have been reflected in the consolidated Directive, but the British Government has gone further in some respects.

In *Spijkers*,[174] the seminal case on the application of the Directive, the European Court of Justice defined a transfer of an undertaking as the transfer of an economic entity that retained

---

[166] Section 188 ERA 1996.
[167] Section 187 ERA 1996.
[168] Section 190 ERA 1996.
[169] Section 189 ERA 1996.
[170] SI 1981/1794.
[171] Directive 77/187/EEC on the approximation of the laws of the Member States relating to the safeguarding of employees' rights in the event of transfers of undertakings; subsequently amended by Directive 98/50/EC and consolidated by Directive 2001/23/EC.
[172] SI 1987/442; s. 33 Trade Union Reform and Employment Rights Act 1993; SI 1995/2587 and SI 1999/1925.
[173] SI 2006/246.
[174] Case 24/85 *JMA Spijkers v Gebroeders Abbatoir CV* [1986] ECR 1119.

its identity. The court looked at the purpose of the Acquired Rights Directive and concluded that its aim was to ensure the continuity of existing employment relationships. Thus, if the operation that is transferred is an identifiable entity before and after the transfer then a relevant transfer is likely to have taken place. One needs to look at the situation before the transfer and identify an economic entity, then after the transfer to consider whether the economic entity has retained its identity.

The ECJ then gave further guidance as to factors which would help in the decision as to whether a transfer had taken place. It was necessary to take all the factual circumstances of the transaction into account, including:

1. The type of undertaking or business in question.

2. The transfer or otherwise of tangible assets such as buildings and stocks.

3. The value of intangible assets at the date of transfer.

4. Whether the majority of staff are taken over by the new employer.

5. The transfer or otherwise of customers.

6. The degree of similarity between activities before and after the transfer.

7. The duration of any interruption in those activities.

The court stated that each of these factors was only part of the assessment. One had to examine what existed before the transfer and then examine the entity after the change in order to decide whether the operation was continued, but these factors might help that consideration.

This approach was further emphasised by the case of *Schmidt*,[175] which concerned the contracting out of a small cleaning operation. Mrs Schmidt complained about her dismissal and eventually her claim ended up in the national court (the Landsarbeitsgericht), which then referred the issue, of whether the transfer of a single person to an outside contractor could be a transfer of an undertaking, to the European Court of Justice. The bank, as well as the German and UK Governments, argued that the answer should be in the negative because the cleaning operation was neither a main function nor an ancillary function of the bank and that there was not a transfer of an economic entity. The fact that it was a small operation was held not to be relevant. What mattered was that there was a stable operation which retained its identity. This was indicated by the fact that before the transfer there was a cleaning operation and, again, after the transfer this continued or was resumed.[176]

In the United Kingdom this approach by the European Court of Justice resulted in the courts finding that contracting out of services, or outsourcing, could amount to a relevant transfer for the purposes of the Transfer Regulations. The case of *Kenny v South Manchester College*,[177] for example, concerned the provision of education services at a young offenders' institution. After a tendering exercise the contract was won by South Manchester College. The question was whether the undertaking had retained its identity. The High Court stated that 'the prisoners and young offenders who attend, say, a carpentry class next Thursday will, save those released from the institution, be likely in the main to be the same as those who attended the same class in the same classroom the day before and will doubtless be using

---

[175] Case 392/92 *Schmidt v Spar und Leikhasse der Fruheren Amter Bordesholm* [1995] ICR 237.

[176] See also *Dudley Bower Building Services Ltd v Lowe* [2003] IRLR 260.

[177] [1993] IRLR 265.

exactly the same tools and machinery'. This was followed by other cases such as those involving the outsourcing of a local authority refuse collection contract[178] and the moving of a hospital cleaning contract from one contractor to another,[179] which were held to be relevant transfers.

It was then that the European Court of Justice appeared to have second thoughts about its approach. In *Süzen*[180] the Court distinguished between the transfer of an entity and the transfer of an activity. As in the case of *Schmidt*, before the transfer there was a cleaning operation and after the transfer there was a cleaning operation. On the face of it, there was a relevant transfer because the entity appeared to retain its identity, as evidenced by its continuation and resumption. The ECJ, however, then stated that an entity could not be reduced to the activity entrusted to it. Thus the Court distinguished between an entity that transferred and an activity that transferred. An entity, according to the court, was

> an organised grouping of persons or assets facilitating the exercise of an economic activity which pursues a specific objective.

There has, therefore, to be something else, other than the activity taking place, which needs to transfer, such as assets or 'an organised grouping' of people. Without these, there appeared to be only the transfer of an activity. This was not enough to provide the protection of the Acquired Rights Directive.

It is from this point that many of the problems concerning the applicability of the Directive and the TUPE Regulations arose. *Süzen* set limits on the applicability of the Directive, but there has been confusion as to where these limits apply and the real difference between an entity and an activity. Both the *Schmidt* case and the *Süzen* case concerned the transfer of cleaning contracts, but in one the court held that an entity transferred and, in the second, it held that the cleaning contract only amounted to an activity and was therefore not protected by the Directive.

It is not surprising that many of those dealing with transfers became confused. The Court of Appeal tackled the problem in *RCO Support Services v Unison*.[181] This concerned the transfer of in-patient care from one hospital to another some three miles away. A new contractor won the cleaning and catering contract at the hospital to which the patients were being transferred. None of the staff at the original hospital transferred to the new one, so there was no transfer of assets or people involved in the change of contractor. Despite this the court held that there had been a relevant transfer of an undertaking. Although it was accepted that *Süzen* had placed limits on the applicability of the Directive, it did not exclude all occasions when none of the workforce transferred. In this case the other circumstances were sufficient to suggest that it was more than just an activity that transferred. Again, one had to adopt the multi-factorial test as in *Spijkers*. More recently in *Klarenberg*[182] the ECJ held that the Directive applied even when the part of the undertaking or business did not retain its organisational autonomy, otherwise it would not apply when an employer decides to integrate the part transferred into their business structure. It is necessary that a 'functional' link be retained only.

[178] *Wren v Eastbourne District Council* [1993] ICR 955.
[179] *Dines v Initial Health Care Services and Pall Mall Services Group Ltd* [1994] IRLR 336.
[180] Case 13/95 *Süzen v Zehnacker Gebäudereinigung* [1997] IRLR 255 ECJ.
[181] [2002] IRLR 401.
[182] Case C-466/07 *Klarenberg v Ferrotron Technologies GMBH* [2009] IRLR 301.

The Government decided to remove uncertainty in the public sector through administrative means (see below) whilst tackling the outsourcing sector with the application of the concept of 'service provision changes'.

Regulation 3(1)(a) of the 2006 TUPE Regulations states that the Regulations apply, first, to a transfer where there is a transfer of an economic entity that retains its identity (the *Spijkers* test), and, secondly, to a service provision change. An economic entity is defined in reg. 3(2) as 'an organised grouping of resources which has the objective of pursuing an economic activity, whether or not that activity is central or ancillary' (the *Süzen* test). There has been an attempt therefore to clarify the meaning of a transfer, using decisions of the European Court of Justice, following art. 1 of the consolidated Directive.

Regulation 3(1)(b) provides that the TUPE Regulations 2006 also apply to a service provision change. These are relevant to outsourcing situations and are meant to ensure a wide coverage of the Regulations. A service provision change takes place when:

1. a person (client) first contracts out some part of its activities to a contractor;
2. such a contract is taken over by another contractor (so-called second generation transfers); and
3. the client takes back the activity in-house from a contractor.

Whereas, however, a relevant transfer consists of an 'organised grouping of resources', a service provision change requires there to be 'an organised grouping of employees, situated in Great Britain, which has, as its principal purpose, the carrying out of activities concerned'.[183] In *Metropolitan Resources Ltd* v *Churchill Dulwich Ltd*[184] a contractor with the Home Office provided accommodation to asylum seekers. The contractor switched provision from one sub-contractor to another. The EAT held that a service provision change had taken place. There was no need for the Tribunal to take a factorial approach as in a transfer situation. A tribunal should ask itself whether, on the facts, one of the three situations contained in reg. 3(1)(b) of the TUPE Regulations existed and whether the conditions set out in reg. 3(3) are satisfied. Minor differences in the task carried out or in the way in which they are carried out should not affect the application of a commonsense and pragmatic approach.

The 2006 Regulations are introduced under powers given by s. 2(2) of the European Communities Act and s. 38 of the Employment Relations Act 1999. This latter power enables the Secretary of State to go beyond just the provisions of the Directive and extend the scope of the Regulations. It is the 1999 Act which allows the Secretary of State to include the provisions relating to service provision changes. Thus, for transfers other than those concerned with outsourcing, the Directive is to be followed. In outsourcing events, however, there appears to be a much broader interpretation so as to avoid the conflicts that have arisen in the past.[185]

9.7.2 Who is to be transferred

Regulation 4(1) of the 2006 Regulations provides that, except where an objection is made, a relevant transfer shall not operate to terminate any contract of employment of any person

---

[183] Regulation 2(1) provides that references to an 'organised grouping of employees' includes a single employee; nor does it apply to single specific events or tasks of a short-term duration: reg. 3(3)(ii).

[184] [2009] IRLR 700.

[185] See Malcolm Sargeant, 'Transfers and Outsourcing' (2000) *Commercial Liability Law Review* 282 and Malcolm Sargeant, 'TUPE: The Final Round' (2006) *Journal of Business Law* 549.

employed by the transferor and assigned to the 'organised grouping of resources or employees that is subject to the relevant transfer'. In reg. 2(1) temporary assignments are excluded. An important addition here is the use of the word 'assigned'.

One problem that has occurred is in deciding who works for the part transferred, when only part of an organisation is transferred to a new employer. If, for example, a business decides to contract out its non-core activities and retain only those parts of the business that are concerned with its primary activities, or if only a part of the business is sold off, there are likely to be a number of employees, such as those in Human Resources, who work in the parts remaining, but whose jobs consisted of servicing those parts transferred. This may be the entire content of their jobs or only a part. If such staff remain with the transferor organisation, they may be faced with the loss of their jobs or, at the very least, a significant change in their job activities. The question then is whether these support staff have the right to transfer also.

It was in the case of *Botzen*[186] that the European Court of Justice first devised the assignment test to deal with such situations. The Advocate General[187] in the case proposed a test for deciding who should be transferred if only a part of a business was sold off:

> A basic working test, it seems to me, is to ask whether, if that part of the business had been separately owned before the transfer, the worker would have been employed by the owners of that part or the owners of the remaining part.

The Advocate General did admit that employees could be involved in work other than for the part transferred, but only on a *de minimus* basis.

Some people, of course, would not have been employed in either part if they were separately owned. It may have been because the whole was a certain size that they were employed. This may be especially true of HR departments as bigger organisations can perhaps have the capacity to employ more specialists, whereas a smaller organisation might demand more generalist abilities. The Court of Justice held that: 'An employment relationship is essentially characterised by the link existing between the employee and the part of the undertaking or business to which he is assigned to carry out his duties.' All that is needed therefore is to establish to which part of the business or undertaking the individual is assigned. This unhelpful conclusion did not establish a satisfactory test because of the need to define what was meant by 'assign'.

Duncan Web Offset (Maidstone) Ltd v *Cooper*[188] concerned three employees who worked at the company's Maidstone office, but spent some of their time working at other offices which were part of the same group. Occasionally this meant a significant amount of time spent away from their office. When the business of the Maidstone office was sold by the receivers these three were not transferred. All three had spent at least 80 per cent of their time on work connected with the Maidstone office. The EAT concluded that the whole of the Maidstone business had been transferred and, unless the employees were also transferred, their contracts of employment would come to an end because they would be left with no employment and no employer. They were, therefore, held to be protected by the TUPE Regulations and the Directive.

---

[186] Case 186/83 *Arie Botzen v Rotterdamsche Droogdok Maatschappij BV* [1986] 2 CMLR 50 ECJ.
[187] The Advocate General investigates cases, summarises the arguments and makes recommendations to the European Court of Justice.
[188] [1995] IRLR 633; see also *Michael Peters Ltd* v *(1) Farnfield and (2) Michael Peters Group plc* [1995] IRLR 190.

The Employment Appeal Tribunal declined to give guidance about when a person was assigned to an undertaking and when they were not. They accepted that there 'will often be difficult questions of fact for employment tribunals when deciding who was assigned and who was not'. It felt, however, that it could not give guidance because the facts may vary markedly from case to case. During the course of argument a number of indicators were suggested and the EAT accepted that they may well help future consideration by tribunals. These suggestions were:

- The amount of time spent on one part of the business or another.
- The amount of value given to each part by the employee.
- The terms of the contract of employment showing what the employee could be required to do.
- How the cost to the employer of the employee's services had been allocated between the different parts of the business.[189]

Regulation 4(3) also provides that it is only persons employed immediately before the transfer and who are assigned to such an organised grouping, or would have been had they not been unfairly dismissed, who are protected.[190]

9.7.3 Contract variations

The ability to vary contracts of employment at the time of transfer, even with the consent of the employees, was considered by the House of Lords in the joined cases of *Wilson* v *St Helens Borough Council* and *British Fuels Ltd* v *Baxendale*.[191] The first case concerned the transfer of a community home from Lancashire County Council to St Helens Borough Council. The County Council had decided that it could no longer afford to run the home and, as a result, gave the trustees of the home two years' notice that it would cease to be involved. St Helens Borough Council agreed to take it over, but only after substantial reorganisation. The result was a reduction in the size of the home and the number of staff needed to run it. Negotiations took place with the trade union concerned and staffing levels were reduced from 162 to 72. In addition, some of the 72 who transferred did so on reduced terms and conditions. All were dismissed for reasons of redundancy by the County Council prior to the move. Subsequently the employees claimed that the Transfer Regulations applied and that they should have been transferred on the same terms and conditions that they enjoyed when employed by Lancashire County Council.

The House of Lords concluded that 'the transfer of the undertaking did not constitute the reason for the variation'. The transfer itself was not the reason for the variation, although deciding when a variation in terms is as a result of a transfer and when it is not seems a difficult question. Lord Slynn, in delivering judgment, stated that:

> It may be difficult to decide whether the variation is due to the transfer or attributable to some separate cause. If, however, the variation is not due to the transfer itself it can in my opinion, on the basis of the authorities to which I have referred, validly be made.

---

[189] This issue is not confined to large organisations only as was shown in *Buchanan-Smith* v *Schleicher & Co International Ltd* [1996] IRLR 547.
[190] *Litster* v *Forth Dry Dock and Engineering Ltd* [1989] IRLR 161 HL.
[191] [1998] IRLR 706.

In the *British Fuels* case, an existing subsidiary company was merged with a newly acquired organisation. The employees concerned were dismissed because of redundancy by the old company and taken on by the newly set up business. They were offered a new contract of employment, which was accepted. The problem for the new enterprise was that the terms and conditions of the two sets of employees were different and the new employer wished to rationalise them. The employees subsequently claimed that their terms and conditions should have been protected. The House of Lords held that their original dismissals had been effective and could not be regarded as a nullity.

It is possible, therefore, to reorganise provided that the reason for the dismissal or variation is not connected with the transfer. Indeed the EAT has distinguished between changes that take place in connection with the transfer and changes that take place 'on the occasion' of the transfer.[192] This is not to say that an employee is barred from taking advantage of a more favourable variation if agreed with the transferee. According to the EAT the case law merely establishes that an employee may rely on the provisions agreed with the transferor. The employee can object to any matters that may be detrimental to him, but this will not stop him taking advantage of any more favourable provisions.[193]

The 2006 TUPE Regulations provide that it is not possible to vary a contract of employment if the sole or main reason was the transfer or any other reason that was not an economic, technical or organisational reason entailing changes in the workforce (ETO reason; reg. 4(4)). The employer and employee are able, however, to agree a variation if it is changed for an ETO reason or 'a reason unconnected to the transfer'.

9.7.4 **Employee choice**

The Directive was silent on the subject of whether an individual employee can decide that they do not wish to transfer. Initially it was left to the European Court of Justice to decide. In *Daddy's Dance Hall*[194] the court suggested that employees had no choice in the matter. Whether the individuals wished it or not there was a public policy reason for not allowing employees to opt out, because this alternative would normally be that they would be worse off by opting out. This position was considerably softened in *Katsikas*[195] when the Court of Justice held that to stop someone objecting to the transfer of his employment would undermine the fundamental rights of the employee who must be free to choose his employer and cannot be obliged to work for an employer whom he has not freely chosen. It followed, therefore, that the Directive does not oblige employees to transfer provided that they choose freely not to continue the employment relationship. It was then left to the Member State to 'decide the fate of the contract of employment or employment relationship with the transferor'.

The 1981 TUPE Regulations were amended by the Trade Union Reform and Employment Rights Act 1993, so that a person's contract of employment will not transfer if the individual informs the transferor or the transferee that he objects to becoming an employee of the transferee.

---

[192] *Ralton v Havering College of Further and Higher Education* [2001] IRLR 738.
[193] See *Regent Security Services Ltd v Power* [2008] IRLR 66.
[194] Case 324/86 *Foreningen of Arbejdsledere I Danmark v Daddy's Dance Hall A/S* [1985] IRLR 315.
[195] Case 132/91 *Katsikas v Konstantidis* [1993] IRLR 179.

The problem for such an employee is that they are left in a sort of employment nether region with no claims against the transferor or the transferee. Regulation 4(7) of the 2006 Regulations repeats that position so that an employee is not transferred if he objects to being so transferred. The current outcome is repeated in reg. 4(8) where the employee is then in a 'no man's land'; they have not been transferred, but the transferor cannot be treated as having dismissed the employee.

The question of how an employee objects to the transfer has also been considered. In *Hay* v *George Hanson*[196] the work of an employee was to be transferred from a district council to a private contractor. The question was whether there needed to be a clear and unequivocal statement from the employee objecting to the transfer. The EAT stated that the 'drafting of the Regulations leaves much to be desired'. In this case the employee was held to have objected. He unsuccessfully sought alternative employment with the council and he tried to obtain a redundancy package, amongst other actions. This led the employment tribunal to conclude that, cumulatively, he had objected to the transfer. There was, therefore, no particular method by which an employee may object, but he is able to communicate his state of mind to the transferee by word or by action. It should not, according to the EAT, be difficult to distinguish between expressing concern, and protesting, about the transfer and withholding consent. It was a matter for the tribunal to decide in each individual case, but the EAT did state:[197]

> ...nor is there any requirement, which seems singularly unfortunate, that the employee intending to object should be informed of the consequences by the transferring employer, given the draconian nature of the result that reg. 5(4B) achieves.

There is a need for care on the part of the employee when objecting as even a short period working for the transferee may result in the loss of the right to object to the transfer. This happened in *Capita Health Solutions Ltd* v *McLean*[198] where the BBC outsourced some of its activities, including its occupational health provision. Mrs McLean was employed as an occupational nurse. She objected to the transfer but agreed to work for Capita for six weeks, helping with the transition. The result was that the EAT held that she could not have objected to the transfer. In fact she had, according to the court, agreed to transfer, but on a six week limited contract.

The situation is unchanged by the 2006 Regulations.

9.7.5 **Insolvency**

Measures to deal with insolvency situations were absent from the original Directive and the problems resulting from this were recognised by the European Court of Justice at an early stage. The perceived problem was that the obligation, imposed by the Directive, upon the transferee enterprise to take over all the debts in relation to the insolvent organisation's employees and, indeed, to transfer all those employees at their current terms and conditions, would act as a disincentive to the 'rescue' of such enterprises.

---

[196] [1996] IRLR 427.
[197] See also *Senior Heat Treatment Ltd* v *Bell* [1997] IRLR 614.
[198] [2008] IRLR 597.

In *Abels*[199] the ECJ tried to distinguish between different types of proceedings in deciding the applicability of the Directive. Mr Abels worked for a company which became insolvent and he and other staff were laid off. The liquidator eventually sold the business to another company which re-employed Mr Abels and others, but did not pay them for the time that they had been laid off. Mr Abels claimed that it was a transfer of an undertaking and that their contracts should have automatically passed to the buyer of the business. If this had happened, then they would have been entitled to continuing pay. The outcome of the case was that the court distinguished between those situations when the insolvency proceedings were aimed at liquidation of the assets and those situations when the aim, at an earlier stage, was to rescue the business. It was an unsatisfactory outcome because it left uncertainty about when the Directive applied.

The consolidated Directive excludes, in art. 5.1, any transfers where the transfer is the subject of bankruptcy proceedings with a view to liquidation of the assets of the transferor. Article 5.2 of the consolidated Directive also gives Member States the option of excluding transfers of liabilities in other types of insolvency proceedings as well as giving them the option of agreed changes to terms and conditions of employees which are 'designed to safeguard employment opportunities by ensuring the survival of the undertaking, business or part of the undertaking or business'.

Unsurprisingly the TUPE Regulations 2006 take advantage of both of these options in regs. 8 and 9. Relevant insolvency proceedings for this purpose in the Regulations repeat the definition stated in the Directive, namely that they are 'insolvency proceedings which have been opened in relation to the transferor not with a view to the liquidation of the assets of the transferor and which are under the supervision of an insolvency practitioner' (reg. 8(6)). In *Oakland* v *Wellswood (Yorkshire) Ltd*[200] the issue was whether the insolvency proceedings were instituted with a view to liquidation of the assets of the transferor is a matter of fact for the employment tribunal. Where joint administrators continue to trade with a view to a sale as a going concern, then any relevant transfer would fall under the protection of the Regulations.

The outcome of the changes was that those elements which the Government would normally be responsible for under its statutory obligations towards the employees of insolvent employers do not transfer. This effectively amounts to a government subsidy to transfers in insolvency situations. The debts owed to employees by the transferor, to the limits of its statutory obligations, will be guaranteed by the Secretary of State. This, of course, includes some arrears of pay, notice periods, holiday pay and any basic award for unfair dismissal compensation.[201] Other debts owed to employees will transfer.

In addition to this subsidy there is provision in reg. 9 for the employer and employee representatives to agree 'permitted variations' to their contracts of employment. Permitted variations are those which are not due to ETO reasons entailing a change in the workforce and are designed to safeguard employment opportunities by ensuring the survival of the undertaking (reg. 9(7)).

Thus the method of dealing with the perceived problem of insolvency transfers is both to provide a potential subsidy and to lessen the protection available to employees. It is difficult to see what employee representatives can use as their case in resisting changes to terms and

---

[199] Case 135/83 *Abels* v *Administrative Board* [1987] 2 CMLR 406.
[200] [2009] IRLR 250.
[201] See, e.g., Part XII of the Employment Rights Act 1996.

conditions when they are negotiating under the threat of unemployment arising from the employer's insolvency.

9.7.6 Information and consultation

Regulations 13 to 15 TUPE Regulations 2006 replaced regs. 10 and 11 of the 1981 Regulations. The obligations to inform and consult employees remain the same apart from the introduction of joint liability between the transferor and the transferee for any compensation awarded as a result of a failure to inform and consult (reg. 15(8) and (9)).

Information should be provided 'long enough before[202] a relevant transfer to enable the employer of any affected employees to consult all the persons who are appropriate representatives of any of those affected employees'. The High Court, in *Institution of Professional and Civil Servants* v *Secretary of State for Defence*,[203] decided that the words 'long enough before' a transfer to enable consultation to take place meant as soon as measures are envisaged and *if possible* long enough before the transfer. The court held that the words did not mean as soon as measures are envisaged and *in any event* long enough before the transfer. This case concerned the introduction of private management into the Royal dockyards at Rosyth and Devonport; a measure which was opposed by the trade unions. Before consultation could take place there needed to be some definite plans or proposals by the employer around which consultation could take place.

The information to be provided should consist of:

1. The fact that a relevant transfer is to take place, approximately when it is to take place and the reasons for it.

2. The legal, economic and social implications for the affected employees. *Royal Mail Group Ltd* v *Communication Workers Union*[204] concerned the transfer of certain post office branches to WH Smith. The EAT held that reg. 13 required an employer to state what it genuinely believed were the legal implications of the transfer. It is not required to warrant that its analysis was correct.

3. The measures which are envisaged to take place in connection with the transfer, in relation to the affected employees or the fact that there are no such measures envisaged.

The rules on who are appropriate representatives and the requirements are identical to those rules concerning the appointment of appropriate representatives for the purposes of consultation in collective redundancies (see above). The representatives are the independent trade union which is recognised by the employer. If there is no such trade union, then there are employee representatives[205] to be elected or appointed by the affected employees, whether for the purpose of these consultations or for some other purpose.

It is, of course, both the transferor and the transferee that need to consult and there is an obligation upon the transferee to provide the transferor with information about their plans,

---

[202] Regulation 13(2) TUPE Regulations 2006.
[203] [1987] IRLR 373.
[204] [2009] IRLR 1046
[205] Regulation 13(3) TUPE Regulations 2006 states that employee representatives are either those who are elected for the purpose of consultation or elected for some other purpose and it is appropriate to consult them.

so that the transferor can carry out their duty to consult.[206] Nor is there any obligation to consult once the transfer has taken place. The need is for consultation prior to the transfer so that agreement may be reached or an individual can object to the transfer. To agree that it should be post transfer also is to impose an open-ended obligation to consult, which would be unnecessarily burdensome.[207]

Where the employer actually envisages taking measures in relation to any of the affected employees, then the employer must consult the appropriate representatives 'with a view to seeking their agreement to the measures to be taken'.[208] In the course of these consultations the employer will consider the representations made by the appropriate representatives and, if any of those representations are rejected, the employer must state the reasons for so doing.[209]

There is a special circumstances defence for the employer if it renders it not reasonably practicable to perform the duty to consult and inform. In such a case the employer must take all such steps as are reasonable in the circumstances.[210] There is also a defence for the employer if the employees fail to elect representatives. In such a case the duty to consult is fulfilled if the employer gives each employee the necessary information.[211]

Complaints to an employment tribunal may be made for a breach of the rules concerning consultation. Complaints must be made to the employment tribunal within three months beginning with the date upon which the transfer was completed.[212] If the complaint is well founded the employment tribunal may order appropriate compensation. Tribunals are expected to adopt a similar approach to that taken concerning failures in consultation concerning collective redundancies (see above). This means that awards should be concerned with punishing the employer rather than with compensating the employee.[213]

There is a further issue related to information, especially the passing of information between contractors. This has been a particular issue especially for those involved in outsourcing. Regulations 11 and 12 of the TUPE Regulations 2006 concern the notification of employee liability information and now provide a statutory duty for the transferor to pass on to the transferee certain information. This includes the identity and age of the employee; their terms and conditions of employment (as required by s. 1 Employment Rights Act 1996); disciplinary or grievance action over the previous two years and details of any claims, cases or action brought in the last two years and any future actions that the transferor might have reasonable grounds to believe are possible. The 2006 Regulations provide for compensation to be paid to the transferee, with a normal minimum of £500 per employee.

---

[206] Regulation 13(4) TUPE Regulations 2006.

[207] See *Amicus* v *City Building (Glasgow) LLP* [2009] IRLR 254.

[208] There is also a common law duty upon the employer to take reasonable care in any statements made to employees with regard to the transfer, to ensure that the information is accurate and that all intentions were capable of being fulfilled: see *Hagen* v *ICI Chemicals Ltd* [2002] IRLR 32 HC.

[209] Regulation 13(7) TUPE Regulations 2006.

[210] Regulation 13(11) TUPE Regulations 2006; the courts have traditionally construed special circumstances very narrowly; see collective redundancies above and *Bakers Union* v *Clarks of Hove* [1978] IRLR 366 CA and *GMB* v *Rankin and Harrison* [1992] IRLR 514, where the shedding of employees to make a sale more attractive was held not to be a special circumstance.

[211] Regulation 15(2) TUPE Regulations 2006.

[212] Regulation 15(12) TUPE Regulations 2006.

[213] *Sweetin* v *Coral Racing* [2006] IRLR 252.

Chapter summary

This chapter has been concerned with when workers are probably at their most vulnerable: when the organisation in which they work is reorganised in some way. It first considered the general obligations to inform and consult workers. Such rights derive from the European Community and are implemented in the form of European Works Councils and the requirement for an information and consultation procedure in all enterprises with 50 or more employees. It then went on to analyse specific situations, including collective redundancies, insolvency and transfers. In respect of transfers it looked at the effect of the Transfers of Undertakings (Protection of Employment) Regulations 2006 and their effect on contracts of employment in transfer situations and where there are service provision changes.

Further reading

Deakin, S. and Morris, G. *Labour Law*: 5th edn, Hart Publishing, 2009, Chapters 3 and 9.

McMullen, J. 'An Analysis of the Transfer of Undertakings (Protection of Employment) Regulations 2006' (2006) 35(2) *Industrial Law Journal* 113.

Sargeant, M. 'TUPE: The Final Round' (2006) *Journal of Business Law* 549.

http://www.berr.gov.uk/files/file20761.pdf for a Government guide to the Transfer Regulations 2006.

Visit **www.mylawchamber.co.uk/sargeant**
to access legal updates, live weblinks and practice
exam questions to test yourself on this chapter.

10 Trade unions

10.1 Introduction

For much of its history the trade union movement in Great Britain has struggled to establish a position within the law which would enable it to organise and make use of the power that comes from size. In the nineteenth century the struggle was with the criminal law, which was used to control and limit the activities of workers' organisations, whilst in the twentieth century the struggle was with the civil law as the courts imposed new tortious liabilities upon them.

The Combination Act 1800, for example, made unlawful any contracts or agreements between certain groups of workers which had, as their purpose, the improvement of wages or working hours or almost anything that interfered with an employer's ability to run their own business. The severity of the oppression varied over time but there were important landmarks, such as the Trade Union Act 1871 which adopted the principle of non-intervention in trade union affairs. Section 2 of that Act provided that trade unions were not to be considered as criminal conspiracies just because their rules were in restraint of trade. Nevertheless, unions suffered a series of setbacks as the civil courts continued to regard them with suspicion. The Trade Disputes Act 1906 was adopted by the last Liberal administration and was partly a reaction to the *Taff Vale* case,[1] which had the effect of limiting opportunities to take strike action and threatened the finances of unions. The 1906 Act provided trade unions with immunities from civil actions, for example the tort of inducing breach of contract when in contemplation or furtherance of a trade dispute.[2]

In more modern times the Conservative Government of 1971–4 introduced the Industrial Relations Act 1971, which repealed the 1906 Act and tried to set up a new legal framework for industrial relations. The National Industrial Relations Court was established to administer this process. It failed because of the lack of co-operation from the union movement and because the Government lacked the authority to enforce its will. The Trade Union and Labour Relations Acts of 1974 and 1976 repealed the Industrial Relations Act 1971 and returned to the system of immunities. After the 'winter of discontent'[3] the

---

[1] *Taff Vale Railway Co v Amalgamated Society of Railway Servants* [1901] AC 426.
[2] This is a very simplistic description. For those who wish a more serious historical analysis there is a wealth of material; see, e.g., Paul Davies and Mark Freedland, *Labour Legislation and Public Policy* (Clarendon Press, 1993).
[3] The 'winter of discontent' was a description given to the winter of 1978/9, where there was a peak in industrial action by trade unions, especially within the public sector.

Conservative Government came to power in 1979 with the intention to reform the union movement. Throughout the 1980s and the early 1990s there was a series of Acts of Parliament which limited the freedom of action of trade unions and their members. It is these legislative measures, mostly incorporated into the Trade Union and Labour Relations (Consolidation) Act 1992 (TULRCA 1992), which largely define the rules governing the right to associate and the rights of members and trade unions in relation to each other. These rules have been amended only in limited ways by subsequent Labour Governments.

10.2 Freedom of association

An important part of the struggle by workers in the past has been to establish the right to associate in unions and not to be discriminated against for doing so. In more recent times the union movement has declined in size and influence. In 1979 it reached its peak membership of over 13.2 million but the latest returns made to the Certification Officer show that this has has declined to some 7.7 million.[4]

The right to associate has been a concern of international organisations and is seen as a basic right of workers in a democratic society. For example, art. 11 European Convention on Human Rights (ECHR) states that everyone has the right of peaceful association and freedom of association.[5] The European Court of Human Rights has recently held that in determining the meaning of the Convention it will take into account elements of international law other than the Convention itself, the interpretation of such elements by competent organs and the practice of European states representing their common values. Thus in *Denmir* v *Turkey*[6] it ruled that the right to bargain collectively with the employer has, in principle, become one of the essential elements of the right to form and join trade unions.[7]

The European Charter of the Fundamental Social Rights of Workers[8] 1989 states:

> 11. Employers and workers of the European Community shall have the right of association in order to constitute professional organisations or trade unions of their choice for the defence of their economic and social interests. Every employer and every worker shall have the freedom to join or not to join such organisations without any personal or occupational damage being thereby suffered by him.

It is interesting that the freedom to join a trade union is linked with the freedom not to join. This dual freedom is reflected in the United Kingdom legislation and results from the perceived coercion resulting from the 'closed shop'. Until their existence became impossible as a result of legislation during the 1980s and 1990s,[9] there were two types of closed shop. These were the pre-entry and the post-entry closed shops. In the former there was a requirement for applicants for job vacancies to be members of the recognised trade union or unions.[10] In the latter there was a requirement for successful job applicants to join a recognised union

---

[4] Annual Report of the Certification Officer 2008/9.

[5] This article was incorporated into national law, from October 2000, by the Human Rights Act 1998.

[6] [2009] IRLR 766.

[7] [2009] IRLR 766.

[8] Signed by all the Member States of the European Community at the time, except the United Kingdom.

[9] Especially the Employment Acts 1980, 1982, 1988 and 1990.

[10] In some instances the trade union had the right to put up candidates from its own known unemployed members before any wider recruitment exercise.

within a specific period of starting employment. This was a widespread practice and one not always opposed by employers. In 1978 about 23 per cent of the workforce (about 5.2 million people) worked in locations where there was a closed shop. The advantage for the management of these companies was that they avoided multi-union situations.

Whether the 'negative right' not to join a trade union can be equated with the 'positive right' to join is debatable. In *Young, James and Webster* v *United Kingdom*[11] three employees of British Rail lost their jobs because they refused to join one of the unions with whom British Rail had concluded a closed shop agreement. In total, 54 individuals were dismissed for refusing to join one of the unions, out of a total workforce of about 250,000. The European Court of Human Rights held that art. 11 ECHR had been breached. The majority of the judges concluded that art. 11 did not put the 'negative' aspect of the freedom of association on the same footing as the 'positive' aspect, although a minority of six judges felt that:

> ... the negative aspect of freedom of association is necessarily complementary to, a correlative of and inseparable from its positive aspect. Protection of freedom of association would be incomplete if it extended to no more than the positive aspect. It is one and the same right that is involved.[12]

This approach is incorporated into s. 137(1) TULRCA 1992, which outlaws the refusal of employment on the grounds that a person is or is not a member of a trade union (see below).

10.3 Meaning of a trade union

Section 1(a) TULRCA 1992 defines a trade union as an organisation

> which consists wholly or mainly of workers of one or more descriptions and whose principal purposes include the regulation of relations between workers of that description or those descriptions and employers or employers' associations.

Similarly it can be an organisation which consists of constituent or affiliated organisations which meet these criteria or an organisation of the representatives of such constituent or affiliated organisations.[13] Thus a trade union is defined by its membership and its purposes. For example, in *Hopkins* v *National Union of Seamen*[14] the objects of the union were shown to include the promotion and provision of funds to extend the adoption of trade union principles and the improvement of the conditions and protection of the interests of all members. According to the court, this might have been enough to justify payments to the National Union of Mineworkers during the miners' strike of 1984 – either keeping pits open might have supplied more work for the seamen involved in transportation or helping miners' families might have promoted the union principle of solidarity.

A list of trade unions is maintained by the Certification Officer (CO)[15] and being on the list is evidence that an organisation is a trade union.[16] An organisation of workers can apply

---

[11] [1981] IRLR 408 ECHR.
[12] *Ibid.* at p. 419.
[13] Section 1(b) TULRCA 1992. Section 122 TULRCA 1992 applies the same purpose to employers' associations.
[14] [1984] ICR 268.
[15] Section 2(1) TULRCA 1992; the CO publishes an annual report containing the list and size of membership; it is available free of charge.
[16] Section 2(4) TULRCA 1992.

to be included in the list and will need to supply the CO with various materials, including a copy of its rules and a list of its officers.[17] If the CO is satisfied with the information, then the organisation will be added.[18] Conversely, the CO may remove an organisation if the CO decides that it is not a trade union or if the organisation so requests it or if the organisation has ceased to exist (for example, where two unions merge). The CO is required to give 28 days' notice of the intention to remove a name from the list.[19]

10.3.1 Independence

An advantage of being on the list maintained by the CO is that any trade union on it may apply to the CO for a certificate that it is independent.[20] The statutory benefits accruing to trade unions usually go to those that are independent. For example, workers cannot have action taken against them because they seek to join, have joined or have taken part in the activities of such a union (see below). The CO may withdraw the certificate if he is of the opinion that the union is no longer independent.[21] However, whilst in force the certificate is conclusive proof of independence.[22] Section 5 TULRCA 1992 defines an independent trade union. There are two tests to be satisfied:

1. the trade union must not be under the domination or control of an employer or an employers' association or of a group of employers or employers' associations; and

2. the trade union must not be liable to interference by an employer, or any such group or association, which tends towards control.

An organisation that is refused a certificate or has one withdrawn may appeal to the EAT on a question of law.[23]

In *Blue Circle Staff Association* v *The Certification Officer*[24] the CO outlined the factors used in assessing the independence of an organisation. These were finance, and whether there was a direct subsidy from the employer; other assistance received, such as free premises, facilities and time off; employer interference; history and the extent to which it has grown away from being a 'creature of management'; rules and the extent to which the employer's senior employees are involved in running it; single company unions are more likely to be under the employer's dominance; organisation; attitude, such as a 'robust attitude in negotiation'. The newness of the Blue Circle Staff Association was a major factor in its failure to gain a certificate.[25]

Interference tending towards control might be as a result of providing financial, material or other support. It is not necessary to show that interference actually takes place, nor is it necessary for the CO to decide on the likelihood of such interference tending towards control. The question for the CO is whether there is a possibility of interference by the employer

---

[17] Section 3(1) and (2) TULRCA 1992.
[18] Section 3(3) and (4) TULRCA 1992.
[19] Section 4 TULRCA 1992.
[20] Section 6(1) TULRCA 1992.
[21] Section 7(1) TULRCA 1992.
[22] Section 8(1) TULRCA 1992.
[23] Section 9(1) TULRCA 1992.
[24] [1977] IRLR 20.
[25] See *Association of HSD (Hatfield) Employees* v *Certification Officer* [1977] IRLR 261, where an organisation was able to satisfy the EAT of its independence.

tending towards control. 'Liable to interference' means 'vulnerable to interference' or being 'exposed to the risk of interference'.[26] This was highlighted in *Government Communications Staff Federation v Certification Officer*.[27] Here a staff association was established at GCHQ after the Government withdrew recognition of the unions and banned GCHQ employees from union membership. The EAT concluded that the Staff Federation was equally vulnerable to interference and that its continuing existence depended upon the approval of the Director of the organisation. It therefore supported the CO's refusal to issue a certificate of independence.

10.4 **Contract of membership**

When an individual joins a trade union he or she enters into a contract of membership. It has not always been entirely clear whether that contract is one that is between the trade union and its members or whether it is one between the members of the trade union. In *Bonsor v Musicians Union*[28] a musician was expelled from the Musicians Union and thereafter found it difficult to obtain work. It was held that, although the trade union was an unincorporated body, it was capable of entering into contracts and being sued as a legal entity, as distinct from its individual members. When Bonsor's application to join was accepted, a contract came into existence with the union. The trade union impliedly agreed that the member would not be excluded by the trade union or its officers otherwise than in accordance with the rules. When the trade union broke this contract by wrongfully expelling the individual, it could be sued as a legal entity. Thus there was no reason why Bonsor should not be granted all the remedies against the union which were appropriate for a breach of contract.

Section 10 TULRCA 1992 gives trade unions a 'quasi corporate status'. The union is not a body corporate, except that it is capable of making contracts and suing or being sued in its own name. Any proceedings for an offence alleged to have been committed by it may be brought against it in its own name. Section 11 TULRCA 1992 excludes the common law rules on restraint of trade (see Chapter 11).

The contract of membership serves as the constitution of the trade union. The primary source of the contract is the union rule book, which is likely to cover the rights and obligations of individual members, the power and composition of various bodies within the union, the purposes for which union funds can be expended and the powers of union officers. The contract between all the members is embodied in the rules of the union. As was stated in *Wise v Union of Shop, Distributive and Allied Workers*,[29] which involved a challenge to a decision of the union executive committee concerning elections:

> A decision which is inconsistent with the rules . . . is a decision . . . to which the member has not given his or her consent. The decision has been made or the election held in a manner which contravenes the contract into which the member has entered by joining the union. Accordingly, as it seems to me, the right of a member to complain of a breach of the rules is a contractual right which is individual to that member; although, of course, that member holds the right in common with all other members having the like right.

[26] See *The Certification Officer v Squibb UK Staff Association* [1979] IRLR 75 CA.
[27] [1993] IRLR 260.
[28] [1956] AC 104.
[29] [1996] IRLR 609 at p. 613.

Thus, by joining a trade union, the member enters into an agreement and joins with all other members in authorising officers or others to carry out certain functions and duties on their collective behalf. The basic terms of the agreement are to be found in the union's rule book.[30]

As with other contracts, the terms may be modified by custom and practice, although not so as to conflict with the union's rules, and terms can be implied with caution.[31] However, the rules are not to be treated as if they were written by parliamentary draftsmen:

> The rules of a trade union are not to be construed literally or like statute, but so as to give them a reasonable interpretation which accords with what, in the court's view, they must have been intended to mean, bearing in mind their authorship, their purpose, and the readership to which they are addressed.[32]

In *Iwanuszezak* v *GMBATU*[33] an individual tried to argue that a trade union had an implied obligation to use its collective strength to safeguard an individual member's terms and conditions. In this case a new agreement between employers and the union had rearranged work shift patterns to this person's detriment. The Court of Appeal refused to imply the term, accepting the argument that, where there was a conflict between collective and individual interests, the collective interest must prevail. In every contract of membership there is also a statutorily implied right for the individual to terminate their membership, subject to reasonable notice and reasonable conditions.[34]

There are three situations considered here in which members have statutory rights that can be exercised against their union. These relate to union membership and discipline; rights arising if a union does not comply with the statutory provisions on ballots; and rights arising from the application of funds for political objects.

10.5 Rights in relation to trade union membership and discipline

Until the Industrial Relations Act 1971 there was little statutory regulation limiting a union's powers to admit, discipline or expel a member.[35] Section 65 of this Act introduced rules dealing with arbitrary exclusions or expulsions and unfair or unreasonable disciplinary action. Although this section was repealed in 1976, it was reintroduced in the Employment Act 1980 as part of the Government's attack on the closed shop.

10.5.1 Exclusion and expulsion

Currently an individual may not be excluded or expelled from a trade union except for the following reasons.[36] (Note that exclusion means not being admitted to membership.)[37]

---

[30] See *Heatons Transport (St Helens) Ltd* v *TGWU* [1972] IRLR 25 HL.
[31] See *Porter* v *National Union of Journalists* [1980] IRLR 404 HL.
[32] *Jacques* v *AUEW (Engineering Section)* [1986] ICR 683.
[33] [1988] IRLR 219 CA.
[34] Section 69 TULRCA 1992.
[35] The Trade Union Act 1913 had established a requirement that a trade union could not refuse admission or discipline solely because of a refusal to contribute to the political fund.
[36] Section 174 TULRCA 1992.
[37] See *NACODS* v *Gluchowski* [1996] IRLR 252.

1. If the individual does not satisfy an enforceable membership requirement.

2. If the individual does not qualify for membership on the grounds that the union only operates in a particular part or parts of Great Britain.

3. If the union's purpose is to regulate the relations with one particular employer, or a number of particular employers, and the individual no longer works for any of those employers.

4. If the exclusion or expulsion is entirely attributable to the individual's conduct (other than 'excluded conduct') and the conduct to which it is wholly or mainly attributable is not 'protected conduct'.

In the first of these exceptions, the 'enforceable membership requirement' means a restriction on membership as a result of employment being in one specific trade, industry or profession; or of an occupational description such as a particular grade or level; or of the need for specific trade, industrial or professional qualifications or work experience. 'Excluded conduct' means:

1. Being or ceasing to be, or having been or ceased to be, a member of another trade union or employed by a particular employer or at a particular place.

2. Conduct to which s. 65 TULRCA 1992 applies.

'Protected conduct' consists of the individual being or ceasing to be, or having been or ceased to be, a member of a political party, unless such membership is contrary to a rule or objective of the trade union.[38] Activities undertaken as a member of a political party are not protected.

These rules necessitated a revision of the 'Bridlington Principles'. These were a set of recommendations agreed at the 1939 Trades Union Congress which were designed to minimise disputes over membership questions.[39] They laid down the procedures by which the TUC dealt with complaints by one union against another and were designed to stop inter-union disputes over membership and representation. In the light of the legislation to inhibit unions from excluding members, introduced by the Trade Union Reform and Employment Rights Act 1993, these principles were revised so as to provide that:

1. Each union should consider developing joint working arrangements with other unions to avoid such conflicts.

2. No union should commence activities at an establishment where another trade union had a majority.

3. There should be no industrial action in an inter-union dispute until the TUC had an opportunity to examine the issue.

The courts have not always been hostile to union autonomy in relation to membership matters. *Cheall v APEX*[40] involved an individual who was excluded from membership on the orders of the TUC's disputes committee. The relevant union rule stated that 'the executive committee may, by giving 6 weeks' notice in writing, terminate the membership of any

---

[38] See s. 174 (4C–4H) TULRCA 1992.

[39] For an example of a TUC disputes committee attempting to resolve issues under the Bridlington Principles, see *Rothwell v APEX* [1975] IRLR 375 CA.

[40] [1983] IRLR 215 HL; see also *Edwards v SOGAT* [1971] Ch 354, where a person's right to work in a closed shop was supported by the court.

member, if necessary to comply with a decision of the disputes committee of the TUC'. The House of Lords rejected the view that this was contrary to public policy. Lord Diplock stated that:

> freedom of association can only be mutual; there can be no right of an individual to associate with other individuals who are not willing to associate with him.

This was clearly not the view of the Government, as shown by its subsequent legislation.[41]

Individuals may present a complaint to an employment tribunal if they have been excluded or expelled in contravention of s. 174.[42] The tribunal is unable to consider the complaint unless it is presented before the end of six months beginning with the date of exclusion or expulsion, unless it is satisfied that it was not reasonably practicable for the claim to be presented in time.[43] Where a tribunal finds the complaint to be well founded it will make a declaration to that effect. A subsequent application for compensation can be made to a tribunal but, in order to give the union time to act, the claimant may not make the application for compensation until after four weeks beginning with the date of the declaration. There is also a limit of six months after which an application cannot be made.[44] If the applicant has not been admitted or readmitted, there is a minimum amount that will be awarded by the EAT of £7,300 (in 2009).

Compensation can be reduced if the union member is partly at fault. In *Howard* v *NGA*[45] an individual was dismissed from a job, in a closed shop environment, for not being a member of a union. The EAT recognised four heads of compensation: loss of earnings during the period of unemployment, the net loss of earnings resulting from his dismissal, loss of earning opportunity generally as a result of being denied union membership, and non-pecuniary loss. However, the individual had contributed by taking the job in a closed shop organisation whilst an application for union membership was still under consideration. This resulted in compensation being reduced by 15 per cent. In *Saunders* v *The Bakers, Food and Allied Workers Union*[46] an applicant resigned from the union over a disagreement about an unofficial strike. The individual later reapplied for membership and was refused. An appeal was made to the national executive committee in writing but the individual failed to attend. The application was rejected and, subsequently, an employment tribunal held this action to be an unreasonable refusal of membership. The EAT agreed with the tribunal when it stated that the individual could have done more to help themselves by attending the meeting of the national executive committee. Compensation was reduced as a result. Similarly, in *Day* v *SOGAT 1982*,[47] it was held that a member's failure to pay their subscription did not contribute to the union's refusal to readmit into membership so as to justify a reduction in compensation. However, the individual's failure to tell the union that he had a new job, which might have led to the return of the union card, had contributed to the situation and this led to a reduction in the amount of compensation.

---

[41] In *ASLEF* v *UK* [2007] IRLR 361 the European Court of Human Rights ruled that there is no general right to join the union of one's choice irrespective of the rules of the union.

[42] Section 174(5) TULRCA 1992.

[43] Section 175(a) and (b) TULRCA 1992.

[44] Section 176(3) TULRCA 1992.

[45] [1985] ICR 101.

[46] [1986] IRLR 16.

[47] [1986] ICR 640.

It is the union's duty to put the member back into the position that they were in before the wrongful expulsion. This might include arranging for the employee to sign a further mandate to authorise the employer to recommence deductions of union subscriptions, rather than placing the onus on the employee to take the initiative.[48]

10.5.2 **Discipline**

The courts have the role of applying union disciplinary rules, often in favour of the individual, especially where the offence is of a broad nature, for example acting in a way which was 'detrimental to the interests of the union'. *Esterman* v *NALGO*[49] involved the following rule: 'a member who disregards any regulation issued by the branch, or is guilty of conduct which, in the opinion of the executive committee, renders him unfit for membership, shall be liable to expulsion'. The member had refused to obey an instruction not to help with local election organisation. The member successfully obtained an injunction on the grounds that, in these circumstances, no committee could find the individual guilty of the offence. The court doubted whether the union had the power in the first place to stop people doing things outside their normal working hours, or from volunteering for duties.

Rules which appear to conflict with public policy can be struck out,[50] as can those requiring action in breach of the rules of natural justice. In *Hamlet* v *GMBATU*[51] an unsuccessful candidate challenged election results using an internal procedure. The individual claimed a breach of the rules of natural justice when an appeal committee was composed of some of the same people as the body against whose decision the appeal was being made. In this case the court held that the individual had expressly agreed to accept a tribunal with this membership and that an individual 'cannot therefore come bleating to the courts complaining of a breach of natural justice when the contract is carried out expressly according to its terms'. Similarly, in *Losinska* v *CPSA*,[52] a union president was able to stop the executive committee and its annual conference from discussing matters critical of themselves on the grounds that both played a part in the union's disciplinary process. They could not therefore be allowed to condemn the individual until that process had taken place.

Section 64(1) TULRCA 1992 states that an individual who is, or has been, a member of a trade union has the right not to be 'unjustifiably disciplined' by that union. A person is disciplined by a union if it takes place under the rules or by a union official or by a number of persons which include an official.[53] Section 64(2) TULRCA 1992 identifies six forms of discipline for these purposes. These include expulsion from the union, payment of a sum to the union, depriving them of access to any services or facilities that they would be entitled to by virtue of belonging to the union, encouraging another union or branch not to accept the individual into membership, and subjecting the individual to some other detriment.[54] Suspension of membership can mean depriving someone of access to the benefits of

---

[48] See *NALGO* v *Courtney-Dunn* [1992] IRLR 114.

[49] [1974] ICR 625.

[50] See *Lee* v *Showmen's Guild* [1952] QB 329, where the court could find no evidence that the members had agreed to a rule which gave an internal body exclusive jurisdiction.

[51] [1986] IRLR 293; see also *Radford* v *National Society of Operative Printers* [1972] ICR 484, where the failure to apply such rules was an issue.

[52] [1976] ICR 473.

[53] Section 64(2) TULRCA 1992.

[54] Section 64(2)(a)–(f) TULRCA 1992.

membership. In *Killorn*[55] an individual was suspended from membership for refusing to cross a picket line. The union also sent out a circular naming her, and others, as being suspended for strike-breaking. Both the suspension and the circular were held to be forms of unjustifiable discipline.

The meaning of 'unjustifiably disciplined' is set out in s. 65 TULRCA 1992. This lists[56] ten types of conduct[57] for which any resulting discipline will be 'unjustified'. This includes failing to participate in or support a strike or other industrial action,[58] or indicating a lack of support for, or opposition to, such action; asserting that the union, an official or a representative of it,[59] has contravened, or is planning to contravene, a requirement under union rules or some other enactment or law;[60] or working with, or proposing to work with, individuals who are not members of the union or who are not members of another union.[61]

An individual who claims to have been unjustifiably disciplined may present a complaint to an employment tribunal within three months of the infringement, unless it was not reasonably practicable for the complaint to be presented in that time.[62] Additionally, if there is a delay resulting from an attempt to appeal against the discipline or have it reviewed or reconsidered,[63] the three-month limit may be extended.[64] This happened in *Killorn*[65] where a letter to the union branch chair, in which the complainant raised a series of questions about the suspension, was held to be a 'reasonable attempt' to appeal in accordance with this section. The EAT held that the statute did not lay down any specific method of appealing, so an employment tribunal should consider the reality of the events, rather than look for formal appeal proceedings. It is also necessary to wait until the union has made a final determination, such as expulsion, before making the complaint to an employment tribunal. If there is only a recommendation to the general executive committee of a union that an individual be expelled, that cannot be seen as the final decision. It is not possible to make a claim in respect of an act that might never take place, no matter how much the individual thinks it is likely to happen.[66]

The employment tribunal may make a declaration that the complaint is well founded.[67] The applicant may then make an application to the tribunal for compensation and repayment of any money unjustifiably paid to the union.[68] The employment tribunal may award

---

[55] *NALGO v Killorn and Simm* [1990] IRLR 464.

[56] Section 65(2)(a)–(j) TULRCA 1992.

[57] Conduct includes statements, acts or omissions; s. 65(7) TULRCA 1992.

[58] See *Knowles v Fire Brigades Union* [1996] IRLR 617 CA, where the complainants failed to prove unjustifiable discipline because the pressure exerted on employers by the union did not amount to industrial action.

[59] Representative means a person acting or purporting to act in their capacity as a member of the union or on the instructions or advice of a person acting, or purporting to act, in the capacity of an official of the union: s. 65(7) TULRCA 1992.

[60] A person is not unjustifiably disciplined if the reason is that they made such assertions vindictively, falsely or in bad faith: s. 65(6) TULRCA 1992.

[61] See *Santer v National Graphical Association* [1973] ICR 60, where a trade union expelled a member for working for a firm which did not recognise the union.

[62] Section 66(1) and (2) TULRCA 1992.

[63] In *McKenzie v NUPE* [1991] ICR 155 it was held to be an implied term of the contract between the union and the member that a disciplinary tribunal should be entitled to reopen it if new evidence came to light.

[64] Section 66(2)(b) TULRCA 1992.

[65] [1990] IRLR 464.

[66] See *TGWU v Webber* [1990] IRLR 462 and *Beaumont v Amicus* [2007] ICR 341.

[67] Section 66(3) TULRCA 1992; s. 66(4) TULRCA 1992 prevents any further proceedings relating to expulsion being brought under this section and s. 174 (see above).

[68] Section 67(1) TULRCA 1992.

compensation in line with that for cases of expulsion or exclusion under s. 174 TULRCA 1992 (see above).[69] This can include injury to feelings.[70] It should be noted that the complaint cannot be made before four weeks from the date of the tribunal's declaration and not more than six months beginning with that date.[71]

10.6 **Statutory obligations in relation to union elections**

Strict statutory rules were introduced during the 1980s concerning the election of certain union officials. The rules stipulated which union offices were to be the subject of regular elections and laid down detailed rules about how those elections were to be conducted. The Government at the time stated its intentions:

> There must also be a proper balance between the interests of the unions and the needs of the community . . . individual unionists themselves [are] . . . entitled to see minimum standards established to ensure that union power is exercised more responsibly, more accountably and more in accordance with the views of their members.[72]

Section 46(2) TULRCA 1992 lists those positions for which there is a duty to hold elections at least every five years.[73] However, there is no requirement for a ballot if the election is uncontested.[74] The positions are: (i) a member of the executive, or any position held as a result of being a member of the executive; (ii) president; and (iii) general secretary. The executive is defined as the principal committee of the union exercising executive powers.[75] However, a member of the executive includes any person who may attend or speak at meetings of the executive, excluding technical or professional advisers.[76]

According to s. 119 TULRCA 1992, presidents and general secretaries are the people that hold those offices or the nearest equivalent to them. Those who hold the position of president on an annual basis and are not voting members of the executive or employees of the union and have not held the position in the 12 months before taking up the position, are excluded from the elections requirements.[77] Similarly, such office holders may stay in office for up to a further six months if they fail to be re-elected. This is a period which may 'reasonably be required' to give effect to the election result and aid the transition between office holders.[78]

---

[69] Sections 67(5)–(7) TULRCA 1992.

[70] See *Bradley* v *NALGO* [1991] IRLR 159.

[71] Section 67(3) TULRCA 1992.

[72] *Democracy in Trade Unions* (HMSO, 1983).

[73] Section 46(1)(b) TULRCA 1992, although there is an exception in s. 58 for those within five years of retirement age. In *GMB* v *Corrigan* [2008] ICR 197 the EAT held that the purpose of s. 46(1) TULRCA 1992 was not to oblige a union to hold an election as soon as a position became vacant but to ensure that anyone in fact holding the position was elected.

[74] Section 53 TULRCA 1992.

[75] Section 119 TULRCA 1992.

[76] Section 46(3) TULRCA 1992. There is a definition of 'voting members of the executive' in s. 46(5) TULRCA 1992.

[77] Section 46(4)–(4A) TULRCA 1992.

[78] See *Paul* v *NALGO* [1987] IRLR 43 CO, where a retiring president who continued on the executive for a further year was held to be covered by the transitional arrangements.

No member of the trade union can be 'unreasonably' excluded from standing as a candidate, although the union can have eligibility conditions that apply to all members.[79] Thus there is a requirement for objective criteria to be applied in relation to eligibility. In *Ecclestone* v *National Union of Journalists*[80] a rule provided that 'the NEC [National Executive Committee] shall prepare a shortlist of applicants who have the required qualifications'. The union argued that this gave the executive committee a discretion to decide on the qualifications appropriate to the post. In this case they imposed the qualification that the candidates should have the confidence of the NEC. According to the court, this amounted to the exclusion of a class of members which was determined by reference to whom the union chose to exclude. It was essentially a subjective test which was in breach of s. 47(3) TULRCA 1992. Good practice requires that selection criteria be laid down in advance of applications so as to avoid arbitrary decisions.

No candidate directly, or indirectly, can be required to be a member of a political party.[81] Although it might be understandable for a Conservative Government to impose such a rule on trade unions, it does seem rather an odd one. Presidents or general secretaries of large trade unions are likely to play an active part in the political party to which their union is affiliated. Those unions that are affiliated to one political party are affiliated to the Labour Party.

Every candidate may provide an election address and the union will distribute it to all members entitled to vote. This will be done at no expense to the candidates. The union can decide the length of the address, subject to a minimum of 100 words. All candidates are to be treated equally in this matter. Their material cannot be changed without consent and it is the candidate that incurs any civil or criminal liability arising from the contents of the election address.[82]

The entitlement to vote should be accorded equally to all members, although the rules can exclude certain classes, such as unemployed members, those in arrears with their subscriptions, new members and students, trainees or apprentices.[83] In *NUM (Yorkshire Area)* v *Millward*[84] an election result was challenged when a group called 'limited members', who were mostly people who had taken early retirement, were excluded from participating. The EAT held that their exclusion was permissible within the union rules, as they were not members for the purpose of voting in ballots. Although they were members of the union and received fringe benefits, they had no right to vote on decisions or stand for office and were only indirect beneficiaries of the purpose of the union.

The union will appoint an independent scrutineer[85] to supervise the production of the ballot papers and their distribution to those entitled to vote. As soon as is reasonably practicable after the end of the ballot period the independent scrutineer will make a report to the union.[86] In *Douglas* v *Graphical, Paper and Media Union*[87] the independent scrutineer issued a certificate

---

[79] In *UNISON* v *Bakhsh* [2009] IRLR 418 the EAT ruled that suspended members are not precluded from standing for office for the purposes of s. 47(3) TULRCA 1992.

[80] [1999] IRLR 166; see also *Wise* v *USDAW* [1996] IRLR 609, where it was held that even if much of the rule governing the election of the general secretary was inconsistent with TULRCA, it would be wrong not to give effect to any of it.

[81] Section 47(1)–(3) TULRCA 1992.

[82] Section 48(1)–(7) TULRCA 1992.

[83] Section 50(1)–(2) TULRCA 1992.

[84] [1995] IRLR 411.

[85] Section 49 TULRCA 1992.

[86] Section 52 TULRCA 1992.

[87] [1995] IRLR 426.

stating that there were no reasonable grounds for believing that there had been any breach of statutory requirements relating to the ballot. Subsequently the scrutineer examined a complaint and decided that there had been a breach of the union rules which might have influenced the outcome of the ballot. The union then attempted to set the ballot aside and call a fresh election. The High Court held that there was nothing in its rules that permitted it to do this so the union was acting outside its powers. It was also doubtful whether it was possible to cancel a ballot once the scrutineer had issued their report approving the ballot.[88]

There are detailed rules on the voting process contained within s. 51 TULRCA 1992. The essential features are that: it is to be done by marking a ballot paper; as far as is reasonably practicable, the ballot is to be conducted by post and at no cost to the individual member; the ballot should, as far as is reasonably practicable, enable votes to be cast in secret. In *Paul v NALGO*[89] the union was held to be in breach of the rule that there should be no cost to the member. Arrangements were made for the ballot papers to be collected from the union district organisers. The responsibility of getting their completed ballot paper to the district organiser was placed on the individual. If a member did not wish to use that system, then they incurred the cost of sending in the vote.

The ballot is to be conducted so as to enable the result to be determined solely by counting the votes cast for each candidate.[90] This does not necessarily mean that those with the highest votes get elected. For example, if there are rules which state that there is a maximum number of elected representatives for each region, then it will be those with the highest votes in that region who are elected. It does not matter that an unsuccessful candidate in one region might have gained more votes than a successful candidate in another.[91] In *AB v CD*[92] two candidates gained identical numbers of votes in an election using the single transferable vote system. The rules did not provide for such an eventuality. The court implied a term into the union's standing orders that the candidate with the most votes in the initial ballot should be declared the winner.

The remedy for a failure to comply with the statutory requirements is for a person who was a member of the trade union at the time of the election, or a person who was a candidate in the election, to make a complaint to the Certification Officer (CO) or to the High Court within one year of the election result being announced.[93] If the application is to the CO[94] in accordance with s. 55 TULRCA 1992, then the CO has an obligation to ensure, so far as is reasonably practicable, that the matter is determined within six months.[95] On receiving the application the CO will make inquiries and give the applicant and the union the opportunity to be heard.[96] The CO may then make a declaration specifying where the union has failed to comply, giving reasons for the decision in writing.[97] This declaration may be accompanied by

---

[88] See also *Brown v AUEW* [1976] ICR 147, where a union called a fresh ballot after some irregularities in the voting process. The new election resulted in a different outcome, but the election was held to be outside the union's powers to call.

[89] [1987] IRLR 43 CO.

[90] Section 51(6) TULRCA 1992, although s. 51(7) allows for the single transferable vote system to be used.

[91] See *R v CO, ex parte Electrical Power Engineers' Association* [1990] IRLR 398 HL.

[92] [2001] IRLR 808.

[93] Section 54(1)–(3) TULRCA 1992.

[94] Similar provisions concerning applications to the court are dealt with in s. 56 TULRCA 1992.

[95] Section 55(6) TULRCA 1992.

[96] Section 55(2) TULRCA 1992.

[97] Section 55(3) and (5) TULRCA 1992.

an enforcement order requiring a new election or rectification of the fault or a requirement to abstain from specified acts in the future.[98] A declaration or enforcement order made by the CO may be relied upon as if it were an order of the court.[99] Appeals on points of law arising from complaints dealt with by the CO are to the EAT.[100]

10.7 Rights related to the application of funds for political objects

The funds of a trade union cannot be used for the furtherance of political objects unless a political resolution is in force. The political resolution needs to be supported by a majority of those voting and needs to be approved at least every ten years.[101] The process of the ballot and the rules governing it are similar to those concerned with ballots for the election of union officials (see above).[102] An individual member may give notice that they object to contributing to the political fund and s. 84(1) TULRCA 1992 contains an example of such a notice. When a political resolution is adopted all members must be given notice of their right to be exempted and where they can obtain a form of exemption.[103] The employee can certify to their employer that they are exempted from such contributions and the employer must then ensure that no deductions are made for that part of the subscription which applies to the political fund.[104]

There also need to be provisions in the union rules for the making of such payments out of a separate fund and for the exemption of any member of the union who objects to contributing to that fund.[105] Section 72 TULRCA 1992 provides some definitions of expenditure for political objects. These are:

1. Any contributions[106] to the funds of a political party, or the payment of expenses incurred directly or indirectly by a political party.

2. The provision of any service or property for use by, or on behalf of, a political party.

3. In connection with the registration of electors or the candidature of any person, including the holding of a ballot by the union in connection with any election.

4. On the maintenance of any holder of a political office.[107]

5. The holding of a conference or meeting by, or on behalf of, a political party, including any meetings whose main purpose is the transaction of business in connection with a political party; this includes, according to s. 72(2) TULRCA 1992, any expenditure incurred by delegates to the conference or meeting.[108]

---

[98] Section 55(5A) TULRCA 1992.
[99] Section 55(8) and (9) TULRCA 1992.
[100] Section 56A TULRCA 1992.
[101] Section 73 TULRCA 1992.
[102] See ss. 75–81 TULRCA 1992.
[103] From the trade union or the CO; see s. 84(2) TULRCA 1992.
[104] Section 86 TULRCA 1992; this applies only if the employer is deducting subscriptions on behalf of the trade union.
[105] Section 71(1) TULRCA 1992.
[106] Contribution includes affiliation fees or loans made to a political party: see s. 72(4) TULRCA 1992.
[107] Political office means the office of Member of Parliament, Member of the European Parliament, or a member of a local authority or any position within a political party: see s. 72(4) TULRCA 1992.
[108] See *Richards v NUM* [1981] IRLR 247, where this was held to include the cost of sending delegates and a colliery band to a lobby of Parliament organised by the Labour Party to protest at government cuts.

6. On the production, publication or distribution of any literature, document, film, sound recording or advertisement concerned with persuading people to vote, or not to vote, for a particular candidate[109] or political party.

A number of these issues were tested in *ASTMS* v *Parkin*,[110] where decisions of the CO were appealed against. These related to donations made by the union and are indicative of how strictly the line between the union's general funds and the political fund are drawn. The donations considered here were a contribution from the union's general fund towards the development of the property then used by the Labour Party as its headquarters and a donation from the general fund to the Leader of the Opposition's office at Parliament. The contribution towards the Labour Party offices was made at commercial rates and, the union argued, was a commercial investment. The EAT supported the CO's conclusions that, despite their commercial nature, they were still payments to a political party and fell within the political objectives as set out in what is now s. 72 TULRCA 1992. Similarly, the EAT supported the CO in deciding that the donation to the Opposition Leader's office should not have been made out of the general fund. The maintenance mentioned in the legislation refers to the support of someone as a politician. The union had argued that this interpretation gave too wide a meaning to the term but the EAT held that maintenance covered expenses incurred in carrying out the functions of being a Member of Parliament. Thus a grant to an MP to enable them to conduct research for the purpose of carrying out parliamentary functions is maintenance as an MP and should come out of the political fund.

It should be noted that a union having its own views on political issues and campaigning for them may not be involved in political activities as defined in the statute. *Coleman* v *Post Office Engineering Union*[111] involved an affiliation fee of £8 to a District Trades Council campaign against Government cuts. The CO decided that 'political' meant 'party political'. It was difficult to draw the line between these two concepts but the legislation applied to support of some kind to a political party or to candidates of political parties.

A member of a trade union who wishes to claim that the union has misapplied its funds in breach of s. 71 TULRCA 1992 may apply to the CO for a declaration to this effect.[112] Where the CO makes a declaration he may order the breach to be remedied.[113] The CO's declaration may be relied upon as if it were a made by a court.[114] If the employer fails to comply with s. 86 TULRCA 1992, the individual may make a complaint to an employment tribunal within three months of the date of the payment, unless the tribunal accepts that this was not reasonably practicable.[115] The tribunal may make a declaration and/or an order to remedy the failure of the employer. If the employer fails to comply with the order then the individual may make a further complaint to the tribunal after four weeks and before six months. The tribunal may then order the employer to provide the claimant with up to two weeks' pay.[116]

---

[109] Candidate also includes 'prospective candidates': see s. 72(4) TULRCA 1992.
[110] [1983] IRLR 448.
[111] [1981] IRLR 427.
[112] Section 72A(1) TULRCA 1992.
[113] Section 72A(4) TULRCA 1992.
[114] Section 72A(7) TULRCA 1992.
[115] Section 87(1)–(8) TULRCA 1992.
[116] Subject to the definition of a week's pay contained in s. 225 ERA 1996.

10.8 Breach of rules

Apart from any common law action for breach of contract, a member of a union[117] may apply to the CO for a declaration that there has been a breach, or threatened breach, of rules relating to the following matters:[118]

1. The appointment or election (or the removal) of a person from any office.
2. Disciplinary proceedings by the union (including expulsion).
3. The balloting of members on any issue other than industrial action.
4. The constitution or proceedings of the executive committee or any other decision-making committee.[119]
5. Any other matters specified by the Secretary of State.[120]

Specifically excluded are the dismissal of an employee of the union or any disciplinary proceedings against such an employee.[121] The application must normally be made within six months from the day in which the breach or alleged breach took place. Alternatively, if an internal appeals procedure is invoked, within six months of the end of that procedure or within one year of the invocation of that procedure.[122] A person may not make a complaint both to the CO and the court but may appeal to the courts against the CO's decisions[123] and to the EAT on points of law.[124]

The CO may refuse to act unless satisfied that the applicant has taken all available steps to make use of the internal complaints procedure. Thereafter the CO may make whatever inquiries the CO thinks fit and give the applicant and the union the right to be heard. The CO may make a declaration with written reasons and may make an enforcement order to remedy the breach and take such action necessary to stop such a breach happening in the future.

10.9 Discrimination against members and officials

10.9.1 Blacklisting

In March 2010 the Employment Relations Act 1999 (Blacklists) Regulations 2010 came into force.[125] Under these Regulations current and former trade union members can claim at an employment tribunal if they are denied employment, subjected to a detriment or unfairly dismissed for a reason relating to a prohibited list. It is unlawful to compile, use, sell or supply blacklists containing details of those who are or have been union members or who are taking

---

[117] Or was a member at the time of the alleged breach: s. 108(3) TULRCA 1992.
[118] Section 108A TULRCA 1992.
[119] Definitions are provided by s. 108A(10)–(12) TULRCA 1992.
[120] Section 108A(2) TULRCA 1992.
[121] Section 108A(5) TULRCA 1992
[122] Section 108A(6)–(7) TULRCA 1992.
[123] Section 108A(14) TULRCA 1992.
[124] Section 108B(9) TULRCA 1992.
[125] S.I. 2010/493.

part or have taken part in union activities.[126] In addition, an employment agency is unable to refuse to provide a service because a worker appears on a blacklist. Where these Regulations are breached, compensation can be awarded, including damages for injury to feelings.[127]

10.9.2 Refusal of employment

Part III TULRCA 1992 deals with refusal of employment related to membership of any trade union or membership of a particular trade union.[128] This part contains a number of measures designed to prevent employers or unions introducing measures related to a closed shop. Thus it is unlawful to refuse employment for belonging to, or not belonging to, any union or a particular union. Pressure exerted by a trade union may also result in the union being joined to any employment tribunal proceedings and being liable to pay compensation (see below). For these purposes 'employment' means employment under a contract of employment.[129]

There is no rigid dividing line between membership of a union and taking part in its activities. Thus an applicant who is refused employment because of trade union activities with a previous employer may have been refused because of their membership of a union.[130] Any requirements that a person must take steps to join a union or make payments in lieu connected with membership or non-membership are also unlawful.[131] Persons offered employment on these conditions who refuse it because they do not meet the conditions, or are unwilling to meet the conditions, are treated as being refused employment for those reasons.[132] Previous practices of putting union membership requirements in advertisements or recruiting from union nominations only are also unlawful.[133]

A person is taken to have been refused employment if, in seeking employment of any description, the potential employer: refuses or deliberately fails to entertain and process the application or inquiry; causes the person to withdraw or cease to pursue the application or inquiry; refuses or deliberately omits to offer employment of that description; makes an offer of such employment on terms which no reasonable employer would offer if they wished to fill the post (and the offer is not accepted); makes an offer of employment, but withdraws it or causes it not to be accepted.[134] Section 138 TULRCA 1992 applies similar rules in respect of employment agencies.

Where a person is refused employment for a reason related to union membership they may make a complaint to an employment tribunal.[135] The claim needs to be made within three months of the date of the conduct which is complained about, unless the tribunal accepts that it was not reasonably practicable to do so.[136] The date of various types of conduct is defined in s. 139(2) TULRCA 1992:

---

[126] Regulation 3.
[127] Regulation 8.
[128] Section 143(3) TULRCA 1992.
[129] Section 143(1) TULRCA 1992.
[130] See *Harrison* v *Kent County Council* [1995] ICR 434; also *Fitzpatrick* v *British Railways Board* [1991] IRLR 376 CA which concerned dismissal for previous trade union activities (see below).
[131] Section 137(1)(b) TULRCA 1992.
[132] Section 137(6) TULRCA 1992.
[133] Section 137(3) and (4) TULRCA 1992; s. 143(1) gives a wide meaning to the term 'advertisement'.
[134] Section 137(5) TULRCA 1992.
[135] Section 137(2) TULRCA 1992.
[136] Section 139(1) TULRCA 1992.

1. In the case of an actual refusal of employment, it is the date of that refusal.

2. In the case of a deliberate omission to entertain or process the application, then the date is the end of a period in which it was reasonable to expect the employer to act.

3. In the case of conduct causing the applicant to withdraw or stop pursuing an application or inquiry, the date is when that conduct took place.

4. In the case when the offer was made and then withdrawn, the date is when it was withdrawn.

5. In any other case where an offer is made, but not accepted, then the date is when the offer was made.[137]

If a tribunal finds that a complaint is justified, then it may award compensation and/or make a recommendation that the employer takes action within a specified period which appears to be reasonable to obviate or reduce the adverse effects on the complainant of the conduct complained of.[138]

10.9.3 Subject to detriment

Section 146 TULRCA provides for workers not to be subject to detriment by any act, or deliberate failure to act, if the act or failure to act takes place for the purpose of:

1. Preventing or deterring them from seeking to become a member of a trade union,[139] or penalising them for doing so.

2. Preventing or deterring them from taking part in the activities of the trade union or from making use of trade union services at an appropriate time, or penalising them for doing so.

3. Compelling them to be or become a member of a trade union, or a particular trade union.[140]

4. Enforcing a requirement that in the event of their failing to become, or their ceasing to remain, members of any trade union or a particular trade union or one of a number of particular trade unions, they must make one or more payments. For this purpose, any deduction from remuneration which is attributable to the employee's failure to become, or his ceasing to be, a union member will be treated as a detriment.

Where either party claims that the employer acted under pressure from a third party, for example a union, they may request that the third party be joined to the proceedings. In these circumstances the tribunal may require that any compensation be paid by the third party.[141]

It is not always easy to identify when the purpose of an act or omission falls within s. 146. For example, in *Gallagher v Department of Transport*[142] an employee was elected group assistant secretary of a union. The individual was a higher executive officer in the civil service, but, with the employer's approval, the union duties were effectively full time. When the employee applied for promotion to the next grade, he was turned down. Previously, in an appraisal, the employee had been told of problems with management skills. As a result of being a union

---

[137] Section 138 TULRCA 1992 applies similar provisions to actions and omissions by employment agencies.

[138] Section 140 TULRCA 1992; s. 141 applies similar provisions in respect of employment agencies.

[139] In *Ridgway and Fairbrother v National Coal Board* [1987] IRLR 80 CA, it was held that this can mean either an individual trade union or any trade union.

[140] Section 146(1) TULRCA 1992.

[141] Section 142 TULRCA 1992.

[142] [1994] IRLR 231 CA.

assistant secretary, it was said that there was no way of telling whether these skills had improved. The job also required more management experience than could be gained by being a union activist. The employment tribunal agreed that there had been discrimination on the grounds of union membership and activities. However, the Court of Appeal held that the tribunal had confused cause and effect. The purpose of the procedure was to ensure that those promoted had management skills, not to deter the employee from continuing with union activities, although this may have been the effect.[143]

The detriment is to be interpreted as action against employees as individuals rather than as trade unionists. In *FW Farnsworth Ltd* v *McCoid*[144] the employee was derecognised by the employer as a shop steward and claimed that this breached s. 146(1)(b) TULRCA 1992. The Court of Appeal held that the words 'as an individual' were inserted into the legislation to exclude collective disputes from the scope of the section. The complainant here was an individual who happened to be a shop steward and so the employer's action was held to be against him as an individual and thus unlawful.[145]

'Penalising' is given a wide meaning and is to be interpreted as subjecting an individual to a disadvantage.[146] Indeed, it is specifically provided that penalising a worker because an independent trade union raises a matter on the member's behalf (with or without the member's consent) falls within the ambit of s. 146 TULRCA 1992. 'Activities' can mean the organising of meetings at an appropriate time. In *British Airways (Engine Overhaul) Ltd* v *Francis*[147] the employee was a shop steward whose members had an ongoing grievance concerning equal pay. They arranged a meeting during their lunch break. It was not a formal meeting of the branch or of a union committee and the discussion was critical of the union. Nevertheless it was held to be an activity of an independent union. 'Trade union services' means the services made available to the worker by virtue of union membership and 'making use' includes consenting to the raising of a matter by the union on his behalf.[148]

'Appropriate time' means either a time outside working hours or a time within working hours where 'in accordance with arrangements agreed with or consent given' by the employer, it is permissible to take part in union activities or make use of their services. 'Working hours' means any time, in accordance with the contract of employment, that the individual is required to be at work.[149] This does not necessarily require the express agreement of an employer and arrangements can be of an informal nature.[150] If workers are able to converse whilst working and discuss union membership and activities, there is no reason why an employment tribunal could not come to the conclusion that there was implied consent or implied arrangements for them to talk about union activities.[151] Additionally, being at work is not necessarily

---

[143] See also *Southwark London Borough Council* v *Whillier* [2001] ICR 142, where a union branch secretary was offered promotion, but no salary increase until she had taken up the new duties; this was held to be a detriment because the individual would have to give up her trade union duties in order to take on these responsibilities.

[144] [1999] IRLR 626 CA.

[145] See also *Ridgway and Fairbrother* v *National Coal Board* [1987] IRLR 80 CA, which was distinguished in this case.

[146] See *Carlson* v *Post Office* [1981] IRLR 158, where the withdrawal of a car parking permit was sufficient to penalise an individual.

[147] [1981] ICR 278.

[148] Section 146(2A) TULRCA 1992.

[149] Section 146(2) TULRCA 1992.

[150] See *Marley Tiles Co Ltd* v *Shaw* [1978] IRLR 238.

[151] See *Zucker* v *Astrid Jewels Ltd* [1978] IRLR 385.

the same as working. An employee is entitled to take part in union activities whilst on the employer's premises, but not actually working.[152] Thus tea breaks might be occasions when an employee is being paid, but is not necessarily at work.[153]

A worker may make a complaint to an employment tribunal if they have been subjected to a detriment contrary to s. 146 TULRCA 1992.[154] The complaint needs to be made within three months of the act or failure to which it relates. If there is a series of acts or failures, then the three months runs from the last of them.[155] There is the usual proviso that where the tribunal is satisfied that it was not reasonably practicable to do so, then the period may be extended.[156] In the absence of evidence to the contrary, the employer will be taken to have decided on a failure to act when they perform an act inconsistent with the failure or when a period expires when they might reasonably be expected to have done the failed act, if it was going to be done.[157] The burden of proof is on the employer to show the purpose of the act or the failure to act.[158]

If the tribunal finds the complaint well founded it may award compensation which reflects any loss suffered by the complainant as a result of the act or failure complained of. This loss will include any expenses reasonably incurred as a result of the act or failure plus the loss of any benefit which the complainant may reasonably be expected to have received but for the act or failure. It may also include compensation for injury to feelings.[159] Compensation is for the injury sustained and is not aimed at punishing the employer.[160] The complainant has a duty to mitigate their losses and the tribunal may take into account any contributory action by the worker towards causing the act or failure complained of.[161]

10.9.4 Inducements relating to membership or activities

Employers may try other ways to influence decisions about joining a trade union. In *Associated Newspapers* v *Wilson*[162] the employer ceased to recognise the union for negotiating purposes and encouraged employees to agree individual contracts. Those who did not agree were given a smaller pay rise than those that did. The question was whether this omission was action aimed at deterring employees from being members of a union. The House of Lords held that the action was not for this purpose but was designed merely to end collective bargaining. The European Court of Human Rights,[163] however, disagreed and held that:

> such conduct constituted a disincentive or restraint on the use by employees of union membership to protect their interests.

---

[152] See *Post Office* v *Union of Post Office Workers* [1974] IRLR 23 HL.
[153] *Zucker* v *Astrid Jewels Ltd* [1978] IRLR 385.
[154] Section 146(5) TULRCA 1992. However, this does not apply to employees who have been dismissed (see below).
[155] In *Adlam* v *Salisbury and Wells Theological College* [1985] ICR 786 continued weekly payments of a disputed settlement were held not to be a series of similar actions.
[156] Section 147(1) TULRCA 1992.
[157] Section 147(3) TULRCA 1992.
[158] Section 148(1) TULRCA 1992.
[159] See *London Borough of Hackney* v *Adams* [2003] IRLR 402 where £5,000 was awarded for injury to feelings after the withdrawal of an offer of promotion.
[160] See *Brassington* v *Cauldon Wholesale Ltd* [1977] IRLR 479.
[161] Section 149 TULRCA 1992.
[162] [1995] IRLR 258 HL; s. 298 TULRCA 1992 also defines act or action as including omission.
[163] [2002] IRLR 568 ECHR.

As a result there was a failure in the State's positive obligation to secure rights under art. 11 of the Convention.

Section 145A TULRCA 1992 now provides workers with the right not to have an offer made to them by their employer for the sole or main purpose of inducing them:

(i)   not to be or seek to become a member of an independent trade union, or
(ii) not to take part in the activities of an independent trade union or make use of union services at an appropiate time, or
(iii) to be or become a member of any trade union at a particular time.[164]

In addition, s. 145B TULRCA 1992 gives members of independent trade unions which are recognised or seeking to be recognised the right not to have an offer made to them if acceptance of the offer would have the 'prohibited result' and the employer's sole or main purpose is to achieve that result. The 'prohibited result' is that any of the worker's terms of employment will not (or no longer) be determined by collective agreement. Claims under s. 145A or 145B TULRCA 1992 must be brought within the usual three-month time period and it will be for the employer to show the main purpose in making the offers.[165] If a complaint is upheld the employment tribunal must make a declaration to that effect and award £3,100 (in 2010) to the complainant. It is also provided that if an offer made in contravention of s. 145A or 145B is accepted, the employer cannot enforce the agreement to vary terms.[166]

10.9.5 Dismissal on grounds related to membership or activities

A dismissal will be unfair if the reason or the principal reason for it was that the employee: (i) was, or proposed to become, a member of a trade union; (ii) had taken part, or proposed to take part, in the activities of a trade union or make use of union services at an appropriate time; (iii) was not a member of a trade union, or had refused or proposed to refuse to become a member; (iv) had failed to accept an offer in contravention of s. 145A or 145B (see 10.9.4 above).[167] Similarly, if one of the reasons in s. 152(1) TULRCA 1992 is a reason for an individual being selected for redundancy, then this is also likely to be an unfair dismissal.[168] Dismissal on the basis of union activities with a previous employer, when that decision was because of a fear that the employee would engage in further union activities, may also be a breach of s. 152 TULRCA 1992.[169] Another example of an employee suffering dismissal as a result of their trade union activities is an individual who spoke on behalf of the union at a company recruitment meeting and made derogatory remarks about the company.[170]

The reasons in s. 152(1) are inadmissible for the purposes of Part X ERA 1996, therefore such a dismissal will be automatically unfair. Section 108 ERA does not apply so there is no

---

[164] 'Appropriate time', 'trade union services' and 'working hours' have the same meaning as in s. 146 TULRCA 1992 (see above).
[165] Sections 145C and 145D TULRCA 1992.
[166] Section 145E TULRCA 1992.
[167] Section 152(1) TULRCA 1992. 'Appropriate time', 'working hours' and 'trade union services' have the same meaning as in s. 146 (see above).
[168] Section 153 TULRCA 1992; see also *Driver v Cleveland Structural Engineering Co Ltd* [1994] IRLR 636.
[169] *Fitzpatrick v British Railways Board* [1991] IRLR 376 CA.
[170] *Bass Taverns Ltd v Burgess* [1995] IRLR 596.

requirement for a qualifying period of service.[171] Where there is a dismissal by virtue of s. 152(1) or 153 TULRCA 1992, then there is a basic minimum award of compensation, before any reductions under s. 122 ERA 1996.[172]

An employee who presents a complaint to an employment tribunal that they have been dismissed by virtue of s. 152 may also apply for interim relief. This application must be made within seven days of the effective date of termination.[173] If the application is in connection with becoming a member of a union or taking part in the activities of a union,[174] then the tribunal will require a certificate signed by an authorised official[175] stating that the individual was or proposed to become a member of the union and there appeared to be reasonable grounds for the complaint.[176] The tribunal has an obligation to determine the application for interim relief as soon as practicable after receiving it and, where appropriate, the certificate. The employer[177] will be given a copy of the notice and certificate at least seven days before the hearing.[178] The tribunal will ask the employer whether they will reinstate or re-engage the employee. If the answer is positive, the tribunal will make an order accordingly. If the employer fails to attend or refuses to reinstate or re-engage, the tribunal can make an order for continuance of the employee's contract.[179] If the employer fails to comply, the tribunal will award compensation to the employee having regard to the infringement of the employee's right to reinstatement or re-engagement and any loss suffered by the employee as a result of the non-compliance.[180]

Chapter summary

This chapter explained the principle of freedom of association and the statutory definition of an independent trade union. It then examined the contract of membership at common law before describing the statutory provisions which impact on both recruitment and termination of this relationship. In addition, a union's obligation to ballot members in particular circumstances was discussed. Finally, it outlined the law protecting members and officials from discrimination by an employer on union grounds.

---

[171] Section 154(1) and (2) TULRCA 1992.
[172] Section 156 TULRCA 1992 (£4,700 in 2010). If the dismissal is unfair by virtue of s. 153, then s. 156(2) (reduction for contributory fault) applies.
[173] Section 161(1) and (2) TULRCA 1992.
[174] Section 152(1)(a)–(b) TULRCA 1992.
[175] Authorised official is an official of the trade union authorised by it to act for these purposes: s. 161(4) TULRCA 1992.
[176] Section 161(3) TULRCA 1992.
[177] And any party joined to the proceedings: s. 160 TULRCA 1992.
[178] Section 162 TULRCA 1992.
[179] Sections 163 and 164 TULRCA 1992.
[180] Section 166 TULRCA 1992.

Further reading

Collins, H., Ewing, K. and McColgan, A. *Labour Law: Text and Materials*: Hart Publishing, 2005, Chapters 7 and 8.

Deakin, S. and Morris, G. *Labour Law*: 5th edn, Hart Publishing, 2009, Chapters 8 and 10.

www.ilo.org

www.tuc.org.uk

Visit **www.mylawchamber.co.uk/sargeant**
to access legal updates, live weblinks and practice
exam questions to test yourself on this chapter.

unrivalled support for legal education

11 Collective bargaining and industrial action

11.1 The trade union role

Any discussion about the relevance, historical or otherwise, of trade unions will include an analysis of the inequalities of the relationship between employer and employee. Whilst the law of contract regards the parties to the contract as being equal and as having willingly entered into a contractual arrangement, the reality is somewhat different. It is only a privileged few that are able to negotiate and agree their terms and conditions of employment. For most the choice is represented by being offered a job by an employer, with associated terms and conditions of employment, and deciding whether to take it or leave it. For many, even this choice may be absent. If there is little alternative employment to be had, then the economic realities for individuals may mean that they have no choice but to accept the contract offered to them.

To some extent, the inequalities in the employment relationship are levelled out by workers joining trade unions that can negotiate with employers on equal terms:

> This system of collective bargaining rests on a balance of the collective forces of management and organised labour . . . However, the common law knows nothing of the balance of collective forces. It is (and this is its strength and its weakness) inspired by a belief in the equality (real or fictitious) of individuals; it operates between individuals and not otherwise.[1]

Perhaps because of the traditional influence of trade unions and the perceived importance of wage levels by governments in their attempts to regulate the economy, collective bargaining and the agreements that are reached are subject to statutory definition.

11.2 Collective agreements

Collective bargaining is a means of achieving a collective agreement. In statutory terms it means any agreement or arrangement made between trade unions and employers relating to a number of specific issues.[2] These issues relate to:

1. Terms and conditions of employment.

2. Engagement, non-engagement, termination or suspension of one or more workers.

---

[1] Otto Kahn-Freund, *Labour and the Law* (Stevens, 1972).
[2] Section 178(1) TULRCA 1992; the issues included are listed in s. 178(2).

3. Allocation of work or duties between workers.

4. Matters of discipline.

5. Membership or non-membership of a trade union.

6. Facilities for officials of trade unions.

7. The machinery for negotiation or consultation.

Sometimes these last two items are treated as a separate 'facilities agreement' between management and trade unions. It should be noted that a collective agreement may be as a result of negotiations in a formal setting or it might be the result of deliberations of a joint consultative committee or other committee which makes recommendations.[3]

11.2.1 Legal enforceability and incorporation

For historical reasons, trade unions have been suspicious of the intervention of the law in industrial relations and, although there is the opportunity for trade unions to enter into legally binding agreements with employers, few actually do so. Collective agreements are presumed not to be legally enforceable contracts, unless the agreement is in writing and contains a provision which states that the parties intend the agreement to be a legally enforceable contract.[4] Any agreement which does satisfy these provisions will be 'conclusively presumed to have been intended by the parties to be a legally enforceable contract'.[5] It is also possible to enter into an agreement where only part is designated as being legally enforceable. In such circumstances the part which is not legally enforceable may be used in interpreting the part that is.[6]

The intentions of the parties appear to be crucial and unless that intention to enter into a legally enforceable agreement is clear, then there is likely not to be such an agreement. The collective agreement needs to show that, at the very least, the parties have directed their minds to the issue of legal enforceability and have decided in favour of such an approach. Without this there will be an insufficient statement of intent for the purposes of the statute.[7] The court may take into account the surrounding circumstances and even the general climate of opinion about this issue when the agreement is made. In *Ford Motor Co Ltd* v *Amalgamated Union of Engineering and Foundry Workers*[8] the court found the generally unanimous climate of opinion as relevant. It cited (from Flanders and Clegg) an extract[9] which described the general view at the time:

> This appears to be the case with collective agreements. They are intended to yield 'rights' and 'duties', but not in the legal sense; they are intended, as it is sometimes put, to be 'binding in honour' only, or (which amounts to very much the same thing) to be enforceable through social sanctions but not through legal sanctions.

---

[3] See *Edinburgh Council* v *Brown* [1999] IRLR 208, which concerned a local authority joint consultative committee.

[4] Section 179(1) TULRCA 1992.

[5] Section 179(2) TULRCA 1992.

[6] Section 179(4) TULRCA 1992.

[7] See *National Coal Board* v *National Union of Mineworkers* [1986] IRLR 439, which concerned whether a 1946 agreement on consultation was legally binding; the court held that there would need to be evidence that the parties had at least directed their minds to the question and decided on legal enforceability.

[8] [1969] 2 QB 303.

[9] A. Flanders and H. Clegg, *The System of Industrial Relations in Britain* (Blackwell, 1954), p. 56.

This view that collective agreements are binding in honour and are subject to social sanctions, rather than legal sanctions, still reflects the climate of opinion.

It is possible for the terms of collective agreements to become legally binding through the route of incorporation into the individual contract of employment (see also Chapter 3). This can be achieved expressly or impliedly. Express incorporation is most effectively achieved by including a term of the contract of employment which refers to the collective agreement.[10] If a collective agreement is not expressly incorporated in this way or by some other form of agreement, then the courts may be prepared to give it legal effect via implied incorporation. It is possible that this may be done on the basis of custom and practice but the collective agreement would need to be well known and established practice and to be 'clear, certain and notorious'.[11]

Alexander v *Standard Telephones & Cables Ltd*[12] concerned a claim that a redundancy procedure had become incorporated into individuals' contracts of employment. The High Court summarised the principles to be applied in deciding whether there had been incorporation of a part of the collective agreement. These were as follows:

1. The relevant contract is that between the individual employee and the employer.

2. It is the contractual intention of these two parties that needs to be ascertained.

3. In so far as that intention is found in the written document, then the document must be construed on ordinary contractual principles.[13]

4. If there is no such document, or if it is unclear, then the contractual intention has to be inferred from other available material, including the collective agreement.

In *Kaur* v *MG Rover Ltd*[14] it was held that a provision in a collective agreement stating that there would be 'no compulsory redundancy' was not incorporated. According to the Court of Appeal, in conjunction with the words of incorporation, it is necessary to consider whether any particular part of the document is apt to be a term of a contract of employment. Looking at the words in their context, it was decided that they were expressing an aspiration rather than a right. However, the fact that a document is presented as a collection of 'policies' does not preclude their having a contractual effect if, by their nature and language, they are apt to be contractual terms. Thus a provision which is part of a remuneration package may be apt for construction as a contractual term even if couched in terms of information or explanation, or expressed in discretionary terms. Provisions for enhanced redundancy pay would seem to be particularly appropriate for incorporation.[15]

Once the collective agreement has become incorporated into the contract it is not open to the employer unilaterally to alter it.[16] It is only when terms are altered by agreement that

[10] See *Whent* v *T Cartledge* [1997] IRLR 153, in which the issue was whether the national agreement had transferred to a new employer as a result of reg. 6 Transfer of Undertakings Regulations 1981, SI 1981/1794 (see Chapter 9). This was subsequently limited to the collective agreement in force at the time of the transfer by the Court of Appeal in *Parkwood Leisure Ltd* v *Alemo-Herron* [2010] IRLR 298.

[11] *Duke* v *Reliance Systems Ltd* [1982] IRLR 347; in *Henry* v *London General Transport Services Ltd* [2002] IRLR 472 CA the court held that there is no requirement for 'strict proof' of custom and practice; the burden is on the balance of probabilities.

[12] [1991] IRLR 286.

[13] See also *Lee* v *GEC Plessey Telecommunications* [1993] IRLR 383, where the court considered whether consideration had passed from the employees for the enhanced redundancy terms contained in a collective agreement which was incorporated into the contract of employment.

[14] [2005] IRLR 40.

[15] *Keeley* v *Fosroc Ltd* [2006] IRLR 961.

[16] See *Gibbons* v *Associated British Ports* [1985] IRLR 376.

individual contracts of employment can be lawfully varied. If the collective agreement is unilaterally varied or the employer withdraws from it, the contracts of employment containing the provisions are likely to remain intact.[17] The possible exception to this is when there are provisions which allow the employer to vary the terms. If there is a collective agreement which allows an employer to vary part of the contents unilaterally, then the fact that it has become part of the contract of employment will not inhibit this option.[18] One issue here is whether the employer's authority is limited as a result of an agreement reached mutually with employee representatives. In *Cadoux* v *Central Regional Council*[19] an employer introduced rules after consultation with the relevant trade unions. This consultation was different from an agreement and the employers retained the right to alter their own rules.

Employees are assumed to know of the contents of a collective agreement negotiated with a trade union. In *Gray Dunn & Co Ltd* v *Edwards*[20] an employee was dismissed only three weeks after the signing of an agreement which included the provision that being at work whilst under the influence of alcohol was a serious misdemeanour which could result in summary dismissal. The EAT stated that there could be no stability in industrial relations if an employee could claim that an agreement did not apply to them on the basis that they had not heard of it or its contents. This suggests that the trade union is acting as the agent of the member in reaching an agreement with an employer that becomes part of the contract of employment. The problem with this approach is, of course, that non-union members would not be bound by such an agreement as the trade union could not act as their agent.[21] Such an approach has not been followed, but it does raise an interesting question in relation to employees who are not members of the trade union with whom the collective agreement is negotiated. In *Singh* v *British Steel Corporation*[22] a group of employees had not received any document which indicated that their system of working could be changed by the employer without consulting them or by consulting a trade union, whether or not they belonged to it. At the time that the employers negotiated a new shift arrangement these particular employees were not members of the trade union concerned. Neither did the employment tribunal find it possible to imply any term entitling the employer to vary the contract. Without an express or implied term binding the individuals to the collective agreement, the variation in working arrangements could not be said to apply to them. The effect is similar to an employer's unilateral variation.

In certain situations the courts are willing to be assertive in their remedies. *Anderson* v *Pringle of Scotland Ltd*[23] concerned a decision about whether an agreed 'last in, first out' redundancy procedure should be followed as a result of incorporation or whether the employer could introduce a different selection method. In order to stop the employees being made redundant under the new procedure the court was willing to grant an interdict (injunction) restraining the employers from changing the selection procedure, even though this might amount to an order for specific performance. In this case the court felt that there was still no

---

[17] See *Robertson and Jackson* v *British Gas Corporation* [1983] IRLR 302; also *Gascol Conversions Ltd* v *JW Mercer* [1974] IRLR 155 CA which concerned conflicting national and local agreements.
[18] See *Airlie* v *City of Edinburgh District Council* [1996] IRLR 516.
[19] [1986] IRLR 131.
[20] [1980] IRLR 23.
[21] See *Heatons Transport (St Helens) Ltd* v *TGWU* [1972] IRLR 25 HL.
[22] [1974] IRLR 131.
[23] [1998] IRLR 64.

lack of trust and confidence in the employee by the employer. There may also be some judicial reluctance to fill gaps in collective agreements. Thus where a collective agreement leaves a topic uncovered the inference is not that there has been an omission so obvious as to require judicial intervention. The assumption should be that it was omitted deliberately for reasons such as the item being too controversial or too complicated.[24]

11.3 **Recognition**

Recognition of a trade union or trade unions by an employer or employers is defined in s. 178(3) TULRCA 1992. It means recognition for the purposes of collective bargaining and, therefore, is likely to be recognition in respect of one or more of the items listed in s. 178(2) (see above). Recognition need not be for the purposes of all these items, but can be partial in the sense that it is only for specific purposes. It appears to require a positive agreement between the parties:

> An act of recognition is such an important matter involving such serious consequences on both sides, both for the employers and the union, that it should not be held to be established unless the evidence is clear upon it, either by agreement or actual conduct clearly showing recognition.[25]

It would be difficult for a trade union to claim implied recognition if the employer had expressly refused recognition for collective bargaining purposes. Recognition is not given because the employer responds to points raised by union representatives, neither is it to be implied from the fact that a union provides health and safety representatives or is a member of a national body, which is not the employer, that is concerned with terms and conditions of employment.[26]

Recognition implies that an employer is willing to recognise a trade union as the legitimate representative of the workforce. There are a number of benefits which accrue to the union as a result of this recognition. There are rights associated with: being given time off for trade union duties and activities;[27] consultation over a number of matters, for example transfers of undertakings, collective redundancies and health and safety matters; and the disclosure of information for collective bargaining purposes.[28]

Prior to the Employment Relations Act 1999, the decision as to whether to recognise a trade union belonged to the employer.[29] Perhaps as a result of this the majority of workplaces in the United Kingdom have no coverage by collective agreement at all.

11.3.1 **A legal framework**

There have been previous attempts at Government intervention to ensure that recognition disputes were settled without disruption. The Industrial Relations Act 1971 was a Conservative

---

[24] See *Ali v Christian Salvesen Food Services Ltd* [1997] IRLR 17 CA.

[25] *National Union of Gold, Silver & Allied Trades v Albury Brothers Ltd* [1978] IRLR 504 CA at p. 506.

[26] See *Cleveland County Council v Springett* [1985] IRLR 131.

[27] See ss. 168–170 TULRCA 1992.

[28] See ss. 181–184 TULRCA 1992.

[29] An exception to this is in the Transfer of Undertakings Regulations 2006, SI 2006/246, where reg. 6 provides for any trade union recognition by the transferor to be transferred to the transferee. This seems a rather strange requirement as it is then open to the transferee to exercise the right to derecognise the union.

Government's attempt to provide a comprehensive legal framework for industrial relations. It allowed employers, trade unions and the Government to refer recognition disputes to a Commission for Industrial Relations.[30] This body was able to make recommendations on whether a union should be recognised for a particular bargaining unit. The legislation largely failed because of the unwillingness of the trade unions to co-operate. The Employment Protection Act 1975, passed by a Labour Government, changed the approach. Section 11 allowed an independent trade union to apply to ACAS to resolve a recognition dispute. ACAS was allowed to organise a workforce ballot and then make recommendations for recognition.[31] Failure to follow an ACAS recommendation could lead to a referral to the CAC, which could then make an award on the terms and conditions that might have been agreed if those negotiations had taken place. This award would be incorporated into the contracts of employment of the employees concerned.[32] This process had only limited success. Between 1976 and 1980 there were 1,610 referrals to ACAS of which some 82 per cent were resolved voluntarily without resort to the s. 11 procedure.

A number of problems were associated with the Employment Protection Act 1975 and inhibited its success. First, some employers refused to co-operate. In one dispute, concerning Grunwick Processing Laboratories Ltd, the employers refused to supply ACAS with the names and addresses of their employees, which resulted in ACAS being unable to carry out its statutory duty under s. 14(1) Employment Protection Act 1975 to ascertain the views of the employees. The result was that the recognition process was thwarted.[33] Secondly, there were difficulties in dealing with inter-union disputes, where more than one trade union claimed recognition on behalf of a group of workers. In *Engineers' and Managers' Association* v *ACAS*[34] there was just such a dispute between two unions. ACAS had deferred its decision on recognition and the House of Lords upheld its right to do so if the deferral would help promote good industrial relations. Thirdly, there were problems associated with defining acceptable bargaining units which would also help foster good industrial relations. ACAS had to deal with situations where there was a demand for representation within a particular unit, but fragmentation of larger units into smaller ones might not be conducive to better industrial relations.[35] Finally, there were problems associated with the length of time the process took[36] and with employers attempting to influence the outcome of the recognition ballots.

All these problems have been addressed in the statutory recognition procedures contained in Sch. A1 TULRCA 1992. An awareness of these potential problems is important in understanding the reasons for some of the procedures contained in the Schedule.

11.3.2 **Statutory recognition**

Section 70A TULRCA 1992 gives effect to Sch. A1 which is concerned with the recognition of trade unions for collective bargaining purposes. Collective bargaining here has a more limited meaning than that contained in s. 178 TULRCA 1992 (see above). For the purpose of

---

[30] See *Ideal Casements Ltd* v *Shamsi* [1972] ICR 408 on the effect of the legislation in a dispute over recognition.
[31] Sections 14 and 15 Employment Protection Act 1975.
[32] Section 16 Employment Protection Act 1975.
[33] See *Grunwick Processing Laboratories Ltd* v *ACAS* [1978] 1 All ER 338 HL.
[34] [1980] ICR 215 HL.
[35] See *ACAS* v *United Kingdom Association of Professional Engineers* [1980] IRLR 124 HL.
[36] *Ibid.*

statutory recognition, collective bargaining means, unless otherwise agreed by the parties, negotiations concerned with pay, hours and holidays only.[37] However, 'pay' does not include terms relating to a person's membership of or rights under, or the employer's contributions to, either an occupational or personal pension scheme.[38]

The schedule was brought into effect on 6 June 2000.[39] The procedures contained in it for claiming recognition are long and complex. Below is a summary of the essentials of part of the recognition process, which shows the underlying principles. The principles underlying the procedures are that:

1. The measures apply to independent trade unions only (see Chapter 10).[40]

2. Trade unions will need to demonstrate 'baseline support'.[41]

3. The subsequent vote must demonstrate widespread support.[42]

4. The bargaining unit needs to be clearly defined.[43]

5. There are exceptions for small businesses.[44]

6. There is a right to derecognition.[45]

7. The time that the process will take should be clear.[46]

11.3.2.1 The request for recognition[47]

The process must begin with the trade union or unions seeking recognition making a request for recognition to the employer.[48] This request must be in writing, it must identify the union or unions concerned and the bargaining unit. It must also state that the request is made under Sch. A1.[49] However, an application is inadmissible if there is already in force a collective agreement under which the employer recognises another union as entitled to conduct collective bargaining on behalf of the workers concerned.[50] If more than one union is applying for recognition the applications will not be admissible unless the unions show that they will co-operate with each other and that, if the employer so wishes, they will enter into collective bargaining arrangements which ensure that they will act together.[51]

Schedule A1 para. 7 provides the exception for small businesses. The employer, together with any associated employers, needs to employ at least 21 workers on the day the request for recognition is received, or an average of 21 workers over the 13 weeks ending with this day.

---

[37] Schedule A1 para. 3 TULRCA 1992.

[38] Schedule A1 para. 171A TULRCA 1992.

[39] Employment Relations Act 1999 (Commencement No 6 and Transitional Provisions) Order 2000, SI 2000/1338.

[40] Schedule A1 para. 6 TULRCA 1992.

[41] Schedule A1 para. 13(5) TULRCA 1992 for a description of 'the 10% test'.

[42] Schedule A1 para. 29 TULRCA 1992.

[43] Schedule A1 paras. 18–19F TULRCA 1992.

[44] Schedule A1 para. 7 TULRCA 1992.

[45] See Sch. A1 Part IV TULRCA 1992.

[46] See, e.g., Sch. A1 para. 10(6) and (7) TULRCA 1992.

[47] Derecognition is covered by similar provisions contained in Sch. A1 Parts IV–VI TULRCA 1992.

[48] Schedule A1 para. 4 TULRCA 1992.

[49] Schedule A1 para. 8 TULRCA 1992.

[50] See Sch. A1 para. 35 TULRCA 1992 and *R v Central Arbitration Committee* [2006] IRLR 54.

[51] Schedule A1 para. 37 TULRCA 1992.

11.3.2.2 **Parties agree**

There are clearly defined periods of time in which events should take place, which are contained in Sch. A1 para. 10(6) and (7). The first period is one of ten working days commencing on the day after the employer received the request for recognition. The second period commences on the day after the first period ends and lasts for 20 working days or such longer time as the parties agree.

Thus, if before the end of the first period the parties agree on the bargaining unit and that the trade union is to be recognised, then there are no further steps to be taken under this schedule. If the employer informs the union, before the end of the first period, that they do not accept the request, but are willing to negotiate, then they may do so. Provided that they reach agreement before the end of the second period, no further steps will need to be taken under this Schedule.

11.3.2.3 **Employer rejects request or negotiations fail**

If, by the end of the first period, the employer has either failed to respond to the request or has rejected the request and refused to negotiate, then the union may apply to the CAC[52] for the determination of two questions. These are:

1. Whether the proposed bargaining unit is appropriate.
2. Whether the union or unions has or have the support of the majority of workers in the proposed bargaining unit.[53]

If the negotiations have not succeeded by the end of the second period, then the union or unions may apply to the CAC for the determination of the same two questions. Additionally, if the parties agree on the bargaining unit, but fail to agree on whether the union or unions should be recognised to represent it, then the union may only apply to the CAC for an answer to the second question on whether it has the majority support of the workers in that bargaining unit.[54]

There is some pressure on the trade union to negotiate as well as the employer. If, within the first period of ten days, the employer requests the help of ACAS during the negotiations and the unions reject that help or fail to accept the employer's proposal for the help of ACAS, then the union will lose its right to put the questions to the CAC.[55]

11.3.2.4 **Acceptance of application**[56]

The CAC must give notice of receipt of an application. The CAC must decide, within the 'acceptance period', whether any of the applications received fulfil the ten per cent test, contained in Sch. A1 para. 14(5) TULRCA 1992. This test is satisfied if at least ten per cent of the workers constituting a relevant bargaining unit are members of the trade union applying for recognition. The acceptance period is ten working days from the receipt of the last application or such longer period as the CAC specifies, giving reasons. If the ten per cent test is

---

[52] In the year 2006/7 the CAC received 64 applications concerning trade union recognition under Sch. A1 Part I. See CAC Annual Report 2006/7.
[53] Schedule A1 para. 11(1) and (2) TULRCA 1992.
[54] Schedule A1 para. 12(1)–(4) TULRCA 1992.
[55] Schedule A1 para. 12(5) TULRCA 1992.
[56] Schedule A1 paras. 13–15 TULRCA 1992.

satisfied by more than one applicant union or none of them, the CAC will not proceed. There is a clear message that there needs to be baseline support for one trade union and that the CAC is not the body to decide which union is to be given recognition where more than one meet this basic test. If the CAC decides that one union meets the test, then it will proceed with that union.

11.3.2.5 **Appropriate bargaining unit**[57]

Once the CAC has decided to accept an application it has an obligation to try to help the parties to reach agreement as to what the appropriate bargaining unit is, if they have not already agreed. This must be done within 20 working days, starting with the day after that on which the CAC has given notice of acceptance, or a longer period specified by the CAC by notice and with reasons.[58] After the end of this period the CAC has ten days in which it must decide on the appropriate bargaining unit, or a longer specified period by notice and with reasons.[59]

There is a set of criteria contained in Sch. A1 para. 19B(2)–(3), which the CAC must use in arriving at its decision. These are the need for the bargaining unit to be compatible with effective management and, so far as they do not conflict with that need:

1. The views of the employer and the trade union or unions.
2. Existing national and local bargaining arrangements.
3. The desirability of avoiding small or fragmented bargaining units within an undertaking.
4. The characteristics of the workers falling within the proposed bargaining unit and any other workers the CAC considers relevant.
5. The location of the workers.

It is expressly provided that the CAC must take into account the employer's view about any other bargaining unit it considers would be appropriate.[60]

In *Graphical, Paper and Media Union* v *Derry Print Ltd*[61] an application was made to the CAC seeking recognition for all production workers employed by the two different companies. Both companies had the same majority shareholder, operated in the same premises and interchanged employees. In considering the most appropriate bargaining unit, the CAC was faced with the choice of deciding whether there should be separate units or whether one should cover all the production workers of both companies. Despite 'employer' being referred to in the singular throughout the Schedule, the CAC held that a bargaining unit that covered both employers would be appropriate. It concluded that the two companies had a long history of separate incorporation, but:

> We consider, however, that the power to lift the veil [of incorporation] in respect of a sham is not intended as a form of punishment but relies on the conclusion that the reality of unity is concealed by the technical appearance of separation . . . This is an exceptional situation, in which the two companies are managed in the interests of asset utilisation and are inextricably intertwined.

---

[57] Schedule A1 paras. 18–19F TULRCA 1992.
[58] Schedule A1 para. 18(2) but note also para. 18(3)–(7) TULRCA 1992. Paragraph 18A introduced a duty on employers to supply information to the union.
[59] Schedule A1 paras. 19(2) and (4) and 19A(2) and (4) TULRCA 1992.
[60] Schedule A1 para. 19(4) TULRCA 1992. See *R* v *CAC, ex parte Kwik-Fit Ltd* [2002] IRLR 395.
[61] [2002] IRLR 380 CAC.

11.3.2.6 **Union recognition**[62]

Once the issue of the bargaining unit is resolved, the CAC may then move on to the question of recognition. If it is satisfied that the majority of the workforce in the bargaining unit are members of the union or unions, the CAC will issue a declaration that the union or unions are recognised for collective bargaining purposes.[63] However, this will not be done if any one of three qualifying conditions are met. These are that:

1. A ballot will be in the interests of good industrial relations.
2. The CAC has credible evidence from a significant number of union members within the bargaining unit that they do not want the union or unions to conduct collective bargaining on their behalf.
3. Evidence is produced that leads the CAC to conclude that a significant number of union members within the bargaining unit do not wish to be represented by the union or unions.[64]

If any of these qualifying conditions are met the CAC will give notice to the parties that it intends to organise a ballot to discover whether the workers in the bargaining unit wish the union or unions to conduct collective bargaining on their behalf. The cost of the ballot is to be borne half by the employer and half by the union or unions.

The ballot must be conducted by a qualified and independent person appointed by the CAC.[65] It will take place within 20 working days starting with the day after the independent person is appointed or longer if the CAC so decides. The CAC may decide whether to organise a workplace ballot or a postal ballot, or a combination of the two. It will determine the method by taking into account the likelihood of a workplace ballot being affected by unfairness or malpractice and the costs and practicality of the alternatives, as well as any other factors it considers appropriate.[66]

There are five duties placed upon an employer who has been informed that a ballot is to take place. These are:

1. To co-operate generally in connection with the ballot, with the union or unions and with the person appointed to conduct the ballot.
2. To give the union or unions access to the workforce constituting the bargaining unit for the purposes of informing them about the ballot and seeking their support. The Government Code of Practice recommends that the parties reach an access agreement which will include the union's programme for when, where and how it will access the workers and will also provide a mechanism for resolving disagreements.[67]
3. To provide the CAC, within ten working days, with the names and home addresses of the workers concerned and to inform the CAC subsequently of the names and addresses of any new workers or those who cease to be employed.

---

[62] Schedule A1 paras. 20–29 TULRCA 1992.
[63] See *Fullarton Computer Industries Ltd* v *Central Arbitration Committee* [2001] IRLR 752.
[64] Schedule A1 para. 22(4) TULRCA 1992.
[65] See the Recognition and Derecognition Ballots (Qualified Persons) Order 2000, SI 2000/1306 which names a number of suitable persons, such as the Association of Electoral Administrators.
[66] Schedule A1 para. 25 TULRCA 1992.
[67] Code of Practice on Access to Workers during Recognition and Derecognition Ballots, issued under s. 203 TULRCA 1992; the Code imposes in itself no legal obligations, but any of its provisions may be taken into account in any proceedings before the CAC or any court or tribunal: s. 207 TULRCA 1992.

4. To refrain from making workers an unreasonable offer which has or is likely to have the effect of inducing them not to attend a meeting between the union and the workers in the bargaining unit.

5. To refrain from taking any action solely or mainly on the grounds that a worker attended or took part in a meeting between the union and workers in the bargaining unit or indicated an intention to attend or take part in such a meeting.[68]

If the employer fails in any of these duties the CAC may order the employer to take steps to remedy the situation within a certain time. If the employer fails to comply with this order, then the CAC may cancel the ballot and declare the union or unions recognised for the purposes of collective bargaining in respect of the bargaining unit.[69]

Once the result of the ballot is known the CAC must inform the parties of the result. If the ballot result is that the union is supported by a majority of the workers voting and at least 40 per cent of the workers constituting the bargaining unit, then the CAC will declare the union recognised. If the result is otherwise, the CAC will issue a declaration stating that the union is not recognised.

11.3.2.7 Consequences of recognition[70]

If the CAC has made a declaration for recognition, the parties have a 'negotiation period' to agree a method by which they will conduct collective bargaining. This negotiation period is 30 working days starting with the day after they have been informed of the declaration, or a longer period if the parties agree. If the parties do not agree in the period then they can ask the CAC for assistance. The CAC will assist for a period of 20 working days or longer, with the agreement of the parties, if the CAC so decides. After this period, if the parties still fail to agree, the CAC will specify the method.[71] Unless the parties agree otherwise, this specified method will have the effect of being a legally binding contract, which can be enforced through an order for specific performance. If, however, the parties negotiate and agree a method of collective bargaining between themselves and one party fails to keep to the agreement, then they may apply to the CAC for assistance. The CAC will then treat the parties in the same way as if they had failed to reach agreement in the first place.[72]

If the CAC has declared that the unions should not be recognised, then those same unions cannot apply again within a period of three years if the bargaining unit remains substantially the same.[73]

11.3.2.8 Changes affecting the bargaining unit

Schedule A1 Part II TULRCA 1992 is concerned with providing the CAC with similar powers for situations where the parties have entered into voluntary arrangements and agreed on recognition and the bargaining unit. Part III is concerned with the issue of a changing

---

[68] Schedule A1 para. 26 TULRCA 1992. See Sch. A1 para. 27A TULRCA 1992 on unfair practices in relation to recognition ballots.

[69] Schedule A1 para. 27 TULRCA 1992.

[70] Schedule A1 paras. 30–32 TULRCA 1992.

[71] In specifying the method the CAC will take into account in exercising its powers the method specified in the Trade Union Recognition (Method of Collective Bargaining) Order 2000, SI 2000/1300.

[72] See UNIFI v Union Bank of Nigeria plc [2001] IRLR 712.

[73] Schedule A1 para. 40 TULRCA 1992; the same rule applies to derecognition claims by employers: see Sch. A1 para. 121 TULRCA 1992.

bargaining unit which can have important consequences for the recognition process. If the employer or the union or unions believe that the original bargaining unit is no longer appropriate they may apply to the CAC to make a decision as to what is an appropriate unit. The CAC will consider such an application only if it decides that the original unit is no longer appropriate because there has been: a change in the organisation or structure of the business; a change in the activities pursued by the employer; or a substantial change in the number of workers employed in the original unit. The CAC will then decide on whether the original unit is still appropriate. If it decides that it is not, then it will decide which new unit is appropriate. If necessary it will then repeat the process of assessing whether a union or unions passes or pass the membership test and proceeding to a new ballot.

11.3.2.9 Detriment and dismissal

Schedule A1 Part VIII TULRCA 1992 provides protection from detriment by any act, or failure to act, of the employer if it takes place, or fails to take place, on the grounds that the worker:

1. Acted with a view to obtaining or preventing recognition of a union.
2. Indicated support or lack of support for recognition.
3. Acted with a view to securing or preventing the ending of bargaining arrangements.
4. Indicated support or lack of support for the ending of bargaining arrangements.
5. Influenced, or sought to influence, the way votes were cast.
6. Influenced, or sought to influence, other workers to vote or abstain.
7. Voted in such a ballot.
8. Proposed to do, failed to do, or proposed to decline to do any of the above.[74]

A ground does not fall within these categories if it constitutes an unreasonable act or omission by the worker.[75] The only remedy is a complaint to an employment tribunal[76] within three months of the act or failure to act to which the complaint relates, or such further period as the tribunal considers reasonable.[77] If the tribunal finds the complaint well founded it may make a declaration and award compensation, which may be reduced if the employee contributed in any way to the action complained of.[78]

The same grounds are contained in Sch. A1 para. 161 in relation to dismissal, with the same proviso that a reason does not fall within these grounds if it constitutes an unreasonable act or omission by the employee. Thus a dismissal for any of these reasons will be automatically unfair for the purposes of Part X ERA 1996. If a worker who is not an employee is dismissed, compensation would be subject to the same rules as those for employees who are unfairly dismissed.[79] Similarly, dismissal for reasons of redundancy will be an unfair dismissal if the grounds are any of those listed above.[80]

---

[74] Schedule A1 para. 156(2) TULRCA 1992.
[75] Schedule A1 para. 156(3) TULRCA 1992.
[76] Schedule A1 para. 156(5) and (6) TULRCA 1992.
[77] Schedule A1 para. 157 TULRCA 1992.
[78] Schedule A1 para. 159 TULRCA 1992.
[79] Schedule A1 para. 160 TULRCA 1992.
[80] Schedule A1 para. 162 TULRCA 1992.

11.3.2.10 **Training**

If a trade union has become recognised as a result of the process in Sch. A1 and the method of collective bargaining has been specified by the CAC, then the employer is under an obligation to invite the trade union to send representatives to a meeting to discuss the employer's policy on the training of workers, together with training plans over the next six months, as well as reporting to them on training since the previous meeting.[81] These meetings are to take place at least every six months and there is an obligation to disclose information in advance[82] (see below on disclosure of information generally). The employer is also obliged to take into account any written representations about matters raised at a meeting, which are received by the employer within four weeks of the meeting.[83] Failure to fulfil these obligations in relation to a bargaining unit will enable the trade union to make a complaint to an employment tribunal. If it finds the complaint well founded, the tribunal may make a declaration and award compensation up to a maximum of two weeks' pay per individual.[84]

11.4 **Prohibition of union recognition requirements**

Despite these new rules enabling a trade union to obtain recognition against an employer's wishes, the provisions stopping recognition being a condition of a contract with a third party remain. Section 186 TULRCA 1992 provides that a term or condition of a contract for the supply of goods and services is void in so far as it requires recognition of a trade union or unions for collective bargaining purposes or to the extent that it requires the other party to negotiate with or consult an official of a trade union or unions. Neither is it permissible to refuse to deal with a supplier or prospective supplier on the grounds that the supplier will not recognise a trade union or negotiate or consult with one.[85] A person refuses to deal with a supplier by failing to include them on a list of approved tenderers, or by excluding them from tendering, or by stopping them from tendering or by terminating a contract for the supply of goods or services.[86] The obligation to comply with this section is to be interpreted as owing a duty to the adversely affected party.[87]

11.5 **Disclosure of information**

A natural consequence of the recognition of a trade union by an employer is the need for both parties to have sufficient information about the undertaking for them to be able to bargain effectively. That there needs to be a statutory requirement, albeit a weak one, to ensure that information is disclosed to the trade union by the employer is an indication that not all employers have regarded it as important that the trade unions with whom they negotiate should be kept informed. One may equally surmise that there have been trade union

---

[81] Section 70B(1) and (2) TULRCA 1992.
[82] Section 70B(3) and (4) TULRCA 1992.
[83] Section 70B(6) TULRCA 1992.
[84] Section 70C(4) TULRCA 1992; a week's pay is subject to the limit in s. 227(1) ERA 1996.
[85] Section 187(1) TULRCA 1992.
[86] Section 187(2) TULRCA 1992.
[87] Section 187(3) TULRCA 1992.

negotiators who, at times, have not wished to know about the employer's financial position, in order to press their claims for a pay rise, regardless of the consequences for the employer.

Section 181(1) TULRCA 1992 provides a general duty for an employer, who recognises an independent trade union, to disclose certain information for the purposes of all stages of collective bargaining. The duty relates to the categories of workers for whom the trade union is recognised as representing for collective bargaining purposes. The information must be disclosed to representatives of the union, who are defined as officials or other persons authorised by the union to carry on such bargaining. According to *R v Central Arbitration Committee, ex parte BTP Oxide Ltd*[88] these provisions contemplate that there may be alternative types of relationship between employers and unions, rather than just collective bargaining that entitled a union to information. These alternatives might be:

- Bargaining between employers and unions which does not amount to collective bargaining because it does not deal with matters referred to in s. 181(2) TULRCA 1992.
- Dealings between employers or unions which do not amount to collective bargaining because they cannot properly be called negotiations.
- Collective bargaining which does not attract the right to information because it is not about matters in respect of which the union is recognised for collective bargaining. In this case the union concerned unsuccessfully asked for information about a job grading structure for which it had representational rights, rather than negotiating rights.

The information to be disclosed is that which relates to the employer's undertaking and is in its possession.[89] There is a twofold test to decide the relevance of the information. It must be:

1. Information without which the trade unions would be 'to a material extent impeded in carrying out collective bargaining'.
2. Information the disclosure of which 'would be in accordance with good industrial relations practice'.

There is an ACAS Code of Practice on the disclosure of information to trade unions for collective bargaining purposes.[90] Paragraph 11 of this Code provides examples of information which might be relevant in certain collective bargaining situations. These examples are information relating to the undertaking about pay and benefits, conditions of service, manpower, performance and finances. Although the ACAS Code is an important guide, it does not exclude other evidence that might be in accord with good industrial relations practice.[91] The request for information by the trade union must be in writing, if the employer so requests, as must the employer's reply, if requested by the trade union.[92]

An employer is not required to disclose information if the disclosure:[93]

1. Would be against the interests of national security.
2. Could not be disclosed without contravening a statutory prohibition.

[88] [1992] IRLR 60.
[89] Section 181(2) TULRCA 1992; employer also includes associated employers.
[90] Originally introduced in 1977; it was last updated in 1997 and was brought into effect by the Employment Protection Code of Practice (Disclosure of Information) Order 1998, SI 1998/45; for the effect of failing to comply with the Code, see s. 207 TULRCA 1992.
[91] Section 181(4) TULRCA 1992.
[92] Section 181(3) and (5) TULRCA 1992.
[93] Section 182(1) TULRCA 1992.

3. Has been communicated to the employer in confidence.

4. Relates specifically to an individual, unless the individual has consented.

5. Could cause substantial injury to the undertaking, other than its effect on collective bargaining.

6. Is information obtained for the purpose of bringing, prosecuting or defending any legal proceedings.

This list of exceptions clearly undermines the effectiveness of the legislation. The confidentiality clause, for example, could result in important and relevant information not being disclosed to a trade union. In *Sun Printers Ltd* v *Westminster Press Ltd*[94] a widely circulated document about the future of a company was held not to be confidential, but it was suggested by Donaldson LJ, *obiter*, that the stamping of the word 'confidential' on the document would have been enough to allow wide circulation, whilst retaining confidentiality. Perhaps of more concern to trade unions is the difficulty in obtaining pay information concerning parts of a business that are put out to competitive tender. In *Civil Service Union* v *CAC*[95] a trade union was stopped from obtaining information about a tenderer's proposed wage rates on the basis that they were given in confidence and that it was information the lack of which could not be held to impede, to a material extent, the union's ability to carry out collective bargaining.

There are further limitations, on the obligations of employers to disclose information, contained in s. 182(2) TULRCA 1992:

1. An employer is not required to produce any documents or extracts from documents unless the document has been prepared for the purposes of conveying or confirming the information.

2. The employer is not required to compile or assemble any information which would involve an amount of work or expenditure out of proportion to the value of the information in the conduct of collective bargaining.

All these exceptions place important limitations on the right of trade unions to make employers disclose information. Indeed, it is significant that during the period of the 1980s and early 1990s, when Conservative Governments were introducing legislation to limit the power of trade unions, this particular piece of legislation remained untouched.

The remedy for failure to disclose information to trade unions is to make a complaint to the CAC. The CAC will refer the matter to ACAS if it thinks that there is a reasonable chance of a conciliated settlement. If this fails, the CAC will decide whether the complaint is well founded. Where it does so, then the employer is given a period of not less than a week to disclose the information. If the employer still fails to disclose, then the trade union may present a further complaint to the CAC, who will decide if the complaint is well founded and specify the information in respect of which it made that decision.[96] The CAC may then make an award in respect of the employees specified in the claim. This award will consist of the terms and conditions being negotiated and specified in the claim, or any other terms and conditions which the CAC considers appropriate. These terms and conditions can only be for matters in which the trade union is recognised for collective bargaining purposes.[97]

---

[94] [1982] IRLR 292 CA.
[95] [1980] IRLR 253.
[96] Section 184 TULRCA 1992.
[97] Section 185 TULRCA 1992.

The ineffectiveness of this legislation is illustrated by the fact that between 1976 and 1997 the CAC received 463 disclosure of information complaints, which was an average of 22 per annum. In the year to 31 March 2007 only 11 complaints were received.[98]

11.6 Industrial action – trade union immunities

It is not appropriate in this book to provide a history of the struggles of individuals and groups to be allowed to join trade unions. Nevertheless, it is worth remembering that, until the latter part of the nineteenth century, it was the criminal law that was used against employees who combined and/or took industrial action in defence of their collective rights. Employees were prosecuted for such offences as obstruction, intimidation and conspiracy. The turning point came in the 1870s with the passing of a number of statutes, notably the Trade Union Act 1871 and the Conspiracy and Protection of Property Act 1875, which protected members of trade unions from the common law doctrine of 'restraint of trade'.

The 1875 Act was a landmark in that it provided immunities from prosecution for those involved in trade disputes. Like subsequent legislation, it did not abolish the offences for which one could be prosecuted. Rather it provided immunity from prosecution if the 'offence' was committed 'in contemplation or furtherance of a trade dispute'. Subsequent protection has followed the pattern of providing immunities, rather than offering positive rights to individuals. In some other Member States of the EU, such as France and Germany, there are constitutions which provide a right for individuals to join trade unions and take part in industrial action. These 'positive rights' are to be contrasted with the 'negative rights' approach in the United Kingdom. Workers do not have positive rights to take part in industrial action; rather they have protection if they do so. The distinction is important because it has allowed the courts and various governments to remove or change the degree of protection provided.

A classic example of this was in *Taff Vale Railway Co v Amalgamated Society of Railway Servants.*[99] This case arose out of a strike in support of an individual alleged to have been victimised by the employer. The trade union organised pickets to stop the employer bringing in non-union labour. The employers applied to the court for an injunction against the union leaders and the union itself. This latter move was a novel one in that it had been assumed that the unions themselves could not be sued in this way for the actions of their officials. Lord Macnaughton stated:

> Has the legislature authorised the creation of numerous bodies of men capable of owning great wealth and acting by agents with absolutely no responsibility for the wrongs they may do to other persons by the use of that wealth and the employment of those agents? In my opinion, Parliament has done nothing of the kind.

Thus trade unions were immediately put at risk if they took industrial action. In this case, damages and fines on the union amounted to £42,000 which, in 1902, amounted to two-thirds of its annual income.

A Royal Commission in 1903 led to the Trade Disputes Act 1906, which provided protection for acts done in 'contemplation or furtherance of a trade dispute'. It provided, in s. 4,

---

[98] See CAC Annual Report 2006/7.
[99] [1901] AC 426.

that an action in tort could not be brought against a trade union for acts of its members or officials, even though carried out on its behalf. It also provided immunity for a person who induced another to break a contract of employment and immunity against a possible tort of interference with trade, business or employment of another person. This Act was to be the foundation of future legislation on industrial action.

11.7 Common law torts

The common law has traditionally regarded a strike as a breach of the contract of employment and the calling or organising of a strike as an inducement to another to breach the contract of employment. The courts have developed a number of torts to limit the actions of workers, both individually and collectively. One perspective is to regard the history of the law regarding industrial action as a series of steps by the courts to introduce new torts to make individuals and unions liable, with the State stepping in from time to time to limit the worst excesses of the judiciary by providing some statutory immunity to individuals and unions for actions in contemplation or furtherance of a trade dispute. These liabilities in tort include the following.

11.7.1 Inducing a breach of contract

This tort derives from the case of *Lumley* v *Gye*.[100] It involved an opera singer, Miss Johanna Wagner, who was induced by a theatre manager to breach her contract with one theatre in order to appear at the defendant's own theatre. The court held that each party has a right to the performance of the contract and that it was wrong for another to procure one of the parties to break it or not perform it.

An inducement to breach an employment contract is when a trade union, for example, instructs its members to take strike action against their employer. Without further intervention the employer may have a case against the trade union for inducing its employees to breach their contracts of employment. A direct inducement to breach of a commercial contract is when A puts pressure on B not to fulfil a contract with C. Thus if trade union A were, for example, to apply pressure on employer B, in order to stop employer B making a delivery to employer C, then C, without further intervention, may be able to take action against B for breach of the supply contract. It is also possible for A indirectly to induce B to break its contract with C. If the trade union instructed its members to take strike action against employer B in order to stop them supplying employer C, then they might be liable for indirectly inducing that breach.

DC Thomson & Co v *Deakin*[101] concerned the delivery of bulk paper from a supplier to a printing firm. The employees of the supplier refused to deliver paper to the printer and an injunction was sought to stop the trade unions concerned from inducing the supplier to breach its contract with the printer. Jenkins LJ listed four categories where there was a direct interference by a third party with the rights of one of the parties to a contract.[102] The four categories were:

---

[100] (1853) 2 E & B 216.
[101] [1952] 2 All ER 361 CA; see also *Merkur Island Shipping Corporation* v *Laughton* [1983] IRLR 218 HL which approved this approach.
[102] The summing up of these categories by Neill LJ in *Middlebrook Mushrooms Ltd* v *TGWU* [1993] IRLR 232 CA is relied upon here.

1. A 'direct persuasion or procurement or inducement by the third party to the contract-breaker, with knowledge of the contract and the intention of bringing about its breach'.[103]

2. Dealings by the third party with the contract-breaker which, to the knowledge of the third party, are inconsistent with the contract between the contract-breaker and the person wronged.[104]

3. An act done by a third party with knowledge of the contract, which, if done by one of the parties to it, would have been a breach of that contract.[105]

4. The imposition by the third party, who has knowledge of the contract, of some physical restraint upon one of the parties to the contract so as to make it impossible for the contract to be performed.

According to Jenkins LJ, the conditions necessary to show that there had been an actionable interference with one of the parties to the contract were:

1. The person charged with the actionable interference knew of the existence of the contract and intended to procure its breach.

2. The person so charged did persuade or induce the employees to break their contracts of employment.

3. The persuaded or induced employees did break their contract of employment.

4. The breach of contract was a natural consequence of the employees' breaches of their contracts of employment.

In relation to this last point, it needs to be shown that, because of the employees' actions, their employer was unable to fulfil the contract.[106]

The difference between direct and indirect inducement to breach a contract is, according to Neill LJ,[107] one of causation. For direct inducement to take place, as in *Lumley v Gye*, the persuasion had to be directed at the parties to the contract. In *Middlebrook Mushrooms Ltd* v *TGWU*[108] the distribution of leaflets by dismissed employees outside a supermarket was aimed at persuading customers not to buy their ex-employer's produce. This amounted to indirect inducement on the parties to the contract, namely the supplier and the shop. There was also the question of knowledge of the contracts. Jenkins LJ concluded that there needed to be knowledge of the contract(s) and an intent to procure its breach.[109] In this case the court held that there was no evidence that contracts existed between the shop and the supplier. It may be possible to infer knowledge, but not in this case.

The knowledge needed, however, may be minimal.[110] In a rather bizarre case in the county court,[111] a railway passenger claimed damages from two rail unions for costs incurred as a result of industrial action. The action had been called without a ballot, resulting in the union

---

[103] *Lumley* v *Gye* (1853) 2 E & B 216 is an example of this.
[104] Jenkins LJ gave *British Motor Trade Association* v *Salvadori* [1949] Ch 556 as an example of this.
[105] Jenkins LJ gave *GWK Ltd* v *Dunlop Rubber Co Ltd* (1926) 42 TLR 376 as an example, where the defendant's employees had removed the tyres from a car, which belonged to a rival, at a motor show.
[106] See *Falconer* v *ASLEF and NUR* [1986] IRLR 331 as an example of a court applying these four steps.
[107] Note 102 above.
[108] [1993] IRLR 232 CA.
[109] *DC Thomson & Co* v *Deakin* [1952] 2 All ER 361 CA.
[110] See *JT Stratford & Sons Ltd* v *Lindley* [1965] AC 269 HL.
[111] *Falconer* v *ASLEF and NUR* [1986] IRLR 331.

being unable to rely on any statutory immunities (see below). The claim was successful because, not only did the union know of the existence of contracts between the railway company and passengers, their intention was to affect the plaintiff and other passengers in order to put pressure on the employer. The county court judge decided that the unions were reckless in their intent, as they knew the effect of the action on the plaintiff, but nevertheless pursued it. More recently, the House of Lords has ruled that for a person to be liable they must know that they are inducing a breach of contract.[112]

There is the possibility of a defence against this tort if the defendant can show that they have an equal or superior right to that of the injured party: for example, where the contract interfered with is inconsistent with a previous contract with the person intervening.[113]

11.7.2 Interference with a contract or with business

This tort is closely connected with the tort of inducing a breach of contract. *Torquay Hotel Co Ltd* v *Cousins*[114] involved an attempt by a trade union to stop the supply of heating oil to a hotel with whom there was a trade dispute. Lord Denning MR extended the principle expounded in *Quinn* v *Leathem*[115] that 'it is a violation of legal right to interfere with contractual relations recognised by law if there be no sufficient justification for the interference'. Lord Denning stated that there were three aspects to the principle:

1. There needed to be interference in the execution of a contract.

2. Interference must be deliberate, meaning that the person interfering must know of the contract.

3. The interference must be direct.

Indirect interference would not be enough and might, according to Lord Denning, take away the right to strike. The conditions were satisfied in this case, where there was direct and deliberate interference in the contractual relations between the hotel and oil supplier.[116]

A further example can be found in *Timeplan Education Group Ltd* v *National Union of Teachers*.[117] This concerned a teachers' union attempting to interfere with the advertising for recruits by a teachers' supply agency. The Court of Appeal held that, in order to establish the tort of wrongful interference with contractual rights, five conditions need to be fulfilled:

1. The defendant persuaded or procured or induced a third party to break a contract.

2. Knowledge of the contract.

3. Intention to procure a breach.

4. The plaintiff suffered more than nominal damages.

5. The plaintiff can rebut a defence of justification.

---

[112] See *Mainstream Properties Ltd* v *Young* [2007] IRLR 608.

[113] See *Smithie's case* [1909] 1 KB 310 HL.

[114] [1969] 2 Ch 106 CA at p. 510.

[115] [1901] AC 495.

[116] See also *Merkur Island Shipping Corporation* v *Laughton* [1983] IRLR 218 HL, where a ship was boycotted. Lord Diplock approved the principle laid down by Denning LJ that interference is not confined to a breach of contract, but includes the prevention or hindering from performing their contract, even though it is not a breach.

[117] [1997] IRLR 457 CA.

In this case no tort was committed because there was a failure to show knowledge of contracts or intention to procure a breach of them.[118]

11.7.3 Intimidation

In its direct form[119] this is committed where an unlawful threat is made directly to the plaintiff with the intention of causing loss to the plaintiff. In its indirect form it is where C suffers as a result of action taken by B following an unlawful threat by A to B. An example of this can be seen in *News Group Newspapers Ltd v SOGAT '82*[120] concerning the breakdown of negotiations between the plaintiff and the union over the employment of union members at its new plant in Wapping – the unions called their members out on strike but they were then dismissed. This was followed by picketing, large-scale rallies and demonstrations outside the Wapping plant. According to the High Court, although the tort of intimidation is not complete unless the person threatened succumbs to the threat and damage results, in this case there were sufficient threats of violence and molestation to justify the granting of injunctive relief.[121]

Rookes v Barnard[122] was a landmark case which caused great alarm to trade unionists by deciding that a threat to breach a contract of employment, by threatening to go on strike, was unlawful for the purposes of a tort of intimidation. In this case an airline company had a closed shop agreement for a part of its operation. The union threatened the airline that it would call its members out on strike if they did not remove an individual employee who had resigned from the union. The House of Lords reacted by making it almost impossible to threaten a strike without being subject to the tort of intimidation. Lord Devlin stated that there was nothing to differentiate a threat of a breach of contract from a threat of physical violence or any other illegal threat. This decision undermined the immunities enjoyed by trade unions in certain circumstances since the 1906 Act. Strikes are often preceded by threats of industrial action which would have fallen foul of the *Rookes v Barnard* decision if immunity had not been restored by the Trade Disputes Act 1965 (see 11.8 below).

11.7.4 Conspiracy

There are two types of conspiracy. One is the conspiracy to injure and the other is the conspiracy to commit an unlawful act.

A conspiracy to injure occurs when two or more people combine to injure a person in their trade by inducing customers or employees to break their contracts or not to deal with that person, which results in damage to that person.[123] *Huntley v Thornton*[124] was about an individual member of a trade union who failed to support a strike. Thereafter there were various

---

[118] See also *Messenger Newspaper Group Ltd v National Graphical Association* [1984] IRLR 397, which concerned pressure on a third party by the union in an attempt to enforce a closed shop and *Union Traffic Ltd v TGWU* [1989] IRLR 127 CA where picketing at a location other than the pickets' own place of work, in an attempt to bring it to a standstill, was considered.

[119] See also s. 240 TULRCA 1992 regarding breach of contract involving injury to persons or property and s. 241 on intimidation or annoyance by violence or otherwise.

[120] [1986] IRLR 337.

[121] See also *Thomas v National Union of Mineworkers (South Wales Area)* [1985] IRLR 136 which partly concerned the intimidatory effect of mass picketing at collieries.

[122] [1964] AC 1129 HL; see also *JT Stratford & Sons v Lindley* [1965] AC 269 HL.

[123] *Quinn v Leathem* [1901] AC 495.

[124] [1957] 1 WLR 321.

successful attempts made to prevent the individual finding other work, by circulating details to shop stewards and others at alternative places of work. The individual then successfully brought an action for damages and conspiracy against a number of members of the trade union, who were held to have combined to injure the plaintiff in his trade and the acts were not done to further the legitimate trade interests of the defendants. Those acts were held to be done without justification. Of importance is the real purpose of the combination. If the predominant purpose was an intention to injure the plaintiff, then the tort is committed, even if the means used to inflict the damage were lawful and not actionable. In *Crofter Hand Woven Harris Tweed Co Ltd v Veitch*[125] the courts recognised that no liability should be attached to a trade union in a genuine trade dispute. It was held that the real purpose of an embargo on Harris Tweed exported by certain crofters was to benefit the members of the trade union. This contrasts with *Huntley v Thornton* where the motives were deemed to be personal rather than in furtherance of a trade dispute.

A conspiracy to commit an unlawful act is when a combination of persons conspires to inflict damage intentionally on another person by an unlawful act. Even if the primary purpose were to further or protect some legitimate interest, it is enough that this was achieved by the use of unlawful means.[126]

11.7.5 Inducing a breach of a statutory duty

It is possible that industrial action may have the effect of applying pressure on an employer to breach a statutory duty imposed on either the employer or the employee. *Associated British Ports v TGWU*[127] concerned proposed industrial action resulting from the Government's decision to abolish the National Dock Labour Scheme. This scheme had the effect of preserving jobs in the docks for registered dock workers. Part of the scheme listed the obligations of workers, which included the requirement to 'work for periods as are reasonable in his particular case'. The issue was whether industrial action would be an inducement to the dock workers to breach a statutory duty to work. The Court of Appeal took the view that this was the case but the House of Lords held that this was incorrect because the relevant provision imposed a contractual duty rather than a statutory one.[128]

11.7.6 Economic duress

Economic duress is when one party is in such a dominant position that they can exercise coercion on the other party. The issue of economic duress has occurred in the context of the boycotting of ships and demands for money and payments to the union or members concerned. *Universe Tankships Inc of Monrovia v ITWF*[129] concerned the boycotting of a ship whilst in a British port and subsequent payments made by the ship owners to obtain the release of the ship. Lord Diplock stated that:

---

[125] [1942] 1 All ER 142 HL.
[126] See *Lonhro plc v Fayed* [1991] 3 All ER 303 HL.
[127] [1989] IRLR 399 HL.
[128] See also *Barrets & Baird (Wholesale) Ltd v IPCS* [1987] IRLR 3, where it was argued that a series of strikes stopped the employer from carrying out their statutory duties. The argument was rejected as no statutory duty was identified.
[129] [1983] AC 366 HL.

The use of economic duress to induce another person to part with property or money is not a tort *per se*; the form that the duress takes may or may not be tortious. The remedy to which economic duress gives rise is not an action for damages but an action for restitution of property or money exacted under such duress . . .

This approach was developed in *Dimskal Shipping Co* v *ITWF*,[130] which also concerned a ship that was confined to port by an industrial dispute. The employers were forced to issue their employees with new contracts with backdated pay as well as to make a payment to the union. As these payments were induced by illegitimate economic pressure, the employer was entitled to restitution.

11.8 Protection from tort liabilities

Protection is given against certain potential liabilities in tort by s. 219 TULRCA 1992. The immunity from liability is on the grounds that the act (i) induces another to break a contract or interferes, or induces another to interfere, with the contract's performance and, (ii) consists in threatening these actions.[131] Any agreement or combination of two or more persons to do, or procure the doing of, an act in contemplation of furtherance of a trade dispute will not be actionable in tort if the act is one that would not have been actionable if done without any agreement or combination.[132]

There are three requirements in respect of this protection:

1. The act done should be in 'contemplation or furtherance of a trade dispute'.
2. It must be a trade dispute between workers[133] and their employer.
3. It must relate, wholly or mainly, to a number of specific issues. These are:
   (a) Terms and conditions of employment,[134] including physical working conditions.
   (b) Engagement, non-engagement, termination or suspension of employment or the duties of employment.
   (c) Allocation of work or the duties of employment between workers.
   (d) Matters of discipline.
   (e) Membership, or non-membership, of a trade union.
   (f) Facilities for trade union officials.
   (g) Machinery for consultation and negotiation in connection with any of the above, including disputes about the right of a trade union to be recognised in representing workers for the purpose of negotiating any of the above.[135]

The phrase 'relates wholly or mainly to' requires a consideration of more than the event that caused the dispute and involves analysis of the reasons why it arose.[136] This means

---

[130] [1992] IRLR 78 HL.
[131] Section 219(1)(a) and (b) TULRCA 1992.
[132] Section 219(2) TULRCA 1992.
[133] Section 244(5) TULRCA 1992 defines a worker as either someone employed by the employer or a person no longer employed by the employer, but who was terminated in connection with the dispute or whose termination is one of the circumstances leading to the dispute.
[134] Section 244(5) TULRCA 1992 provides that employment includes any relationship where one person personally does work or performs services for another.
[135] Section 244(1) TULRCA 1992.
[136] *Mercury Communications Ltd* v *Scott-Garner* [1983] IRLR 494 CA.

investigating the motives of a trade union and whether there are other reasons which might be perceived as the real ones.[137]

The term 'in contemplation or furtherance of a trade dispute' requires a subjective judgment as to how widely it should be interpreted. For example, is the collection of information about an employer's business performance and the terms and conditions of their employees an act in contemplation or furtherance of a dispute? In *Bent's Brewery Co Ltd v Luke Hogan*[138] a union attempted to collect such information. The court held that the union was inducing employees to breach their contracts of employment by revealing confidential information. The union was not entitled to statutory protection, because there was no imminent or existing dispute. There was a possibility of a future dispute, but no certainty that such a dispute would arise. The court relied upon a judgment given in *Conway v Wade*,[139] where Lord Loreburn LC discussed the words 'in contemplation or furtherance':

> I think they mean that either a dispute is imminent and the act is done in expectation of and with a view to it, or that the dispute is already existing and that the act is done in support of one side to it. In either case the act must be genuinely done as described and the dispute must be a real thing imminent or existing.

A trade dispute needs to be related to the contractual or other relationship between workers and the employer. In *British Broadcasting Corporation v DA Hearn*[140] the trade union attempted to stop the employer broadcasting the football cup final via a satellite which would allow it to be seen in South Africa. The court held that this could not be seen as a trade dispute in itself. If the unions had requested a change in the contract of employment to include a term that the union's members would not be required to take part in broadcasts to South Africa, then a subsequent dispute about whether to include that term might have been interpreted as a trade dispute about terms and conditions of employment. Without such a link, the dispute could not qualify for protection.

According to the House of Lords, a dispute about the reasonableness of instructions from an employer can be a dispute about terms and conditions of employment.[141] In this case an individual was excluded from school for disruptive behaviour. The school governors allowed the mother's appeal and reinstated the pupil, and, subsequently, the headmaster issued an instruction that he should be taught in class. The trade union balloted its members and the union gave notice that it would not comply with the instruction. The court held that the reality was that the dispute was about the working conditions of teachers and therefore related to terms and conditions of employment.

The dispute must be between existing workers and their current employer. Thus it is not possible to conduct a dispute, within the protection of s. 219 TULRCA 1992, about the contracts of employment of future workers. This unfortunate outcome was confirmed in *University College London Hospital v UNISON*.[142] Here the trade union balloted its members on

---

[137] Perhaps a wider political motivation. Such motivation was considered in *University College London Hospital v UNISON* [1999] IRLR 31 CA where the court held that it was possible to have a wider political objective and, simultaneously, a specific objective of alleviating adverse consequences in a particular situation. See also *UNISON v UK* [2002] IRLR 497 where the ECHR considered the impact of art. 11 of the European Convention on Human Rights.

[138] [1945] 2 All ER 570.

[139] [1909] AC 506 HL.

[140] [1977] IRLR 273 CA.

[141] *P v National Association of Schoolmasters/Union of Women Teachers* [2003] IRLR 307.

[142] [1999] IRLR 31 CA.

a strike over the employer's refusal to guarantee the protection of the Transfer of Undertakings Regulations 1981[143] for the duration of a 30-year PFI[144] scheme. The Court of Appeal held that there were three requirements of a trade dispute: (i) that it must be a dispute between workers and their employer; (ii) that the dispute must relate wholly or mainly to one of the activities in s. 244 TULRCA 1992; and (iii) that the act must be carried out in contemplation or furtherance of a trade dispute. This was a dispute about terms and conditions between workers and a future employer and about workers as yet to be employed. It is difficult to see how this latter point is different from all other industrial disputes, which not only protect the contracts of current workers, but also future ones yet to be employed.[145]

11.9 Exceptions to statutory immunity

There are a number of actions which will not qualify for the immunity provided by s. 219 TULRCA 1992.

11.9.1 Picketing

As well as the economic torts, pickets are potentially liable for other torts. Possible torts include: trespass to the highway, which would need to be enforced by the owner of the soil; the tort of private nuisance, which suggests an unlawful interference with a person's right to enjoy or use land or some right in connection with it;[146] and the tort of public nuisance which consists of an act or omission which causes inconvenience to the public in the exercise of their common rights, such as the unreasonable obstruction of the highway.[147]

There is no immunity from actions in tort for acts done in the course of picketing unless they are done in accordance with s. 220 TULRCA 1992.[148] This provides that it is lawful for a person, in contemplation or furtherance of a trade dispute, to attend at or near their own place of work for the purpose of either peacefully obtaining or communicating information, or peacefully persuading any person to either work or abstain from working. The same provision allows an official of a trade union to accompany, for the same purposes, a member of the union, whom the official represents, at or near their place of work.[149] There is no precise definition of what is meant by 'at' or 'near' the place of work. May LJ declined to give one as the number of circumstances that one might have to provide for were so variable as to make it impossible to lay down a test.[150] He suggested the use of a commonsense approach, as did Woolf LJ in *R v East Sussex Coroner, ex parte Healy*:[151]

---

[143] SI 1981/1794.
[144] Private Finance Initiative to build and run a new hospital.
[145] In *Westminster City Council* v *UNISON* [2001] IRLR 524 CA the court held that a dispute about a proposed transfer was a trade dispute because it was about the change in the identity of the employer, rather than about the public policy issue of privatisation.
[146] See *Thomas* v *NUM (South Wales)* [1985] IRLR 136, which considered mass picketing of collieries and held that the way in which it was carried out amounted to harassment of working miners in using the highway for the purpose of going to work; see also *Mersey Docks* v *Verrinder* [1982] IRLR 152.
[147] See *News Group Newspapers* v *SOGAT '82* [1986] IRLR 337, which discussed the torts of public and private nuisance.
[148] Section 219(3) TULRCA 1992.
[149] Section 220(1) TULRCA 1992.
[150] See *Rayware Ltd* v *TGWU* [1989] IRLR 134 CA.
[151] [1988] 1 WLR 1194.

The word 'near' being an ordinary word of the English language indicating a short distance or at close proximity is to be applied . . . in a common sense manner . . . it seems to me that it is not for the courts to define what is precisely meant by the word.

In *Rayware Ltd* v *TGWU*[152] the issue had been whether a group of workers picketing at the entrance to a private trading estate, about 7/10ths of a mile from the workplace, were 'at' or 'near' the place of work. According to the Court of Appeal, the word 'near' was an expanding word and not a restraining one, i.e. its meaning was to be expanded to give effect to the purpose of the legislation. This purpose was to give a right to picket. This right was not to be taken away by holding that the nearest point where picketing could take place, even though it was 7/10ths of a mile away, was not 'at or near'.[153]

If a person normally works at a number of different locations or at a location where it would be impracticable to picket, then the place of work can be any location at which that employee works or otherwise at the location from which the work is administered.[154] The same rules apply for ex-employees whose termination is related to the dispute. They may treat their last place of work as their location for picketing purposes.[155]

The legislation does not prescribe the number of pickets that are to be allowed at or near the place of work. However, the requirement is for the picketing to be peaceful and it may be that the presence of large numbers of individuals may be too intimidating for it to be seen as peaceful. In *Thomas* v *NUM (South Wales Area)*[156] there was mass picketing at the gates of a number of collieries in South Wales during the 1984 miners' strike. It was held to be tortious because of its nature and the way that it was carried out. It represented an unreasonable harassment of those miners who were working. Mass picketing by trying to block the entry to the workplace may be a common law nuisance. The court relied on the existing Code of Practice on Picketing[157] which recommended that the number of pickets should be limited to six and issued an injunction restricting the number of pickets to that number.

11.9.2 Action taken because of dismissal for unofficial action

An act is not protected if the reason, or one of the reasons, for it is in connection with the dismissal of one or more employees who are not entitled to protection from unfair dismissal by reason of their taking unofficial action.[158]

11.9.3 Secondary action

Secondary action is not lawful picketing.[159] It is defined as an inducement, or a threat, to break or interfere with a contract of employment where the employer in that contract is not

---

[152] [1989] IRLR 134 CA.

[153] In *Union Traffic* v *TGWU* [1989] IRLR 127 CA, picketing at a depot some 14 miles away was held to be too far, even though the 'home' depot had closed down.

[154] Section 220(2) TULRCA 1992.

[155] Section 220(3) TULRCA 1992; if a reason for the dispute is a change of work locations, ex-employees will not be protected if they picket at the new location where they have not worked; they are confined to the old location even if it has been closed down. See *News Group Newspapers* v *SOGAT '82* [1986] IRLR 337.

[156] [1985] IRLR 136.

[157] This Code was made by the Secretary of State for Employment and came into force on 1 May 1992; SI 1992/476.

[158] See below, s. 237 TULRCA 1992.

[159] Section 224(1) TULRCA 1992.

party to the dispute.[160] An employer shall not be regarded as party to a dispute between another employer and the workers of that employer; and where more than one employer is in dispute with its workers, the dispute between each employer and its workers is to be treated as a separate dispute.[161] Finally a primary action in one dispute, which is protected if in contemplation or furtherance of a trade dispute, cannot be relied upon as secondary action in another dispute.[162]

11.9.4 Pressure to impose a union recognition requirement

An act is not protected if it constitutes an inducement or an attempt to induce a person to incorporate into a contract a requirement to recognise or consult with a trade union[163] or is an act that interferes with the supply of goods and services in an attempt to achieve the same with the supplier.[164]

11.10 Ballots and notices of industrial action

Detailed rules on the need for trade unions to conduct ballots before taking industrial action were introduced by successive Conservative Governments during the 1980s and early 1990s. Currently s. 219 TULRCA 1992 provides that if industrial action takes place without a ballot complying with the rules then there will be no immunity from actions in tort.

An underlying assumption on the need for such ballots was that many strikes were organised and led against the wishes of the majority of members of a particular trade union. Compulsory balloting of the membership would stop this happening. It would also reduce or eliminate 'wildcat' strikes.[165] It was intended to stop public voting at mass meetings where, it was suggested, individuals might feel coerced into showing solidarity and voting for industrial action. The arguments against formalised balloting procedures include: (i) the fact that once a ballot has been held which is in favour of industrial action, then that action may be given greater legitimacy; and (ii) negotiators may have less flexibility to come to a deal with the employer if there is a ballot result which is binding upon them. It is worth noting that, although a ballot is required before protected industrial action can take place, no ballot is required to stop the action.

Although there was an unsuccessful attempt to introduce ballots and 'cooling-off' periods in the Industrial Relations Act 1971, the current legislation stems from the Trade Union Act 1984.[166] The rules were added to and amended in the Employment Acts 1988 and 1990, with

---

[160] Section 224(2) TULRCA 1992.
[161] Section 224(4) TULRCA 1992.
[162] Section 224(5) TULRCA 1992.
[163] As in ss. 186 and 187 TULRCA 1992; see above under 11.3 'Recognition'.
[164] Section 225 TULRCA 1992.
[165] A wildcat strike is where members of a group of workers stop work and take industrial action without notice to the employer or, possibly, their own trade union.
[166] The Trade Union Act 1984 only withdrew immunity for disputes concerning contractual matters. If the action did not concern contractual matters then, it could be argued, no ballot was required. This was the argument unsuccessfully used by teachers in *Metropolitan Borough of Solihull* v *NUT* [1985] IRLR 211, who refused to cover for colleagues' absences and to cover school lunches, amongst other actions. They claimed that these were of a voluntary nature and not contractual, so a ballot was not required.

the current law contained in TULRCA 1992. There is also a Code of Practice on Industrial Action Ballots and Notice to Employers.[167]

One must be careful about introducing causal relationships where none may exist, but it is certainly true that the number of industrial disputes has declined significantly. In 1986 (after the 1980s' miners' strike) the number of working days lost through strikes in the United Kingdom was 1,920,000. This figure increased during the next three years, but then started to decline again. In 1991 the figure was 761,000 and by 1997[168] it had fallen to 235,000 working days lost. Perhaps more remarkable is the number of working days lost per 1,000 employees. In 1986 this figure was 90 working days, in 1991 it was 34 days and, by 1997, it had become ten working days lost per 1,000 employees.[169]

A trade union will lose its protection under s. 219 TULRCA 1992 if it induces a person to take part or to continue to take part in industrial action that is not supported by a ballot and the rules about notifying the employer about the ballot contained in s. 226A TULRCA 1992.[170] This is so even if the inducement is unsuccessful, whether because the individual is not interested or for some other reason.[171]

A failure to hold a ballot will deprive the union of protection against legal action taken by members under s. 62 TULRCA 1992; by employers, or customers or suppliers of that employer, relying on s. 226 TULRCA 199; or by an individual deprived, or likely to be deprived, of goods and services under s. 235A TULRCA 1992 but relying on s. 62 or 226 TUL-RCA 1992. Section 62 TULRCA 1992 deals with the rights of members of a trade union who have been, or are likely to be, induced into taking industrial action, which does not have the support of a ballot.[172] Industrial action shall only be seen to have the support of a ballot if all the requirements of ss. 226–234A TULRCA 1992 have been fulfilled (see below).[173] The member or members of the trade union concerned may apply to an employment tribunal. If the tribunal finds that the claim is well founded, it may make such orders as are necessary to ensure that the trade union stops inducing members to continue or take part in industrial action.[174]

11.10.1 Notifying the employer of the ballot

The trade union must take such steps as are reasonably necessary to notify the employer of persons entitled to vote in the ballot, that the union intends to hold a ballot and the date which the union reasonably believes will be the opening day of the ballot.[175] The notice, which is to be in writing, must also contain: a list of the categories of employee to which the employees concerned belong and a list of their workplaces; the total number of employees concerned, the number in each of the categories listed and the number at each workplace, together with an explanation of how these figures were arrived at. Alternatively, where some

---

[167] The current Code came into effect on 1 September 2005, SI 2005/2420.

[168] The year that the Conservative Government lost office.

[169] Office for National Statistics, *Labour Market Trends*, June 1998, p. 299.

[170] Section 226(1) TULRCA 1992.

[171] Section 226(4) TULRCA 1992.

[172] In ss. 226–234A TULRCA 1992, a reference to a contract of employment includes any contract under which one person personally does work or performs services for another; see s. 235 TULRCA 1992.

[173] Section 62(2) TULRCA 1992.

[174] Section 62(3) TULRCA 1992.

[175] Section 226A(2)(a)–(b) TULRCA 1992.

or all of the employees concerned have union deductions made from their wages, the union can supply 'such information as will enable the employer readily to deduce': the total number of employees concerned, the categories to which they belong and the number in each of the categories; and the number who work at the workplaces concerned.[176] This notice must be given not later than the seventh day before the opening day of the ballot.[177]

It is still unlikely, however, that the statement of an intention to hold a ballot amongst 'all our members in your institution' would fulfil the requirements of the legislation. This statement was contained in *Blackpool and Fylde College* v *NATFHE*[178] which involved the introduction of flexible contracts for new members of staff. Of the 330 members of staff, 288 were members of the union. Only 109 had subscriptions deducted through the payroll, so it was not possible for the employer to ascertain which employees would be entitled to take part in the ballot.[179] The rule now is that if the trade union possesses information as to the number, category or workplace of the employees concerned, that is the minimum information that must be supplied. The fact that it is not necessary to give names of individuals to an employer[180] is an important safeguard for employees, both in terms of privacy and in terms of protection from potential harassment by the employer.

Not later than the third day before the opening day of the ballot, the trade union must also submit a sample of the ballot paper to the employer of the persons likely to be entitled to vote.[181] If, for some reason, not all the ballot papers are the same, then a sample of all of the different versions must be given to the employer.[182]

11.10.2 Appointment of a scrutineer

Before the ballot takes place, the trade union needs to appoint a suitably qualified[183] person as a scrutineer. The functions of the scrutineer are to take all the steps necessary to prepare a report on the ballot for the trade union stating whether the ballot was satisfactory or not and providing a free copy to employers and voters on request.[184] This report is to be made as soon as possible after the ballot and, in any event, not more than four weeks after the date of the ballot.[185] There is an obligation for the trade union to comply with all reasonable requests made by the scrutineer in relation to the ballot.[186]

There is an exception for small ballots, as there is no requirement for the appointment of a scrutineer where the number of members entitled to vote does not exceed 50.[187]

---

[176] Sections 226A(2)(c) and 226A(2A)–(2C) TULRCA 1992.
[177] Section 226A(1)(a) TULRCA 1992; s. 226A(4) defines the opening day of the ballot as the first day when a voting paper is sent to any person entitled to vote.
[178] [1994] IRLR 227.
[179] See also *National Union of Rail, Maritime and Transport Workers* v *London Underground* [2001] IRLR 228 CA, where the phrase 'all members of the union employed in all categories at all workplaces' was held not to comply with the Act's requirements; and *British Telecom* v *CWU* [2004] IRLR 58.
[180] Section 226A(2G) TULRCA 1992.
[181] Section 226A(1)(b) TULRCA 1992.
[182] Section 226A(2F) TULRCA 1992.
[183] Section 226B(2) TULRCA 1992 provides information on who is a qualified person.
[184] Section 231B TULRCA 1992 describes the contents of the scrutineer's report: it is to state whether the ballot met statutory requirements, that the arrangements for the ballot were fair and that the scrutineer has been able to carry out the required duties without interference.
[185] Section 226B(1) TULRCA 1992.
[186] Section 226B(2), (4) TULRCA 1992.
[187] Section 226C TULRCA 1992.

11.10.3 **Entitlement to vote**

The entitlement to vote is to be given only to those members of the trade union whom it is reasonable at the time of the ballot for the union to believe will be induced to take part in, or to continue to take part in, the industrial action. No one else has any entitlement to vote.[188]

Subject to exceptions, a separate ballot is to be held for each workplace. If there is a single set of premises, a person's workplace is the premises the person works at, or, in any other case, the premises to which the person's employment has the closest connection.[189] The exceptions to the requirement for separate workplace ballots include, first, if the entitlement to vote is limited to all those members who have an occupation of a particular kind or have any number of particular kinds of occupation; secondly, where the entitlement to vote is limited to members employed by a particular employer, or by any number of particular employers, with whom the union is in dispute.[190] In *University of Central England* v *NALGO*[191] the ballot covered a number of colleges, in which the union had members entitled to vote. As the negotiations were with an employers' association and the vote covered all the colleges concerned, it was held that there was no requirement for separate workplace ballots. The potential absurdity of the rules on separate workplace ballots is shown in *Inter City West Coast* v *NURMTW*.[192] In this case there were two railway companies owned by the British Railways Board occupying separate office sites. The dispute concerned train conductors who worked from Manchester Piccadilly station, but the employers claimed that two separate ballots should have been held. The court rejected their arguments and held that the conductors had one place of work, i.e. the railway station.[193]

Industrial action will not be regarded as having the support of a ballot if a member of a trade union, whom it was reasonable to assume would be induced to take part in the industrial action, was not accorded their entitlement to vote and was subsequently induced to take part in the action.[194] Small accidental failures in the process are to be ignored if the failure was unlikely to have an effect on the result of the ballot.[195] There are problems for trade unions in organising ballots that meet the statutory requirements. These are connected with maintaining a centralised register of members when membership can be in a state of flux. *London Underground* v *NURMTW*[196] involved the recruitment of some 600–700 new members after the ballot for industrial action had been completed. The employers were unsuccessful in their attempt to obtain an injunction, because the Court of Appeal accepted that industrial action was not the action of the individual who voted, but was a collective action in which the individual took part. It is the collective industrial action that must have the support of the ballot.[197]

---

[188] Section 227 TULRCA 1992. In *RMT* v *Midland Mainline Ltd* [2001] IRLR 813 the union omitted to ballot a significant number of members in the grades concerned.

[189] Section 228 TULRCA 1992.

[190] Section 228A(1)–(4) TULRCA 1992; s. 228A(5) defines who are the particular members of a trade union affected by different types of disputes.

[191] [1993] IRLR 81.

[192] [1996] IRLR 583.

[193] See also *RJB Mining (UK) Ltd* v *NUM* [1997] IRLR 621, where the union decided to hold an aggregate ballot, but then omitted one location.

[194] Section 232A TULRCA 1992; see also *National Union of Rail, Maritime and Transport Workers* v *Midland Mainline Ltd* [2001] IRLR 813 CA, which concerned the missing out of some of those entitled to vote.

[195] Section 232B TULRCA 1992.

[196] [1995] IRLR 636 CA.

[197] See also *British Railways Board* v *NURMTW* [1989] IRLR 349 CA where the number of ballot papers issued appeared to be less than the membership of the union entitled to vote.

11.10.4 **The voting paper**

We have seen that voting at mass meetings is no longer permissible. Every member entitled to vote must be given a voting paper which must state the name of the independent scrutineer and clearly specify the address to which it is to be sent and the date by which it must be sent. In addition it must have a unique whole number which is one of a series of numbers.[198] The voting paper must also contain at least one of two questions, depending upon the industrial action envisaged. The first question is whether the voter is prepared to take part in, or continue, a strike. The second is whether they are prepared to take part in, or continue, industrial action short of a strike.[199] If the union wishes to pursue both options, then they must ask both questions.[200] The questions need to be in such a form that the members can vote either yes or no. Prior to the ERELA 1999 the only definition of a strike was contained in s. 246 TUL-RCA 1992, which defined it as 'any concerted stoppage of work'. In *Connex South Eastern Ltd v NURMTW*[201] this was held to include any refusal by employees to work for periods of time for which they are employed to work, provided it was 'concerted'. Concerted was taken to mean mutually planned. Such action could therefore include a ban on rest-day working and overtime when people might normally be working. The ERELA 1999 changed this view and included a section stating that, for the purposes of s. 229(2) TULRCA 1999, an overtime ban and a call-out ban constituted action short of a strike.[202]

In addition, the voting paper must also specify, in the event of a yes vote, who is authorised to call upon members to take industrial action.[203] The person specified must be one of those included in s. 20(2) TULRCA 1992, which defines those whose acts are to be taken as being authorised or endorsed by a trade union. Finally, the following statement needs to appear on the ballot paper:

> If you take part in strike or other industrial action, you may be in breach of your contract of employment.
>
> However, if you are dismissed for taking part in strike or other industrial action which is called officially and is otherwise lawful, the dismissal will be unfair if it takes place fewer than eight weeks after you started taking part in the action, and depending on the circumstances may be unfair if it takes place later.[204]

The second paragraph, perhaps making it less intimidatory, was added by the ERELA 1999.

11.10.5 **The ballot**

There are also strict rules applied to the ballot itself. As far as is reasonably practicable, voting must be done in secret.[205] Every person who is entitled to vote in the ballot must be allowed to do so without interference from the trade union or its officials and must be able

---

[198] Section 229(1) TULRCA 1992.
[199] Section 229(2) TULRCA 1992.
[200] See *West Midlands Travel* v *TGWU* [1994] IRLR 578, which considered that each question had to be voted on individually and the majority in respect of each question considered separately.
[201] [1999] IRLR 249 CA.
[202] Section 229(2A) TULRCA 1992.
[203] Section 229(3) TULRCA 1992.
[204] Section 229(4) TULRCA 1992; see 11.14 below.
[205] Section 230(4)(a) TULRCA 1992.

to do so, as far as is reasonably practicable, without incurring any direct costs themselves.[206] Members must have a voting paper sent to them by post to their home address, or any other address to which the individual has requested the union to send it.[207] *London Borough of Newham v NALGO*[208] involved a strike ballot which the trade union thought would take one month to organise and hold. The union funded a campaign, and provided speakers, to rally support for a yes vote. The courts held that the statute did not require trade unions to adopt a neutral stance. The union is perfectly entitled to be partisan so long as it complies with the legislation.

There is an obligation that the votes in a ballot are to be fairly and accurately counted, although this does not mean that inaccuracies in the counting will necessarily invalidate the result. So long as the inaccuracies are accidental and do not affect the result, they are to be disregarded.[209] As soon as reasonably practicable after the ballot, the union must inform both those entitled to vote and all the employers concerned of the result.[210] The scrutineer will also produce a report on the ballot.[211] In *Metrobus v Unite*[212] the union claimed that there was no need to inform the employer of the ballot result unless the union decided in favour of industrial action, because the need to inform the employer of the result only arose in order for the union to have statutory immunity for the action. The Court of Appeal did not accept this argument, stating that the need to inform the employer of the ballot result was a free-standing obligation. The union could wait for the best part of three weeks before it called industrial action, but there was an obligation to inform the employer of the ballot result as soon as reasonably practicable.

The ballot will cease to be effective if action has not been called, by a specified person,[213] or taken place within a period of four weeks from the date of the ballot. This period can be extended to a maximum of eight weeks if such an extension is agreed between the employer or employers concerned and the trade union.[214] If there has been legal action by the employer during this period, which has resulted in a court order stopping the trade union from calling or taking industrial action, then, when such an order lapses or is discharged, the union may apply to the court for an order that this period does not count towards the four weeks or longer.[215]

11.10.6 Notice to the employer

An act done by a trade union to induce a person to take part in, or continue, industrial action will not be regarded as protected unless the trade union gives a relevant notice to the affected

---

[206] See *Paul v NALGO* [1987] IRLR 43 CO. Although this case did not concern industrial action, it did show that even minor costs incurred, i.e. the cost of posting a ballot paper, would be sufficient to breach the requirement that there should be no direct costs falling upon the member.

[207] Section 230(1) and (2) TULRCA 1992.

[208] [1993] IRLR 83 CA.

[209] Section 230(4)(b) TULRCA 1992.

[210] Sections 231–231A TULRCA 1992.

[211] Section 231B TULRCA 1992; see above.

[212] [2009] IRLR 851.

[213] See s. 233 TULRCA 1992 which states that action will only be regarded as having the support of a ballot if called by a specified person; see above.

[214] Section 234(1) TULRCA 1992; the possible extension to eight weeks was added by the ERELA 1999, presumably to allow more time for a negotiated settlement.

[215] Section 234(2)–(6) TULRCA 1992; although there is an absolute maximum of 12 weeks after which the effect of the ballot is removed.

employer or employers, within seven days of having notified the employer of the result as required by s. 231A TULRCA 1992.[216] A relevant notice is one that is in writing and contains: a list of the categories of employee to which the affected employees belong and a list of their workplaces; the total number of affected employees, the number in each of the categories listed and the number at each workplace, together with an explanation of how these figures were arrived at. Alternatively, where some or all of the employees affected have union deductions made from their wages, the union can supply 'such information as will enable the employer readily to deduce': the total number of affected employees, the categories to which they belong and the number in each of the categories; and the number who work at the workplaces concerned.[217] The relevant notice must also state whether the action is going to be continuous or discontinuous; the dates on which continuous action will commence and, if relevant, the dates on which discontinuous action will take place.[218] Discontinuous action is that which takes place on some days only.[219]

One of the problems with the legislation prior to the ERELA 1999 was that the rules were so rigid that if a trade union wished to cease or suspend action in order to negotiate, they were then required to go through the notice provisions again in order to restart the whole process.[220] The ERELA 1999 added subsections (7A) and (7B) to s. 234A TULRCA 1992. These additions have the effect of allowing a suspension of the action and therefore of the requirement to notify the employer again of intended action. These suspensions can take place so that the union can comply with a court order or undertaking or if the employer and the union agree to the suspension.

11.10.7 Industrial action affecting the supply of goods and services

Where an individual claims that, as a result of an unlawful act to induce any person to take part in industrial action, there has been a delay or failure in the supply of goods or that there has been a reduction in the quality of goods or services supplied, that individual may apply to the High Court for an order. An act to induce any person to take part in or continue such industrial action is unlawful if it is actionable in tort and does not have the support of a ballot. The High Court may grant interlocutory relief or make an order requiring that there is no further inducement to take part in industrial action and that no person should engage in conduct after the order as a result of inducement before the order.[221]

11.11 Union responsibility for the actions of their members

Where proceedings in tort are brought against a trade union on the grounds that it is inducing, or threatening to induce, another to break a contract of employment or interfere with its

---

[216] Section 234A(1) TULRCA 1992.
[217] Section 234A(3)–(3C) TULRCA 1992; see also s. 234A(5A) which describes the information that must be given to the employer, although not giving the names of any employees is not a ground for holding that there has been a breach of the condition. This provision was added by the ERELA 1999; for an example of the position before this amendment see *Blackpool and Fylde College* v *NATFHE* [1994] IRLR 227.
[218] Section 234A(3)(b) TULRCA 1992.
[219] Section 234A(6) TULRCA 1992.
[220] See s. 234A(7) TULRCA 1992.
[221] Section 235A TULRCA 1992.

performance, then the union is to be treated as liable if it has endorsed or authorised the act in question.[222] One of the perceived problems that this measure attempts to solve is that of unofficial action, where individual groups or parts of a trade union take action without the express approval of their trade union.

Trade unions are to be taken as having endorsed or authorised an act if it was done, or was authorised or endorsed: by any person who is empowered by the rules[223] of the union to authorise or endorse such action; or by the executive committee or the president or general secretary of the union; or by any other committee or official of the union.[224] For the purpose of this latter category a committee of the union is any group of persons constituted in accordance with the union's rules and an act is to be taken as authorised or endorsed by an official if it was authorised or endorsed by a committee of which the official was a member and the committee had as one of its purposes the organising or co-ordinating of industrial action.[225] *Heatons Transport (St Helens) Ltd* v *TGWU*[226] discussed the derivation of a shop steward's authority in order to assess the union's liability for the shop steward's actions. The court concluded that such authority could come from the rules expressly or by implication; or may come under the rules by express or implied delegation; or by virtue of the office held; or otherwise by such means as custom and practice. There is no need to look for specific authority in a particular case if the authority to act has been expressly or impliedly delegated to different levels of the organisation. A court may grant an injunction requiring the union to ensure that there is no further inducement to take part in industrial action and that no person continues to act as if they had been induced to take part.[227]

It is possible for a trade union to avoid liability for the actions of its members if the executive, president or general secretary repudiates the act as soon as is reasonably practicable after it came to their knowledge. For such a repudiation to be effective, the union must give, without delay, a written notice to the committee or official in question and do its best, without delay, to give the notice to every member that the union believes might be involved in the action and to the employer of every such member.[228] The notice must, according to s. 21(3) TULRCA 1992, contain the following statement:

> Your union has repudiated the call (or calls) for industrial action to which this notice relates and will give no support to unofficial industrial action taken in response to it (or them). If you are dismissed while taking unofficial industrial action, you will have no right to complain of unfair dismissal.

It is only by following this procedure that the union can avoid liability for the act and its consequences. There is a requirement for strict compliance with a repudiation, for the union not to be held liable for further breaches. Section 21(5) TULRCA 1992 provides that an act

---

[222] Section 20(1) TULRCA 1992. See *Gate Gourmet Ltd* v *TGWU* [2005] IRLR 881.

[223] Rules means the written rules of the union or any other written provision between members: s. 20(7) TULRCA 1992.

[224] Section 20(2) TULRCA 1992; an official need not be employed by the union; see *Express & Star Ltd* v *NGA* [1985] IRLR 455 where the West Midlands Secretary was held to be an official for whose actions, in this respect, the union was vicariously liable.

[225] Section 20(3) TULRCA 1992.

[226] [1972] IRLR 25 HL.

[227] Section 20(6) TULRCA 1992; the provisions relating to union liability above also relate to complying with court injunctions; proceedings against the trade union do not affect the liability of any other person in respect of the act: s. 20(5) TULRCA 1992.

[228] Section 21(1)–(2) TULRCA 1992.

will not be treated as being repudiated if, subsequently, the executive, president or general secretary of the union acts in a way that is inconsistent with it. Thus it is not enough to issue a written repudiation and then continue as before. In *Richard Read (Transport) Ltd* v *NUM (South Wales Area)*[229] there was a failure to comply with an injunction stopping mass picketing. Although the union president had said that the union would comply, there was no evidence that instructions to pickets had changed at all. The court cited a statement by Sir John Donaldson to the effect that it was not sufficient, when complying with an injunction, to say that one had done one's best (unless that was what was required by the injunction). Strict compliance was necessary.[230] In *Read*, the officials had shown an indifference as to whether or not the injunction was complied with.[231] As a result the union was held liable and fined.[232]

The union will be held not to have repudiated if, within three months of the repudiation, there is a request from a party to a commercial contract (i.e. not an employment contract) whose performance has been, or is being, interfered with and who has not been given the necessary written notification, and the union has not provided written confirmation that the act has been repudiated.[233]

11.12 **Prohibition on use of funds to indemnify unlawful conduct**

Section 15(1) TULRCA 1992 prohibits trade unions from using their property in the following ways. First, towards the payment of a fine imposed by a court for an offence or for contempt of court. Secondly, towards the securing of any such payment and, finally, towards indemnifying an individual in respect of such a penalty. This reflects a view of the courts that such payments or indemnities are against public policy. *Drake* v *Morgan*[234] concerned the ability of the National Union of Journalists to pay the fines that its members incurred on the picket line. The court refused to make a declaration that such payments were not lawful. The resolution indemnifying the pickets had been made after the event and could not be seen as a way of indemnifying future unlawful acts. Thus it was not contrary to public policy because it could not be seen as either an incitement to commit an offence or aiding or abetting the securing of an offence. By way of contrast, in *Thomas* v *NUM (South Wales Area)*[235] an injunction was granted to stop the union indemnifying pickets against possible future fines. According to the court, even this did not stop the union from considering individual cases of hardship if it was in the interests of the union and the members as a whole. The court distinguished *Taylor* v *NUM (Derbyshire Area)*,[236] where payments had been made to pickets and

---

[229] [1985] IRLR 67.
[230] *Howitt Transport Ltd* v *TGWU* [1973] IRLR 25.
[231] See also *Express & Star Ltd* v *NGA* [1985] IRLR 455, where the relationship of the statutory provisions on repudiation and contempt proceedings for failure to abide by an injunction were considered.
[232] Section 22 TULRCA 1992 provides limits as to the amount of fines that can be levied on trade unions in actions in tort and s. 23 provides that certain property of the union is protected with regard to the enforcement of fines.
[233] Section 21(6) TULRCA 1992.
[234] [1978] ICR 56.
[235] [1985] IRLR 136.
[236] [1985] IRLR 99.

striking miners, on the grounds that the strike was not authorised and was in breach of the union's rules.

11.13 Remedies

The remedies that may be available to the courts include specific performance, injunctions and damages.

Specific performance is an order of the court which compels the party in breach of contract to fulfil its obligations under that contract. Like all equitable remedies it is discretionary and is unlikely to be used in the context of industrial relations. In fact s. 236 TULRCA 1992 stops the courts making orders for specific performance in relation to the contract of employment. It establishes an important statutory principle that an employee cannot be made to work or attend at any place for the purpose of doing so. The dividing line between an order for specific performance and an injunction may sometimes be unclear. It is possible that an injunction stopping an employer from, for example, dismissing an employee with one month's notice, rather than the six months' notice to which they were entitled, has the effect of ordering the continuation of the contract of employment.[237]

Injunctions can be interim or permanent in nature. The advantage of interim injunctions is the speed with which they can be obtained, although s. 221 TULRCA 1992 does place some restrictions on their availability. First, where there is a without notice application for an injunction and the likely defence is that the action was in contemplation or furtherance of a trade dispute, the court cannot grant the injunction unless it is satisfied that all reasonable steps have been taken to give the other side the opportunity of being heard. Secondly, where there is an application for an interim injunction pending a full trial of the action, and the party against whom the injunction is sought claims that they acted in the furtherance or contemplation of a trade dispute, then the court is to exercise its discretion as to whether it will be possible to establish a defence. Issues to be considered are whether there is a possibility of establishing a defence under ss. 219 and 220 TULRCA 1992; whether it can be established that there is a trade dispute;[238] whether there is a serious issue to be tried: where the balance of convenience lies between the plaintiff and the defendant; and whether the granting of an order is in the public interest.

The standard authority for the approach to be taken in granting interim injunctions is set out in *American Cyanamid Co v Ethicon Ltd*.[239] Lord Diplock stated that the object of such an injunction was to protect the plaintiff against injury for which there could not be sufficient compensation in damages, if successful at the trial. However, this protection had to be weighed against the defendant's need to be protected from injury resulting from being stopped from exercising their own legal rights. Thus the test to be used is the balance of convenience. In particular, the court needs to decide whether the granting of an interim injunction is tantamount to giving final judgment against the defendant.[240] The courts will also need to ask

---

[237] *Hill v CA Parsons Ltd* [1972] 1 Ch 305 CA.
[238] See *University College London Hospital v UNISON* [1999] IRLR 31 CA, which set out three conditions for establishing whether there was a trade dispute (see above).
[239] [1975] AC 396 HL.
[240] *NWL Ltd v Nelson and Laughton* [1979] IRLR 478 HL, *per* Lord Diplock.

whether there is a serious question to be tried.[241] For example, in *Associated British Ports* v *TGWU*,[242] the employers failed to show that a strike by registered dock workers would be in breach of their statutory duty under the National Dock Labour Scheme. Having failed in this argument there was no serious issue to be tried, so there was no basis for granting an injunction.

An injunction must be complied with by the person to whom it is addressed and must be obeyed from the moment that the defendant knows of its existence. It is not enough to claim that the order was not formally served and therefore could not be followed, as this would open the door to abuse. A telephone call or letter informing the defendant should be enough.[243]

Most disputes are resolved at, or soon after, the interim injunction stage and it is rare for a dispute to go all the way to obtaining a permanent injunction. If proceedings do continue, the appropriate remedy by then is likely to be damages rather than an injunction. In *Messenger Newspapers* v *NGA*[244] the plaintiffs were awarded: sums for liquidated damages for all the expenditure that they had incurred as a result of the tort; compensatory damages for the loss of revenue; aggravated damages as a result of the injury being caused by malice or by the manner of doing the injury; and exemplary damages for the necessity of teaching the wrongdoer that tort does not pay.[245]

11.14 Dismissals during industrial action

An employee who is sacked is only able to claim unfair dismissal in limited circumstances. The circumstances that need to be taken into account are: whether the action is official or unofficial; whether all or some of the employees taking part have been dismissed or re-engaged; and whether the employee is taking part in protected industrial action.

11.14.1 Unofficial action

An employee has no right to complain of unfair dismissal if, at the time of the dismissal, the employee was taking part in unofficial industrial action.[246] Industrial action is unofficial unless the employee is:

1. a member of a trade union and the action is authorised or endorsed[247] by that trade union; or

2. not a member of a trade union, but there are members taking part in the action whose union has authorised or endorsed the action.[248]

There are exceptions to this rule, which include the dismissals being for a reason related to pregnancy, maternity leave, parental leave, time off for dependants, health and safety, being or planning to be an employee representative, or making a protected disclosure.[249]

---

[241] See *Dimbleby & Sons Ltd* v *NUJ* [1984] IRLR 161 HL.
[242] [1989] IRLR 399 HL.
[243] See *Kent Free Press* v *NGA* [1987] IRLR 267, where such an event happened.
[244] [1984] IRLR 397.
[245] See *Rookes* v *Barnard* [1964] AC 1129 HL, *per* Lord Devlin.
[246] Section 237(1) TULRCA 1992.
[247] Authorised or endorsed in accordance with s. 20(2) TULRCA 1992 – see note 224 above.
[248] Section 237(2) TULRCA 1992.
[249] Section 237(1A) TULRCA 1992.

11.14.2 **Official action**

Where an employee has a right to complain of unfair dismissal during industrial action or a lock-out, the employment tribunal will not be able to entertain the claim unless:

1. one or more of the relevant[250] employees has not been dismissed;[251] or

2. a relevant employee has been offered re-engagement within a period of three months, beginning with the date of dismissal, and the complainant has not been offered re-engagement.[252] Re-engagement means the same job as before the dispute or in a different reasonably suitable job.[253]

Even a re-engagement made in error might be enough to bring these provisions into effect. In *Bigham and Keogh* v *GKN Quickform Ltd*[254] an employee working on a site was dismissed as a result of going on strike. Less than three months later he applied for and was successful in obtaining a job at the employer's main office elsewhere. He revealed his previous employment but not the dismissal. After two weeks the connection with the dismissal was made and the employee was dismissed from the new position. This was sufficient to bring into effect s. 238(2)(b) TULRCA 1992 as the employer had constructive knowledge of the employee's previous employment, even though they had not connected this to the previous industrial dispute.[255]

There are the same exceptions to this rule as are applied in unofficial industrial action above.

11.14.3 **Protected action**

A person takes protected industrial action if that person commits an act, or is induced to commit an act, which is protected from action in tort by s. 219 TULRCA 1992 (see above). Such a person will be unfairly dismissed[256] if the reason, or the principal reason, for the dismissal is that the individual took protected industrial action, provided that the dismissal takes place within a basic period of 12 weeks beginning with the day that the employee started to take protected action. This basic period can be extended by the number of days on which an employee is locked out by the employer.[257]

The provisions will continue to apply to dismissals that take place after the protected period if:

---

[250] Section 238(3) TULRCA 1992 states that a relevant employee is an employee, at the establishment of the employer, who is taking part in the industrial action; in the case of a lock-out, a relevant employee is an employee who was directly interested in the dispute leading to the lock-out.

[251] The material time for deciding whether a relevant employee has not been dismissed is at the conclusion of the hearing determining jurisdiction of the complaint; see *P & O European Ferries (Dover) Ltd* v *Byrne* [1989] IRLR 254 CA and *Manifold Industries* v *Sims* [1991] IRLR 242.

[252] Section 238(1) TULRCA 1992.

[253] Section 238(4) TULRCA 1992.

[254] [1992] IRLR 4.

[255] See also *Crosville Wales Ltd* v *Tracey* [1993] IRLR 60, which concerned the dismissal of an entire workforce and the recruitment of a new one on different terms and conditions; some of the old workforce were recruited into this new workforce.

[256] The rules on length of service do not apply in respect of dismissals for taking a protected action: s. 239(1) TULRCA 1992.

[257] Section 238A(7A)–(7C) TULRCA 1992.

1. The employee had stopped the industrial action during or before the end of the period.

2. The employee had not stopped industrial action during that period but the employer had not taken 'such procedural steps as would have been reasonable for the purposes of resolving the dispute to which the protected industrial action relates'.[258]

The protection is linked to applying pressure to both parties to act in a way that might lead to the resolution of the dispute, because, in deciding whether an employer has taken such steps, regard is to be had as to whether:

1. There had been compliance by the union or the employer with any procedures agreed in a collective agreement or other agreement.

2. The employer or the union had offered or agreed to negotiate after the start of the protected action.

3. Either party had unreasonably refused, after the start of the protected action, a request for the use of conciliation services.

4. The employer or union had unreasonably refused mediation services in relation to the procedures to be adopted for ending the dispute.[259]

The remedies for an unfair dismissal in respect of taking protected industrial action are as for other unfair dismissal cases, except that the remedies of reinstatement and re-engagement are not available until the end of the protected industrial action.[260]

Chapter summary

This chapter continued the consideration of trade union issues from the last chapter. It focused on collective bargaining and industrial action. It considered the voluntarist nature of collective bargaining and how the law defines the framework of bargaining. Then it looked at the rules concerning recognition of trade unions and especially the rules concerning the statutory recognition of trade unions by employers. The chapter examined statutory immunity from common law torts in relation to industrial action, provided that the action is taken in contemplation or furtherance of a trade dispute. The common law torts analysed include inducing a breach of contract, interference with a contract or business, intimidation and conspiracy.

---

[258] Section 238A(4)–(5) TULRCA 1992.
[259] Sections 238A(6) and 238B TULRCA 1992.
[260] Section 239(4)(a) TULRCA 1992.

Further reading

Barrow, C. *Industrial Relations Law*: Cavendish, 2002, Chapters 8–17.

Brown, W. and Oxenbridge, S. 'Trade Unions and Collective Bargaining: Law and the Future of Collectivism' in **Barnard, C., Deakin, S. and Morris, G.** (eds) *The Future of Labour Law*: Hart Publishing, 2004, Chapter 3.

Collins, H., Ewing, K. and McColgan, A. *Labour Law: Text and Materials*: Hart Publishing, 2005, Chapters 8 and 9.

Deakin, S. and Morris, G. *Labour Law*: 5th edn, Hart Publishing, 2009, Chapters 9 and 11.

Ewing, K. 'Laws against Strikes Revisited' in **Barnard, C., Deakin, S. and Morris, G.** (eds) *The Future of Labour Law*: Hart Publishing, 2004, Chapter 2.

Novitz, T. *International and European Protection of the Right to Strike*: Oxford University Press, 2003.

www.acas.org.uk

www.cac.gov.uk

www.ilo.org.uk

www.tuc.org.uk

Visit **www.mylawchamber.co.uk/sargeant**
to access legal updates, live weblinks and practice
exam questions to test yourself on this chapter.

Index

Get more support with study and revision than you ever thought possible …